CONSTITUTIONAL AND ADMINIS ~~~~ V

Third Edition

This book is supported by an online subscription to give you access to periodic updates. To gain access to this area, you need to enter the unique password printed below. The password is protected and your free subscription to the site is valid for 12 months from the date of registration.

1   Go to http://www.cavendishpublishing.com.

2   If you are a registered user of the Cavendish website, log in as usual (with your email address and your personal password). Then click the Constitutional and Administrative Law button on the home page. You will now see a box next to Constitutional and Administrative Law. Enter the unique passcode printed below. Once you've done that, the word 'Enter' appears. Click Enter and that's where you'll find your updates.

3   If you are not yet a registered user of the Cavendish website, you will first need to register. Registration is completely free. Click on the 'Registration' button at the top of your screen, then type in your email address and a password. You should use something personal and memorable to you. Then click the Constitutional and Administrative Law button on the home page. You will now see a box next to Constitutional and Administrative Law. Enter the unique passcode printed below. Once you've done that, the word 'Enter' appears. Click Enter and that's where you'll find your updates

4   Cavendish will email you each time updates are uploaded. All you need to do to obtain any past or future updates is to go to http://www.cavendishpublishing.com and follow the instructions in point 2 above. You no longer need the unique passcode printed below. It is protected the moment you register it.

Congratulations! You now have access to periodic updates to help you stay current with legal developments. Your unique passcode is:

5520TKMXLSUZMB

Cavendish
Publishing
Limited

London • Sydney

CONSTITUTIONAL AND ADMINISTRATIVE LAW

Third Edition

Cavendish
Publishing
Limited

London • Sydney

CONSTITUTIONAL AND ADMINISTRATIVE LAW

Third Edition

Hilaire Barnett, BA, LLM
Queen Mary and Westfield College
University of London

Cavendish
Publishing
Limited

London • Sydney

Third edition first published in Great Britain 2000 by Cavendish Publishing
Limited, The Glass House, Wharton Street, London WC1X 9PX, United
Kingdom

Telephone: + 44 (0)20 7278 8000   Facsimile: + 44 (0)20 7278 8080

Email: info@cavendishpublishing.com
Website: www.cavendishpublishing.com

© Barnett, H	2000
First edition	1995
Second edition	1998
Third edition	2000
Reprinted with amendments	2001

Barnett, Hilaire A
Constitutional and Administrative Law – 3rd edition
1. Constitutional law – Great Britain
2. Administrative law – Great Britain
I. Title
342.4'1

ISBN 1 85941 552 0

Printed and bound in Great Britain

For Matthew

PREFACE

The United Kingdom's constitution, while of ancient origins, remains both dynamic and vibrant. As every public lawyer is only too aware, nowadays, the proper boundaries of constitutional and administrative law are both increasingly wide and subject to debate. In compiling any textbook on this subject, one of the principal preliminary tasks lies in defining the scope of material to be included and the approach to be adopted in relation to that material. The task of writing is made more problematic by the many and varied depths in which, and the means by which, the subject is taught both in the United Kingdom and overseas. Full time students; part time students; students on long distance learning programmes such as the University of London's Programme for External Students and students combining both constitutional and administrative law within a one year course, all have differing needs. The aim in this book has been to provide sufficient detail to meet all such needs in a user-friendly manner.

As emphasised in the introductory chapters, the study of the United Kingdom's constitutional and administrative law involves rather more than a learning of rules of law, and necessarily encompasses – over and above an understanding of legal rules – an understanding of history, government, politics and conventional practices which form the foundations of the contemporary constitution. As a result, any constitutional and administrative law textbook must incorporate sufficient information relating to such matters so as to enable students to view the constitution in its historical, political and conventional context. In this work, I have addressed the subject in this manner in order to provide a rounded, contextual explanation of the United Kingdom's constitution, which goes beyond pure law while also adequately covering the law.

The 1998 second edition was published against a background of significant constitutional reform introduced by the Labour government elected in 1997. Two years on, many of the proposals have become law: the House of Lords has undergone its first stage of reform, the Human Rights Act 1998 is about to come into effect in England (having become effective in Scotland in 1998) and devolution to Scotland and Wales has been implemented.

As previously, the text is divided into seven main parts. Part I provides a general introduction to the scope of constitutional law, the sources of the constitution and the structure of the United Kingdom. In Part II, the fundamental concepts of the constitution are considered: the rule of law, separation of powers, the royal prerogative and parliamentary sovereignty. In Part III, the European Union and Community is discussed. The material is divided into two chapters. Chapter 8 considers the evolution, aims and structure of the Union and Community and the principal institutions and their respective powers. In Chapter 9, the sources of Community law and the relationship between national and Community law are discussed.

In Part IV, the structure of government is discussed, Chapter 10 considering the role of Prime Minister, Cabinet and the Civil Service, Chapter 11 discussing the concept of responsible government and ministerial responsibility and Chapter 12 the devolution of power to the Northern Ireland Assembly, Scottish Parliament and Welsh Assembly and local government.

Part V is devoted to the United Kingdom Parliament: 'Westminster'. Chapter 13 discusses the electoral system, Chapter 14 introduces students to the House of Commons. Chapters 15 and 16 are devoted to parliamentary procedures for the scrutiny of legislative proposals and scrutiny of government administration. The House of Lords, its role, functions and the current reform proposals are considered in Chapter 17. Parliamentary privilege is discussed in Chapter 18. Notwithstanding the devolution of powers to regional and local government, Westminster remains technically sovereign in its law making powers and central to ensuring the accountability of the United Kingdom government to the electorate. Nevertheless, the impact of devolution and other constitutional reforms – most notably the Human Rights Act 1998 – is considerable, and introduces new restraints on the scope of Parliament's powers, an issue addressed in Chapter 15 in relation to the legislative competence of Parliament and also Chapter 7 which addresses the concept of sovereignty.

Part VI focuses on the individual and the State. The materials on civil liberties are organised into three separate chapters. The protection of human rights under the European Convention is discussed in Chapter 22, as is the incorporation of the Convention into domestic law, and its constitutional significance. The subject of State security is discussed in Chapter 23.

Part VII introduces administrative law. Judicial review of administrative action comprises two chapters, the first dealing with the role and scope of judicial review and procedural matters; the second analysing the grounds for judicial review. The complementary role, functions and powers of Commissioners for Administration are considered in Chapter 26.

This third edition could not have been prepared so effectively without the help of colleagues. My thanks are due once more to Bob Burns, the Law Librarian at Queen Mary and Westfield College for his patience and help, and to Jules Winterton of the Institute of Advanced Legal Studies. Thanks go also to my colleagues Joanne Scott and Ian Yeats for their constructive contributions to various chapters, and to Richard Stone of the Inns of Court School of Law for his helpful comments and suggestions. Special thanks to Robert Jago, without whose energetic and valued contribution this edition could not have been produced in time. As before, the usual disclaimer applies – any errors remain my sole responsibility. Repeated thanks are also due to Jo Reddy, Sonny Leong and their team at Cavendish Publishing, with whom as before, it has been a pleasure to work.

I would also like to thank all the students, past and present – both at home and, particularly, in the Far East – who, over the years, have deepened my understanding of the difficulties they face in studying such a rich, varied and essentially protean subject as that of the constitution of the United Kingdom. Family and all friends are again owed a large and unquantifiable debt of gratitude, not just for all their support, but also for allowing me the necessary time and solitude in which to complete this text.

Hilaire Barnett
Faculty of Laws
Queen Mary and Westfield College
University of London
July 2000

CONTENTS

PART II

FUNDAMENTAL CONSTITUTIONAL CONCEPTS

Contents

PART III

THE EUROPEAN COMMUNITY AND UNION

PART IV

CENTRAL, REGIONAL AND LOCAL GOVERNMENT

Contents

PART V

PARLIAMENT

13 THE ELECTORAL SYSTEM   523

Contents

PART VI

THE INDIVIDUAL AND THE STATE

Contents

Contents

PART VII

INTRODUCTION TO ADMINISTRATIVE LAW

Contents

Contents

TABLE OF CASES

TABLE OF LEGISLATION

TABLE OF INTERNATIONAL LEGISLATION

Table of International Legislation

TABLE OF ABBREVIATIONS

Anglo-American L Rev	Anglo-American Law Review
BYIL	British Yearbook of International Law
California UL Rev	California University Law Review
Canadian Bar Rev	Canadian Bar Review
CLJ	Cambridge Law Journal
CLP	Current Legal Problems
CLP Annual Review	Current Legal Problems Annual Review
CML Rev	Common Market Law Review
CMLR	Common Market Law Reports
Crim LR	Criminal Law Review
EHRLR	European Human Rights Law Review
ELJ	European Law Journal
EL Rev	European Law Review
Harv L Rev	Harvard Law Review
Industrial LJ	Industrial Law Journal
ICCLR	International Company and Commercial Law Review
ICLQ	International and Comparative Law Quarterly
Int J Soc L	International Journal of Society and Law
J of Child Law	Journal of Child Law
JLS	Journal of Law and Society
J of Social Welfare and Family Law	Journal of Social Welfare and Family Law
JSPTL	Journal of the Society of Public Teachers of Law
J of the International Commission of Jurists	Journal of the International Commission of Jurists
Law Soc Gazette	Law Society's Gazette
LQR	Law Quarterly Review
Melbourne UL Rev	Melbourne University Law Review
MLR	Modern Law Review
NILQ	Northern Ireland Legal Quarterly
NLJ	New Law Journal
OJLS	Oxford Journal of Legal Studies
Parl Aff	Parliamentary Affairs
PL	Public Law
Public Admin	Public Administration
SJ	Solicitor's Journal
Toronto ULJ	Toronto University law Journal
YBEL	Yearbook of European Law

PART I

GENERAL INTRODUCTION

CHAPTER 1

INTRODUCTION:
THE SCOPE OF CONSTITUTIONAL LAW

Constitutional law is concerned with the role and powers of the institutions within the State and with the relationship between the citizen and the State. The constitution is a living, dynamic organism which at any point in time will reflect the moral and political values of the people it governs, and accordingly, the law of the constitution must be appreciated within the socio-political context in which it operates.

The study of the constitution of the United Kingdom involves acquiring an understanding of a variety of historical, legal, philosophical and political factors which have, over the centuries, shaped the organisation of the State. The United Kingdom appears to be almost unique in not having a constitution which is conveniently set out in a single written document.[1] However, not too much weight should be given to the 'unwritten' nature of the constitution. Under all constitutions, not all of the rules will be written, and still less will they be collected within a single document.

In the United Kingdom, by contrast with most other States, the constitution is the product of many centuries of continuous and, mostly, gradual, peaceful evolution. With the exception of the constitutional turmoils of the seventeenth century,[2] the United Kingdom's constitutional development has an unbroken history dating from 1066. Accordingly, historical origins form the background for the study of the contemporary constitution, and no meaningful appreciation of the present constitution can be acquired without understanding this historical backcloth which reveals the moral and political influences which have shaped the constitution as it exists today. That said, it must always be remembered that the principal emphasis of study is on the contemporary constitution of the United Kingdom rather than on the many centuries of development which underlie it. With that point in mind, it is necessary to draw on historical sources and events with a view to understanding the contribution made to an evaluation of the many constitutional issues which present themselves today.

It is particularly true of the United Kingdom's constitution, which is more the product of evolution than conscious rational thought, that it is difficult to see clearly the demarcation lines between constitutional law, history, philosophy and political science. In order, therefore, to study the United Kingdom's constitution successfully, it is necessary to gain an insight into the history, politics and political philosophy which underpin the constitution.

---

1   Israel and New Zealand share this constitutional feature.
2   See, in particular, Chapters 2, 6 and 7.

This task is not easy, particularly as many students will come to constitutional law without a background in history, politics or political philosophy. It is, however, an essential component of constitutional study, without which the structure, law and policies of the State cannot be understood. More than any other area of legal study except jurisprudence, constitutional law in the United Kingdom involves far more than a learning of legal rules. Indeed, it may be said, without exaggeration, that the non-legal rules and practices within the constitution are at least as important – if not more important on many occasions – as the legal rules. For example, in analysing and evaluating the extent to which the individual citizen enjoys constitutional protection of individual rights, it is necessary to appreciate the timeless and tireless quest to ensure the legal protection of the rights of individuals. This study involves, *inter alia*, an appreciation of natural law and social contract theories[3] which underpin the constitutional limitations on government power in order that the rights of individuals are protected against the power of the State.

Also, by way of example, the study of the constitutional relationship between the government and the legislature today encompasses a knowledge of the political backcloth, the rules of parliamentary practice and the non-legal or conventional rules which apply in a given situation. By way of further illustration, when studying the legislative supremacy of Parliament, it is of fundamental importance to grasp that, in terms of classical constitutional legal theory, the power of Parliament in the absence of a written constitution is omnipotent or sovereign.[4] However, the constitutional and legal fact that Parliament has the ultimate law making power within the State, does not mean that there are no restraints on what Parliament may do. The law making powers of Parliament, while theoretically and legally unlimited, are in fact constrained by the electorate to which Parliament is accountable, and by economic, moral and political necessities. In terms of accountability to the electorate and the limits which this imposes on Parliament's powers, it is necessary to appreciate the philosophical and historical foundations of democracy and the idea of individual rights. Notwithstanding the lack of a codified constituent document, under the constitution of the United Kingdom, the principles on which the government operates today are precisely those which govern the relationship between the government and the people under a written constitution. Here, an understanding of the idea of 'social contract'[5] makes it possible to understand the complex relationship between 'sovereign power' and the power of the people to determine who holds that sovereign power and the manner in which it may – and may not – be exercised.

Nowadays, the 'supremacy' of Parliament in the United Kingdom must also be considered against the United Kingdom's membership of the

---

3 See Chapters 4 and 19.
4 See Chapter 7.
5 See Chapters 4 and 19.

European Community and European Union,[6] which has significant implications for the classical doctrine of sovereignty. Since 1972, when the United Kingdom acceded to the European Community,[7] the United Kingdom has in many respects ceased to be an autonomous, independent State and has become a member of an ever-expanding European political, economic and legal order, the impact of which reaches to the heart of the constitution. In legal terms, it is undeniable that the United Kingdom Parliament could decide to withdraw from the European Community and Union. It is, however, arguable that, as time passes, and the United Kingdom becomes more subject to and influenced by membership of the Union, that, in light of the non-legal restraints – political and economic – there exists little real power to withdraw from the Community and Union. The non-legal restraints are in fact more important in this regard than the simple legal rule that Parliament is sovereign in its law making powers.

To illustrate further the distinction between absolute legal power and practical power, in terms of law, the Crown has the right to appoint the Prime Minister of its choice, and the power to dissolve Parliament when it chooses.[8] To know these rules, however, is not to know very much, for the legal powers of the Crown are restricted – constrained – by non-legal, 'conventional' rules which determine the conditions under which the Crown has a discretion to exercise its powers. In order, therefore, to understand issues such as the appointment of a Prime Minister and the rules regulating the dissolution of Parliament, it is necessary to understand the conventional rules which have developed over time and have taken on binding force.

THE CONCEPT OF CONSTITUTIONALISM[9]

'Constitutionalism' is the doctrine which governs the legitimacy of government action. By constitutionalism is meant – in relation to constitutions written and unwritten – conformity with the broad philosophical values within a State. Constitutionalism implies something far more important than the idea of 'legality' which requires official conduct to be in accordance with pre-fixed legal rules. A power may be exercised on legal authority; however, that fact is not necessarily determinative of whether or not the action was

---

6   See Chapters 8 and 9.

7   The original three Communities are now referred to as the European Community.

8   See Chapter 6.

9   See Bogdanor, V, 'Introduction', in *Constitutions in Democratic Politics*, 1988, London: Policy Studies Institute; McAuslan, P and McEldowney, JF, *Legitimacy and the Constitution: The Dissonance between Theory and Practice in Law*, 1985, London: Sweet & Maxwell, p 11ff.

'constitutional'. The doctrine of constitutionalism suggests, at least, the following:

(a) that the exercise of power be within the legal limits conferred by Parliament on those with power – the concept of *intra vires* – and that those who exercise power are accountable to law;

(b) the exercise of power – irrespective of legal authority – must conform to the notion of respect for the individual and the individual citizen's rights;

(c) that the powers conferred on institutions within a State – whether legislative, executive or judicial – be sufficiently dispersed between the various institutions so as to avoid the abuse of power; and

(d) that the government, in formulating policy, and the legislature, in legitimating that policy, are accountable to the electorate on whose trust power is held.

In summary, constitutionalism suggests the limitation of power,[10] the separation of powers[11] and the doctrine of responsible accountable government. It is against these conceptual and practical requirements that the constitution of the United Kingdom must be studied and evaluated.

WHAT IS A CONSTITUTION?

In lay terms, a constitution is a set of rules which governs an organisation. Every organisation, whether social club, trade union or nation State, which has defined objectives and departments or offices established to accomplish those objectives, needs a constitution to define the powers, rights and duties of the organisation's members. This set of rules, in addition to regulating the internal working of the organisation, will also make provision for the manner in which the organisation relates to outside bodies. It can therefore be said that a constitution looks both to internal and external regulation of the body to which it relates.

In addition to the function of defining powers and duties and relationships with other bodies, a constitution fulfils two related purposes – those of definition and evaluation. In its defining function, the constitution is both descriptive and prescriptive (or normative). Differently expressed, the constitution will both define the manner in which the rules in fact operate and dictate what ought to happen in a given situation. As such, the rule or normative statement in question sets a standard of conduct or behaviour which is regarded as correct and which is expected to be adhered to by those

---

10 See Chapter 4.
11 See Chapter 5.

to whom the rules are addressed. These constitutional rules – whether written or unwritten – facilitate the stability and predictability of behaviour. Further, when such normative rules exist, they provide a standard against which actual conduct can be judged or evaluated. If the accusation is made that a member of an organisation has acted 'unconstitutionally', the speaker is claiming that those accused have acted in a manner which breaches the required standards of behaviour as laid down in the body of generally accepted pre-determined normative rules. In this sense, a constitutional rule, in addition to being descriptive, normative and predictive, is evaluative and judgmental.

When examining the rules of any organisation, it becomes apparent that individual rules have differing levels of importance and, moreover, that rules may have differing degrees of specificity or generality. The manner in which the rules are expressed may also differ; some may be written down, whereas some may be discernible only through observation of actual conduct. And thus it is with the constitution of a State, and particularly that of the United Kingdom, in which the sources of constitutional law are varied. The legal sources are represented by a mixture of statute and judicial precedent, and these legal sources are supplemented by the binding, non-legal, conventional rules and practices.[12] The rules of constitutional law will also reveal differences in the manner in which they may be changed to adapt to changing circumstances. Under a written constitution, the constitution will itself define the procedure for amendment and may provide for varying degrees of ease or difficulty in amendment in relation to particular rules. The rules regarded as the most important are characterised by the greatest degree of difficulty in the process of amendment. Under the United Kingdom's constitution, by way of contrast, the manner in which constitutional change is effected will be dependent not upon clearly defined written rules but, rather, by accepted constitutional practice which has evolved over time.

DEFINING CONSTITUTIONS

Professor KC Wheare[13] defines the constitution of a State as:

> ... the whole system of government of a country, the collection of rules which establish and regulate or govern the government.

An older definition, that of Thomas Paine,[14] reveals a more complex set of ideas:

---

12 See Chapter 2.
13 See Wheare, KC, *Modern Constitutions*, 2nd edn, 1966, Oxford: OUP, p 1.
14 Paine, T, *Rights of Man* (1792, Pt II), 1984, rep 1998, Collins, H (ed), New York: Penguin, p 93.

> A constitution is not the act of a government, but of a people constituting a
> government, and a government without a constitution is power without right
> ... A constitution is a thing antecedent to a government; and a government is
> only the creature of a constitution.

From this second definition, it can be discerned that a constitution is
something which is prior to government, or, as Paine expresses it, 'antecedent'
to government, giving legitimacy to the government and defining the powers
under which a government may act. As such, the constitution sets limits both
to the powers which can be exercised and to the manner in which they may be
exercised. Accordingly, the constitution defines the legality of power. This
notion is particularly apposite in a country with a written constitution and a
Supreme Court which is conferred with jurisdiction to rule on the legality of
government action. Under such a constitutional arrangement, it can be said
that everything which the government does is either lawful or unlawful
depending upon whether or not the contested conduct is held to be
'constitutional' or not. Under a largely unwritten constitution, the position is
less clear-cut, and it may often be the case that conduct will be adjudged to be
'unconstitutional' and yet not be 'unlawful'. This distinction will be returned
to in a subsequent discussion of the legal and non-legal sources of the
constitution.[15] At this introductory stage, it need only be noted that the
unwritten nature of the United Kingdom's constitution has given rise to
argument as to whether or not a constitution – as generally understood in the
majority of States – exists. Sir Ivor Jennings, author of *The Law and the
Constitution*, offers a balanced evaluation of this apparent paradox:[16]

> If a constitution means a written document, then obviously Great Britain has
> no constitution. In countries where such a document exists, the word has that
> meaning. But the document itself merely sets out rules determining the
> creation and operation of governmental institutions, and obviously Great
> Britain has such institutions and such rules. The phrase 'British constitution' is
> used to describe those rules.[17]

CLASSIFYING CONSTITUTIONS

When looking for the salient characteristics of the constitution, it is helpful to
bear in mind the range of possible classifications which can be applied to any
constitution. Professor KC Wheare identifies the following classifications:

---

15 See Chapter 2.

16 Jennings, I (Sir), *The Law and the Constitution*, 5th edn, 1959, London: Hodder &
    Stoughton, p 36.

17 See, also, McIlwain, CH, *Constitutionalism, Ancient and Modern*, 1958, Ithaca, New York:
    Great Seal; Ridley, FF, 'There is no British Constitution: a dangerous case of the
    Emperor's clothes' (1988) 41 Parl Aff 340.

(a) written and unwritten;

(b) rigid and flexible;

(c) supreme and subordinate;

(d) federal and unitary;

(e) separated powers and fused powers; and

(f) republican and monarchical.[18]

Written and unwritten constitutions

A written constitution is one contained within a single document or a series of documents, with or without amendments, defining the basic rules of the State. The origins of written constitutions lie in the American War of Independence[19] and French Revolution.[20] More recent written constitutions derive from the grant – or devolution – of legislative power from previously imperial powers to former colonies and dominions,[21] whether secured as a result of peaceful settlement or violent revolution.[22]

The feature which characterises all States with a written constitution is that there has been a clear historical break with a previously pertaining constitutional arrangement, thus providing the opportunity for a fresh constitutional start. As Wheare explains:

> If we investigate the origins of modern constitutions, we find that, practically without exception, they were drawn up and adopted because people wished to make a fresh start, so far as the statement of their system of government was concerned ... The circumstances in which a break with the past and the need for a fresh start come about vary from country to country, but in almost every case in modern times, countries have a constitution for the very simple and elementary reason that they wanted, for some reason, to begin again ... This has been the practice certainly since 1787 when the American constitution was drafted, and as the years passed, no doubt imitation and the force of example have led all countries to think it necessary to have a constitution.[23]

The absence of any such break in continuity in British history, from 1066 to the current time,[24] more than any other factor, explains the mainly unwritten nature of the United Kingdom's constitution.

---

18 *Op cit*, Wheare, fn 13, Chapter 1.

19 1775–83.

20 1789.

21 See, eg, the South Africa Act 1909, the British North America Act 1867 (now, the Constitution Act 1867) and the Canada Act 1982.

22 See, eg, the Nigeria Independence Act 1960 and the Zimbabwe Act 1979. See, also, de Smith, SA, *The New Commonwealth and its Constitutions*, 1964, London: Stevens, Chapter 5.

23 See *op cit*, Wheare, fn 13, p 4.

24 With the exception of the seventeenth century constitutional upheavals (see Chapters 6 and 7).

The characterisation of constitutions into 'written' and 'unwritten' is, however, too limited, for such classification tells neither the whole constitutional story nor necessarily makes the constitution accessible to those seeking to understand it. A written constitution will provide the basic rules, but, for an understanding of the whole constitutional picture, it is also necessary to examine subsequent interpretations of the constitution contained in case law and the political practices which reveal the actual operation of the constitution. At the heart of this matter lies one simple fact: all constitutions – howsoever defined and categorised – are dynamic organisms. They are dependent for much of their meaning and relevance on the societal framework which surrounds them. Nowhere is this more apparent than in relation to individual rights and liberties. The vast majority of States have adopted both written constitutions and Bills of Rights stipulating the inviolable rights of citizens – nevertheless, the political reality for many citizens' rights around the world is very different from the formally drafted constitution. Irrespective of whether or not a State has a written constitution and a Bill of Rights, it must be recognised that the actual protection of individual rights, as with so much of the constitution, is explained not solely by reference to written rules. Regardless of the form in which rights are protected, in any society, it will be the democratic political process, political practice and norms of acceptable governmental conduct[25] which, while not having the force of law, provide constitutional standards which determine the respect accorded to individual rights.[26] These constitutional features also establish standards against which the probity of official conduct may be measured. It is for this reason that a true understanding of constitutions and the concept of constitutionalism requires a deeper understanding than that provided for by an analysis of the formal written rules.

Rigid and flexible constitutions

This classification rests primarily on the question whether or not constitutions can be amended with ease. The framers of a written constitution, endeavouring to provide a comprehensive legal framework for the State, will naturally seek to protect its constitutional provisions from subsequent repeal or amendment. Towards this end, all or many of the rules will be 'entrenched', that is to say the constitution will stipulate stringent procedures to be followed in any attempt to amend the provision in question. As will be seen later, entrenchment may take several forms,[27] but its central characteristic is that it either prevents, or makes difficult, amendment or

---

25 See Chapter 2.
26 See *op cit*, Bogdanor, fn 9.
27 See Chapter 7.

repeal. By way of example, the federal Commonwealth of Australia Constitution Act of 1900 specifies the procedure to be adopted for its own alteration. An amending Bill must pass through at least one House of Parliament by a specified majority and the proposed amendment must be endorsed in a referendum which approves the measure by an overall majority in at least four of the six States.[28] In the 90 years between 1900 and 1990, 42 proposals for constitutional amendment had been put forward. Of these, only eight were approved by a majority of electors nationally and a majority of electors in a majority of States. In this regard, it has been observed that 'constitutionally speaking, Australia is a frozen continent'.[29] As a further example, under the United States' constitution, constitutional amendments may be proposed either by a two-thirds majority of both Houses of Congress or, following a request by the legislatures of two-thirds of the States, by the convention summoned by Congress. To be accepted, the proposed amendments must then be approved by the legislatures of three-quarters of the States, or by conventions in three-quarters of the States. Between 1813 and 1913, only three amendments had been accepted; between 1913 and 1933 six amendments; and by 1951, only one further amendment.[30]

The United Kingdom's constitution, by comparison with the constitutions of the United States and Australia, represents the height of flexibility. Under the doctrine of Parliamentary sovereignty examined in Chapter 7, Parliament is the supreme law making body and can pass any law, by a simple majority vote in Parliament, on any subject matter whatsoever. Moreover, no court may hold an Act of Parliament to be void.[31] Note for now, therefore, that under the United Kingdom's constitution, no legal constraints can – under the traditional doctrine of sovereignty – fetter Parliament's powers.[32] Of particular importance in this regard is the fact that no Parliament may lay down irreversible rules regulating future legislative procedures which must be followed. The constitutional import of this lies in flexibility. It has been argued, controversially, and continues to be argued, that the legislative supremacy of Parliament is constrained by various constitutional devices and Acts of constitutional importance. However, it is significant that none of these challenges has succeeded in limiting Parliament's theoretical power.

The issue of flexibility, however, should not be exaggerated. That there are no legal restraints on what Parliament does, does not mean that there are no

---

28 Commonwealth of Australia Constitution Act 1900 (UK), s 128.

29 Sawer, G, *Australian Federalism in the Courts,* 1967, Melbourne: Melbourne UP, p 208. See Lee, HP, 'Reforming the Australian Constitution – the frozen continent refuses to thaw' [1988] PL 535.

30 See Wheare, KC, *Federal Government,* 4th edn, 1963, Oxford: OUP, Chapters 4 and 12.

31 *Edinburgh and Dalkeith Railway v Wauchope* (1842) 8 Cl & F 710; *Sillars v Smith* 1982 SLT 539.

32 Complications arise in relation to the European Community, to be examined in Chapters 8 and 9.

non-legal constraints. In practical terms, such 'extra-legal' constraints may be as important as legal controls. By way of illustration of the distinction between legal and non-legal constraints, Sir Ivor Jennings offers the example of Parliament passing an Act which bans smoking in the streets of Paris. As he states, there is nothing in the constitution which prevents Parliament from doing precisely that: 'If it enacts that smoking in the streets of Paris is an offence, then it is an offence.'[33] The relevant Act so passed would be valid and recognised by the English courts. However, the Act would be totally ineffective and ignored by the courts and everyone else in France. Equally, as Jennings states, 'if Parliament enacted that all men should be women, they would be women so far as the law is concerned'. Sir Leslie Stephens, writing in the nineteenth century,[34] asks what restrains Parliament from passing an Act providing that all blue-eyed babies be put to death? The response to this question is that in legal-theoretical terms, of course Parliament could pass such a law, but in political terms, it neither could nor would do so, for ultimately, Parliament is dependent upon the support of the electorate.

Supreme and subordinate constitutions

This constitutional category overlaps in many respects, although not totally, with the classification into federal and unitary States. A 'supreme' constitution refers to a State in which the legislative powers of the governing body are unlimited. Conversely, a subordinate constitution is one whose powers are limited by some higher authority.[35]

Federal and unitary constitutions

In many States, for example, the United States of America, Canada, Australia and Malaysia, there exists a division of powers between central government and the individual States or Provinces which make up the federation. The powers divided between the federal government and States or Provinces will be clearly set down in the constituent document. Some powers will be reserved exclusively to the federal government (most notably, such matters as defence and State security); some powers will be allocated exclusively to the regional government (such as planning and the raising of local taxation); and others will be held on the basis of partnership, powers being given to each level of government with overriding power, perhaps, reserved for central government. The common feature of all federal States is the sharing of power

---

33 See *op cit*, Jennings, fn 16, p 170.

34 Stephens, L, *The Science of Ethics* (1882), 1972, Newton Abbot: David and Charles.

35 See Chapter 7 for discussion in relation to New South Wales, Australia and South Africa.

between centre and region – each having an area of exclusive power, other powers being shared on some defined basis. Equally common to all federations is the idea that the written constitution is sovereign over government and legislature and that their respective powers are not only defined by the constitution but are also controlled by the constitution, which will be interpreted and upheld by a Supreme Court.

The constitution of the United Kingdom presents a very different arrangement from that outlined above. The State is unitary and there is no defining written constitution controlling the powers of government or of the legislature.[36] Instead of a written constitution, there exists a sovereign legislative body, which represents the ultimate law making power in the State. Power is given to the Scottish parliament and regional assemblies and to local government, under Acts of the United Kingdom Parliament, to fulfil defined functions such as the provision of services and raising of local revenue to finance such services.[37] However, no power is given to the regions or to local government other than that decreed by Parliament. Regional parliaments and assemblies and local authorities are entirely creatures of Acts of Parliament, and any power given can subsequently – subject only to political acceptability to the electorate – be withdrawn. An illustration of this point can be seen in relation to the statutory abolition of the Greater London Council and other Metropolitan Borough Councils in 1985.[38] An example on a larger scale can be seen in the grant of limited legislative authority to the Northern Ireland Assembly under the Government of Ireland Act 1920. The law making power given in 1920 was later revoked by the United Kingdom Parliament by the Northern Ireland Constitution Act 1973. Similarly, during the 1970s, the Labour government planned to devolve limited legislative power to Scotland and Wales, and Acts of Parliament were passed to this effect.[39] Neither of those Acts was, however, brought into force, and legislative power in relation to both Scotland and Wales thus remained with the Westminster Parliament.[40] In 1998, however, devolution of power was again on the constitutional agenda.[41] The Scotland Act 1998, the Government of Wales Act 1998 and Northern Ireland Act 1998 each involve a decentralisation of power, although ultimate sovereign power remains with the Westminster Parliament.[42]

---

36 But note the issue of devolution to Northern Ireland, Scotland and Wales; see below, p 17, and see, further, Chapter 12.

37 See Chapter 12.

38 Local Government Act 1985.

39 Scotland Act 1978; Wales Act 1978.

40 The phrase 'Westminster Parliament' refers to the United Kingdom Parliament. Westminster is the geographical area in which Parliament is sited.

41 See, further, Chapter 3.

42 The Northern Ireland Act 2000 suspended the operation of the Northern Ireland Assembly and Executive. See, further, Chapter 12.

Separated powers and fused powers

The separation of powers is a fundamental constitutional concept which will be discussed more fully in Chapter 5. With respect to the classification of constitutions, the concept here requires outline consideration. The doctrine is of great antiquity, dating back at least to Aristotle.[43] John Locke,[44] Viscount Bolingbroke[45] and Baron Montesquieu[46] gave further expression to the idea.

The essence of the doctrine is that the powers vested in the principal institutions of the State – legislature, executive and judiciary – should not be concentrated in the hands of any one institution.[47] The object of such separation is to provide checks on the exercise of power by each institution and to prevent the potential for tyranny which might otherwise exist. A constitution with clearly defined boundaries to power, and provisions restraining one institution from exercising the power of another, is one in conformity with the doctrine of separation of powers. This arrangement is most readily achievable under a written constitution, although it is arguable whether, under any constitution, a pure separation of powers is possible, or indeed desirable, a point which will be returned to later. At the other end of the spectrum of constitutional arrangements from a nearly 'pure' separation of powers is a totalitarian State or a purely monarchical State. Under such a constitution will be found a single figure, or single body, possessed with the sole power to propose and enact law, to administer the State, and both to apply and to adjudicate upon the law.

Under the largely unwritten constitution of the United Kingdom, the separation of powers is difficult to ascertain and evaluate. There is undeniably a distinct legislative body, executive, and judiciary, each exercising differing powers. On further examination, however, it will be found that, in practice, there are so many exceptions to the 'pure' doctrine that the significance of separation of powers is called into question. Suffice to say at this introductory stage that it is a doctrine which is respected under the constitution, despite many apparent anomalies.

Republican and monarchical constitutions

A republic is a State having as its figurehead a (usually) democratically elected President, answerable to the electorate and to the constitution.

---

43 384–323BC; Aristotle, *The Politics*, 1962, Sinclair, TA (trans), London: Penguin.

44 Locke, J, 'Second treatise of civil government', in *Two Treatises of Government* (1690), 1977, London: JM Dent, Chapter XII, para 143.

45 Bolingbroke, H, *Remarks on the History of England*, 3rd edn, 1748, London: Francklin.

46 Montesquieu, C, *De l'Esprit des Lois* (1748), 1989, Cambridge: CUP, Bk XI.

47 See Vile, MJC, *Constitutionalism and the Separation of Powers*, 1967, Oxford: Clarendon, Chapter IV.

Presidential office is both a symbol of statehood and the repository of many powers. In the name of the State, the President will enter into treaties, make declarations of war, and represent the State on formal international and domestic occasions. Additionally, as with the President of the United States of America, the President has responsibility for proposing legislation to give effect to the political programme which gave him the mandate of the people. The President, however, has no formal power to initiate legislation, and it is the Congress of the United States which will ultimately determine the acceptability of legislative proposals. It may well be that the elected President is from a different political party than that which dominates Congress.[48] When that political situation pertains, the prospects for successful implementation of Presidential election promises is weakened, and although the President has a veto power over legislation passed by Congress, that veto can be overridden by Congress voting with a two-thirds majority.

Looking at the United Kingdom as an example of a sophisticated Western democracy based on constitutional monarchy, the position of the head of State is very different.[49] Queen Elizabeth II is the head of State, and all acts of government are undertaken in the name of the Crown. This statement implies that great power is accorded to the Queen. In reality, however, and with the exception of important residual powers, this is not the case. As with the President of the United States of America, the Queen is the figurehead – the symbol of nationhood – on a domestic and international level. The Crown also represents the continuity of the State. From an historical constitutional viewpoint, it matters little which leader of which political party at any one time occupies the office of Prime Minister, or whether he or she is a Labour or Conservative Prime Minister, for he or she will be exercising all powers in the Queen's name. Unlike the position of the head of State under the United State's constitution, however, the Queen is, by definition, unelected and unaccountable to the electorate in any democratic sense. The Crown enjoys enormous legal-theoretical power but little practical power, save in exceptional circumstances.

The legal powers held by the Crown are, for the most part,[50] exercised in her name by the elected government of the day. The rules which restrict the monarch's powers are for the most part non-legal. The restrictions comprise the all-important conventional rules of constitutional practice which regulate so much of the United Kingdom's constitution.[51] Thus, for example, the Crown has the legal power to withhold the royal assent from Bills passed by

---

48 As was the position under President Clinton (Democrat) and Congress (Republican).

49 See Chapter 10.

50 See, however, Chapter 6 for discussion of the circumstances under which this theoretical power may become real power.

51 See Chapter 2.

Parliament but, by convention, this assent will never be withheld (and has not been withheld since 1708) unless so advised by the government.

In addition to representing the symbolic figurehead, the role of the Crown may be said to be protective. The Queen, it has been said, has the power to 'warn and advise' the Prime Minister of the day.[52] Queen Elizabeth II, since her accession in 1952, has seen many Prime Ministers, both Conservative and Labour, enter and leave office. Throughout that 48 year reign, the Queen has quietly influenced government,[53] and garnered vast experience in domestic, international and particularly Commonwealth affairs. That experience represents a wealth of knowledge at the disposal of the government in power. While the role of the monarchy is a matter for contemporary debate, the continuity and longevity of monarchy remains a distinguishing feature of the United Kingdom's constitution.

CHARACTERISTICS OF THE UNITED KINGDOM'S CONSTITUTION

From the discussion of classification above, some conclusions can now be reached about the characteristics of the United Kingdom's constitution. In summary, it can be said that it:

(a) is largely unwritten in character;

(b) is flexible in nature;

(c) is supreme;

(d) is unitary in structure, but, following the 1998 reforms, with some powers devolved to a Scottish Parliament, to a Welsh Assembly, to the new Northern Ireland Assembly and to local government;

(e) exhibits mainly but not completely separated powers; and

(f) is monarchical.

Each of these features will become clearer as we examine the constitution in more detail.

THE CONSTITUTION IN FLUX

The absence of a written constitution, allied to the doctrine of parliamentary sovereignty, enables constitutional change to be brought about within the

---

52 Bagehot, W, *The English Constitution* (1867), 1993, London: Fontana, Chapter II.

53 See Macmillan, H, *At the End of the Day* (1961–63), 1973, London: Macmillan; Wilson, H, *The Governance of Britain*, 1976, London: Weidenfeld & Nicolson.

United Kingdom with the minimum of constitutional formality. The constitution has evolved in a pragmatic and gradual manner over the centuries. At the current time, however, the constitution is undergoing perhaps more change, and more major change, than in previous decades. The last and greatest constitutional change occurred in 1973 when the United Kingdom joined the European Communities (now European Community).[54] Joining the Community, which has now evolved as but one part of the wider European Union, involved not only entering into an agreement which affected the economic life of the country, but also joining a unique legal order under which rights and obligations in matters regulated by the treaties are ultimately defined and enforced by the European Court of Justice. Moreover, the Treaty on European Union 1992 (the Maastricht Treaty) and the Treaty on European Union 1997 (the Treaty of Amsterdam) mark new and significant developments within the European Union in relation to economic, monetary and political union and the evolution of common policies in relation to justice and home affairs and security and foreign affairs policies.

It was the general election of 1997 which presaged further significant constitutional change. The incoming Labour government had committed itself to several constitutional reforms. Devolution of limited, but nonetheless wide ranging, law making powers to Scotland and Wales was the first issue to be addressed by the government.[55] An elected 'strategic authority' for London was also on the agenda, as was regional devolution in England. Reform of the membership of the House of Lords, the 'upper House' of the United Kingdom's bicameral Parliament, has already been effected, although the ultimate role and powers of the Lords remains to be determined. The settlement reached in April 1998 with regard to Northern Ireland has culminated in devolved powers to a new Northern Ireland Assembly.[56] The government is also committed to the better protection of rights and freedoms, and in order to achieve this objective, the Human Rights Act 1998 'incorporated' the European Convention on Human Rights into domestic law, thereby for the first time providing a 'code' of human rights which is not only binding on public authorities and the courts and compels ministers to make declarations of compatibility or incompatibility with Convention requirements when presenting Bills to Parliament, but also provides citizens with the legal means by which to challenge the legality of administrative action. As significantly, the Human Rights Act will mark a change in perception about freedoms and rights among the British people who, by contrast with citizens living under written constitutions and Bills of Rights, have hitherto been largely unaware of their rights and freedoms. Moreover,

---

54 See Chapters 8 and 9.
55 On devolution to Northern Ireland, Scotland and Wales, see Chapter 12.
56 See, further, Chapters 3 and 12.

the government is intent on improving further the openness of government. While openness in government was greatly improved under the former Conservative government, the Labour government's proposals mark a movement further towards openness, a movement which will provide greater, but still limited, transparency in government for all affected by its actions.

CHAPTER 2

SOURCES OF THE CONSTITUTION

As has been seen in Chapter 1, the United Kingdom's constitution is classified as 'unwritten'. However, while there is no single constituent document, many constitutional sources are of a written nature, albeit not conveniently compiled within any one document. In order to give meaning to the constitution as a whole, it is necessary to study the many fundamental documents, statutes and cases together with the non-legal conventional rules which surround and give meaning to the legal rules. In undertaking this exercise, it must be remembered that what is being sought is not a rote-learned catalogue of sources, but rather a broad appreciation of the constituent elements of the constitution.

DEFINITIONAL DIFFICULTIES

Defining the scope of sources which are correctly labelled 'constitutional' under an unwritten constitution is an inherently difficult exercise. Were the United Kingdom to have a written constitution, all of the rules now contained within various sources would be contained within it. By this means, a clear picture would be obtained as to those rules which the framers of the constitution regarded as being of 'constitutional importance'. In the absence of such a document, matters are less clear-cut and doubt exists as to precisely which rules – statutory, common law or conventional – are correctly defined as 'constitutional' rules. As Geoffrey Marshall explains:

> [N]o easy logical limit can be set to the labour of the constitutional lawyers ...
> any branch of the law, whether it deals *prima facie* with finance or crime or local
> government, may throw up constitutional questions.[1]

The disadvantage of such a lack of precision may be illustrated in relation to the legal protection of civil liberties and human rights before incorporation of the European Convention on Human Rights under the Human Rights Act 1998. Hitherto, in the United Kingdom, having neither a domestically enforceable Bill of Rights nor a written constitution, doubts as to such sensitive matters had been resolvable under an application under the European Convention on Human Rights[2] and, in some instances, by the Court

---

1 Marshall, G, *Constitutional Theory*, 1971, Oxford: Clarendon, p 6.
2 See Chapter 22.

of Justice of the European Community.[3] However, because the European Convention was not enacted into English law until the Human Rights Act 1998, no domestic court could provide a remedy for alleged abuses of rights protected under the European Convention unless statute, common law or rights under European Community law provided a remedy. As a result, an individual citizen seeking to discover precisely what legal rights he or she had was obliged to scrutinise the statute book, the text of the European Convention on Human Rights, and the treaties and case law relating to European Community Law. The Human Rights Act 1998 remedied this deficiency by conferring jurisdiction on domestic courts of law to rule on Convention rights. The status of the Human Rights Act 1998 and its scope are considered in Chapter 22.

It is even more difficult, in the absence of a written constitution, for the citizen to discern, at a conceptual level, precisely what is and what is not a 'constitutional issue'. As Marshall observes, all legal issues in the United Kingdom are potentially capable of being interpreted as constitutional issues. That fact is not, however, reassuring to the student of the constitution who is trying to define its scope and limits.

To illustrate this definitional difficulty, questions as to the status of many and differing statutes may be briefly examined.

Employment law

Statutes regulating relations between workers and employers define the extent to which an employee is free to withdraw his or her labour, to act in support of a dispute between him or herself and his or her employer, and to act in support of other workers in support of a dispute with employers. Such matters raise the fundamental question of the individual's right to withdraw his or her labour and the conditions under which this is lawful. Are such statutes 'constitutional' in nature?

Pornography

Also by way of illustration, in the United Kingdom, the Obscene Publications Act 1959,[4] an ordinary Act of Parliament having no particular 'constitutional status', provides the legal rules relating to pornographic literature. In contrast, in the United States of America, legal challenges to the availability of and access to allegedly pornographic material fall under the First Amendment to

---

3   See Chapters 8 and 9.

4   As amended.

the Constitution.[5] The subject of pornography in the United States may accordingly be classified as a clearly constitutional issue, being regarded as a question of freedom of 'speech'.

Abortion

In the United Kingdom, the right to abortion is defined under the Abortion Act 1967.[6] In the United States of America, by contrast, the right to abortion falls under the constitutional right to privacy provisions of the constitution. The constitution of the Republic of Ireland prohibits abortion under its right to life provisions, and a recent challenge to that prohibition was launched under the guise of restrictions on equal access to information and the right to free movement to receive services under the law of the European Community.[7]

These examples are not intended to lead to an analysis of the substantive legal and constitutional issues, but rather to demonstrate a very real and important point of principle. That point is that under a written constitution, a particular issue may be defined as a 'constitutional' issue. Under an unwritten constitution, matters are far less certain. Pornography and abortion are clearly regarded as constitutional matters in some jurisdictions.

There are obvious limitations to the utility of merely listing statutory and common law sources of the constitution. It is, however, important at an early stage of study to be familiar with the major statutory sources of the constitution.

STATUTORY SOURCES

The Magna Carta[8]

One starting point is the Magna Carta of 1215.[9] Historically, the Magna Carta represented a formal settlement between the Crown[10] and the barons. The Charter represented settlement of the grievances of citizens and challenged the untrammelled powers of the king. The settlement provided for freedom of

---

5   *Roth v US* 354 US 476 (1957).

6   As amended by the Human Fertilisation and Embryology Act 1990.

7   *The Society of the Unborn Children Ireland Ltd v Grogan* [1991] 3 CMLR 849. See Spalin, E, 'Abortion, speech and the European Community' [1992] J of Social Welfare and Family Law 17.

8   Statute 25 Edw I (1297). See Holt, J, *Magna Carta*, 1965, Cambridge: CUP.

9   Subsequently reaffirmed many times, eg, 1225 (Henry II), 1297 (Edward I), 1324 (Edward III).

10   Statute 25 Edw I (1297).

the Church, and the right of merchants to be free from exorbitant taxation. Today, the document's importance lies in its declaration of the confirmation of the liberties enjoyed by 'freemen of the realm' and their future protection,[11] and in the protection to be given to the enjoyment of these liberties by the requirement for trial by jury:

> No freeman shall be taken or imprisoned, or be disseised of his freehold, or liberties, or free customs, or be outlawed, or exiled, or any other wise destroyed; nor will we pass upon him, nor condemn him, but by lawful judgment of his peers, or by the law of the land. We will sell to no man, we will not deny or defer to any man either justice or right.[12]

While of little legal importance today – for much of the original Magna Carta has been repealed – the document has symbolic value as an early assertion of the limits of monarchical power and the rights of individuals.

The Petition of Right 1628

The Petition of Right 1628 arose as a result of *Darnel's Case* (the *Five Knights's Case*)[13] in which the defendants had been convicted and imprisoned as a result of refusing to pay a loan imposed – a forced loan – by King Charles I.[14] The Petition forbade such loans, taxes and other monetary demands without the consent of Parliament. The Petition, while still in force, was superseded by the Bill of Rights 1689.

The Bill of Rights 1689

The background

The Bill of Rights 1689 is of greater contemporary constitutional importance than the Magna Carta and the Petition of Right. The source of the Bill of Rights lies, in large measure, in the tensions between Roman Catholicism and the State, originating with the conflict between the Holy See of Rome and Henry VIII.[15] The Succession Act, Act of Supremacy and the Treason Act 1534 had established the supremacy of the king as head of the Church of England and destroyed formal papal authority in England. Catholicism did not die out, but over the next 150 years, suspicion and fear of 'popery' remained high at a

---

11   See *op cit*, Holt, fn 8, Chapter I.
12   *Op cit*, Holt, fn 8, Chapter XXIX.
13   (1627) 3 St Tr 1.
14   1625–49.
15   1491–1547.

public level. The death of Charles II[16] in 1685 heralded the succession of James II, an avowed Roman Catholic, who nevertheless publicly declared himself bound 'to preserve this government both in Church and State as it is now by law established'.[17] Despite such assurances, in subsequent years James II strove to remove discrimination against Catholics and to place Catholics in prominent public administrative offices at both central and local level. Prominent Anglicans, dismayed by James's promotion of Catholicism, entered into negotiations with William of Orange, the Protestant husband of James's daughter Mary, with a view to their seizing the throne. In the absence of a male heir, Mary was next in line to the English Crown. However, in 1688, James's wife gave birth to a son, thus providing a Catholic heir. In July of that year, James dissolved Parliament. William of Orange landed in England with his army on 5 November 1688 and James II fled the country, landing in France in December 1688.

The 'Convention' Parliament

William summoned an assembly of peers, previous Members of Parliament and aldermen of London. William, not yet king, had no legal power to summon the assembly, and the assembly itself had no legal powers. The assembly advised Prince William to summon a Convention of peers and commoners. The Convention, meeting in January 1689, declared that James II had subverted the constitution and abdicated and that, accordingly, the throne was 'vacant'. The House of Lords subsequently agreed with the Convention, and on 13 February 1689, the Crown was offered to William and Mary. The Convention then proceeded to declare itself to be the Parliament of England. The Parliament had no authority to issue such a declaration: the only lawful manner in which a Parliament can come into being is by Writ of Summons from the Crown, and it is for this reason that the Convention Parliament is widely regarded as having no law making powers:

> ... it is difficult for a lawyer to regard the Convention Parliament as a lawfully constituted assembly. By whom was it summoned? Not by a king of England, but by a Prince of Orange. Even if we go back three centuries, we find no precedent ... If, when the Convention met, it was no Parliament, its own act could not turn it into a Parliament. The act which declares it to be a Parliament depends for its validity on the assent of William and Mary. The validity of that assent depends on their being king and queen; but how do they come to be king and queen? Indeed, this statute very forcibly brings out the difficulty – an incurable defect.[18]

---

16 1630–85.

17 Quoted in Lockyer, R, *Tudor and Stuart Britain 1472–1714*, 2nd edn, 1985, Harlow: Longman, p 351.

18 Maitland, FW, *The Constitutional History of England*, 1908, Cambridge: CUP, pp 284–85.

Nevertheless, the Convention Parliament passed the Bill of Rights, which incorporated the Declaration of Right which set out the terms under which the Crown was offered to William and Mary. The Convention Parliament continued in being until 1690 when a new Parliament, correctly summoned by the Crown, met.

William and Mary's accession was not to be unconditional.[19] The Declaration of Right sought to resolve the actual and potential tensions between Crown and Parliament, Church and State. The terms of the Bill of Rights marked a sharp alteration in the balance of power between Crown and Parliament – in Parliament's favour.[20]

The substance of the Bill of Rights

The principal provisions of contemporary importance are:

Article I	... the pretended power of suspending ... or executing laws by the Crown without Parliamentary consent is illegal;
Article IV	... the levying of money for use of the Crown under the prerogative without Parliamentary consent is illegal;
Article VI	... the raising or keeping of an army in peacetime without Parliamentary consent is illegal;
Article VIII	... elections of Members of Parliament ought to be free;
Article IX	... freedom of speech and debates in proceedings in Parliament ought not to be impeached or questioned in any court or place out of Parliament;
Article X	... excessive bail ought not to be required, nor excessive fines imposed, nor cruel and unusual punishments inflicted;
Article XI	... jury trial is available; and
Article XIII	... for the redress of grievances, Parliament ought to meet frequently.

Subsequent to the Bill of Rights – and to give effect to its provisions – the Crown and Parliament Recognition Act 1689[21] gave statutory force to the Bill of Rights, and the Meeting of Parliament Act 1694[22] provided that Parliament must be summoned to meet at least once in three years.

---

19   As had been that of Charles II in 1660.
20   1 Will & Mar sess 2 c 2. In Scotland, the Claim of Right 1689.
21   2 Will & Mar c 1.
22   6 and 7 Will & Mar c 2.

The Act of Settlement 1700[23]

The Act of Settlement 1700[24] clarified the line of succession to the throne. The Act also provided for security of tenure for the judiciary 'during good behaviour',[25] thus ending the power of the Crown to dismiss judges at will. In relation to succession to the throne, the Act tied the succession to Protestant heirs, thus prohibiting accession to the throne by persons who are Roman Catholics, or who marry a Roman Catholic:

> ... that the Crown and regall government of the kingdoms of England, France and Ireland and the dominions thereunto belonging should be and continue to your Majestie and the said late Queen during the joynt lives of your Majesty and the said Queen and to the survivor and after the decease of your Majesty and of the said Queen the said crown and regall government should be and remain to the heirs of the body of the said late Queen and for default of such issue to her royal Highness the Princess Ann of Denmark and the heirs of her body and for default of such issue to the heirs of the body of your Majesty.

> And it was thereby further enacted that all and every person and persons that then were or afterwards should be reconciled to or shall hold communion with the see or church of Rome or should professe the popish religion or marry a papist should be excluded and are by that Act made for ever incapable to inherit possess or enjoy the crown and government of this realm and Ireland and the dominions thereunto belonging or any part of the same or to have use or exercise any regall power authority or jurisdiction within the same and in all and every such case and cases the people of these realms shall be and are thereby absolved of their allegiance and that the said crown and government shall from time to time descend to and be enjoyed by such person or persons being protestants as should have inherited and enjoyed the same in case the said person or persons so reconciled holding communion professing or marrying as aforesaid were naturally dead.

As must be evident, the seventeenth century was a time of immense constitutional reform. The statutes of this era remain relevant today and will be discussed further in Chapter 6.

The Treaty of Union 1706[26]

The Treaty of Union also has enduring constitutional effect. The Treaty united England and Scotland under a single Parliament of Great Britain. Prior to the Treaty, each country enjoyed independent sovereign status. Scotland had its own Parliament and its own system of private law. Decades earlier, James VI,

---

23   10 Halsbury's Statutes, p 51.
24   12 and 13 Will 3 c 2.
25   On the independence of the judiciary, see Chapter 4.
26   See, further, Chapter 7.

king of Scotland and subsequently king of England,[27] had attempted but failed to bring about a union between Scotland and England. By the late seventeenth century, negotiations were continuing with a view to ending the historical conflicts between the two countries,[28] and the Treaty of Union represented the culmination of this process.

The major provisions of the Treaty of Union 1706

For current purposes, the most important provisions are:

Article I	That the two kingdoms of England and Scotland shall be united in one kingdom by the name of Great Britain;
Article II	That succession to the united throne be according to the Act of Settlement 1700;
Article III	That there be a single Parliament;
Article XVIII	That no alteration be made in laws which concern Scottish private rights except for the evident utility of the subjects; and
Article XVIX	That the Court of Session in Scotland remain 'in all time being as now constituted', and that lower courts remain subject to alteration in their powers by Parliament.

Further illustrations

Further statutes of major constitutional importance – and the list is by no means exhaustive – include the following:

(a) the Statute of Westminster 1931 gave statutory force to the conventions regulating relations between the sovereign United Kingdom Parliament and legislatures of the Dominions;

(b) His Majesty's Declaration of Abdication Act 1936[29] varied the succession to the throne established under the Act of Settlement 1700;

(c) the Regency Acts 1937–53 provided that if the Sovereign is under the age of 18, regal powers shall be exercised through a Regent appointed under the Acts;

(d) the Royal Titles Act 1953,[30] which founded a challenge from Scottish lawyers to its compatibility with the Act of Union,[31] provided that the

---

27 As James I (1603–25).

28 For a succinct account of the history, see *op cit*, Maitland, fn 18, pp 331–32.

29 1 Edw 8 and 1 Geo 6 c 3.

30 1 and 2 Eliz 2 c 9.

31 *MacCormick v Lord Advocate* 1953 SC 396. See, further, Chapter 7.

Sovereign may by Proclamation adopt such a style and titles as she may think fit;

(e) the European Communities Act 1972, as amended, together with the Treaties on European Union 1992 and 1997, regulate the United Kingdom's membership of the European Community and Union and will continue to have immense significance for the constitution of the United Kingdom;[32]

(f) the Treaty of Union with Ireland Act 1800, the Government of Ireland Act 1920, the Ireland Act 1949 and the Northern Ireland Constitution Act 1973 have all reflected the changing constitutional relationship between Ireland, Northern Ireland and the United Kingdom;[33]

(g) more recently, the Acts establishing a Scottish Parliament and Welsh Assembly and re-establishing a Northern Ireland Assembly will ensure greater regional involvement in legislation; and

(h) finally, the Human Rights Act 1998, which incorporates the rights enshrined in the European Convention on Human Rights and Freedoms into domestic law represents a fundamental change in the domestic protection of rights.

COMMON LAW SOURCES

Throughout history, the judiciary has, through case law, defined the relationship between the institutions of the State – the Crown, the executive, Parliament and the judiciary – and defined the relationship between the State and the individual. Nowadays, much interest focuses on the relationship between the law of the European Community and the domestic law of the United Kingdom and the manner in which the judges are able to accommodate the requirements of the law of the Community within domestic law.[34] As with statutory sources of the constitution, the entire study of constitutional and administrative law concerns the examination and analysis of judicial precedents, and it is thus impossible at this introductory stage to give more than a few seminal illustrations.

The Crown and the judiciary

Prior to the Act of Settlement 1700, which provided security of tenure for the senior judges, the king had power to dismiss judges at his pleasure.[35] For

32 See Chapters 8 and 9.
33 See, further, Chapter 2.
34 See Chapter 9.
35 See, further, Chapter 6.

example, when Coke CJ told King James I that monarchical power derived from the law alone,[36] and that the judges alone and not the king had the power to rule on the law, he was dismissed from the Bench.

Acts of Parliament are supreme

With the rise in Parliamentary supremacy in the seventeenth century, the role of the judges changed significantly, and it has long been accepted that the *dictum* of Coke CJ in *Dr Bonham's Case*, to the effect that the judges could declare an Act of Parliament void, does not – if indeed it ever did[37] – represent the law. The judiciary today has no power to question the validity of an Act of Parliament.[38]

Delegated powers

However, whilst Acts of Parliament are unchallengeable as to their validity, delegated or secondary legislation is not immune from such review.[39] Furthermore, the judges have the power to review the legality of acts of persons and organisations acting under powers conferred by Act of Parliament in order to ensure that they act *intra vires* the powers conferred by Parliament.[40]

Parliamentary privilege

In relation to the conduct of its business, Parliament claims many privileges and immunities.[41] As will be seen, judicial deference to Parliament extends to the judges declining jurisdiction over any matter of Parliamentary privilege, other than to rule whether or not a matter is in fact a matter of privilege. Article IX of the Bill of Rights 1689 confers the absolute privilege of freedom of speech in parliamentary proceedings. Accordingly, a Member of Parliament is free from any threat from the law of defamation by any person harmed by his exercise of free speech.[42]

---

36 *Case of Proclamations* (1611) 12 Co Rep 74.
37 See 4 Co Inst 36; Plucknett, TFT, '*Dr Bonham's Case* and judicial review' (1926) 40 Harv L Rev 30; Thorne, SE, '*Dr Bonham's Case*' (1938) 54 LQR 543.
38 *Edinburgh and Dalkeith Railway v Wauchope* (1842) 8 Cl & F 710; *Pickin v British Railways Board* [1974] AC 765. But see Chapters 7 and 9 on the position in relation to the law of the European Community.
39 See Chapters 7, 24 and 25.
40 See Chapters 5 and 25.
41 See Chapter 18.
42 See *Church of Scientology of California v Johnson-Smith* [1972] 1 QB 522; Mummery, DR, 'The privilege of freedom of speech in Parliament' (1978) 94 LQR 276; Leopold, PM, 'Freedom of speech in Parliament: its misuse and proposals for reform' [1981] PL 30.

The State and the individual

Domestic law

Traditionally, the United Kingdom had no Bill of Rights in so far as such a document provides a written source of protection for certain fundamental rights and freedoms.[43] In the absence of such guaranteed protection – protection which would prevail even against an Act of Parliament – the citizen remains dependent either upon ad hoc statutory provisions – such as the Habeas Corpus Acts,[44] the Race Relations Act 1976 or the Sex Discrimination Act 1975 – or upon judicial protection under the common law. The extent to which such protection is accorded to the individual is discussed in Chapters 19 to 21. By way of introductory illustration, the very differing cases of *Entick v Carrington*[45] and *Liversidge v Anderson*[46] may be cited. In the former case, the court ruled that a general warrant issued by a Home Secretary for the entry into private property and seizure of allegedly seditious material was contrary to law and amounted to a trespass to property. This bold assertion of judicial power to rule on the legality of acts of the executive and to control such acts is in stark contrast to the ruling in *Liversidge v Anderson*. Here, in the context of a challenge to the legality of detention without warrant under the order of the Home Secretary, the House of Lords held that the courts could not, in times of emergency, review the Home Secretary's belief that detention was justified. Such conflicting outcomes demonstrate that reliance on judicial protection from executive action, under common law, is by no means certain, let alone guaranteed. The Human Rights Act 1998, however, 'incorporated' the European Convention on Human Rights into domestic law, and now enables citizens to challenge the legality of government action against the provisions of the Convention. As will be discussed in Chapter 22, the Act does not empower the courts to challenge the *validity* of Acts of Parliament, but rather preserves Parliament's traditional sovereignty by empowering the courts to make declarations of the incompatibility of a statute with the Convention requirements. Thereafter, it is for the government and Parliament to change the law if it wishes to comply with the Convention requirements.

European Community law

Nowadays, the protection of individual rights in the United Kingdom must also be viewed in the context of Britain's membership of the European Community and Union.. Since accession to the European Community (and, now, European Union), the United Kingdom has been subject to the

---

43 See Chapter 22.
44 1679, 1816, 1862.
45 (1765) 19 St Tr 1019.
46 [1942] AC 206.

jurisdiction of the European Court of Justice[47] which has steadily expanded its jurisprudence to provide greater protection of individual rights. Whilst, for the most part, this is confined to the protection of equality and non-discrimination in fields of employment, it is clear that the European Court is committed to furthering the protection of other rights and freedoms.

NON-LEGAL SOURCES OF THE CONSTITUTION

Constitutional conventions

> The short explanation of the constitutional conventions is that they provide the flesh which clothes the dry bones of the law; they make the legal constitution work; they keep it in touch with the growth of ideas.[48]

Constitutional conventions form the most significant class of non-legal constitutional rules[49] A clear understanding of their nature, scope and manner of application is essential to the study of the United Kingdom's constitution. Conventions supplement the legal rules of the constitution and define the practices of the constitution. Conventions, as Jennings states, 'provide the flesh which clothes the dry bones of the law' and represent the 'unwritten maxims' of the constitution.[50] Conventions apply to virtually all aspects of the constitution, and for this reason it is, in part, unrealistic and unsatisfactory to attempt adequately to consider their role in a 'vacuum'. Nevertheless, given their central importance, conventions must be considered at this early stage, while bearing in mind that many and varied further illustrations will emerge throughout the course of study.

Conventions defined

Conventions are defined by AV Dicey[51] as:

> ... conventions, understandings, habits or practices which, though they may regulate the ... conduct of the several members of the sovereign power ... are not in reality laws at all since they are not enforced by the courts.

---

47 See Chapters 8 and 9.

48 Jennings, I (Sir), *The Law of the Constitution*, 5th edn, 1959, London: Hodder & Stoughton, pp 81–82.

49 See, *inter alia*, Dicey, AV, *Introduction to the Study of the Law of the Constitution*, 10th edn, 1959, London: Macmillan, Chapter 14; *ibid*, Jennings, Chapter 3; Marshall, G and Moodie, G, *Some Problems of the Constitution*, 5th edn, 1971, London: Hutchinson, Chapter 2; Marshall, G, *Constitutional Conventions*, 1984, Oxford: Clarendon, esp Chapters 1 and 13; Munro, CR, *Studies in Constitutional Law*, 1987, London: Butterworths, Chapter 3.

50 Mill, JS, *Representative Government* (1865), 1958, Indianapolis: Bobbs-Merrill, Chapter 5.

51 *Ibid*, Dicey, p clii.

Marshall and Moodie[52] offer an alternative definition:

> … rules of constitutional behaviour which are considered to be binding by and upon those who operate the constitution but which are not enforced by the law courts … nor by the presiding officers in the Houses of Parliament.

A number of important questions arise concerning these non-legal rules, namely:

(a) What are the characteristics of a conventional rule?

(b) What is the source or origin of the rule?

(c) In what manner are conventions distinguishable from laws?

(d) Who is bound by the conventional rules?

(e) What is the consequence of a breach of the rule?

(f) Does the distinction between law and convention really matter?

(g) What is the attitude of the courts to conventional rules?

(h) How do conventions change?

(i) How best can these rules be analysed and understood? and

(j) Should conventions be codified?

Each of these questions, many of which overlap, must be addressed and answered.

Conventions illustrated

Before turning attention to the task of further analysis, some examples of constitutional conventions will aid understanding. Each of these conventions will be discussed in greater detail later in this book:

(a) Acts of Parliament are technically enacted by the Queen in Parliament – the Crown, Commons and Lords. The Queen has the legal right to refuse to give the royal assent to Bills passed by the House of Commons and Lords. By convention, the Queen must assent to such Bills unless advised to the contrary by her government;[53]

(b) the Queen will appoint as Prime Minister the leader of the political party with the majority of seats in the House of Commons;[54]

(c) the Prime Minister must be a member of the House of Commons;[55]

---

52 *Op cit*, Marshall and Moodie, fn 49, pp 23–24.
53 See Chapter 6.
54 *Ibid*.
55 *Ibid*.

(d) the government must maintain the confidence of the House of Commons. If a 'vote of confidence' on a matter central to government policy is lost, the government must resign or advise the Queen to dissolve Parliament;[56]

(e) the Crown exercises its right to dissolve Parliament on the advice of ministers;[57]

(f) Ministers of the Crown are individually and collectively responsible to Parliament;[58]

(g) Ministers must be members of either the House of Commons or the House of Lords;[59]

(h) Parliament must be summoned to meet at least once a year;[60]

(i) judges shall not play an active part in political life;[61]

(j) Members of Parliament shall not criticise the judiciary;[62]

(k) the opinion of the law officers of the Crown is confidential; and[63]

(l) when speaking for the government in the House of Lords, the Lord Chancellor physically moves from the Woolsack which he occupies in his capacity as Lord Chancellor and Speaker of the House of Lords.

This list is not intended to be exhaustive, but is sufficient to give a flavour of the nature and scope of constitutional conventions.

The binding nature of conventions

The characteristics of conventions are suggested both by Dicey and by Marshall and Moodie. The latter authors correctly introduce the concept of a 'rule', and it is this concept which is central to our understanding and which requires further analysis. What is a rule? A rule may be defined as a statement prescribing the conduct which is required in a given situation and which imposes an obligation on those who are regulated by the rule.[64] The idea of obligation is of prime importance here, for if a person is under an obligation which is recognised by observers of the constitution, and that person fails to act in accordance with the obligation, then that failure will give rise to legitimate criticism which will invariably be phrased in terms of 'constitutionality'. To reiterate, the obligation imposes a standard of conduct

---

56 See Chapter 6.
57 *Ibid*.
58 See Chapter 11.
59 See Chapter 10.
60 See Chapter 14.
61 See Chapter 5.
62 *Ibid*.
63 See Chapter 11.
64 Hart, HLA, *The Concept of Law*, 1961, Oxford: Clarendon, pp 79–88.

which is expected to be followed. The obligation is 'normative': by that is meant that the rule is 'prescriptive' – that it dictates the appropriate form of action in a particular situation. As Sir Ivor Jennings states, conventions 'not only are followed but have to be followed'.[65]

Dicey's definition suggests that conventions are of the same quality as 'understandings, habits or practices'. This view is inaccurate in so far as none of these words conveys the idea of obligation – the normative (or prescriptive) – the idea of what ought to be done in particular circumstances.

Conventions distinguished from habits

Conventions are conceptually different from 'habits' or 'practices' in that these concepts do not prescribe or dictate what ought to happen but are merely descriptive of what in fact does happen. To offer a simple but possibly outdated example, consider the statement that 'the English drink tea in the afternoon'. Drinking tea is a habit: the statement is simply reflective of actual observable conduct. There is nothing in the statement which requires that conduct, or which states that it ought to happen. Accordingly, it is a descriptive and not a normative statement. If the English fail to drink tea in the afternoon, or drink coffee instead, that action is not going to give rise to any criticism because a mere habit imposes no obligation. The observation is a statement of what 'is', and not what 'ought to be'. There is no obligation imposed on the English to drink tea and hence no criticism will follow from failure to do so. It is very different with a breach of a constitutional convention, which will invariably give rise to adverse criticism. Conventions are thus distinguishable from habits.

Conventions distinguished from understandings

To what extent is Dicey correct in equating conventions with 'understandings'? Once more, it is helpful to resort to definitions. The word 'understanding' connotes a mutual agreement between relevant actors as to the pertinent subject matter, or the manner in which it is appropriate to respond or react to a given situation. As such, any understanding rests on a meeting of minds, and is capable of being the subject of *mis*understanding, as in cases where the actors, through a lack of understanding of the situation (or as a result of a differing interpretation of the situation), fail to be of 'one mind'. An 'understanding' may well be relied on by the parties, as are conventions. Understandings may also be brought about by some form of precedent conduct or mutual recognition: but this is not a prerequisite for their existence or nature. Most importantly, an understanding, while imposing some weak form of moral obligation will not, in the case of failure to comply with its

---

65   Jennings, I (Sir), *Cabinet Government*, 3rd edn, 1959, Cambridge: CUP, p 2.

terms, give rise to a sanction in the form of criticism of the same magnitude as that of a breach of a constitutional convention. The explanation for this lies in the fact that an understanding – as opposed to a convention – does not amount to a rule, and accordingly is not obligation-imposing to the same degree as a convention.

Conventions distinguished from practices

The concept of a practice remains for consideration. A practice may be defined as being 'a usual or customary action or proceeding'.[66] A practice, therefore, is the normal manner in which a person or body will react to a factual situation on the basis of some previous, or precedent, form of conduct. In everyday life – whether in commercial offices or in the professions of medicine or law – it is a commonplace assertion that 'it is our practice to do ...'. That statement conveys the message that past experience of doing something in a particular way is the correct way of proceeding, and that – unless there are justifiable reasons for not so doing – the practice will be adhered to. A practice, therefore, may be distinguished from a mere habit on the basis that it imports a notion of reflectiveness, the idea of the 'right' way of reacting to a situation. How, then, is a practice distinguishable from a convention? The borderline between the two is admittedly fine. It may be, however, that the correct dividing line is drawn on the basis of the concept of obligation and rule, and that it is legitimate to argue that whilst a practice imposes some form of weak obligation – and requires some justification for departure from the practice – the practice is no more than an emergent or potential convention and has not yet acquired the binding characteristic of a rule.

Conventions distinguished from laws

Conventions are distinguishable from laws in a number of important respects. First, the source of a legal rule is, for the most part, identifiable and certain. In searching for a legal rule, its source will normally be found within a judicial decision or within an Act of Parliament. Conventions are far less certain in their origins, and it may at times be difficult to see whether a particular form of conduct is, for example, one of practice or convention. Secondly, the core content of a legal rule will generally have a settled meaning. One often-cited example illustrates the point. In *The Concept of Law*,[67] Professor HLA Hart offers the example of the correct interpretation of the word 'vehicle' in a statute or delegated legislation.[68] A judge, interpreting the word within the context of a trial concerning an alleged violation of a bylaw prohibiting the

---

66 Adams, D (ed), *Collins English Dictionary*, 3rd edn, 1991, London: Collins, p 1221.
67 *Op cit*, Hart, fn 64, Chapter VII.
68 Eg, in local authority bylaws. See, further, Chapters 12, 24 and 25.

use of vehicles in a public park, will be clear, for example, that a motor car, van or armoured truck will fall within the meaning of the word 'vehicle'. But what of a skateboard or its successor, rollerblades? A skateboard shares some of the characteristics of the other examples given: a skateboard is a wheeled object and capable of conveying a person from point A to point B. Is it then a 'vehicle'? Professor Hart makes two important points here. The first point is that to make sense of the word 'vehicle', the word must be placed within its broader context. That is to say, the question must be asked: 'For what purpose was the rule devised?' In other words, can the judge provide an interpretation which is meaningful within the context of the legislature's intention?

The second point, of greater significance to this discussion, is that most words – legal or non-legal – have a 'core of certainty and penumbra of doubt',[69] and that while a motorised wheeled object designed for the carriage of persons and goods is clearly a vehicle, an object designed for purely recreational purposes may, or may not, subject to the court's interpretation of the purpose of the legislation, fall within the meaning of a particular word.

The foregoing discussion can be presented – albeit with recognition of overlaps between, and ambiguities in, the concepts – in the following tabular form:

	HABITS	UNDERSTANDINGS	PRACTICES	CONVENTIONS	LAWS
Regularity of conduct	yes	not necessarily	yes	yes	yes
Reflectiveness	no	yes	yes	yes	yes
Degree of obligation imposed	none	weak	strong	absolute	absolute
Sanction attending breach	none	justification required	justification required	charge of unconstitutional conduct	unlawful conduct

Summary of the meaning of constitutional conventions

A constitutional convention is a non-legal rule which imposes an obligation on those bound by the convention, breach or violation of which will give rise to legitimate criticism: and that criticism will generally take the form of an accusation of 'unconstitutional conduct'.

---

69 *Op cit*, Hart, fn 64, Chapter VII.

The source of conventions

The question concerning the source of the constitutional convention is in part interwoven with the characteristics of the convention. A conventional rule may be said to exist when a traditional practice has been consciously adopted and recognised by those who operate the constitution as the correct manner in which to act in a given circumstance. A practice will be seen to have become a convention at the point at which failure to act in accordance with it gives rise to legitimate criticism.

Sir Ivor Jennings once suggested that three questions must be asked in order to determine whether a convention exists.[70] First, are there any precedents for the convention? 'Mere practice', he tells us, 'is not enough. The fact that an authority has always behaved in a certain way is no warrant for saying that it ought to behave in that way'. What more, then, is required? According to Jennings, that turns on the normativity of the practice:

> ... if the authority itself and those connected with it believe that they ought to do so [behave in a certain way], then the convention does exist ... Practice alone is not enough. It must be normative.[71]

Finally, Jennings argues that neither practice nor precedent is sufficient. In addition, there must be a reason for the rule: '... the creation of a convention must be due to the reason of the thing because it accords with the prevailing political philosophy.'[72] This point is supported by JP Mackintosh. Accepting Viscount Esher's view that 'precedent, like analogy, is rarely conclusive',[73] Mackintosh argues that precedents have 'no independent existence or validity'. Rather, the precedent represents 'a correct decision or action in certain political circumstances'. Accordingly:

> ... searching for a precedent is really looking for a case where previous exponents of the constitution have solved a similar difficulty in an approved fashion.[74]

Situations will arise for which there is no apparent precedent and where accordingly there is no firm convention regulating a situation. Mackintosh illustrates this phenomenon by reference to the dilemma in which George V found himself in 1923 when the general election failed to produce a clear majority for any one party, and thus left the King with a real choice as to who should be appointed Prime Minister:

---

70 *Op cit*, Dicey, fn 49, Chapter III.
71 *Op cit*, Dicey, fn 49, p 135.
72 *Op cit*, Dicey, fn 49, p 136.
73 Esher, RBB, *The Influence of King Edward: And Essays on Other Subjects*, 1915, London: John Murray, p 167.
74 Mackintosh, JP, *The British Cabinet*, 3rd edn, 1977, London: Stevens, p 13.

... the King noted that 'there are really no precedents for the present situation. I must use my own judgment as each case arises'.[75]

Whether the outcome is deemed to be correct or not will depend on the acceptability of that action in light of current political practice.

With this brief discussion in mind, it can be said that, while the meaning and scope of conventions frequently display a lack of certainty, it does not necessarily follow that this is a conclusively distinguishing characteristic from rules of law which may also display uncertainty as to their meaning. Nonetheless, it must be conceded that the requirements of some conventional rules are often difficult to discern. Sir Ivor Jennings cites Mr Stanley Baldwin:[76]

> The historian can tell you probably perfectly clearly what the constitutional practice was at any given period in the past, but it would be very difficult for a living writer to tell you at any given period in his lifetime what the constitution of the country is in all respects, and for this reason, that almost at any given moment ... there maybe one practice called 'constitutional' which is falling into desuetude and there may be another practice which is creeping into use but is not yet constitutional.[77]

Who is bound by constitutional conventions?

The question as to who is bound by the rules, for the most part, gives rise to little practical difficulty. For example, it is a convention that the doctrine of collective responsibility of ministers to Parliament be observed. The convention requires that all members of Cabinet, the inner core of government, must speak in public with a united voice, and further, in order to reinforce public confidence in government, Cabinet members may not disclose the contents of Cabinet discussions. This issue will be discussed in detail subsequently in Chapter 11; for current illustrative purposes, it is sufficient to indicate the doubts which have been voiced as to the scope of this convention. Members of Cabinet are appointed predominantly from the elected House of Commons, but may also be appointed from the House of Lords. In this manner, members of Cabinet are made accountable to Parliament, and through Parliament to the electorate. Does the convention, for instance, require that not only members of Cabinet – the Prime Minister and 16 to 20 senior ministers – but also junior ministers[78] and their Parliamentary Private Secretaries[79] follow the decisions taken in Cabinet and refrain from speaking against them? That would appear to be the consensus view, but no

---

75 *Op cit*, Mackintosh, fn 74, p 13.
76 Prime Minister 1912–24, 1924–29, 1935–37.
77 *Op cit*, Jennings, fn 65, p 12, cited from 261 HC Deb 5s, 531.
78 Ministers who are not in Cabinet.
79 Elected members of Parliament on the most junior rung of the ministerial ladder.

definitive rule exists. For the most part, however, it is clear that the conventional rules are understood by those actors on the constitutional stage.

For collective Cabinet responsibility to be a reality, it is essential that there be full and frank discussion between its members and – in order that consensus appears to exist – that decisions are collectively reached. The doctrine was put under much strain during Mrs Thatcher's government.[80] Professor Peter Hennessy has observed that:

> Mrs Thatcher moved into Downing Street and subjected the conventions of Cabinet government to their greatest hammering since David Lloyd George refashioned the Cabinet system at the height of the First World War.[81]

During Mrs Thatcher's premiership, two practices emerged.[82] The first was that increasing use was made of decision making by a small group of Cabinet members, an 'inner Cabinet', whose decisions were then, under the convention of collective responsibility, made binding of all other members, even though they had not participated in the decision making process. The second practice was that the Prime Minister took advice on financial and economic policy from an economist who was neither a member of Cabinet nor even a Member of Parliament. Accordingly, a non-elected and democratically unaccountable individual was involved in decision making with the Prime Minister, whose decision – provided that she could secure the support of Cabinet – would bind all ministers and others outside the Cabinet but holding government office.[83] One effect of this practice was to reduce the power and influence of the then Chancellor of the Exchequer.[84] The constitutional convention of collective responsibility is silent as to a situation such as this, and doubts were expressed as to the propriety of the Prime Minister's conduct.[85]

The effects of breaching constitutional conventions

The consequences which flow from a breach of a conventional rule is both a simple and a complex issue. If – as a starting point for discussion – the consequence of breaking a rule of law is examined, two basic points must be recognised. The first point is that a breach of law normally, but not invariably, leads to enforcement of the rule by the courts. The second point is that when a rule of law is breached, the rule remains valid and in force, unless repealed by

---

80 1979–89.

81 Hennessy, P, *Cabinet*, 1986: Oxford: Blackwells, p viii.

82 Neither practice was original, but Mrs Thatcher made notably more use of them than had previous Prime Ministers.

83 Non-Cabinet ministers, junior ministers and Parliamentary Private Secretaries

84 Then Nigel Lawson.

85 Partly in consequence of the Prime Minister's style of government, the Chancellor of the Exchequer resigned: see, further, Chapter 11.

Parliament or overruled by the judges. With conventional rules, the situation is very different. Being non-legal rules, there is no question of a breach of convention being enforced by the courts: the courts do not have the jurisdiction to enforce conventional rules, although they may give recognition to them.[86] However, it is also the case, as Dicey argued, that breach of a convention may lead to a breach of law. The most often cited example offered is that if Parliament, in breach of convention, did not meet annually, the consequence would be that money granted on an annual basis by Parliament for the maintenance of the armed forces would not be forthcoming. Accordingly, maintenance of the army would become unlawful by virtue of Article VI of the Bill of Rights 1689, which provides that the raising and keeping of an army in peacetime, without Parliament's consent, is unlawful. Such consequences are the exception. For the most part, the consequence of violating a conventional rule is political rather than legal.

That said, it is not possible to offer a single consequence. Much will turn on the particular convention 'broken', the extent of the 'breach' and the political mood of the country at the time. Conventions are obeyed because of the potential political difficulties which would arise if a firmly established convention was departed from without constitutional justification.

Two introductory illustrations of the very differing effects of breaching conventional rules are provided by the doctrine of collective ministerial responsibility (discussed more fully in Chapter 11) and the House of Lords (discussed more fully in Chapter 17).

Collective ministerial responsibility

The doctrine of collective ministerial responsibility provides an example of the uncertainties entailed in the scope and binding nature of conventional rules. In two situations the doctrine has been 'waived' in order to respond effectively to political circumstances. In 1932, a coalition government was in office.[87] Following Cabinet disagreements over economic policy, the government adopted an 'agreement to differ', whereby members of Cabinet were free to express their divergent views both in Parliament and in public. Within months, the dissident members resigned from the Cabinet and collective responsibility was reinstated. In 1975, the Labour government was divided as to the benefits of continued membership of the European Community. It was decided that the matter should be put to the electorate in a referendum. The Cabinet itself was deeply divided on the question and the Prime Minister decided to 'lift' the convention of collective responsibility in order to facilitate full and free public debate. Thus, a convention was set aside

---

86   *Attorney General v Jonathan Cape Ltd* [1976] 1 QB 752; *Manuel v Attorney General* [1983] Ch 77.

87   See *op cit*, Marshall, fn 49, Chapter 4; see, further, Chapter 11.

for a particular purpose, for a defined period of time and for a specific matter. The convention remained effective in respect of other matters before the Cabinet, and upon resolution of the issue, the convention was fully reinstated.[88] No adverse political consequences flowed from this, despite criticisms that such a move was unconstitutional. It is arguable whether this action represented a breach of convention at all, but it was clearly a departure from normal constitutional practice. Above all, these situations demonstrate the point that conventions can be adjusted, under certain circumstances which are undefined, to suit the exigencies of a particular situation.

The House of Lords 1908–10

A very different consequence followed a breach of convention by the House of Lords in 1908–10.[89] Prior to the Parliament Act 1911, one major conventional rule regulated the relationship between the House of Lords and the House of Commons in legislative matters and most particularly in financial matters: namely, that the Lords would ultimately give way to the will of the elected House. This convention broke down in 1908 when the House of Lords rejected the Finance Bill of the Commons. After a deadlock between the two Houses, and a threat by the King to 'flood' the House of Lords with sufficient new peers to secure a majority for the Bill, the government introduced the Parliament Bill 1911. The Parliament Act, which will be looked at in detail in Chapter 17, provided that the House of Lords would no longer enjoy equal powers to approve or reject legislative proposals and that its power would be restricted to a power to delay legislation subject to strict time limits.[90] It can be seen from this that where the breach of a convention is deemed to be sufficiently grave, Parliament can – in the exercise of its sovereign power – place a convention on a statutory basis.

Further illustrations will present themselves throughout the course of this book: conventional rules are of such fundamental importance that they regulate virtually every aspect of constitutional law. The main point to be understood here is that breaches of conventions have no automatic or defined ramifications.

The differing importance of individual conventions

A related factor which should also be understood is that not all conventions are of equal certainty or importance, and it is in part for this reason that the consequences of a breach will vary. For example, in legal terms, the right to

---

88 The referendum produced a vote in favour of continued membership, although the government had indicated that, in any event, it would not be bound by the result.

89 See Jennings, I (Sir), *Parliament*, 2nd edn, 1969, Cambridge: CUP, Chapter 12.4.

90 Money Bills, one month; non-Money Bills, two years over three Parliamentary sessions.

assent or to refuse to assent to Bills passed by Parliament rests with the Crown. However, by convention, the Crown must assent to Bills passed by Parliament whenever so advised by the Prime Minister. So settled is the convention that the Crown must assent to Bills passed by Parliament that it is difficult to foresee circumstances under which it would be broken.[91] Perhaps, a political situation could present itself where a Bill had been duly passed by Parliament and where the government had a change of heart and, despite parliamentary opposition, refused to present the Bill for assent. Would this represent a breach of convention? Arguably not, for the convention requires that the monarch give assent on the advice of her government. A situation such as this would undoubtedly cause a political furore; but it is doubtful that it would represent unconstitutional conduct on the part of the government, and still less so by the Crown. It could also be asked, speculatively, what the position would be if a Bill was duly passed by Parliament, the Bill was presented for the royal assent and refused on the basis that public opinion was so firmly set against the Bill that to assent would amount to defeating the rights of the electorate. Such a situation raises some fundamental questions about democracy and the relationship between the electorate and the elected government. Geoffrey Marshall questions whether the power to refuse assent to legislation is 'now a dead letter', and states that, 'under present constitutional arrangements, it may well be so',[92] while recognising that the issue is not closed.

At the other end of the spectrum of the certainty of conventions and their meaning, is the doctrine of individual ministerial responsibility.[93] In essence, individual ministerial responsibility requires that ministers of the Crown are accountable to Parliament, and through Parliament to the electorate, for their personal conduct and for the conduct of their departments.[94] The doctrine is expressed in practical terms at Parliamentary Question Time, in debates, and in committee proceedings, whereby Parliament ensures that ministers explain and, if necessary, defend their actions.[95] In theory, if a minister's personal conduct falls below the high standard required of public figures, he or she should resign. Equally, if the government department under a minister's authority is found to have misused or mismanaged its powers, it is the minister who takes the responsibility in Parliament. If the matter is of sufficient gravity and the minister loses the support of his party and Prime Minister, he or she may be forced to resign. But, as with responsibility for personal conduct, there are no hard and fast rules. There exist no fixed criteria from which it can be predicted in advance the consequence which will flow

91   See *op cit*, Marshall, fn 49, p 22.
92   *Op cit*, Marshall, fn 49, p 22.
93   For further discussion, see Chapter 11.
94   On the structure of government, see Chapter 10.
95   See Chapter 16.

from a breach of convention. In terms of consequences, this convention is the most uncertain of all conventional rules.

Evolution and change

Implicit in the above discussion lies the answer to a further question: how do conventions change? It has been seen that conventions come into being, unlike legal rules, when a habit or practice becomes so established that it imposes obligations on those to whom it applies, and takes on the characteristics of a rule. And so it is with changes in conventions. A convention may change with changing circumstances: individual ministerial responsibility is a prime example of this feature of conventions. Conventions may adapt to meet particular needs, as with collective responsibility in relation to the European Community in 1975, discussed above. Conventions may be breached and placed on a statutory basis, as with the House of Lords in 1911. A legal rule has a relatively fixed and certain quality while in existence. If a legal rule is changed, either by judicial decision or by Parliament, the previous rule will be superseded by the new: it will 'go out with a bang'. The same cannot be said of conventions. For the most part, they evolve, adapt in amoeba-like fashion to meet the constitutional needs of the time. It is for this reason that they present the student of the constitution with such a fascinating challenge.

The courts and conventions

Given that conventional rules are non-legal rules, the attitude of the courts towards constitutional conventions is inevitably different from their attitude to legal rules. The courts do not have jurisdiction to adjudicate upon conventions. This is not to say that the court must take no cognisance of conventional rules, but rather, as Dicey asserted, conventions are not 'court enforceable'. The courts will give recognition to conventions, although they are rarely called upon to do so. Two cases are illustrative. The first is that of *Attorney General v Jonathan Cape Ltd.*[96] In 1976, the executors of the late Richard Crossman, a former Cabinet minister, decided to proceed with publication of the diaries he had kept while in government. The diaries included records of Cabinet discussions which, under the doctrine of collective ministerial responsibility, may never be revealed other than under the conditions specified by law or on the authority of the Cabinet Secretary. The government sought an injunction to restrain publication on the basis that Cabinet meetings are, by convention, confidential and that the diaries, accordingly, represented a breach of confidentiality.

This litigation required that the court recognise the convention, and it did so. However, having no jurisdiction over conventional rules, the court could

---

96   [1976] 1 QB 752.

not enforce the convention. The court ruled in favour of the government in relation to the doctrine of confidentiality. In the event, however, the court declined to suppress 'secrets' which were over 10 years old. The court ruled that, unless national security[97] was involved, an eight to 10 year embargo was the maximum period that such material would be protected.

Lord Widgery CJ recited the opposing arguments:

> The Attorney General contends that all Cabinet papers and discussions are *prima facie* confidential, and that the court should restrain any disclosure thereof if the public interest in concealment outweighs the public interest in a right to free publication. The Attorney General further contends that, if it is shown that the public interest is involved, he has the right and duty to bring the matter before the court.

> The defendants' main contention is that, whatever the limits of the convention of joint Cabinet responsibility may be, there is no obligation enforceable at law to prevent the publication of Cabinet papers and proceedings, except in extreme cases where national security is involved. In other words, the defendants submit that the confidential character of Cabinet papers and discussion is based on a true convention as defined in the evidence of Professor Wade, namely, an obligation founded in conscience only. Accordingly, the defendants contend that publication of these diaries is not capable of control by any order of this court.[98]

In reaching judgment, the Lord Chief Justice evaluated the doctrine of collective responsibility, finding that there was 'overwhelming evidence that the doctrine ... is generally understood and practised and equally strong evidence that it is on occasion ignored'.[99] He recognised also that the Attorney General's submissions as to the duty of confidence owed by ministers to the Crown were correct. Notwithstanding that acceptance, the Lord Chief Justice opined that there was no one dominant rule to be applied to the situation. Three factors had to be weighed in the balance, and in order to succeed, the Attorney General had to establish three matters:

(a) that such publication would be a breach of confidence;

(b) that the public interest requires that the publication be restrained; and

(c) that there are no other facts of the public interest contradictory of and more compelling than that relied upon.

Moreover, the court, when asked to restrain such a publication, must closely examine the extent to which relief is necessary to ensure that restrictions are not imposed beyond the strict requirement of public need.[100]

The injunction was refused.

---

97 See Chapter 23.
98 [1976] 1 QB 752, p 765.
99 *Ibid*, p 756.
100 *Ibid*, p 755.

In 1982, in the Canadian case of *Reference re Amendment of the Constitution of Canada*,[101] detailed consideration was given to the relationship between law and convention. The principal question for decision by the Supreme Court of Canada was whether, as a matter of law, the constitution of Canada could be amended without the consent of the Provinces. A second question was whether the consent of the Provinces was required as a matter of convention. The British North America Act 1867 created the Dominion of Canada and set out the legislative and executive powers of the provincial and federal legislatures. Amendment to the 1867 Act was possible only by a further Act of the Westminster Parliament. At that time, the Statute of Westminster 1931[102] provided, *inter alia,* that the United Kingdom Parliament would not legislate for a Dominion 'unless it is declared in that Act that that Dominion has requested, and consented to, the enactment thereof'.[103] Section 7 of the Statute, however, prohibited changes to the British North America Act 1867, which affected the competence of provincial or federal legislatures. In 1949, the United Kingdom Parliament passed the British North America (No 2) Act, which gave substantial powers of amendment to the 1867 Act to the Canadian Federal Parliament. However, the power conferred was not absolute, and the Canadian Parliament lacked the competence to enact amendments altering the distribution of powers between the respective legislatures without the request and consent of the provincial legislatures. One of the principles intended to regulate amendments to the constitution, agreed by all the Provinces and set out in a Canadian White Paper in 1965, stated that:

> ... the Canadian Parliament will not request an amendment directly affecting federal-provincial relationships without prior consultation and agreement with the Provinces. This principle did not emerge as early as others but came in 1907, and particularly since 1930, has gained increasing recognition and acceptance. The nature and the degree of provincial participation in the amending process, however, have not lent themselves to easy definition.

It was argued by the Provinces that the 'request and consent' declaration required under the Statute of Westminster meant the 'request and consent' of both the Dominion and the Provinces if the Act were one affecting provincial or federal competence.

By a majority, the Canadian Supreme Court – adopting Jennings's test for the existence of a convention – recognised the constitutional convention that the Canadian Parliament would not request the Queen to lay before the United Kingdom Parliament an Act to amend the constitution of Canada in a manner affecting federal-provincial relationships and their respective powers and rights without first obtaining the agreement of the Provinces.

---

101 (1982) 125 DLR (3d) 1.
102 See, further, Chapter 7.
103 Statute of Westminster 1931, s 4.

Nevertheless, the court went on to hold that the Diceyan distinction between convention and law remained and that the court could not accordingly go beyond recognition of the convention and enforce it. Judicial approval was given to Professor Colin Munro's view that:

> The validity of conventions cannot be the subject of proceedings in a court of law. Reparation for breach of such rules will not be effected by any legal sanction. There are no cases which contradict these propositions. In fact, the idea of a court enforcing a mere convention is so strange that the question hardly arises.
>
> If, in fact, laws and conventions are different in kind, as is my argument, then an accurate and meaningful picture of the constitution may only be obtained if this distinction is made. If the distinction is blurred, analysis of the constitution is less complete; this is not only dangerous for the lawyer, but less than helpful to the political scientist.[104]

By a majority, the Supreme Court ruled that consent of the Provinces was not required by law and, again by a majority, that consent was required by convention, but that the convention could not be enforced by a court of law. The court declared that:

> The main purpose of constitutional conventions is to ensure that the legal framework of the Constitution will be operated in accordance with the prevailing constitutional values or principles of the period.
>
> Being based on custom and precedent, constitutional conventions are usually unwritten rules ...
>
> The conventional rules of the constitution present one striking peculiarity. In contradistinction to the laws of the constitution, they are not enforced by the courts. One reason for this situation is that, unlike common law rules, conventions are not judge-made rules. They are not based on judicial precedents but on precedents established by the institutions of government themselves. Nor are they in the nature of statutory commands which it is the function and duty of the courts to obey and enforce. Furthermore, to enforce them would mean to administer some formal sanction when they are breached. But, the legal system from which they are distinct does not contemplate formal sanctions for their breach.
>
> It should be borne in mind, however, that, while they are not laws, some conventions may be more important than some laws. Their importance depends on that of the value or principle which they are meant to safeguard. Also, they form an integral part of the constitution of the constitutional system.
>
> ... constitutional conventions plus constitutional law equal the total constitution of the country.

---

104 Munro, C, 'Laws and conventions distinguished' (1975) 91 LQR 224, p 228.

Is the distinction between law and convention important?

Both Sir Ivor Jennings and John Mackintosh have suggested that the distinction between conventions and laws is ultimately of little significance. In *The Law and the Constitution*, Jennings asserts that:

> ... there is no distinction of substance or nature. The conventions are like most fundamental rules of any constitution in that they rest essentially upon general acquiescence.[105]

In *The British Cabinet*, John Mackintosh argues that:

> There is a distinction between law and convention both from the view of the practical politician and the student of government, but in the long term development of the constitution, it is of no great importance. Both rest on the necessities of political life. Laws can be repealed or conventions changed if this is found to be desirable. The real difference between law and convention is just that there is no formal procedure for enacting or enforcing conventions, though some conventions (for example, the monarch shall not veto laws passed by both Houses; the Prime Minister shall resign if he is defeated on a major issue in the Commons) are as important as any laws and perhaps even more difficult to alter.[106]

Such views, while having merit from a political perspective, are overly dismissive from a legal, constitutional standpoint. The significant difference between laws and conventions is well demonstrated in both *Attorney General v Jonathan Cape Ltd*[107] and *Reference re Amendment of the Constitution of Canada*.[108] In both cases, the lack of a legal remedy is explained by the strict distinction between law and convention, and by the courts' refusal to go beyond recognition of the convention to enforcement thereof.[109]

Should conventions be codified?

One question asked earlier was whether or not constitutional conventions should be codified. Again, no straightforward or simple answer to this question presents itself. Much will turn on the perception of the value of the status quo. Much also turns on the constitutional implications of attempting to provide a comprehensive, binding code of constitutional conventions.

---

105 *Op cit*, Jennings, fn 48, p 117.

106 *Op cit*, Mackintosh, fn 74, p 12.

107 [1976] 1 QB 752.

108 (1982) 125 DLR (3d) 1, and see *First Report of the Foreign Affairs Committee*, HC 42 (1980–81), London: HMSO.

109 For a strong, if controversial, argument against this orthodox position, see Allan, TRS, 'Law, convention, prerogative: reflections prompted by the Canadian constitutional case' [1986] CLJ 305.

The Australian experiment

In Australia, a constitutional crisis in 1975 contributed to the experiment in codification of conventions into an authoritative but non-legally binding text. The crisis involved the prerogative power of the Crown in the person of the Governor General to dismiss the Prime Minister and appoint a caretaker Prime Minister on the condition of ensuring the passage of financial legislation and the holding of a general election. One outcome of the crisis – in which the inherent vagueness of the conventional rules was revealed – was formal consideration of the 'codification' of conventions, albeit in a non-legal form. During the crisis, conventions had been 'creatively interpreted and ignored in a successful attempt to unseat the Labour government during the depths of an international recession'.[110] In 1983, a plenary session of the Constitutional Convention adopted a set of 34 practices which were to be 'recognised and declared' as conventions of the Australian constitution. Among those 'recognised' were the powers of the Crown in relation to the Governor General, and his powers in relation to the dismissal of ministers and powers over Parliament, and the relationship between the Prime Minister and the Governor General in relation to the dissolution of Parliament.[111]

Professor Charles Sampford has analysed comprehensively the merits and demerits of the codification of conventions.[112] Among the many unanswered questions raised are the following. Under what authority did the Constitutional Convention act? What is the effect of the resolution? Is it merely declaratory of the existing rules? If there is a conflict with the restatement and actual practice, which should be authoritative? Professor Sampford contends that there exist three possibilities here. If the code is followed in preference to conventional practice, then the codification goes beyond clarification and becomes a source of the rules themselves. This raises the question as to 'why should the old rules and old sources give way to the new?'.[113] The second approach is that the 'declaration' has whatever force the constitutional actors accord to it: it would be absurd if the declaration were to have no authority. Thirdly, it could be argued that the declaration is merely evidence of the rule. This latter possibility, however, is unsatisfactory in so far as the declaration was intended to be 'sole and conclusive evidence for the existence of the recognised convention. This effectively makes the Constitutional Convention a new source for conventions'.[114] Furthermore, what is the position where a convention was agreed to only by a small

---

110 Sampford, CJG, '"Recognize and declare": an Australian experiment in codifying constitutional conventions' (1987) 7 OJLS 369.

111 A previous convention in 1983 had adopted resolutions relating to the conventions regulating the powers of the Queen and the Governor General.

112 *Ibid*, Sampford.

113 *Ibid*, Sampford, p 385.

114 *Ibid*, Sampford, p 386.

majority? What then happens to its authority? To what extent will the new conventions be observed? What is the status of those pre-existing conventions which were not 'recognised and declared'? As can be seen, codification is – even if desirable – by no means a simple matter.

Conclusion

It is clear from the analysis thus far that conventions comprise a set of binding rules, non-legal in nature, which supplement and inform the legal rules of the constitution and which can adapt to meet changing circumstances. Viewed in that light, their primary importance lies in their flexibility. On the other hand, it may be argued cogently that for rules of such importance to be ill-defined, uncertain in application and unenforceable by the courts is, at best, anomalous, and at worst, a threat to the principle of government according to law.[115]

Further considerations intrude upon the discussion. It has been seen that conventions are flexible. In this feature lies much of their value, and it is to be doubted whether, in relation to such a dynamic organism as the constitution, it would be possible to identify, define and formalise conventions in such a manner both to provide a comprehensive code and to allow for subsequent constitutional development. It may prove to be the case that codification would stultify the growth of the constitution. On the other hand, such codification would undoubtedly provide greater insight into the rules regulating government and thereby act as some check on the power of government. Professor SA de Smith[116] states that codification of conventions would purchase certainty at the expense of flexibility, and this point must carry great weight in evaluating the desirability of codification.

The relationship between the government and the courts must also be weighed in the balance in this regard. It has been seen that the courts give recognition to, but cannot enforce, conventions. If the effect of codification were to give jurisdiction to the courts, this would represent a very real and problematic shift in the balance of authority and power between the government and the courts. In Chapter 5, the doctrine of the separation of powers is considered in detail. Sufficient has been said by way of introduction for it to be apparent that if the courts were to be given jurisdiction to adjudicate upon and enforce, by way of legal sanction, the conventional rules of the constitution, this would impinge greatly upon the concept of the separation of powers.

For these reasons, the loss of flexibility and the separation of powers doctrine, it can be argued that conventions should not be codified.

---

115 On the rule of law, see Chapter 4.

116 de Smith, SA and Brazier, R, *Constitutional and Administrative Law*, 8th edn, 1998, London: Penguin, Chapter 2.

The royal prerogative

The prerogative powers of the Crown are those powers which arise out of the common law which are unique to the Crown. Two definitions may be given by way of introduction. To Dicey,[117] the prerogative powers were 'the residue of arbitrary and discretionary powers legally left in the hands of the Crown' which, being exercised by the government in the name of the Crown entails 'every act which the executive government can do without the authority of an Act of Parliament'.

Blackstone[118] offers a more limited definition:

> ... that special pre-eminence which the King hath over and above all persons, and out of the ordinary course of the common law ... And ... only applied to those rights and capacities which the King enjoys in contradistinction to others.

The prerogative will be discussed in detail in Chapter 6.

The law of the European Union and Community

The law of the European Union and Community represents an increasingly significant source of constitutional law. By acceding to the European Community, and subsequently the Union, the United Kingdom has undertaken the obligation to accept the law of the Community. To understand the constitutional implications of membership of the European Union, it is necessary to understand the scope of the Treaties and the law making institutions of the Community, and the manner in which laws are made and enter into force within the legal systems of the Member States. It is also necessary to understand clearly the relationship between the law of the Community and domestic law and the question as to which law has supremacy should a conflict between them arise. Under the traditional doctrine of parliamentary sovereignty,[119] the law of the United Kingdom Parliament alone has sovereign power. The perception of the European Court of Justice – the highest court of the European Community – is much different. As will be seen, the European Court has long asserted the supremacy of Community law[120] over the laws of Member States, thus providing a fertile source for constitutional speculation about the Diceyan theory of sovereignty. The law of the Community is also making an ever-increasing impact on the protection of individual rights under national law.[121]

---

117 *Op cit*, Dicey, fn 49, p 425.

118 Blackstone, W (Sir), *Commentaries on the Laws of England* (1765–69), Chicago: Chicago UP, p 239.

119 See Chapter 7.

120 *Costa v ENEL* [1964] CMLR 425.

121 See Chapters 8 and 9.

The law and custom of Parliament

Parliament being the sovereign legislative body has sole jurisdiction over its composition and procedure. Both of these aspects will be considered subsequently. It is sufficient here to note that, where Parliament has jurisdiction, it is exclusive and the courts will accordingly have no jurisdiction to rule on matters within Parliament's authority. This rule has implications for the doctrine of separation of powers and for parliamentary sovereignty. One important aspect of this area of the law is the privileges which Parliament claims, and the manner in which these are enforced. This topic will be considered in Chapter 18.

Authoritative works

Finally and in brief, mention should be made of the writings of eminent jurists such as Blackstone, Dicey, Jennings and later commentators to whose works the actors on the constitutional stage, including the judges, may make reference for elucidation of matters of constitutional law.

CHAPTER 3

THE EVOLUTION OF THE STRUCTURE OF THE UNITED KINGDOM

The United Kingdom comprises England, Wales, Scotland (which together comprise Great Britain) and Northern Ireland.[1] The Channel Islands and the Isle of Man while not forming part of the United Kingdom other than for the purposes of nationality law[2] are represented by the United Kingdom government in international affairs.

While it is correct to speak of the constitution of the United Kingdom, it should not be assumed that there is a single legal system within the constitutionally defined area. The English legal system extends to England and Wales. Scotland has its own system of private law which is distinct from English law. Equally, in Northern Ireland, there exists a quite distinct legal system. Nevertheless, it is the Westminster Parliament which has hitherto legislated for each jurisdiction, and been supreme or 'sovereign'. Nineteen ninety-eight brought change, with devolution of law making powers to a Scottish Parliament, a Northern Ireland Assembly and administrative powers to a Welsh Assembly. Each enjoys limited legislative powers, which must be considered alongside the legislative powers which remain with Westminster. The United Kingdom will remain in being: the object of devolution is to provide more representative and accountable regional government, and to strengthen rather than undermine the union with England. Devolution is discussed in Chapter 12.

To understand the constitutional arrangements, it is necessary to revert to history, for the contemporary structure of the United Kingdom is the product of forces of the past. While the 'kingdom' is now 'united', it has not always been so. Rather, the United Kingdom has been forged in part out of conquest (in the case of Wales and what is now the Republic of Ireland) and out of Treaty (for example, with Scotland in 1706). As will be seen, in relation to each part of the United Kingdom, the union with England has not always been smooth, and the history of the United Kingdom is one marked by conflict, with demands at different times in history from Ireland, Scotland and Wales for self-governing status. Devolution – the granting of self-regulating legislative powers – as mentioned above, has become a reality for Scotland and Northern Ireland and, to a lesser extent, Wales.

---

1   Interpretation Act 1978, Sched 1.
2   British Nationality Act 1981, s 50(1).

WALES[3]

Wales covers an area of some 8,000 square miles, having a population approximately five per cent of that of the United Kingdom.

The early history: an overview

Wales was conquered by the English in 1282, and from 1284,[4] Wales was subject to English law. A rebellion in the early fifteenth century sought to overthrow English rule, but after initial success, collapsed. The enduring union between England and Wales was formally effected by Act of Parliament in 1536.[5] English became the official language for Wales, and use of the Welsh language officially banned, although in 1563, Elizabeth I ordered that the bible be translated into Welsh in order to ensure compliance with the Protestant religion, and by this means ensured that the Welsh language survived.[6] All Acts of Parliament were deemed to extend to Wales. Throughout the nineteenth and twentieth centuries, nationalist feeling increased, with demands for greater recognition and representation of Welsh interests. Nationalism became an overtly political issue at the end of the nineteenth century with the establishment of the Wales of the Future Movement (Cymru Fydd), although separatism was not a demand. Welsh Liberals sought national educational institutions[7] and disestablishment of the Welsh Church rather than a Welsh Parliament.[8] In 1925, Plaid Cymru was established to promote the Welsh language and further Welsh interests and parliamentary representation, although its electoral success was slight.

Administrative decentralisation to Wales has taken place in a number of areas. In addition to education,[9] national insurance was to be separately administered in Wales,[10] and agricultural interests separately represented.[11]

---

3   See the *Report of the Royal Commission on the Constitution 1969–73*, Cmnd 5460, 1973, London: HMSO, Vol 1.

4   Statute of Rhuddlan 1284.

5   27 Hen VIII c 26 (variously labelled the Laws in Wales Act 1535 and the Act of Union 1536). The Tudor Act of 1542 established the court structure.

6   See, now, the Welsh Language Act 1967, which provides, *inter alia*, that the Welsh language may be used in legal proceedings in Wales.

7   Intermediate Education Act 1889; Education Act 1902. In 1893, the University of Wales was established by Charter and, in 1896, a Welsh Examination Board established. See, further, Bogdanor, V, *Devolution*, 1979, Oxford: OUP.

8   *Ibid*, Bogdanor, Chapter 5.

9   In relation to which, a Welsh Department of the Board of Education was established in 1907.

10   National Insurance Act 1911.

11   An Agricultural Commissioner for Wales and an Agricultural Council for Wales were established in 1912.

In 1951, the office of Minister for Welsh Affairs was established and, in 1964, the first Secretary of State for Wales was appointed with the responsibility for overseeing the execution of national policy in Wales.

The Royal Commission on the Constitution 1969–73

The Royal Commission on the Constitution, established in 1969, recommended by a majority that there should be greater devolution of power to Wales.[12] The scheme envisaged establishing a Welsh legislature (a Senate) with the power to legislate on specifically defined matters. Existing legislation of the United Kingdom Parliament would continue to apply in Wales, but future legislation – provided that the subject matter fell within the area of power devolved – would be for the Welsh Parliament. The United Kingdom Parliament would retain power to legislate over certain matters and the United Kingdom government would retain sovereignty and the ultimate power in exceptional circumstances to override legislation passed by the Welsh Senate. The Senate would comprise a single, 100 member chamber, elected on the basis of proportional representation and having a fixed term of four years. Welsh interests would, however, continue to be represented in the United Kingdom Parliament.

The election of the Labour Party to government in 1974 heralded the opportunity to further the cause of devolution recommended by the majority of the Royal Commission. A White Paper, *Democracy and Devolution: Proposals for Scotland and Wales*,[13] proposed a directly elected assembly for Wales with executive – rather than legislative – powers. A further White Paper, published in 1975,[14] proposed restricting the powers to be enjoyed by the Assembly. Economic matters, revenue, industry, energy and agriculture were to remain within the purview of the United Kingdom Parliament. The Wales Bill 1976 represented the outcome of deliberations.

The government, fearing that the Bill would be defeated in Parliament, decided to introduce a referendum to secure the approval of the people with the outcome of the referendum being conclusive. In the event, the Wales Bill 1976 failed to pass in that parliamentary session.[15]

Legislative success was achieved in the following parliamentary session, with the Wales Bill receiving the Royal Assent in July 1978, only to be rejected by the people in a referendum. In order that the Wales Act 1978 would come

---

12 *Report of the Royal Commission on the Constitution 1969–73*, Cmnd 5460, 1973, London: HMSO, Vol 1.

13 Cmnd 5732, 1874, London: HMSO.

14 *Our Changing Democracy: Devolution to Scotland and Wales*, Cmnd 6348, 1975, London: HMSO.

15 The government was in a minority: an attempt to guillotine the Bill failed as a result of defections and abstentions on the part of Labour MPs.

into effect, it was necessary for those voting in favour of devolution to be in a majority of the votes cast and to represent a minimum of 40 per cent of those entitled to vote. The voting in Wales was 11.9 per cent in favour, 46.6 per cent against with 41.7 per cent abstaining. Accordingly, the Act was not to be brought into effect.

DEVOLUTION: THE GOVERNMENT OF WALES ACT 1998

The Labour government, elected in 1997, committed itself to devolution to both Scotland and Wales. In the case of Wales, the proposal was for the establishment of a Welsh Assembly, with principally administrative powers, and subject to the overriding sovereignty of the United Kingdom Parliament. The reforms effected in 1998, are discussed in Chapter 12.

SCOTLAND[16]

Scotland has a total area of some 30,000 square miles representing an area three-fifths the size of England, with a population of some 10 per cent of the United Kingdom total.

The early history: an overview

The historical relationship between England and Scotland is one marked by conflict and war resulting from English attempts at seizing sovereignty over Scotland. Perhaps the original force uniting the two countries was the marriage, in 1503, of James IV of Scotland to Margaret, Henry VII's daughter. When Elizabeth I of England died in 1603, without leaving an heir to the throne, Henry VII's great-great-grandson – then James VI of Scotland – succeeded to the throne of England as James I.[17] Despite this union, each country retained its own constitution and Parliament and – separated by religious differences and economic rivalry – the two countries were to remain separate for a further century.

In *Calvin's Case*,[18] it was held that persons born in either of the kingdoms, after James's accession to the English throne, held dual nationality, all owing allegiance to the same Crown. James's accession was not, however, to lay past conflicts to rest. James ruled Scotland from London, much of government in

---

16 *Report of the Royal Commission on the Constitution 1969–73*, Cmnd 5460, 1973, London: HMSO.

17 See Wormald, J, 'James VI and I: two Kings or one?' (1983) 68 History 187.

18 (1608) 7 Co Rep 1a.

practice being conducted by the Scottish Privy Council acting on the King's orders. The Scottish Parliament seldom met and was dominated by the Lords of the Articles, who were royal nominees. Within Scotland, conflict arose in the form of religious dispute with the King, who attempted to curb the power of the Presbyterian Kirk in Scotland, in 1606 exiling one of its leaders.[19] In 1608, in the *Five Articles of Perth*, the King ordered certain religious practices to be undertaken which were regarded by the puritans as 'popery',[20] as was the Prayer Book drawn up at James's command in 1619.

It was in the reign of Charles I[21] that open conflict on the religious question emerged. Charles attempted to impose James's Prayer Book on the Kirk (the Scottish Church). The end result, in brief, was that the Scots opponents of his attempted reforms – the Covenanters – played a significant role in Charles's defeat in the Civil War which led to his trial, conviction and execution as 'a tyrant, traitor, murderer and public enemy to the good people of this nation'.[22]

From 1649–60, during the 'interregnum'[23] (the period between the execution of Charles I and the restoration of the monarchy), Scotland was to be ruled by the military, whilst theoretically integrated into the Cromwellian united Republic of England and Scotland. On restoration of the monarchy, religious persecution of the Scottish Presbyterians was rife. The Scottish Parliament, under the control of the Lords of the Articles, proved impotent, and was dissolved by Charles II.[24] In 1666, provoked by persecution, the Pentland Rising against the Crown occurred. While unsuccessful, it prompted Charles towards greater religious tolerance.

In 1688, when James II[25] was forced to flee England,[26] the Scots took the opportunity to assert their constitutional and religious liberties against William and Mary.[27] The Claim of Right – the Scottish constitutional settlement with the Crown – went much further than its English counterpart, the Petition of Right. The Scots claimed that Parliament had the right to depose any King who violated the trust on which his powers were held, and William was not to establish his supremacy in Scotland without blood being shed. Rebellious highland chiefs, who refused to submit to William's authority, were massacred at Glencoe in 1692, as an example to others.

19 Andrew Melville.
20 Adherence to the Roman Catholic faith.
21 1625–49.
22 Cited in Lockyer, R, *Tudor and Stuart Britain 1471–1714*, 2nd edn, 1985, Harlow: Longman, p 288.
23 1649–60.
24 1649–85 (in exile until 1660).
25 1685–89.
26 1688.
27 1689–1702.

Scottish hostility towards the Crown was further exacerbated by the Navigation Acts, which treated Scotland and England as separate entities. As a response, acting alone, and without royal support, the Scots raised revenues for an expedition to Panama. Three expeditions set out but failed, being decimated either by disease or military opposition from the Spanish Armada. The English, meanwhile, continued to exclude Scotland from its commercial empire. The Scottish response to such discrimination was to declare that Scotland would not be committed to either war or peace by English policy[28] and that the succession to the Hanoverian Crown[29] would not be accepted by Scotland unless and until constitutional, economic and religious liberties were guaranteed to the Scottish people.

The only long term solution to such conflicts of interest was the full union of England and Scotland. The Act of Union with Scotland[30] was passed in 1707, 'abolishing' the respective sovereign Parliaments which became united under the title of the Parliament of Great Britain. The Act of Union represented the culmination of years of negotiations between the two countries following centuries of intermittent hostilities. As will be seen in Chapter 6, when union came about, it was to be subject to strict conditions and terms. In particular, the Act of Union protects the separate Scottish legal system – both in relation to private law and to the court structure – and provided special protection for the Presbyterian Church. There was, however, to be a common Parliament, common flag, taxation and coinage: by this, meaningful political and economic union was secured.

The Wars of Independence between England and Scotland in the Middle Ages, culminating in the recognition of an independent Scotland in 1328, had resulted in a complete break between English law and Scottish law. The Scottish looked to continental Europe for their training and law, and thus adopted the civil law system based originally on Roman law, which had never been fully adopted in England. Under the terms of the union, the highest civil and criminal courts – the Court of Session and the High Court of Justiciary – were to remain outside the jurisdiction of the English courts. The High Court of Justiciary has remained the final court of appeal in Scottish criminal cases, while in civil cases the House of Lords has appellate jurisdiction.[31]

Following the union, Scottish interests were represented by a Secretary of State for Scotland. From 1745, responsibility for Scotland passed to a Secretary of State who also held other responsibilities.[32] In 1885, the office of Secretary

---

28 Act anent Peace and War 1703.
29 As provided by the Act of Security 1704.
30 See, further, Chapter 7.
31 By custom, two Lords of Appeal in Ordinary are from Scotland.
32 Such as Home Affairs.

for Scotland was established, which, from 1892, became a Cabinet[33] post. Administrative devolution to Scotland included Boards created to administer agriculture, fisheries, local government, prisons, health and education, each operating under the supervision of the Scottish Secretary of State.

In 1952, a Royal Commission on Scottish Affairs[34] was appointed to review government functions in relation to Scotland. Further responsibilities were transferred to the Scottish Secretary of State: appointment of Justices of the Peace, animal health, highways and electricity. Subsequently, road passenger transport, ancient monuments, royal parks and palaces have been transferred. The Scottish Office, established in 1945, comprises five departments: Agriculture and Fisheries, Development, Education, Home and Health. The administration is based in Edinburgh and headed by the Secretary of State, Ministers of State and Under Secretaries.

Responsibility for the administration of the criminal law in Scotland lies with the Lord Advocate who is normally a Member of the House of Commons but may, alternatively, be a member of the House of Lords, having been conferred a life peerage. The Lord Advocate has responsibility for aspects of government business affecting Scotland. Representation in Parliament was determined by the Act of Union at 45, but has since increased to 72.[35]

The Royal Commission on the Constitution 1969–73[36] recommended the devolution of legislative power to Scotland. As with Wales, the legislation could only come into effect following a referendum which returned a majority of voters in favour, having secured a minimum of 40 per cent of all eligible voters.[37] The results of the referendum in Scotland were 32.5 per cent in favour of devolution, 30.4 per cent against, with 37.1 per cent of voters abstaining. The statutory requirements for an electoral majority being unmet, the Scotland Act 1978 was repealed.

The Royal Commission had not been unanimous in its support of devolution for either Wales or Scotland, and a powerful Memorandum of Dissent was published with the report.[38] The objections of the dissenters[39] may be summarised as being:

(a) that devolving 'sovereignty' over certain matters to the legislative assembly from Westminster takes too little account of the impact of the

---

33 See, further, Chapter 10.

34 *Report of the Royal Commission on Scottish Affairs 1952–54*, Cmnd 9212, 1954, London: HMSO.

35 See the Parliamentary Constituencies Act 1986.

36 *Report of the Royal Commission on the Constitution 1969–73*, Cmnd 5460, 1973, London: HMSO, Vol 1.

37 See Bogdanor, V, 'The forty per cent rule' (1980) 33 Parl Aff 249.

38 *Report of the Royal Commission on the Constitution 1969–73*, Cmnd 5460, 1973, London: HMSO, Vol 2.

39 Lord Crowther-Hunt and Professor AT Peacock.

European Community towards which 'sovereignty' appeared to be moving;

(b) that devolution would confer on the peoples of Scotland and Wales greater political rights than those enjoyed by citizens in other regions; and

(c) that to deny Westminster power to legislate over certain matters in relation to Scotland and at the same time retain Scottish (and Welsh) representation at Westminster, where MPs could vote on matters pertaining solely to England, was wrong in principle.

Nevertheless, the devolution issue – particularly in relation to Scotland – had not been finally laid to rest. Following the general election in 1987, the Conservative government, despite having a majority of seats in England, won only 10 out of 72 seats in Scotland. The results of the 1992 election, whilst slightly better in terms of government representation, still resulted in Scotland being under-represented in Parliament.

The by-election of May 1995, following the death of a Conservative Member of Parliament, resulted in the Scottish Nationalist Party winning the seat. The Conservative government therefore had little electoral support north of the border in general elections or by-elections, a fact which was also reflected in local government elections. This 'democratic deficit' of the Conservative government continued to fuel the fires of the demand for greater devolution of power to Scotland. The 1997 general election resulted in there being no Scottish Conservative Members of Parliament.

Devolution to Scotland[40]

The general election of 1997 presaged the devolution of power to a Scottish Parliament. The government's White Paper, *Scotland's Parliament*,[41] while retaining the sovereignty of the Westminster Parliament,[42] envisaged devolution of law making power to the Scottish Parliament, and a limited power to vary levels of taxation, while also reserving to the United Kingdom Parliament legislative capacity in relation to certain matters. Whether or not powers are devolved or reserved, the Scottish Parliament is entitled to debate all matters.[43] The Scotland Act 1998 gave effect to the proposals for devolution, approved by the people through a referendum. The Scottish Parliament and the Executive are discussed in Chapter 12.

---

40 See, generally, Bogdanor, V, *Power and the People*, 1997, London: Gollancz; Bates, St JT, *Devolution to Scotland: The Legal Aspects*, 1997, Edinburgh: T & T Clark.

41 Cmnd 3658, 1997, London: HMSO.

42 *Ibid*, para 4.2.

43 *Ibid*, para 2.5.

NORTHERN IRELAND[44]

Northern Ireland has a land area of some 5,000 square miles and a population amounting to three per cent of the United Kingdom population. The constitutional position of Northern Ireland cannot be understood without some appreciation of the history of Ireland as a whole – a matter which remains of contemporary constitutional importance given the recent initiatives to end the sectarian bloodshed and to achieve a lasting constitutional settlement in relation to the status of Northern Ireland. Space does not permit more than a brief overview of the rich and troubled history of Ireland.

Ireland: the early history – an overview

Ireland first came under the control of the English in the twelfth century when, in 1155, Henry II[45] had been awarded the overlordship of Ireland by the English Pope, Adrian IV, for the specific purpose of reforming the Irish Church. An Irish Parliament was established by the end of the thirteenth century, although representation was confined to English settlers, thereby excluding the native Irish population. At the time of Henry VII's reign[46] English rule in Ireland was confined to the Pale, a stretch of coastal land running some 50 miles north of Dublin and 20 miles inland. An early attempt at a form of self-government entailed the Irish Parliament's assertion that Acts of the English Parliament would extend to Ireland only in so far as the Irish Parliament ratified the statute. The outcome of this claim to independence was the reassertion of royal power and the passage of Poyning's Law[47] in 1494, which provided that all Irish legislative proposals must be approved by the King and his Council.

When Henry VIII[48] broke with Rome[49] and established himself as Head of the Church of England, he ran the risk of incurring Irish Roman Catholic hostility. In 1534, rebellion broke out, the leaders of which called on the Pope and the Spanish Emperor for support against the King of England. The result

---

44 See, *inter alia*, Foster, RF, *Modern Ireland 1600–1972*, 1989, London: Penguin; Foster, RF (ed), *The Oxford History of Ireland*, 1989, Oxford: OUP; *Report of the Royal Commission on the Constitution 1969–73*, Cmnd 5460, 1973, London: HMSO; Calvert, H, *Constitutional Law in Northern Ireland*, 1968, London: Stevens; *op cit*, Bogdanor, fn 7; Ranelagh, J, *A Short History of Ireland*, 1983, Cambridge: CUP; Lee, JJ, *Ireland 1912–85: Politics and Society*, 1990, Cambridge: CUP; Hughes, M, *Ireland Divided: The Roots of the Modern Irish Problem*, 1994, Cardiff: Wales UP.

45 1154–89.

46 1485–1509.

47 Named after Sir Edward Poyning, the envoy sent by Henry VII to secure obedience to English authority.

48 1509–47.

49 Act of Supremacy 1534; Treason Act 1534.

was military suppression of the rebellion by an invasion of an English army under the leadership of Sir William Skeffington. Direct rule was to be introduced with Skeffington appointed as the King's Lord Deputy. In 1540, with the fall from favour of Henry's Chancellor, Cromwell, Henry VIII decided on conciliation with the Irish, and in 1541, the Irish Parliament finally recognised Henry as King of Ireland.

The province of Ulster – then the nine northern counties of Ireland – was largely unaffected by English rule until the sixteenth century, when Elizabeth I[50] sought to extend her power beyond the Pale. On the advice of the Privy Council, the Queen decided that government in Ireland should be approximated as far as possible to that of England rather than allowing governance on the basis of Ireland's own history and experience. The Queen's decision was to alter the course of history. Beyond the Pale, the 'Irishry' had enjoyed their own language, customs and law. English was now to become the official language and English law and administrative practices were to extend to the whole territory of Ireland. In Munster, in the South, an earlier rebellion against English rule – supported by Spanish and Italian troops and financed by the Pope – started in 1569, and was finally suppressed in 1583.

Relations between the English and the Irish remained uneasy. Ireland adhered to the Roman Catholic faith,[51] whereas the immigrants from Scotland and England were staunchly Protestant. The native tongue was Gaelic, a language neither understood nor spoken by the English. When the Earl of Tyrone[52] demanded that traditional rule by chieftains be allowed and that there should be official tolerance of Roman Catholicism, Elizabeth rejected these demands. In consequence of this rejection, a Spanish armada set forth in support of Catholicism. The armada, whilst unsuccessful, heightened the sense of Irish nationalism and antagonism towards the English. In 1603, the rebellion was ultimately suppressed: Tyrone and others fled to France in 'the flight of the Earls'. The province was taken over by the Crown and, in 1607, with the exile of the native aristocracy, was divided into counties on the English model.

One effect of Irish suppression was to further English settlement of the area, with land being confiscated and distributed to English and Scots immigrants. In 1609, under James I,[53] a comprehensive scheme of 'plantation' began in Ulster, and by 1622, some 21,000 English, Scottish and Welsh immigrants had settled in Northern Ireland. Fortified towns were built by the incoming settlers as 'control points' across the province.

---

50   1558–1603.
51   Religious faith was reinforced by missionaries from the Continent.
52   Hugh O'Neill.
53   1603–25.

As the number of Protestant immigrants increased, so too did the potential for religious strife. Immigrants to Ulster changed its character into that of a Protestant society, and the dispossessed Irish found themselves outsiders in their own country. In 1641, the native Irish rebelled against the settlers. Unable to send troops to suppress the rebellion, King Charles I accepted a proposal whereby 10 million acres of Irish land would be confiscated and used to repay those who would lend money to suppress the rebellion.

In the Interregnum,[54] during which time England was governed by the Cromwellian Commonwealth, the Treaty of Kilkenny 1649 was agreed, which guaranteed religious toleration and an independent Parliament for Ireland. However, in light of continuing opposition to English rule, Cromwell landed in Ireland in July 1649 with an army intent on suppressing dissent. By May 1652, the conquest was complete. The terms of settlement were set out in the Act for Settlement of Ireland, and included the provision that every Irish landowner would have his estate forfeited unless he could prove that he had shown 'constant good affection to the interests of the Commonwealth of England'. During the Commonwealth, an estimated 36,000 immigrant settlers were given land, much of it in Ulster. An estimated 8,000 Catholic landowners were thus displaced from their lands, to be replaced by English soldiers, who accepted land in lieu of pay, and by those who had lent money to the government for suppression of the rebellion. By 1660, when Charles II was restored to the throne, the share of land owned by native Catholics had declined from 60 per cent to 20 per cent of the total. An attempt – under the Act of Settlement of 1661 – to preserve the land of existing landowners and to restore land to those who had suffered in the Crown's cause was doomed to fail because, quite simply, there was insufficient land to meet the claims. Notwithstanding such attempts to redress past injustices, the Act of Explanation of 1665 declared that, in disputes between Catholics and Protestants, Protestants were to be favoured. The Act of Settlement was to be a continuing source of conflict.

James II, having fled England for Catholic France in 1688, arrived in Ireland in 1689 in an attempt to restore his English Crown. The Irish Parliament – in which, at that time, Roman Catholics formed a majority – repealed the Act of Settlement and restored freedom of religion. In response, William III despatched an army to Ireland, and at the Battle of the Boyne in 1690, James was defeated. Protestants were once again in the ascendancy. Following James's defeat, and the repression which followed, some 12,000 Roman Catholics went into exile.

Throughout the reign of William and Mary,[55] and that of Queen Anne,[56] further measures were introduced to confirm Protestant supremacy. Catholics

54 1649–60.
55 1689–1702.
56 1702–14.

were excluded from Parliament, the civil service, armed forces, local government and the professions. An Act of 1728 deprived Catholics of the electoral franchise. Roman Catholics were prohibited from acquiring land and from sending their children to university. On the death of a Catholic, by law his lands were compulsorily divided between all his children, but if there was a Protestant heir, he was to take precedence. By these various means, Catholics were excluded from participation in public life. Some redress occurred in 1792 when the Relief Act allowed Roman Catholics to practise law and to vote, although not to stand for election to Parliament which by now had become a Protestant body.

From 1541, when Henry VIII took the title of King of Ireland and Supreme Head of the Church of Ireland, Ireland was subject to the King's rule. In William's reign, however, the issue which became contentious was whether Ireland was also subject to the English Parliament. From the standpoint of England, Ireland was a colony and thus subject to the supremacy of the English Parliament. In 1719, a clash between the two Houses of Lords brought the matter to the fore. Each House claimed the sovereign right to adjudicate upon Irish law. An Act of the English Parliament[57] gave full power to the English Parliament to legislate for Ireland and denied the Irish House of Lords jurisdiction to hear appeals from the Irish courts. The Declaratory Act was repealed in 1782, and the right of the Irish to be bound only by law enacted by the Irish Parliament and the King was established.

In 1791, the Society of United Irishmen was established in Belfast, with Republicanism – full independence from England for an Irish State – as its political platform. Although the majority of its membership was Protestant, the Society favoured Catholic emancipation.[58] In the north, however, in 1794, the Protestant and staunchly unionist Orange Order was established. Mounting religious and political instability in Ireland culminated in the Great Rising of 1798.

The Act of Union 1800

In an attempt to quell unrest and reach a lasting settlement, negotiations were undertaken towards establishing political union between Ireland and England. The British Prime Minister, William Pitt, promised full Catholic emancipation. The resulting Act of Union 1800 effected the union between Ireland and England on the theoretical basis of equal independence for the two countries.[59] The Kingdom of Ireland and the Kingdom of Great Britain were united under the United Kingdom of Great Britain and Ireland. Irish

---

57 Declaratory Act, 6 Geo I c 5.
58 Official suppression of the Society took place in 1794.
59 The Act came into effect on 1 January 1801.

interests were to be represented in the United Kingdom's House of Lords by 28 Irish peers and four bishops. Representation in the House of Commons was by 100 Irish members. The House of Lords of the United Kingdom was the court of last resort. Demands for the repeal of the Act of Union were soon to be heard from Catholics when the promised emancipation was blocked by George III[60] and demands made for reforms in relation to land law and education. These claims, in turn, were resisted by Protestants who feared that dissolution of the union and a revived Irish Parliament would favour the Catholics.

The movement towards Home Rule[61]

Following the Napoleonic War in 1815, economic disaster was to strike Ireland. The economy was traditionally heavily dependent upon the potato crop: in the mid 1800s, the crop failed. The effect of famine – starvation and emigration – was to decimate the Irish population.[62] Demands for Home Rule began following the famine when many felt that the British government had taken inadequate steps to deal with the economic crisis. The famine once again heightened demands for independence from England.

Some reforms were introduced: in 1829, a Catholic Relief Act removed discrimination in education and property and provided for Roman Catholic entry to civic and military offices. This emancipation in turn gave rise to increased solidarity in the Unionist communities of the north and to further sectarian violence. In 1836, a paramilitary national police force was set up, to be known from 1867 as the Royal Irish Constabulary.[63]

In 1869, the Anglican Church in Ireland was disestablished,[64] and in 1870 and 1881, Acts were introduced to regulate land rents and tenure.[65] Electoral reforms in 1868, 1872 and 1884–85 introduced the secret ballot and extended the franchise. These measures, however, were not enough to quell Irish Catholic discontent. The land question was converted into a full scale campaign for Home Rule for Ireland. Charles Stewart Parnell and Michael

---

60 1738–1820. The King's veto resulted in Pitt's resignation.

61 See Morton, G, *Home Rule and the Irish Question*, 1980, Harlow: Longman; Jalland, P, *The Liberals and Ireland: The Ulster Question in British Politics to 1914*, 1980, Hemel Hempstead: Harvester; O'Halpin, E, *The Decline of the Union: British Government in Ireland 1892–1920*, 1987, Dublin: Gill and Macmillan.

62 In 1841, the population was 8,175,124; in 1881, 5,174,836 and, by 1901, 4,458,775: census figures.

63 Between 1800 and 1921, some 105 Coercion Acts were passed, increasing the powers of the military and police.

64 Irish Church Disestablishment Act 1869.

65 Land Acts 1870, 1881.

Davitt[66] created the United Irish League, an organisation designed to back Irish Home Rule members of the United Kingdom Parliament. Between 1879 and 1882, a violent campaign against landlords was undertaken. The government's response was to suspend habeas corpus, but at the same time to introduce further land reforms. The violence nevertheless continued: Irish republican leaders were arrested but subsequently released in order to try to stop the bloodshed. In 1881, the brutal murder of the Chief Secretary for Ireland, Lord Frederick Cavendish, and Chief Under Secretary Thomas Burke was to turn public opinion in England against the Irish and put back the cause of Home Rule.

With a total of 100 members, the Irish represented a significant block in the Westminster Parliament. Following the 1885 general election, 85 of the 100 elected members supported Home Rule in Ireland. They proceeded to exercise their power, blocking government legislation and campaigning for Irish independence from Westminster. The Liberal Prime Minister, William Ewart Gladstone,[67] sponsored the cause of Home Rule, but not that of a fully independent Irish State. The aim, for the Liberals, was to introduce constitutional reform which would ensure a degree of autonomy for an Irish Parliament whilst retaining the supremacy of Westminster. By this means, it was hoped that some form of devolution of power would be acceptable to the Unionists.

This compromise solution was one adopted in other attempts at devolution of power from Westminster. In 1867, limited powers were devolved to Canada,[68] as was later to be the case in relation also to Australia[69] and South Africa.[70] In each instance, the Westminster Parliament retained ultimate sovereignty over the laws of each country whilst conferring broad grants of legislative power to the colonial legislature.[71]

Home Rule Bills were introduced in the British Parliament in 1886[72] and 1893,[73] but both were defeated. The defeat of the Bills both disappointed the Nationalists and increased the insecurity of the Unionists. Substantive defects in the Bills proved insurmountable, with the central dilemma turning on taxation and representation. If Ireland was to have its own legislature – albeit subordinate to Westminster – it followed that Irish Members of Parliament should be excluded from Westminster, since they should not be allowed to sit

---

66   Member of Parliament for Meath.
67   1809–98: Prime Minister 1868–74; 1880–85; 1892–94.
68   British North America Act 1867.
69   Commonwealth of Australia Constitution Act 1900 (UK).
70   South Africa Act 1909.
71   See, *inter alia*, the Colonial Laws Validity Act 1865 and Chapter 7.
72   The Bill failed to pass the House of Commons.
73   The Bill was rejected by the House of Lords.

and vote on purely English and Scottish affairs.[74] Yet, if this were to be the case, it raised the spectre of the Westminster Parliament legislating for Irish taxation – a power reserved to the United Kingdom Parliament – without Irish representation.

Relations between England and Ireland were to deteriorate throughout the first 20 years of the twentieth century. In 1905, Sinn Fein was established, with strongly nationalist objectives. In the years 1911–12, there was industrial unrest in Ireland. By the outbreak of the First World War in 1914, the scene was set for Civil War in Ireland, an event only postponed by the War.

With Home Rule so firmly on the political agenda, Unionist opposition intensified. For example, in 1912, some 400,000 Ulster Protestants signed the Covenant on Ulster Day,[75] committing themselves to use 'all means which may be found necessary to defeat the present conspiracy to set up a Home Rule Parliament in Ireland' and 'to refuse to recognise its authority'.[76] In 1913, the Ulster Volunteer Force (UVF), a private army of over 100,000 men, was formed to protect Unionist interests against Republican demands. The forming of the UVF led directly to the foundation of the Irish Volunteers, the forerunners of the Irish Republican Army (IRA).

The issue of Home Rule for Ireland became, for the British, an issue which demanded the separation of Ulster from the remainder of Ireland, rather than Home Rule for the entire country. A Bill passed through Parliament in 1914, but with the outbreak of the First World War was never put into effect, and the intractable issue of separation of north from south was thus delayed.[77] At Westminster, the question of Home Rule had by now become a straight and passionate party political issue, with the Conservatives and Ulster Unionists opposing devolution and the Liberals and Irish Members proposing devolution.

The Easter Rising 1916[78]

In 1916, an event occurred which was to prove to be a decisive factor in the Home Rule story. Nationalists in Dublin, under the leadership of Patrick Pearse, James Connolly and Michael Collins, initiated an uprising. On Easter

---

74 This same issue bedevilled devolution to Scotland in 1978.

75 28 September 1912.

76 Cited by Fitzpatrick, D, 'Ireland since 1870', in *op cit*, Foster (ed), fn 44, p 191.

77 Attempts were made to implement the Home Rule Bill following the Easter Rising in 1916 but failed.

78 See Thompson, WI, *The Imagination of an Insurrection: Dublin, Easter 1916*, 1967, Oxford: OUP; Martin, FX (ed), *Leaders and Men of the Easter Rising: Dublin 1916*, 1967, London: Methuen; O'Connor, U, *The Troubles: The Struggle for Irish Freedom 1912–1922*, 1989, London: Mandarin.

Monday, some 1,600 members of the Irish Volunteers and Irish Citizen Army embarked on a rebellion, proclaiming republican status for Ireland.[79]

Six days later, the rebels surrendered with a loss of life of 132 soldiers and policemen and 397 wounded, and 318 civilian deaths and 2,217 wounded. Three thousand five hundred people were arrested and court-martialled. Fifteen men were executed: 14 in Dublin and one in Cork. While the uprising was unsuccessful, its effect, and the brutal response of the British, was to consolidate the nationalist cause and to win the support of the Catholic Church. Sinn Fein membership grew and electoral success followed in the 1918 general election, with Sinn Fein members having a majority throughout the country except in the staunchly Unionist area of the north east. Sinn Fein secured 73 seats and 48 per cent of the votes cast. The Unionists secured only 29 per cent of votes.

Civil War: 1919–22

Sinn Fein was banned in 1918, and its leader, Eamon De Valera, arrested. Members of Sinn Fein refused to take their seats in Westminster and instead issued a Declaration of Independence and established the first Irish Parliament – the *Dail Eireann*. Civil unrest again erupted, with the Irish war of independence[80] lasting until 1921. The war was, essentially, a programme of terrorism directed against the authorities. The government passed the Restoration of Order in Ireland Act in 1920, providing for internment of suspects while at the same time seeking to implement Home Rule. The savagery with which the army and Royal Irish Constabulary dealt with the troubles provoked disgust and outrage: pressure on the government from public opinion at home and overseas necessitated a truce.

Partition: the Government of Ireland Act 1920

By 1919, it had become clear that there could be no single Home Rule Parliament for a united Republic of Ireland. In light of the continuing and increasing sectarian bitterness and civil unrest, the British government became resigned to a divided Ireland. In 1920, the United Kingdom Parliament passed the Government of Ireland Act under which the country was partitioned, with six of the original nine Ulster counties being separated from the remainder of Ireland.[81] Under the Government of Ireland Act, a Council of Ireland was to

---

79 *The Proclamation of the Irish Republic 24 April 1916*, National Museum of Ireland, cited in *op cit*, Hughes, fn 44, pp 97–99.

80 Variously called the Anglo-Irish War, Irish War of Independence or the Black and Tan War.

81 Cavan, Monaghan and Donegal were excluded from the newly created Northern Ireland.

be established, having exclusive jurisdiction over a number of all Ireland matters.[82]

Six northern counties,[83] characterised by a majority population of Protestants, were henceforth to be separately represented by a separate Parliament from that of southern Ireland. The Act provided for two Home Rule Parliaments, with Westminster retaining ultimate sovereignty:

> Notwithstanding ... anything contained in this Act, the supreme authority of the Parliament of the United Kingdom shall remain unaffected and undiminished over all persons, matters, and things in Ireland and every part thereof.[84]

The Parliament of Southern Ireland – the Dail – rejected the Act, and the war of independence continued. In Northern Ireland, however, the Home Rule Parliament opened in 1921. In December 1921, following intensive negotiations, Articles of Agreement were signed by Irish delegates. The Articles provided for the partition of Ireland; for the creation of an Irish Free State with Dominion status[85] under the Crown, to be represented by a Governor General. By a narrow majority, the Irish Parliament, the Dail, accepted the agreement.

The Anglo-Irish Treaty 1921

The Anglo-Irish Treaty gave to southern Ireland (the 'Irish Free State') self-governing dominion status, equivalent to that of Canada, within the Commonwealth. The Parliament of Northern Ireland was given the choice as to whether or not it should be part of the Irish Free State. When it decided that it should not, the Irish Free State (Consequential Provisions) Act of 1922 provided that the 1920 Act, which regulated the respective powers of the southern and northern Parliaments and their relationships with Westminster should cease to apply to any part of the Irish Free State and that its operation was confined to Northern Ireland.

In 1922, the Irish Free State Constitution was published, and ratified by the Westminster Parliament in the Irish Free State (Constitution) Act 1922. War was not to end, however, and, on 28 June 1922, the Irish Civil War began, with the IRA leading the campaign against the Treaty. The war ended in 1923, but the anti-treaty forces refused to surrender their arms.[86]

---

82 Railways, fisheries and contagious diseases in animals.
83 Antrim, Armagh, Down, Fermanagh, Londonderry and Tyrone.
84 Government of Ireland Act 1920, s 75.
85 As enjoyed by Canada, Australia, New Zealand and South Africa.
86 The same position pertained in 1999.

Within the newly separated north, with a Protestant Unionist population of 56.4 per cent of the total, sectarian strife continued. In two years, over 400 people died, the majority being Catholics. The government responded with the Civil Authorities (Special Powers) Act of 1922, which provided for internment of suspected terrorists without trial. The Act was to remain in force until 1972.[87]

The Constitution of the Irish Free State 1937

In 1931, the Statute of Westminster conferred greater freedom on the powers of Dominions. In Ireland, the Prime Minister (the *Taoiseach*), Eamon de Valera,[88] introduced major changes: in 1933, it was announced that Ireland was to become a *de facto* Republic. The Senate – the upper House of Parliament – was abolished; the Governor General was stripped of his powers. In addition, Irish citizens lost their British citizenship. The right of appeal to the Privy Council was abolished.

In 1937, de Valera drafted and published the constitution of the Irish Free State. The constitution declared independence from the United Kingdom, declaring that:

> The Irish nation hereby affirms its inalienable, indefeasible, and sovereign right to choose its own form of government, to determine its relations with other nations, and to develop its life, political, economic and cultural, in accordance with its own genius and traditions.[89]

Under Article 2, the constitution declared Ireland to be a unitary, not divided, State, thus refusing to accept the constitutional position of Northern Ireland as established under the 1920 Act:

> The national territory consists of the whole island of Ireland, its islands and the territorial seas.

Furthermore, it was declared in Article 5 that:

> Ireland is a sovereign, independent, democratic State.

It was not, however, until 1949 that the United Kingdom Parliament was to accept separation and pass the Ireland Act 1949, which formally severed constitutional ties. The Republic withdrew from the Commonwealth in the same year.

---

87 See, further, Chapter 23.
88 1882–1975.
89 Constitution, Art I.

Self-government in Northern Ireland 1920–72

From 1920 until 1972, Northern Ireland enjoyed a measure of self-government represented by the Parliament at Stormont. The Northern Ireland Parliament had powers to make laws for 'the peace, order and good government of Northern Ireland'. In effect, this meant law and order, the police and lower courts, local government, health and social services, education, planning and internal trade, agriculture and finance.[90] Westminster retained reserved powers and ultimate sovereignty over the territory.[91] Sectarian strife, in addition to the reserved legislative powers, ensured that the United Kingdom government continued to play a role in Northern Ireland.

The Northern Ireland Parliament was bicameral, the House of Commons being elected by the people, the Senate being elected by Members of the House of Commons. The Executive was headed by the Governor, appointed by the Crown. In the first elected Parliament of 1921, the Unionists held a majority and thus formed the government, a feature which was to be repeated in every election until the constitution was suspended in 1972.

Not only was there a continuous Unionist majority in the House of Commons, but there was also Unionist dominance in local government: a contributing factor to the discontent of the Catholic community. Further disquiet arose over the composition of the Royal Ulster Constabulary, and in particular the force of 'B Specials',[92] all Protestant, which gained a reputation for violence. Catholic membership of the entire police force in Northern Ireland was never to be above 20 per cent of the total. The allocation of public housing also became a matter of discontent. In the attempt to separate Catholics from Protestants, the housing allocated to Catholics proved to be of a poorer standard than that offered to the Protestants. Education was segregated, again on religious grounds. Mutual distrust between the two communities within Northern Ireland intensified as a result of religion.

The 'Troubles': 1968–98

In 1968, a campaign of civil disobedience and unrest began. The target for the violence was twofold: the discrimination which existed against Catholics in many sectors of life – such as housing, employment and the local government franchise – and the continued union with the mainland. The civil disturbances led to a Commission of Inquiry which reported a 'widespread sense of political and social grievances for long unaudited and therefore ignored by

---

90 See Palley, C, 'The evolution, disintegration and possible reconstruction of the Northern Ireland Constitution' (1972) 1 Anglo-American L Rev 368.
91 Government of Ireland Act 1920, s 75.
92 Part time policemen.

successive governments of Northern Ireland'.[93] By the summer of 1969, British troops were deployed in support of the police, whose operational control over security matters became subject to military control. In 1970, the Provisional Sinn Fein Party was formed and, in 1971, the Reverend Ian Paisley founded the Democratic Unionist Party. The Civil Authorities Special Powers Act (Northern Ireland) 1922 was used to intern suspected Irish Republican terrorists without trial – a factor which increased rather than decreased sympathy for the nationalist cause. On 30 January 1972, 13 Catholic civilians were shot dead by British paratroopers in the course of a banned civil rights march in Derry ('Bloody Sunday'). By the end of 1972, 474 deaths had occurred in the escalation of sectarian killings by Protestant murderers and the IRA.

Internment and allegations of ill treatment of detainees led to legal proceedings being initiated against the United Kingdom by the Republic of Ireland government under the European Convention on Human Rights.[94] The Crompton Report of 1971[95] outlined the interrogation methods used as including continuous noise, deprivation of food, water and sleep, and wall standing. Three Privy Counsellors[96] were appointed to examine the procedures. Unable to reach agreement, two differing reports were published.[97] The majority report concluded that the techniques would be acceptable provided adequate safeguards were introduced in relation to their use. Lord Gardiner, however, a former Labour Lord Chancellor, ruled that the procedures used were unlawful:

> If it is to be made legal to employ methods not now legal against a man whom the police believe to have, but who may not have, information which the police desire to obtain, I, like many of our witnesses, have searched for, but been unable to find, either in logic or in morals, any limit to the degree of ill treatment to be legalised. The only logical limit to the degree of ill treatment would appear to be whatever degree of ill treatment proves to be necessary to get the information out of him, which would include, if necessary, extreme torture. I cannot think that Parliament should, or would, so legislate.

The government accepted Lord Gardiner's view, and the interrogation procedures were abandoned. The European Court of Human Rights ruled that the procedures amounted to inhuman and degrading treatment contrary

---

93 *Report of the Cameron Commission: Disturbances in Northern Ireland*, Cmnd 532, 1969, London: HMSO.

94 *Republic of Ireland v United Kingdom* (1978) 2 EHRR 25. See, further, McCrudden, C, 'Northern Ireland', in Jowell, J and Oliver, D (eds), *The Changing Constitution*, 3rd edn, 1994, Oxford: Clarendon, esp pp 317–27. See, also, Chapter 22.

95 Cmnd 4823, 1971, London: HMSO.

96 Lord Parker of Waddington, JA Carpenter and Lord Gardiner.

97 *Report of the Committee of Privy Counsellors appointed to Consider Authorised Procedures for the Interrogation of Persons Suspected of Terrorism*, Cmnd 4901, 1972, London: HMSO.

to Article 3 of the Convention on Human Rights but that they did not amount to torture.

Some reforms designed to improve relations between the Catholic community and the Unionists were introduced by the Northern Ireland Parliament. A Northern Ireland Parliamentary Commissioner for Administration was appointed to deal with complaints against public authorities,[98] and a Commissioner for Complaints[99] established to investigate allegations based on discrimination in employment.

Prorogation of the Northern Ireland Parliament 1972

In 1972, with the violence unabated and the civilian death toll mounting, the United Kingdom government once again assumed responsibility for the province.[100] The Northern Ireland Parliament was prorogued indefinitely and the powers of the Northern Ireland government transferred to a Secretary of State for Northern Ireland. A review of the Special Powers Act and internment was undertaken in 1972.[101] Confirming the need for detention without trial as a short term measure for certain alleged offences, the Committee recommended the introduction of special courts which would sit without a jury: the 'Diplock Courts'.[102]

Power sharing 1973

In 1973, following the prorogation of Stormont and a referendum, a new system of power sharing between the Northern Ireland Assembly and the Westminster Parliament was introduced.[103] Under the Northern Ireland Assembly Act 1973 and the Northern Ireland Constitution Act 1973, an Assembly was to be established, having 78 members elected under the single transferable vote system.[104] The Northern Ireland Constitution Act 1973 provided a statutory guarantee that Northern Ireland should remain part of the United Kingdom until the time at which a majority of the people, voting in a referendum, should determine otherwise.[105] Representation of Northern

---

98 Parliamentary Commissioner (Northern Ireland) Act 1969.

99 Commissioner for Complaints (Northern Ireland) Act 1969; see Poole, KP, 'The Northern Ireland Commissioner for Complaints' [1972] PL 131.

100 Northern Ireland (Temporary Provisions) Act 1972.

101 *Report of the Commission to Consider Legal Procedures to deal with Terrorist Activities in Northern Ireland*, Cmnd 5185, 1972, London: HMSO (the 'Diplock Inquiry').

102 Northern Ireland (Emergency Provisions) Act 1973.

103 *Northern Ireland Constitutional Proposals*, Cmnd 5259, 1973, London: HMSO.

104 See Chapter 13.

105 See Hadfield, B, *The Constitution of Northern Ireland*, 1989, Belfast: SLS.

Ireland at Westminster was increased to 17 Members of Parliament. In a referendum held in 1973[106] on the question of union with the United Kingdom, a majority favoured continuation of the union.[107] The Executive in Northern Ireland.

Direct rule 1974

The breakdown of that system resulted in the Northern Ireland Act of 1974, the result of which was the restoration of direct rule by Westminster over Northern Ireland.

Further attempts were made to dismantle the discrimination which continued to exist in fields of housing and employment.[108] Section 17 of the Northern Ireland Constitution Act 1973 provided that any Northern Ireland legislation which discriminated against persons on the basis of religion or political belief was void.[109] The attempts proved largely ineffective and the Policy Studies Institute reported that the legislation had little impact on the attitudes of employers.[110]

Throughout the 1970s and 1980s, a virtual civil war existed.[111] From 1971 to 1977, 'an average of 252 persons were killed and 3,269 shootings have occurred each year; for the years 1978–81, the averages have fallen, respectively, to 82 and 1,574'.[112] In 1975, a further attempt to devolve power to the province was made when a Constitutional Convention was elected.[113] The attempt failed as a result of the Unionists' insistence that they retain a majority in any new Assembly. The Northern Ireland Act 1982 nevertheless provided for a new Assembly, to be elected by proportional representation, which initially was designed to be a debating and deliberative forum which would, in the future, propose plans for a new form of devolved government in Northern Ireland.[114] The Social Democratic and Labour Party and Sinn Fein members refused to take their seats. Faced with political deadlock, the

---

106 Under the Northern Ireland (Border Poll) Act 1972.

107 Although only 58.7 per cent of the electorate voted.

108 See *op cit*, McCrudden, fn 94, esp pp 327–31.

109 The Fair Employment (Northern Ireland) Act 1976 makes discrimination in the fields of either public or private employment void.

110 Chambers, G, *Equality and Inequality in Northern Ireland, Part 2: The Workplace*, 1987, London: Policy Studies Institute; Smith, DJ, 'Policy and research: employment discrimination in Northern Ireland' (1988) 9(1) Policy Studies 41, cited in *op cit*, McCrudden, fn 94.

111 See Gearty, G, *Terror*, 1991, London: Faber & Faber, Chapter 8.

112 Dickson, B, 'Northern Ireland's emergency legislation: the wrong medicine' [1993] PL 592.

113 Under the Northern Ireland Act 1974.

114 *Northern Ireland: A Framework for Devolution*, Cmnd 8541, 1982, London: HMSO.

Assembly was dissolved in 1986. In 1983, the New Ireland Forum was established, in which the major political parties in the south and north were represented. The outcome of deliberations was the Anglo-Irish Agreement, signed by the Prime Ministers of the United Kingdom and the Republic of Ireland in 1985.[115]

The Anglo-Irish Agreement 1985

The Agreement endorsed the principle that no constitutional change concerning the relationship between the north and south could come about other than with the consent of a majority of the people in Northern Ireland. That majority did not currently exist. In the absence of such consent, it was agreed that there should be closer co-operation in relation to security, economic, social and cultural matters and the promotion of reconciliation between the two parts of Ireland. An Inter-governmental Conference was established with a membership drawn from representatives of both south and north to consider reforms across a range of issues. The British government undertook to consider any recommendations made, although the ultimate sovereignty over Northern Ireland remained firmly in the United Kingdom. Under the Anglo-Irish Agreement, the work of the Inter-governmental Conference was to be reviewed after three years. Reforms implemented since the Agreement included the Fair Employment (Northern Ireland) Act 1989, which aimed at removing discrimination in employment, and the introduction of an independent Commission for Police Complaints.

The Unionists of Northern Ireland opposed the Agreement, regarding the involvement of the Republic in the Intergovernmental Conference as an unwarranted interference with the affairs of the north and an indication that unification with the Republic remained on the agenda. In *Ex parte Molyneaux and Others*,[116] a challenge was issued over the legality of the Agreement. In an application for judicial review,[117] it was claimed that the Agreement would fetter the powers and duties of the Secretary of State for Northern Ireland, created a distinction between the rights of citizens of Northern Ireland and those of the rest of the United Kingdom contrary to Article 6 of the Union with Ireland Act 1800, and that the Executive – as opposed to the Queen in Council – had no power to exercise the prerogative and enter into agreements with the Republic of Ireland. The application was dismissed.

---

115 See Connolly, M and Loughlin, J, 'Reflections on the Anglo-Irish Agreement' (1986) 21 Government and Opposition 146; Hadfield, B, 'The Anglo-Irish Agreement 1985 – blue print or green print' (1986) 37 NILQ 1; Harvey Cox, W, 'The Anglo-Irish Agreement' (1987) 40 Parl Aff 80; McGarry, J, 'The Anglo-Irish Agreement and the prospects for power sharing in Northern Ireland?' (1988) 59 Political Quarterly 236.

116 [1986] 1 WLR 331.

117 See Chapters 24 and 25.

The Joint Declaration 1993

In 1993, a Joint Declaration was signed between the British and Irish governments. The Declaration recognised and renewed the commitment to preservation of the union with the United Kingdom for as long as a majority of the people of Northern Ireland so wished. The Declaration also, however, indicated for the first time that the British government had 'no selfish, strategic or economic interest' in Northern Ireland, thus officially giving recognition to the neutrality of the government's position over the long term future of the province. In September 1994, the IRA announced a ceasefire of hostilities. The British government responded with cautious optimism. In the same month, and as a response to the ceasefire, the government announced that the ban on live sound broadcasts by members of Sinn Fein would be lifted. The exclusion order on the President of Sinn Fein, Mr Gerry Adams, was also lifted.[118]

In 1995, with the lasting of the ceasefire in Northern Ireland, the prospects for peace in Northern Ireland were higher than at any time in the past. Full negotiations between Sinn Fein and the British government were, however, delayed, in part by a dispute over the terms for negotiation and in part over the refusal of the IRA to relinquish its armoury of weapons[119] in advance of peace talks.

The fragile hopes of 1995 were dashed in February 1996 when the IRA bombed Canary Wharf in London, thus ending the ceasefire. Further IRA action took place on the mainland, but not initially in Northern Ireland itself. In December 1996, the British government announced the terms for including Sinn Fein in all party discussions for the purpose of reaching a settlement. These included the announcement of a permanent ceasefire – proof that the IRA would bring the violence permanently to an end. The government's demands were rejected by Gerry Adams, President of Sinn Fein, and criticised by the Prime Minister of the Irish Republic.

The election of the Labour government in May 1997 led to renewed efforts to revitalise the peace talks.

In September 1997, following a renewal of the ceasefire by the IRA, and Sinn Fein's renunciation of the use of force, peace talks commenced between all parties. In February 1998, however, following renewed violence, Sinn Fein was expelled from the talks, but told that it could return if violence ceased. The Chairman of the talks, George Mitchell, in March set a 15 day deadline on the talks, which culminated in formal proposals being drawn up. On Good Friday, 10 April 1998, agreement was finally reached.

---

118 On emergency legislation in respect of Northern Ireland, see Chapter 23.
119 As the IRA refused to do in 1923: see above, p 67.

The agreement centred on five principal points. First, the principle that Northern Ireland would remain part of the United Kingdom was endorsed, and the Republic of Ireland agreed to amend its constitution to remove its claim to Northern Ireland.[120] Secondly, a Northern Ireland Assembly of 108 members was to be elected under a system of proportional representation. The Assembly is to be run by an executive of 12 members. Thirdly, a North-South ministerial council was to be established by the Assembly in order to coordinate relations between Ireland and Ulster. Fourthly, a Council of the Isles was to be established, its membership to be drawn from the Parliaments at Westminster, Dublin, Edinburgh and the Welsh Assembly. Finally, all participants expressed the commitment to the disarmament of paramilitary organisations, a commitment the fulfilment of which was a condition for the devolution of power.

In order for the agreement to take effect, referendums were held in both the Republic of Ireland and Northern Ireland. In Northern Ireland, the vote in favour of the agreement was 71.12 per cent, with a turnout of 80.98 per cent. In the Irish Republic, 94.40 per cent voted for the agreement, the turnout being 55.47 per cent. In June 1998, elections were held for membership of the Northern Ireland Assembly.

The results of the election produced an Assembly with power shared by the four main political parties, with five minority parties winning 18 seats between them. The Ulster Unionists won 28 seats with 21.3 per cent of the vote; the Social Democratic and Labour Party 14 seats with 22.2 per cent of the vote; the Democratic Unionist Party 20 seats with 18.1 per cent of the vote and *Sinn Fein* 18 seats with 17.6 per cent of the vote.

In 1999, the devolution of power was complete, the Assembly elected and a power sharing executive in place. As noted above, however, the full devolution of power was conditional on agreement being reached over the decommissioning of paramilitary weapons. When the IRA refused to co-operate and it became clear that decommissioning was not to occur, the Assembly was suspended, and power returned to Westminster under the Northern Ireland Act 2000, to be restored once again following further negotiations. The position relating to the Northern Ireland Assembly will be returned to in Chapter 12.

THE BRITISH ISLANDS

The United Kingdom, the Channel Islands and the Isle of Man, together, comprise the British Islands.[121] Accordingly, while the islands are not part of

---

120 Constitution, Arts 2 and 3.
121 Interpretation Act 1978, s 5 and Sched 1.

the United Kingdom, they are part of Her Majesty's dominions. Citizens of the islands are treated as citizens of the United Kingdom for the purposes of the British Nationality Act 1981.

The Channel Islands[122]

The Channel Islands comprise the islands of Jersey, Guernsey, Alderney and Sark. Historically part of the Duchy of Normandy, the Channel Islands remained in allegiance to the King of England when Normandy was lost by the English in 1204. The islands are organised under two separate Bailiwicks: the Bailiwick of Jersey and the Bailiwick of Guernsey, which includes Alderney and Sark. Each Bailiwick enjoys its own legislature, court structure and system of law. Alderney and Sark, whilst part of the Guernsey Bailiwick, enjoy a large measure of independence, having their own legislative assemblies.

The States of Jersey comprises 52 elected members and five non-elected members. The States of Guernsey comprises 61 members. Official links between the Crown and the United Kingdom government are through the Lieutenant Governor of the Bailiwicks. The legislature – the States – is headed by the Bailiff and Deputy Bailiff.

The Isle of Man

The Isle of Man became formally linked with England in 1405. From that time until 1765, it was ruled by 'Kings' or 'Lords' of Man. Under Acts of Parliament of 1765[123] and 1825,[124] the Westminster Parliament assumed, in the name of the Crown, the rights of the Lords. In 1958, under the Isle of Man Act of that year, much control over the Isle was relinquished by Westminster. The Isle enjoys full powers of self-government and has its own system of courts and law. The head of the Executive, the Lieutenant Governor of the Isle of Man, is the formal link between the local administration and the Crown and United Kingdom government. The Parliament (the Court of Tynwald) has executive and legislative functions. It comprises the Lieutenant Governor, the Legislative Council and the House of Keys. The lower House – the House of Keys – has 24 members elected on a constituency basis for a five year term of office. The Legislative Council comprises the senior Bishop, the Attorney General, a judge and seven members elected by the House of Keys.

---

122 See, *inter alia, Report of the Royal Commission on the Constitution*, Cmnd 5460, 1973, London: HMSO, Vol 1, Pt XI.

123 Isle of Man Purchase Act 1765.

124 Duke of Atholl's Rights, Isle of Man, Act 1825.

The constitutional relationship between the islands and the United Kingdom

> The constitutional position of the islands is thus unique. In some respects, they are like miniature States with wide powers of self-government ...[125]

The Crown has ultimate responsibility for the islands. Under international law, the United Kingdom government is responsible both for the islands' international relations and for their defence. Where legislative measures are to extend to the islands, these are effected through the Privy Council. Acts of Parliament only extend to the islands if the statute expressly so provides, or where the Act applies to all Her Majesty's dominions 'by necessary implication'.[126] The Bailiwicks of Jersey and Guernsey do not accept that either the United Kingdom Parliament or the Queen in Council have the power to legislate for them without the consent of the local legislatures and registration in the Royal Court. Contrary to the accepted doctrine of parliamentary supremacy, the Channel Islands deny that Acts of Parliament or prerogative acts, under Orders in Council, can take effect without local registration.

THE ISLANDS AND EUROPE

The European Community and Union

When the United Kingdom signed the Treaty of Rome, special arrangements had to be effected for the islands.[127] Under Article 227(4) of the Treaty of Rome, the Treaty extends to all territories for which Member States have responsibility for their international relations. Were the Treaty to extend automatically to the islands, it would confer power of the institutions of the Community to legislate for the islands in matters such as taxation which the United Kingdom Parliament, consistent with the convention, would have no *de facto* power to legislate. Accordingly the islands sought special terms in relation to membership of the Community. The resulting solution was that the United Kingdom government negotiated special status for the islands in relation to the Community: the islands are part of the Community for the purpose of free movement of industrial and agricultural goods but not for the purpose of free movement of persons or taxation provisions.

---

125 *Report of the Royal Commission on the Constitution*, Cmnd 5460, 1973, London: HMSO, Vol 1, para 1360.

126 *Sodor and Man (Bishop) v Derby (Earl)* (1751) 2 Ves Sen 337.

127 See Simmonds, KR, 'The British Islands and the Community: II Isle of Man' (1970) 7 CMLR 454 and 'The British Islands and the Community: III Guernsey' (1971) 8 CMLR 475.

The European Convention on Human Rights

While the position of the Channel Islands and the Isle of Man vis à vis the European Community is the same, the position is different in relation to the Convention. Initially, the Convention on Human Rights extended to both the Channel Islands and the Isle of Man, and nowadays it continues to apply to the Channel Islands.[128] While the Convention initially applied to the Isle of Man, the case of *Tyrer v United Kingdom*[129] brought about a change. In *Tyrer's* case, the European Court of Human Rights held that judicial birching in the Isle of Man of a juvenile amounted to degrading punishment in violation of Article 3 of the Convention. As a result, the Isle of Man government requested that the right of individual petition under the Convention be withdrawn. The United Kingdom government acceded to the request.

LOCAL GOVERNMENT IN ENGLAND AND WALES[130]

Local government antecedes central government by many centuries. Consideration will be given to local government in Chapter 12. Suffice here to note that the country is divided into local authorities, each having law making and administrative powers as delegated by Parliament. Local authorities are entirely creatures of statute: accordingly, the only powers which they have are those conferred by the sovereign Westminster Parliament. Increasingly, however, the law of the European Community requires action at local authority level.

With the devolution of legislative power to the Scottish Parliament, Northern Ireland Assembly and Welsh Assembly, and the government's commitment to give further consideration to extending the principle of regional government to English regions, significant changes have occurred to the governmental structure of the United Kingdom.

THE EUROPEAN COMMUNITY AND UNION

The United Kingdom's membership of the European Community and Union represents perhaps the most significant challenge to the constitution. It is no longer possible, realistically, to view the United Kingdom as an isolated constitutional entity. Rather, it must be viewed as a distinctive nation (or union of distinctive nations) within the larger union formed by the European

---

128 See *Gillow v United Kingdom* (1986) 11 EHRR 335.
129 (1978) 2 EHRR 1.
130 Local government in Scotland and Northern Ireland is differently arranged.

Community and Union. The aims and institutions of the Community, its law making powers and the relationship between the law of the United Kingdom and European law will be discussed in Chapters 8 and 9.

THE UNITED KINGDOM AND THE COMMONWEALTH[131]

From Empire to Commonwealth

In the sixteenth and seventeenth centuries, Britain embarked on empire building, although the original expansion of British interests overseas was essentially undertaken by private commercial companies. Where territory was taken over by conquest, it became the property of the Crown.[132] Legal authority over such territories vested in the Crown and political control lay with the Privy Council.[133]

The earliest 'revolution' against colonisation came with the American Declaration of Independence in 1776 in which Britain was deprived of 13 North American colonies. By the end of the nineteenth century, vast swathes of the world's map were 'coloured pink' – that is to say, under British power and control. The relationship between Britain and its colonies may be characterised as the movement from full British sovereignty over the territories through to increasing self-government and independence. In 1865, the Colonial Laws Validity Act was passed by the British Parliament in order to clarify the relationship between British law and colonial law and the capacity of colonial legislatures for self-regulation.[134] While the Act confirmed self-regulating legislative capacity, it also affirmed the principle that such devolved powers were subject to the overriding sovereignty of the imperial Parliament.

In 1867, Canada became the first self-governing Dominion, (a status implying equality with rather than subordination to Britain), to be followed by Australia in 1900, New Zealand in 1907, South Africa in 1910 and the Irish Free State in 1921. The recognition that the Empire was being transformed into a Commonwealth of Nations came in 1884.

The desire for formal recognition and explication of the constitutional relationship between Britain and the Dominions led to four-yearly Prime Ministerial conferences, commenced in 1887. The Imperial Conference of 1926 adopted the Balfour Report which defined the Dominions as:

---

131 See, *inter alia*, Roberts-Wray, K, *Commonwealth and Colonial Law*, 1966, London: Stevens; Dale, W, *The Modern Commonwealth*, 1983, London: Butterworths; Wheare, KC, *The Constitutional Structure of the Commonwealth*, 1960, Oxford: Clarendon; de Smith, SA, *The New Commonwealth and its Constitutions*, 1964, London: Stevens.

132 *Calvin's Case* (1608) 7 Co Rep 1a.

133 On which, see, further, Chapter 10.

134 See, further, Chapter 7.

> ... autonomous communities within the British Empire, equal in status, in no way subordinate one to another in any aspect of their domestic or external affairs, though united by common allegiance to the Crown, and freely associated as members of the British Commonwealth of Nations.

The Statute of Westminster 1931 gave formal recognition to this definition. Section 2 of the Act extended the powers of Dominion legislatures to amend or repeal Acts of the United Kingdom Parliament, although this power did not extend to going against the limits on the Dominion's legislative capacity as laid down in the Acts containing that country's constitution.[135, 136]

By the end of the Second World War in 1945, much of the remaining British power had been repossessed by its rightful owners, either through direct resistance to British rule[137] or negotiated constitutional settlements between the British Crown and the formerly dependent territory.[138] From this time, what remained of the British Empire was transformed into a loosely defined, voluntary Commonwealth of nations, of which the British monarch represents the formal Head.[139] While the Commonwealth was originally characterised by its members' allegiance to the British Crown, the movement towards republicanism forced a change in direction for the Commonwealth. It was Indian independence which represented the catalyst for change. India had remained a Dominion under the India Act of 1935, until independence in 1947. In 1949, India's desire to become a republic and yet remain within the Commonwealth posed a novel question concerning the allegiance to the British Crown. The London Declaration of 1949 revised the position and enabled India to enter as the first republican member. Heads of government also agreed, however, at this meeting, that members would continue to recognise the Crown as the 'symbol of their free association and thus Head of the Commonwealth', the position which still pertains.

The Commonwealth today

Unlike the European Union and Community, the Commonwealth is undefined by legal texts; it is not established nor regulated by Treaty; nor do

---

135 See *Harris v Minister of the Interior* (1952)(2) SA 428; *British Coal Corporation v R* [1935] AC 500; *Ndlwana v Hofmeyer* [1937] AD 229; and see, further, Chapter 7.

136 The constitutional position in relation to Canada was defined by the British North America Act 1867, which contained no amendment provisions. Accordingly, it remained for the United Kingdom Parliament to amend the Canadian Constitution. This anomalous position was resolved in 1982 by the Canada Act which 'repatriated' the Canadian Constitution. For a challenge to the Act, see *Re Amendment of the Constitution of Canada* (1981) 125 DLR (3d) 1, discussed in Chapter 2.

137 As in India.

138 The constitutional relationship between the United Kingdom Parliament and Australia was finally resolved in 1986 under the Australia Act, which severed the legislative links with Westminster and terminated appeals from the Australian courts to the Privy Council.

139 See, further, *op cit*, Dale, fn 132; *op cit*, Roberts-Wray, fn 132.

formal legal procedures regulate its inter-governmental relations. Rather, the Commonwealth is characterised by 'bonds of common origin, history and legal traditions'. The Commonwealth is made up of 54 countries,[140] ranging from monarchies – either under Queen Elizabeth II or national monarchs – to republics.[141] Nowadays, 32 members are republics and five have national monarchies of their own, while 16 are constitutional monarchies which recognise Queen Elizabeth II as Head of State. The total population of the Commonwealth is 1.7 billion. The shared history and traditions of Britain and other Commonwealth members, including legal traditions, provides the basis for this voluntary association of States, which spans six continents and five oceans, and which operates without a formal Charter or Constitution.

The Commonwealth was defined in 1971 at the Commonwealth Heads of Government Meeting (CHOGM) (CHOGMs take place every two years) as:

> ... a voluntary association of independent sovereign States, each responsible for its own policies, consulting and cooperating in the common interests of their peoples and in the promotion of international understanding and world peace.[142]

Further, at the 1971 CHOGM held in Singapore, Heads of Government issued the Declaration of Commonwealth Principles. The principles include:

(a) the commitment to international peace in order to ensure the security and prosperity of mankind;

(b) commitments to the liberty of the individual, irrespective of race, colour, creed or political belief and the individual's democratic right to participate in democratic political processes;

(c) a commitment to combatting racial discrimination;

(d) an opposition to all forms of colonial domination;

(e) a commitment to removal of disparities in wealth between nations and to raising standards of living; and

(f) a commitment to international co-operation.

These principles were reaffirmed and extended at the Harare CHOGM in 1991, which declared the Commonwealth's commitment to promoting democracy, good government, human rights and the rule of law and gender equality within the context of sustainable economic and social development. Commonwealth members provide assistance to other countries in their transition to democracy by drafting legislation and reviewing electoral procedures.

---

140 Nigeria's membership of the Commonwealth was suspended in 1995.
141 See Appendix III, pp 1031–32, for a full list of Member States.
142 Commonwealth Declaration, 22 January 1971.

The Commonwealth Secretariat

The Commonwealth is headed by a Secretary General. Under his stewardship, the Commonwealth Secretariat has been refashioned to enable it better to achieve Commonwealth objectives. The Secretariat was formed in 1965 and now has 12 separate divisions.[143] The operational arm of the secretariat is the Commonwealth Fund for Technical Co-operation, established in 1971,[144] which, at the request of Commonwealth governments, provides: '... technical assistance and expert advice on all issues within the Commonwealth's agenda.'[145]

Appeals from Commonwealth courts to the Privy Council

The Judicial Committee of the Privy Council has jurisdiction to hear appeals from 'dependencies of the Crown'. Deriving from the royal prerogative,[146] the jurisdiction was given statutory force under the Judicial Committee Acts of 1833 and 1844. Appeals may be with special leave of the Privy Council, or without leave. Appeals with special leave are predominantly criminal cases. Appeals against the death penalty represent the majority of appeals.[147]

While, before independence, colonies had no power to abolish appeals to the Privy Council, on independence, this power arose. As a result, a majority of Commonwealth countries have abolished the right of appeal. The Privy Council, however, continues to hear appeals from the Bahamas, Barbados, Belize, the Gambia, Guyana, Jamaica, Malaysia, Mauritius, New Zealand, Singapore, and Trinidad and Tobago.[148]

---

143 The Secretariat is funded by an assessed budget (in 1996–97, amounting to £120.4 million), contributed to by member governments on an agreed scale based on each country's population and income. In addition to the assessed budget are the Commonwealth Fund for Technical Co-operation, the Commonwealth Youth Programme, and the Commonwealth Science Council, each of which has its own budget.

144 In 1996–97, the CFTC had an annual budget of £25 million.

145 The CFTC has four principal divisions: Economic and Legal Advisory Services Division; the Export and Industrial Development Division; the General Technical Assistance Services Division and the Management and Training Services Division.

146 On which, see Chapter 6.

147 See *Hector v Attorney General of Antigua* [1990] 2 AC 312; *Runyowa v R* [1967] 1 AC 26; *Ong Ah Chuan v Public Prosecutor* [1981] AC 648; *Riley v Attorney General of Jamaica* [1983] 1 AC 719; *Pratt v Attorney General of Jamaica* [1994] 2 AC 1; *Reckley v Minister of Public Safety (No 2)* [1996] 2 WLR 281.

148 Barbados, Guyana, Jamaica and Trinidad are reported to be in the process of establishing a Caribbean Court of Justice to replace the jurisdiction of the Privy Council: Harding, R, 'Caribbeans reject Privy Council jurisdiction' (1998) The Lawyer, 14 July.

PART II

FUNDAMENTAL CONSTITUTIONAL CONCEPTS

CHAPTER 4

THE RULE OF LAW

Where laws do not rule, there is no constitution.[1]

INTRODUCTION

The rule of law represents one of the most challenging concepts of the constitution. The rule of law is a concept which is capable of different interpretations by different people, and it is this feature which renders an understanding of the doctrine elusive. Of all constitutional concepts, the rule of law is also the most subjective and value laden. The apparent uncertainties in the rule of law and its variable nature should not cause concern, although, inevitably, it will cause some insecurity. In the study of the rule of law, it is more important to recognise and appreciate the many rich and varied interpretations which have been given to it, and to recognise the potential of the rule of law for ensuring limited governmental power and the protection of individual rights, than to be able to offer an authoritative, definitive explanation of the concept.

The rule of law may be interpreted either as a *philosophy* or *political theory* which lays down fundamental requirements for law, or as a *procedural device* by which those with power rule under the law. The essence of the rule of law is that of the sovereignty or supremacy of law over man. The rule of law insists that every person – irrespective of rank and status in society – be subject to the law. For the citizen, the rule of law is both *prescriptive* – dictating the conduct required by law – and *protective* of citizens – demanding that government acts according to law. This central theme recurs whether the doctrine is examined from the perspective of philosophy, or political theory, or from the more pragmatic vantage point of the rule of law as a procedural device. The rule of law underlies the entire constitution and, in one sense, all constitutional law is concerned with the rule of law. The concept is of great antiquity and continues to exercise legal and political philosophers today.

The rule of law cannot be viewed in isolation from political society. The emphasis on the rule of law as a yardstick for measuring both the extent to which government acts under the law and the extent to which individual rights are recognised and protected by law, is inextricably linked with

---

1 Aristotle, *The Politics*, 1962, Sinclair, TA (trans), London: Penguin, Bk iv, para 1292a31.

Western democratic liberalism.[2] In this respect, it is only meaningful to speak of the rule of law in a society which exhibits the features of a democratically elected, responsible – and responsive – government and a separation of powers, which will result in a judiciary which is independent of government. In liberal democracies, therefore, the concept of the rule of law implies an acceptance that law itself represents a 'good'; that law and its governance is a demonstrable asset to society.

CONTRASTING ATTITUDES TO THE RULE OF LAW

It should not be assumed that this acceptance of law as a benevolent ruling force is universally accepted. In differing societies, subscribing to very different political philosophies, the insistence on the rule of law – in the Western liberal sense – has little application. For example, from a Marxist perspective,[3] the law serves not to restrict government and protect individual rights but rather to conceal the injustices inherent in the capitalist system. Accordingly, the concept of the rule of law – denoting some form of morality in law – represents no more than a false idealisation of law designed to reinforce the political structure and economic status quo in society. Echoes of this thesis dominate the more moderate socialist conceptions of the rule of law and the critique of liberalism. It can be argued – from the socialist perspective – that liberalism plays too little regard to true equality between persons and too great attention to the protection of property interests. The liberal domain thus becomes one which, again, masks true social and economic inequality while at the same time proclaiming equality and justice under the rule of law.[4]

The rule of law, as understood in liberal democracies, also has little relevance in a totalitarian State. While it is true that such a State will be closely regulated by law, there will not be government under the law – as adjudicated upon by an independent judiciary – which is insisted upon under the liberal tradition.

In traditional Oriental society, the Western preference for law is an alien notion. By way of example, in relation to traditional Chinese society, David and Brierley write:

> For the Chinese, legislation was not the normal means of guaranteeing a harmonious and smooth-working society. Laws, abstract in nature, could not

---

2   See, *inter alia*, Fine, R, *Democracy and the Rule of Law: Liberal Ideals and Marxist Critiques*, 1984, London: Pluto; Hutchinson, AP and Monahan, P (eds), *The Rule of Law: Ideal or Ideology*, 1987, Toronto: Carswell; Neumann, F, *The Rule of Law: Political Theory and the Legal System in Modern Society*, 1986, Leamington Spa: Berg.

3   See, further, below, pp 97–98.

4   For a critical account of the liberal tradition, see Lustgarten, L, 'Socialism and the rule of law' (1988) 15 JLS 25.

take into account the infinite variety of possible situations. Their strict application was apt to affect man's innate sense of justice. To enact laws was therefore considered a bad policy by traditional Chinese doctrine. The very exactitude which laws establish in social relations, and the way in which they fix the rights and obligations of each individual, were considered evils, according to the Chinese, not benefits. The idea of 'rights', an inevitable development of the laws themselves, ran counter to the natural order. Once individuals think of their 'rights' there is, it was thought, some form of social illness; the only true matter of concern is one's duty to society and one's fellow men.

> The enactment of laws is an evil, since individuals, once familiar with them, will conclude that they have rights and will then be inclined to assert them, thereby abandoning the traditional rules of propriety and morality which should be the only guides to conduct. Legal disputes become numerous, and a trial, by reason of its very existence, is a scandalous disturbance of the natural order which may then lead to further disturbances of the social order to the detriment of all society.[5]

In Japan, despite the nineteenth century adoption of codes based on French and German models,[6] law, in the Western sense, remained largely irrelevant to traditional Japanese life:

> Still essential for the Japanese are the rules of behaviour (*giri-ninjo*) for each type of personal relation established by tradition and founded, at least in appearance, on the feelings of affection (*ninjo*) uniting those in such relationships. A person who does not observe these rules is seeking his own interest rather than obeying the nobler part of his nature; he brings scorn upon himself and his family. Apart from the contracts arising between important but depersonalised business and industrial concerns, one does not attempt to have one's rights enforced in a court of law even though this is permitted by the various codes ...[7]

As the notion of the rule of law is dependent upon the political foundations of a State, so, too, it is dependent – according to the approach adopted to the concept – upon a nation's economic resources. It may be that law, as a mere regulator of individual behaviour, is perfectly feasible in an impoverished State, and accordingly, a State which maintains law and order, and no more, can conform to a narrow interpretation of the rule of law which insists simply on a citizen's unquestioning compliance with rules of the law. However, if the rule of law implies more than mere regulation by law and is elevated to a theory guaranteeing freedom from hunger and homelessness and entitlement to a basic decent standard of life, then economic conditions are of paramount

---

5   David, R and Brierley, JEC, *Major Legal Systems*, 1st edn, 1966, London: Stevens, p 442, and see 3rd edn, 1985, London: Sweet & Maxwell, Title III, Chapter 1 for the persistence of traditional ideas.

6   Penal Code and Code of Criminal Procedure enacted in 1882; Codes on Judicial Organisation and Civil Procedure 1890; Commercial Code 1899.

7   *Ibid*, David and Brierley, 1st edn, p 458, and see 3rd edn, Title III, Chapter 2.

importance to conformity with the rule of law. Such an approach is adopted by the International Commission of Jurists, which in the New Delhi Declaration of 1959, included – alongside traditional civil and political rights – the realisation of social, economic, cultural and educational standards under which the individual could enjoy a fuller life within the ambit of the rule of law.[8] On the other hand, reasoning such as this is anathema to radical conservatives such as Friedrich von Hayek,[9] who viewed the correct role of government as being best confined to establishing clear, fixed rules of law which ensure maximum economic freedom for individuals, unimpeded either by planning controls or ideas of redistributive justice.[10] From von Hayek's perspective, the rule of law requires no more than the existence of a stable set of minimum rules which are to be applied in a uniform, non-discretionary manner. A legal system is viewed as just – and in conformity with the rule of law – if it exhibits both these features and an absence of discretionary rules or practices.

UNCERTAINTY IN THE WESTERN RULE OF LAW

An understanding and appreciation of the rule of law is both politically and culturally dependent. Moreover, it is also clear that the rule of law has more than one meaning, even within the Western liberal tradition. To some theorists, the rule of law represents an aspirational philosophy; to others, no more than a device under which compliance with law – good or bad in content – is secured. It has been remarked that:

> It would not be very difficult to show that the phrase 'the rule of law' has become meaningless thanks to ideological abuse and general over-use.[11]

Partly as a result of such 'over-use', some writers have refuted the claim that the rule of law represents anything other than a purely procedural or formalistic device. By way of example, Raz writes that the rule of law:

> ... says nothing about how the law is to be made: by tyrants, democratic majorities, or any other way. It says nothing about fundamental rights, about equality, or justice.[12]

Other writers have gone further. SA de Smith and R Brazier confine discussion of the rule of law to a few paragraphs and, having acknowledged

---

8   On this aspect, see, further, below, pp 121–22.

9   von Hayek, F, *The Road to Serfdom*, 1994, London: Routledge and Kegan Paul; von Hayek, F, *The Constitution of Liberty*, 1960, London: Routledge and Kegan Paul.

10 See, further, below, pp 98–99, and cf Rawls, J, *A Theory of Justice*, 1973, Oxford: OUP.

11 Shklar, JN, 'Political theory and the rule of law', in *op cit*, Hutchinson and Monahan, fn 2, p 1.

12 Raz, J, 'The rule of law and its virtue' (1977) 93 LQR 195 and *The Authority of Law*, 1979, Oxford: OUP, p 210.

the past influence of Dicey's ideas (but denied their contemporary relevance),[13] state that it would not be 'justifiable to examine the general concept of the rule of law at length in this book'.[14]

Contrast such a dismissive view with that expressed in the following statement:

> The rule of law is a rare and protean principle of our political tradition. Unlike other ideals, it has withstood the ravages of constitutional time and remains a contemporary clarion-call to political justice. Apparently transcending partisan concern, it is embraced and venerated by virtually all shades of political opinion. The rule of law's central core comprises the enduring values of regularity and restraint, embodied in the slogan of 'a government of laws, not ... men'.[15]

In light of such divergent assessments, it must be recognised that any attempt to align the rule of law with a broad philosophical doctrine – or indeed with any other interpretation – is likely to meet with opposition from some quarters. Notwithstanding such criticisms, the rule of law retains a secure grasp on political and legal thinking: it has 'enduring importance as a central artefact in our legal and political culture'.[16]

THE RULE OF LAW AS PHILOSOPHICAL DOCTRINE

The rule of law is an aspect of ancient and modern natural law thought.[17] In essence, the natural law tradition – of which there are many strands – insists that the authority of law derives not from the power of any political ruler, but from a higher source, either theological or secular. The laws of man must be evaluated against the dictates of this 'higher' form of law. It is impossible to provide more than a mere sketch of the rich history of natural law in Western philosophy and political thought and the legacy it gives to modern constitutions. Nevertheless, a basic understanding of its nature and evolution is instructive, for it reveals the manner in which the requirements of good law – morally worthwhile law – have been stipulated over centuries.

---

13 On which, see, further, below, pp 105–20.

14 de Smith, SA and Brazier, R, *Constitutional and Administrative Law*, 6th edn, 1989, London: Penguin, p 18 (see, now, 8th edn, 1998).

15 *Op cit*, Hutchinson and Monahan, fn 2, p ix.

16 *Op cit*, Raz, 1979, fn 12, p xiii.

17 On natural law, see d'Entrèves, AP, *Natural Law*, 2nd edn, 1970, London: Hutchinson; and Finnis, J, *Natural Law and Natural Rights*, 1980, Oxford: Clarendon.

Natural law in ancient Greece and Rome

Aristotle[18] stated that 'the rule of law is preferable to that of any individual'. The appeal to law as a control over naked power has been apparent throughout history. At a philosophical level, the natural law tradition, whether theological or secular, instructs that the power of man is not absolute, but is rather controlled and limited by the requirements of a higher law. To the ancient Greeks, man was under the governance of the laws of nature – the natural forces which controlled the universe – although this view is more closely aligned to the 'law of nature' than 'natural law' as it came to be understood in later times. However, from the time of Socrates, Plato[19] and Aristotle,[20] the quest for virtue – or goodness or justice under the law – has been a recurrent theme. Socrates, teacher and philosopher, was accused, tried and convicted by the grand jury of Athens for corrupting youth with his teachings. Despite the possibility of escape, Socrates chose to accept the verdict of death which had been imposed upon him, in order to demonstrate his fidelity to law. When pressed by Crito to escape, Socrates considered the questions which would be put to him by the laws and constitution of Athens were he to succumb to the temptation to escape the penalty of the law:

> Can you deny that by this act [of escaping] which you are contemplating you intend, so far as you have the power, to destroy us, the laws, and the whole State as well? Do you imagine that a city can continue to exist and not be turned upside down, if the legal judgments which are pronounced in it have no force but are nullified and destroyed by private persons?[21]

In submitting to death, Socrates was doing nothing other than giving recognition to the supremacy of law: to the rule of law. An early – and famous – formulation of the dictates of natural law was offered by Cicero:[22]

> True law is right reason in agreement with nature; it is of universal application, unchanging and everlasting; it summons to duty by its commands, and averts from wrongdoing by its prohibitions. And it does not lay its commands or prohibitions upon good men in vain, though neither have any effect on the wicked. It is a sin to try to alter this law, nor is it allowable to attempt to repeal any part of it, and it is impossible to abolish it entirely. We cannot be freed from its obligations by Senate or People, and we need not look outside ourselves for an expounder or interpreter of it. And there will not be different laws at Rome and at Athens, or different laws now and in the future, but one eternal and unchangeable law will be valid for all nations and for all times, and

---

18 *Op cit*, Aristotle, fn 1, p 16.
19 427–347 BC.
20 384–322 BC.
21 Crito, in Hamilton, E and Cairns, H (eds), *Plato's Collected Dialogues*, 1989, Ewing, New Jersey: Princeton UP, p 50b.
22 106–43 BC.

there will be one master and one ruler, that is, God, over us all, for He is the author of this law, its promulgator, and its enforcing judge.[23]

It is from ancient Greek philosophy that natural law enters into Roman law. From the *Corpus Iuris Civilis*[24] is derived *ius civilis*, *ius gentium* and *ius naturale*. *Ius civilis* denotes the law of the State; *ius gentium* the law of nations; and *ius naturale* 'a law which expresses a higher and more permanent standard'. It is the law of nature (*ius naturale*), which corresponds to 'that which is always good and equitable'.[25]

Christian natural law thought

The scriptures and gospel provided the basis for Christian natural law thought which developed in the Middle Ages. Natural law was perceived as God-given, communicated to man by Revelation, and remaining absolutely binding upon man and unchanging in its content. As a result, the dictates of natural law take precedence over man made laws. If the demands of the State conflict with the laws of God, the obligation to God must prevail. Undoubtedly, the most powerful writing of the Middle Ages comes from St Thomas Aquinas:[26]

> This rational guidance of created things on the part of God ... we can call the Eternal Law.

> But, of all others, rational creatures are subject to divine Providence in a very special way; being themselves made participators in Providence itself, in that they control their own actions and the actions of others. So they have a share in the divine reason itself, deriving therefrom a natural inclination to such actions and ends as are fitting. This participation in the Eternal Law by rational creatures is called Natural Law.[27]

In the thirteenth century, Bracton[28] proclaimed that 'the King himself ought not be subject to man but subject to God and to the law, because the law makes him King'. In 1534, Thomas More[29] – at the cost of his life – refused to recognise Henry VIII as head of the Church, thereby acknowledging the higher duty of obedience to God rather than the rule of his temporal King.

---

23 Cicero, *De Republica*, III, xxii, 33, cited in *op cit*, d'Entrèves, fn 17, p 25.

24 AD 534.

25 *Op cit*, d'Entrèves, fn 17, p 24.

26 1225–74.

27 Aquinas, T (St), *Summa Theologica*, 1947–48, Fathers of the English Dominican Province (trans), London: Burns & Oates, 1a 2ae, quae 91, arts 1 and 2, cited in *op cit*, d'Entrèves, fn 17, p 43.

28 Bracton, H, *The Laws and Customs of England* (1200–68), 1968–77, Thorne, SE (trans), Cambridge, Mass: Harvard UP, f5 b.

29 1478–1535.

Natural law and international law

On an international level, natural law thought played a significant role in establishing the overarching dictates of international law. Grotius,[30] for example, maintained that natural law was discernible by man by virtue of his rationality and that a system of natural law would accordingly exist independently of theological perceptions and dictates. In short, natural law would exist even if God did not exist. In addition to the insistence on rationalism, the emphasis of natural law at this time started to focus on the individual, and from this period is discerned the origins of assertions of the rights of man. AP d'Entrèves writes that:

> ... when we read the American or the French Declarations we know that we are confronted with a complete architecture, about the style of which there can be no mistake. It is a political philosophy based upon a particular notion of the individual, of society and of their mutual relationship.[31]

The idea of social contract

It is from these beginnings that the theories of social contract and the rights of man derive.[32] The writings of John Locke,[33] Jean-Jacques Rousseau[34] and Thomas Paine[35] are all infused with the doctrine of the inalienability of individual human rights – rights which transcend the law of the State, which cannot be overridden by the State, and which affirm the supremacy of the law of the State with the important proviso that the law of the State is in compliance with natural law.

Natural law and common law

In the West, the sovereignty of law became inextricably linked with the Christian faith. As seen above, in the thirteenth century, Aquinas asserted the overriding obligation to God, as opposed to any temporal power. In England, the break with the Roman Catholic Church in 1535 established Henry VIII as head of the English Church. By assuming supreme power over both spiritual and secular matters, Henry VIII ostensibly broke the logical separation of duty towards God and the duty owed to the King: obedience to the sovereign now became a religious as well as a political duty. The execution of Sir Thomas

---

30 1583–1645.
31 *Op cit*, d'Entrèves, fn 17, p 57.
32 See, further, Chapter 19.
33 Locke, J, *Two Treatises on Government* (1690), 1977, London: JM Dent.
34 Rousseau, J, *The Social Contract and Discourses* (1762), 1977, London: JM Dent.
35 Paine, T, *Rights of Man* (1791, Pt I), 1984, rep 1998, Collins, H (ed), New York: Penguin.

More in 1534 is illustrative of the King's reaction to an individual refusal to recognise the absolute supremacy of the King. Nevertheless, natural law thought continued to permeate the common law of England before the settlement of 1688 and the rise of Parliamentary sovereignty.

One of the classic exponents of the demand for the King to be subject to the law – rather than above it – was Sir Edward Coke,[36] whose struggle with the King led to his dismissal as Chief Justice in 1616. James I[37] viewed himself as imbued with ultimate power, derived from God under the prerogative. To Coke, laws derived from Parliament – comprising the King and the three estates of the realm, that is of the Lords Spiritual, the Lords Temporal and the Commons.[38] The power of Parliament was subject to the common law, and hence it was that Coke declared:

> It appears in our books that in many cases the common law will control the Acts of Parliament and sometimes adjudge them to be utterly void; for when an Act of Parliament is against the common right or repugnant or impossible to be performed the common law will control it and adjudge such Act to be void.[39]

When, in 1608, Coke told the King that the common law protected the King, the King regarded his speech as traitorous, proclaiming that 'The King protecteth the law, and not the law the King'.[40] Coke's insistence on the supremacy of common law was not pure natural law thought, but rather the philosophical view of the power of legal reasoning deriving from precedent. Indeed it was the King who claimed natural law as being on his side, claiming that the King was not 'ignorant of any points [of law] which belong to a King to know'.[41] Sir Francis Bacon[42] favoured the King's view, seeking to limit the power of the judges: it was for the King to formulate policy and make law.[43] Coke's view nevertheless expresses an idea which is central to natural law thought, namely that there is a higher authority – based on moral judgment – than the law of man. The control of the prerogative power of the King was to dominate English constitutional development until 1688.[44] With the settlement of 1688 and the Bill of Rights 1689, the doctrine of parliamentary supremacy over the King, the prerogative and common law was established.

---

36 1552–1634.

37 King of Scotland 1567–1625; King of England and Scotland 1603–25.

38 Coke, E (Sir), *Institutes of the Laws of England; Concerning the Jurisdiction of the Courts*, 1644, Bk IV, Chapter 1.

39 *Dr Bonham's Case* (1610) 8 Co Rep 114a; 2 Brown 255. But see the contrary explanation offered by Thorne, SE, '*Dr Bonham's Case*' (1938) 54 LQR 543. See, also, Chapter 7.

40 Bowen, CD, *The Lion and the Throne*, 1957, London: Hamish Hamilton.

41 *Ibid*.

42 1561–1626.

43 Bacon, F, *Advancement of Learning*, 1951, Oxford: OUP.

44 See Chapters 6 and 7.

Thereafter, there were to be no assertions of any overriding higher law. The judges bowed to the sovereignty of Parliament.

THE RULE OF LAW AS POLITICAL THEORY

Liberalism, conservatism and the rule of law

The rule of law has been subjected to analysis by political theorists of all persuasions. From the vantage point of the liberal democrat, the rule of law will ensure the minimum rules in society to enable man to fulfil his life plan according to law, but with the minimum interference of law.

AV Dicey's writing on the rule of law has had a lasting influence on constitutional thought.[45] His writing will be considered in detail below.[46] However, Dicey has been criticised by Sir Ivor Jennings for being motivated, in his writings, by his conservative views. Dicey, in expressing his preference for clear and stable rules and the minimum of discretion within the legal process, was, according to Jennings, revealing his conservative preference for certainty within law rather than concern for the law being directed towards social justice which necessarily entails much discretionary power in the application of broad rules. Jennings writes that Dicey was 'concerned not with clearing up of the nasty industrial sections of the towns, but with the liberty of the subject'.[47] For Jennings, Dicey's view that 'Englishmen are ruled by the law, and by the law alone'[48] is 'not enough':[49]

> The powers of Louis XIV, of Napoleon I, of Hitler, and of Mussolini were derived from the law, even though that law be only 'The Leader may do and order what he pleases'. The doctrine involves some considerable limitation on the powers of every political authority, except possibly (for this is open to dispute) those of a representative legislature. Indeed it contains, as we shall see, something more, though it is not capable of precise definition. It is an attitude, an expression of liberal and democratic principles, in themselves vague when it is sought to analyse them, but clear enough in their results.[50]

For Jennings, the doctrine implies, first, that the State as a whole must be regulated by law; secondly, that the separation of powers is implied within the doctrine in order to prevent dictatorship or absolutism. Accordingly, there

---

45 Dicey, AC, *Introduction to the Study of the Law of the Constitution*, 10th edn, 1959, London: Macmillan, Chapter IV.

46 See pp 108–22.

47 Jennings, I (Sir), *The Law and the Constitution*, 5th edn, 1959, London: Hodder & Stoughton, p 311.

48 Cited in *ibid*, Appendix II.

49 *Ibid*, p 47.

50 *Ibid*, p 48.

are incorporated certain basic requirements[51] of the law: equality before the law; clearly defined police powers; clear general rules adjudicated upon by the courts; non-retrospectivity in penal statutes; and the strict construction of penal statutes. Thirdly, the doctrine incorporates the principle of *equality*: a notion which Jennings concedes is as vague as that of the rule of law itself.[52] Moreover, and of prime importance, the rule of law implies the notion of *liberty*.

Marxism and the rule of law

Arguments against a formalistic perception of the rule of law adopted by, *inter alia*, Dicey and von Hayek present a formidable target for attack from a Marxist perspective. Where liberalism insists that law is neutral as between persons and classes and favours maximum liberty for all under the law, Marxism insists that law represents the interests of the powerful within society. Law is an ideological device engaged by those with power to mask the reality of that power in society, and the correlative powerlessness of the ordinary citizen. The rule of law is thus portrayed as a means of subterfuge: it is a mere pretence which hides injustice. Marxism stands in opposition to liberalism and yet, paradoxically, seeks as its end result the complete liberty of man. Law, from a Marxist perspective, is the reflection of economic power within society, a power which is used to exploit the powerless. Thus it is that, under capitalism, the worker is not rewarded with the full value of his labour: rather, he receives a price for his labour to which is added production costs and profits and together comprise the final price of a product. The laws which regulate factories and employment terms are all underpinned by the acceptance of the capitalist ideal. Laws which ameliorate the conditions of the poor do not represent – as appears at first sight – real social justice, but rather they represent a calculated means by which the poor are kept compliant within their powerlessness.[53] Accordingly, the Welfare State is but a cynical mask for maintenance of the status quo which defeats the movement towards revolutionary economic and social change:

> Far from hastening the revolution, the Welfare State undermines efforts to create working class solidarity. By preventing the fullest development of the material degradation of the working class and by providing a limited immunity from the vicissitudes of economic crises, a Welfare State delays the formation of class consciousness and thus prevents a revolutionary situation from arising ... Many of these benefits, and hosts of others, have been won by political struggles aimed at the introduction of legislation. But from the

---

51   Cf *op cit*, Raz, 1977, fn 12; *op cit*, Raz, 1979, fn 12, Chapter 11; and Fuller, L, *The Morality of Law*, 1964, New Haven: Yale UP.

52   *Op cit*, Jennings, fn 47, p 49.

53   See Cain, M and Hunt, A, *Marx and Engels on Law*, 1979, London: Academic.

Marxist perspective, they are a mixed blessing. Immediate results are traded for long term disabilities in forming a dynamic, working class movement. Welfare legislation obscures the structure of class domination based on the relations of production and reduces the asperity of class antagonisms.[54]

Whether law serves to oppress or merely to uphold the economic status quo – and there exists dispute on this matter between Marxists themselves – law, from a Marxist perspective, does not serve the interests of all in society. The rule of law thus becomes a grand slogan under which is hidden the reality of oppression and absence of liberty. The capitalist's insistence on the rule of law is seen as a 'fetishism' which must be removed along with economic oppression.[55] Only when the capitalist system breaks down, and the law which serves it 'withers away', will society become truly free. When that occurs, there will be no need for law and man will achieve true freedom.

Professor Joseph Raz and the rule of law

Professor Joseph Raz approaches the rule of law from a morally neutral but conceptual standpoint, and asserts that:

> The rule of law is a political ideal which a legal system may lack or may possess to a greater or lesser degree. That much is common ground. It is also to be insisted that the rule of law is just one of the virtues which a legal system may possess and by which it is to be judged. It is not to be confused with democracy, justice, equality (before the law or otherwise), human rights of any kind or respect for persons or for the dignity of man. A non-democratic legal system, based on the denial of human rights, on extensive poverty, on racial segregation, sexual inequalities, and religious persecution may, in principle, conform to the requirements of the rule of law better than any of the legal systems of the more enlightened Western democracies.[56]

Raz acknowledges that his claim will 'alarm many',[57] but insists that it presents 'a coherent view of one important virtue which legal systems should possess'. In seeking to elucidate the ideal of the rule of law, Raz draws the analogy between the rule of law and a knife. One quality of a good knife is sharpness. However, the quality of sharpness says nothing as to the use to which the knife might be put: beneficial surgery or murder. Sharpness is morally neutral. And thus it is with the rule of law. However, the purpose of law is to enable citizens to live within the law. Accordingly, there are certain principles which must be respected if that goal is to be fulfilled. For the rule of law to exist in society, certain qualities must be present. The law must be clear

---

54 Collins, H, *Marxism and Law*, 1982, Oxford: Clarendon, pp 126–27.

55 *Ibid*, Chapter 5.

56 *Op cit*, Raz, 1977, fn 12, p 211.

57 *Op cit*, Raz, 1977, fn 12.

if it is to be capable of being obeyed. In *Merkur Island Shipping Corporation v Laughton and Others*,[58] for example, Lord Donaldson MR stated that:

> The efficacy and maintenance of the rule of law, which is the foundation of any parliamentary democracy, has at least two pre-requisites. First, people must understand that it is in their interests, as well as in that of the community as a whole, that they should live their lives in accordance with the rules and all the rules. Secondly, they must know what those rules are ...

Lord Donaldson's view was endorsed by Lord Diplock in the House of Lords:

> Absence of clarity is destructive of the rule of law; it is unfair to those who wish to preserve the rule of law; it encourages those who wish to undermine it.[59]

The law must be publicised in order that citizens are aware of its demands; reasonably stable in order that citizens can plan their lives according to law; prospective so that the law does not require the impossible;[60] non-contradictory for the same reason, and, in addition, the courts must be accessible and staffed by an independent judiciary. Compliance with each of these requirements will indicate that a society respects the rule of law. To make such a statement is not to say that the legal system is one which is necessarily morally 'good'. As seen in Raz's illustration with the quality of sharpness in relation to the knife, the fact of sharpness does not dictate the morality of the purposes to which the knife will be put. It is possible, accordingly, for the rule of law to exist without the legal system necessarily pursuing morally good ends.

Professor Lon Fuller and the rule of law

The writing of Professor Lon Fuller[61] – who stands in contrast to Raz – may be invoked here in order to develop further this idea. Fuller's focus is on the 'morality of law'. For Fuller, the requirements of law, which are substantially the same as those of Raz, lay down the basic minimum requirements, not just of a system in accordance with the rule of law, but for the very existence of a system to which he would accord the label 'legal'. These basic prerequisites form the 'morality of duty' or 'inner morality of law'. These principles provide the basic foundations of a legal system. To draw an analogy with building construction, failure to lay sound foundations will result in the edifice resting on an insecure and fragile base. In addition to a secure foundation, for a legal

---

58 [1983] 2 AC 570.

59 *Ibid*, p 612.

60 A principle endorsed in *Phillips v Eyre* (1870) LR 6 QB 1 and *Waddington v Miah* [1974] 2 All ER 377. See, however, the War Damage Act 1965 and the War Crimes Act 1991 for illustrations of Parliament's power to legislate retrospectively.

61 *Op cit*, Fuller, fn 51.

system to be worthy of recognition – and to impose the duty of obedience upon its members – it must serve the needs of the people. Law does not exist in a vacuum separate from the society it regulates. Recognition of this vital characteristic of law demands that the legal system be directed towards altruistic, beneficial ends. This is the 'morality of aspiration' towards which each valid legal system must strive. Thus, a government must seek to provide the environment in which each citizen may realise to his maximum potential the rational plan of life to which he aspires. Society must be free and directed to the good of each of its members. Any government which fails in a material degree to meet these requirements may fail to deserve the label of a 'legal system'.

The important point here is that Fuller is quite prepared to argue that a system of government which contravened the basic requirements of a 'good' system of law might be recognised as some form of governmental regime but would not be a government according to law, and hence would not be a 'legal' system. In order to deserve recognition as a system of law, the system must respect the very fundamental moral requirements which Fuller identifies.

Professor HLA Hart[62] has argued that even a dictatorial regime with no respect for morality or fundamental rights would be capable of meeting Fuller's requirements. Fuller disputes this, arguing that an evil regime, such as that of Nazi Germany, sooner or later would be compelled to pass retrospective law or secret laws in order to pursue its evil objectives. Moreover, Fuller argues that there is an additional quality of morality which must be present in a system of law: that the law serves the interests of the people it governs. Thus, the law must be pursuing altruistic moral ends if it is to have recognition. If it is not, then Fuller would have no difficulty in denying that a 'legal system' existed at all.

Raz rejects the linkage between the rule of law and morality and claims that Fuller's thesis fails to establish a necessary connection between law and morals. And yet, for some, the distinction may be a fine one.

Friedrich von Hayek and the rule of law

A further perspective of the rule of law is provided by Friedrich von Hayek.[63] *The Road to Serfdom* was written against the background of the Second World War, and expressed von Hayek's fundamental concern with the prospect of the expansion of the State. This von Hayek opposed, other than at a basic level necessary to guarantee freedom, and von Hayek describes the rule of law in the following manner:

---

62 See Hart, HLA, 'Positivism and the separation of law and morals' (1958) 71 Harv L Rev 593.

63 *Op cit*, von Hayek, 1994, fn 9.

> ... stripped of all technicalities this means that government in all its action is bound by rules fixed and announced beforehand – rules which make it possible to foresee with fair certainty how the authority will use its coercive powers in given circumstances, and to plan one's individual affairs on the basis of this knowledge.[64]

The idea of a Welfare State and the entailed notion of distributive justice which entails the State operating under discretionary rules in order to provide a minimum standard of living was firmly opposed by von Hayek. The rule of law, for von Hayek, should be confined to the provision of clear, certain rules which would enable people to plan their lives in a free society. To require that people should contribute to the less well off in society through a system of graduated taxation, coupled with discretion to determine entitlement and quantum of recipients, violated his perceived ideal State.

Modern expression of many of von Hayek's ideas is to be found in the writings of Robert Nozick,[65] a clear and forceful advocate of the 'minimal State'. Nozick rejects any concept of distributive justice. Instead, he argues for perceptions of justice based on the concept of rights expressed in the name of entitlements. A state of affairs – and hence a State – will be 'just' if it respects the principle of entitlement. As Nozick puts it:

> Things come into the world already attached to people having entitlements over them. From the point of view of the historical entitlement conception of justice in holdings, those who start afresh to complete 'to each according his ...' treats objects as if they appeared from nowhere, out of nothing.[66]

Justice therefore lies in the recognition of the justice of holdings. If the manner in which property is acquired is lawful, if the manner in which property is transferred is lawful, the society will be just. To deny the justice of this situation – from a Nozickian perspective – and to argue for the forced redistribution of wealth in society, is to defeat the rights of the individual property holder.

John Rawls's theory of justice and the rule of law

Opposed to von Hayek and Nozick stands John Rawls, whose *Theory of Justice*[67] provides a detailed exposition of, and justification for, the interventionist State committed to distributive justice. In essence, a society will be 'just' if it is organised according to principles established by all its members in the 'original position' behind a 'veil of ignorance'. Suffice to note here that the 'original position' and 'veil of ignorance' relate to a stage of decision

---

64 *Op cit,* von Hayek, 1994, fn 9, p 54.
65 Nozick, R, *Anarchy, State and Utopia,* 1974, Oxford: Blackwells.
66 *Ibid,* p 160.
67 *Op cit,* Rawls, fn 10.

making about constitutional arrangements wherein the participants know nothing of their own personal attributes and wants and little of the society in which they live. They will accordingly choose principles of justice which are not self-interested but based on maximising the position of those persons (of whom the decision maker may turn out to be but one) who are in the least enviable position in society. The principles which they will choose will be, first, the priority of liberty for all, subject to the need to redistribute goods in society in order to improve the lot of the 'worst off'.

The rule of law, according to Rawls, is 'obviously closely related to liberty'.[68] Rawls calls for the 'regular and impartial administration of public rules' which is the essence of a just legal system characterised by the 'legitimate expectations' of the people. Several requirements must be met: rules of law must only command action which is possible; those who enact laws must do so in good faith; like cases must be treated alike. Echoing Dicey, Rawls states that there is no offence without a law,[69] and this requirement in turn demands that laws be known, that they be general, and that penal laws should not be retroactive to the disadvantage of those to whom they apply. Finally, the legal system must respect the dictates of natural justice.[70]

'Law and order' and the rule of law: the obligation to obey law

An alternative perception of the rule of law may be labelled the 'law and order' model.[71] This view emphasises the peaceful settlement of disputes without recourse to violence, armed force or terrorism. In legal philosophy, the idea of absolute obedience to law is compatible with the analytical, positivist school of thought which dominated much jurisprudential thought from the nineteenth century until after the Second World War. Positivism is the antithesis of natural law. The primary quest for positivists is to separate legal and moral issues: to distinguish between the 'is' (that which exists as fact) and the 'ought' (that which is desirable). Under positivist theory – which is primarily concerned to explain law as it exists in fact – where valid law exists, that is to say law which is accorded validity under the fundamental constitutional rule in a State, there is an obligation on each citizen to obey that law. Hans Kelsen and other legal positivists regard the duty to obey validly created norms as absolute.[72]

---

68 *Op cit*, Rawls, fn 10, p 235.

69 *Nulla poena sine lege.*

70 See Chapter 25.

71 See Wade, ECS and Bradley, AW, *Constitutional and Administrative Law*, 11th edn, 1993, Harlow: Longman, Chapter 6 (see, now, Bradley, AW and Ewing, KD, *Constitutional and Administrative Law*, 12th edn, 1997, Harlow: Longman).

72 Kelsen, H, *The General Theory of Law and State*, 1961, New York: Russell; Kelsen, H, *The Pure Theory of Law*, 1967, Berkeley, California: California UP.

Taken to its logical conclusion, however, the 'law and order' view can lead to the repression of freedom. By way of illustration, it is a common cry of politicians that a demonstration by, for example, trades union members or students, contravenes the 'rule of law'. In a strict sense, any action which involves protest will almost inevitably violate some legal rule – whether it is the rule protested against or otherwise.[73] Public protest, for example, will often involve breach of rules against obstruction of the highway, of the police in the execution of their duty, trespass, or criminal damage, even though those laws are not the object of the protest. It becomes necessary, therefore, to consider – albeit in outline – the nature of an individual's obligation to obey valid law. The fundamental question in this regard lies in the extent to which citizens should be coerced into obedience to 'unjust laws'. Is there an absolute obligation to obey, irrespective of the quality of the law? Is the duty only *prima facie*? Is there ever a duty to disobey the law in pursuit of a higher ideal? Each of these vast and timeless philosophical questions underpins the concept of the rule of law.

Is there a duty to obey law?

To be balanced against the arguments for absolute obedience to law is the legitimacy of protest within society. Since the time of Aristotle, it has been argued that the law must be tempered with equity, which dictates the standards of justice and rightness in society. Law derives its authority from the obedience of the people.[74] Laws must be directed to the 'good', not only to comply with the dictates of morality, but also for the more pragmatic reason of ensuring voluntary compliance with law. It may be argued that nowadays in a responsive, democratic State, any dispute as to the rights of individuals and grievances against government action will be dealt with through the provided channels of complaint, for example through the individual's Member of Parliament or through an investigation by the Commissioners for Administration.[75] Alternatively, it may be argued that if many citizens are commonly aggrieved, the media can be employed to influence government and that, ultimately, at least once every five years,[76] the electorate can express its views through the ballot box. None of these avenues, however, may yield the desired result, particularly if the aggrieved individual or group is a minority without popular support.

---

73 On 'direct' and 'indirect' civil disobedience, see *op cit*, Rawls, fn 10, Chapter 7.

74 *Op cit*, Aristotle, fn 1, 1269a.

75 See Chapter 26.

76 Under the Parliament Act 1911, the maximum life of a Parliament is five years. See, further, Chapter 14.

Is there a right to disobey law?

The question which then arises is whether the individual has a 'right' to disobey the law?[77] A government true to democratic precepts of representativeness and fairness must be sensitive to demands for change. If it fails in that regard, it is at least arguable that demands for change, while entailing technical breaches of the law, should be accommodated within the constitutional framework.

In the nineteenth century, Henry Thoreau refused to pay taxes to support the slavery laws and declared that: '... the place for a just man in such a community is in jail.'[78]

In the same century, the suffragette movement resorted to unlawful behaviour in the ultimately successful pursuit of the right to enfranchisement – the right to vote.[79] Mahatma Gandhi's peaceful civil disobedience campaign led to the independence of India in 1947. The Civil Rights movement in the United States in the 1950s, led by Martin Luther King, resulted in reforms of the law concerning racial segregation.[80] The tide of protest over American involvement in the Vietnam war had a direct impact on government policy and further raised legal and political interest in civil disobedience. Major social changes of such magnitude would have been impossible without recognition that under certain limited conditions there exists a right of legitimate protest, however inconvenient and uncomfortable this is for governments. The 'law and order' model of the rule of law would fail to respect any such 'right', and the reaction may be one of repression.[81] However, it is not necessary to look to such major societal changes brought about by defiance of law in order to refute the 'law and order' model and proclaim some entitlement to dissent.

John Rawls concedes a right to disobedience in pursuit of changing a society's 'sense of justice', but confines civil disobedience to peaceful protest.[82] Rawls's thesis is founded on the notion of social contract. That concept, as has been seen above, involves the mutual recognition, *inter alia*, of the rights of citizens and the rights of the State. The extent to which citizens participate in the law making process is critical to an understanding of the extent to which there exists an obligation to obey the law. Participation in the democratic

---

77 See *op cit*, Rawls, fn 10, Chapter 7.

78 Thoreau, HD, *Resistance to Civil Government* (1848), 2nd edn, 1992, Rossi, W (ed), New York, London: Norton.

79 See, *inter alia*, Kent, SK, *Sex and Suffrage in Britain 1860–1914*, 1987, Ewing, New Jersey: Princeton UP (rep 1990, London: Routledge).

80 *Brown v Board of Education of Topeka* 347 US 483 (1954); and see King, ML, *Why We Can't Wait*, 1963, New York: Signet.

81 As in Tiananmen Square 1989.

82 *Op cit*, Rawls, fn 10, Chapter 6.

process may, however, be used as a means to deny any right to disobey. That is to say, it may be argued that democratic participation implies the individual's acceptance of all laws within the State. Here it must be considered what it is that citizens consent to when electing a government. It seems implausible to argue that we each consent to every action of government throughout a possible five year term of office, irrespective of its merits. However, Professor Plamenatz states that when a vote is cast:

> ... you put yourself by your vote under an obligation to obey whatever government comes legally to power under the system, and this can properly be called giving consent. For the purpose of an election is to give authority to the people who win it and if you vote, knowing what you are doing and without being compelled to do it, you voluntarily take part in the process, which gives authority to those people.[83]

This argument surely is contentious and represents a very limited view of the requirement that a government should have moral authority to govern. Richard Wasserstrom, on the other hand, argues that, by the participatory democratic process, a *prima facie* obligation to obey law is imposed, but this *prima facie* duty can be overridden by the demands of conscience.[84]

Professor JM Finnis offers a contemporary natural law thesis.[85] On the relationship between authority, law and the duty to obey, Finnis writes:

> ... the ruler has, very strictly speaking, no right to be obeyed; but he has the authority to give directions and make laws that are morally obligatory and he has the responsibility of enforcing. He has this authority for the sake of the common good ... Therefore, if he uses his authority to make stipulations against the common good, or against any of the basic principles of practical reasonableness, those stipulations altogether lack the authority they would otherwise have by virtue of being his. More precisely, stipulations made for partisan advantage, or (without emergency justification) in excess of legally defined authority, or imposing inequitable burdens on their subjects, or directing the doing of things that should never be done, simply fail, of themselves, to create any moral obligation whatever.[86]

Finnis, however, is equivocal about the duty to obey unjust laws and silent as to the dilemma such laws pose for judges and other officials. There is an obligation to obey the law – not for the sake of 'being law abiding' but, rather, in order to – and to the extent to which obedience will – ensure that the 'just parts of the legal system' will not be rendered 'ineffective'.[87] Such an approach follows closely that of St Thomas Aquinas who argued that bad laws do not bind the conscience of man, but that in considering whether or

---

83 Plamenatz, J, *Man and Society*, 1963, New York: Longman, Vol 1, p 239.
84 Wasserstrom, R, 'The obligation to obey the law' (1963) California UL Rev 780.
85 *Op cit*, Finnis, fn 17, Chapter XII.
86 *Op cit*, Finnis, fn 17, p 359.
87 *Op cit*, Finnis, fn 17, p 361.

not to obey such laws, the citizen must weigh up the consequences of his actions for law as a whole. If, in the act of disobeying immoral law, the citizen undermines the legal system as a whole – which is not morally bad – then the act of civil disobedience itself would be morally culpable.[88]

The appropriate response of the State to acts of civil disobedience is a difficult matter. Professor Ronald Dworkin, for example, argues for official tolerance in the face of dissent and law breaking which is undertaken in pursuit of rights – even where violence is employed.[89] In *Taking Rights Seriously*, Dworkin argues that the State should act with caution in prosecuting civilly disobedient acts. First, the State should respect the stand taken in the defence of rights, even if that stand should prove misguided when the matter ultimately comes before the Supreme Court for a ruling on the validity of the contentious legislation. The decision to prosecute should be decided on the basis of utilitarianism.[90] As Dworkin states:

> Utilitarianism may be a poor general theory of justice, but it states an excellent necessary condition for just punishment. Nobody should ever be punished unless punishing him will do some good on the whole in the long run all things considered.[91]

By prosecuting disobedience to law, the State upholds the positive law and reinforces it. On the other hand, in prosecuting, the State may reveal the defects in the law and may be seen to be enforcing that for which there exists little or no popular support. By way of example, the acquittal of Clive Ponting on charges of breaching section 2 of the Official Secrets Act 1911[92] is illustrative: the jury refusing to convict despite a clear ruling by the judge as to the illegality of Ponting's conduct.[93] It may also be argued that by rigid enforcement the State enhances the moral claims advanced by the civilly disobedient. In part, this was the view adopted by Socrates in submitting to his fate. He drank the hemlock to show respect to the law and constitution of Athens, although he must have known that in so doing he would bring the positive law of the State into disrepute. What he could not foresee was the timeless example that Athens, in executing Socrates, set for humanity.[94]

---

88 *Op cit*, Aquinas, fn 27, I-II, q 96.

89 Dworkin, R, *Taking Rights Seriously*, 1977, London: Duckworth, Chapters 7 and 8; and see MacGuigan, MR, 'Obligation and obedience', in Pennock, JR and Chapman, JW (eds), *Political and Legal Obligation*, 1970, New York: Atherton, Nomos 12.

90 The doctrine which assesses the justification for a particular action according to the overall increase in the sum of benefit to society as a whole.

91 Dworkin, R, *A Matter of Principle*, 1986, Oxford: Clarendon, p 114.

92 Discussed in Chapter 23.

93 *R v Ponting* [1985] Crim LR 318; and see Barker, R, *Political Legitimacy and the State*, 1990, Oxford: Clarendon, pp 183–84.

94 See Plato, 'Socrates' defence and Crito', in *op cit*, Hamilton and Cairns, fn 21.

Is there a duty to disobey?

The converse position must also be considered: if a State violates the requirements of the rule of law, to what extent is it the duty of citizens to disobey the law? Furthermore, what justification, if any, is there for another State or the international community taking action against the 'guilty' State? The Nazi regime in Germany provides the most obvious – but not unique – example. On individual duty, Professor Lon Fuller maintained that the citizen is under no obligation to obey unjust law: 'A mere respect for constituted authority must not be confused with fidelity to law.' Fuller goes further and asserts that an evil regime, which grossly violates the basic precepts of morality, is incapable of creating law at all.[95] In HLA Hart's view, this represents confused thinking on Fuller's part. His preferred approach is to recognise the validity of Nazi laws – however abhorrent in moral terms – but also to recognise that moral obligations can outweigh the legal obligation to obey.[96] In addition to facilitating clarity about law, this approach enables the regime to be held to account for its actions. Simply to deny – as does Professor Fuller – that there was no law during Nazi rule is to remove the basis for international legal sanctions.

AV Dicey and the rule of law[97]

In *Introduction to the Study of the Law of the Constitution*, AV Dicey[98] offered a prosaic description of the rule of law. Here, there are none of the ringing proclamations of the theological or political philosophers. Nevertheless, Dicey's views have continued to exert their influence, despite many challenges, and it is this influence which requires examination.

Dicey argued that the rule of law – in its practical manifestation – has three main aspects:

- no man is punishable or can be lawfully made to suffer in body or goods except for a distinct breach of law established in the ordinary legal manner before the ordinary courts of the land. In this sense, the rule of law is contrasted with every system of government based on the exercise by persons in authority of wide, arbitrary, or discretionary powers of constraint;

- no man is above the law; every man and woman, whatever be his or her rank or condition, is subject to the ordinary law of the realm and amenable to the jurisdiction of the ordinary tribunals; and

---

95 Fuller, L, 'Positivism and fidelity to law – a reply to Professor Hart' (1958) 11 Harv L Rev 630.

96 *Op cit*, Hart, fn 62, p 593 – a view echoing that of St Thomas Aquinas.

97 See *op cit*, Jennings, fn 47, p 54; Heuston, RFV, 'The rule of law', in *Essays in Constitutional Law*, 2nd edn, 1964, London: Stevens, p 40.

98 *Op cit*, Dicey, fn 45.

- the general principles of the constitution (as, for example, the right to personal liberty, or the right of public meeting) are, with us, the result of judicial decisions determining the rights of private persons in particular cases brought before the courts.[99]

Each of these requirements requires examination.

Lack of arbitrariness and retrospectivity

The first element of this analysis is self-explanatory. It requires that no one be punished except for conduct which represents a clear breach of law.[100] Designed to deny to governments any right to make secret or arbitrary laws, or retrospective penal laws, and to limit the discretionary powers of government, the rule protects the individual. In order to comply fully with this requirement, laws should be open and accessible, clear and certain. In part, this idea ties in with that of the 'social contract'[101] and the reciprocal relationship between the State and the individual. Under social contract theories, the individual citizen transfers his autonomous individual rights to the government, to be held by that government on trust. To express the matter differently, the citizen owes allegiance to the Crown in return for which he is under the protection of the Crown.[102] The doctrine of allegiance incorporates the idea of obedience to law – both on the part of the citizen and on the part of government. Laws which are arbitrary or secret are incapable of justification on the basis of the mandate of the people and, accordingly, offend against the reciprocal relationship on which constitutional democracy depends. Where wide discretionary powers are conferred on the executive – whether it be in the form of granting power to a minister of the Crown to act 'as he thinks fit' or on civil servants administering the social welfare system – it will be impossible for the individual to know what rights he or she has. Moreover, the delegation of broad discretionary power – albeit on the authority of the sovereign Parliament – renders such power difficult, if not impossible, to challenge before a court of law or other adjudicatory tribunal.[103]

If retrospective penal liability is imposed, the individual is placed in the position where his conduct was lawful at the time of his action but, subsequently, he is held responsible as if his conduct was then unlawful. An examination and evaluation of the relevance of this first proposition entails drawing on relevant illustrations from both statute and case law. For example,

---

99 *Op cit*, Dicey, fn 45, pp 188, 193, 195, respectively. And see Craig, PP, 'Dicey: unitary, self-correcting democracy and public law' (1990) 106 LQR 105.

100 The principle of *nulla poena sine lege*.

101 See, further, Chapter 19.

102 See Chitty, J, *Law of the Prerogatives of the Crown*, 1820, London: Butterworths, discussed in Chapter 7.

103 See Smith, ATH, 'Dicey and civil liberties: comment' [1985] PL 608.

the courts construe penal statutes narrowly and will be slow to find that Parliament intended to impose retrospective liability. So important is the concept of *mens rea* in the criminal law[104] that it will rarely be appropriate for a prosecution to succeed in its absence, and it is for this reason that the courts employ the presumption of statutory interpretation against retrospectivity:

> Perhaps no rule of construction is more firmly established than this – that a retrospective operation is not to be given to a statute so as to impair an existing right or obligation, otherwise than as regards matters of procedure, unless that effect cannot be avoided without doing violence to the language of the enactment. If the enactment is expressed in language which is fairly capable of either interpretation, it ought to be construed as prospective only.[105]

In *Waddington v Miah*,[106] the House of Lords interpreted the Immigration Act 1971 in a manner which denied retrospective effect in relation to criminal offences, using, as an aid to construction, Article 7 of the European Convention on Human Rights, which guarantees freedom from retrospectivity. Nonetheless, the presumption will not be available where Parliament expressly provides for retrospectivity, as, for example, in the War Damage Act 1965 and the War Crimes Act 1991.[107] In *Burmah Oil v Lord Advocate*,[108] where the House of Lords had awarded compensation to be paid for the destruction of oil installations in wartime, the government speedily introduced legislation nullifying the effect of the decision under the War Damage Act 1965.[109] This case demonstrates clearly the subordination of the judiciary to parliamentary supremacy and the limits thereby imposed on the judges' capacity to uphold rights.

Notwithstanding the general prohibition against retrospectivity, there may be instances where a decision which imposes, for example, criminal liability may be upheld by the courts. For example, until 1990, there existed a time honoured exemption from the law of rape for husbands who 'raped' their wives. In the case of *R v R*,[110] however, the House of Lords upheld the conviction of a husband for the rape of his wife, arguing that the rule against liability for rape within marriage was anachronistic. In a challenge to this decision under the European Convention on Human Rights, on the basis that it infringed Article 7 of the Convention, which makes retrospectivity unlawful, the Court of Human Rights ruled that the sweeping away of husbands' immunity from criminal prosecution and conviction for rape

---

104 *Sweet v Parsley* [1970] AC 132.
105 Wright J in *Re Athlumney* [1898] 2 QB 547, pp 551–52.
106 [1974] 1 WLR 683.
107 See Chapter 7.
108 [1965] AC 75.
109 See, further, Chapter 7.
110 [1991] 2 WLR 1065; 2 All ER 257, CA; [1991] 3 WLR 767, HL.

represented an evolution towards greater equality between the sexes and was consistent with that equality.[111]

Equality before the law: government under the law

Dicey's second limb emphasises the notion that government itself is subject to law and that everyone, irrespective of rank, whether official or individual, shall be subject to the law,[112] and subject to the same courts. Dicey viewed the French system of special courts to deal with complaints against government as abhorrent, fearing that specially constituted courts would unduly favour the government over the citizen. Dicey has often been interpreted as requiring that there be actual equality in terms of legal rights, powers and capacities. Such an interpretation is, however, misguided. The idea of equality before the law, irrespective of status, is subject to so many exceptions 'that the statement is of doubtful value'.[113] In so far as equal powers are concerned, it must be recognised that the police have powers over and above the citizen,[114] that ministers have power to enact delegated legislation (but subject to Parliamentary approval), that the Crown enjoys immunities under the law, that the government acting in the name of the Crown may exercise prerogative powers which may defeat the rights of individuals,[115] that Members of Parliament have immunity from the law of defamation under the privileges of Parliament,[116] and that diplomats enjoy immunities not available to citizens. And, as Sir Ivor Jennings points out, no two citizens are entirely equal:

> ... pawnbrokers, money lenders, landlords, drivers of motor cars, married women, and indeed most other classes have special rights and duties.[117]

Against this catalogue, which is not exhaustive, must be set the extent to which government and public officials are subject to law in the sense of being accountable for their actions before the ordinary courts, for this, indeed, was Dicey's real argument. The doctrine acknowledges the need of a consistent application of the law irrespective of status. No one is immune from criminal prosecution (other than the monarch: 'Against the King law has no coercive power').[118] Official accountability to law is one of the foundations of the rule

---

111 Case 48/1994/495/577: *SW v United Kingdom; C v United Kingdom*, judgment of 22 November 1995; (1995) 21 EHRR 404.

112 See Zellick, GJ, 'Government beyond law' [1985] PL 283.

113 Hood Phillips, O and Jackson, P, *Constitutional and Administrative Law*, 7th edn, 1987, London: Sweet & Maxwell, p 37.

114 Under common law and the Police and Criminal Evidence Act 1984.

115 See *Malone v Metropolitan Police Commissioner* [1979] Ch 344, discussed in Chapter 5.

116 See Chapter 18.

117 *Op cit*, Jennings, fn 47, Appendix II, p 311.

118 Maitland, FW, *The Constitutional History of England*, 1908, Cambridge: CUP, p 100.

of law. Dicey has been much criticised for his limited view on this aspect – although the criticism is in some respects too strong. Wade and Bradley – recognising the limited procedural approach Dicey adopted – assert that the discussion on the rule of law 'should no longer be cast in the Diceyan mould'.[119] On the other hand, following a detailed analysis of Dicey's writing, Professor Jeffrey Jowell concludes that:

> ... its ghost has refused to rest. It rises still to haunt a minister who publishes 'guidelines' that cut across the powers of the statute under which he operates, the minister who penalises local authorities for overspending without giving them a fair hearing, a government department which decides in accordance with a secret code not available to the public, or a Prime Minister who seeks to deprive civil servants of their rights to remain members of a trade union.[120]

Sir Ivor Jennings criticises Dicey's emphasis on government according to law on the basis that it is too narrow an interpretation:

> ... it is a small point upon which to base a doctrine called by the magnificent name of 'rule of law', particularly when it is generally used in a very different sense.[121]

TRS Allan subjects Dicey's analysis to detailed scrutiny which is devoid of the dismissiveness of de Smith and Brazier or the scepticism of Sir Ivor Jennings, and focuses on Dicey's second principle: that of equality before the law.[122] Allan seeks a solution to the apparent paradox presented by Dicey's insistence that both parliamentary sovereignty and the rule of law comprise the fundamental doctrines of the constitution – given that the former concept is inherently capable of damaging the latter. Towards this end, Allan presents a wealth of evidence directed to establishing a middle way between the formalism of the 'principle of legality' and the vagueness of the 'broad political ideal'. In other words, what is sought is an explanation of the means by which the power of sovereignty is restrained or restricted without expounding a 'complete social philosophy'.[123] The key to such an understanding, according to Allan, lies in the role of the judiciary and in an acceptance that it is the judges who – in applying the 'juristic principle' of the rule of law – limit the power of Parliament. To summarise, Allan draws on the principles of statutory interpretation (non-retrospectivity, clarity, *mens rea* in penal statutes, etc); on the independence of the judiciary as ensured by the separation of powers; on the right of access to the courts for all citizens; and

---

119 *Op cit*, Wade and Bradley, fn 71, p 105.
120 Jowell, J, 'The rule of law today', in Jowell, J and Oliver, D (eds), *The Changing Constitution*, 2nd edn, 1989, Oxford: Clarendon, p 23 (see, now, 4th edn, 2000).
121 *Op cit*, Jennings, fn 47, p 312.
122 Allan, TRS, 'Legislative supremacy and the rule of law: democracy and constitutionalism' [1985] CLJ 111 and 'The rule of law', in *Law, Liberty and Justice*, 1993, Oxford: Clarendon, Chapter 2.
123 *Ibid*, 1985, p 114.

on the judiciary's reluctance for the jurisdiction of judicial review to be limited. By these and other means, Allan seeks to demonstrate that:

> ... the rule of law strengthens democracy by ensuring that government operates only within rules adopted or sanctioned by Parliament ...

and that:

> The constitutional principle of the rule of law serves, however, to bridge the gap between the legal doctrine of parliamentary sovereignty and the political doctrine of the sovereignty of the people. In interpreting statutes in conformity, so far as possible, with general notions of fairness and justice – in seeking to apply those common standards of morality which are taken for granted in the community – the judge respects the natural expectations of the citizen.

> The rule of law therefore assists in preventing the subversion of the political sovereignty of the people by manipulation of the legal sovereignty of Parliament.[124]

In order to evaluate such contrasting views as those expressed above, consideration of some evidence becomes necessary.

Judicial review

Actions for judicial review of administrative action, employing concepts of *intra* and *ultra vires* and the rules of natural justice, ensure that the executive acts within the law. Judicial review – in its infancy in Dicey's time – represents the means by which the sovereignty of Parliament is upheld and the rule of law applied. Dicey[125] analysed the significance of the *Board of Education v Rice*[126] and *Local Government Board v Arlidge*,[127] claiming that:

> ... each case finally lays down, as far as the courts of England are concerned, a clear and distinct principle by which any department of the government, such for example as the Board of Education, must be guarded in the exercise of powers conferred upon it by statute.[128]

The means by which, and grounds upon which, judicial review may be granted are considered in Chapters 24 and 25. It is sufficient for current purposes to note that judicial review is the means by which administrative authorities – whether ministers of the Crown, government departments, local authorities or others with law-making and administrative powers – are confined by the courts within the powers granted to them by Parliament. It is for a court to determine – following the granting of an application for judicial

---

124 *Op cit*, Allan, 1985, fn 122, p 130.

125 Writing in 1915. On these cases, see, further, Chapter 25.

126 [1911] AC 179; (1911) 80 LJ KB 796.

127 [1915] AC 120.

128 Dicey, AV, 'The development of administrative law in England', in *op cit*, fn 45, Appendix 2, p 493.

review – whether the body in question has acted *intra vires* or *ultra vires* (that is, inside or outside its powers). Judicial review is confined to matters of public, rather than private law. Thus, where a relationship between an aggrieved citizen and a body is based, for example, on the law of contract, judicial review will not lie.[129] It is also necessary – in the interests of good administration – that aggrieved individuals have 'sufficient interest' – or *locus standi* – in the matter to bring it to court.[130] There are numerous grounds on which judicial review may be sought. By way of illustration, a body may act *ultra vires* if it uses its powers for the wrong purpose,[131] or if it abuses its powers,[132] or if it adopts a policy which is so rigid that it fails to exercise a discretion with which it has been invested.[133] The law imposes standards of reasonableness upon administrative bodies, and failure to act in a reasonable manner may cause a body to act *ultra vires*.[134] A body may act *ultra vires* if it is conferred with delegated powers but delegates them further to another.[135] Statute may require that administrators adopt particular procedures in the exercise of these powers: should they not do so, and the procedures are judicially deemed to be 'mandatory' (compulsory) rather than 'directory' (advisory), a body will be held to be acting *ultra vires*. If a public body under a duty to act fails to act at all, the court can order it to do so.[136] The rules of natural justice must also be observed in decision making: where an individual has a right or interest at stake because of an administrative decision, he is entitled to fair treatment.[137] All of these grounds for review have been rationalised by the House of Lords into three principal categories: irrationality, illegality and procedural impropriety.[138] The powers of the court can only be exercised over a matter which it is competent to determine. This introduces the concept of justiciability,[139] and it is this latter doctrine which most particularly undermines the concept of the rule of law.

In *Council of Civil Service Unions v Minister for the Civil Service*, the House of Lords identified the categories of decision which would be immune from

---

129 See, eg, *R v City Panel on Takeovers and Mergers ex parte Datafin plc* [1987] QB 815; *O'Reilly v Mackman* [1983] 2 AC 237.

130 See, *inter alia*, *Inland Revenue Commissioner v National Federation of Self-Employed and Small Businesses Ltd* [1982] AC 617.

131 *Attorney General v Fulham Corporation* [1921] 1 Ch 440.

132 *Webb v Minister of Housing and Local Government* [1965] 1 WLR 755; *Westminster Bank v Minister of Housing and Local Government* [1971] AC 508.

133 *Padfield v Minister of Agriculture Fisheries and Food* [1968] AC 997.

134 *Associated Provincial Picture Houses Ltd v Wednesbury Corporation* [1948] 1 KB 223.

135 *Barnard v National Dock Labour Board* [1953] 2 QB 18; *Vine v National Dock Labour Board* [1957] AC 488.

136 By an order of mandamus. See, further, Chapter 25.

137 *R v IRC ex parte Preston* [1985] AC 835; *Wheeler v Leicester City Council* [1985] AC 1054.

138 *Council of Civil Service Unions v Minister for the Civil Service* [1985] AC 374.

139 *Ibid*.

judicial review – that is to say – non-justiciable. Amongst these – and the list is not exhaustive[140] – are the making of treaties, the dissolution of Parliament, the appointment of ministers, declarations of war and peace, and matters relating to the granting of honours. What unites these categories is the fact that each involves matters of high policy which is most appropriately determined – in the eyes of the judiciary – not by the courts but by the executive. Where this applies, it may be said that the rule of law is undermined by respect for the doctrine of the separation of powers: an ironic consequence.

The doctrine of judicial review nevertheless represents a bedrock for the application of the rule of law, keeping those with law making and discretionary powers within the law. From *Entick v Carrington*[141] to *R v Secretary of State for the Home Department ex parte Fire Brigades' Union and Others*,[142] wherein the Home Secretary[143] was held to be acting *ultra vires* when attempting to introduce a new tariff for compensation under the Criminal Injuries Compensation Scheme under the royal prerogative rather than under power conferred by statute, the principle is established and reiterated.

The legal process

For the rule of law to be respected and applied, the legal process – civil and criminal – must exhibit certain features. These features may be categorised as accessibility and procedural fairness.

Accessibility

The law must be accessible to all if rights are to be enforced. Accordingly, there must not only exist a system of courts available locally but the cost of having recourse to the courts must be such that there is real – rather than symbolic – access to the courts. For the law to be attainable, adequate legal advice and assistance must be provided at a cost affordable by all.[144] The cost of litigation in the United Kingdom is high. The cost of counsel defending in a criminal trial is high. The statutory legal aid scheme is designed to mitigate

---

140 See Chapter 6.

141 (1765) 19 St Tr 1029.

142 [1993] 3 WLR 433.

143 Kenneth Baker.

144 See, *inter alia*, Smith, P and Bailey, SH, *The Modern English Legal System*, 2nd edn, 1991, London: Sweet & Maxwell, Chapter 9 (see, now, Bailey, SH and Gunn, M (eds), *Smith & Bailey on The Modern English Legal System*, 3rd edn, 1996, London: Sweet & Maxwell); Zander, M, *Cases and Materials on the English Legal System*, 6th edn, 1993, London: Butterworths, Chapters 6 and 9; Slapper, G and Kelly, D, *The English Legal System*, 4th edn, 1999, London: Cavendish Publishing, Chapter 12.

the cost of access to the law by providing financial assistance to defendants and litigants who are unable to meet the full costs of a legal action.[145] The principles put forward by the Royal Commission on Legal Services[146] were that:

> Financial assistance out of public funds should be available for every individual (not corporations) who, without it, would suffer an undue financial burden in properly pursuing or defending his or her legal rights;
>
> All those who receive legal services are entitled to expect the same standard of legal service irrespective of their personal circumstances.[147]

The legal aid scheme, however, fell far short of these objectives. In 1972, the green form scheme came into existence, designed to ensure the provision of free legal advice to those in need.[148] The scheme was originally limited to the giving of advice and assistance, but not representation, although, in 1979, 'assistance by way of representation' (ABWOR) was introduced for certain restricted proceedings.[149] Traditionally, legal aid was unavailable for tribunal hearings, and thus many persons in need were excluded from pre-hearing advice under the scheme.[150] It is, however, the financial limits on the availability of legal aid which bedevils the system and excludes many from access to law. Eligibility is determined by both a merits test and a means test. Under the civil legal aid scheme, the proportion of persons eligible has declined in recent years. In 1979, 74 per cent of the population were eligible; in 1990, 66 per cent. Of the 75 per cent of adults eligible in 1979, only 29 per cent were eligible for free legal aid, while 46 per cent were eligible subject to a contribution being made towards costs.[151] In 1990, the proportion of eligible adults had decreased to 56 per cent, with 22 per cent being eligible for free legal aid and 34 per cent eligible but subject to a contribution. As with civil legal aid, the criminal legal aid scheme employs the merits and means tests. In terms of merits, the test is whether it is 'in the interests of justice' for aid to be granted.[152] The means test is administered by the court clerks, and may result in a contribution being ordered, although, in 1990, of 510,000 legal aid applications granted by magistrates, only 47,000 (nine per cent) had contribution orders attached.[153]

---

145 Legal Aid Act 1988, now Access to Justice Act 1999.

146 *Report of the Royal Commission on Legal Services*, Cmnd 7648, 1979, London: HMSO.

147 *Ibid*, Vol I, pp 50–54.

148 Legal Advice and Assistance Act 1972.

149 Legal Aid Act 1979.

150 ABWOR is now available for hearings before certain tribunals: see *op cit*, Smith and Bailey, fn 144, Chapter 9.

151 *Lord Chancellor's Review of Legal Aid Eligibility for Civil Legal Aid: A Consultation Paper*, 1991, London: HMSO; and see Legal Aid Board, *Report to the Lord Chancellor on the Operation and Finance of the Legal Aid Act 1988 for the Year 1989–90*, 1990, London: HMSO.

152 Legal Aid Act 1988, s 21(2).

153 *Op cit*, Zander, fn 144, p 518.

The right to a fair trial is protected under Article 6 of the European Convention on Human Rights, and includes the right of the citizen:

> ... to defend himself in person or through legal assistance of his own choosing or, if he has not sufficient means to pay for legal assistance, to be given it free when the interests of justice so require.[154]

In *Granger v United Kingdom*,[155] the defendant had been denied further legal aid to pursue an appeal against conviction. Granger, unable to afford legal representation, acted in person. Representing the Crown were senior government counsel. On an application under the Convention, Granger alleged that he had been denied the protection of law. The Court of Human Rights ruled that the denial of legal aid infringed Granger's rights.

The current government intended to continue the former government's plans to reduce further the availability of legal aid.[156] Reforms included removing the right to legal aid for personal injury work; extending 'no win, no fee' schemes in relation to disputes over money and damages; losers to pay opponent solicitor's 'success fee'; and means by which to encourage the insurance market and group or company schemes to develop 'legal cover' products. In relation to personal injury claims, the government intends to set up a 'safety net' fund for 'deserving but costly' cases or those which it is in the public interest to pursue. Further reforms are under consideration. Legal aid will be retained for housing claims, judicial review proceedings and for those forced to defend a claim for money or damages.

Procedural fairness

Justice and the rule of law demand that, in the conduct of legal proceedings, procedural fairness be observed. Subsumed within this requirement are many subsidiary conditions. The judge must be impartial: *nemo iudex in sua causa*.[157] Where jurors are involved, they, too, must be free from bias. In addition, jurors should be reasonably representative of the society they serve. Evidence gathered by the police, must be acquired by lawful means. The evidence admitted into court must be both of an admissible nature and fairly presented. The proceedings should be conducted in such a manner as to be intelligible to the parties, witnesses and jurors.[158]

---

154 See Chapter 22.

155 (1990) 12 EHRR 469.

156 Access to Justice Act 1999. See *op cit*, Slapper and Kelly, fn 144, Chapter 12.

157 See Chapter 25 and see, further, Chapter 5.

158 See, *inter alia*, Kafka, F, *Trial*, Muir, E and Muir, W (trans), 1956, London: Secker & Warburg. See Keedy, ER, '*R v Sinnisiak*: a remarkable murder trial' (1951) 100 Pennsylvannia UL Rev 48 for illustrations of breaches of this requirement.

The jury

The precise origins of trial by jury in its modern form are shrouded in mist.[159] It is thought that by the end of the fifteenth century, the jury, as triers of fact, was established in what today would be a recognisable form. Trial by jury for serious criminal offences, and in civil cases where defamation, malicious prosecution, false imprisonment and allegations of fraud are at issue,[160] is regarded as the 'bulwark of our liberties'.[161] The decision of the jury is regarded as conclusive and unimpeachable. Criticisms have long been made of the lack of representativeness of the jury. Several factors militate against representativeness: the accuracy of the electoral register from which jurors are selected; the relative lack of randomness in jury selection; the vetting of jurors;[162] and challenges to members of the jury. Moreover, a wide range of persons are either ineligible for jury service, or disqualified from sitting or may be excused from jury service.[163] When a jury is summoned, the presence of a juror may be challenged 'for cause' – that is, where some fact relating to the juror is known and gives rise to a challenge. Little is known about the individual juror – only the names and addresses are given.[164] This relative anonymity of jurors contrasts starkly with the position in the United States of America, where the selection of a jury entails a prolonged inquiry into the lives and attitudes of prospective jurors. While the process is protracted,[165] it is designed to ensure that the jury ultimately selected will be one free from bias in relation to the defendant. In the United Kingdom, a person may be excused from service on the basis of personal knowledge of the case, bias, personal hardship or conscientious objection to jury service. A juror should not be excused on general grounds such as race, religion, political beliefs or occupation.[166]

Evidence

For the rule of law to be observed, it is of central importance that the evidence before the court be both complete and reliable. Contravention of this requirement undermines the concept of a fair trial. Subsumed within this question is the complex and controversial matter of the manner in which

---

159 See *op cit*, Maitland, fn 118, pp 115–30. See, also, Denning (Lord), *What Next in the Law?*, 1982, London: Butterworths, Pt 2.

160 Supreme Court Act 1981, subject to the proviso in s 69(1) which permits the court to refuse trial by jury in cases of complexity or impracticality.

161 *Ward v James* [1966] 1 QB 273, p 295, *per* Lord Denning MR.

162 *R v Mason* [1980] 3 All ER 780; *Attorney General's Guidelines on Jury Checks* [1988] 3 All ER 1086.

163 Jury Act 1974; Juries' Disqualification Act 1984.

164 Prior to 1973, jurors' occupations were made known.

165 Jury selection for the trial of John de Lorean took five weeks.

166 *Practice Direction* [1988] 3 All ER 177.

evidence is obtained and the question of admissibility. While the Police and Criminal Evidence Act 1984[167] went some way to improving the safeguards for the accused and was introduced, in part, to rectify deficiencies which had come to light,[168] the cases of the Birmingham Six,[169] the Guildford Four and the Maguire Seven[170] illustrated the deficiencies in the criminal justice system. In each of these cases, the defendants had served long terms of imprisonment for alleged Irish Republican Army (IRA) terrorist acts. In each case, the evidence relied upon was unreliable. Their convictions were quashed by the Court of Appeal following years of campaigning by relatives and friends for a review of their cases. In each case, a serious miscarriage of justice had occurred and as a result the integrity of the criminal justice system tarnished.

At common law, a confession which is improperly obtained is inadmissible.[171] The Police and Criminal Evidence Act 1984 places this rule on a statutory basis, providing that if a confession has been obtained 'by oppression', the court shall not allow the confession to be given in evidence unless satisfied beyond reasonable doubt that the confession – even if true – has not been obtained improperly.[172]

Whereas the rules on the admissibility of improperly obtained confessions are relatively clear, the admissibility of other evidence obtained by either dubious or unlawful means has proved less clear and less satisfactory. Until 1979, the judges exercised their discretion as to whether or not evidence improperly acquired would be admissible.[173] However, in *R v Sang*,[174] the House of Lords ruled that no discretion existed to exclude evidence which had been obtained by unlawful or improper means. The only basis on which evidence could be excluded would be where the effect of admitting it would prove unduly 'prejudicial' to the defence or 'unfair' to admit it. The fact that the evidence was unlawfully acquired does not amount to 'unfairness' *per se*.[175] This position compares unfavourably with that pertaining in the United States, where evidence improperly obtained is excluded,[176] and that, in

---

167 See, *inter alia*, Zander, M, *The Police and Criminal Evidence Act 1984*, 3rd edn, 1995, London: Sweet & Maxwell.

168 See McConville, M and Baldwin, J, 'Confessions: the dubious fruit of police interrogation' (1980) 130 NLJ 993.

169 *R v McIlkenny and Others* [1992] 2 All ER 417.

170 See May, J, *Interim Report on the Maguire Case*, HC 556 (1990–91), London: HMSO.

171 *Marks v Beyfus* (1890) 25 QBD 494.

172 Police and Criminal Evidence Act 1984, s 76.

173 *Kuruma Son of Kaniu v R* [1955] AC 197; *Jeffrey v Black* [1978] 1 All ER 555.

174 [1979] 2 WLR 263.

175 See Heydon, JD, 'Illegally obtained evidence' [1973] Crim LR 690; Ashworth, A, 'Excluding evidence and protecting rights' [1977] Crim LR 723.

176 See Driscoll, J, 'Excluding illegally obtained evidence – can we learn from the United States?' (1981) Legal Action Group Bulletin, June, p 131 and 'Excluding illegally obtained evidence in the United States' [1987] Crim LR 553.

Australia, where such evidence is inadmissible unless the judge is satisfied that there is some special reason why the impropriety should be excused.

The Royal Commission on Criminal Procedure[177] confirmed the test propounded in *R v Sang*. However, the government rejected the Commission's view, and the position as to admissibility of such evidence is now governed by section 78 of the Police and Criminal Evidence Act 1984, which provides that the court may refuse to allow evidence if:

> ... it appears to the court that, having regard to all the circumstances, including the circumstances in which the evidence was obtained, the admission of the evidence would have such adverse effect on the fairness of the proceedings that the court ought not to admit it.[178]

Professor Michael Zander describes the effect of section 78 as 'nothing less than startling'.[179] He records that, from 1986 (when the Act came into force) until early 1991:

> ... there had been close to a hundred reported decisions in which the courts had given rulings under section 78 and that in the 'great majority' of these cases the decision had been in favour of the accused.

The following are offered by Zander as illustrations of Court of Appeal decisions in that time:

> *R v Absolam*,[180] where the Court of Appeal quashed a conviction for supplying cannabis where A had not been told of his right to legal advice and the Code rules about recording of interviews had been broken. In *Delaney*,[181] the Court of Appeal quashed a conviction for indecent assault on a small child because the police had misled D, who had a low IQ, about the gravity of the case and the rules about the recording of interviews had been broken. See, to like effect, *Keenan*.[182] In *Kanale*,[183] the Court of Appeal quashed a conviction for conspiracy to rob for which the accused was sentenced to six years' imprisonment after finding 'flagrant, deliberate and cynical' breaches of the rules in Code C regarding the recording of interviews. But see *Dunn*,[184] in which similar breaches were cured in the view of the Court of Appeal because a solicitors' clerk had been present during the interview.[185]

---

177 *Report of the Royal Commission on Criminal Procedure*, Cmnd 8092, 1981, London: HMSO.
178 Police and Criminal Evidence Act 1984, s 78(1).
179 *Op cit*, Zander, fn 144, p 414.
180 (1989) 88 Cr App R 332.
181 (1989) 88 Cr App R 338.
182 [1989] 3 All ER 598.
183 [1990] 2 All ER 187.
184 (1990) 91 Cr App R 237.
185 *Op cit*, Zander, fn 144, p 414.

Evaluation of Dicey's 'equality before the law'

The evidence for the notion of equality before the law is neither clear nor uncontentious. As with so much of the constitution, there remains room for doubt and argument. Nevertheless, it is submitted that there exists sufficient evidence to suggest that Dicey's approach remains a fruitful avenue for inquiry and exploration. To dismiss – as some writers do – this aspect of Dicey's exposition of the rule of law, is to deprive the student of the constitution of a valuable tool for analysis.

The protection of rights under common law

The third limb of Dicey's description of the rule of law reveals his preference for common law protection of human rights over and above a specially formulated code of rights, thus demonstrating a faith in the judiciary which may not be sustainable nowadays. Evaluation of this aspect of the definition must await analysis of the European Convention on Human Rights[186] and the scope of the protection which it gives to individual citizens. Nevertheless, some broad overview of the protection of rights will promote understanding of Dicey's third requirement. The position of individual rights in the United Kingdom has traditionally been that protection is not provided within any code, but rather within specific statutes enacted to deal with specific problems,[187] and by judicial decisions. Over and above such protection is the European Convention on Human Rights, established in 1951, to which citizens of the United Kingdom have the right of petition. The Convention gives protection against a range of violations of rights,[188] but is essentially limited to the protection of civil and political – as opposed to economic and social – rights. Before 2000, the Convention was not directly enforceable in the domestic courts, and consistent with the classic constitutional dualist concept,[189] judges did no more than look to the Convention as an aid to interpretation,[190] and on occasion declined so to do.[191] This position changed substantially under the Human Rights Act 1998.[192] In addition, the protection of certain rights is being enhanced under the jurisprudence of the European Court of Justice of the European Community. At the domestic level, however, the rights that are protected are at the mercy of the sovereignty of Parliament. Even if and when the judges take a bold stand and assert the rights of

---

186 See Chapter 22.
187 Eg, Sex Discrimination Act 1975; Race Relations Act 1976.
188 See the text in Chapter 22.
189 See Chapter 9.
190 *Waddington v Miah* [1974] 2 All ER 377.
191 *R v Home Secretary ex parte Brind* [1991] 1 AC 696.
192 On this, see, further, Chapter 22.

individuals against the government, there is no guarantee that Parliament will not intervene to *nullify* that right.[193] By way of example, in *Entick v Carrington*,[194] the court held that a general warrant issued by the Home Secretary for the entry and search of premises for unspecified documents was a violation of the rule of law and unlawful. That general principle, clearly and firmly established, has, however, been violated by Parliament. The Taxes Management Act 1970, for example, provides for warrants to be granted for the entry into premises and the seizure of property. Section 20C provides that on the issue of a warrant, an officer may enter premises:

> ... if necessary by force, at any time within 14 days from the time of issue of the warrant, and search them ... (3) On entering the premises with a warrant ... the officer may seize and remove any things whatsoever found there which he has reasonable cause to believe may be required as evidence for the purposes of proceedings ...

When the lawfulness of the warrant was tested, the House of Lords upheld the validity thereof, declaring that Parliament's clearly stated will must be given effect.[195] Furthermore, the Child Support Act 1991 conferred on Child Support Inspectors wide powers of entry without warrant and the right to search for evidence,[196] contrary to the principle established in *Entick v Carrington*.[197]

Prior to the 'incorporation' of the European Convention on Human Rights, the consequences of this ad hoc statutory scheme and the common law were several. First, the rights were not enunciated in any comprehensive or comprehensible manner. To identify the possible existence of a right, it might be necessary to research hundreds of years of case law. Secondly, the scope of such rights as can be identified was undefined. To know that one has a 'right' of free passage on the highway is not to know very much without an understanding of all the potential exceptions to that 'right' and the legal limitations upon its exercise. Thirdly, the opportunity was never taken to consider, formulate and reach agreement on the rights of citizens as a whole. Law making proceeds on an ad hoc basis, with government responding to demand as a situation arises which requires legislation. Fourthly, without a right on which to found litigation, there was no means by which an aggrieved citizen can get a matter into court: where there is no right there is no remedy.

---

193 See, eg, the War Damage Act 1965, discussed in Chapter 7.

194 (1765) 19 St Tr 1029.

195 See *R v Inland Revenue Commissioners ex parte Rossminster Ltd* [1980] AC 952; and see, further, Chapter 20.

196 Child Support Act 1991, s 15. See, also, Police and Criminal Evidence Act 1984, s 8; Theft Act 1968, s 26(1); Criminal Damage Act 1971, s 6(1); Firearms Act 1968, s 46; Misuse of Drugs Act 1971, s 23(3); Obscene Publications Act 1959, s 3, which all illustrate broad grants of rights of entry.

197 (1765) 19 St Tr 1030.

Malone v Metropolitan Commissioner of Police provides but one illustration.[198] In *Malone's* case,[199] the defendant in criminal proceedings had had his telephone 'tapped' on the authority of the Home Secretary. Malone sought a declaration on the legality of this intrusion. The Home Secretary had no statutory basis for the exercise of such power. Despite this invasion of privacy and the apparent contradiction with the principle established in *Entick v Carrington*,[200] the court felt compelled to accept that telephone tapping disclosed no illegality. Sir Robert Megarry VC ruled that in the absence of statute – the need for which he saw as 'a subject which cries out for legislation' – there was nothing illegal in the telephone tap. No right to privacy existed in English law, and the judge was not prepared to establish a precedent which would create such a right.[201]

The evidence for and against Dicey's faith in the common law as the principal protector of rights is examined in Part VI. Suffice it to say here that the evidence is at best equivocal, and that – considered alongside the record of the United Kingdom under the European Convention – cannot nowadays be supported with any conviction. Notwithstanding such reservations, the protection of human rights under the European Convention on Human Rights must be weighed in the balance: in each case where a finding against the government is made, the rule of law is upheld by the judges in favour of the citizen irrespective of his status.[202]

The European Convention on Human Rights is considered in detail in Chapter 22. It must be noted here, however, that the Human Rights Act 1998 for the first time 'incorporates' the Convention into domestic law. Accordingly, citizens no longer have to undertake the lengthy process of applying to the Commission on Human Rights in Strasbourg, but are able to seek a remedy in the domestic courts. The method of incorporation adopted, however, falls far short of enabling the judges to invalidate or set aside domestic legislation. Instead, the judges of the higher courts will be empowered to make 'declarations of incompatibility' with Convention rights. Once such a declaration has been made, it remains for Parliament to approve an amendment to the law. As a result, the Human Rights Act, far from elevating individual rights proclaimed in the Convention to a higher status than statute, will preserve Parliament's sovereign law making and amending power, and also preserve the separation of powers.

---

198 [1979] Ch 344; and see *Malone v United Kingdom* (1982) 5 EHRR 385 and the Interception of Communications Act 1985.

199 Discussed more fully in Chapter 22.

200 (1765) 19 St Tr 1030.

201 See Harlow, C, 'Comment' [1980] PL 1; Bevan, V, 'Is anybody there?' [1980] PL 431.

202 See, *inter alia*, *Ireland v UK* (1978) 2 EHRR 25 on freedom from inhumane treatment for detainees in Northern Ireland; *Golder v UK* (1975) 1 EHRR 524 on prisoners' right to access to a solicitor.

The rule of law in international dimension

The Universal Declaration of Human Rights of the United Nations, published in 1948, declares that:

> It is essential, if man is not to be compelled to have recourse, as a last resort, to rebellion against tyranny and oppression, that human rights should be protected by the rule of law.

The European Convention for the Protection of Human Rights and Fundamental Freedoms of 1950 also recognises the concept of the rule of law. The preamble states that:

> The governments of European countries which are like-minded and have a common heritage of political traditions, ideals, freedom and the rule of law ... have agreed as follows ...

On an international level, the rule of law is also advanced by the International Commission of Jurists, which strives to uphold and improve the rule of law within the legal systems of its members. The Declaration of Delhi, issued under the auspices of the International Commission of Jurists, affirms the rule of law and its value in promoting the protection of civil and political rights and linked such rights with the development and protection of social and economic rights. The Congress of the International Commission of Jurists met in 1959 in order to 'clarify and formulate a supranational concept of the rule of law'.[203] The Declaration of Delhi 1959 recognised that:

> ... the rule of law is a dynamic concept for the expansion and fulfilment of which jurists are primarily responsible and which should be employed not only to safeguard and advance the civil and political rights of the individual in a free society, but also to establish social, economic, educational and cultural conditions under which his legitimate aspirations and dignity may be realised ...

Accordingly, clause I of the report of the committee stipulates that:

> The function of the legislature in a free society under the rule of law is to create and maintain the conditions which will uphold the dignity of man as an individual. This dignity requires not only the recognition of his civil and political rights but also the establishment of the social, economic, educational and cultural conditions which are essential to the full development of his personality.[204]

Such aspirational statements recognise the need for the economic foundations to be such that the dignity of man can be a reality in society. It is meaningless

---

203 Marsh, NS, 'The rule of law as a supranational concept', in Guest, AG (ed), *Oxford Essays in Jurisprudence*, 1961, Oxford: OUP, p 240 and 'The declaration of Delhi' (1959) 2 J of the International Commission of Jurists 7.

204 Cited in *Executive Action and the Rule of Law (A Report on the Proceedings of the International Congress of Jurists)*, December 1962.

to speak of the rule of law as insisting on decent, or even minimal, standards of living within the context of poverty and disease. In order to secure any such standards, a sufficient level of economic wealth must be achieved. Even where such standards do exist, there will remain resistances to any formulation of social and economic rights as enforceable positive legal rights, for such formulations require the allocation of resources within society. Whereas governments may be willing – indeed obliged – to respect civil and political rights in a democracy, the protection of such rights generally will be effected without significant national resource implications. The protection of freedoms, such as freedom of speech and association, requires no more than a restraint on government. The protection of social and economic rights requires positive action, at a high cost.[205]

Conclusion

The rule of law – in its many guises – represents a challenge to State authority and power, demanding that powers both be granted legitimately and that their exercise is according to law. 'According to law' means both according to the legal rules and something over and above purely formal *legality* and imputes the concepts of *legitimacy* and constitutionality. In its turn, legitimacy implies *rightness* or *morality* of law. The law is not autonomous but rests on the support of those it governs. The law is the servant of the sense of rightness in the community, and whilst the rule of law places law above every individual – irrespective of rank and station – it remains, paradoxically, subject to the ultimate judgment of the people.

---

205 See Aubert, V, *In Search of Law*, 1983, Oxford: Martin Robertson, Chapters 2 and 7.

CHAPTER 5

THE SEPARATION OF POWERS

The separation of powers, together with the rule of law[1] and parliamentary sovereignty,[2] runs like a thread throughout the constitution of the United Kingdom. It is a doctrine which is fundamental to the organisation of a State – and to the concept of constitutionalism[3] – in so far as it prescribes the appropriate allocation of powers, and the limits of those powers, to differing institutions. The concept has played a major role in the formation of constitutions. The extent to which powers can be, and should be, separate and distinct was a central feature in formulating, for example, both the American and French revolutionary constitutions. In any State, three essential bodies exist: the executive, the legislature and the judiciary. It is the relationship between these bodies which must be evaluated against the backcloth of the principle. The essence of the doctrine is that there should be, ideally, a clear demarcation in function between the legislature, executive and judiciary in order that none should have excessive power and that there should be in place a system of checks and balances between the institutions. However, as will be seen, there are significant departures from the pure doctrine under the United Kingdom's constitution, and it must be conceded that, while the doctrine is accorded respect, it is by no means absolute. It is for this reason, for example, that it has been commented that 'no writer of repute would claim that it is a central feature of the modern British constitution'[4] and that:

> ... there is not, and never has been, a strict separation of powers in the English constitution in the sense that legislative, executive and judicial powers are assigned respectively to different organs, nor have checks and balances between them been devised as a result of theoretical analysis. Development of our public institutions has been mainly empirical.[5]

However, before accepting such a critical judgment, it is necessary to examine the evidence for and against the concept of separation of powers. The separation of powers interacts with both the rule of law and parliamentary sovereignty. The independence of the judiciary ensures that the executive will be kept within the legal powers conferred by Parliament, thus simultaneously upholding the rule of law and sovereignty.

---

1   See Chapter 4.
2   See Chapter 7.
3   See the discussion in Chapter 1.
4   de Smith, SA and Brazier, R, *Constitutional and Administrative Law*, 6th edn, 1989, London: Penguin, p 19 (see, now, 8th edn, 1998).
5   Hood-Phillips, O and Jackson, P, *Constitutional and Administrative Law*, 7th edn, 1987, London: Sweet & Maxwell, p 29.

HISTORICAL DEVELOPMENT

The identification of the three elements of the constitution derives from Aristotle.[6] In *The Politics*, Aristotle proclaimed that:

> There are three elements in each constitution in respect of which every serious lawgiver must look for what is advantageous to it; if these are well arranged, the constitution is bound to be well arranged, and the differences in constitutions are bound to correspond to the differences between each of these elements. The three are, first, the deliberative, which discusses everything of common importance; second, the officials; and third, the judicial element.[7]

The constitutional seeds of the doctrine were thus sown early, reflecting the need for government according to and under the law, a requirement encouraged by some degree of a separation of functions between the institutions of the State.

The constitutional historian FW Maitland traces the separation of powers in England to the reign of Edward I:[8]

> In Edward's day all becomes definite – there is the Parliament of the three estates, there is the King's Council, there are the well known courts of law.

Viscount Henry St John Bolingbroke,[9] in *Remarks on the History of England*,[10] advanced the idea of separation of powers. Bolingbroke was concerned with the necessary balance of powers within a constitution, arguing that the protection of liberty and security within the State depended upon achieving and maintaining an equilibrium between the Crown, Parliament and the people. Addressing the respective powers of the King and Parliament, Bolingbroke observed that:

> Since this division of power, and these different privileges constitute and maintain our government, it follows that the confusion of them tends to destroy it. This proposition is therefore true; that, in a constitution like ours, the safety of the whole depends on the balance of the parts.[11]

Baron Montesquieu[12] stressed the importance of the independence of the judiciary:

> When the legislative and executive powers are united in the same person, or in the same body of magistrates, there can be no liberty ... Again, there is no liberty if the power of judging is not separated from the legislative and

---

6   384–322 BC.

7   Aristotle, *The Politics*, 1962, Sinclair, TA (trans), London: Penguin, Bk iv, xiv 1297b35.

8   1272–1307. Maitland, FW, *The Constitutional History of England*, 1908, Cambridge: CUP, p 20.

9   1678–1751.

10 Bolingbroke, H, *Remarks on the History of England*, 3rd edn, 1748, London: Francklin.

11 *Ibid*, pp 80–83.

12 1689–1755, living in England from 1729–31.

executive. If it were joined with the legislative, the life and liberty of the subject would be exposed to arbitrary control; for the judge would then be the legislator. If it were joined to the executive power, the judge might behave with violence and oppression. There would be an end to everything, if the same man, or the same body, whether of the nobles or the people, were to exercise those three powers, that of enacting laws, that of executing public affairs, and that of trying crimes or individual causes.[13]

Here is the clearest expression of the demand for a separation of functions. It has been remarked that Montesquieu's observations on the English constitution were inaccurate at the time, representing more a description of an idealised State than reality.[14] Moreover, it should not be assumed that Montesquieu's preferred arrangement of a pure separation of powers is uncontroversial. Throughout history, there has been exhibited a tension between the doctrine of separation of powers and the need for balanced government – an arrangement depending more on checks and balances within the system (as emphasised by Bolingbroke) than on a formalistic separation of powers. Sir Ivor Jennings has interpreted Montesquieu's words to mean not that the legislature and the executive should have no influence over the other, but rather that neither should exercise the power of the other.[15] Sir William Blackstone, a disciple of Montesquieu, adopted and adapted Montesquieu's strict doctrine, reworking his central idea to incorporate the theory of mixed government. While it was of central importance to Blackstone that, for example, the executive and legislature should be sufficiently separate to avoid 'tyranny', he nevertheless viewed their total separation as potentially leading to dominance of the executive by the legislature.[16] Thus, partial separation of powers was required to achieve a mixed and balanced constitutional structure.

THE CONTEMPORARY DOCTRINE

The separation of powers doctrine does not insist that there should be three institutions of government each operating in isolation from each other. Indeed, such an arrangement would be unworkable, particularly under a constitution dominated by the sovereignty of Parliament. Under such an arrangement, it is essential that there be a sufficient interplay between each

---

13 Montesquieu, C, *De l'Esprit des Lois* (1748), 1989, Cambridge: CUP.
14 Vile, MJC, *Constitutionalism and the Separation of Powers*, 1967, Oxford: Clarendon, pp 84–85.
15 Jennings, I (Sir), *The Law and the Constitution*, 5th edn, 1959, London: Hodder & Stoughton, Appendix I.
16 Blackstone, W (Sir), *Commentaries on the Laws of England* (1765–69), Chicago: Chicago UP, p 50.

institution of the State. For example, it is for the executive,[17] for the most part, to propose legislation for Parliament's approval. Once passed into law, Acts of Parliament are upheld by the judiciary. A complete separation of the three institutions could result in legal and constitutional deadlock. Rather than a pure separation of powers, the concept insists that the primary functions of the State should be allocated clearly and that there should be checks to ensure that no institution encroaches significantly upon the function of the other. If hypothetical constitutional arrangements within a State are considered, a range of possibilities exists:

(a) absolute power residing in one person or body exercising executive, legislative and judicial powers: no separation of powers;

(b) power being diffused between three separate bodies exercising separate functions with no overlaps in function or personnel: pure separation of powers; and

(c) powers and personnel being largely – but not totally – separated with checks and balances in the system to prevent abuse: mixed government and weak separation of powers.

It is to this third category that the constitution of the United Kingdom most clearly subscribes.

Geoffrey Marshall states that the phrase 'separation of powers' is 'one of the most confusing in the vocabulary of political and constitutional thought'. In part, as Marshall explains, this is because it has been used 'with varying implication' by historians and political scientists, and because the concept manifests itself in so many arenas: '... judicial independence, delegation of legislative powers, executive responsibility to legislatures, judicial review, and constitutionality of arbitral bodies exercising mixed functions.'[18] In Marshall's view, the separation of powers comprises a 'cluster of overlapping ideas', which he identifies as follows:

(a) the differentiation of the concepts 'legislative', 'executive', and 'judicial';

(b) the legal incompatibility of office holding as between members of one branch of government and those of another, with or without physical separation of persons;

(c) the isolation, immunity, or independence of one branch of government from the actions or interference of another;

(d) the checking or balancing of one branch of government by the action of another; and

(e) the co-ordinate status and lack of accountability of one branch to another.[19]

---

17 See Chapters 10 and 15.

18 Marshall, G, *Constitutional Theory*, 1971, Oxford: Clarendon, p 97.

19 *Ibid*.

DEFINING THE INSTITUTIONS

The executive[20]

The executive may be defined as that branch of the State which formulates policy and is responsible for its execution. In formal terms, the sovereign is the head of the executive. The Prime Minister, Cabinet and other ministers, for the most part, are elected Members of Parliament.[21] In addition, the Civil Service, local authorities, police and armed forces, constitute the executive in practical terms.

The legislature[22]

The Queen in Parliament is the sovereign law making body within the United Kingdom. Formally expressed, Parliament comprises the Queen, House of Lords and House of Commons. All Bills[23] must be passed by each House and receive the royal assent.

Parliament is bicameral, that is to say there are two chambers, each exercising a legislative role – although not having equal powers – and each playing a part in ensuring the accountability of the government. By way of introduction, it should be noted that membership of the House of Lords is not secured by election and is accordingly not accountable in any direct sense to the electorate. The House of Commons is directly elected,[24] and a parliamentary term is limited under the Parliament Act 1911 to a maximum of five years. In practice, the average life of a Parliament is between three and four years. The House is made up of the majority party: the political party which secures the highest number of seats at the election, which will form the government. The head of that party will be invited by the Queen to take office as Prime Minister. In turn, it is for the Prime Minister to select his or her Cabinet. The opposition parties[25] comprise the remainder of the now 659 Members of Parliament.[26] The official Opposition is the party which represents the second largest party in terms of elected Members. In principle, the role of the official Opposition is to act as a government in waiting, ready at

---

20 See Chapters 10 and 11.
21 Note that some Ministers are drawn from the unelected House of Lords. See, further, Chapter 17.
22 See Chapters 14–17.
23 With the exception provided by the Parliament Acts 1911–49.
24 See Chapter 13.
25 Conservative, Liberal Democrat, Scottish Nationalists, Ulster Unionists, Democratic Unionists and Plaid Cymru.
26 The number of Members of Parliament was increased to 659 for the 1997 General Election.

any time to take office should the government seek a dissolution of Parliament.[27]

The judiciary

The judiciary is that branch of the State which adjudicates upon conflicts between State institutions, between State and individual, and between individuals. The judiciary is independent of both Parliament and the executive. It is the feature of judicial independence which is of prime importance both in relation to government according to law and in the protection of liberty of the citizen against the executive. As Blackstone observed:

> ... in this distinct and separate existence of the judicial power in a peculiar body of men, nominated indeed, but not removable at pleasure by the Crown, consists one main preservative of the public liberty which cannot subsist long in any State unless the administration of common justice be in some degree separated both from the legislative and from the executive power.[28]

It is apparent, however, that, whilst a high degree of judicial independence is secured under the constitution, there are several aspects of the judicial function which reveal an overlap between the judiciary, Parliament and the executive. The first of these lies in the office of Lord Chancellor.

The office of Lord Chancellor[29]

It is the office of Lord Chancellor[30] which is most frequently cited as being a violation of the doctrine of separation of powers. It is certainly a most notable exception to that doctrine. The office derives from the Norman Conquest when the King's secretary became known as the royal 'chancellor'. The first Chancellor is recorded in 1068. In the Middle Ages, the primary role of the Chancellor was to preside over Parliament. From the fourteenth century, his functions have been both parliamentary and judicial, in the latter role presiding over the Court of Chancery until 1875.[31] A glance at the several roles he undertakes reveals why the office is claimed to breach the doctrine of separation of powers.

---

27 For consideration of the role of the Opposition, see Chapters 14–16.

28 *Op cit*, Blackstone, fn 16, Vol I, p 269.

29 See, *inter alia*, Heuston, RFV, *Lives of the Lord Chancellors 1885–1940*, 1964, Oxford: Clarendon and *1940–70*, 1987, Oxford: Clarendon; Bradney, A, 'The judicial activity of the Lord Chancellor 1946–87' (1989) 16 JLS 360; Drewry, G, 'The Lord Chancellor as judge' (1972) 122 NLJ 855.

30 The title Lord Chancellor is first recorded in 1461.

31 When reorganisation of the superior courts was effected: Supreme Court of Judicature Acts 1873 and 1875.

Functions in relation to the courts

The Lord Chancellor is head of the judiciary and is formally recognised as President of the Supreme Court under the Supreme Court Act 1981. The administration of the Supreme Court (Court of Appeal, High Court and Crown Courts) and the county courts is the responsibility of the Lord Chancellor.[32] Magistrates are appointed by the Lord Chancellor. High Court judges, circuit judges and recorders are appointed by the Crown on his advice.[33] The dismissal of magistrates,[34] without showing cause, and circuit judges for incapacity and misbehaviour is within the Lord Chancellor's powers.[35]

The Lord Chancellor has responsibility for the court service,[36] legal aid and advice schemes, the Land Registry[37] and the Public Records Office.[38] He also presides over the Court of Protection.[39]

Law reform

The Lord Chancellor works closely with the Law Commission of England and Wales[40] established in 1965.[41] The task of the Law Commission is to:

> ... take and keep under review all the law with which [it is] concerned with a view to its systematic development and reform, including in particular the codification of such law, the elimination of anomalies, the repeal of obsolete and unnecessary enactments, the reduction of the number of separate enactments and generally the simplification and modernisation of the law.[42]

The Lord Chancellor may refer matters to the Law Commission for investigation, or the Commission may investigate issues of its own motion.

Member of the executive

The Lord Chancellor is a member of the executive arm of government. He is a senior member of Cabinet and, as such, may be dismissed by the Prime Minister.[43] It is perhaps this feature of the Lord Chancellor's office which

---

32 On funding and the courts, see Browne-Wilkinson (Lord), 'The independence of the judiciary in the 1980s' [1988] PL 44.
33 Supreme Court Act 1981, s 10.
34 Justices of the Peace Act 1979, s 6.
35 Courts Act 1971, s 17(4).
36 *Ibid*, s 27(1).
37 Land Registry Act 1862.
38 Public Records Act 1958.
39 Mental Health Act 1959.
40 But not the Scottish Law Commission.
41 Law Commissions Act 1965.
42 *Ibid*, s 3(1).
43 As was Viscount Kilmuir in 1962.

gives rise to the greatest disquiet when evaluated against the doctrine of the separation of powers, for the obvious impression is given that there is too close an association between the head of the judiciary and the central body of the executive – the Cabinet. Nevertheless, there is some justification for this arrangement. Lord Chancellor Birkenhead,[44] for example, defended the link between the head of the judiciary and the Cabinet in 1922:

> ... it is difficult to believe that there is no necessity for the existence of such a personality, imbued on the one hand with legal ideas and habits of thought, and aware on the other of the problems which engage the attention of the executive government. In the absence of such a person, the judiciary and the executive are likely enough to drift asunder to the point of a violent separation, followed by a still more violent and disastrous collision.[45]

More recently, Lord Hailsham[46] has argued that it is vital that:

> ... the independence of the judiciary and the rule of law should be defended inside the Cabinet as well as in Parliament. The Lord Chancellor must be, and must be seen to be, a loyal colleague, not seeking to dodge responsibility for controversial policies, and prepared to give to Parliament a justification for his own acts of administration.[47]

Equally strong support for this constitutionally unusual relationship between the judiciary and the executive came from Lord Mackay of Clashfern, the former Conservative Lord Chancellor. Lord Mackay conceded that there is an inevitable tension between the role of Lord Chancellor as a judge and his role as a member of the executive.[48] Nevertheless, Lord Mackay argued that these tensions are offset by the benefits which are perceived to flow from the close relationship. First, he supported Lord Hailsham's view that the Lord Chancellor should be able to advance and defend the cause of the administration of justice within Cabinet. Secondly, Lord Mackay stated that the linkage promotes a realisation that:

> ... both the judiciary and the executive are parts of the total government of the country with functions which are distinct but which must work together in a proper relationship if the country is to be properly governed.[49]

Speaker of the House of Lords

The Lord Chancellor is a member of the House of Lords and presides over its proceedings as *ex officio* Speaker. He is the principal spokesman for the

---

44 1872–1930.
45 Birkenhead (Lord), *Points of View*, Vol 1, 1922, London: Hodder & Stoughton, Chapter 4.
46 Lord Chancellor 1979 and 1987.
47 Hailsham (Lord), *The Door Wherein I Went*, 1975, London: Collins.
48 Mackay (Lord), *The Administration of Justice*, 1994, London: Stevens, p 18.
49 *Ibid*.

government in the Lords.[50] The Lord Chancellor's salary as Speaker is paid under the Ministerial and Other Salaries Act 1975.

As a member of Cabinet, the Lord Chancellor cannot be a politically impartial figure, nor can he be politically impartial when acting in his capacity of government spokesman and head of the House of Lords in its legislative capacity. Some separation of function in this latter regard is secured by convention. When speaking for the government in debate, the Chancellor removes himself from the Woolsack[51] and speaks from a spot appointed by King Henry VIII.[52] It is by this means that he can be identified as having changed from the impartial Speaker of the House of Lords to government spokesman.

The Lord Chancellor and judicial proceedings

The Lord Chancellor is a member of the House of Lords Appellate Committee and the Judicial Committee of the Privy Council, and, accordingly, will participate in decisions which affect both common law and statutory interpretation. In relation to his judicial functions as member of the House of Lords, it is by convention that the Chancellor will not preside over, or be judicially involved in, cases which involve the government or are overtly political in nature. Some Lord Chancellors sit rarely in their judicial capacity; others are judicially active. Lord Gardiner, for example, presided over only two appeals in six years, whereas Lord Hailsham presided over 37 appeals in eight years. Lord Mackay of Clashfern presided over five appeals in the first five months of entering office, although in each case the appeals were argued before he assumed the office of Lord Chancellor, the judgments being handed down after he had taken office.[53] The extent to which Lord Chancellors ought to participate in appeals – and the type of appeals they should hear – is a matter for debate. It is clear that the Lord Chancellor should not sit on appeals in which the government is a party to the proceedings, or where the government has a clear interest in the matter litigated.

The requirements of judicial impartiality, however, were recently tested before the European Court of Human Rights in a judgment which has implications for the role of the Lord Chancellor. In *McGonnell v United Kingdom*,[54] a case relating to the position of the Deputy Bailiff of Guernsey as President of the States of Deliberation (Guernsey's legislative body) and subsequently as the sole judge of law in proceedings relating to the applicant's

---

50 See, further, below.
51 Literally, a sack of wool which represents the Lord Chancellor's seat in the House of Lords.
52 The House of Lords Precedence Act 1539.
53 Bradley, AW, 'Constitutional change and the Lord Chancellor' [1988] PL 165.
54 (2000) *The Times*, 22 February.

planning application which had been refused, the Court of Human Rights held that the Deputy Bailiff's position was 'capable of casting doubt' on his 'impartiality' and as a result was in violation of Article 6(1) of the European Convention of Human Rights, which guarantees 'a fair and public hearing ... by an independent and impartial tribunal established by law'. The Bailiff in Guernsey occupies a number of positions. He is a senior judge of the Royal Court and is *ex officio* President of the Guernsey Court of Appeal. In his non-judicial capacity, the Bailiff is President of the States of Election, of the States of Deliberation, of four States committees (the Appointments Board, the Emergency Council, the Legislation Committee and the Rules of Procedure Committee). He also has a role in communications between the Guernsey authorities and the United Kingdom Government and the Privy Council. Referring to its earlier decision in *Findlay v United Kingdom*,[55] the Court re-stated the requirements of 'independence' and 'impartiality'. On independence, the Court declared that, in establishing whether the court or tribunal was independent, regard had to be had, *inter alia*, to the 'manner of appointment of its members and their term of office, the existence of guarantees against outside pressures and the question whether the body present an appearance of independence'. On impartiality, the Court re-stated the proposition that the tribunal:

> ... must [first] be subjectively free of personal prejudice or bias. Second, it must also be impartial from an objective viewpoint, that is, it must offer sufficient guarantees to exclude any legitimate doubt in this respect ...

In the instant case, there was no question of actual bias on the part of the Bailiff; nevertheless, the Court considered that 'any direct involvement in the passage of legislation', or of executive rules, was likely to be sufficient to cast doubt on the judicial impartiality of a person subsequently called on to determine a dispute over whether reasons exist to permit a variation from the wording of the legislation or rules at issue. Accordingly, 'the mere fact that the Deputy Bailiff presided over the court ... was capable of casting doubt on his impartiality...'. There was, accordingly, a violation of the requirements of fair trial before an independent and impartial tribunal.

The Lord Chancellor's Department

The Lord Chancellor is assisted in his work by the Lord Chancellor's Department with a staff of approximately 11,000. The Department is divided into divisions dealing with judicial appointments and legislation, court service management, policy and legal services, establishment and finance.

Concerns over the democratic accountability of the Department and the Lord Chancellor have long been voiced.[56] The Lord Chancellor's membership

---

55 (1997) *The Times*, 27 February.
56 See, further, below.

of the House of Lords precludes any personal accountability to the House of Commons. The Attorney General, until 1992, deputised for the Lord Chancellor in the Commons and acted as a 'courier' between the Commons and the Lords. Since that time, there has been a Parliamentary Under Secretary of State to the Lord Chancellor in the House of Commons, and it is hoped that, by this means, the Commons will be able to ensure enhanced accountability. From 1991, the House of Commons Home Affairs Select Committee has included review of the work of the Lord Chancellor's Department. In addition, the Department is subject to the scrutiny of the Public Accounts Committee of the House of Commons.

A Minister of Justice?

The parliamentary accountability of the Lord Chancellor has long been criticised and various proposals made to introduce the office of a Minister of Justice. Rodney Brazier points to the 'undesirable' consequences which flow from the separation of responsibility for criminal law reform, which is a matter for the Home Office, and civil law reform, which is for the Lord Chancellor's Department, but for which there is no Minister with responsibility accountable to the House of Commons.[57] Brazier calls for nothing less than fundamental reform of the present arrangements with abolition of the office of Lord Chancellor and the Lord Chancellor's Office and the introduction of a new Department of Law.[58] The term 'Ministry of Justice' is avoided deliberately by Brazier on the basis that, whenever the phrase is used, the reaction of the judiciary is one of alarm. Lord Chancellor Hailsham, for example, regarded the proposal[59] by the Social Democratic Party and Liberal Party Alliance (now merged into the Liberal Democrat Party) for a new Department of Justice[60] as 'constitutionally very dangerous' and 'a menace to the independence of the judiciary'.[61] Lord Mackay of Clashfern rejected the need for a Ministry of Justice, arguing that the new forms of accountability in the House of Commons – through the Parliamentary Under Secretary and the Home Affairs Select Committee – would prove sufficient in securing adequate accountability.[62]

---

57   Brazier, R, *Constitutional Reform*, 1991, Oxford: Clarendon, p 146.

58   *Ibid*, p 149.

59   *Government, Law and Justice: The Case for a Ministry of Justice*, Alliance Papers No I, 1986, London, SDP/Liberal Alliance.

60   The Labour Party has, in the past, called for a Department of Legal Administration: *Looking to the Future*, 1990, London: Labour Party, p 40.

61   (1986) *The Guardian*, 26 May.

62   *Op cit*, Mackay, fn 48, p 23.

The judiciary

Appointment

The Lord Chief Justice, Master of the Rolls, President of the Family Division, Vice Chancellor, Lords of Appeal in Ordinary and Lord Justices of Appeal are appointed by the Queen.[63] By convention, the appointments are made on consultation with the Prime Minister, who will have consulted the Lord Chancellor. The Lord Chancellor makes appointments to the High Court bench. Candidates must meet the qualification requirements. For appointments to the High Court, the candidate must be a barrister of 10 years' standing or a solicitor with rights of audience in the High Court or a circuit judge of two years' standing.[64] For appointment to the Court of Appeal, the candidate must either be a barrister of 10 years' standing, a solicitor with rights of audience in the High Court, or a current member of the High Court Bench.[65]

The socio-economic and educational background of the judiciary has been subjected to much research. In brief, the picture presented is one of a middle and upper class, middle aged, white, predominantly male, judiciary dominated by public school and Oxford or Cambridge University education.[66] In profile, the judiciary is staffed by persons having a very similar background to most Members of Parliament in general, and more specifically, to the majority of the executive. Such a feature inevitably raises questions as to the capacity of the judges for true intellectual independence from government. The process of selection has traditionally been shrouded in secrecy, with records of eligible candidates, who in practice will be successful practitioners, being maintained by the Lord Chancellor's Department. The criteria for selection are ability, experience, standing, integrity and physical health.[67] It has been argued that the appointment of senior judges should be made by a Judicial Commission rather than on the recommendation of the Lord Chancellor alone.[68] From 1994, in order to attempt to redress the imbalance in terms of class, sex and race, judicial vacancies are advertised in the press. Whether the outcome will be to broaden the base from which judges are selected remains to be seen.

---

63 Supreme Court Act 1981, s 10(1), (2).

64 Courts and Legal Services Act 1990, s 71.

65 *Ibid*, s 71.

66 See, *inter alia*, Griffith, JAG, *The Politics of the Judiciary*, 4th edn, 1991, London: Fontana, pp 25–29 (see, now, 5th edn, 1997); Blom-Cooper, L and Drewry, G, *Final Appeal*, 1972, Oxford: Clarendon, pp 158–69.

67 *Judicial Appointments*, 1985, London: Lord Chancellor's Department.

68 Harlow, C (ed), *Public Law and Politics*, 1986, London: Sweet & Maxwell, Chapter 10; Brazier, R, 'Government and the law' [1989] PL 64. See, also, Gilvarry, E, 'Selection changes to be urged' (1991) 88 Law Soc Gazette 6, pp 6–7.

Tenure

The Act of Settlement 1700[69] secured a senior[70] judge's tenure of office during 'good behaviour'. More modern expression is given to this protection under the Supreme Court Act 1981,[71] which provides that a person appointed shall hold office during good behaviour, removable only by Her Majesty on an address presented to her by both Houses of Parliament. Senior judges cannot be dismissed for political reasons. They can be removed by compulsory retirement if they are incapacitated or unable to resign through incapacity.[72] Judges can be dismissed for misbehaviour, and under an Address to the Crown made by the two Houses of Parliament. 'Misbehaviour' relates to the performance of a judge's official duties or the commission of a criminal offence. Not every judge convicted of an offence will be dismissed: six judges have been convicted for driving with an excess of alcohol in their blood but have continued in office. In 1830, Sir Jonah Barrington was removed from office in Ireland under the Address procedure for the embezzlement of monies paid into court. Theoretically, a judge can also be removed by 'impeachment' for 'high crimes and misdemeanours', although this procedure has not been used since 1805[73] and is thought to be obsolete.[74] In Scotland, judges can only be removed on the grounds of misconduct.[75]

The Judicial Pensions and Retirement Act 1993 introduced the retirement age of 70, which may be extended to 75 if in the public interest. From 1959, the retirement ages were set at 75 for a High Court judge and 72 for a circuit judge, although judges appointed before this date were permitted to remain in office.[76]

Salaries

In order further to protect the judiciary from political debate, judicial salaries are charged on the Consolidated Fund.[77] Judicial salaries are relatively high,

---

69   See Chapter 2.

70   Lords of Appeal in Ordinary, Lords Justices of Appeal, Justices of the High Court.

71   Supreme Court Act 1981, s 11(3).

72   *Ibid*, s 11(8), (9).

73   The trial of Lord Melville. The previous trial was that of Warren Hastings in 1788. Two Lord Chancellors, Bacon (1620) and Macclesfield (1725), have been removed by impeachment.

74   Impeachment is not obsolete in the United States of America where President Nixon was threatened with impeachment and resigned and President Clinton was acquitted in impeachment proceedings.

75   Claim of Right 1689, Art 13; *Mackay and Esslemont v Lord Advocate* 1937 SC 860.

76   As did Lord Denning, who retired at the age of 83.

77   Supreme Court Act 1981, s 12(5). The Consolidated Fund provides payments under the Civil List, the salaries of the Speaker, the judiciary, the Comptroller and Auditor General and the Parliamentary Commissioner. The Consolidated Fund Bill is passed without parliamentary debate. See, further, Chapter 13.

on the basis that it is in the national interest 'to ensure an adequate supply of candidates of sufficient calibre for appointment to judicial office'.[78]

Disqualifications

Holders of full time judicial appointments are barred from legal practice,[79] and may not hold paid appointments as directors or undertake any professional or business work. Judges are also disqualified from membership of the House of Commons.[80] Membership of the House of Commons does not, however, disqualify that person from appointment to the Bench.

Immunity from suit

All judges have immunity from legal action in the performance of their judicial functions. Provided that a judge acts within jurisdiction, or honestly believes he is acting within his jurisdiction, no action for damages may lie. Judges are immune from the law of defamation and, even if 'actuated by envy, hatred and malice and all uncharitableness', he is protected.[81] In *Sirros v Moore*,[82] Lord Denning MR and Ormrod LJ ruled that every judge – irrespective of rank and including the lay magistracy – is protected from liability in respect of his judicial function provided that he honestly believed that the action taken was within his jurisdiction.[83] The Crown Proceedings Act 1947 also provides protection for the Crown from liability for conduct of any person discharging 'responsibilities of a judicial nature vested in him' or in executing the judicial process.[84]

Bias or personal interest

A judge is under a duty not to adjudicate on cases in which he has either an interest – whether personal or financial – or where he may be influenced by bias. A fundamental doctrine of natural justice[85] is that 'no man should be judge in his own cause': *nemo iudex in sua causa*.

---

78   HC Deb Vol 23 Cols 257–61.

79   Courts and Legal Services Act 1990, s 75 and Sched 11.

80   House of Commons Disqualification Act 1975, s 1 and Sched 1.

81   *Sirros v Moore* [1975] QB 118, p 132, *per* Lord Denning MR. See, also, *Fray v Blackburn* (1863) 3 B & S 576; 122 ER 217; *Anderson v Gorrie* [1895] 1 QB 668. Jury verdicts are similarly protected (*Bushell's Case* (1670) 6 St Tr 999), as are words spoken by participants in legal proceedings (*Munster v Lamb* (1883) 11 QBD 588). Barristers cannot be sued for negligence in the presentation of a client's case (*Rondel v Worsley* [1969] 1 AC 191).

82   [1975] QB 118.

83   See Brazier, M, 'Judicial immunity and the independence of the judiciary' [1976] PL 397.

84   Crown Proceedings Act 1947, s 2(5).

85   See Chapter 25.

Financial interests

In *Dr Bonham's Case*[86] Lord Coke held that members of a board which determined physicians' fines could not both impose and receive the fines, thus giving early judicial expression to the requirement of freedom from bias. Rather more recently, in *Dimes v Grand Junction Canal Proprietors*,[87] the propriety of Lord Cottenham LC adjudicating was challenged on the basis that the Lord Chancellor held shares in the canal company involved in litigation. The House of Lords set aside the decision of the court despite the fact that:

> No one can suppose that Lord Cottenham could be in the remotest degree influenced by the interest ... It is of the last importance that the maxim that no man is to be judge in his own cause should be held sacred.[88]

Thus, the mere existence of a financial interest, even where it does not in fact result in actual bias but may present the appearance of bias, will be sufficient to disqualify a judge from adjudication.[89] The same position prevails in the United States of America,[90] where the issue of financial interests of federal judges is expressly covered by law. The Ethics in Government Act 1978 requires that Supreme Court and Federal judges must make a public declaration of 'income, gifts, shares, liabilities and transactions in securities and real estate',[91] a protection which is conspicuously absent in the United Kingdom.

A financial interest in a case which does not go beyond the financial interest of any other citizen does not disqualify judges from sitting. Thus, in *Bromley London Borough Council v Greater London Council*,[92] for example, the fact that all the judges in the Court of Appeal were taxpayers and users of public transport in London did not disqualify them from hearing the case.

Other bias

Judges, like everyone else, may be biased by virtue of race, sex, politics, background, association and opinions.[93] When adjudicating they must, however, be demonstrably impartial. This impartiality involves:

> ... the judge listening to each side with equal attention, and coming to a decision on the argument, irrespective of his personal view about the litigants ...

and, further, that:

---

86 (1609) 77 ER 646.
87 (1852) 3 HL Cas 759.
88 *Ibid*, p 793.
89 See, further, Chapter 25.
90 28 USC §455(b).
91 See Cranston, R, 'Disqualification of judges for interest or opinion' [1979] PL 237.
92 [1983] 1 AC 768.
93 See *op cit*, Griffith, fn 66.

Whatever his personal beliefs, the judge should seek to give effect to the common values of the community, rather than any sectional system of values to which he may adhere.[94]

There has, however, been uncertainty and inconsistency in the interpretation of 'bias'. In *R v Gough*,[95] opposing counsel presented two different tests for bias. The first suggested criterion was whether a reasonable and fair minded person sitting in the court and knowing all the relevant facts would have had a reasonable suspicion that a fair trial of the defendant was not possible – the 'reasonable suspicion' test. The second suggested test was whether there was a real likelihood of bias. The question to be asked is whether there was a 'real danger' that a trial may not have been fair as a result of bias – the 'real likelihood' test.[96] The House of Lords declared that the correct test was whether there was a real likelihood, in the sense of a real possibility, of bias of the part of a justice or member of a tribunal.

Where a judge himself feels that he has a bias against one of the parties to litigation he may disqualify himself from sitting on the case, as did Lord Denning MR in *Ex parte Church of Scientology of California*.[97] There, counsel for the Church requested that he disqualify himself as a result of eight previous cases involving the Church on which he had adjudicated, and in which, in the eyes of the Church, he displayed bias against them.

Nineteen eighty-nine witnessed the start of a high profile case in which the doctrine of judicial impartiality was re-stated by the House of Lords. Earlier in the year, the former President of Chile, Senator Pinochet, arrived in Britain on a private visit for medical tests. The Spanish government sought the arrest and extradition of Pinochet on charges involving the murder, torture and the hostage-taking of Spanish citizens in Chile between 1973 and 1979. Two provisional warrants for Pinochet's arrest had been granted following the Spanish proceedings. Pinochet then sought judicial review of the decision to grant an arrest warrant and an order of certiorari to quash the decision. At first instance, the Queen's Bench Division ruled that Pinochet enjoyed sovereign immunity as a former Head of State.[98] On appeal to the House of Lords, the court ruled – by a majority of three to two judges – that former Heads of State enjoyed immunity from arrest and extradition proceedings in the United Kingdom only in respect of official acts performed in the exercise of their functions as a Head of State. Torture and hostage-taking could not be

---

94 Bell, J, *Policy Arguments in Judicial Decisions*, 1983, Oxford, Clarendon, pp 4 and 8.

95 [1993] 2 All ER 724.

96 *Ibid*, p 727; see, also, *R v Spencer* [1987] AC 128.

97 (1978) *The Times*, 21 February.

98 *R v Evans and Another ex parte Pinochet Ugarte; R v Bartle ex parte Pinochet Ugarte: In re Pinochet Ugarte* (1998) *The Times*, 3 November.

regarded as part of Pinochet's official functions and therefore were excluded from immunity. In the course of the hearing before the House of Lords, several organisations – including Amnesty International – had been granted leave to intervene and submit evidence to the court. Following the decision, Senator Pinochet's lawyers complained to the Home Secretary that one of the judges, Lord Hoffmann, was a director of the Amnesty International Charitable Trust and, as a result, was disqualified from sitting, on the basis that his participation raised the question of bias: of a judge 'sitting on his own cause'. Senator Pinochet accordingly applied for the decision to be set aside. Lord Hoffmann had been one of the three majority judges. In an unprecedented move, and in the light of extensive national and international publicity, Lord Browne-Wilkinson, the most senior of the 12 Law Lords, convened a differently constituted panel of judges to reconsider the case. All five judges agreed that the earlier decision could not stand. Lord Browne-Wilkinson, reiterating the principle that it was 'of fundamental importance that justice should not only be done, but should manifestly and undoubtedly be seen to be done',[99] stated that 'once it was shown that the judge was himself a party to the cause, or had a relevant interest in its subject matter, he was disqualified without any investigation into whether there was a likelihood or suspicion of bias. The mere fact of his interest was sufficient to disqualify him unless he made sufficient disclosure'.[100]

The *Pinochet* case, a unique and unprecedented case which brought the highest domestic court under public scrutiny, spawned further challenges against judges, alleging bias of one form or another. It also led to calls for a register of judges' interests, in which any interests which might raise the question of bias could be recorded and made public, a proposal rejected by Lord Browne-Wilkinson as unworkable: whereas it was generally clear when Members of Parliament's interests conflict with their professional duties, as he put it, 'a judge [unlike Members of Parliament] may be dealing with anything, any local club or society ... there's no end to it'.[101]

THE RELATIONSHIP BETWEEN EXECUTIVE AND LEGISLATURE; LEGISLATURE AND JUDICIARY; EXECUTIVE AND JUDICIARY

In light of the doctrine of separation of powers, it is necessary to evaluate the manner in which, and extent to which, separate functions are allocated

---

99 *Per* Lord Hewart in *R v Sussex Justices ex parte McCarthy* [1924] KB 256, p 259.

100 *In re Pinochet Ugarte* (1999) *The Times*, 18 January.

101 See Gibb, F, 'The Law Lord who took the rap over Pinochet' (1999) *The Times*, 19 October, p 3.

between the differing bodies and kept separate. This task is most conveniently undertaken by examining the relationship between first, the executive and legislature, secondly, the legislature and judiciary and, thirdly, the executive and judiciary.

Executive and legislature

The personnel of government

Parliament provides the personnel of government. Ministers of the Crown, including the Prime Minister, must be Members of either House of Parliament. By convention,[102] the Prime Minister must be a member of the House of Commons and it is for this reason that Lord Home renounced his peerage in 1963[103] to revert to being Sir Alec Douglas-Home, Leader of the Conservative Party and subsequently Prime Minister. It is thus immediately apparent that the executive, far from being separated from the legislature, is drawn from within its ranks. It is for this reason that Walter Bagehot in *The English Constitution* denounced the theory of the separation of powers under the English constitution. For Bagehot, this feature of the constitution, however, far from being a dangerous divergence from an ideal separation of powers, had clear merits. To Bagehot, the close relationship between executive and Parliament represented 'the efficient secret of the English constitution' which:

> ... may be described as the close union, the nearly complete fusion, of the executive and legislative powers. No doubt by the traditional theory, as it exists in all the books, the goodness of our constitution lies in the entire separation of the legislative and executive authorities, but in truth its merit consists in their singular approximation. The connecting link [between the executive and Parliament] is the Cabinet.[104]

There are, however, opposing views. Lord Hailsham, the Lord Chancellor in the 1979–87 Parliament, asserted[105] that the current electoral process[106] which, generally, but not invariably, returns a government with a large majority of seats in Parliament, contributes to what he termed an 'elective dictatorship' – that is to say, a situation in which the executive controls the legislature. While Bagehot's view may have been tenable at the time in which

---

102 See Chapters 2 and 14.
103 Under the Peerage Act 1963.
104 Bagehot, W, *The English Constitution* (1867), 1993, London: Fontana, pp 67–68.
105 (1976) 120 SJ 693.
106 See Chapter 13.

he wrote, it is nowadays too simplistic and inaccurate a description of the working of the constitution.[107]

Prima facie, this close union of executive and legislature would suggest that the potential for abuse against which Montesquieu warned exists at the heart of the constitution. This would be so if it were to be demonstrated that the executive controls Parliament. Judgment on that matter must be suspended until the working of Parliament has been examined in detail.[108] There exist, however, tenable grounds for such an argument, but these must be set against the extent to which procedural mechanisms in Parliament avoid an actual or potential abuse of power by the executive. The constitutional principle entailed in this close union between executive and legislature, deriving from historical practice, is that of 'responsible government': that is to say, that the powers of government are scrutinised adequately by a democratically elected Parliament to whom every member of government is individually and collectively responsible.[109]

Statutory limits on membership

There exist statutory limits on the extent to which the executive can dominate Parliament. The House of Commons Disqualification Act 1975 preserves the separation between the executive and legislature by providing that certain categories of people are disqualified from holding parliamentary office. Under section 2, holders of judicial office, civil servants, members of the armed forces and the police and members of foreign legislatures are debarred from office.

The Act also limits the number of government ministers in the House of Commons to 95.[110] Despite this limitation, 95 ministers, when considered together with their loyal parliamentary Private Secretaries,[111] ensures that the government will generally enjoy the automatic support of some 120 Members of Parliament. Where the government has been elected with a strong majority of seats – as in 1983, when the Conservative Party had a majority of 144, and in 1997, when the electorate returned a Labour government with a majority of 179 – it must be conceded that the potential for parliamentary dominance exists. An evaluation of this matter depends upon the adequacy of parliamentary procedure.

---

107 Richard Crossman states that Bagehot provides a correct description of Cabinet government as it was between 1832 and 1867: Crossman, R, *Introduction to the English Constitution*, 1993, London: Fontana; but see the opposing view expressed by Vile, *op cit*, fn 14.

108 See Chapters 14–16.

109 See Chapter 2 on constitutional conventions and Chapters 14 and 16 on scrutiny of government.

110 House of Commons Disqualification Act 1975, s 2.

111 Who are elected Members of Parliament.

Political and procedural checks on government

The government, it must be recognised, irrespective of the size of its majority of seats in Parliament, is dependent upon Parliament for its continuance in office. The loss of a vote of confidence on a matter of policy central to a government's programme will cause the government to fall, as occurred in 1979 when the Labour Prime Minister, Mr James Callaghan, was forced to seek a dissolution of Parliament and call a general election.[112] Furthermore, parliamentary procedures are devised to secure adequate scrutiny for legislative proposals, and it cannot merely be assumed that the government will always get its legislation through in the form which it envisaged.[113] By way of example, in 1983–84, the Police and Criminal Evidence Bill was substantially amended following pressure from politicians of all parties, pressure groups, academics and lawyers. In 1986, the government – despite having a strong majority in Parliament – was forced to abandon its plans for legislation to deregulate Sunday trading due to parliamentary pressure. In 1994, the Conservative government faced unprecedented opposition over membership of the European Community and Union.[114] While the government narrowly won a vote of confidence in the Commons, eight of its own Members refused to support the government and the Conservative Party whip[115] was withdrawn. The constitutional effect of losing eight Members under the whip was to place the government in the position of a minority government.[116] In the following week, the government lost a vote[117] when eight of its Members supported the Opposition and a further seven Members abstained from voting. As a result, the government became dependent upon the uncertain support of Members of Parliament not subject to party discipline and of support from Members of opposition parties. The Chancellor of the Exchequer immediately announced that the Bill would be dropped and that the requisite revenue would be raised through other means.[118]

The Opposition

The role of the official Opposition must also be considered. Her Majesty's Loyal Opposition is, constitutionally speaking, a 'government in waiting'. Not

---

112 See Chapter 6.

113 See Chapter 15.

114 See, further, Chapter 15.

115 The organisational and disciplinary government Members who control and co-ordinate parliamentary business. Loss of the whip, in effect, renders Members of Parliament without a political party.

116 In the 1992 election, the government had a majority of 21 seats.

117 On an increase in the level of Value Added Tax on domestic fuel in the European Finance Bill.

118 Through the introduction of a 'mini budget' in December 1994.

only is it the function of the Opposition to question, challenge and oppose the government, but it also puts forward alternative policies and solutions to problems. In order to ensure that there is adequate opportunity for the Opposition to fulfil its constitutional role, 20 days per session are set aside for debate on subjects chosen by the opposition.[119]

Question Time, debates and select committees[120]

Question Time and debates in Parliament ensure the accountability of government to Parliament. The administration of the State is scrutinised by a system of select committees in Parliament with wide powers of inquiry.

The House of Lords[121]

In addition to checks within the House of Commons, the House of Lords may cause government to modify or abandon proposed legislation. The House of Lords has the power to amend and delay non-Money Bills for approximately a year before the Bill can receive the royal assent under the Parliament Acts 1911 and 1949. Rather than risk the delay of legislation, the government may prefer to compromise its proposals and accept proposed amendments from the Lords.

The electorate

Finally, the electorate, in addition to its role in a general election, can also express its displeasure with government policies during a parliamentary term at by-elections and local government elections. In the 1993 county council elections,[122] the government lost control of many of the councils which had been its traditional supporters – clear evidence that no government can afford to ignore the views of the people. Subsequent by-elections confirmed the government's loss of electoral support, as did the general election on 1 May 1997, when the Conservative government suffered a humiliating defeat.

Delegated legislation and the separation of powers

Delegated – or secondary – legislation raises important questions relating to the separation of powers. Delegated legislation[123] refers to laws, rules and regulations, made by government departments, local authorities and other

---

119 Standing Order No 13.
120 See Chapter 16.
121 See Chapter 17.
122 For the structure of local government, see Chapter 12.
123 See, further, Chapter 15.

public bodies, under the authority of an Act of Parliament: '... every exercise of a power to legislate conferred by or under an Act of Parliament.'[124]

The principal justification for the delegation of such law making power is efficiency. By granting delegated power, Parliament is freed from scrutinising every technical detail of a Bill. Delegated power also enables ministers and others to 'fill in the details' after the parent Act is in force. AV Dicey approved of delegated powers on this basis.[125] Delegated power has, however, been questioned. In 1929, Chief Justice Hewart[126] criticised delegated legislation as being an abuse of power. An Interdepartmental Committee of Inquiry on Ministers' Powers,[127] exonerated ministers from this charge and defended both the necessity and desirability of delegated legislation.

In any parliamentary year, some 60 to 70 Acts of Parliament will be passed. The volume of delegated legislation, however, may amount to some 2,000 statutory instruments per year. While general Bills – public and private – are subjected to full parliamentary scrutiny, it will be seen[128] that delegated legislation receives far more cursory examination by Parliament as a whole. The implication of delegated legislation in constitutional terms is that a legislative function is being exercised by the executive and not Parliament. The delegation of law making power is a necessity given the heavy legislative programme and the modern complexity of legal regulation. Provided that parliamentary scrutiny is adequate, and that the courts are vigilant and effective in ensuring that delegated powers are exercised consistently with the law,[129] it may be concluded that this ostensible breach of the separation of powers is unavoidable, although whether it is subject to adequate scrutiny and control remains questionable.

Legislature and judiciary

It has been stated above that Parliament is sovereign and that the judiciary is subordinate to Parliament. It has also been stated, perhaps paradoxically, that the judiciary is independent. This raises the question of how such apparently conflicting assertions can be reconciled. At the head of the judiciary is the Crown. The Crown represents the 'fountain of justice' and all judicial acts are carried out in the name of the Crown. In law, it is the Crown which appoints

---

124 *Joint Committee on Delegated Legislation*, HL 184, HC 475 (1971–72), London: HMSO, para 6.

125 Dicey, AV, *Introduction to the Study of the Law of the Constitution*, 10th edn, 1959, London: Macmillan, p 52.

126 Hewart, CJ, *The New Despotism*, 1929, London: Benn.

127 Donoughmore-Scott Committee, Cmnd 4046, 1932, London: HMSO.

128 See Chapter 15.

129 *Intra vires*. See Chapters 24 and 25.

all senior judges, acting on the advice of the Prime Minister and the Lord Chancellor.

Rules against criticism of the judiciary

To reinforce the independence of judges, convention dictates that there should be no criticism levelled at them from members of the executive – but not from other Members of Parliament. Parliamentary practice prohibits the criticism of judges other than under a motion expressing specific criticism or leading to an Address to the Crown for the removal of a judge. It was not, however, regarded as a breach of conventional rules when the then Prime Minister, Mrs Thatcher, in Parliament, criticised the light sentence imposed on a child molester.[130] There have, however, been other incidents where judges have been criticised in Parliament. In 1977, for example, motions were tabled for the dismissal of judges who had reduced a sentence for rape.[131] Further, a judge who described a rape victim as guilty of contributory negligence was criticised in Parliament.[132] The manner in which Members of Parliament are controlled in terms of what they may, or may not, say is through the powers of the Speaker of the House of Commons. These powers will be considered in Chapters 14 and 18.

The subjudice rule

Where civil proceedings are either before a court or awaiting trial, Members of Parliament are barred from raising them in debate. If the matter has not yet reached the courts, debate may be barred if the Speaker considers that there would result a real and substantial danger of prejudice to the trial arising as a consequence.[133] No reference may be made to criminal proceedings from the time of the charge being made until the final appeal is determined.[134]

Parliamentary supremacy and the judicial function

The doctrine of parliamentary supremacy[135] entails the necessary constitutional subordination of judges to Parliament and has several implications. First, it is well established that the sovereign Parliament can overturn any court decision by way of legislation.[136] Secondly, the judiciary's

---

130 HC Deb Vol 34 Cols 123–25, 285–86.

131 (1979) *The Times*, 20 and 21 December; (1980) *The Times*, 17 January and 1 February.

132 (1982) *The Times*, 6 and 21 January.

133 See Erskine May, T, *Parliamentary Practice*, 21st edn, 1989, London: Butterworths, pp 378–79 (see, now, 22nd edn, 1997).

134 *Ibid*, 1989, p 378.

135 See Chapter 7.

136 Eg, the War Damage Act 1965.

primary role in relation to the interpretation of statutes is to give effect to the latest expression of the will of Parliament.[137]

Judges as legislators

One of the most debated aspects of the relationship between the legislature and the judges lies in the question: 'Do judges make law?' In constitutional terms, the issue is whether by making law – either by virtue of the doctrine of precedent or through the interpretation of statutes – the judges are usurping the legislative function or, in other words, violating the separation of powers.[138]

The rules of statutory interpretation, devised by the judges themselves, are designed to limit judicial creativity. Statutory interpretation is not straightforward, even though Acts of Parliament are couched in detailed language in order to maximise clarity and minimise vagueness or obscurity. Despite this attempt to achieve clarity in statutory language, it is artificial to deny that judges 'make law'. Every new meaning conferred on a word, every application of a rule to a new situation, whether by way of statutory interpretation or under common law, 'creates' new law. Judges have themselves abandoned the fiction of the 'declaratory theory' which asserts that they do not 'make' law but merely discover its true meaning. From the separation of powers perspective, judicial law making should cause disquiet only if judges display overtly dynamic law making tendencies. By way of illustration, in *Magor and St Mellons Rural District Council v Newport Corporation*,[139] Lord Denning MR was accused by Lord Simonds in the House of Lords of 'naked usurpation of the legislative function'.

Lord Simonds, in the House of Lords, reviewing Lord Denning's approach, roundly rejected Lord Denning's broad 'gap filling' attitude to interpretation:

> The court, having discovered the intention of Parliament and of ministers too, must proceed to fill in the gaps. What the legislature has not written, the court must write. This proposition, which restates in a new form the view expressed ... in the earlier case ... cannot be supported. It appears to me to be a naked usurpation of the legislative function under the thin disguise of interpretation. And it is less justifiable when it is guesswork with what material the legislature would, if it had discovered the gap, have filled it in. If a gap is disclosed, the remedy lies in an amending Act.[140]

---

137 *Vauxhall Estates Ltd v Liverpool Corporation* [1932] 1 KB 733; *Ellen Street Estates Ltd v Minister of Health* [1934] 1 KB 590.

138 This issue is complex and outside the scope of this work. See, for detailed discussion, Bailey, SH and Gunn, M (eds), *Smith & Bailey on The Modern English Legal System*, 3rd edn, 1996, London: Sweet & Maxwell. See, also, Reid (Lord), 'The judge as lawmaker' [1972] JSPTL 22.

139 [1965] AC 1175.

140 See Denning (Lord), *The Discipline of Law*, 1979, London: Butterworths, pp 13–14.

Lord Denning's contribution to developing the law was marked in many areas. His judicial 'campaign' to protect the occupational rights of deserted wives[141] ultimately led to enactment of the Matrimonial Homes Act 1967, giving statutory protection to rights of occupation in the matrimonial home. Placed within the context of separation of powers and the position of judges as subordinate to Parliament, it can be seen that the courts developed the common law to a point where Parliament felt it necessary to legislate. *Burmah Oil v Lord Advocate*[142] further illustrates the point. The government, being dismayed at the implications of the House of Lords decision over compensation rights for property destroyed in wartime, passed the War Damage Act 1965 to nullify the decision retrospectively. Such is the sovereignty of Parliament.

The reference by judges to government publications and records of parliamentary proceedings, for the purposes of interpreting statutes, has traditionally been regarded as improper. In *Davis v Johnson,* Lord Denning MR stated that privately he looked at *Hansard* in order to establish the true construction of a statute, a revelation not approved of by the House of Lords.[143] The Renton Committee's *Report on the Preparation of Legislation*[144] and the Law Commission's *Report on the Interpretation of Statutes*[145] had both ruled against any relaxation of the rules on the basis, *inter alia,* that such reference was of doubtful benefit, difficult in practice and costly. Exceptions to this rule existed. For example, in *Black-Clawson International Ltd v Papierwerke AG,*[146] the House of Lords accepted that reference could be made to Law Commission reports and to the reports of parliamentary committees in order to establish the defect in the previous law which Parliament was seeking to redress. Further, in *Pickstone v Freemans plc,*[147] reference to *Hansard* was regarded as justified for the purpose of determining the purpose of the legislation and government policy. Until the case of *Pepper v Hart,*[148] it had been widely accepted that the courts should not, except under these circumstances, consult materials preparatory to the enactment of the statute or the records of parliamentary proceedings in connection with its passage in order to assist with the task of interpretation. In *Pepper v Hart,* however, the House of Lords conceded the limited right to resort to *Hansard* as an aid to interpretation. The Attorney General had argued that any relaxation in the rules would amount to a questioning of the freedom of speech in debate in

---

141 *National Provincial Bank v Ainsworth* [1965] AC 1175.
142 [1965] AC 75.
143 [1979] AC 264.
144 Cmnd 6053, 1975, London: HMSO.
145 Law Com No 21, 1969, London: HMSO.
146 [1975] AC 591.
147 [1989] AC 66.
148 [1992] 3 WLR 1032. See, further, Chapter 18.

Parliament contrary to Article IX of the Bill of Rights 1689. Lord Browne-Wilkinson, for the majority, rejected that reasoning, declaring that far from 'questioning the independence of Parliament and its debates, the courts would be giving effect to what is said and done there'.[149]

The High Court of Parliament

Parliament has the sovereign power to regulate its own composition and procedure. Under parliamentary privilege[150] – derived from the law and custom of Parliament and thus part of the common law – Parliament, and not the courts, has jurisdiction to rule on its own powers. Parliament cannot, however – other than by an Act of Parliament – extend its own privileges.[151] The role of the judges in relation to privilege is to rule on its existence and extent. Once the court is satisfied that a particular matter falls within Parliament's domain, it will defer to Parliament. Accordingly, if, for example, a citizen is defamed by the absolute privilege of free speech in parliamentary proceedings,[152] there is no legal redress. Privilege will thus protect the Member of Parliament from the law of defamation and leave the aggrieved individual without a legal remedy.

Privilege also extends to regulating the legislative process. It is for Parliament alone to determine the procedure by which an Act of Parliament should come into being. It is clearly established that, in order to become an Act of Parliament, a Bill must pass its legislative stages in the Commons and Lords[153] before receiving the royal assent. Once that process is complete, it is not for the judiciary to inquire behind the parliamentary roll.[154]

Executive and judiciary

With regard to the relationship between the executive and the judiciary, several matters having implications for the separation of powers require examination: the attitude of the courts in matters entailing the exercise of the royal prerogative; parliamentary privilege; judicial review; the role of judges in non-judicial functions; and the role of the Law Officers of the Crown.

---

149 See, further, Oliver, D, 'Pepper v Hart: a suitable case for reference to Hansard?' [1993] PL 5. For post-Pepper v Hart developments, see Chapter 18.
150 See Chapter 18.
151 Stockdale v Hansard (1839) 9 Ad & E 1.
152 Bill of Rights 1689, Art IX.
153 Except where the Parliament Acts apply.
154 Pickin v British Railways Board [1974] AC 765.

The royal prerogative

Detailed consideration of the royal prerogative will be undertaken in Chapter 6. The royal prerogative has significant implications for the separation of powers. Being the residue of monarchical power, the prerogative is part of the common law and thus amenable to the jurisdiction of the courts. Today, the vast majority of prerogative powers are exercised by the government in the name of the Crown. As will be seen later, the substance of many prerogative powers is political, entailing matters of policy which the judges are not competent to decide or – to phrase it differently – matters which, if ruled on by the judges in a manner inconsistent with the interpretation of the executive, would place the judges in a sensitive constitutional position and open to accusations of a violation of the separation of powers. That is not to suggest, however, that the courts have no role to play with respect to the royal prerogative. The traditional role of the courts is to rule on the existence and scope of the prerogative, but – having defined its existence and scope – to decline thereafter to rule on the exercise of the power. However, in *Council of Civil Service Unions v Minister of State for Civil Service*[155] (the *GCHQ* case), the House of Lords made it clear that the courts have jurisdiction to review the exercise of executive power irrespective of whether the source of power is statutory or under the prerogative. Having seemingly extended the jurisdiction of the courts in relation to the prerogative, the House of Lords, nevertheless, proceeded to rule that there exists a wide range of 'non-justiciable' matters which should be decided by the executive rather than the courts: a clear expression of the separation of powers.

By way of further example of the relationship between the executive and the courts in prerogative matters, the power to enter treaties under international law is a hallmark of a sovereign State and derives from the royal prerogative. The courts have consistently declined to become involved in matters of treaty making or its implications. When, in 1993, Lord Rees-Mogg sought to challenge ratification of the Maastricht Treaty under the prerogative by an application for judicial review, the court declined jurisdiction.[156] At the time, the Speaker of the House warned the courts against interference with the business of Parliament.[157] To claim and exercise jurisdiction over such a matter would place the judges above the executive – effectively alter the balance within the constitution – and place ultimate power in an unelected, unaccountable judiciary. It is for this reason that the judges are traditionally cautious when matters of prerogative are involved, and that caution is

---

155 [1985] AC 374.

156 *R v Secretary of State for Foreign and Commonwealth Affairs ex parte Rees-Mogg* [1994] 2 WLR 115; [1994] 1 All ER 457.

157 (1993) *The Times*, 24 July.

protective of the separation of powers, but may also prove to be detrimental to the concept of the rule of law.[158]

Law Officers of the Crown

The Law Officers of the Crown – the Attorney General and the Solicitor General – are members of the government. The Attorney General may also be a member of Cabinet. The Attorney General is bound by conventions which serve to limit the overlap in functions. Thus, where his consent to prosecution is required, by convention the Attorney General must avoid party political considerations, and may not take orders from government. This is a particularly delicate matter when essentially political prosecutions are being contemplated.[159]

The Law Officers are advisers to government and its ministers, and, by convention, this advice must never be disclosed. In 1986, this convention was breached when Leon Brittan, then Secretary of State for Trade and Industry, revealed advice given on the Westland Helicopter rescue plan.[160]

Judicial review

Judicial review of administrative action is designed to keep those persons and bodies with delegated powers within the scope of the power conferred upon them by Parliament: the doctrine of *intra vires*.[161] Thus, if a minister of the Crown or a local authority exceeds the power granted, the courts will nullify the decision taken and require that the decision maker reach a decision according to the correct procedure. Judicial review is concerned with the process by which decisions are made, not with the merits of the decision itself, nor with the merits of the legal rules which are being applied by the administrator. From this perspective, it may be said that the judges are merely upholding the will of Parliament in controlling the exercise of powers delegated by it to subordinate bodies. It could be said that the judges are here upholding both the rule of law and the sovereignty of Parliament. From another perspective, however, serious questions are raised for the separation of powers. If Parliament confers on a minister of the Crown the power to decide a matter 'as he thinks fit', to what extent is it constitutionally proper for a court of law to intervene and question the manner of the exercise of his decision making power? Does this represent an intrusion into executive power on the part of the judiciary? Does it amount to judicial supremacy over the executive?

---

158 See Chapter 4.
159 See *R v Ponting* [1985] Crim LR 318.
160 See, further, Chapter 16.
161 See Chapters 24 and 25.

Judicial review thus presents a constitutional paradox, representing, on the one hand, a check on the executive – arguably infringing the doctrine of separation of powers – and, on the other hand, keeping the executive within its legal powers, thus buttressing the sovereignty of Parliament and the rule of law. Public and press criticism of the judiciary's role in keeping the executive under check led to the former Lord Chief Justice, Lord Taylor of Gosforth, publicly defending the role of the judges. Speaking at an annual judges' dinner, Lord Taylor rejected recent charges that the 'senior judiciary have decided to mount a bloodless coup and seize the commanding heights of the constitution'. Recent cases involving the government – for example, the ratification of the Maastricht Treaty,[162] the declaration that the government had acted unlawfully in relation to funding the Pergau Dam project in Malaysia,[163] the appointment of Scott LJ to inquire and report on the *arms to Iraq* affair,[164] and the appointment of Nolan LJ to inquire and report on standards in public life[165] – have all recently raised the public profile of the judges. Lord Taylor rejected the criticisms, stating that:

> ... nothing could be further from the truth. Indeed their [the judges'] aim and function is quite the reverse. It is to ensure that powers are exercised by those to whom Parliament has given them and in the way in which Parliament has specified.

Lord Taylor added that the judiciary was conscious that it must avoid usurping the functions of the legislature or the executive – thus, reaffirming the doctrine of separation of powers.[166]

Contemporary issues for the separation of powers doctrine

Two of the Labour government's constitutional reform measures raise particularly difficult questions for the separation of powers, namely, the Human Rights Act 1998, which 'incorporates' the European Convention on Human Rights into domestic law, and the devolution of legislative and administrative powers to regional assemblies.[167]

In relation to the Human Rights Act, the legislation was consciously drafted in such a manner as to preserve the balance of power – and separation of power – between the judiciary and Parliament. As will be seen more fully in Chapter 22, this is accomplished by providing that primary (but not

---

162 *R v Secretary of State for Foreign and Commonwealth Affairs ex parte Rees-Mogg* [1994] 1 All ER 457; [1994] 2 WLR 115.

163 See *R v Secretary of State for Foreign and Commonwealth Affairs ex parte World Development Movement* [1995] 1 All ER 611.

164 See, further, Chapters 11 and 16.

165 See, further, Chapters 11 and 18.

166 (1995) *The Times*, 6 July.

167 For full discussion, see Chapters 22 and 12, respectively.

secondary) legislation remains immune from judicial invalidation even where that legislation is ruled to be incompatible with Convention rights. Where judges in the higher courts make 'declarations of incompatibility', the matter is referred back to the executive to determine whether, and in what form, amending primary legislation should be enacted by Parliament. While the Human Rights Act is in force in England from October 2000, it was in effect in Scotland on the devolution of power to the Scottish Parliament in 1998, and it is from Scotland that early indications of the impact of the Act are to be discerned. Specifically relevant to the position of judges and their independence – a crucial aspect of the separation of powers – is the appointments system. In *Starrs and Chalmers v Procurator Fiscal*,[168] the Court of Session ruled that the right to a fair trial before an independent and impartial tribunal, guaranteed under Article 6(1) of the Convention, would be violated where the presiding judge held a temporary position with no guarantee of permanent appointment and security of tenure, unless so offered by the Lord Advocate who enjoys discretion. In the case of Scotland, temporary sheriffs are appointed to serve one year, renewable terms, and they hear a large proportion of Scottish criminal cases. The Court of Session ruled that such an appointments system, the lack of security of office and the discretion of the Lord Advocate was incompatible with the right to fair trial. The sheriffs were not sufficiently independent of the executive, and could only be so if there were 'adequate guarantees that the appointed judge enjoys security of tenure'. The court recognised that the fact that the Executive appoints judges does not, of itself, signify a threat to judicial independence. Nevertheless, where a judge is appointed on a temporary basis, and his or her re-appointment lies at the discretion of the Executive, judicial independence may be threatened by a judge's awareness of the power the Executive holds over his or her judicial career. The *Starrs and Chalmers* case has widespread implications for the system of judicial appointments throughout the United Kingdom and the Lord Chancellor's power to appoint tribunal members, Assistant Recorders and deputy High Court judges who lack security of tenure.

The Convention right to a fair trial before an independent and impartial tribunal raises a further questions concerning judicial independence, questions which were highlighted in the course of the *Pinochet* case, discussed above (pp 138–39), which in turn re-invigorated interest in the issue of judicial bias.[169] At the root of the problem of judicial independence and public confidence in the impartiality of the judiciary, lies the system of appointments and promotions. As noted above, while appointments are theoretically made

---

168 (1999) *The Times*, 17 November.
169 See, *inter alia*, *Locabail (UK) Ltd v Bayfield Properties Ltd*; *Locabail (UK) Ltd v Waldord Investment Corporation*; *Timmins v Gormley*; *Williams v Inspector of Taxes*; *R v Bristol Betting and Gaming Licensing Committee ex parte O'Callaghan* (1999) *The Times*, 19 November, CA.

by the Crown, in practice, the Prime Minister and Lord Chancellor enjoy virtually untrammelled powers. The British appointments system is inherently secret, relying for the most part on the knowledge of the Lord Chancellor gleaned from 'soundings' taken within the profession.[170] Despite attempts to broaden the base from which judges are drawn, for example, through public advertisements introduced in 1994, and official encouragement to women and people from ethnic minorities to apply, the profile of judges remains predominantly white, Oxbridge educated and male. The selection procedure remains immune from public gaze and from independent scrutiny from a body, such as a Judicial Appointments Commission, which could ensure impartiality in appointments and promotions, and thereby dispel the disquiet which arises from a closed system, controlled by the Lord Chancellor, who is himself a political appointee.

The devolution of power to the Northern Ireland Assembly, Scottish Parliament and Welsh Assembly also raises issues for the separation of powers. The legislative and administrative powers devolved must not only comply with the Human Rights Act 1998, but must also be *intra vires* the scope of power devolved. Each of the Acts devolving power specifies the power which is 'excepted', 'reserved' or 'devolved' to the body in question. While the Government of Scotland Act 1998 includes a limited list of reserved matters ('reserved' meaning that the United Kingdom Parliament retains legislative power over the matter), and provides an extensive list of devolved power, the Northern Ireland Act 1998 is less clear in relation to those powers reserved or excluded than it is in legislative powers devolved which in effect are the sum of those subjects not excluded or reserved. The position under the Government of Wales Act 1998 is more straightforward: the Act devolves primarily administrative powers and not legislative power. Notwithstanding the scope of power devolved, and its nature, however, disputes concerning devolved issues will fall to the courts. In 1999, a Practice Direction was issued, laying down the procedure to be followed where a challenge arose over whether a devolved body had acted or proposed to act within its powers, which includes not acting incompatibly with the Convention on Human Rights and Community law, or whether it had failed to comply with a duty imposed on it. The effect of the dispute resolution procedure is to highlight further the role of the judges. Given that challenges to competence may be motivated by political forces, and the consequence of a ruling adverse to the devolved body being inherently political, the public profile of the judiciary will inevitably be raised. It may be argued that, in essence, there is little novel about the judiciary keeping constitutionally subordinate bodies (such as local authorities) within the power granted by Parliament, and there is much force

---

170 For a critical evaluation, see Slapper, G and Kelly, D, *The English Legal System*, 4th edn, 1999, London: Cavendish Publishing, Chapter 6.

in this. On the other hand, the political stakes in devolution matters are rather higher than in relation to local government and, as high profile cases of judicial review in relation to local government have shown in the past, controversial decisions – such as the House of Lords' decision in relation to the then Greater London Council's transport subsidy policy – give rise to criticism and allegations of political bias. All the more important then that the independence of the judiciary from the Executive, its policies and the politics of devolved institutions, be put and maintained beyond any doubt.

Judges as fact finders

It has become increasingly common for the executive to appoint judges as chairmen of tribunals of inquiry.[171] That this should be so is unsurprising. Judges are equipped by training and experience to review evidence with impartiality and rigour and to present findings in a logical manner. In recent years, inquiries have been conducted by judges in the following matters:

- Interception of communications (Birkett LJ);[172]

- Security matters: security in the public service (Lord Radcliffe);[173]

- Vassall (Lord Radcliffe);[174]

- Profumo (Lord Denning);[175]

- 'D Notices' (Lord Radcliffe);[176]

- Industrial disputes: miners and electricity supply industry (Lord Wilberforce);[177]

- Disturbances in Northern Ireland in 1969 (Scarman J);[178]

- Interrogation methods (Lord Parker);[179]

- Collapse of Vehicle and General Insurance Company (James J);[180]

- Legal procedures in relation to terrorism (Lord Diplock);[181]

---

171 See Drewry, G, 'Judicial inquiries and public reassurance' [1996] PL 368.
172 Cmnd 283, 1957, London: HMSO.
173 Cmnd 1681, 1962, London: HMSO.
174 Cmnd 2009, 1963, London: HMSO.
175 Cmnd 2125, 1963, London: HMSO.
176 Cmnd 3312, 1967, London: HMSO.
177 Cmnd 4594, 1971, London: HMSO.
178 Cmnd 566 (NI), 1972, London: HMSO.
179 Cmnd 4801, 1972, London: HMSO.
180 HC 133 (1971–72), London: HMSO.
181 Cmnd 5158, 1972, London: HMSO.

- 'Bloody Sunday' in Londonderry (Lord Widgery CJ);[182]
- Anti-terrorist legislation (Lord Gardiner);[183]
- Public disorder: Red Lion Square,[184] Brixton[185] (Lord Scarman);
- Industrial dispute: Grunwick (Scarman LJ);[186]
- Interrogation methods (Bennett J);[187]
- Crown agents (Croom-Johnson);[188]
- Bradford City Football Club disaster (Taylor J);[189]
- Hillsborough Football Club disaster (Popplewell J);[190]
- Arms to Iraq (Scott LJ);[191]
- Standards in public life (Lord Nolan/Lord Neill);[192]
- Dunblane shootings (Lord Cullen);[193] and
- BSE in cattle (Lord Phillips).

Many of these inquiries involve sensitive political issues. As a result, it is inevitable that judges will attract criticism from one quarter or another. There exists the potential for charges of political bias in the report, or that the judge has avoided the issue and effected a 'whitewash', or that the inquiry has not been conducted properly. To place judges in the position where criticism is likely to ensue is to create the possibility that their independence and impartiality will be damaged.

Conclusion

It was seen at the outset of this chapter that some academic constitutional authorities either deny, or minimise, the relevance of the doctrine of

---

182 HC 220 (1971–72), London: HMSO. See Boyle, K, Hadden, T and Hillyard, P, *Law and State*, 1975, London: Martin Robertson, pp 126–29.
183 Cmnd 5847, 1975, London: HMSO.
184 Cmnd 5919, 1975, London: HMSO.
185 Cmnd 8427, 1981, London: HMSO.
186 Cmnd 6922, 1977, London: HMSO.
187 Cmnd 7497, 1979, London: HMSO.
188 HC 364 (1981–82), London: HMSO.
189 Cmnd 9710, 1986, London: HMSO.
190 Cmnd 962 , 1990, London: HMSO.
191 See, further, Chapters 11 and 16.
192 Announced 25 October 1994. See, further, Chapter 16.
193 Established March 1996 under the Tribunals and Inquiries Act 1921.

separation of powers under the United Kingdom's constitution. The critical voice of Geoffrey Marshall is also to be considered:

> To sum up: the notion of the Separation of Powers seems to suffer from the following deficiencies:
>
> First, it is rarely clear whether, and in what sense, there is such a separation. The argument that legislative, executive, and judicial powers are constitutionally declared to be vested in particular persons is inconclusive.
>
> Secondly, if there is a separation of powers, it is unclear what it is that is separated, since the notions of 'legislation', 'adjudication', and 'execution' have not proved capable of precise definition ...
>
> In short, the principle is infected with so much imprecision and inconsistency that it may be counted little more than a jumbled portmanteau of arguments for policies which ought to be supported or rejected on other grounds.[194]

On the other hand, it has been judicially asserted by Lord Diplock that:

> ... it cannot be too strongly emphasised that the British constitution, though largely unwritten, is firmly based on the separation of powers: Parliament makes the laws, the judiciary interprets them.[195]

Equally, Sir John Donaldson MR has stated that:

> ... it is a constitutional convention of the highest importance that the legislature and the judicature are separate and independent of one another, subject to certain ultimate rights of Parliament over the judicature ...[196]

As Professor Munro has said, 'there is something of a puzzle here ...'.[197]

The separation of powers is certainly neither an absolute nor a predominant feature of the British constitution. Nevertheless, it is a concept which is firmly rooted in constitutional tradition and thought. Judicial assertions of the importance of the doctrine are explainable in light of the constitutional position of judges in relation to Parliament. The concept of separation of powers offers the judiciary a protective device both for the protection of the independence of the judiciary and against allegations of judicial intrusion into matters more appropriate to Parliament or the executive. The reluctance of judges to be drawn into such matters is reflected particularly strongly in relation to matters of the royal prerogative[198] and parliamentary privilege.[199] Accordingly, to deny the relevance of some form of separation of powers would be to misconstrue the evidence. The separation of powers is a principle respected under the constitution which exerts its

---

194 *Op cit*, Marshall, fn 18, p 124.

195 *Duport Steels Ltd v Sirs* [1980] 1 WLR 142, p 157.

196 *R v HM Treasury ex parte Smedley* [1985] 1 All ER 589, p 306.

197 Munro, CR, *Studies in Constitutional Law*, 2nd edn, 1999, London: Butterworths, p 195.

198 See Chapter 6.

199 See Chapter 18.

influence on each of the fundamental institutions of the State. While the separation of powers is ill defined, and is not accorded absolute respect, it ought not to 'be lightly dismissed'.[200]

---

200 *Op cit*, Munro, fn 197, pp 328–32.

THE ROYAL PREROGATIVE

The King should not be over man, but under God and the law.[1]

INTRODUCTION

Under the constitution of the United Kingdom, all actions of government are undertaken in the name of the Crown. Any account of the prerogative is an account of power, and the prerogative, historically and contemporarily, concerns the power of the Crown.[2] The prerogative today represents one of the most intriguing aspects of the unwritten constitution. In order fully to appreciate the meaning of the term 'the Crown', an analysis of both who in fact exercises various powers in the name of the Crown, and the source of the power exercised, needs to be examined. The question to be asked is: is the power (to be exercised) a prerogative power or is it the outcome of statute? As will be seen, there is no certainty as to either the existing prerogative powers or manner in which these may be extinguished. It is, however, clear that no new prerogative powers can be created.

THE PREROGATIVE DEFINED

Blackstone[3] defines the prerogative as:

> ... that special pre-eminence which the King hath over and above all other persons, and out of the ordinary course of the common law, in right of his regal dignity. It signifies, in its etymology (from *prae* and *rogo*) something that is required or demanded before, or in preference to, all others.

Dicey,[4] on the other hand, describes the prerogative in the following manner:

> ... the residue of discretionary or arbitrary authority, which at any time is legally left in the hands of the Crown ... Every act which the executive government can lawfully do without the authority of an Act of Parliament is done in virtue of this prerogative.

---

1   Bracton, H, *The Laws and Customs of England* (1200–68), 1968–77, Thorne, SE (trans), Cambridge, Mass: Harvard UP.

2   On the distinctions between the monarch and the Crown, see Marshall, G, *Constitutional Theory*, 1971, Oxford: Clarendon, pp 17–24.

3   Blackstone, W (Sir), *Commentaries on the Laws of England* (1765–69), Chicago: Chicago UP.

4   Dicey, AV, *Introduction to the Study of the Law of the Constitution*, 10th edn, 1959, London: Macmillan, p 424.

From these differing definitions, the following can be deduced: first, that these are powers which are inherent in, and peculiar to, the Crown; secondly, that the powers derive from common law; thirdly, that the powers are residual; fourthly, that the majority of the powers are exercised by the executive government in the name of the Crown; and, finally, that no Act of Parliament is necessary to confer authority on the exercise of such powers.

Joseph Chitty,[5] whose work remains the most comprehensive account of the prerogative, explains the need for prerogative power in the following manner:

> The rights of sovereignty, or supreme power, are of a legislative and executive nature, and must, under any form of government, be vested exclusively in a body or bodies, distinct from the people at large.[6]

In Chitty's analysis, the power of the King is but part of a reciprocal relationship between monarch and subject. To the King is owed a duty of allegiance on the part of all subjects; to the subjects is owed the duty of protection.

THE PREROGATIVE BEFORE 1688

The King and Parliament

It was for the King to summon Parliament and to prorogue it. The King could suspend Parliament's sittings and dissolve it. Parliaments were held regularly from 1295, and in 1311, it was decreed that Parliament should meet twice a year.[7] In 1330, the first statute was passed requiring that Parliament meet at least once a year – and more frequently if necessary.[8] At that time, Parliament did not sit for a term of years, but rather was summoned to meet *de novo* each year. The record was by no means constant: there were, for example, no Parliaments in the years 1364, 1367, 1370, 1373–76, 1387, 1389, 1392, 1396 or between 1407–10. Under Edward IV,[9] only six Parliaments met in the course of his 22 year reign. Under Henry VII,[10] there were but seven Parliaments, despite the Act of Edward III remaining on the statute book. Whether and when a Parliament should meet was much dependent upon the King's need for revenue, for it had been established by the middle of the fourteenth

---

5   Chitty, J, *Law of the Prerogatives of the Crown*, 1820, London: Butterworths.
6   *Ibid*, p 2.
7   See Maitland, FW, *The Constitutional History of England*, 1908, Cambridge: CUP.
8   4 Edw III, c 14.
9   1442–83.
10 1457–1509.

century that it was unlawful for the King to impose direct taxes without Parliament's consent.[11]

In the reign of Henry VIII,[12] nine Parliaments met in 38 years, although one of these lasted for seven years between 1529–36; under Edward VI,[13] two Parliaments met, the second of which lasted four and a half years. Mary reigned for over five years[14] and Parliament met annually throughout her reign. Under Elizabeth I,[15] by way of comparison, a mere 10 Parliaments met, although one Parliament lasted for 11 years. In the reign of James I,[16] four Parliaments met in 22 years, one lasting for nearly seven years.

The absoluteness of the King's power came to a head in the reign of Charles I[17] when Charles confronted Parliament over taxation to meet the cost of war, imprisoning over 70 people who refused to pay the forced loan, including the 'five knights'[18] who sought a writ of habeas corpus against the King. Sir Edward Coke supported Members of the Commons who sought to petition the King against unparliamentary taxation, imprisonment without good cause, the billeting of troops and the imposition of martial law. Charles accepted the Petition of Right but, faced with continued opposition from Parliament, prorogued Parliament in June 1628. Parliament was again summoned in 1629 but confrontation was again rife, with the Commons criticising the King's religious policy and refusing to vote supply for the Crown. Charles decided to adjourn Parliament in 1629 and there commenced an 11 year period of personal monarchical rule. In 1641, under the leadership of Pym, the 'Grand Remonstrance' was drafted – listing the grievances of the country under the rule of prerogative. While the Commons was divided over the Remonstrance, it represented a starting point in history, one which was to lead to the Civil War, Charles's execution and the rule of Oliver Cromwell under the only Republican constitution Britain has ever experienced.[19]

The Crown and the Council

Members of the King's Council were appointed and dismissed by the King at pleasure. While most matters of government and administration were decided

---

11 On taxation, see, further, below, pp 165–67.

12 1491–1547.

13 1547–53.

14 1553–58.

15 1558–1603.

16 1603–25.

17 1600–49.

18 *Darnel's Case* (1627) 3 St Tr 1.

19 See Lockyer, R, *Tudor and Stuart Britain 1471–1714*, 2nd edn, 1985, Harlow: Longman, Chapters 12–13.

by the Council, the King was under no duty to heed their advice, and, under a strong King, the Council had little real power. Under a weak King, however, real power vested in the Council, and in the course of a King's minority, the 'Council has ruled England'.[20] Under King Edward II,[21] the Council became a more formal body, with members being sworn in. The King in Council legislated, raised taxes and dispensed justice. FW Maitland observed that it is difficult to discern, during that time, whether a particular act of government was effected by Parliament or the King in Council. From 1386, the proceedings of the Council were recorded, and the Council was established as a permanent part of the machinery of government.

Law making powers of the Crown

Proclamations

In Chapter 2, the constitutional upheavals of the seventeenth century were discussed, and it is in this period of history, and in particular with the constitutional settlement of 1689, that the origins of parliamentary sovereignty are to be discovered. It will be recalled that it was Henry VIII[22] who asserted the power to make law by way of proclamations:[23] '... the most extraordinary act in the Statute Book.'[24] The statute did not affect the common law or existing Acts of Parliament, and it prohibited the use of the death penalty for breach of proclamations. This, nevertheless, left a wide – and ill defined – scope for the Crown to legislate without Parliament. The Act was repealed in the reign of Edward VI.[25] Its repeal was of great constitutional and symbolic importance in that it denied, by implication, the supremacy of the King over Parliament and declared that it was the 'King in Parliament' which represented the lawful legislature. Nevertheless, both Mary I[26] and Elizabeth I[27] continued to rule by proclamation. However, when James I[28] asserted his right to rule by proclamation, his assumed power was challenged by an application from the King's Council to the courts.[29] In the *Case of Proclamations*,[30] Chief Coke CJ declared that:

---

20 *Op cit*, Maitland, fn 7, p 200.
21 1307–27.
22 1509–47.
23 Statute of Proclamations 1539.
24 *Op cit*, Maitland, fn 7, p 253.
25 1461–83.
26 1553–58.
27 1558–1603.
28 1603–25.
29 *Case of Proclamations* (1611) 12 Co Rep 74.
30 *Ibid*.

... the King by his proclamation or other ways cannot change any part of the common law, or statute law, or the customs of the realm.

... the King cannot create any offence by his prohibition or proclamation, which was not an offence before, for that was to change the law, and to make an offence which was not.

Also, it was resolved that the King hath no prerogative but that which the law of the land allows him.

Dispensing and suspending powers of the Crown

The King's assent was needed for the enactment of statutes, but he also had the power to dispense with statutes and suspend their application. According to Coke, where statute affected the prerogative power, the King could suspend the Act.[31] The conflict between Crown and the courts in the seventeenth century is illustrated by the cases of *Thomas v Sorrell*[32] and *Godden v Hales*.[33] In *Thomas v Sorrell*, it was declared that the King could not dispense with a penal law made for the good of the public. However, in *Godden v Hales*, the court accepted that the King could dispense with a penal law – under specific circumstances – where that law fell within his jurisdiction. In 1687, James II, intent on removing obstacles to Roman Catholics holding public office, issued a Declaration of Indulgence which condemned the principle of religious compulsion and announced that all penal laws in ecclesiastical matters be suspended. In 1688, he went further, issuing a second Declaration of Indulgence which he instructed all Anglican clergy to read from the pulpit. On an appeal from the seven bishops who questioned the legality of such a dispensing power, James II ordered their arrest on a charge of seditious libel. In the *Seven Bishops' Case*,[34] they were acquitted.

The King and the courts

It was within the King's prerogative to establish new courts of justice. The Court of Star Chamber, exercising extensive criminal jurisdiction with little of the formality of judicial proceedings and without the use of juries, was established either under the Statute of 1487[35] or under the Crown's inherent prerogative: doubt exists as to its source. Unlike the ordinary courts, the Court of Star Chamber used torture. It became one of the most feared and powerful weapons under the control of the Crown until its abolition in 1641.

---

31 *Case of Proclamations* (1611) 12 Co Rep 74.
32 (1674) Vaughan 330.
33 (1686) 11 St Tr 1165.
34 (1688) 12 St Tr 183.
35 3 Hen VII c 1.

The King's claim to dispense justice in his own right and without the judges was dispelled in 1607. In *Prohibitions Del Roy (Case of Prohibitions)*,[36] the King sought to settle a dispute concerning land. In the Resolution of the Judges, Coke declared:

> ... it was answered by me, in the presence, and with the clear consent of all the Judges of England, and Barons of the Exchequer, that the King in his own person cannot adjudge any case, either criminal, as treason, felony, etc, or betwixt party and party, concerning his inheritance, chattels, or goods, etc, but this ought to be determined and adjudged in some Court of Justice, according to the law and custom of England; and always judgments are given ... so that the Court gives the judgment ...

> His Majesty was not learned in the laws of his realm of England, and causes which concern the life, or inheritance, or goods, or fortunes of his subjects are not to be decided by natural reason [which the King claimed] but by the artificial reason and judgment of the law, which law is an art which requires long study and experience, before that a man can attain to the cognisance of it ...

When, in 1617, the King ordered the Court of King's Bench to adjourn proceedings until he had been consulted, Chief Justice Coke refused, declaring that:

> Obedience to His Majesty's command to stay proceedings would have been a delay of justice, contrary to the law, and contrary to oaths of the judges.[37]

Coke was dismissed from the Bench.

Whether a writ of habeas corpus would lie against the King was determined in 1627. In *Darnel's Case* (the *Five Knights's Case*),[38] it was held that, where the King detained a prisoner under special order, the court would not look behind the order. Thus, while the King could not determine cases, he could nevertheless hold a subject free from interference by the judges. The Petition of Right 1628 declared such power to be unlawful, and in 1640, the Habeas Corpus Act guaranteed that habeas corpus would lie against the Crown.

Regulation of trade and defence of the realm

Historically, much of the commerce and trade of the country was under the prerogative of the Crown: according to Sir William Blackstone, the King 'is the arbiter of commerce'.[39] But, if such a prerogative ever existed in relation to

---

36   (1607) 12 Co Rep 63.

37   *John Colt and Glover v Bishop of Coventry and Lichfield* (the *Commendam* case) (1617) Hob 140.

38   (1627) 3 St Tr 1.

39   *Op cit,* Blackstone, fn 3.

foreign trade, it was effectively abolished by various statutes and, today, no commentator on the prerogative includes trade and commerce as being within its ambit. The King's duty as to the protection of the realm encompassed the powers to restrict imports of the raw materials of war, and the right to erect ports and havens. As Chitty observed, in 1820:

> It is indisputably established, that the right to erect ports and havens is in general vested exclusively in the Crown ...

> The King has not merely the prerogative power of erecting ports and havens, but he possesses *prima facie* the priority of ownership in all ports and havens within his dominions, though the public have the right to use them; and even though the right to a port or haven be vested by charter or prescription in a subject, yet he holds it charged or affected with the *jus regium* or royal prerogative, as it relates to ports and havens.[40]

As a corollary, the King had the prerogative power of erecting beacons and lighthouses. Under statute, Elizabeth I vested power to erect beacons and lighthouses for the protection of seafarers in Trinity House at Deptford, but the Act did not affect the King's prerogative powers over beacons and lighthouses on the shores of non-coastal waters.

The Crown and taxation

The early history of finance for the Crown is inextricably linked to the notion of the King as ultimate lord of all land. The King was the largest landowner in the Kingdom and exercised his right to collect revenues from the land. In addition, the King received profits from legal proceedings in the form of fees paid by litigants and fines. Pardons were also sold. FW Maitland records that in the twelfth century:

> ... the King's revenue was the King's revenue, no matter the source whence it came; it was his to spend or to save, as pleased him best; all was his pocket money; it is to later times that we must look for any machinery for compelling the King to spend his money upon national objects.[41]

The granting of supply to the King by Parliament from direct taxation had been established in 1215, from which time it was accepted that the King had no power to levy direct taxation without parliamentary consent.[42] The position of indirect taxation was, however, unclear. The power to regulate trade, including the power to establish, open and close ports, was within the royal prerogative. Accordingly, it could be argued that the correlative power to levy taxes on imports and exports was within the power of the Crown. In Mary I's reign, the Queen imposed indirect taxes on the exportation of cloth,

---

40   *Op cit*, Chitty, fn 5, p 174.
41   *Op cit*, Maitland, fn 7, p 94.
42   In the reign of Edward I, 1271–1307.

and, in Elizabeth I's reign, a tax was imposed on the importation of wine. A legal challenge to this assumed power of the Crown was instigated in James I's[43] reign over the increased taxation on currants. In *Bate's Case*,[44] the Court of Exchequer ruled in the King's favour, accepting that:

> The matter in question is a material matter of State, and ought to be ruled by the rules of policy; and, if so, the King has done well to execute his extraordinary powers. All customs, old or new, are effects of commerce with foreign nations; but commerce and affairs with foreigners, war and peace, the admitting of foreign coin, all treaties whatsoever, are made by the absolute power of the King. The King may shut the ports altogether; therefore he may take toll at the ports.

The indirect taxation issue was again to be tried in the courts in the reign of Charles I.[45] In 1628, Charles had announced that in future all counties would contribute towards the cost of the navy: the contribution being either in the form of the provision of ships or money in lieu thereof. In 1634, this scheme was put into effect, and thereafter Ship Money was levied annually. Whilst this undoubtedly was within the King's prerogative, it enabled the King to avoid the constitutional convention that there should be no taxation without Parliament's approval. In the *Case of Ship Money (R v Hampden)*,[46] Hampden had refused to pay taxes levied by Charles I to raise money for the navy in times of emergency. The King argued that it was for the Crown to determine whether or not an emergency situation existed and that this determination was conclusive of his right to exercise his prerogative power to raise revenue. The courts upheld the power of the Crown:

> The King *pro bono publico* may charge his subjects for the safety and defence of the Kingdom, notwithstanding any Act of Parliament, and a statute derogatory from the prerogative doth not bind the King and the King may dispense with any law in cases of necessity.
>
> ... Acts of Parliament to take away his royal power in the defence of the Kingdom are void; they are void Acts of Parliament to bind the King not to command the subjects, their persons and goods, and I say their money too; for no Acts of Parliament made any difference.[47]

The Shipmoney Act of 1640 reversed the decision, and Article IV of the Bill of Rights 1689 declared it illegal for the Crown to raise money without parliamentary approval. The King's power included the right to debase the coinage,[48] although Blackstone was doubtful whether such a power was

---

43 1603–25.

44 (1606) 2 St Tr 371.

45 1625–49.

46 (1637) 3 St Tr 825.

47 *Ibid*, pp 826–1315.

48 Hale, M (Sir), *The History of the Pleas of the Crown*, 1736, Emlyn, S (ed), London: E and R Nott and R Gosling, Vol 1, p 194.

lawful.[49] Establishing markets for trading and granting monopolies over their usage was within the King's power, generating much income for the Crown.

Protest against Charles I's reign by prerogative was fuelled by a rebellion in Ireland, during which an estimated 2,000 English settlers were massacred.[50] The Grand Remonstrance of 1641 listed the grievances of the country ruled under the prerogative. The House of Commons, following debate, voted in favour of the Remonstrance by 159 votes to 148.[51]

In 1685, James II inherited a Crown which was in debt. The question of indirect taxation had not been fully resolved. James, though granting generous sums for the army, requested an increased grant. When Parliament refused, in 1685, James prorogued Parliament. When James II fled to France in 1688, the throne was offered to William and Mary of Orange under the terms set out in a Declaration of Right. Following acceptance of its terms, the Crown and Parliament Recognition Act 1689 was passed by the Convention established to reach a settlement. Parliament, as then constituted, proceeded to enact the Bill of Rights 1689,[52] providing, *inter alia*, that there should be regular meetings of Parliament; that elections should be free; that the Crown's power to raise taxation[53] was subject to Parliament's approval, as was the power to maintain an army; that the powers of suspending or dispensing with laws by the Crown[54] were illegal; and of the greatest significance, that the 'freedom of speech and debates or proceedings in Parliament ought not to be impeached or questioned in any court or place out of Parliament'.[55]

From this time, the supremacy of Parliament over the Crown was established and the prerogative powers of the Crown continued in existence or were abolished or curtailed as Parliament determined. No new prerogative powers may be claimed by the Crown: as Diplock LJ stated in *BBC v Johns*:[56] '... it is 350 years and a civil war too late for the Queen's courts to broaden the prerogative.'

Miscellaneous prerogatives

Miscellaneous prerogatives included the right to raise revenue from the demesne lands of the Crown as 'lord paramount of the soil',[57] to the

---

49 *Op cit*, Blackstone, fn 3. See, now, Coinage Act 1971 and Currency Act 1983.

50 See Foster, RF, *Modern Ireland 1660–1972*, 1989, London: Penguin, Chapter 4.

51 Thus leading to the arrest by the King of one Member of the House of Lords and five Members of the House of Commons.

52 See, further, Chapter 18.

53 *R v Hampden* (1637) 3 St Tr 825.

54 *Godden v Hales* (1686) 11 St Tr 1165.

55 Bill of Rights, 1689, Art IX, discussed in Chapter 18.

56 [1965] Ch 32. See, further, Chapter 5.

57 *Op cit*, Chitty, fn 5, p 206.

ownership of tidal riverbeds, and to the land beneath a non-tidal riverbed – provided that it had not become a dry riverbed, whereupon the ownership of the soil is equally owned by the owners of the adjoining banks. Equally, the King, by virtue of his prerogative, was owner of the shores – the land lying between the high and low water mark – of seas and navigable rivers within his dominions. The ancient right of the King to wild creatures, to franchises of forest, 'free chase', park or free warren have been abolished[58] with the exception of the right to royal fish (sturgeon) and swans, which is expressly reserved by the Act. Additionally, the Crown had the right to treasure trove, now regulated under the Treasure Act 1996.[59]

THE PREROGATIVE TODAY

The constitutional questions requiring answer include those relating to the relationship between statute and prerogative and the control, judicial or political, of the prerogative. The most significant question which continues to intrigue and to concern constitutional theorists today relates to the very existence and scope of the powers themselves, together with the constitutional implications of this ill defined reservoir of power. As Maitland observed in 1888, and as remains true in the late twentieth century, examination of the prerogative is:

> ... set about with difficulties, with prerogatives disused, with prerogatives of doubtful existence, with prerogatives which exist by sufferance, merely because no one has thought it worthwhile to abolish them.[60]

Under the United Kingdom's constitutional monarchy, the Queen is part of the legislature: Parliament comprises the Crown, Lords and Commons. the Queen is the 'fountain of justice' – and while the Queen has no power to make laws[61] or suspend laws[62] or to act in a judicial capacity,[63] the entire administration of justice is conducted in the name of the Crown. The Queen is Supreme Head of the Church of England.[64] The Queen is head of State in relation to foreign affairs. The Queen is head of the executive, and all acts of government, whether domestic or foreign, are conducted in the name of the Crown. The right to summon and dissolve Parliament remains a legal power vested in the Crown. The Queen is the Fountain of Honour, and all honours in the United Kingdom are conferred by the Crown.

---

58 Wild Creatures and Forest Laws Act 1971.
59 See MacMillan, CA, 'Burying treasure trove' (1996) 146 NLJ 1346.
60 *Op cit*, Maitland, fn 7, p 421.
61 *Case of Proclamations* (1611) 12 Co Rep 74.
62 Bill of Rights 1689.
63 *Case of Prohibitions* (1607) 12 Co Rep 63.
64 Act of Supremacy 1558.

While regal powers are exercised in the name of the Crown by the government of the day, the Crown nevertheless retains important residual powers. Of these, the dissolution of Parliament and the appointment of Prime Minister are the most significant. These are discussed below. It must also be recognised that a few powers remain the personal prerogative of the Crown. Illustrations include the grant of honours such as the Order of Merit, and the Orders of the Garter and Thistle. More importantly, there still remains the prerogative notion that the Crown never dies and that the Crown is never an infant (thus, ensuring continuity of monarchy), and that the Crown can 'do no wrong', thus, placing the Queen outside the jurisdiction of the courts and guaranteeing immunity from prosecution in her own courts. Beyond these limited powers and immunities, the sovereign has, in the words of Bagehot:[65] '... under a constitutional monarchy such as ours, three rights – the right to be consulted, the right to encourage, the right to warn.' The influence of the monarch should not be underestimated: and will be returned to below.

In legal theory, however, the position is much different. As Bagehot stated:

> Not to mention other things, she could disband the army (by law, she cannot engage more than a certain number of men, but she is not obliged to engage any men); she could dismiss all the officers, from the General Commander in Chief downwards; she could dismiss all the sailors too; she could sell off all our ships of war and all our naval stores; she could make a peace by the sacrifice of Cornwall, and begin a war for the conquest of Brittany. She could make every parish in the United Kingdom a 'university'; she could dismiss most of the civil servants; she could pardon all offenders. In a word, the Queen could by prerogative upset all the action of civil government within the government, could disgrace the nation by a bad war or peace, and could, by disbanding our forces, whether land or sea, leave us defenceless against foreign nations.[66]

On the other hand, FW Maitland observes:

> There is one term against which I wish to warn you, and that is the term 'the crown'. You will certainly read that the crown does this and the crown does that. As a matter of fact, we know that the crown does nothing but lie in the Tower of London to be gazed at by sightseers.[67]

Maitland's warning is apt, but cannot be taken at face value. The point being made is that, in order to understand the power of the Crown, it is necessary to look beyond the superficial phrase 'in the name of the Crown'. The actual power which is exercisable by the Crown is limited in two ways. First, by convention, the majority of powers are exercised by Her Majesty's government or Her Majesty's judges in her name. Secondly, the existence and scope of a purported prerogative power is subjected to the scrutiny of the

---

65   Bagehot, W, *The English Constitution* (1867), 1993, London: Fontana, p 111.
66   *Ibid*, 'Introduction' and pp 287–88.
67   *Op cit*, Maitland, fn 7, p 418.

courts: 'The King has no power save that allowed by law.'[68] However, that should not be considered as equivalent to a power to control the prerogative.[69]

THE PREROGATIVE ILLUSTRATED

Before examining the nature, scope and constitutional significance of the prerogative, some examples are necessary to indicate the areas of power which fall under the prerogative. Under the United Kingdom's unwritten constitution, there exists no formal and agreed text as to the prerogative. In order, therefore, to ascertain the contents of the prerogative, an examination of the historical attributes of the Crown and the attitude of the courts to the prerogative is required. It is paradoxical – but undeniable – in a modern democracy, that there is no comprehensive, authoritative 'catalogue' of prerogative powers.[70]

To make an analysis of prerogative powers manageable, they may be separated into two categories:[71] those relating to foreign affairs and those relating to domestic affairs. Under foreign affairs can be subsumed:

- the power to make declarations of war and peace;
- power to enter into treaties;
- the recognition of foreign States;
- diplomatic relations; and
- disposition of the armed forces overseas.

Within the domestic category falls:

- the summoning and dissolution of Parliament;
- appointment of ministers;
- royal assent to Bills;
- the granting of honours;
- defence of the realm;
- the keeping of the peace;
- the *parens patriae* jurisdiction of the courts;
- the power to stop criminal prosecutions – *nolle prosequi*;

---

68 *Case of Proclamations* (1611) 12 Co Rep 74.
69 See *Council of Civil Service Unions v Minister for Civil Service* [1985] AC 374, discussed below, pp 198–99.
70 The most recent authoritative account remains that of Chitty, *op cit*, fn 5.
71 As does Blackstone, *op cit*, fn 3.

- the prerogative of mercy;
- reduction of sentences;
- pardoning of offenders;
- regulation of the terms and conditions of the Civil Service; and
- the right to royal fish and swans.[72]

It can be seen from this list, which is by no means exhaustive, that the powers are wide and diverse.

THE PREROGATIVE AND DOMESTIC AFFAIRS

The dissolution of Parliament

The dissolution of Parliament refers to the process by which an existing Parliament is brought to an end with a new Parliament coming into being following a general election. The dissolution of Parliament lies within the prerogative of the Crown.[73] It is perhaps the most important residual prerogative exercised personally by the sovereign, and represents the greatest potential for controversy. Three aspects of the right to dissolve Parliament require consideration: first, whether the Crown has the right to dissolve Parliament on its own initiative; secondly, whether the Crown has the right to refuse a dissolution when requested by the Prime Minister or other ministers; and thirdly, whether, by refusing to assent to a Bill contrary to the advice of the Prime Minister, the Crown can indirectly force a dissolution.

Royal dissolution on the initiative of the Crown

The last occasion on which the Crown – on its own initiative – dissolved Parliament was in 1835. The dismissal of his government by William IV in 1834–35 reveals the constitutional dangers of the exercise of monarchical power. The government had lost its leader, but was nonetheless viable as a continuing ministry. The King, misjudging the strength of public opinion against the government, forced it out of office only to be replaced by an unsuccessful successor. Bagehot evaluates the 1834–35 situation thus:

---

72 A right expressly preserved by the Wild Creatures and Forest Laws Act 1971. Formerly, the right to treasure trove also vested in the Crown: *Attorney General of Duchy of Lancaster v GE Overton (Farms) Ltd* [1982] Ch 277. The right to treasure trove is now regulated by the Treasure Act 1996. Treasure found must be reported within 14 days to the local coroner. Failure to do so will be a criminal offence. A Treasure Valuation Committee has been established which has the duty to value treasure and advise on *ex gratia* payments to the finder.

73 See, further, Chapter 5.

So that the last precedent for a royal onslaught on a ministry ended thus: in opposing the right principles, in aiding the wrong principles, in hurting the party it was meant to help. After such a warning, it is likely that our monarchs will pursue the policy which a long course of quiet precedent at present directs – they will leave a ministry trusted by Parliament to the judgment of Parliament.[74]

It has been suggested that 'a royal dissolution in our times would not merely be unpolitical; it would also be unconstitutional'.[75] This view has the support of Sir Ivor Jennings, who argues that, since the dissolution involves 'the acquiescence of ministers',[76] the Queen is accordingly unable to achieve a dissolution without advice. In Jennings's view, 'if ministers refuse to give such advice, she can do no more than dismiss them'.[77] The matter cannot be left there, however, for uncertainty remains over this issue. Walter Bagehot, writing in 1867, observed that the Crown's power to dissolve Parliament, other than following a Prime Ministerial request 'has almost, if not quite, dropped out of the reality of our Constitution'.[78] Bagehot continued:

> Nothing, perhaps, would more surprise the English people than if the Queen by a *coup d'etat* and of a sudden destroyed a ministry firm in the allegiance and secure of a majority in Parliament. That power, indisputably, in theory, belongs to her; but it has passed so far away from the minds of men that it would terrify them, if she used it, like a volcanic eruption from Primrose Hill.

Dicey was of a different view. In Dicey's judgment, the Crown has the right – in certain circumstances – to 'dismiss a ministry who commands a Parliamentary majority, and to dissolve the Parliament by which the ministry are supported'.[79] Dicey continued:

> The prerogative, in short, of dissolution may constitutionally be so employed as to override the will of the representative body, or, as it is popularly called, 'The People's House of Parliament'. This looks at first sight like saying that in certain cases the prerogative can be so used as to set at nought the will of the nation. But in reality it is far otherwise. The discretionary power of the Crown occasionally may be, and according to constitutional precedents sometimes ought to be, used to strip an existing House of Commons of its authority. But the reason why the House can in accordance with the constitution be deprived of power and of existence is that an occasion has arisen on which there is fair reason to suppose that the opinion of the House is not the opinion of the

---

74 *Op cit*, Bagehot, fn 65, p 231.

75 Markesinis, BS, *The Theory and Practice of Dissolution of Parliament*, 1972, Cambridge: CUP, p 115; see, also, Marshall, G, *Constitutional Conventions*, 1984, Oxford: Clarendon, Chapter III.

76 In so far as an Order in Council is required, the Lord President of the Council must summon the Council and a Proclamation and writs of summons must be issued, for which the Lord Chancellor has responsibility.

77 Jennings, I (Sir), *Cabinet Government*, 3rd edn, 1959, Cambridge: CUP, p 413.

78 *Op cit*, Bagehot, fn 65, p 230.

79 *Op cit*, Dicey, fn 4, p 433.

electors. A dissolution is in its essence an appeal from the legal to the political sovereign. A dissolution is allowable, or necessary, whenever the wishes of the legislature are, or may fairly be presumed to be, different from the wishes of the nation.[80]

Dicey recognised, however, that the dissolution of 1834–35 was 'a mistake', the King wrongly interpreting the will of the nation. That judgment is not conclusive of the constitutionality of the King's action, although Dicey conceded that it 'is hard to speak with decision' over that dissolution. As Dicey argued, if there is a constitutional right to appeal directly to the people by dissolving Parliament, then that right cannot itself be defeated merely because of a mistaken judgment. The precedent of 1834[81] is cited as authority for the proposition that the Crown has the right to dissolve Parliament, other than on the advice of ministers, where the main objective of dissolution is to 'ascertain that the will of Parliament coincides with the will of the nation'.[82]

> Whatever may be the answer given by historians to this inquiry, the precedents of 1784 and 1834 are decisive; they determine the principle on which the prerogative of dissolution ought to be exercised, and show that in modern times the rules as to the dissolution of Parliament are, like other conventions of the constitution, intended to secure the ultimate supremacy of the electorate as the true political sovereign of the State; that, in short, the validity of constitutional maxims is subordinate and subservient to the fundamental principle of popular sovereignty.[83]

Queen Victoria[84] was in little doubt that she retained the power to dissolve Parliament without the advice of her ministers. Lord Salisbury summarised the consequences of such use of the prerogative:

> A dissolution by the Queen, against the advice of her ministers, would, of course, involve their resignation. Their party could hardly help going to the country as the opponents of the royal authority; or, at least, as the severe crisis of the mode in which it had been exerted ... There must be some hazard that, in the end, such a step would injure the authority of the Queen. It ought not, therefore, to be taken unless there is an urgent reason for taking it. No such reason exists at present. It may ultimately be necessary in order to escape from a deadlock.[85]

Whether such a power continues to exist as a practical reality is, accordingly, in doubt. However, in so far as prerogatives continue in existence until expressly abolished by Parliament, in legal-theoretical terms, Dicey's view

---

80 *Op cit*, Dicey, fn 4.
81 And the earlier precedent of 1784, when George III dissolved Parliament.
82 *Op cit*, Dicey, fn 4, p 435.
83 *Op cit*, Dicey, fn 4, p 437.
84 1837–1901.
85 *Letters of Queen Victoria*, 3rd series, Vol II, pp 297–99, cited in *op cit*, Jennings, fn 77, pp 413–14.

would appear to be correct. There are, however, principled objections to this position. The power of control over the executive lies within Parliament and the parliamentary process. With the parliamentary process of government and opposition functioning correctly, there should never be a situation arising in which an exercise of prerogative power would become necessary. A situation in which the Crown felt obliged to protect the 'sovereignty of the people' against its democratically elected Parliament would represent an extreme paradox.

Refusal of dissolution on Prime Ministerial request

Two illustrations of refusal of a dissolution can be drawn from the Commonwealth. In 1926, the Governor General of Canada refused a dissolution to the Prime Minister, Mackenzie King, who resigned. The Governor General wrongly believed that the Leader of the Opposition could form a viable government with the support of Parliament. After only four days in office, the incoming government was defeated and the Prime Minister requested, and was granted, a dissolution. A similar situation arose in 1939 in South Africa. In each case, the Governor General was much criticised. It is, however, by no means clear whether the position of a Governor General is identical to that of the Crown. A Governor General is appointed by the Crown, on the advice of Commonwealth ministers, for a fixed term of office. Once appointed, the Governor General acts on the advice of Commonwealth ministers. His position is therefore not identical to that of the monarch, and it cannot be assumed that the precedents of 1926 and 1939 can be invoked unqualifiedly to demonstrate the position of the Queen.[86]

Professor Markesinis questions whether the Crown retains the right – if it ever existed – to refuse a dissolution on the request of a Prime Minister. On the other hand, he states that:

> ... no one in particular was or is quite sure whether a convention has emerged that virtually allows the Prime Minister a free hand in the matter.[87]

What does appear clear is that the Crown – if it is to exercise this personal prerogative – must at least have the support of some ministers.[88] The claim that the advice on which the Crown acts to dissolve Parliament is Prime Ministerial advice appears to derive only from 1918.[89] However, the situation could arise whereby the Prime Minister wishes a dissolution to take place, but other ministers do not. The Queen would then have to exercise a personal

---

86 See Marshall, G and Moodie, G, *Some Problems of the Constitution*, 5th edn, 1971, London: Hutchinson, Chapter 3.4.

87 *Op cit*, Markesinis, fn 75, p 116.

88 See Anson, W (Sir), *Law and Custom of the Constitution*, 4th edn, 1933, Oxford: Clarendon, Vol 1, p 327.

89 *Op cit*, Jennings, fn 77, Chapter XIII.3.

choice. In this regard, Geoffrey Marshall, cites *The Times* newspaper's editorial view, expressed in relation to the Labour government of 1966–70:

> If a Prime Minister defeated in Cabinet, unable to carry his policy in the party meeting, were to ask for a dissolution for the apparent purpose of unnecessarily involving his party in his own downfall, the Queen would have ample grounds for refusing and dismissing him, provided an alternative leader of the majority party was in sight.[90]

It is arguable that if there is no discretion remaining, then the prerogative is at least in abeyance, or at most, is no longer truly a prerogative power.[91] It could be argued, alternatively, that the supposed convention that the responsibility of the Prime Minister for the exercise of this prerogative is no true convention at all. As Geoffrey Marshall puts it:

> It can be argued that it lacks the essential quality that should mark a constitutional convention, namely the combination of consistent historical precedents, and a convincing *raison d'être*.[92]

Sir Ivor Jennings was of the opinion that, while 'the Queen's personal prerogative is maintained in theory, it can hardly be exercised in practice'.[93]

Dissolution following refusal of the royal assent

A 'forced' dissolution would inevitably come about if the Queen were to refuse to assent to a Bill against the wishes of her Prime Minister. During the Home Rule for Ireland debate,[94] King George V[95] was encouraged to veto the Home Rule Bill. In legal theory, the Queen has the right to refuse her assent to Bills, but by convention, assent is always given. The right to refuse assent has not been exercised since the reign of Queen Anne in 1704. George V, however, believed that he had the power to refuse assent to the Irish Home Rule Bill under the Parliament Act 1911 in 1913 and 1914.[96] In relation to this, Sir Ivor Jennings states that:

> It was assumed by the King throughout that he had not only the legal power but the constitutional right to refuse assent. On the other hand, he recognised that his exercise of the power would involve the resignation of ministers, a dissolution of Parliament, and a general election in which the main issue would be the prerogatives of the Crown. There is something to be said for a power to dismiss an unconstitutional ministry or to dissolve a corrupt

---

90 *Op cit*, Marshall, fn 75, p 46.

91 Following Blackstone's view that for a prerogative to exist it must be a power unique to the Crown.

92 *Op cit*, Marshall, fn 75, p 45.

93 *Op cit*, Jennings, fn 77, p 428.

94 On Home Rule, see Chapter 3.

95 1910–36.

96 *Op cit*, Jennings, fn 77, Chapter XIII.

Parliament, but nothing to be said for a power to refuse assent to a Bill because the King thinks it wrong.[97]

Doubt exists as to whether the Queen can refuse the royal assent, dissolve Parliament against the government's will, and dismiss the government. No government has been dismissed by the Crown since 1783, although the question arose in 1913–14 over the issue of Irish Home Rule, and the right to dismiss ministers was claimed to exist by George V, but not exercised. Sir Ivor Jennings[98] states that:

> The Queen's function is ... to see that the constitution functions in the normal manner. It functions in the normal manner so long as the electors are asked to decide between competing parties at intervals of reasonable length. She would be justified in refusing to assent to a policy which subverted the democratic basis of the constitution, by unnecessary or indefinite prolongations of the life of Parliament, by a gerrymandering of the constituencies in the interests of one party, or by fundamental modifications of the electoral system to the same end. She would not be justified in other circumstances; and certainly the King would not have been justified in 1913.

On this alleged right to withhold assent to Bills, Geoffrey Marshall[99] speculates as to whether the Queen could refuse to follow the advice of ministers if a Private Members' Bill was approved by both Houses but opposed by government, and whether, if Parliament approved a Bill in a manner required by procedural rules, the Queen could refuse assent – but there is no definitive answer to these questions.

As can be seen, many doubts surround the prerogative of the dissolution of Parliament. It is claimed nowadays that, whilst the dissolution of Parliament is technically for the Queen, it is exclusively within the Prime Minister's domain to request a dissolution at a time of his or her choice. This alleged exclusivity of Prime Ministerial – rather than Cabinet – choice stems only from the 1920s. Until 1918, when the convention was first challenged, it was thought that the decision rested with Cabinet. However, in 1935, Prime Minister Baldwin asserted his independent right to decide on the date of dissolution, resulting in criticism that the Prime Minister had unilaterally increased the importance of the Prime Ministerial office by assuming the discretionary power of the Crown.[100] Sir Ivor Jennings states that:

> No dissolution since 1918 has been brought before the Cabinet, and all Prime Ministers since Mr Lloyd George have assumed the right to give the advice.[101]

---

97 *Op cit*, Jennings, fn 77, p 400.
98 *Op cit*, Jennings, fn 77, pp 403, 407–12.
99 *Op cit*, Marshall, fn 75, pp 21–23.
100 Keith, B, *The King, the Constitution, the Empire and Foreign Affairs: Letters and Essays 1936–37*, 1936, London: Longman, Green.
101 *Op cit*, Jennings, fn 77, p 419.

Geoffrey Marshall doubts the accuracy of this assertion, citing 1950, 1966 and 1970 as dates on which the Cabinet was consulted before a decision was reached, whilst also citing Harold Wilson's statement that 'there is no obligation on the Prime Minister to consult'.[102]

While, for the most part, the timing of a dissolution will be within the Prime Minister's discretion, there may arise situations where the Crown may have a constitutional duty to exercise its powers. By way of example, a minority government – shortly after a general election – might form a pact with an opposition party on whose co-operation it depended for a working majority in Parliament. If, as a result of political disagreement, the pact broke down and the opposition party united with other opposition parties, the resultant situation would cause the Prime Minister either to resign or to seek a dissolution of Parliament in order to test the support of the electorate. However, if the newly combined opposition parties had a leader who could command a majority in the House of Commons, it is by no means certain that the Queen would grant the dissolution requested. The Queen would, in effect, be confronted by two opposing constitutional principles. The first of these is that the dissolution of Parliament is a matter for the Prime Minister and accordingly must be granted. The second principle is that the Queen should appoint as Prime Minister the leader of that party – or parties – which could command a majority in the House of Commons. In such a situation, the Crown clearly would have to exercise its powers of decision making, and might, in the interests of continuity of Parliament and the avoidance of another general election, refuse a dissolution and call the leader of the opposition parties to form a government.[103]

The Labour government of 1974 reveals the potential difficulties and uncertainties concerning the power of dissolution. It also reveals the inherent vagueness in the concept of votes of confidence following the loss of which governments – by convention – are expected to seek a dissolution of Parliament. The general election resulted in the Labour Party holding 301 (37 per cent) seats, the Conservative Party 297 (38 per cent), the Liberal Party 14 and the other parties 23 seats. The Labour Party was accordingly 34 seats short of an overall majority.[104] Given the indeterminate election result, neither the Labour Party nor Conservative Party was keen for there to be a dissolution in the near future. The Labour government accordingly made it clear that a defeat in the Commons would not force the government to seek a dissolution, other than where the government had made it clear to all members of the House that it was treating the matter as one of confidence. Between March

---

102 *Op cit*, Marshall, fn 75, p 52, citing Wilson, H, *The Governance of Britain*, 1976, London: Weidenfeld & Nicolson, p 37.

103 See *op cit*, Marshall, fn 75, Chapter III; and, on this specific point, see Brazier, R, 'Choosing a Prime Minister' [1982] PL 395.

104 See Butler, D, *British General Elections since 1945*, 1989, Oxford: Blackwells, Chapter II.

and October 1974, the government suffered 17 defeats in the Commons.[105] A general election took place in October 1974 when the opinion polls appeared favourable to Labour. The resulting election results produced an overall majority of three seats for the Labour Party.[106]

Between 1977 and 1978, the Labour government entered into a pact with the Liberal Party. While the Labour Party had won a narrow overall majority in the general election of October 1974, by 1976 this majority had been lost. Having failed to reach agreement with the Ulster Unionist Party, the Prime Minister, James Callaghan, entered negotiations with the Liberal Party leader, David Steel, out of which the 'Lib-Lab Pact' was born. The pact did not amount to a coalition government; no Liberals held government posts, nor was the government committed to accommodate Liberal policy within its legislative programme. Despite the government's lack of a majority (from 1976) and its dependency on the Liberal Party for its survival in office, the Party asserted the constitutional right of the Prime Minister – and no one else – to determine the dissolution of Parliament. The matter should not be regarded as so certain. SA de Smith and R Brazier have written:

> Perhaps the following proposition would command a wide measure of support: the Queen may properly refuse a Prime Minister's request for a dissolution if she has substantial grounds for believing (i) that an alternative government, enjoying the confidence of a majority of the House of Commons, can be formed without a general election, and (ii) that a general election held at that time would be clearly prejudicial to the national interest.[107]

An illustration from the Republic of Ireland

There is no precedent within the United Kingdom from which firm conclusions can be drawn. However, in the Republic of Ireland, the matter has been recently tested. In November 1994, following a controversial appointment of a former Attorney General[108] to the position of President of the High Court, the 22 month coalition government of *Fianna Fail* and the Labour Party collapsed. Article 13.2.2 of the Constitution provides that:

> The President[109] may in his absolute discretion refuse to dissolve *Dail Eirann* on the advice of a *Taoiseach* who has ceased to retain the support of a majority in *Dail Eirann*.

---

105 Between October 1974 and March 1979, the government was defeated 42 times, three of which were defeats on matters central to government policy.

106 Labour 319, Conservative 277, Liberal 13, others 26.

107 de Smith, SA and Brazier, R, *Constitutional and Administrative Law*, 7th edn, 1994, London, Penguin, p 129 (see, now, 8th edn, 1998).

108 Harry Whelehan.

109 Then Mary Robinson.

It is also clear, however, that the President cannot refuse a dissolution to a Prime Minister who retains the support of a majority in the Parliament (*Dail*). Three possible solutions could be sought. First, the President could grant a dissolution on Prime Ministerial request and a general election would take place. Secondly, the opposition parties could try to form a coalition and the President appoint its leader as Prime Minister. Thirdly, the *Fianna Fail* (the governing party) ministers could replace the Prime Minister with another leader who could secure a continued coalition government, in which case neither a dissolution nor a general election would be required. Should the Prime Minister (the *Taoiseach*) lose majority support by losing a formal vote of confidence, he would be obliged to resign.[110] When the Deputy Prime Minister, Dick Spring, announced that he would vote against the Prime Minister, Albert Reynolds, in a vote of confidence, the Prime Minister resigned.[111]

On 15 December, after five weeks of political turmoil, John Bruton, Leader of the *Fine Gael* Party, with the support of the Labour and Democratic Left Party, was elected Prime Minister. The new coalition government had a majority of four in the *Dail*. Dick Spring, Leader of the Labour Party, was reappointed as Deputy Prime Minister and Foreign Minister.[112] Thus, the second option had been favoured and a new government – albeit fragile – formed without a dissolution of Parliament (the *Dail*).

An illustration from Australia

The Australian political crisis in 1975 provides a further example of this uncertain constitutional situation.[113] Under section 2 of the Commonwealth of Australia Constitution Act 1900, the Governor General:

> ... shall have and may exercise in the Commonwealth during the Queen's pleasure, but subject to this Constitution, such powers and functions of the Queen as Her Majesty may be pleased to assign to him.

Section 5 states that:

> The Governor General may appoint such times for holding the sessions of the Parliament as he thinks fit, and may also from time to time, by proclamation or otherwise, prorogue the Parliament, and may in like manner dissolve the House of Representatives.

Section 64 provides that:

> The Governor General may appoint officers to administer such Departments of State of the Commonwealth as the Governor General in Council may establish. Such officers shall hold office during the pleasure of the Governor General.

---

110 Constitution, Art 28.10.

111 17 November 1994.

112 (1994) *The Times*, 16 December .

113 Sawer, G, *Federation Under Strain*, 1977, Melbourne: Melbourne UP.

In October 1975, the Senate refused supply to the government by resolving not to proceed with legislation giving effect to the Labour government's financial programme until the government agreed to a general election for the House of Representatives. When the Prime Minister, Gough Whitlam, refused to accede to this demand, supply was denied. On 11 November 1975 the Prime Minister called on the Governor General, Sir John Kerr, to request that writs be issued for elections to be held for 50 per cent of the Senate seats. Rather than granting the writs, the Governor General informed the Prime Minister that his commission had been withdrawn. In so doing – among other things – the Governor General prevented the Prime Minister from telephoning the Queen, as was his right whilst in office. Subsequently, the Governor General called for the Opposition Leader to act as caretaker Prime Minister, subject to two conditions. The first related to ensuring the granting of supply; the second to advising the Governor General to dissolve both Houses. In the ensuing general election the Opposition Leader, Malcolm Fraser, was returned with a majority of seats and the impasse ended.

One cause of the problem was the constitution itself, for while ministers must be in the lower House – the House of Representatives – the Senate had been given the power to withhold finance from a ministry formed from the House of Representatives. Compare this situation with the pre-1911 position of the House of Lords in the United Kingdom whereby – by convention – the House of Lords traditionally gave way to the Commons on matters of supply, and now the Parliament Acts 1911 and 1949 which regulate the position. In Australia, there had been no serious conflict until the situation of 1975.[114]

The intervention of – and actions of – the Governor General was much criticised, and whilst acting within his constitutional powers, the Governor General was seen to be directly involved in a political controversy. The criticisms were the greater for the fact that, in so acting, he was dismissing a Labour Prime Minister and the ministry of the House of Representatives and was seen to be favouring the upper House.[115]

David Butler identified four questions implicit in the crises of 1975, two of which have immediate relevance:

(1) What should the Queen have done if Mr Whitlam had the chance to 'phone her to demand the instant dismissal of the Governor General?

(2) Is 'the Governor General in Council' the only power that can dissolve Parliament, necessarily the Governor General and ministers of the Crown: or could the Governor General have called an Executive Council composed of Councillors not currently 'on summons' as ministers?

---

114 Hanks, PJ, *Constitutional Law in Australia*, 1991, Sydney: Butterworths, p 163.
115 *Ibid*, p 164.

To neither of these questions were answers forthcoming to David Butler in his discussions.[116] More than anything else, the Australian saga reveals that the constitutional position of the monarch – in the representative form of a Governor General – can be as uncertain under a written constitution as under a largely unwritten one.

Circumstances requiring dissolution

Loss of confidence vote

By convention, a government must resign or seek a dissolution of Parliament from the Queen if a confidence vote is lost in the House of Commons. A vote of confidence was described by Prime Minister Ramsey MacDonald in 1924 as being a vote on 'substantial issues, issues of principle, issues which really matter, a matter which strikes at the root of proposals made'. In 1979, the Labour government had been defeated by two votes in a vote over its economic policy. The then Leader of the Opposition, Mrs Margaret Thatcher, said that:

> The government has been decisively defeated and discredited on a matter central to their whole economic policy. Such a defeat is unprecedented in modern times.

> In the light of the decision of the House of Commons, I call upon the government to resign or seek a vote of confidence forthwith.

The Prime Minister, James Callaghan, tabled a vote of confidence and won the vote. Nevertheless, in light of the political uncertainty, the Prime Minister sought and was granted a dissolution, and a general election followed at which the Labour Party was defeated.

During the first term of the incoming Conservative government's tenure of office, many 'votes of no confidence' were tabled (put down) by the Opposition, yet none led to a dissolution of Parliament.

Professor Basil Markesinis identifies eight aspects of the convention on the dissolution of Parliament:

(a) The Crown cannot force a dissolution upon a government; this would also imply its dismissal.

(b) The Crown, in the vast majority of cases, must act on the advice of the Prime Minister of the time.

(c) The Crown cannot refuse a dissolution to a majority Prime Minister. The size of his party's majority is irrelevant.

(d) The timing of and reason for the dissolution is left to the Prime Minister's discretion.

---

116 Butler, D, 'The Australian crisis of 1975' (1976) 29 Parl Aff 201.

(e) The Crown may, under certain circumstances, refuse a dissolution to a minority government (whether defeated or undefeated) provided an alternative government is possible and able to carry on with the existing House. If the government is censured, it is advisable that the Crown recall its predecessor and grant its request to dissolve.

(f) Though an appeal to the electorate is always proper, a series of dissolutions, particularly if they are based on the same reason, might represent a triumph over and not a triumph of the electorate.

(g) A government which has been granted a dissolution may not proceed to a second dissolution until the new Parliament proves unworkable and no other government is likely and willing to carry on with the existing House.

(h) The question as to which party was granted the previous dissolution and the timing of the dissolution (first or last session of Parliament) are matters which may be taken into account but are not in themselves decisive.[117]

THE APPOINTMENT OF PRIME MINISTER

In constitutional theory, the Queen – under the royal prerogative – may appoint whomsoever she pleases to the office of Prime Minister.[118] In practice, the position is governed by convention and the Queen must appoint the person who can command a majority in the House of Commons who, under normal circumstances, will be the leader of the political party which secures the greatest number of parliamentary seats at a general election. Several differing situations present themselves: the government of the day may be returned by the electorate with a majority and the Prime Minister will remain in office. Alternatively, the government may lose the election, and the incoming Prime Minister will be the leader of that political party which commands a majority of seats in the House of Commons. More difficult is the position where the election produces no outright winner, resulting in no one party having an overall majority. Here, the spectre of a 'hung Parliament' arises. The situation may also arise where a Prime Minister resigns from old age or ill health during the course of his term of office – as was the case in 1935 (Ramsey MacDonald), 1955 (Winston Churchill) and 1957 (Anthony Eden) – or dies in office (Campbell-Bannerman).[119] Finally, it may be the case that a Prime Minister chooses to retire, as occurred in 1937 (Stanley Baldwin) and 1976 (Harold Wilson).

---

117 *Op cit*, Markesinis, fn 75, p 120.

118 See, *inter alia, op cit*, Jennings, fn 77; *op cit*, Marshall and Moodie, fn 86; Laski, H, *Reflections on the Constitution*, 1951, Manchester: Manchester UP; Brazier, R, *Constitutional Texts*, 1990, Oxford: Clarendon, Chapters 1 and 2; *op cit*, Marshall, fn 75, Chapter II.

119 1905–08.

Appointment of Prime Minister following a general election

Where general elections are involved, for the most part, as will be seen later, the electoral system in the United Kingdom returns a single party with an overall majority, and so no question arises as to whom the Queen should appoint as Prime Minister. It is not out of the question, however, for a different political scenario to present itself. Should the Queen send for the leader of the party having the largest number of seats, or the leader of the party which will hold the balance of power? There is much debate over this issue,[120] but once again no clear cut answer.

In February 1974, the Conservative Party lost the general election by a small number of seats and could command no overall majority in the House of Commons. Following the election results, the Prime Minister, Edward Heath, did not tender his resignation immediately but rather entered into negotiations over the following weekend with the Liberal Party, with a view to forming a political pact which would ensure a majority over the opposition parties. When those negotiations broke down, Mr Heath immediately resigned, and the Queen invited the Leader of the Labour Party to become Prime Minister. The question arising at the time was whether there had been any unconstitutional conduct involved in Mr Heath not relinquishing office the moment the election results were known.[121] The answer would appear to be that Mr Heath had the constitutional right to attempt to form a coalition which would avoid the need for a further election.

Appointment of Prime Minister following retirement of the incumbent

When the Prime Minister retires, the government still retains the mandate of the people and hence the choice of the new Prime Minister will be dictated by the wishes of the Party. It may be that there is a 'Prime Minister in waiting' who commands the support of the Party and will hence be appointed without delay. Under such circumstances, it is unrealistic to speak of the Crown having any choice in the matter. Where no Party consensus as to a successor exists, the political process will come into play. Nowadays, each of the major political parties utilises a method of election of its leader, and it is that process which will determine the successor: again, the Queen has no practical 'say' in the matter. It was not always thus.

---

120 See, *inter alia, op cit*, Jennings, fn 77, Chapter II; *op cit*, Marshall, fn 75, Chapter II, pp 29–35; *op cit*, Marshall and Moodie, fn 86, pp 44–51; *op cit*, Brazier, fn 103.
121 See, *inter alia*, Bogdanor, V, *Multi-Party Politics and the Constitution*, 1983, Cambridge: CUP, Chapters 5–8, Butler, D, *Governing Without a Majority: Dilemmas for Hung Parliaments in Britain*, 1983, London: Collins.

In 1957, Sir Anthony Eden resigned office, and there was no obvious successor – nor was there in place at that time an electoral process within the governing Conservative Party which would produce a successor. The Queen was thus left with a choice. The Queen consulted elder statesmen of the Conservative Party and acted upon their advice that Harold Macmillan be appointed. Had she not acted upon impartial advice, the Crown could have been damaged by charges of political decision making. One consequence of the 1957 dilemma was that the Labour Party announced its intention to introduce a selection procedure for its leader: a move designed to remove any discretion from the Crown. The Conservative Party did not react in this manner until after the difficulties revealed in 1963. The resignation of Harold Macmillan fell at a time when there were several contenders for leadership of the Party. The matter was resolved by the appointment of Lord Home, a Conservative peer, and the passage of the Peerage Act 1963,[122] which enabled Lord Home to relinquish his peerage and take a seat in the House of Commons as Sir Alec Douglas-Home. However, the saga emphasised the uncertainties in the choice of Party Leader and an electoral system for the leadership of the Party was subsequently introduced.

In 1976, Harold Wilson resigned office. In *The Governance of Britain*, Wilson describes the theory and practice in the handover of power:

> In the relatively simple handover of what is in fact, though not constitutionally, a continuing government, the test, given the normal circumstances of a party majority, is whether A or B can in fact command a majority in the House of Commons. Where the party's procedure for selecting a leader is laid down and is seen to have worked, for example, the eliminating ballot procedure used by the Parliamentary Labour Party in March–April 1976, the selection is fairly clear, though it still has to be made. The Parliamentary Party was not in fact electing a Prime Minister; it was electing a new party leader.

> When the process is complete, the outgoing Prime Minister goes straight to the Palace and formally tenders his resignation; the most he needs to do is to inform the monarch, who will have been given the figures already, that the ballot has produced a given result, probably adding that, in his view, the newly elected leader can command a majority in Parliament ...

> Contrary to widespread belief, there is no duty on the Prime Minister, still less any inherent right, to recommend the man to be sent for. *It is the sovereign who decides whom to send for and invite to form a government.*[123]

---

122 See Chapter 17.
123 *Op cit*, Wilson, fn 102, pp 21–22, emphasis added.

THE PREROGATIVE OF MERCY

Nowadays, the prerogative of mercy entails two aspects: the power to grant pardons which in turn has two elements and the power to enter a *nolle prosequi*.

Pardons and commutation of sentence

A complete pardon is used to remove the 'pains, penalties and punishments' which flow from a conviction for a criminal offence, but does not eliminate the conviction itself.[124] The right of pardon does not extend to civil matters. The power is exercisable in England and Wales on the advice of the Secretary of State for the Home Department, who is accountable to Parliament. The Crown therefore has no personal involvement in its exercise. Commutation of sentence is a limited – or conditional – form of pardon. The sentence will be reduced on conditions: '... a condemned murderer is pardoned on condition of his going into penal servitude.' As Maitland comments: 'It is a nice question whether he might not insist on being hanged.'[125] Commutation is distinguishable from remission of sentence. The latter reduces the sentence imposed but does not alter its form.

RFV Heuston examines the unusual situation which arose in 1948. The Criminal Justice Bill included a clause – accepted by the Commons on amendment – abolishing the death penalty for a period of five years. The government was clear that the House of Lords would reject the amendment. The Home Secretary announced that he proposed to advise the Crown 'to exercise the prerogative of mercy in every case of the death sentence being pronounced until a definite decision had been come to by Parliament'.[126] In debate in the House of Lords, Lord Goddard CJ took the view that the proposal of the Home Secretary came close to 'being an exercise of the suspending and dispensing powers claimed by the Stuarts and prohibited by the Bill of Rights'. In Heuston's view, the dispensing and suspending powers are distinguishable from the power of pardon: the former affects the legality of the act, the latter simply 'frees a guilty person from the legal consequences of his admittedly illegal act'.[127]

The prerogative of mercy has traditionally been regarded as unreviewable by the courts. In 1976, in *De Freitas v Benny*,[128] Lord Diplock was to state that:

---

124 *R v Foster* [1985] QB 115.
125 *Op cit*, Maitland, fn 7, p 480.
126 Heuston, RFV, *Essays in Constitutional Law*, 2nd edn, 1964, London: Stevens, p 7.
127 *Ibid*, p 71.
128 [1976] AC 239.

> At common law, this has always been a matter which lies solely in the discretion of the sovereign, who by constitutional convention exercises it in respect of England on the advice of the Home Secretary to whom Her Majesty delegates her discretion. Mercy is not the subject of legal rights. It begins where legal rights end.[129]

In *Council of Civil Service Unions v Minister for the Civil Service*,[130] Lord Roskill confirmed that the prerogative of mercy was not 'susceptible to judicial review'. However, as will be seen further below, the review of the prerogative is not a static matter, and is one which evolves over time. Judicial doubt on refusal to review the prerogative was expressed in the New Zealand Court of Appeal in *Burt v Governor General*.[131] In that case, while the court ruled that, in light of the safeguards which existed under the New Zealand criminal justice system, there was in the instant case no good reason to review the exercise of the prerogative of mercy; nevertheless, the court stated that 'it would be inconsistent with the contemporary approach to say that, merely because it is a pure and strict prerogative power, its exercise or non-exercise must be immune from curial challenge'.[132]

The case of *Bentley* illustrates the contemporary position regarding the review of the prerogative of mercy in the United Kingdom. In 1952, Derek Bentley, aged 19, and with a mental age of an 11 year old, was convicted of the murder of a policeman. At the time, the death penalty was the mandatory sentence for murder. Derek Bentley was hanged in 1953, a mere three months after the murder. His co-defendant, Christopher Craig, who fired the fatal shot at the police officer who died, was also convicted of murder, but escaped execution because he was aged only 16. Despite a recommendation by the jury that mercy be exercised, the Home Secretary decided not to exercise the prerogative. In 1992, the then Home Secretary refused to recommend a posthumous free pardon on the grounds that, while he personally agreed with the view that the death sentence should not have been carried out, it was the long established policy of Home Secretaries not to grant a free pardon unless the person concerned was both 'morally and technically innocent' of any crime and that his review of the case did not establish Bentley's innocence. In an application for judicial review brought by Derek Bentley's family, the court considered the question whether the prerogative of mercy was amenable to judicial review.[133] The applicant sought a declaration that the Home Secretary had erred in law in declining to recommend a posthumous free pardon, and mandamus to require the Home Secretary to reconsider the matter. Counsel for the Home Secretary argued that the exercise of the royal prerogative of

---

129 [1976] AC 239, p 247. See, also, *R v Allen* (1862) 1 B & S 850; 121 ER 929; *Hanratty v Lord Butler* (1971) 115 SJ 386.

130 [1985] AC 374. For discussion of this case, see, further, below, pp 198–99.

131 [1992] 3 NZLR 672.

132 *Ibid*, p 678.

133 *R v Secretary of State for the Home Department ex parte Bentley* [1993] 4 All ER 442.

mercy was not reviewable in the instant case, in so far as the applicant sought to challenge the criteria upon which the pardon should be granted was a question of policy which was not justiciable. Counsel for the applicant argued that the prerogative of mercy is an important feature of the criminal justice system, and that 'it would be surprising and regrettable ... were the decision of the Home Secretary to be immune from legal challenge irrespective of the gravity of the legal errors which infected such a decision'.[134] The court ruled that the view that 'the formulation of the criteria for the exercise of the prerogative by the grant of a free pardon was entirely a matter of policy which is not justiciable' was 'probably right'.[135] However, the court ruled that the Home Secretary failed to recognise that the prerogative of mercy is 'capable of being exercised in many different circumstances and over a wide range', and should have considered the form of pardon which might be appropriate to the facts of the case. This the Home Secretary did not do, and this failure was reviewable by the courts. The court, citing *Burt v Governor General*, endorsed the view that the prerogative of mercy is now 'a constitutional safeguard against mistakes'. The court also ruled, however, that it had no power to direct the way in which the prerogative of mercy should be exercised, but that it had a role to play by way of judicial review. The court declined to make any formal order, but invited the Home Secretary to reconsider the matter 'in light of the now generally accepted view that this young man should have been reprieved'.[136]

In 1998, the Court of Appeal, Criminal Division, on a reference by the Criminal Cases Review Commission under section 9 of the Criminal Appeal Act 1995, quashed Derek Bentley's conviction for murder. In a powerful judgment, the Court of Appeal criticised a number of aspects of Bentley's trial. In particular, the court ruled that the then Lord Chief Justice, Lord Goddard, had failed to direct the jury adequately on the standard of proof to be met; had, in effect, reversed the burden of proof from the prosecution to the defence; had shown partiality to the police evidence over that of the defence; that the summing up by the Lord Chief Justice represented 'a highly rhetorical and strongly worded denunciation of both defendants and their defence'; and that, by failing adequately to direct the jury on the law then in force as to 'joint enterprises', the judge had 'failed to grapple with that ground of appeal', which should have succeeded. As a result, the effect was to deprive Bentley of the protection which jury trial should have afforded: 'The summing up here was such as to deny Bentley that fair trial which was the birthright of every British citizen.' The Court of Appeal ruled that the conviction had been unsafe, and the conviction for murder was quashed.[137] Thus, 45 years after

---

134 [1993] 4 All ER 442, p 452, *per* Watkins LJ.
135 *Ibid*, p 453.
136 *Ibid*, p 455.
137 *R v Bentley* (1998) *The Times*, 31 July.

the event, Bentley's name was cleared by the courts on the basis that his conviction had been unsafe, the royal prerogative of mercy in the hands of the politicians having failed to provide a remedy.

Nolle prosequi

On proceedings on indictment, the Attorney General, in the name of the Crown, can enter a *nolle prosequi*, the effect of which stops the legal proceedings. The power is not subject to the control of the courts: *R v Comptroller of Patents*.[138] The grant of a *nolle prosequi* does not amount to an acquittal, and accordingly, the accused may be brought before the court on the same charge. The effect of this would be to invite a further application for a *nolle prosequi*.

LAW ENFORCEMENT

For many legal proceedings, the consent of the Attorney General is required.[139] The rationale behind this requirements lies in the public interest in pursuing offenders and the doctrine of ministerial responsibility to Parliament. In 1982, the Royal Commission on Criminal Procedure identified 39 statutes requiring his consent to prosecute, including offences under the Public Order Act 1936, the Hijacking Act 1971 and the Suppression of Terrorism Act 1978.[140] The Attorney General has a discretion whether or not to institute proceedings. In *Gouriet v Union of Post Office Workers*,[141] this discretion was tested.

The Union of Post Office Workers and the Post Office Engineering Union (POEU) intended to call on their members not to handle mail to South Africa, in protest against South Africa's policy of apartheid. The Secretary of the National Association for Freedom, Gouriet, applied to the Attorney General for permission to act as plaintiff in relator proceedings for an injunction against the Post Office Workers. The Attorney General refused his consent. Gouriet then applied to the court for an injunction in his own name. On appeal to the Court of Appeal, an interim injunction was granted and permission given for the POEU and the Attorney General to be joined as defendants. Gouriet then sought a permanent injunction against the unions

---

138 [1899] 1 QB 909.

139 On instituting proceedings, see Smith, P and Bailey, SH, *The Modern English Legal System*, 2nd edn, 1991, London: Sweet & Maxwell, Chapter 13B–C (see, now, Bailey, SH and Gunn, M (eds), *Smith & Bailey on The Modern English Legal System*, 3rd edn, 1996, London: Sweet & Maxwell).

140 *Ibid*, Smith and Bailey, p 619.

141 [1978] AC 435.

and a declaration that the Attorney General had wrongfully exercised his discretion. The Court of Appeal held that there was no power to review the exercise of the Attorney General's discretion and that a permanent injunction could not be granted.

Lord Denning MR, in the minority, held that the refusal by the Attorney General to give his reasons for withholding his consent was contrary to the rule of law. He held further that, while the giving of consent by the Attorney General to a relator action was unreviewable, his refusal to give consent was subject to review by the court – a finding rejected by Lawton LJ and Ormrod LJ. Behind Lord Denning's dissenting view apparently lay the fear that the Attorney General, in refusing his consent to a relator action, was rendering it impossible for a private individual to invoke the legal process to prevent a breach of the criminal law. On appeal to the House of Lords, Lord Wilberforce analysed the function of the Attorney General:

> The Attorney General has many powers and duties. He may stop any prosecution on indictment by entering a *nolle prosequi*. He merely has to sign a piece of paper saying that he does not wish the prosecution to continue. He need not give any reasons. He can direct the institution of a prosecution and direct the Director of Public Prosecutions to take over the conduct of any criminal proceedings and he may tell him to offer no evidence. In the exercise of these powers, he is not subject to direction by his ministerial colleagues or to control and supervision by the courts. If the court can review his refusal of consent to a relator action, it is an exception to the general rule. No authority was cited which supports the conclusion that the courts can do so. Indeed such authority as there is points strongly in the opposite direction.

> ... the main question to be decided in this appeal ... was that it was wrong in principle that the Attorney General should, by the refusal of his consent to a relator action, be able to block recourse to the civil courts when a widespread breach of the criminal law was threatened ... This would appear to be the basis for Lord Denning MR's observation that his refusal of consent in this case was a direct challenge to the rule of law ...

> Mr Gouriet does not ... assert any private right of any kind ... The conclusion to which I have come ... is that ... only the Attorney General can sue on behalf of the public for the purpose of preventing public wrongs and that a private individual cannot do so on behalf of the public though he may be able to do so if he will sustain injury as a result of a public wrong ...

> If these conclusions are right, then when the Attorney General gives his consent to a relator action, he is enabling an action to be brought which an individual alone could not bring. When he refuses his consent, he is not denying the right of any individual and barring his access to the courts, for the courts have no jurisdiction to entertain a claim by an individual whose only interest is as a member of the public in relation to a public right. Consequently, any suggestion that his refusal constitutes a challenge to the rule of law appears to me to be entirely misconceived, and though views may differ as to where the balance of public interest lies, it should not be lightly assumed that

his refusal of consent in a particular case was unjustified and not grounded on considerations of public interest.

POWER TO ESTABLISH NON-STATUTORY AGENCIES

The Criminal Injuries Compensation Board was established under the prerogative in 1964. Its objective was to provide compensation for the victims of criminal offences[142] through *ex gratia* payments calculated on the same principles as compensation paid to victims of tort. The Board was reconstituted under statute in 1988,[143] although the provisions had not been brought into force. Was the setting up of the Board in 1964 the exercise of a true prerogative? Reverting to Blackstone's definition, the answer must be negative. The power to establish such a scheme clearly fell within Parliament's jurisdiction, as the Criminal Justice Act 1988 proves. However, under Dicey's definition, the government is effectively given a choice in the manner of establishing such bodies: a surely questionable prerogative? In *R v Criminal Injuries Board ex parte Lain*,[144] Lord Diplock stated:

> It may be a novel development in constitutional practice to govern by public statement of intention made by the executive government instead of by legislation. This is no more, however, than a reversion to the ancient practice of government by royal proclamation, although it is now subject to the limitations imposed on that practice by the development of constitutional law in the seventeenth century.[145]

Professor HWR Wade denies that this was an exercise of a true prerogative:

> So far as the Crown came into the picture at all, it was exercising its ordinary powers as a natural person, which, of course, includes the power to transfer property, make contracts and so on. Blackstone was quite right, in my opinion, in saying that such powers are not prerogative at all.[146]

> The truth seems to be that judges have fallen into the habit of describing as 'prerogative' any and every sort of government action which is not statutory. It may be, also, that the responsibility for this solecism can be loaded onto that popular scapegoat, Dicey.[147]

In 1993, when the relevant provisions of the Criminal Justice Act 1988 had still not been brought into force – despite a statutory obligation being imposed on

---

142 See Newburn, T, *The Settlement of Claims at the Criminal Injuries Compensation Board*, Home Office Research Study No 112, 1989, London: HMSO.

143 Criminal Justice Act 1988, ss 108–17 and Scheds 6–7.

144 [1967] 2 QB 864.

145 *Ibid*, p 886.

146 Wade, HWR, *Constitutional Fundamentals*, rev edn, 1989, London: Stevens, p 61.

147 *Ibid*.

the Home Secretary by section 171 – the government published a White Paper announcing its intention to implement a different scheme. In June 1993, the House of Lords introduced – and passed – an amendment to the Criminal Justice and Public Order Bill which would have required the Home Secretary to perform his statutory duty under the 1988 Act. The House of Commons removed the amendment.[148] When the Home Secretary introduced changes to the Criminal Injuries Compensation Scheme – claiming to act under the royal prerogative – proceedings for judicial review of his decision were instigated. The outcome was the judicial verdict that the Home Secretary had acted *ultra vires*.[149] For discussion, see, further, below.[150]

THE GRANTING OF HONOURS

Whilst legally still in the hands of the Crown, the effective control over the granting of the majority of honours lies with the executive. The Queen has the personal right to confer the Order of the Garter, the Order of the Thistle, the Royal Victoria Order and the Order of Merit. Otherwise, the conferment of honours is by the Queen, acting on the advice of the Prime Minister who is, in turn, advised by a Political Honours Scrutiny Committee comprising three Privy Councillors.[151]

REGULATION OF THE CIVIL SERVICE[152]

The control of the Civil Service is vested in the Crown and civil servants, like ministers, are servants of the Crown. However, the appointments are permanent, subject to 'good behaviour', although, in practice, a civil servant will not be dismissed other than for misconduct.[153] Civil servants have no contractual relationship with the Crown.[154] Salaries and other benefits are

---

148 For comment see Riddell, P, 'Quality control deficiency that lets down the law' (1994) *The Times*, 16 December, p 9.

149 *R v Secretary of State for the Home Department ex parte Fire Brigades' Union and Others* [1995] 2 WLR 1; 2 All ER 244.

150 See pp 199–202. Within 24 hours of this verdict, the government suffered another defeat when the Secretary of State for Foreign Affairs, Mr Douglas Hurd, was held to have acted unlawfully in relation to aid granted for the Pergau Dam project in Malaysia. See, further, Chapter 25.

151 Cmnd 1789, 1922, London: HMSO; Honours (Prevention of Abuses) Act 1925; and see Wagner, A and Squibb, GD, 'Precedence and courtesy titles' (1973) 89 LQR 352.

152 See, further, Chapter 8. The structure and conditions of employment are outside the scope of this work: see Hood-Phillips, O and Jackson, P, *Constitutional and Administrative Law*, 7th edn, 1987, London: Sweet & Maxwell, Chapter 17.

153 Fulton Committee Report, Cmnd 3638, 1971, London: HMSO.

154 *CCSU v Minister for the Civil Service* [1985] AC 374, p 419.

prescribed by statute, but for the most part, the Civil Service is governed under the prerogative.[155]

REGULATION OF THE ARMED FORCES

As with the Civil Service, members of the armed forces are regulated under the royal prerogative, and statutory protection of employment in, for example, the Employment Protection (Consolidation) Act 1978, does not apply to members of the armed forces.[156]

The sovereign is Commander in Chief of the armed forces. The Bill of Rights 1689[157] prohibits the maintenance of an army by the Crown in peacetime without the consent of Parliament. The control, organisation and disposition of the forces are within the prerogative and cannot be questioned in a court of law.[158]

IMMUNITIES AND PRIVILEGES OF THE CROWN

These are considered in outline in Chapter 10.

THE PREROGATIVE AND FOREIGN AFFAIRS

Acts of State[159]

An act of the executive as a matter of policy performed in the course of its relations with another State, including its relations with the subjects of that State, unless they are temporarily within the allegiance of the Crown.[160]

Acts of State in relation to foreign States

The recognition of foreign States and government, diplomatic relations – including the sending of diplomats and the reception of foreign diplomats –

---

155 For a detailed and critical analysis of the Civil Service, see Hennessy, P, *Whitehall*, 1990, London: Fontana.

156 For details of the organisation and control of the armed forces, see *op cit*, Hood-Phillips and Jackson, fn 152, Chapter 18.

157 See, further, Chapter 2.

158 *China Navigation Company Ltd v Attorney General* [1932] 2 KB 197; *Chandler v Director of Public Prosecutions* [1964] AC 763. See, also, Crown Proceedings Act 1947, s 11.

159 See *op cit*, Anson, fn 88, Vol II, Pt I, Chapter 6.8.

160 Wade, ECS, 'Act of State in English law' (1934) 15 BYIL 98, p 103.

declarations of war and peace, and the annexation of cession of territory fall within this part of the definition.

Recognition of foreign States

The recognition of foreign States is within the prerogative of the Crown. Several statutes regulate the privilege and immunities enjoyed by heads of foreign States[161] and their diplomatic representatives.[162]

Diplomatic relations

In 1708, the Diplomatic Privileges Act was passed after a Russian Ambassador had been arrested for debt. The Russian Czar, Peter the Great, regarded this action as a criminal offence. The Court of Queen's Bench was uncertain as to the legal position.[163] The Act of 1708, provided that no judicial proceedings could be brought against diplomats or their servants and that it was an offence to commence proceedings.

Under the Diplomatic Privileges Act 1964, diplomatic staff enjoy full immunity – both civil and criminal – whereas administrative and technical staff have immunity for actions taken in the course of their duties but are otherwise civilly – but not criminally – liable for other acts. Members of service staff are only immune for official acts. Whether a particular member of diplomatic staff falls within a certain category is determined by the Foreign Secretary by means of a certificate. The court will determine whether the action performed is within – or without – the individual's official duties.

Where an individual enjoys immunity from the courts, the only redress will be for the Foreign Secretary to request the diplomat's government to recall him as *persona non grata*.

Declarations of war and peace

Where a declaration of war has been made, the status of nationals of the enemy State within the United Kingdom is altered. If the Secretary of State for Foreign and Commonwealth Affairs issues a certificate to the effect that a state of war exists, this must be accepted by the courts.[164]

---

161 State Immunity Act 1978.

162 Diplomatic Privileges Act 1964. On immunities and privilege accorded to international and commonwealth organisations, see the International Organisations Acts 1968 and 1981; Diplomatic Immunities (Conferences with Commonwealth Countries and Republic of Ireland) Acts 1952 and 1961; International Headquarters and Defence Organisations Act 1964.

163 *Mattueof's Case* (1709) 10 Mod Rep 4.

164 *R v Bottrill ex parte Kuechenmeister* [1947] KB 41.

Annexation and cession of territory

In 1955, the Crown exercised its prerogative power to take possession of the island of Rockall, which subsequently was incorporated into the United Kingdom as part of Scotland.[165] Once territory has been annexed, the Crown has a discretion as to the extent to which it will take over the liabilities of the former government of the State.[166]

The Crown also has the power to alter the limits of British territorial waters.[167] However, while this prerogative seems firmly established, there are doubts as to the power of the Crown – without parliamentary approval – to cede territory and thereby deprive British citizens of their nationality and other rights under[168] United Kingdom law.[169] When the Crown sought to cede Heligoland to Germany in 1890, parliamentary approval was sought. While the law may be doubtful, there is at least a convention that Parliament's approval will be sought and granted.

Issue of passports[170]

Consistent with the Crown's power to regulate its boundaries and those who enter and leave is the power to issue passports: again, under Blackstone's definition, this is a questionable prerogative power, for the government is doing no more than what it is free to do under statute and the power has no legal effect as such. Nevertheless, the conventional classification of the right to issue and withhold passports is that of the prerogative. At common law, citizens have the right to enter and leave the realm. It is nevertheless extremely difficult in practice to travel without a passport, which is issued under the prerogative. In *R v Foreign Secretary ex parte Everett*,[171] the court for the first time held that the granting and withholding passports was subject to review by the courts. The position in the United Kingdom – both uncertain and unsatisfactory – may be contrasted with that in the United States of America where the Supreme Court has held that freedom of travel is a basic constitutional liberty.

---

165 Island of Rockall Act 1972.

166 *West Rand Central Gold Mining Company v The King* [1905] 2 KB 391.

167 *R v Kent Justices ex parte Lye* [1967] 2 QB 153; *Post Office v Estuary Radio* [1968] 2 QB 740.

168 *Op cit*, Anson, fn 88, pp 137–42; Holdsworth, W, 'The treaty making power of the Crown' (1942) 58 LQR 177.

169 See, further, Chapter 21.

170 [1989] QB 811.

171 See, *inter alia, Aptheker v Secretary of State* 378 US 500 (1964); *Kent v Dulles* 375 US 116 (1958).

The ancient right to issue the writ *ne exeat regno* – forbidding a person from leaving the realm – is declared by Hood-Phillips and Jackson,[172] relying on *Felton v Callis*,[173] to be 'obsolescent', and is so accepted to be by de Smith and Brazier. However, as the latter authors point out, the doctrine of obsolescence has never been one accepted in English law. The rationale for such acceptance in relation to the writ *ne exeat regno*, and that of impressment into naval service, is that offered by Lord Simon of Glaisdale in *McKendrick v Sinclair*[174] to the effect that:

> ... a rule of English common law, once clearly established, does not become extinct merely by disuse ... but may 'go into a cataleptic trance' ... and revive in propitious circumstances ... but not revive if it is 'grossly anomalous and anachronistic'.

That it is not obsolete is confirmed by two recent cases. In *Al Nahkel for Contracting Ltd v Lowe*,[175] the writ was used to prevent a defendant leaving the country to avoid a judgment of the court. In *Parsons v Burk*,[176] an unsuccessful attempt was made to prevent the New Zealand rugby team from leaving the country to play in South Africa.

Treaty making powers

The power to enter into treaties under international law is a feature of the sovereignty of a State. In the United Kingdom, it is generally accepted that such power is an emanation of the prerogative. As such, the entry into treaties is regarded as a matter solely for the executive and not for Parliament. A treaty is defined as a written agreement between States governed by international law.[177] It will be seen[178] that under the doctrine of parliamentary sovereignty, an Act of Parliament alone can alter domestic law. Accordingly, a treaty – being a creature of international law – cannot alter national law without being given effect by an Act of Parliament.[179] It is for this reason that, *inter alia*, the European Communities Act 1972 was enacted to provide for the entry and application of European Community law into the United Kingdom.

---

172 *Op cit*, Hood-Phillips and Jackson, fn 152, p 132.

173 [1969] 1 QB 1 (Megarry J).

174 1972 SLT 110, pp 116–17.

175 [1986] QB 235.

176 [1971] NZLR 244.

177 Vienna Convention on the Law of Treaties, Cmnd 4848, 1969, London: HMSO.

178 See Chapter 7.

179 *Walker v Baird* [1982] AC 491; *The Parlement Belge* (1879) 4 PD 129; *JH Rayner (Mincing Lane) Ltd v Department of Trade and Industry* [1990] 2 AC 418.

There is debate as to whether treaty making power is truly a prerogative power. Blackstone's definition insists that a prerogative power be unique to the Crown: if it is exercisable by anyone else, it ceases to be a prerogative. The second aspect is – according to HWR Wade – whether the prerogative produces 'legal effects at common law'.[180] It follows, therefore, that a treaty – having no legal effect in the absence of statute – is not a true prerogative. However, the preferred judicial view is in line with Dicey: a prerogative act is any action of government not authorised by statute.

The treaty making power of the executive was challenged in *R v Secretary of State for Foreign and Commonwealth Affairs ex parte Rees-Mogg*.[181] In February 1991, the Heads of Government of the Member States of the European Community signed the Treaty on European Union – the Maastricht Treaty.[182] The Treaty was to come into effect on ratification by the Member States. In some countries, ratification was dependent upon the approval of the majority of the people voting in a referendum, as for example in France and Denmark. Under the constitution of the United States of America, treaties are ratified by the President with the advice and consent of two-thirds of the Senators present and voting.

In the United Kingdom, no such constitutional arrangements exists. Under constitutional practice, a treaty need only be approved by Parliament if it requires a change in legislation or the grant of public money. Otherwise, the power of Parliament is confined to the political process, and in the last resort, the forcing of a government's resignation through the withdrawal of the confidence of the House of Commons. However, a convention has been established whereby Parliament approves certain treaties. Under the Ponsonby Rule,[183] the government undertakes to lay every treaty, when signed, for a 21 day period before ratification, and secondly to inform the House of all other 'international agreements and commitments which may bind the nation to specific action in certain circumstances'.

Erskine May records the convention as follows:

> When a treaty requires ratification, the government does not usually proceed with ratification until a period of 21 days has elapsed from the date on which the text of such a treaty was laid before Parliament by Her Majesty's command. This practice is subject to modification, if necessary, when urgent or other important considerations arise.[184]

The Ponsonby undertaking also included the commitment on the part of government to make time for debate on a treaty if there is a formal demand

---

180 Wade, HWR, 'Procedure and prerogative in public law' (1985) 101 LQR 180.

181 [1994] 1 All ER 457.

182 See Chapter 8.

183 Under Secretary of State for Foreign Affairs. See HC Deb Vol 171 Cols 2001–04.

184 Erskine May, T, *Parliamentary Practice*, 21st edn, 1989, London: Butterworths, p 215 (see, now, 22nd edn, 1997).

from the Opposition or other party. The issue raised in *Rees-Mogg* was whether the government had the power to ratify the Maastricht Treaty without the approval of the House of Commons. It was clear that there was substantial opposition to the Treaty on all sides of the House, and the government was not confident that any vote would approve the Treaty. As a result, or as a failsafe device, the Prime Minister announced that, if necessary, the Treaty would be ratified under the prerogative: thus avoiding the risk of parliamentary disapproval. The Queen's Bench Division refused to grant an application for judicial review: the matter was within the prerogative of the Crown. In the long run, the Bill bringing the Treaty into effect in the law of the United Kingdom was passed by the Commons and Lords.

JUDICIAL CONTROL OF THE PREROGATIVE

... the King hath no prerogative, but that which the law of the land allows him.[185]

Statute and the prerogative

Although there is a degree of certainty as to the existence and scope of the prerogatives discussed above, the discussion of all prerogatives must be regarded as overlain with a degree of doubt. Consistent with the doctrine of parliamentary sovereignty, Parliament has the right and power to abolish, restrict or preserve prerogative powers. For example, historically, the Crown owed the duty of protection to those under a duty of allegiance to the Crown who were either under the age of majority[186] or suffering mental incapacity. This duty of protection – the concept of *parens patriae* – manifested itself in the wardship jurisdiction conferred on the Court of Chancery.[187] The Law Reform (Miscellaneous Provisions) Act 1949 gave statutory force to the jurisdiction, which was further amended under the Supreme Court Act 1981. The Children Act 1989, while not affecting the entire wardship jurisdiction, removes the right of local authorities to apply to ward a child.[188] However, the Act also makes provision for local authorities to apply to the court[189] for an order under the inherent jurisdiction. The effect of this provision is still unclear, but the constitutional implication is that, whilst the prerogative of *parens patriae* in wardship has been placed on a statutory footing (under the

---

185 *Case of Proclamations* (1611) 12 Co Rep 74.
186 Now age 18 (Family Law Reform Act 1969, s 1).
187 Now the Family Division of the High Court.
188 Children Act 1989, s 100.
189 *Ibid*, s 100(4).

1949 and 1981 Acts), the Children Act 1989 nevertheless recognises and preserves a form of prerogative inherent jurisdiction.

Where an Act of Parliament seeks to regulate a matter previously falling under the prerogative but does not expressly abolish the prerogative, the statute will prevail. In *Attorney General v de Keyser's Royal Hotel Ltd*,[190] the court was faced with a claim for compensation by the owners of the hotel, under the Defence of the Realm Act 1914, for compensation due as a result of occupation by the armed forces in wartime. The government sought to rely on the prerogative under which a lesser discretionary sum of compensation would be payable. The House of Lords rejected the government's right to rely on the prerogative, holding that, once a statute had been enacted, the prerogative power fell into 'abeyance', that is to say, it was set aside for the duration of the life of the statute. Should the statute be repealed, the prerogative would once more come into operation.

In *Laker Airways v Department of Trade*,[191] statute and prerogative were considered once again. The facts involved regulation of the trans-Atlantic air route. Under the Bermuda Agreement of 1946, the United States and United Kingdom governments agreed that air carriers should be approved by both governments: the 'designation' requirement. In 1971, the Civil Aviation Act was passed by Parliament, providing for the licensing of airlines by the Civil Aviation Authority (the CAA). The Act provided that the Secretary of State could give 'guidance' to the CAA as to the policy to be followed in the consideration of licence applications. Mr Freddie Laker had both applied for designation under the Bermuda Treaty and had been granted a licence under the Civil Aviation Act 1971.

A change in government led to a change in policy, and it was decided that British Airways should have a monopoly on the trans-Atlantic route. Accordingly, the Secretary of State issued 'guidance' to the CAA to the effect that Mr Laker's licence should be withdrawn. The Secretary of State also requested that the United States government did not proceed to grant designation to Laker Airways under the Treaty. In an application for judicial review by Mr Laker, it was argued that the Secretary of State's 'guidance' was *ultra vires*. The court agreed, regarding the instruction given to the CAA as beyond the normal meaning of the word 'guidance'. The court also rejected the government's argument that it had the right, under the prerogative, to deny Laker Airway's right to fly the Atlantic route. The government could not, it was held, defeat a statutory right by use of a prerogative power.

In *Council of Civil Service Unions v Minister of State for Civil Service*,[192] the prerogative returned to the courts. The Prime Minister, as the Minister for the

---

190 [1920] AC 508.
191 [1977] QB 643.
192 [1985] AC 374.

Civil Service, by a prerogative order,[193] terminated the right of workers at the Government Communications Headquarters (GCHQ) to belong to trade unions. The order followed industrial unrest which threatened to disrupt the interception of signals intelligence. The Union challenged the order under judicial review proceedings, claiming that they had a legitimate expectation to be consulted prior to their rights to membership being withdrawn. The Unions won at first instance, but lost both before the Court of Appeal and the House of Lords.

The House of Lords accepted that the terms and conditions of employment of civil servants were within the prerogative powers of the Crown.[194] Their Lordships likewise accepted that the employees had a legitimate expectation to be consulted before their rights were adversely affected. Nevertheless, the government's plea of national security trumped the interests of the union members.[195]

The significance of the GCHQ case in relation to prerogative power is twofold. On the question of the reviewability of the royal prerogative, the House of Lords declared that the exercise of the prerogatives of the Crown were, in principle, as reviewable as powers exercised under statute. However, having boldly declared the principle, the court proceeded to qualify the approach by stating that a number of matters would not be subjected to review. Utilising the concept of 'justiciability', the court held that matters such as the appointment of ministers, dissolution of Parliament, grant of honours, treaties, and *par excellence* matters of national security were not appropriate subjects for review by the courts. Each of these matters was regarded as involving matters of high policy which it should be for ministers to decide, and by implication for Parliament to control.[196] It remains the case after GCHQ that many significant attributes of the prerogative remain immune from judicial review.

The case of *R v Secretary of State for the Home Department ex parte Northumbria Police Authority*[197] reveals a far less robust judicial attitude towards the control of the prerogative than did the *Laker Airways* case. Once again, the issue involved was the relationship between statute and the prerogative. The Police Act 1964[198] sets out the respective powers of the

---

193 An Order in Council.

194 On HWR Wade's doubts concerning the accuracy of this classification, see *op cit*, Wade, fn 180, p 180.

195 The Labour government has reinstated the right of workers to join trade unions.

196 See, also, *Patriotic Front – ZAPU v Minister of Justice, Legal and Parliamentary Affairs* 1986 (1) SA 532, discussed by Walker, C, 'Review of the prerogative' [1987] PL 63.

197 [1988] 1 All ER 556.

198 Police Act 1964, ss 4 and 5.

Home Secretary, the police authorities and the Chief Constables of police with regard to, *inter alia*, the supply of equipment to police forces.

The Secretary of State, by way of a Circular, advised that the Secretary of State would be making available supplies of riot control equipment to police forces, irrespective of approval by the police authorities. The Northumbria Police Authority sought judicial review of the legality of the Circular. The Home Secretary argued first that, as a matter of statutory interpretation, he had power to issue the equipment, and that, independent of the statutory power which he claimed, he had the power under the prerogative to issue the weapons. On the point of statutory interpretation, the Court of Appeal held that no monopoly was reserved to the Police Authority and that, accordingly, the Secretary of State had not acted *ultra vires*.

On the prerogative aspect, the court's reasoning was both surprising and interesting. First, the Court of Appeal accepted that the Police Act 1964 left unaffected the prerogative powers to keep the peace. Little evidence was adduced as to the existence of such a prerogative, but nevertheless, Croom-Johnson LJ felt able to hold that he had 'no doubt' that the Crown had such a prerogative. Nourse LJ stated that there was no historical or other basis for denying that a prerogative to keep the peace could be viewed as a 'sister' prerogative to the power to declare war, without making any reference to Blackstone's division of prerogatives into 'foreign' and 'domestic' categories. Recalling that it had never been possible to identify all the prerogatives of the Crown and that their existence could be ascertained only by means of piecemeal decisions, Nourse LJ declared that there had never been 'a comparable occasion for investigating a prerogative of keeping the peace within the realm':

> The Crown's prerogative of making war and peace, the war prerogative, has never been doubted ... it is natural to suppose that it was founded, at least in part, on the wider prerogative of protection ...

> The wider prerogative must have extended as much to unlawful acts within the realm as to the menaces of a foreign power. There is no historical or other reason for denying to the war prerogative a sister prerogative of keeping the peace within the realm ...

More surprisingly, the judge argued that the fact that no evidence existed was almost conclusive proof that it did exist. In the seminal case of *Entick v Carrington*,[199] Lord Camden had asserted that, if there existed authority for the lawful exercise of power, it would be found 'in the books'. It might be thought that in passing the Police Act, Parliament considered that it was providing comprehensive regulation of the terms and conditions under which each regulatory body could act. It cannot have been contemplated that, by

---

199 (1765) 19 St Tr 1030; see Chapters 2 and 20.

plea of a previously unconsidered prerogative, the provisions of the Act could be circumvented. Nevertheless, Purchas LJ was clear that:

> ... the prerogative powers to take all reasonable steps to preserve the Queen's peace remain unaffected by the Act and these include the supply of equipment to police forces which is reasonably required for the more efficient discharge of their duties.

The *Northumbria Police Authority* case is indicative of the fine line to be drawn between updating a prerogative and creating a new prerogative. Prerogatives, being a feature of monarchical power are, as Dicey stated, residual. Accordingly, for the judges to give recognition to an alleged prerogative, it must be shown that the prerogative claimed existed before 1688. In *BBC v Johns*,[200] Lord Diplock gave judicial expression to this in the statement: '... it is 350 years and a civil war too late for the Queen's courts to broaden the prerogative.'

In *R v Secretary of State for the Home Department ex parte Fire Brigades' Union and Others*,[201] the matter in issue was whether the Secretary of State, having failed to implement the statutory scheme provided in the Criminal Justice Act 1988, was free to implement a different scheme under the royal prerogative.[202] The scheme introduced a 'tariff' for compensation for injuries at a substantially lower rate than provided for under the statute.[203] In the Queen's Bench Division, the court had declined to grant a declaration that the Home Secretary, by failing to bring into force the relevant provision of the Act, had acted unlawfully and that, by introducing the Tariff Scheme (under the royal prerogative), he had acted unlawfully and in abuse of his common law powers. On appeal to the Court of Appeal, the Master of the Rolls, Sir Thomas Bingham, in the minority on the first point as to whether the Home Secretary had acted lawfully in refusing to implement the statutory scheme, ruled that Parliament could not have intended to give the Home Secretary unfettered discretion as to whether and when he would bring the provisions into effect:

> His Lordship confessed to surprise at the suggestion that Parliament, having formally enacted provisions, should intend to entrust to a member of the executive a complete and unfettered discretion as to whether those provisions should ever take effect ...

> The effect of section 171(1) was to impose a legal duty on the Home Secretary to bring the provisions into force as soon as he might properly judge it

---

200 [1965] Ch 32.
201 [1995] 2 WLR 1.
202 As announced in the White Paper, *Compensating Victims of Violent Crime: Changes to the Criminal Injuries Compensation Scheme*, Cmnd 2434, 1993, London: HMSO.
203 The new scheme was implemented on 1 April 1994.

appropriate to do so. In making that judgment, he would be entitled to have regard to all relevant factors, including the escalating cost of the non-statutory and the enacted statutory scheme ...

However, the Master of the Rolls went on to agree with the Divisional Court and would refuse to grant the declaration sought, conceding that the question of the costs of implementing the scheme provided the Home Secretary with good grounds for not bringing the statutory provisions into effect. Hobhouse LJ and Morritt LJ agreed on the first point.

With respect to the second point as to whether, in the absence of implementation of the statutory provisions, the Home Secretary had a prerogative power to introduce a Tariff Scheme different from the statutory provisions, the Master of the Rolls and Morritt LJ were in agreement that he had no such power. Hobhouse LJ disagreed. Sir Thomas Bingham ruled that:

> ... the old non-statutory scheme was established by a proper exercise of prerogative power. In the absence of statute, there would not, in law, have been anything to prevent the Home Secretary exercising his prerogative powers to modify the old scheme or to revoke it and substitute a new one devised on different principles.
>
> Even after the 1988 Act had been passed, he would not have been open to legal challenge had he continued the old scheme without bringing the new statutory provisions into force, so long as his reasons for postponement fell within the wide discretion accorded him.
>
> But was he, while those provisions remained unrepealed, legally free to exercise prerogative powers to establish a scheme radically different from those provisions?
>
> *Attorney General v de Keyser's Royal Hotel Ltd* ([1920] AC 508) and *Laker Airways Ltd v Department of Trade* ([1977] QB 643) did not concern statutory provisions not brought into force and so provided no direct answer to the question.
>
> Again, the Home Secretary's argument had given too little weight to the overriding legislative role of Parliament. It had approved detailed provisions governing the form which, underpinned by statute, the scheme should take. The 1988 provisions were not a discussion paper but a blueprint approved in the most solemn form for which our constitution provided ...

The Master of the Rolls accepted that the Home Secretary had the power to invite Parliament to repeal the provisions or to seek enactment of the Tariff provisions in statute or, alternatively, to seek to have the statutory provisions abolished and then implement the Tariff provisions under the royal prerogative. But:

> ... what he could not do, so long as the 1988 provisions stood unrepealed as an enduring statement of Parliament's will, was to exercise prerogative powers to introduce a scheme radically different from what Parliament had approved ...

Accordingly, the Secretary of State could not avoid the requirements of the 1988 Act and introduce – by means of the prerogative – a different scheme.

The Home Secretary had two choices. First, he could persuade Parliament to repeal the unimplemented sections of the 1988 Act, whereupon the prerogative power would be restored in full and he could proceed to introduce the new scheme under the prerogative. Alternatively, and secondly, the Secretary of State could comply with his statutory duty and implement the scheme provided for by the 1988 Act. What he was not free to do – while the 1988 statutory duty remained in force – was ignore that duty and act under the prerogative, using the prerogative as an alternative legal authority. This decision – analogous in some respects to the decision in *de Keyser's Royal Hotel* – reaffirms the doctrine of the supremacy of statute over the prerogative.[204]

While the case may be compared with *de Keyser's Royal Hotel*, it can be contrasted with the *Northumbria Police Authority* case, where the Court of Appeal apparently had little difficulty in accepting that statutory powers could coexist with a prerogative power.

On appeal to the House of Lords, the decision of the Court of Appeal was upheld.[205] The House of Lords ruled, by a majority,[206] that the decisions of the Secretary of State not to implement the statutory scheme, and to introduce an alternative scheme under the prerogative, were unlawful. The House of Lords refused, however, to rule that the Secretary of State was under a legally enforceable duty to bring the statutory scheme into effect at a particular date. Lord Browne-Wilkinson, for the majority, ruled that the court:

> ... should not intervene in the legislative process by requiring an Act of Parliament to be brought into effect. That would be for the courts to tread dangerously close to the area over which Parliament enjoyed exclusive jurisdiction.

However, the Secretary of State did not enjoy an unfettered discretion as to whether to bring the scheme into effect, and he could not, through use of the prerogative, defeat the purpose of the statute. Lord Keith, dissenting, argued that the court should not become involved in a matter which was for Parliament to determine. Lord Mustill was of the same mind, relying specifically on the Bill of Rights 1689:

> Absent a written constitution, much sensitivity was required of the parliamentarian, administrator and judge if the delicate balance of the unwritten rules evolved successfully in recent years was not to be disturbed and all the recent advances undone.

> Some of the argument addressed would have the court push to the very boundaries of the distinction between court and Parliament established in, and recognised ever since, the Bill of Rights 1689.

---

204 See also, *Re W's Application* [1998] NI 19, in which the Queen's Bench Division in Northern Ireland applied, *inter alia*, the *Fire Brigades Union* case.

205 [1995] 2 All ER 244; *The Times*, 6 April; .

206 Lord Keith of Kinkel and Lord Mustill dissenting.

Three hundred years had passed since then and the political and social landscape had changed beyond recognition, but the boundaries remained.

Here, within one case, is seen differing considerations weighing on the judges in the House of Lords. The majority decision rests squarely on the rule of law and the preference for statute over the prerogative. The minority view, however, leans far more clearly in favour of the doctrine of separation of powers and the supremacy of Parliament in regulating its own affairs and in calling ministers to account.[207]

POLITICAL CONTROL OF THE PREROGATIVE

Political control over the exercise of the prerogative, while preserving the separation of powers between the executive and judiciary, may in practice prove to be inadequate. In theory, the prerogative, as is the case with any other act of government, is capable of being subjected to the full range of parliamentary procedure.[208] Thus, Question Time, debates and select committees may be utilised in order to scrutinise prerogative acts. However, under parliamentary practice, there exists a number of issues on which ministers conventionally decline to provide information, and many of these matters are precisely those which fall within the scope of the prerogative. The dissolution of Parliament is a matter for Prime Ministerial determination alone: not even a duty to consult Cabinet is imposed, and the matter will certainly not be for parliamentary scrutiny. Likewise, the grant of honours is a matter not for parliamentary discussion. On matters of the disposition of the armed forces, weaponry for the armed forces, government contracts, judicial appointments, and investigations by the Director of Public Prosecutions, the government will decline to answer questions. Aside from such specific matters, the government may plead such wide notions as national security, confidentiality or the public interest in order to avoid scrutiny.

EVALUATION AND CONCLUSION

Under all constitutions, written or unwritten, there will be a number of powers reserved to the executive, powers which are exercisable without the passage of legislation. Such powers may include the entering into treaties, declarations of war and peace, recognition of foreign States and diplomats.

---

207 Note that, following the decision of the House of Lords, the Criminal Injuries Compensation Act 1995 repealed the Criminal Justice Act 1988, ss 108–17, and made provision for a scheme of payments of a standard amount of compensation calculated in accordance with a tariff prepared by the Secretary of State.

208 To be discussed in more detail in Chapters 15 and 16.

Such powers are referred to as 'inherent executive powers', or 'prerogative power'. Section 2 of the Commonwealth of Australia Constitution Act 1900 confers on the Governor General 'such powers and functions ... as Her Majesty may be pleased to assign to him'. In 1900, these powers entailed the power to summon, prorogue or dissolve Parliament, to appoint judges and other public officials. Section 61 of the Constitution confers the executive power of the Commonwealth in the Queen and declares that this executive power is vested in the Governor General. Other powers were expressly assigned to the Governor General in 1954 and 1973, implying that, for such powers to exist, they must be express and cannot exist by implication or by analogy with the prerogative powers of the Crown.

The scope of the powers has been the subject of judicial disagreement in the High Court of Australia, some judges adopting a narrow view of the powers, others a broader interpretation. In *Commonwealth v Colonial Combing Spinning and Weaving Co Ltd*,[209] Higgins J adopted the narrow approach:

> ... the Governor General is not a general agent of His Majesty, with power to exercise all His Majesty's prerogatives; he is a special agent with power to carry out the Constitution and the laws, and such powers and functions as the King may assign to him.

In *Barton v Commonwealth*,[210] Mason J took a broader view of the powers conferred under section 61:

> ... enables the Crown to undertake all executive action which is appropriate to the position of the Commonwealth under the Constitution and to the spheres of responsibility vested in it by the Constitution. It includes the prerogative powers of the Crown, that is, the powers accorded to the Crown by the common law.

These two brief examples illustrate the point that, even under a written constitution, the scope of prerogative power is capable of differing interpretations.[211]

Under the United Kingdom constitution, it may be concluded, quite reasonably, that parliamentary control over the exercise of prerogative power is less than adequate. Set alongside or juxtapositioned with the excluded areas of judicial review under the concept of justiciability, it can be seen that there exists a reservoir of power, much of which is undefined or at best ill defined, which is not amenable either to judicial or to parliamentary control.

---

209 (1922) 31 CLR 421.
210 (1974) 131 CLR 477.
211 *Op cit*, Marshall and Moodie, fn 86, Chapter 3.

REFORM OF THE PREROGATIVE?

It is precisely for the reasons discussed above that, in 1988, the Rt Hon Tony Benn MP introduced a Private Members' Bill to place prerogative powers under statutory authority. That Bill did not proceed through the legislative process but such a proposal requires careful consideration.

The Preamble to the 1988 Crown Prerogatives (House of Commons Control) Bill stated that:

... whereas the people of the United Kingdom have an inherent right of self-government, through their elected representatives, over all decisions made by government and Parliament;

... and whereas those rights of self-government are seriously limited by the secret exercise of executive power, without any statutory basis, under Crown prerogatives, for which ministers are not individually accountable to the House of Commons or to the electorate;

... and whereas the use of the Crown prerogatives is on such a scale, and of such a nature, as to constitute a major obstacle to the realisation of the legitimate needs of the people, and may involve a denial of civil liberty and democratic rights and the rights of Parliament itself ...

There then followed[212] a listing of prerogative powers which would require the assent of the House of Commons before having legal effect. Most significant of these are the power to declare war, to make peace, to recognise foreign governments, to sign or ratify treaties, to grant pardons, to confer honours, and more generally to exercise all other executive powers not conferred by statute. Clause 2 of the Bill conferred on the Speaker of the House the sole responsibility for advising on the dissolution of Parliament and the issue of an invitation to a person to attempt to form a government. In respect of both of these matters, the assent of the House of Commons was required and that assent binding on the Crown. The power of the Crown to assent to Bills and of the House of Lords to approve legislation would have been removed under clause 4 of the Bill.

The extent to which such a proposal would clarify questions as to the existence and control of the prerogative is necessarily a matter for speculation. Nowhere in the Bill was the role of the courts mentioned. Once the House of Commons had given its assent to the proposed exercise of power, the courts would be precluded from examining the parliamentary process leading up to that assent.[213] The power of judicial review, however, would remain, and it would be within the courts' jurisdiction to determine whether the power exercised was a power authorised by the assent. It has been seen in relation to

---

212 Crown Prerogatives (House of Commons Control) Bill 1988, cl 1.
213 *Pickin v British Railways Board* [1974] AC 765.

the *GCHQ* case that the courts have now developed a category of non-justiciable matters, and the majority of the powers identified in the Bill fall within this category. To that extent, placing the prerogatives under statutory authority, would, arguably, make little difference. Remaining powers, covered in the general power 'to issue all other executive powers not conferred by statute', would continue to be reviewable according to their subject matter.

However, the prerogative has been seen to be an elusive constitutional animal which is capable of appearing in novel form under unforeseen circumstances. Recalling the *Northumbria Police Authority* case, it was there seen that the prerogative 'to keep the peace' was pleaded as an alternative to the existence of power within the Police Act 1964: a reserve power claimed as insurance against the court finding that the minister had acted *ultra vires* the statute. That the Court of Appeal upheld the minister's claim was by no means a foregone conclusion, and to do so in the virtual absence of authority and precedent, and with little analysis, quite remarkable.

The *Northumbria Police Authority* case illustrates the fundamental difficulty of prerogative power: that of identification and definition. In March 1993, the Prime Minister, in a written reply to a request for a list of the occasions of which the prerogative had been exercised over an 18 month period, declined to provide the list, on the basis of 'the complexity of the relationship between statutory and prerogative power'.[214] The Prime Minister could have confined his excuse to 'the complexity of the prerogative'.

It can be agreed that there is little to suggest that replacing such powers by statute, even if they could be identified, would lead to fewer abuses of power. Further, it may be added that, even if the powers could be identified, given their wraith-like nature, it would be impossible, conclusively, to define their scope and application. For this reason, the prerogative – a paradox in a modern democratic State – is likely to retain its uncertain form, thus leaving to government a residue of largely uncontrolled power.

214 HC, *Official Report,* 1 March 1993.

CHAPTER 7

PARLIAMENTARY SOVEREIGNTY

INTRODUCTION

The sovereignty, or supremacy, of Parliament is 'the dominant characteristic of our political institutions'.[1] Sovereignty as a doctrine has long caused controversy amongst philosophers, lawyers and political scientists and is a concept which assumes – as does the rule of law – differing interpretations according to the perspective being adopted. By way of example, international lawyers are concerned with the attributes which render a State independent and sovereign within the international community. Political scientists are concerned with the source of political power within the State. Legal theorists and constitutional lawyers, particularly in the United Kingdom where the matter remains contentious, are concerned to identify the ultimate legal power within a State.

DIFFERING INTERPRETATIONS OF 'SOVEREIGNTY'

Political and legal sovereignty – from the standpoint of sovereignty within the State as opposed to sovereignty as understood in international law – may be analysed as meaning either the supreme legal authority within a State or the supreme political authority within a State.[2]

Sovereignty as supreme legal authority

It is this interpretation with which AV Dicey and later constitutional writers are concerned. As this meaning is the central focus of our concern in understanding legislative – or parliamentary – sovereignty, consideration will be postponed until other interpretations of the concept have been considered.

---

1   Dicey, AV, *Introduction to the Study of the Law of the Constitution*, 10th edn, 1959, London: Macmillan, p 39.
2   For a more elaborate categorisation, see Rees, WJ, 'The theory of sovereignty restated', in Laslett, P (ed), *Philosophy, Politics and Society*, 1975, Oxford: Blackwells, Chapter IV.

Sovereignty as supreme political authority

The essence of this idea is that lawful power and authority must be in conformity with moral dictates: some form of 'higher law' or 'natural law'. Political theorists of the eighteenth century contributed much to an understanding of the idea of ultimate authority. Four broadly similar approaches, each entailing the idea of a 'social contract', may be outlined here.

Thomas Hobbes[3] offered the most extreme version of the social contract theory, arguing that man by nature is incapable of regulating his life in peace and harmony with his fellow man. Hobbes's view of man in a society lacking a restraining all-powerful sovereign was inherently pessimistic, an attitude encapsulated in the often quoted phrase that life is 'solitary, poor, nasty, brutish and short'.[4] In order for there to be civil order, it was necessary for each man to surrender to the State his own sovereignty in exchange for security. Such a surrender was revocable only if the State abused its trust. The requirement of obedience to law is strict: and yet there are limits:

> If the Soveraign command a man (though justly condemned) to kill, wound, or mayme himselfe; or not to resist those that assault him; or to abstain from the use of food, ayre, medicine, or any other thing, without which he cannot live; yet hath that man the Liberty to disobey.

Further, Hobbes states that:

> The Obligation of Subjects to the Soveraign, is understood to last as long, and no longer, than the power lasteth, by which he is able to protect them. For the right men have by Nature to protect themselves, when none else can protect them, can by no Covenant be relinquished.[5]

According to Jean-Jacques Rousseau,[6] the citizen enters into a 'contract' with the State, surrendering to the State individual rights in exchange for the protection of the State. The State, according to Rousseau, is thus embodied in the 'general will' of the people and becomes both the agent and ruler of the people in the peoples' name. Rousseau's vision of man differs markedly from that of Thomas Hobbes – far from living in a state of 'war' with one another, men in the 'natural state' of primitive society would have nothing to fight over and would be united in a community of endeavour to secure the essential provisions of life. Man comes together – from necessity – within civil society, and, through participation in the decision making processes, produces a democratic society. Rousseau distinguishes between supreme power – sovereignty – and the government. Sovereignty lies with the people, and is absolute and inalienable. The government's power is less absolute, established

---

3   Hobbes, T, *The Leviathan* (1651), 1973, London: JM Dent.
4   *Ibid*, p 65.
5   *Ibid*, pp 114–16.
6   Rousseau, J, *The Social Contract and Discourses* (1762), 1977, London: JM Dent.

to implement the will of the people and accountable to the people. The government is dependent upon the sovereign people for the continuation of its power, and the people retain the right to revoke the power devolved.

Thus, for Rousseau, sovereignty is a concept which entails moral approval and acceptance by the people whose 'collective will' sovereignty represents.[7] Indeed, for Rousseau:

> ... the sovereign, being formed wholly of the individuals who compose it, neither has nor can have any interest contrary to theirs; and consequently the sovereign power need give no guarantee to its subjects, because it is impossible for the body to wish to hurt all its members. We shall also see later on that it cannot hurt any in particular. The sovereign, merely by virtue of what it is, is always what it should be.[8]

Thomas Paine advances a social contract theory in which the rights of the individual are given central importance.[9] Paine both influenced and was influenced by the French and American Revolutions. In *Rights of Man*, Paine argued that the citizen gives up his rights to the State, but on a conditional basis. The State is placed in the position of trustee of the rights of man, and should that trust be broken, the citizen has the ultimate – or sovereign – right to depose the government. Paine argues that man has natural rights, 'those which appertain to man in right of his existence'. These rights are both individualistic and civil. The former category includes:

> ... all the intellectual rights, or rights of the mind, and also all those rights of acting as an individual for his own comfort and happiness, which are not injurious to the natural rights of others.

By way of distinction:

> Civil rights are those which appertain to man in right of his being a member of society. Every civil right has for its foundation, some natural right pre-existing in the individual.[10]

These natural and civil rights are held by government on trust for the people, and should – under an ideal constitution – be protected from governmental abuse by a Bill of Rights.[11] Such an approach is also taken by John Locke[12] who regards the people, as a collectivity, holding the sovereign power which is in some sense delegated to the government on trust, and who may accordingly exert their sovereign power to remove the government if it violates its sacred trust.

---

7   *Op cit*, Rousseau, fn 6, Bk I, Chapter VII, and Bk II.
8   *Op cit*, Rousseau, fn 6, p 177.
9   Paine, T, *Rights of Man* (1791, Pt 1), 1984, rep 1998, Collins, H (ed), New York: Penguin.
10 *Ibid*, p 90.
11 See, further, Chapter 22.
12 Locke, J, *Two Treatises of Government* (1690), 1977, London: JM Dent, Bk II.

In *Two Treatises of Government*,[13] John Locke advances powerful arguments for the limits of governmental power and the ultimate political sovereignty of the people. In Book II,[14] Locke argues that men come together in civil society and tacitly consent to be ruled by government directed to 'the peace, safety, and public good of the people'.[15] Hence, the power accorded to government is not absolute, but whilst in existence, the legislative power is the 'supreme power'. Nevertheless, Locke concludes that if the people:

> ... have set limits to the duration of their legislative, and made this supreme power in any person or assembly only temporary, it is forfeited; upon the forfeiture of their rules, or at the determination of the time set, it reverts to the society, and the people have a right to act as supreme, and continue the legislative in themselves or place it in a new form, or new hands, as they think good.[16]

Sovereignty, then, is limited and conditional: government holds supreme power on trust for the people. On this view, the authority of the constitution will be dependent upon its conformity with a higher law. As KC Wheare explains:

> This view of government limited by the natural rights of man lies at the basis of the American Constitution and finds a place ... in many modern constitutions. It provides a moral basis upon which a government's actions can be judged and, what is more, upon which the validity of a constitution can be tested. A constitution binds in so far as it is in accordance with natural law. Neither a government nor a citizen may disregard the authority of a constitution except in so far as the action can be justified by the law of nature. This is indeed a 'higher law' than a constitution.[17]

DISTINGUISHING LEGAL AND POLITICAL SOVEREIGNTY

It is often difficult to distinguish clearly between legal and political sovereignty. The distinction is nevertheless one insisted upon by authorities such as Sir Edward Coke, Sir William Blackstone and, in particular, AV Dicey. As with so much of the United Kingdom's constitutional law, contemporary thinking about sovereignty remains influenced by the legacy of Dicey. Dicey's interpretation of parliamentary sovereignty will be examined below (pp 225–52). At this introductory stage, however, it is necessary to note that

---

13   *Op cit*, Locke, fn 12.

14   'An essay concerning the true original extent and end of civil government', in *op cit*, Locke, fn 12, Bk II.

15   *Op cit*, Locke, fn 12, p 182.

16   *Op cit*, Locke, fn 12, p 242.

17   Wheare, KC, *Modern Constitutions*, 2nd edn, 1966, Oxford: OUP, p 65.

Dicey drew a strict separation between legal sovereignty and political sovereignty.[18] In Dicey's view, the people hold political sovereignty whilst legal sovereignty rests with the 'Queen in Parliament'. In large measure, this clear demarcation between the political and the legal is explained by the unwritten nature of the United Kingdom's constitution. In the majority of States having a written constitution, the constitution defines the limits of governmental power. In the United Kingdom, by way of contrast, the powers of government – whilst ultimately dependent upon the electoral 'mandate' – remain unconstrained by any fundamental written document and subject only to Parliament's approval. All law making power thus derives, not from the power conferring and power delimiting constitutional document, endorsed by the people, but from the sovereignty of the legislature: Parliament.

LEGAL THEORY AND SOVEREIGNTY

Legal theory contributes to an understanding of legal and political sovereignty within the constitution. In the overview of the theories of John Austin, Hans Kelsen and HLA Hart which follow, it will be seen that, in each case, the jurist is seeking an explanation of the source of ultimate authority, its identifying characteristics and the manner in which sovereignty is upheld within a legal order. By revealing the characteristics of valid law, it becomes easier to understand the distinction between laws and other rules in society – such as moral rules – which have binding effect, but which do not have the force – and enforceability – of legal rules.

John Austin

Within every civil society – or polity – there will be found, as a social and political fact, one supreme power. The nineteenth century jurist John Austin[19] was one of the earliest 'modern' theorists to offer an in depth analysis of sovereignty, and his work – while much criticised by later writers – still marks a useful starting point for analysis of the concept. Austin's theory was an attempt to define law in the positivist tradition.[20] Law is nothing more or less than the commands of the identifiable, illimitable and indivisible sovereign body. The sovereignty conferred exhibits itself in the habit of obedience of the

---

18 As do Coke and Blackstone.

19 1790–1859. See Austin, J, *The Province of Jurisprudence Determined* (1832), 1954, London: Weidenfeld and Nicolson.

20 Positivism being defined as man made law – as opposed to divine or natural law – enacted by a political superior within the State for the governance of citizens: the law which is posited or laid down.

people, which in turn is instilled by the fear of sanctions which attach to all laws and thus underpin the legal system. Laws are nothing more nor less than the general commands of this sovereign, to which sanctions are attached:

> ... every positive law, or every law strictly so called, is a direct or circuitous command of a monarch or sovereign number in the character of a political superior: that is to say, a direct or circuitous command of a monarch or sovereign number to a person or persons in a state of subjection to its author. And, being a command (and, therefore, flowing from a determinate source), every positive law is a law proper, or a law properly so called.[21]

While the model most closely accords with the criminal statute, it is difficult to endorse in relation to much of the civil law and in relation to those laws which regulate the law making and law enforcing institutions within the State. However, in every State, whether monarchical or parliamentary, unitary or federal, there must be some body which demonstrates the characteristics of a sovereign. For Austin, sovereignty as a legal concept within the United Kingdom lies with the Queen in Parliament: as a political concept, the ultimate sovereignty vested in the people.

Austin's analysis of both sovereignty and law is somewhat crude. It is difficult, for example, to adapt his idea of sovereignty to a federal State where, to cite but one example, the distribution of power may confer co-equal legislative powers on both the individual provincial legislatures and the federal government and provide for judicial review of the constitutionality of primary legislation.[22] Today, his theory is the more difficult to apply when considered in light of the United Kingdom's membership of the European Community and Union.[23]

HLA Hart

A thorough critique of Austin's analysis is offered by Professor HLA Hart.[24] Hart portrays the legal system as being one of rules rather than commands. For Hart, Austin's jurisprudence is tainted by its overtly coercive nature, as exemplified in the command plus sanction portrayal of law. Austin has missed, according to Hart, an important dimension of law: the concept of a rule. Rules, for Hart, are distinguishable from commands in several significant respects. Legal rules may, as with the criminal law, lay down specific prohibitions, breach of which will be met with punishment. Nevertheless, there are laws which do not exhibit the characteristics of prohibition and

---

21 *Op cit*, Austin, fn 19, p 134.
22 As, eg, the Commonwealth of Australia Constitution Act 1900.
23 See, further, below, pp 252–57, and Chapters 8 and 9.
24 Hart, HLA, *The Concept of Law*, 1961, Oxford: Clarendon.

sanction. Many rules of law confer the power on individuals and groups to act, but evince no element of coercion: rules of contract, of making wills, of entering into marriage, fall within this category. These rules Hart labels 'power conferring rules': rules which are permissive and the breach of which will result in a 'nullity', a concept which is difficult to conceptualise as an Austinian 'sanction'.

By distinguishing between rules which stipulate prohibitions and rules which confer powers, Hart is able to construct a theory of law which is represented as a union of primary and secondary rules. Each legal rule within the system is identified according to accepted criteria: what Hart calls the 'rule of recognition'. At the apex of the hierarchy of laws – whether bylaws of a local authority, judicial decisions, delegated legislation or statute – is the 'ultimate rule of recognition'. This ultimate rule, while involving some complexity and uncertainty,[25] is mostly explained in the form that 'what the Queen in Parliament enacts is law'.

Hart analyses the problems surrounding the nature of sovereignty. In *The Concept of Law*,[26] Hart discusses the concepts of *continuing sovereignty* and *self-embracing sovereignty*, an issue which, as will be seen further below, has attracted continuing academic debate. Hart argues that the conventionally understood Diceyan concept of sovereignty is an interpretation which has been accepted as the criterion of legal validity, but that that interpretation is 'only one arrangement among others, equally conceivable'.[27] The Diceyan view is that Parliament enjoys continuing sovereignty – that is to say, that each Parliament, irrespective of time, has equal legislative competence to that of any other Parliament. However, Hart argues, Parliament's sovereignty could be interpreted to be a form of *self-embracing* sovereignty – a sovereignty which would permit the exercise of power to delimit Parliament's legislative powers in the future. This power, however, being the ultimate power, would be exercisable only once. Hart draws the analogy with God in the following manner:

> ... on the one hand, a God who at every moment of his existence enjoys the same powers and so is incapable of cutting down those powers, and, on the other, a God whose powers include the power to destroy for the future his omnicompetence.[28]

In the former case, God enjoys continuing sovereignty; in the latter, self-embracing sovereignty. Furthermore, neither of these interpretations, Hart instructs:

---

25 *Op cit*, Hart, fn 24, Chapter VII.
26 *Op cit*, Hart, fn 24, Chapter VII.
27 *Op cit*, Hart, fn 24, p 145.
28 *Op cit*, Hart, fn 24, p 146.

... can be ruled out as wrong or accepted with confidence as right; for we are in the area of open texture of the system's most fundamental rule. Here at any moment a question may arise to which there is no answer – only answers.[29]

Hans Kelsen

Hans Kelsen analysed sovereignty both within a State and within the international legal order.[30] Kelsen's theory involves nothing less than an attempt to formulate a scientific global analysis of law. For Kelsen positive, man made, law is best expressed as a 'norm':

> By 'norm' we mean that something ought to be or ought to happen, especially that a human being ought to behave in a specific way.[31]

Each norm will be a valid legal rule if it is validated by a higher norm. Thus, a bylaw will be valid if it is properly enacted under an Act of Parliament. A legal decision will be valid provided that the judge is acting within his jurisdiction. An Act of Parliament will be valid if enacted in the constitutionally accepted correct manner. Taken together, the individual legal norms will form a system which itself is validated according to the 'basic norm' or 'grundnorm'. While for Kelsen, unlike Austin, it is not necessary that every legal rule have an attendant sanction, it is crucial that the legal order as a whole is a coercive order:

> As a coercive order, the law is distinguished from other social orders. The decisive criterion is the element of force – that means that the act prescribed by the order as a consequence of socially detrimental facts ought to be executed even against the will of the individual and, if he resist, by physical force.[32]

At an international level, Kelsen recognises that the existence of a valid national legal order is dependent upon the recognition of the State under international law. Where a revolution occurs within a State, it is international law which will determine the validity of claims to exercise legitimate power and hence law making power. Thus, by this means, it is possible to view law globally.

THE VALIDITY OF LAW AND THE EFFECTIVENESS OF LAW

In addition to identifying the characteristics of valid law, each of the above theorists also seeks to explain the relationship between – and distinctions

---

29 *Op cit*, Hart, fn 24, p 147

30 1881–1973. See Kelsen, H, *The Pure Theory of Law*, 1967, Berkeley: California UP and *The General Theory of Law and State*, 1961, New York: Russell.

31 *Ibid*, Kelsen, 1967, pp 4–5.

32 *Ibid*, Kelsen, 1967, pp 33–34.

between – the concepts of validity and effectiveness. The importance of the distinction between validity and effectiveness of law lies in explaining the ultimate source of authority or Sovereignty within a State. One question which frequently arises is whether, if a law is ineffective (perhaps because it is morally disapproved of by a majority of citizens, or because it is regarded as futile), that law loses its validity within the legal order. The commonly agreed position adopted by Austin and Hart is that such a law – provided that it conforms with the constitutional criteria for law – remains valid despite being ineffective. However, it is also a point of agreement that if a legal system were to cease to be effective overall – that is to say, if a state of anarchy existed – then the ultimate sovereign power would be under threat, and would probably be forced to change. The people, in rejecting the ultimate power within the State, would be taking back the power which they had entrusted to the sovereign. Accordingly, it can be seen that the legal sovereign is dependent ultimately upon the political sovereign power in society – the people.

The effectiveness of law, while it does not *per se* determine legal validity, nevertheless interrelates with law's validity. Under the constitutional theory of the United Kingdom, an Act of Parliament does not become invalid under the doctrine of *desuetude* (disuse). As a result, statutes of great antiquity – although never or seldom used – retain the force of law, and may be relied upon at any time.[33] Equally, a statute – of whatever date – is valid if it meets the criteria of validity, irrespective of whether or not it is effective in achieving its objectives. This is the point made by Sir Ivor Jennings in relation to the banning of smoking on the streets of Paris (discussed below, pp 228–29). A more realistic example of the relationship between the effectiveness and validity of law stems from the system of local taxation in the 1980s. The government decided that the existing system of taxation based on the rateable value of properties – irrespective of the number of persons living in the property – was inequitable. Accordingly, the government introduced the Community Charge[34] (or Poll Tax) which levied a flat rate of tax on each person within a local government area. The system was first introduced in Scotland and was met with condemnation and evasion. As a result of its ineffectiveness – based on the rejection of the law by the people – the government was forced to change the law. The law did not become invalid as a result of its ineffectiveness: rather, the ineffectiveness created a political reason as to why the law should be repealed.

If that one instance of an ineffective law is extrapolated to the legal system as a whole, the manner in which effectiveness affects validity can be seen more clearly. If a legal system comes under strain to a significant degree, a

---

33 Unless expressly repealed. See, eg, the Statute Repeals Act 1998, which repeals ecclesiastical leases legislation dating from the early sixteenth century.

34 Under the Local Government Finance Act 1988.

point will be reached at which there is civil unrest, anarchy or revolution. The law will cease to be effective. The law, however, under the theory of sovereignty, remains valid. At some point on the scale between general effectiveness and more or less total ineffectiveness – and the point cannot be precisely determined – the underlying explanation for the validity of law will cease. Effectiveness, accordingly, can be seen to be the prime condition for meaningful statements about validity.[35]

In a revolutionary situation – as explained by Kelsen – there is a point where the basic norm – or sovereign power – changes. The ultimate validity of law depends on its effectiveness. When there is a revolution, the basic norm may change, brought about by a change in the power structure within a society ultimately creating a new basic norm.

Ultimate validity and effectiveness: an illustration

The relationship between the ultimate validity of a legal system and effectiveness is well illustrated by the position in Rhodesia, as it then was, in the 1960s. Until 1965, the governance of Rhodesia was under the sovereignty of the United Kingdom, with Rhodesia enjoying self-governing powers to the extent allowed under the Constitution of Rhodesia. By convention, the United Kingdom Parliament would not legislate for the colony without the express request or consent of the Rhodesian Parliament. In 1965, however, the Prime Minister of Rhodesia, Mr Ian Smith, issued a unilateral declaration of independence from the United Kingdom and asserted the full right of self-government. The response of the United Kingdom's government was to reassert its own powers, reaffirming its right to legislate for Rhodesia in the Southern Rhodesia Act 1965 and thus overriding the convention. Between 1965 and 1979, when a constitutional conference resulted in full independence being conferred on the renamed Zimbabwe,[36] there was thus doubt as to which Parliament represented sovereignty within the State of Rhodesia.

Jurisprudentially, Hans Kelsen had argued that one of the conditions for change in the sovereignty of the State – or, in his phraseology, the 'basic norm' of a State – lay in revolution, whether by act of force or change in the allegiance of the judiciary. The case of *Madzimbamuto v Lardner Burke*[37] provided the opportunity to test the revolutionary position in relation to sovereignty.

Madzimbamuto had been detained on order of the government of Rhodesia under a provision enacted by the Rhodesian government post-UDI (the unilateral declaration of independence). Challenging the legality of his

---

35 See *op cit*, Kelsen, 1967, fn 30, p 214; *op cit*, Hart, fn 24, Chapter VI.
36 Under the Zimbabwe Act 1979 and SI 1979/1600.
37 [1969] 1 AC 645.

detention, Madzimbamuto claimed that the Act was *ultra vires* the powers of the Rhodesian government. On appeal to the Privy Council, the traditional doctrine of parliamentary sovereignty was affirmed. Lord Reid declared that:

> It is often said that it would be unconstitutional for the United Kingdom Parliament to do certain things, meaning that the moral, political and other reasons against doing them are so strong that most people would regard it as highly improper if Parliament did these things. But that does not mean that it is beyond the power of Parliament to do these things. If Parliament chose to do any of them, the courts could not hold the Act of Parliament invalid.

Accordingly, the sovereignty over Rhodesia remained – from the English courts' point of view – that of the United Kingdom Parliament. The Rhodesian government had *de facto* power; *de jure* power remained in the United Kingdom. An impasse was thus reached: to the government of Rhodesia – and ultimately the Rhodesian courts – the alleged sovereignty of the United Kingdom was an irrelevance. To the United Kingdom, however – as illustrated by *Madzimbamuto's* case before the Privy Council – the 'basic norm' of the constitution of Rhodesia remained the sovereign power of Westminster.[38] Nevertheless, from the point of view of the judges within Rhodesia, there was a dilemma: how to react to legislation promulgated by the *de facto* sovereign power. From 1965 to 1968, the Rhodesian courts refused to acknowledge the lawfulness of the Smith government, following the view of the Privy Council that, since the government was unlawful, so too were all of its acts. However, to continue to deny the force of law to any acts of the unlawful government was to produce uncertainty and doubt. The doctrine of necessity was employed by the judges to give legal effect to what was constitutionally invalid. Gradually, the continuing effectiveness of the Smith regime was to result in recognition of the validity of its Acts, thus further revealing the complexities in maintaining a clear separation between the criterion of legal validity and effectiveness.[39]

In a revolutionary situation, a change in the basic norm, or grundnorm, will take place when the judges accept the new source of sovereign power. As JW Harris explains:

> Being merely a hypothesis of juristic thinking, the grundnorm does not change the moment the revolutionaries shoot the King. It cannot change until jurists change their thinking, that is, until lawyers begin to make post-revolutionary assertions to the effect: 'The law in the country now is ...' where 'now' refers to some revolutionary, established source of law.[40]

---

38 See, *inter alia*, Harris, J, *Legal Philosophies*, 1980, London: Butterworths, p 125; Raz, J, *The Authority of Law*, 1979, Oxford: OUP, Chapter 7; Stone, J, 'Mystery and mystique in the basic norm' (1963) 26 MLR 34; Brookfield, FM, 'The courts, Kelsen, and the Rhodesian revolution' (1969) 19 Toronto ULJ 326.

39 See Dias, RWM, 'Legal politics: norms behind the grundnorm' [1968] CLJ 233.

40 [1971] CLJ 110.

Kelsen's theory of revolutionary change in the grundnorm has not been universally accepted, but it marks an effort to deal with the difficult issue of change and continuity in a legal order. By way of example, in *The State v Dosso*,[41] the Supreme Court of Pakistan, applying Kelsenian theory, accepted the validity of a coup and that the successful coup conferred sovereign power on the victors. However, in *Asma Jilani v Government of Punjab*,[42] the Supreme Court rejected the notion that any person seizing power could claim the authority of sovereign power. Rather, sovereign power could only be conferred on the successful revolutionary party under the constitution of the State expressing the will of the people through the medium of chosen representatives.[43]

THE ULTIMATE RULE IS EXTRA-LEGAL

When one comes to search for the ultimate higher authority which itself validates the basic norm, a logical impasse is reached. Accordingly, it is necessary to look outside this discrete structural system in order to find the authority which confers ultimate validity. On a domestic basis,[44] we find this validating force in 'juristic consciousness' – in other words, the acceptance of legal validity by the judges. Kelsen's view on the source of ultimate sovereign power is analysed by HLA Hart in *The Concept of Law*. While keen to distinguish his own theory of law from that of Kelsen and that of John Austin, there are similarities between Kelsen's and Hart's view of the ultimate validity within a legal system. For Hart, the ultimate rule of recognition is validated by the sociologically observable fact of official acceptance. By this, Hart means that the officials' – and most importantly the judges' – acceptance of authority can be seen in operation whenever one observes a court of law. A judge may perhaps personally disapprove of a precedent case or of a statutory provision, but his acceptance of its validity is demonstrated by his application of the law. Expressed differently, it is the judges who uphold and reinforce the sovereignty of Parliament – the basic norm of the constitution.

In Kelsen's analysis, the 'basic norm' within any State will be the historically traceable first constitution. In many instances, this will prove a workable test. In the United States of America, the Constitution of 1787 will be the basic norm; in the Republic of Ireland, the Constitution of 1937, and in Australia, the Commonwealth Constitution of 1900, as amended. The position in the United Kingdom is less clear cut on this analysis, which will assume

---

41 Pak Leg, December 1958, S Ct 533.
42 Pak Leg, December 1972, S Ct 139.
43 See Iyer, TKK, 'Constitutional law in Pakistan: Kelsen in the courts' (1973) 21 AJCL 759.
44 And Kelsen seeks to establish a global 'pure theory' for law, but that need not be considered here.

importance when considering the status of the Acts of Union with Scotland and Ireland.[45] Since the Norman Conquest in 1066, there has been an unrivalled continuity in constitutional development in the United Kingdom, interrupted by only two major historical events and a fundamentally important, more contemporary, change. The first of these, the Civil War of 1642–46, resulted in the execution of Charles I in 1649, and the abolition of the monarchy and rule by Cromwell until the restoration of the monarchy in 1660. The second significant constitutional change came with the uniting of the sovereign Parliaments of Scotland and England under the Act of Union 1707, creating the State of Great Britain, and later the Union with Ireland, 1800, by which Act the State of the United Kingdom came into being. The third change, which has wide ranging implications for the constitution and law was Britain's accession to the European Community which took effect from 1973. Most recently, the government's constitutional reform programme entails two significant changes – devolution to regional assemblies and 'incorporation' of the European Convention on Human Rights. While neither of these affect the *ultimate* sovereignty of the United Kingdom Parliament, each has significant implications for the scope of legislative power which Parliament retains while these measures remain in force. These issues are discussed below at pp 252–62.

SOVEREIGNTY AND WRITTEN CONSTITUTIONS

Where a written constitution exists, it will have come into being either by a grant of independence from a previously sovereign power or through a revolution – peaceful or otherwise. Where the constitution arises from the native authority of the people, it is 'autochthonous':

> ... [the people] assert not the principle of autonomy only; they assert also a principle of something stronger, of self-sufficiency, of constitutional autarky ... of being constitutionally rooted in their own soil.[46]

Where autochthony[47] exists, the authority for the constitution arises from the people. The phrase 'We the People' has powerful psychological – and legal – force, and the resultant document, the constitution, will be supreme. As KC Wheare explains in relation to the United States of America:

> The constitution of the United States expresses the essential supremacy of a constitution in a federal government in the passage: 'This Constitution and the Laws of the United States which shall be made in pursuance thereof ... shall be

---

45 See, further, below, pp 235–41.

46 Wheare, KC, *The Constitutional Structure of the Commonwealth*, 1960, Oxford: Clarendon, Chapter 4.

47 See Marshall, G, *Constitutional Theory*, 1971, Oxford: Clarendon, Chapter III.4.

the supreme law of the land; and the judges in every State shall be bound thereby, anything in the constitution or laws of any State to the contrary notwithstanding.'[48]

All power entrusted to government comes from the people: it is accordingly understandable that, under such a constitutional arrangement, there is a strongly held belief that government holds its power on 'trust' for the people. It may be said, as a result, that both law making and executive powers are conditionally conferred on those who hold public office, subject to the doctrine of trust which will be enforced by the courts in the name of the people. All constitutions – written and unwritten – exist against the backcloth of the historical, political and moral evolution: none exists in a vacuum. However, under a written constitution, this background has a particular significance. The constitution, being the expression of the political morality of its age – updated by the judiciary through interpretative methods – is a constant reflection and reminder of the will of the people and the restraints which that will imposes on government.

Chief Justice Marshall, in *Marbury v Madison*,[49] explained the power of the constitution:

> It is a proposition too plain to be contested that the constitution controls any legislative act repugnant to it; or, that the legislature may alter the constitution by an ordinary act. Between these two alternatives, there is no middle ground. The constitution is either a superior, paramount law, unchangeable by ordinary means, or it is on a level with ordinary legislative acts, and, like other acts, is alterable when the legislature shall please to alter it. If the former part of the alternative is true, then a legislative act contrary to the constitution is not law; if the latter part be true, then written constitutions are absurd attempts, on the part of the people, to limit a power in its own nature illimitable.

It is possible, accordingly, under such a constitutional arrangement, for the constitutional court[50] effectively to redefine the relationship between the governors and the governed, the State and its citizens. By this means, the constitution is renewed and reinvigorated. By way of example, the American Bill of Rights, enacted as amendments to the 1787 Constitution, provides that:

> All persons born or naturalised in the United States, and subject to the jurisdiction thereof, are citizens of the United States and of the State wherein they reside. No State shall make or enforce any law which shall abridge the privileges or immunities of citizens of the United States; nor shall any State deprive any person of life, liberty, or property, without due process of law; nor deny to any person within its jurisdiction the equal protection of the laws ...[51]

---

48 Wheare, KC, *Federal Government*, 4th edn, 1963, Oxford: OUP, p 54.

49 1 Cranch 137 (1803).

50 Howsoever labelled: in the United States of America, the Supreme Court; in Australia, the High Court.

51 Bill of Rights, Art XIV, s 1, ratified 9 July 1868.

This 'equal protection' clause has been the focus of the development of equal civil and political rights in the United States of America. In 1896, the Supreme Court was called upon to determine whether the policy of segregation of black and white citizens was lawful under the Constitution. The court ruled that 'separate but equal treatment' laws did not amount to a denial of the equal protection of law.[52] When, however, in 1954, the question of 'equal protection' came before the Supreme Court concerning segregation in the schools of the States of Kansas, South Carolina, Virginia and Delaware, the court was to rule that such 'treatment' violated the Fourteenth Amendment of the constitution.[53]

THE SOURCE OF SOVEREIGNTY IN THE UNITED KINGDOM

The sovereignty of Parliament is not itself laid down in statute: nor could it be, for the ultimate law maker cannot confer upon itself the ultimate power. As legal theorists[54] have demonstrated, when searching for ultimate legal power, there comes a point of inquiry beyond which one cannot logically move. In order to understand the ultimate authority of law, whether expressed in terms of the 'basic norm' (Hans Kelsen)[55] or the 'ultimate rule of recognition' (HLA Hart)[56] or sovereignty, the inquirer must move beyond the law itself. As has been seen above, for both Kelsen and Hart, the key to ultimate power lies in its acceptance – but not necessarily moral approval – by the judges within the legal system. Each theorist expresses a similar idea in different terms. To reiterate: for Kelsen, the acceptance of sovereign power can be seen in 'juristic consciousness'. Hart is rather less mysterious, although still abstruse, stating that the existence of sovereign power can be demonstrated in the everyday workings of the machinery of the law. The test for acceptance, according to Professor Hart, lies in the attitude of the officials in the legal system and most importantly the judges, what Hart terms the 'internal aspect' of law. This internal aspect entails acceptance by the judges that the existence and acceptance of the authority of a legal rule is justification for acting in a particular manner: that is to say, for reaching a judgment in a particular case.

---

52 *Plessey v Ferguson* 163 US 537 (1896).

53 *Brown v Board of Education of Topeka* 347 US 483 (1954). The ruling did not end segregation on other grounds. See King, ML, *Why We Can't Wait*, 1964, New York: Signet; see, further, the Civil Rights Acts 1964 and 1968.

54 See *op cit*, Kelsen, 1961, fn 30, p 116; *op cit*, Hart, fn 24, p 104. See, also, Kelsen, H, 'The function of a constitution', in Tur, R and Twining, W (eds), *Essays on Kelsen*, 1986, Oxford: Clarendon.

55 See *op cit*, Kelsen, 1967, fn 30; and *op cit*, Kelsen, 1961, fn 30.

56 *Op cit*, Hart, fn 24.

SOVEREIGNTY AS A RULE OF COMMON LAW

Sovereignty is thus the fundamental rule of the common law, for it is the judges who uphold Parliament's sovereignty. For as long as the judges accept the sovereignty of Parliament, sovereignty will remain the ultimate rule of the constitution. As Salmond explains:

> All rules of law have historical sources. As a matter of fact and history they have their origin somewhere, though we may not know what it is. But not all of them have legal sources. Were this so, it would be necessary for the law to proceed *ad infinitum* in tracing the descent of its principles. It is requisite that the law should postulate one or more first causes, whose operation is ultimate and whose authority is underived ... The rule that a man may not ride a bicycle on the footpath may have its source in the bylaws of a municipal council; the rule that these bylaws have the force of law has its source in an Act of Parliament. But whence comes the rule that Acts of Parliament have the force of law? This is legally ultimate; its source is historical only, not legal ... It is the law because it is the law, and for no other reason that it is possible for the law to take notice of. No statute can confer this power upon Parliament, for this would be to assume and act on the very power that is to be conferred.[57]

Accordingly, the rule which confers validity on legislation is 'logically superior to the sovereign'.[58] The logical consequence of this is stated by HWR Wade:

> ... if no statute can establish the rule that the courts obey Acts of Parliament, similarly no statute can alter or abolish that rule. The rule is above and beyond the reach of statute ... because it is itself the source of the authority of statute.[59]

The sovereignty of Parliament will only be lost under two conditions. The first condition would be where Parliament decided – perhaps on the authority of the people tested in a referendum – to abolish its sovereignty and to place its residual authority under that of a written constitution to be adjudicated upon by the judiciary. The second condition would be where the judiciary itself underwent a 'revolution' in attitude, and accepted that Parliament was no longer the sovereign lawmaking body and that the judges owed allegiance to an alternative – or different – sovereign power. These points will be returned to when considering challenges to the traditional Diceyan view of sovereignty (discussed below, pp 225–52).

In the United Kingdom, in the absence of a written constitution which asserts the sovereignty of the people and the sovereignty of the constitution – as interpreted by the judiciary – over the legislature and executive, the 'vacuum' is filled by the doctrine of parliamentary sovereignty, or supremacy.

---

57 Williams, G (ed), *Jurisprudence*, 10th edn, p 155, cited by Wade, HWR, in 'The basis of legal sovereignty' [1955] CLJ 177, p 187.

58 Wade, HWR, 'Introduction', in *op cit*, Dicey, fn 1.

59 *Ibid*, Wade, 1955, p 187.

Under this doctrine, political sovereignty vests in the people: legal sovereignty vests with Parliament over which no legal controls are exerted, but which remains responsible to the electorate for the continued, and regularly renewed, grant of law making and executive authority. The means by which the constitution is renewed is through the democratic process and the concept of a responsive responsible government, rather than through the means of a Supreme Court reinterpreting the constitution according to judicial perceptions of the mores in society. This is not to suggest that under a written constitution, there is no responsive, accountable and democratic government or that the evolution of the constitution lies solely within the domain of the judges. Rather, the point to be emphasised is that, under a written constitution, there is an additional element in effecting constitutional change. Depending upon the independence, integrity and motivation of the courts, acts of the executive and legislature can be subjected to the control of the constitution.

The origins of parliamentary sovereignty

In Chapter 6, the manner in which the near absolute powers of the Crown[60] were reduced by the courts and Parliament was discussed. With the reduction in the King's prerogative powers, there came about the correlative rise in the sovereignty of Parliament. From 1688, the supremacy of Parliament over the Crown was established. From this time, the prerogative powers of the Crown continued in existence or were abolished or curtailed as Parliament determined. No new prerogative powers may be claimed by the Crown, as Diplock LJ stated in *BBC v Johns*,[61] discussed in Chapter 6.

AV DICEY AND SOVEREIGNTY

The classical definition of sovereignty, offered from a constitutional law rather than a jurisprudential perspective, is that of AV Dicey.[62] Dicey had been critical of John Austin's account of sovereignty, arguing that Austin confused political and legal sovereignty. From a legal-theoretical point of view, it remains imperative to separate the political from the legal and to recognise that, as matters stand, legal sovereignty remains with the United Kingdom

---

60 To make laws by proclamation, to rule under the prerogative without Parliament, and to participate in the judicial process.

61 [1965] Ch 32.

62 *Op cit*, Dicey, fn 1.

Parliament, although there may be political restraints which effectively inhibit the exercise of those powers.[63] On sovereignty, Dicey stated that:

> The principle of parliamentary sovereignty means neither more nor less than this: namely, that Parliament thus defined has, under the English constitution, the right to make or unmake any law whatever; and, further, that no person or body is recognised by the law of England as having a right to override or set aside the legislation of Parliament.

> A law may, for our present purpose, be defined as 'any rule which will be enforced by the courts'. The principle, then, of parliamentary sovereignty may, looked at from its positive side, be thus described: any Act of Parliament, or any part of an Act of Parliament, which makes a new law, or repeals or modifies an existing law, will be obeyed by the court. The same principle, looked at from its negative side, may be thus stated: there is no person or body of persons who can, under the English constitution, make rules which override or derogate from an Act of Parliament, or which (to express the same thing in other words) will be enforced by the courts in contravention of an Act of Parliament.[64]

From this description can be deduced three basic rules:

(a) Parliament is the supreme law making body and may enact laws on any subject matter;

(b) no Parliament may be bound by a predecessor or bind a successor;

(c) no person or body – including a court of law – may question the validity of Parliament's enactments.

It is the correctness of this definition which must be tested and evaluated. Having considered the concept of sovereignty in theoretical terms, examination of the manner in which this is translated into a practical legal doctrine is required. Dicey's description of sovereignty will provide the framework for discussion.

Parliament's unlimited law making power

This aspect of sovereignty is the easiest both to explain and to understand: the rule means that there is no limit on the subject matter on which Parliament may legislate. Thus Parliament may legislate to alter its term of office. In 1716, the life of a Parliament was limited to three years under the Act of 1694. Fearing the effects of an election, the government introduced, and Parliament passed, the Septennial Act, extending the life of Parliament to seven years. The consequence of this Act was to confer authority on the Commons to legislate without the express consent of the electorate: thus usurping the rights of the

---

63 On extrinsic and intrinsic limitations, see below, pp 230–31.

64 *Op cit*, Dicey, fn 1, p 39.

people.[65] The Septennial Act, under a written constitution such as that of the United States, would be legally invalid. Nevertheless, as Dicey argued, 'Parliament made a legal though unprecedented use of its powers'.[66] Parliament also extended its own life between 1910 and 1918, and the Parliament elected in 1935 was to endure until 1945.[67] Parliament may also legislate to alter the succession to the throne, as with the Act of Settlement 1700 and His Majesty's Declaration of Abdication Act 1936. Parliament may 'abolish' itself and reconstitute itself as a different body, as occurred with the Union with Scotland Act 1706.[68] Parliament may also legislate to alter its own powers, as with the Parliament Acts 1911 and 1949,[69] whereby the powers of the House of Lords in respect of legislation were curtailed. Parliament may grant independence to dependent States, whether dominions or colonies, as with the Nigeria Independence Act 1960 and the Zimbabwe Independence Act 1979. Furthermore, Parliament may legislate to limit its own powers in relation to dependent territories, as shown by the Colonial Laws Validity Act 1865 and the Statute of Westminster 1931.[70]

Parliament may also legislate with retrospective effect, as with the War Damage Act 1965. The War Damage Act effectively overruled the decision of the House of Lords in *Burmah Oil Company v Lord Advocate*.[71] In 1942, British troops had destroyed oil installations in Rangoon, with the intention of preventing them from falling into the hands of the Japanese. The British government made an *ex gratia* payment of some £4 million to the company. Burmah Oil sued the government for some £31 million compensation. The House of Lords held that compensation was payable by the Crown for the destruction of property caused by the exercise of the prerogative power in relation to war.[72] The government immediately introduced into Parliament the War Damage Bill to nullify the effect of the decision.

Parliament may legislate with extra-territorial effect, that is to say, Parliament may enact laws affecting the rights and duties of citizens and non-citizens outside the territorial jurisdiction of the United Kingdom. For example, certain offences committed in a foreign State will be triable in this country. Thus, murder, manslaughter, treason, bigamy and tax offences

---

65 See Priestley, J, *An Essay on the First Principles of Government; and on the Nature of Political, Civil, and Religious Liberty, including remarks on Dr Brown's Code of Education, and on Dr Balguy's Sermon on Church Authority*, 2nd edn, 1771, London: J Johnson, cited in *op cit*, Dicey, fn 1, p 47.

66 *Op cit*, Dicey, fn 1, p 47.

67 Prolongation of Parliament Act 1944.

68 See, further, below, pp 235–38.

69 See Chapter 17.

70 See, further, below, pp 233–35.

71 [1965] AC 75.

72 See Chapter 6.

committed abroad will not render the accused immune from prosecution in this country.[73] Parliament may expressly legislate for overseas territory, as in the Continental Shelf Act 1964, under which exploration and exploitation rights of the continental shelf vest in the Crown. However, it is a presumption of statutory interpretation that statutes will not be given extra-territorial effect other than where it is expressly or impliedly provided for under the Act.[74] Such statutes will normally be passed in order to give effect to obligations undertaken under an international treaty.[75] The Hijacking Act 1971, for example, gave legislative effect to the Convention for the Suppression on Unlawful Seizure of Aircraft. Section 1 of the Aviation Security Act 1982, which succeeded the Hijacking Act 1971, provides that the crime of hijacking is committed when a person on board an aircraft in flight unlawfully seizes control of the aircraft and exercises control over it by the use of force or by threats. The jurisdiction of the United Kingdom courts, with limited exceptions, extends to an act of hijacking, wherever it occurs, and irrespective of the nationality of the hijacker.[76]

The most often quoted and best remembered examples of Parliament's theoretically untrammelled legislative powers are those offered by Sir Ivor Jennings: Parliament can legislate to ban smoking on the streets of Paris; Parliament can legally make a man into a woman; and Sir Leslie Stephens:[77] Parliament could legislate to have a blue eyed babies put to death. In *The Law and the Constitution*,[78] Jennings writes:

> Parliamentary supremacy means essentially two things. It means, first, that Parliament can legally enact legislation dealing with any subject matter whatever. There are no limitations except political expedience and constitutional convention ... if Parliament enacted that all men should be women, they would be women so far as the law is concerned. In speaking of the power of Parliament, we are dealing with legal principles, not the facts. Though it is true that Parliament cannot in fact change the course of nature, it is equally true that it cannot in fact do all sorts of things. The supremacy of Parliament is a legal fiction, and legal fiction can assume anything.

> Parliamentary supremacy means, secondly, that Parliament can legislate for all persons and all places. If it enacts that smoking in the streets of Paris is an offence, then it is an offence. Naturally, it is an offence by English law and not by French law, and therefore it would be regarded as an offence only by those

---

73 Law Com No 91, *Territorial and Extra-territorial Extent of Criminal Law*, 1978, London: HMSO.

74 *Treacey v DPP* [1971] AC 537; *R v Kelly* [1982] AC 665.

75 Parliament may, however, legislate contrary to the requirements of international law. See *Mortensen v Peters* (1906) 8 F (J) 93; *Cheney v Conn* [1968] 1 All ER 779.

76 See, also, the Taking of Hostages Act 1982 giving effect to the International Convention Against the Taking of Hostages.

77 Stephens, L, *The Science of Ethics* (1882), 1972, Newton Abbot: David and Charles.

78 Jennings, I (Sir), *The Law and the Constitution*, 5th edn, 1959, London: Hodder & Stoughton, pp 170–71.

who paid attention to English law. The Paris police would not at once begin arresting all smokers, nor would French criminal courts begin inflicting punishments upon them. But if any Frenchman came into any place where attention was paid to English law, proceedings might be taken against him. If, for instance, a Frenchman who had smoked in the streets of Paris spent a few hours in Folkestone, he might be brought before a court of summary jurisdiction for having committed an offence against English law.

These extreme, hypothetical examples illustrate the distinction between what is theoretically possible and what is practically possible, or to express it differently, the distinction between *validity* and *effectiveness* discussed above. The distinction is important and helps to explain the apparent paradox of unlimited legislative power.

An Act of Parliament will be valid if it has passed through the requisite parliamentary stages and received the royal assent. The manner in which the judges deal with this 'enrolled Bill' rule is discussed further below. All that need be noted for now is that, provided an Act of Parliament is 'on the parliamentary roll', it will be held to be good law. That is not to say that every rule making power exercised by Parliament results in an 'Act of Parliament' which alone can alter the law, and is thus 'sovereign'.

Acts of Parliament alone are supreme

Resolutions of Parliament

Resolutions of either House of Parliament – for example, decisions of the House of Commons – do not have the force of law and cannot alter the law of the land and thereby affect individual rights and duties.[79] For a resolution to have the force of law, it must be placed on a statutory basis.

Proclamations

Proclamations of the Crown, issued under the royal prerogative, do not have the force of law. To understand the status of proclamations, it is necessary to turn to the reign of Henry VIII. Under the Statute of Proclamations 1539, the King was given wide – though not unlimited – power to make law without Parliament's consent. The Act was repealed in 1547, although monarchs continued to 'legislate' by proclamation. The *Case of Proclamations*[80] clarified the constitutional position. The most significant aspects of the case lay in the findings, first, that the King could not by proclamation create an offence

---

79   *Stockdale v Hansard* (1839) 9 Ad & E 1; 3 St Tr (NS) 723; *Bowles v Bank of England* [1913] 1 Ch 57.

80   (1611) 12 Co Rep 74.

previously unknown to law, and secondly, that the King had only such prerogative power as was granted under law.

Treaties

Treaties entered into under the royal prerogative cannot alter the law of the land. The courts have made it clear that treaties can take legal effect only under the authority of an Act of Parliament.[81] This point will be returned to when the constitutional relationship between the United Kingdom and the European Community is examined in Chapters 8 and 9. It is sufficient to note here that a treaty has no legal force under domestic law unless and until its provisions are incorporated into law by way of statute.

Resolutions, proclamations and treaties are but three species of 'law making' which are distinguishable from statute: and it is the statute alone which will be valid, provided that the required parliamentary procedures have been followed.

Intrinsic and extrinsic limits on Parliament's power

As seen above, the criterion of effectiveness underlies the supremacy of Parliament and represents one important – albeit extra-legal – constraint on Parliament's power. As Dicey says, sovereignty 'is limited on every side by the possibility of popular resistance'.[82] Leslie Stephens makes the same point and is quoted at length by Dicey:

> Lawyers are apt to speak as though the legislature were omnipotent, as they do not require to go beyond its decision. It is, of course, omnipotent in the sense that it can make whatever law it please, in as much as a law means any rule which has been made by the legislature. But, from the scientific point of view, the power of the legislature is of course strictly limited. It is limited, so to speak, both from within and from without; from within, because the legislature is the product of a certain social conditions, and determined by whatever determines the society; and from without, because the power of imposing laws is dependent upon the instinct of subordination, which is itself limited. If a legislature decided that all blue eyed babies should be murdered, the preservation of blue eyed babies would be illegal; but legislators must go mad before they could pass such a law, and subjects be idiotic before they could submit to it.[83]

---

81 See, *inter alia, The Parlement Belge* (1879) 4 PD 129; *AG for Canada v AG for Ontario* [1937] AC 326; *R v Home Secretary ex parte McWhirter* (1969) *The Times*, 20 October; *Blackburn v AG* [1971] 2 All ER 1380.

82 *Op cit*, Dicey, fn 1, p 79.

83 *Op cit*, Stephens, fn 77, p 143, cited in *op cit*, Dicey, fn 1, p 81.

These views are indicative of the constitutional role of government today. In a representative democracy, the proper purpose of government is to serve the people. In former times, when government was conducted by the King in Council, this was not necessarily the case. But even then, there were limits on monarchical and aristocratic power: ultimately, law cannot be enforced against the will of the governed. Compliance – in the absence of a military or police State – depends for the most part on voluntary acquiescence, not on the application of power. One of Hart's principal objections to Austin's 'command backed by sanction' theory of law turns on this point. As Hart explains, the law is largely 'self-enforcing' and 'self-enforced'. By this, he means that it rests on acceptance, by and large, by the people. Nowadays, with a more or less democratic House of Commons,[84] the internal and external constraints discussed by Dicey and Stephens coalesce. As Dicey explains:

> The aim and effect of such (representative) government is to produce a coincidence, or at any rate diminish the divergence, between the external and the internal limitations on the exercise of sovereign power.

> Where a Parliament truly represents the people, the divergence between the external and the internal limit to the exercise of sovereign power can hardly arise, or if it arises, must soon disappear.[85]

No Parliament may be bound by its predecessor or bind its successor

The rationale for this aspect of Dicey's definition of sovereignty lies in the recognition that for a body to be sovereign it must be, in Austin's word, illimitable. For a sovereign body to be subordinate to another body would be a logical contradiction:

> The logical reason why Parliament has failed in its endeavours to enact unchangeable enactments is that a sovereign power cannot, while retaining its sovereign character, restrict its own powers by any particular enactment ... 'Limited sovereignty', in short, as in the case of a parliamentary as of every other sovereign, is a contradiction in terms.[86]

It follows, therefore, that each Parliament must enjoy the same unlimited power as any Parliament before it. No Parliament can enact rules which limit future Parliaments.[87] It is this aspect of Dicey's definition which gives rise to the most argument and which requires the most careful analysis.

---

84 See, further, Chapters 13–16.

85 *Op cit*, Dicey, fn 1, pp 82–83.

86 *Op cit*, Dicey, fn 1, p 68.

87 On the distinction between 'continuing' and 'self-embracing' sovereignty, see the discussion in *op cit*, Hart, fn 24, and see, further, below, pp 247–52.

The doctrine of implied repeal

The doctrine of implied repeal provides the mechanism by which the judge gives effect to the rule against Parliament being bound by previous Parliaments or being able to bind subsequent Parliaments, and thereby guarantees contemporary sovereignty. Parliament may, of course, repeal any previous law by expressly declaring that law to be repealed. The position of the judiciary is then clear: they must give effect to the latest expression of sovereign will and judges are not free to apply the earlier statute. The position, however, may not always be so clear cut. Parliament may pass, perhaps through inadvertence, a statute, which while not expressly repealing an earlier Act, is inconsistent with it. When the judges are thus faced with two apparently conflicting statutes, the doctrine of implied repeal will come into play, the judges applying the latest statute in time and deeming the earlier provisions to be impliedly repealed.

Two cases which illustrate the principle in operation are *Vauxhall Estates Ltd v Liverpool Corporation*[88] and *Ellen Street Estates Ltd v Minister of Health*,[89] each of which entailed similar facts. Section 7(1) of the Acquisition of Land (Assessment of Compensation) Act 1919 provided that:

> The provisions of the Act or order by which the land is authorised to be acquired ... shall ... have effect subject to this Act and so far as inconsistent with this Act those provisions shall cease to have or shall not have effect ...

The Housing Act 1925 provided for a less generous scheme for compensation on the compulsory acquisition of land than the 1919 Act. In both cases, the plaintiffs argued that section 7(1) of the 1919 Act was binding on the courts and should be applied in preference to the Housing Act 1925. If that claim were to succeed, the constitutional position would be that the provisions of the 1919 Act were effectively 'entrenched' – that is to say, have a superior legal status to that of other Acts of Parliament and therefore binding – on a future Parliament. In the *Vauxhall Estates* case, the Divisional Court held that the 1925 Act impliedly repealed the conflicting provisions in the 1919 Act and, in the *Ellen Street Estates* case, the Court of Appeal again ruled that the 1919 Act must give way to the 1925 legislation. Maugham LJ stated that:

> The legislature cannot, according to our constitution, bind itself as to the form of subsequent legislation, and it is impossible for Parliament to enact that in a subsequent statute dealing with the same subject matter there can be no implied repeal. If, in a subsequent Act, Parliament chooses to make it plain that

---

88 [1932] 1 KB 733.
89 [1934] 1 KB 590.

the earlier statute is being to some extent repealed, effect must be given to that intention just because it is the will of the legislature.[90]

With the doctrines of express and implied repeal firmly in mind, consideration must now be given to the special problems allegedly posed for legislative supremacy by grants of independence, the Acts of Union with Scotland and Ireland, 'manner and form' and 'redefinition' theories. The impact of membership of the European Community and Union also requires careful consideration, as does the recent devolution of power to the Scottish Parliament and the Northern Ireland and Welsh Assemblies, and the Human Rights Act 1998.

Grants of independence

The Statute of Westminster 1931 was enacted to give statutory force to the constitutional convention that the United Kingdom Parliament would not legislate for Dominions without their consent. Section 4 provides:

> No Act of Parliament of the United Kingdom passed after the commencement of this Act shall extend, or be deemed to extend, to a Dominion as part of the law of that Dominion unless it is expressly declared in that Act that that Dominion has requested, and consented to, the enactment thereof.

Where Parliament confers partial competence on a subordinate legislature, the question arises as to whether the United Kingdom Parliament can revoke that grant of power. The principle that Parliament cannot be bound by the Acts of its predecessor has already been established. The issue here is the relationship between the sovereign Parliament and a Parliament dependent for its powers upon Westminster. This issue arose in *British Coal Corporation v The King*.[91] The Judicial Committee of the Privy Council had to determine whether or not

---

90 See, however, the earlier case of *Nairn and Others v University of St Andrews and Others* [1909] AC 147, in which the House of Lords ruled that the Universities (Scotland) Act 1889, which empowered commissioners to make ordinances, *inter alia*, to enable universities to confer degrees on women, did not impliedly repeal the Representation of the People (Scotland) Act 1868, s 27, which provided for the right to vote, *inter alia*, 'every person whose name is for the time being on the register, ... if of full age, and not subject to any legal incapacity'. In *Jex-Blake v Senatus of the University of Edinburgh* (1873) 11 M 784, following *Chorlton v Lings* (1868) LR 4 CP 374, the court ruled that 'women' were not 'persons' within the meaning to be applied to the right to vote. The House of Lords in *Nairn* ruled that the 1889 Act, empowering universities to grant degrees to women could not be taken to impliedly repeal the 1868 Act so as to confer the right to vote on women. Only Parliament, in the most express terms, could 'effect a constitutional change so momentous and far-reaching', and it could not be taken to have done so by 'so furtive a process' as this later Act ([1909] AC 147, p 161, *per* Lord Loreburn LC). Given the date of this case, and its positioning in the continuing struggle for women's right to vote, which was so consistently obstructed by the courts, the decision is perhaps best understood within the political climate of the time rather than as an illustration of objective legal analysis.

91 [1935] AC 500.

the Canadian legislature had the power to regulate or prohibit appeals in criminal matters to the King in Council. A determination of that matter entailed consideration of the scope of legislative competence of the legislature. The relevant Acts were the British North America Act 1867, the Colonial Laws Validity Act 1865, the Statute of Westminster 1931 and the Canadian Criminal Code which prohibited appeal to the courts of the United Kingdom. The Statute of Westminster had removed any legislative incompetence from the Canadian legislature and accordingly the legislature had full power to enact the section in question. It was accepted by the Judicial Committee of the Privy Council that, whilst the power of the Imperial Parliament remained 'in theory unimpaired' and that, 'as a matter of abstract law', section 4 of the Statute of Westminster could be repealed by the Parliament of the United Kingdom, in practice it could not be: '... legal theory must march alongside practical reality.' *British Coal Corporation v The King* is, however, no more than a recognition of the extrinsic or practical limitations on the exercise of sovereignty, and not of any legal limitations on Parliament's supremacy.

In *Ndlwana v Hofmeyer*,[92] the Appellate Division of the South African High Court adopted the view that such a restriction amounted to a fetter on Parliament's powers: '... freedom once conferred cannot be revoked.'[93] Again, however, it is to be noted that such judicial utterances do no more than recognise the practical political restraints which are imposed on Parliament, not its legal powers. It is correct, therefore, to view such *obiter* as reflecting the distinction between legal and political sovereignty: a point emphasised by Dicey himself.

The question of the status and effect of section 4 of the Statute of Westminster arose once more in *Manuel and Others v Attorney General*.[94] The issue concerned was whether the Canada Act 1982 passed by the United Kingdom Parliament, at the request and consent of Canada, was a valid enactment. The plaintiffs' argument was that the United Kingdom Parliament had no power to amend the Constitution of Canada to the detriment of the native population without their consent. It was argued that section 4 of the Statute of Westminster required not just the consent of the federal Parliament but also that of all the provincial legislatures and the native minority population. The application failed: the Statute of Westminster, as interpreted by the Court of Appeal, did not require the actual consent of a Dominion, but rather the mere recital on the face of the request that the United Kingdom legislate for the Dominion. Having thus failed on that point, the plaintiffs proceeded to argue that the conventional rule, which predated the Statute of

---

92   [1937] AD 229; see, also, *Ibralebbe v R* [1964] AC 900; *Blackburn v AG* [1971] 2 All ER 1380.
93   *Ibid*, p 237. See, also, Owen Dixon, J, 'The law and the constitution' (1935) 51 LQR 611, but cf his later view expressed in *Hughes and Vale Property Ltd v Gair* (1954) 90 CLR 203.
94   [1982] 3 All ER 822.

Westminster 1931, had hardened into a rule of law and was thus as effective as section 4 of the statute. The Court of Appeal rejected that reasoning,[95] maintaining the traditional distinction between conventions and rules of law.

The Acts of Union with Scotland 1706 and Ireland 1800

The Acts of Union, their status and their effect on Parliament's sovereignty have provided a fertile source for academic debate which represents a powerful argument against the unlimited freedom of any Parliament at any time to legislate as it pleases. The whole debate centres on the notion that the new United Kingdom Parliament was, in the words of Professor JDB Mitchell,[96] 'born unfree'. The idea being conveyed here is that the Acts of Union have some form of 'higher law' status which binds and limits the powers of Parliament.

The Union with Scotland Act 1706

As discussed in Chapter 3, prior to the accession to the throne of James I (James VI of Scotland), England and Scotland were both independent sovereign States, each having its own monarch and Parliament. With James's accession to the English throne in 1603, the two countries were united under one monarch but retained their sovereign Parliaments until 1706. The Treaty of Union 1706 effected, conceptually, the abolition of both Parliaments and the birth of the Parliament of Great Britain.

Article I of the Act of Union provides:

> That the two kingdoms of England and Scotland shall upon the first day of May which shall be in the year one thousand seven hundred and seven and for ever after be united into one Kingdom by the name of Great Britain ...

The sovereignty issue has been argued in three cases concerning the Act of Union with Scotland. In *MacCormick v Lord Advocate*,[97] MacCormick sought an injunction against the Lord Advocate, as representative of the Crown, preventing the use of the title Queen Elizabeth II of the United Kingdom of Great Britain. The objection to the use of the title was based on historical inaccuracy[98] and a contravention of Article I of the Treaty of Union which provided for the union of the two countries from 1707. The petition was dismissed as was the subsequent appeal. Lord Cooper, the Lord President, however, proceeded to discuss the doctrine of sovereignty:

---

95 See Marshall, G, *Constitutional Conventions*, 1984, Oxford: Clarendon, Chapter XII.

96 Mitchell, JDB, 'Sovereignty of Parliament – yet again' (1963) 79 LQR 196; and see Munro, CR, *Studies in Constitutional Law*, 1987, London: Butterworths (see, now, 2nd edn, 1999).

97 [1953] SC 396.

98 Queen Elizabeth I was Queen of England, not of Scotland.

The principle of the unlimited sovereignty of Parliament is a distinctively English principle which has no counterpart in Scottish constitutional law. It derives from Coke and Blackstone, and was widely popularised during the 19th century by Bagehot and Dicey, the latter having stated the doctrine in its classic form in his *The Law of the Constitution*. Considering that the Union legislation extinguished the Parliaments of Scotland and England and replaced them by a new Parliament, I have difficulty in seeing why it should have been supposed that the new Parliament of Great Britain must inherit all the peculiar characteristics of the English Parliament but none of the Scottish Parliament, as if all that happened in 1707 was that Scottish representatives were admitted to the Parliament of England. That is not what was done. Further, the Treaty and the associated legislation, by which the Parliament of Great Britain was brought into being as the successor of the separate Parliaments of Scotland and England, contain some clauses which expressly reserve to the Parliament of Great Britain powers of subsequent modification, and other clauses which either contain no such power or emphatically exclude subsequent alteration by declarations that the provision shall be fundamental and unalterable in all time coming, or declarations of a like effect.

I have not found in the Union legislation any provision that the Parliament of Great Britain should be 'absolutely sovereign' in the sense that that Parliament should be free to alter the Treaty at will.

In *Gibson v The Lord Advocate*,[99] the issue tested was whether allowing fishermen of Member States of the European Community to fish in Scottish coastal waters infringed Article XVIII of the Act of Union. Article XVIII provides that:

... no alteration be made in laws which concern private right except for the evident utility of the subjects within Scotland.

The claim was dismissed, Lord Keith ruling that the European Community Regulations did not confer rights or obligations on individual citizens and accordingly were matters of public and not private law and, accordingly, that Article XVIII could not be invoked. On the sovereignty question, Lord Keith stated that:

There were addressed to me interesting arguments upon the question of jurisdiction and the competency of the action. These arguments raised constitutional issues of great potential importance, in particular whether the Court of Session has power to declare an Act of the United Kingdom Parliament to be void, whether an alleged discrepancy between an Act of that Parliament and the Treaty or Act of Union is a justiciable issue in this court, and whether, with particular reference to Article XVIII of the Act of Union, this court has power to decide whether an alteration of private law bearing to be effected by an Act of the United Kingdom Parliament is 'for the evident utility' of the subjects in Scotland. Having regard to my decision on relevancy, these are not live issues in the present case ...

---

99   [1975] 1 CMLR 563.

Like Lord President Cooper, I prefer to reserve my opinion what the position would be if the United Kingdom Parliament passed an Act purporting to abolish the Court of Session or the Church of Scotland or to substitute English law for the whole body of Scots law. I am, however, of the opinion that the question whether a particular Act of the United Kingdom Parliament altering a particular aspect of Scots private law is or is not 'for the evident utility' of the subjects within Scotland is not a justiciable issue in this court. The making of decisions upon what must essentially be a political matter is no part of the function of the court, and it is highly undesirable that it should be. The function of the court is to adjudicate upon the rights and obligations of the individual person, natural or corporate, in relation to other persons or, in certain instances, to the State. A general inquiry into the utility of certain legislative measures as regards the population generally is quite outside its competence.

In *Sillars v Smith*,[100] a similar challenge was lodged over the validity of the Criminal Justice (Scotland) Act 1980, on the basis that the United Kingdom Parliament, which had passed the Scotland Act 1978, which created a legislative Assembly for Scotland, had no power to repeal that Act – as had been done – and accordingly, Parliament, it was argued, had no power to pass the Criminal Justice (Scotland) Act. The claim was dismissed, the court adopting the classical view expressed in *Edinburgh and Dalkeith Railway Company v Wauchope*[101] by Lord Campbell:

> All that a court of justice can look to is the parliamentary roll; they see that an Act has passed both Houses of Parliament, and that it has received the royal assent, and no court of justice can enquire into the manner in which it was introduced into Parliament, what was done previously to its being introduced, or what passed in Parliament during the various stages of its progress through both Houses of Parliament. I therefore trust that no such enquiry will hereafter be entered into in Scotland, and that due effect will be given to every Act of Parliament, both private as well as public, upon the just construction which appears to arise upon it.

Despite the questioning *dicta* of Lords Cooper and Keith on sovereignty, the evidence to date goes clearly against the notion that the Act of Union is legally unalterable. To take but one example, the Protestant Religion and Presbyterian Church Act 1707 provided that 'the true Protestant religion and the worship, discipline and government' of the established church were 'to continue without any alteration to the people of this land in all succeeding generations' was incorporated into the Treaty of Union and declared to be 'a fundamental and essential condition of the ... Union in all times coming'. The Act also required that teachers in universities and schools had to subscribe to the faith. Yet, in 1711, the Scottish Episcopalians Act and the Church Patronage (Scotland) Act were passed to reflect greater religious toleration, and by the Universities (Scotland) Act 1853 and the Parochial and Burgh Schoolmasters

---

100 1982 SLT 539.
101 (1842) 8 Cl & F 710.

(Scotland) Act 1861, the requirement that teachers must subscribe to the Protestant faith was removed.

Further changes in the organisation of the Church were made in the Church of Scotland Act 1921. As Colin Munro asserts, 'this adds up to a substantial number of amendments and repeals in supposedly unalterable legislation'.[102]

The Union with Ireland Act 1800

The Act of Union with Ireland 1800 has given rise to similar arguments, although these arguments are even less convincing than those addressed to the Act of Union with Scotland. The Act of Union was declared to 'last forever'. Article 5 provided for a United Church of England and Ireland that 'shall be and shall remain in full force for ever, and that this be deemed and taken to be an essential and fundamental part of the Union'. Nevertheless, in 1869 the Irish Church was disestablished under the Irish Church Act of that year. In *Ex parte Canon Selwyn*,[103] a clergyman sought an order of mandamus against the Lord President of the Council ordering him to petition the Queen for adjudication of the question whether the giving of the royal assent to the Irish Church Act 1869 was contrary to the coronation oath and the Act of Settlement. The coronation oath contained a commitment to maintain a unified and established Church of England and Ireland. The court dismissed the petition on the basis that the statute was supreme and could not be questioned in a court of law.

The Acts of Union[104] provided for the permanent union between Ireland and Great Britain. However, the Ireland Act 1949 recognised republican status and independence of southern Ireland, thereby terminating the union. The 1949 Act also provided that Northern Ireland:

> ... remains part of His Majesty's dominions and of the United Kingdom and it is hereby affirmed that in no event will Northern Ireland or any part thereof cease to be part of His Majesty's dominions and of the United Kingdom without consent of the Parliament of Northern Ireland.[105]

Under the Northern Ireland Constitution (Amendment) Act 1973, the United Kingdom Parliament reiterated the statutory guarantee that Northern Ireland would not cease to be part of the United Kingdom unless and until a majority of voters should determine otherwise. That commitment is reiterated in section 1 of the Northern Ireland Act 1998. However, such assurances, whilst morally and politically binding on the government, do not amount – under Diceyan theory – to a legal restriction on Parliament's powers. Parliament

---

102 *Op cit*, Munro, fn 96, p 69. See, now, 2nd edn, 1999, Chapter 5.
103 (1872) 36 JP 54.
104 The Act of Union (Ireland) 1800; the Act of Union with Ireland Act 1800.
105 Ireland Act 1949, s 1(2).

remains free, in legal theoretical terms, to legislate contrary to such undertakings, although the political implications of so doing guarantee that Parliament will not do so.

AV Dicey and the Acts of Union

AV Dicey had argued that the Acts of Union had no greater legal status than the Dentists Act 1878, or indeed any other unimportant Act.[106] Moreover, as has been seen, Dicey viewed the Acts of Unions as being ordinary Acts of Parliament by which – in the case of the Union with Scotland – the English and Scottish Parliaments 'abolished' themselves, to be reconstituted as the Parliament of Great Britain, and in the case of the Act of Union with Ireland, were reconstituted as the Parliament of the United Kingdom. The key passage which reveals his view is the following:

> Let the reader, however, note that the impossibility of placing a limit on the exercise of sovereignty does not in any way prohibit either logically, or in matter of fact, the abdication of sovereignty ... A sovereign power can divest itself of authority in two ways, and (it is submitted) in two ways only. It may simply put an end to its own existence. Parliament could extinguish itself by legally dissolving itself and leaving no means whereby a subsequent Parliament could be legally summoned ... The Parliament of England went very near doing this when, in 1539, the Crown was empowered to legislate by proclamation; and though the fact is often overlooked, the Parliaments both of England and of Scotland did, at the time of the Union, each transfer sovereign power to a new sovereign body, namely, the Parliament of Great Britain. This Parliament, however, just because it acquired the full authority of the two legislatures by which it was constituted, became in its turn a legally supreme or sovereign legislature, authorised therefore, though contrary perhaps to the intention of its creators, to modify or abrogate the Act of Union by which it was constituted. If indeed the Act of Union had left alive the Parliaments of England and Scotland, though for one purpose only, namely, to modify when necessary the Act of Union, and had conferred upon the Parliament of Great Britain authority to pass any law which did not infringe upon or repeal the Act of Union, then the Act of Union would have been a fundamental law unchangeable legally by the British Parliament: but in this case, the Parliament of Great Britain would have been, not a sovereign, but a subordinate, legislature, and the ultimate sovereign body, in the technical sense of that term, would have been the two Parliaments of England and of Scotland respectively.[107]

Alternative interpretations of the Acts of Union

The power of Parliament to 'abolish itself' and to be reconstituted as a 'new Parliament' is one of the principal matters to which opponents to Diceyan

---

106 *Op cit*, Dicey, fn 1, p 145.
107 *Op cit*, Dicey, fn 1, p 69.

theory address their arguments. Professor JDB Mitchell, for example, questions Dicey's insistence on the equal legal status of Acts of Parliament, distinguishing between rules which create and represent the foundation of the State, and other derivative rules of law: '... the one set of rules creates or is the legal foundation of the State, the other is built upon that foundation.'[108]

The Acts of Union of Scotland and England creating the unified Parliament of Great Britain represents a 'fresh starting point'. In Mitchell's view, the Acts of Union, being antecedent to the Parliament of Great Britain, imposed valid legal limitations on its powers. Conceding that many legislative changes have been made to the provisions of the Acts of Union, Mitchell nevertheless argues that the provisions, at least in relation to the Church of Scotland and the Court of Session, are essential limitations on Parliament's powers.

Professor Neil MacCormick also challenges Diceyan orthodoxy.[109] In MacCormick's view, the Acts of Union amounted to a rudimentary written constitution. Adopting Kelsenian terminology, the Anglo-Scottish Treaty of 1706 and the Union with Ireland 1800 represent the 'historically first constitution' of Great Britain and the United Kingdom respectively, and accordingly have a very special status in constitutional law. MacCormick is not alone in this thinking: Professors SA de Smith and R Brazier, whom MacCormick cites, accept that the Articles of Union 'provided a rudimentary framework of a written constitution and that the Acts of Union were "constituent Acts"'.[110] Harry Calvert specifically rejects Dicey's view of the effects of the Acts of Union as 'untenable'.[111] Calvert adopts Professor RVF Heuston's[112] arguments regarding the legal status of the Acts of Union and proceeds to argue that the royal assent could be denied – in a departure from constitutional convention – to a Bill purporting to sever the union between Northern Ireland and the rest of the United Kingdom against the wishes of the people, the expression of which has been provided for by statute. Such a severance would, in Calvert's view, be unconstitutional. Accordingly, it would be for the Crown to defeat any attempt to act unconstitutionally:

> [A]t all events, it cannot readily be conceded that a constitutional monarch has no constitutional power to resist being implicated in unconstitutionality by his ministers. The bounds of the British constitution are very widely drawn. There

---

108 *Op cit*, Mitchell, fn 96.

109 MacCormick, N, 'Does the United Kingdom have a constitution? Reflections on *MacCormick v Lord Advocate*' (1978) 29 NILQ 1.

110 de Smith, SA and Brazier, R, *Constitutional and Administrative Law*, 7th edn, 1994, London: Penguin, p 10 (see, now, 8th edn, 1998). See, also, Upton, M, 'Marriage vows of the elephant: the constitution of 1707' (1989) 105 LQR 79.

111 Calvert, H, *Constitutional Law in Northern Ireland*, 1968, London: Stevens, p 21.

112 Heuston, RVF, *Essays in Constitutional Law*, 2nd edn, 1964, London: Stevens, pp 20–30.

is very little that a Prime Minister, supported by his Cabinet and a majority of the House of Commons, cannot do. But if there is nothing that he cannot do, there is no constitution at all.[113]

Manner and form and redefinition theories

Parliament, in the exercise of its sovereign power, may specify particular procedures which must be undertaken in order to enact legislation. It has been seen, for example, that the Northern Ireland Constitution (Amendment) Act 1973[114] provided that the six counties of Northern Ireland shall not cease to be part of the United Kingdom unless the proposed separation is approved by a majority of the electorate in a border poll (referendum). This may be interpreted to mean either that Parliament has specified the procedure – or manner and form – for enacting laws, or that Parliament has 'redefined' itself for the purposes of enacting laws, by including in the definition of Parliament the electorate of Northern Ireland. Any provision relating solely to procedure but not affecting the composition of Parliament may be termed a 'manner and form' provision; whereas when the actual composition of Parliament is altered, the appropriate term is 'redefinition'. The Northern Ireland (Amendment) Act straddles both theories.

The essential question to be asked is whether such provisions, however labelled, are capable of binding a future Parliament. If that were to be the case – and, as will be seen, there are supporters for that view – two possible conclusions would follow: first, that Parliament has unlimited power – exercisable, as HLA Hart argues,[115] only at one single point in time, forever after to limit the sovereignty of future parliaments; and, secondly, that future Parliaments would be less than sovereign – a contradiction in terms, for it would not then be correct to speak of Parliament having unlimited sovereignty.

A seminal case illustrating manner and form theory is that of the *Attorney General for New South Wales v Trethowan*.[116] In 1929, the government of New South Wales, Australia, sought to prevent a subsequent government from abolishing the Legislative Council (the upper chamber). An Act of Parliament was passed, amending the Constitution Act 1902, providing that any Bill purporting to abolish the upper House must have the approval of both legislative chambers and of two-thirds of the members of each chamber. Further, there had to be popular electoral support for the abolition, to be determined in a referendum. In addition, to prevent a subsequent Parliament

---

113 *Op cit*, Calvert, fn 111, p 32.
114 Discussed above, pp 238–39, and see, further, Chapter 3.
115 See above, pp 214–16.
116 [1932] AC 526; (1931) 44 CLR 394.

ignoring the provisions of the 1929 Act, it was provided that any Bill attempting to repeal the 1929 Act must follow the same procedure: a device known as 'double entrenchment'. In 1930, following an election, the incoming government decided to abolish the upper chamber and to do so by ignoring the provisions of the 1929 Act. Members of the Legislative Council sought an injunction restraining the grant of the royal assent to the Bill, and a declaration that such a grant of assent would be unlawful.[117] The High Court of Australia ruled that the provisions of the 1929 Act could not be avoided, and that the royal assent could not be given to the Bill.[118] The matter was referred to the Privy Council which affirmed the judgment of the High Court of Australia.

The constitutional reason underlying the court's rejection of the government's claim that the 1932 Bill could lawfully receive the royal assent was that the Parliament in New South Wales was a legislative body having subordinate and not supreme power. Such powers as the legislature enjoyed were derived from the sovereign United Kingdom Parliament under the Constitution Acts 1902–29 and the Colonial Laws Validity Act 1865. The Colonial Laws Validity Act 1865 represented a landmark in the clarification of powers between the sovereign United Kingdom Parliament and subordinate colonial legislatures. The Act gave statutory affirmation to the non-legal conventional rule that laws enacted in the colony which were contradictory to statute or the common law of the United Kingdom would not be held to be invalid by the courts of the United Kingdom. The Act further clarified the extent to which the colonial legislature had power to amend its own composition and procedure. Section 5 is the all-important provision for current purposes. Section 5 provides that:

> ... every representative legislature shall ... have and be deemed at all times to have had, full power to make laws respecting the constitution, power, and procedure of such legislature; provided that such laws shall have been passed in such manner and form as may from time to time be required by any Act of Parliament, letters patent, Order in Council, or colonial law, for the time being in force in the said colony.

It is this section which dictated the decision in *Attorney General for New South Wales v Trethowan*.[119] The government of New South Wales was not free to introduce the 1931 Bill and to attempt to enact it other than in conformity with the requirements of section 5. Section 5 required that the legislature complied with the 'manner and form' provisions in force. The specific 'manner and form' provisions were those laid down in the 1929 Constitution Act, and these requirements could not merely be ignored by the subordinate legislature.[120]

---

117 Being *ultra vires* the lower House.

118 [1932] AC 526; (1931) 44 CLR 394.

119 *Ibid*.

120 Australia Act 1986 (Commonwealth and UK), s 3(1), provides that the Colonial Laws Validity Act 1865 shall not apply 'to any law made after the commencement of this Act by the Parliament of a State'.

In the High Court of Australia in the *Trethowan* case, Rich J denied the proposition that the New South Wales Parliament had unlimited sovereign power.

A similar constitutional arrangement can be seen demonstrated by the South African case of *Harris v The Minister of the Interior*,[121] which tested the validity of the Separate Representation of Voters Act 1951. The South Africa Act 1909, an Act of the United Kingdom Parliament, established the constitution of South Africa. Section 152 of the South Africa Act provided that no repeal or alteration of section 35 (relating to the qualification of Cape coloured voters) should be valid unless the Bill was passed by both Houses of Parliament sitting together, and the third reading was agreed to by not less than two-thirds of the members of each House.

In 1931, the United Kingdom Parliament passed the Statute of Westminster. The Statute of Westminster gave statutory effect to the constitutional convention which previously governed the relationship between the United Kingdom and its Dominions.[122] Section 2 of the Act provided that:

(1) The Colonial Laws Validity Act 1865 shall not apply to any law made after the commencement of this Act by the Parliament of a Dominion.

(2) No law and no provision of any law made after the commencement of this Act by the Parliament of a Dominion shall be void or inoperative on the ground that it is repugnant to the law of England, or to the provisions of any existing or future Act of Parliament of the United Kingdom, or to any order, rule or regulation made under any such Act, and the power of the Parliament of a Dominion shall include the power to repeal or amend any such Act, order, rule or regulation in so far as the same is part of the law of the Dominion.

Section 4 of the Act provided that:

An Act of the United Kingdom Parliament passed thereafter shall not extend, or be deemed to extend, to a Dominion as part of the law of that Dominion unless it expressly declared in the Act that that Dominion has requested, and consented, to its enactment.

In 1951, the South African Parliament purported to pass the Separate Representation of Voters Act, depriving voters in the Cape of the right to vote, disregarding the provisions of section 152 of the South Africa Act. It was argued before the Appellate Division of the Supreme Court of South Africa that the Statute of Westminster had conferred full legislative authority, or sovereignty, on the South African Parliament and that, accordingly, Parliament was no longer bound by the South Africa Act 1909. The Supreme Court rejected that argument, stating that the South Africa Act was a

---

121 1952 (2) AD 428; 1 TLR 1245.
122 Canada, South Africa, Australia, New Zealand and Eire (the Republic of Ireland).

constitutional Act whose provisions could not be indirectly amended by the Statute of Westminster. The Court held that the Statute of Westminster was not intended to alter the South Africa Act, but rather to confer additional powers on the legislature. Cantilevres CJ drew a distinction between a truly sovereign legislative body, such as the United Kingdom Parliament, and a legislative body which was less than sovereign: '... a State can be unquestionably sovereign although it has no legislature which is completely sovereign.'

In *Bribery Commissioner v Ranasinghe*,[123] section 55 of the 1946 Constitution of Ceylon (now Sri Lanka) required that the appointment and dismissal of the holders of judicial office be vested in a Judicial Services Commission. Section 29(4) of the constitution required that amendments to the constitution required a certificate stating that the amendments had been passed by the requisite two-thirds majority.

In 1954, a Bribery Act was passed (with the necessary certificate) giving to the Attorney General powers to investigate and prosecute allegations of bribery. In 1958, a Bribery Tribunal was established, headed by a Bribery Commissioner. No certificate was produced as required under section 29(4). The central issue was whether or not the legislature was free to avoid provisions of the constitution. The Supreme Court held that it could not. On appeal to the Privy Council, Lord Pearce stated:

> ... it has been argued that the court, when faced with an official copy of an Act of Parliament, cannot inquire into any procedural matter and cannot now properly consider whether a certificate was endorsed on the Bill. That argument seems to their Lordships unsubstantial and it was rightly rejected by the Supreme Court. Once it is shown that an Act conflicts with a provision in the constitution, the certificate is an essential part of the legislative process ... The English authorities have taken a narrow view of the court's power to look behind an authentic copy of the Act. But, in the constitution of the United Kingdom, there is no governing instrument which prescribes the law making powers and the forms which are essential to those powers ... The courts have a duty to look for the certificate in order to ascertain whether the constitution has been validly amended. Where the certificate is not apparent, there is lacking an essential part of the process necessary for amendment ...

These cases demonstrate one fundamental principle: that legislative bodies do not necessarily enjoy full sovereign power, and that some form of 'higher law' may control their powers. In each of these cases, the powers of the legislatures of New South Wales, South Africa and Ceylon (as it then was) had been established under an Act of the sovereign United Kingdom Parliament. That being so, the legislative bodies had to comply with the constitutional laws in force, and failure to do so would give the courts the jurisdiction to declare a legislative act void.

---

123 [1965] AC 172.

No one may question the validity of an Act of Parliament

True it is, that what the Parliament doth, no authority on earth can undo.[124]

As has been seen, an Act will be accepted as valid by the courts provided that it has passed through the requisite legislative stages and received the royal assent. Early evidence of this fundamental rule is revealed in *The Prince's Case:*[125]

> If an Act of Parliament be penned by assent of the King, and of the Lords Spiritual and Temporal, and of the Commons, or, it is enacted by authority of Parliament, it is a good Act; but the most usual way is, that it is enacted by the King by the assent of the Lords, Spiritual and Temporal and of the Commons ... but if an Act be penned, that the King, with the assent of the Lords, or with the assent of the Commons, it is no Act of Parliament, for three ought to assent to it, [namely] the King, the Lords, and the Commons, or otherwise, it is not an Act of Parliament ...

Regardless of the subject matter of the Act, it will be upheld by the judges.[126] In the time before the 1688 settlement, it was not uncommon for judges to proclaim that an Act of Parliament could be held to be invalid because it conflicted with some higher form of divine law. Blackstone[127] expressed the view that a human law which conflicted with the law of nature would be invalid.

In *Dr Bonham's Case,*[128] there is the often-cited *obiter dictum* of Coke CJ to the effect that:

> When an Act of Parliament is against common right and reason, or repugnant, or impossible to be performed, the common law will control it, and adjudge such act to be void.

Such views, while appealing to the senses, were of doubtful validity when expressed and have no authority today. The opinion of Lord Reid expressed in *Pickin v British Railways Board*[129] represents the correct contemporary judicial view on the authority of statute:

> In earlier times many learned lawyers seem to have believed that an Act of Parliament could be disregarded in so far as it was contrary to the law of God or the law of nature or natural justice, but since the supremacy of Parliament was finally demonstrated by the revolution of 1688 any such idea has become obsolete.

---

124 Blackstone, W (Sir), *Commentaries on the Laws of England* (1765–69), Chicago: Chicago UP, Vol I, pp 160–61.

125 (1606) 8 Co Rep 1a, p 20b.

126 But, see, further, below, and Chapter 9, on the complexity arising by virtue of membership of the European Community.

127 *Ibid*, Blackstone, Vol I, p 41.

128 (1610) 8 Co Rep 114, p 118, discussed in Chapter 6.

129 [1974] AC 765, p 782.

Non-legal constraints on Parliament powers

Political acceptability to the electorate represents the strongest external basis of restraint. All governments are accountable to the electorate, albeit in terms of a direct vote only periodically.[130] But elections do not of themselves always provide the means of sanctioning governments, nor do they guarantee that government invariably acts in accordance with the electorate's wishes. Still less can the electorate be regarded as exercising any power to enact law. Whilst the electorate may be correctly regarded as politically sovereign, and can, at the 'end of the day', oust a government which violates its trust, on the exercise of the franchise the electorate conditionally transfers sovereign legislative power to Parliament. As Dicey puts it:

> The electors can in the long run always enforce their will. But the courts will take no notice of the will of the electors. The judges know nothing about any will of the people except in so far as that will is expressed by an Act of Parliament, and would never suffer the validity of a statute to be questioned on the ground of having been passed or being kept alive in opposition to the wishes of the electors.[131]

Whereas, therefore, the power of the electorate is great at the time of a general election, it is a more limited power during a government's term of office – most particularly where the government has a strong majority in Parliament. It will be seen in Chapters 14–17 that it is the task of Parliament as a whole, both Commons and Lords, to scrutinise government policy and legislative proposals, and that a range of procedural devices exists which facilitate such inquiry. It is through Parliament that the will or wishes of the electorate for the most part find expression. Parliament may be seen as the sounding board of the nation. As John Stuart Mill observed:

> Parliament ... [is] at once the nation's Committee of Grievances, and its Congress of Opinions: an arena in which not only the general opinion of the nation, but that of every section of it, and as far as possible of every eminent individual whom it contains, can produce itself in full light and challenge discussion; where every person in the country may count upon finding some body who speaks his mind, as well as or better than he could speak it himself – not to friends and partisans exclusively, but in the face of opponents, to be tested by adverse controversy; where those whose opinion is overruled, feel satisfied that it is heard, and set aside not by a mere act of will, but for what are thought superior reasons, and commend themselves as such to the representatives of the majority of the nation ...[132]

No government can afford to ignore Parliament and, ultimately, a government can be brought down if its policies are such that it loses the

---

130 See Chapters 13–16.

131 *Op cit*, Dicey, fn 1, pp 73–74.

132 Mill, JS, *Representative Government* (1865), 1958, Indianapolis: Bobbs-Merrill, Chapter V, pp 99–100.

confidence of the House as a whole.[133] If Parliament is truly the 'sounding board of the nation', Parliament must reflect the political morality within society.[134]

A further political restraint imposed on governments relates to international relations. No State today exists in isolation from its neighbours. The United Kingdom, as with most States, is bound by numerous treaties under international law which impose restrictions on the freedom of government action. Across virtually every aspect of government, such restraints are visible: environmental protection, protection of human rights, the protection of children from abduction, the regulation of currency exchanges, agreements on trade and tariffs and so on. In addition to such treaties, the United Kingdom is bound in practical terms by membership of the European Community and Union and the United Nations. In theoretical terms, therefore, Parliament may remain free to enact laws violating any or all of the United Kingdom's international obligations: in practice, it would not and could not.

ACADEMIC ARGUMENTS AGAINST THE TRADITIONAL DOCTRINE OF SOVEREIGNTY

We have seen above that there are a number of sophisticated academic arguments concerning the traditional doctrine of sovereignty. In this brief section, the differing approaches are brought together for further consideration.[135]

In *Bribery Commissioner v Ranasinghe*,[136] Lord Pearce had asserted that:

The proposition which is not acceptable is that a legislature, once established, has some inherent power derived from the mere fact of establishment to make a valid law by the resolution of a bare majority which its own constituent instrument has said shall not be a valid law unless made by a different type of majority or by a different legislative process.

Geoffrey Marshall seizes upon this *dictum* and argues that Lord Pearce:

... seemed to imply equally that both non-sovereign and sovereign legislatures may be made subject to procedural rules entrenching parts of the law from simple majority repeal.

Marshall goes further and states that:

---

133 On votes of confidence, see Chapter 6.

134 See Allan, TRS, 'The limits of parliamentary sovereignty' [1985] PL 614; and Lee, S, 'The limits of parliamentary sovereignty' [1985] PL 633.

135 And see the views of HLA Hart, discussed above, pp 214–16.

136 [1965] AC 172, p 198.

What can be certainly inferred from *Ranasinghe* is that a legislature whose constitutional instrument places procedural restraints upon the forms of law making may not ignore them simply because it is sovereign in the sense of having plenary power to make law for the peace, order and good government of the territory.[137]

His conclusion from an examination of *Ranasinghe* is significant:

It helps to confirm that existing English authority does not rule out the possibility that the Queen in Parliament might legislate so as to provide a special manner and form for specified types of legislation.[138]

Sir Ivor Jennings has also questioned the orthodox Diceyan view. In *The Law and the Constitution*,[139] Jennings distinguishes two situations:

If a prince has supreme power, and continues to have supreme power, he can do anything, even to the extent of undoing the things which he has previously done. If he grants a constitution, binding himself not to make laws except with the consent of an elected legislature, he has power immediately afterwards to abolish the legislature without its consent and to continue legislating by his personal decree.

But if the prince has not supreme power, but the rule is that the courts accept as law that which is in the proper legal form, the result is different. For when the prince enacts that henceforth no rule shall be law unless it is enacted by him with the consent of the legislature, the law has been altered, and the courts will not admit as law any rule which is not made in that form. Consequently a rule subsequently made by the prince alone abolishing the legislature is not law, for the legislature has not consented to it, and the rule has not been enacted according to the manner and form required by the law for the time being.

The difference is this. In the one case, there is sovereignty. In the other, the courts have no concern with sovereignty, but only with the established law. 'Legal sovereignty' is merely a name indicating that the legislature has for the time being power to make laws of any kind in the manner required by law. That is, a rule expressed to be made by the Queen, 'with the advice and consent of the Lords spiritual and temporal, and Commons in this present Parliament assembled, and by the authority of the same', will be recognised by the courts, including a rule which alters this law itself. If this is so, the 'legal sovereign' may impose legal limitations upon itself, because its power to change the law includes the power to change the law affecting itself.

Sir Ivor Jennings then illustrates his thesis by reference to *Attorney General for New South Wales v Trethowan*,[140] *Ndlwana v Hofmeyer*[141] and *Harris v The*

---

137 *Op cit*, Marshall, fn 47, pp 55–56.
138 *Op cit*, Marshall, fn 47, p 57.
139 *Op cit*, Jennings, fn 78, p 152.
140 [1932] AC 526; (1931) 44 CLR 394.
141 [1937] AD 229.

Minister of the Interior.[142] Jennings concedes that the decisions do not necessarily 'determine the law as it applies in the United Kingdom', and leaps from that proposition to one which claims that Dicey 'failed to prove that that law made the King in Parliament a sovereign law making body'.[143] Such a view is unconvincing. The constitutional justification for the decisions examined lay precisely in the fact that both the legislatures of New South Wales and South Africa had legislative powers conferred upon them by a fully sovereign superior sovereign body – the United Kingdom Parliament. Only once such complete sovereignty was conferred would the legislative fetters be removed. No such controlling device pertains to the Parliament of the United Kingdom itself.

Arguing from the proposition that Parliament may redefine itself – as in the Parliament Act 1911[144] – and may alter its own composition – as in the Life Peerages Act 1958,[145] Professor JDB Mitchell turns to 'the purported self-limitations of Parliament'.[146] On section 4 of the Statute of Westminster, Mitchell argues that there are two possible interpretations when looked at from the point of view of the United Kingdom judges. The first is that section 4 amounts to a rule of construction directed to the courts, which does not raise the problem of limitation on Parliament. If, however, section 4 is understood to mean that Parliament has forfeited its legislative capacity – by conferring that capacity on the recipient legislature – then there 'is quite clearly a purported limitation of the United Kingdom Parliament'.[147] Parliament has redefined itself in a manner which excludes its power to legislate for the Dominion.

Mitchell cites in support of the argument the *dictum* of Lord Radcliffe in *Ibralebbe v The Queen* in which Lord Radcliffe argues that while the United Kingdom Parliament has the legal power to legislate for Ceylon (as it then was), to use such power would be 'wholly inconsistent' with the powers of legislation conferred on the legislature of Ceylon.[148]

Further authorities could be offered in support of this view. As seen above, in *British Coal Corporation v The King*,[149] Lord Sankey LC said, in relation to section 4, that:

---

142 1952 (2) SA 428.

143 *Op cit*, Jennings, fn 78, p 156.

144 The Parliament Act 1911 reduced the powers of the House of Lords with respect to legislation. See Chapter 17.

145 See Chapter 17.

146 Mitchell, JDB, *Constitutional Law*, 2nd edn, 1968, Edinburgh: Green, p 78.

147 *Ibid*, p 79.

148 [1964] AC 900.

149 [1935] AC 500.

... indeed, the Imperial Parliament could, as a matter of abstract law, repeal or disregard section 4 of the statute. But that is theory and has no relation to realities.[150]

Further, in *Ndlwana v Hofmeyer*,[151] Lord Denning asserted that 'freedom once given cannot be revoked'. How should such claims be evaluated? First, as Dicey made clear, the United Kingdom Parliament – in the exercise of its sovereign power – clearly has the power to abolish itself, or to surrender its sovereignty in favour of another legislature, as in grants of independence. In political terms, it is, of course, unthinkable that Parliament would attempt to revoke such independence. The more troublesome question is whether Parliament retains the capacity to revoke such grants of freedom in legal terms. On this, Dicey was very clear:

'Limited sovereignty', in short, is, in the case of a Parliamentary as of every other sovereign, a contradiction in terms.[152]

Dicey exemplifies his view by reference to the Taxation of Colonies Act 1778. Section 1 of the Act provides that Parliament:

... will not impose any duty, tax, or assessment whatever, payable in any of His Majesty's colonies, provinces, and plantations in North America ...

Is this a self-limiting ordinance which fetters sovereignty? Dicey continues:

The point calling for attention is that, though policy and prudence condemn the repeal of the Taxation of Colonies Act 1778 or the enactment of any law inconsistent with its spirit, there is, under our constitution, no legal difficulty in the way of repealing or overriding this Act. If Parliament were tomorrow to impose a tax, say, on New Zealand or on the Canadian Dominion, the statute imposing it would be a legal valid enactment.[153]

Professor RVF Heuston has put forward a 'new view' of sovereignty.[154] This view is summarised as follows:

(a) sovereignty is a legal concept: the rules which identify the sovereign and prescribe its composition and functions are logically prior to it;

(b) there is a distinction between rules which govern, on the one hand: (i) the composition; and (ii) the procedure, and, on the other hand; (iii) the area of power, of a sovereign legislature;

(c) the courts have jurisdiction to question the validity of an alleged Act of Parliament on grounds b(i) and b(ii), but not on ground b(iii); and

---

150 [1935] AC 500, p 520.
151 [1937] AD 229.
152 *Op cit*, Dicey, fn 1, p 68.
153 *Op cit*, Dicey, fn 1, p 67.
154 *Op cit*, Heuston, fn 112, Chapter I. See, also, *op cit*, Munro, fn 96, Chapter 4.

(d) this jurisdiction is exercisable either before or after the royal assent has been signified – in the former case by way of injunction, in the latter by way of declaratory judgment.[155]

To what extent is it correct to state that the judiciary may 'question the validity of an alleged Act of Parliament' on the grounds of the composition and the procedure adopted within Parliament? Clearly, as demonstrated by *Attorney General for New South Wales v Trethowan*[156] and other comparable cases, under certain circumstances, it is within the jurisdiction of the courts to question whether or not an Act is valid. Those circumstances invariably arise within jurisdictions having subordinate rather than supreme legislatures.

In this regard, it may be said that the judges are protecting the sovereignty of the United Kingdom Parliament by keeping subordinate legislatures within the powers conferred. In the United Kingdom, however, Parliament is distinguishable by the absence of any such controlling powers. The orthodox position is that expressed in *British Railways Board v Pickin*,[157] where the House of Lords, affirming its earlier decision,[158] endorsed the 'enrolled Bill rule'. Thus, once the Bill has proceeded through Parliament, either under the normal legislative process[159] or under the Parliament Acts 1911 and 1949,[160] and received the royal assent, the Bill becomes a validly enacted Act of Parliament and will not be impugned by the courts. The courts have jurisdiction to determine what is an Act of Parliament. As has been seen earlier, the courts have held, by way of illustration, that mere resolutions of the House of Commons are incapable of having legal effect in the same manner as an Act: *Stockdale v Hansard*[161] and *Bowles v Bank of England*[162] are clear authorities for that view. Nevertheless, the procedure adopted by Parliament is not a matter within the jurisdiction of the courts and, on the authority of *Pickin's* case, it is not for the courts to go behind the 'parliamentary roll' and inquire into procedural aspects of law making. Sovereign power entails the right to determine composition and procedure.[163]

The central distinguishing feature between the jurisdictions concerned in the 'manner and form' cases and the United Kingdom lies in the existence of a

---

155 *Op cit*, Heuston, fn 112, p 7. Professor Heuston is supported in his approach by Jennings, *op cit*, fn 78, Chapter 4, Appendix III; Cowen, DV, *Parliamentary Sovereignty and the Entrenched Sections of the South Africa Act*, 1951, Cape Town: Juta; Marshall, G, *Parliamentary Sovereignty and the Commonwealth*, 1957, Oxford: Clarendon, Chapters 2–4.

156 [1932] AC 526; (1931) 44 CLR 394.

157 [1974] AC 765.

158 *Edinburgh and Dalkeith Railway Co v Wauchope* (1842) 8 Cl & F 710.

159 See Chapter 15.

160 See Chapter 17.

161 (1839) 9 Ad & E 1, p 108.

162 [1913] 1 Ch 57.

163 See, further, Chapter 18.

higher legislative authority. In each case, it was the United Kingdom Parliament which defined and limited the powers of a subordinate legislative body. Only once a Parliament enjoys full sovereignty can it be free of such constraints. The United Kingdom Parliament, by contrast, is 'uncontrolled': there exists no higher source of legal authority than Parliament itself. For this reason, to draw an analogy between the legislatures of New South Wales or South Africa and the United Kingdom misses the vital dimension of unlimited power which is enjoyed by the United Kingdom Parliament.

The last words on the manner and form arguments shall be left to Professors Wade[164] and Munro.[165] Professor Wade summarises his views on manner and form theorists as follows:

> But, in the end, what is the substance of their argument? It is simply their prediction, made with varying degrees of dogmatism, that the judges will, or should, enforce restrictions about manner and form and abandon their clear and settled rule that the traditional manner and form is what counts. But if it is vain for Parliament to command the judges to transfer their allegiance to some new system of legislation if the judges are resolved to remain loyal to the old one, it is still more vain for professors to assert that they should. The judicial loyalty is the foundation of the legal system and, at the same time, a political fact.

Professor Munro finds the arguments as to manner and form equally unconvincing, stating that 'the cases cited by the "manner and form" school do not, in the end, seem very helpful'.

PARLIAMENTARY SOVEREIGNTY AND THE EUROPEAN UNION AND COMMUNITY

In Chapters 8 and 9, the aims, organisation and law making power of the institutions of the European Community are considered, and the relationship between the law of the United Kingdom and the European Community will become clearer after that chapter has been studied. Nonetheless, it is necessary to consider here, in outline, the impact of membership of the European Community on the doctrine of parliamentary supremacy.

The United Kingdom became a member of the European Communities[166] in 1973. The original Communities – now termed European Community – have their own constitutional structure as defined in the Treaties. The Court of Justice of the Communities has, since the 1960s, asserted the supremacy of

---

164 Wade, HWR, *Constitutional Fundamentals*, rev edn, 1989, London: Stevens.

165 Munro, CR, *Studies in Constitutional Law*, 2nd edn, 1999, p 160.

166 European Economic Community, European Coal and Steel Community, European Community for Atomic Energy.

Community law over the laws of any Member State.[167] As will be seen later, the Court of Justice has adopted the view that, by becoming signatories to the Treaties, Member States have limited their own legislative competence in Community matters, conferring the supreme power to legislate on these matters on the law making institutions of the Community.

The laws of the Community – the Treaties, laws enacted by the Commission, Council of Ministers and the European Parliament together with the judicial decisions of the European Court – are binding on all Member States. In the United Kingdom, the acceptance of Community law is under the European Communities Act 1972 – an Act of the United Kingdom Parliament. Accordingly, all Community law derives its force and authority under this Act, which, as with any Act, has no special legal status within the constitution. However, membership of the Community raises some unique questions for the sovereignty of Parliament.

The principal issue for consideration is the attitude of the judges – both domestic and Community – towards Community law. It is clear that, from the perspective of the European Court, Community law prevails over domestic law, and that domestic legislatures have no power to enact binding legislation contrary to the requirements of Community law. From the domestic perspective, however, the issue is not so clear-cut. The issues which require explanation are:

(a) the extent to which the judges are prepared to accept and apply Community law;

(b) the manner in which, and extent to which, inadvertent or deliberate parliamentary Acts are reconciled with the requirements of Community law; and

(c) whether membership of the Community entails an irrevocable relinquishment of parliamentary supremacy.

The application of Community law

Section 2 of the European Communities Act 1972 provides that Community law shall have direct applicability in the United Kingdom:

(1) All such rights, powers, liabilities, obligations and restrictions from time to time created or arising by or under the Treaties, and all such remedies and procedures from time to time provided for by or under the Treaties, as in accordance with the Treaties are without further enactment to be given legal effect or used in the United Kingdom shall be recognised and available in law, and be enforced, allowed and followed accordingly; and

---

167 See the early cases of *Costa v ENEL* [1964] CMLR 425; *Van Gend en Loos* [1963] CMLR 105; *Simmenthal* [1977] 2 CMLR 1; *Internationale Handelgesellschaft* [1972] CMLR 255.

> the expression 'enforceable Community right' and similar expressions shall be read as referring to one to which this sub-section applies.

Section 2(4) provides for the primacy of Community law, without expressly stating that the law of the Community is supreme:

> The provision that may be made under sub-section (2) above[168] includes, subject to Schedule 2 of this Act, any such provision (of any such extent) as might be made by Act of Parliament, and any enactment passed or to be passed, other than one contained in this part of this Act, shall be construed and have effect subject to the foregoing provisions of this section.

Accordingly, all the rights, powers, liabilities, obligations and restrictions provided for under section 2(1) are to be given effect by the courts, and section 2(4) operates as a rule of construction to the courts to interpret law in accordance with the requirements of Community law. The manner in which the courts have achieved the objectives expressed in the European Communities Act 1972 are considered in Chapters 8 and 9 as is the view of the European Court of Justice on the supremacy of Community law. However, it would be misleading to leave this chapter on the traditional Diceyan theory of sovereignty without giving some introductory overview of the challenge which European Community law has posed. The European Court of Justice (the ECJ) adopts as its guiding principle the supremacy of the law of the Community. In the Court of Justice's view, a new legal order has been founded, a sovereign legal order within its sphere of competence. The sovereignty of Community law must, according to the ECJ, be respected by Member States, because through accession to the European Community, Member States have 'surrendered' their sovereign power in relation to those matters now regulated by the Community and Union.

The European Court of Justice has adopted several means by which to expand the applicability of Community law and to assert its supremacy. First, as will be seen in Chapters 8 and 9, the Treaty of Rome, as amended, under Article 10,[169] imposes a duty on all Member States to comply with Community law and not to impede the application of Community law. Secondly, Article 249 of the EC Treaty[170] provides that regulations[171] made under the Treaty (in part) 'shall be binding in its entirety and directly applicable in all Member States'. This principle of 'direct effect' has been adapted and developed by the ECJ to ensure the harmonious application of Community law throughout the legal systems of the now 15 Member States. The doctrine of 'indirect effect' is also a concept developed and expanded by

---

168 Which provides for implementation of Community obligations by secondary legislation.
169 Formerly, Art 5.
170 Formerly, Art 189.
171 A form of secondary legislation.

the ECJ, and, as will be seen, has far-reaching implications for the courts and legislatures of each Member State. Where provisions of Community law have direct or indirect effect, the individual citizen of that State has a right of redress against the Member State, or against bodies which the ECJ deems to be 'emanations of the State', and, under certain circumstances, the right to compensation from the State. Moreover, while the ECJ does not expressly rule on the validity of domestic legislation, it will, when its jurisdiction is raised, rule on the requirements of Community law as interpreted by the Court, and, once that interpretation is received by the domestic courts, that interpretation *must* be given effect – notwithstanding incompatible domestic law.

While it would be premature to reach firm judgment on the fate of conventional Diceyan theory before studying the structure, organisation and objectives of the European Community and Union (on which, see Chapters 8 and 9), some tentative conclusions may be suggested. Without rehearsing the arguments set out above, there are two differing approaches which may be taken to this conundrum. First, it may be argued that unreconstructed Diceyan theory remains unimpaired, despite all appearances and arguments to the contrary, on the basis that the United Kingdom voluntarily acceded to the European Community, the force of Community law within domestic law deriving from the 1972 European Communities Act. That Act, as seen, is consistent with constitutional law and convention – not entrenched (nor could it be) – and remains, in legal theory, repealable. From this perspective, parliamentary sovereignty remains the fundamental rule of the common law, and the key to the source of sovereignty lies with the judges. While the judges continue to cling to the rationale that Community law is given effect – even to the point of setting aside legislation[172] – because of the rule of construction provided under section 2 of the European Communities Act 1972, judicial loyalty remains unaffected. The clearest evidence for this view is expressed by Lord Bridge, when he states that:

> By virtue of section 2(4) of the Act of 1972, Part II of the Act of 1988 [the Merchant Shipping Act] is to be construed and take effect subject to enforceable Community rights – this has precisely the same effect as if a section were incorporated in Part II of the Act 1988 ...[173]

Moreover, it will be seen from the cases of *Macarthys v Smith*[174] and *Garland v British Rail Engineering Ltd*[175] that both the Court of Appeal and House of Lords, respectively, endorsed the view that, while effect must, in accordance with section 2(4) of the European Communities Act 1972, be given to Community law, if Parliament chose expressly to legislate contrary to

---

172 This issue being central to the *Factortame* cases, discussed in Chapter 9.

173 *R v Secretary of State for Transport ex parte Factortame (No 2)* [1991] 1 AC 603.

174 [1979] 3 All ER 325.

175 [1983] 2 AC 751. Both cases are discussed in Chapter 9.

Community law, that intention would be given effect by the judges. No more so would this be clearer than if Parliament, implausible though this hypothesis may seem, chose to repeal the 1972 Act.

Alternatively, it could possibly be argued, as HWR Wade has argued,[176] that, for the first time in constitutional history, Parliament succeeded in 'entrenching' a provision (section 2(4) of the 1972 Act), so as to bind future parliaments. This position, Wade submits, is more than evolutionary: it represents more than a rule of construction to be applied by the courts, and is rather an illustration of the Parliament of 1972 imposing 'a restriction upon the Parliament of 1988'.[177] If this argument had substance, there would indeed have been a 'revolution' in the constitution. However, the argument does not convince in light of the *dicta* of the judges, exemplified by that of Lord Bridge cited above, which confirms the conventional allegiance of the judiciary to the United Kingdom Parliament. Moreover, as will be seen in Chapter 9, successive cases raising questions on Community law have come before the Court of Appeal and House of Lords in which the courts have found the requisite interpretative mechanism to accommodate the requirements of Community law as interpreted by the Court of Justice. Judicial interpretative techniques are the essence of the common law, and the essence of the common law is its capacity to evolve in accordance with the socio-political and legal domain within which it resides. There is little that is 'revolutionary' – in relation to the ultimate 'rule of recognition' of the constitution – in the seminal cases which have, for example, in the development of judicial review,[178] incorporated into statutory requirements the common law rules of natural justice, and restricted Parliament's capacity to exclude (or oust) the jurisdiction of the courts, even in the face of apparently clear statutory language to the opposite effect. In this light, the insistence on the part of the domestic courts that section 2(4) of the European Communities Act 1972 is a rule of construction to be applied to future legislation is hardly 'revolutionary' but rather more a recognition of the requirements of the European legal order and the overriding force of Community law for which the 1972 Act provided.

The preoccupation with parliamentary sovereignty is understandable given that conventionally sovereignty has, in the absence of a written constitution, represented the 'cornerstone' or foundation of the British constitution. Membership of the European Community and Union, and the insistence of the European Court of Justice on the supremacy of Community law, inevitably challenges traditional understandings of that concept, and

---

176 See Wade, HWR, 'Sovereignty – revolution or evolution' (1996) 112 LQR 568, but see the counter-arguments put forward by TRS Allan, responding to Wade's analysis, in Allan, TRS, 'Parliamentary sovereignty: law, politics and revolution' (1997) 113 LQR 443.

177 *Ibid*, Wade, p 570.

178 On which, see Chapters 24 and 25.

raises hitherto unforeseen questions. While traditional Diceyan theory can accommodate membership of the Community and Union, it can do so only by clearly demarcating, as did its author, the realms of the legal and political. Legal theory resides against the backcloth of the political. Political sovereignty, while the United Kingdom remains a member of the Community and Union, may (arguably) lie in the institutions and law making processes of the Community and Union, in which every Member State participates, and which is supported by the political will of the citizens of the Member States. That political sovereignty, while membership continues, has a profound impact on the extent to which the domestic legislature may legislate over areas within the ambit of the treaties establishing the Community and Union. Thus, as Dicey himself argued, back in the nineteenth century under fundamentally different socio-economic and political conditions, the extra-legal may de facto limit the exercise of sovereign power. This de facto limitation on *legal sovereignty* remains ultimately conditional on the political commitment of the United Kingdom government and people to continued membership of that unique legal order which it voluntarily joined in 1972.

Constitutional reform and parliamentary sovereignty

As noted above, the devolution of power to regional assemblies (in the case of Wales and Northern Ireland) and the Scottish Parliament and the Human Rights Act 1998 which 'incorporates' the European Convention on Human Rights into domestic law both raise the issue of sovereignty. While full discussion of these matters is found in Chapters 12 and 22 respectively, it is useful here to consider the sovereignty issue.

Devolution

The Scotland Act, Government of Wales Act and Northern Ireland Act 1998 each establish a system of self-government, in differing degrees, for the nations of the United Kingdom other than England. In London, as a pilot project, a new layer of government has been introduced with the new Greater London Authority and the office of Mayor for London. Since the powers devolved are the will of Parliament, the continued existence of such power remains dependent upon Parliament's will. This ultimate power to confer and rescind powers granted to subordinate bodies is nothing new: at a lower governmental level, there is the granting of limited autonomy, defined by Act of Parliament and controlled by the courts, whereby local authorities have long enjoyed a measure of self-governance. This statement, however, and the legal provisions which give it expression, disguise a fundamentally important factor in the devolution debate: the dependence of legal-theoretical sovereignty upon the political sovereignty of the people of the nations.

It is the devolution of legislative power to the Scottish Parliament which illustrates the complexity of the sovereignty issue most starkly. Northern Ireland, which has enjoyed devolved power in the past (from 1922 to 1972), and, in practice, extensive autonomy from Westminster, has, because of its troubled history, always been a special case: the partition of the North from the South and the Protestant majority in the North has resulted in a highly Unionist state, notwithstanding the republican ambitions of the Irish Republican Army and its political arm, *Sinn Fein*. Wales, on the other hand, although demonstrating varying degrees of nationalism, has never in recent history previously enjoyed self-government, nor expressed a majority opinion in favour of separation from the United Kingdom. By contrast with Northern Ireland and Wales, Scotland has retained a strong sense of national identity since the union with England in 1707, has a memory of national independence and a distinctive identity expressed through its own legal system.

Politically, the Scottish electorate was disaffected by the Conservative government which ruled from 1979 until 1997, which enhanced a sense of isolation from central government and an increase in nationalist demands for devolution. Whereas in the mid-1950s, Conservative candidates polled over 50 per cent of the vote, by 1987 this was down to 24 per cent[179] and by the 1997 general election, the Conservative Party had not a single Member of Parliament from north of the border. With Conservative support dwindling, Labour became the dominant party in Scotland, in 1992, securing 49 seats with 39 per cent of the vote. By contrast, the overtly nationalist and separatist Scottish National Party (SNP) won only three seats with 21.5 per cent of the vote. When Tony Blair succeeded John Smith in 1994 as Leader of the Labour Party, his sights were set on devolution. Mindful of the failures of previous attempts at devolution, most particularly in 1978 when the Scotland Act passed but failed to come into effect because there was insufficient support expressed by the people of Scotland in a referendum, Tony Blair insisted that referendums be held prior to introducing legislation in order to test public opinion. Once in office, the Scottish referendum held in 1997 gave the people's clear view: 74.3 per cent voting in favour of a Scottish Parliament, and 63.5 per cent voting in favour of the Parliament having tax-varying powers.

The Labour Government, while enthusiastic about devolution to the regions, was also intent on preserving the United Kingdom and the sovereignty of the United Kingdom Parliament. This was expressed strongly in the Government's White Paper, *Scotland's Parliament*:[180] '... the United Kingdom Parliament is and will remain sovereign in all matters.' Section 28(7) of the Government of Scotland Act gives clear expression to this intention: '... this section does not affect the power of the Parliament of the United

---

179 See, Thatcher, M, *The Downing Street Years*, 1993, London: HarperCollins, pp 618–24.
180 Cm 3648, para 42.

Kingdom to make laws for Scotland.' In order to reinforce the Union with Scotland, Scottish representation was not, in the short term, to be reduced at Westminster. The Scotland Act did, however, provide for a future reduction in Scottish representation — with section 86 of the Act providing that the rule that Scotland is to have no less than 71 parliamentary constituencies in the Parliamentary Constituencies Act 1986 be amended to remove the over-representation of Scotland at Westminster.

However, notwithstanding expressions of intent as to continued sovereignty and adjustments to Scottish representation at Westminster, the political reality of the transfer of legislative power and the authority given to the Scottish Parliament by virtue of the referendum result paints a rather different picture. While Westminster retains the right to legislate over 'reserved matters', which are adjudged to be of United Kingdom-wide concern rather than national concern, the legislative powers devolved are considerable. The theoretical stance that Westminster remains free to legislate for Scotland over such matters must be in doubt. While Northern Ireland enjoyed devolved power, the convention developed that Westminster would not legislate over areas devolved and, moreover, that domestic affairs of Northern Ireland would not even be debated at Westminster. Were the United Kingdom Parliament to attempt to legislate over Scottish domestic affairs which have been devolved to Edinburgh, against Scottish wishes, real conflict would arise — and no assertions of the sterile sovereignty of Westminster would quell political dissent from north of the border. Further, while the government chose to continue the office of Secretary of State for Scotland, his or her role is purely one which facilitates communication and co-operation between Edinburgh and London. Real power lies with the First Secretary — in effect, if not in name, the 'Prime Minister' of Scotland — and it is to him that the people look for political leadership in relation to Scottish affairs. The First Secretary's role extends to direct participation in European Union matters, thus giving Scotland an individual voice separate from that of the rest of the United Kingdom and one which can represent particular Scottish concerns over all issues falling within the European Union remit.

All of this adds up to considerable legislative and political autonomy for Scotland and its people. What, then, is left of 'the sovereignty of the United Kingdom Parliament' in conventional Diceyan terms? *Theoretically*, two aspects of sovereignty remain. The first is the ability – notwithstanding the political unreality – to legislate for Scotland contrary to Scottish wishes. The second is the power to abolish the Scottish Parliament and to reclaim the powers devolved. Given that the government chose first to seek the endorsement of the people for devolution before devolving power, the likelihood of either theoretical power being exercised, *without the support and consent of the people of Scotland*, is negligible. It will be recalled that, in

MacCormick v Lord Advocate,[181] Lord Cooper questioned the notion that the Treaty of Union resulted in the adoption of the 'distinctively English principle [of sovereignty] which has no counterpart in Scottish constitutional law'. Under Scottish constitutional law, it has always been the case that it is the people, and not a Parliament, which is sovereign: the Scottish people exercised their sovereignty in choosing to have their own Parliament. Whether the future entails an independent Scotland outside the United Kingdom, or Scotland within some form of quasi-federal relationship with the rest of the United Kingdom, must be a matter for the political judgment of the Scottish people.

The use of referendum[182]

The use of referendum raises the question of whether or not Parliament redefines itself to include the people – in a direct expression of their views – for the purpose of legislating. The referendum has been used in relation to constitutional matters in Northern Ireland in 1973 and 1998; in relation to devolution to Scotland and Wales in 1977 and 1997; in London in 1998 in relation to the establishment of a directly elected mayor the re-establishment of a London-wide elected authority; and in the United Kingdom as a whole in 1975 in relation to the United Kingdom's continued membership of the European Communities. The Labour government elected in 1997 is committed to the use of referendum in relation to constitutional reform. Accordingly, further referendums are planned in relation to devolution to English regions, and are expected to be used in relation to reform of the House of Lords and a single European currency. However, referendum, as conceived in the United Kingdom, does not affect Parliament's legal sovereignty. While the opinion of the people may be regarded as morally binding on government, Parliament's sovereignty is preserved through regarding the result of a referendum as not legally binding the government or Parliament.

The Human Rights Act 1998

As with the devolution of power to the nations, the manner in which the government chose to incorporate the European Convention on Human Rights into domestic law is based on the premise of ensuring the Parliament retains its sovereignty over law making. Whereas under most constitutions which include fundamental guarantees protecting human rights, those rights are

---

181 1953 SC 396.

182 See Butler, D and Ranney, A (eds), *Referendums around the World*, 1994, Basingstoke: Macmillan; Marshall, G, 'The referendum: what? when? how?' (1997) 50 Parl Aff 307; Munro, CR, 'Power to the people' [1997] PL 579.

protected from encroachment by the legislature, and the legislature thereby limited in what it may enact – and subject to the rulings of a constitutional court – the Human Rights Act 1998 utilises a peculiarly British device which preserves Parliament's theoretical sovereignty. As discussed in more detail in Chapter 22, the Act provides that judges in the higher courts may issue 'declarations of incompatibility' between statute and the Convention rights incorporated under the Act. Where such a declaration is made, the matter is then transferred to the Executive, which may choose whether and how to amend the law to bring it into line with Convention rights. Further, where proposals for legislation are introduced into Parliament, the relevant Minister must declare whether the Bill in question accords with Convention rights. If it does not, an explanation as to the necessity for the legislation must be given. While both of these measures will undoubtedly improve the protection of rights and generate a more rights conscious society, they fall far short of making individual rights and freedoms immune from legislative change. Moreover, consistent with conventional constitutional theory, the Human Rights Act 1998 has not been accorded any special status: its existence and scope remains – as with other seminal acts of constitutional import – subject to Parliament's will.

However, the traditional theory of sovereignty, as applied to the Human Rights Act 1998, disguises the importance of the constitutional change which the Act represents. The delay in implementing the Act in England until 2000 was in large measure dictated by the need for all governmental and other public bodies, private bodies exercising public functions and judges, to be conversant with the scope for the Act and to have reviewed policies and practices so as to avoid challenges under the Act. As has already been seen in Scotland, where the Act came into force in 1998, the Act has brought about successful challenges reaching to the heart of the criminal justice system. The ruling in *Starrs and Chalmers v Lord Advocate*,[183] requires a basic reconsideration of the position of temporary sheriffs, whose re-appointment and security of tenure lies in the discretion of the Executive, in relation to Article 6 of the Convention which guarantees the right to a fair trial before an independent and impartial tribunal. Within the English legal system, the position of temporary High Court judges and Assistant Recorders will require review in light of the Scottish decision. The role of lay magistrates – before whom over 90 per cent of criminal cases are determined – has also fallen for review in advance of the Act coming into effect in England.[184] Lay magistrates (who now number some 30,000) determine criminal cases according to the evidence and are advised on points of law by the justices' clerk, who plays no role in the decision. No reasons for the decision are given, and the legal advice of the clerk is not subject to scrutiny. The requirements of

---

183 (1999) *The Times*, 17 November. Discussed in Chapter 5, pp 152–53.
184 Under the chairmanship of Auld LJ.

Article 6 of the Convention include a duty to give reasons for decisions. The role of the clerk may become more prominent, possibly becoming a full member of the bench and thereby ensuring that magistrates reach decisions in accordance with the legal advice of the clerk.

Over and above the criminal justice system, all aspects of policy and practices of public and quasi-public bodies will fall for scrutiny in accordance with Convention requirements. The right to respect for 'private and family life' under Article 8 is likely to spawn challenges to laws which discriminate between married and unmarried couples, and between same sex couples who are denied equal parental rights over children of the family. The powers of local authorities to restrict the exercise of parental rights over children in their care will also fall for scrutiny. The ban on gays and lesbians serving in the armed forces has already been abandoned in light of rulings by the European Court of Human Rights and in advance of implementation of the Human Rights Act 1998. Surveillance techniques employed by the police may also be challenged under the right to respect for private and family life. These are but speculative illustrations of the potential scope of the Human Rights Act which will become entrenched at the heart of the legal system, providing a yardstick against which all actions of government and other public bodies may be judged. Of immediate concern here is the issue of sovereignty.

While the government adopted a constitutional mechanism which preserves Parliament's sovereignty, and maintains the conventional (and subordinate) role of the judiciary, the working of the Act is more subtle than the re-statement of sovereignty implies. The judges are under a duty to interpret legislation in a manner which gives effect to Convention requirements, save where such an interpretation is impossible. Here, there is a significant shift in the process of judicial reasoning which traditionally focuses on interpreting the 'latest will of Parliament' as expressed in legislation. The requirement that Ministers must state that legislative proposals are in compliance with Convention requirements, coupled with the directive to judges to interpret in line with Convention rights, gives rights a special constitutional, moral and legal status. That the ultimate decision to amend the law in line with a declaration of incompatibility rests with the executive and Parliament does not suggest a lessening in the importance of rights so much as an ingenious device by which to keep constitutional fundamentals – sovereignty and separation of powers – intact, rather than turning the constitution on its head by reversing the balance of power between judges and Parliament. Nevertheless, the Act does give to judges an unprecedented scope for statutory interpretation and development of the common law in line with Convention rights: the extent to which judges grasp the opportunity remains a matter for future evaluation, as does the judgment as to the extent to which moral prior restraints have been imposed on the Executive and Parliament.

PART III

THE EUROPEAN COMMUNITY AND UNION

CHAPTER 8

STRUCTURE AND INSTITUTIONS[1]

The law relating to the European Community is now a wide ranging subject. European Community law intrudes upon, and affects, an ever increasing volume of domestic law and now represents an important source of law in the United Kingdom.[2] The original treaties establishing the three European Communities have been much amended. Moreover, in 1992, the Treaty on European Union was signed by the heads of the governments of Member States. The 1992 Treaty brought into being[3] the European Union, the aims of which go far beyond the original objectives of the European Economic Community and seek to provide the further integration of the laws and policies of Member States. The 1992 Treaty (TEU 1992) also extended the competence of the institutions of the Community. The Treaty on European Union 1997 (TEU 1997, the Treaty of Amsterdam) marks the latest stage in the development of the Union, representing:

> ... a new stage in the process of European integration undertaken with the establishment of the European Communities.[4]

The Treaty of Amsterdam 1997 confirms the Union's 'attachment to the principles of liberty, democracy and respect for human rights and fundamental freedoms and of the rule of law'.[5] The political objectives of the Union are extensive, seeking to achieve European economic and monetary union, the promotion of economic and social progress, 'taking into account the principle of sustainable development and within the context of the accomplishment of the internal market and of reinforced cohesion and environmental protection', common defence and foreign policy,[6] and the

---

1   See, *inter alia*, Hartley, T, *The Foundations of European Community Law*, 4th edn, 1998, Oxford: Clarendon; Rudden, R and Wyatt, D, *Basic Community Laws*, 5th edn, 1994, Oxford: Clarendon; Mathijsen, PSRF, *A Guide to European Union Law*, 1995, London: Sweet & Maxwell, 1995; Steiner, J, *Textbook on EEC Law*, 5th edn, 1996, London: Blackstone and *Enforcing EC Law*, 1995, London: Blackstone; Charlesworth, A and Cullen, H, *European Community Law*, 1994, London: Pitman; Craig, P and de Búrca, G, *European Community Law*, 2nd edn, 1998, Oxford: OUP; Weatherill, S and Beaumont, P, *EU Law*, 3rd edn, 1999, Harmondsworth: Penguin.

2   See Chapter 2.

3   Entering into force in November 1993.

4   TEU 1997, Preamble.

5   Note that the Treaty of Amsterdam revises all the Articles of the EC Treaty, and those of the TEU 1992. For the sake of clarity, both the new and the former Treaty provisions will be referred to in the text. The new Article numbers are cited first, with the former numbers in brackets, except in relation to case law relating to EC Treaty Articles before revision of the Treaty, where the new Article numbers are shown in brackets.

6   TEU 1997, Art 11 (formerly, TEU 1992, Art J.1).

complete elimination of border controls within the Union. These objectives are expressed in Article 2 of the 1997 Treaty (formerly, Article B of the Treaty on European Union 1992) as follows:

The Union shall set itself the following objectives:

- to promote economic and social progress and a high level of employment and to achieve balanced and sustainable development, in particular through the creation of an area without internal frontiers, through the strengthening of economic and social cohesion and through the establishment of economic and monetary union, ultimately including a single currency in accordance with the provisions of this Treaty;

- to assert its identity on the international scene, in particular through the implementation of a common foreign and security policy including the progressive framing of a common defence policy, which might lead to a common defence, in accordance with the provisions of Article 17;

- to strengthen the protection of rights and interests of the nationals of its Member States through the introduction of a citizenship of the Union;

- to maintain and develop the Union as an area of freedom, security and justice, in which the free movement of persons is assured in conjunction with appropriate measures with respect to external border controls, asylum, immigration and the prevention and combating of crime;

- to maintain in full the *acquis communautaire* and build on it with a view to considering to what extent the policies and forms of co-operation introduced by this Treaty may need to be revised with the aim of ensuring the effectiveness of the mechanisms and the institutions of the Community.

The objectives of the Union shall be achieved as provided in this Treaty and in accordance with the conditions and the timetable set out therein while respecting the principle of subsidiarity as defined in Article 5 of the Treaty establishing the European Community.

The principles on which the Union is based are set out in Article 6 of the 1997 Treaty (formerly, Article F of the Treaty on European Union 1992):

1   The Union is founded on the principles of liberty, democracy, respect for human rights and fundamental freedoms, and the rule of law, principles which are common to the Member States.

2   The Union shall respect fundamental rights, as guaranteed by the European Convention for the Protection of Human Rights and Fundamental Freedoms signed in Rome on 4 November 1950 and as they result from the constitutional traditions common to the Member States, as general principles of Community law.

3   The Union shall respect the national identities of its Member States.

4   The Union shall provide itself with the means necessary to attain its objectives and carry through its policies.

The current membership of the Union, with dates of accession, is as follows: Austria (1995), Belgium (1957), Denmark (1972), Finland (1995), France (1957),

Germany (1957), Greece (1981), Ireland (1972), Italy (1957), Luxembourg (1957), Netherlands (1957), Portugal (1985), Spain (1985), Sweden (1995), United Kingdom (1973).[7]

HISTORICAL ORIGINS

To understand the origins of the Union, it is necessary to look back to 1945 and a Europe which had been devastated by war: economically, politically and socially. In the desire to attain some form of harmony in order to guarantee peace and to rebuild Europe, the movement towards the integration of European countries was started. The movement took several forms. In 1948, the Organisation for Economic Co-operation and Development (OECD) was established with financial aid from the United States of America in order to restructure the European economies. In 1949, the North Atlantic Treaty Organisation (NATO) was formed as a military alliance between the United States, Canada and Europe.

In 1949, the Council of Europe was established, out of which the European Convention of Human Rights was born.[8] In 1950, under the leadership of the French Foreign Minister, Robert Schuman, a plan was devised whereby the raw materials of war, coal and steel, would be placed under the control of a supra-national organisation and, thus, the European Coal and Steel Community (ECSC) was established under the Treaty of Paris, signed in 1951. The original Member States were Germany, France, Belgium, Italy, Luxembourg and the Netherlands. Initiatives were being introduced to provide supra-national regulation of the non-military use of atomic energy. At the same time, the move towards greater economic co-operation and the creation of a European trading area was underway. The results of these developments took the form of the Treaties of Rome signed in 1957, establishing the European Economic Community (EEC) and the European Atomic Energy Community (Euratom).

The EEC had the broadest aims of the three communities, seeking to create a European common market and close co-operation between Member States. The Community is based on four basic principles: freedom of persons, goods, capital and services.

---

7   Norway was a signatory to the TEU, but ratification of the Treaty, and hence membership of the Union, was rejected by the people of Norway in a referendum in 1994. Proposals are under consideration for an expansion of the European Union from 15 Member States to 26 or possibly 28: the majority of applicants are Eastern European States. Poland, the Czech Republic, Slovenia, Hungary, Cyprus and Estonia are candidates for early entry into the Union. Romania, Bulgaria, Slovakia, Latvia and Lithuania have also applied for membership. Malta announced, in 1996, that its request to accede to the Union was suspended. Special arrangements for co-operation between Malta and the EU are under negotiation.

8   See Chapter 22, and, further, below.

THE ORIGINAL INSTITUTIONS

The Treaty establishing the ECSC provided for four institutions which today form the nucleus of the institutional framework of the Community: the High Authority, being the executive body serving the interests of the Community; the Council, being the executive representing the interests of Member States; the Assembly (a non-elected Parliament), and the European Court of Justice (ECJ). On the introduction of Euratom and the EEC, separate High Authorities and Councils were established, all three Communities sharing the Assembly and the Court.

Having established three Treaties with different organs and differing powers, the next logical step was to merge the institutions. This merger came about in 1965,[9] under a Treaty establishing a single Council and single Commission of the European Community: the Merger Treaty.

The current organisation of the Community derives from the increasingly dynamic movement towards greater economic and political union between the now 15 Member States. A brief examination of the evolutionary stages in the Community makes the position clearer.

1957–87

The original Common Market, created under the European Economic Community Treaty (EEC Treaty) signed in 1957 – which the United Kingdom joined in 1973 – has changed markedly. From 1957 until 1987, the EEC Treaty remained unchanged, although membership of the Community expanded from the original six[10] Members to 12.[11]

The Single European Act 1986[12]

In 1986, the Single European Act (SEA) was passed.[13] This Act – a European Treaty – provided a timetable for realising the objectives of the original treaties – namely the free movement of capital, goods, persons and services – by 31 December 1992. In addition, the Single European Act increased the powers of the European Parliament. The Single European Act also changed

---

9   Coming into force in 1967.

10 France, Germany, Italy, Luxembourg, Belgium and Holland.

11 The United Kingdom, Ireland and Denmark joined in 1973, Greece in 1981, Spain and Portugal in 1986.

12 See Campbell, A, 'The SEA and its implications' (1988) 35 ICLQ 932 and Pescatore, P, 'Some critical remarks on the Single European Act' (1987) 24 CML Rev 9.

13 The European Communities (Amendment) Act 1986.

the voting procedure to be adopted in many areas of decision making in Europe. It did this by weakening the requirement of unanimous voting for decisions made by the Council of Ministers and increasing the extent to which the 'qualified majority voting system' would apply (see, further, pp 296–99). By doing this, the Single European Act provided that individual Member States could be outvoted in decision making, thus making Europe stronger and the power of the Member States to block European legislation weaker.[14] Furthermore, the Single European Act increased the competence of the Community institutions, including new areas such as the environment and regional development policy,[15] consolidated the legal basis of the European Monetary System,[16] and took steps towards greater political co-operation and foreign policy making.

The Treaty on European Union 1992 (Maastricht)

In December 1991, a new agreement was reached by Heads of Governments in Maastricht which significantly expanded the aims and objectives of the Community. This agreement resulted in the Treaty on European Union (TEU) – the Maastricht Treaty – which was signed in February 1992. It was to come into force once ratified (approved) by individual Member States, according to their own constitutional arrangements. Because of difficulties with ratification,[17] it was to be November 1993 before the Treaty came into force.

The Treaty, resulting from inter-governmental negotiations, represented a compromise between the federalists (or 'integrationists') and the anti-federalists (or 'inter-governmentalists'). It needs to be understood that, in the development of the Community, there has been exhibited a constant tension between those Member States who see the movement towards almost total political and economic union, whereby the Community would take on the characteristics of a federal State, and those Member States (particularly the United Kingdom) who have reservations about greater fusion in Europe and wish to retain a higher degree of autonomy from Europe than the federalists would wish to see. These Member States, the anti-federalists or inter-governmentalists, accordingly resist the drive towards federalism, preferring development to proceed along more piecemeal lines and to be pursued

---

14 See EC Treaty, Art 205 (formerly, EC Treaty, Art 148(2)), discussed below, p 297.

15 See Krämer, L, *The EEC Treaty and Environmental Protection*, 1992, London: Sweet & Maxwell; Scott, J, *Development Dilemmas in the EC: Rethinking Regional Development Policy*, 1995, Milton Keynes: OU Press; Scott, J, *European Community Environmental Law*, 1998, London: Longman.

16 In *de facto* operation since 1979.

17 In the United Kingdom, the government, fearing that Parliament would fail to approve ratification, threatened to ratify under the royal prerogative – a decision which led to an unsuccessful application for judicial review: see *R v Secretary of State for Foreign and Commonwealth Affairs ex parte Rees-Mogg* [1994] 2 WLR 115 and, further, Chapter 6.

through inter-governmental agreement rather than movements from the centre of the Community.

As a result of these tensions, rather than drafting a Treaty to supplement the existing Treaties and to provide a coherent working 'constitution' for Europe, based on the principle of a more federalist Union, the Treaty has produced a structure in which the Union is 'founded on the European Community, supplemented by the policies and forms of co-operation'[18] laid down by the Treaty on European Union. The Treaty has two main sections. The first group of provisions represent a series of amendments to the EEC Treaty (and the ECSC and Euratom Treaties). The provisions make it clear that, in future, the EEC Treaty is to be known as the EC Treaty and the European Economic Community as the European Community. The EC Treaty now comprises the original Treaty of Rome, as amended by the Single European Act, as further amended by the Treaty on European Union 1992 (Maastricht Treaty) and the Treaty on European Union 1997 (Treaty of Amsterdam).[19] Once again, the aims and powers – or competence – of the Community are extended, and changes are made in the relationship between the various Community institutions. Consumer protection, culture and public health represent three areas over which Community powers have been extended. There is further consolidation in some areas, for example, regional development and the environment. The Treaty also provides a framework and timetable for progress towards economic and monetary union. Article 17 of the revised EC Treaty (amended by the Treaty on European Union 1997) confers citizenship of the European Union on all nationals of Member States within the Union.

The Treaty on European Union 1992 involved the creation of the European Union, which has far wider aims than the EC, which is now part of the Union. Accordingly, the second part of the Treaty on European Union, as now amended by the Treaty on European Union 1997, provided a framework for co-operation on future developments. The areas concerned are common foreign and security policy and justice and home affairs. There are now three 'pillars' which represent the structure of the Union. The first pillar amends the EEC Treaty (and renames it the EC Treaty). The second pillar introduces and regulates common foreign and security policy. The third pillar concerns justice and home affairs. The Common Foreign and Security Policy and Justice and Home Affairs (now called Police and Judicial Co-operation in Criminal Matters) pillars are, however, fundamentally different from the first. The first pillar, comprising European Community law, is regulated by the institutions of the Community – the Council of Ministers, the European Commission, European Parliament and the European Court of Justice. In relation to the

---

18   TEU 1997, Art 1 (formerly, TEU 1992, Art A); see Curtin, D, 'The constitutional structure of the Union: a Europe of bits and pieces' (1993) 30 CML Rev 17 for a critical account.

19   On which, see below, p 273.

second and third pillars, the decision making process is quite different. In relation to both foreign and security policy and justice and home affairs (the latter of which includes immigration policy), decisions are to be reached by way of inter-governmental co-operation. This means that decisions will be reached through agreements to co-operate and co-ordinate policy – agreements which will require ratification or implementation at national level. In relation to these matters, in pillars two and three, the European Court of Justice will have no jurisdiction other than where the Council of the European Community decides that it should have. There are thus two differing sets of laws: the laws of the European Community and the law of the European Union, with the court involved only in relation to the Community, other than where the Council of the Community determines otherwise. Accordingly, the role of both the Commission and the European Parliament is substantially diminished in relation to the second and third pillars of the Union.[20] However, as discussed below, the 1997 Treaty amends the pillar structure, placing much of Justice and Home Affairs into the European Community pillar, while leaving parts of Justice and Home Affairs in pillar three and regulated as noted above.

Monetary union

The Maastricht Treaty involved economic and monetary union as a central process towards further European integration. Jacques Delors[21] envisaged economic and monetary union as the 'left boot and right boot for Europe to wear in its advance towards the ever closer union of the peoples of Europe'.[22]

The Maastricht Treaty also introduced two new Community institutions which are discussed further below. The European Central Bank is given law making and other powers[23] and will play a pivotal role in economic and monetary union. The Court of Auditors, having responsibility for scrutinising Community administration, becomes the fifth institution of the EC, its members having a six year renewable term of office and being under the same requirements of independence from governments as the Commission.[24]

---

20 For an overview, see d'Oliveira, HUJ, 'Expanding external and shrinking internal borders: Europe's defence mechanisms in the areas of free movement, immigration and asylum', in O'Keefe, D and Twomey, PM (eds), *Legal Issues of the Maastricht Treaty*, 1994, London: Chancery.

21 Former President of the Commission.

22 Delors Report: *Report on Economic and Monetary Union in the Community* (1989) cited by Dunnett, DRR, 'Legal and institutional issues affecting economic and monetary union', in *ibid*, O'Keefe and Twomey, Chapter 9.

23 EC Treaty, Arts 105–09; Art 237 (formerly, EC Treaty, Art 180(d)); Art 230 (formerly, EC Treaty, Art 173); Arts 232–34 (formerly, EC Treaty, Arts 175–77); Art 288 (formerly, EC Treaty, Art 215); Protocol 3. Protocol annexed to the EC Treaty on certain provisions relating to the United Kingdom of Great Britain and Ireland, 1997.

24 *Ibid*, Art 246 (formerly, EC Treaty, Art 188).

Article 8 of the EC Treaty (formerly, Article 4a) provides that a European System of Central Banks (ESCB) shall be established, and a European Central Bank (ECB), whose powers are derived from the Treaty and from the Statute of the ESCB and of the ECB. The timetable for monetary union was set by the Treaty on European Union 1992, which anticipated that Member States satisfying the 'convergence criteria' should withdraw their own currencies[25] and adopt the euro in 1999[26] – unless the Member State has derogated (or opted out) from this provision. Central to this process is the role of the European Central Bank, which was established under the Maastricht Treaty.[27] The Bank is under a duty to 'translate the objective [of economic and monetary union] into monetary targets and to work towards their achievement'. Member States are under a duty not to have 'excessive government deficits',[28] and the Commission has a duty to monitor Member States' compliance. If a Member State fails to comply with its duty, the Commission will make recommendations to the State concerned. If the State does not correct matters, the Council may then impose sanctions.[29] The Council also has the power to decide 'whether a Member State shall have a derogation from entry into the third stage of monetary union and whether to abrogate [formally cancel or annul] such a derogation'.[30] In reaching such decisions, the Council acts by a qualified majority – not unanimously. Thus, an individual Member State cannot block the decision. The Council is given wide powers in relation to the European Bank, which will become the primary financial institution of the Community. For example, the European Bank will be involved in fixing the exchange rates in the stages up to adoption of the single currency, reaching agreements concerning the exchange rate for the ECU and between the ECU and non-EC currencies. The United Kingdom, while meeting the convergence criteria for joining, has opted out of this scheme,[31] but is free to opt in in the future, and the Labour government intends to take Britain into the economic and monetary union at the earliest appropriate moment, having established first how the initial stage of monetary union is working.

---

25 TEU 1992, Art 109j(3). The date set for certifying compliance with the criteria was 27 February 1998. On that date, 11 Member States were deemed to be qualified to join monetary union in January 1999.

26 EC Treaty, Art 121 (formerly, EC Treaty, Art 109j).

27 *Ibid*, Art 8 (formerly, EC Treaty, Art 4a).

28 *Ibid*, Art 104(1) (formerly, EC Treaty, Art 104c).

29 *Ibid*, Art 104(11) (formerly, EC Treaty, Art 104c(11)).

30 *Ibid*, Art 111 (formerly, EC Treaty, Art 109).

31 Protocol annexed to the EC Treaty on certain provisions relating to the United Kingdom of Great Britain and Ireland 1997, para 1.

The Treaty on European Union 1997 (Treaty of Amsterdam)[32]

Since the creation of the European Union, the original Communities exist side by side with the expanded objectives of seeking common policies on justice and home affairs, and foreign and security policy. The Treaty on European Union 1997 introduced significant alterations to the three pillars, in addition to making a number of other important changes which are discussed below. In relation to the structure of the Union, the 1997 Treaty transfers aspects of free movement of persons, asylum and immigration to the European Community, while crime and the police remain in pillar three.

While the 1992 Maastricht Treaty established the Union and the principles on which it is based, many matters remained unresolved and for future determination. As a result, the Treaty provided for an inter-governmental conference to be convened in 1996 in order to reach decisions on matters which remained outstanding. Moreover, it was perceived by many that, in relation to Justice and Home Affairs, the inter-governmental decision making process introduced at Maastricht was deficient. Paradoxically, while the Maastricht Treaty, particularly in the United Kingdom, was attended by great political debate and controversy, the Treaty of Amsterdam,[33] which gives substance to many of the commitments undertaken in principle at Maastricht, was concluded with relatively little public debate.

The objectives determined for the 1996 inter-governmental conference were both to remedy some of the perceived defects of the Maastricht Treaty and to prepare the Union for its proposed expansion to 26 Members. In summary, the Treaty of Amsterdam marks significant changes in respect of four principal areas:

(a) freedom, security and justice;

(b) the Union and the citizen;

(c) common foreign and security policy;

(d) the Union's institutions.

Each of these is considered below.

Closer co-operation

The difficulties experienced in accommodating differing perceptions concerning the Union, and incorporation into domestic systems of all Union

---

32 See *European Union Consolidated Treaties*, 1997, Luxembourg: Office for Official Publications of the European Communities; Petite, M, 'The Treaty of Amsterdam' (www.law.harvard.edu/programs/JeanMonnet/papers/98/98-2-.html); Editorial, 'The Treaty of Amsterdam: neither a bang nor a whimper' (1997) 34 CML Rev 767.

33 Incorporated into domestic law under the European Communities (Amendment) Act 1998.

and Community measures, has led to the adoption of flexibility, under the guise of 'closer co-operation'. Difficulties over the social protocol, European monetary union, border controls and common defence policy represent some of the areas over which a lack of unity exists. The Treaty of Amsterdam formalises the concept by inserting a general flexibility clause into the common provisions of the Treaty on European Union and also makes provision for Member States to avail themselves of Community institutions and procedures, in order to establish closer co-operation between themselves, subsequent to authorisation by the Council, acting on a qualified majority on a proposal from the Commission and after consulting the European Parliament.[34]

Limitations on the degree of flexibility permissible are provided in Article 11 of the EC Treaty (formerly, Article 5a), which provides, in part, that action taken by Member States in pursuit of closer co-operation:

(a) does not concern areas which fall within the exclusive competence of the Community;

(b) does not affect Community policies, actions or programmes;

(c) does not concern the citizenship of the Union or discriminate between nationals of Member States;

(d) remains within the limits of the powers conferred upon the Community by this Treaty; and

(e) does not constitute a discrimination or a restriction of trade between Member States and does not distort the conditions of competition between the latter.

Special rules apply to the situation where a Member State considers that the proposed action would adversely affect important aspects of national policy. Where that arises, a vote in Council shall not be taken on a qualified majority, but rather the Council may request that the matter be referred to the European Council of Heads of Government for a decision to be taken unanimously. In effect, this formalises the Luxembourg Accords, on which, see, further, below, and enables a single Member State to block proposals for closer co-operation.

Freedom, security and justice

Fundamental rights and freedoms

Article 6 of the EC Treaty (formerly, Article F of the Treaty on European Union 1992), provides that:

---

34 See de Búrca, G and Scott, J (eds), 'Constitutional change in the European Union', in *From Uniformity to Flexibility*, 2000, London: Hart.

1   The Union is founded on the principles of liberty, democracy, respect for human rights and fundamental freedoms, and the rules of law, principles which are common to the Member States.

2   The Union shall respect fundamental rights, as guaranteed by the European Convention for the Protection of Human Rights and Fundamental Freedoms signed in Rome on 4 November 1950 and as they result from the constitutional traditions common to the Member States, as general principles of Community law.

3   The Union shall respect the national identities of its Member States.

4   The Union shall provide itself with the means necessary to attain its objectives and carry through its policies.

The Maastricht Treaty had reaffirmed the commitment of the Union to fundamental rights and freedoms as secured under the European Convention on Human Rights. In order further to advance the protection of rights, the Treaty of Amsterdam introduces three new elements. First, the Treaty confirms that the European Court of Justice has the power to review respect for fundamental rights by the Community institutions. In relation to the European Convention, to which all Member States of the Union, but not the Union itself are signatories, the Treaty provides that Community law is subject to the European Convention, but as applied by the Court of Human Rights in Strasbourg. Limited judicial review is also available in respect of the third pillar. In relation to matters pertaining to foreign and security policy, however, judicial review does not lie, this issue having proved too contentious at the Conference.

In addition to affirming respect for fundamental rights and freedoms, the Treaty of Amsterdam introduces a system of penalties for Member States that fail to respect rights. If the Heads of Government discern a breach of the principles of liberty, democracy and respect for human rights and fundamental freedoms, following a proposal by one third of Member States or by the Commission, and after obtaining the assent of the European Parliament, the Council may decide, by a qualified majority, to suspend some of the Member States' rights, including its voting rights in the Council.[35] In addition, admission to membership of the Union is dependant upon applicant States demonstrating a commitment to individual rights.

Freedom from discrimination

Article 13 of the EC Treaty (formerly, Article 6a) provides for non-discrimination in relation to sex, racial or ethnic origin, religion or belief, disability, age or sexual orientation. Measures to combat discrimination under Article 13 are to be undertaken by the Council of Ministers, acting

---

35   EC Treaty, Art 7 (formerly, TEU 1992, Art F.1).

unanimously on a proposal from the Commission, and after consulting the European Parliament. Measures adopted under this Article will not have direct effect. Together with the requirement of unanimity in the Council, the potential for this Article is limited. Article 13 must also be distinguished from Article 12 (formerly, Article 6), which provides that discrimination on grounds of nationality is prohibited, and which has direct effect.

Freedom of movement

Under the Maastricht Treaty, Justice and Home Affairs represented the third pillar, and were, accordingly, to be regulated under the inter-governmental decision making process, rather than under Community law. Under the Maastricht Treaty, 11 areas of policy fell for decision:

(a) asylum policy;

(b) rules on external borders of the Member States;

(c) immigration policy and policy regarding nationals of third countries;

(d) conditions of entry and movement by non-EU citizens within the EU;

(e) conditions of residence of the above;

(f) combating drug addiction;

(g) combating fraud on an international scale;

(h) judicial co-operation in civil matters;

(i) judicial co-operation in criminal matters;

(j) customs co-operation;

(k) police co-operation in relation to terrorism, drugs and other international crime.

In relation to Justice and Home Affairs, the 1997 Treaty transfers many powers from the Union to the European Community. Title IV of the EC Treaty (formerly, Title IIIa) regulates visas, asylum, immigration and other policies related to the free movement of persons. Article 61 of the EC Treaty (formerly, Article 73i) provides that the Council, within five years from the coming into force of the Treaty of Amsterdam, adopt measures aimed at ensuring the free movement of persons, in accordance with Article 14 (formerly, Article 7a). The Council will also adopt provisions relating to directly related matters with respect to external border controls, asylum and immigration, in accordance with Articles 62 and 63 of the EC Treaty (formerly, Articles 73j, 73k and 37), and measures to prevent and combat crime, in accordance with Article 31 of the EC Treaty (formerly, Article 37). The latter Article relates to the free movement of goods. The provisions relating to the free movement of persons are outlined here. Article 14, in part, provides that:

> The internal market shall comprise an area without internal frontiers in which the free movement of goods, persons, services and capital is ensured in accordance with the provisions of this Treaty.

Article 62 provides, in part, that:

The Council, acting in accordance with the procedure referred to in Article 67, shall, within a period of five years after the entry into force of the Treaty of Amsterdam, adopt:

(1) measures with a view to ensuring, in compliance with Article 14, the absence of any controls on persons, be they citizens of the Union or nationals of third countries, when crossing internal borders;

(2) measures on the crossing of external borders of the Member States which shall establish:

   (a) standards and procedures to be followed by Member States in carrying out checks on persons at such borders;

   (b) rules on visas for intended stays of no more than three months, including:

      (i) the list of third countries whose nationals must be in possession of visas when crossing the external borders and those whose nationals are exempt from that requirement;

      (ii) the procedures and conditions for issuing visas by Member States;

      (iii) a uniform format for visas;

      (iv) rules on a uniform visa ...

Article 63 provides that:

The Council, acting in accordance with the procedure referred to in Article 67, shall, within a period of five years after the entry into force of the Treaty of Amsterdam, adopt:

(1) measures on asylum, in accordance with the Geneva Convention of 28 July 1965 and the Protocol of 31 January 1967 relating to the status of refugees and other relevant treaties, within the following areas:

   (a) criteria and mechanisms for determining which Member State is responsible for considering an application for asylum submitted by a national of a third country in one of the Member States;

   (b) minimum standards on the reception of asylum seekers in Member States;

   (c) minimum standards with respect to the qualification of nationals of third countries as refugees;

   (d) minimum standards on procedures in Member States for granting or withdrawing refugee status.

(2) measures on refugees and displaced persons within the following areas:

   (a) minimum standards for giving temporary protection to displaced persons from third countries who cannot return to their country of origin and for persons who otherwise need international protection;

   (b) promoting a balance of effort between Member States in receiving and bearing the consequences of receiving refugees and displaced persons.

(3) measures on immigration policy within the following areas:

(a) conditions of entry and residence, and standards on procedures for the issue by Member States of long term visas and residence permits, including those for the purpose of family reunion;

(b) illegal immigration and illegal residence, including repatriation of illegal residents.

(4) measures defining the rights and conditions under which nationals of third countries who are legally resident in a Member State may reside in other Member States ...

The transfer of power from the third pillar to the Community represents one of the most significant changes introduced under the Treaty of Amsterdam. Whereas under the third pillar, regulation is by way of conventions agreed through the inter-governmental process, the transfer means that, once the Treaty is ratified, this area will be regulated under Community law by way of regulations or directives. The European Court of Justice will also have jurisdiction, albeit limited, to review the decisions of domestic courts of last instance, in relation to these matters. On the role of the ECJ, see, further, below.[36] Furthermore, the Commission – following a five year period in which there will be joint Member State/Commission initiative – will have the sole right of initiative in respect of such issues, with the exception of matters relating to the abolition of controls at internal borders.

The Schengen Agreement, which provided for the abolition of border controls between Member States, discussed further below, has been formally incorporated into Community law via a protocol annexed to the Treaty of Amsterdam. Before the Treaty entered into force, it was necessary to identify those issues of the Schengen *acquis*[37] which relate to crime and police matters, which are accommodated in the third pillar, and those relating to free movement of persons, which become matters of Community law in the first pillar. Special provisions relate to Denmark, Ireland and the United Kingdom. All three countries have formally derogated from Article 14 of the Treaty (formerly, Article 7a of the EC Treaty), because of their special geographical boundaries. Iceland and Norway are to be associated with the provisions on the basis of their existing agreements with Schengen members, but are free to revoke all or part of the protocol. In relation to Table IV of the EC Treaty, on an area of freedom, security and justice, and on police and judicial co-operation in criminal matters, Denmark, Ireland and the United Kingdom

---

36 On the changing nature of the jurisdiction of the Court in relation to freedom, security and justice and police and criminal matters, see Lyons,C, 'Variable geometry in the Court of Justice', in de Búrca and Scott, *op cit*, fn 34.

37 The Schengen *acquis* is defined in an Annex to the Treaty as comprising: the Schengen Agreement of 1985; the implementing Convention of 1990; Accession Protocols and Agreements; decisions and declarations adopted by the Executive committee; acts adopted by the organs on which the Community has conferred decision making powers.

have negotiated special conditions. They may join in the future and may decide to participate in Union initiatives.

The Court of Justice has examined the compatibility with Community law of national legislation governing identity checks on citizens when crossing frontiers. It has ruled that the right of freedom of movement is not unconditional, and that, until all Member States are required, through harmonisation of laws provisions, to abolish all controls at frontiers, they are entitled to require that the person seeking entry is able to establish that he or she has the nationality of the Member State.[38]

The transfer of powers to the European Community was purchased at the cost of the requirement that decisions relating to Justice and Home Affairs, with the exception of visas, will be taken by the Council following a unanimous, rather than qualified majority, vote. After a five year period from the coming into force of the Treaty, the Council will decide, unanimously, whether some or all of the areas should become subject to the qualified majority voting system.

The third pillar as amended: Justice and Home Affairs

Under the Treaty of Amsterdam, all matters relating to the movement of persons are now in the first pillar, while the third pillar now relates solely to criminal law and the police. In respect of the third pillar, following reform, a number of amendments under the Treaty of Amsterdam may be noted. First, the European Parliament is to have a role through the requirement to consult. Secondly, the European Commission now has the sole right of initiative. Thirdly, the Court of Justice is given limited jurisdiction to review the legality and interpretation of acts, and to give preliminary rulings, provided that each Member State has individually accepted its jurisdiction.

Furthermore, the Treaty of Amsterdam introduces a new form of law making in respect of the third pillar. Formerly, aspects of Justice and Home Affairs were regulated under Conventions signed by the Member States, but rarely ratified, and hence of limited value. Under the new arrangements, a 'framework decision' is to be introduced. Similar to a directive, a framework decision is aimed at harmonising laws between Member States, and is binding on the objective to be achieved, whilst leaving a measure of discretion in relation to the methods adopted to achieve the objective. However, unlike directives, the framework decision is stated not to have direct effect.[39]

---

38 Case C-378/97: Press Release of the European Court of Justice No 69/99.
39 On which, see, further, Chapter 9.

The Union and the citizen

The Treaty of Amsterdam reaffirms citizenship of the Union introduced by the Maastricht Treaty: 'Citizenship of the Union shall complement and not replace national citizenship.'[40]

Citizenship of the Union, and its consequences as determined by the European Court of Justice, are likely to have an increasingly significant impact on domestic rules, and on the supremacy of Community law. In *Maria Martinez Sala v Freistaat Bayern*,[41] the Court, on a reference under Article 177 (now, Article 234), was called upon to rule on the definition of worker, and the impact of citizenship of the Union on the rights of workers to family benefits. Mrs Sala, a Spanish national, had lived in Germany since 1989. When not in employment, she received social assistance under the Federal Social Welfare law. In 1993, at a time when she did not have a resident permit, Mrs Sala applied for a child-raising allowance. Her application was rejected on the ground that she did not have German nationality, a residence entitlement or a resident permit. On appeal, the court referred a series of questions to the Court of Justice for interpretation. The Court of Justice ruled that Community law does not prevent a Member State from requiring nationals from other Member States lawfully resident in its territory to carry a document certifying their right of residence *provided that* the Member State imposes the same requirement on its own nationals. However, to require non-nationals, but not nationals, to possess a residence permit in order to qualify for benefit represented unequal treatment which amounted to discrimination under Article 6 of the EC Treaty (now, Article 12). The Court ruled that:

> Article 8(2) [now, Article 17] of the Treaty attaches to the status of citizen of the Union the rights and duties laid down by the Treaty, including the right, laid down in Article 6 of the Treaty, not to suffer discrimination on grounds of nationality within the scope of application *ratione materiae* of the Treaty ...
>
> Since the unequal treatment in question thus comes within the scope of the Treaty, it cannot be considered to be justified: it is discrimination directly based on the appellant's nationality and, in any event, nothing to justify such unequal treatment has been put before the Court.[42]

One of the principal concerns over the relationship between the citizen and the Union has been the perception that the Union is remote, lacking in sufficient democracy, and overly complex. The principle of subsidiarity, discussed below, is one means by which Member States may retain a measure of control over decision making in areas which otherwise would fall to Community control. In order to clarify the principle of subsidiarity, and the

---

40 EC Treaty, Art 17 (formerly, EC Treaty, Art 8).

41 Case C-85/86, 1998, not yet reported.

42 Judgment, paras 61 and 64. See, also, Cases 2134/92 and 2159/92: *B v R; Brunner v European Union Treaty* [1994] 1 CMLR 57. And see MacCormick, N, 'The Maastricht-Urteil: sovereignty now' [1995] 1 ELJ 259.

related concept of proportionality, the Treaty of Amsterdam introduces a protocol which has legal status. Accordingly, subsidiarity is now a legal concept, whereas, it was formerly considered to be a guiding, but non-legal, and unenforceable, principle.[43]

The Treaty of Amsterdam also strives to promote openness and accessibility for the citizen. A right of access to Council, Parliament and Commission documents has been provided.

The right of access to information founded the basis for an application for annulment of a Commission decision in 1996 confirming its refusal to grant access to certain documents.[44] The Code of Conduct drawn up to give effect to the right of access states that 'the public will have the widest possible access to documents held by the Commission and the Council'. The factors which may be relied on for rejecting a request for access include refusal where disclosure would undermine the protection of the public interest (public security, international relations, monetary stability, court proceedings, inspections and investigations, the protection of the individual and of privacy, the protection of commercial and industrial secrecy, the protection of Community financial interests, and the protection of confidentiality, including the confidentiality of the institutions' proceedings. The Court ruled that, where exceptions are pleaded by an institution, those exceptions must be interpreted strictly. Further, reasons must be given for the refusal. Merely to state that the institution relies on an exception is inadequate. The Court annulled the decision. In *Interpoc Import und Export GmbH v Commission*,[45] the Court had occasion to again rule on the refusal to disclose information by the Commission which relied on the public interest in relation to court proceedings. The Court ruled that the access to information provisions were designed to make:

> ... the Community more open, the transparency of the decision making process being a means of strengthening the democratic nature of the institution and the public's confidence in the administration.

Where the Commission relied on the exception relating to court proceedings, it could not use that exception to exclude documents drawn up in connection with a purely administrative matter. The decision was annulled.

Common foreign and security policy

The second pillar of the Union structure established under the Maastricht Treaty 1992 is that of Common Foreign and Security Policy, and represents

---

43 See de Búrca, G, 'The principle of subsidiarity and the Court of Justice as an institutional actor' (1998) 36(2) JCMS 217.

44 Case T-124/96: *Interporc Import und Export Gmbh v Commission* [1998] ECH II-231.

45 Case T-92/98.

one of the most politically difficult areas of the Union. Title V of the Treaty of Amsterdam regulates the area. Article 13 of the Treaty on European Union 1997 (formerly, Article J.3 of the Treaty on European Union 1992) provides, in part, that:

1   The European Council shall define the principles of and general guidelines for the common foreign and security policy, including matters with defence implications.

2   The European Council shall decide on common strategies to be implemented by the Union in areas where the Member States have important interests in common.

Decisions are to be taken by the Council acting unanimously.[46] However, in light of political sensitivities, the Treaty of Amsterdam also makes two concessions to Member States. First, Article 23 of the Treaty on European Union (formerly, Article J.13(1)) provides for abstentions, which will not prohibit the Union reaching decisions by a qualified majority. Member States who abstain are under a duty not to impede the action. Secondly, as noted above, a Member State may attempt to block decisions on the basis of important national interests. Where this occurs, the matter is referred to the European Council for unanimous decision.

The Treaty of Amsterdam also furthers the goal of a common foreign and security policy. The Secretary General of the Council is to act as High Representative for foreign and security policy issues. The Secretary General is to continue to be appointed by governments. In relation to security and defence and enforcement capabilities, difficulties arise due to the differing memberships of the European Union, the North Atlantic Treaty Alliance (NATO) and the Western European Union (WEU). The Amsterdam Treaty enables the Council to take decisions for the Union in relation to humanitarian and rescue tasks and peacekeeping tasks, and enables the Union to avail itself of the WEU to implement the political decisions relating to these tasks.

The United Kingdom and Europe

The United Kingdom stood aloof from the early development of the Community, rejecting the call of Sir Winston Churchill in 1949 for a 'United States of Europe'.[47] Instead, Britain formed the European Free Trade Area (EFTA) together with Austria, Denmark, Norway, Portugal, Sweden and Switzerland. In part, EFTA was formed as a defensive action to fend off the potentially adverse effects of the free trading area established under the EEC.

---

46   TEU 1997, Art 23(1) (formerly, TEU 1992, Art J.13(1)).
47   Speech at University of Zurich, 19 September 1946.

By 1961, the Conservative government of Mr Harold Macmillan had decided to seek entry to the Community, an application which was initially blocked by France. It was not until 1972 that the Final Act was signed containing the instruments of accession of the United Kingdom along with Ireland, Denmark and Norway.[48, 49]

THE OBJECTIVES OF THE COMMUNITY

The original aims of the EEC (now, EC) were set out in a Resolution of Foreign Ministers of the ECSC in June 1955:

> The governments of Belgium, France, the Federal Republic of Germany, Italy, Luxembourg and The Netherlands consider that the moment has arrived to initiate a new phase on the path of constructing Europe. They believe that this has to be done principally in the economic sphere and regard it as necessary to continue the creation of a united Europe through an expansion of joint institutions, the gradual fusion of national economies, the creation of a common market and the gradual co-ordination of social policies. Such a policy seems indispensable if Europe is to maintain her position in the world, regain her influence and achieve a steady increase in the living standards of her population.

These broadly expressed objectives found expression in Article 2 of the EC Treaty, which provides that:

> The Community shall have as its task, by establishing a common market and an economic and monetary union and by implementing the common policies or activities referred to in Articles 3 and 4, to promote throughout the Community a harmonious and balanced development of economic activities, a high level of employment and of social protection, equality between men and women, sustainable and non-inflationary growth, a high degree of competitiveness and convergence of economic performance, a high level of protection and improvement of the quality of the environment, the raising of the standard of living and quality of life, and economic and social cohesion and solidarity among Member States.

Article 3 of the EC Treaty now provides that the activities of the Community shall include:

---

48   The people of Norway rejected EC membership in a referendum.
49   At the time of publication, a European Union (Implications of Withdrawal) Bill 2000 was before Parliament. The Bill provides for the establishment of a Committee of Inquiry into withdrawal from the European Union. The implications defined are those relating to the economy, national security and the constitution of the United Kingdom, and impact costs and other public expenditure in the United Kingdom as a result of its membership of the Union. The Committee is to report to the Chancellor of the Exchequer before 1 February 2001. The report will be laid before each House of Parliament.

(a) the prohibition, as between Member States, of customs duties and quantitative restrictions on the import and export of goods, and of all other measures having equivalent effect;

(b) a common commercial policy;

(c) an internal market characterised by the abolition, as between Member States, of obstacles to the free movement of goods, persons, services and capital;

(d) measures concerning the entry and movement of persons in the internal market as provided for in Title IV;

(e) a common policy in the sphere of agriculture and fisheries;

(f) a common policy in the sphere of transport;

(g) a system ensuring that competition in the internal market is not distorted;

(h) the approximation of the laws of the Member States to the extent required for the functioning of the common market;

(i) the promotion of co-ordination between employment policies of the Member States with a view to enhancing their effectiveness by developing a co-ordinated strategy for employment;

(j) a policy in the social sphere comprising a European Social Fund;

(k) the strengthening of economic and social cohesion;

(l) a policy in the sphere of the environment;

(m) the strengthening of the competitiveness of Community industry;

(n) the promotion of research and technological development;

(o) encouragement for the establishment and development of trans-European networks;

(p) a contribution to the attainment of a high level of health protection;

(q) a contribution to education and training of quality and to the flowering of the cultures of the Member States;

(r) a policy in the sphere of development co-operation;

(s) the association of the overseas countries and territories in order to increase trade and promote jointly economic and social development;

(t) a contribution to the strengthening of consumer protection;

(u) measures in the spheres of energy, civil protection and tourism.

In all the above activities, the Community 'shall aim to eliminate inequalities, and to promote equality, between men and women'.[50]

---

50 EC Treaty, Art 3(2) (formerly, EC Treaty, Art 3).

The proposed Charter of Fundamental Rights

In 2000, the European Council approved the setting up of a convention consisting of representatives of the 15 national governments, 30 national parliamentarians, 16 MEPs and the Commission, charged with drafting a Charter of Fundamental Rights for the European Union. The European Court of Justice and the Council of Europe have observer status at the Convention. The draft Charter covers 50 basic rights, including:

> The dignity of the human person and equality before the law; the right to life; right to respect for the integrity of the human person, which includes a ban of eugenic practices, informed consent, ban on financial gain from the human body and a ban on reproductive cloning; prohibition of torture and inhuman treatment and the right not to be expelled or extradited to a State where there would be a danger of the death penalty or torture; prohibition of slavery and forced labour; right to liberty and security; right to an effective remedy for violations of rights and freedoms; right to a fair trial; presumption of innocence; no retrospective criminal liability; the right not to be tried twice; respect for private life; the right to marry and found a family, and enjoy legal, economic and social protection of the family; freedom of thought, conscience and religious; freedom of expression; the right to education; freedom of assembly and association; the right of access to documents of the European Parliament, Council and Commission; data protection; the right to property; right to asylum in accordance with the Geneva Convention of 1951; the right to equality and non-discrimination; children's rights; the principle of democracy; the right to form political parties; the right to vote and stand for elections; the right to fair administration; the right to refer to the European Ombudsman allegations of maladministration; the right to petition the European Parliament; freedom of movement; social rights; freedom to choose an occupation; workers' rights to information and consultation; rights of collective bargaining action; right to rest periods and annual leave; safe and healthy working conditions; protection of young people in employment; right to protection against unjustified or abusive termination of employment; right to reconcile family and professional life, including parental leave after the birth of a child; right of migrant workers to equal rights; social security and social assistance; health protection; social and vocational integration for the disabled; environmental protection; consumer protection; the prohibition against the destruction of Charter rights.

The draft Charter is to be submitted to heads of government at the December 2000 summit in Nice and, if approved, will be incorporated into a treaty which must be ratified by all Member States according to their constitutional requirements. The political decision which remains open is whether the Charter will be legally binding, and enforced by the Court of Justice, or not.

A UNIQUE LEGAL ORDER

The European Community is the creation of the original EEC Treaty, as amended by the Single European Act 1986 and the Treaty on European Union (Maastricht), its Protocols and Declarations, and the Treaty on European Union 1997 (Treaty of Amsterdam). Community law, however, is not international law as normally understood in the sense of merely establishing mutual obligations between contracting States. Community law involves not only mutual obligations between Member States but also the transfer of sovereign rights to the institutions of that system and the creation of rights and obligations for their citizens, 'who thereby became subjects of the Community'.[51] The Community is, therefore, a unique constitutional entity, having its own institutions and law making powers, capable of creating rights and duties within the legal systems of the Member States, and represents far more than a mere form of institutionalised inter-governmental co-operation, the success of which rests on the full approval of each Member State. The law making powers of the Community's institutions, as will be seen below, are far reaching. When duties are imposed on Member States, these may imply rights for individuals which may be enforced in the domestic courts and, in respect of the duties of Member States, also ultimately in the European Court of Justice (ECJ), the Community's judicial forum.

In constitutional terms, the Community is not a 'State', neither is it a 'federation', rather it is a unique supranational organisation. When new Member States are admitted to the Union, they become automatically bound by the entire law of the Community – in European terminology, the *acquis communautaire*.[52] Under international law, when a State becomes a signatory to a Treaty, it becomes bound by the provisions of that Treaty, but not bound by any acts done under the Treaty before that State's accession. It is different with the Community, and new Member States become automatically committed to the Community Treaties, all secondary legislation, judicial and non-judicial decisions made by the institutions of the Community, together with non-binding opinions and resolutions of institutions. The concept of *acquis communautaire* has been given prominence in the Treaty on European Union, which provides that:

> The Union shall set itself the following objectives:
>
> – to maintain in full the *acquis communautaire* and build upon it with a view to considering, through the procedure referred to in Article N(2), to what extent the policies and forms of co-operation introduced by this Treaty

---

51 *Op cit*, Mathijsen, fn 1, p 7.
52 Which, literally translated, means 'Community patrimony'.

> may need to be revised with the aim of ensuring the effectiveness of the mechanisms and institutions of the Community.[53]

- The Union shall be served by a single institutional framework which shall ensure the consistency and the continuity of the activities carried out in order to attain its objectives while respecting and building on the *acquis communautaire*.[54]

The status of the Community will become clearer as its structure is examined in more detail.

The major constitutional issues

From the constitutional law perspective, the issues which require scrutiny are:

(a) the nature of the Community, the institutions and their law making powers;

(b) the nature and sources of community law;

(c) the effect of membership of the Union on the constitution of the United Kingdom;

(d) the relationship between Community law and domestic law.

The allocation of functions between Community institutions and Member States

In any federal or quasi-federal State or organisation, the functions of the federal government and the regional governments must be allocated. As discussed in Chapter 1, the concept of federalism involves the allocation of powers which may reserve some powers to the exclusive competence of the federal government, some powers which will be concurrently held by the federal and regional governments, and some powers over which the regional government has exclusive competence. In the European Community, the manner in which powers are allocated and exercised is largely determined by the Treaty provisions. However, in order to achieve a realistic balance between Community competence and the autonomy of Member States, the principle of subsidiarity has come to play a major role and requires examination. While subsidiarity does not effect competence *per se*, it significantly affects the manner in which it is to be exercised.

---

53 TEU 1997, Art 2 (formerly, TEU 1992, Art B).
54 *Ibid*, Art 3 (formerly, TEU 1992, Art C).

The principle of subsidiarity[55]

Subsidiarity is a fundamental concept in federal States and the approach to subsidiarity taken in the Community has been said to be very like the approach adopted in Germany. The principle of subsidiarity is enshrined in the treaties, although the precise allocation of powers is not laid down as one might expect in a constitutional text such as this. The principle of subsidiarity is central to Community law, although doubts remain as to its precise meaning, as shown below.

Discussion of the principle in the Community context, even before its incorporation into the Maastricht Treaty, reveal that it is capable of no less than 30 different meanings. Designed to determine the appropriate level of action across the whole spectrum of public activity, international (in the widest sense), Community, national, regional and local, it has been invoked in the Community context to assist in determining the appropriate allocation of powers between the Community and its Member States, and to control the exercise of Community powers. In this context, it has been described, variously, as 'the principle of necessity, or proportionality, of effectiveness, an elementary principle of good government, or simply a principle of good sense'. It has been interpreted as meaning that the Community should only act:

(a) where the objective cannot be achieved by regulation at national level;

(b) where the objective can be better, or more effectively, achieved by action at Community level (the 'efficiency by better results' criterion); or

(c) where the matter in question can be more effectively regulated at Community level (the 'administrative efficiency' criterion).[56]

Failure to formulate specific detailed rules regarding subsidiarity led the late Lord Mackenzie Stuart[57] in 1991 to argue that the inter-governmental conference at Maastricht should be 'getting down to the detailed rules of detailed competence', rather than leaving subsidiarity as a 'hopelessly ill defined concept',[58] but his words were not heeded. Article 5 of the EC Treaty (formerly, Article 3b of the EC Treaty),[59] as revised by the Treaty of Amsterdam, provides:

---

55 See Emiliou, N, 'Subsidiarity: an effective barrier against "the enterprises of ambition"?' (1991) 17 EL Rev 383 and 'Subsidiarity: panacea or fig leaf?', in *op cit*, O'Keefe and Twomey, fn 20, Chapter 5; Toth, AG, 'The principle of subsidiarity in the Maastricht Treaty' (1992) CML Rev 1079.

56 Steiner, J, 'Subsidiarity under the Maastricht Treaty', and references therein, in *op cit*, O'Keefe and Twomey, fn 20.

57 President of the Court of Justice from 1984 to 1988.

58 Mackenzie Stuart (Lord), 'Subsidiarity and the challenge of change 1991', in the Proceedings of the Jacques Delors Colloquium, cited in *ibid*, Steiner.

59 Inserted by the Treaty on European Union 1997.

The Community shall act within the limits of the powers conferred upon it by this Treaty and of the objectives assigned to it therein.

In areas which do not fall within its exclusive competence, the Community shall take action, in accordance with the principle of subsidiarity, only if and so far as the objectives of the proposed action cannot be sufficiently achieved by the Member States and can therefore, by reason of the scale or effects of the proposed action, be better achieved by the Community.

Any action by the Community shall not go beyond what is necessary to achieve the objectives of this Treaty.

The closely related principles of subsidiarity and proportionality are thus both provided for under Article 5. A protocol on the application of subsidiarity restates the principles, listing guidelines to be followed in reaching decisions as to whether action should be taken at Community level or at national level. Now a clear legal concept, it will be for the Court of Justice to adjudicate on its scope and application. The Protocol also makes clear that subsidiarity is a concept which is dynamic and flexible, allowing decisions on the appropriate level at which action should be taken to develop on a case by case basis. The doctrine of proportionality is one which is largely alien to – until recently – English lawyers,[60] but one familiar to European lawyers and one utilised by the ECJ. Sir William Wade explains that the principle of proportionality 'ordains that administrative measures must not be more drastic than is necessary for attaining the desired result'.[61] The protocol on the application of subsidiarity also clarifies the distinction between subsidiarity and proportionality.[62]

The application of subsidiarity

Exclusive competence

As the text of Article 5 makes clear, where the Community has 'exclusive competence', the subsidiarity principle has no application. The Community has sole power of decision and therefore no question arises as to whether others share that power, or the extent to which they should be entitled to act. However, many issues remain unclear from the text of the Treaty. For example, there is no definition as to what areas fall within the Community's exclusive competence, and the Commission itself has accepted that there was 'no clear line of demarcation between exclusive and shared power'. On the

---

60 See, also, Chapter 25.

61 Citing Schwarze, J, *European Administrative Law*, Luxembourg: Office for Official Publications of the European Communities, p 680; see, also, Boyron, S, 'Proportionality in English administrative law: a faulty translation?' (1992) 12 OJLS 237.

62 See de Búrca, G, 'The principle of proportionality and its application in EC law' [1993] 13 YBEL 105.

other hand, it is generally accepted that common agricultural and commercial policies and aspects of common fisheries policies fall within the exclusive competence of the Union. Furthermore, the Commission argued that even where exclusive power exists, it does not mean that 'all responsibility for the activity in question is covered by exclusive competence. The text of the Treaty cannot be interpreted so broadly as to leave common sense out of account'.[63]

Concurrent powers

Notwithstanding the above observation, it is the concept of subsidiarity which lies at the heart of the distribution of powers between Member States and the Community – and thus determines the scope of Community powers. Where a Member State has a concurrent power, the power to act remains, so long as the Community has not exercised that power. However, if the Community takes action itself, the power of the Member State is pre-empted, and the power to act – once pre-empted – remains with the Community.[64] Where the Community has exclusive power, the Member State has no power to act unless the legislation in question contains a specific authorisation by the Community in favour of the Member States.[65] Secondly, the Court has ruled that, where the Community has exclusive competence to act but has not so acted and urgent action is needed, the Member States may act as 'trustees of the common interest'.[66] Only time, political practice and the jurisprudence of the European Court of Justice, will reveal which view is correct. Josephine Steiner provides a further argument as to the need for subsidiarity, stating that the principle of subsidiarity is an essential safeguard to protect the interests of differing groups and regions within the Community, and that any transfer of power away from Member States to Europe requires justification:

> ... if competence is to be transferred to centralised authorities, the transfer must be justified. The burden is on the Community institutions to show that there is a real need for Community action, by reference to the scale or effects of the problem, and that the particular action proposed is appropriate and necessary to achieve specific Community goals.[67]

The concept of subsidiarity was debated at the meeting of the European Council at its summit meeting in December 1992,[68] which resulted in guidelines being laid down, guidelines which now have a legal basis under the protocol to the Treaty of Amsterdam. These are summarised by Nicholas Emiliou in the following manner:

---

63 Communication to the Council and Parliament outlining proposals for the Subsidiarity Principle Bulletin EC 10-1992, Pt 2.2.1, cited in *op cit*, Steiner, fn 56.

64 See Weatherill, S, 'Beyond pre-emption', in *op cit*, O'Keefe and Twomey, fn 20.

65 Case 41/76: *Donckerwolcke v Procureur de la Republic* [1976] ECR 1921.

66 Case 804/79: *Commission v United Kingdom* [1981] ECR 1045.

67 *Op cit*, Steiner, 1996, fn 1, p 63.

68 The Edinburgh Summit.

1 Is the proposed action within the limits of the powers conferred on the Community by the Treaty and aimed at meeting one or more of the Treaty objectives?

2 If so, can the objectives of the proposed action not be sufficiently achieved by Member States?

3 If not, what should be the nature and the intensity of Community actions?[69]

Issues of subsidiarity will inevitably fall for the Court to consider. For example, if the Community legislates on a particular area, a Member State may wish to resist that legislation by invoking subsidiarity, and thus the Court will be obliged to make a decision. The power to do so has been criticised on the basis that subsidiarity is a political, rather than a legal concept.[70]

THE INSTITUTIONS OF THE COMMUNITY

The European Commission[71]

Originally called the High Authority, the Commission is centrally concerned with all aspects of Community decision making at all levels and on all fronts: the Commission is the very heart of the Community, exercising both powers of initiative and powers of enforcement. As envisaged by the authors of the original treaties, the Commission, while acting independently of governments and in pursuit of the objectives of the Community, would help preserve the interests of individual Member States.[72] The Commission is the engine which drives the Community forward.

Articles 211–19 of the EC Treaty, as revised by the 1997 Treaty, (formerly, Articles 155–63 of the EC Treaty) established the powers of the Commission. Article 211 sets out the basic powers:

In order to ensure the proper functioning and development of the common market, the Commission shall:

(a) ensure that the provisions of this Treaty and the measures taken by the institutions pursuant thereto are applied;

(b) formulate recommendations or deliver opinions on matters dealt with in this Treaty, if it expressly so provides or if the Commission considers it necessary;

---

69 *Op cit*, Emiliou, 1994, fn 55, p 76.

70 Mackenzie Stuart (Lord), 'Letter' (1992) *The Independent*, 15 June, cited by *op cit*, Emiliou, 1994, fn 55, p 77.

71 EC Treaty, Arts 211–19 (formerly, EC Treaty, Arts 155–63).

72 See, further, below.

(c) have its own power of decision and participate in the shaping of measures taken by the Council and by the Assembly [Parliament] in the manner provided for in this Treaty;

(d) exercise the powers conferred on it by the Council for the implementation of the rules laid down by the latter.

The Commission accordingly has powers of initiative and powers of supervision and enforcement.

The Commission consists of 20 Members, appointed by the governments of Member States in consultation with one another.[73] The number of Commissioners may be altered by the Council, acting unanimously. Commissioners must be nationals of one of the Member States and no more than two may be nationals of the same Member State.[74] The five largest Member States (Germany, France, Italy, Spain and the United Kingdom) each have two Commissioners, other Member States one. Commissioners are appointed for a renewable five year term of office, and cannot be dismissed during their term of office by governments.[75] Commissioners remain in office until replaced, or compulsorily retired.[76] The Commission has a staff of approximately 15,000. Decisions in the Commission are reached by majority voting.[77]

The increasing size of the Community – and its projected further expansion to a membership of 26 – has led to an examination of the size of the Commission.[78] This issue was again debated at the inter-governmental conference leading to the Treaty of Amsterdam, although no firm conclusions were agreed as to its appropriate size. A protocol to the Treaty of Amsterdam provides that, at the time of enlargement, the Commission will comprise one national from each Member State, *providing that* agreement has been reached on the reweighting of votes in the Council of Ministers, on which see, further, below, pp 295–96. Agreement was, however, reached that a new inter-governmental conference will be convened one year before the Union exceeds 20 Member States, in order to review the composition and operation of the institutions. The European Parliament has the power to pass a motion of

---

73 EC Treaty, Art 213 (formerly, EC Treaty, Art 157(1)).

74 *Ibid*, Art 213 (formerly, EC Treaty, Art 157(1)).

75 *Ibid*, Art 214 (formerly, EC Treaty, Art 158). Commissioners can, however, have their reappointment blocked by a government, as occurred in 1989 when the Prime Minister felt that Lord Cockfield had been over-zealous in his support of the Community.

76 *Ibid*, Art 216 (formerly, EC Treaty, Art 160) provides that, if a Commissioner no longer fulfils the conditions required for the performance of his duties, or if he has been guilty of serious misconduct, the Court of Justice may, on an application of the Council or the Commission, compulsorily retire him.

77 *Ibid*, Art 219 (formerly, EC Treaty, Art 163).

78 See Proposals for Reform of the Commission of the European Community and its Services, 1979; and Report on European Institutions, 1979.

censure to remove the Commission *en bloc*.[79] However, when, in 1999, allegations of waste and mismanagement in the Commission surfaced, Parliament failed to pass a motion of sanction. In the event, the entire Commission, including the President, resigned.

Once appointed, Commissioners must act entirely independently of government: they are not representatives of government. Article 213(2) of the EC Treaty, as revised (formerly, Article 157(2) of the EC Treaty), provides:

> The Members of the Commission shall, in the general interests of the Community, be completely independent in the performance of their duties.
>
> In the performance of these duties they shall neither seek nor take instructions from any government or from any other body. They shall refrain from any action incompatible with their duties. Each Member State undertakes to respect this principle and not to seek to influence the Members of the Commission in the performance of their tasks.
>
> The Members of the Commission may not, during their term of office, engage in any other occupation, whether gainful or not.

The Commission is headed by a President, appointed from among the Commission in common agreement with Member States. The office is held for a renewable two year term. The Presidency is the most prestigious job in the EC, carrying with it the responsibility for the sense of direction and co-ordination of effort within the Community. The Commission may appoint a Vice President or two Vice Presidents from among its number.[80] The Treaty of Amsterdam has strengthened the role of the President in several respects. First, in the appointment of Commissioners by Member States, the President has a right to object to a nominee. Secondly, Article 219 of the EC Treaty (formerly, Article 163) provides that the Commission shall work under the political guidance of its President.

Organisationally, the Commission is divided into Directorates General, each headed by a Director responsible to the relevant Commissioner. Each Commissioner holds one or more portfolios, that is to say, special responsibility for some area of Community policy, and is assisted by a Cabinet of six.

The broad and ill defined power conferred under Article 211 of the EC Treaty and the role of the Commission can only be understood within the framework of the European Union as a whole. It is clear that it is the Commission which is charged with the duty to act in the interests of the objectives of the Community as expressed in the treaties. It is the Commission which puts forward proposals for decision by the Council of Ministers (see below), having negotiated widely with representatives of Member States' governments and with interest groups within the Community. The Council of

79 EC Treaty, Art 201 (formerly, EC Treaty, Art 144).
80 *Ibid*, Art 217 (formerly, EC Treaty, Art 161).

Ministers may, in some instances, request the Commission to draft proposals,[81] and the Treaty on European Union has given the European Parliament the right to request the Commission to submit a proposal for legislation.[82] Where the Commission is under an obligation to submit legislative proposals within a certain time laid down in the Treaty, failure to act within that time will render the Commission liable to a challenge before the ECJ.[83] When such proposals assume the force of law, it is again the Commission which is charged primarily with the task of law enforcement.

The Commission's broad powers of initiative should not be understood to mean that the Commission has total freedom of action. The working of the EC depends on a variety of factors, actors and forces. In the final analysis, the Community can only be effective in achieving the goals set out in the treaties if its proposals can carry the support of the Member States. The effectiveness of Community law within the legal systems of all Member States is ultimately dependent upon the political acceptability of that law. It is for this reason that the role of the Commission is so important, for the Commission – having the sole power to formulate proposals for the implementation of Treaty objectives – is responsible for ensuring that proposals have the support of Member States before they are hardened into law. As originally envisaged by the drafters of the original treaties, only a body acting with complete independence was competent to negotiate with Member States and formulate acceptable policies. It must be remembered that the Community comprises 15 States of vastly differing sizes and populations, and that, within these States, there are regions with differing interests and needs. It is vital, therefore, that there is some guarantee that the interests of the smaller Member States, and regions in all Member States, are protected against the power of the larger States. Accordingly, in the process of formulating policies, one of the Commission's principal tasks is to reconcile the differing interests at stake and to make the resulting law acceptable to all.[84] It is for this reason that, where the Commission drafts a proposal, the Council of Ministers, which has the formal law making power, may adopt a proposal of the Commission by a 'qualified majority vote' (on which see, further, below), but may amend the proposal only by a unanimous vote.

The Treaty of Amsterdam extends the Commission's right of initiative. First, the Commission now has the right of initiative in relation to policies and actions in relation to employment and health. Secondly, with the transfer of areas of competence to the Community in relation to the free movement of persons (from the Justice and Home Affairs pillar), the Commission has a joint

---

81 EC Treaty, Art 208 (formerly, EC Treaty, Art 152).

82 *Ibid*, Art 192 (formerly, EC Treaty, Art 138b).

83 *Ibid*, Arts 232, 233 (formerly, EC Treaty, Arts 175, 176).

84 Temple-Lang, J, 'The European Commission: safeguard for Member States', European Law Lecture (Queen Mary and Westfield College, University of London, 5 June 1995).

right of initiative with Member States for the first five years, after which the Commission will have exclusive competence. Thirdly, whereas formerly, the Commission had no right of initiative in respect of the third pillar, now confined to crime and the police, the Treaty extends the right of initiative to the Commission to act jointly with Member States.

Where a Member State is in default of Treaty obligations, the Commission has the power to deal with the breach. Article 226 of the EC Treaty, as revised (formerly, Article 169), specifies the procedure to be followed:

> If the Commission considers that a Member State has failed to fulfil an obligation under this Treaty, it shall deliver a reasoned opinion on the matter after giving the State concerned the opportunity to submit its observations.
>
> If the State concerned does not comply with the opinion within the period laid down by the Commission, the latter may bring the matter before the Court of Justice.

In an average year, the Commission might issue 500 letters of notice of violation, deliver 150 reasoned opinions and make 50 references to the ECJ. Most matters are settled at an early stage – infringements being due not to wilful disregard of the law, but rather from genuine differences of opinion as to the meaning of requirements, or from administrative delay. Where, however, a Member State fails to fulfil its Community obligations and the Commission brings the case before the Court of Justice, the Commission must specify an amount of a lump sum or penalty payment to be paid by the Member State.[85] Where the Court rules that the Member State is in default of its obligations, the Court may impose the penalty on the Member State.[86]

The Council of Ministers[87]

The Council of Ministers has legislative and executive powers and functions. It is the Council of Ministers which defends the interests of Member States. The Council of Ministers has no fixed membership and its composition varies depending upon the subject matter under discussion. Accordingly, when the subject on the Agenda is agriculture, the Council will consist of the Ministers of Agriculture from all Member States, when the subject is transport, the membership will be made up of the respective Ministers of Transport. Article 202 of the EC Treaty, as revised (formerly, Article 145 of the EC Treaty), sets out the powers of the Council:

> To ensure that the objectives set out in this Treaty are attained, the Council shall, in accordance with the provisions of this Treaty:

---

85 EC Treaty, Art 228 (formerly, EC Treaty, Art 171(2)).
86 *Ibid*, Art 228 (formerly, EC Treaty, Art 171(2)).
87 *Ibid*, Arts 202–10 (formerly, EC Treaty, Arts 145–54).

(a) ensure co-ordination of the general economic policies of the Member States;

(b) have power to take decisions;

(c) confer on the Commission powers for implementation of rules which the Council lays down. The Council may impose certain requirements in respect of the exercise of these powers. The Council may also reserve the right, in specific cases, to exercise directly implementing powers itself. The procedures referred to above must be consonant with principles and rules to be laid down in advance by the Council, acting unanimously on a proposal from the Commission and after obtaining the opinion of the European Parliament.

Article 203 of the EC Treaty (formerly, Article 146) provides that:

The Council shall consist of a representative of each Member State at ministerial level, authorised to commit the government of that Member State.

The Office of President shall be held in turn by each Member State for a six month term ...

The Council is the most powerful political institution of the EC, and the Council has interpreted and developed its role in such a manner so as to increase its powers. As seen from Article 203, it is the Council which has power to take decisions, and this represents the law making power in the Community. While the Council of Minister has the majority of power in the law making process, the Single European Act 1986 and the Treaty on European Union have extended the powers of the European Parliament in relation to legislation.[88]

When the Communities (now, Community) were originally established, it was envisaged that the role of the Council would decline as Member States developed mutual trust, and that much of the running of the Communities would be in the hands of the Commission. It was also felt that governments would become less concerned about their own State's sovereignty and let the Communities grow in a supra-national way under the direction of the Commission. Neither of these two predictions has fully taken place, and the increase in the power of the Council has been at the expense of the power of the Commission.

---

88 See, further, below.

The voting system for decision making[89]

Central to Community development is the voting system used in the Council of Ministers. The Treaty provides for three basic methods by which the Council can reach a decision: unanimously, by qualified majority vote or by a simple majority vote. Unanimity is normally required where a new policy is to be initiated or the existing policy framework is to be developed or modified. Unanimity is also required when the Council wishes to amend a Commission proposal against the wishes of the Commission. While the Union and Community rests on consensus, and there is little point in adopting a procedure which will cause national Parliaments' resentment or reluctance on the part of State authorities to implement decisions, a balance is needed between respecting the interests of the Member States while not impeding Community development.

Article 205 of the EC Treaty (formerly, Article 148) states that, unless otherwise provided in the Treaty, that is to say, under specific articles, the Council shall act by majority vote. In some specific cases the Council is required to act by a qualified majority, for which purpose the votes of Member States are weighted, the largest States having a weighting of 10, the remaining, according to size, eight, five, four, three or two. Where the Council adopts a matter on a proposal from the Commission, 62 votes are required.[90] Where unanimity is required, the abstention of a Member State shall not prevent the Council adopting a matter.[91] The voting system was designed in order to minimise the circumstances in which one State could block Community progress. It became clear in the 1960s, however, that this was unworkable – most notably when France refused to co-operate in any decisions and caused a constitutional crisis.

The outcome of the crisis was an agreement contained in what is known as the *Luxembourg Accord* of 1966, which provided that:

> Where in the case of decisions which may be taken by majority vote on a proposal from the Commission, very important interests of one or more partners are at stake, the Members of the Council will endeavour, within a reasonable time, to reach solutions which can be adopted by all Members of the Council while respecting their mutual interests and those of the Community in accordance with Article 2 of the Treaty.[92]

---

89 See Morner, A, 'The conflicts inherent in enlargement – is history catching up with the European Union?', in Butterworths European Information Services, *Butterworths' Annual European Review*, 1994, London: Butterworths.

90 EC Treaty, Art 205 (formerly, EC Treaty, Art 148(2)).

91 *Ibid*, Art 205 (formerly, EC Treaty, Art 148(2)).

92 *Bulletin of the European Community* 3/66, p 5.

The French government insisted that where very important State interests are at stake, the discussion should continue until unanimous agreement is reached.

This *Accord* had no formal legal status. It was an informal agreement, and probably unlawful. However, the *Accord* profoundly affected decision making, and the French amendment has been interpreted to mean that any State has the right to exercise a veto on questions which affect its vital national interests, and it is for the States themselves to determine when such interests are at stake. However, this does not mean that whenever a Member State asserts that a matter is a 'matter of vital national interest' that the Community will accept the statement. For example, in 1982, the United Kingdom was opposed to a decision on agricultural prices, and claimed that this was a matter of vital national interest: the Council, however, refused to accept the plea.[93] Under the Treaty of Amsterdam, however, the issue of important national interests has been resurrected and formalised in the EC Treaty in relation to the provisions for closer co-operation. As noted above, Article 11 of the EC Treaty (formerly, Article 5a), provides that, in relation to authorisation by the Council for measures aimed at closer co-operation between Member States, where a Member State raises the objection of important national interests, the Council shall refer the matter to the European Council for unanimous decision. As the Editorial notes, 'predictions of the demise of the Luxembourg Compromise were thus distinctly premature: it has been given a new lease of life, no longer in the demi-monde of political deals but as part of the legal machinery of the EC Treaty'.[94]

The Treaty of Amsterdam made limited reforms to the voting system. The use of qualified majority voting is extended to most of the new Treaty provisions: those relating to incentives in employment and social matters, equal opportunities, social exclusion, public health, anti-fraud measures, openness and the outermost regions. Of the major existing provisions of the Treaty, the research framework programme is under qualified majority voting, and qualified majority voting may be used in relation to decisions under the second pillar, common foreign and security policy. These limited reforms mark one of the failings of the Amsterdam Treaty, under which the Commission had hoped to gain major advances in the application of qualified majority voting.

With the predicted expansion of the Union to 26 Member States, the issue of voting in Council has become a matter for debate and review, although the inter-governmental conference leading to the Treaty of Amsterdam 1997 failed to reach consensus on the matter, which remains for future resolution. Given that no agreement was forthcoming, the reweighting of votes has been linked to the issue of the size of the Commission, and deferred, as noted above, in a protocol for decision of both matters after the next enlargement of the Union.

---

93   See (1982) *The Times*, 19 May.
94   *Op cit*, Editorial, fn 32, p 769.

The Council represents the principal law making body within the Community. The legislative capacity of Council is limited by the Commission's power of proposal, although Article 208 (formerly, Article 152) does provide the means whereby the Council may request the Commission to undertake enquiries the Council considers desirable for the attainment of common objectives, and to submit proposals to the Council.

Because the Council has a fluctuating membership and is not permanently in session,[95] the Committee of Permanent Representatives (COREPER) acts as the permanent body engaged in Council work.[96] The Committee is divided into two: the first Committee dealing with social affairs and transport, and the second dealing with foreign affairs, economic and financial affairs. Because agriculture is so central to the Community, it is served by a separate Committee on Agriculture. Beneath this structure is a complex structure of committees, dealing with every subject.

The European Parliament[97]

Originally called the Assembly, Article 189 of the revised EC Treaty (formerly, Article 137) provides that:

> The Assembly which shall consist of the peoples of the States brought together in the Community, shall exercise the advisory and supervisory powers which are conferred upon it by this Treaty.

Members of the Assembly, now Parliament, were initially delegates designated by the Parliaments of Member States.[98] In constitutional terms, the delegates had a dual mandate: that of membership of both the domestic and European Parliaments. The Treaty, however, envisaged[99] that the Assembly should draw up proposals for direct elections and that the Council would lay down the appropriate provisions, which it would recommend to Member States for adoption. It was to be in 1976 that agreement could be reached on the proposals drawn up in 1960, and only in 1979 did direct election take place in the United Kingdom. The Council Decision and Act of September 1976 on Direct Elections[100] simply stated that the representatives in the European Parliament of the peoples of the States brought together in the Community

---

95 Some 80 Council meetings take place each year.
96 EC Treaty, Art 207 (formerly, EC Treaty, Art 151).
97 *Ibid*, Arts 189–210 (formerly, EC Treaty, Arts 137–44).
98 *Ibid*, Art 190 (formerly, EC Treaty, Art 138).
99 *Ibid*, Art 190(2) (formerly, EC Treaty, Art 138(2)).
100 OJ L278, 1976.

shall be elected by direct universal suffrage.[101] The European Parliamentary Elections Act 1999 regulates elections to the European Parliament.

Article 189 of the EC Treaty (formerly, Article 137) provides that the number of members shall not exceed 700. Seats in the European Parliament, the name formally adopted in 1962, are allocated according to the size of population of the Member States, although there is no absolute equality in voting powers. For example, Germany now has 99 seats and France, Italy and the United Kingdom now have 87 seats, whereas Luxembourg has six seats; although the population of the United Kingdom is 150 times that of Luxembourg, yet the number of seats is less than 14 times that of Luxembourg.[102] Representative are elected for a term of five years.[103]

An elected European Member of Parliament may also be a Member of the national Parliament. This arrangement has both advantages and disadvantages. On the one hand, it facilitates close links being maintained between the two Parliaments, on the other hand, retaining a dual mandate may involve a conflict of interests.[104]

Under the European Parliamentary Elections Act 1999, the United Kingdom is divided into electoral regions. England is divided into nine, Scotland, Wales and Northern Ireland each constitute a single electoral region. The number of MEPs elected in the United Kingdom is 87, of whom 71 are elected for England, eight for Scotland, five for Wales and three for Northern Ireland.[105] The voting system employed in England, Wales and Scotland is the regional list system[106] and, in relation to Northern Ireland, the single transferable vote.[107]

The Members of Parliament do not sit in groupings organised by nationality but rather by political party groupings. Article 191 of the Treaty (formerly, Article 138a) recognises the importance of political parties as 'a factor for integration within the Union. They contribute to forming a European awareness and to expressing the political will of the citizens of the Union'. The major political parties are the Socialists, European Peoples' Party, European Democrats, Communists and Liberals. Unless otherwise provided

---

101 Council Decision and Act of September 1976 on Direct Elections, OJ L278, 1976, Art 1.

102 EC Treaty, Art 190 (formerly, EC Treaty, Art 138).

103 *Ibid*, Art 190(3) (formerly, EC Treaty, Art 138).

104 See the House of Lords' Report, *Relations Between the United Kingdom Parliament and the European Parliament After Direct Elections*, HL 256 (1977–78), London: HMSO. In 1997, three Members of Parliament were also Members of the European Parliament.

105 European Parliamentary Elections Act 1999, s 1.

106 *Ibid*, s 3.

107 *Ibid*, s 3A.

for under the Treaty, the Parliament acts by an absolute majority of the votes cast.[108]

The European Parliament is required to hold an annual session, and may meet in extraordinary session at the request of a majority of its Members or at the request of the Council or of the Commission.[109] In practice, the Parliament meets approximately 12–14 times a year for a few days per session. Members of the Commission may attend all parliamentary meetings and are entitled to address the Parliament.[110] The Parliament holds plenary sessions in Strasbourg, Committee meetings in Brussels and has its secretariat based in Luxembourg. Much of the work of Parliament is undertaken by committees on, for example, agriculture, legal affairs and so on. Before a matter goes before Parliament sitting in plenary session, it will normally be considered by the relevant standing committee.

The original intention in relation to Parliament's function was that it would be a 'supervisory and advisory' body, with no legal effect being attached to its deliberations. Under specific Treaty articles, the Council of Ministers is obliged to seek the advice of the Parliament, and failure to consider Parliament's view would cause the Council to be in violation of an essential procedural requirement of Community law, and could cause the decision of the Council to be declared void by the European Court of Justice.[111] As will be seen, the powers of the European Parliament have been increasing since 1986 (under the Single European Act 1986), but even now it remains a very different constitutional institution from that of domestic Parliaments.

As originally provided, the Parliament had advisory and supervisory functions. When the Commission is devising proposals it will consult with the relevant standing committee: many of the Articles require that this consultation take place. When the Treaty does so specify, failure to consult will mean that a legislative measure subsequently adopted can be declared invalid by the European Court of Justice. However, neither the Commission nor the Council is obliged to accept an opinion or recommendations of the Parliament.

The European Parliament can adopt its own ideas and try to persuade the Commission to adopt them. Usually this takes the form of an initiative report – around 100 per annum are approved by the European Parliament. However, Parliament has no power to insist that the Commission adopt a proposal from Parliament – the right of initiative is firmly in the hands of the Commission itself, other than where the Council of Ministers requests a proposal from the Commission.

---

108 EC Treaty, Art 198 (formerly, EC Treaty, Art 141).
109 *Ibid*, Art 196 (formerly, EC Treaty, Art 139).
110 *Ibid*, Art 196 (formerly, EC Treaty, Art 139).
111 Case 138/79: *Roquettes Frere SA v Council*; and Case 139/79: *Maizena GmbH v Council* [1980] ECR 3393.

The European Parliament has decision making powers regarding the annual budget. This power in relation to the Community budget has always been of significance. The revenue of the Community comes primarily from agricultural levies, customs duties on imports from outside the Community and value added tax (VAT) levied within the Community. When the draft budget is drawn up by the Council, after receiving proposals from the Commission, it is then submitted to Parliament which has power to accept, amend or reject the budget. The right of amendment depends on the type of expenditure proposed. There are two categories of expenditure: compulsory expenditure, which necessarily arises from Treaty provisions, and non-compulsory expenditure. The non-compulsory expenditure can be amended but, in relation to compulsory expenditure, Parliament may suggest amendments but the Council of Ministers has the last word.

Parliament has the power to reject the Community budget in total if there are 'important reasons to do so'.[112] There must be a majority of votes in Parliament and also two thirds of the votes cast. Rejection of the budget occurred in 1979, when a new budget was subsequently drawn up.

Parliament has the right to question the Commission and Council,[113] and replies are given both orally and in writing, and published in the *Official Journal of the European Communities*. Parliament also has the power to dismiss the entire Commission on a vote of censure if the vote is carried by a two thirds majority of the votes cast, a vote which must represent an overall majority of the votes in Parliament.[114] If the vote is carried, the Commission resigns as a body. However, in one sense, the power is too great to be effective, for Parliament has no power to force the incoming Commission to adopt a different policy from that of its predecessor. Under the Treaty on European Union 1997, however, nominations for appointment to the Commission must hereafter be approved by Parliament.[115]

Extension of Parliament's powers: the Single European Act 1986,
Treaty on European Union 1992 and Treaty on European Union 1997

The powers of the European Parliament have been extended by the Single European Act 1986 and, further, by the Treaty on European Union 1992. The Treaty on European Union 1997 also affects Parliament's powers. The legislative process is now more complex and, in specific instances, it is necessary to consult the substantive Articles of the Treaty in order to establish the precise procedure to be followed.

---

112 EC Treaty, Art 272 (formerly, EC Treaty, Art 203).
113 *Ibid*, Art 197 (formerly, EC Treaty, Art 140).
114 *Ibid*, Art 201 (formerly, EC Treaty, Art 144).
115 *Ibid*, Art 214(2) (formerly, EC Treaty, Art 158(2)).

The co-operation and conciliation procedures

Under the Single European Act 1986,[116] Articles 6 and 7 provided for a new 'co-operation procedure', which applies to many, but not all, instances in which the Treaties require Parliament to be consulted. This complex procedure has been considerably modified under the Treaty of Amsterdam, and has been largely superceded by the conciliation procedure and co-decision powers. The co-operation procedure does continue to apply, however, to some issues relating to European monetary union.

Under the Treaty on European Union 1992, Parliament was given legal powers in addition to its consultative powers.[117] The Parliament was also given powers of co-decision in relation to the internal market, education, consumer affairs and other areas. The Treaty on European Union 1992 further extended Parliament's role in the legislative process.[118] The procedure adopted extends the role and power of Parliament to a considerable extent – although not to the point where it can be equated with the normally understood meaning of a democratic legislature. Articles 251–54 of the Treaty on European Union 1997 (the Treaty of Amsterdam) regulates the legislative process and consolidates the provisions relating to the European Parliament.

Articles 251 and 252 of the EC Treaty, as revised by the Treaty of Amsterdam (formerly, Article 189b of the EC Treaty) defines the procedure to be followed where references are made to it in the substantive Treaty articles. The 1997 Treaty has considerably extended the Parliament's right to co-decision with the Council. The new areas to which the co-decision procedure applies include: non-discrimination on the grounds of nationality (Article 12 – formerly, Article 6); freedom of movement and residence (Article 19 – formerly, Article 8a(2)); social security for migrant workers (Article 42 – formerly, Article 51); right of establishment for foreign nationals (Article 46 – formerly, Article 56(2)); rules governing professions (Article 47 – formerly, Article 57(2)); implementation of transport policy (Article 71 – formerly, Article 75, and Article 80 – formerly, Article 84); provisions arising from the social protocol; decisions implementing the Social Fund (Article 148 – formerly, Article 125); vocational training (Article 150 – formerly, Article 127(4)); public health (Article 152 – formerly, Article 129); provisions relating to trans-European networks (Article 153 – formerly, Article 129d); decisions implementing the European Regional Development Fund (Article 157 – formerly, Article 130e); research (Article 157 – formerly, Article 130o); the

---

116 Given effect in the United Kingdom by the European Community (Amendment) Act 1986.

117 EC Treaty, Art 189 (formerly, EC Treaty, Art 137).

118 On Parliament's powers under the TEU, see Bradley, KStC, '"Better rusty than missing"? The institutional reforms of the Maastricht Treaty and the European Parliament', in *op cit*, O'Keefe and Twomey, fn 20.

environment (Article 157 – formerly, Article 130s(1)); development co-operation (Article 157 – formerly, Article 130w); equal opportunities and equal treatment (Article 141 – formerly, Article 119); openness (Article 254 – formerly, Article 191a); measures to counter fraud (Article 279 – formerly, Article 209a); statistics (Article 285 – formerly, Article 213a); creation of an advisory body on data protection (Article 286 – formerly, Article 213b); incentive measures for employment (Article 129 – formerly, Article 109r); customs co-operation (Article 136 – formerly, Article 116); incentive measures for combating social exclusion (Article 137 – formerly, Article 118(2))).[119]

Where Parliament is given a role in the decision making process, Parliament is required to complete its first reading of a proposal within a strict time limit. Thus, for example, under Article 251 (formerly, Article 189b), if Parliament 'has not taken a decision' within three months,[120] and the period has not been extended, the Council 'shall adopt the act in question in accordance with its common position'.

Article 251 also requires that, at second reading, Parliament must act by an absolute majority of its Members in order to reject or amend the common position adopted by the Council. This is a far weaker power than it would have been had the suggestion of Parliament been adopted, namely that Parliament could reject or amend the Council's position by a simple majority. Where Parliament does reject or amend the proposal by an absolute majority, the 'conciliation procedure' comes into play. This process involves convening a Conciliation Committee which is made up of an equal number of Members of the Council and Parliament.[121] The Committee meets in order to attempt to reconcile the two opposing views within a six week time limit.[122] The Commission attends and is charged with the task of securing reconciliation and agreement.[123] If the conciliation is successful, the Council, acting by a qualified majority, and Parliament, acting by an absolute majority of its Members, may adopt the measure in question within a six week period.[124] Under reforms introduced by the Treaty of Amsterdam, the former requirement of a third reading by Parliament has been dropped, thus simplifying the procedure and securing greater equality between the Council and Parliament. If the conciliation procedure is unsuccessful under these new arrangements, the proposed instrument will not be adopted.

---

119 Under EC Treaty, Arts 40, 54(2), 57(1), 95, 149, 151, 152, 157 (formerly, EC Treaty, Arts 49, 54(2), 57(1), 100a(1), 100b(1), 126(4), 128(5), 129(4), 129a(2), 129(d) 130i(1), 130s(3))).

120 The period is extendable; see EC Treaty, Art 251(7) (formerly, EC Treaty, Art 189b(7)).

121 EC Treaty, Art 251(3) (formerly, EC Treaty, Art 189b(3)).

122 *Ibid*, Art 251(5) (formerly, EC Treaty, Art 189b(5)). The six week time limit may be extended by two weeks: EC Treaty, Art 251(7) (formerly, EC Treaty, Art 189b(7)).

123 *Ibid*, Art 251(4) (formerly, EC Treaty, Art 189b(4)).

124 *Ibid*, Art 251(5) (formerly, EC Treaty, Art 189b(5)).

Parliament also has the right to request the Commission to submit legislative proposals, although this power is limited.[125] There is no power given to Parliament to draft a proposal itself if the Commission does not act within the time limit suggested by the Parliament.

The Treaty on European Union 1992 provided that Parliament shall appoint an ombudsman to inquire into allegations of maladministration within the Community.[126] Article 195 of the EC Treaty, as revised by the 1997 Treaty, now regulates this matter. Parliament may also establish committees of inquiry to investigate allegations of maladministration.[127]

How should the Parliament's role be evaluated? Prior to the extension of Parliament's legislative role under the Single European Act, the Treaty on European Union 1992 and the Amsterdam Treaty 1997, in many instances, the European Parliament had limited control over what happened after it had been consulted. The Council of Ministers could in many areas, if acting unanimously, ignore the views of Parliament. Nor was the Council bound by Opinions issued by the Parliament. If a matter required urgent attention, the Council might act without gaining Parliament's opinion. Parliament was not consulted on all Council legislation. For example, traditionally, no consultation was required on external trade agreements which the Council concluded on behalf of the Member States.

The Single European Act gave the Parliament power to agree or to veto special trade agreements. The Single European Act also extended Parliament's role in the admission of new Member States, whose admission must be approved by a majority, thus giving the Parliament a power of veto. Where Parliament is given a role in the legislative process under Article 251, as revised (formerly, Article 189b), its role is subject to the limitations of being required to act by an absolute majority – rather than simple majority – of its Members, and the time limits imposed, although extendable,[128] represent a real restriction on what Parliament may be expected to accomplish – particularly given the relative infrequency of its meetings, and the short duration of its sessions.

With the powers of Parliament enhanced under the Single European Act and the Treaties on European Union 1992 and 1997 and, most significantly, the extensive increase in the areas over which the Parliament has a right of co-decision with the Council introduced by the Maastricht Treaty but reformed under the 1997 Treaty, the European Parliament has gradually been given the powers needed to offset the perception that the Parliament lacked a real role in legislation, including a properly functioning veto power.

---

125 EC Treaty, Art 190 (formerly, EC Treaty, Art 138b).
126 See, further, Chapter 26. By inserting a new Art 138e into the EC Treaty.
127 EC Treaty, Art 193 (formerly, EC Treaty, Art 138c).
128 *Ibid*, Art 249 (formerly, EC Treaty, Art 189b(7)).

The European Council

The year 1974 saw the formalisation of an informal arrangement which had pertained from the 1960s. A communiqué was issued at the Paris Summit of Heads of Government and Foreign Ministers of Member States, of which the following is the most important:

> Recognising the need for an overall approach to the internal problems involved in achieving European unity and the external problems facing Europe, the Heads of Government consider it essential to ensure progress and overall consistency in the activities of the Community and in the work on political co-operation.

> The Heads of Government have therefore decided to meet, accompanied by Ministers of Foreign Affairs, three times a year and, whenever necessary, in the Council of the Community and in the context of political co-operation.

The constitutional implications of the communiqué are twofold. In the first place, the communiqué represented an adjustment of the institutional arrangements of the Community (now, Union) which were brought about without recourse to the formal Treaty amending provisions, a mechanism demonstrating the dynamic and flexible means by which the Community and Union can evolve. Secondly, the motivation behind the communiqué lay in the perception that the role of the Commission had been reduced by the Member States' insistence on protection of their national interests, as exemplified in the increasing use of the unanimous vote in Council which had the effect of stultifying the growth of the Community. The first official recognition of the communiqué, which had no legal standing, is found in the Single European Act 1986,[129] which specified the membership of the European Council and reduces the minimum number of annual meetings from three to two. The Treaty on European Union 1997 confirms this arrangement and Article 4 of the Treaty (formerly, Article D of the Treaty on Union 1992) states that:

> The European Council shall provide the Union with the necessary impetus for its development and shall define the general political guidelines thereof.

> ...

> The European Council shall submit to the European Parliament a report after each of its meetings and a yearly written report on the progress achieved by the Union.

The Heads of Government and Foreign Ministers accordingly meet twice a year, together with the President of the Commission, two Members of the Commission and officials. A primary purpose of the meetings is to review economic and social matters such as inflation, economic growth, unemployment, the European monetary system, international political issues,

---

129 EC Treaty, Art 28 (formerly, EC Treaty, Art 30).

reform of the Common Agriculture Policy and constitutional issues such as applications for membership of the Union and political integration.

The decisions reached are political, the European Council having no law making powers. The impact on the Commission, Council of Ministers and Parliament are of constitutional significance. The Commission loses its own power of initiative, the Council of Ministers loses power because decisions are reached at Head of State level, and the Parliament is bypassed in the decision making process.

The Court of Auditors[130]

The Court of Auditors originates in the Financial Provisions Treaty of 1975 but has now been given formal recognition as an institution of the European Union under the Treaty on European Union 1992. The Court of Auditors comprises 15 members, appointed under similar terms and conditions to judges of the European Court of Justice. The term of years is six, and Members are under a duty to act completely independently in the performance of their duties and to act in the general interests of the Community. A President of the Court, appointed for a renewable term of three years, heads the Court of Auditors. It is the Court of Auditors which has responsibility for monitoring the expenditure of the Community. It carries out audits, examining the accounts of all revenue and expenditure of the Community. At the end of each financial year, the Court of Auditors is under a duty to draw up an Annual Report which is forwarded to the other institutions of the Community and published, with replies from these institutions, in the *Official Journal of the European Communities*.

The significance of the Court of Auditors being given the status of a Community institution under the Maastricht Treaty is that it makes available to the Court the full range of legal remedies available to other institutions, thus reinforcing the safeguards which ensure that it is able to perform effectively. The Court of Auditor's task is to assist the European Parliament and the Council of the European Union in exercising their powers of control over the implementation of the budget. The Court may also submit observations on specific questions and deliver opinions at the request of one of the European institutions.

The Court of Auditors is required to provide the Council and Parliament with a Statement of Assurance relating to the reliability of accounts and the legality of the underlying transactions. In its auditing function, the Court of Auditors may examine records in the European institutions and the Member States. The Court of Auditors examines the accounts of Community revenue

---

130 EC Treaty, Arts 246–48 (formerly, EC Treaty, Art 188).

and expenditure and considers whether these have been received and incurred in a lawful manner and whether the financial management has been sound. The Court of Auditors is independent and has the power to carry out its audits at any level. In addition to monitoring the internal revenues and expenditure of the Union, the Court of Auditors also monitors co-operation agreements between the European Union and many developing countries, and the system of Community aid to Central and Eastern Europe.

The Economic and Social Committee

The Economic and Social Committee is appointed by the Council, and has 222 members, appointed on the basis of the populations of Members States. The Member States submit lists of nominees for appointment, and are required to nominate twice as many persons as will be appointed.[131] Members of the Committee are representative of different occupational and social groups. Article 257 of the EC Treaty (formerly, Article 193) stipulates that the Committee has advisory status. Article 257 also stipulates that, in particular, the Committee shall have representatives of producers, farmers, carriers, workers, dealers, craftsmen, professional occupations and representatives of the general public.

The Committee of the Regions

Under the Treaty on European Union 1992, the Committee of the Regions, comprising 222 representatives of regional and local bodies, was established, with advisory status.[132] It advises the Council and Commission on education, culture and regional development. The Committee, headed by a Chairman, meets at the request of the Council or Commission, and may also meet on its own initiative. The Committee must be consulted by the Council or the Commission where the Treaty so provides.

The European Investment Bank[133]

Established under the Treaty on European Union 1992, the European Investment Bank is charged with the task of promoting the 'balanced and steady development of the common market in the interest of the Community'.

---

131 EC Treaty, Art 259 (formerly, EC Treaty, Art 195).
132 *Ibid*, Arts 263–65 (formerly, EC Treaty, Art 198a, b, c).
133 *Ibid*, Arts 266–67 (formerly, EC Treaty, Art 198d, e).

The Bank operates on a non-profit making basis, and grants loans and can give guarantees which facilitate the financing of a number of projects, including projects for developing less developed regions, modernising or conversion projects and projects of common interest to several Member States.

The European Court of Justice[134]

The judges in the European Court of Justice (ECJ) are appointed by 'common accord of the governments of Member States'. Each State makes one nomination. Unlike superior judges in the United Kingdom, the qualification for appointment to judicial office in the ECJ is that candidates are 'persons whose independence is beyond doubt and who possess the qualifications required for appointment to the highest judicial offices in their respective countries or who are jurisconsults of recognised competence'.[135] Judges are appointed for a six year term of office.[136]

The Court is presided over by a President who holds office for a three year term. Assisting the judges are eight Advocates General,[137] whose duties are defined in the Treaty[138] as 'acting with complete impartiality and independence, to make, in open court, reasoned submissions on cases brought before the Court of Justice ...'. It is the Advocates General who will examine each case and present the legal arguments to the Court for its decision.

Pressure on the ECJ resulted in a Court of First Instance being introduced under the Single European Act 1986. Starting work in 1989, the Court of First Instance consists of 12 Members with the majority of cases being heard in Chambers comprising three or five judges. The Court of First Instance is not empowered to hear and determine questions referred for a preliminary ruling under Article 234 of the EC Treaty (formerly, Article 177), on which see further, Chapter 9.[139]

The role of the ECJ is provided for in the most general terms by Article 220 of the EC Treaty (formerly, Article 164): 'The Court of Justice shall ensure that in the interpretation and application of this Treaty, the law is observed.'

At first sight, given that the jurisdiction of the Court is derived solely from the treaties, Article 220 would seem to confine the ECJ to consideration of

---

134 EC Treaty, Arts 220–24 (formerly, EC Treaty, Arts 164–68).
135 *Ibid*, Art 223 (formerly, EC Treaty, Art 167).
136 *Ibid*, Art 223 (formerly, EC Treaty, Art 167).
137 See *ibid*, Art 222 (formerly, EC Treaty, Art 166).
138 *Ibid*, Art 222 (formerly, EC Treaty, Art 166).
139 *Ibid*, Art 225 (formerly, EC Treaty, Art 168a).

Community law, a point reinforced by the wording of Article 234 of the Treaty (formerly, Article 177).[140] In the early days, the Court adopted this narrow interpretation of its jurisdiction and the Court rejected any invitation to draw on the law of Member States in the forming of decisions. From the 1970s at least, a change in attitude can be discerned in the reasoning of the Court. From that time, judges felt able, indeed compelled, to make recourse to domestic law of Member States in order to ensure both the effectiveness of Community law within a particular Member State and to produce harmony between the laws of all Member States. The Court accordingly draws particularly on fundamental concepts existing in the laws of Member States in order to enable common legal concepts to be incorporated into Community law.[141] It is the need for uniformity of the law within the legal systems of Member States which represents a major function of the Court.

Under Article 226 of the Treaty (formerly, Article 169), the Court of Justice may make rulings on a matter brought before it by the Commission alleging breach of the treaties by a Member State. Prior to bringing the matter to the ECJ, the Commission exercises a quasi-judicial function. The Commission must first consider that a Member State has failed to fulfil a Treaty obligation and, secondly, give a reasoned opinion to that State and advise as to the action which must be taken, and the time limit for action to be taken to comply with the opinion. Only if a Member State fails to comply with the opinion will the matter be taken to the ECJ.

Two early examples of the circumstances giving rise to the use of this power are provided in *Commission v Italy*[142] and *Commission v United Kingdom*.[143] In the latter case, a Regulation issued by the Council came into effect on 1 January 1976, requiring Member States to introduce tachographs[144] into certain commercial vehicles. In February 1976, the United Kingdom government sent a draft statutory instrument, which showed the intention to introduce a voluntary rather than compulsory scheme. The Commission reiterated the compulsory nature of the scheme and, in May 1977, the government indicated that it would not comply. In October 1977, the Commission initiated action under Article 169 of the EC Treaty (now, Article 226). In January 1978, the government stated that, due to trades union objections, it was unable to comply. In February 1978, the Commission gave its reasoned opinion requiring compliance and a two month period in which to comply. In June 1978, the matter went to the European Court. In February

---

140 On which, see below, p 314.

141 See Mendelsen, M, 'The European Court of Justice and human rights' (1981) 1 YBEL 126; Dauses, M, 'The protection of fundamental right in the Community legal order' (1985) 10 EL Rev 398.

142 [1979] 1 CMLR 206.

143 [1979] 2 CMLR 45.

144 Devices which monitor a driver's speed, hours and distance travelled.

1979, the ECJ ruled that the United Kingdom was in breach of the Treaty. Failure to transpose a Directive into national law by the stipulated date will not be excused on the basis that transposition required revision of provisions of a Member State's constitution. The Court of Justice so held in *Commission v Kingdom of Belgium*,[145] in which an action was lodged under Article 169 of the EC Treaty for a declaration that Belgium had failed to bring into force within the prescribed period the laws, regulations and administrative provisions necessary to comply with Council Directive 94/80/EC, which laid down detailed arrangements for the exercise of the right to vote and to stand as a candidate in municipal elections by citizens of the Union residing in a Member State of which they are not nationals.

Under Article 227 of the Treaty (formerly, Article 170), one Member State may bring a fellow Member State before the Court. Again, a procedure is specified which gives the Commission a quasi-judicial function. Before an action is brought before the Court the aggrieved Member State must bring the matter to the attention of the Commission. Once again, the Commission must give a reasoned opinion, the Member State having been given the opportunity to make oral and written submissions on the allegation. Once this procedure has been completed, the Member State has a discretion whether or not to bring the matter before the Court. If the Commission fails to act and deliver its opinion within three months from the date of the allegation, then the aggrieved State may proceed with the action before the Court.

Article 228 of the Treaty (formerly, Article 171) provides that, if the ECJ finds that a Member State has failed to fulfil its obligations, the State shall be required to take the necessary measures to comply with the judgment of the Court. However, one of the principal defects in the ECJ's power lay in its inability to impose sanctions.

The Treaty of Amsterdam introduced two significant reforms. In relation to policies relating to free movement of persons, visas, asylum and immigration, the Court of Justice is given jurisdiction to make rulings on questions of interpretation of the relevant Treaty provision and to rule on the validity or interpretation of acts of the institutions of the Community. This right is confined to courts or tribunals against which there is no judicial remedy, and provides that that tribunal or court *must* refer the matter for a ruling. The Court may also give rulings on the interpretation of these matters when requested by the Council, Commission or a Member State. The Court does not have jurisdiction, however, to rule on any measure relating to the maintenance of law and order and the safeguarding of internal security.[146] The Court's jurisdiction is also extended in relation to the third pillar (Police and Judicial Co-operation in Criminal Matters, formerly, Justice and Home

---

145 Case C-323/97: judgment 9 July 1998.
146 EC Treaty, Art 68 (formerly, EC Treaty, Art 73p).

Affairs), to give preliminary rulings, in respect of which, Member States have made a declaration stating that they accept this jurisdiction. The Court also has jurisdiction to rule on any dispute between Member States or between the Member States and the Commission in respect of the third pillar.

The increasing volume of work undertaken by the Court of Justice and the Court of First Instance, has led the Court to propose reforms designed to improve efficiency. The Court had advocated a form of accelerated or simplified procedure for dealing with cases of a 'manifestly urgent nature', and for dealing with certain cases on the basis of written procedure alone. In relation to preliminary rulings (under Article 234 – formerly Article 177, on which see below), while the system should remain, the Court has proposed that where an answer to a question is apparent from existing case law, it should rule more frequently by way of simple order, and that Member States could set up judicial bodies with responsibility for dealing with references for preliminary rulings within their territorial jurisdiction.

With the future membership of the Union being set to increase, the Court has expressed concern that the increasing number of judges would 'cross the invisible boundary between a collegiate court and a deliberative assembly', a development which could pose a threat to efficiency and the consistency of case law.

Penalties for failure to comply with rulings of the European Court

The Treaty on European Union 1992 empowered the Court to impose a lump sum or penalty payment against a Member State which fails to respect the judgment of the Court.[147] In January 1997, the Commission agreed the procedures for the imposition of fines on Member States who fail to comply with rulings of the European Court of Justice. Where a Member State is in breach of Community law, the Commission will apply to the Court for a determination of the fine. The levels of fines will be relative to the size of the economy of the State.

Article 230 of the EC Treaty (formerly, Article 173) provides the ECJ's jurisdiction to review the legality of acts adopted 'jointly by the European Parliament and the Council, of acts of the Council [and] of the Commission ...'. The Court is also given jurisdiction to rule on complaints brought by Members States, the Council or the Commission on grounds of 'lack of competence, infringement of an essential procedural requirement, infringement of this Treaty or of any rule of law relating to its application, or misuse of powers'. If an action is well founded, the Court may declare the act concerned to be

---

147 EC Treaty, Art 228 (formerly, EC Treaty, Art 171).

void.[148] It is by these means that the ECJ controls the exercise of powers by the institutions of the Community.[149]

The European Court has ruled that a natural or legal person may challenge the validity of provisions in Directives before a national court, even though that person has not brought an action for annulment under Article 230 of the Treaty, and even though another Member State has already been given judgment in separate proceedings.[150] However, in *Stichting Greenpeace (Greenpeace International) v EC Commission*,[151] the Court ruled that a body who is not individually concerned by a decision and whose situation was not taken into consideration in the adoption of an act, in this case, granting financial assistance to Spain for the construction of power stations, does not have *locus standi* to bring an action seeking annulment under Article 230 of the Commission decision. The decision to build the power station affected environmental rights under the Directive, those rights were protected by the national courts, and the national court, if necessary, could make a reference for a preliminary ruling under Article 234 (formerly, Article 177).

Article 232 of the Treaty (formerly, Article 175) provides the means whereby Member States and institutions of the Community can challenge the Council and Commission on the basis that they have failed to act as required under the Treaty. The use of Article 232 (formerly, Article 175) is illustrated by the European Parliament's attempt to push the Council over the implementation of direct elections to Parliament. Article 138(3) of the original EC Treaty (now, Article 190(4)) stated that the Assembly shall draw up proposals for direct elections, which it did in 1960. Article 138(3)(2) stated that the Council shall, acting unanimously, lay down the appropriate measures for the elections and make recommendations to Members States for their implementation. The Council failed to act and in 1969 the Assembly again requested action, threatening the Council with an action under Article 175 (now, Article 232) for failure to act. Agreement was finally reached and direct elections took place in 1979. Article 138 also provided that the voting procedure employed within Member States for the election of Members of the European Parliament would be 'uniform'. This measure lapsed in 1979, when it became clear that uniformity would not be achievable.[152] Article 138 now simply provides that representatives in the European Parliament 'shall be elected by direct universal suffrage'.[153]

---

148 EC Treaty, Art 231 (formerly, EC Treaty, Art 174).

149 See *op cit*, Steiner, 1995, fn 1, and references therein. Most recently, see Case C-42/97: *European Parliament v Council of the European Union*, judgment 23 February 1999.

150 Case C-408/95: *Eurotunnel SA v Seafrance* [1998] 2 CMLR 293.

151 Case C-321/95P: [1998] 3 CMLR 1

152 Council Decision and Act of 20 September 1976 on Direct Elections.

153 EC Treaty, Art 190 (formerly, EC Treaty, Art 138).

In *Commission of the European Communities, supported by Kingdom of Spain and United Kingdom v French Republic,*[154] the Court of Justice ruled that France had failed to fulfil its obligations under the Treaty (Article 30, in conjunction with Article 5), in that it had failed to adopt appropriate measures to prevent farmers and others from obstructing the free movement of fruit and vegetables. The Court ruled that the free movement of goods was one of the fundamental principles of the Treaty. The French government had failed to prevent violent and obstructive behaviour by farmers and others and therefore its failure placed it in breach of the Treaty requirements.

The Treaty of Amsterdam 1997 introduces penalties for the failure of Member States to respect fundamental rights and freedoms as guaranteed by the European Convention of Human Rights. This issue is discussed further below.

Article 234 of the EC Treaty (formerly, Article 177)[155]

The single most important jurisdiction in terms of the harmonisation of laws is that conferred on the Court to give preliminary rulings under Article 234. The Court may rule on the interpretation of the Treaty, and on the validity and interpretation of acts of the institutions of the Community. Article 234 provides that:

The Court of Justice shall have jurisdiction to give preliminary rulings concerning:

(a) the interpretation of this Treaty;

(b) the validity and interpretation of acts of the institutions of the Community and of the European Central Bank (ECB);

(c) the interpretation of the statutes of bodies established by an act of the Council, where those statutes so provide.

Where such a question is raised before any court or tribunal of a Member State that court or tribunal may, if it considers that a decision on the question is necessary to enable it to give judgment, request the Court of Justice to give a ruling thereon.

Where any such question is raised in a case pending before a court or tribunal of a Member State against whose decision there is no judicial remedy under national law, that court or tribunal shall bring the matter before the Court of Justice.

It is this Article which raises directly the nature of the legal system of the Community and the relationship between Community law, the European Court of Justice and domestic law and the role of judges in national courts.

---

154 Case C-265/95: (1997) *The Times,* 11 December.

155 See Arnull, A, 'The scope of Article 177' (1988) 13 EL Rev 40, 'The uses and abuses of Article 177 EEC' (1989) 52 MLR 622 and 'References to the European Court' (1990) 15 EL Rev 375.

Article 234 is crucial to the development of Community law and the Treaty of Rome (the EEC Treaty, now the EC Treaty) extended the jurisdiction of the Court in a significant manner. Under the European Coal and Steel Treaty, the Court had power to rule on the validity of Community actions when the issue was in question before the national court – but it did not, unlike the Court of Justice under the EEC Treaty, have jurisdiction to interpret the Treaty. There is a vast difference in power between being able to rule on the *vires* of an action of an institution and the power to interpret the Treaty provisions themselves.

The latter power gives to the Court a dynamic function as opposed to the more limited review function, which, whilst important, did not entail any development of substantive law by interpretative methods. Under Article 234, the ECJ has been given a role in the creation of law at least as important as the legislative powers of the Commission and Council. This power, as utilised, is a matter of some controversy with the European Court being both criticised and praised for adopting a deliberate policy making stance which goes beyond that of interpretation of the Treaty.[156]

Article 234 envisages a partnership approach between the domestic courts and the European Court of Justice. It is important both as a matter of principle and as a practical matter that the domestic courts are actively involved in the application of Community law, and that a measure of discretion is left to domestic courts in the matter of referring a matter to the ECJ under Article 234. It must also be recognised, however, that the discretion left to domestic courts carries with it the potential for a distortion of the meaning of Community law within the 15 legal systems. A particular difficulty faces the courts in the United Kingdom, whose traditional approach to the interpretation of statutes has been one very much constrained by the detailed wording of statutes and the pedantic literal, golden and mischief rules. By contrast, in civil law systems,[157] the judges are experienced in interpreting broadly phrased statutory provisions, using the teleological[158] interpretative method. Lord Diplock explained the approach of the European Court in *Henn and Darby v Director of Public Prosecutions*:[159]

> The European Court, in contrast to English courts, applies teleological rather than historical methods to the interpretation of the Treaties and other Community legislation. It seeks to give effect to what it conceives to be the spirit rather than the letter of the Treaties; sometimes, indeed, to an English judge, it may seem to the exclusion of the letter. It views the Community as living and expanding organisms and the interpretation of the provisions of the Treaties as changing to match their growth.[160]

156 See Rasmussen, H, 'Between self-restraint and activism; a judicial policy for the European Court' (1988) 13 EL Rev 28; Slynn, G, 'The Court of Justice of the European Community' (1984) 33 ICLQ 409.

157 Defined as those deriving primarily from Roman law.

158 That is to say, seeking the interpretation which most closely fits the objective sought by the legislature.

159 [1981] AC 850.

160 *Ibid*, p 852.

Under Community law, both the common law and civil law systems must coexist in a manner which best promotes the harmony of the new legal system created by the treaties. For harmony to be achieved, it is axiomatic that judges with very differing backgrounds and experience adopt a common approach both to interpretation and to the circumstances under which it is appropriate and necessary to refer a matter to the European Court of Justice for interpretation. In order to understand the relationship between the European Court of Justice and national courts, and the issue of the supremacy of Community law, it is first necessary to examine the sources of Community law, and the manner in which Community law comes into effect in domestic law. This matter is discussed in the next chapter.

THE EUROPEAN UNION AND THE EUROPEAN CONVENTION ON HUMAN RIGHTS

The Convention for the Protection of Human Rights and Fundamental Freedoms – drafted and enacted in 1950 under the aegis of the Council of Europe[161] – establishes a charter of rights and freedoms which are protected by the Commission and Court of Human Rights in Strasbourg.[162] Article 230 of the Treaty of Rome 1957 (now, Article 303 of the EC Treaty)[163] envisaged close links with the Council of Europe.[164] The EC itself, however, has not as such been bound by the Convention.[165]

In 1979 the Commission of the European Community adopted a Memorandum endorsing the option of accession by the EC to the Convention.[166] A number of obstacles lie in the way of such accession. First, it would enable the rights enshrined in the Convention to enter indirectly into those dualist States[167] which had not incorporated the Convention into domestic law. Secondly, it would further increase the workload of the already stretched Strasbourg machinery. Thirdly, it would pose problems for the enforcement of rights in those States seeking admission to the European Community which do not yet conform to the principle of the rule of law and

---

161 Of which, all Member States of the European Community are Members.

162 Institutional changes have been effected to unify the Commission and the Court; see, further, Chapter 22.

163 Establishing the European Economic Community.

164 Article 230 states that 'The Community shall establish all appropriate forms of co-operation with the Council of Europe'.

165 *Confederation Française Democratique du Travail v European Community* [1979] 25 CMLR 229.

166 2/79 Bulletin EC Supp.

167 The United Kingdom, Ireland and Denmark.

protection of rights which underlies membership of the European Community and Union.[168]

The Preamble to the Single European Act 1986 had already made explicit the concern for the protection of human rights within the Community. The Preamble stated a:

> ... determination to promote Democracy on the basis of the Fundamental Rights recognised in the constitutions of the Member States, in the Convention for the Protection of Human Rights and the European Social Charter, notably freedom, equality and social justice.

Article 6 of the Treaty on European Union 1997 (formerly, Article F of the TEU 1992) goes further, and states that:

> The Union shall respect fundamental rights, as guaranteed by the European Convention for the Protection of Human Rights and Fundamental Freedoms signed in Rome on 4 November 1950 and as they result from the constitutional traditions common to the Member States, as general principles of Community law.

The original Treaties gave no explicit reference to the protection of individual rights in their entirety, although Treaty articles such as Article 119[169] provide for equal treatment of men and women in matters of employment. The manner in which the ECJ has developed the jurisprudence on rights is linked inextricably with its insistence on the supremacy of Community law over the domestic law of Member States. That evolution has been considered above, where it was seen from cases such as *Costa v ENEL*,[170] and *Internationale Handelsgesellschaft GmbH v EVST*[171] that, in conflicts between the laws of Member States – even laws protecting fundamental rights – Community law must prevail. In 1969, the Court of Justice turned its attention specifically to the status of fundamental individual rights in relation to the principles of Community law. In *Stauder v City of Ulm*,[172] the ECJ stated that it had a duty to protect the rights of individuals as provided for by the constitution of the Member State, and that such provisions formed part of the general principles of Community law. The *Handelsgesellschaft* case clarified the relationship between domestic constitutional law and Community law in matters of rights. The ECJ expressed its opinion that respect for fundamental rights 'forms an integral part of the general principles of law protected by the Court of Justice. The protection of such rights, whilst inspired by the constitutional traditions common to the Member States, must be ensured within the framework of the

---

168 Eg, the former Yugoslavia. Turkey's application for membership was rejected in 1989 because of alleged violations of human rights.

169 Now, Art 141, and amended under the TEU 1997.

170 Case 6/64: [1964] ECR 585.

171 Case 11/70: [1970] ECR 1125.

172 Case 29/69: [1969] ECR 419.

structures and objectives of the Community'.[173] In *Nold v Commission*,[174] a case concerning a person's status as a wholesaler, the ECJ ruled that, consistent with its earlier judgment in *Handelsgesellschaft*, constitutional rights protected under Member States' constitutions must be respected, but also declared that 'international treaties for the protection of human rights' can 'supply guidelines which should be followed within the framework of Community law'.[175] The European Convention on Human Rights,[176] the International Labour Organisation treaties,[177] the Council of Europe's European Social Charter, the International Covenants on Civil and Political and Economic, Social and Cultural Rights[178] have all been cited by the ECJ as aids to interpretation of Community law.

On a piecemeal, case by case basis, the ECJ has gradually and steadily incorporated the protection of individual rights into its case law. However, while all Member States of the Community are signatories to the European Convention on Human Rights (ECHR), the EC is not a party to the ECHR, and the relationship between the EC and ECHR remains indistinct. The ECJ accepts the significance of the ECHR, and regards the ECHR provisions as part of the general principles of Community law. However, that position does not go so far as to amount to the ECHR being regarded as a central, integral part of Community law. Academics disagree as to whether the ECHR is binding on the law of the EC. HG Schermers has argued that the EC is bound by the ECHR.[179] Conversely, A Dremczewski argues that the ECHR does not bind the EC.[180] Whatever the precise status of the ECHR, and its relationship with the Community, it is clear that the ECJ is committed to the protection of rights. What remains unclear, is the breadth of the protection which the ECJ will afford to provisions of the ECHR. On the question of whether accession by the Community to the European Convention on Human Rights was compatible with the Treaty establishing the Community, the European Court of Justice has itself ruled that there is no legal basis in the Treaty for such

---

173 Case 11/70: [1970] ECR 1125, p 1134.

174 Case 4/73: [1974] ECR 491.

175 *Ibid*, para 13.

176 Discussed in Chapter 22. See *Rutili v Ministre de L'Interieur* [1975] ECR 1219.

177 See Case 43/75: *Defrenne v SABENA* [1978] ECR 1365.

178 See Case C-262/88: *Barber v Guardian Royal Exchange Insurance Company* [1990] 2 CMLR 513.

179 See Schermers, HG, 'The European Community bound by fundamental human rights' (1990) 27 CML Rev 249 and *Judicial Protection in the European Community*, 4th edn, 1987, Dordrecht: Kluwer.

180 Dremczewski, A, 'The domestic application of the European Human Rights Convention as European Community law' (1981) ICLQ 118.

accession, and that accession could only be brought about by amendment of the Treaty.[181]

The Treaty of Amsterdam 1997, reiterating the fundamental commitment of the Union to human rights and fundamental freedoms, introduces the power to issue penalties to Member States who are in breach of rights. Aware of the potential problems entailed in the enlargement of the Union and the admission of Member States with a poor record on human rights, the Treaty provides for a penalty falling short of expulsion from the Union, a penalty which itself could undermine the protection of rights of that Member State's citizens. Article 7 of the Treaty on European Union (formerly, Article F.1) provides that:

> The Council, meeting in the composition of the Heads of State or Government and acting by unanimity on a proposal by one third of the Member States or by the Commission and after obtaining the assent of the European Parliament, may determine the existence of a serious and persistent breach by a Member State of principles mentioned in Article 6(1), after inviting the government of the Member State in question to submit its observations.

> Where such a determination has been made, the Council, acting by a qualified majority, may decide to suspend certain of the rights deriving from the application of this Treaty to the Member State in question, including the voting rights of the representative of the government of that Member State in the Council. In doing so, the Council shall take into account the possible consequences of such a suspension on the rights and obligations of natural and legal persons.

The principle of respect for human rights is also binding on Member States when acting within the scope of Community law, namely when implementing an EC measure,[182] or seeking to derogate from a fundamental freedom.[183] On the draft Charter of Fundamental Rights, see above, p 285.

---

181 Opinion No 2/94: (1996) *The Times*, 16 April, [1996] ECR I-1759.

182 Case C-5/1998: *Wauchauf v Bundescourt für Ernährung und Fortwistschalt* [1989] ECR 2609.

183 Case C-260/1989: *ERT v Dimotiki* [1991] ECR I-2925.

CHAPTER 9

EUROPEAN COMMUNITY LAW AND NATIONAL LAW

SOURCES OF COMMUNITY LAW

Having examined the structure, institutions and law making process of the European Union and Community in the previous chapter, it is now necessary to turn attention to the forms of Community law and the interaction between Community law and domestic law. The primary sources of Community law are the Treaties, as amended. These include the original EEC Treaty and its Protocols as amended by later Treaties – the Merger Treaty 1965, Acts of Accession, budgetary Treaties, the Single European Act 1986, the Treaty on European Union 1992, and the Treaty on European Union 1997 (the Treaty of Amsterdam).[1]

Secondary legislation is law made by the Community institutions, and includes the interpretation of both primary and secondary sources by the European Court of Justice (ECJ). Secondary legislation comprises regulations, directives and decisions. Article 249 of the EC Treaty (formerly, Article 189) defines these terms as follows:

> In order to carry out the task, the Council and Commission shall, in accordance with the provisions of this Treaty, make regulations, issue directives, take decisions, make recommendations or deliver opinions ...
>
> A regulation shall have general application. It shall be binding in its entirety and directly applicable in all Member States;
>
> A directive shall be binding, as to the result to be achieved, upon each Member State to which it is addressed, but shall leave to the national authorities the choice of form or methods;
>
> A decision shall be binding in its entirety upon those to whom it is addressed;
>
> Recommendations and opinions shall have no binding force.

---

1   It should be noted that the 1997 Treaty changes the Article numbers in the Treaties. In this text, the new Article number is cited first, with the former number in brackets, except in relation to case law relating to EC Treaty Articles before revision of the Treaty, where the new Article numbers are shown in brackets.

DIRECT APPLICABILITY AND DIRECT EFFECT[2]

The principles of direct applicability and direct effect[3]

As can be seen from the text of Article 249, a regulation is 'binding in its entirety' and has direct applicability. By 'direct applicability' it is meant that the measure leaves no discretion to the Member States but, rather, confers rights and duties within the Member States without further legislative participation. In other words, the provision is self-executing.[4] On the other hand, a directive, whilst binding in its objective, leaves to the Member State some leeway in its introduction and the manner in which a Member State implements and achieves the objectives set by the Council and Commission.

In order to understand the way in which Community law operates within Member States' legal systems, the principle of direct effect must be examined. The basic principle of direct effect of Community measures is that nationals of Member States may invoke certain provisions as conferring direct rights, which individuals may rely in national courts. While Article 249 states specifically that regulations are directly applicable, the Article is silent as to the legal *consequence* of this applicability, and as to whether a Treaty provision itself, or regulations or directives, can have direct legal effect on individuals.

The principle of direct effect is linked to Article 10 of the EC Treaty (formerly, Article 5). Article 10 provides, in part, that:

> Member States shall take all appropriate measures, whether general or particular, to ensure fulfilment of the obligations arising out of this Treaty or resulting from action taken by institutions of the Community. They shall facilitate the achievement of Community tasks. They shall abstain from any measure which could jeopardise the attainment of the objectives of this Treaty.[5]

As can be seen from Article 10, Member States are under a legal duty both to take action to ensure compliance with Community law and to refrain from any action which might impede the application and effectiveness of Community law. Article 10 forms the basis for much of the jurisprudence of

---

2   See, *inter alia*, Steiner, J, 'From direct effects to *Francovich*: shifting means of enforcement of Community law' (1993) 18(3) EL Rev 3; Ross, M, 'Beyond *Francovich*' (1993) 56 MLR 55.

3   The two terms are used synonymously by the Court of Justice of the European Communities. See Winter, T, 'Direct applicability and direct effect: two distinct and different concepts in Community law' (1972) 9 CML Rev 425; Eleftheriadis, P, 'The direct effect of Community law: conceptual issues' (1996) 16 YBEL 205.

4   See *Consorzio del Prosciutto di Parma v Asda Food Stores Ltd* [1999] 1 CMLR 696; [1999] Eu LR 437, in which the Court of Appeal ruled that a regulation did not have direct effect, *inter alia*, since it was not sufficiently clear and precise and itself indicated that it was not intended to have direct effect.

5   See Temple-Lang, J, 'Community constitutional law: Article 5 EC Treaty' (1990) 27 CML Rev 645.

the ECJ, and the foundation for the enforcement of individual rights against Member States.

Direct effect and Articles of the Treaty

In 1963, the ECJ articulated the theoretical basis for the principle of direct effect in *Van Gend en Loos*,[6] a case which involved a reference to the ECJ from the Dutch courts. From this case, virtually all significant later developments of Community law can be seen to originate. Under Article 25 of the EC Treaty (formerly, Article 12):

> Customs duties on imports and exports and charges having equivalent effect shall be prohibited between Member States. This prohibition shall also apply to customs duties of a fiscal nature.

Before 1958, and the coming into force of the EC Treaty, the Dutch firm of Van Gend en Loos had been importing glue from Germany, applying a customs duty of three per cent. In 1959, the Dutch ratified an agreement with other countries establishing an eight per cent duty. The company protested to the Customs Court, relying on the direct effect of Article 12 of the EC Treaty (now, Article 25). The Court referred the matter to the ECJ under Article 177 (now, Article 234). The principal question for the court was whether, as claimed, Article 12 had direct effect on the legal position on the company. The Treaty Article did not stipulate its legal effect, and Article 189 of the EC Treaty (now, Article 249) refers only to regulations having direct effect. The ECJ held, first, that, if a Treaty provision is to confer individual enforceable rights, it must indicate that it applies not just to Member States but also to individuals within the State. Secondly, the provision must be clear and precise. Thirdly, the provision must be unconditional and unqualified and not subject to any further measures on the part of Member States. Finally, the provision must be one which does not leave any substantial latitude or discretion to Member States.

Specifically in relation to Article 12, as it then was, the ECJ held that the text was clear and unconditional, that it required no legislative intervention by the Member State and that the Member State had no power to subordinate Article 12 to its own law. Thus, it can be seen that both provisions in the Treaty and regulations are capable of having direct effect if they satisfy the requirements laid down by the ECJ.

The principle of direct effect of Treaty provisions was examined by the House of Lords and the ECJ in *Henn and Darby v the Director of Public Prosecutions*.[7] In that case, the accused defended a criminal prosecution on the basis that the subject matter of the charge offended against Treaty provisions.

---

6   Case 26/62: [1963] CMLR 105.
7   [1981] AC 850.

The accused were charged with conspiracy to import obscene materials contrary to the law of the United Kingdom. Article 28 of the EC Treaty (formerly, Article 30), however, prohibits quantitative restrictions on imports. The House of Lords referred the matter to the ECJ under Article 177 (now, Article 234), asking the ECJ to interpret Article 30 (now, Article 28) in order to establish whether English law was bound by the restriction in Article 30. In response, the ECJ ruled that English law infringed Article 30 but that lawful restrictions on pornography could be imposed by a Member State under Article 36 of the EC Treaty (now, Article 30), which provides that restrictions on imports otherwise contrary to Article 30 are justified on the grounds of, *inter alia*, public morality, public policy or public security. Accordingly, the prosecution was able to proceed, but the point was established that the defendants could raise the direct effect of Article 30 in their defence.[8]

Directives and direct effect[9]

A further question which arises is whether directives are similarly capable of having direct effect. It has been seen from Article 249 that directives leave no discretion as to their objectives, but do leave some discretion as to manner of implementation. The reasoning of the ECJ is revealed in *Van Duyn v Home Office*.[10] Article 39 of the EC Treaty (formerly, Article 48) provides (in part) that:

1   Freedom of movement for workers shall be secured within the Community.

2   Such freedom of movement shall entail the abolition of any discrimination based on nationality ... as regards employment, remuneration, conditions of work and employment.

3   It shall entail the right, subject to limitations justified on grounds of public policy, public security and public health ...

Yvonne Van Duyn, a Dutch national, arrived in England in May 1973, having accepted a job as a secretary with the Church of Scientology. Immigration Officials refused Ms Van Duyn admission to the United Kingdom on the basis that the Secretary of State considered employment with the Church undesirable. In an action against the Home Office, Ms Van Duyn sought to rely on Article 48 of the EC Treaty and a reference was made to the ECJ under Article 177 (now, Article 234 of the EC Treaty).

---

8   See, also, *Erich Ciola v Land Vorarlberg* [1999] 2 SMLR 1220.

9   See Craig, PP, 'Directives: direct effect, indirect effect and the construction of national legislation' (1997) 22 EL Rev 519.

10 Case 41/74: [1975] 1 CMLR 1.

The directive in question was that of the Council[11] which set out the objective of co-ordinating measures concerning movement and residence. The public policy issue, relied on by the Home Office, was set out in Article 3(1) of Directive 64/221, which stipulates that: '... measures taken on grounds of public policy and public security shall be based exclusively on the personal conduct of the individual concerned.'

The ECJ held that it would be incompatible with the binding effect attributed to a directive by Article 189 (now, Article 249) to exclude in principle – as the United Kingdom government sought to argue – the possibility that the obligation which it imposed might be invoked by those concerned, that usefulness would be weakened if an individual could not rely on it before national courts. Since the directive laid down an obligation which was not subject to any exception or condition, and by its nature did not require intervention on the part of the Community or Member States, it followed that the directive was to be regarded as directly effective and conferred enforceable individual rights which national courts must protect.

Thus, it can be seen that, in some cases, directives, as well as regulations and Treaty provisions, may have direct effect – depending on their wording and clarity and whether or not Member State action is required as a prerequisite to implementation, or whether the deadline for implementation has passed.[12] Where a directive is not precise, and a right insufficiently defined, it will not have direct effect. The Court of Appeal so ruled in *Gibson v East Riding of Yorkshire Council*.[13] At issue was Article 7 of the Working Time Directive,[14] which requires Member States to take necessary measures to ensure that workers are entitled to 'paid annual leave of at least four weeks' in accordance with relevant national legislation. Mummery LJ stated that the right the applicant wished to assert against the council was quite simply not sufficiently defined in Article 7 to be enforceable by an individual in national courts and tribunals.

Vertical and horizontal effect of Community law

In addition to the concept of direct effect, Community law utilises the notion of vertical and horizontal effect of legal provisions, and this complicating factor is one which is the subject of a good deal of argument. In essence, the concept of vertical effect means that a Community measure – whether a regulation or directive (depending on whether the qualifying criteria are met) – is directly enforceable by an individual against the Member State. In other words, the rights conferred and obligations imposed by Community law are enforceable at the suit of an individual against his or her own Member State,

---

11   EC 64/221, Art 3.
12   See Case 148/78: *Pubblico Ministero v Ratti* [1979] ECR 1629.
13   (2000) *The Times*, 6 July.
14   (93/104/EC) OJ L307/18, 1993.

which is responsible for giving effect to the Community provision. For example, in *Van Duyn v The Home Office* (above), the citizen was challenging the decision of a government Minister: the action was thus vertical in nature and the Directive could be invoked. Of greater difficulty is the question of whether an enforceable obligation exists which entitles an individual to pursue his or her rights, not directly against the Member State, but against institutions, organisations or individuals within the Member State other than the government of the State. The form of direct effect – that is to say, vertical or horizontal – will determine the liable body concerned.

With vertical effect, Community law imposes a duty on the Member State to comply and confers an enforceable right on the citizen. The Member State is thus responsible to the citizen for the enforcement of his or her Community rights. Directives enjoy vertical, but not horizontal, effect and can only be invoked against the State and emanations of the State. The Court of Justice denies the possibility of horizontal direct effect, which would extend the liability for failure to comply with Community law requirements to non-State bodies or individuals. However, the concept of indirect effect (on which, see below) of directives complicates this theoretically straightforward position. Under the concept of indirect effect, the Court of Justice insists that national courts have a duty to interpret national law in a manner consistent with Community law directives so far as possible. This doctrine applies even in actions between two individuals, and regardless of whether the directive or national law is earlier in time. Where indirect effect applies, therefore, a directive appears to have been given horizontal effect.

PUBLIC AND QUASI-PUBLIC BODIES

In *Defrenne v SABENA*,[15] the ECJ confirmed the principle of horizontal direct effect of Treaty provisions. In that case, the provision in question was Article 119 of the EC Treaty (now, Article 141). Gabrielle Defrenne, an air hostess with the Belgian airline SABENA, was required, under the contract of employment, to retire at the age of 40, whereas men did not have to retire at that age. Moreover, she was paid less than male employees, and would receive a smaller State pension then men. The State pension question went to the ECJ, which ruled that the EC Treaty did not cover pension rights.[16] Ms Defrenne then commenced actions against her employer, on the issue of equal pay and on the discriminatory retirement ages. In relation to the question of equal pay (but not retirement age), the action was successful.[17] The matter was referred to the ECJ, which ruled that Member States were obliged to implement Article

---

15 [1974] ECR 455.
16 *Defrenne v Belgian State* [1971] ECR 445. See, now, State Social Security Directive 79/7/EEC.
17 Case 149/77: *Defrenne v SABENA* [1978] ECR 1365.

119 by the end of a transitional period, and that the principle of direct effect of the Article entitled individuals to rely on Article 119, (now, Article 141 of the EC Treaty) against both public and private sector employers, even where the provisions implementing the principle of equal pay had not been implemented by the State.[18]

The duty imposed on Member States under Article 10 of the EC Treaty (formerly, Article 5) is clear, and forms the basis for the European Court's jurisprudence on direct effect. The question of whether Article 119 (now, Article 141) could be relied on by individuals against employers was tested in the English courts in *Marshall v Southampton and South West Hampshire Area Health Authority*.[19] The English Sex Discrimination Act 1975 enabled differing retirement ages to be fixed for men and women. Mrs Marshall challenged the legality of the requirement for women to retire at the age of 60, alleging that the Act was contrary to the European Community's Equal Treatment Directive.[20] Two issues, therefore, fell for consideration by the court. First, were different retirements ages in breach of the EC Directive? and, secondly, if so, could an individual rely on the Directive to challenge an Area Health Authority? In other words, the issue was whether the Directive was directly effective against an 'emanation of the State'. An Area Health Authority was deemed to be a public (as opposed to a private) body, and accordingly bound by Community law.

In *Foster v British Gas plc*,[21] however, which also entailed differing retirement ages for employees, the Court of Appeal had held that British Gas, a statutory corporation, was not a public body against whom the Directive could be enforced. The House of Lords sought clarification on this issue from the ECJ under Article 177 (now, Article 234). The ECJ refused to accept British Gas's argument that there was a distinction between a nationalised undertaking and a State agency and ruled that a directive might be relied on against organisations or bodies which were 'subject to the authority or control of the State or had special powers beyond those which result from the normal relations between individuals'. The Court accordingly ruled that a directive might be invoked against 'a body, whatever its legal form, which has been made responsible, pursuant to a measure adopted by the State, for providing a public service under the control of the State and has for that purpose special powers beyond those which result from the normal rules applicable in relations between individuals'. Therefore, British Gas was a public body against which a directive might be enforced, a ruling which the House of Lords subsequently accepted. In *Doughty v Rolls Royce plc*,[22] however, the

---

18 For further discussion of the ECJ's decisions in relations to equality between men and women, see, also, Chapter 19.

19 Case 152/84: [1986] QB 401; 1 CMLR 688; ECR 723.

20 Directive 76/207.

21 Case C-118/89: [1991] 2 AC 306.

22 [1992] IRLR 126.

Court of Appeal distinguished *Foster* and held that Rolls Royce plc, although 'under the control of the State' had not been 'made responsible pursuant to a measure adopted by the State for providing a public service'. Rolls Royce was at the time a nationalised body, responsible for providing defence equipment. However the court distinguished between services for the public, and services provided to the State, and thereby ruled Rolls Royce not to be a public body for the purposes of the effectiveness of directives.

The European Court of Justice, in *Faccini Dori v Recreb srl*,[23] re-examined the principle of the horizontal effect of directives. An EC consumer directive,[24] which had not yet been implemented by the Italian authorities, founded a claim against a private undertaking. The Advocate General argued that the ECJ should extend the principle of direct effect of directives to claims against all parties (irrespective of their public or private nature). The ECJ declined to do this, and reasserted its view that directives could not be invoked directly against private bodies. However, the ECJ referred to the possibility that directives could be deemed to be indirectly effective and also that they might be enforceable via the principle of the liability of the State to give effect to Community measures, as seen in *Francovich and Bonifaci v Italy*[25] (on which, see below).

In relation to directives, the Court of Justice has ruled that these can, at best, have vertical effect against an emanation of the State as laid down in *Marshall v Southampton Area Health Authority (No 1)* and subsequently confirmed, as in *Faccini Dori v Recreb srl*[26] and not horizontal effect. The role of directives in ensuring the harmonisation and approximation of laws within the legal systems of the Member States of the Union, and the manner in which direct effect ensures harmonisation is illustrated by the case of *CIA Security International SA v Signalson SA and Securitel SPRL*,[27] which also has significant implications on the direct effect of directives. Involved in this case was the interpretation of Article 30 of the EC Treaty (free movement of goods) and of Directive 83/189/EEC, which came before the European Court of Justice under a reference under Article 177 (now, Article 234 of the EC Treaty).[28]

Articles 8 and 9 of Directive 83/189 lay down procedures for the provision of information in the field of technical standards and regulations. Under these provisions, Members States must notify the Commission of all draft technical regulations, and, except in particularly urgent cases, suspend their adoption

---

23 Case C-91/92: [1994] ECR I-3325; [1995] 1 CMLR 665.

24 EC 85/577.

25 [1992] IRLR 84; [1993] 2 CMLR 833.

26 [1994] ECR I-3325.

27 Case C-194/94. See Slot, PJ, 'Case C-194/94: *CIA Security International SA v Signalson SA and Securitel SPRL*' (1996) 33 CML Rev 1035; Coppel, J, 'Horizontal effect of directives' [1997] Industrial LJ 69.

28 The reference was made by the Tribunal de Commerce, Commercial Court, Liège.

and implementation for specified periods until the requirement of notification has been complied with. The provisions are unconditional and sufficiently precise in terms of their content to have direct effect and so enable an individual to rely on them before a national court, which *must* decline to apply a national technical regulation which has not been notified in advance in accordance with the directive. The purpose of making such regulations inapplicable is in order to ensure the effectiveness of Community control for which the directive is made. The Court of Justice ruled that:

> It is settled law that, wherever provisions of a directive appear to be, from the point of view of their content, unconditional and sufficiently precise, they may be relied on against any national provision which is not in accordance with the directive.[29]

This decision appears to undermine the clear rule against the horizontal effect of directives as expressed in *Faccini Dori*. Where previously an individual who suffers from the failure of a Member State to implement a directive could resort to a claim for compensation, the decision in *CIA Security* enables an individual to claim in a national court that the directive in question is unenforceable, even in proceedings between private parties. However, the Court of Justice, in its judgment, does not avert to the decision in *Faccini Dori* and certainly does not in express terms state that it is either overruling its former position on the direct effect of directives or that it is departing significantly from its own established jurisprudence.

Subsequent to *CIA Security* came a reference from the District Court of Maastricht for a preliminary ruling in criminal proceedings before the court against Johannes Lemmens.[30] The case also involved Directive 83/189/EEC regarding the provision of information in the field of technical standards and regulations. Mr Lemmens had been charged with driving a vehicle while under the influence of alcohol. Following the decision in *CIA Security*, the Netherlands government drafted a list of national measures which should possibly have been notified to the Commission in accordance with the directive, which included the national regulations concerning equipment for breath analysis. Mr Lemmens had raised the question in court as to the effect of a failure by the government to notify the Commission on his case. The court accordingly made a reference under Article 177 of the EC Treaty (now, Article 234), requesting a preliminary ruling on whether the defendant could successfully rely on the failure of the government to notify the domestic regulations in his defence, and whether a court in criminal proceedings could disapply the regulation of its own motion on account of the failing to notify it as required.

---

29 Case C-194/94: *CIA Security International SA v Signalson SA* (1996) 33 CML Rev 1035; judgment, para 42.

30 Case C-226/97: judgment 16 June 1998.

The Netherlands government contended, in part, that the domestic regulation applied in the field of criminal law which falls outside the sphere of Community law, whereas the French government argued that products concerned with the exercise of public authority and criminal proceedings instituted by Member States fell outside the scope of the directive. The Court of Justice refused to accept those arguments, stating that:

> Although in principle criminal legislation and the rules of criminal procedure are matters for which the Member States are responsible, it does not follow that this branch of the law cannot be affected by Community law.

However, the Court, having reiterated the principle reaffirmed in *CIA Securities* concerning the right of an individual to rely on the directive and the duty of a national court to set aside conflicting domestic legislation, drew a distinction in relation to criminal proceedings such as these. Despite the breach of the obligation to notify in accordance with the directive, the failure to notify did not 'have the effect of making it impossible for evidence obtained by means of such apparatus, authorised in accordance with regulations which have not been notified, to be relied upon against an individual charged with driving while under the influence of alcohol'.[31]

The principle of indirect effect

Whereas the principle of direct effect entails rights which are directly enforceable against the Member State or an emanation of the State, indirect effect provides a more subtle mechanism for ensuring compliance with Community law. Indirect effect involves the application of the duty imposed on Member States under Article 10 of the EC Treaty (formerly, Article 5). Article 10 provides that:

> Member States shall take all appropriate measures, whether general or particular, to ensure fulfilment of the obligations arising out of this Treaty or resulting from action taken by the institutions of the Community. They shall facilitate the achievement of the Community's tasks. They shall refrain from any measure which could jeopardise the attainment of the objectives of this Treaty.

In securing the uniformity of the application of Community law within Member States, the European Court of Justice has utilised Article 10 to great effect. Where, under particular circumstances as defined by the Court of Justice, a Member State fails to comply with its Article 10 duty, that Member State may be held liable for loss incurred by an individual as a direct result of its failure. When indirect effect applies, as in relation to directives,

---

31 See, also, Case C-129/94: *Criminal Proceedings Against Cruz Bernaldez* [1996] ECR I-1829; and Craig, P and de Búrca, G, *European Community Law*, 2nd edn, 1998, Oxford: OUP, pp 206–10, for further indication that all is not yet settled as regards the 'horizontal effect' of directives.

Community law imposes a duty on the Member State to implement the directive by the stipulated time. The citizen is conferred a potential right to the rights arising under the implemented directive. Should the Member State fail, by the date set, to implement the directive, the citizen has a legal right to the benefits conferred under the directive – a right which is enforceable against the Member State,[32] and for which compensation in defined circumstances may be payable.[33]

In *Von Colson v Land Nordrhein-Westfalen*,[34] Article 5 of the EC Treaty (now, Article 10) and the Equal Treatment Directive 76/207 fell for consideration by the ECJ. As seen above, Article 10 of the Treaty provides that Member States are under a duty to 'take all appropriate measures' to ensure fulfilment of their Community obligations. Ms Von Colson's application for employment in the prison service was rejected. The rejection was based on gender, and was justifiable according to the German court. Under German law, the only compensation payable to Ms Von Colson was her travelling expenses. The question arose as to whether such compensation gave effect to the requirements of Article 5, as it then was. On a reference under Article 177 (now, Article 234), the ECJ examined Article 5 (now, Article 10) of EC Treaty. The ECJ ruled that Article 5 imposed a duty not just on the governments of Member States, but on all national authorities, including the courts. It is therefore the duty of the domestic courts to interpret national law in such a way as to ensure that the obligations imposed by Community law are achieved. The result is that, although a provision is not directly effective, it may be applied indirectly as law by means of interpretation.

The question of the relationship between domestic law and subsequently introduced Community law came before the ECJ in the *Marleasing* case in 1989. In *Marleasing SA v La Comercial Internacional de Alimentacion SA*,[35] the ECJ, on a reference from a Spanish court, had ruled that, whereas a directive cannot of itself impose obligations on private parties, national courts must as far as possible interpret national law in order to achieve a result pursued by a directive, and that this must be done whether the national provisions in

---

32 See, *inter alia*, Case 14/83: *Von Colson* [1984] ECR 1891; [1986] 2 CMLR 430 (EC Treaty, Art 5 – now, Art 10); Case C-106/89: *Marleasing* [1992] 1 CMLR 305; Cases C-6, C-9/90: *Francovich* [1993] 2 CMLR 66 (EC Treaty, Art 5 – now, EC Treaty, Art 10). See, also, *Webb v EMO Cargo (UK) Ltd* [1995] 4 All ER 577, HL; Case C-168/95: *Criminal Proceedings Against Arcaro* [1996] ECR I-4705, paras 41–41, where the ECJ observes that indirect effect reaches its limit where the interpretation 'leads to the imposition on an individual of an obligation laid down by a directive which has not been transposed'.

33 *Brasserie du Pêcheur; Factortame* [1996] 2 WLR 506, ECJ: conditions under which compensation payable; *Dillenkofer v Federal Republic of Germany* (1996) *The Times*, 14 October.

34 Case 14/83: [1984] ECR 1891; [1986] 2 CMLR 430. See, also, *Harz v Deutsche Tradax GmbH* [1984] ECR 1921.

35 Case 106/89: [1992] 1 CMLR 305. See, also, Case C-168/95: *Criminal Proceedings Against Arcaro* [1997] 2 All ER (EC) 82; [1998] Env LR 39; and *Perceval-Price v Department of Economic Development* (2000) *The Times*, 28 April, CA NI.

question were adopted before or after the directive. In *Marleasing*, no legislation had been passed to comply with the directive: the duty was nevertheless on the courts to give effect to the *Von Colson* principle, that is to say, the court must interpret domestic law in accordance with Community law. This principle enables directives to have horizontal direct effect 'by the back door'. A gap in protection, however, still remained. Where there was no domestic law on a Community matter and where, as a result, there was no domestic provision to construe in line with Community law, a problem would remain. That problem was resolved in *Francovich and Bonifaci v Italy*.[36]

The decision of the ECJ in *Francovich and Bonifaci v Italy*,[37] has far reaching implications for the supremacy of Community law over domestic law. In *Francovich*, employees were seeking compensation against Italy for failure to implement a directive which was designed to guarantee the payment of arrears of wages to employees in the event of their employer's insolvency. The time limit set down by the Community for implementation of the directive had expired and, as a result, Italy was held to be in breach of its Community obligations under Article 5 (now, Article 10).[38]

The ECJ held that, while the directive was not sufficiently clear to be directly effective against the State, as regards the identity of institutions responsible for payments, Italy was under an obligation to implement the directive under Article 5 of the EC Treaty. Accordingly, since Italy had failed in its obligation, it was under a duty to compensate individuals for damage suffered as a result of its failure.[39] The ECJ laid down three conditions which applied to the issue of compensation for loss, namely that:

(a) the directive confers individual rights;

(b) the content of those rights can be identified on the basis of the provisions of the directive; and

(c) there is a causal link between the State's failure and the damage suffered by individuals affected.[40]

Under such conditions, an individual may proceed directly against the State. Accordingly, the importance of the principle of direct effect diminishes, and liability falls not on the employer – whether public or private – but on the State, by virtue of its obligations under the Treaty.

---

36 Cases C-6, C-9/90: [1993] 2 CMLR 66. See Lasok, P, '*Francovich* overrules *Bourgoin*: State liability for breach of Community law' [1992] ICCLR 186.

37 Cases C-6, C-9/90: [1993] 2 CMLR 66.

38 See *Gibson v East Riding of Yorkshire DC* [1999] 3 CMLR 190; [1999] ICR 622; [1999] IRLR 358.

39 Cf *Evans v Motor Insurers Bureau* [1999] Lloyd's Rep IR 30; (1998) *The Times*, 12 October, CA.

40 See, also, *Marks & Spencer plc v Customs and Excise Commissioners (No 1)* [2000] 1 CMLR 256; (2000) *The Times*, 19 January, CA; and *R v Durham County Council ex parte Huddleston* [2000] Env LR 20; (2000) *The Times*, 15 March, CA.

However, many questions remained unanswered. Was the State liable only for failure to implement the directive? Was the State liable, irrespective of whether there was any fault involved on the part of the State? Furthermore, was the State liable for loss incurred prior to the ECJ finding the Member State in breach of its obligations? What form of compensation is recoverable? Does it include loss of profits? Is compensation confined to economic loss?

In *Brasserie du Pêcheur SA v Federal Republic of Germany*[41] and *R v Secretary of State for Transport ex parte Factortame Ltd (No 4)*,[42] the European Court of Justice ruled on the principles which regulate the grant of compensation to bodies suffering damage as a result of Member States' breach of Community law. Member States are obliged to make good the loss suffered by individuals when:

(a) the national legislature is responsible for the breach of Community law;

(b) where the national legislature has discretion as to the means by which its Community obligations will be fulfilled, three conditions are met:

- the rule of law breached must be intended to confer rights on individuals;
- the breach must be sufficiently serious; and
- there must be a direct causal link between the breach of the obligation and the damage suffered.

The conditions correspond to those defined by the Court in relation to Article 215 (now, Article 288) in its case law on liability of the Community for damage caused by individuals by unlawful legislative measures adopted by its institutions. As to the degree of seriousness of the breach, the considerations to be taken into account by the court considering the issue of compensation, as stipulated by the Court of Justice, are:

> ... whether the Member State [or the Community institution] concerned manifestly and gravely disregarded the limits on its discretion.

> ... the clarity and precision of the rule breached; the measure of discretion left by that rule ...; whether the infringement and the damage caused was intentional or involuntary; whether any error of law was excusable or inexcusable; the fact that the position taken by a Community institution may have contributed towards the omission, and the adoption or retention of national measures or practices contrary to Community law.

> On any view, a breach of Community law will clearly be sufficiently serious if it has persisted despite a judgment finding the infringement in question to be established, or a preliminary ruling or settled case law of the court on the

---

41 Case C-46/93: [1996] 2 WLR 506. For the development of this case, see *R v Secretary of State for Transport ex parte Factortame Ltd (No 1)* [1989] 2 CMLR 353; *(No 2)* [1991] AC 603; *(No 3)* [1992] QB 680; *(No 5)* (1998) *The Times,* 28 April.

42 Case C-48/93: [1996] 2 WLR 506, ECJ.

matter from which it is clear that the conduct in question constituted an infringement.[43]

Member States must compensate individuals at a level which is commensurate with the loss or damage suffered. Further, if damages could be awarded under English law to similar claims based on domestic law, it is possible to award exemplary damages for the breach of Community law.

The question of compensation was also considered by the Court of Justice in *R v HM Treasury ex parte British Telecommunications plc*.[44] The United Kingdom had incorrectly transposed a directive into domestic law. The Divisional Court referred the matter to the Court of Justice which ruled that compensation for loss caused was only payable under the circumstances laid down in *Factortame (No 4)* (above). In the instant case, no reparation was payable because the breach was not sufficiently serious. The directive was imprecisely worded and was reasonably capable of being interpreted in the manner adopted by the United Kingdom.

In *R v Ministry of Agriculture, Fisheries and Food ex parte Hedley Lomas (Ireland) Ltd*,[45] the European Court of Justice ruled that the United Kingdom had an obligation to pay compensation for damage caused to an individual by its failure to comply with Community law. The United Kingdom authorities decided that they would not issue export licences for the export of live animals intended for slaughter in Spain, on the basis that Spain did not comply with the directive on the welfare of animals and that, if the export licence was granted, the animals would suffer treatment contrary to the directive. However, the export licence was intended to enable the export to a specific slaughterhouse in Spain, which complied with Community directives on animal welfare, and the United Kingdom authorities had no evidence that it did not so comply. As a result, the United Kingdom was in breach of Article 34 of the Treaty, and its action could not be justified under Article 36 (justifications for quantitative restrictions on exports) (now, Article 30). The breach was sufficiently serious and there was a direct causal link between the breach and the damage sustained by the individuals.

In *Dillenkofer and Others v Federal Republic of Germany*,[46] the European Court ruled, once again, that, if a Member State failed to take 'timeous' (timely) action to implement a Community directive, individuals injured by

---

43 Joined Cases C-46/93 and C-48/93: *Secretary of State for Transport ex parte Factortame (No 4)* [1996] 2 WLR 506, ECJ.

44 Case C-392/93: [1996] 3 WLR 203.

45 (1996) *The Times*, 6 June.

46 (1996) *The Times*, 14 October.

that failure were entitled to seek reparation from the Member State. Member States had been required to bring a directive[47] into effect before 31 December 1992. Germany brought the directive into effect as from July 1994. Travellers adversely affected by this delay sought compensation for their loss. The Court of Justice held that:

> The first question to be answered concerned the conditions under which a state incurred liability towards individuals where a directive has not been transposed within the prescribed period.
>
> The crux of that question was whether such a failure was sufficient *per se* to afford individuals who had suffered injury a right to reparation, or whether other conditions had to be taken into account ...

Reciting *Francovich and Bonifaci v Italy*,[48] *Brasserie du Pêcheur SA v Federal Republic of Germany*,[49] *R v HM Treasury ex parte British Telecommunications plc*[50] and *R v Ministry of Agriculture, Fisheries and Food ex parte Hedley Lomas (Ireland) Ltd*,[51] the Court stated that individuals who had suffered damage were entitled to compensation where the three conditions set out above were met. Germany had argued in its defence that the time allowed for full implementation of the directive was too short. This argument, however, did not succeed and the Court ruled clearly that failure to take the necessary measures under Community law *per se* constituted a serious breach of Community law.

In *Aannemersbedrijf PK Kraaijeveld BV ea v Gedeputeerde Staten van Zuid-Holland*[52] and *World Wildlife Fund (WWF) v Autonome Provinz Bozen*[53] the Court of Justice considered the question of whether directives could be invoked by individuals in their national courts in the context of judicial review applications, and accepted that this could be the case, without enquiring into their capacity for direct effect. The implication of this is that directives may have an effect distinct from direct effect, which is labelled the 'public law effect'.[54]

---

47 Council Directive 90/314/EEC of 13 June 1990, Art 9.

48 (1991) *The Times*, 20 November.

49 (1996) *The Times*, 7 March; [1996] 2 WLR 506.

50 (1996) *The Times*, 15 April; [1996] QB 615.

51 (1996) *The Times*, 6 June.

52 Case C-72/95: [1996] ECR I-5403.

53 Case C-435/97: judgment 16 September 1999.

54 See Scott, J, *European Community Environmental Law*, 1998, London: Longman, pp 123, 157.

THE INTERACTION BETWEEN NATIONAL COURTS AND THE EUROPEAN COURT OF JUSTICE: ARTICLE 234 OF THE EC TREATY (FORMERLY, ARTICLE 177)[55]

Article 234 (formerly, Article 177) represents a vital means by which the harmony of laws between Member States is achieved. The European Court of Justice is insistent both that Community law has supremacy and that it be uniformly applied within Member States. And yet, the treaties establish a partnership between the judges within the national legal systems and the European Court. It is not difficult to see that the task of uniformity is a difficult one as 15 nation States adopt and adapt to the requirements of Community law. For optimum effectiveness, a balance needs to be struck between making references to the ECJ where necessary and the domestic courts being able to apply Community law without undue delay or cost.

The text of Article 234 is set out in Chapter 8[56] and, from this, it can be seen that courts or tribunals may refer a question, provided that it is a question of Community law – and not national law – which requires interpretation, and provided also that a decision of the ECJ is necessary to enable the national court to reach a decision in the case.[57] A reference becomes mandatory when the question of Community law is before a court or tribunal of last resort, that is to say, a court or tribunal from which there is no further appeal. This does not always mean the House of Lords: in many cases, the appeal structure will end lower in the hierarchy, or leave to appeal may be needed and be refused. Accordingly the court of last resort may effectively be at any level in the judicial hierarchy. If no appeal is possible and the other criteria of a question of Community law and the necessity for interpretation exist, a reference must be made. In *Costa v ENEL*,[58] the reference was from a magistrates' court and involved a claim of less than £2.00 in value: no right of appeal existed because the amount in issue was so small. The English Court of Appeal, in *Bulmer v Bollinger*,[59] considered the question of when references to the ECJ should be made and Lord Denning laid down the following guidelines for English courts to apply when a reference was a matter of discretion:

---

55 See Watson, J, 'Experience and problems in applying Article 177 EEC' (1986) 23 CML Rev 207. See *op cit*, Winter, fn 3. See Curtin, D, 'The province of government: delimiting the direct effect of directives in the common law context' (1990) 15 EL Rev 195; Pescatore, P, 'The "doctrine of direct effect": an infant disease of Community law' (1983) 8 EL Rev 155.

56 See p 314.

57 The office of immigration adjudicator has been held to be within the meaning of 'court or tribunal' for the purposes of Art 234: *El-Yassni v Secretary of State for the Home Department* [1999] All ER (EC) 193; [1999] 2 CMLR 32.

58 Case 6/64: [1964] ECR 585; CMLR 425.

59 [1974] Ch 401.

(a) the decision must be necessary to enable the court to give judgment – a court must feel that it cannot reach a decision unless a reference is made;

(b) the decision of the question must be conclusive to the case – not just a peripheral issue;

(c) even if the court considers a reference to be necessary, regard must still be paid to:

- the delay involved;
- the expense;
- the difficulty of the point of law;
- the burden on the European Court.

These 'guidelines' are questionable in so far as they may impede the willingness of a court to refer matters to the ECJ, and they represent a gloss on the wording of Article 234. A further impediment to referral may arise from the doctrine of *acte clair* – the concept which states that if a matter is so obvious in its meaning to the domestic court, then no reference need be made. As with the *Bulmer v Bollinger* guidelines, the doctrine of *acte clair* can lead to distortions in interpretation within domestic legal systems. The ECJ has itself considered the circumstances under which courts should refer, and the doctrine of *acte clair*,[60] in the *CILFIT* case of 1983.[61] The Court was asked to consider the meaning of Article 177(3) which relates to mandatory references from a court of last resort. The Court ruled that:

(a) there is no duty to refer where a question of Community law was irrelevant – that is, if the interpretation can have no effect on the outcome of the case;

(b) there is no duty of refer when the question is one substantially the same as one previously answered by the ECJ;

(c) there is no need to refer where no real doubt about the law exists. The national court must, however, be satisfied that the matter is equally obvious to courts of other Member States and to the ECJ. To this extent, the doctrine of *acte clair* is endorsed.

In *CILFIT*, the ECJ emphasised that the purpose of Article 177 (now, Article 234 of the EC Treaty), in general, was to ensure the proper application and uniform interpretation of Community law in all Member States and to prevent divergencies occurring within Member States.

Whereas national courts have some discretion as to whether to refer a matter to the ECJ, the position is different in relation to matters of validity – as opposed to interpretation – of Community law. It is clear that the ECJ has the sole power to rule on whether a measure of Community law is invalid. It is

---

60 The concept derives from French law.

61 Case 283/81: *CILFIT S & I Ministro della Sanita* [1982] ECR 3415; [1983] 1 CMLR 337. See Rasmussen, H, 'The European Court's *acte clair* strategy in *CILFIT*' (1984) 9 EL Rev 242.

not for national courts to rule on that question. National courts only have the power to uphold the validity of Community legislation.[62]

The House of Lords had adopted a similar approach to that endorsed by the ECJ in the *CILFIT* case, in *Henn and Darby v Director of Public Prosecutions* in 1981.[63] The Court of Appeal had ruled that quantitative restrictions on imports prohibited by Article 30 did not amount to a total ban on such imports, and had refused to refer the case to the ECJ. On appeal to the House of Lords, a reference was made to the ECJ, which ruled that a total ban could be within Article 30 of the EC Treaty (now, Article 28). The House of Lords warned that lower courts should be slow to assume that a matter was 'clear'. As Lord Diplock put it:

> ... judicial minds can differ on questions of interpretation ... this serves as a timely reminder to English judges not to be too ready to hold that because the meaning of the English text (one of the nine equally authoritative EC languages) seems plain to them that no question of interpretation can be involved.

As seen from the text of Article 234 of the EC Treaty (formerly, Article 177), the questions which may be referred are set out in Article 234:

(a) interpretation of the treaties;

(b) the validity and interpretation of acts of institutions of the Community: regulations, directives, etc;

(c) the interpretation of statutes of bodies established by acts of the Council.

Once the ECJ accepts jurisdiction – and a discretion is conferred on the ECJ over whether or not to accept jurisdiction – and gives a ruling, the matter is then returned to the domestic court for application, thus preserving the partnership ideal.

THE QUESTION OF LEGAL SUPREMACY

The question of legal supremacy can be examined both from the standpoint of the Community itself and from that of national law.

The European Court of Justice's view

The ECJ claims that Community law is supreme over national law. This claim carries the following implications:

---

62 See Case 314/85: *Foto-Frost v Hauptzollamt Lubeck Ost* [1987] ECR 4199. See, also, Arnull, A, 'National courts and the validity of Community acts' (1988) 13 EL Rev 125; and Bebr, G, 'The reinforcement of the constitutional review of Community acts under Article 177 EEC Treaty' (1988) 25 CML Rev 667.

63 [1981] AC 580.

(a) Community law confers rights on individuals to which national law must give effect;

(b) national law cannot prevail over Community law;

(c) the effectiveness of Community law must be the same in all Member States – it cannot vary in effect from one Member State to another;

(d) courts of Member States cannot interpret Community law but must follow the interpretation of laws given by the ECJ or, where there is no authority, and under certain conditions, must refer the matter to the ECJ under Article 234 of the Treaty (formerly, Article 177);

(e) where the ECJ gives a ruling, Member States are under an obligation to amend their national laws so as to conform to Community law.[64]

The ECJ has asserted the supremacy which Community law assumes on many occasions. The early cases lay the foundations for the current relationship between domestic law and Community law. The starting point is once again the case of *Van Gend en Loos v Nederlandse Tariefcommissie*,[65] in which the ECJ enunciated the view that, by signing the treaties, the Member States had created a new legal order, in which individual States had limited their sovereign rights. In *Costa v ENEL*,[66] this view was reaffirmed by the ECJ:

> The transfer by the States from their domestic legal system to the Community legal system of the rights and obligations arising under the Treaty carries with it a permanent limitation of their sovereign rights against which a subsequent unilateral act incompatible with the concept of Community law cannot prevail.

Internationale Handelsgesellschaft GmbH v EVST[67] takes the principle of Community supremacy further. Under Community law, in order to export produce, the company was required to obtain a licence, for which a 'permanent deposit' had to be paid. If the goods were not exported within the licence period, the deposit was to be forfeited. The company paid the deposit, failed to complete the export, and forfeiture was made. The firm sued the agency involved for return of the deposit, arguing that the forfeiture was contrary to the Constitution of the Federal Republic of Germany. The Constitution[68] provided that powers could be transferred to international organisations, but that no transfer could be made of powers which the central government itself did not have. Since the retention of the deposit was contrary to the Federal Constitution, it could not, according to German law, be lawful

---

64 In January 1997, the Commission agreed the procedures for the imposition of fines on Member States who fail to comply with rulings of the European Court of Justice. Where a Member State is in breach of Community law, the Commission will apply to the Court for a determination of the fine. The levels of fines will be relative to the size of the economy of the State.

65 Case 26/62: [1963] CMLR 105.

66 Case 6/64: [1964] CMLR 425.

67 Case 11/70: [1970] ECR 1125; [1972] CMLR 255.

68 Under the EC Treaty, Art 24.

under the law of the Community. The matter was referred to the ECJ under Article 177 (now, Article 234).

The ECJ declared that giving effect to rules or concepts of national law contained even within the constitution of a State, for the purposes of judging the validity of Community measures, would have an adverse effect on the uniformity and efficacy of Community law. The validity of Community measures could be judged only in the light of Community law and could not be affected by allegations that the measures ran counter to fundamental rights as formulated by the constitution of the Member State. Having made this unequivocal and controversial statement, the ECJ softened its tone, ruling that the respect for fundamental rights forms an integral part of the 'general principles of law' protected by the Court of Justice, and that the protection of such rights, inspired by traditions common to Member States, must be ensured within the framework of the structure and objectives of the Community.

The *Simmenthal* case[69] further developed the jurisprudence of the ECJ in relation to supremacy. Simmenthal imported beef from France into Italy. Under Italian legislation of 1970, fees for veterinary and health checks had to be paid by the importer at the frontier. Simmenthal sued the Italian Minister of Finance for return of the money, arguing that the fee was equivalent to a customs duty and was contrary to both Article 25 of the Treaty (formerly, Article 12) and Community regulations on the common organisation on beef imports. The national court ordered the Ministry to return the money. The Minister pleaded that the domestic 1970 Act was binding unless and until set aside by the Italian Constitutional Court.

The Italian court was thus faced with a conflict between Article 12, as it then was, of the Treaty and a later Italian statute. A reference was made under Article 177 (now, Article 234), the question at issue being whether directly applicable regulations issued under Article 189 (now, Article 249) required national courts to disregard subsequently passed domestic legislation, without waiting for the Constitutional Court to declare it invalid. The ECJ held that regulations take precedence over previous and subsequent domestic legislation and that a national court must set aside any provision which conflicts with Community law and apply Community law in its entirety, without waiting until the domestic legislation had been set aside by the Constitutional Court.

The *European Road Transport Agreement (ERTA)* case[70] offers another perspective.[71] In 1962, several European States, five of which were EC

---

69 Case 35/76: *Simmenthal v Italian Minister of Finance* [1976] ECR 1871; [1977] 2 CMLR 1; and *Simmenthal v Italian Ministry of Finance* [1978] ECR 1453; 3 CMLR 670; and Case 92/87: *Simmenthal v Commission* [1979] ECR 777; [1980] 1 CMLR 25.

70 Case 22/71: *Commission v Council* [1971] CMLR 335.

71 See Mancini, G and Keeling, D, 'From *CILFIT* to *ERTA*: the constitutional challenge facing the European Court' (1991) 11 YBEL 1.

Member States, others being Eastern European States, signed the European Road Transport Agreement, which sought to establish common rules concerning conditions of work of long distance lorry drivers crossing several State boundaries. As such, the Agreement was not an EC agreement. In 1969, the EC had acted for the (then) six Member States by issuing a regulation covering the same issue. In 1970, the matter was further complicated by the Council meeting to attempt to find a common basis for a new transport agreement. The Commission attempted to have the proceedings of the Council annulled on the basis that the Council was not competent to reach agreements of this kind.[72]

At the heart of the matter lay the question as to who had the power – Member States, the Council or the Commission – to make such 'international' agreements. If Member States retained the power to enter into international agreements (and such a power is a basic attribute of sovereignty), then the Council proceedings were merely recommendatory; if the Council had power then the proceedings took on more of a law making character, which deprived the Member States of competence to act either unilaterally or collectively.

Article 281 of the Treaty (formerly, Article 210) provides that the Community shall have legal personality and so has capacity to make international agreements. Where then does this leave the capacity of Member States? The Court held that the sole power to enter into such agreements lay with the Community institutions, thus depriving Member States of any capacity in this regard. The ECJ's decision had thereby conferred an implied external relations power on the Community.

Under the EC Treaty, express powers to enter into treaties is provided under Article 310 (formerly, Article 238). It might have been thought that, given such powers, there would be no need for the ECJ to confirm that the Community has implied powers, as in *ERTA*. In summary, the effect of these early cases is that, since 1962, the ECJ has declared the existence of a new legal order, one to which Member States have limited their sovereign rights by transferring these to the Community. These rights include even the protection of constitutionally guaranteed individual rights. Further, it matters not whether a domestic law in conflict with Community law was passed prior to accession to the EC or subsequently: neither can prevail over Community law. Thirdly, where the Community has the power to act on behalf of Member States in the making of international agreements, Member States have lost that capacity.

It is clear that Community law prevails not only over domestic law, but also over issues of domestic policy. In *R v Secretary of State for the Environment ex parte Royal Society for the Protection of Birds; the Port of Sheerness Ltd,*

---

72 Acting under the EC Treaty, Art 173 (now, EC Treaty, Art 230).

intervener,[73] for example, a Council directive[74] on the conservation of wild birds fell for interpretation by the Court of Justice on a reference from the House of Lords under Article 177 of the EC Treaty (now, Article 234).[75] The questions referred by the House of Lords were:

(a) whether a Member State was authorised to take account of the economic requirements mentioned in Article 2 of the Birds Directive when designating a special protection area and defining its boundaries;

(b) whether a Member State, when designating a special protection area and defining its boundaries, was allowed to take account of economic requirements as constituting a general interest superior to that represented by the ecological objectives of the Directive;

(c) whether a Member State could take account of economic requirements to the extent that they reflected imperative reasons of overriding public interest of the kind referred to in Council Directive 92/43/EEC on the conservation of the natural habitats of wild fauna and flora.[76]

The Court of Justice ruled that the Secretary of State was not entitled to take economic considerations into account when designating a special protection area for wild birds and defining its boundaries.

Before examining the position of the English courts, it is necessary to consider the means by which Community law is received into English law.

THE RECEPTION OF COMMUNITY
LAW INTO THE UNITED KINGDOM

The concepts of monism and dualism

At a conceptual level, the manner in which international law, of which Community law may be regarded as a *sui generis* (that is to say, unique) example, is dependent upon whether a particular State adopts a monist or dualist approach to international law. Monism is the doctrine whereby international law and national law form a single whole, or part of the same conceptual structure, in which international law takes precedence. Under this doctrine, adhered to by, *inter alia*, France and Italy, the obligations of international law, once assumed, enter automatically into the legal system, needing no domestic legislative acts. Once entered, the obligations take precedence over national law.

---

73 Case C-44/95.

74 Directive 79/409/EEC (OJ L103pl, 2 April 1979).

75 On the Royal Society for the Protection of Birds standing in judicial review proceedings, see Chapter 24.

76 21 May 1992 (OJ L206, 1992, p 7).

Dualism, on the other hand, regards the systems of international law and national law as separate: in order for international law to enter into national law, some domestic legislative action must be enacted by the national Parliament. This is the view adopted by the United Kingdom and is one consistent with the sovereignty of Parliament.[77] Treaties are part of international law, and can have no effect in domestic law unless and until a statute of the sovereign United Kingdom Parliament is enacted to give them effect.[78]

The principle was given early expression by Lord Atkin in *Attorney General for Canada v Attorney General for Ontario* in 1937:[79]

> Within the British Empire, there is a well established rule that the making of a Treaty is an executive act, while the performance of its obligations, if they entail alteration of the existing domestic law, requires legislative action.

> The stipulations of a Treaty do not, by virtue of the Treaty alone, have the force of law. If the government of the day decides to incur the obligations of a Treaty which involves alteration of law they have to run the risk of obtaining the assent of Parliament to the necessary statute or statutes.

In 1972, Lord Denning MR gave further expression to this view in *Blackburn v Attorney General*:[80]

> Even if a Treaty is signed, it is elementary that these courts take no notice of treaties as such. We take no notice of treaties until they are embodied in laws enacted by Parliament, and then only to the extent that Parliament tells us.

Accordingly, the signing of the EC treaties, without any further parliamentary action, had no effect in English law. In order to have effect, it was necessary for Parliament to pass the European Communities Act 1972.

The European Communities Act 1972

Section 2 of the European Communities Act 1972 provides that:

> (1) All such rights powers liberties obligations and restrictions from time to time created or arising by or under the treaties, and all such remedies and procedures from time to time provided for by or under the treaties ... are without further enactment to be given legal effect or used in the United Kingdom shall be recognised and available in law and be enforced, allowed and followed accordingly ...

---

77 See Chapter 7.

78 This matter assumed prime importance in the debate over the ratification of the Treaty on European Union, the Maastricht Treaty, in 1993.

79 [1937] AC 326.

80 [1971] 2 All ER 1380, p 1382.

(2) Subject to Schedule 2 of this Act, at any time after its passing Her Majesty may by Order in Council and any designated Minister or Department may by regulations make provision:

   (a) for the purpose of implementing any Community obligation of the United Kingdom, or of enabling any rights enjoyed or to be enjoyed by the United Kingdom under or by virtue of the treaties to be exercised ...

(4) The provisions that may be made under section 2(2) include, subject to Schedule 2, any such provision (of any such extent) as might be made by Act of Parliament, and any enactment passed or to be passed ... shall be construed and have effect subject to the foregoing provisions of this section ...

Section 3(1) provides that:

For the purposes of all legal proceedings any question as to the meaning and effect of any of the treaties, or as to the validity, meaning or effect of any Community instrument, shall be treated as a question of law (and if not referred to the European Court of Justice, be for determination as such in accordance with the principles laid down by and any relevant decision of the European Court).

Here, then, are the most fundamental provisions of the Act – specifying that rights and duties which are directly applicable or effective are to be given legal effect within the United Kingdom; that the executive has the power to give effect to Community obligations, and that existing and future enactments are to be interpreted and have effect and that the meaning or effect of Treaty provisions is to be decided according to Community law.

The view of the United Kingdom courts

The manner in which, and extent to which, the United Kingdom courts have accommodated Community obligations requires consideration. First, it should be noted that nothing in the European Communities Act (ECA) 1972 represents an attempt to entrench its provisions, that is to say, to make them immune from amendment or repeal. There is no statement in the Act purporting that EC law is a 'higher form of law', or that it cannot be repealed, or could be repealed but only by some specified 'manner and form'.

Nevertheless, section 2(4) has produced controversy among commentators, given that it directs the courts to interpret Acts of Parliament passed in the future in conformity with the principle expressed in section 2(1). The dominant view is that this section does not achieve entrenchment as such, but rather should be viewed as a directive to the courts in the form of a rule of construction (interpretation) which must give way to a contrary intention expressed by Parliament.

Two early challenges were made to the signing of the Treaty on the basis of the potential or actual loss of parliamentary sovereignty. In *Blackburn v Attorney General* in 1971,[81] the plaintiff sought a declaration that the government, by signing the Treaty of Rome, would surrender part of Parliament's sovereignty which it could not lawfully do, as no Parliament could bind another. In *R v Home Secretary ex parte McWhirter*,[82] the plaintiff adduced that joining the EC was contrary to the Bill of Rights 1689, which declared that all powers of government are vested in the Crown and Parliament could not, therefore, by means of a Treaty, transfer those rights.

In both cases, the arguments were disposed of with speed. In *Blackburn*, Lord Denning MR stated that 'even if the Treaty is signed, it is elementary that the courts take no notice of them until embodied in an Act of Parliament'. Further, in *McWhirter*, Lord Denning stated that 'even though the Treaty of Rome has been signed, it has no effect as far as the courts are concerned until implemented by Act of Parliament. Until that day, we take no notice of it'.

A challenge to the government's Treaty making power also came *in R v Secretary of State for Foreign and Commonwealth Affairs ex parte Rees-Mogg*.[83] Lord Rees-Mogg sought a declaration from the court to the effect that the government could not lawfully ratify the Treaty on European Union 1992, the Maastricht Treaty, without the consent of Parliament. The Court of Appeal gave short shrift to the argument, relying on the earlier precedents, and no appeal was made to the House of Lords.

Conflicts between Community law and domestic law[84]

One area of law which has given rise to an instructive array of case law concerning the relationship between English law and Community law is that of sex discrimination. There are, of course, a variety of ways in which discrimination on the basis of sex may arise: in relation to equal pay or equal treatment in respect of access to employment, promotion, training, working conditions, social security and retirement ages. Article 141 (formerly Article 119) and directives[85] form the framework of the law of the Community.

In *Macarthys v Smith*,[86] Mrs Smith was employed by Macarthys as a stockroom manageress. The man who had previously held the position had

---

81 [1971] 1 WLR 1037.

82 (1969) *The Times*, 20 October.

83 [1994] 2 WLR 115; 1 All ER 457.

84 See, *inter alia*, Szyszczack, E, 'Sovereignty: crisis, compliance, confusion, complacency?' (1990) 15(6) EL Rev 483; de Búrca, G, 'A community of interests? Making the most of European law' (1992) 55 MLR 346 and 'Giving effect to European Community directives' (1992) 55 MLR 215.

85 75/117, 76/207, 79/7, 86/378, 86/613.

86 [1981] QB 180; [1979] 3 All ER 325.

been paid a higher wage than Mrs Smith. The applicable domestic legislation was that of the Equal Pay Act 1970, as amended by the Sex Discrimination Act 1975, which provided, *inter alia*, that men and women employed in the same job should be paid equal amounts. The Act was silent, however, as to whether employers were required to pay the same wage to a woman who came to the job after the man had left their employment. The relevant point for interpretation, therefore, was whether men and women, employed at differing times for the same job, were required to be paid equally.

Article 141 of the Treaty (formerly, Article 119) provides for equal pay for men and women. Article 141 is couched in far broader terms than those used by the Equal Pay Act 1970. The matter was referred by the Court of Appeal to the European Court of Justice under Article 177 (now, Article 234). The ECJ held that Article 119 (now, Article 141) required equal pay for men and women whether they were employed contemporaneously or in succession. On receiving the judgment of the ECJ, the Court of Appeal ruled in favour of Mrs Smith. Lord Denning's judgment is of particular significance:

> We should, I think, look to see what those [EC] provisions require about equal pay for men and women. Then we should look at our own legislation on the point – giving it, of course, full faith and credit – assuming that it does fully comply with the obligations under the Treaty. In construing our statute, we are entitled to look to the Treaty as an aid in its construction: and even more, not only as an aid, but as an overriding force. If on close investigation it should appear that our legislation is deficient – or is inconsistent with Community law – by some oversight of our draftsmen – then it is our bounden duty to give priority to Community law. Such is the result of section 2(1) and (4) of the European Communities Act 1972.

> Thus far, I have assumed that our Parliament, whenever it passes legislation, intends to fulfil its obligations under the Treaty. If the time should come when our Parliament deliberately passes an Act with the intention of repudiating the Treaty or any provision in it – or intentionally of acting inconsistently with it – and says so in express terms – then I should have thought that it would be the duty of our courts to follow the statute of our Parliament.

Article 141 (formerly, Article 119) fell for further consideration in *Garland v British Rail Engineering Ltd* in 1983,[87] this time by the House of Lords. British Rail made concessionary travel facilities available to the children of male employees reaching retirement, but not to the children of women reaching retirement. The question was whether this policy amounted to discrimination contrary to Article 119, as it then was, of the Treaty, and whether the courts in the England should construe the Sex Discrimination Act 1975 in a manner so as to make it compatible with the requirements of Article 119. The House of Lords referred the matter to the ECJ, which ruled that the policy amounted to discrimination contrary to Article 119, and that Article 119 must prevail.

---

87   Case 12/81: [1983] 2 AC 751; [1982] ECR 359.

In *Duke v GEC Reliance Ltd*,[88] the House of Lords considered the construction of section 6(4) of the Sex Discrimination Act 1975. In the *Duke* case, the plaintiff's claim for damages based on unequal treatment was for a period prior to Parliament's amendment of the Sex Discrimination Act to bring English law into line with the requirements of Community law. The House of Lords declined to give retrospective effect to the amendment in light of Parliament's express decision not to amend the Act retrospectively. One interpretation of *Duke* is that, being a pre-*Marleasing* case – which makes it clear that the Article 5 duty is imposed on national courts – the House of Lords was in line with the ECJ's interpretation of the Community law at the time.

In *Litster v Forth Dry Dock Ltd*,[89] however, the House of Lords interpreted a domestic regulation contrary to its clear meaning in order to comply with a directive as interpreted by the Court of Justice. The domestic regulation had been introduced for the purpose of complying with the directive and, accordingly, the House of Lords was complying with its duty under section 2(4) of the European Communities Act 1972[90] to give effect to Community law.[91] Thus, from the House of Lords' perspective, one important factor in the matter of the interpretation and application of Community law is the response which Parliament has made to the Community measure. If Parliament had implemented a measure before a directive was made, or if Parliament has responded to the requirements of Community law by not amending domestic law in line with Community law, the judges may hold that domestic law prevails over Community law. Where, however, Parliament has responded by amending the law, with the intention of bringing English law into line with Community law, the English courts would undoubtedly give effect to the Community law, even where the wording of a domestic regulation required imaginative interpretation to give primacy to Community law.[92]

For example, in *Pickstone v Freemans plc*,[93] the applicants were female warehouse workers – operatives – who were paid the same as male operatives but claimed that their work was of equal value to that of warehouse checkers, who were paid more than they were. The Equal Pay Act 1970 did not encompass the concept of equal value, but had been amended in 1983, by statutory instrument under section 2(2) of the ECA 1972, following a ruling by the ECJ that the Equal Pay Act was in breach of a Community directive. The

---

88 [1988] 1 All ER 626.
89 [1990] 1 AC 546.
90 On which, see, further, below.
91 See, also, *Finnegan v Clowney Youth Training Programme Ltd* [1990] 2 AC 407.
92 As in *Litster v Forth Dry Dock and Engineering Company Ltd* [1989] 1 All ER 1134.
93 [1989] AC 66.

1983 amendment was intended to bring the Equal Pay Act protection in line with Article 119 (now, Article 141) and the Community directive, but had been obscurely worded. The result was that the House of Lords was forced to strain to achieve an interpretation which could give effect to what Lord Oliver described as the 'compulsive provision of section 2(4)' of the ECA 1972. The required result was achieved by the House of Lords departing from the strict literal interpretation of the text and implying words to fill the legislative gap in order to reach conformity with Community law.

In *Webb v EMO Cargo (UK) Ltd*,[94] the issue of dismissal on the basis of pregnancy was considered in relation to the EC's Directive on Equal Treatment.[95] The English Trades Union Reform and Employment Rights Act 1993 provides that dismissal on the grounds of pregnancy is unfair.[96] However, in *Webb v EMO Cargo (UK) Ltd*,[97] the Court of Appeal ruled, and the House of Lords affirmed, that a woman who was dismissed from employment because of her pregnancy was not unlawfully dismissed, since – comparing her to a man with a temporary physical disability who would also have been unable to work – the man would also have been dismissed. Under Article 177 (now, Article 234), a reference was made to the European Court of Justice. The ECJ ruled that English law was inadequate. As further discussed in Chapter 19, the European Court of Justice ruled, first, that pregnancy was not a pathological condition to be compared with illness and, secondly, that a pregnant woman's inability to work was temporary and not permanent. Accordingly, the dismissal had amounted to sex discrimination.[98] The Court ruled that the Article 'precludes dismissal of an employee who is recruited for an unlimited term with a view, initially, to replacing another employee during the latter's maternity leave and who cannot do so, because, shortly after recruitment, she is herself found to be pregnant'.[99] The House of Lords, in *Webb v EMO Air Cargo (UK) Ltd (No 2)*,[100] ruled that sections 1(1)(a) and 5(3) of the 1975 Act were to be construed in accordance with the ECJ's ruling and that in the case where a woman was engaged for an indefinite period, the fact that the reason why she would be temporarily unavailable for work at a time when her services would be particularly required was pregnancy was a

---

94 [1992] ICR 445.

95 See, further, Chapter 19.

96 Trades Union Reform and Employment Rights Act 1993, ss 23–25 and Scheds 2 and 3; EC Pregnancy Directive 92/85.

97 [1992] ICR 445.

98 Case C-177/88: *Dekker v VJV Centrum* [1991] IRLR 27; [1990] ECR I-3841.

99 [1994] QB 718.

100 [1995] 1 WLR 1454.

circumstance relevant to her case, being a circumstance that could not be present in the case of the hypothetical man.[101] Maternity pay conditions fell for consideration by the ECJ in *Boyle and Others v Equal Opportunities Commission*.[102] The Court ruled that a clause in a contract of employment, which made the payment, during the period of maternity leave, of higher maternity pay than the statutory entitlement conditional upon the worker's undertaking to return to work after the birth of the child for at least one month, failing which she was required to repay the difference between the amount of pay she would have received during maternity leave and the actual amount paid, was not contrary to Article 119 (now, Article 141), and associated Council directives.[103]

In *Grant v South West Trains Ltd*,[104] the Court of Justice apparently reached the limits of its respect for equality. A Southampton industrial tribunal had referred a question under Article 234 of the Treaty (formerly, Article 177) concerning whether the female partner of a lesbian woman was entitled to the same employment benefits enjoyed by married or cohabiting heterosexual couples. The applicant had enjoyed a stable relationship for over two years. When she applied for the same benefits as heterosexual couples enjoy for her partner, she was refused on the basis that concessions were only granted to cohabiting couples who were heterosexual. The Court of Justice ruled that there had been no violation of the Treaty on the basis of sexual inequality. The Court of Justice referred to the jurisprudence of the European Court of Human Rights which did not yet accord the same protection to same sex relationships in respect of marriage.[105] However, the Court also noted that the Treaty of Amsterdam 1997, when in force, would allow the Council, under certain conditions, to take action to eliminate, *inter alia*, discrimination based on gender orientation. As matters stood, however, the Court did not find a violation of Article 119 (now, Article 141 of the EC Treaty).

Undoubtedly, the most constitutionally significant British case revealing the relationship between Community law and domestic law is that *of R v Secretary of State for Transport ex parte Factortame*.[106] In 1970, the Council of

---

101 In *Strathclyde Regional Council and Others v Wallace and Others* (1998) *The Times*, 24 January, the House of Lords ruled that an objectively-justifiable employment practice which was not 'tainted' by sexual discrimination, which resulted in unequal pay, did not contravene the Equal Pay Act 1970, relying on Case 170/84: *Bilka-Kaufhaus GmbH v Weber von Hartz* [1987] ICR 110, EC Treaty, Art 119 (now, Art 141). In a significant ruling by a tribunal on equal pay in March 1998, a former female teacher at an independent school, Eileen Halloran, in an action brought by the Association of Teachers and Lecturers, was found to have been discriminated against in receiving less pay than male teachers.

102 Case C-411/96: (1998) *The Times*, 29 October.

103 Directive 75/117/EEC, Directive 76/207/EEC, Council Directive 92/85/EEC.

104 Case C-249/96: (1998) *The Times*, 23 February.

105 See, for discussion, Chapter 22.

106 [1991] 3 CMLR 769; [1991] 2 Lloyd's Rep 648; AC 603.

Ministers passed a regulation relating to the common organisation of the market in fishery products. The basic principle employed was that, subject to certain exceptions, there should be equal access for the fishing vessels of all Member States to the fishing grounds of fellow Member States. In 1983, due to fears of over-fishing caused by such open access, the Council established, by way of regulation, a system for the conservation and management of resources. This entailed, in part, setting limits to the amount of fish to be caught in certain periods by way of 'total allowable catches' – the allocation of total allowable catches being fairly distributed among the Member States by way of national quotas. The quotas were based on the number of ships flying the flag of a Member State or registered in a Member State.

Spain acceded to the EC in 1986. Before 1986, the extent to which Spanish vessels could ship in British waters was determined under agreements between the Spanish and United Kingdom governments. Under English law, the Merchant Shipping Act 1894 prohibited non-British nationals from owning British fishing vessels but did permit corporate ownership by British companies. Thus, directors/ shareholders of Spanish vessels were able to register under the 1894 Act. Some 96 Spanish fishing boats were registered under the Act, and each of these vessels counted as part of the United Kingdom's quota under Community law.

The United Kingdom government, understandably alarmed at the restrictions imposed on the domestic fishing industry and the ability of foreign companies to register and therefore take up part of the United Kingdom's quota, imposed additional conditions for registration which came into force in 1986.[107] The three principal conditions for registration were to be that a proportion of the catch was to be sold in the United Kingdom; that 75 per cent of the crews were to be EC nationals ordinarily resident in the United Kingdom; and that all crew were to be required to contribute to the National Insurance Scheme.

In 1988, the United Kingdom Parliament passed the Merchant Shipping Act and enacted fresh merchant shipping regulations. The new system of registration[108] entailed qualification on the basis of a 'genuine and substantial connection with the United Kingdom'. The revised conditions required that not less than 75 per cent of vessels be owned by United Kingdom citizens resident in the United Kingdom; or wholly owned in the United Kingdom, with 75 per cent of shareholders and directors in the United Kingdom; or part owned, with 75 per cent of owners in the United Kingdom; and, further, that vessels be effectively operated from the United Kingdom. Registration would be lost with effect from 31 March 1989 until vessel owners could satisfy the government that they were eligible for registration.

---

107 Under the Sea Fish (Conservation) Act 1967.
108 SI 1988/1926.

As a result, Factortame, which did not comply with these more stringent requirements, challenged the domestic requirements as incompatible with EC law, on the grounds of discrimination on the grounds of nationality contrary to Article 7 (now, Article 14) of the Treaty and the rights of companies to establishment under Articles 43–48 (formerly, Articles 52–58 of the EC Treaty). The Divisional Court wanted to refer the matter to the ECJ under Article 177 (now, Article 234) – a move opposed by the plaintiffs unless the Divisional Court was prepared to grant an interim order protecting their putative Community rights by way of an injunction restraining the government from imposing the requirements of the new regulations. The Divisional Court, in 1990, granted an interim injunction against the government restraining it from applying the Merchant Shipping Act regulations until final judgment was made following a reference to the ECJ under Article 177 (now, Article 234).

The government appealed to the Court of Appeal, which ruled that the court had no jurisdiction to grant interim relief disapplying an Act of Parliament. On appeal to the House of Lords, the decision of the Court of Appeal was upheld: injunctive relief against the Crown was not within the court's jurisdiction.

Lord Bridge of Harwich stated that:

> In this situation, the difficulty which faces the applicants is that the presumption that an Act of Parliament is compatible with Community law unless and until declared incompatible must be at least as strong as the presumption that delegated legislation is valid until declared invalid.

> ... if the applicants fail to establish their claim before the European Court of Justice, the effect of interim relief granted would be to have conferred upon them rights directly contrary to Parliament's will ... I am clearly of the opinion that, as a matter of English law, the court has no power to make an order which has these consequences.

It has been seen previously that Community law is supreme and requires the protection – by domestic courts – of Community rights and that English courts cannot rely on parliamentary sovereignty to justify the denial of protection unless there is a clear and unequivocal parliamentary intention to defeat Community law.[109] Three complicating and constitutionally significant factors arose in *Factortame*. First, whether the court could protect alleged rather than established rights under Community law; secondly, whether – contrary to all previous precedent – the provisions of Community law could confer jurisdiction on the English courts to grant injunctive relief against the Crown; and, thirdly, the conditions under which, should such jurisdiction exist, such relief could be granted.

---

109 See *Macarthys v Smith* [1979] 3 All ER 32; *Garland v British Rail Engineering* [1983] 2 AC 751.

The ECJ, in its preliminary ruling on the first point,[110] held that the offending provisions of the Merchant Shipping Act should be suspended, pending a full determination of Factortame's claim, stating that:

> The full effectiveness of Community law would be impaired if a rule of national law could prevent a court seized of a dispute governed by Community law from granting interim relief in order to ensure the full effectiveness of the judicial decision to be given on the existence of rights claimed under Community law.

The ECJ reverted to its decision in *Simmenthal*,[111] reiterating that directly applicable rules were to be fully and uniformly applied in all Member States in accordance with the principle of precedence of Community law over national law. Article 5 of the EC Treaty (now, Article 10 of the EC Treaty) imposes an obligation, as has been seen above, to ensure the legal protection which is provided for under the principle of direct effect. The House of Lords in *R v Secretary of State for Transport ex parte Factortame Ltd (No 2)* accepted the ECJ's ruling and granted interim relief.

While legal action being pursued by Factortame was in progress, a separate action was commenced by the Commission, alleging that the United Kingdom was in breach of its Treaty obligation, and seeking an order that the United Kingdom should suspend the Merchant Shipping Act in respect of fishing vessels.[112] The ECJ held that an interim order could be granted, on the basis that the Act could be in breach of the prohibition against discrimination on the grounds of nationality under Articles 43 and 294 (formerly, Articles 52 and 221).[113]

In *R v HM Treasury ex parte British Telecommunications plc*[114] (the *BT* case), the applicant sought an interim injunction which would have had the effect – as in *Factortame* – of causing national legislation to be disapplied while the substantive issue was being considered by the ECJ. In *Factortame*, great weight was attached to the very strong *prima facie* case put forward by the applicants. In the *BT* case, the Court of Appeal cautioned against over-reliance on the likelihood of success in the ECJ as a basis for granting relief. In part, this caution was based on the fact that a reference had been made to the ECJ under

---

110 Case 213/89.

111 Case 92/87: *Simmenthal SpA v Commission* [1979] ECR 777; [1980] 1 CMLR 25.

112 Case C-246/89: *Re Nationality of Fishermen: EC Commission (Spain intervening) v United Kingdom (Ireland intervening)* [1991] 3 CMLR 706.

113 In *R v Secretary of State for Transport ex parte Factortame Ltd and Others (No 5)* (1999) *The Times*, the House of Lords ruled that the United Kingdom's breach of Community law was sufficiently serious as to warrant damages. For contrasting interpretations of the *Factortame* case, see Craig, PP, 'Sovereignty of the United Kingdom after *Factortame*' (1991) 11 YBEL 221; Wade, HWR, 'Sovereignty – revolution or evolution' (1996) 112 LQR 568; Allan, TRS, 'Parliamentary sovereignty: law, politics and revolution' (1997) 113 LQR 443, and see Chapter 8.

114 (1993) *The Times*, 2 December.

Article 177 (now, Article 234), and that to give great weight to the prognosis for success was to pre-judge the interpretation to be given by the ECJ. The fact that a reference had been made – as discussed above – meant that the English court was uncertain as to the question in issue. Accordingly it would be inappropriate to prejudge the issue by granting relief at an interim stage. The Court of Appeal also warned of the difficulties in disapplying domestic legislation. As the court stated, there should be a distinction drawn between a 'major piece of primary legislation' and a 'minor piece of subordinate legislation'. In relation to the former, the court ruled that it would be far more circumspect than in relation to secondary legislation. In the instant case, unlike *Factortame*, the issues were not clear-cut. The court, ruling that it would only grant a interim order 'in the most compelling circumstances', declined to grant the injunction.[115]

The question of the compatibility of domestic law with Community law arose once more in the case of *R v Secretary of State for Employment ex parte Equal Opportunities Commission and Another* (the *EOC* case).[116] There, the Equal Opportunities Commission had brought an action challenging allegedly discriminatory employment protection provisions in English law, arguing that these contravened European Community legislation. The House of Lords, in a bold decision, granted a declaration to the effect that national law was incompatible with Community law. However, the House of Lords did not go so far as to rule that the English provisions were void, rather, the House confined its ruling to the compatibility issue – thus avoiding any potential conflict with Parliament and the concept of sovereignty.

In *Ratcliffe and Others v North Yorkshire County Council*,[117] the House of Lords ruled that the County Council had violated section 1 of the Equal Pay Act 1970. The action had been brought by Unison, the public service union, on behalf of 1,300 dinner ladies employed by the Council, whose pay had been reduced from £3.31 per hour to £3.00 per hour, a rate below that of dustmen, gardeners, cleaners and street sweepers, with whom they had been compared for equal pay purposes. Section 1 of the Equal Pay Act 1970[118] provides that: 'An equality clause shall not operate in relation to a variation between the women's contract and the man's contract if the employer proves that the

---

115 In a challenge to a directive, a company sought to restrain the United Kingdom government from laying before Parliament regulations to implement a Council Directive. Proceedings were already before the Court of Justice which was not expected to give judgment until some four months after the time limit for implementation by Member States. The Court of Appeal declined to interfere, stating that interim relief could only be given in cases where there would be irreparable damage and that, in any case, the UK government should not be constrained from making regulations: *R v Secretary of State for Health ex parte Imperial Tobacco Ltd* [2000] 1 All ER 572.

116 (1994) *The Times*, 4 March.

117 (1995) *The Times*, 7 July.

118 Substituted by the Equal Pay (Amendment) Regulations SI 1983/1794, reg 2.

variation is genuinely due to a material factor which is not the difference of sex ...' Under the Local Government Act 1988, local councils were obliged to put the provision of school meals out to tender, and could only lawfully continue to provide such services if their own tender was accepted. In order to render its bid competitive, the Council had made a number of women redundant and re-employed them at lower hourly rates of pay. The House of Lords ruled that the Council 'had paid women less than men engaged on work rated as equivalent'. There was no material difference between the case of the women and that of their male comparators and, accordingly, the Council had discriminated against the women.

The Equal Opportunities Commission welcomed the decision, pointing out that women still received wages which on average were only 79 per cent of those earned by men, and that any clarification which would eliminate inequalities was a step forward.

In a significant case for part time women workers, the European Court of Justice, in *Magorrian and Another v Eastern Health and Social Services Board and Another*,[119] ruled that national provisions which limited access to occupational pensions for part time workers amounted to indirect sexual discrimination and were contrary to the Treaty. The Occupational Pension Schemes (Equal Access to Membership) Regulations (Northern Ireland) 1976, violated the right to equality enshrined in Article 141 (formerly, Article 119), in specifying limited rights to membership of pension schemes.

In *R v Secretary of State for Employment ex parte Seymour-Smith and Another*,[120] under English law, protection against unfair dismissal from employment commences after a period of two years' continuous employment. The applicants had both been employed for some 15 months before being dismissed by their employers. They had complained to an industrial tribunal and sought compensation, but were denied the right to redress because they had not been employed for a continuous two year period. In an application for judicial review, the applicants sought an order to quash the 1985 order and declarations.

The applicants' case was that the order indirectly discriminated against women, on the basis that the proportion of women who could comply with the qualifying period was substantially smaller than that of men, and that the order violated the principle of equal treatment enshrined in the EC Directive.[121] Neill LJ declared that the most difficult decision for the court to reach concerned the question of 'whether the applicants had established that the 1985 Order had a disparate adverse impact on women so as to lead to the conclusion that the prescribed qualifying period was incompatible with the

119 Case C-246/96: [1998] All ER (EC) 38.
120 Case C-167/97: (1995) *The Times*, 3 August.
121 76/207/EEC, OJ L39/40, 1976.

equal treatment directive'. However, the Court held that the principle of equal treatment meant 'that there should be no discrimination whatsoever on the ground of sex either directly or indirectly', and that the only margin of appreciation [discretion] which the Court of Justice adopted was that of 'considerable difference'.

The case went to the House of Lords,[122] which stayed proceedings and referred to the Court of Justice for a preliminary ruling questions concerning the interpretation of the EC Treaty and the Equal Pay and Equal Treatment Directives. The ECJ considered the legal test to be used for establishing whether a measure adopted by a Member State has a disparate effect on men and women to such an extent as to amount to indirect discrimination prohibited by the Treaty. The Court stated that:

> The best approach is to compare the relevant statistics by considering, on the one hand, the respective proportions of men in the workforce able to satisfy the requirement of two years' employment under the disputed rule and of those unable to do so, and, on the other, to compare those proportions as regards women in the workforce. It is for the national court hearing the case to assess the relevance and validity of the statistics presented, the degree of disparity between the men and women affected, and the length of time the disparity has existed.

> It is also for the national court to establish whether, and to what extent, a rule which has a more detrimental impact on women than on men is justified by objective reasons unrelated to any discrimination based on sex.

Finally, the Court pointed out that while Member States were free to pursue a social policy aim, that policy cannot have the effect of frustrating the implementation of a fundamental principle of Community law, namely that of equal pay for men and women.[123] The matter having been referred back to the House of Lords, their Lordships ruled that the figures demonstrated that the 1985 Order had considerably greater adverse impact on women than men. However, the government had shown that the Order was objectively justified as a measure adopted in pursuance of a legitimate aim of its social and economic policy unrelated to any sex discrimination, namely the encouragement of recruitment by employers. Accordingly, the Order when disqualifying the applicants from bringing claims for unfair dismissal, had not infringed Article 118 (now, Article 137).[124]

Article 119 (now, Article 141) extends to pensions schemes, entitlements from which constitute pay. In *Deutsche Telekom AG v Vick*, the Court of Justice ruled that national legislation which prohibited discrimination and thereby furthered the principle of equality enshrined in Article 119 was not affected by

---

122 [1997] 1 WLR 473.
123 Case C-167/97: [1999] 2 AC 554, Press Release of the Court of Justice No 06/99.
124 [1999] 2 AC 554.

time limits imposed on making claims.[125] However, in *Preston and Others v Wolverhamptom Healthcare NHS Trust and Others; Fletcher and Others v Midland Bank plc*,[126] in which pension entitlements were also at issue, the European Court, on a reference from the House of Lords under Article 177 (now, Article 234 EC), ruled that a national rule – that pensionable service could be calculated only by reference to service after a date no earlier than two years before the date of the claim – was contrary to Community law.[127] In its examination, the Court of Justice once again considered the doctrine of direct effect. Two facets of direct effect are the principles of effectiveness and the principle of equivalence against which national law must be measured vis à vis the requirements of Community law. In the absence of Community rules, it was for the national legal order of each Member State to designate the competent courts and to lay down the procedural rules for proceedings designed to ensure the protection of rights which individuals acquired through the direct effect of Community law. Those national rules, if they are to satisfy the principle of equivalence, must be framed in such a way as to be no less favourable than those governing similar domestic actions. To satisfy the principle of effectiveness, the national rules must be such that they do not render impossible in practice the exercise of rights conferred by Community law. In the instant case, the claimants had sought entitlement to retroactive membership of pension schemes for the periods of part time employment completed by them before amendments to the law designed to enable all part time workers, previously wholly or partially excluded, to join them. The purpose of section 2(5) of the Equal Pay Act 1970, as amended, was not to obtain, with retroactive effect, arrears of benefits under the occupational pension scheme, but to secure recognition of the right to retroactive membership of that scheme for the purpose of evaluating the benefits to be paid in the future. Such a rule, the ECJ held, prevented the entire record of service completed before the two years preceding the date on which proceedings were commenced from being taken into account for the purposes of calculating the benefits which would be payable even after the date of the claim. Since the 1970 Act constituted the legislation by means of which the United Kingdom discharged its obligations under the Community equal pay legislation, Article 119 of the Treaty and, subsequently, Directive 75/117/EEC, the Act could not provide an appropriate ground of comparison against which to measure compliance with the principle of equivalence. Under the 1970 Act, the relevant period in relation to claims started to run was at the end of each contract of employment and not at the end of the employment

---

125 (2000) *The Times*, 28 March.

126 Case C-78/96: (2000) *The Times*, 19 May.

127 On the other hand, a rule that a claim to membership of an occupational pension scheme was time-barred if it was brought later than six months after the end of employment was not contrary to Community law.

relationship. It followed that workers who were employed under successive short term contracts of employment were unable to secure recognition of periods of part time work for the purpose of calculating their pension rights unless they had instituted proceedings within six months after the end of each contract under which the work concerned was performed: that rendered the exercise of rights conferred by Article 119 excessively difficult and was contrary to Community law.

The ECJ has also ruled that the principle of equal treatment for men and women applies in matters of social security, in the instant case, in relation to the grant of a winter fuel payment in the United Kingdom.[128]

In *Meyers v Adjudication Officer*,[129] the European Court of Justice held that social security benefit, in the form of family credit, was concerned with access to employment and working conditions and therefore fell within the scope of Council Directive 76/207/EEC on the implementation of the principle of equal treatment for men and women as regards access to employment, vocational training and promotion and working conditions. The United Kingdom argued that family credit was excluded from the Directive. Under section 20 of the Social Security Act 1986, family credit was payable to a person whose income did not exceed a specified amount when he or his spouse or partner was normally engaged in remunerative work and he or his spouse or partner was responsible for, among other things, a child in the same household. Miss Meyers, a single parent, had applied for family credit. In calculating her eligibility, no deduction had been made for child care costs. As a result, she was ruled to be ineligible on the basis that her income exceeded the specified level. Miss Meyers argued on appeal, that non-deduction of child care costs discriminated against single parents, who found it more difficult to organise child care than couples and amounted to indirect discrimination against women. The question for the European Court of Justice, on a reference under Article 177 (now, Article 234), was whether family credit fell within the scope of the Directive. The Court ruled that it did. The purpose of family credit was to enable low income persons in employment to be able to continue to work, and to encourage poorly paid workers to remain in employment by ensuring that there were not worse off in work than out of work. Accordingly, family credit was concerned with access to employment, referred to in Article 3 of the Directive. Further, the principle of equal treatment presupposed that a benefit such as family credit, which was linked to an employment relationship, constituted a working condition within the meaning of Article 5 of the Directive. The European Court accordingly ruled that a benefit with the characteristics and purpose of family credit was concerned with both access to

---

128 Case C-382/98: *R v Secretary of State for Social Security ex parte John Henry Taylor*; Press Release of the Court of Justice No 100/99.
129 Case C-116/94: (1995) *The Times*, 19 July.

employment and working conditions and fell within the scope of Directive 76/207.

In *Marschall v Land Nordrhein-Westfalen*,[130] the Court of Justice ruled that the equal treatment directives of the Community were not breached where a national rule allowed female candidates for promotion to be favoured over equally qualified male applicants, where women were under-represented in a particular field of employment, provided certain conditions were met. The purpose of the national legislation was to correct the imbalance in employment opportunities, which discriminated against women. The goal was accordingly to achieve greater gender based equality, not to discriminate against men.

In 1994 and 1995, public concern over animal welfare in the export of live animals to Europe for slaughter on the point of destination led to incidents of public disorder and the disruption of exports of animals. In April 1995, the Chief Constable of Sussex decided that no policing would be provided to protect the transport of livestock to the port of Shoreham other than on two consecutive days a week or four consecutive days per fortnight, excluding Fridays, weekends or bank holidays. The Chief Constable later resolved not to change the earlier decision or to delay its implementation. International Traders' Ferry Ltd challenged the decision in an application for judicial review.

In *R v Chief Constable of Sussex ex parte International Trader's Ferry Ltd*, the Court of Appeal ruled that the Chief Constable's restrictions on policing could be justified under Article 30 (formerly Article 36), and was proportionate.[131] The export of live animals from the United Kingdom was considered by the Court of Justice on a reference to the Court by the High Court in *R v Minister of Agriculture, Fisheries and Food ex parte Compassion in World Farming Ltd*.[132] The Royal Society for the Prevention of Cruelty to Animals (RSPCA) and Compassion in World Farming Ltd (CIWF) had asked the Minister to prohibit the export of veal calves for rearing in veal crates. They contended that the Government had power under Community law to restrict exports to other Member States where the system of rearing calves was contrary to the standards in force in the United Kingdom[133] and the international standards laid down by the European Convention for the Protection of Animals Kept for Farming Purposes, to which all the Member States and the Community had agreed to adhere. Council Directive 91/629/EEC laid down minimum standards for the protection of calves, which were lower than the standards laid down by the Convention. CIWF accepted that a ban or restriction on the

---

130 Case C-409/95: [1997] ECR I-6363.

131 [1995] 3 CMLR 485.

132 Case C-1/96: judgment 19 March 1998.

133 Welfare of Livestock Regulations SI 1994/2126 and Welfare of Livestock Regulations (Northern Ireland) SI 1995/172.

export of live calves would constitute a quantitative restriction on exports contrary to Article 34 of the Treaty, but nevertheless maintained that such a restriction would be justified having regard to Article 36 (*inter alia*, restrictions justified on the grounds of public morality, public policy or the protection of health or life of animals). The Court ruled that a Member State cannot rely on Article 36 in order to justify restrictions. The Directive laid down standards and, even though these were less stringent than the national provisions, the Directive overrode the national requirements.

CONCLUSION

As the discussion of the aims, development and structure of the European Union and Community in Chapter 8 demonstrates, the original aims of the Community established under the Treaty of Rome have been expanded and developed into an ambitious, expansive and vigorous Union and Community, founded on the principles of individual rights and the rule of law. European integration has extended from the limited goals of a common market to incorporate full economic and monetary union and towards every closer co-operation in relation to matters relating to common defence and security policies and matters relating to justice and home affairs. As the aims and objectives of the Union have expanded, so too has the law of the Community. The European Court of Justice, through its dynamic approach, has ensured the supremacy of Community law over domestic law, to the extent that the Court of Justice's early statement that the Community represents a 'unique legal order' is now a reality which touches on increasingly wide aspects of domestic law.

PART IV

CENTRAL, REGIONAL AND LOCAL GOVERNMENT

CHAPTER 10

CENTRAL GOVERNMENT

INTRODUCTION

In this chapter, the structure and roles of the institutions of central government – the Crown, Privy Council, Prime Minister, Cabinet, Ministers and government departments – are examined. In Chapter 11, the concept of responsible government is introduced, and the fundamentally important concept of ministerial responsibility is considered. If government is to be conducted under the law, and in line with the principles of democracy and constitutionalism, it is of the utmost importance that those holding power should be accountable to citizens through their elected legislature. The responsibility of Ministers of the Crown is thus fundamental to the constitution, and the more so in the absence of an authoritative constitutional document which defines the scope and limits of ministerial power. Note that the procedural means by which Parliament scrutinises government action is considered in Chapter 16.

THE STRUCTURE OF GOVERNMENT

THE CROWN

> It is commonly hidden like a mystery, and sometimes paraded like a pageant, but in neither case is it contentious. The nation is divided into parties, but the Crown is of no party. Its apparent separation from business is that which removes it both from enmities and from desecration, which preserves its mystery, which enables it to combine the affection of conflicting parties – to be a visible symbol of unity to those still so imperfectly educated as to need a symbol.[1]

While the Monarch is titular head of the government and all governmental acts are carried out in the name of the Crown, the role of the Queen is largely, but not completely, formal and ceremonial. In the study of the government it is necessary to bear in mind that the United Kingdom remains a constitutional monarchy[2] and that the Crown is the symbolic head of the executive,

---

1   Bagehot, W, *The English Constitution* (1867), 1993, London: Fontana, p 90; Maitland, FW, *The Constitutional History of England*, 1908, Cambridge: CUP.

2   See Chapter 1.

legislature and judiciary. The remaining prerogatives of the Crown have been discussed in Chapter 6, which should be referred to for discussion of the Crown's role in the appointment of the Prime Minister and the dissolution of Parliament.

Succession to the Crown

The Act of Settlement 1700 provides that succession to the throne is confined to members of the Protestant religion and specifically excludes Roman Catholics, or those married to Roman Catholics, from succession to the throne.[3] This religious exclusion has been under recent discussion. Any amendment to the Act of Settlement would require the consent of the Parliaments of the United Kingdom's Dominions,[4] and may also require the assent of the Parliaments of all independent member countries of the Commonwealth which recognise the Queen as Head of State.

The line of succession

Succession to the Crown traditionally devolves according to the principles of *primogeniture*, that is to say, that male heirs, and their children (irrespective of sex), take precedence over female heirs. Again, this matter is said to be under current discussion with a view to reform. Because of *primogeniture*, the current line of succession is Prince Charles, his sons Prince William and Prince Henry, Andrew, Duke of York, his daughters, Princess Beatrice and Princess Eugenie, Prince Edward, Princess Anne, the Princess Royal, and then her children, Peter and Zara Phillips, and thereafter to other members of the Royal Family in a predetermined line of succession.

Were the Queen to abdicate, in favour of an early succession by Prince Charles, the assent of the Parliaments of the Dominions would be required. The only precedent case is that of King Edward VIII, who abdicated in 1936 in order to avoid the constitutional crisis which was perceived to be imminent if he persisted in his intention to marry the Roman Catholic American divorcee, Wallace Simpson.[5]

---

3   For this reason, Prince Michael of Kent was excluded from the line of succession upon his marriage to a Catholic in 1978.

4   Statute of Westminster 1931. Australia and Canada have Dominion status. New Zealand ceased to be a Dominion in 1987: see the Constitution Act 1986 (NZ), s 26.

5   See His Majesty's Declaration of Abdication Act 1936.

The Regency Acts

Should the Crown fall 'vacant', through death or (more rarely) abdication, or the Monarch becomes too ill to fulfil his or her constitutional duties,[6] and the successor has not yet reached the age of majority, there will be a need for the appointment of an adult with responsibility for the Crown's duties during the successor's minority. This situation is regulated under the Regency Acts 1937–53.

The Regency Act 1937 provides that the Sovereign may appoint Counsellors of State, charged with the responsibility of carrying out the Sovereign's duties whenever he or she is either absent from the United Kingdom, or suffering from temporary physical or mental illness. Those eligible to be appointed include the Monarch's spouse and the next four persons in line of succession.

Where there is the need to appoint a Regent, the Regency Act 1937 provides that, until the heir to the Throne reaches the age of 18, his or her duties will be carried out by a Regent.[7] The appointment of a Regent continues until it is declared to be no longer necessary by the wife or husband of the Monarch, the Lord Chancellor, the Speaker, the Lord Chief Justice and the Master of the Rolls.

The Royal Titles Act 1953

By statute, the Monarch may assume whatever title she thinks fit, with the assent of member governments of the Commonwealth. The Royal Titles Act provides the title:

> Elizabeth II by the Grace of God of the United Kingdom of Great Britain and Northern Ireland and of her other Realms and Territories Queen, Head of the Commonwealth, Defender of the Faith.

Within the Commonwealth, it was agreed in 1952[8] that the title of the Monarch within the Commonwealth was for each Member State to determine.[9] Accordingly, the only title of the Monarch which is uniform throughout the Commonwealth is that of 'Head of the Commonwealth'.

Prince Charles has recently made it known that he would prefer, on succession, to be known as 'Defender of Faith', rather than Defender of the (Protestant) Faith.

---

6   As occurred in the reigns of George III (in 1811) and George VI (in 1928).
7   The 1953 Regency Act provided that if one of Queen Elizabeth II's minor children succeeded to the throne, the Queen and the Duke of Edinburgh would be appointed Regent.
8   At a meeting of Commonwealth Prime Ministers.
9   See Cmd 8748, 1952, London: HMSO.

The Civil List

The Civil List is a fund provided by Parliament for the financing of expenditure on official business by the Monarch and specified members of her family. The Civil List is designed to offset expenditure incurred on official business; the cost of maintaining royal residences and the salaries and pensions payable to employees of the Crown.[10] The List was established in the reign of George III[11] and represents an agreement whereby Parliament will vote monies for the official business of the Royal Family in exchange for the surrender of hereditary revenues held by the Crown.[12] The revenues are paid directly into the Exchequer and become part of the Consolidated Fund.[13] Payments under the Civil List are provided for by the Civil List Act 1952, as amended.[14] The Civil List Act 1972 made separate provision for the Duke of Edinburgh and other members of the Royal Family who undertake public duties in the name of the Crown. In 1992, the Queen took over financial responsibility for members of the Royal Family, although the Duke of Edinburgh and the Queen Mother still receive separate provision under the Civil List. Financial provision for the Prince of Wales is made from the revenues accruing from the Duchy of Cornwall.

Taxation and the Sovereign

Until 1992, the Sovereign was not liable to pay tax on her private property[15] unless an Act of Parliament so determined. From 1993, the Queen, on her own undertaking, has paid tax on her private income.

The Crown Estate

Revenues from Crown lands and from other sources are managed by the Crown Estate Commissioners[16] under the authority of the Chancellor of the Exchequer and the Secretary of State for Scotland. The Commissioners lay an annual report before Parliament. It is these revenues which are exchanged for provision under the Civil List.

---

10 The amount awarded is variable: see the Civil List Act 1972, which provides that sums may be increased from time to time by statutory instrument, s 6; and the Civil List Act 1975.

11 1760–1820.

12 With the exception of revenues from the Duchies of Cornwall and Lancaster.

13 On which, see, further, Chapter 15.

14 Civil List Act 1972; Civil List Act 1975.

15 Other than on revenues from Balmoral and Sandringham estates which are liable to tax under the Crown Private Estates Act 1862.

16 Crown Estates Act 1961.

The role of the Monarch in the United Kingdom's constitutional democracy

In Chapter 6, the prerogative powers of the Crown were discussed, and that chapter should be consulted in order to appreciate the several important reserve powers which the Crown retains. In this section, the role of the Monarch in the practical administration of the State is considered. In Walter Bagehot's often-quoted phrase, the Monarch has the right to 'be consulted, the right to encourage, the right to warn'.[17] As such, the Queen must be fully informed of the actions of her government, and given adequate opportunity to express her views.

If the role of the Monarch is to remain respected by governments of all political persuasions, and the nation, it is axiomatic that the Queen be seen formally to be immune from party-political differences and to fulfil her duties in an even-handed manner. This is not to suggest that the Queen has no views on her government's policies or that she should not express them to the Prime Minister. What is required, however, is the absolute confidentiality of discussions between herself and the Prime Minister, and, should there be a disagreement over policy, it is required that, once the Monarch's views are made known, irrespective of her approval or otherwise, she follows the advice of her Prime Minister on policy matters.[18]

Queen Elizabeth II, since her accession to the throne in 1952, has presided over 35 years of Conservative rule and 13 years of Labour rule. She thus has accumulated a wealth of experience in political matters unmatched by her individual Prime Ministers.

The 'modernisation' of the monarchy?

Public perceptions that the monarchy is out-dated and needs reform have been recognised by the Royal Family. The Queen heads the 'Way Ahead Group', which comprises senior members of the Royal Family and meets to consider reform. Among recent proposals, none yet agreed,[19] are that the use of the royal title HRH should be confined to the monarch and his or her immediate successors; that, in the future, the right of those members of the Royal Family entitled to take their seats in the House of Lords should be removed;[20] and that the State opening of Parliament should be less formal. It

---

17 *Op cit*, Bagehot, fn 1.
18 See the letter to *The Times*, by the Queen's Press Secretary, Sir William Heseltine, 29 July 1986.
19 As at June 2000.
20 This proposed reform is consistent with the government's plans to abolish the right of hereditary peers to sit in the House of Lords. See, further, Chapter 17.

has also been suggested that Kensington Palace, former home of Diana, Princess of Wales, and home to other members of the Royal Family, should become an art gallery housing the royal art collection. On the matter of style, the Queen supports the view that people should not be required either to curtsey or bow on meeting the monarchy.

The State opening of Parliament

At the start of each new parliamentary session,[21] the Monarch formally opens Parliament.

The Queen's Speech is formally delivered to the House of Lords with members of the House of Commons having been summoned to the Lords by Black Rod. The Speech outlines the government of the day's proposals for legislation in the forthcoming session. Thereafter, there is a four or five day debate on the Speech in the Commons.

THE CHANNELS OF COMMUNICATION BETWEEN CROWN AND GOVERNMENT

Government papers

The Monarch receives copies of all significant government papers. She also receives copies of reports from ambassadors abroad and Commonwealth High Commissioners. All Cabinet papers and the minutes of Cabinet meetings are received by the Queen.

The weekly prime ministerial audience

Whatever the pressure of work, the Prime Minister attends a weekly half to one hour audience with the Queen. It is at this weekly meeting that issues will be discussed and the Queen's views made known to the Prime Minister.[22] Channels of communication are facilitated by the Queen's Private Secretary, whose appointment is the choice of the Queen, and who on appointment will become a Member of the Privy Council. The Private Secretary may not belong to any political party. Very rarely will the Queen's Private Secretary be drawn into public debate although, in 1986, the then Private Secretary, Sir William Heseltine, wrote to *The Times* (following public claims that the Queen and

---

21 On which, see Chapter 14.
22 See, further, Brazier, R, *Constitutional Texts*, 1990, Oxford: Clarendon, Chapter 8 and *Constitutional Practice*, 2nd edn, 1994, Oxford: Clarendon, Chapter 9.

Prime Minister (then Mrs Thatcher) disagreed on policy matters. In his letter, Sir William Heseltine spelled out three main points concerning the relationship between the Crown and the Prime Minister:

(a) the Sovereign has the right and duty to counsel, encourage and warn her government. She is thus entitled to have opinions on government policy and to express them to the Prime Minister;

(b) whatever the Queen's personal opinions may be, she is bound to accept and act on the advice of her Ministers;

(c) the Sovereign is obliged to treat communications with the Prime Minister as entirely confidential.[23]

Privy Council meetings

See below.

THE PRIVY COUNCIL

Historical origins

Since 1066, the monarch has appointed a Chancellor, who was head of the King's administration and had custody of the Great Seal. The Chancellor had responsibility for the administration of law, drawing up royal writs and exercising judicial powers. The Chancellor has always been a Member of the King's Council. The Privy Council may be viewed as the successor to the *Curia Regis*, the supreme legislative, executive and judicial body. The Council is traceable to the thirteenth century. It was through the Privy Council that monarchs would rule without recourse to Parliament. Under Edward I,[24] it was difficult to discern whether legislative acts emanated from the King-in-Parliament or the King-in-Council.[25] Throughout the fourteenth century, however, there were serious conflicts between the Council and Parliament and, in the reigns of Henry IV[26] and Henry V,[27] there is evidence of the Commons petitioning the King against the jurisdiction seized by the Council. The Council by this time was exercising judicial powers in relation to both criminal and civil litigation. Enforcement of the criminal law, where offences against the State were alleged or officers of State were involved, was effected

---

23 (1986) *The Times*, 29 July; see, also, Marshall, G, 'The Queen's press relations' [1986] PL 505.

24 1271–1307.

25 *Op cit*, Maitland, fn 1, p 136.

26 1399–1413.

27 1413–22.

by the feared Court of Star Chamber.[28] To this claim to wide civil and criminal jurisdiction came parliamentary objection on the basis that the Star Chamber was usurping the function of the common law courts. FW Maitland writes of the Council at this time that:

> The Tudor reigns are, we may say, the golden age of the Council: the Council exercises enormous powers of the most various kinds; but it is not an independent body – as against the King it has little power or none at all.[29]

By the reign of Henry VIII,[30] the Council comprised Privy Councillors – the elite King's advisers – and ordinary Councillors – lawyers and administrators. Over time, the Council fragmented into committees dealing with specified matters. The Council survived the abolition of the Star Chamber, although its powers were much weakened. Following the restoration of the monarchy, it became the body on which the King relied for advice. With the abolition of the Star Chamber, did the Council lose all its judicial powers? From early times the Council had asserted jurisdiction over territory overseas which fell under the suzerainty of the English Crown. With the Channel Islands and the Isle of Man coming under the Crown's protection in the thirteenth century, the seeds were sown for the Privy Council's jurisdiction over civil and criminal appeals from the British Empire and Commonwealth.

With the Glorious Revolution of 1688 and the rise of parliamentary sovereignty, the role of the Council changed. Under William, the inner circle of the Council became known as the Cabinet Council. Through this Cabinet, the King could exercise all his powers, although he had to have recourse to the wider membership of the Privy Council in order to undertake acts which required Orders in Council, the formal means by which such prerogative acts came into effect. It was the Privy Council which determined the summoning and dissolution of Parliament, although it seems clear that the King would act through Orders in Council published after consultation with an inner circle of the Privy Council. The early origins of Cabinet government can be seen here. As FW Maitland observed:

> We now see how it is legally possible for the work of government to fall into the hands of a small number of the Council – those Members who hold the high offices of State and who have control over the seals of office. If the King has with him the Chancellor, the Treasurer or First Lord of the Treasury, the Lord Privy Seal, and the Secretaries of State, he can get his work done without consulting the mass of Privy Councillors. If, for any purpose, an Order in Council is required, a meeting of the King with just these few intimate advisers will be a good enough meeting of the Privy Council at which Orders in

---

28 Abolished in 1640.
29 *Op cit*, Maitland, fn 1, p 256.
30 1509–47.

Council can be made. So much is the legal possibility of Cabinet government.[31]

While King William and Queen Anne attended Council meetings regularly, a change of practice occurred with the reign of George I[32] and George II.[33] Neither could speak English, and nor were they particularly concerned with English matters. Accordingly, the Cabinet began to meet without the King. Under George III,[34] the same situation prevailed, the Cabinet meeting without the King and communicating its decision to the King. Again, we find the origins of today's Cabinet, with the three principles of Cabinet government becoming apparent: those of 'political unanimity, common responsibility to Parliament and a common leader'.[35] With the rise of the Cabinet system of government in the eighteenth century, the Privy Council gradually lost much of its power.[36]

Composition of the Privy Council

The Privy Council has some 420 members, half of whom are peers, half commoners. There is no fixed number of members. Appointments are made by the Crown, with the advice of the Prime Minister. By convention, all present and past Cabinet members are appointed to the Privy Council. Also included in the membership are members of the Royal Family, senior judges, two Archbishops, British Ambassadors, the Speaker of the House of Commons, present and former leaders of the Opposition, and leading Commonwealth spokesmen and judges. On appointment, a new member of the Council takes the oath of allegiance, or affirms loyalty. The Privy Council oath binds the member to secrecy in relation to any matters discussed in the Council.[37]

Meetings of the Privy Council

The Privy Council may meet wherever the Queen so decides although, normally, the Council will meet at Buckingham Palace. The quorum is three.

---

31 *Op cit*, Maitland, fn 1, p 394.

32 1714–27.

33 1727–60.

34 1738–1820.

35 *Op cit*, Maitland, fn 1, p 395.

36 See Mackintosh, JP, *The British Cabinet*, 3rd edn, 1977, London: Stevens, Chapter 2. On the constitutional struggles between King, courts and Parliament, see Chapter 6.

37 Privy Councillors would in any event be prevented from disclosing confidential information by virtue of the Official Secrets Acts 1911–89.

FUNCTIONS OF THE PRIVY COUNCIL

Proclamations and Orders in Council

Proclamations are used for the summoning, proroguing and dissolving of Parliament and declarations of war and peace. Orders in Council give effect to decisions reached under the royal prerogative and under statute. Orders in Council may be legislative, executive or judicial.

Committees of the Privy Council

The majority of Privy Council functions are undertaken in committees. Miscellaneous committees have been established. These include committees dealing with scientific research, universities and the granting of charters. The most important committee is the Judicial Committee.

The Judicial Committee was established under statute by the Judicial Committee Act 1833. The Judicial Committee Act 1844 provided that the Queen may, by Order in Council, admit appeals from courts of British colonies or overseas territories. The Judicial Committee is composed of the Lord Chancellor, Lord President and former Lord Presidents of the Council, Lords of Appeal in Ordinary and the Lord Justices of Appeal, former Lord Chancellors and retired Lords of Appeal; senior judges or former judges of those Commonwealth countries from which a right of appeal still lies.[38]

In addition to its appellate jurisdiction, the Judicial Committee will on occasion examine and report on matters of constitutional importance. It has, for example, examined the legality of telephone tapping, issues of State security, and British policy in relation to the Falkland Islands.

THE OFFICE OF PRIME MINISTER[39]

As with so much of the United Kingdom's constitution the office of Prime Minister is one which developed by convention rather than by law. The office dates from the early eighteenth century,[40] but had become firmly established as a necessary and inevitable post in the latter half of the nineteenth century, when the extension of the franchise[41] combined with the growth of political

---

38   Appellate Jurisdiction Acts 1876, 1887, 1908; Judicial Committee Amendment Act 1895.

39   See Blake (Lord), *The Office of Prime Minister*, 1975, Oxford: OUP. For a listing of prime ministers and their political parties, see Appendix II.

40   Sir Robert Walpole, 1721–42.

41   See Chapter 13.

parties to produce both a (reasonably) accountable government and an opposition party. The first official recognition of the post of Prime Minister derives from the Treaty of Berlin 1878, and statutory and other formal references to the office remain scant.[42]

In 1889, Lord Morley[43] stated that:

... the Prime Minister is the keystone of the Cabinet arch. Although in Cabinet all its members stand on an equal footing, speak with an equal voice, and, on the rare occasions when a division is taken, are counted on the fraternal principle of one man, one vote, yet the head of the Cabinet is *primus inter pares*, and occupies a position which, so long as it lasts, is one of exceptional and peculiar authority.

Little has changed over the intervening century and the judgment expressed above remains true today. Sir Anthony Eden[44] has written that:

A Prime Minister is still nominally *primus inter pares*, but in fact his authority is stronger than that. The right to choose his colleagues, to ask for a dissolution of Parliament and, if he is a Conservative, to appoint the Chairman of the party organisation, add up to a formidable total of power.[45]

Contemporary interest focuses on the power of the office, the relationship between the Prime Minister and the Cabinet and the occasional dominance – as was apparent with Mrs Thatcher's premiership – of the Prime Minister over Cabinet colleagues.[46] One question which inevitably arises is whether government has changed from being parliamentary government, through to being best described as Cabinet government and now through to prime ministerial government.[47] The assessment of this question is a matter for evaluation on consideration of the evidence. It must be recognised, however, that the extent to which there exists prime ministerial dominance will depend very much upon the individual personality of the incumbent Prime Minister: there can be no broad generalisations. It must also be recognised that, whatever the personal power of the Prime Minister, he or she is ultimately dependent upon the support of Cabinet, party and Parliament; and, in turn, that support is dependent upon the support of the electorate expressed not just through the vote at a general election, but continually expressed in that

---

42 *Inter alia*, the Chequers Estates Act 1917, Chevening Estate Act 1959, the Parliamentary and Other Pensions Act 1972, the House of Commons Disqualification Act 1975, Ministerial and Other Pensions and Salaries Act 1991.

43 Cited in Gwynn, SL, *The Life of Walpole*, 1932, London: Butterworths.

44 Prime Minister from April 1955 to January 1957.

45 Cited in *op cit*, Mackintosh, fn 36, p 628.

46 See Hennessy, P, *Cabinet*, 1986, Oxford: Blackwells, Chapter 3.

47 See Wolf-Phillips, L, 'A long look at the British Constitution' (1984) 37 Parl Aff 385; Brazier, R, 'The downfall of Margaret Thatcher' (1991) 54 MLR 471. On this question and the role of Mrs Thatcher, see Doherty, M, 'Prime ministerial power and ministerial responsibility in the Thatcher era' (1988) 41 Parl Aff 49; Marshall, G, 'The end of prime ministerial government?' [1991] PL 1.

amorphous concept 'the mood of the people'. As the resignation of Mrs Margaret Thatcher in 1990 demonstrated,[48] even a seemingly invincible Prime Minister, who had enjoyed success at three general elections, can fall victim to the loss of the vital support of Cabinet and consequently the loss of office.

The Prime Minister, in addition to being the figurehead of government both within the United Kingdom and internationally, holds more than one office. The Prime Minister holds office as First Lord of the Treasury[49] and is formally in charge of the Treasury, although in practical terms it is the Chancellor of the Exchequer who runs the Treasury. It is in part because of the role of First Lord of the Treasury that the Prime Minister must be a Member of the House of Commons which has parliamentary supremacy over financial matters.[50] Since 1937, the Ministers of the Crown Act has assumed that the office of Prime Minister and First Lord are held by the same person. Since 1968, the Prime Minister has also held responsibility for the Civil Service as Minister for the Civil Service.[51] On occasions, Prime Ministers will assume other offices. For example, Ramsey MacDonald also held office as Foreign Secretary;[52] Winston Churchill was also Minister of Defence.[53]

The Prime Minister and membership of the House of Commons

Between 1837 and 1902, six Prime Ministers were peers.[54] However, as early as 1839, the Duke of Wellington expressed the view that:

> I have long entertained the opinion that the Prime Minister of this country, under existing circumstances, ought to have a seat in the other House of Parliament, and that he would have great advantage in carrying on the business of the Sovereign by being there.[55]

With the extension of the franchise in 1832, 1867 and 1884,[56] the supremacy of the Commons over the Lords was firmly established. The role of the House of

---

48 See, *inter alia*, Alderman, RK and Carter, N, 'A very Tory coup: the ousting of Mrs Thatcher' (1991) 44 Parl Aff 126; Alderman, RK and Smith, MJ, 'Can prime ministers be pushed out?' (1990) 43 Parl Aff 260; *op cit*, Marshall, fn 47; Blackburn, RW, 'Margaret Thatcher's resignation as Prime Minister', in *Constitutional Studies*, 1992, London: Mansell.

49 Ministerial and Other Salaries Act 1975. As First Lord of the Treasury the Prime Minister has responsibility for the civil service which is controlled by the Treasury.

50 No Prime Minister has been a member of the House of Lords since 1902.

51 SI 1968/1656; SI 1971/2099. See *Council of Civil Service Unions v Minister for Civil Service* [1985] AC 374.

52 Labour government, 1924.

53 1940–45.

54 Lords Melbourne, John Russell, Derby, Aberdeen, Beaconsfield, Salisbury.

55 Parl Debs 3rd Ser Vol 47 Col 1016, cited in Jennings, I (Sir), *Cabinet Government*, 3rd edn, 1959, Cambridge: CUP, p 21.

56 See Chapter 13.

Lords in legislation was reduced significantly by the Parliament Acts of 1911 and 1949.[57] Sir Ivor Jennings writes:

> No peer has been Prime Minister since the resignation of Lord Salisbury in 1902. In 1923, the question, whether it was then possible for a peer to become Prime Minister, was definitely raised. The resignation of Mr Bonar Law left George V with a choice between Lord Curzon and Mr Baldwin. Lord Curzon's experience and party standing were greater. It is doubtful if Mr Baldwin would have become prominent in the councils of the Conservative Party but for the fact that most of the Coalition Unionists remained faithful to Mr Lloyd George in 1922. The King nevertheless chose Mr Baldwin. Lord Stamfordham on his behalf explained to Lord Curzon that 'since the Labour Party constituted the official Opposition in the House of Commons and were unrepresented in the House of Lords, the objections to a Prime Minister in the Upper Chamber were insuperable.[58]

There are good reasons – aside from the office of First Lord of the Treasury – for arguing that the Prime Minister must be a member of the House of Commons. First, he is today the elected leader of the parliamentary party and must lead that party into a general election for an affirmation – or denial – of the party's, and hence his own, mandate. Secondly, the doctrine of individual and collective ministerial responsibility applies to the Prime Minister as it does to all other holders of office. Above all, the doctrines require that a Minister is accountable to the electorate through Parliament. For the Prime Minister not to be accountable to the democratically-elected House of Commons would effectively defeat the concept of collective responsibility and would be an affront to democracy and the very idea of constitutionalism. Certainly, no breach of law would follow if the Queen invited a peer to take office as Prime Minister and First Lord of the Treasury: but it would clearly fly in the face of convention.

The choice of Prime Minister[59]

A change in Prime Minister will be brought about by either resignation or death or – rarely – dismissal of the office holder. Resignation from office may stem from electoral defeat at a general election,[60] from conflict within the government,[61] from losing the support of the party,[62] from losing a vote of

---

57 See Chapter 17.

58 *Op cit*, Jennings, fn 55, p 23, citing the Rt Hon the Earl of Ronaldshay, *The Life of Lord Curzon*, 1928.

59 See, *inter alia, op cit*, Jennings, fn 55, Chapter II; *op cit*, Mackintosh, fn 36, Chapter 20; Brazier, R, 'Choosing a Prime Minister' [1982] PL 395; *op cit*, Brazier, 1990, fn 22, Chapter 4.

60 1945, 1951, 1964, 1970, 1974, 1979.

61 As in 1931.

62 As occurred in 1990 when Mrs Margaret Thatcher resigned.

confidence in the House,[63] from a challenge to the leadership of the party,[64] from illness[65] or old age,[66] from death, from voluntary retirement[67] or from loss of support of the Cabinet.[68]

Whatever the explanation for a change in Prime Minister, it is for the monarch to appoint the succeeding Prime Minister. It was seen in Chapter 6 that it is the prerogative right of the Crown to appoint whosoever she please, but that by convention rather than law the Queen appoints as Prime Minister the leader of the political party who can command a majority in the House of Commons. In the days before the major parties chose their leaders by some form of election, some discretion was left to the Queen as to the choice of Prime Minister. Nowadays, such discretion is all but dead, other than where a general election produces a situation where there is no overall majority party in the House of Commons.

The actual choice of Prime Minister will thus be dictated by the election process within the major political parties[69] and, where relevant, by the result of a general election.[70] The three major parties, Conservative, Labour and Liberal Democrat, all differ in their approach to choice of leadership. The Conservative Party elects its leader annually, by ballot, at the start of the new parliamentary session. If there is only one nomination, as may occur where there is unity as to the choice of a new leader, or where the incumbent leader continues to enjoy the support of the Party, that person is declared leader. Should there be a contest for the leadership,[71] the choice will be determined by up to three secret ballots among the Party's Members of Parliament. In order to win on the first ballot the candidate must receive an overall majority of the votes cast and 15 per cent more votes than any other candidate.[72] If the matter goes to a second ballot, all candidates must resubmit their names and the result will be determined by a simple majority. If no candidate wins an outright majority of votes on the second ballot, a third ballot will be held on which Members choose between the three candidates who secured the highest number of votes on the second ballot. At this final ballot, each Member has two votes, the first for the candidate of his preference, the other for his second preference. By a system of redistributing the votes cast for the candidate with

---

63 1895, 1923, 1979.

64 Thatcher, 1990.

65 Campbell-Bannerman, 1908, Bonar Law, 1923, Eden, 1957, Macmillan, 1963.

66 Salisbury, 1902, MacDonald, 1935, Churchill, 1955.

67 Baldwin, 1937, Wilson, 1976.

68 Mrs Thatcher in 1990.

69 See *op cit*, Brazier, 1990, fn 22, Chapter 1.

70 As in 1906, 1918, 1922, 1931, 1935, 1950, 1955, 1959, 1966, October 1974, 1983, 1987, 1992 where the Government was returned with a clear majority in the House of Commons.

71 As in 1990.

72 See Procedure for the Selection of the Leader of the Conservative Party.

the least votes among the other candidates according to their second preference, an overall winner will emerge.[73]

The Conservative Party leadership elections 1990 and 1995

In the leadership contest of 1990,[74] Mrs Thatcher[75] won 54.8 per cent of the votes cast in the first round of the contest but failed by 1.1 per cent to achieve the 15 per cent hurdle. Having announced her intention to contest the leadership in the second round, Mrs Thatcher was advised by members of her Cabinet that she would be defeated and she announced her resignation the following morning.[76] Following her resignation two further contestants entered the race:[77] John Major[78] and Douglas Hurd.[79] Both Michael Heseltine and Douglas Hurd withdrew their candidacies when John Major won a majority of votes cast among the parliamentary Party but failed to secure the necessary 15 per cent overall majority.

On 22 June 1995, the Prime Minister, John Major, resigned as Leader of the Conservative Party in order to force a leadership election in advance of the normal annual cycle. Major's objective was to force the election early in order to settle finally the arguments within the Conservative Party over his leadership.[80] In July 1995, the then Prime Minister received the endorsement of 66 per cent of the parliamentary party. John Major's resignation from leadership of the Conservative Party, following electoral defeat in May 1997, led to the election of William Hague as Party Leader.

The Labour and Liberal Democrat leadership

Until 1993, the Labour Party's arrangements were complex and involved not only Members of Parliament. The Party's Constitution provided that the Leader and Deputy Leader of the Party shall be elected from members of the

---

73 Four contested elections have taken place: 1965, Edward Heath elected; 1975, Margaret Thatcher elected; 1990, John Major elected; 1997, William Hague elected.

74 See Watkins, A, *A Conservative Coup*, 1992, London: Duckworth.

75 On Mrs Thatcher's premiership, see Young, H, *One of Us*, 1989, London: Macmillan.

76 22 November 1990. See *op cit*, Blackburn, fn 48.

77 Michael Heseltine, President of the Board of Trade, had challenged Mrs Thatcher's leadership on 15 November 1990.

78 Then Chancellor of the Exchequer.

79 Then Foreign Secretary.

80 Two further resignations from Cabinet were announced. The Rt Hon Douglas Hurd, Secretary of State for Foreign and Commonwealth Affairs resigned (his retirement had been expected); and on 5 July 1995 Jonathan Aitken announced his resignation from the post of Chief Secretary to the Treasury, to enable him better to concentrate on a number of libel actions he was pursuing against the press.

Parliamentary Labour Party at the annual Party Conference, with votes given to Members of Parliament, Trade Unions (but not their individual members) and members of local parties, each being proportionally determined. The procedure for the election of Leader of the Labour Party was reviewed in 1992–93, with John Smith being determined to reform the system in order to give one vote to each member of trade unions, thus replacing the 'block' union vote. Following John Smith's death in 1994, Tony Blair was elected under the reformed system.

The Constitution of the Liberal Democrats provides the circumstances under which a leadership election may be called for, and the rules for election, which include entitlement to vote by Liberal Democrat Members of Parliament and members of local parties and specified associated organisations.[81]

THE FUNCTIONS OF THE PRIME MINISTER

Formation of Cabinet[82]

Once in office, the first task of the Prime Minister is to form his Cabinet. Constitutionally, the appointment of all Ministers is a decision for the monarch but, in practice, it is the Prime Minister who determines who shall be appointed. The Prime Minister decides which government departments should be represented in Cabinet although, by convention, certain Departments are always represented. Thus, the Chancellor of the Exchequer, the Secretary of State for Foreign and Commonwealth Affairs, the Home Secretary, the Lord Chancellor, the Secretary of State for Defence, the Secretary of State for Scotland and the Leader of the House of Commons always hold a seat in Cabinet. Further constraints on membership exist. For example, under the Ministers of the Crown Act 1975, certain Cabinet positions are allocated to Members of the House of Lords. Accordingly, the Lord Chancellor and three other Ministers are appointed from that House. Further, under the Ministerial and Other Salaries Act 1975, the size of Cabinet is effectively controlled – if indirectly – by limiting the number of Ministers who may draw a ministerial salary.

It is also for the Prime Minister to decide whether Cabinet Members should remain in office, and he has the right to require a member to resign and, if he refuses, to request the Queen to dismiss him. This form of control

---

81 Only two elections have been held under the constitution of the new merged Liberal Democrat Party, electing first Paddy Ashdown and, subsequently, Charles Kennedy as Leader of the Party.

82 See *op cit*, Jennings, fn 55, Chapter III.

was most strikingly seen in 1962 when Harold Macmillan in 'the night of the long knives' removed seven Ministers (from a Cabinet of 20) overnight. The Cabinet normally comprises approximately 20 senior members of the government of the day. The actual membership is not fixed, and is (subject to convention) for the Prime Minister to determine.

THE CABINET

Organisation of the Cabinet in Tony Blair's government[83] is as follows:

OFFICE

Prime Minister, First Lord of the Treasury and Minister for Civil Service

Deputy Prime Minister

Chancellor of the Exchequer

Secretary of State for Foreign and Commonwealth Affairs

Lord Chancellor

Secretary of State for Home Department

Secretary of State for Education and Skills

Secretary of State for Trade and Industry

Secretary of State for Environment, Food and Rural Affairs

Secretary of State for Scotland

Secretary of State for Defence

Secretary of State for Health

Leader of the House of Commons

Secretary of State for Culture, Media and Sport

Secretary of State for Work and Pensions

Secretary of State for Northern Ireland

Secretary of State for Wales

Secretary of State for International Development

---

83   As at July 2001.

Lord Privy Seal, Leader of the Lords and Minister for Women

Minister for the Cabinet office and Chancellor of the Duchy of Lancaster

Parliamentary Secretary to the Treasury and Chief Whip

Chief Secretary to the Treasury

Cabinet meetings

The Prime Minister has almost total control over the conduct of Cabinet. The holding and conduct of Cabinet meetings is a matter for the Prime Minister to decide. Traditionally, but not invariably, full meetings of Cabinet are held twice a week. Under the leadership of Mrs Thatcher, the number of full Cabinet meetings was reduced, and the number of Cabinet Committees increased. Matters which are to be discussed in Cabinet are for the Prime Minister to determine.[84] In the course of the 'Westland affair' (discussed below, pp 395–98) the Secretary of State for Defence, Michael Heseltine, was expecting to be able to put his case for the European rescue bid of the helicopter company to a Cabinet meeting. The Prime Minister, however, allegedly cancelled that meeting, thus precipitating Heseltine's resignation from office.[85]

Timing of dissolution of Parliament

The timing of the dissolution of Parliament is within the Prime Minister's discretion and there is no requirement, either in law or convention, that the Prime Minister submit his choice of date to the Cabinet.[86]

Appointments

The Prime Minister has significant powers and influence over the appointment of persons to senior positions. For example, it is the Prime Minister who is responsible for the appointment of a Commission to oversee the work of the Security Service, and his consent is required for the

---

84 See *op cit*, Mackintosh, fn 36, Chapter 21. Cf Wilson, H, *The Governance of Britain*, 1976, London: Weidenfeld & Nicolson.

85 See *op cit*, Young, fn 75, Chapter 19.

86 On the dissolution of Parliament, see, further, Chapter 6.

appointment of most senior civil servants. Prime Ministerial nomination leads to the appointment of, *inter alia*, senior judges, bishops, and the Parliamentary Commissioner for Administration. His advice is given to the Queen on the granting of new peerages, on honours and on appointments to the Privy Council.

The role and functions of Cabinet[87]

A Cabinet is a combining committee – a hyphen which joins, a buckle which fastens the legislative part of the State to the executive part of the State. In its origins, it belongs to the one and in its functions, it belongs to the other.[88]

The Cabinet represents the nucleus of government. It is the Cabinet as a whole which, at least in theoretical terms, formulates, initiates and implements the policy of the government. Because there is no written constitution defining and controlling the working of Cabinet, it is not possible to give a fixed picture of its role. The use and working of Cabinets will vary with different governments and the different style and personality of the Prime Minister of the day.

As the central decision making body, the Cabinet has great power in relation to Parliament as a whole, in relation to the political party it represents and in relation to the Prime Minister. While the Prime Minister may control the composition and working of Cabinet, no Prime Minister can ultimately survive in office without the support of Cabinet and party.[89] The style of leadership will depend upon the personality of the premier, and an evaluation of whether it is parliamentary government, Cabinet government or Prime Ministerial government will also depend upon the strength of the Prime Minister vis à vis his or her colleagues.

Cabinet committees

In order to facilitate efficiency, the Cabinet is supported by a system of committees which, again, is largely determined by the Prime Minister.[90] Some of these are standing committees which will exist for the life of the government. Mrs Thatcher established four such committees on taking office in 1979: defence and overseas policy; economic strategy; home and social

---

87 See, *inter alia, op cit*, Jennings, fn 55; *op cit*, Mackintosh, fn 36; *op cit*, Hennessy, fn 46.

88 *Op cit*, Bagehot, fn 1, p 68; see, also, Jones, GW, 'Cabinet government since Bagehot', in *op cit*, Blackburn, fn 48.

89 See *op cit*, Brazier, 1994, fn 22; and *op cit*, Alderman and Carter, fn 48; *op cit*, Alderman and Smith, fn 48.

90 See *op cit*, Jennings, fn 55, Chapter IX; *op cit*, Mackintosh, fn 36, Chapter 21; *op cit*, Hennessy, fn 46.

affairs and a legislation committee.[91] The first two of these were chaired by the Prime Minister herself. Ad hoc committees may be established to consider particular matters. In addition, a whole range of official committees staffed by civil servants exist to complement the work of Ministers. Professor Peter Hennessy has analysed the pattern of committee formation under several governments:[92]

> Attlee accumulated 148 standing and 313 ad hoc groups in six and a quarter years, and Churchill 137 and 109 respectively in three and a half years. The figures for Eden are incomplete, and those for Macmillan and Home remain a mystery which the current Cabinet Secretary refuses to resolve. Thanks to Mrs Castle's *Diary* we have some intelligence on Wilson Mark I. Elected in October 1964, he had by early 1969 (that is, after four and a quarter years) reached his 236th ad hoc group. The Heath era is another unknown. Wilson Mark II, between March 1974 and March 1976, ran up a total of somewhere around 120 ad hoc groups. Callaghan, in the three years between April 1976 and April 1979, commissioned about 160 ad hoc committees, a similar growth rate to Attlee's. Judging by the Cabinet committee criterion, Mrs Thatcher has done exceedingly well. Under her, there have been 30–35 standing committees and just over 120 ad hocs in six and a half years. So Cabinet *and* Cabinet committee discussion is down.[93]

While the use of committees is both necessary and inevitable, it raises important constitutional questions concerning the doctrine of collective responsibility. Collective responsibility (discussed in Chapter 11) requires that each member of Cabinet, and all government Ministers and Parliamentary Private Secretaries, is bound by the decision of the Cabinet. The extent to which the doctrine will in practice be binding will depend upon the extent government members are prepared to maintain confidentiality and unanimity over decisions in which they may have played no part.

The former Prime Minister, John Major, announced a streamlining of the Cabinet committee structure in July 1995.[94] The number of committees was reduced from 27 to 19, with the objective of achieving greater efficiency in government business. The Prime Minister chaired the committees on economic and domestic policy, and those on overseas, defence, nuclear and intelligence issues. The then Deputy Prime Minister, Michael Heseltine, chaired four committees: those on competitiveness, co ordination and presentation of government policy, the environment and local government.

---

91 Official Reports, HC 967 Deb 179.
92 *Op cit*, Hennessy, fn 46.
93 *Op cit*, Hennessy, fn 46, pp 100–01.
94 18 July 1995; (1995) *The Times*, 19 July.

Under the Labour government elected in 1997, the following ministerial Cabinet committees were formed:

Committee	Chairperson
Economic Affairs	Chancellor of the Exchequer
Public Services and Public Expenditure	Chancellor of the Exchequer
Environment	Deputy Prime Minister and Secretary of State for the Environment, Transport and the Regions
Local Government	Deputy Prime Minister
Intelligence Services	Prime Minister
Northern Ireland	Prime Minister
Joint Consultative Committee with Liberal Democrat Party	Prime Minister
Defence and Overseas Policy	Prime Minister
Devolution Policy	Lord Chancellor
Legislation	Leader of the House of Commons
Constitutional Reform Policy	Prime Minister
Queen's Speeches and Future Legislation	Leader of the House of Commons
Home and Social Affairs	Prime Minister

The Prime Minister's Private Office

While often mooted, and its absence an apparent anomaly in a sophisticated system of government, there has never been a 'Prime Minister's Department' dedicated to the task of organising, co-ordinating and liaising on behalf of the Prime Minister. Instead, a British Prime Minister's team comprises civil service support and non-civil service political support in the form of a specially appointed team of advisers. Heading the Prime Minister's support system is his Principal Private Secretary who heads the Private Office, who has close relations with both the Cabinet Secretary and the Queen's Private Secretary. A civil servant, usually seconded from the Treasury for a three year period, it is the Private Secretary who co-ordinates the work of the Prime Minister, controlling the flow of paper into Number 10, and prioritising matters for prime ministerial attention. In addition to the Private Secretary, there is a Private Secretary for Overseas and Defence Affairs, Economic and Home Affairs, Europe, Central and Constitutional Affairs and Security and Intelligence. The Private Secretaries link the Prime Minister with Cabinet, other government Ministers and civil servants, and attend prime ministerial meetings and Cabinet meetings. The Prime Minister's Diary Secretary – a political appointment since 1979 – also plays a key role in the inner corpus of prime ministerial support, controlling the Prime Minister's time and engagements. A Duty Clerk is responsible for maintaining links between Number 10 and the outside world, and manning the Prime Minister's office in the absence of the Private Secretary. The Prime Minister's secretariat, known as the 'Garden Room Girls' (*sic*) since Lloyd George's premiership, completes the support staff at Number 10. These appointments represent the Prime Minister's staff in his role as head of government. In addition, the Prime Minister must maintain close links with his parliamentary party and with the party in the country. Given the requirement of political neutrality in civil servants, this would be an inappropriate task for the Private Office and, as a result, this responsibility falls on the Prime Minister's Political Secretary, a post funded by the party rather than the taxpayer. Harold Wilson was the first Prime Minister to formally appoint a Political Secretary, Marcia Williams, and all subsequent Prime Ministers have felt the need for this particular support mechanism. A Parliamentary Private Secretary, a Member of Parliament, assists in liaison with the party, meeting members of Parliament, accompanying the Prime Minister for Prime Minister's Question Time and generally facilitating lines of communication between the party and its leader.

The Cabinet Office[95]

The daily working of Cabinet is assisted by the Cabinet Office,[96] established in 1917, headed by the Secretary to the Cabinet. It is the Secretary to the Cabinet who is responsible for the recording of Cabinet meetings and circulation of the agreed conclusions. Within the Cabinet Office, there exists a number of secretariats, including the Economic Secretariat; Overseas and Defence Secretariat; European Secretariat and Home and Social Affairs Secretariat.[97]

---

95 See *op cit*, Wilson, fn 84, Chapter 4; Mosley, RK, *The Story of the Cabinet Office*, 1969, London: Routledge and Kegan Paul; *op cit*, Jennings, fn 55, Chapter 9.

96 See *op cit*, Mackintosh, fn 36, Chapter 21.

97 See Hennessy, P, *Whitehall*, 1990, London: Fontana, pp 390–91.

Between 1970 and 1983, there existed within the Cabinet Office the Central Policy Review staff whose principal task was to keep policy choices and implementation under review and to advise Ministers.[98] The Central Policy Review staff – or 'Think Tank' – stood between the Civil Service and the Cabinet and was regarded as invaluable by Prime Minister James Callaghan.[99] However, in Mrs Thatcher's first administration,[100] some of the Think Tank's proposals were too radical and the unit was destined to be closed down,[101] to be replaced with a Policy Unit whose function is to serve the Prime Minister rather than Cabinet as a whole.

THE CIVIL SERVICE[102]

A civil servant has been defined as: '... a servant of the Crown, other than holders of political or judicial offices, who is employed in a civil capacity and whose remuneration is paid wholly and directly out of monies voted by Parliament.'[103]

---

98 Cmnd 4506, 1970, London: HMSO, paras 44–48.

99 Callaghan, J, *Time and Chance*, 1987, London: Collins, pp 404–08.

100 *Op cit*, Young, fn 75, pp 300–01.

101 (1993) *The Times*, 14 June.

102 See *Report of the Committee on the Civil Service 1966–68*, Cmnd 3638, 1968, London: HMSO; Drewry, G and Butcher, T, *The Civil Service Today*, 1988, Oxford: Blackwells; *op cit*, Hennessy, fn 97.

103 Report of the Royal Commission on the Civil Service, 1929–31, Cmd 3909, 1931, London: HMSO.

The constitutional relationship between the Civil Service and the government of the day is a matter directly linked to Ministers' responsibility to the electorate – through Parliament – and the extent to which that responsibility is affected by the role of civil servants. Before considering the relationship between Ministers and departments, some preliminary points require attention. Some doubt exists as to the precise number of personnel in the Civil Service, doubts which arise from the difficulties concerning the appropriate classification of some occupations within the public service. For example, employees of the National Health Service are not technically employees of the Crown – and therefore not civil servants – although responsibility for the Health Service lies with the Secretary of State.

One further difficulty in evaluating the operation of the Civil Service arises from the disparity in size between government departments, with some departments having a staff of over 100,000, while others may have less than 10,000. The size of a department has a practical bearing on the extent to which Ministers can realistically be said to be making decisions. Added to that difficulty is the preference of some governments for large departments of State. Moreover, recent changes to the structure of the Civil Service to enhance its efficiency[104] have led to a proliferation of government agencies.

By way of example of the disparity in size of departments, in 1951, the Prime Minister, Winston Churchill, appointed Lord Leathers as Secretary of State with responsibility for the co-ordination of transport, fuel and power and Lord Woolton as Lord President of the council with special responsibility for the co-ordination of food and agriculture. These two Ministers became known as the 'Overlords' and the appointments were much criticised by the Opposition as weakening the responsibility of Ministers running the Departments and also on the basis that both 'Overlords' were Members of the House of Lords and not the Commons.

In debate,[105] the Prime Minister defended the appointments, emphasising the close links between collective and individual responsibility, and asserting

---

104 Discussed below, pp 388–90.
105 6 May 1952.

that the co-ordinating Minister's role could best be viewed as an aspect of collective responsibility. In 1970, the Prime Minister, Mr Edward Heath, regarded the merging of departments as a means of achieving greater efficiency in both management and in the implementation of government policy.[106] As a result, the Ministry of Housing and Local Government, Ministry of Transport, Ministry of Public Building and Works were amalgamated to form the Department of the Environment with some 72,000 civil servants.[107]

When considering responsibility for the Civil Service and accountability to Parliament, a further feature of political life must be borne in mind: that of ministerial mobility. The average tenure of responsibility for a department is two years. The Department of Education and Science, between 1944 and 1986, had 21 ministerial heads. During the Thatcher administration (1979–90), Cabinet reshuffles were frequent with several Ministers holding a number of portfolios during that government.

A final practical preliminary point to consider is the sheer volume of work entailed in government. An estimated[108] two-thirds of a Minister's working week is taken up by non-departmental business: Cabinet meetings, Cabinet committees, parliamentary party meetings, debates and questions in the House, official visits, and constituency duties. The task of heading a major department of State in addition to all the other duties is a major one, and the practical impact of regular government 're-shuffles', the size of departments and non-departmental duties is great. Such considerations lead the observer to wonder whether Ministers, rather than senior civil servants, can truly be said to be in charge of their Departments.

Not too much must be made of this matter, but it can be noted that senior politicians such as Tony Benn, Richard Crossman, Michael Meacher and Barbara Castle (each of whom has held Cabinet office) have all given some credence to what may be dubbed the 'conspiracy theory of government'. Tony Benn advances this criticism of the Civil Service:

> The Civil Service sees itself as being above party battle, with a political position of its own to defend against all-comers, including incoming governments armed with their philosophy and programme.

However, Peter Hennessy warns that:

> It is easy but wrong to take away the impression from reading the literature on Whitehall that officials do behave rather like keepers at the zoo watching the

---

106 White Paper, *The Reorganisation of Central Government*.

107 The Ministry of Transport subsequently became independent once more, but is now linked with the Environment and the regions.

108 Headey, BW, *British Cabinet Ministers: The Roles of Politicians in Executive Office*, 1974, London: Allen & Unwin.

antics of their charges – Ministers – with a mixture of familiarity, superiority and detachment.[109]

THE CHANGING STRUCTURE OF THE CIVIL SERVICE

Improving efficiency in the Civil Service

From November 1986 to March 1987, the Efficiency Unit, under the supervision of Sir Robin Ibbs, inquired into the future of the Civil Service. Its report to the Prime Minister, *Improving Management in Government: The Next Steps*,[110] was published in 1988. The terms of reference of the inquiry were:

(a) to assess progress in improving management in the Civil Service;

(b) to identify measures which have been successful in changing attitudes and practice;

(c) to identify institutional, administrative, political and attitudinal obstacles to better management and efficiency;

(d) to report to the Prime Minister on what further measures should be taken.[111]

A principal interest of the Unit was expressed to be not so much the detailed working of the Civil Service or its efficiency, but rather the relationship between the Civil Service and ministerial responsibility, and the impact which any recommendations as to the improvement of efficiency within the Civil Service might have on this constitutional relationship.

On the management and efficiency front, the Unit reported several difficulties, *inter alia:* that there was a lack of clear and accountable management responsibility within departments; that there was a lack of clarity as to what was expected of individuals; that the size and diversity of the Civil Service made it difficult to impose a uniform system; that there was a need to reorganise the Civil Service in such a way that efficiency would improve so as to ensure 'value for money'.

The report recommended that agencies be established – either within or outside of the departments – charged with the responsibility of overall management of the Department. By 1996, 130 agencies had been created.

The main controls would continue to lie with Ministers or the Permanent Secretary but, once policy objectives and budgets had been established, the Agency should have as much independence as possible in deciding how objectives should be met. The crucial question was that of the line of

---

109 *Op cit*, Hennessy, fn 97, p 499.

110 1988, London: HMSO.

111 Annex C, para 1.

responsibility. The Head of the Agency should be given personal responsibility to achieve the best results.

As to the future role of Ministers, the report recommended that Ministers continue to be wholly responsible for policy but that it was unrealistic to suppose that they could have in-depth knowledge about every operational question:

> ... the convention that they do is part of the cause of the overload which we observed. We believe it is possible for Parliament, through Ministers, to regard managers as directly responsible for operational matters.

A development such as this, while apparently aimed purely at the efficiency of management of the Civil Service, has serious implications for ministerial accountability. The Head of the Agency is directly accountable to parliamentary committees for operational matters: the Minister taking the constitutionally conventional responsibility for policy.[112]

In February 1988, the Prime Minister announced that the government had accepted the main recommendations of the Efficiency Unit. In response, the Treasury and Civil Service Select Committee emphasised the importance of the Head of Agency being directly accountable to select committees, and the government accepted that in relation to operational matters. The extent to which such a new line of responsibility affects the responsibility of Ministers to Parliament remains to be seen – what is clear is that this move represents a very clear dilution in the overall responsibility of Ministers.

The (Social Security) Benefits Agency is the largest. Others include the Child Support Agency,[113] the Driver and Vehicle Licensing Agency, Her Majesty's Stationary Office, the Land Registry, Ordinance Survey, Patent Office and United Kingdom Passport Agency. Issues of responsibility of Ministers are also raised in respect of non-departmental public bodies – 'quangos' – whereby State enterprises are privatised.[114] A non-departmental public body is defined as a body 'which has a role in the processes of national government but is not a government department'.[115] The movement towards increased government involvement in commerce and industry stems from 1945, although public corporations had been earlier established.[116] Today, the

---

112 On the growth in administration, see, also, Chapter 24.

113 In 1998, the government announced that the Agency is to be disbanded due to inefficiency.

114 See, *inter alia*, Lewis, N, 'Regulating non-governmental bodies: privatization, accountability and the public-private divide', in Jowell, J and Oliver, D (eds), *The Changing Constitution*, 2nd edn, 1989, Oxford: Clarendon, Chapter 9 (see, now, 3rd edn, 1994).

115 *Non-Departmental Public Bodies: Guide for Departments*, 1986, Cabinet Office/MPO, London: HMSO.

116 Eg, the Port of London Authority 1908; Central Electricity Board 1926; London Passenger Transport Board 1933; British Overseas Airways Corporation and British European Airways 1939.

movement is towards privatisation, with, among others, British Rail, British Gas, British Telecom, Her Majesty's Stationery Office, and the Naval Dockyards being sold into private ownership. Accountability for such organisations, when publicly owned, was weak. Today the question is to what extent these organisations are truly private; to what extent Ministers exert control over them, whether via financial power or the power to issue policy guidance; and, more importantly, the extent to which Parliament assures that Ministers are accountable for the implementation of policies.

The Labour government and the civil service

When the government entered into office in May 1997, it arrived not only with a radical mandate to reform the constitution, but also to improve efficiency in the civil service. In March 1999, the government published its White Paper, *Modernising Government*, described by Cabinet Secretary Sir Richard Wilson as 'a key document which signals a change of course for the Civil Service for the next 10 years as important as Next Steps 10 years ago'.[117] The aim, he said, was 'modernisation with a purpose: better policy making, better responsiveness to what people want, and more effective public services'. The White Paper introduces a range of reforms, including the commitment to make public services available on a 24 hour a day, seven day a week basis; removing unnecessary regulation and requiring departments which are preparing policies involving new regulations to submit Regulatory Impact Assessments following consultation with the Cabinet Office; creating greater incentives for civil servants, which includes considering financial rewards for staff who identify financial savings or service improvements. In Whitehall, all Permanent Secretaries are required to 'ensure that their Department has the capacity to drive through achievement of the key government targets and to take a personal responsibility for ensuring that this happens'. To facilitate this, the government calls for the introduction of more people from outside the civil service. While the focus is on improved management and the delivery of service to the consumer, sight has not been lost of the core civil service values. Selection and promotion will remain based on merit; political impartiality and the giving of best independent advice to government will be maintained.

Five key commitments are presented in the White Paper. The first relates to policy making which is designed to 'deliver outcomes that matter', rather than simply reacting to short term pressures. A new Centre for Management and Policy Studies is introduced to identify and spread best practice throughout the service. There is to be a refocus on the delivery of public services to ensure that services meet the needs of citizens, rather than the

---

117 Wilson, R (Sir), *The Civil Service in the New Millennium*, May 1999. See www.cabinet-office.gov.uk/1999/senior/rw_speech.htm.

service providers – 'joined-up working' of departments to ensure that the citizen is not faced with bureaucratic barriers to responsibility for services. To eliminate 'mediocrity' in government, all central and local government department services are to be reviewed over a five year period to identify the best suppliers of services. All public bodies will be set new targets for improving quality and effectiveness, and there will be closer monitoring to ensure the maintenance of quality. The government's information technology systems will be geared to meeting the needs of citizens and business. A People's Panel, 5,000 randomly selected individuals, will be appointed to advise government on all aspects of the provision and delivery of services. Equality, on the basis of gender, race and physical disabilities, within the service has been highlighted. In 1999, only 18 per cent of senior civil servants were women, and 1.6 per cent from ethnic minority backgrounds. By 2004–05, the target is to have 35 per cent women and 3.2 per cent ethnic minorities, and targets are to be set for people with disabilities.

In January 2000, the Prime Minister's Performance and Innovation Unit's report, *Wiring It Up*, reinforced the White Paper's aims on modernisation while focusing on the need for departments to engage in closer co-operation over issues which cross departmental boundaries, and the introduction of bonuses and promotion for those who work on multi-faceted problems such as social deprivation, crime reduction, young people at risk and rural issues. In the Prime Minister's 'Foreword to the Report', Tony Blair stated that 'many of the challenges facing government do not fit easily into traditional Whitehall structures', and that drug addiction, the criminal justice system and dealing with run-down areas all required a range of departments and agencies to work together.

PERMANENCE, POLITICAL NEUTRALITY AND ANONYMITY

The role of the Civil Service must be considered against the constitutional features of permanence, political neutrality and anonymity.

Permanence

In many countries, such as the United States of America, the Civil Service is a semi-permanent body, the most senior posts of which change hands with a change in government. A variation on this model, which is employed in Germany and France, involves incoming Ministers bringing into the department with them a small body of hand picked professional advisers. Under the constitution of the United Kingdom, Civil Servants hold permanent posts, in law 'holding office at the pleasure of the Crown'. Many aspects of employment protection legislation[118] apply to the Civil Service, but such rights as, for example, the right of appeal against unfair dismissal and the right to belong to a trades union, may be revoked, under the royal prerogative.[119] Moreover, at common law, the position of civil servants is precarious. Being a servant of the Crown, they may be dismissed with no common law action for wrongful dismissal.[120] However, while the formal position is insecure, in practical terms civil servants enjoy a high degree of security. Terms and conditions of employment are regulated under the prerogative, and the Minister for the Civil Service has power to make regulations relating to the conditions of service of all civil servants.[121]

The constitutional significance of permanency lies in the development of expertise and the natural growth of a Civil Service 'ethos'. Most importantly, permanency ensures the availability of such expertise to governments of differing political persuasions. The Private Secretary is a Minister's closest contact with a department, and his adviser. Of his Private Secretary, Richard Crossman[122] wrote:

> I have got to face it that his main job is to get across to me what the department wants. The Private Office is the department's way of keeping a watch on me, of making sure that I run along the lines they want me to run on, of dividing my time and getting the department's policies and attitudes brought to my notice.

Political neutrality

The Civil Service owes its loyalty to the government of the day, irrespective of political party, and it is imperative that the Civil Service avoids creating the impression of political bias. While the writings of leading Labour Party politicians referred to above reveal scepticism as to this, its theoretical importance cannot be underestimated.

The dilemma posed for an individual civil servant in terms of neutrality and loyalty can be seen in the circumstances of the case of *R v Ponting*. Clive Ponting OBE was Assistant Secretary in charge of the defence secretariat dealing with naval operations at the Ministry of Defence. In May 1982, during the course of the Falklands War, an Argentine ship, the *General Belgrano* was sunk by a British torpedo with the loss of thousands of lives. Mr Tam Dalyell

---

118 Employment Protection (Consolidation) Act 1978.

119 *Council of Civil Service Unions v Minister for the Civil Service* [1985] AC 374, discussed in Chapter 6.

120 *Dunn v R* [1896] 1 QB 116; *Riordan v War Office* [1959] 1 WLR 1046.

121 Civil Service Order in Council 1995.

122 Crossman, R, *The Diaries of a Cabinet Minister*, 1977, London: Jonathan Cape, Vol 2, p 385.

MP[123] persistently asked the Prime Minister questions on the matter in the House of Commons, but felt that the information given was inaccurate. At the time, the Defence Select Committee was examining the conduct of the Falklands War.[124]

Clive Ponting was responsible for preparing a report on the circumstances surrounding the sinking of the *Belgrano* and, in breach of section 2 of the Official Secrets Act 1911, sent documents to Tam Dalyell anonymously. Ponting was charged under section 2 with communicating information to an unauthorised person. At his trial in 1985, defence counsel admitted that Dalyell was not a person to whom Ponting was authorised to disclose information, but argued that Dalyell was 'a person to whom it was, in the interests of the State, his duty to communicate it'. Mr Justice McCowan directed the jury that the word 'duty' meant the official duty imposed on Ponting by his position and that 'interests of the State' meant the policy of the State as laid down by the government: not as perceived by Ponting, Dalyell or anyone else. Notwithstanding the clear direction as to Ponting's guilt, the jury acquitted him. Following Ponting's acquittal, the Head of the Home Civil Service, Sir Robert Armstrong, issued *Notes of Guidance on the Duties and Responsibilities of Civil Servants in Relation to Ministers*[125] in which, *inter alia*, it was stated that:

> The Civil Service has no constitutional personality or responsibility separate from the duly elected government of the day.

The Note of Guidance on the Duties and Responsibilities of Civil Servants issued by the Head of the Home Civil Service in 1985, and revised in December 1987 (following the *Westland* affair), emphasised the duty of civil servants to the Minister of the day, and advised on the manner in which actual or potential conflicts of interest should be dealt with:

> A civil servant should not decline to take, or abstain from taking, an action because to do so would conflict with his or her personal opinions on matters of political choice or judgment between alternative or competing objectives and benefits; he or she should consider the possibility of declining only if taking or abstaining from the action in question is felt to be directly contrary to deeply held personal conviction on a fundamental issue of conscience.

> A civil servant who feels that to act or to abstain from acting in a particular way, or to acquiesce in a particular decision or course of action, would raise for him or her a fundamental issue of conscience, or is so profoundly opposed to a policy as to feel unable conscientiously to administer it in accordance with the standards described in this note, should consult a senior officer. If necessary, and if the matter cannot be resolved by any other means, the civil servant may take the matter up with the Permanent Head of the Department and also has a

---

123 Labour Member for West Lothian.
124 See HC 11 (1984–1985), London: HMSO.
125 February 1985.

right, in the last resort, to have the matter referred to the Head of the Home Civil Service through the Permanent Head of the Department. If the matter still cannot be resolved on a basis which the civil servant concerned is able to accept, he or she must either carry out his or her instructions or resign from the public service – though, even after resignation, he or she will still be bound to keep the confidence to which he or she has become privy as a civil servant.

The anonymity and political neutrality of civil servants is reinforced by the rules restricting political activity. If the Civil Service is to serve governments of all political persuasions, it is imperative that civil servants, whatever their private political views, should not be seen to be politically active in a manner which would inevitably compromise their neutrality under one political party or another.

The Civil Service is divided, for the purpose of control over political activity, into three groups:

(a) the 'politically free' category which comprises industrial staff and non-officer grades, which may freely engage in either national and local politics;

(b) the 'politically restricted' category, comprising higher staff grades who are debarred from participating in national political activities, but may be permitted to engage in local politics;

(c) an intermediate group which comprises those who are neither employed in the highest or lowest grades.

Political activities which are subject to restriction are divided into activities at both national and local level. Those activities subject to restriction at national level include standing as a candidate for election to the European Parliament; holding office in party political organisations which relate to party politics in relation to the United Kingdom or the European Parliament; and speaking on matters of national political controversy, or expressing such views to the press or in books, articles or leaflets. Canvassing on behalf of a candidate for election to the United Kingdom Parliament or the European Parliament, or on behalf of a political party in respect of such elections, is also prohibited. At local level, civil servants in the restricted category may not stand as candidates for local elections; hold office in party political organisations relating to local government; speak on local politically controversial matters or express such views in the media or other publications; and may not canvass on behalf of either a candidate or a political party in the course of local elections.[126]

---

126 *Pay and Conditions of Service Code.*

Anonymity

In order that the Minister be seen to be responsible and accountable for the working of his Department, the Civil Service has traditionally been shielded from the public gaze and protected from public inquiry. By protecting the Civil Service, its impartiality and integrity is enhanced. Further, if civil servants become public figures scrutinised in Parliament or the media, their capacity for maintaining the appearance of political impartiality, so important to the concept of permanence, would be damaged.

It has been seen that the Minister in charge of a particular government department is absolutely responsible to Parliament for the conduct of civil servants, and that this responsibility in turn involves two aspects. The first of these is that the Minister has an obligation to explain and answer for the work of his department to Parliament; the second is that the Minister is responsible in constitutional terms for any failure of departmental policy and administration. As a corollary to ministerial responsibility, the Civil Service is not accountable to Parliament and is protected by the concept of anonymity.

While, in theoretical constitutional terms, the anonymity of civil servants is important in buttressing the responsibility of Ministers of the Crown, it is becoming, as will be seen below, an increasingly less notable feature of the Civil Service. The explanations for the decrease in anonymity are manifold: the vagaries of individual ministerial responsibility, the increasing strength of departmental select committees and the televising of those proceedings and recent developments in the management of government departments.

If any single event is responsible for raising the profile of the Civil Service, it must be the Westland affair, the facts of which are outlined in Chapter 11. Constitutionally, the saga is significant for the light it throws on the conventions of ministerial responsibility. The Secretary of State for Trade and Industry Mr Leon Brittan was individually responsible for the leaking of the Solicitor General's letter; the Secretary of State for Defence Mr Michael Heseltine's allegations that he had been deprived of the opportunity to put his case for the European rescue bid and publicly going against the decision of Cabinet represented an aspect of collective responsibility and also concerned was ministerial responsibility for the actions of civil servants.

In January 1986, Miss Colette Bowe, the Head of Information at the Department of Trade and Industry, leaked part of Sir Patrick Mayhew's letter in which the accuracy of information contained in Mr Michael Heseltine's letter to Lloyds Merchant Bank (advisers to the European group) was questioned. Miss Bowe had cleared the release of the information with Mr Bernard Ingham, the Prime Minister's Chief Press Secretary and Mr Charles Powell, the Prime Minister's Private Secretary on foreign and defence issues.[127] Nevertheless, Leon Britton was held ultimately responsible for the 'leak'.

The identification of civil servants by the Prime Minister in parliamentary debate and the publicity surrounding Collette Bowe breached the principle of anonymity. The Defence and Trade and Industry Select Committee's inquiries further raised the profile of the Civil Service, not least when the five named civil servants were forbidden to give evidence to the Defence Select Committee.[128]

The issue of whether, and the extent to which, civil servants are entitled to give evidence before select committees was governed by the *Memorandum of Guidance for Officials Appearing before Select Committees* issued by the Cabinet Office in 1980.[129] In summary, the *Memorandum* instructed that:

> ... the general principle to be followed is that it is the duty of officials to be as helpful as possible to Committees, and that any withholding of information should be limited to reservations that are necessary in the interests of good government or to safeguard national security ... However, Ministers are ultimately responsible for deciding what information is to be given and for defending their decisions if necessary, and Ministers' views should always be sought if any question arises of withholding information which Committees are known to be seeking ...

> Officials should not give evidence about or discuss the following topics:

> (i)   In order to preserve the collective responsibility to Ministers, the advice given to Ministers by their departments should not be disclosed ...

> (ii) Advice given by a Law Officer ...

> Officials should also, where possible, avoid giving written evidence about or discussing the following matters:

> (iii) Questions in the field of political controversy ...

> (iv) Sensitive information of a commercial or economic nature ...

> (v) Matters which are, or may become, the subject of sensitive negotiations with governments or other bodies, including the European Community ...

In the course of the inquiries into the Westland affair,[130] negotiations between the government and the Select Committee Chairman resulted in the government allowing Sir Robert Armstrong, then Head of the Civil Service, to give evidence. Following this conflict between the government and the Defence Select Committee, the Treasury and Civil Service Select Committee embarked on its own inquiry into the relationship between Parliament, Ministers and civil servants. As a result of this enquiry, fresh guidelines were

---

127 See Marshall, G (ed), *Ministerial Responsibility*, 1989, Oxford: OUP.

128 See HC 518, 519 (1985–86); HC 176 (1986–87); HC 92 (1985–86), London: HMSO.

129 The 'Osmotherly Rules'.

130 See, further, Chapter 16.

published, designed to clarify and regulate the extent to which civil servants could co-operate with select committees. The *Memorandum Guidelines for Officials Giving Evidence* emphasised the following points:

(a) that civil servants give evidence on behalf of Ministers (and not on their own behalf);

(b) that civil servants are accountable to Ministers alone and not to Parliament: it is the Minister who is so accountable;

(c) that civil servants are subject to the instructions given by Ministers and bound to observe the requisite confidentiality;

(d) that witnesses should be 'as helpful as possible' (subject to the above guidelines);

(e) that where a select committee questions was directed to the conduct of a civil servant, as opposed to a departmental policy, the matter did not lie within the remit of the select committee. Select committees are not disciplinary tribunals. Where Civil Service conduct was concerned, it was for the Minister to set up his own enquiry and, if appropriate, for the Minister to report the result of the enquiry to the Committee.

In the aftermath of the Westland affair, a third select committee – the Treasury and Civil Service Committee – reconsidered the role of civil servants. In its report,[131] it was stated:

> The issue of accountability is of crucial importance in considering the relationship between civil servants, Ministers and Parliament. The traditional view, exemplified in the famous Crichel Down case, is that Ministers are responsible and accountable to Parliament for all that occurs within their Departments. It followed from this that if a significant mistake were made by the department, the Minister should resign.

> We start by reaffirming two basic propositions. First, that Ministers, and not officials, are responsible and accountable for policy; and secondly, that officials' advice to Ministers is and should remain confidential.

Considering the available options, the Committee recommended that:

> ... the government and other interested parties should produce for reconsideration specific proposals on how the crucial question of accountability should be dealt with in future.

In response to the report, the government published *Civil Servants and Ministers: Duties and Responsibilities*.[132] Concerning accountability, the government stated that:

> The government endorses the Committee's two basic propositions on accountability: that Ministers and not officials are responsible and accountable for policy; and that officials' advice to Ministers is and should remain confidential. Constitutionally, Ministers are responsible and accountable for all

---

131 HC 92 (1985–86), London: HMSO.
132 Cmnd 9841, 1986, London: HMSO.

actions carried out by civil servants of their departments in pursuit of government policies or in the discharge of responsibilities laid upon them by Parliament ... Any attempt to make civil servants directly accountable to Parliament ... would be difficult to reconcile with Ministers' responsibility for their departments and civil servants' duty to their Ministers.

It is impossible, and would be unwise to try, to lay down detailed guidelines about the implications of ministerial accountability for individual conduct in particular situations: the variety of situations that can arise is infinite, and there must be room for the exercise of discretion and judgment having regard to particular circumstances. It has never been the case that Ministers were required or expected to resign in respect of every mistake made by their departments, though they are clearly responsible to Parliament for ensuring that action is taken to put matters right and prevent a recurrence. The principle is clear: Ministers are accountable to Parliament for the policies and actions of their departments. The implications of applying that principle can only be a matter of judgment in each case ...

THE CIVIL SERVICE MANAGEMENT CODE

In 1994, the Treasury and Civil Service Committee reviewed the position of civil servants.[133] In its report, *The Role of the Civil Service*, it concluded that a new Civil Service Code should be drafted to clarify the position of civil servants. The Nolan Committee also recommended clarification in the constitutional framework within which civil servants work and 'the values they are expected to uphold'.[134] The new Code was introduced under the royal prerogative,[135] and came into force in 1996, replacing Sir Robert Armstrong's statement. The *Civil Service Management Code*, as amended, now states that:

... the constitutional and practical role of the Civil Service is, with integrity, honesty, impartiality and objectivity, to assist the duly constituted government, of whatever political complexion, in formulating policies of government, carrying out decisions of the government and in administering public services for which the government is responsible.

Civil servants are under a duty to give honest and impartial advice to Ministers and to:

... endeavour to deal with the affairs of the public sympathetically, effectively, promptly and without bias or maladministration of public money.

---

133 HC 27-I (1993–94), London: HMSO.

134 Nolan Report, *Standards in Public Life*, Cm 2850-I, 1995, London: HMSO.

135 See the Civil Service Management Code issued under the Civil Service Order in Council 1995, as amended by the Civil Service (Amendment) Order 1995 and the Civil Service (Amendment) Order 1996.

They are also required to conduct themselves in such a manner as to:

> ... deserve and retain the confidence of Ministers and to be able to establish the same relationship with those whom they may be required to serve in some future administration.

The *Code* also states that civil servants must not misuse their official position to further their own, or another's, personal interests.

Openness in government

As discussed in Chapter 11, the former Conservative government announced that it intended to make the administration of government more open, and thus more accountable to the public. The Labour government, elected in May 1997, has taken this matter further with the publication of a White Paper, *Your Right to Know: The Government's Proposals for a Freedom of Information Act* and a Freedom of Information Bill. Because this issue is intimately connected with the concept of responsible government, it is considered in the next chapter.

CHAPTER 11

RESPONSIBLE GOVERNMENT

MINISTERIAL RESPONSIBILITY

The convention of ministerial responsibility is central to the constitution, and plays a fundamental role in the relationship between the executive and Parliament. For the doctrine of government under the law to be observed, it is essential that government be both accountable to Parliament and to the electorate, and that government be conducted in a manner sufficiently open, subject to the requirements of the national interest, to inspire public confidence. The origins of ministerial responsibility are traced by FW Maitland to the principle that 'for every exercise of royal power some minister is answerable'.[1] Marshall and Moodie[2] describe ministerial responsibility as follows:

> Ministers are responsible for the general conduct of government, including the exercise of many powers legally vested in the Monarch; and ultimately, through Parliament and parties, to the electorate.

The doctrine thus has two limbs – individual and collective responsibility. As with so much of the constitution, there is vagueness on occasion as to the distinction between the two limbs which are both closely related and also complementary of one another. In order to facilitate analysis, the topic may be broken down into three aspects:

(a) the collective responsibility of the Cabinet to Parliament, and ultimately the electorate, for policy and administration;

(b) the individual responsibility of Ministers for the policy and administration of his or her Department;

(c) the individual responsibility of Ministers for their personal conduct.

---

1 Maitland, FW, *The Constitutional History of England*, 1908, Cambridge: CUP, p 203.
2 Marshall, G and Moodie, G, *Some Problems of the Constitution*, 5th edn, 1971, London: Hutchinson, Chapter 4.

COLLECTIVE RESPONSIBILITY[3]

The convention of collective Cabinet responsibility emphasises the unanimity of government and its accountability to Parliament. The classic expression of collective responsibility remains that of Lord Salisbury:[4]

> For all that passes in Cabinet every member of it who does not resign is absolutely and irretrievably responsible and has no right afterwards to say that he agreed in one case to a compromise, while in another he was persuaded by his colleagues ... It is only on the principle that absolute responsibility is undertaken by every member of the Cabinet, who, after a decision is arrived at, remains a member of it, that the joint responsibility of Ministers to Parliament can be upheld and one of the essential principles of parliamentary responsibility established.

The rationale for the convention lies in the need for government to present a united front to Parliament and the public in order to maintain confidence. A government which exhibits public disagreements over policy matters is one which will be regarded as weak, and will be subjected to challenges to its authority to continue in office.

Two principal sub-rules underlie collective responsibility. The first rule is that, once an agreement is reached in Cabinet, all members of Cabinet – and many outside Cabinet (see Chapter 10) – are bound to speak in support of the decision. There should be no criticism or dissent from the decision in public – irrespective of whether or not the particular member of Cabinet was party to the discussion. Equally, if a decision is reached by the Prime Minister in Cabinet Committee or the Inner Cabinet when only a small handful of members are present, the decision binds all. The second supporting rule is that records of Cabinet discussions are absolutely secret. The knowledge that Cabinet records are protected by confidentiality, enhances the opportunity for members of Cabinet to discuss matters freely, secure in the knowledge that their personal point of view, whatever the decision, will be protected from the public gaze.

These principles are expressed in *Questions of Procedure for Ministers*[5] in the following manner:

> Collective responsibility requires that Ministers should be able to express their views frankly in the expectation that they can argue freely in private while maintaining a united front when decisions have been reached. This in turn requires that the privacy of opinions expressed in Cabinet and Ministerial Committees should be maintained. Moreover, Cabinet and Committee

---

3   See Mackintosh, JP, *The British Cabinet*, 3rd edn, 1977, London: Stevens, Chapter 2; Marshall, G, *Constitutional Conventions*, 1984, Oxford: Clarendon, Chapter IV.

4   *Official Report*, HC Cols 833–34, 8 April 1878.

5   Cabinet Office, 1992.

documents will often contain information which needs to be protected in the national interest. It is therefore essential that Ministers take the necessary steps to ensure that they and their staff preserve the privacy of Cabinet business and protect the security of government documents.[6]

As with the convention of individual responsibility, there is dispute about the status and scope of collective responsibility. So many exceptions to the classic doctrine can be discerned that it is possible to question whether it is a convention at all within the classical definition, or whether the term convention should be discarded and replaced by the words practice or usage.

Alternatively, it may be argued that the variations which can be observed in the working of the convention merely illustrate one of the greatest strengths of conventional rules – their flexibility.

Agreements to differ

It is possible for the convention of collective responsibility to be waived when the circumstances are such that the political disagreements within Cabinet are of such magnitude that the Prime Minister finds it more expedient to set aside the convention than to have the convention broken by members of Cabinet. Two illustrations of waiver can be given. In 1931–32, the National (coalition) government contained bitterly opposing views over economic policy.[7] Four members of Cabinet handed in their resignations, and withdrew them only after the Prime Minister, Mr Ramsey MacDonald, decided to waive the convention and allow the dissident members to express their views publicly.

In 1975, the Labour government of Mr Harold Wilson was faced with an equally intransigent faction in Cabinet on the matter of the United Kingdom's continued membership of the European Community. The government had decided to put the question to the people in a referendum, although, in advance of the referendum, the government announced that it would not be bound by the result.

Rather than face a public display of disunity in contravention of collective responsibility, Mr Wilson announced a limited waiver of the convention, in the guise of an 'agreement to differ':[8]

> ... those Ministers who do not agree with the government's recommendation in favour of continued membership of the European Community are, in the unique circumstances of the referendum, now free to advocate a different view during the referendum campaign.

---

6 Cabinet Office, 1992, para 18.
7 In particular, over the levy of tariff duties.
8 HC Deb Col 1745, 23 January 1975; Col 351, 7 April 1975; Cmnd 6003, 1975; Wilson, H, *The Governance of Britain*, 1976, London: Weidenfeld & Nicolson, pp 194–97.

This freedom does not extend to parliamentary proceedings and official business ... At meetings of the Council of Ministers of the European Community and at other Community meetings, the United Kingdom position in all fields will continue to reflect government policy.

I have asked all Ministers ... not to allow themselves to appear in direct confrontation, on the same platform or programme, with another Minister who takes a different view on the government recommendation.

In the event, one Minister[9] flouted the limited waiver, and two senior Cabinet members, Mr Roy Jenkins and Mr Tony Benn, opposed each other in a public televised debate shortly before the referendum took place.

Cabinet papers[10]

The confidentiality of Cabinet discussion is protected by the prohibition against disclosure by members of Cabinet. In addition, the rules regarding the confidentiality of Cabinet papers include the rule that the government of the day may not release the papers of a previous government without the consent of the former Prime Minister.[11] Furthermore, the papers of the previous government may not be disclosed to a government of a different political persuasion. It may at first sight appear curious that an incoming government cannot gain access to the papers of the previous government, and it may be wondered how the government is supposed to act effectively in any policy area if denied so much data. Nevertheless, the rule is justified on the basis that an outgoing government might be tempted to remove politically sensitive documentation if it feared that a new government would make political capital out of it. Three categories of papers are excepted from the convention:[12]

(a) papers which, even if not publicly available, can be deemed to be in the public domain, for example, letters sent by former Ministers to trade associations, trade unions, etc, or to Members of Parliament about constituency cases, or to members of the public;

(b) papers, other than genuinely personal messages, dealing with matters which are known to foreign governments, for example, messages about inter-governmental negotiations;

(c) written opinions of the Law Officers, which are essentially legal rather than political documents.

---

9   Mr Eric Heffer.

10 On secrecy in government, see, further, below.

11 HC Deb Col 1039, 1 July 1982; Cols 468, 8 July 1982; 474; Hunt (Lord), 'Access to a previous government's papers' [1982] PL 514.

12 Hunt (Lord), 'Access to a previous government's papers', in Marshall, G (ed), *Ministerial Responsibility*, 1989, Oxford: OUP.

Ministerial memoirs

The publication of a former Minister's memoirs of his political life poses problems for the rules relating to Cabinet secrecy. In 1976, the Radcliffe Committee Report[13] stated that:

> The author should be free to use his ministerial experience for the purpose of giving an account of his own work, subject to restrictions on three separate categories of information:
>
> (a) he must not reveal anything that contravenes the requirements of national security operative at the time of his proposed publication;
>
> (b) he must not make disclosures injurious to this country's relations with other nations;
>
> (c) he must refrain from publishing information destructive of the confidential relationships on which our system of government is based.
>
> The final restriction relates to opinions or attitudes of Cabinet colleagues, advice given to him by colleagues and criticism of those working for him in office.

In *Attorney General v Jonathan Cape Ltd*,[14] the issue of the publication of the diaries of Richard Crossman, a former Labour Cabinet *member*, was considered. Executors of the estate of Richard Crossman sought to publish his *Diaries*; the government sought an injunction restraining publication. Recognising the convention of collective responsibility, Lord Widgery CJ stated that:

> I find overwhelming evidence that the doctrine of joint responsibility is generally understood and practised, and equally strong evidence that it is on occasion ignored.

Having given such ambivalent recognition to the convention, which in any event was not court-enforceable, the injunction was denied.

INDIVIDUAL MINISTERIAL RESPONSIBILITY[15]

In *Questions of Procedure for Ministers*,[16] individual responsibility is defined as:

> Each Minister is responsible to Parliament for the conduct of his or her department, and for the actions carried out by the department in pursuit of

---

13 *Report of the Committee of Privy Councillors*, Cmnd 6386, 1976, London: HMSO, Appendix 2.

14 [1976] QB 752.

15 See Turpin, C, 'Ministerial responsibility: myth or reality?', in Jowell, J and Oliver, D (eds), *The Changing Constitution*, 2nd edn, 1989, Oxford: Clarendon, Chapter 3 (see, now, 3rd edn, 1994).

16 Cabinet Office, 1992. See, also, *Civil Servants and Ministers: Duties and Responsibilities*, Cmnd 9841, 1986, London: HMSO, para 11.

government policies or in the discharge of responsibilities laid upon him or her as a Minister. Ministers are accountable to Parliament, in the sense that they have a duty to explain in Parliament the exercise of their powers and duties and to give an account to Parliament of what is done by them in their capacity as Ministers or by their departments. This includes the duty to give Parliament, including its select committees, and the public as full information as possible about the policies, decisions and actions of the government, and not to deceive or mislead Parliament and the public.[17]

Ministerial responsibility for the department

The classic doctrine of this limb of ministerial responsibility states that a Minister is responsible for every action of his department. As AV Dicey expressed it, the responsibility of Ministers means, where used in its strict sense, the legal responsibility of every Minister for every act of the Crown in which he takes part.[18]

Lord Morrison viewed the doctrine equally strictly:

... a Minister is accountable to Parliament for anything he or his department does or for anything he has powers to do, whether he does it or not. That is to say, if the action or possible action is within the field of ministerial power or competence, the Minister is answerable to Parliament.[19]

It is the Minister who represents the public face of the department and who speaks for the department in Parliament. The doctrine is underpinned by Parliamentary Question Time and in debates in Parliament and in committees.[20] During the passage of legislation relating to a particular department's responsibilities, it is the Minister who will introduce the Bill and who will defend the Bill throughout its passage through the House of Commons. The Minister thus stands as the link between the Civil Service and Parliament, assuming full responsibility for the department. As seen in Chapter 10, the conventionally-recognised characteristics of the Civil Service are permanence, political neutrality and anonymity. The civil servant owes his or her duty to the government of the day, and is directly accountable to his or her Secretary of State. The principle of ministerial responsibility to Parliament not only underpins the doctrine of democratic responsibility of Ministers to the people through Parliament, but also facilitates the distinction between the responsibility of elected representatives and the civil servants who are responsible for the practical implementation of policy.

---

17 *Civil Servants and Ministers: Duties and Responsibilities*, Cmnd 9841, 1986, London: HMSO, para 27.

18 Dicey, AV, *Introduction to the Study of the Law of the Constitution*, 10th edn, 1959, London: Macmillan.

19 Morrison (Lord), *Government and Parliament*, 3rd edn, 1964, London: OUP, p 265.

20 See, further, Chapter 16.

As noted in Chapter 10, in practical terms nowadays, several factors diminish the extent to which a Minister can assume responsibility for every action of the department. The size of departments, the usually short ministerial tenure of office in any one department and the complexity of modern government have long made the pure doctrine unworkable. As the Home Secretary, Mr Reginald Maudling, stated in 1973, the classic doctrine of responsibility must be viewed in the light of modern conditions, with large departments of State. Furthermore, the complexity of defining the scope of ministerial responsibility must also be seen in light of the rapid and extensive administrative framework under the system of Next Steps agencies which are designed to increase efficiency in administration by establishing specialist agencies, each with its own executive.

Crichel Down

The classic doctrine was seen to operate most clearly in the Crichel Down affair in 1954.[21] Crichel Down, an area of some 725 acres in Dorset, had been compulsorily acquired by the Air Ministry in 1937 for use as a bombing range. After the Second World War, the land was no longer needed and it was transferred to the Ministry of Agriculture and administered by the Agriculture Land Commission. In 1950, the Commission decided that the best way of disposing of the land was to equip it as a single farm unit and lease it.

Three hundred and twenty eight acres of Crichel Down had been part of the Crichel Estates owned by a Mrs Marten. Her husband wanted to reclaim the land. In both 1950 and 1952 he asked the Commission whether he could buy back the land. The Commission wrongly thought that they had no power of sale and declined to investigate his request. Mr Marten raised the matter with his Member of Parliament who referred the matter to the Parliamentary Secretary to the Minister of Agriculture who requested a report from the Land Commission. The official in charge of making the report was instructed not to approach the previous owners or to inspect the land, and to treat the matter as one of great confidentiality. The resulting report was full of inaccuracies, and went unchecked by the Ministry which decided to adhere to its original plan for the land.

Mr Marten was informed of the decision in 1953, and advised the Ministry that he would rent the whole of the land. Meanwhile, the Ministry had committed itself to another course of action. Mr Marten's letters to the authorities went unanswered and he pressed for a public inquiry. The inquiry found that there had been inaccuracies in the report on the land, muddle and

---

21   Cmnd 9220, 1954, London: HMSO.

inefficiency in handling the matter and hostility to Mr Marten. In July 1954, the Minister Thomas Dugdale accepted responsibility and resigned.[22]

In parliamentary debate on ministerial responsibility following the Crichel Down affair, the Home Secretary, Sir David Maxwell-Fyfe,[23] stated that:

> Without ministerial responsibility it would be impossible to have a Civil Service which would be able to serve Ministries and governments of different political faiths and persuasions with the same zeal and honesty which we have always found ...

> The position of the civil servant is that he is wholly and directly accountable to his Minister ...

> Different categories [of responsibility] apply to different considerations:

> (a) where an explicit order has been given by a Minister, the Minister must protect the civil servant;

> (b) where a civil servant acts properly in accordance with policy laid down by the Minister, the Minister must protect and defend the civil servant;

> (c) where an official makes a mistake or causes delay but where no individual rights are seriously involved, the Minister must accept responsibility although not personally involved and must take corrective action in the Department;

> (d) the Minister is not bound to defend actions of which he did not know or of which he disapproves, but nevertheless he remains constitutionally accountable to Parliament and he alone can tell Parliament what has occurred and render an account of his stewardship.

Ministerial responsibility after Crichel Down

It is notable that, between 1954 and 1982, there were no instances of ministerial resignation following allegations of and inquiries into serious defects in departmental administration. In 1959, 52 people were killed by security forces in Nyasaland but the Colonial Secretary Mr Lennox-Boyd did not resign. In 1964, due to a lack of co-ordination within the Ministry of Aviation, an overpayment of some £4 million pounds was made to the Ferranti company, but the Minister did not resign. In 1968, the Foreign Secretary, Mr George Brown, did not resign over the Sachsenhausen affair in which 12 former detainees in a Nazi prison camp were wrongly denied

---

22 See, *inter alia*, Nicolson, IF, *The Mystery of Crichel Down*, 1986, Oxford: Clarendon; Griffith, JAG, 'Crichel Down: the most famous farm in British constitutional history' (1987) 1 Contemporary Record 35.

23 HC Deb Cols 1286–87, 20 July 1954; and see Griffith, JAG, 'Statutory restriction of judicial review' (1955) 18 MLR 557.

compensation under a scheme set up to compensate victims of Nazi persecution.[24]

In 1971, the Vehicle and General Insurance Company collapsed leaving over a million policy holders uninsured. The Department of Trade and Industry had supervisory responsibility for insurance companies. An inquiry report placed the blame on a civil servant, Mr Jardine, an Under Secretary in the Department, and the Minister did not resign.[25] In 1982, the Home Secretary, Mr William Whitelaw, did not resign over a breach of security at Buckingham Palace which resulted in an intruder entering the Queen's bedroom, nor did Mr James Prior (as he then was), the Northern Ireland Minister, resign in 1984, following the escape of terrorists from the Maze Prison. The exchange in Parliament revealed divergent views about accountability. In debate, Mr Prior distinguished carefully between responsibility for policy – for which he accepted responsibility – and the failure of officials to follow the correct orders and procedures – for which he denied responsibility:

> However, I do not accept – and I do not think it right for the House to accept – that there is any constitutional or other principle that requires ministerial resignations in the face of failure, either by others to carry out orders or procedures or by their supervisors to ensure that staff carried out those orders
>
> ...
>
> Of course, I have looked carefully at the precedents. There are those who quote the *Crichel Down* case. I do not believe that it is a precedent or that it establishes a firm convention. It is the only case of its sort in the past 50 years, and constitutional lawyers have concluded that the resignation was not required by convention and was exceptional.[26]

Mr Enoch Powell MP was of a different view:

> What happened was an immense administrative disaster. It was not a disaster in a peripheral area of the responsibilities of the Northern Ireland Department. It was a disaster that occurred in an area which was quite clearly central to the department's responsibilities. If the responsibility for administration so central to a department can be abjured by a Minister, a great deal of our proceedings in the House is a beating of the air because we are talking to people who, in the last resort, disclaim the responsibility for the administration.[27]

The Falklands War provided the scenario for three ministerial resignations. Lord Carrington, the Foreign Secretary, resigned following allegations, which

24 *Third Report of the Parliamentary Commissioner for Administration*, HC 54 (1967–68), London: HMSO; *Select Committee Report*, HC 258 (1967–68); Fry, GK, 'The Sachsenhausen concentration camp case and the convention of ministerial responsibility?' [1970] PL 336.

25 HL Deb 80; HC Deb 133 (1971–72), para 344.

26 HC Deb Vol 53 Cols 1042, 1060–61, 9 February 1984 and see HM Chief Inspector of Prisons Report, HC 203 (1983–84), London: HMSO.

27 *Ibid.*

he denied, over the lack of preparation of the British forces when the Argentinians attacked; Mr Luce and Mr Atkins also resigned from the Foreign Office.[28]

In 1986 came the Westland Helicopter saga.[29] Westland, a helicopter manufacturing company, was threatened with closure. The government sought to promote a rescue bid for the company. Two alternative plans were put forward; one from an American consortium, the other from Europe. Mr Heseltine, Secretary of State for Trade and Industry, wanted the European option to be taken up. Mrs Thatcher, however, favoured the American plan. Mr Heseltine had been informed that he would be able to put his preferred plan to a Cabinet meeting. In the event, however, Mrs Thatcher cancelled that meeting. The conduct of the affair resulted in the resignations of Mr Michael Heseltine, more on the basis of a breakdown in collective responsibility than of individual responsibility, and of Mr Leon Brittan for the breach of convention in the leak of the Solicitor General's letter.

In 1989, Mrs Edwina Currie resigned over the furore caused by her claim that the majority of eggs in the United Kingdom were infected by the salmonella virus[30] and, in 1990, Mr Nicholas Ridley resigned from the Department of Trade and Industry, having accepted responsibility for making intemperate remarks about a fellow Member State of the European Community.

In 1994, the Home Secretary, Michael Howard, faced several calls for his resignation over escapes from Whitemore prison and over the finding of escape equipment and weapons in prisons. Mr Howard refused to resign, citing in his support the precedent set by Mr James Prior (as he then was) over escapes from the Maze prison in Ulster, and the distinction between responsibility for operational matters and matters of policy.

Evaluating the evidence

From the above evidence, how is the working of the doctrine of individual ministerial responsibility to be evaluated? First, it is arguable that the doctrine represents one of the most significant conventions of the constitution, enhancing the accountability of the government to Parliament and the electorate. However, as has been seen above, the existence and acceptance of responsibility does not inevitably lead to the consequence of the resignation of a Minister for the failures within his department. No hard and fast rules exist

---

28   See Cmnd 8787, 1983, London: HMSO.

29   See Oliver, D and Austin, R, 'Political and constitutional aspects of the *Westland* affair' (1987) 40 Parl Aff 20; and Hennessy, P, 'Helicopter crashes into Cabinet: Prime Minister and constitution hurt' (1986) 13 JLS 423; *op cit*, Marshall, fn 12, Chapter 18.

30   See, further, Chapter 16.

which will determine whether and when a Minister should resign, and accordingly it cannot clearly be said that resignation forms a part of the convention itself. As Professor Geoffrey Marshall has written in relation to the convention:

> ... uncertainty about the conventional rule and the degree to which there existed an obligation to shoulder culpability, and with it an implied duty of resignation, continues to plague the textbooks and to cloud the issue of political accountability.[31]

Evidence from 1954 to the current time adds increased weight to that view. On the question of the circumstances under which a Minister will resign as a result of departmental mismanagement, Professor SE Finer[32] considered that:

> ... whether a Minister is forced to resign depends on three factors: on himself, his Prime Minister and his party.
>
> For a resignation to occur, all three factors have to be just so: the Minister compliant, the Prime Minister firm, the party clamorous. This conjuncture is rare, and is in fact fortuitous. Above all, it is indiscriminate – which Ministers escape and which do not is decided neither by the circumstances of the offence nor by its gravity.

Professor Finer went on to question whether in fact there is a 'convention' of resignation at all, and concluded that the convention is so haphazard in operation that it cannot amount to a rule.[33]

INDIVIDUAL RESPONSIBILITY FOR PERSONAL CONDUCT

Personal conduct

While responsibility for the implementation and execution of policy of course entails 'personal conduct', one aspect of ministerial responsibility which has also given rise to particular concern is the conduct of Ministers in relation to their private lives. The personal relationships of Ministers are also matters which fall under intense public scrutiny. In 1963, the Minister of Defence, Mr John Profumo, was found to have been having a sexual relationship with a prostitute, Christine Keeler. Ms Keeler, it was found, also enjoyed a close personal relationship with Mr Stephen Ward, an attaché at the Soviet Embassy. When questioned in the House of Commons about the affair, Mr Profumo lied to the House. When the truth emerged, Mr Profumo resigned office. The cause of his resignation was not so much the sexual affair, but the

---

31 'Introduction', in *op cit*, Marshall, fn 12, p 9.

32 Finer, SE, 'The individual responsibility of ministers' (1956) 34 Public Admin 377.

33 See, also, Woodhouse, D, 'Ministerial responsibility in the 1990s: when do ministers resign?' (1993) 46 Parl Aff 277. For discussion of the arms to Iraq affair and the Scott Report, see pp 425–33.

contempt of the House committed through lying. The potential security aspects of the affair led to a judicial inquiry headed by Lord Denning MR.[34]

In 1973, Lords Lambton and Jellicoe resigned office. Earl Jellicoe, Lord Privy Seal and Leader of the House of Lords, resigned after it had been revealed that he had been associating with prostitutes. Lord Lambton, Parliamentary Under-Secretary of State for Defence for the Royal Air Force, resigned over allegations of involvement with illegal drugs. The government requested an inquiry by the Security Commission[35] into any security aspects of the affairs, which resulted in the finding that no classified information had in fact been revealed either directly or indirectly to 'any potentially hostile power'.[36]

In 1983, Cecil Parkinson MP, the Secretary of State for Trade and Industry and Conservative Party Chairman, resigned following revelations about a long standing relationship with his secretary, Sarah Keays, who became pregnant. For some time, the Prime Minister, Mrs Thatcher,[37] and the Party maintained their support for Mr Parkinson,[38] as did his wife throughout the public attention focused on the affair. When Sarah Keays published a series of articles in the national press about the matter, and alleged that Mr Parkinson had said that he wanted to marry her, public and political support began to wane, and Mr Parkinson resigned.

More recently, in 1992, Alan Amos MP resigned after allegations of indecency with another man. Also in 1992, the Heritage Secretary Mr David Mellor was forced to resign following revelations of a sexual relationship with an actress (and the receipt of gifts). The majority of the revelations had been brought about through the illicit bugging of an apartment used by Mr Mellor. While this affair alone may not have caused his downfall, the revelation that Mr Mellor and his family had enjoyed the hospitality, while on holiday, of the wife of a Palestinian Liberation organisation official, sealed his fate. Despite being regarded as an excellent Heritage Secretary, the intense and hostile coverage by the media ensured his resignation.[39] In January 1994, Tim Yeo MP, Minister of State for the Environment, resigned after admitting fathering a child out of wedlock, as did Alan Duncan MP after allegations that he had used the 'right to buy' legislation to make money in property deals with a

---

34 Statement to the House 674 HC Deb 809–10, 21 March 1963; Lord Denning's Report, Cmnd 2152, 1963, London: HMSO; Macmillan, H, *At the End of the Day* (1961–63), 1973, London: Macmillan, pp 436–41; Denning (Lord), *The Due Process of Law*, 1980, London: Butterworths, Pt 2, Chapter II; *op cit*, Marshall, fn 3, Chapter VI.

35 On which, see Chapter 23.

36 *Report of the Security Commission*, Cmnd 5367, 1973, London: HMSO, para 5; *op cit*, Marshall, fn 3, Chapter VI. On the role of the Security Commission, see, further, Chapter 23.

37 Thatcher, M, *The Downing Street Years*, 1993, London: HarperCollins, pp 310–11.

38 Tebbitt, N, *Upwardly Mobile*, 1988, London: Weidenfeld & Nicolson, pp 205, 208–11.

39 Statement of Resignation 212 HC Deb 139, 25 September 1992.

neighbour. In February 1994, Hartley Booth MP resigned after a 'close relationship' with a research assistant; in May 1994, Michael Brown MP resigned following newspaper reports of a 'friendship' with a male civil servant. Most recently Ron Davies, the Welsh Secretary, resigned immediately after being discovered in still unexplained but curious circumstances on Clapham Common. The message is, if you are caught out resign sooner rather than later in order to spare the government embarrassment and loss of public confidence.

Premature disclosure of confidential information

In 1936, the Colonial Secretary, JH Thomas, resigned after revealing information relating to Budget proposals before they had been announced in Parliament. As a consequence, two friends, Alfred Bates and Sir Alfred Butt MP, made financial gains. A 'leak' of information was suspected and a Tribunal of Inquiry was established. The Prime Minister described Thomas's conduct as 'letting his tongue wag when he was in his cups'.[40] The Attorney General refused to prosecute under the Official Secrets Act, and the Minister resigned. In 1947, the Chancellor of the Exchequer, Sir Hugh Dalton, resigned after revealing Budget proposals to a journalist.

Nowadays, the contents of the Budget are regarded as being far less secret, and it is not uncommon for the Chancellor to discuss proposals publicly prior to revealing the precise details to Parliament. Nevertheless, the convention of secrecy of the Budget is such that the exact proposals need not be, and are not, revealed even to the Cabinet before being disclosed in Parliament.

THE MORALITY OF PUBLIC OFFICE

Qualification for ministerial office

Given the fundamental importance of ministerial responsibility, it is perhaps surprising that there are neither formal qualifications for office nor formal means by which the suitability for office is scrutinised in advance. Sir Ivor Jennings states that:

> ... the most elementary qualification demanded of a Minister is honesty and incorruptibility. It is, however, necessary not only that he should possess this qualification but also that he should appear to possess it.[41]

---

40   That is to say 'drunk'.
41   Jennings, I (Sir), *Cabinet Government*, 3rd edn, 1959, Cambridge: CUP, Chapter V, p 106.

Lord Hailsham expresses the same sentiment as follows:

> A politician must be trustworthy, and if he is found out telling a lie or if he is discovered in even a small financial dishonesty, he can only bow himself out of public life.[42]

If a Minister of the Crown or Member of Parliament conducts his personal or financial affairs in such a manner that falls below an 'acceptable standard', the Minister may be required to resign. Professor SE Finer[43] describes such conduct as being:

> ... a personal misadventure of the Minister which raises such doubt about his personal prudence or integrity as to cause him to resign.

Financial probity

The personal financial probity of Ministers, their Parliamentary Private Secretaries and other Members of Parliament is regarded with seriousness. Under the law and custom of Parliament, Members must declare their financial interests in the Register of Members' Interests and make public declarations in debate or committee proceedings of any interests they hold which may affect their impartiality.[44] The holding of directorships, ownership of shares, consultancy positions and receipt of gifts all raise issues concerning integrity and fitness for office. Ministers of the Crown must give up any public appointments or directorships on assuming office. Further, they must divest themselves of any financial interests on assuming office where that interest might give rise to conflict with his or her ministerial responsibilities.[45]

There is an inherent vagueness in such criteria, yet relatively few Ministers and other Members of Parliament have fallen from grace as a result of imprudent (or dishonest) financial dealings. In 1913, the issue of Ministers holding shares was raised in debate following allegations of improper ministerial involvement in the Marconi Company.[46] It was rumoured that Ministers[47] had used information received as Ministers for their own personal advantage. All three Ministers involved denied any share dealings. A select committee inquiry exonerated the Ministers of all charges of corruption and from charges that they had used their Ministerial positions for personal gain. In debate, the Prime Minister, Herbert Asquith ruled, *inter alia*, that:

---

42 Hailsham (Lord), *The Door Wherein I Went*, 1975, London: Collins, p 199.

43 *Op cit*, Finer, fn 32.

44 On alleged payments for parliamentary questions, see Chapter 18.

45 *Questions of Procedure for Ministers*, Cabinet Office, 1992, paras 103–27.

46 54 HC Deb 5 Ser 391–514, 543–664. See Donaldson, F, *The Marconi Scandal*, 1962, London: R Hart-Davis.

47 Attorney General, Sir Rufus Isaacs, Chancellor of the Exchequer, D Lloyd George, and Postmaster General, Sir Herbert Samuel.

The first ... and the most obvious [proposition] is that Ministers ought not to enter into any transaction whereby their private pecuniary interest might, even conceivably, come into conflict with their public duty ... Again, no Minister is justified under any circumstances in using official information, information which has come to him as a Minister, for his own private profit or for that of his friends. Further, no Minister ought to allow or to put himself into a position to be tempted to use his official influence in support of any scheme or in furtherance of any contract in regard to which he has an undisclosed private interest ... Again, no Minister ought to accept from persons who are in negotiation with or seeking to enter into contractual or proprietary or pecuniary relations with the State any kind of favour ... I will add a further proposition, which I am not sure has been completely formulated, though it has no doubt been adumbrated in the course of these debates, and that is that Ministers should scrupulously avoid speculative investments in securities as to which, from their special means of early or confidential information, they have or may have an advantage over other people in anticipating market changes.[48]

In 1949, a Tribunal of Inquiry[49] was established to inquire into allegations of payments and other benefits being made to John Belcher MP.[50] Mr Belcher had received gifts offered with a view to securing favourable treatment in relation to licences granted by the Board of Trade. He resigned office and his parliamentary seat as a result.[51]

Recent ministerial resignations involving allegations of financial imprudence – although in each case there were additional factors involved in the resignations – include, as noted above, p 398, David Mellor, the Heritage Secretary, who resigned following a mixture of allegations, one of which involved the receipt of a free holiday from a woman with Palestinian Liberation Organisation associations.[52] In 1992, it was revealed that the Chancellor of the Exchequer, Norman Lamont, had received £4,700 of public money for legal fees involved in the eviction of a tenant from his apartment.[53] In June 1993, the Minister for Northern Ireland, Michael Mates MP, resigned office after it had been revealed that Mr Mates gave to the fugitive businessman Asil Nadir, who faces prosecution on charges of theft and fraud, an inexpensive watch, shortly before Mr Nadir fled the United Kingdom. The Prime Minister described the gift as 'an error of judgment' and 'not a hanging matter'. The matter might have been allowed to rest if it were not for the subsequent allegation that Mr Mates accepted the loan of a car from Mr Nadir for his ex-wife's use, and that Mr Mates had dined with Mr Nadir shortly

---

48   Cited in *op cit*, Jennings, fn 41, p 109.
49   Under the Tribunals of Inquiry (Evidence) Act 1921.
50   Parliamentary Secretary to the Board of Trade.
51   *Report of the Tribunal*, Cmnd 2616, 1949, London: HMSO.
52   HC Deb Col 139, 25 September 1992.
53   See Brazier, R, 'Regulating ministers' and ex-ministers' finances' (1992) 43 NILQ 19 and 'Ministers in court: the personal legal liability of ministers' (1993) 44 NILQ 317.

before he left the country. Mr Mates[54] claimed to have the full support of the Prime Minister and said that he would not resign over the matter: nevertheless, he ultimately resigned. Further embarrassment was caused to the government in 1994, when it was alleged that Jeffrey Archer, former Conservative Party Chairman, had been involved in share-dealing in Anglia Television, on whose Board of Directors his wife held a directorship. In 1994, allegations were made that Members of Parliament had accepted payment for asking parliamentary questions. This affair escalated into a full-scale judicial inquiry into 'standards in public life', and to a tightening of the rules regulating the financial interests of all members of the House of Commons. This matter is discussed further in Chapter 18.

The Nolan Committee

The result of continued and intensive media interest in ministerial conduct has caused a loss of public confidence in Members of Parliament as a whole, and in the conduct and probity of Ministers. The Nolan Committee, appointed to inquire into standards in public life, examined in general the standards of conduct expected of Ministers. More specifically, the Committee has investigated the question of the rules relating to Ministers who retire from office and subsequently take up employment with organisations with whom they had dealings whilst in ministerial office. In addition, the Committee considered the organisation, regulation and personnel employed in non-departmental public bodies (NDPBs or 'quangos').[55]

The conduct of Ministers of the Crown

The Nolan Committee endorsed the view that the 'public is entitled to expect very high standards of behaviour from Ministers, as they have profound influence over the daily lives of us all'.[56] The Committee distinguished between the need for clear enforceable rules regulating financial conduct and those regulating sexual conduct. In respect of the latter, the Committee, whilst recognising that sexual improprieties may on occasion be relevant to the performance of a Minister's public duties, took the view that it was not possible to lay down hard and fast rules to regulate such private conduct.

In respect to financial matters, however, the Committee took a very different view. The Committee recommended that *Questions of Procedure for*

---

54 Interview, *BBC News*, 22 June 1993.

55 Quasi-autonomous non-governmental organisations, on which, see, further, below and Chapter 24.

56 Nolan Report, *Standards in Public Life*, Cm 2850-I, 1995, London: HMSO, Chapter 3, para 4.

Ministers,[57] the document issued by the Prime Minister for the regulation of public conduct, should be redrafted and the rules relating to Ministers more clearly and forcefully expressed. *Questions of Procedure*, while having no formal constitutional status, is nevertheless, in practice, binding on all members of the government.[58] The Committee recommended that the Prime Minister should be given explicit power to determine whether Ministers – who are responsible for complying with the standards of conduct – have in fact upheld the required standard.[59] While the Committee accepted that it is for the Prime Minister to draft the document, the Committee recommended that it include the following essential principles, supported where necessary by detailed rules:

> Ministers of the Crown are expected to behave according to the highest standards of constitutional and personal conduct. In particular, they must observe the following principles of ministerial conduct:
>
> (a) Ministers must ensure that no conflict arises, or appears to arise, between their public duties and their private interests;
>
> (b) Ministers must not mislead Parliament. They must be as open as possible with Parliament and the public;
>
> (c) Ministers are accountable to Parliament for the policies and operations of their departments and agencies;
>
> (d) Ministers should avoid accepting any gift or hospitality which might, or might appear to, compromise their judgment or place them under an improper obligation;
>
> (e) Ministers in the House of Commons must keep separate their roles as Minister and constituency Member;
>
> (f) Ministers must keep their party and ministerial roles separate. They must not ask civil servants to carry out party political duties or to act in any other way that would conflict with the Civil Service Code.[60]

As discussed in Chapter 18, the appointment of a Commissioner for Standards, as recommended by the Nolan Committee, the refashioning of the Committee of Privileges as the Committee on Standards and Privileges and the renewed emphasis on the duty to formally register interests, has resulted in a tightening of parliamentary scrutiny of, and control over, ministerial conduct. In 1997, the Commissioner ruled that the former Chancellor of the Exchequer should have registered his sponsored attendance at a conference in Greece. One early inquiry also undertaken by the Commissioner, Sir Gordon Downey, was into allegations that the Labour Party had accepted, during the election campaign, a donation of over £1 million from the head of Formula

---

57 In existence since 1945, but made public only in 1992.
58 *Op cit*, Nolan Report, fn 56, para 9.
59 *Op cit*, Nolan Report, fn 56, para 13.
60 *Op cit*, Nolan Report, fn 56, para 16.

One racing. Controversy heightened when, subsequent to the election, the government exempted Formula One from the proposed ban on the tobacco industry sponsoring sporting events. Following some delay, the money was returned. The Commissioner has also examined allegations concerning the Paymaster General, Geoffrey Robinson, who, it was alleged, failed to register his substantial interests in offshore trusts. While the Commissioner was critical of Robinson's failure to register, Sir Gordon Downey and the Committee on Standards and Privileges cleared him of breaking any House of Commons rules. The Commissioner stated that in future, where there was doubt as the requirement of registration, the advice of the Commissioner should be sought.[61] Nineteen ninety-eight saw the culmination of the long running inquiry into the financial affairs of the former Paymaster General, Geoffrey Robinson, when in December both Robinson and Peter Mandelson, Secretary of State for Trade and Industry, resigned. Peter Mandelson had been a leading architect in making the Labour Party 'electable' and a pivotal figure is the general election campaign. However, it was revealed that Mandelson had accepted a personal loan from Robinson to finance the purchase of a London home, and that the loan had not been disclosed. While protesting that he had done nothing 'wrong', Mandelson resigned. He returned to ministerial office in 1999 as Secretary of State for Northern Ireland.

Vetting of prospective Ministers?

In the United States of America, appointment to Cabinet office is undertaken only after the 'advice and consent' of the Senate has been obtained.[62] By this means, it is intended to test the suitability of candidates prior to appointment and to avoid the inevitable embarrassment which occurs when resignation is forced through disclosure of some financial, sexual or other impropriety. In the United Kingdom, by contrast, appointment is entirely at the discretion of the Prime Minister and will be made on information which is publicly available and from the personal and political reputation of the candidate. As has been seen above, the standard of conduct required for public life and the reality frequently part company. It is thus at least arguable that some form of 'vetting' – such as occurs with prospective holders of senior Civil Service posts – should be introduced. Professor Rodney Brazier has advocated this course of action,[63] favouring some form of pre-appointment formal inquiry into fitness for office. Such an approach has not found favour with others who have considered it. In the inquiry following the Profumo scandal, Lord Denning stated that there should be no inquiry into politicians' private lives by the

---

61   (1998) *The Times*, 21 January.

62   Constitution, Art II, s 2.

63   Brazier, R, *Constitutional Reform*, 1991, Oxford: Clarendon, Chapter 3 and 'It is a constitutional issue: fitness for ministerial office in the 1990s' [1994] PL 431.

Security Service other than where State security was under threat, a view endorsed by the Security Commission in its report following the resignations of Lords Lambton and Jellicoe.[64] Lord Hailsham has expressed the view that, in a democracy, there should be no such invasive advance inquiries into the private lives of public figures,[65] while recognising the real risks of corruption in public life which 'is hard to define ... harder to detect, and almost as catching as smallpox'.[66] It must, however, be conceded that when the standard of conduct is lowered and the esteem of a government damaged by lack of integrity, then some action is needed.

GOVERNMENT OPENNESS AND GOVERNMENT SECRECY

The issue of the confidentiality of Cabinet papers has been discussed above, p 404. More generally, the issue of confidentiality of government papers gives rise to questions about the extent to which the government in the United Kingdom operates with an unnecessary degree of secrecy. Secrecy in government raises important questions for the individual citizen over the right of access to personal information stored by the government and also to the right of access of citizens more generally to documents concerning government of the State and of access to information about the policies and standards of service of public bodies. The issue of access to personal data held by government is discussed later in this chapter. A further question arises as to the disclosure of government documents to courts of law and the use of public interest immunity certificates by the government to conceal evidence.

THE GOVERNMENT AND THE COURTS

The government, acting in the name of the Crown, has a historic right to privileges and immunities[67] Before the Crown Proceedings Act 1947, two main principles governed the question of the legal liability of the Crown. The first principle was that 'the King could do no wrong' and, accordingly, could not be held liable for any actions which would be unlawful if committed by individuals.[68] The second rule was that the King could not be sued in his own courts. Designed to protect the unique constitutional position of the Crown, as

---

64 *Op cit*, Lord Denning's Report, fn 34, para 230; Report of the Security Commission, Cmnd 5367, 1973, London: HMSO, para 42.

65 *Op cit*, Hailsham, fn 42, Chapter 29.

66 *Op cit*, Hailsham, fn 42, p 201.

67 An aspect of the royal prerogative. See Chapter 6.

68 See, further, Chapter 6.

State regulation increased, Crown privilege extended to a wide range of central government activities, thereby weakening the legal protection given to individuals aggrieved by government action. In 1947, the Crown Proceedings Act extended the liability of the Crown to areas of tort and contract. In relation to tortious liability, the Crown is placed in the same legal position as any other adult individual, and has the same liability for the tortious acts of its employees and agents as do private persons and organisations. Two important exceptions to liability remain: liability in respect of actions of members of the armed forces while on duty or on premises used for the purposes of the armed forces, and liability for tortious actions committed by the Post Office.[69] In respect of a breach of statutory duties imposed on private persons, the Crown is liable where the statute in question is one which binds the Crown.[70] It was originally thought that the unique position of the Crown meant that the remedies of specific performance and injunctions were not available against the Crown. In *M v Home Office*,[71] however, the Home Secretary was held to be liable in his official, but not personal, capacity for his failure to obey an order of the court and it was declared by the House of Lords that injunctions could be issued against officers of the Crown.

Public interest immunity[72]

The phrase 'Crown privilege' has been superseded by the term 'public interest immunity' or more colloquially 'gagging orders'. One aspect of the immunity which is of contemporary and continuing concern is the extent to which governments – and agencies of government – may be required to disclose information to a court of law. The matter was examined by Sir Richard Scott in his inquiry into the Matrix Churchill affair (the arms to Iraq affair), in the course of which, the government refused to disclose information to a court, information which would, if it had been disclosed earlier, have resulted in stopping the prosecution of directors of Matrix Churchill for breaching Customs and Excise Export Regulations. While the immunity from disclosure of information relates principally to the government, it extends to other persons and organisations. Public interest immunity was raised, for example, in *D v NSPCC*[73] in order to protect the sources of information given to the National Society for the Prevention of Cruelty to Children.

---

69 The Post Office ceased to be a government department and became a public corporation in 1969. The restrictions on liability were nevertheless retained.

70 Eg, the Occupiers' Liability Act 1957.

71 [1993] 3 WLR 433.

72 See, *inter alia*, Jacob, JM, 'From privileged Crown to interested public' [1993] PL 121; Simon Brown LJ, 'Public interest immunity' [1994] PL 579. See Zuckerman, AAS, 'Public interest immunity – a matter of prime judicial responsibility' (1994) 57 MLR 703.

73 [1978] AC 171.

Under the Crown Proceedings Act 1947, a court may order the disclosure of documents in the interests of justice. Section 28, however, also provides that the power of the court in civil proceedings does not extend to disclosures which it would not be in the public interest to make:

(1) Subject to and in accordance with rules of court and county court rules:

    (a) in any civil proceedings in the High Court or a county court to which the Crown is a party, the Crown may be required by the court to make discovery of documents and produce documents for inspection; and

    (b) in any such proceedings as aforesaid, the Crown may be required by the court to answer interrogatories:

Provided that this section shall be without prejudice to any rule of law which authorises or requires the withholding of any document or the refusal to answer any question on the ground that the disclosure of the document or the answering of the question would be injurious to the public interest. Any order of the court made under the powers conferred by paragraph (b) of this sub-section shall direct by which officer of the Crown the interrogatories are to be answered.

(2) Without prejudice to the proviso to the preceding sub-section, any rules made for the purposes of this section shall be such as to secure that the existence of a document will not be disclosed if, in the opinion of a Minister of the Crown, it would be injurious to the public interest to disclose the existence thereof.

There are thus two aspects of public interest entailed within this area of the law: the public interest in the administration of justice and the public interest in non-disclosure of damaging information. The questions which arise are, who it is who has the power to decide whether disclosure would or would not be in the public interest, and on what basis the 'public interest' is to be evaluated?[74]

In *Duncan v Cammell Laird*,[75] dependants of victims who died in the submarine *Thetis*, which sank during trials, sued the builders of the submarine. Disclosure was sought of documents relating to contracts between the Admiralty and the building contractors, and salvage reports on the submarine. The Admiralty refused to disclose the information, relying on national security, and the Minister certified that disclosure was against the public interest. The House of Lords held that the Minister's certificate was conclusive and could not be questioned. Accordingly, the rule emerged that a court of law could never question a claim of Crown privilege (or public interest immunity), irrespective of the type of documents being sought. The House of Lords ruled that public interest immunity could lie in respect of the contents of a particular document, or to a class of documents which ought to

---

74 On evidence generally in criminal trials, see Chapters 4 and 20.
75 [1942] AC 264.

be withheld in the interests of the proper functioning of the public service.[76] This decision altered the law and, in the words of Professor Wade, gave the Crown the right to withhold information and thereby 'to override the rights of litigants not only in cases of genuine necessity but in any case where a government department thought fit'.[77]

In 1957, the Lord Chancellor[78] issued a Statement.[79] The Lord Chancellor drew a distinction between such documents which were absolutely necessary to protect the 'proper functioning of the civil service', and documents which are relevant to litigation but which do not require 'the highest degree of confidentiality ... in the public interest', and stated that privilege relating to medical and other documents relevant to the defence in criminal proceedings should not be routinely claimed.[80] The rule in *Duncan v Cammell Laird*, however, prevailed until 1967. In *Conway v Rimmer*,[81] the House of Lords took a more robust attitude to a claim of public interest immunity, reversing its own decision in *Duncan v Cammell Laird*. In an action for malicious prosecution against his former Superintendent of Police, the Home Secretary objected to the disclosure of reports made on the former police probationary officer. The court refused to follow the broad ruling in *Duncan v Cammell Laird* and ruled that it was for the court – and not the person seeking to prevent disclosure – to rule on the competing public interests in the administration of justice and confidential information. Accordingly, it is for the person seeking to withhold information to assert – through the use of a public interest immunity certificate – the right to non-disclosure, and for the court to determine whether or not non-disclosure is in the public interest. Lord Reid, in rejecting that the power of decision lay solely with Ministers of the Crown, stated that he did not doubt that:

> There were certain classes of documents[82] which ought not to be disclosed whatever their content may be ... To my mind the most important reason is that such disclosure would create or fan ill informed or captious public or political criticism. The business of government is difficult enough as it is, and no government could contemplate with equanimity the inner workings of the government machine being exposed to the gaze of those ready to criticise

---

76 [1942] AC 264, pp 941–42.

77 Wade, HWR and Forsyth, CF, *Administrative Law*, 7th edn, 1994, Oxford: Clarendon, p 847.

78 Lord Kilmuir.

79 HL Deb Col 741–48, 6 June 1956.

80 On guidelines issued by the Court of Appeal in relation to disclosure in criminal proceedings, see *R v Keane* [1994] 1 WLR 746; *The Times*, 15 March.

81 [1968] AC 910.

82 Lord Reid refers here specifically to Cabinet minutes.

without adequate knowledge of the background and perhaps with an axe to grind.[83]

In *Burmah Oil Co v Bank of England*,[84] the oil company sought disclosure of information relating to the rescue of the company by the bank, in exchange for low-priced stock in the company. The Attorney General produced a public interest immunity certificate from the Chief Secretary to the Treasury, in which objection was made against producing documents sought on the basis that it related to government policy. The House of Lords inspected the documents, but felt that their disclosure was unnecessary.

A question relating to public interest immunity certificates (PIIs) which assumed particular importance in the *Arms to Iraq* affair, was whether the Minister was under a duty to sign the certificate when advised to do so by the Attorney General. The notion of duty arose in *Air Canada v Secretary of State for Trade*[85] in which Lord Scarman (in the minority) stated that, whilst it was for the court to accept or deny the claim, in claiming public interest immunity, the Crown was not 'claiming a privilege but discharging a duty'. In the *Air Canada* case, the House of Lords ruled, by a majority, that the government was entitled to immunity. At issue were the circumstances under which, in judicial review proceedings, the court would examine documents for which immunity was claimed. No order for disclosure can be made unless the documents are inspected by the court. The majority in the House of Lords ruled that the party seeking disclosure of documents had to show that 'the documents are very likely to contain material which would give substantial support to his contention on an issue which arises in the case'.[86] It was not sufficient that the documents might reveal information relevant to the case, it had to be established by the person seeking disclosure, that it was 'very likely' that the information would assist his case.

The House of Lords had the opportunity to re-examine the issue in *R v Chief Constable of West Midlands Police ex parte Wiley; Chief Constable of Nottinghamshire Police ex parte Sunderland*.[87] In that case, the defendant, Mr Wiley, was charged with robbery, but at his trial the prosecution offered no evidence. He subsequently made formal complaints against the police and commenced a civil action against the Chief Constable. Mr Sunderland had been charged with assault but, again, no evidence was offered at trial by the prosecution. He also made a formal complaint against the police. He alleged assault by the police and indicated that he would institute civil proceedings

---

83 [1968] AC 910, p 953.
84 [1980] AC 1090.
85 [1983] 2 AC 394.
86 *Per* Lord Fraser [1983] 1 All ER 910, p 917e.
87 [1995] 1 AC 274.

against them. The problem faced by both complainants was that the police had documents which it was thought would attract public interest immunity on behalf of the police, thereby making them unavailable to the complainants. The Chief Constables concerned refused to give undertakings that the documents would not be used to the detriment of the complainants, and the complainants secured a declaration that the Chief Constables had acted unlawfully in refusing to give the undertakings. The Chief Constables appealed against the declarations to the House of Lords. In the earlier case of *Neilson v Laugharne*,[88] the House of Lords had ruled that public interest immunity attached to police complaints documents, on the basis that if it did not the complaints procedure would be damaged. However, the House of Lords ruled that, in principle, documents which are relevant to litigation should be disclosed, unless that disclosure would cause 'substantial harm'. In particular, Lord Templeman stated that 'a rubber stamp approach to public interest immunity by the holder of a document is neither necessary nor appropriate ...'.[89]

One aspect of the law as previously understood, and which was the cause of much criticism in the Scott Inquiry, discussed below, pp 426–34, was the issue of whether public interest immunity was a 'right' or a 'duty'. The perceived distinction was analysed in *Makanjuola v Metropolitan Police Commissioner*.[90] In that case, Bingham LJ stated that:

> ... where a litigant asserts that documents are immune from production or disclosure on public interest grounds he is not (if the claim is well founded) claiming a right but observing a duty ...

Bingham LJ went on to state that:

> ... it [the distinction between a right and a duty] does, I think, mean: (1) that public interest immunity cannot in any ordinary sense be waived, since, although one can waive rights, one cannot waive duties; (2) that, where a litigant holds documents in a class *prima facie* immune, he should (save perhaps in a very exceptional case) assert that the documents are immune and decline to disclose them, since the ultimate judge of where the balance of public interest lies is not him but the court; and (3) that, where a document is, or is held to be, in an immune class, it may not be used for any purpose whatever in the proceedings to which the immunity applies, and certainly cannot (for instance) be used for the purpose of cross-examination.

---

88 [1981] QB 736; applied in *Halford v Sharples* [1992] 1 WLR 736 in proceedings alleging unlawful sexual discrimination; distinguished in *Peach v Metropolitan Police Commissioner* [1986] 1 QB 1064 on the basis that the allegation is of a serious crime committed by the police, and *Ex parte Coventry Newspapers Ltd* [1993] QB 278.

89 [1995] 1 AC 274, p 281.

90 [1992] 3 All ER 617.

Woolf LJ, while endorsing much of this analysis, noted that *Makanjuola* did not involve a Department of State, represented by a Secretary of State. He stated that:

> If a Secretary of State on behalf of his department, as opposed to any ordinary litigant, concludes that any public interest in the documents being withheld from production is outweighed by the public interest in the documents being available for purposes of litigation, it is difficult to conceive that, unless the documents do not relate to an area for which the Secretary of State was responsible, the court would feel it appropriate to come to any different conclusion from that of the Secretary of State. The position would be the same if the Attorney General was of the opinion that the documents should be disclosed.

However, that situation did not pertain to other bodies or persons, and it could not be left to individuals to decide that documents should be disclosed. The court retained the ultimate right to determine disclosure and would 'intervene to protect the public interest'. The decision in *Neilson*, and those cases in which it had been applied, was wrong and could no longer be justified. It was not, Woolf LJ stated, that 'there had been a change in attitudes since the *Neilson* decision' but rather that 'establishing a class of public interest immunity of this nature was never justified'. In *Wiley*, the House of Lords ruled that in *Neilson* and the subsequent cases in which it had been applied, the law was incorrectly stated. The House of Lords did not, however, go so far as to say that material which came to light in investigations against the police could never be entitled to class immunity. The European Court of Human Rights has ruled that the use of Public Interest Immunity Certificates which prevent a judge from considering whether or not evidence should be disclosed in the court of a murder trial violates Article 6 of the Convention.[91]

Matrix Churchill and arms to Iraq[92]

Between 1987 and 1989, the Matrix Churchill company exported machine tools to Iraq. It was alleged by Customs and Excise (which brought the prosecution against the directors of the company) that those exports breached the export regulations in place at the time. In defence, it was argued that the government knew about the exports and had in fact authorised them, and that MI6 (the Secret Intelligence Service) was aware of the exports. When the

---

91 *Rowe and Others v United Kingdom* (2000) *The Times*, 1 March.
92 See Leigh, D, *Betrayed: The Real Story of the Matrix Churchill Trial*, 1993, London: Bloomsbury; Norton-Taylor, R, *Truth is a Difficult Concept: Inside the Scott Inquiry*, 1995, London: Fourth Estate; Tomkins, A, *The Constitution after Scott: Government Unwrapped*, 1998, Oxford: Clarendon.

matter came to trial, four government Ministers[93] signed public interest immunity certificates, refusing disclosure of documents relating to, *inter alia*, records of meetings and communications between the Department of Trade and Industry and the Foreign and Commonwealth Office. The trial of the directors of Matrix Churchill collapsed after a former government Minister, Alan Clark, revealed to the court that the government had – as the defence claimed – in fact known of the exports. The Prime Minister established the inquiry the day after the collapse of the trial.

The Scott Inquiry: arms to Iraq

The inquiry chaired by Sir Richard Scott[94] into the *arms to Iraq* affair provided the most in-depth analysis of ministerial responsibility in recent years.[95]

The background to the inquiry

The Iran-Iraq war lasted from 1980 to 1988. Sales of weaponry to these countries were regulated by government guidance[96] on the use of criteria to be used to evaluate requests for export licences to sell equipment to Iran or Iraq. The guidance[97] stated that:

(a) we should maintain our consistent refusal to supply any lethal equipment to either side;

(b) subject to that overriding consideration, we should attempt to fulfil existing contracts and obligations;

(c) we should not, in future, approve new orders for any defence equipment which in our view would significantly enhance the capability of either side to prolong or exacerbate the conflict;

(d) in line with this policy, we should continue to scrutinise rigorously all applications for export licences for the supply of defence equipment to Iran and Iraq.[98]

---

93 Tristan Garel-Jones (Foreign and Commonwealth Office on behalf of Douglas Hurd, the Foreign Secretary); Malcolm Rifkind (Defence Secretary); Michael Heseltine (President of the Board of Trade); Kenneth Clarke (Home Secretary).

94 At the time of his appointment, Scott LJ; during the course of the Inquiry, he was appointed as Vice Chancellor and resumed the title Sir Richard Scott.

95 See *Report of the Inquiry into the Export of Defence Equipment and Dual-Use Goods to Iraq and Related Prosecution,* HC 115 (1995–96), 15 February 1996 (the 'Scott Report').

96 Issued under the Import, Export and Customs Powers (Defence) Act 1939.

97 Drawn up in December 1984.

98 HC Deb Col 46, 29 October 1985, para D1.155.

The government was thus prohibiting absolutely the sale of lethal weapons, and pursuing a policy of neutrality and even-handedness in relation to the two countries in the supply of other defence equipment.[99] The body scrutinising applications for export licences comprised officials from the Foreign and Commonwealth Office, Ministry of Defence and the Department of Trade and Industry. At the end of the war, the guidelines were revised and a more liberal policy pursued in relation to equipment to Iraq, but the revision not reported to Parliament.

Three directors of Matrix Churchill, a manufacturer of, *inter alia*, weapons components, were prosecuted by Customs and Excise for irregularities in relation to the export of machinery capable of being assembled by Iraq as lethal weapons. Prosecuting counsel did not have all the relevant government documentation on which to base a sound decision as to whether the prosecution should proceed.[100] Counsel for the defendants sought to acquire documents from government departments which it was hoped would reveal vital information as to whether the government knew of the exports by Matrix Churchill and the role of Paul Henderson, one of the defendants, in relation to information gathering on behalf of the British security services.

The response of the government was to sign public interest immunity certificates[101] which denied access to the requested documents on the basis that their disclosure would be contrary to the public interest. Three Ministers, Kenneth Clarke, Malcolm Rifkind and Gareth Jones, signed the Certificates. Michael Heseltine[102] refused to sign the certificates on the basis that the interests of justice required their disclosure. His disquiet over the signing of the certificates was not, however, made known to the court until a much later date. Subsequently, Mr Heseltine signed a modified version of the certificate, having sought further advice from the Attorney General. Each of the Ministers had acted upon the advice of the Attorney General, then Sir Patrick Mayhew.[103]

The effect of the certificates was to deny to the court the evidence which might have led to the acquittal of the defendants, each of whom was facing a significant term of imprisonment if convicted. In 1992, however, it was revealed, by Alan Clark, that evidence which affected the defence was not before the court. The effect of this revelation was the collapse of the prosecution's case and the announcement the following day of a judicial

---

99 For analysis, see Freedman, L, 'Even-handedness, guidelines and defence sales to Iraq' [1996] PL 391.

100 *Op cit*, Scott Report, fn 95, p 1108, para G2.8; p 1245, para G9.5.

101 On which, see, further, pp 423–25.

102 President of the Board of Trade.

103 Sir Nicholas Lyell was appointed Attorney General in April 1992.

inquiry into the circumstances surrounding the prosecution. The decision to establish a judicial inquiry was brought about in large measure through the failure of select committee inquiries to unravel the full facts surrounding the issue.[104]

Sir Richard Scott's Report[105] represented the most wide ranging judicial inquiry into a number of important constitutional issues, including:

(a) whether the relevant government departments, agencies and responsible Ministers operated in accordance with the policies of Her Majesty's government;

(b) an examination of decisions taken by the prosecuting authority and those signing public interest immunity certificates;

(c) an examination of similar cases relevant to the issues of the inquiry and to making recommendations.[106]

The change in policy over exports

In 1989, government Minister, William Waldegrave, in response to inquiries from Members of Parliament, advised that government policy in respect of exports had not changed. However, in Sir Richard Scott's view, the answers given were not accurate and were apt to mislead. Sir Richard accepted, however, that William Waldegrave had not in fact noticed the changed wording in the letters which, if noticed, would have alerted him to the fact that the policy had in fact changed, and that there was no intention 'to be misleading'.[107]

In relation to parliamentary questions concerning the policy being applied, Sir Richard found that the government had deliberately failed to 'inform Parliament of the current state of government policy on non-lethal arms sales to Iraq'.[108]

---

104 See the Trade and Industry Select Committee, *Second Report, Exports to Iraq: Project Babylon and Long Range Guns*, HC 86 (1991–92), London: HMSO; see, also, Leigh, I, 'Matrix Churchill, supergun and the Scott Inquiry' [1993] PL 630, pp 635–41; Tomkins, A, 'Public interest immunity after Matrix Churchill' [1993] PL 650; Bradley, AW, 'Good government and public interest immunity' [1992] PL 514.

105 *Op cit*, Scott Report, fn 95.

106 Terms of reference: *op cit*, Scott Report, fn 95, Vol 1, para A2.2.

107 *Op cit*, Scott Report, fn 95, para D4.12.

108 *Op cit*, Scott Report, fn 95, para D4.25.

The use of public interest immunity certificates[109]

As discussed above, the rules regulating the disclosure of documents in civil and criminal cases vary, but in each case there are common rules. First, a document may or may not fall within a category of documents which *prima facie* must be disclosed. Secondly, disclosure may be denied on the basis that the contents of the documents falls within a particular category of disclosure or non-disclosure,[110] or that the documents fall within a class of documents which may or may not be disclosed.[111] Thirdly, disclosure involves the evaluation of the relevance of the information or documents, which in some cases will be clear, but in other cases less clear until disclosed and evaluated by counsel and the court. Over and above these rules is the public interest immunity certificate. The public interest immunity certificate may be used to claim that it is contrary to the public interest for information or documents to be disclosed irrespective of the first two rules, and may be claimed on the basis of either contents or class.

Where the government would prefer not to disclose information, and the information falls into a 'grey area', there is a temptation to claim public interest immunity to protect the information, whereby its actual relevance to the case in hand may go undetected.

In the case of criminal trials, it has been well established that it is the judge who has the final say as to whether the documents in question should be produced.[112] Where, in a criminal trial, disclosure might risk the identity of a police informant, for example, the judge must weight in the balance the public interest of non-disclosure and the public interest in a fair trial for the defendant. To come down on the side of non-disclosure where there is a risk of a miscarriage of justice for the defendant has been ruled unacceptable.[113] However, the approach taken in civil cases has differed, with the court holding in *Duncan v Cammell Laird*[114] that a Minister's certificate to the effect that disclosure would be contrary to the public interest was conclusive.

---

109 *Op cit*, Scott Report, fn 95.

110 Eg, non-disclosure is in the public interest if the contents reveal the identity of a police informer, or the workings of the security services.

111 Eg, non-disclosure of Cabinet proceedings, or intergovernmental negotiations, or documents relating to military operations. See *Duncan v Cammell Laird* [1942] AC 624; *Conway v Rimmer* [1968] AC 910; *Burmah Oil v Bank of England* [1980] AC 1090; *Air Canada* [1983] 2 AC 394; *R v Chief Constable of West Midlands Police ex parte Wiley* [1995] 1 AC 274; [1994] 1 WLR 114, discussed above.

112 See *R v Hardy* (1794) 24 St Tr 199; cf *Duncan v Cammell Laird* [1942] AC 624, and see, now, *R v Chief Constable of West Midlands Police ex parte Wiley* [1995] 1 AC 274; [1994] 1 WLR 114.

113 See *R v Hallett* [1986] Crim LR 462; *R v Agar* [1990] 2 All ER 442; *R v Keane* [1994] 1 WLR 746; *R v Winston Brown* [1994] 1 WLR 599.

114 [1942] AC 624.

In the Matrix Churchill trial, the government claimed that it had the absolute right, in the name of the public interest, to withhold information which was central to the defendants' case. Accordingly, there was a confusion of the test to be applied to civil and criminal cases, to the detriment of the defendants. Furthermore, by relying on immunity from disclosure on the basis of a 'class claim', the government strengthened its case against the duty to disclose.

It has been argued that class claims are unnecessary, in so far as all the material concerned could equally be protected under a contents claim. In the government's view, however, class claims were essential to maintain 'candour' between Ministers and civil servants in the development of policy, and that it would be 'wrong and inimical to the proper functioning of the public service if the public were to learn of these high level communications'.[115]

Class claims, therefore, are supposedly to do with matters of 'high policy' and yet it was a class claim which the government relied on in the Matrix Churchill case although, in the view of Sir Richard Scott, many of these documents 'could not possibly have been described as relating to "high policy"'.[116]

In Sir Richard Scott's view, 'it had become the practice in the Treasury Solicitor's Department that PII class protection for all documents relating directly or indirectly to advice to ministers should be sought, whether in a civil case or in a criminal trial'.[117] Moreover, he found that the documents which the government was so keen to protect caused no damage to the Intelligence and Security Agencies, and that, in any event, if sensitive material was contained within the documents this could have been 'blacked out' on the basis of a contents claim. Moreover:

> It is, I suggest, unacceptable for PII class claims to be made covering such relatively routine and, in terms of 'high policy', unimportant documents as many of those for which protection was sought in the Matrix Churchill case.[118]

The analysis of ministerial responsibility

As noted above, when the guidelines on defence equipment exports were relaxed following the ceasefire, these were not reported to Parliament. Nor

---

115 See *Public Interest Immunity: Government Response to the Scott Report*, February 1996, House of Commons Library. See, also, Lord Upjohn in *Conway v Rimmer* [1968] AC 910, pp 993–94.

116 Scott, R (Sir), 'The acceptable and unacceptable use of public interest immunity' [1996] PL 427, p 439.

117 *Ibid*.

118 *Ibid*. On the government's response, see below, p 433.

was the information given in response to parliamentary questions in 1989 and 1990, or in correspondence with members of the public seeking information. Sir Richard Scott endorsed the proposals made in Nolan LJ's *First Report*,[119] recommending amendments to *Questions of Procedure for Ministers* to emphasise that 'Ministers must not knowingly mislead Parliament and the public ... They must be as open as possible with parliament and the public, withholding information only when disclosure would not be in the public interest'. In his report, Sir Richard Scott stated that 'the withholding of information by an accountable Minister should never be based on reasons of convenience or for the avoidance of political embarrassment, but should always require special and carefully considered justification'.[120]

In 'Ministerial accountability',[121] Sir Richard Scott developed the themes analysed by Sir David Maxwell-Fyfe in his report on the Crichel Down affair,[122] and evidence given to the Scott Inquiry by Sir Robin Butler, the Cabinet Secretary. Referring to the distinction increasingly frequently made in recent years between ministerial constitutional responsibility and ministerial constitutional accountability, Sir Richard Scott cited Sir Robin's evidence as follows:

> I am using 'accountability' to mean that the Minister must always answer questions and give an account to Parliament for the action of his department, whether he is 'responsible' in the sense of attracting personal criticism himself, or not. So I am using 'accountability' to leave out, as it were, the blame element of it. The blame element is an open question. There are cases where he is accountable in which he may be personally blameworthy, and there will be occasions when he is not personally blameworthy.[123]

The 'divorce' between the acceptance of responsibility and the consequence of resignation is not, in Sir Richard's expressed view, the 'heart of an effective system of Parliamentary accountability' as the Treasury and Civil Service Select Committee regarded it to be.[124] In Sir Richard's view, what does lie at the heart of the constitutional doctrine is rather the:

> ... obligation of ministers to give, or to facilitate the giving, of information about the activities of their departments and about the actions and omission of their civil servants.[125]

---

119 *Op cit*, Nolan Report, fn 56. On which, see, further, Chapter 18.

120 *Op cit*, Scott Report, fn 95, para K8.5.

121 Scott, R (Sir), 'Ministerial accountability' [1996] PL 410.

122 On which, see above.

123 Evidence given to the Inquiry on 9 February 1994: transcript, pp 22–23, cited in *ibid*, Scott.

124 *Fifth Report of the Treasury and Civil Service Committee: The Role of the Civil Service*, HC 27-I (1993–94), London: HMSO, para 133; cited in *ibid*, Scott, p 415.

125 *Ibid*, Scott, p 415.

This obligation to provide information came into conflict in relation to defence sales with the government's insistence on following the practice of not disclosing to Parliament information concerning individual export licensing matters, a practice which did not, in Sir Richard's view, constitute any departure from the practice adopted by all other post-war administrations. However, in 1991, the British government supported the introduction by the United Nations of a voluntary register identifying the movement of, and quantities of, conventional weaponry between supplier and recipient nations. On this basis, Sir Richard Scott called for an abandonment of the blanket refusal to answer parliamentary questions, at least in relation to conventional weaponry.

The refusal to answer questions at all is but part of the problem of the duty to give information. A further cause for concern lay in the failure of Ministers to give full answers to questions and, in relation to the Scott Inquiry, in the failure of witnesses to provide the full picture. 'Commercial confidentiality' is an accepted reason for the denial of information, but that, in Sir Richard's view, did not excuse the refusal of information or the provision of information about weapons supply. National security is another justified exception to the duty to make full disclosure. Nevertheless:

> ... setting those rare cases aside, the proposition that it is acceptable for a Minister to give an answer that is deliberately incomplete is one which, in my opinion, is inconsistent with the requirements of the constitutional principle of ministerial accountability. Half the picture can be true ... But the audience does not know that it is seeing only half the picture. If it did know, it would protest.[126]

A strong democracy can only be a legitimate label if the electors are able to express their view on the basis of adequate knowledge of government activities:

> A failure by Ministers to meet the obligations of ministerial accountability by providing information about the activities of their departments engenders cynicism about government and undermines, in my opinion, the democratic process.[127]

Sir Richard Scott's recommendations

Sir Richard called for the appointment a parliamentary officer, independent of the executive, charged with the task of scrutinising claims by Ministers that information should not be revealed 'in the public interest'. Such an officer

---

126 *Op cit*, Scott, fn 121, p 422. See Tomkins, A, 'Government information and Parliament: misleading by design or by default?' [1996] PL 472.

127 *Op cit*, Scott, fn 121, p 425.

would require free access to government documents and would report to Parliament twice yearly. In addition, Parliament needed to tighten up on the rules requiring witnesses to give evidence by a more robust use of the concept of contempt of Parliament.[128]

Moreover, Sir Richard called for a 'comprehensive review' of the subjects on which governments refuse to answer questions, and of the obligation of Ministers 'to provide and facilitate the provision of information to select committees'.[129] This task was been undertaken by the Public Service Committee which reported in July 1996.

The Public Service Committee report: ministerial accountability and responsibility[130]

Reviewing the doctrine of ministerial responsibility from the *Crichel Down* affair in 1954 to the current time, the Committee produced 34 conclusions and recommendations. In the Committee's view, it was not possible to distinguish absolutely between areas in which a Minister is personally responsible (and blameworthy) and areas in which the Minister is constitutionally accountable.[131] Further, the Committee concluded that 'proper and rigorous scrutiny and accountability' is the more important feature of ministerial responsibility than is Parliament's ability to force that Minister's resignation.

The government's response

In *Government Response to the Report*,[132] the government accepted the Committee's view on the difficulty of a clear distinction between responsibility and accountability but, nevertheless, agreed that the distinction was one which, in some circumstances, remained useful. The government also accepted that Ministers must account to Parliament for their, and their department's actions, and must respond to criticisms made in Parliament. Further, the government accepted that Parliament had the right to determine whether to impose and what sanctions were to be imposed on Ministers.

The Public Service Committee had been critical of the fact that the definition and scope of ministerial responsibility was formulated by the

128 See, further, Chapter 18.

129 *Op cit*, Scott, fn 121, p 424.

130 *Second Report from the Public Service Committee*, HC 313 (1995–96), London: HMSO.

131 See HC Deb Vol 290 Col 273, 12 February 1997; and see *Government Response to the Report of the Public Service Committee on Ministerial Accountability*, HC 67 (1996–97), London: HMSO, November 1996, p vi.

132 *Government Response to the Report of the Public Service Committee on Ministerial Accountability*, HC 67 (1996–97), London: HMSO.

government of the day, via *Question of Procedures for Ministers*, rather than by Parliament, which alone had the right to demand and enforce ministerial responsibility. As a result, and after much inter-Party debate, the House resolved in 1997 that:

In the opinion of the House, the following principles should govern the conduct of ministers of the Crown in relation to Parliament:

(1) Ministers have a duty to Parliament to account, and be held to account, for the policies, decisions and actions of their departments and next step agencies;

(2) It is of paramount importance that ministers should give accurate and truthful information to Parliament, correcting any inadvertent error at the earliest opportunity. Ministers who knowingly mislead Parliament will be expected to offer their resignation to the Prime Minister;

(3) Ministers should be as open as possible with Parliament, refusing to provide information only when disclosure would not be in the public interest;

(4) Ministers should require civil servants who give evidence before parliamentary committees on their behalf and under their directions to be as helpful as possible in providing accurate, truthful and full information;

(5) The interpretation of 'public interest' in paragraph (3) shall be decided in accordance with statute and the government's Code of Practice on Access to Government Information ...; and compliance with the duty in paragraph (4) shall be in accordance with the duties and responsibilities of civil services set out in the Civil Service Code ...[133]

In 1996, the Attorney General announced that, having reviewed the operation of public interest immunity certificates, the government would not longer utilise the distinction between 'class' and 'contents' claims but rather, in future, the government would only claim public interest immunity when the government 'believed that disclosure of a document would cause real harm to the public interest'. The certificate will explain the nature of the harm, and the manner in which disclosure would harm the public interest,[134] thereby allowing for 'even closer scrutiny of claims by the court, which is always the final arbiter'.

---

133 See HC Deb Vol 292 Cols 1046–47, 19 March 1997. See, also, Woodhouse, D, 'Ministerial responsibility: something old, something new' [1997] PL 262.

134 HL Deb Vol 576 Col 1507 and HC Deb Vol 287 Cols 949–58, 18 December 1996; and see HL Deb Vol 576 Cols 1507–17, 18 December 1996.

STANDARDS OF PUBLIC SERVICE AND THE OPENNESS OF GOVERNMENT

Access to information[135]

The balance to be struck between the right of authorities to maintain confidential records and the right of individuals to access to that information is increasingly a matter of concern. There is no general right of access to data stored by the State, for example, records maintained by the Police, Inland Revenue, National Health Service and Department of Social Security. Under the Official Secrets Act 1989,[136] categories of information can never be disclosed. A limited right of access to personal files is granted under the Data Protection Act 1984.[137] Citizens in the United Kingdom are entitled to access to official records in certain categories of cases.[138] The information which can be disclosed is currently confined to computerised records, and not to manually created files, although access to these will be introduced in the future.

In any heavily regulated State, government departments will have access to large amounts of personal data on its citizens. Tax authorities, Social Security offices, local authorities and driving licence authorities are but four major holders of personal information. The individual has two interests in personal records. The first is that information held about the individual should be accessible to him or her. The second is that the individual should be protected against disclosure of such personal data to third parties.

In the United Kingdom – unlike in many other countries – there is no general right of access to such data. In many other jurisdictions, a Freedom of Information Act guarantees access to data stored by the government. A movement towards a more open form of government has begun in the United Kingdom, but goes nowhere near to ensuring 'open government'. Clearly, there is much information which it is not in the public interest – perhaps on grounds of national security – for the government to reveal. However, a balance needs to be struck between adequate secrecy and appropriate openness. The balance has tilted in favour of greater openness with the Labour government's proposed Freedom of Information Act. This proposal is considered below.

---

135 See Savage, N and Edwards, C, *A Guide to the Data Protection Act 1985*, 1985, London: Financial Training; Tapper, C, *Computer Law*, 4th edn, 1989, London: Longman; Reed, C (ed), *Computer Law*, 2nd edn, 1993, London: Blackstone.

136 See Chapter 23.

137 As extended by the Data Protection (Subject Access Modifications) Health Order SI 1987/1903.

138 On current proposals for greater access to information, see, further, below.

The protection of personal data

A range of statutes prohibit the unauthorised disclosure of personal data to third parties. Local authority records (relating to, *inter alia*, adoption, education, child support, housing, medical records and social security) are protected. Equally, in the financial industry, there is protection given to confidential information. In relation to such information, the government does not accept that there is a need to relax the restrictions on disclosure.

Access to personal data

The Data Protection Act 1984 provides that computer-held personal information should be made available to individuals, in order that the person concerned may check the accuracy of the data. The Access to Personal Files Act 1987 provides that individuals have the right to inspect records relating to social services and housing tenancies. Medical records prepared for insurance or employment purposes are accessible under the Access to Medical Reports Act 1988. The Access to Health Records Act 1990 gives patients the right to see records held by general practitioners, health authorities or NHS trusts. The government intends to extend the range of data to which individuals have a right of access. Consultation is taking place on matters such as government departments and agencies, non-departmental public bodies, regulatory authorities and inspectorates, the National Health Service, local authorities, police forces, schools and other educational bodies. The proposed access right would not be confined to computer-held records, and would thus extend the range of records to which individuals have a right of access.

Access to public records

The Public Records Acts 1958 and 1967 provide for the inspection of public records at the Public Records Office after 30 years, unless there is justification for withholding them. The Lord Chancellor also has the power under the Act to order the release of documents at an earlier period if in the public interest. Under the 1958 Act,[139] records may be kept closed for a longer period.[140] The main classes of information not disclosed relate to population census returns, Ministry of Pensions First World War war pensions awards files and the Inland Revenue Stamps and Taxes Division registered files.

---

139 Public Records Act 1958, s 5.
140 Only 1–2% of records remain closed for longer periods.

Standards of service: the 'Citizen's Charter'

In 1991, the government published the 'Citizen's Charter'.[141] The objective was to provide information for the citizen on the standards of service which can be expected from government departments and public bodies. The Charter reflects the government's commitment to openness and provides that there should be no secrecy in public service administration, its cost, and the relevant department's quality of service.[142] The Charter also provided for the establishments of internal complaints procedures, with lay persons having a role to play in the handling of complaints. There exists an overlap with the role of the Commissioners for Administration,[143] and the Select Committee on the Parliamentary Commissioner for Administration expressed disquiet over the proposed complaints procedure,[144] particularly where there is evidence of maladministration, which it is within the Commissioner's jurisdiction to investigate.

The government's 1993 White Paper, *Open Government*[145]

In order to redress the balance in favour of openness, the government, in 1993, issued a White Paper, *Open Government*.[146] The White Paper declared that it was the government's 'commitment to make government in the United Kingdom more open and accountable'.[147] At the same time, the government recognised that it was under a duty to keep some 'secrets' and to protect the privacy of individuals in their dealings with government. The government's approach was stated to be:

(a) handling information in a way which promotes informed policy making and debate, and efficient service delivery;

(b) providing timely and accessible information to the citizen to explain the government's policies, actions and decisions; and

(c) restricting access to information only where there are good reasons for so doing.[148]

---

141 *The Citizen's Charter: Raising the Standard*, Cmnd 1599, 1991, London: HMSO. See Drewry, G, 'Mr Major's Charter: empowering the consumer' [1993] PL 248; Barron, A and Scott, C, 'The Citizen's Charter programme' (1992) 55 MLR 526.

142 Cm 1599, 1991, London: HMSO.

143 See Chapter 26.

144 *Second Report on the Implications of the Citizen's Charter for the Work of the Parliamentary Commissioner for Administration*, HC 158 (1991–92), London: HMSO.

145 Cmnd 2290, 1993, London: HMSO; see Birkinshaw, P, 'I only ask for information: the White Paper on *Open Government*' [1993] PL 557.

146 Cmnd 2290, 1993, London: HMSO.

147 *Ibid*, para 1.3.

148 *Ibid*, para 1.7.

On the need for confidentiality, the government recognised that the right of a person of access to information is always a limited right. Areas which require a degree of secrecy include defence and national security; international relations; law enforcement and legal proceedings; internal opinion, discussion and advice; management of the economy and the collection of taxes; public authorities' commercial and negotiating interests; personal privacy; commercial confidentiality; information given in confidence. Further, there was a need to avoid 'unreasonable or voluminous requests' for information and to prevent premature disclosure of information.[149]

As the government also recognised, there is a public interest in disclosure of information and also a public interest in confidentiality. The problem is to find the correct balance between the two interests. As at 1993, 179 statutes and a further 60 pieces of secondary legislation prohibited the disclosure of official information.[150] A further 48 statutes and 25 pieces of secondary legislation provided for discretionary disclosure of information.[151]

The Code of Practice

The Code of Practice on Government Information[152] seeks to extend access to official information, unless such disclosure would be contrary to the public interest. The Code came into force in 1994, with a second edition published in 1997. With the exception of the matters listed above which it would not be in the public interest to disclose, information, in response to reasonable requests, must be provided within 20 working days. The Code extends to all government departments and other bodies within the jurisdiction of the Parliamentary Commissioner for Administration.[153] The Parliamentary Commissioner's jurisdiction has thus been extended, without amending the Parliamentary Commissioner Act 1967, to deal with complaints concerning access to information. If information is not disclosed, individuals may complain in the first instance to the department concerned, and thereafter to the Parliamentary Commissioner for Administration, through a Member of Parliament.

On the routine publication of data held by government, the White Paper laid down one basic principle. All records not retained in departments should be released after 30 years unless (a) it is possible to establish that actual damage would be caused by release, and (b) that the damage would fall within the listed criteria in the *Guidelines on Extended Disclosure*.[154] The criteria

---

149 Cmnd 2290, 1993, London: HMSO, para 3.2.
150 *Ibid*, Annex B, Pt I.
151 *Ibid*, Pt II.
152 *Ibid*, Annex A.
153 See Chapter 26.
154 *Ibid*, Annex C.

for extended non-disclosure include sensitive documents which would harm defence, international relations, national security (including the maintenance of law and order) or the economic interests of the United Kingdom. Such records should remain undisclosed for a 40 year period. Documents containing information given in confidence where disclosure would amount to a breach of that confidence should be disclosed only after the following periods. Records including commercial and personal data: 40 years; tax information: 75 years; records subject to a statutory bar during the lifetime of the individual: 75 years; population census: 100 years. Documents containing information, the disclosure of which would cause either substantial distress or endangerment from third parties should, depending upon their sensitivity, be retained for a 40 to 100 year period.

The right to information from government departments and public bodies does not, however, include a right of access to the files on which information is based. Moreover, the 'right' to information is not a legal right, but rather establishes a formal ground for complaint if the information being sought is withheld. There also exist a number of excluded categories of information. Thus, information concerning defence, security and international relations is exempt if the provision of that information would be harmful; confidential communications and advice between departments is also excluded, as is information which, if disclosed, would prejudice the administration of justice, the management of the economy or the management of the public service. Also exempt is information relating to personnel records and public appointments. Further, non-disclosure is permissible in the interests of avoiding invasion of privacy or breach of confidentiality: broad grounds concerning the truth of which would prove difficult. Notwithstanding the exclusions, which seek to balance the principles of open government and efficient administration, there is a presumption in favour of disclosure: the Code now provides[155] that 'the presumption remains that information should be disclosed unless the harm likely to arise from disclosure would outweigh the public interest in making the information available'.[156]

The Freedom of Information Bill 2000[157]

In 1997, the incoming Labour government promised to inject greater openness into the machinery of government. Towards this end, a White Paper, *Your*

---

155 Following a recommendation from the Public Service Committee of the House of Commons: HC 3413-I (1995–96), London: HMSO.

156 HC 67 (1996–97), London: HMSO.

157 At the time of publication, the Bill was still before Parliament. Section numbers and details may therefore be amended.

Right to Know: White Paper on Freedom of Information, was published in December 1997.[158]

The proposals: an overview

The government intends that, for the first time, citizens will have a legal right to information and to the records in which that information is contained. In addition, an independent Information Commissioner will be appointed, who will be answerable not to Parliament, but to the courts. The new legal right will apply throughout the public sector, as well as to some private organisations carrying out duties on behalf of government and privatised utilities. Citizens will be entitled to information, subject to 'harm tests'. The Freedom of Information Act will supercede the Code of Practice on Access to Government Information and amend the Data Protection Act 1998 and the Public Records Act 1958.

The 'right to know'

The right of access to information held by public authorities has existed in other jurisdictions for some considerable time. In Sweden, for example, such a right has been in existence since the eighteenth century. More recently, the right to know has existed in the United States of American since 1966, in France since 1978, in Canada, Australia and New Zealand since 1982 and in the Netherlands since 1991.

As noted above, while the Code of Practice introduced in 1994 provides for a 'right' to information, that 'right' is not a legal right, and does not entail access to the records containing information. Moreover, there are a large number of exemptions provided for under the Code. For these reasons, the government is of the view that there should be legislation to create a legal right of access, not just to information, but to records. In contrast to the Code, therefore, the Freedom of Information Act will guarantee access to information and records, subject to exceptions, a right which will be enforceable, if needs be, by an application to the Information Commissioner who will be conferred wide powers of entry and search.

Requests for information

Under section 7 a request for information must be made in writing, stating the name and address of the applicant and describing the information requested. Under section 1(1), any person making a request for information is entitled

---

158 Cm 3818, London: HMSO.

(a) to be informed in writing by the public authority whether it holds information of the description specified in the request, and (b) if that is the case, to have that information communicated to him. However, section 1(1) has effect subject to limitations in section 1, and further sections 8, 11 and 12 (on which see below). Under section 1, the authority may request further information relating to the request. In addition, the right is subject to the limitations imposed under Part II relating to exempt information. The public authority must comply with the request for information due under section 1(1) within 20 working days of receipt.[159] Section 1(1) does not oblige a public authority to comply with a request if the authority estimates that the cost of complying with the request would exceed the 'appropriate limit'. The appropriate limit means such amount as may be prescribed, and different amounts may be prescribed in relation to difference cases.[160] An authority has no duty to comply with requests which are vexatious, or to reply to identical or substantially similar requests made by the same person, unless a reasonable interval has elapsed between compliance with the previous request and the making of the current request.[161]

Disclosure in the public interest

Where disclosure would be required under section 1(1) but for the fact that the information is exempt under Part II (other than the provisions specified in sub-section (2))[162] and, under section 34(6), is not otherwise required by law, the public authority must inform the applicant whether it does or does not hold information, where it appears to the authority that the public interest in disclosure outweighs the public interest in maintaining the exemption in question.[163] Under section 13(4), where an authority holds the information requested and has informed or intends to inform the applicant that it does so, then if it appears to the authority that the public interest in disclosing the information outweighs the public interest in maintaining the exemption in question, the public authority shall communicate the information to the applicant.

The public interest disclosure provisions do not apply to the following categories of exempt information. Under section 19, information which is reasonably accessible to the applicant is exempt, even though it may only be accessible through payment. Under section 21, information relating to the Security Service, Secret Intelligence Service, GCHQ, the special forces, tribunals established under the Interception of Communications Act 1985, Security Service Act 1989, Intelligence Services Act 1994 (see now the

---

159 Freedom of Information Act 2000, s 9.
160 *Ibid*, s 11(1), (3).
161 *Ibid*, s 12(1), (2).
162 Namely, *ibid*, ss 19, 21, 30, 32, 38(1), (2), 39, 42 and 43(2).
163 *Ibid*, s 13(1), (3).

Regulation of Supervisory Powers Bill 2000), the Security Vetting appeals Panel, the Security Commission, the National Criminal Intelligence Service and the Service Authority for the National Criminal Intelligence Service is exempt. Under section 30, information is exempt information if it relates to court proceedings, inquiries or arbitration proceedings. Under section 32, information is exempt if exemption is required for the purpose of avoiding an infringement of the privileges of either House of Parliament, and the duty to confirm or deny does not apply if such exemption is required. A certificate from the Speaker of the House of Commons or the Clerk of the Parliaments in relation to the House of Lords is conclusive. The duty to confirm or deny also does not arise in relation to personal information of which the applicant is the data subject, and information which would contravene data protection principles or section 10 of the Data Protection Act 1998. Section 39 exempts from the duty to confirm or deny information which is held by a public authority in confidence and disclosure would constitute an actionable breach of confidence. Under section 42, the duty to confirm or deny does not arise if disclosure is prohibited by any other enactment, is incompatible with any Community obligation, or would constitute or be punishable as a contempt of court. Section 43(2) provides that the Secretary of State may, if it appears to him that the public interest in exempting information from disclosure outweighs the public interest in allowing access to the information, by order provide that the information is to be exempt. The duty to confirm or deny does not arise in relation to matters certificated under section 34(6) as being prejudicial to the effective conduct of public affairs, and relating to disclosure of information held by either House of Parliament or compliance with section 1(1)(a) by either House.

Cost

Under section 8, authorities are entitled to charge fees and are exempt from the duty to provide information until the fee is paid. The applicant has three months from the date of notification to pay the fee before the application lapses. It is proposed that regulations governing fees will specify that up to 10 per cent of the reasonable marginal costs of complying with the request may be charged.

The information requested may be supplied in different ways. The applicant may request provision of a copy of the information in permanent form or in another acceptable form, or to inspect a record or a digest or summary of the information. So far as reasonably practicable, the authority shall give effect to the applicant's preference, having regard to all the circumstances and the cost involved.

Refusal of a request

A public authority which relies on a claim that information is exempt or that the duty to confirm or deny does not arise must give the applicant a notice which states that fact and specifies the exemption in question, and state why the exemption applies.

The bodies covered by the proposed Act

Section 2 defines a public authority as being a body listed in Schedule 1 or designated by order under section 4 (designation by the Secretary of State), or a publicly owned company as defined by section 5. Section 5(1) states that a publicly owned company is such if it is wholly owned by the Crown, or wholly owned by any public authority listed in Schedule 1 other than a government department or any authority which is listed only in relation to particular information. Section 5(2) defines a company wholly owned by the Crown as a company having no members except Minister, government departments or companies wholly owned by the Crown, or any person acting on behalf of the above. A company wholly owned by a public authority other than a government department is defined as having no members except that public authority or companies owned by that public authority, or any person acting on behalf of the above. Public authorities are designated in four ways. First, in Schedule 1, using general descriptions where appropriate, which specifies the principal authorities in national and local government, together with the principal public authorities relating to the armed forces, National Health Service, education, the police and other public bodies and offices. Secondly, under section 4, which confers power on the Secretary of State to amend Schedule 1. Thirdly, under section 4 and designation by the Secretary of State. And, fourthly, publicly owned companies under section 5.

Some public authorities in Schedule 1 are designated as being listed in relation to information of a specified description. In relation to these, nothing in Parts I to V of the Act applies to any other information held by the Authority. For example, in relation to the Bank of England, it is listed in respect of information held for purposes other than those of its functions with respect to (a) monetary policy; (b) financial operations intended to support financial institutions for the purposes of maintaining stability; and (c) the provision of private banking services and related services, and the British Broadcasting Corporation, Channel Four Television Corporation listed in respect of information held for purposes other than those of journalism, art or literature. The Secretary of State has power by order, under sub-section (3) to amend Schedule 1 by limiting the information in relation to any public authority and by removing or amending that limitation. Such an order is subject to the parliamentary resolution procedure.[164]

The Secretary of State and Lord Chancellor have duties relating to giving guidance to public authorities through Codes of Practice.[165] The Information Commissioner is under a general duty to promote the following of good practice by public authorities and to perform his functions so as to promote the observance by public authorities of the requirements of the Act.[166]

Exempt information

Part II of the Act regulates exemptions. Information which is reasonably accessible, albeit at a cost, is exempt, as is information which is held with a view to publication.[167] Information relating to the security forces and security matters are exempted under section 21, and information not falling within section 21 is exempt if exemption is required for the purpose of safeguarding national security under section 22. Matters relating to the defence of the British Islands or of any colony, or the capability, effectiveness or security of any relevant forces is exempt information if disclosure would be like to cause prejudice to defence.[168] Under section 25, information is exempt if its disclosure would or would be likely to prejudice international relations, or the interests of the United Kingdom abroad or the promotion or protection by the United Kingdom of its interests abroad. Confidential information obtained from another State or international organisation or court is also exempt.

Relations within the United Kingdom are protected under section 26, which provides that information is exempt if its disclosure would or would be likely to prejudice relations between the government of the United Kingdom, the Scottish Administration, the Executive Committee of the Northern Ireland Assembly or the National Assembly for Wales. Information is exempt if its disclosure would or would be likely to prejudice the economic interests of the United Kingdom or any part of the United Kingdom or the financial interests of any administration.[169]

Information relating to investigations or criminal proceedings and law enforcement are protected under sections 28 and 29. In respect of investigations, the exemption covers those which an authority has a duty to conduct to ascertain whether a person should be charged with an offence or whether the person charged is guilty, and investigations which may lead to a

---

164 Freedom of Information Act 2000, s 80(3).
165 *Ibid*, ss 44 and 45.
166 *Ibid*, s 46.
167 *Ibid*, s 19 and 20.
168 *Ibid*, s 24.
169 *Ibid*, s 27.

decision to institute criminal proceedings and criminal proceedings. In relation to law enforcement, the prejudice test is employed. Information which is not exempt under section 28 is exempt under section 29 if its disclosure would or would be likely to prejudice the prevention or detection of crime, the apprehension or prosecution of offenders, the administration of justice, assessment or collection of taxes or duties, operation of immigration controls, maintenance of security and good order in prisons and other detention institutions. The exercise by any public authority of its functions in relation to matters specified in sub-section 2 are exempted, as are civil proceedings brought by or on behalf of a public authority and enquiries held under the Fatal Accidents and Sudden Deaths Inquiries (Scotland) Act 1976. Information is exempt if it is held in court documents.[170]

Information relating to public authorities which have audit functions in relation to other public authorities are exempt under section 31.

As seen above, information is exempt information if exemption is required for the purpose of avoiding an infringement of the privileges of either House of Parliament.[171] There is also an exemption relating to information held by government departments relating to the formulation or development of government policy, ministerial communications, the provision of advice by any of the Law Officers or any request for the provision of such advice and the operation of any ministerial private office.[172] This controversial provision ensures that the advice of the civil service to government is kept protected from public scrutiny, and seriously limits the ability to scrutinise the range of alternative policy options put to government in the formulation and development of its policies. Information held by a government department which is not exempt by virtue of section 33 and information held by any other public authority is exempt information if, 'in the reasonable opinion of a qualified person', disclosure would or would be likely to prejudice the maintenance of the collective responsibility of Ministers, the work of the Executive Committee of the Northern Ireland Assembly, or would be likely to inhibit the free and frank provision of advice, or the free and frank exchange of views for the purposes of deliberation or would otherwise prejudice the effective conduct of public affairs. The 'qualified person' means, in relation to a government department, any Minister of the Crown, or, in relation to the Northern Ireland Department, the Northern Ireland Minister in charge of the department. In relation to other government departments, it means the commissioners or other person in charge of that department, in relation to the House of Commons, the Speaker, and in relation to information held by the House of Lords, the Clerk of the Parliament. In relation to information held by

---

170 Freedom of Information Act 2000, s 30.
171 *Ibid*, s 32.
172 *Ibid*, s 33.

the Northern Ireland Assembly, the qualified person is the Presiding Officer, and, in relation to the National Assembly for Wales, it is the Assembly First Secretary. In relation to information held by the National Audit Office, the qualified person is the Comptroller and Auditor General and his or her equivalent in relation to Northern Ireland. The qualified person in relation to information held by the Greater London Authority is the Mayor of London, and, in relation to functional bodies under the Greater London Authority Act, the chairperson of that functional body. Under section 35, information is exempt if it relates to communications with Her Majesty, with other members of the Royal Family or with the Royal Household or the conferring by the Crown of any honour.

Further exemptions relate to information the disclosure of which would or would be likely to endanger the physical or mental health of any individual or his or her safety,[173] information held by a public authority in relation to environmental matters connected with the Convention on Access to Information, Public Participation in Decision Making and Access to Justice in Environmental Matters of 1998. As seen above, personal data is protected under section 38, and confidential information is covered by section 39. Information in relation to which a claim to legal professional privilege or confidentiality is made is exempt information under section 40. Information which constitutes a trade secret, and information the disclosure of which would prejudice the commercial interests of any person, including the public authority holding it, is exempt under section 41. Information is also exempt if its disclosure is prohibited under any other enactment, is incompatible with any Community obligations or would constitute or be punishable as a contempt of court.[174]

The Information Commissioner and Tribunal

The Data Protection Commissioner is renamed the Information Commissioner. The general duties of the Commissioner are set out in section 47. It is the general duty of the Commissioner to promote good practice in public authorities in relation to their responsibilities under the Act. The Commissioner has a duty to disseminate information to the public about the operation of the Act, good practice and other matters, and to give advice. The Commissioner may, with the consent of any public authority, assess whether the authority is following good practice. The Commissioner is permitted to charge fees for such services with the consent of the Secretary of State. If the

---

173 Freedom of Information Act 2000, s 36.
174 *Ibid*, s 42.

Commissioner considers that an authority is not conforming with good practice, the Commissioner may make recommendations to the authority under section 47. The Commissioner must lay before each House of Parliament a general report on the exercise of his functions under the Act.[175]

Any person may apply for a decision whether, in any specified respect, a request for information made to a public authority by the complainant has been dealt with in accordance with the requirements of Part I of the Act.[176] The Commissioner must make a decision regarding the complaint unless the complainant has not exhausted any complaints procedure provided by the relevant public authority, there has been undue delay in making the application, the application is frivolous or vexatious or the application has been withdrawn or abandoned.[177] The Act specifies the investigative and enforcement powers of the Commissioner. Where the Commissioner decides that a public authority has failed to communicate information, or to provide confirmation or denial, in a case where it is required to do so, the Commissioner may issue a decision notice specifying the steps which must be taken by the authority in order to comply.[178] The Commissioner may also issue enforcement notices requiring the authority to take, within a specified time, such steps as required to comply. Where the Commissioner has issued a decision or enforcement notice in respect of the disclosure of information under section 13, a certificate may be issued by an 'accountable person' as defined in the Act, the effect of this is that a public authority need not comply with the Commissioner's notice.[179] If an authority fails to comply with the Commissioner's notice, the Commissioner may so certify to the High Court or, in Scotland, the Court of Session, and the court may, having conducted a hearing, deal with the authority as if it had committed a contempt of court.[180]

Appeals

Either the complainant or the pubic authority may appeal against a decision notice to the Tribunal under section 56. The Tribunal shall either allow the appeal or substitute such other notice as could have been served by the Commissioner and, in other cases, must dismiss the appeal. Appeals from the decision of the Tribunal on a point of law lie to the High Court or to the Court of Session in relation to Scotland and to the High Court of Justice in Northern Ireland.

---

175 Freedom of Information Act 2000, s 48.
176 *Ibid*, s 49.
177 *Ibid*, s 49(2).
178 *Ibid*, s 49(4).
179 *Ibid*, s 52.
180 *Ibid*, s 53.

Amendments relating to public records

Part VI of the Act provides a statutory regime for access to public records, replacing the provisions of the Public Records Act 1958 relating to discretionary disclosure. It also provides for increased access to information contained in records more than 30 years old.

Amendments to the Data Protection Act 1998

Part VII extends the Data Protection Act 1998 in relation to subject access and data accuracy on information held by public authorities. Schedule 6 extends the 1998 Act to include relevant personal information processed by or on behalf of both Houses of Parliament. Personal data is, however, exempt if the exemption is required for the purpose of avoiding an infringement of the privileges of either House of Parliament.[181]

---

181 Freedom of Information Act 2000, Sched 6, inserting s 35A into the Data Protection Act 1998.

CHAPTER 12

REGIONAL AND LOCAL GOVERNMENT

PART I – REGIONAL GOVERNMENT: THE DEVOLUTION OF POWER

As discussed in Chapters 1 to 3, the constitution of the United Kingdom has traditionally been characterised by the unity of its several parts, with centralised government. Wales became united with England through being conquered in 1262, while the Acts of Union 1706 and 1707 marked the end of the separation of Scotland and England under two sovereign parliaments. Despite the former attempt at devolution of power to both Wales and Scotland in 1978, discussed in Chapter 3, the population of neither country then expressed – according to the terms of the referendum – the desire for greater separation from centralised government. Two decades later, however, the political position is much changed. A disenchantment with the extent to which the national Parliament reflected the views of the people of Scotland, in particular, and Wales, and a rising tide of nationalist regional sentiment, has led to change and power being devolved from the centre to the nations. In addition, settlement reached in Northern Ireland under the 1998 Good Friday agreement facilitated the re-establishment of the Northern Ireland Assembly.

NORTHERN IRELAND

The Belfast Agreement of April 1998 signalled the prospect for peace in Northern Ireland and the re-establishment of a legislative authority for Northern Ireland. The Agreement focused on five principal points. First, Northern Ireland would remain a part of the United Kingdom; and the Republic of Ireland agreed to formally amend its constitution to remove its claim to Northern Ireland. Secondly, a Northern Ireland Assembly of 108 members was to be elected, and run by an executive of 12 members drawn from all political parties. Thirdly, a North-South Ministerial Council was to be established to co-ordinate relations between Ireland and Ulster. Fourthly, a British-Irish Council was to be set up, its membership drawn from the parliaments at Westminster, Dublin, Edinburgh and the Welsh Assembly, with representatives of the Isle of Man and the Channel Isles to consider matters of mutual interest. Finally, implementation of the Agreement was conditional upon the decommissioning of all paramilitary weapons. The Agreement required ratification by the people and, in May 1998, was approved by a referendum. In Northern Ireland, on a turnout of 81.1 per cent, 71.1 per cent voted for peace, while in the Republic, on a turn out of 56 per cent, 94 per cent voted for peace. Parliament passed the Northern Ireland (Elections) Act 1998 to establish elections for the new Assembly of 108 members representing the existing Westminster constituencies, under the single transferable voting system, which were held in June 1998.

The Northern Ireland Act 1998 regulates the Northern Ireland Assembly and Executive. The Act includes many significant distinguishing features unique to the situation pertaining in Northern Ireland before the Belfast Agreement was reached. In particular, the Act provides for a power sharing executive, with offices allocated between differing political parties according to their electoral support. As discussed in more detail at p 454, the Assembly is given statutory power to exclude a Minister or junior Minister, or a political party, from holding office for a 12 month period if the Assembly resolves that he, she or it no longer enjoys the confidence of the Assembly on the basis that he or she is not committed to non-violence and exclusively peaceful and democratic means. The Act also provides for the protection of all citizens of Northern Ireland from discrimination on the grounds of religious belief and introduces a Human Rights Commission and Equal Opportunities Commission. The Act repeals, *inter alia*, in full, the Government of Ireland Act 1920, the Northern Ireland (Temporary Provisions) Act 1972, the Northern Ireland Assembly Act 1973, the Northern Ireland Constitution (Amendment) Act 1973, the Northern Ireland Act 1974, and, in part, the Northern Ireland Constitution Act 1973 and all of the Northern Ireland Act 1982 and the Northern Ireland (Elections) Act 1998.

As noted above, the completion of the devolution of power to the new Assembly was conditional upon the decommissioning of weaponry by the paramilitary organisations, under the terms of the Belfast Agreement. As a result of the failure of the IRA to decommission its arms, power reverted to the United Kingdom Parliament under the Northern Ireland Act 2000. Following further negotiations on the arms issue, power was once again transferred to the Northern Ireland Assembly and Executive. During the brief period of suspension, the Northern Ireland Assembly was suspended and no Acts could be passed by the Assembly, nor could the Assembly or any Committee hold meetings or conduct any business during the period of revocation. Ministers and chairpersons of statutory committees did not hold office during the revocation period. The functions of the North-South Ministerial Council and the British-Irish Intergovernmental Conference were not to be exercised. Following suspension, the Secretary of State had a statutory duty to initiate a review of the situation as required under the Belfast Agreement. The Secretary of State ended suspension through the making of a restoration order, taking into account the result of the review. When a restoration order is made, the persons holding office as First Minister and Deputy First Minister, and Ministers or junior Ministers and chairpersons of statutory committees, remain eligible to hold office and resume office on the effective date. If a restoration order is revoked by the Secretary of State, section 1 of the Northern Ireland Act 2000 comes into force once again.[1] The Secretary of State's powers are exercisable by statutory instrument.[2] While a suspension order is in effect, the functions of the First Minister and Deputy First Minister are exercisable by the Secretary of State, and the functions of Northern Ireland Ministers are exercised by a Northern Ireland Department.

The status of Northern Ireland

Section 1 of the Northern Ireland Act 1998 reiterates earlier pledges regarding the status of Northern Ireland, stating that:

> ... Northern Ireland in its entirety remains part of the United Kingdom and shall not cease to be so without the consent of a majority of the people of Northern Ireland voting in a poll held for the purposes of this section ...

Giving recognition to long held Republican ambitions, section 1 commits the government of the United Kingdom to give effect to the wishes of the people should a majority express the wish to cease to be part of the United Kingdom and form part of a united Ireland, following such agreement as may be made between the United Kingdom government and the government of Ireland.

The Executive

Part III of the Northern Ireland Act 1998 regulates the executive authorities. Within six weeks of the date of the first meeting of the Assembly, the Assembly elected the First Minister and Deputy First Minister. Each candidate for the post of First Minister and Deputy First Minister must stand for election jointly with the other candidate, and the two candidates must be elected by a majority of members voting in the election, requiring a majority of designated Nationalists voting and a majority of designated Unionists voting. If either the

---

1   Northern Ireland Act 2000, s 4.
2   *Ibid*, s 7.

First Minister or Deputy First Minister resigns or otherwise ceases to hold office, the other Minister shall also cease to hold office at that time, but may continue in office until a new election is held.[3] The Leader of the Ulster Unionists, David Trimble became First Minister and Seamus Mallon, the Social Democratic and Labour Party's (SDLP) deputy leader became Deputy First Minister.

Ministerial offices

The number of ministerial offices is determined by the First Minister and deputy First Minister acting jointly, but may not exceed 10, or such greater number as is approved by the Secretary of State.[4] The allocation of ministerial offices provided for under the Act is one designed to achieve power sharing between the political parties, in proportion to the number of seats held in the Assembly. The formula, the 'd'Hondt system' devised by the eighteenth century Belgian political scientist, is the number of seats in the Assembly held by members of the party on the day the Assembly first met following its election, divided by the number of Ministerial offices (if any) held by members of the party, plus one. Where this results in the same total for two parties, the party with the bigger number of first preference votes in the Assembly elections has the first choice of offices.[5] In the 1998 elections, the Ulster Unionist Party won 28 seats in the Assembly, the SDLP 24, the Democratic Unionist Party (DUP) 20 and Sinn Fein 18. The formula resulted in the Ulster Unionists having three seats on the Executive, the SDLP three, the DUP and Sinn Fein each having two.

An Executive Committee is established, comprising the First Minister, the Deputy First Minister and the Northern Ireland Ministers. The First Minister and Deputy First Minister are chairmen of the Committee.[6]

Ministers or Northern Ireland Departments have no power to make, confirm or approve any subordinate legislation, or do any act, so far as the legislation or act is incompatible with Convention rights or Community law, or discriminates against, or aids or incites another person to discriminate against, a person or class of person on the ground of religious belief or political opinion.[7] If any subordinate legislation made, confirmed or approved by a Minister or Northern Ireland Department contains provisions dealing with excepted or reserved matters, the Secretary of State may revoke the

---

3   Northern Ireland Act 1998, s 16.
4   *Ibid*, s 17.
5   *Ibid*, s 18.
6   *Ibid*, s 20.
7   *Ibid*, s 24.

legislation.[8] Section 26 provides that the Secretary of State may prohibit any action proposed to be taken by a Minister or Northern Ireland Department where it would be incompatible with international obligations, the interests of defence or national security or with the protection of public safety or public order. Equally, where the Secretary of State considers that action should be taken to give effect to international obligations, safeguard interests of defence or national security or protect public safety or public order, he may by order direct that the action shall be taken. Any subordinate legislation made which conflicts with the above interests may be revoked by the Secretary of State.[9]

Elections

Assembly elections are to be held in May every four years.[10] Provision is made for extraordinary elections, whereby, if the Assembly passes a resolution that it should be dissolved, the Secretary of State must propose a date for the election of the next Assembly.[11] Constituencies are those for parliamentary elections and each constituency returns six members.[12] Voting is by single transferable vote, defined under section 34(3) as being a vote:

(a) capable of being given so as to indicate the voter's order of preference for the candidates for election as members for the constituency; and

(b) capable of being transferred to the next choice when the vote is not needed to give a prior choice the necessary quota of votes or when a prior choice is eliminated from the list of candidates because of a deficiency in the number of votes given for him.

The Northern Ireland Assembly Disqualification Act 1975 regulates eligibility for membership, and a person claiming that a person purporting to be a member of the Assembly is disqualified may apply to the High Court of Justice in Northern Ireland for a declaration to that effect.[13]

The Assembly

The first task of the elected Assembly was to elect from among its members a Presiding Officer and deputies, positions analogous to the Speaker of the House of Commons and his or her deputy.[14] Consistent also with the Scotland

---

8   Northern Ireland Act 1998, s 25.
9   *Ibid*, s 26.
10   *Ibid*, s 31.
11   *Ibid*, s 32.
12   *Ibid*, s 33.
13   *Ibid*, ss 37 and 38.
14   *Ibid*, s 39.

Act 1998, there is established a corporate body, known as the Northern Ireland Assembly Commission, comprising the Presiding Officer and members of the Assembly, to perform the functions of providing property, staff and services, and other contractual functions.

All proceedings of the Assembly are regulated by Standing Orders. *Inter alia*, Standing Orders are to make provision for a register of members interests, and provisions requiring a member to declare any financial or other interest as specified in Standing Orders before taking part in any Assembly proceedings. Provision may be made for the prevention of a member with a registrable interest from participating in proceedings. A member who advocates or initiates any cause on behalf of another in consideration of any payment or benefit in kind, or urging another member so to act, may be excluded from Assembly proceedings. Any member who fails to comply with Assembly requirements may have his or her rights and privileges as a member withdrawn. A member contravening the provisions is guilty of an offence, and liable on summary conviction to a fine not exceeding level 5. Proceedings may not be taken without the consent of the Director of Public Prosecutions for Northern Ireland.[15]

As noted earlier, the Assembly has the power to exclude a Minister or junior Minister, or a political party, from the Assembly if that Minister or party does not enjoy the confidence of the Assembly. The Assembly may resolve that a person or party no longer enjoys its confidence on the basis that the person or party is not committed to non-violence and exclusively peaceful and democratic means; or because of any failure to observe any other terms of the pledge of office. If a resolution is passed, the Assembly may exclude that person or party from the Assembly or members of the political party may be excluded from holding office as Ministers or junior Ministers for a period of 12 months, which may be extended for a further period of 12 months. A motion for a resolution shall not be moved unless it is supported by at least 30 members of the Assembly, the First Minister and deputy First Minister acting jointly, or by the Presiding Officer. If the Secretary of State is of the opinion that the Assembly ought to consider such a resolution, he may serve a notice on the Presiding Officer requiring him to move a motion for the resolution. In forming an opinion, the Secretary of State must take into account whether the Minister or party:

(a) is committed to the use now and in the future of only democratic and peaceful means to achieve his, her or its objectives;

(b) has ceased to be involved in any acts of violence or of preparation for violence;

(c) is directing or promoting acts of violence by other persons;

---

15   Northern Ireland Act 1998, s 43.

(d) is co-operating fully with any Commission involved in decommissioning.

A resolution under section 30 'shall not be passed without cross-community support'.[16]

Legislation

The Northern Ireland Act 1998, section 5 provides for the making of Acts of the Assembly, but reserves for the United Kingdom Parliament the right to make laws for Northern Ireland, subject to the right of the Assembly to modify provisions made by Act of Parliament in so far as it is part of the law of Northern Ireland. The legislative competence of the Assembly is regulated by sections 6 and 7, and section 6(1) states that a provision of an Act is not law if it is outside the legislative competence of the Assembly. Provisions defined as outside legislative competence include those forming part of the law of a country or territory other than Northern Ireland, matters which are excepted and not ancillary to other provisions dealing with reserved or transferred matters,[17] provisions incompatible with Convention rights or Community law, matters discriminating against any person or class of person on the ground of religious belief or political opinion. The Minister in charge of the Bill shall make a statement to the effect that the Bill is within the legislative competence of the Assembly.[18] In addition, if the Presiding Officer decides that any provision of a Bill would not be within the legislative competence of the Assembly, that Bill is not to be introduced. The Presiding Officer must consider a Bill both on its introduction and before the Assembly reaches its final legislative stage, and if he considers that any provision is outside the Assembly's competence, he shall refer it to the Secretary of State and the Assembly shall not proceed with the Bill. The Attorney General for Northern Ireland may refer a Bill to the Judicial Committee of the Privy Council for a ruling as to whether a provision is within the legislative competence of the Assembly,[19] and the Judicial Committee may refer a question for a preliminary ruling of the European Court of Justice. Where such a reference is made, and the reference has not been disposed of, the Assembly may resolve to reconsider the Bill and the Presiding Officer must notify the Attorney General and the Attorney General request the withdrawal of the reference.[20] Bills shall not be submitted for the royal assent at any time when the Attorney General is entitled to make a reference under section 11 or such a reference has been made but not decided by the Judicial Committee, or if the Judicial

16 Northern Ireland Act 1998, s 30(8).
17 On reserved and excepted matters, see *ibid*, Scheds 2 and 3, respectively.
18 *Ibid*, s 9.
19 *Ibid*, s 12.
20 *Ibid*, s 12.

Committee has decided that any provision of a Bill is not within the legislative competence of the Assembly or a reference made has been withdrawn under section 12. If the Secretary of State considers that a Bill contains provisions which are incompatible with international obligations, the interests of defence or national security or the protection of public safety or public order, or would have an adverse effect on the operation of the single market within the United Kingdom, he may decide not to submit the Bill for royal assent.[21]

Resolving devolution issues

Schedule 10 defines and regulates proceedings in relation to devolution issues. A devolution issue is one relating to the legislative competence of the Assembly, whether the purported or proposed exercise of a function would be invalid by virtue of section 24 (discussed above), failures to comply with Convention rights or Community law or questions relating to excepted or reserved matters. In relation to proceedings in Northern Ireland, these may be initiated or defended by the Attorney General or the Attorney General for Northern Ireland. The First Minister and deputy First Minister acting jointly may defend proceedings.[22] A court, other than the House of Lords or Court of Appeal in Northern Ireland, may refer a devolution issue to the Court of Appeal in Northern Ireland.[23] A tribunal from which there is no appeal must refer any devolution issue to the Court of Appeal in Northern Ireland, and any other tribunal may make such a reference.[24] The Court of Appeal in Northern Ireland may refer any devolution issue to the Judicial Committee of the Privy Council.[25] Appeals from decisions on a devolution issue by the Court of Appeal in Northern Ireland lie to the Judicial Committee, but only with leave of the Court of Appeal in Northern Ireland or special leave of the Judicial Committee.[26] Devolution issues arising in England and Wales are similarly regulated, with references being made to the High Court, Court of Appeal and ultimately the Judicial Committee.[27] Devolution issues arising in proceedings in Scotland follow a similar process, references being made to the Inner House of the Court of Session or, in relation to criminal proceedings, to the High Court of Justiciary, with ultimate determination being made by the Judicial Committee.[28]

---

21 Northern Ireland Act 1998, s 14.
22 *Ibid*, Sched 10, paras 1, 3, 4.
23 *Ibid*, para 7.
24 *Ibid*, para 8.
25 *Ibid*, para 9.
26 *Ibid*, para 10.
27 *Ibid*, Pt III.
28 *Ibid*, Pt IV.

Witnesses and documents

The Assembly has the power to call for witnesses and documents, and may require any person to attend to give evidence or produce documents in relation to transferred matters concerning Northern Ireland and matters concerning statutory functions exercisable by Ministers or Northern Ireland Departments. Exceptions are made in relation to Ministers of the Crown or those in Crown employment and those discharging functions relating to excepted or reserved matters, and judges or members of tribunals exercising judicial power. A person is not obliged to answer questions or produce documents which he or she would be entitled to refuse to answer or produce in court proceedings in Northern Ireland.[29] A person failing or refusing to attend, or answer questions, or produce documents or who deliberately alters, suppresses, conceals of destroys any document is guilty of an offence carrying a fine not exceeding level 5 on the standard scale or to imprisonment for a period not exceeding three months.[30] It is a defence to prove that he or she had a reasonable excuse for the refusal or failure.[31] Standing orders may provide that the Presiding Officer administer an oath to a person giving evidence in proceedings, and requiring that person to take the oath. It is an offence to refuse, carrying the same penalty as above[32] For the purposes of the law of defamation, absolute privilege attaches to the making of statements in Assembly proceedings and the publication of a statement under the Assembly's authority.[33]

Members' interests

A register of members' interests is provided for under section 43. Members having a financial or other interest must declare that interest before participating in Assembly proceedings, and standing orders may include a provision preventing or restricting participation in proceedings of a member with a registrable interest. It is an offence to advocate or initiate any cause, or urge another member to do so, in consideration of any payment or benefit in kind. A person guilty of an offence is liable to a fine not exceeding level 5 on the standard scale. Proceedings may only be brought with the consent of the Director of Public Prosecutions for Northern Ireland.

---

29 Northern Ireland Act 1998, s 44.
30 *Ibid*, s 45.
31 *Ibid*, s 45(2).
32 *Ibid*, s 46.
33 *Ibid*, s 50.

Privilege

For the purposes of the law of defamation, absolute privilege attaches to the making of a statement in Assembly proceedings, and the publication of a statement under the Assembly's authority.[34]

Human rights and equal opportunities

The Act establishes a Human Rights Commission,[35] consisting of a Chief Commissioner and other Commissioners appointed by the Secretary of State, who, in making the appointments, must ensure so far as practicable that the Commissioners, as a group, are representative of the community in Northern Ireland.[36] The functions of the Commission include ensuring the adequacy and effectiveness of law and practice in relation to the protection of human rights, and reporting to the Secretary of State such recommendations as are considered necessary to improve law and practice. The Commission has a duty to advise the Assembly on the compatibility of Bills with human rights. The Commission is also under a duty to promote understanding and awareness of the importance of human rights in Northern Ireland. The Commission may conduct such investigations as it considers necessary or expedient. The Commission may also give assistance to individuals and bring proceedings in relation to human rights law and practice.[37] Where a person applies for assistance, the Commission may grant the application on the grounds that the case raises a question of principle; that it would be unreasonable to expect the person to deal with the case without assistance, or that there are other special circumstances warranting assistance. Assistance includes the provision of legal advice, arrangements for legal representation and any other assistance the Commission thinks appropriate.[38] No person, excepting the Attorney General, Attorney General for Northern Ireland, the Advocate General for Scotland or the Lord Advocate, may challenge the compatibility of legislation with Convention rights, or rely on Convention rights in legal proceedings, unless he or she is a 'victim' as interpreted by the European Court of Human Rights.[39]

The Act also establishes an Equality Commission for Northern Ireland, consisting of between 14 and 20 Commissioners appointed by the Secretary of State who, so far as is practicable, shall ensure that the Commissioners as a

---

34 Northern Ireland Act 1998, s 50.
35 See, also, *ibid*, Sched 7.
36 *Ibid*, s 68.
37 *Ibid*, s 69.
38 *Ibid*, s 70.
39 *Ibid*, s 71.

group are representative of the community in Northern Ireland.[40] The Equality Commission replaces bodies formerly promoting equal opportunities.[41] A statutory duty is imposed on all public authorities to 'have due regard to the need to promote equality of opportunity between persons of different religious belief, political opinion, racial group, age, marital status or sexual orientation; between men and women generally; between persons with a disability and those without and between those with dependants and those without. It is unlawful for a public authority to discriminate, or aid or incite another to discriminate, against a person or class of persons on the ground of religious belief or political opinion.[42]

North-South Ministerial Council and British-Irish Council

The Belfast Agreement established two new bodies, designed to facilitate and promote co-operative relations between the United Kingdom and the Republic of Ireland. The North-South Ministerial Council is to comprise representatives of the Irish government and the Northern Ireland Executive with a view to fostering cross-community participation in the Council. The First Minister and deputy First Minister acting jointly nominate Ministers to the Council. Agreements reached by meetings of the North-South Ministerial Council will be given effect by the Assembly, and no agreement entered into shall come into effect without the approval of the Assembly.[43]

A British-Irish Council is also established, which provides a forum for debate on matters of mutual interest between the British and Irish governments and representatives of the devolved institutions in Northern Ireland, Scotland and Wales, together with representatives from the Isle of Man and the Channel Islands.

In relation to both Councils, the First Minister and deputy First Minister acting jointly shall give the Executive Committee and the Assembly details of the date and agenda of meetings, and participating Ministers or junior Ministers will report to the Executive committee and to the Assembly on the proceedings in Council.

SCOTLAND

In 1989, a Scottish Constitutional Convention was set up, following the publication of *A Claim of Right for Scotland* by the Campaign for a Scottish

---

40   See, also, Northern Ireland Act 1998, Scheds 8 and 9.

41   *Ibid*, s 74.

42   *Ibid*, s 76.

43   *Ibid*, ss 52 and 53.

Assembly. It was argued that the people of Scotland had the right to govern themselves, and that the conventional doctrine of parliamentary sovereignty, as understood south of the border, had no basis in Scottish political thought. In Scotland, the preferred view is that the people, not Parliament, are sovereign. The final report of the Convention, *Scotland's Parliament, Scotland's Right* was published in November 1995.

While the former Conservative government was opposed to any devolution of power to either Scotland or Wales, the Labour government elected in 1997 declared in its election *Manifesto* that it favoured the devolution of power. In the words of the *Manifesto*, 'our proposal is for devolution not federation. A sovereign Westminster Parliament will devolve power to Scotland and Wales. The Union will be strengthened and the threat of separatism removed'.

The referendum

The Referendums (Scotland and Wales) Act 1997 provided the mechanisms for testing the wishes of the people. The Scottish people were asked to vote both for or against a Scottish Parliament, and for or against the proposition that the Scottish Parliament should have tax varying powers. The referendum in Scotland took place in September 1997. In favour of the establishment of a Scottish Parliament were 74.3 per cent of voters, and in favour of tax varying powers, 63.5 per cent.

Devolution and the Treaty of Union

The Union with Scotland Act 1706 and Union with England Act 1707 remain in force and have effect subject to the provisions of the Scotland Act 1998.[44] The government is firmly committed to strengthening the Union, and makes it clear that Scotland continues to form an integral part of the United Kingdom:

> The government want a United Kingdom which everyone feels part of, can contribute to, and in whose future all have a stake. The Union will be strengthened by recognising the claims of Scotland, Wales and the regions with strong identities of their own. The government's devolution proposals, by meeting these aspirations, will not only safeguard but also enhance the Union.[45]

---

44 Scotland Act 1998, s 37.
45 *Scotland's Parliament*, Cm 3658, 1997, London: HMSO, para 3.1.

THE SCOTTISH PARLIAMENT

The meeting of Parliament

The Scottish Parliament is unicameral and has a fixed four year term of office. The first general election for Parliament was held in May 1999 and subsequent general elections will be held on the first Thursday in May in the fourth calendar year following that in which the previous ordinary general election was held.[46]

Provision is made for the holding of extraordinary general elections under section 3. If Parliament resolves that it should be dissolved, and on the vote taken, not less than two-thirds of the total number of Members of Parliament vote in favour, then by proclamation the Queen may dissolve Parliament and require an extraordinary general election to be held. If an ordinary general election would otherwise take place within six months, that election shall not take place, but subsequent ordinary general elections will not be affected.

The electoral process

In the government's White Paper,[47] the government stated that:

> The government believe that electoral arrangements for the Scottish Parliament should reflect the will of the Scottish people. A constituency link will be the essential foundation of the new Scottish Parliament. However, it is also important to provide for greater proportionality to build stability into the overall settlement. It is therefore proposed that there be a significant number of additional members elected on a wider and proportional basis, in order to bring a closer relationship between votes cast and seats won.[48]

On the voting system, the government stated that:

> Members will be known as Members of the Scottish Parliament (MSPs). They will be elected in two different ways. The majority will be elected from constituencies which are the same as the constituencies of the Westminster Parliament except that Orkney and Shetland (which at the moment form one constituency) will become two separate constituencies thus making 73 in total. The remaining 56 Members – 'additional members' – will be selected from party lists drawn up for each of the current European Parliament constituencies. There will be seven additional members from each constituency.[49]

---

46 Scotland Act 1998, s 2(1).

47 HC Deb Vol 298 Col 1041, 24 July 1997; Vol 299 Col 456, 31 July 1997; HL Deb Vol 581 Col 1526, 24 July 1997; Vol 582 Col 185, 31 July 1997.

48 *Scotland's Parliament*, Cm 3658, 1997, London: HMSO, para 8.1.

49 *Ibid*, para 8.2.

The Scottish Parliament is established under section 1 of the Scotland Act 1998. The 129 seat Parliament is based in Edinburgh. The Parliament's first task was to elect a Presiding Officer and two deputies.[50] The role of Presiding Officer is analogous to that of the Speaker of the House of Commons, although distinctions between the two offices exist. For example, the Presiding Officer has been given statutory functions under the Act, *inter alia* in relation to the holding of general elections and by-elections,[51] notifications of filling of vacancies of regional seats,[52] notice of member's resignation,[53] administering oaths to witnesses,[54] the scrutiny of Bills to ensure they fall within the Parliament's legislative competence,[55] and making recommendations to the Queen in respect of the choice of First Minister and any person designated to exercise the functions of the First Minister.[56]

A Clerk of the Parliament, and Assistant Clerks, are appointed by the Scottish Parliamentary Corporate Body, comprising the Presiding Officer and four members of Parliament. The Parliamentary Corporation has functions defined under the Act, including the provision of property, staff and services required for Parliament's purposes,[57] entering into contracts, and bringing or defending proceedings against the Scottish Parliament.[58]

Parliamentary proceedings

Parliamentary proceedings are regulated by standing orders.[59] The Act confers on the Scottish Parliament the power to call for witnesses and documents, and provides for criminal penalties in the event of failure to comply with Parliament's directions. Under section 23, 'any person' may be required to attend Parliament to give evidence, or to produce documents 'in his custody or under his control', relating to any subject for which a member of the Executive has general responsibility. Section 23(3), (4), (5) and (6) limits the requirements to give evidence by Ministers of the Crown and civil servants, in order to avoid the situation where Ministers and civil servants find themselves accountable to both the United Kingdom and Scottish Parliament. Under sub-section (7), Parliament cannot require judges or

---

50   Scotland Act 1998, s 19. Standing orders will provide that persons holding office of Presiding Officer or Deputy do not represent the same political party: Sched 3, para 5.

51   *Ibid*, ss 2, 3 and 9.

52   *Ibid*, s 10.

53   *Ibid*, s 14.

54   *Ibid*, s 26.

55   *Ibid*, ss 32–35.

56   *Ibid*, ss 45 and 46.

57   *Ibid*, ss 19, 20 and 21.

58   See *ibid*, s 40.

59   *Ibid*, s 22.

members of tribunals to attend and give evidence. Where a person is required to attend, the Clerk will give written notice of the time and place at which the persons to attend, and the particular subjects concerning which he is required to give evidence, or the documents or type of documents which are to be produced, and the date by which they must be produced.[60] A person served with such notice, who refuses or fails to attend, or to answer questions, or who 'alters, suppresses, conceals or destroys any document which he is required to produce', or fails or refuses to produce such a document is guilty of an offence.[61] It is a defence to prove that the person concerned had a reasonable excuse for the refusal or failure. If found guilty, the person is liable to a fine not exceeding level 5 or to imprisonment for a period not exceeding three months.[62] Section 25 extends to Scotland only.[63] The Presiding Officer may administer an oath to any person giving evidence in proceedings of Parliament, and require that person to take the oath. A person refusing to take the oath when so required is guilty of an offence carrying the same penalty as under section 25(4).[64]

Legislation

The Scottish Parliament has the power to make Acts of Parliament within the sphere of competence laid down in the Act. Any Act which is outside the legislative competence of the Parliament is not law.[65] Section 28(7) makes clear that the legislative competence of the Scottish Parliament does not affect the power of the Parliament of the United Kingdom to make laws for Scotland. The member of the Scottish Executive in charge of a Bill must state, on or before its introduction in Parliament, that the provisions of the Bill are within the legislative competence of Parliament.[66] Additionally, the Presiding Officer must, on or before the introduction of a Bill in the Parliament, decide whether or not the provisions of the bill are within the legislative competence of Parliament.[67] It is for the Presiding Office to submit Bills for the Royal Assent, but he may not do so at any time when the Advocate General, Lord Advocate or Attorney General is entitled to refer the Bill to the Judicial Committee of the Privy Council to determine whether or not a Bill, or any of

---

60   Scotland Act 1998, s 24.
61   *Ibid*, s 25.
62   *Ibid*, s 25(3), 25(4).
63   *Ibid*, s 131.
64   *Ibid*, s 26.
65   *Ibid*, ss 28 and 29.
66   *Ibid*, s 31(1).
67   *Ibid*, s 31(2).

its provisions, are within the legislative competence of the Parliament.[68] A reference to the Judicial Committee may be made at any time during the four week period beginning with the passing of the Bill.[69] The Judicial Committee may request a preliminary ruling from the European Court of Justice under Article 177 (now, Article 234) of the Treaty of Rome.[70] To avoid excessive delay in the enactment of Bills, Parliament may resolve that it intends to reconsider a Bill which has been referred to the Privy Council and if it does so the person who referred it to the Privy Council must request the withdrawal of the reference from the European Court.[71] Where the Secretary of State for Scotland has reasonable grounds to believe that a Bill would be incompatible with international obligations or the interests of defence or national security, or would adversely modify the law relating to reserved matters, the Secretary of State may make an order prohibiting the Presiding Officer from submitting the Bill for Royal Assent.[72]

Section 29 stipulates that an Act is not law if it is outside the Parliament's legislative competence and states that a provision is outside its competence if it relates to the law of a country or territory other than Scotland; it relates to reserved matters; its is in breach of the restrictions in Schedule 4; it is incompatible with Convention rights or with Community law, or would remove the Lord Advocate from his position as head of the systems of criminal prosecution and investigation of deaths in Scotland. The most complex provisions relate to reserved matters and incompatibility with the restrictions in Schedule 4 of the Act, and these in turn must be read in conjunction with Schedule 5 which lists the matters reserved to the United Kingdom Parliament.

Schedule 4: enactments protected from modification

Paragraphs 4 to 6 prohibit the Scottish Parliament from amending or modifying the Scotland Act 1998. In addition, the Acts of Union are immune from amendment, as is the European Communities Act 1972 and assorted other specified Acts. Further there is a prohibition on modification of reserved matters.

---

68 Scotland Act 1998, ss 32 and 33.
69 *Ibid*, s 33(1).
70 *Ibid*, s 34.
71 *Ibid*, s 34(2).
72 *Ibid*, s 35.

Schedule 5: reserved matters

Part I of Schedule 5 lays down five general categories of matters reserved to the United Kingdom Parliament: the constitution; the registration of political parties; foreign affairs; Civil Service, defence and treason. Part II lists specific reservations under eleven broad heads, namely: financial and economic matters; home affairs, trade and industry; energy; transport; social security; regulation of the professions; employment; health and medicines; media and culture and miscellaneous. Matters reserved facilitate United Kingdom-wide uniformity, while devolving to the Scottish Parliament the power to regulate non-reserved matters according to national requirements. Schedule 5 also provides for certain exceptions to apply to particular reserved matters. For example under Head A: Financial and Economic Matters, which in turn has five sections covering fiscal, economic and monetary policy, the currency, financial services, financial markets and money laundering, an exception to fiscal, economic and monetary policy is provided for local taxes to fund local authority expenditure in Scotland, and in relation to financial services, an exception is made in relation to the dates of bank holidays. Accordingly, the scope of the legislative power devolved is defined within the Act, to the extent that precision and foreseeability allow. Inevitably, however, these detailed and complex provisions will give rise to questions as to the power devolved.

Schedule 6: devolution issues

A devolution issue is defined as:

(a) a question whether an Act of the Scottish Parliament or any provision of an Act of the Scottish Parliament is within the legislative competence of the Parliament;[73]

(b) a question whether any function (being a function which any person has purported, or proposing, to exercise) is a function of the Scottish Ministers, the First Minister or the Lord Advocate;

(c) a question whether the purported or proposed exercise of a function by a member of the Scottish Executive is, or would be, within devolved competence;

(d) a question whether a purported or proposed exercise of a function by a member of the Scottish Executive is, or would be, incompatible with any of the Convention rights or with Community law;

(e) a question whether a failure to act by a member of the Scottish Executive is incompatible with any of the Convention rights or with Community law;

---

73 Scotland Act 1998, Sched 6, Pt I, para 1.

(f) any other question about whether a function is exercisable within devolved competence or in or as regards Scotland and any other question arising by virtue of this Act about reserved matters.

It was seen above that section 29 of the Act states that an Act of the Scottish Parliament is not law so far as it is outside the legislative competence of the Parliament, and that provision is made for references to be made to the Judicial Committee of the Privy Council before a Bill receives the Royal Assent.[74] Challenges may arise by virtue of judicial review proceedings, or in the course of civil or criminal proceedings.

Part II of Schedule 6 details the procedures relating to proceedings in Scotland. Either the Advocate General or the Lord Advocate may institute proceedings, and the Lord Advocate may defend proceedings instituted by the Advocate General. This power is without prejudice to any power to institute or defend proceedings exercisable by any person.[75] Where a devolution issue is intimated in any legal proceedings, notice must be given to the Advocate General and the Lord Advocate.

Members' interests

Section 39 of the Scotland Act regulates Members' interests. It provides for a Register of interests and requires Members to register financial interests, including benefits in kind, and for Members to declare interests before taking part in any proceedings in Parliament relating to that matter. Members of Parliament are prohibited from 'advocating or initiating any cause or matter ... in consideration of any payment or benefit in kind ...' or from 'urging, in consideration of any such payment or benefit in kind, any other Member of the Parliament to advocate or initiate any cause or matter ...'. A Member of Parliament failing to comply with, or in contravention of the prohibition, is guilty of an offence, and liable on summary conviction to a fine not exceeding level 5 on the standard scale.

Parliamentary committees

A Parliamentary Bureau is established with the task of proposing the establishment, membership, remit and duration of committees. The Bureau also proposes the political party whose members are eligible to be the convenor (chairperson) and deputy convenor of the committee. The Bureau's proposals are subject to parliamentary approval. A number of mandatory committees have been established, which sit for the duration of a

---

74 Scotland Act 1998, ss 32–36.
75 *Ibid*, Sched 6, Pt II, para 4.

parliamentary session. these include the Procedures Committee, the Standards Committee, Finance Committee, Audit Committee, European Committee, Equal Opportunities Committee, Public Petitions Committee and Subordinate Legislation Committee. The functions of committees, set out in Standing Orders, are broadly to examine any matters which fall within their remit and regarded as 'competent matters'. In relation to such competent matters, Committees consider and report on the policy and administration of the Scottish Administration; consider proposals for legislation, primary or secondary, whether before the Scottish or United Kingdom Parliament, including pre-legislative scrutiny; consider European Community legislation; consider and report on any petitions referred to it by the Petitions Committee; consider the need for reform of the law; initiate legislation and consider financial proposals and the financial administration of the Scottish Administration. Committees have between five and fifteen members. In proposing the membership of committees the Bureau must have regard to the balance of the parties within the Parliament, and have regard to the qualifications and experience of potential members

A number of additional committees have been established, including Education Culture and Sport, Enterprise and Lifelong Learning, Finance, Health and Community Care, Justice and Home Affairs, Local Government, Procedures, Rural Affairs, Social Inclusion, Housing and Voluntary Sector, Standards, Subordinate Legislation and Transport and the Environment.

Parliamentary privilege

Section 41 provides that for the purposes of the law of defamation any statement made in proceedings of the Parliament and the publication of any statement under the authority of Parliament is absolutely privileged.

Maladministration

Section 91 of the Scotland Act makes provision for the investigation of complaints made to Members in respect of the exercise of functions by the Scottish Executive.

THE EXECUTIVE

Under section 44 of the Scotland Act 1998, there is established a Scottish Executive, whose members shall be the First Minister, and such Ministers as the First Minister may appoint, and the Lord Advocate and the Solicitor

General for Scotland. The First Minister is appointed by Her Majesty from among members of the Parliament, and holds office at Her Majesty's pleasure.[76] Members of the Executive are responsible to the Scottish Parliament.

The continuing role of the Secretary of State for Scotland

The Secretary of State for Scotland is responsible for focusing on promoting communication between the Scottish Parliament and Executive and between the United Kingdom Parliament and government on matters of mutual interests, and on representing Scottish interests in reserved matters.[77] The Secretary of State and the Scottish Executive meet in order to monitor progress.

Law Officers

The Law Officers of the Scottish Executive are the Lord Advocate and the Solicitor General for Scotland. The United Kingdom government also needs advice on Scottish law, and a new office of Scottish Law Officer to the United Kingdom government has been created.[78]

Scottish representation at Westminster

The problematic issue of continued Scottish representation at Westminster after devolution, particularly in relation to matters exclusively English (the 'West Lothian question'), has been addressed by initially continuing the same level of Scottish representation as hitherto. However, section 86 of the Scotland Act 1998 amends Schedule 2 to the Parliamentary Constituencies Act 1986 by omitting rule 1(2) requiring Scotland to have not less than 71 constituencies, and providing for Scottish representation in the future to be based on the same electoral quota as for England.

The West Lothian question

The government avoided the complexities of the West Lothian question which bedevilled the debate about devolution in previous times. The term derives from the Member of Parliament for West Lothian, Tam Dalyell, although the problem posed had been equally difficult in the nineteenth century in relation

---

76   Scotland Act 1998, s 45.
77   *Scotland's Parliament*, Cm 3658, 1997, London: HMSO, para 4.12.
78   *Ibid*, paras 4.8, 4.9.

to Irish Home Rule (on which, see Chapter 3), and later in relation to the devolution of legislative power to Northern Ireland between 1921 and 1972. In essence, the West Lothian question concerns over- or under-representation in the Westminster Parliament once legislative power is devolved to a regional Parliament.

The difficulty stems from continued regional representation in the Westminster Parliament. The first problem is that of regional representative participation in the legislative process as it relates exclusively to England. In simple terms, the argument made is that, if the Scottish Parliament has exclusive competence in relation to health matters, on what legitimate basis should Scottish Members of the Westminster Parliament have the right to influence health matters which relate exclusively to English people? On the other side of that particular coin, lies the fact that, whereas the Scottish Members of the Westminster Parliament may exert influence on purely English health issues, the Westminster Parliament and its Members, by contrast, have no equal right to influence the decisions of the Scottish Parliament in relation to the same matters.

When a government has a large majority, as the current government enjoys – or even a workable majority – the issue is less problematic. However, in a situation where a government has no clear and workable majority within the Westminster Parliament, the difficulty is more pronounced. In the latter situation, it may well be that the government of the day becomes dependent on Scottish representatives at Westminster in order to enact legislation. The question of legitimacy becomes more acute when the proposed legislation relates exclusively to an English matter and the correlative legislative power over that matter in relation to Scotland has been devolved to the Scottish Parliament.

This position was precisely that which faced the Labour government in the 1960s. In 1964, the Labour government was returned to Parliament with a majority of three. At that time, Northern Ireland enjoyed a degree of legislative autonomy from the rest of the United Kingdom, and Northern Irish representation at Westminster included 12 Ulster Unionist Members. In 1965, Parliament was considering the Manchester Corporation Bill and Rent Bill, which did not relate to Northern Ireland. The Ulster Unionist Members opposed the Bill and aligned themselves with the Conservative Opposition. The same position arose in relation to the Labour government's proposals to nationalise the steel industry. The Labour Prime Minister, Harold Wilson, addressed the issue directly when he stated that he:

> ... would hope that Northern Ireland Members who are here, and who are welcomed here, for the duties they have to perform on behalf of the United Kingdom in many matters affecting Northern Ireland, would consider their position in matters where we have no equivalent right in Northern Ireland.[79]

---

79   HC Deb Vol 711 Col 1561, 6 May 1965.

Possible solutions to the West Lothian question

A number of solutions have been proposed to the West Lothian question, each of which must be considered. First, it would be theoretically possible to exclude Scottish representation at Westminster. Secondly, it would be possible to reduce the strength of Scottish representation at Westminster in order to reduce the possibility of Scottish representatives alone having real power in a situation of a small majority, or minority, government. Thirdly, it would be possible to legislate to ensure that Scottish representatives only have a legislative role in relation to legislation concerning Scotland, and none in relation to legislation which has a purely English dimension (the 'in and out' approach).

Exclusion of Scottish representation

Short of devolution taking the form of a dismantling of the Union, which has endured for nearly 300 years, and conferring complete legal and political independence upon Scotland, this solution is not viable. The devolution of power falls far short of complete legislative independence. The Scottish Parliament enjoys legislative competence in relation to matters which are not reserved to the Westminster Parliament. Accordingly, in matters reserved to the Westminster Parliament, it is not tenable to argue that there should be no Scottish representation at Westminster and, *a fortiori*, that there should be no representation in relation to matters relating to Scotland which have been reserved to the Westminster Parliament. To adopt such a policy would ensure not the strengthening of the Union, but its rapid and ultimate demise and the break up of the United Kingdom.

The 'in and out' solution

This possible solution was one ruled out under the present government's insistence that the Union with Scotland be strengthened rather than weakened, and that Scottish Members of Parliament should continue to play a full role in the proceedings of the House of Commons. However, it is a solution which has long been considered in relation to solving the difficulties inherent in devolving legislative power to one region alone.

The 'in and out' solution was mooted in relation to Irish Home Rule,[80] but rejected by Gladstone as unworkable. The 'in and out' solution requires a mechanism whereby legislation is classified as applying to either the United Kingdom as a whole, or to Scotland in matters reserved to the United

---

80   On which, see Chapter 3.

Kingdom Parliament, or solely to England. Where legislative proposals relate to either the United Kingdom as a whole, or to Scotland in reserved matters, the 'in and out' solution would enable Scottish representatives to vote. However, if a matter related solely to England or England and Wales, (legislative competence over that matter in relation to Scotland having been devolved) Scottish representatives would be ineligible to vote on the matter. In relation to Irish Home Rule, it was suggested that it should be the Speaker of the House of Commons who classifies Bills for this purpose. If 'in and out' was not viable in the nineteenth century, it is likely not to be viable in the twenty-first century.

There also exists a different objection to this solution, which is less based on practicality, and is more principled. The problem involves governments with a small majority in Parliament and minority governments. In both cases the government may find itself dependent upon Scottish representation (and/or on other minority groups). Were the government to find itself in a position of dependence on Scottish representation, and the 'in and out' solution had been adopted, the Scottish representation on which the government was dependent would be absent in relation to legislation on a matter solely relating to England. Thus, the 'in and out' solution could lead to an otherwise, albeit barely, viable government being defeated. Moreover, in a situation where a government had no electoral support in Scotland, and the government has a weak majority, as occurred under the last Conservative government, that government could be held to ransom by Scottish representatives who support alternative policies.

Devolved and reserved powers

When power was devolved to the Northern Ireland Parliament, Stormont, which enjoyed limited legislative power between 1921[81] and 1972,[82] the legislation was framed in such a way that it was the powers to be devolved to Stormont, rather than the powers reserved to the Westminster Parliament, which were the principal focus of the legislation. In relation to devolution to Scotland, this process is reversed, the White Paper stating that 'all matters that are not specifically reserved ... will be devolved',[83] and further that:

> There are many matters which can be more effectively and beneficially handled on a United Kingdom basis. By preserving the integrity of the United Kingdom, the Union secures for its people participation in an economic unit which benefits business and provides access to wider markets and investment

---

81 Government of Ireland Act 1920.
82 Northern Ireland (Temporary Provisions) Act 1972; Northern Ireland Constitution Act 1973. See, now, the Northern Ireland Act 1998.
83 *Scotland's Parliament*, Cm 3658, 1997, London: HMSO, para 2.4.

and increases prosperity for all. Scotland also benefits from strong and effective defence and foreign policies and a sense of belonging to a United Kingdom.[84]

Powers devolved to the Scottish Parliament

The major areas over which the Scottish Parliament has legislative power were set out in the White Paper and include:

- *health* generally, including overall responsibility for the NHS in Scotland and public and mental health; also the education and training of health professionals and the terms and conditions of service of NHS staff and general practitioners;
- *school education,* including pre-five, primary and secondary education, the functions of Her Majesty's Inspectorate of Schools and teacher supply, training and conditions of service;
- *further and higher education,* including policy, funding, the functions of the Scottish Higher Education Funding Council (SHEFC) and student support;
- *science and research funding,* where supported through SHEFC and where it is undertaken in support of other devolved matters;
- *training policy and lifelong learning,* including all the training responsibilities presently exercised by the Scottish Office;
- *vocational qualifications,* including the functions of the Scottish Qualifications Authority;
- *careers advice and guidance;*
- *local government,* including local government finance and domestic and non-domestic taxation;
- *social work,* including the Children's Hearings system;
- *voluntary sector issues;*
- *housing,* including the functions of Scottish Homes;
- *area regeneration,* including the designation of enterprise zones;
- *land-use planning* and *building control;*
- *economic development,* including the functions of Scottish Enterprise, Highlands and Islands Enterprise and the local enterprise companies;
- *financial assistance to industry,* subject to common UK guidelines and consultation arrangements to be set out in a published concordat;
- *inward investment,* including the functions of Locate in Scotland;

---

84   *Scotland's Parliament,* Cm 3658, 1997, London: HMSO, para 3.2.

- promotion of *trade and exports* including the functions of Scottish Trade International;
- promotion of *tourism* including the functions of the Scottish Tourist Board;
- *passenger and road transport,* covering the Scottish road network, the promotion of road safety, bus policy, concessionary fares, cycling, taxis and minicabs, non-technical aspects of disability and transport, some rail grant powers, the Strathclyde Passenger Transport Executive and consultative arrangements in respect of public transport;
- appropriate *air and sea transport* powers, covering ports, harbours and piers, the provisions of freight shipping and ferry services, the activities of Highland and Islands Airports Ltd and planning and environmental issues relating to airports;
- *inland waterways;*
- *criminal law* and procedure, except for offences created in statute law relating to reserved matters including drugs and firearms;
- *civil law,* except in relation to matters which are reserved;
- *electoral law* in relation to local government elections;
- *judicial appointments,* subject to the appointments of the Lord President of the Court of Session and the Lord Justice Clerk being made by the Queen on the advice of the Prime Minister, on the basis of nominations from the Scottish Executive;
- the *criminal justice* and prosecution system;
- the *civil and criminal courts,* including the functions of the Scottish Courts Administration and the Court of Lord Lyon;
- *tribunals* concerned with devolved matters and the Scottish Council on Tribunals;
- *legal aid;*
- *parole,* the release of life sentence prisoners and alleged miscarriages of justice;
- *prisons,* including the functions of the Scottish Prison Service and the treatment of offenders;
- the *police and fire services,* including fire safety;
- *civil defence* and *emergency planning;*
- functions under various *international legal agreements* in devolved areas, for example relating to child abduction and the reciprocal enforcement of Maintenance Orders;
- *liquor licensing;*
- *protection of animals,* including protection against cruelty to domestic, captive and wild animals, zoo licensing, controlling dangerous wild animals and game;

- the *environment*, including environmental protection, matters relating to air, land and water pollution and the functions of the Scottish Environment Protection Agency; water supplies and sewerage; and policies designed to promote sustainable development within the international commitments agreed by the United Kingdom;

- *national heritage*, including countryside issues and the functions of Scottish Natural Heritage;

- *built heritage*, including the functions of Historic Scotland;

- *flood prevention, coast protection* and *reservoir safety*;

- *agriculture*, including responsibility for implementing measures under the Common Agricultural Policy, and for domestic agriculture including crofting, animal and plant health and animal welfare subject to suitable co-ordination arrangements to ensure consistency with the United Kingdom where required under European law or to protect the public, animal or plant health or animal welfare;

- *food standards*: the relationship between the powers to be exercised by the Scottish Executive and the proposed Food Agency, and the degree of United Kingdom co-ordination required to protect the public will be considered in the White Paper on the Agency to be issued in the autumn of 1998;

- *forestry*, including responsibility for implementing measures under the Common Fisheries Policy, subject to suitable co-ordination arrangements to ensure effective discharge of United Kingdom obligations; domestic fisheries matters including inshore sea fisheries, salmon and freshwater fisheries and aquaculture;

- *sport*, including the activities of the Scottish Sports Council;

- the *arts*, including the functions of the National Library of Scotland, the National Museums of Scotland, the National Galleries of Scotland, the Scottish Museums Council, the Scottish Arts Council, Scottish Screen and support for Gaelic;

- *statistics, public registers and records*, including the responsibilities of the Keeper of the Registers, the Keeper of the Records, and the Registrar General for Scotland.[85]

---

85 *Scotland's Parliament*, Cm 3658, 1997, London: HMSO, para 2.4.

Financial arrangements[86]

The Scottish Parliament has the power to increase or decrease the basic rate of income tax set by the United Kingdom Parliament by up to three pence in the pound.[87] The Inland Revenue will continue to administer tax variations.

Since the 1970s, there has existed a 'block and formula' system of funding Scotland's public expenditure programmes. There have been adjustments made to this arrangement, and the Scottish Parliament also has tax varying powers which enable it to raise revenue independently. The Parliament is entitled to determine its own expenditure priorities. The Parliament has powers to control Scottish local government expenditure and to finance local government. The Parliament also has control over the form of local taxation, both domestic and non-domestic. There is a statutory duty to maintain effective scrutiny and audit arrangements.

Debating powers

The Scottish Parliament is able to examine devolved matters, and debate all matters irrespective of whether they are devolved or reserved.[88]

Scotland and the European Union and Community

While relations with Europe are the responsibility of the United Kingdom Parliament and government, the Scottish Parliament and Executive plays an important role in relation to those aspects of European Union affairs which affect devolved areas. The government has promised to ensure that Scottish Office Ministers play a full role in European Union Councils. Scottish Office officials will participate in discussion with the relevant Whitehall department. The Scottish Executive and officials will be directly involved in the government's decision making and formulation of policy in relation to European Union matters.

The Scottish Parliament scrutinises European Union legislative proposals 'to ensure that Scotland's interests are properly reflected'. Responsibility for ensuring the implementation of European Union obligations lies with the Scottish Executive. The overall approach to be pursued is as follows:

---

86 See Scotland Act 1998, Pts III and IV.
87 *Ibid*, Pt IV.
88 *Scotland's Parliament*, Cm 3658, 1997, London: HMSO, para 2.5.

The guiding principle which the United Kingdom government sets out to establish in the relationship with the Scottish Executive on European Union matters is that there should be the closest possible working relationship and involvement. Provided the Scottish Executive is willing to work in that spirit of collaboration and trust, there will be an integrated process which will build upon the benefits of the current role of the Scottish Office within government. Taken together, these arrangements will allow Scotland, within the United Kingdom, to develop its role in the European Union.[89]

The Scottish Parliament and local government and other bodies

Relations with local government and other public bodies are based on the following principles:

(a) the Scottish Parliament should set the national framework within which other Scottish public bodies operate;

(b) local authorities, non-departmental public bodies and other Scottish public bodies should be open and accountable to the Scottish people through the Scottish Parliament and its Executive or, in the case of local authorities, directly through local elections.[90]

General responsibility for legislation and policy relating to local government lie with the Scottish Parliament.[91] The Scottish Parliament has responsibility for all Scottish public bodies whose functions and services are devolved.[92]

WALES

The previous attempt to devolve power to Wales has been discussed in Chapter 3. Consistent with the Labour government's commitment to greater accountability of government and closer links between government and the people through enhanced regional decision making, an Assembly for Wales has been established. However, whereas the Scottish Parliament has full legislative powers in relation to devolved matters, the Welsh Assembly's role and functions are more limited.

Rather than devolve legislative power to a Welsh Parliament, the Government of Wales Act 1998 provides for a directly elected Assembly which has the responsibilities currently exercised by the Secretary of State for Wales. The devolution is thus conferring administrative rather than legislative

---

89 *Scotland's Parliament*, Cm 3658, 1997, London: HMSO, para 5.12.

90 *Ibid*, para 6.3.

91 *Ibid*, para 6.5.

92 *Ibid*, para 6.8.

competence. The government's White Paper,[93] *A Voice for Wales: The Government's Proposals for a Welsh Assembly*,[94] perceived a 'democratic deficit' in the administrative arrangements for Wales. Until devolution, the majority of administrative matters were the responsibility of the Welsh Office. Other bodies, such as health authorities and National Health Service Trusts, and unelected bodies, such as the Welsh Development Agency and Further and Higher Education Funding Councils and *Tai Cymru*, were not accountable to the Welsh people. The only directly accountable bodies were local authorities. The devolution of administrative competence to the Welsh Assembly to redresses this lack of local accountability.

The referendum

The result of the referendum held to determine the people's wishes in respect of devolved powers was less clear-cut than that of the Scottish referendum. Only 50 per cent of the electorate voted, as compared with 60 per cent in the Scottish referendum, and 50.3 per cent voted in favour of the establishment of an Assembly. A majority of voters in 11 of the 22 local government areas voted in favour.

THE WELSH ASSEMBLY

Meetings of the Assembly

The Government of Wales Act 1998 established the Welsh Assembly.[95] As with the Scottish Parliament, the Assembly sits for a fixed four year term of office. The Assembly has 60 Members. Unlike the Scottish Parliament, however, the Assembly has no power to dissolve itself before the end of the four year term of office. The Assembly is staffed by existing Welsh Office staff. The first Assembly met in 1999. Initial Standing Orders for the Assembly have been drawn up by an all-party Commission. The Assembly runs under a committee system. An Executive Committee provides the overall direction for the Assembly and comprises members of the majority party alone. Regional Committees have been established to ensure that the needs of each area of

---

93 Debated in the House of Commons, HC Deb Vol 298 Col 753, 22 July 1997, Vol 298 Col 1119, 25 July 1997; HL Deb Vol 581 Col 1322, 22 July 1997.
94 *A Voice for Wales: The Government's Proposals for a Welsh Assembly*, Cm 3718, 1997, London: HMSO.
95 Government of Wales Act 1998, s 1.

Wales are properly considered. The Regional Committees are advisory bodies only and do not have specific functions or decision making powers.

Members of the Assembly are salaried, and allowances are payable.[96]

The electoral system

The additional member electoral system is employed for elections.[97] There are 40 constituency Members, elected on the simple majority system, and 20 additional members elected from the party list. Each voter has two votes – one for the constituency Member and one for the additional member. The first elections took place in the spring of 1999. Thereafter, elections take place every four years, on the first Thursday in May.[98]

THE LEADER AND EXECUTIVE COMMITTEE

The overall political direction of the Assembly is provided by a Leader of the Assembly, elected by the Assembly, and an Executive Committee.[99] The Executive Committee, headed by the Leader, comprises leaders of differing subject committees. The Act allows for the Executive Committee to be made up of members of a single political party, and to sit in private. The Committee is thus envisaged to be the equivalent of the British Cabinet. The Leader of the Committee faces questions in the Assembly concerning all issues.

Welsh representation at Westminster

Because the Assembly does not have devolved legislative powers, the West Lothian question does not arise. The Secretary of State for Wales and Welsh Members of Parliament continue to play a full role at Westminster, but one which also involves a new partnership with the Assembly.[100] The number of Welsh Members remains unchanged.

---

96 Government of Wales Act 1998, s 16.
97 *Ibid*, s 4.
98 *Ibid*, s 3.
99 *Ibid*, s 56.
100 *A Voice for Wales: The Government's Proposals for a Welsh Assembly*, Cm 3718, 1997, London: HMSO, para 3.33.

The relationship between Westminster and the Assembly

The United Kingdom Parliament at Westminster continues to legislate for Wales. Members of the Assembly need to develop a close partnership with Welsh Members of Parliament. The White Paper stated that the government intended that the Assembly should be able to 'seek to influence legislation which is being considered at Westminster'.[101] The Secretary of State for Wales is under a statutory duty to consult the Assembly about the government's legislative programme, after it has been announced in the Queen's Speech, and the Assembly, following debate, may draft its response. The Secretary of State is able to attend Assembly debates, but not entitled to vote.

In relation to subordinate legislation, however, the Executive Committee and subject committees have power to prepare secondary legislation for submission to the Assembly for debate and approval. Such pieces of secondary legislation are known as Assembly Orders. A subordinate legislation scrutiny committee has been established to consider draft statutory instruments and to report to the Assembly.[102] The Assembly has the power to revoke, replace or amend such legislation in the same manner as the Secretary of State had formerly been able to do. Proposed Orders relating to Wales are scrutinised by the Assembly's subject committees.[103]

The powers of the Welsh Assembly

As stated above, the Assembly takes over many of the responsibilities which formerly lay with the Secretary of State for Wales. Part II of the Government of Wales Act 1998 defines the functions of the Assembly. Section 22 provides for the transfer of ministerial functions to the Assembly, by the means of Orders in Council. Any ministerial function exercisable by a Minister of the Crown in relation to Wales may be transferred. The Order in Council may also direct that any function transferred may be exercisable by the Assembly concurrently with the Minister of the Crown, or alternatively direct that a function exercisable by a Minister of the Crown in relation to Wales shall be exercisable by the Minister only with the agreement of, or after consultation with, the Assembly.[104]

Schedule 2 of the Act specifies the matters which are to be devolved and for which subject committees are to be established. These are:

---

101 Government of Wales Act 1998, para 3.38.

102 *Ibid*, s 58.

103 *A Voice for Wales: The Government's Proposals for a Welsh Assembly,* Cm 3718, 1997, London: HMSO, paras 4.22–4.24.

104 Government of Wales Act 1998, s 22.

- agriculture, forestry, fisheries and food;
- ancient monuments and historic buildings;
- culture (including museums, galleries and libraries);
- economic development;
- education and training;
- the environment;
- health and health services;
- highways;
- housing;
- industry;
- local government;
- social services;
- sport and tourism;
- town and country planning;
- transport;
- water and flood defence;
- the Welsh language.

The Committee structure

In addition to the Executive Committee, the Assembly is required to establish Committees required under the Act, and other such Committees and sub-committees as the Assembly considers appropriate.[105]

Subject committees are established with responsibilities to the fields in which the Assembly has functions. A member of the Executive Committee who has responsibility for a particular matter is a member of the Subject Committee. In addition, a Subordinate Legislation Committee is established to consider 'relevant Welsh subordinate legislation' and 'Assembly general subordinate legislation'. Members of the Committee are elected by the Assembly from its members and so far as practicable shall ensure the balance of the parties in the Assembly is reflected in the Committee.[106] An Audit Committee is established under section 60, its members elected from Assembly members, again reflecting, so far as practicable, party political representation in the Assembly. Section 61 provides for the establishment of

---

105 Government of Wales Act 1998, ss 54 and 55.
106 *Ibid*, ss 58 and 59.

regional committees. A Committee for North Wales is established, and the Assembly may also establish a committee for each of the other regions of Wales.

Members' interests

A register of interest is established, requiring any Assembly member who has financial interest or other interest in any matter to be registered and for declarations of interest to be made before participating in Assembly proceedings. Members are prohibited from advocating any cause on behalf of any person in consideration of payments or benefits in kind, or to urge another Assembly member to advocate or initiate any cause in consideration of any payment or benefit in kind.[107] It is an offence to act in violation of the section 72 procedures, and a person found guilty of an offence is liable on summary conviction to a fine. Prosecutions may only be instituted by or with the consent of the Director of Public Prosecutions. Similar provisions to those in the Scotland Act relate to the attendance of witnesses, giving of evidence and production of documents.[108]

Privilege

Section 77 provides that any statement made for the purposes of, or for purposes incidental to proceedings of the Assembly (including committee proceedings), and the publication of reports of such proceedings, are absolutely qualified for the purposes of the law of defamation.

The continuing role of the Secretary of State for Wales

While many of the powers exercised by the Secretary of State are transferred to the Assembly, the Executive Committee and its Subject Committees, the Secretary of State continues to play a pivotal role. The Secretary of State continues to represent Wales in Cabinet, having listened to the views of the Assembly, although he or she is not bound by the Assembly's views. The Secretary of State also meets regularly with the Executive Committee to exchange views about government policy. The Secretary of State is entitled to attend and participate in proceedings of the Assembly, but not to vote or to attend committee proceedings.[109]

---

107 Government of Wales Act 1998, s 72.
108 *Ibid*, ss 74 and 75.
109 *Ibid*, s 76.

The Assembly and the Welsh economy

A principal thrust behind the government's devolution of power is economic. The economy of Wales was formerly dominated by heavy industry – coal and steel – but has now diversified into more modern manufacturing industries. Nevertheless, as the White Paper made clear, economic prosperity is not evenly spread in Wales and there remain areas with high unemployment, poor health, poor housing and social deprivation. As a result, Welsh gross domestic product per head remains fixed at around 84 per cent of the UK average.[110]

The government considered that the Assembly would provide the driving force in relation to economic growth and recovery. The government summarised the role of the Assembly in relation to economic affairs as follows:

The Assembly will:

(a) provide leadership in setting a new economic agenda for Wales attuned to the needs of Wales;

(b) deliver its programmes through a new economic powerhouse – the expanded Welsh Development Agency, which will take on the functions of the Development Board for Rural Wales and the Land Authority for Wales;

(c) develop its policies in partnership with local authorities, industry, further and higher education, Training and Enterprise Councils and the voluntary sector;

(d) seek further inward investment, widening the Welsh industrial and commercial base;

(e) forge close and dynamic international links with other regions in Europe.[111]

Financial matters[112]

Wales had been managed under a block formula, with the Secretary of State for Wales responsible for over half of government expenditure in Wales. The 1997–98 provision for the block, including central government support for local authorities, was £6,636 billion. Now that the Assembly is established, these arrangements will continue, save that the Secretary of State determines how much of the block should be reserved for his office's costs, and the

---

110 *A Voice for Wales: The Government's Proposals for a Welsh Assembly*, Cm 3718, 1997, London: HMSO, para 1.26.

111 *Ibid*, Chapter 2.

112 See Government of Wales Act 1998, Pt IV.

remainder is available to the Assembly. The Assembly manages its own spending priorities, and reports annually on expenditure. Wales continues to receive an agriculture allocation under the European Union's Common Agriculture Policy.

Resolving disputes about devolution issues

The White Paper stated that if the Assembly exceeded its powers, the government would be able to challenge the *ultra vires* use of power in the courts. In addition, where devolution issues arise in civil or criminal proceedings before either courts or tribunal, the Act stipulates the procedure to be followed. Section 109 and Schedule 7 of the Act regulate such challenges. A devolution issue is defined as:

> (a) a question whether a purported or proposed exercise of any function by the Assembly is, or would be, within the powers of the Assembly (including a question whether a purported or proposed exercise of a function by the Assembly is, or would be, incompatible with Community law or any of the Convention rights); or
>
> (b) a question whether the Assembly has failed to comply with any Community obligation which is an obligation of the Assembly.[113]

Under paragraph 2, a devolution issue shall not be taken to arise:

> ... in any proceedings merely because of any contention of a party to the proceedings which appears to the court or tribunal before which the proceedings take place to be frivolous or vexatious.

Proceedings to determine a devolution issue may be instigated by the Attorney General, but that right does not preclude the right of any other person to institute proceedings. Where a devolution issue arises in judicial proceedings, a court or tribunal shall order notice of the issue to be given to the Attorney General and the Assembly, unless the Assembly is party to the proceedings. A magistrates' court may refer any devolution issue which arises before it in civil proceedings to the High Court. A court may refer a devolution issue which arises in civil proceedings to the Court of Appeal.[114] This paragraph does not apply to a magistrates' court, the Court of Appeal or the House of Lords, or to the High Court if the devolution issue arises in proceedings on a reference under paragraph 6 (which provides for references from the magistrates' court as above).[115] A tribunal from which there is no appeal must refer any devolution issue to the Court of Appeal, and any other tribunal may so refer a devolution issue.

---

113 Government of Wales Act 1998, Sched 7, para 1.
114 *Ibid*, Sched 7, paras 4, 5, 6.
115 *Ibid*, Sched 7, para 7(2).

Where a devolution issue arises in criminal proceedings, a court, other than the Court of Appeal or the House of Lords, may refer any devolution issue which arises before it to the High Court, if the proceedings are summary proceedings, or to the Court of Appeal if the proceedings are proceedings on indictment.[116]

Where a devolution issue in *any* proceedings arises before the Court of Appeal, the issue may be referred to the Judicial Committee of the Privy Council.[117] An appeal against a determination of a devolution issue by the High Court or the Court of Appeal on a reference under paragraphs 6, 7, 8 or 9 shall lie to the Judicial Committee, but only with the leave of the High Court or the Court of Appeal or, failing such leave, with special leave of the Judicial Committee.[118]

The Welsh Assembly and the European Union and Community

While the United Kingdom government remains responsible for issues arising out of membership of the European Union, it is recognised that Wales needs a strong voice in Europe.[119] The Assembly is able to scrutinise legislative proposals and other European documents. The Assembly also has the responsibility for ensuring that European Union obligations are implemented and enforced, and to meet any financial penalties which may arise out of failure to implement or enforce Union obligations. Within the framework of the Council of Ministers, the Secretary of State for Wales participates in meetings of the Council. The Wales European Centre in Brussels continues to act as a facilitator and source of advice on European matters. Members of the Assembly represent Wales on the Committee of the Regions. European Structural Funds are an important source of funding for the regeneration of the Welsh economy. It is estimated that payments under these funds amount to £1,280 million in the five years to 1995 to 2000. The Welsh Office had formerly been responsible for negotiations over the funds, and for their implementation and management. The role of the Welsh Office in these matters has been transferred to the Assembly.[120]

---

116 Government of Wales Act 1998, Sched 7, para 9(a), (b).

117 *Ibid*, Sched 7, para 10.

118 *Ibid*, Sched 7, para 11.

119 *A Voice for Wales: The Government's Proposals for a Welsh Assembly*, Cm 3718, 1997, London: HMSO, para 3.46.

120 *Ibid*, paras 3.46–3.55.

The Assembly and local authorities and other public bodies[121]

The Assembly works in partnership with local authorities, other public bodies and voluntary bodies, in order to ensure greater local democracy and accountability. The funding of local authorities has been taken over by the Assembly from the Welsh Office.[122]

The Assembly has been given significant powers in relation to appointments to Welsh public bodies, taking over responsibility from the Secretary of State for Wales. The Assembly also has power to issue directions to various bodies (quangos) and to monitor their performance. In relation to unelected bodies in Wales, such as the Welsh Tourist Board, the Assembly has power to restructure bodies in order to ensure improved economic effectiveness and efficient working.[123] In a major rationalisation of public bodies, the Welsh Development Agency, which plays a pivotal role in economic matters, has been reformed and takes over the responsibilities of the Development Board for Rural Wales, which has been abolished.[124] The Agency also assumes the powers and functions formerly vested in the Land Authority for Wales.[125]

LONDON: THE GREATER LONDON AUTHORITY AND MAYOR

In addition to the government's firm commitment to devolution to Scotland and Wales, and the future consideration of devolution to the English regions, the government intended to introduce an elected 'strategic authority' for London. As noted below, the Greater London Council (GLC), which formerly represented a centralising focus for the capital city, was abolished in 1985. Many of the GLC's functions reverted to the individual London councils. London was unique in being a capital city without an elected Mayor and centralised area government. This perceived deficiency has been redressed. The government's White Paper, *A Mayor and Assembly for London*, proposed an elected Mayor and 25 seat Greater London Authority. The Authority does not have direct tax raising powers, but revenue will be raised from road tolls and parking fees. In addition, the Authority is funded by central government. A

---

121 See *A Voice for Wales: The Government's Proposals for a Welsh Assembly*, Cm 3718, 1997, London: HMSO, Chapter 3.

122 Government of Wales Act 1998, ss 111 and 112.

123 *Ibid*, *A Voice for Wales*, para 3.23.

124 Government of Wales Act 1998, ss 121–28.

125 *Ibid*, ss 129–35.

referendum held in the spring of 1998 established popular support for the proposal.[126] The Greater London Authority Act 1999 regulates the Authority.

Elections

The first election was held in May 2000, electing an Assembly and Mayor for a four-year term of office.[127] Every eligible elector has one vote for the mayoral candidate, one vote for an Assembly member and one vote – a 'London vote' – for a registered political party.

The simple majority voting system is used for the mayoral election unless there are three or more candidates. Where three or more candidates stand, the Mayor is elected under the supplementary vote system, a vote which indicates the voter's first and second preferences from among the candidates.[128] The Assembly members are elected under the simple majority system.[129] The London vote, for a registered political party which has submitted a list of candidates to be London members, or an individual who is a candidate to be a London member, is calculated according to Part II of Schedule 2 of the Act. The qualifications for election to be Mayor or an Assembly member are that the person must be a Commonwealth citizen; citizen of the Republic of Ireland or citizen of the European Union and be 21 years of age.[130] In addition, the candidate must have demonstrable links with Greater London, either by being a local government elector for Greater London, or through residency or through principal employment in Greater London throughout the preceding 12 months.

The Greater London Authority

The general power of the Assembly, as defined in Part II of the Act, is to 'do anything which it considers will further any one or more of its principal purposes, which are defined as being:

(a) promoting economic development and wealth creation in Greater London;

(b) promoting social development in Greater London; and

(c) promoting the improvement of the environment in Greater London.

In deciding whether or how to exercise these powers, the Authority must comply with the general principles of exercising power so as to also further

---

126 Under the Greater London Authority (Referendum) Act 1998.
127 Greater London Authority Act 1999, s 3.
128 *Ibid*, s 4(2), (3) and Sched 2, Pt I.
129 *Ibid*, s 4(4).
130 *Ibid*, s 20.

the remaining principal purpose(s) and securing, over a period of time, a reasonable balance between furthering each of its principal purposes, and have regard to the effect of its exercise of power on the health of persons in Greater London and the achievement of sustainable development in the United Kingdom, and shall act in such a way as to promote these objectives, unless such action would 'not reasonably practicable in all the circumstances of the case'. The Secretary of State may issue guidance to the Authority in relation to the above general power.[131] The requirements of consultation with London councils and representative voluntary bodies and interest groups are defined in section 32. Functions conferred on the Authority under section 32 are exercisable by the Mayor acting on behalf of the Authority. All functions conferred on the Mayor acting on behalf of the Authority, or on the Authority alone, or on the Mayor and Authority jointly are exercisable only by the Mayor acting on behalf of the Authority, subject to any express provision to the contrary in the Act. Section 38 makes provision for the delegation of functions exercisable by the Mayor to designated bodies.

The Authority is regulated by Standing Orders defining its procedures, which are made in consultation with the Mayor. The office of Chair and Deputy Chair of the London Assembly is created. The function of the Chair is to chair meetings of the Assembly and exercise any other functions imposed under the Act.[132] The Chair and Deputy Chair are elected by the Assembly from members of the Assembly.[133] The Assembly is required to meet initially within 10 days of an election for the purpose of electing the Chair and Deputy Chair and thereafter on 10 occasions in each calendar year, the first meeting being held within 25 days of the election.[134] The Assembly may arrange for any of its functions to be exercised by a committee or sub-committee of the Assembly, and may delegate functions relating to staff appointments and terms and conditions of appointment (under sections 67 and 70 respectively) to an appointed member of staff of the Authority. No delegation of functions under section 20A of the Police Act 1996 is permitted.[135] The Local Government Act 1972, Part VA, regulating access to meetings and documents, applies to the Assembly and its committees, with the exception of confidential information and exempt information which may be withheld from the press and the public.

The Assembly is under a statutory duty to keep under review the Mayor's exercise of statutory functions, and has the power to investigate and report on any actions and decision of the Mayor, actions and decisions of any member

---

131 Greater London Authority Act 1999, s 30.

132 *Ibid*, s 50.

133 *Ibid*, s 51.

134 *Ibid*, s 52.

135 *Ibid*, s 54.

of staff of the Authority, matters relating to the principal purposes of the Authority and any other matters which the Assembly considers to be of importance to Greater London.[136] The Assembly may submit proposals to the Mayor, but this function cannot be delegated to a committee or sub-committee.[137]

Witnesses and documents

The Assembly has the power to call for witnesses and documents. Consistent with section 23 of the Scotland Act 1998 and sections 74 and 75 of the Government of Wales Act 1998, the Assembly may require certain categories of person to attend, and the power may also be exercised by Assembly committees, but not by an individual committee member or member of staff of the Authority.[138] Certain categories of information, and documents, which a person required to attend may refuse to disclose may be prescribed by the Secretary of State.[139] Refusal or failure to attend proceedings as required, or failure to answer questions, or produce required documents, or the alteration, suppression, concealment or destruction of documents required to be produced is an office. On conviction a person is liable to a fine not exceeding level 5 on the standard scale, or a term of imprisonment not exceeding three months. A person is not obliged to answer questions or produce documents which he would be entitled to refuse to answer or produce before court proceedings in England and Wales.[140]

Ethical standards

Under section 66, the Secretary of State may issue guidance to the Authority regarding the ethical standards for the Mayor, Assembly members and member of the Authority's staff, and other persons who are members of advisory committees or sub-committees of the Assembly. Such guidance may include the disclosure and registration of interests, the exercise of functions in relation to which the relevant person has an interest in the matter in question, and voting. The Secretary of State may also issue guidance on the establishment and functions of committees concerned with ethical standards and the prescription of model codes of conduct.[141]

---

136 Greater London Authority Act 1999, s 59.
137 *Ibid,,* s 60.
138 *Ibid,* s 61 and 62.
139 *Ibid,* s 63.
140 *Ibid,* s 64.
141 *Ibid,* s 66.

Bills in Parliament

The Authority may promote a local Bill in Parliament, or oppose any local Bill which affects inhabitants of Greater London. The Mayor acts on behalf of the Authority, having consulted the Assembly.[142] In addition, the Mayor on behalf of the Assembly, and following consultation with it, may request a London local authority to include provisions in local Bills. A local Bill promoted in Parliament by a London local authority may include provisions which affect the exercise of statutory functions by the Authority or any of the functional bodies, only if the Authority gives its written consent.[143]

The London Mayor

The Mayor is under a duty to prepare, keep under review and revise strategies relating to transport, the London Development Agency, spatial development,[144] the London Biodiversity Action Plan, municipal waste management, air quality, ambient noise and culture.[145] In preparing or revising any strategy the Mayor must have regard to the principal purposes of the Authority, the effect which the strategy would have on the health of persons in Greater London and the achievement of sustainable development in the United Kingdom. In addition, the strategy must be consistent with national policies and international obligations as notified by the Secretary of State, available resources and the desirability of promoting and encouraging the use of the River Thames safely, in particular for the provision of passenger transport services and freight.[146]

In preparing or revising strategies, the Mayor must consult the Assembly, the functional bodies, each London borough council, the Common Council of the City of London and any other 'appropriate person or body'.[147] Adequate publicity must be given to the strategies, and copies provided to the Common Council and each London borough council.[148] The Secretary of State may issue directions to the Mayor to prepare and publish any strategy which the Mayor has not prepared and to stipulate the period in which the strategy must be prepared.[149]

---

142 Greater London Authority Act 1999, s 77.

143 *Ibid*, ss 78 and 79.

144 Separate provision is made for revision of spatial development strategy under s 340.

145 *Ibid*, ss 41, 142; Regional Development Agencies Act 1998, s 7A(2); Greater London Authority Act 1999, Pt VIII; Greater London Authority Act 1999, ss 352, 353, 362, 370 and 376, respectively.

146 Greater London Authority Act 1999, s 41(4), (5).

147 *Ibid*, s 42.

148 *Ibid*, s 43.

149 *Ibid*, s 44.

The appointment of staff

The Mayor may appoint not more than two persons as his political advisers, and not more than 10 other members of staff. The Assembly may also appoint such staff as it considers necessary for the proper discharge of functions of the Authority.[150] Political restrictions and disqualifications are regulated by section 68. Sections 1 and 2 of the Local Government and Housing Act 1989 have effect in relation to the Authority, Transport for London and the London Development Agency.

Accountability

The Mayor is under a duty to report to the Assembly, not less than three clear working days before each meeting of the Assembly, on significant decisions taken and the reasons for them, and his response to proposals submitted by the Assembly under section 60. The Mayor must attend every meeting of the Assembly and answer questions put to him about matters relating to his statutory functions.[151] Questions will be answered orally 'so far as practicable to do so', or in writing before the end of the third working day following the day on which the question was asked at the meeting.[152] An Annual Report is to be prepared by the Mayor as soon as practicable after the end of each financial year, reporting on his mayoral activities during the year.[153]

Once in each financial year the Mayor must hold and attend a 'State of London debate', open to all members of the public.[154] In addition, twice in every financial year, a 'People's Question Time' shall be held, open to all members of the public, for the purpose of putting questions to the Mayor and Assembly members. People's Question Time is to be held within one month of the State of London debate.[155]

Transport functions of the Authority

Part IV of the Act regulates transport. The Mayor is under a duty to develop and implement policies for the 'promotion and encouragement of safe,

---

150 Greater London Authority Act 1999, s 67.
151 Should the Mayor be absent from six consecutive monthly Assembly meetings, he or she is disqualified from office: s 13.
152 *Ibid*, s 45.
153 *Ibid*, s 46.
154 *Ibid*, s 47.
155 *Ibid*, s 48.

integrated, efficient and economic transport facilities and services to, from and within Greater London'.[156] The Act stipulates the respective powers and duties of the Secretary of State, the Mayor and London borough councils. 'Transport for London' is the functional body established to implement the Mayor's transport strategy, and will assume the functions previously exercised by a number of differing bodies. Transport for London will have wide-ranging responsibilities, including traffic management, maintenance of roads, the London Underground, the regulation of bus services and rail services, road safety and parking, including the fixing of parking and other charges for London. The making of public-private partnership agreements (PPP agreement) is provided for, enabling contracts between the London Authority bodies and private companies for the provision, construction, improvement or maintenance of railways.[157]

Transport for London will comprise a Board of between eight and 15 members, all of whom are appointed by the Mayor. The Mayor will designate one of the members to be Chairman of Transport for London. The Mayor may be a member, and if he elects to be so, shall be the chairman.[158] The Mayor may issue guidance, general directions and specific directions as to the exercise of its functions.[159]

The London Development Agency

Part V of the Act establishes the London Development Agency and amends the Regional Development Agencies Act 1998 in relation to London. The Mayor is responsible for appointing the 15 members of the London Development Agency, and must ensure that at least four members are elected members of the Assembly, a London borough council or the Common Council of the City of London. The Mayor must consult the London Assembly before making appointments. The Chairman is designated by the Mayor, and must be a 'person who has experience of running a business'.[160] The functions of the London Development Agency is to further economic development, promote business efficiency, investment and competitiveness, promote employment and to enhance the development and application of skills relevant to employment and to contribute to sustainable development.

The Mayor is responsible for preparing and publishing the London Development Agency strategy, assisted by the Agency.

---

156 Greater London Authority Act 1999, s 141.
157 *Ibid*, s 210.
158 *Ibid*, Sched 10, paras 2 and 3.
159 *Ibid*, s 155. See, also, Scheds 10–24.
160 *Ibid*, s 304.

The Metropolitan Police

Section 310 of the Act inserts into section 5 of the Police Act 1996, section 5A: 'A police force shall be maintained for the metropolitan police district', and section 5B: 'There shall be a police authority for the metropolitan police district', known as the Metropolitan Police Authority.[161] Formerly, the Police Authority for the Metropolitan Police District was the Home Secretary. Whereas other police forces in England and Wales were accountable to a local police authority, the Home Secretary's responsibility as police authority meant that London lacked the degree of local accountability existing outside London. The establishment of the Metropolitan Police Authority redresses this lack of accountability, and also ensures that the Mayor and Assembly have a role to play in the combating of crime in the capital. The Metropolitan Police Authority is to consist of 23 members, 12 of whom are members of the London Assembly appointed by the Mayor, one of whom must be the deputy Mayor, one appointed by the Secretary of State, six appointed by members of the Metropolitan Police Authority from persons on a shortlist prepared by the Secretary of State, and four magistrates for commission areas which are wholly or partly within the metropolitan police district. Members generally serve a four-year renewable term. The Authority shall appoint a chairman from among its members.[162]

The Authority is responsible for ensuring the maintenance of an efficient and effective police force.[163] The metropolitan police force is under the direction and control of the Commissioner of Police of the Metropolis,[164] appointed by Her Majesty on the recommendation of the Secretary of State following any recommendations made to him by the Metropolitan Police Authority and representations made by the Mayor.

London Fire and Emergency Planning Authority

The Fire and Emergency Planning Authority replaces the London Fire and Civil Defence Authority as established under the Local Government Act 1985.[165] The reconstituted Authority is responsible to the Mayor. The Fire and Emergency Planning Authority consists of 17 members, of whom nine are Assembly members appointed by the Mayor and the remainder members of

---

161 Greater London Authority Act 1999, s 312.
162 *Ibid*, Sched 26.
163 *Ibid*, s 311, inserting new sub-s (5)to the Police Act 1996, s 6.
164 *Ibid*, s 314.
165 *Ibid*, s 328.

London borough councils appointed by the Mayor on the nomination of the London borough councils acting jointly. The Mayor is under a duty to ensure, so far as practicable, that members for whose appointment he is responsible reflect the balance of parties for the time being prevailing among the members of those councils taken as a whole.[166] Members are appointed for a renewable one-year term of office. The Mayor is also responsible for appointing a chairman from among the members of the Authority.

Planning

Part VIII of the Act gives to the Mayor a role in planning, although neither the Mayor nor Assembly is a local planning authority for the purposes of the Town and Country Planning Act 1990, and the local planning authorities for the Greater London area remain. The Mayor has a duty to prepare and publish a 'spatial development strategy' (SDS) document for Greater London,[167] which includes his general policies in respect of the development and use of land in Greater London. The Secretary of State has the power to direct the Mayor to prepare and publish either such alterations of the Spatial Development Strategy as he directs, or a new SDS to replace the existing one.[168] When preparing the SDS, the Mayor must consult the Assembly and the functional bodies.[169] Copies of the SDS must be sent to the Secretary of State, every London borough council, councils whose area adjoins Greater London and is affected by the proposed SDS, bodies or persons designated by the Secretary of State under section 343 and any other body or person to whom the Mayor considers it appropriate to send a copy. They Mayor is under a duty to keep the SDS under review, and if the Secretary of State so directs, the Mayor shall review the strategy as specified in directions from the Secretary of State.[170]

Environmental functions

Within three years of the first election, and within four years from the date of the previous report, the Mayor must produce and publish a Report on the environment in Greater London, known as the 'state of the environment

---

166 Greater London Authority Act 1999, Sched 28, para 1.

167 *Ibid*, s 334.

168 *Ibid*, s 341.

169 Defined as Transport for London, the London Development Agency, the Metropolitan Police Agency and the London Fire and Emergency Planning Authority: s 424.

170 *Ibid*, ss 339 and 340.

report'.[171] The Report must contain information about: air quality and emissions to air, including in particular emissions from road traffic; road traffic levels; water quality and emissions to water; ground water levels; energy consumption and the emission of substances which contribute to climate changes; land quality; biodiversity; the production, minimisation, recycling and disposal of waste; noise; national resources, and litter.[172]

The Mayor is also to prepare and publish a 'London Biodiversity Action Plan', containing information concerning the ecology of Greater London, wildlife, conservation proposals and commitments made as to conservation and promotion of biodiversity within Greater London.[173]

The Mayor must also prepare and publish a 'Municipal Waste Management Strategy', containing proposals and policies for the recovery, treatment and disposal of municipal waste,[174] and a 'London Air Quality Strategy' detailing implementation of policies on national air quality strategy and the achievement of air quality standards provided for under the Environment Act 1995. In addition, the Mayor must prepare and publish a 'London Ambient Noise Strategy', detailing information about noise and the impact of noise and proposals to counteract the effect of noise, including aircraft noise.[175]

Culture, media and sport

A Cultural Strategy Group for London (CSGL) is established under the Act, which has the function of advising the Mayor on the implementation of culture strategy.[176] The CSGL will formulate and submit to the Mayor a draft strategy containing proposed policies relating to culture, media and sport. The policies may relate to arts, tourism and sport; ancient monuments and sites; buildings of historical or architectural interest; museums and galleries; library services; archives; treasure and movable antiquities; broadcasting, film production and other media of communication.[177] The Authority may

---

171 Greater London Authority Act 1999, s 351.
172 *Ibid*, s 351(3)(a)–(k).
173 *Ibid*, s 352.
174 *Ibid*, s 353.
175 *Ibid*, s 370 and 371.
176 *Ibid*, s 375.
177 *Ibid*, s 376.

provide financial or other assistance for the purposes of any museum, gallery, library, archive or other cultural institution in Greater London.[178] The functions of the Authority include the duty to promote tourism to Greater London.[179]

The Cultural Strategy Group for London shall consist of not fewer than 10 and not more than 25 members, appointed by the Mayor, following consultation with such bodies or persons as he considers appropriate, and for such term of office as the Mayor determines.[180]

---

178 Greater London Authority Act 1999, s 377.
179 *Ibid*, s 378.
180 *Ibid*, Sched 30, para 2.

PART II – LOCAL GOVERNMENT IN ENGLAND AND WALES: AN OUTLINE[181]

Local government represents both a form of decentralisation of power from central government and a basis for local democracy. Local government predates central government by many centuries. Historically, local government represented an early form of localised self-regulation. The country is divided into local authorities – either county or district – each having law making and administrative powers as delegated by Parliament. Local authorities nowadays are entirely creatures of statute: accordingly, the only powers which they have are those conferred by the sovereign United Kingdom Parliament. Increasingly, however, the law of the European Union and Community also requires action at local authority level.

THE ADVANTAGES OF LOCAL GOVERNMENT

Central government is ill equipped to deal with many matters which require special local knowledge and regulation on the basis of local needs. The devolution of power to directly elected local authorities enables those with local knowledge and expertise to regulate the provision of services, such as public housing, public sanitation, educational and recreational facilities. Local government, therefore, is justified on the basis of efficiency. Local government also represents the citizen's closest contact with a democratic institution and enables individuals to play a role in the administration of their geographical area. The merits of local government were summarised by the Widdicombe Committee[182] as follows:

The value of local government stems from its three attributes of:

(a) pluralism, through which it contributes to the national political system;

---

181 See, *inter alia*, Sharpe, LG, 'Theories and values of local government' (1970) 18 Political Studies 153; Bailey, S, *Cross on Principles of Local Government Law*, 2nd edn, 1997, London: Sweet & Maxwell; Davies, K, *Local Government Law*, 1983, London: Butterworths; Loughlin, M, *Local Government in the Modern State*, 1986, London: Sweet & Maxwell; Jones, G and Stewart, J, *The Case for Local Government*, 2nd edn, 1985, London: Allen & Unwin; Byrne, A, *Local Government in Britain*, 6th edn, 1994, Harmondsworth: Penguin; Stewart, J and Stoker, J (eds), *The Future of Local Government*, 1989, Basingstoke: Macmillan; Newton, K and Karran, TJ (eds), *The Politics of Local Expenditure*, 1985, London: Macmillan; Leach, S, Stewart, J and Walsh, K (eds), *The Changing Organisation and Management of Local Government*, 1994, London: Macmillan; Jones, G (ed), *The New Government Agenda*, 1997, Hemel Hempstead: ICSA. Note that local government in Scotland and Northern Ireland is differently arranged.

182 *The Conduct of Local Authority Business*, Cmnd 9797, 1986, London: HMSO, and see McAuslan, P, 'The Widdicombe Report: local government business or politics?' [1987] PL 154. See, also, *inter alia*, Keith-Lucas, B and Richards, PG, *A History of Local Government in the Twentieth Century*, 1979, London: Allen & Unwin.

(b) participation, through which it contributes to local democracy;

(c) responsiveness, through which it contributes to the provision of local needs through the delivery of services.[183]

Local authority boundaries

In order to revise boundaries and to adjust them to reflect changes in population the Local Government Act 1972 introduced the Local Government Boundary Commissions. One Commission exists for England, Scotland and Wales. The present structure was established following a lengthy inquiry into the structure, role and functions of local authorities.[184]

In 1992, a Local Government Commission,[185] appointed by the Secretary of State for the Environment, was established,[186] under the Chairmanship of John Banham, to review the structure, boundaries and electoral arrangements of all areas except London and the metropolitan areas. The government's intention was to seek to increase the efficiency of local government and reduce overlapping functions and bureaucracy. Accordingly, it was the government's objective to introduce unitary authorities which would replace the previous two tier structure. The government's guidance to the Commission was to consider using districts as 'building blocks' and merging authorities. The proposals proved controversial. In December 1993, Sir John Boynton, first president of the Society of Local Authority Chief Executives, criticised the reforms as being 'unwanted and unnecessary' and queried the need to revise the radical reforms introduced in 1974.[187] The question was also asked as to why the government was prepared to spend the estimated £1 billion for the cost of change. The reason for the proposed reforms was cost saving in the long term. However, cost saving was the prediction and motivation behind the 1972 reforms, when it was expected that reduced overheads would cut costs, and that there would be a saving in relation to salaries alone of some £9 million annually, an expectation which was not realised.

The proposed changes came about at the end of a period marked by radical change in the functions local government.[188] As will be seen, the

---

183 Cmnd 9797, 1986, London: HMSO, p 47.

184 See, *inter alia, Report of the Royal Commission on Local Government in England,* Cmnd 4040, 1969, London: HMSO (the 'Redcliffe-Maud Report'); *Report of the Royal Commission on Local Government* in Scotland, Cmnd 4150, 1969, London: HMSO (the 'Wheatley Report'); *Local Government in England,* Cmnd 4585, 1971, London: HMSO; *The Reform of Local Government in Wales,* 1971, London: HMSO.

185 Comprising 13 people including business, councillors, administrators and academics.

186 Local Government Act 1992.

187 Under *ibid.*

188 See, further, below.

thrust of development over the period from 1979 to 1997, under the former Conservative government, was one towards compulsory competitive tendering for services and the privatisation of local government departments, reducing the role of Local Education Authorities. In the view of Sir John Boynton:[189] '... for good or ill the whole concept of local government as a public service is being transformed.' The reviews, however, ended in compromise. The Commission recommended the retention of the two tier system in many areas, but also proposed unitary councils in some areas. In 1994, unitary councils were introduced in Scotland and Wales, with respectively 32 and 22 unitary councils being established.[190] In England, no uniformity was achieved.[191, 192]

Before the review began in 1992, the structure of local government in Great Britain comprised some 515 councils, made up of the following:

In England:

    32 London boroughs

    the Corporation of London

    36 metropolitan districts

    39 county councils

    296 district councils

In Scotland:

    nine regional councils

    53 district councils

    three island councils

In Wales:

    37 district councils

    eight county councils

Following the review, the total number of councils in Britain was reduced between 1994 and 1998 from 515 to 442. The number of authorities in Scotland was reduced from 62 to 32 unitary councils; whereas in Wales, 45 councils were reduced to 22 unitary councils. In England, in 1998, there are 238 district councils, 34 county councils and 46 new unitary authorities.

---

189 First President of the Society of Local Authority Chief Executives.

190 Scotland (Local Government) Act 1994; Local Government Wales Act 1994.

191 The counties of Avon, Cleveland and Humberside which had been created in 1972 but lacked public support were abolished with effect from 1996.

192 Ministerial guidance to the Commission was successfully challenged in judicial review proceedings on the basis that the guidance undermined the statutory criterion: *R v Secretary of State for the Environment ex parte Lancashire County Council* [1994] 4 All ER 165.

The current structure of local government

The structure of local government was substantially revised by the Local Government Act 1972 and, further, by the Local Government Act 1985. Under the 1972 Act, England was divided into six metropolitan counties outside London.[193] London was governed by the Greater London Council. In addition to the metropolitan counties, 39 non-metropolitan counties were established. In 1983, the Conservative government abolished the Greater London Council and the metropolitan county councils.[194] As seen above, the current government has introduced an elected Mayor and Assembly for London.

The size of local government

In comparison with other nations, local government in the United Kingdom is represented by substantially larger units, representing a substantially greater number of people. Before the latest reorganisation of local government, statistics reveal the average population per local authority.[195] The figures reveal that whereas the United Kingdom had an average population per local authority of 118,400, the corresponding figure for France is 1,580; Germany is 4,925; Norway, 9,000; Denmark 18,760 and Sweden 30,040. The population size of authorities naturally affects the number of constituents a local councillor will represent. Accordingly, in France, one elected representative represents 116 people, in Germany 250, in Denmark 783, in Sweden 667 and in the United Kingdom, 2,605.

THE FUNCTIONS OF LOCAL GOVERNMENT

Local government has no powers other than those conferred by Parliament. The powers conferred must be exercised according to law, and judicial review of local authority decisions may be made to ensure that the rule of law is respected.[196] Some discretion exists, however, as to the means by which local authorities achieve the goals set by central government.

However, the freedom of local authorities to raise finance, to undertake expenditure and to provide services was substantially reduced under the

---

193 Greater Manchester, Merseyside, South Yorkshire, Tyne and Wear, West Midlands, and West Yorkshire.

194 Local Government (Interim Provisions) Act 1984 and Local Government Act 1985.

195 See, more fully, *The Size of Municipalities, Efficiency and Citizen Participation,* Council of Europe: Local and Regional Authorities in Europe, No 56, cited in *op cit,* Jones, fn 181, p 9.

196 See Chapters 4, 24 and 25.

Conservative government which assumed office in 1979 and lasted until 1997. During that time, as will be seen, the government altered the manner in which local taxation was raised, set clear limits on expenditure and imposed sanctions on local authorities who exceeded the expenditure approved by central government. Moreover, the provision of services by local authorities has been significantly curtailed. Intent on improving efficiency and on privatising many aspects of government previously performed either by local authorities or by central government, 'market forces' were introduced to many local authority services. Local authorities are now required to put many services out to tender to the private sector, and may provide services themselves only if they can do so in a manner which is competitive with private companies and organisations.[197]

In addition to taxation and the provision of services, local authorities have a regulatory and law making role. Local councils have wide powers to regulate, for example, the granting of licences of taxis, market trading, the approval of child care facilities and private welfare homes for the elderly, disabled or sick. In relation to law making, local authorities, acting under the authority of Acts of Parliament, have the power to make bylaws – local laws which regulate the area. For example, footpaths, parks and recreational facilities are controlled by local bylaws. In the exercise of all such power, the local authority is subject to control by the courts: all local authorities must act *intra vires* (within their powers), or their decisions will be declared null and void by the courts.

The allocation of functions between authorities in England and Wales

Functions are allocated between local authorities principally on the basis of 'operational efficiency and cost-effectiveness'.[198] The provision of certain services, for example, education, is clearly a matter for regulation on a large scale, whereas the provision of local libraries and refuse collection may be appropriate for smaller councils to administer. However, there can be no generalisations about the distribution of functions: there are variations throughout. From the point of view of local democracy, and the accountability and responsiveness of local councillors, however, the larger the local government unit, and the more diffuse the provision of services between differing levels of local government, the more difficult it becomes for the individual to apportion responsibility. In Byrne's analysis, the allocation of responsibilities is made the more complex by the sharing of responsibilities,

---

197 See, further, below.
198 *Op cit*, Byrne, fn 181, p 80.

which of itself takes several forms. Shared responsibilities in this analysis may include *concurrent provision*, whereby all local authorities provide the same service in their area; or *joint provision*, where two or more local authorities combine to provide a common service to all within their common area; or *shared but divided provision*, in which different levels of local authority provide differing aspects of the same service; *reserve powers*, under which larger authorities reserve the power to provide particular aspects of a service otherwise provided by smaller authorities; *claimed powers*, through which individual, small authorities assume responsibility for a service or function formally allocated to a larger authority, and *agency powers*, whereby one authority will act as the agent of another authority in the provision of a service or exercise of certain functions.[199]

In addition to the complexity in the allocation of functions between local authorities must be considered the movement, discussed further below, towards compulsory competitive tendering (CCT), which obliges local authorities to put the provision of services out to tender and, in the event that they wish to continue to make provision for a particular service, demonstrate that they can do so in a manner competitive with private companies. What is evident from this movement is that local authorities nowadays are far less the actual providers of services and more bodies which, through contract, enable services to be provided by those in the private sector. Moreover, no picture of local government can be complete without recognition of the increased, and increasing, functions formerly undertaken by local authorities, which are now undertaken by boards and trusts under provisions introduced by the Conservative government in relation to education and housing (discussed, further, below) which further fragments local government, accountability and democracy.

THE ELECTION OF COUNCILLORS

Councillors are elected for a four year term of office and represent 'wards' within the local government area. In metropolitan districts, one third of councillors retire each year, other than in a year in which there will be county council elections. In other, non-metropolitan districts, councillors retire every four years, or may choose to adopt the metropolitan model. The electoral system reflects that used for general elections, being the simple majority or 'first past the post' system.[200]

---

199 *Op cit*, Byrne, fn 181, pp 82–83.
200 See Chapter 13.

Detailed rules regulate election expenditure and, as with general elections, a number of corrupt and illegal practices are proscribed. An election challenge may be presented by way of a petition to the Queen's Bench Division of the High Court.[201] The petition is heard by the election courts which consists of a commissioner appointed by the judges who are nominated to try election petitions.

Qualification and disqualification for election

A candidate must – unlike candidates for Parliament – be able to demonstrate a close connection with the locality. Accordingly, he or she must either be on the local register of electors, or have been resident or occupied property or have his place of employment within the local authority area for a 12 month period preceding 'nomination day'.[202] Bankruptcy, conviction for corrupt or illegal practices, a conviction and sentence of three months' imprisonment within five years of the election or the imposition of a surcharge by the Audit Commission for unlawful local government expenditure[203] will all disqualify a person from standing for election.

The fact of regular local elections during the life of a Parliament enables the people not only to express their preferences for those who will govern them until the next set of local elections, but also to express their approval or disapproval of central government policies. In the May 1995, local elections, in which the Conservative Party lost control of a large number of local councils, the Conservative government was given a clear indication of the people's judgment on its stewardship of power.

Payments for councillors

Councillors are not salaried. Chief Executives are salaried, whereas the chairman and vice chairman of county and district councils receive expense allowances as approved by the council. Other councillors receive travelling and subsistence allowances, attendance allowances and reimbursement for loss of earnings.

---

201 Representation of the People Act 1983, ss 127–63, as amended.

202 Local Government Act 1972, s 79.

203 Audit of local authority accounts is undertaken under the Local Government Finance Act 1982.

Standards of conduct

The Prevention of Corruption Acts 1906 and 1916[204] made it a criminal offence for a member of the council to accept payments, in money or kind, for services. Under the Local Government Act 1972,[205] Councillors must disclose the existence of any direct or indirect financial interest in council business. In 1974, following a scandal involving councillors in the North of England concerning contracts for a private architect,[206] official inquiries were launched into the standard of conduct in public life.[207] While it was found that, in general, local government members' conduct was 'honest', a number of reforms have been introduced. A statutory Register of Members' Interests has been established[208] and a Code of Conduct introduced relating to non-pecuniary interests.

The conduct of local government came under review from the Committee of Standards in Public Life, chaired by Lord Nolan.[209] The inquiry examined the 'seven principles of public life' – selflessness, integrity, objectivity, accountability, openness, honesty and leadership – identified by the Committee in its inquiries to parliamentary standards.[210] Lord Nolan's frame of reference included the issue of the manner in which, and extent to which, local government operates these principles. Moreover, the Committee examined codes of conduct, including the declaration of financial and non-pecuniary interests; the role of councillors and officers of local authorities; the role of auditors and ombudsmen; the relationships between councils and contractors and/or consultants; the management of planning permissions; local authority allowances and access to information by the public into local authority work.

---

204 And, previously, the Public Bodies Corrupt Practices Act 1889.

205 Local Government Act 1972, ss 94–98.

206 John Poulson.

207 *Conduct in Local Government*, Cmnd 5636, 1974, London: HMSO; *Report of the Royal Commission on Standards in Public Life 1974–76*, Cmnd 6524, 1976, London: HMSO. See, also, *The Conduct of Local Authority Business*, Cmnd 9797, 1986, London: HMSO. On the 1994–95 Inquiry into Standards of Conduct in Public Life in relation to Central Government, see Chapters 11 and 16.

208 Local Government and Housing Act 1989, s 18.

209 See Nolan (Lord), 'Lord Nolan's shopping list', in *op cit*, Jones, fn 181, p 58.

210 See, further, Chapter 16.

THE MANAGEMENT OF LOCAL GOVERNMENT[211]

Unlike central government, there is no 'cabinet' which formulates policy. All councils employ officers, some of which are required to be appointed under statute.[212] Officials hold office on 'such reasonable terms and conditions, including conditions as to remuneration' at the discretion of the council.[213] Local authorities appoint a salaried chief officer or executive and employ senior administrators, clerical officers and secretarial and office staff. In addition, a local authority will employ teachers, police and firemen and personnel related to their specific services.[214]

Local authorities have some discretion to decide on their management arrangements.[215] For the most part, committees undertake the majority of decision making, with their decisions being ratified by a meeting of the full council which may meet as frequently as the council thinks fit. By law, councils are required to have at least one annual meeting, but in practice these are usually far more frequent.

Meetings of the council must be publicised[216] and council meetings[217] are open to the public, unless the council rules that the meeting should be conducted in private because of the confidential nature of the business.[218]

CENTRAL GOVERNMENT AND LOCAL GOVERNMENT[219]

Parliament is supreme and can control both the structure of local government, and the extent of local government powers and functions. The major forms of control are through general legislation and through delegated legislation. Local authorities have statutory power to make bylaws but these are subject to confirmation by the Minister. Central government policy and standard-setting control the manner in which local authorities may exercise their powers. Schemes for town planning, transport and education must have central approval and, in town planning, appeals will ultimately lie to the Secretary of

---

211 See *op cit*, Leach, Stewart and Walsh, fn 181.

212 Eg, the Chief Education Officer. See Local Government Act 1972, s 112(1), (3), (4).

213 *Ibid*, s 112(2).

214 In 1997, local government employed some 2.5 million persons.

215 Under statute, however, certain committees must be established, eg, an Education Committee, Police Committee and Social Service Committee.

216 Local Government (Access to Information) Act 1985.

217 And meetings of the Education Committees.

218 Public Bodies (Admission to Meetings) Act 1960.

219 See Loughlin, M, 'The restructuring of central-local government legal relations' (1985) Local Government Studies 61; Grant, M, 'Knee-capping local government', in *op cit*, Newton and Karran, fn 181.

State, and his approval will be needed in relation to compulsory purchase orders. In relation to fire, education and the police, regular inspections are made by central government inspectors.

The Department of State most closely associated with local government is the Department of the Environment, created in 1970. There are also other departments such as the Department of Education and Employment, the Home Office,[220] and the Social Security Department which have powers over local government.

Financial controls over local government

In order to understand the current status of local government and its relationship with central government, it is necessary to understand the recent history of local government finance, which is one characterised by increasing controls being imposed by central government. The Royal Commission on Local Government, 1966–69, discussed finance but made no proposals for change in financial arrangements. The genesis of increased control on local government spending by central government generally can be seen in the 1970s under the Labour government. The oil crisis of 1973 increased government alarm over public spending in general. In 1976–77, the government fixed grants at a level of projected price levels for the financial year without any adjustment for inflation.

Throughout the 1979 general election campaign, Ministers criticised local government as wasteful, irresponsible and unaccountable. The Conservative Party came into government promising reform of the rating system and added to its promises the commitment to introduce a fairer and more simple grant system.

Local government revenue[221]

Some 60 per cent of local government revenue comes from central government grants. These are either specific grants – for example, for particular services such as fire or police (50 per cent), or general grants – a central government contribution to local authority funds. In addition, local authorities may borrow money, subject to strict control by the Treasury, and raise money from the imposition of charges, for example, for services (swimming pools and recreational facilities) and the sale of council houses, for transport services.

---

220 With powers in relation to the police, fire services, local government elections and the approval of bylaws.

221 See *Report of the Layfield Committee of Inquiry into Local Government Finance*, Cmnd 6453, 1976, London: HMSO.

The financial needs of local government are thus met by a mixture of local and central revenues. In terms of local revenue, from around 1600 until 1988, local domestic rates had been in existence. The rates, calculated according to the value of the property, were cheap and easy to collect, and the public were used to them. Rates applied to a property irrespective of the number of persons living in it. During the 1960s and 1970s, high spending councils led to pressure for reform of the rating system. As the position stood then, a local authority raised the annual local rates and central government, through the Rate Support Grant – a 'top-up' grant – provided the short-fall between revenue and expenditure.

By 1974, the Conservative Party was committed to abolishing local rates, and at that time adopted the view that a local income tax to replace the property tax was the best way forward. However, by 1979, the Conservative government was committed to reducing all forms of direct taxation and it therefore became undesirable to continue to entrust local authorities with the ultimate power to raise local direct taxation. A further alternative to the rating system presented itself – and found favour with the then Prime Minister, Margaret Thatcher – that of the local sales tax. That idea, however, proved to be short lived, with the recognition that it would be anomalous to have differing rates of sales tax within different parts of the country. In addition, there were fears that local sales taxes might in any event contravene European Community law.

The politically conservative Adam Smith Institute promoted the flat rate Community Charge – Poll Tax – a tax which would be imposed on every adult within a local authority area and would be unrelated to the value of a particular property. The perceived advantages of such a tax were those of fairness and accountability. The same rate within a local authority area would apply to every person: it was a person based rather than property based tax. Accordingly, each resident in a local area would contribute to the costs of services which were enjoyed by all. Equally, such a tax would ensure that each voter in the area felt the impact of local authority spending and, accordingly, the local authority would be more accountable to the voters. The community charge found favour with the government and was introduced – amidst widespread public disorder – under the Local Government Finance Act 1988. In addition to that personal tax, the government was keen to reform business rates, and introduced the National Non-Domestic Rate, to be set by government and outside local authority control.

The conflict and disquiet over the introduction of the community charge led to rapid reform.[222] Whilst in principle the tax would serve the needs of fairness and accountability, in practice, the tax was rapidly regarded as iniquitous and, as a result, uncollectable. The backtrack once again centred on

---

222 Local Government Finance Act 1992.

property values. From 1993, the Council Tax payable is based on values of property within differing price bands and is payable irrespective of the numbers of people living within the house although, to mitigate the perceived unfairness of the old rating system, a 25 per cent discount is allowable for single person households.

Local authority expenditure

Before 1980, the Rate Support Grant was designed to top up the needs of a local authority where the income from domestic rates fell short of their expenditure requirements. The sum payable by central government annually was fixed by the Secretary of State for the Environment following discussion with local authority associations. Prior to the Local Government Planning and Land Act 1980, the majority of the grant was based on what was needed: and what was needed was dependent upon the local authorities' perception of need. By the 1970s, the Conservative Party had come to the view that local government was 'profligate, wasteful and out of control'. The result was the introduction[223] of a new Block Grant, distributed according to grant related expenditure assessments (GREAs) and those were to be determined by central, and not local, government. Overspending councils were to be penalised by a grant taper. Simply expressed, the taper represented a reduction in the central government grant where the Secretary of State considered that a local authority was spending too much. By 1981, it was realised by the government that this initiative was ineffective. Accordingly, the government introduced the grant holdback.[224] Henceforth, overspending local authorities were to have their grant withheld. In order to prevent the local authority from simply levying a mid term supplementary rate to make up the short fall, the right to impose a supplementary rate was removed. However, these controls also proved ineffective. In order to circumvent the consequences of grant being withheld, some local authorities increased the amount of the annual rate levied to make up the short fall. The Rates Act 1984 introduced further central government powers: those of rate capping. Rate capping sought to prevent rate increases above a target set by central government, and conferred a broad discretion on the Secretary of State for the Environment to impose sanctions.[225] Those opposed to rate capping claimed that it represented an interference in local government affairs and an erosion of local democracy. For each one per cent of overspend, the offending local authority would lose a proportion of its allowable rate figure.

---

223 Local Government Planning and Land Act 1980.
224 Local Government Finance Act 1982.
225 Rates Act 1984, s 2.

An illustration of the political conflict which ensued involved Liverpool City Council. The City Council, a Labour Party controlled council, decided to take illegal action to safeguard vital services, and set their own rate outside the limits set by government. Between 1985 and 1986, unemployment was running at 27 per cent; the City Council had enough money for only nine months' administration. The government refused to come to the City Council's assistance. The City Council resolved to close down for three months and to make employees redundant, while the Council was moving towards bankruptcy. Eventually, the City Council set a legal rate financed, ironically, by Swiss banks. One response to such restraints by local authorities was the attempt to raise money through the financial markets in interest swaps. The House of Lords, however, ruled such transactions to be *ultra vires*.[226]

With the demise of the Poll Tax and introduction of the council tax in 1993,[227] came a change in the manner in which central government calculated and allocated the Revenue Support Grant.[228] In an attempt to ensure standard levels of service throughout the country, the Grant Related Expenditure Allocation gave way to the Standard Spending Assessment (SSA). In brief, the Department of the Environment (DoE) calculates the level of resource which each local authority needs in order to achieve the 'standard level of service' across the range of services which a local authority is statutorily required to provide. In part, this figure is determined by the previous expenditure of the local authority. In calculating the resource needs, the DoE operates a formula based on statistical data on each authority, comprising a number of variables, such as population, property prices, demographic factors, level of social deprivation and so on. Based on this, the DoE calculated the resource needs in relation to particular services – education, social services, etc. The DoE combines this calculation with the amount which it deems it appropriate for a local authority to raise through the imposition of the council tax, and the amount which the local authority will be given from government from the National Non-Domestic (Business) Rate (NNDR). The combination of the amount to be levied via the council tax plus the receipts from the NNDR, subtracted from the DoE's assessment of resource need, equals the government's Revenue Support Grant for a particular authority. Over and above that final calculation, and based on former expenditure, the government set for each authority the percentage level at which the authority

---

226 *Hazell v Hammersmith London Borough Council* [1992] 2 AC 1; and see Loughlin, M, 'Innovative financing in local government: the limits of legal instrumentalism: Part 1' [1990] PL 372 and 'Part 2' [1991] PL 568.

227 Local Government (Finance) Act 1992.

228 My thanks to Councillor Stephen Knight, Political Assistant at the Association of London Government, for his help in unravelling the complexities of the current financial system.

is 'capped' – that is to say, the absolute maximum budget which that authority was permitted to spend in the financial year. If a local authority decided that it needs to spend more than the cap figure, the revenue needed could only come from an increase in local council tax. The government would not provide monies over the cap, and local authorities exceeding the cap are liable to the full range of penalties available under statute.

A CHANGED GOVERNMENT PHILOSOPHY TOWARDS LOCAL GOVERNMENT 1979 TO 1997[229]

The philosophy of the Conservative government under the premiership of Mrs Margaret Thatcher[230] was one dominated by limited central government provision for local government allied to the principles of competition, market forces, efficiency and accountability. This philosophy was felt keenly by local authorities and represented a fundamental change in the relationship between central and local government. Central government policy was reflected at a local level in a number of ways, some examples of which are discussed below.

Public housing policy

The provision of housing by local authorities has been a central function of local government since the turn of the century. By 1980, there were 6.8 million dwelling properties owned by local authorities. By 1986, however, the number of dwellings owned by local authorities had declined to six million. The explanation for the decrease in available public housing is two fold. The first relates to the 'right to buy' legislation introduced in 1980, which provided that council tenants had a right to buy council property at a reduced cost.[231] The second explanation relates to cuts in public expenditure and restrictions imposed on the right of local authorities to direct the proceeds of sales to new building which has made it impossible for local authorities to replenish their depleted stocks of housing.

A further reduction in local authority control over housing is seen in the Housing Act 1988, which provides that local authority tenants living in multiple housing units may resolve, by a majority, to opt out of local authority control and for their tenancies to be transferred to a private landlord.

---

229 See Mather, G, 'Thatcherism and local government: an evaluation' and Stewart, J, 'A future for local authorities as community government', in *op cit*, Stewart and Stoker, fn 181.

230 Prime Minister, 1979–90.

231 Housing Act 1980.

Local authorities retain important responsibilities for providing housing for the homeless,[232] but do so in the face of increasing difficulties over housing stock.

Reforms in education[233]

Local government is responsible for the implementation of central government education policy, but it remains central government which controls the policy to be pursued. Thus, if a government decides to phase out Grammar Schools and introduce comprehensive education, it can do so. If it decides, as provided under the Education Reform Act 1988, that schools would be better run by giving more control to parents than to local government, it can do so, and make school funding dependent upon central government grants rather than on the local authority. Equally, under the Education Reform Act 1988, the government has the power to determine what is taught in schools under a centrally determined national curriculum.

The Education Reform Act 1988 provides that schools which opt out of local authority control may choose whether to use local authority provided services or to supply their own.

The Education Reform Act 1988 provided for the introduction of a national curriculum with national assessment of performance and greater emphasis on parental choice of schools. The Act effectively redefined the relationship between central and local government, parents and teachers. From 1969, concern has been expressed at the falling educational standards, the inadequacies of comprehensive schools, the lack of parental rights and choice and the monopolisation of education by local authorities.

The emphasis of would be reformers was on public (parental) choice and direct accountability of the producer (schools) to the consumers. The opt out provisions of the Act enabled both the ownership and management of schools, under certain conditions, to be transferred from local authorities to independent trusts or boards. The introduction of Grant Maintained Schools enabled the governors of all secondary schools and primary schools with over 300 pupils to apply to the Secretary of State for maintenance from central government, thereby ceasing to be owned or maintained by the local education authority. Twenty per cent of parents' support, secured by ballot, is required as a prerequisite. School governors are given powers over budgets and the appointment and dismissal of staff, thus further reducing the role of local authorities.

---

232 Housing Act 1985.

233 See Ranson, S and Thomas, H, 'Education reform: consumer democracy or social democracy?', in *op cit*, Stewart and Stoker, fn 181.

The Act also ends the control of local authorities over setting limits to admission to schools and provides that schools can recruit pupils up to available capacity, and that the schools can appeal to the Secretary of State for Education to expand the availability of places in individual schools. The Act also introduced City Technology Colleges established under the aegis of the Secretary of State but sponsored by the private sector.

The introduction of competition and the national curriculum have the greatest impact on local authorities. The introduction of Grant Maintained Schools and City Technology Colleges fragments local public (democratic) control of schools. The prognosis for local authorities as providers of education may be bleak. With better schools choosing to become independent of local government, the education authority may be left with control over schools in the poorest areas with the least advantaged pupils. While local authorities retain important functions in respect of education, central government has intervened to such an extent that the role remaining for local government may be regarded as almost residual.

Competitive tendering for service[234]

As stated earlier, the government pursued a policy of reducing the role of central government, enhancing the efficiency of local authorities and requiring a more competitive basis for the provision of local services. Part of this philosophy was reflected in the requirements that local authorities, rather than providing all services for the community themselves, subject various services to competition through tendering.

The Local Government Planning and Land Act 1980 required that tendering of jobs with high value be made for construction works and maintenance of buildings and highways. The Transport Act 1985 required bus undertakings to operate commercially.

In 1983, tendering was extended to the NHS in relation to catering, domestic and laundry services. In 1985, the government announced its intention to extend tendering to local authority services such as refuse collection, street cleaning, catering, building cleaning, and grounds and vehicle maintenance. The Local Government Act 1988 made provision for this and gave power to the Secretary of State, by statutory instrument, to add other activities which must be put out to tender. Jobs of small value, emergency situations and the maintenance and cleaning of police buildings were exempted.

---

234 See Walsh, K, 'Competition and service in local government', in *op cit*, Stewart and Stoker, fn 181.

If local authorities wanted to use their own labour for services they must win the right to do so in competition with commercial enterprises. Research studies showed that refuse collection costs have been reduced by 22 per cent when private firms undertake the service.[235]

The Local Government Act 1988[236] required local authorities 'not to act in a manner having the effect or intended or likely to have the effect of restricting, disturbing or preventing competition', and the private sector was given the right to challenge local authorities through the courts or by appealing to the Secretary of State.

The Local Government Act 1999

The Labour Government entered power in 1997 with a pledge to reform local government. The Local Government Act 1999 represents the first stage of reform, removing the requirement of compulsory competitive tendering imposed by the 1988 Local Government Act, and introducing the concept of best value (on which, see below, p 515), and amending the scheme of rate capping in place under the 1992 Local Government Finance Act. The 1999 Act introduces greater flexibility into the rate-capping mechanisms. Under the 1992 Act, local authorities were classified according to type and the same principles applied to all local authorities within a particular class, which prevented the particular circumstances of individual authorities from being taken into consideration when making the decision in relation to capping. Section 30 and Schedule 1 to the 1999 Act enable the Secretary of State to apply different capping principles to individual authorities. The Act also introduces the power of the Secretary of State to 'nominate' a local authority. The nomination power is one enabling the Secretary of State to warn a local authority that its spending is becoming excessive.[237] Where an authority's spending is becoming excessive, the Secretary of State may either designate the authority or nominate the authority. Paragraph 52B sets out the principles to be applied by the Secretary of State in reaching the decision as to whether or not spending is excessive. Where an authority is designated, the Secretary of State notifies the authority of the amount which he proposes should be the maximum for the amount calculated by the authority as its budget requirement for the year, and the target amount for the year which the Secretary of State proposes the authority could calculate as its budget

---

235 See the research findings of Domberger, S, Meadowcroft, S and Thompson, D, cited in *op cit*, Walsh, fn 234.

236 Local Government Act 1988, s 7(7).

237 Local Government Act 1999, Sched 1, para 52B, 52D. Schedule 1 inserts a new Chapter IVA into the Local Government Finance Act 1992, Pt I.

requirement for the year without the amount calculated being excessive.[238] Where an authority is nominated, the Secretary of State may decide to designate the authority for the following financial year, or to set a notional sum for its budget requirement, against which the authority's budget requirement for the following year will be compared.[239]

Audit

The government controls local authorities by way of audit. The Audit Commission Act 1998 consolidates the former provisions relating to audit. The Audit Commission[240] of Local Authorities and the National Health Service in England and Wales is the principle body responsible for supervising local government and heal service audits. The Commission consists of not less than 15 and not more than 20 members appointed by the Secretary of State.[241] The accounts of bodies subject to the Act are required to be compiled at the end of March annually and audited by auditors appointed by the Commission.[242]

The Commission is responsible for preparing and keeping under review a Code of Audit Practice.[243] Auditors have a right of access to every document relating to a body which appears to him necessary for the purposes of his functions under the Act.[244] It is an offence to fail to comply, without reasonable excuse, with any requirement of the auditor.[245]

If in the course of an audit of a local government body, other than a health service body, that an item of account is contrary to law and has not been sanctioned by the Secretary of State, the auditor may apply to High Court for a declaration that the item is contrary to law.[246] If the High Court makes such a declaration, it may also require the responsible person to repay the unlawful expenditure in whole or in part. If the unlawful expenditure exceeds £2,000, and at the time the person responsible was a member of a local authority, the Court may order him to be disqualified from being a member of a local authority for a specified period and may order rectification of the accounts. The High Court must not make an order if it is satisfied that the responsible person 'acted reasonably or in the belief that the expenditure was authorised

---

238 Local Government Act 1999, para 52E.

239 *Ibid*, para 52L, 52M.

240 The Audit Commission was established in 1982 to supervise local government audit. Its role was extended to the NHS in 1990.

241 Audit Commission Act 1998, s 1, and see Sched 1.

242 *Ibid*, s 2 and see Sched 2.

243 *Ibid*, s 4.

244 *Ibid*, s 6.

245 *Ibid*, s 6.

246 As in *Hazell v Hammersmith LBC* [1992] 2 AC 1, discussed above.

by law', and in any other case shall 'have regard to all the circumstances, including that person's means and ability to repay the expenditure or any part of it.[247] If a person has failed to bring into account a sum, and that failure has not been sanctioned by the Secretary of State and a 'loss has been incurred or deficiency caused by the wilful misconduct of any person' the auditor must certify that the sum, or the amount of the loss or deficiency, is due from that person.[248] Wilful misconduct has been held to include the failure to collect fees which were due,[249] and a delay in setting the rate resulting in the authority losing interest on money which would otherwise have been collected.[250] A person aggrieved by the auditor's decision to certify a sum or amount due may appeal to the High Court.[251] In relation to health service bodies, section 19 provides that if the auditor has reason to believe that the body or an officer of the body, has made or is about to make a decision which involves incurring unlawful expenditure, or undertake a course of action which would be unlawful and likely to cause a loss or deficiency, the auditor must refer the matter to the Secretary of State.

In relation to authorities, other than a health service body, the auditor may issue a prohibition notice if he has reason to believe that the body is about to make or has made a decision which involves incurring unlawful expenditure, or has taken, or is about to take, action which is unlawful and likely to cause a loss or deficiency, or is about to enter in the accounts an item of unlawful expenditure.[252] If the authority's chief finance officer has already made a report on unlawful expenditure,[253] no prohibition order may be made in relation to the period covered by the report. Where a prohibition order is issued, it is not lawful for the body concerned to make or implement the relevant decision or undertake the course of action to which the prohibition order relates. The body concerned may appeal against the prohibition order to the High Court.[254] The auditor has power to apply for judicial review of local authority, but not health service bodies, decision or failure to act.[255]

The Commission has the power to direct an auditor to undertake an extraordinary audit, and the Secretary of State may require the Commission to direct such an audit.[256]

---

247 Audit Commission Act 1998, s 17.
248 *Ibid*, s 18(1).
249 *R v Roberts* [1901] 2 KB 117.
250 *Lloyd v McMahon* [1987] 2 WLR 821.
251 Audit Commission Act 1998, s 18(10).
252 *Ibid*, s 20.
253 Under the Local Government Finance Act 1988, s 114(2).
254 Audit Commission Act 1998, s 22.
255 *Ibid*, s 24.
256 *Ibid*, s 25.

Under Part III of the Act, the Commission has responsibility for undertaking or promoting comparative or other studies for the improving economy, efficiency and effectiveness of local authority services, and of other bodies covered by the Act, and for improving the financial or other management of bodies subject to audit.[257] Bodies subject to the Act may require the Commission to undertake such studies.[258] The right to make studies and receive requests for studies extends to higher education funding councils, the governing bodies of institutions within the higher education sector and further education sector, the Funding Agency for Schools and the governing body of a grant-maintained school.[259] The Secretary of State may request the Commission's assistance in studies designed to improve the economy, efficiency, effectiveness and quality of performance in relation to social services functions of local authorities.[260]

The abolition of compulsory competitive tendering and the best value concept

As noted above, the Labour government entered office intent on substantial local government reform, part of which involved the abolition of compulsory competitive tendering. The 1999 Local Government Act, gives effect to this intention.[261] Tendering, however, while no longer compulsory continues to form one part of the government's quest for value and efficiency in the provision of local authority services. Section 1 defines the local authorities to which the best value duty will apply, which extends beyond local authorities proper and includes such bodies as the police authorities, Transport for London and other metropolitan transport authorities, waste disposal authorities, fire authorities and the London Development Agency.

The general duty imposed on best value authorities is to 'make arrangements to secure continuous improvement in the way in which its functions are exercised, having regard to a combination of economy, efficiency and effectiveness'.[262] In deciding how to fulfil its duty under section 3, authorities must consult local tax payers, service users and representatives of persons appearing to have an interest in any area in which the authority

---

257 Audit Commission Act 1998, s 33.

258 *Ibid*, s 35.

259 *Ibid*, s 36.

260 *Ibid*, s 37

261 Local Government Act 1999, s 21 repeals the compulsory competitive tendering requirements in the Local Government, Planning and Land Act 1980, the Local Government Act 1988 and the Local Government Act 1992 with effect from January 2000.

262 Local Government Act 1999, s 3.

carries out functions. The Secretary of State may by order specify factors 'performance indicators' by reference to which best value authority's performance can be measured and standards 'performance standards' to be met in relation to the performance indicators. Differing performance indicators or standards may be set for different functions and different functions and may apply at different times.[263] A best value authority must conduct reviews of its functions with the aim to improving the way its functions are exercised, and the Secretary of State may by order specify matters which an authority must include in a review of functions. In particular an order may require an authority to consider whether it should carry out a particular function, the level at which it should be exercising the function, and its objectives in relation to the exercise of the function. It should also assess its performance, and the competitiveness of its performance by reference to other best value authorities and by commercial or other businesses, and consult other authorities and commercial operations about the exercise of the function. It must also assess its progress towards meeting performance standards, which have been specified.[264]

Each authority must prepare a best value performance plan for each financial year, and the Secretary of State may by order specify matters which an authority must include in its plan.[265] The performance plan published for a financial year is to be audited by the authority's auditor.[266] The authority must respond to the auditor's report, and where recommendations have been made, must make a statement of action it intends to take as a result of the report and its proposed timetable, within 30 days of receiving the report or earlier if the report so specifies.[267] The Audit Commission may carry out inspections of an authority's compliance with the requirements, and inspectors have a right of access and may require responsible persons to give such information, explanation or documentation as is required.[268] Where an inspection has been carried out, the Audit Commission must issue a report stipulating areas in which the Commission believes the authority is failing to comply with requirements and may recommend that the Secretary of State give directions to the authority. Where the Commission issues a report stating failure to comply with requirements, the authority must, in its next performance plan, record that fact and any action taken by the authority as a result of the report.[269] Under section 15, the Secretary of State has the power to intervene where he or she is satisfied that an authority is failing to meet the

---

263 Local Government Act 1999, s 4.
264 *Ibid*, s 5.
265 *Ibid*, s 6.
266 *Ibid*, s 7.
267 *Ibid*, s 9.
268 *Ibid*, s 11.
269 *Ibid*, s 13.

requirements relating to best value. The Secretary of State may require an authority to amend a performance plan, to follow specified procedures in relation to the plan and to carry out a review of its exercise of specified functions. The Secretary of State may also direct a local inquiry to be held in relation to the exercise of functions.

Section 15 also gives to the Secretary of State the power to direct an authority to take any action which he considers necessary or expedient to secure compliance with best value requirements. The Secretary of State may direct that a specified function of an authority shall be exercised by the Secretary of State or a person nominated by him, thereby removing that function, for the period specified, from the authority.[270] Where the Secretary of State takes over the function of an authority, regulations may be made to avoid the situation where, for example, planning functions have been taken over. The Secretary of State is also the final arbiter of an appeal against that planning decision.[271]

COMPLAINTS ABOUT LOCAL GOVERNMENT

Complaints against local government may be made to the authority itself and, if such a complaint does not receive satisfactory treatment, a complaint may be made to the Commissioner for Local Administration. The jurisdiction, role and powers of Commissioners for Administration are considered in Chapter 26.

The reforms introduced after 1980 radically altered the role of local government. It is no longer assumed that local authorities have the democratic right to set local taxation at a level unrestrained by Parliament, or that local authorities are the most efficient providers of local services. The spirit of privatisation and market forces, so prevalent throughout the former Conservative government's tenure of office, severely reduced the traditional role of local authorities and altered the balance of power between central and local government.

While the role and function of local government is defined, controlled and restrained by central government, local government must also be seen within the wider context of the European Union and Community.[272] Since the United Kingdom acceded to the European Community in 1973, and the

---

270 Local Government Act 1999, s 15(6).
271 *Ibid*, s 15(7), (8).
272 On which, see, further, Chapters 8 and 9.

formation of the European Union under the Treaty on European Union 1992, an increasing volume of European law affects not only the legislative sphere of competence of Parliament in relation to matters within the competence of the Union, but also affects both national and local policies and standards. The Community was founded on the four freedoms – of persons, goods, capital and services – which affect all levels of government. In addition, the community and Union has expanded its sphere of competence over the years to include such diverse matters as environmental protection, health and hygiene standards and weights and measures. Many of the Community laws on these areas fall on local authorities to implement. The freedom of movement and right of establishment of European citizens[273] has implications for local authority housing, as does the European Court of Justice's development of the law of gender equality in the workplace.

The European Union's relationship to local government is not limited to the imposition of regulations and directives imposing duties on local authorities, but extends to the provision of regional aid. The Committee of the Regions of the European Union[274] provides the means by which the views and interests of local authorities may be taken into account. Furthermore, the provision of financial aids and grants through the Social Fund, European Investment Bank and Regional Development Fund provides an additional source of finance for local authorities.

Local government and the courts

Local authorities, being bodies to whom powers are delegated by Parliament, may exercise their powers and spend money only for the purposes authorised by statute. In order to ensure that bodies with delegated law making, administrative and/or judicial powers act within those powers (*intra vires*), the courts are seized with jurisdiction to review any action challenged by a person or body aggrieved by that action. The jurisdictional rules are laid down in Order 53 of the Rules of the Supreme Court pursuant to the Supreme Court Act 1981.[275] Applications for judicial review proceed by way of an application for leave to apply for judicial review. Applicants must have sufficient interest (*locus standi*) in the matter to apply, and the matter challenged must be one falling under public law as opposed to private law.

---

273 Union citizenship was conferred on all nationals of Member States under the Treaty on European Union 1992.

274 Formerly, the Consultative Council of Regional and Local Authorities.

275 See, further, Chapters 24 and 25.

Furthermore, the matter must be one which is justiciable, that is to say, a matter which the courts deem themselves to be the appropriate body to adjudicate on the matter.[276]

Local government is a regular participant in judicial review proceedings. As seen earlier, all the powers which they exercise are powers delegated by statute; local authorities have no inherent jurisdiction. Accordingly, the courts may rule on the *'vires'* of their activities. Judicial review is considered in Chapters 24 and 25 and those chapters should be consulted for discussion of the case law. In relation to control over the exercise of local government powers, the courts employ the concept of fiduciary duty. Local government is in a fiduciary position of trustee of resources to be exercised for the benefit of the consumers of those resources, council tax payers.[277]

THE LOCAL GOVERNMENT ACT 2000[278]

The Local Government Act 2000 provides for new executive arrangements to be introduced into local government, and empowers a local authority to decide whether to introduce the executive arrangements,[279] consisting of an elected mayor and two or more councillors of the authority appointed by the elected may to the Executive. The Executive is to be referred to as the Mayor and Cabinet Executive.[280] The Act introduces a further layer of management to local government, and is subject to the approval of electors expressed at a referendum.[281] Where a local authority, with referendum approval, introduces an executive, the Secretary of State may by regulations provide for any functions of a local authority to be the responsibility of the Executive.[282] Every local authority must draw up proposals for the operation of executive arrangements and send a copy of the proposals to the Secretary of State. The proposals must indicate the form the Executive is to take, having consulted local government electors and other interested persons.[283] Where the executive arrangement include a mayor and cabinet executive a referendum is required.[284] In other cases, where a referendum is not required, the authority

---

276 *Council of Civil Service Unions v Minister for Civil Service* [1985] AC 374.

277 *Roberts v Hopwood* [1925] AC 578; *Bromley London Borough Council v Greater London Council* [1982] 2 WLR 62; *Hazell v Hammersmith London Borough Council* [1992] 2 AC 1.

278 Introducing the Bill, the Secretary of State declared that he was unable to state that the Bill was compatible with the Human Rights Act 1998.

279 Local Government Act 2000, s 10; Pt II regulates executive arrangments.

280 See *ibid*, Pt II.

281 *Ibid*.

282 *Ibid*.

283 *Ibid*.

284 *Ibid*.

must implement the proposals in accordance with a timetable included in the proposals.[285] The Secretary of State may direct a local authority to hold a referendum in relation to the election of a mayor and executive cabinet.

Part III of the Act relates to standards of conduct in local government, and empowers the Secretary of State to specify the principles which are to govern the conduct of members of relevant authorities in England in a model code. In relation to Wales, the National Assembly may specify standards. Local authorities will be under a duty to adopt a code of conduct, and incorporate such mandatory provisions of a model code as apply to that authority. Every local authority, other than a parish council or community council, must establish a standards committee,[286] the functions of which are to promote and maintain high standards of conduct and assist members of the authority to observe the code of conduct. The standards committee also has power to advise the authority on the adoption or revision of a code, monitoring the operation of the code, and advising, training or arranging to train members of the authority in relation to the code of conduct. Adjudication tribunals are to be established to consider allegations of non-compliance with the code, and to report to the standards committee. Every local authority must establish and maintain a register of members' interests.[287]

Part I of the Act regulates the duty of local authorities to promote the economic, social or environmental well being of the relevant area. Every local authority is to have power to prepare a strategy for promoting or improving the economic, social and environmental well being of their area. The authority must consult or seek the participation of appropriate persons and must have regard to any guidance issued by the Secretary of State. The Secretary of State has the power to amend, repeal or revoke enactments relating to the strategy.[288]

---

285 See Local Government Act 2000, Pt II.
286 *Ibid*, s 53.
287 *Ibid*, s 81.
288 *Ibid*, s 5.

PART V

PARLIAMENT

CHAPTER 13

THE ELECTORAL SYSTEM

The first variety of democracy is that which is so called because it is based chiefly on the principle of equality. In such a democracy, the law interprets equality as meaning that the poor shall not enjoy any more advantage than the rich, that neither shall be sovereign, but both shall be exactly similar. For if, as is held by some, freedom is especially to be found in democracy, and also equality, this condition is most fully realised when all alike share most fully in the constitution. But, since the people are a majority, and the decision of the majority is sovereign, this must be a democracy.[1]

INTRODUCTION

In a democratic State, the electoral process exercises determining power over those who hold political office. It is the electorate which confers the power to govern and calls government to account. If the electorate is to enjoy true equality in constitutional participation, it is of fundamental constitutional importance that the electoral system ensures four principles:

(a) that there is a full franchise, subject to limited restrictions;

(b) that the value of each vote cast is equal to that of every other vote;

(c) that the conduct of election campaigns is regulated to ensure legality and fairness;

(d) that the voting system is such as to produce both a legislative body representative of the electorate and a government with sufficient democratic support to be able to govern effectively.

It is against these four principal objectives that the law must be evaluated. However, it must be recognised that these elements are in large measure inseparable from each other. Each aspect of the electoral process combines to form a system:

> Any code of electoral law includes a number of essential sections of almost equal importance ... Each of these sections is meaningless in isolation from the others. A wide and equal suffrage loses its value if political bosses are able to gerrymander constituencies so as to suit their own interests; there is no point in having an elaborate system of proportional representation if the electors are all driven in one direction by a preponderance of bribes and threats; legal

---

1   Aristotle, *The Politics*, 1962, Sinclair, TA (trans), London: Penguin, Bk iv, 1291b30.

provisions mean nothing if enforcement is left wholly in the hands of those who profit by breaking it.

That is why it is right to speak of the 'electoral system'. Procedure for elections is systematic in that its parts are interdependent; it is impossible to advance on one 'front' without regard to others.[2]

THE FRANCHISE[3]

Evolution of the franchise

Prior to the Reform Acts of 1832 and 1867, the right to vote was limited and based on rights in property. The 1832 Act – the Representation of the People Act – increased the franchise by 50 per cent, which represented only seven per cent of the population. The Reform Act of 1867 doubled the number of people entitled to vote. The debate as to who should participate in the franchise goes back to ancient Greece. Aristotle argued for maximum involvement of all citizens in the decision making processes of the City State, arguing *inter alia* that, while the individual citizen acting alone may be of unsound judgment, decisions reached collectively will be better – or at any rate no worse – than those made by 'experts'.[4]

In Great Britain, the right to vote – by the nineteenth century – was based on property holdings. Men without property, and all women, were excluded from the franchise. The extension of the franchise in 1867 to skilled and unskilled male labourers was not a matter greeted with universal approval. Walter Bagehot retorted that:

> ... no one will contend that the ordinary working man who has no special skill, and who is only rated because he has a house, can judge much of intellectual matters.[5]

Bagehot feared the potential power of the working class: should they combine as a class, the 'higher orders' might have to consider whether to concede to their demands or 'risk the effect of the working men's combination'.[6]

---

2   Mackenzie, R, *Free Elections*, 1967, London: Allen & Unwin, p 19, cited in Rawlings, H, *Law and the Electoral Process*, 1988, London: Sweet & Maxwell, p 2.

3   For a full history of the franchise, see, *inter alia*, Anson, W (Sir), *Law and Custom of the Constitution*, 4th edn, 1933, Oxford: Clarendon; Maitland, FW, *The Constitutional History of England*, 1908, Cambridge: CUP, pp 352–64.

4   *Op cit*, Aristotle, fn 1, Bk III xi, pp 204–05.

5   Bagehot, W, *The English Constitution* (1867), 1993, London: Fontana, p 273.

6   *Ibid*, p 278.

Women and the right to vote

Women were to remain disenfranchised until 1928, but the movement for women's right to vote predates the 1867 Act.[7] In 1851, Harriet Taylor Mill had published *Enfranchisement of Women* in the *Westminster Review*. In 1886, John Stuart Mill[8] presented a petition to Parliament calling for the enfranchisement of women. The following year, the Manchester Women's Suffrage Committee was formed, soon to be united in a National Committee based in London. When the Reform Bill was before Parliament, John Stuart Mill introduced an amendment – changing the word 'man' to 'person' – thereby entitling women to vote. The amendment was defeated.

A legal challenge to disenfranchisement came in *Chorlton v Lings*.[9] It was argued before the Court of Common Pleas that the Representation of the People Act 1867 had conferred on women a right to vote. The argument centred on the use of the word 'man' in the Act. It was contended that Lord Brougham's Act[10] which stipulated that the word 'man' included 'women' applied to an interpretation of the Representation of the People Act. Bovill CJ rejected such a view:

> The conclusion at which I have arrived is, that the legislature used the word 'man' in the Act of 1867 in the same sense as 'male person' in the former Act; that this word was intentionally used, in order to designate expressly the male sex; and that it amounts to an express enactment and provision that every man, as distinguished from women, possessing the qualification, is to have the franchise. In that view, Lord Brougham's Act does not apply to the present case, and does not extend the meaning of the word 'man' so as to include women.[11]

Mr Justice Willis, Byles J and Keating J agreed. In accepting Bovill CJ's interpretation, Willis J turned to comment on the wider issue. In declaring himself opposed to any view that women were excluded from the franchise on the basis of 'fickleness of judgment and liability to influence', which would be quite inconsistent 'with one of the glories of our civilisation – the respect and honour in which women are held', Willis J declared, concerning the prohibition against voting – and the prohibition against peeresses in the House of Lords – that 'out of respect to women, and a sense of decorum, and not from their want of intellect, or their being for any other reason unfit to

---

7   See Kent, SK, *Sex and Suffrage in Britain 1860–1914*, 1987, Ewing, New Jersey: Princeton UP (rep 1990, London: Routledge).

8   A Member of Parliament and radical reformer. See, *inter alia*, Mill, JS, *Representative Government* (1865), 1958, Indianapolis: Bobbs-Merrill; see, also, Mill, JS, *On Liberty* (1859), 1989, Cambridge: CUP and *The Subjection of Women* (1869), 1989, Cambridge: CUP.

9   (1868) LR 4 CP 374. See, also, Chapter 7, p 233, fn 90.

10 13 & 14 Vict c 21.

11 (1868) LR 4 CP 374, p 387.

take part in the government of the country, they have been excused from taking any share in this department of public affairs'.[12]

In 1869, Mill published *The Subjection of Women*. The right to vote was but one campaign. Women were also seeking equal rights in education, in politics and in the medical profession. In 1897, the differing suffrage movements were to be united under the National Union of Women's Suffrage Societies. By 1913, the number of affiliated societies had reached 400. The leadership of Emmeline and Christabel Pankhurst injected new energy into the campaign and the age of militancy in support of the right to vote began. The tide of public opinion started to turn in women's favour in 1909, when the authorities started to force feed hunger striking suffragettes imprisoned as a result of their campaign. A Bill to give women the right to vote passed second reading in 1910, but was defeated by the Prime Minister, Asquith, acting in concert with Lloyd George, the Opposition Leader. The failure of a second Bill in 1911 sparked violent protest all over London: 217 women were arrested. A Bill of 1913 met with a similar fate and reaction. Fearful of the consequences of imprisonment and hunger strikes, the government passed the 'Cat and Mouse' Act,[13] which enabled the authorities to release hunger striking prisoners who were in medical danger and rearrest them on their physical recovery.

The persistence of the suffragettes, combined with the involvement of women in industry during the 1914–18 World War, acted as catalysts for winning the right to vote. In 1916, an all-party conference on electoral reform was established under the chairmanship of the Speaker of the House of Commons.

The Representation of the People Act 1918, which implemented the conference's proposals, introduced a full franchise of all men in parliamentary elections and conferred the right to vote in Parliament on all women over the age of 30 who were either local government electors or the wives of local government electors.[14] Full equality with men was delayed until 1928. A full franchise, on the basis of equality, and respecting the principle of 'one person, one vote', was finally achieved under the Representation of the People Act 1948.

---

12 (1868) LR 4 CP 374, p 392.

13 Prisoners (Temporary Discharge for Ill Health) Act 1913.

14 In addition, the Parliament (Qualification of Women) Act 1918 provided that: 'A woman shall not be disqualified by sex or marriage from being elected to or sitting or voting as a Member of the Commons House of Parliament.'

The current franchise

The right to vote is defined in the Representation of the People Act 1983, as amended, which consolidates earlier Representation Acts. Prior to enactment of the Representation of the People Act 2000, eligibility was based solely on residency in a constituency.[15] The Representation of the People Act 2000 extends the right to vote in both parliamentary elections and local government elections by supplementing the residency requirement with registration on the register of parliamentary electors for that constituency.[16] In addition, a person's eligibility depends on citizenship,[17] voting age (now 18 years and over),[18] and not being subject to any legal incapacity — including minors (those under the age of 18), aliens, peers other than Irish peers, mental patients who are compulsorily detained,[19] convicted persons in detention[20] and, for a period of five years, anyone found guilty of election offences.[21] Section 2 of the 2000 Act inserts into section 3 of the 1983 Act provisions relating to the disenfranchisement of offenders detained in mental hospitals.

Section 5 of the 1983 Act defined 'residence' for the purposes of inclusion on the electoral register. Section 3 of the 2000 Act extends those requirements. Section 6 of the 2000 Act[22] extends eligibility to vote in parliamentary or local elections, other than for those disenfranchised by virtue of mental incapacity or detention pursuant to criminal conviction, to those who have no fixed residence, through 'declarations of local connection'. A declaration of local connection must state the name of the declarant and either an address to which election correspondence can be delivered, or that he or she is willing to collect such correspondence periodically from the registration officer's office. The declaration must state the required address and also be dated, and, on the date of declaration, the declarant must also be otherwise qualified to vote by virtue of relevant citizenship and age. A declaration of local connection may be cancelled at any time by the declarant. The declaration is of no effect unless it is received by the relevant registration officer within the period of three months beginning with the date of the declaration.

---

15 Representation of the People Act 1983, ss 1 and 2.
16 Representation of the People Act 2000, ss 1 and 2, substituting ss 1 and 2 of the 1983 Act.
17 In relation to parliamentary elections, relevant citizenship is British citizenship, a qualifying Commonwealth citizen, or a citizen of the Republic of Ireland. In relation to local government elections, relevant citizens of the European Union are also eligible to vote: Representation of the People Act 1984, ss 1, 2 and 4; as amended by the Representation of the People Act 2000, ss 1, 2 and 4.
18 Representation of the People Act 1983, s 1.
19 *Ibid*, s 7, as substituted by s 4 of the 2000 Act.
20 *Ibid*, s 3, as amended by the Representation of the People Act 1985, Sched 4.
21 *Ibid*, s 60.
22 Inserting s 7B into the 1983 Act.

Section 7 of the 2000 Act provides that section 12(3) and (4) of the 1983 Act, which provides that persons with service qualifications may only be registered in pursuance of a service declaration, even where they would otherwise be entitled to vote by virtue of residence in the United Kingdom, shall cease to have effect.[23]

Constituencies

The United Kingdom is divided for electoral purposes into 659 constituencies, or voting areas. The number of constituencies was increased from 651 to 659 for the 1997 general election as a result of the Boundary Commissions' review, completed in 1994.[24] Each constituency is represented in Parliament by just one member, who has secured a majority of votes in a general election or by-election.[25] The regulation of constituency sizes is under the authority of four separate Boundary Commissions: one each for England, Scotland, Wales and Northern Ireland.[26]

The Boundary Commissions

The principle of 'one man, one vote, one value' is given formal recognition in the rules regulating the work of the Boundary Commissions[27] contained in the Parliamentary Constituencies Act 1986,[28] which consolidates the House of Commons (Redistribution of Seats) Acts 1949–79. Equality is not, however, as will be seen below, the sole, or even dominant, criterion. By way of comparison, in the United States of America, the principle was judicially considered by the Supreme Court in *Baker v Carr*, in 1962.[29] In that case, the principle was regarded as of such constitutional importance that the Supreme Court held that the Fourteenth Amendment of the Constitution – the 'equal protection' clause – required that electoral districts had to have an approximately equal number of electors to prevent over or under-representation and inequality in voting power.

---

23 Representation of the People Act 2000, Sched 2 extends the parliamentary franchise in relation to overseas voters, amending the Representation of the People Act 1985. On the right to vote and the European Convention of Human Rights, see *Matthews v United Kingdom* (1999) *The Times*, 3 February.

24 See the Boundary Commission Reports for England, Scotland and Wales, HC 433–I (1994–95), London: HMSO; SIs 1995/1626, 1037 and 1036.

25 An election in a single constituency, conducted as a result of the seat falling vacant during the life of a Parliament.

26 Parliamentary Constituencies Act 1986, s 2.

27 *Ibid*, Sched 2.

28 As amended by the Boundary Commissions Act 1992.

29 369 US 186 (1962).

Each Boundary Commission is headed by the Speaker of the House of Commons, and comprises a senior judge, as Deputy, and two other members who are not Members of Parliament. The duty of the Commissions is to review, and report to the Home Secretary, the representation within constituencies, reports being submitted not less than eight years or more than 12 years[30] from the date of the submission of their last report.[31]

The rules regulating the work of the Commissions are contained in Schedule 2 of the Parliamentary Constituencies Act 1986, from which it can be seen that the principle of 'one man, one vote, one value' is, under the United Kingdom's constitution, but one of several considerations. Schedule 2 provides, in part, that:

1   (i)   The number of constituencies in Great Britain shall not be substantially greater or less than 613;

    (ii) the number of constituencies in Scotland shall not be less than 71;[32]

    (iii) the number of constituencies in Wales shall not be less than 35;

    (iv) the number of constituencies in Northern Ireland shall not be greater than 18 or less than 16 ...

2   Every constituency shall return a single member.

...

4   So far as is practicable, having regard to rules 1–3:

    (a) in England and Wales,

      (i)   no county or part of a county shall be included in a constituency which includes the whole or part of any other county or the whole or part of a London borough;

      (ii) no London borough or any part of a London borough shall be included in a constituency which includes the whole or part of any other London borough.

5   The electorate of any constituency shall be as near the electoral quota as is practicable having regard to rules 1–4; and a Boundary Commission may depart from the strict application of rule 4 if it appears to them that a departure is desirable to avoid an excessive disparity between the electorate of any constituency and the electoral quota, or between the electorate of any constituency and that of neighbouring constituencies in the part of the United Kingdom with which they are concerned.

6   A Boundary Commission may depart from the strict application of rules 4 and 5 if special geographical considerations, including in particular the

---

30   Boundary Commissions Act 1992 reduced the period from intervals of 10 to 15 years.

31   Parliamentary Constituencies Act 1986, s 3, as amended by Boundary Commissions Act 1992.

32   The Scotland Act 1998 removes this minimum figure. In future, Scottish representation at Westminster will be calculated on the basis of population.

size, shape and accessibility of a constituency, appear to them to render a departure desirable.

In 1983, the English Boundary Commission proposals affected 468 out of the total of 516 constituencies, and seven new constituencies were added, bringing the total in England to 523. The largest constituency was Buckinghamshire, having an electorate of 122,036. By contrast, Newcastle Central had a mere 24,574 electors. Such a disparity effectively resulted in a vote in Buckinghamshire being worth one fifth of the value of a vote cast in Newcastle Central. The Commission recommended that two extra constituencies be created in Buckinghamshire to iron out the discrepancies. As a result of the Commission's report, 366 out of 523 constituencies had electorates within 10 per cent of the national average of 68,534 per seat. The average number of voters in constituencies in 1991 were: England, 69,279; Wales, 58,086; and Scotland, 54,369.

The Commission starts its work on the basis of the population count at the start of its inquiry – the 'enumeration date'. The 1983 report was thus based on the population of 1976.

The target figure for constituency electorates is based on the simple division of the eligible voting population in the country divided by the number of constituencies. The Commission aims to achieve a result which brings the majority of constituencies within a narrow band of this target figure, bearing in mind the other criteria contained within the rules. Between 1976 and 1983, the total electorate in England rose by 13 per cent, in part as a result of the lowering of the voting age to 18 years.[33] The Greater London electorate, by contrast, shrank by 3.7 per cent, and this factor would have justified a reduction in the capital's allocation of seats by 13. The report recommended, however, through according respect to local authority boundaries, a reduction of eight seats, to a total of 84 seats. In part, the Commission was concerned to redraw parliamentary boundaries in line with the revised local government boundaries established in 1974. A further important factor in the large number of changes recommended was the large population shift away from the cities and into the shires which had occurred since the previous review in 1969. The 1982 electoral register revealed 13 seats in non-metropolitan counties with more than 100,000 voters, a figure which may be contrasted with 15 constituencies wholly in metropolitan counties with fewer than 40,000 voters. On the 1976 electoral quota, the Commission found that 165 existing seats had electorates more than 20 per cent higher or lower than the quota. As a result of the 1983 changes, only 17 out of 523, or 3.25 per cent of constituencies, had more than 20 per cent above or below the quota.

---

33   Family Law Reform Act 1969.

When the new boundaries came into effect, the largest constituency was the Isle of Wight, with 94,768 electors, and the smallest, Surbiton, with 47,313. Over two-thirds of the new seats, 366 out of 523, had electorates within 10 per cent of the national average of 68,534 voters per seat. The discrepancies become even more stark when the 1992 figures are considered. In 1992, the Isle of Wight had 101,492 electors and Huntingdon, 94,077. By contrast, the Western Isles of Scotland had 23,015 electors, Meirionnydd Nan Conwy in Wales, 32,779 and Kensington, 42,327.[34]

The review commencing in 1983, and completed in 1994, led to an increase in the number of English seats from 524 to 529.[35]

Legal challenges to Boundary Commission reports

The political difficulties – generally the loss of a number of 'safe' seats by one party – which arise from boundary changes have given rise to challenges in the courts. In *R v Home Secretary ex parte McWhirter*,[36] the Labour Party feared the loss of up to 10 constituencies as a result of the Commission's recommendations. The Home Secretary laid the report before Parliament, without the draft Orders in Council which were necessary to implement the changes. The reason given for failure to produce the draft Orders was that it made little sense to implement changes, given that local government boundaries were under review at the time.

The Home Secretary introduced the House of Commons Redistribution of Seats Bill, implementing some of the recommendations regarding large urban areas, but not the remaining recommendations. The House of Lords introduced amendments, which the Home Secretary rejected. The Home Secretary then suggested compromise amendments, which the House of Lords rejected. Subsequently, the Home Secretary introduced the draft Orders in Council, leaving the Lords' amendments intact, but inviting the House of Commons to reject the Orders. The application for mandamus was withdrawn. In 1970, however, the incoming Conservative government reintroduced and passed the Orders.

In *R v Boundary Commission for England ex parte Foot*,[37] the Labour Party, having been aggrieved by the Boundary Commission's recommendations, instituted legal proceedings. The Rt Hon Michael Foot MP sought an order of prohibition and injunctions to restrain the Commission from putting the

---

34 Office of Population Censuses and Surveys, *Electoral Statistics 1992*, 1992, London: HMSO, Series EL No 19, p 2, cited in Blackburn, RW, *The Electoral System in Britain*, 1995, London: Macmillan, pp 114–15.

35 See HC 433-i (1994–95), London: HMSO; SIs 1995/1626, 1037, 1036.

36 (1969) *The Times*, 21 October.

37 [1983] QB 600.

recommendations to the Home Secretary, alleging that the Commission had misinterpreted the rules.[38] The court rejected the argument, relying on the considerable discretion built into the rules by the Parliamentary Constituencies Act. Sir John Donaldson MR, having referred to the constitutional role of judicial review, and accepted that jurisdiction lay to review the decision of the Boundary Commission, turned to the merits of the case:

> ... the issue in this appeal is quite simply whether there is any sufficient evidence that the commission is intent upon making recommendations which go beyond, or differ from, what any reasonable body of men in their position could properly make, exercising the best of their skill and judgment in the light of the instructions given to them by Parliament. If there is such sufficient evidence, it will or may be the duty of this court to intervene in order to ensure either that the commission's breach of duty is made known or, possibly, that it is remedied. If there is not, it must be the court's duty to leave the commission to get on with the process entrusted to them, that being their business and not that of the courts.

On the relationship between the different rules within Schedule 2 of the Act, the Master of the Rolls stated that:

> We are prepared to accept the theoretical possibility that in a given instance the disparity between the electorate of a proposed constituency and the electoral quota might be so grotesquely large as to make it obvious on the figures that no reasonable commission which had paid any attention at all to rule 5 could possibly have made such a proposal ...

> For all this, the submission that the statistics on their face reveal an error on the part of the commission seems to us totally unsustainable on the facts of the present case, for two reasons if no others. First, as we have already pointed out, the guidelines designed to achieve the broad equality of electorates, which are to be found in the opening limb of rule 5, have been deliberately expressed by the legislature in such a manner as to render them subordinate to the guidelines given by rule 4, designed to prevent the crossing of boundaries and not vice versa ... Even if a strict adherence to the principles of rule 4 will produce what is a *prima facie* excessive disparity between the electorate of any constituency and the electoral quota, the wording of the second limb of rule 5 implicitly makes it clear that the commission are to be left with a discretion not to depart from the strict application of rule 4 if, in all the particular circumstances of the case, they consider such departure undesirable ... From a bare reference to the statistics in the present case, we see no reason to assume that the commission did not, consciously and on sufficient grounds, conclude that departure from the strict application of rule 4 was not desirable in any of the particular cases where 'excessive disparity' is alleged.

> Secondly, and quite apart from this first reason, rule 6 expressly confers on the commission a discretion to depart from the strict application of either rule 4 or

---

38 Parliamentary Constituencies Act 1986, Sched 2.

rule 5 itself, if special geographical considerations, including in particular the size, shape and accessibility of a constituency, appear to them to render a departure desirable. We are wholly unable to say that any of the discrepancies in the cases of Stoke-on-Trent North and South East Staffordshire, already referred to ... are so great that they could not have been justifiable simply by a conscious exercise of the commission's discretion under rule 6 alone. There is no evidence that such a discretion was not exercised.

In all these circumstances, the burden of proof falls fairly and squarely on the applicants to show good grounds on the available evidence for saying that no reasonable commission, if properly instructed as to the relevant facts, could have arrived at the same decisions or proposals.

The reluctant attitude of the courts towards controlling the Boundary Commissions' exercise of power is understandable, given the politically charged nature of the subject matter. Judicial inquiry in this matter comes very close to questioning a matter which is more appropriately dealt with in Parliament,[39] and to thereby infringing the privileges of Parliament.[40] Nevertheless, such an attitude is thrown into sharp relief when compared with the position in the United States of America, where the constitutional guarantee of 'the equal protection of the law'[41] has been utilised to ensure real equality in voting power. As noted above, in *Baker v Carr*,[42] the Supreme Court held that such inequality (as is permitted under United Kingdom law) was a violation of the Fourteenth Amendment, which guarantees the equal protection of the law.

In Australia, a system of determining boundary sizes exists for each of the State Parliaments and for the Commonwealth Parliament. Under the Commonwealth Electoral Act 1918 (Cth), the Electoral Commission is under a duty to undertake a reassessment of the allocation of seats between the States between 11 and 12 months after the opening of the House of Representatives following a general election, in order that the review may be completed and recommendations implemented and 'available for use at the next election'. In relation to the House of Representatives, section 24 of the Commonwealth Constitution states:

... that the number of members chosen in the several States shall be in proportion to the respective numbers of their people. It has been held that this question of proportionality is to exist on each occasion when the members are chosen, that is, at each time an election is held.[43]

---

39   See Chapter 5 on separation of powers.
40   See Chapter 18 on privilege.
41   The Fourteenth Amendment to the Constitution.
42   369 US 186 (1962).
43   *Per* Gibbs J in *Attorney General (Cth); ex rel McKinlay v Commonwealth* (1975) 135 CLR 1, p 51.

Any legislation which impedes the review or implementation of its recommendations is invalid.[44] Despite these requirements, it has been held that total equality was not the objective. Rather, equality was to be measured on a scale of deviation from absolute equality: a 10 per cent variance would not contravene the requirements of section 24, whereas one of over 100 per cent clearly would.[45] The Constitutional Commission reviewing electoral law in 1988, while acknowledging the fundamental importance of 'one vote, one value', nevertheless conceded that such variation was acceptable.[46]

Reform of the Boundary Commissions?

There are a number of criticisms which may be levelled at the current arrangements concerning the number and size of constituencies. The first relates to the inherent conflict in principles enshrined in the legislation. The principle of equality in constituency size and hence voting power is too often sacrificed to the requirement to respect local government boundaries and to have regard to special geographical considerations. The second criticism relates to the time-lag between the enumeration date for the Commissions' reviews and the ultimate Report and recommendations. Were the Commissions required to complete their reviews on a fixed date and within a prescribed period from that date this problem could be alleviated. Professor Robert Blackburn has addressed this issue, calling for reforms which would require the Commissions to complete their work within a two year period from the fixed date of report.[47] Not only would this reform diminish the problem of population changes within the time taken to complete the review, but the fixed term for submission of the Report would also avoid much of the uncertainty which surrounds the implementation of boundary changes, and encourages party-political controversy.

Robert Blackburn also calls for the appointment of a single Boundary Commission, rather than the existing four Commissions which, although there is some liaison, operate largely autonomously. The advantages of a single Commission, in Blackburn's view, would include:

> ... rationalisation of working practices and criteria across the United Kingdom; the greater professionalism and independence which would attend a permanent body of experts; the opportunity for the Commission to take on the role of reviewing all matters relating to elections, including financial matters, broadcasting and advertising. The Commission, should, the author argues, be headed by an independent Chairman rather than the Speaker of the House of

---

44 *Attorney General (Cth); ex rel McKinlay v Commonwealth* (1975) 135 CLR 1.
45 *Ibid*, pp 37, 39.
46 Constitutional Commission, Final Report, 1988, p 154.
47 See *op cit*, Blackburn, fn 34, Chapter 4.

Commons, who, in any event, plays no role in the actual working of the Boundary Commissions.[48]

INITIATING THE ELECTION PROCESS

General elections

General elections must be held every five years, the maximum life of any Parliament.[49] Section 7 of the Septennial Act 1715, as amended by the Parliament Act 1911, provides that a Parliament shall 'have continuance for five years, and no longer ...'. A royal proclamation dissolves Parliament and orders the issue of writs for the election of a new Parliament.

The Prime Minister controls the timing of general elections although, in theory, the dissolution of Parliament lies within the prerogative of the Crown.[50] The Crown's powers in relation to the dissolution of Parliament are discussed in Chapter 6. Within the context of electoral law, what is of significance is the inexactitude relating to the actual date of a general election, and the extent to which Prime Ministers control the timing of elections. While a Parliament may run for a full five year term, there are often political reasons against this, which result in Prime Ministers choosing a politically convenient date for his or her own party. While there is a maximum time limit on the life of a Parliament, there is no minimum period which a government must serve before calling an election.[51] In 1974, for example, the Parliament lasted less than one year, whereas Parliament's life extended to four years and nine months between 1987 and 1992. The Parliament elected in 1992, would have ceased to exist on Saturday 26 April 1997, had it not been previously dissolved. In the absence of firm rules, Prime Ministers also have latitude over the amount of notice which is given before the election is held. In 1974, Edward Heath gave just one day's notice before Parliament was dissolved; later that year, Harold Wilson gave just two day's notice before the dissolution; whereas Margaret Thatcher gave seven days' notice before the 1987 dissolution and, in 1992, John Major gave five days' notice.[52]

---

48 See *op cit*, Blackburn, fn 34, Chapter 4.

49 Parliament Act 1911, s 7.

50 For detailed discussion of the dissolution of Parliament, see Chapter 6.

51 Although, as discussed in Chapter 6, the Crown could, in theory, refuse the dissolution of Parliament if it were considered that a second election within a short period of time would run counter to the public interest.

52 See *op cit*, Blackburn, fn 34, Chapter 2; Gay, O and Winetrobe, B, 'Putting out the writs' [1997] PL 385.

By-elections

By-elections take place following the death or retirement of a Member of Parliament. Any Member of Parliament may put down a motion to the House, which if successful, orders the Speaker to make a warrant for the issue of a writ commencing the election procedure. In practice, the Chief Whip of the party which held the seat of the Member moves the motion for a writ. There is a limit laid down by law as to the time period in which a by-election must be held. In 1973, a Speaker's Conference recommended that the motion initiating the by-election process should be moved within three months of the vacancy arising.

Eligibility of candidates

There is no statutory or other authority defining the qualifications for membership of the House of Commons. However, under the House of Commons Disqualification Act 1975, certain categories of persons are eligible for election and others are disqualified under the Act.

Under the House of Commons Disqualification Act 1975,[53] the following classes of persons are disqualified from membership of the Commons:

(a) holders of judicial office;[54]

(b) civil servants;

(c) members of the armed forces;

(d) members of the police;

(e) members of non-Commonwealth legislatures;

(f) members of Boards of Nationalised Industries, Commissions, Tribunals and other bodies whose members are appointed by the Crown.[55]

In addition, a number of general restrictions on eligibility apply.

Persons under the age of 21

While the age of majority was reduced in 1969,[56] eligibility for election to Parliament does not arise until the age of 21.[57]

---

53 House of Commons Disqualification Act 1975, s 1 and Sched 1.
54 As specified in *ibid*, Sched 1.
55 See *ibid*, Sched 1, Pt II.
56 Family Law Reform Act 1969.
57 *Ibid*, Sched 2, para 1.

Persons suffering from mental illness

Mental illness is a common law disqualification. If an already elected Member of Parliament is authorised to be detained on grounds of mental illness, the Speaker of the House is notified and, following confirmation of the illness, the Member's seat is declared vacant.[58]

Peers

Members of the House of Lords, or persons succeeding to a peerage, are not eligible for office. Under the Peerage Act 1963, a person succeeding to a peerage has a limited right to disclaim his peerage.[59] If a member of the House of Commons succeeds to a peerage, he has one month in which to disclaim his peerage or resign from the House of Commons.

Members of the clergy

No person who has been ordained 'to the office of priest or deacon' or who is a Minister of the Church of Scotland may stand for election.[60] A clergyman may relinquish his office and thereby become eligible to stand for election.[61] The disqualification of the clergy is preserved by section 10(2) of the House of Commons Disqualification Act 1975. A select Committee examined the issue of the clergy, but recommended that no change should be introduced.[62]

Bankrupts

Persons declared bankrupt are ineligible for election to the House of Commons and, if already a Member, may not either sit or vote in Parliament until the bankruptcy is discharged by a court or the adjudication annulled.[63]

Treason

Persons convicted of treason are disqualified for election to the House and, if already a Member of the House, may not sit or vote until a pardon has been received or the sentence of the court has expired.[64]

---

58 Mental Health Act 1983, s 141.
59 See, further, Chapter 17.
60 House of Commons (Clergy Disqualification) Act 1801; Roman Catholic Relief Act 1929; Welsh Church Act 1914.
61 Clerical Disabilities Act 1870.
62 HC 200 (1952–53), London: HMSO.
63 Insolvency Act 1986, s 427.
64 Forfeiture Act 1870, ss 2 and 7.

Corrupt practices at elections

Any person found guilty of corrupt practices in the course of an election may be disqualified from membership of the House of Commons. If the corrupt practices come to light only after the election, the Member may be disqualified from sitting in Parliament.[65] The disqualification commences from the date of the report of the Election Court on the practices and will last, in relation to any constituency, for a period of five years and, in relation to the constituency in which the practices occurred, for a 10 year period.

The conduct of election campaigns

The Representation of the People Act 1983 governs the law relating to election campaigns, controlling both the amounts of expenditure and the manner in which it can lawfully be spent, proscribing certain unlawful practices and providing for challenges to the legality of a campaign.[66] Corrupt practices include exceeding the lawful expenditure limits, bribery, treating, and undue influence which includes making threats or attempts to intimidate electors.[67] A bribe is defined as 'any money, gift, loan or valuable consideration, office, place or employment, in order to influence how an elector will cast his or her vote'.[68] 'Treating' occurs where a candidate offers or gives food, drink or entertainment with a view to influencing how the elector will vote.[69] A corrupt practice may be committed by any person, not just the candidate or his or her election agent. While minor infringement of the strict rules may be excused by a court,[70] a finding of corrupt practices may cause the election of the candidate to be invalidated.[71]

It may be noted at this point that the law closely regulates the conduct of constituency campaigns, but virtually ignores regulation of the national political party campaigns. In an age of mass communication, and ever increasing personality politics in terms of political party leaders, the absence of regulation at national level – other than via broadcasting controls – is a matter for concern.[72]

---

65 Representation of the People Act 1983, ss 159 and 160.

66 In December 1997, it was reported that charges of election fraud were made against the Labour Members for Glasgow Govan, Mohammed Sarwar, who was suspended. The criminal charges related to late registration of voters, attempting to pervert the course of justice and contravention of the Representation of the People Act in connection with election expenses. Mr Sarwar was acquitted of all charges.

67 Originally, the Corrupt and Illegal Practices Prevention Act 1883. See, now, the Representation of the People Act 1983, ss 72–75, 107, 109, 111, 115.

68 Representation of the People Act 1983, s 113.

69 *Ibid*, s 114.

70 *Ibid*, s 167.

71 *Ibid*, s 159.

72 See, further, below.

Section 10 of the Representation of the People Act 2000 makes provision for greater flexibility in the voting arrangements for local government elections. A local authority may submit to the Secretary of State proposals for a scheme relating to when, where and how voting is to take place, how the votes cast are to be counted and the sending by candidates of election communications free of postage charges. The scheme may make provision for voting to take place on more than one day, and at places other than polling booths. The Secretary of State has power to approve the proposals either without modification or with such modifications as, after consulting the authority, he considers appropriate, and may by order make provision for and in connection with the implementation of the scheme in relation to those elections he considers appropriate. Once elections under the scheme have taken place, the authority concerned must prepare a report on the scheme, detailing its provisions and assessing the scheme's success or otherwise in facilitating voting at the elections in question and, if relevant, the counting of votes, or in encouraging voting at the elections in question or enabling voters to make informed decisions at those elections. The assessment must also include a statement by the authority as to whether in their opinion:

(a) the turnout was higher than it would have been if the scheme was not applied;

(b) the voters found the procedures provided for their assistance by the scheme easy to use;

(c) the procedures provided for by the scheme led to any increase in personation or other electoral offences or in any other malpractice in connection with elections;

(d) those procedures led to any increase in expenditure, or to any savings, by the authority.[73]

A copy of the report must be sent to the Secretary of State, and published in the relevant area, by the end of the period of three months beginning with the date of the declaration of the result. If it appears to the Secretary of State that it would be desirable for provision to be made to apply generally and on a permanent basis to local government elections in England and Wales, he may by order make such provision as he considers appropriate, which power includes the power to modify or disapply any provision of an Act of Parliament including the 2000 Act. Such an order must be made by statutory instrument, and laid before and approved by a resolution of each House of Parliament.[74]

---

73 Representation of the People Act 2000, s 10(8).
74 *Ibid*, s 11.

The 2000 Act makes special provision for assistance with voting for persons with disabilities, whether by virtue of partial sight, blindness or other physical incapacity or inability to read.[75, 76]

Expenditure

Section 75 of the Representation of the People Act 1983 provides that no expenditure shall be made other than by the candidate or through his or her election agent. Each candidate is obliged to appoint an election agent.[77] The rationale for this rule lies in establishing and maintaining fairness between candidates and providing a mechanism for accountability as to election expenses. All accounts relating to election expenses must be reported, within 21 days of the election result, to the Returning Officer. Section 76 of the Act[78] permits the Secretary of State to set and raise the permitted amounts of expenditure, in line with inflation, by way of statutory instrument. The allowable amounts are £4,642 per candidate per borough (urban) constituency, plus 3.9 pence for each voter in the constituency and 5.2 pence for each voter in a county (country) constituency. The amounts were increased by 6.9 per cent in 1997.[79] Any expenditure exceeding the prescribed limits amounts to a corrupt practice under section 75(1). Expenditure on national party election broadcasts is met by central party funds. Broadcasting is controlled by sections 92 and 93 of the Act, and is confined to broadcasts made by the British Broadcasting Corporation and Independent Broadcasting Authority. No broadcast may be made without the consent of the participating candidate.[80]

Several challenges to expenditure have been presented to the courts. In *R v Tronoh Mines Ltd*,[81] Tronoh Mines placed an advertisement in *The Times* newspaper urging voters not to vote socialist. The company and *The Times* were charged under the Act. The court held that the expenditure had been incurred with a view to promoting the interests of a Party generally, rather than an individual candidate; that any advantage incurred was incidental and not direct; and that accordingly the expenditure did not fall within section 75.

---

75 Representation of the People Act 2000, s 13, amending the 1983 Act, Sched 1, the parliamentary elections rules.

76 The Act also makes provision for the free delivery of election addresses by candidates at the first election for London Mayor: s 14 of the 2000 Act amending the Greater London Authority Act 1999, s 17, on which, see Chapter 12.

77 Representation of the People Act 1983, s 67(2).

78 As amended by the Representation of the People Act 1985.

79 The Presentation of the People (Variation of Limits of Candidates' Election Expenses) Order SI 1997/879. See HC Deb Vol 291 Col 659, 3 March 1997 and HL Deb Vol 579 Col 564, 14 March 1997.

80 *Marshall v BBC* [1979] 3 All ER 80. See, further, below.

81 [1952] 1 All ER 697.

Conversely, in *DPP v Luft*,[82] an anti-fascist group had distributed pamphlets in three constituencies urging voters not to vote for National Front (extreme right wing) candidates. The group was prosecuted under section 75 of the 1983 Act for incurring expenditure with a view to promoting the election of a candidate without the authority of an election agent. It was held that an offence had been committed, even though the promoters were seeking to prevent election of a candidate, rather than directly promote the election of a preferred candidate. In *Walker v Unison*,[83] the court ruled that section 75(1) of the Representation of the People Act 1983 had not been breached. During local elections in Scotland, Unison, a trades union, placed advertisements in national newspapers and on billboards, urging voters not to vote Conservative. The advertisements were placed without the authorisation of an election agent. Two Conservative candidates argued that there had been an illegal expenditure. The court ruled that the advertisements were a generalised attack on a political party, and not a direct attack on the candidates and, accordingly, the advertisements did not contravene the Act.

Section 75 of the Representation of the People Act has come under the scrutiny of the European Court of Human Rights.[84] In *Bowman v United Kingdom*, the applicant had been prosecuted under section 75, as being an 'unauthorised person' for the purpose of election expenditure incurred 'with a view to promoting or procuring the election of a candidate' in the 1992 general election, over the allowable £5 limit. She was acquitted because the summons had been issued out of time. On an application under the European Convention on Human Rights, the applicant alleged a breach of Article 10, which protects freedom of expression, by section 75 of the Representation of the People Act. The Court of Human Rights noted that section 75 did not directly limit freedom of expression but, rather, was directed to prohibit unauthorised expenditure during election campaigns for the purpose of promoting a candidate's election. The Court also accepted that the aims of the legislation – the promotion of equality between candidates – was a legitimate aim. However, one of the fundamental requirements of a democratic society is the promotion of freedom of expression and, in particular, freedom of political debate within the context of the election process. The requirement of freedom of expression had to be balanced against the legitimacy of the State's interest in promoting equality in the election campaign. The Court ruled, by a majority of 14 to six, however, that Mrs Bowman had no other effective means, within the period the election campaign, of communicating information to the electorate on the candidates' attitudes to, and voting record on, abortion. Section 75 therefore operated as a total ban on Mrs Bowman's freedom of expression, albeit within a narrow time frame. It was not necessary, to achieve

---

82　[1977] AC 962.

83　1995 SLT 1225.

84　Case 141/1996/762/959: *Bowman v United Kingdom* (1998) *The Times*, 23 February.

equality between the candidates, to limit the applicant's expenditure to £5, especially in light of the lack of financial controls at national party-political level. The restriction was accordingly disproportionate to the aim pursued, and represented a violation of Article 10 of the Convention. The Committee on Standards in Public Life recommended that the £5 limit should be raised to £500, and section 75 amended accordingly.[85]

In *Grieve v Douglas-Home*,[86] Alec Douglas-Home's election was alleged to be void on the basis that he had participated in a national Party Political Broadcast on behalf of the Conservative Party and had not declared the cost of this expenditure within his election expenses. The court held that no offence had been committed either by the candidate, the British Broadcasting Corporation (BBC) or the Independent Broadcasting Authority (IBA). The court accepted the contention that the intention behind the broadcast was not to promote the candidature of Douglas-Home in his own constituency but to provide general information about the Party to the general public.

Broadcasting and elections

No broadcast may be made other than through the BBC or the ITC. The role of these two organisations is unregulated by statute. There exists a non-statutory body, the Committee on Party Political Broadcasts, which comprises representatives from the broadcasting authorities and from the main political parties. Broadcasting time is allocated on the basis of the number of votes cast for each party at the last general election, and at by-elections between general elections. This arrangement disadvantages the Liberal Democrats, who have wide popular support throughout the country, and other smaller parties, such as the Scottish National Party and the Green Party, which enjoy much popular support nationwide which rarely – because of the voting system employed[87] – translates into electoral success.

The ITC is under a statutory duty[88] to ensure that news is accurate and impartial, and that political parties are given a fair allocation of time for party political broadcasts and news coverage of their campaigns. The BBC is not controlled by statute, but by Charter, and is under a duty to preserve impartiality. Judicial review will lie if either body infringes the rules. This general duty of fairness was raised by the Rt Hon David Owen MP,[89] in *R v*

---

85 Fifth Report of the Committee of Standards in Public Life, *The Funding of Political Parties in the United Kingdom*, Cm 4057-1, 1998, London: The Stationery Office, Vol I, para 9.6; see, also, White Paper, Cm 4413, 1999 and Political Parties, Elections and Referendums Bill 2000, discussed below.

86 1965 SLT 186.

87 See below.

88 Broadcasting Act 1981, s 4.

89 Now, Lord Owen.

Broadcasting Complaints Commission ex parte Owen.[90] David Owen had complained to the Commission that the allocation of time to various parties, principally the Social Democratic Party, was unjust or unfair under section 54 of the Broadcasting Act 1981. On an appeal to the court, it was held that the Commission had jurisdiction to consider complaints about general fairness, rather than just the unfairness, or otherwise, of particular programmes, but that the Commission had acted lawfully in allocating time on the basis of the number of seats won rather than votes cast. A further challenge to the allocation of broadcasting time came in *R v British Broadcasting Corporation ex parte Referendum Party.*[91] The Referendum Party was founded in 1994 and contested 547 seats at the general election. The broadcasting authorities allocated the party one five-minute broadcast on each network. The Conservative and Labour parties each were allocated four broadcasts. The Referendum Party sought judicial review, claiming that it had three per cent support in public opinion polls and that, given that it was a new party, the broadcasting authorities should not have relied on past electoral support. The Divisional Court held that former electoral support must not be determinative, but that the authorities were allowed to include it as a criterion. The decision was not irrational.

It has been noted above, p 542, that the law[92] requires the consent of participants in broadcasts. In addition to that requirement, if a candidate participates in a broadcast with a view to promoting his own election, every other candidate in the constituency must consent to the broadcast. This rule was tested in *Marshall v BBC.*[93] The candidate, having refused to participate in a debate, was filmed while canvassing in the streets. On a challenge to the legality of the broadcast, it was held that no offence had been committed. To 'take part' in a constituency item, means to take active part in.

Disputed elections

Any challenge to an election campaign must be made within three weeks of the result being declared. The complaint may be made by a registered elector, by unsuccessful candidates or by their nominees. Since 1868, such challenges go to the Election Court, a Divisional Court of the Queen's Bench Division of the High Court. The court has the power to order a recount; declare corrupt or illegal practices; disqualify a candidate from membership of the House of Commons and declare the runner-up duly elected; or to order a fresh election. Two cases illustrate this aspect of the law. In *Re Parliamentary Election for*

90   [1985] QB 1153.
91   (1997) *The Times*, 29 April.
92   Representation of the People Act 1983, s 93(1).
93   [1979] 3 All ER 80.

Bristol South East,[94] Tony Benn MP, who had recently succeeded to a peerage as Viscount Stansgate, stood for re-election. The election was declared void and awarded to the runner-up. In *Ruffle v Rogers*,[95] the election papers were incorrectly counted and affected the outcome of the election. The election was declared void, but the court made clear that had the miscount not affected the result, the election would have been upheld. A fresh election was ordered in 1997, following allegations concerning the accuracy of the count of the vote which returned a Member of Parliament with a majority of just two votes.

The Registration of Political Parties Act 1998

The Act introduces for the first time a register of political parties. A political party is entitled to be entered on the Register of Political Parties if that party intends to have one or more candidates at parliamentary elections, elections to the European Parliament, Scottish Parliament, National Assembly for Wales, the Northern Ireland Assembly or local government elections. Registration is intended to clarify the identity of *bona fide* political parties and thereby make regulation more certain. No party political broadcast may be made by broadcasters other than on behalf of a registered political party.[96]

Political party funding[97]

In the United Kingdom, there is no provision for State aid for political parties for the conduct of election campaigns. Political parties do, however, receive public funds for their parliamentary work. Under the system, generally known as 'Short Money',[98] the money allocated is to be spent exclusively in relation to the party's parliamentary business, and not for election expenses. The amounts allocated are indicated below. A similar scheme operates in the House of Lords. Introduced in 1996 by the then Leader of the House of Lords, Viscount Cranborne, 'Cranborne Money' is paid to the first two opposition parties. From 1997 to 1998, the total allocation in the Lords was £134,000. The Committee on Standards in Public Life has recommended that both the Commons and the Lords consider considerable increases of the amounts paid to opposition parties. In addition to financial support for parliamentary

---

94 [1964] 2 QB 257.

95 [1982] 3 WLR 143.

96 Registration of Political Parties Act 1998, s 14.

97 See Ewing, K, *The Funding of Political Parties*, 1987, Cambridge: CUP; Oliver, D, 'Fairness and political finance: the case of election campaigns', in Blackburn, RW (ed), *Constitutional Studies*, 1992, London: Mansell.

98 After the Rt Hon Edward Short (now Lord Glenamara), the Leader of the House of Commons in 1975 when the system was introduced.

business, candidates at parliamentary elections or elections to the European Parliament are entitled to free postage for one election communication to every elector within the constituency. Candidates are also entitled to the free use of publicly funded premises for an election meeting. Indirect State assistance is provided through political broadcasts during election campaigns.

TABLE I: PAYMENTS TO OPPOSITION PARTIES IN THE HOUSE OF COMMONS BETWEEN MAY 1987 AND MARCH 1998

Party	Grant
Conservative	£986,762
Liberal Democrat	£371,997
Ulster Unionists	£ 47,580
Scottish National	£ 46,167
SDLP	£ 18,553
Plaid Cymru	£ 21,210
Democratic Unionist	£ 11,618[99]

For election purposes, parties are dependent upon the support of the membership and, more importantly, from companies and trades unions. Approximately 30 per cent of Conservative Party funds come from companies, whereas almost 55 per cent of Labour Party funds have traditionally come from trades union donations, although this pattern has recently changed. In 1976, the Houghton Committee recommended that State aid be given to parties in proportion to the success at the previous election. In 1982, the Commission recommended State funding equivalent to individual contributions to local constituency parties. Neither proposal has been adopted. Payments are, however, made to opposition parties in Parliament on the basis of a fixed sum for every seat won, plus an amount for every 100 votes cast, up to a fixed maximum for any one party.

The issue of party funding was brought to the forefront of debate in June 1993. Senior Conservative Members of Parliament joined in the criticism of donations in evidence to the Home Affairs Select Committee on Party Funding. Sir Norman Fowler, Conservative Party Chairman, was under pressure to disclose party funds. In debate on 22 June, heated exchanges took place – including an accusation by Margaret Beckett, then Labour's Deputy Leader that there existed an 'atmosphere of sleaze and odour of corruption' in relation to party funding. In the course of debate, Sir Norman Fowler dismissed claims that the Party had received £7 million from sources close to

---

99 Fifth Report of the Committee of Standards in Public Life, *The Funding of Political Parties in the United Kingdom*, Cm 4057-1, 1998, London: The Stationery Office, Vol I, para 9.6.

the Saudi Arabian government: '... the Conservative Party did not, does not and will not accept donations from foreign governments and that also applies to foreign royal families.' In a vote in the Commons, the government won its motion supporting the principle of voluntary contribution to political parties by 284 votes to 249, a majority of 35.

State funding of political parties?[100]

Any limitation on the rights of parties to accept funds, disclosed or undisclosed, increases the arguments in favour of State funding of political parties. State funding in Europe is an accepted commonplace. Austria, Denmark, France, Germany, Greece, Italy, Portugal and Spain all have publicly funded political parties. This issue is, however, contentious in the United Kingdom on a number of grounds. First, it is argued by the Conservative Party that state funding potentially undermines the cohesiveness of the party, and introduces the possibility of politically inspired changes to the bases of funding. Moreover, it is argued that State funding would encourage the formation and growth of extremist parties. Opposition is also voiced on the constitutional basis that, to compel citizens to finance political parties, through taxation, especially those with which they have no sympathy, would cause dissent. Set against these objections, however, are the benefits which would accrue from public funding. First, depending on the method used to calculate entitlement, greater equality and fairness would be achieved among the political parties. Secondly, party political finances would become most clearly a matter of open public record. Thirdly, the elimination of contributions from individuals and organisations would eradicate the public's suspicions about the integrity of party political finance and thus enhance confidence in the political process. Fourthly, the ability of parties to conduct their official duties would be enhanced by improving the level of contributions made. The Houghton Committee commented, in its 1976 report, that, at a local level, party organisation was weak and 'generally exists on a pitifully inadequate scale of accommodation, equipment, trained staff and resources'.[101] Thus, improved funding would facilitate an enhanced level of efficiency at the grass roots level of democracy.

In November 1997, the Labour Government extended the terms of reference of the Committee on Standards in Public Life to include political party funding. Recognising that 'political parties are essential to democracy',[102] the Committee identified three of the seven 'principles of

---

100 See *Report of the Committee on Financial Aid to Political Parties*, Cmd 6601, 1976, London: HMSO (the 'Houghton Report'); Hansard Society Commission, *The Financing of Political Parties*, 1981; the Home Affairs Select Committee, *Funding of Political Parties*, HC 301 (1993–94), London: HMSO.

101 *Ibid*, Houghton Report, p 54.

102 *Ibid*, Houghton Report, para 2.1.

public life', namely, integrity, accountability and openness, as particularly relevant to the funding of political parties. Increasing election spending by the two main parties, who between them spent some £54 million on the last general election, and the issue of large donations to political parties by persons known or unknown, gave rise to the public perception that election results can be affected by spending and that wealthy organisations or individuals could effectively influence public policy. Undisclosed foreign donations to the Conservative Party also caused concern. Whereas the Conservative Party accepted 47 overseas donations worth a total of £16.2 million between 1992 and 1997, the Labour Party received none. In the same period, the Conservative Party received over 1,300 donations of over £5,000 while the Labour Party received almost 300.

In the Committee's view, it was 'undesirable that a political party should be dependent for its financial survival on funds provided by a few well endowed individuals, corporations or organisations', irrespective of 'whether or not the suspicion [that he who pays the piper calls the tune] is justified'. The problem of public confidence in the political system was compounded when such donations came from undisclosed sources.

On the issue of State funding for political parties, the Committee considered the arguments for and against increasing aid. The principal argument in favour was that public funding would 'purify' the political process by eliminating the need for parties to be reliant on donations. State aid would also enable the parties to fulfil their functions more effectively, both ensuring that sufficient funds were available to cover costs and that parties were not reliant on individuals or organisations for finance. On the other hand, it was argued, *inter alia*, that individual taxpayers should not be obliged to contribute to financing political parties with whose views they disagreed. There was also the problem of the criteria for State aid, which, if dependent upon success at elections, could deter new parties from access to funding. The Committee found the arguments for and against State funding 'finely balanced', but the arguments in favour were not conclusive. The Committee considered that its proposals for limits on campaign expenditure coupled with the requirements of disclosure and registration would meet the concerns expressed about the current system of party funding.

Controls over donations and expenditure: the recommendations

The Committee proposed significant changes to the funding of political parties. Under the recommendations, political parties will be limited in future to £20 million expenditure on national general elections. Rules will be introduced to regulate the preparation and auditing of a political party's annual accounts and election expenditure. The proposals call for public disclosure of donations, including benefits in kind, to political parties of £5,000 or more nationally and of £1,000 or more in a constituency in any one financial year, from any one person or source. Anonymous donations to political parties over the sum of £50 will be prohibited. In order to encourage small donations to political parties, tax relief on donations of up to £500 is recommended. Donations to parties will only be allowed from a 'permissible source', which is defined as being registered voters in the United Kingdom and those who are eligible to be put on the electoral register. Those eligible include British subjects, Commonwealth citizens, citizens of the Republic of Ireland and citizens of the European Union resident in the United Kingdom and overseas voters. Companies registered in the United Kingdom would be regarded as a permissible source, as would partnerships based in the United Kingdom and operating principally in the United Kingdom. Trade unions registered in the United Kingdom would also be a permissible source, as would other organisations, voluntary associations and trusts if genuinely based in the United Kingdom and operating principally in the United Kingdom. The setting up of blind trusts – trusts created to fund the private offices of Opposition members, the beneficiaries of which do not know the identity of the donor – is to be prohibited, as being inconsistent with transparency and openness. Open trusts, however, will be permitted, subject to the disclosure of donations and their registration in the Register of Members' Interests. If the amount of money payable to the opposition parties for their parliamentary duties is increased, as the Committee recommends, the need for donations to trusts should be diminished considerably.

It will be the responsibility of the political parties to ensure that donations are received only from a permissible source, and the party will be required to certify the legality of sources to the Election Commission. The definition of permissible sources is designed to prohibit in effect, foreign donations.

Regulating party funding, elections and referendums: the Election Commission

The requirements of openness and transparency can only be met through the disclosure of the identity of donors and the amount of donations to political parties and their registration. The Committee recommended that there be established an Election Commission, independent of both government and political parties, charged with the tasks of regulating party funds and overseeing the conduct of elections and referendums. The Commission will have a number of roles. It will receive the audited accounts of political parties and receive and publish details of 'substantial donations to political parties', stipulated to be £5,000 or more nationally and of £1,000 or more in a constituency. The Commission will have investigative powers, enabling it to enquire into allegations of improper election expenditure, or illegal donations. The Commission will also be responsible for the registration of political parties. In addition, the Commission will act as an advisory body for political parties. It will also have the responsibility for keeping election practices and law under review, and to make recommendations for reform.

The Committee recommends that the Commission have five part time members, holding office for a 'considerable period of years' and enjoying substantial security of tenure. The Commission's terms of reference will extend to the whole of the United Kingdom, with individual Commissioners taking responsibility for overseeing electoral matters in Scotland, Wales and Northern Ireland. Responsibility for the conduct of elections, currently overseen by local Acting Returning Officers, will fall within the Commission's responsibility, with a brief report on the conduct of elections and referendums being drawn up and published within six months of the election or referendum date.

The Political Parties, Elections and Referendums Act 2000

The Political Parties, Elections and Referendums Act 2000 gives effect to the recommendations. The Act provides for the establishment of the Electoral Commission, comprising not less than five but not more than nine Electoral Commissioners, appointed by Her Majesty. The Commission is not to be regarded as the servant or agent of the Crown, or as enjoying any status, immunity or privilege of the Crown. Schedule 1 makes detailed provision for the terms of office. The Commission regulates its own procedure, and may appoint a chief executive and such other staff as the Commission considers necessary.

The Commission's functions include preparing and publishing reports relating to parliamentary general elections and elections to the European Parliament, Scottish Parliament, National Assembly for Wales and Northern Ireland Assembly.[103] The Commission must keep under review such matters relating to elections and referendums as the Commission determines, the redistribution of seats at parliamentary elections, the registration of political parties and the regulation of their income and expenditure and political advertising.[104] The Commission assumes responsibility for the registration of political parties.[105] No nomination may be made in relation to an election in the name of a party unless that party is registered, or the candidate is a person who does not propose to represent any party.[106]

The Commission may provide advice and assistance in relation to elections.[107] The Commission is also to be under a duty to promote public

---

103 Political Parties, Elections and Referendums Act 2000, s 5.
104 *Ibid*, Part II.
105 Currently regulated under the Registration of Political Parties Act 1998.
106 Political Parties, Elections and Referendums Act 2000, s 22.
107 *Ibid*, s 10.

awareness about electoral and democratic systems, including the institutions of the European Union.[108] The Act also provides that the functions of the Boundary Committees, as they are labelled in the Act, are transferred to the Electoral Commission.[109] Under Part II of the Act, the registration of political parties falls under the Commission's terms of reference, and Part III provides for accounting requirements for registered parties, and provides for annual audits for parties whose gross income or total expenditure exceeds £250,000 in any financial year, and in relation to those with less income or total expenditure, where the Commission requires an audit to be carried out. Failure to submit a proper statement of accounts incurs criminal liability.

There is established a Speaker's Committee, consisting of the Speaker and the Chairman of the Home Affairs Select Committee of the House of Commons, the Secretary of State for the Home Department, whether or not a Member of the Commons, a member of the Commons who is the Minister with responsibilities in relation to local government and five Members of the Commons who are not Ministers.[110] The Speaker's Committee scrutinises the annual estimates of the Commission, and decides whether the estimated level of income and expenditure is consistent with the economical, efficient and effective discharge by the Commission of their functions. If the Committee is not satisfied, it may modify the estimates. Having concluded examination of the estimate, the estimate is laid before the House of Commons. The Commission is also to submit to the Speaker's Committee a five year plan, setting out the aims and objectives for the period and estimated requirements for resources during that five year period. The Speaker's Committee examines the plan, and may make modifications. The Speaker's Committee is assisted by the Comptroller and Auditor General, who, each year, is to carry out an examination into the economy, efficiency and effectiveness with which the Commission has used its resources in discharging its functions, and report to the Speaker's Committee, including such recommendations as he considers appropriate.[111]

Part IV of the Act provides for the control of donations to registered parties and their members, defining permissible donors and providing rules regulating the acceptance or return of donations, and providing for forfeiture of donations by impermissible or unidentifiable donors, under a court order, on an application of the Commission. A person commits an offence if he or she knowingly enters into, or does any act in furtherance of, any arrangement which facilitates or is likely to facilitate the making of donations by any person or donor other than a permissible donor. The Act provides for quarterly

108 Political Parties, Elections and Referendums Act 2000, s 13.
109 *Ibid*, ss 14–20.
0 *Ibid*, s 2.
bid, Sched 1.

donation reports to be made,[112] and, in the period of general elections, for weekly reports.[113] The Commission is to maintain a register of donations.[114]

Part V of the Act relates to campaign expenditure. No expenditure may be incurred by or on behalf of the registered party unless it is incurred with the authority of the treasurer or deputy treasurer of the party, or a person authorised by the treasurer or deputy treasurer. No campaign expenditure may be incurred unless it is made by the above.[115] Section 74 and Schedule 8 impose limits on campaign expenditure in relation to parliamentary general elections and general elections to the European Parliament, Scottish Parliament, National Assembly for Wales and the Northern Ireland Assembly. In relation to a parliamentary general elections, the limit applying to campaign expenditure in England, Scotland and Wales is £30,000 multiplied by the number of constituencies contested by the party in that part of the United Kingdom, of, if greater, in relation to England, £810,000, Scotland, £120,000 and Wales, £60,000. In relation to Northern Ireland, the limit is £30,000 multiplied by the number of constituencies contested by the party there. In relation to general elections to the European Parliament, the limit is £45,000 multiplied by the number of MEPs to be returned for that part of the United Kingdom at the election. In relation to general elections to the Scottish Parliament, the limits on campaign expenditure incurred by or on behalf of a registered party in the relevant period are £12,000 for each constituency contested by the party, plus £80,000 for each region contested by the party. In relation to elections to the Welsh Assembly, the limits are £10,000 for each constituency and £40,000 for each region contested by the party. In relation to Northern Ireland, the limit is £17,000 for each constituency. Special provision is made where there is a combination of elections to the European Parliament and a devolved legislature.

Part VII and Schedule 13 regulate expenditure at referendums. The amount persons or bodies designated by the Commission under section 103 and registered parties within section 100(1)(a) but not designated under section 103 may expend is related to the percentage of votes cast for a party's candidates at the last parliamentary general election, and ranges between £500,000 and £5 million.

Schedule 18 of the Act makes new provision for the control of political donations by companies and amends the Companies Act 1985, inserting a new Part XA. *Inter alia*, a company is prohibited from making any donation to any registered party to any other EU political organisation, or incurring any EU political expenditure unless the donation or expenditure is authorised by

---

112 Political Parties, Elections and Referendums Act 2000, s 62.
113 *Ibid*, s 63.
114 *Ibid*, s 69.
115 *Ibid*, ss 75–77.

virtue of an approval resolution passed by the company in general meeting before the relevant time. An approval resolution is a resolution passed by special resolution procedure or a resolution passed by any percentage of the members greater than that required for an ordinary resolution.

The Act provides for 69 offences, with liability ranging from a fine at level 5 or six months' imprisonment on summary conviction to a fine or one year's imprisonment on conviction on indictment.[116]

VOTING SYSTEMS[117]

The first and foremost object of reforming zeal ought, in my opinion, to be the system of parliamentary representation, or rather misrepresentation.[118]

The Labour Government came to power in 1997 committed to major electoral reform, and to holding a referendum to ascertain the people's view. Substantial reform has taken place. The 1999 elections to the new Scottish Parliament employed the additional member system, as did election to the new National Assembly for Wales. The 1999 elections to the new Northern Ireland Assembly employed the single transferable vote system, one already utilised for elections in Northern Ireland to the European Parliament and for local elections. The 1999 elections for the European Parliament in the rest of the United Kingdom saw the introduction of a new system of proportional representation based on Party Lists. Despite these reforms, no move has yet been made to reform the simple majority system employed for elections to the United Kingdom Parliament. In this section, the merits and demerits of differing systems are considered.

Vernon Bogdanor categorises voting systems under three heads: plurality systems; majority systems; and proportional systems.[119] Under the heading of proportional systems, there exists a range of differing systems:

Proportional representation' is in fact a generic term denoting a number of different systems sharing only the common aim of proportionality between seats and votes. This common aim, however, does not prevent the various proportional systems diverging considerably, one from another; and their political consequences, therefore, can be quite different.[120]

---

116 Political Parties, Elections and Referendums Act 2000.

117 See Finer, SE, *Adversary Politics and Electoral Reform*, 1975, London: Anthony Wigram; Bogdanor, V, *The People and the Party System*, 1981, Cambridge: CUP and *Multi-party Politics and the Constitution*, 1983, Cambridge: CUP; Bogdanor, V and Butler, D, *Democracy and Elections*, 1983, Cambridge: CUP; Chandler, JA, 'The plurality vote: a reappraisal' (1982) 30 Political Studies 87; Oliver, D, 'Reform of the electoral system' [1983] PL 108; Butler, D, 'Electoral reform', in Jowell, J and Oliver, D (eds), *The Changing Constitution*, 3rd edn, 1994, Oxford: Clarendon.

118 Wade, HWR, *Constitutional Fundamentals*, rev edn, 1989, London: Stevens.

119 *Ibid*, Bogdanor and Butler, p 1.

120 *Ibid*, Bogdanor and Butler, p 2.

Despite recent reforms, the United Kingdom is out of step with much of the rest of the world in terms of systems employed for electing its national Parliament. As a generalisation, it can be said that those countries influenced by English common law are the countries which retain the majority system of voting. The majority of States on the continent of Europe employ a list system; France by contrast employs a system which involves two ballots. In France, when no candidate wins an absolute majority of the vote in the first ballot, a second ballot is held to determine which of those candidates who have gained 12.5 per cent of the registered electorate in the first ballot are to be elected. In Australia, two electoral systems are employed. For election to the House of Representatives, a system of compulsory preferential voting is used. For election to the Senate, a proportional representation system is employed.

The simple majority system

If it is accepted that a democratic Parliament ought to represent so far as possible the preferences of the voters, this system is probably the worst that could be devised.[121]

For elections to the United Kingdom Parliament, the system of election remains the simple majority (colloquially, 'first past the post') system. The origins of the voting system lie in tradition, and it should be noted that the voting system is not a matter of law, but of past political practice. One principal merit of the system lies in its simplicity. The candidate who gains the largest number of votes in the election wins the seat – irrespective of the proportion of votes cast for himself or his opponents. Thus, to illustrate, if the votes cast for individual candidates at an election are:

CANDIDATE	NUMBER OF VOTES
Smith	3,200
Jones	2,700
Brown	2,500
TOTAL	7,400

Smith wins the election, even though 5,200, or 70 per cent, voters have voted for the other candidates. This lack of representativeness – when viewed from the perspective of proportionality of votes cast to seats won – is reflected in the results nationwide. The results of the 1992 general election, for the three main parties, were as follows:

---

121 *Op cit*, Wade, fn 118, p 9.

THE 1992 GENERAL ELECTION

Party	Number of seats	Percentage of vote	Percentage of seats
Conservative	336	41.9%	51.6%
Labour	271	34.4%	41.6%
Liberal Democrat	20	17.8%	3.1%
Other	24	5.9%	3.7%
TOTAL	651	100.0%	100.0%

Looking at the overall percentage change in the vote since 1987, the Conservative Party lost 0.5 per cent, Labour gained 3.7 per cent, Liberal Democrat lost 4.8 per cent, and other parties gained 0.16 per cent. Considered in another way, it can be seen that it took 32,777 votes to elect a Conservative Member of Parliament; 40,482 to elect a Labour Member; and 338,089 to elect a Liberal Democrat member.

The 1997 and 2001 general elections

The general election of 1 May 1997 resulted in a landslide victory for the Labour Party.[122] Tony Blair MP became the youngest Prime Minister, at the age of 43, since 1812, and only the fifth Labour Prime Minister in this century.[123] The electoral turnout was 71.3 per cent in 1997, but only 59 per cent in 2001.

The 2001 election results were as follows:

Party	Number of seats	Percentage of vote	Percentage of seats
Labour	413	42.0%	62.7%
Conservative	166	32.7%	25.2%
Liberal Democrat	52	18.8%	7.9%
Other	28	6.5%	4.2%
TOTAL	659	100.0%	100.0%

---

122 The 1997 election resulted in a significant increase in women Members of Parliament. Of 659 Members, 120, or 18.2 per cent.

123 The others being Ramsey MacDonald, 1924, 1929–31, Clement Attlee, 1945–51, Harold Wilson, 1974–76, James Callaghan, 1976–79.

The Electoral Reform Society calculated that had there been a system of proportional representation in place for the 1997 election, the results would have been much different, namely:

Party	Number of seats	Percentage of vote	Percentage of seats
Labour	286	44.4%	43.4%
Conservative	199	31.4%	30.2%
Liberal Democrat	109	17.2%	16.5%
Other	65	7.0%	9.9%
TOTAL	659	100.0%	100.0%

Far from having a commanding majority in the House of Commons, the Labour government would have had 286 seats, the opposition parties 308.

It is figures such as these which explain the demands for reform of the electoral system. Several alternatives present themselves, some of which offer proportional representation, others of which do not, but do represent an improvement of the representativeness of Parliament when compared with the simple majority system. The alternative vote, the supplementary vote, the additional member system and the single transferable vote are all alternative systems. The alternative vote and supplementary vote are both majoritarian systems. The latter two – the additional member system and the single transferable vote, along with the party list system – are proportional representation systems. Simply stated, proportional representation means that Members should be elected to Parliament on a party basis which reflects the proportion of votes cast for a party in the election: thus, if 40 per cent of the population vote Liberal Democrat, then 40 per cent of the parliamentary seats should be held by that party; not as under the present system, where the 1987 election revealed that 15 per cent of the population voted Liberal Democrat but, in terms of seats in Parliament, the party only won three per cent of seats.

Alternative voting systems

The alternative vote

This system retains individual constituencies, but introduces the notion of multiple votes in order of preference. As noted above, it is a majoritarian system, not a proportional representation system. The voter marks his ballot paper with preferences expressed in numerical order. The candidate who wins 50 per cent of the first preference vote is declared elected. Should no candidate achieve 50 per cent, the votes of the candidate who achieves the lowest number of first preference votes are redistributed in accordance with that candidate's supporters' second preferences. The process is continued until one candidate achieves an overall majority of votes compared with all other candidates. Where the system fails is from the point of view of proportional representation, since the overall result will bear little or no resemblance to proportionality. It would also potentially have the effect of returning to Parliament candidates who have achieved no clear support (or mandate) from the people. The system does, however, ensure that, within each constituency, the candidate with most support overall is returned to Parliament.

The advantages of the alternative vote are, first, that the traditional one member, one constituency principle is retained and, secondly, that the elected candidate has a majority of votes, as compared with other candidates.

The supplementary vote

This system is very similar to the alternative vote system, and is the system recommended by the working party on electoral systems set up by the Labour Party, under the chairmanship of Lord Plant, which reported in 1993.[124] The system allows voters to express a preference through voting for two candidates. If no candidate secures 50 per cent of the vote, the second preferences cast for all candidates other than the top two are redistributed between the two leading candidates until a clear winner emerges. Where there are only three candidates, this system would work smoothly. However, the system becomes more complex in constituencies where a greater number of candidates is standing for election, for the electorate would not be clear as to who the leading two candidates will be, and may therefore vote tactically in order to ensure, as far as possible, that a candidate who they did not want elected, would not be in either of the two top positions.

The additional member system (AMS)[125]

This is the system adopted for the 1999 elections to the Scottish Parliament and Welsh Assembly. The additional member system seeks to combine the advantages of the single member constituency, with overall proportionality between votes and seats. The system has been used in West Germany since 1945. Under AMS, three quarters of the United Kingdom's Members of Parliament (487 seats) would be elected in single member constituencies, using the first past the post system. The remaining one quarter (163 seats) would be 'additional members', elected from party lists on a regional party

---

124 *Report of the Working Party on Electoral Systems*, 1993, London: Labour Party.
125 Employed in Germany.

basis, employing a formula based on the largest average of votes cast between the parties. The additional Members thus top up the total for each party in order to give overall proportionality.

Under AMS, each voter would thus have two votes: one for the candidate of his choice in the constituency, one for the party of his choice on a regional basis. The additional member system has the advantage of remaining close to the system which is currently in place, while departing from it sufficiently to ensure proportionality. The system would necessitate a reduction of the number of constituency Members of Parliament in order to accommodate the regionally elected Members. If the division between constituency and regional Members is to be equal, this would necessitate doubling the size of current constituencies. However, the additional member system also confers wide powers on political parties who would control who is to be included on the regional list, and in what order of priority. For this reason, the Hansard Society Commission on Electoral Reform, chaired by Lord Blake, concluded that the German model of AMS was not suitable for Britain.[126]

There is a variant of this system which is employed in local elections in Germany which avoids the problem of party control. Under this variant of AMS, all candidates stand directly as constituency candidates, but only three quarters, or some other percentage, are elected in single member constituencies. The remaining one quarter of seats would be allocated to those who had been runners up in the election contest, who would sit as additional members.

Single transferable vote (STV)[127]

Employed in Northern Ireland for the European Parliament elections and elections to the new Northern Ireland Assembly, the single transferable vote offers both proportionality between votes and seats and a constituency based, but multi-member, system of election. The STV was recommended for introduction in urban constituencies as long ago as 1917. The STV would involve a rearrangement of the current single member constituencies into far larger regional units, each returning several Members of Parliament. The method of calculation varies, but is based on a quota of the votes cast that is achieved either by first preference voting producing the required quota or the redistribution of votes cast for losing candidates. The STV offers both proportionality and the greatest range of choice to electors. The system used

---

126 Hansard Society, *Report of the Commission on Electoral Reform*, 1976, London: Hansard Society, para 93.
127 Employed in the Republic of Ireland and in Northern Ireland.

for local elections and elections to the European Parliament in Northern Ireland[128] requires that the total number of votes be divided by one more than the number of vacant seats, plus one. The current constituencies would require alteration in order to increase their size to accommodate three Members (or four or five, as favoured by the Liberal Democrats),[129] which would require a fresh look at the criteria for constituency boundaries. The current requirement to respect local authority boundaries is the most obvious criteria which would be compromised if such a system were to be adopted.

This is the most complex of alternative systems and, for that reason alone, is not favoured by many, although, despite the complexity, the system works well in Northern Ireland. The voter expresses his or her preferences for candidates in numerical order. A quota is predetermined. Thus, in a five member constituency, the quota would be approximate to one sixth of the votes cast. Successful candidates are those reaching the quota, and those who on a redistribution of second, third and more remote preferences reach the quota. If less than the required number of candidates reach the quota figure, then redistribution of second preferences will take place until the required number of elected Members is reached. If, on the other hand, the required number of elected Members is not achieved by the redistribution of second preferences, then a third stage comes into play. The candidate who polled the lowest number of votes is then eliminated, and the votes for that candidate distributed among the other remaining candidates in order of preferences expressed. This process of elimination continues until the quota is reached for all five required elected Members.

The party list system[130]

This system requires that a list of candidates be nominated by each political party. The votes for each party's list are calculated on a nationwide basis – rather than a constituency basis – and the parties obtain the number of seats in the legislature in direct proportion to the votes in the country. The party list system is not a serious contender for adoption in the United Kingdom. Two principal defects are perceived with the system: first, that it destroys election on the basis of constituencies, and secondly, that too much patronage is placed in the hands of party leaders. Within the two principal political parties in the United Kingdom – Conservative and Labour – there exists a broad spectrum of political opinion: from the political left to the political right in each party. To leave the power of nomination, and the positioning of candidates on the 'list', to political leaders would potentially exclude some of the best candidates – most likely, those whose views are incompatible with, or troublesome to, the leadership.

---

128 European Assembly Elections Act 1978, Sched 1, para 2(2)(b).
129 Liberal/SDP Alliance, 1982.
130 Employed in Belgium, Denmark, Greece, Netherlands, Portugal, Spain.

THE CASE FOR AND AGAINST
REFORMING THE SIMPLE MAJORITY SYSTEM

Most of the arguments for reform of the electoral system centre on the alleged defects of the present system. Reformers argue that the status quo results in a government which does not represent the majority of the voters' wishes. Since the Second World War, no government has been elected with a majority of votes overall. The Liberal Democrats have been arguing for reform for many years, and they are not alone in this. Lord Hailsham, former Conservative Lord Chancellor and Cabinet Minister,[131] and Angus Maude[132] have both questioned the democratic basis of the current system. Professor SE Finer,[133] Vernon Bogdanor[134] and Professor HWR Wade[135] have all questioned the status quo.

The case for reform therefore centres on the principle of democracy and equality in voting power. For democracy to have real meaning, it is argued that the government of the day, and the composition of the legislature as a whole, must reflect the wishes of the electors. Under such a system, it can be argued that the government would have enhanced authority to pursue its electoral mandate. In answer to the charge that proportional representation can result in weak government, reformers argue that less extreme, rather than weak, government would be the result. Such an outcome would force a 'rethink' in radical politics, with governments being keenly aware that with a slim majority in Parliament, and possibly the balance of power being held by a third party (both outcomes which are common to proportional representation systems), certain radical policies would have to be modified. Thus many of the more politically contentious subjects, such as education and health, might be largely removed from party political conflict: consensus would become the only way in which to make legislative progress.

Reformers also point to the inequity of the distribution of the vote between the parties under the current system. The simple majority system invariable favours a two party system, and leaves little room for the adequate representation of smaller parties. The Liberal Democrat Party regularly

---

131 In Hailsham (Lord), *The Dilemmas of Democracy*, 1978, London: Collins.
132 Maude, A, *Why Electoral Change? Proportional Representation Examined*, 1982, London: Conservative Political Centre.
133 Finer, SE, *The Changing British Party System*, 1980, Washington: AEI Studies.
134 *Op cit*, Bogdanor, fn 117.
135 *Op cit*, Wade, fn 118.

achieves approximately 25 per cent of the popular vote at general elections (and has a high success rate at by-elections), but that overall popularity does not translate itself into a proportionally related number of parliamentary seats. One explanation for this result is that votes for the Liberal Democrats are spread fairly evenly over the United Kingdom, and not concentrated in one geographic area (although the south west of England is becoming a Liberal stronghold). It is otherwise with the Conservative and Labour Parties. For the most part, the United Kingdom is subject to an electoral north-south divide, with the Labour Party holding a majority of seats in the north, the Conservatives dominating the southern seats (and being unrepresented in Scotland).

The case for the status quo is linked to the point made above. The simple majority system generally, although not invariably, produces a government with a strong parliamentary majority which is able to implement its electoral programme without undue hindrance. This argument requires careful evaluation. One of the often experienced effects of proportional representation based systems is that governments are returned with either a very small majority of seats or with a minority of seats overall in the legislature. One of the most significant effects of this result is that minority parties with few seats and relatively small electoral support may hold a disproportionate amount of power, making governments dependent upon their wishes in order to implement their legislative programme. As a result of such dependence, governments are also subject to the risk of defeats on motions of no confidence,[136] thus producing general political insecurity and the potential for frequent elections.

A further, related effect is that a government may be required to compromise substantially upon its electoral promises in order to govern. Under the current system, it is generally the case that the elected government – always depending upon its majority in Parliament – is relatively free to implement its electoral programme. In other words, the voter knows what he is getting in terms of policies and proposals for legislation. Under proportional representation, where less strong government is the frequent result, voters can be far less certain either that the policies for which they are voting will be implemented or of the policies which will be pursued after the election. In countries where politics are less polarised than has traditionally been the case in the United Kingdom, this consequence may be of little practical significance: in the United Kingdom, the political spectrum is still sufficiently diverse and conflicting as to cause disquiet and to compromise government.

---

136 See Chapters 6 and 11.

There also exist doubts as to the effects of a reformed system on the convention of collective ministerial responsibility.[137] Under current constitutional arrangements, the convention of collective responsibility requires that the Cabinet 'speaks with one voice' in order to maintain parliamentary, and electoral, confidence. The rule accordingly requires that, where a decision has been made by the Cabinet, each member of Cabinet and non-Cabinet Ministers and all their Parliamentary Private Secretaries, adhere to the decision and do not speak out against it. Such a show of unity would prove difficult to sustain in governments which were either coalition or minority governments. The sister doctrine of individual ministerial responsibility might also prove more difficult to adhere to, particularly where a Minister felt unable to support and pursue a policy with which he or she disagreed on political principle. One consequence, therefore, which could flow from the introduction of some form of proportional representation could be that governments become less cohesive and, as a result, less commanding of the confidence of the people.

A further argument is put for the status quo: that of the close links currently established between the constituency Member and his or her electorate. Irrespective of the proportion of votes won in an election, the Member of Parliament, once duly elected, and irrespective of political party, represents each and every one of his or her constituents in Parliament. Constituencies are relatively small and Members of Parliament are accessible – through surgeries and other contact – to the voters. A Member is thus able to gain a detailed knowledge of his or her constituency, its geography, industry and economy, environment and populace. With large constituencies, such a detailed working knowledge of an area becomes more difficult, with the attendant possibility that a Member is less effective in his representation of that constituency in Parliament.

As can be seen, the issue of electoral reform is by no means clear-cut, and real potential constitutional problems could be encountered as a result of its introduction. At the end of the day, the quest for an alternative system is rooted in the paramountcy of the principle of real democracy and equality of representation of the people in Parliament. Against that ideal must be set the constitutional implications of introducing reform.

As noted above, one of the manifesto pledges of the Labour Party before the 1997 election was a review of the electoral system for the Westminster Parliament and, once in office, the government appointed Liberal peer Lord Jenkins to review the system. The Jenkins Commission reported in October

---

137 See Chapter 11.

1998, and recommended a novel, if complex, solution. The Commission, wanting to retain single member constituencies but also inject a greater degree of proportionality into the system, opted for a 'mixed system' made up of the alternative vote and regional list systems. Constituency members would be elected on the alternative vote system, and comprise 80–85 per cent of members, with additional members, 15–20 per cent elected on the regional list basis. Greater proportionality would be achieved, while the traditional strong link between a member and his or her constituency would be retained. The system would also, the Commission claimed, avoid coalition governments and in its estimation would have produced a single party majority government in three out of the four last general elections.[138]

The current position is that the United Kingdom now employs a number of differing systems: a new system of proportional representation was used in May 1999 for elections to the European Parliament, for elections to the Scottish Parliament and National Assembly for Wales the additional member system was used, and for elections to the Northern Ireland Assembly, the single transferable vote system. The issue which remains unresolved is the voting system for elections to the United Kingdom Parliament. The government had promised to hold a referendum on that matter and as seen above, the Jenkins Commission recommended a mixed system of voting. The government has however deferred both issues until after the next general election. Despite the experimentation with reform, the government appears unconvinced of wholesale reform of the system employed for elections to the Westminster Parliament.

---

138 Cm 4090-I, para 161. This claim has been disputed by M Pinto-Duschinsky who calculates that coalition would have been the outcome in nine of the last 14 elections: (1998) *The Times*, 29 October.

CHAPTER 14

INTRODUCTION TO THE HOUSE OF COMMONS

Parliament is composed of the Sovereign, the House of Lords and the House of Commons. Its origins lie in the King's Council – the assembly of advisers summoned by the King – and the term 'Parliament' can be traced to the thirteenth century.[1]

In order to evaluate Parliament, it is necessary to examine its composition and procedure. The former task may be accomplished by looking at the actual membership of Parliament by party allegiance at a fixed point in time or by looking at it in a more sociological manner in order to analyse the class and educational background of Members and their employment status. The undertaking is complicated by the bicameral nature of Parliament and the fact that the House of Commons is elected and the House of Lords unelected. The importance of procedure, particularly in the House of Commons, cannot be overemphasised. Only by acquiring an understanding of the procedural rules can sense be made of the functions of Parliament and its importance, or otherwise, in the process of government. In the absence of a written constitution which clearly defines and allocates powers and functions, the manner in which the legislative proposals of government are examined, and the administration of the State scrutinised, assumes central importance to the notion of democratic control of the executive. The doctrine of constitutionalism[2] can only be effective if the procedures adopted by Parliament are effective in controlling the government.

THE FUNCTIONS OF PARLIAMENT

In 1861, John Stuart Mill wrote of Parliament:[3]

> Instead of the function of governing, for which it is radically unfit, the proper office of a representative assembly is to watch and control the government; to throw the light of publicity on its acts; to compel a full exposition and justification of all of them which anyone considers questionable; to censure them if found condemnable; and if the men who compose the government abuse their trust, or fulfil it in a manner which conflicts with the deliberate sense of the nation, to expel them from office, and either expressly or virtually appoint their successors.

---

1 The role of the Sovereign is discussed in Chapter 6. The House of Lords is discussed in Chapter 17.
2 See Chapter 1.
3 Mill, JS, *Representative Government* (1865), 1958, Indianapolis: Bobbs-Merrill, p 99.

> The House of Commons is the sounding board of the nation – an arena in which not only the general opinion of the nation, but that of every section of it can produce itself in full light and challenge discussion.

Very little has changed. Parliament is not there to govern: that is for the executive. Parliament exists to represent the views and opinions of the people and to influence, constrain and demand justification for the actions of government and to give them legitimacy.

Accordingly, the functions of Parliament may be summarised as being:[4]

(a) to provide the personnel of government;

(b) to legitimise government actions; and

(c) to subject matters of public policy to scrutiny and influence.

As discussed in Chapters 7 and 12, the devolution of legislative power to the Northern Ireland Assembly and Scottish Parliament and, to a lesser extent, the Welsh Assembly affects the scope of the United Kingdom Parliament's role and functions. In terms of debating and scrutinising government policy and administration and the passage of legislation, while the United Kingdom Parliament (Westminster) remains the sovereign legislature in the United Kingdom, there is now a diffusion of power – differing in nature and scope – between Westminster and the devolved institutions.

THE LIFE OF A PARLIAMENT

A Parliament is summoned to meet by the sovereign following a general election, and the life of the Parliament will run until the subsequent general election. Under section 7 of the Parliament Act 1911, the life of a Parliament is restricted to five years from the day on which first appointed to meet, unless previously dissolved. Parliaments are summoned and dissolved by Proclamation of the Crown on the advice of the Privy Council.[5] The average life of a Parliament is three years, one month. The Parliament elected in June 1983 lasted for three years 11 months; that of June 1987 for four years 10 months. By contrast, the previous Parliament elected in 1992 existed for just under the maximum five year term.

---

4   Norton, P, *Parliament in the 1980s*, 1985, Oxford: Blackwells and see *Does Parliament Matter?*, 1993, Hemel Hempstead: Harvester.

5   See Chapter 6.

The parliamentary session

A parliamentary session is the parliamentary year, which commences in November. There is no legal requirement as to the length of a session. At the end of the session, Parliament is formally closed by the Queen and stands 'prorogued' until the new session begins. The significance of prorogation lies in the fact that all business is suspended until the new session.

The number of sitting days per session varies from year to year. In 1979–80, there were 244 sitting days, in 1985–86, 172, in 1990–91, 160 and, in 1991–92 (a short session terminated by the dissolution of Parliament), 83. The figure for the 1992–93 session was 240 days. The average session length is 168 days. In 1995–96, the House of Commons sat for 146 days. There were no sittings on seven Fridays. The House sat for 1,278 hours and 29 minutes. The average length of a sitting was eight hours and 45 minutes. The 1996–97 session was short, Parliament being dissolved prior to the general election in May, and there were only 86 sitting days, lasting an average of 8 hours and 21 minutes per sitting. In the 1998–99 session, there were 149 sitting days, the daily average sitting being nine hours and 15 minutes.

Parliamentary sittings

The term 'parliamentary sitting' relates to the daily business of the House. Under Standing Orders, the rules of the House, Parliament meets at 2.30 pm from Monday to Thursday, and from 9.30 am on Fridays. The House is adjourned for three weeks at Christmas, one week at Easter, for the whole of August and for most of September. In emergency situations, the House may be recalled for urgent debate during a recess or at a weekend, as occurred in 1982 for debate on the invasion of the Falkland Islands.[6] The daily proceedings of the House generally cease at 10.00 pm[7] but frequently will extend beyond this time. The average duration of a sitting is eight and three quarter hours, Monday to Thursday, and on Fridays, five and a half hours.

The length of parliamentary sittings varies according to the pressure of time on the House. In the 1980s, for example, seven sittings lasted over 24 hours, the longest recorded in that decade, being 32 hours and 12 minutes.[8] Where the House sits beyond the normal time of the commencement of business the following day, the business of that day (with the exception of Questions put down for written answer for that day) will be lost. It is a matter of constant concern that Parliament sits unsocial hours and, for this reason,

---

6   3 April 1982.
7   Standing Order No 9.
8   Debate on the Local Government (Interim Provisions) Bill, 22 May 1984.

reforms have been introduced, in 1995, to limit the number of occasions on which Parliament sits after 10.00 pm. Under Standing Orders, the normal business of Parliament should end at 10.00 pm. However, certain business is exempted from that rule, which results in lengthy sittings.[9] The House resolved not to sit on eight Fridays, in order to facilitate the constituency work of Members of Parliament which is traditionally undertaken on Fridays and at weekends. Further, the House resolved to meet on Wednesdays at 10.00 am and to hold debates until 2.30 pm, when the normal business of the House will commence. The House of Commons Modernisation Select Committee recommended in July 2000 that a strict finishing time of 10 pm should be introduced, and that daily business should begin at 9.30 am.

SUMMONING, ADJOURNMENT, PROROGATION,[10] AND DISSOLUTION OF PARLIAMENT

Summoning

It is within the Crown's prerogative to determine when Parliament should be summoned. However, under statute, the Queen is bound to issue writs within three years of the ending of a Parliament.[11] In practice, a Parliament must be summoned to meet every year in order that approval can be given for monies to be provided for public services. Parliament is summoned to meet by proclamation of the Queen. The proclamation dissolves the previous Parliament, orders the issue of writs by the Lord Chancellor and appoints the day and place for the meeting of the new Parliament.[12]

Adjournment

During a parliamentary session, Parliament will be adjourned on many occasions. The adjournment is no more than an 'interruption in the course of one and the same session'.[13] Up to a quarter of the time in the House of Commons is spent debating the question: '... that this House do not adjourn.'[14] The effect of adjournment is to suspend the sitting of the House for

---

9   Under Standing Order No 14.

10 From the Latin, *prorogare*, literally to ask publicly, from *pro* in public and *rogare* to ask.

11 16 Cha 2 c 1 and 6 & 7 Will & Mary c 2.

12 Erskine May, T, *Parliamentary Practice*, 21st edn, 1989, London: Butterworths, p 221 (see, now, 22nd edn, 1997).

13 *Ibid*, Erskine May.

14 Silk, P and Walters, R, *How Parliament Works*, 1987, London: Longman, p 210.

a period, but to leave unaffected the business of the House. Adjournments take place for a number of reasons and to effect a number of consequences.

A motion for adjournment can be used in debate to interrupt proceedings. The motion will take the form 'that the debate be now adjourned'. The device may be used as an alternative to moving an amendment to the question before the House, and will be used to determine consideration of the matter under consideration. The Speaker has a discretion whether to decline to put the matter to the House.[15] The business which has been interrupted can be brought before the House at the next sitting day, provided that notice is given.

Daily adjournment debates

There is a daily motion for adjournment which suspends the day's sitting. Under Standing Order No 9(7):

> The House shall not be adjourned except in pursuance of a resolution or by Mr [or Madam] Speaker in pursuance of paragraph (3) of Standing Order No 10 (Sittings of the House (suspended sittings)) or Standing Order No 45 (Power of Mr Speaker to adjourn House or suspend sitting [on the basis of grave disorder within the House]):

> Provided that, when a substantive motion for the adjournment of the House has been made at or after 10 o'clock Mr Speaker shall after the expiration of half an hour after that motion has been made, adjourn the House without putting any question.

Once the motion for adjournment has been moved, the daily adjournment debate takes place.[16] The adjournment debate enables one Member to speak on a topic, previously notified, for 15 minutes, and to receive a ministerial reply. Topics may include any matter other than a request for legislation. There is a weekly ballot held at which successful Members are chosen for the adjournment debate, other than for the debate on Thursdays when the choice of Member is made by the Speaker.

Adjournment debates before holidays

Adjournment debates also take place before the House adjourns for holidays.[17] No ballot is held for participation: five backbenchers speak for half an hour each and the Leader of the House replies to the debate.

---

15 Standing Order No 34.
16 See, further, Chapter 16.
17 Four times a year.

Adjournment debates following consideration of Consolidated Fund Bills

In any session, there will be three Consolidated Fund Bills before Parliament. Second reading consideration is purely formal, with no debate.[18] When proceedings are finished, any Member of the government may move a motion 'that this House do now adjourn'. The ensuing debate may last until 9.00 am the following day, 8.00 am on Fridays. Private Members can raise any matter, but their names are balloted. One and a half or three hours may be allocated to any topic, at the discretion of the speaker.

Adjournments for emergency debates[19]

Provision is made under Standing Order No 20 for urgent matters to be brought to the attention of the House for early debate. A Member may, at the start of business of the day, propose that the House be adjourned for consideration of an urgent matter. It is within the discretion of the Speaker as to whether the matter should be discussed. If satisfied, it is then for the House to give leave for the debate. If refused, the support of not more than 40 Members of the House is required in order for leave to be granted.[20] The debate will take place at the start of business the following day.

Prorogation

Prorogation is effected under the prerogative, by the announcement of the Queen's command. The effect of prorogation is that all business before Parliament is suspended. Any Bill which has not concluded its parliamentary stages must be brought anew to the future Parliament. Parliament will be prorogued until a specified date. The prorogation of Parliament has not been effected in person by the Crown since 1854: the normal procedure is for Parliament to be prorogued by a commission under the Great Seal. The period between prorogation and the summoning of a new Parliament is known as the 'recess'.

---

18 Standing Order No 54.
19 See, further, Chapter 16.
20 If fewer than 40 Members, but not less than 10 Members, support the motion, the House will determine the matter by a vote.

Dissolution[21]

Parliament is dissolved prior to a general election. Under the Parliament Act 1911, the maximum duration of the life of a Parliament is five years. Dissolution is therefore required before the expiry of this period. For the most part, the Prime Minister will seek a dissolution – effected by the Crown under the royal prerogative – at a date which is politically favourable to his or her party. It is entirely within the Prime Minister's personal discretion when to seek a dissolution. Alternatively, dissolution may be sought when the government loses the support of the House of Commons. Governments may suffer defeats in the Commons on a range of issues which will not force a dissolution. However, if the government is defeated on a motion of confidence on a matter central to its administration a dissolution will be forced.

When a dissolution is granted, the government does not resign until after a defeat in the general election. It has been seen[22] that, in 1974, the Prime Minister, Edward Heath, did not resign until it was clear that he could not form a pact with the Liberal Party which would secure a working majority in the Commons.

THE ORGANISATION OF BUSINESS

The business in a typical parliamentary session is as follows. The session opens with the State Opening of Parliament and the Queen's Speech, which outlines the government's proposals for legislation in the session. The following five days are spent in Debate on the Address, including two days on which the Opposition proposes – 'moves' – amendments to specific areas of policy. The government then introduces the most important Bills and, until Christmas, most of the time of the House will be spent on second reading debates on these Bills (see, further, Chapter 15). Between Christmas and Easter, the majority of the time of the House will be spent in second reading debates and the committee stage of Bills. Before the end of July, the remaining legislative stages of Bills take place. The budget is introduced in November each year. Prior to 1994, the budget was introduced annually in March.[23]

---

21 For detailed discussion, see Chapter 6.
22 Chapter 6.
23 See, further, Chapter 7.

ALLOCATION OF TIME IN THE HOUSE OF COMMONS: Session 1998–99	
Type of business	Hours : minutes
Addresses, other than Prayers	38 : 21
Adjournment Debates	350 : 20
Finance	66 : 72
Government Bills	388 : 19
Government Motions	27 : 70
Opposition Day Motions	131 : 94
Oral Questions and Private Notice Questions	124 : 78
Prayers	12 : 25
Private Members' Bills	70 : 45
Statements	68 : 32
Affirmative Statutory Instruments	35 : 19
Prayers against Statutory Instruments	1 : 43
Miscellaneous	63 : 12
TOTAL	1,378 : 50

PERSONNEL OF THE HOUSE OF COMMONS

The office of Speaker

The office of Speaker is traceable to 1377 and the appointment of Sir Thomas Hungerford although, from 1258, Parliaments had similar officers.[24] The Speaker of the House featured in the constitutional struggles between King and Parliament in the seventeenth century. When Charles I arrived in the Commons to arrest the Five Knights, the Speaker declared:

> May it please Your Majesty, I have neither eyes to see, nor tongue to speak in this place, but as the House is pleased to direct me, whose servant I am here, and I humbly beg Your Majesty's pardon that I cannot give any other answer than this to what Your Majesty is pleased to demand of me.

Henceforth, the independence of the Speaker from the Crown was established.

The Speaker regulates the proceedings of the House. The Speaker is a senior Member appointed by common agreement of all Members and is generally a Member of the Opposition Party. The election of the Speaker is the

---

24 Known as parlour or prolocutor.

first task undertaken by Parliament following a general election. The Speaker acts with political impartiality and controls the business of the House.

The Speaker is the presiding officer of the House and ensures that the rules of conduct and order are observed. The Speaker is also the representative of the Commons in relations with the Crown – it is through the Speaker that the privilege of access to the Sovereign is effected – and the House of Lords and other bodies outside Parliament. When the House of Lords amends Commons' Bills, the Speaker checks the amendments to ensure that they do not infringe the financial privileges of the lower House. It is also the function of the Speaker to certify Bills under the Parliament Act 1911.[25]

The Speaker has a discretion in relation to the granting of an application for an emergency debate,[26] whether to allow private notice questions or grant requests for emergency debates,[27] and whether a *prima facie* case of a breach of the privileges of the House has been established.[28] It is also for the Speaker to rule on matters of procedure. Furthermore, the Speaker will decide whether a proposed amendment to a motion will be accepted.

Disciplinary powers of the Speaker

The control of debate lies in the Speaker, who chooses who is allowed to speak. Advance notice of the wish to participate in debate is given and the Speaker calls each side (government and Opposition) alternately, and respects the rights of minority parties to participate. The Speaker has powers under Standing Orders to control the following:

(a) irrelevance or tedious repetition;

(b) minor breaches of order;

(c) the use of disorderly or unparliamentary expressions;

(d) grossly disorderly conduct;

(e) grave disorder;

(f) obstruction of the business of the House by other means.[29]

Disorderly conduct – such as damaging the Mace[30] – may result in the Member, if a suitable apology is not given to the House, being suspended from the House for a period determined by the House on a motion.[31] Suspension from the House in the first instance will be for five sitting days, on a second occasion for 20 days and in the event of a further repetition, for the

---

25 See Chapter 17.
26 Under Standing Order No 24.
27 See Chapter 17.
28 See Chapter 18.
29 *Op cit*, Erskine May, fn 12, p 393.
30 The ceremonial staff of office of the Commons.
31 As in 1988, Member suspended for 20 days.

remainder of the session. Any Member refusing to withdraw from the chamber of the House may be forcibly removed by the Serjeant at Arms.[32] In such an event, the Member will be suspended for the remainder of the parliamentary session.

If a Member persists in a speech after being ordered to discontinue on the basis of irrelevance or tedious repetition, the Speaker may direct him to withdraw from the House for the remainder of the sitting, or 'name' him for disregarding the authority of the Speaker's Chair. The same penalty may befall a Member who uses unparliamentary language. Unparliamentary language includes:

(a) the imputation of false or unavowed motives;

(b) the misrepresentation of the language of another and the accusation of misrepresentation;

(c) charges of uttering a deliberate falsehood;

(d) abusive and insulting language likely to create disorder.[33]

The Leader of the House

The Leader of the House is responsible to the Prime Minister for the organisation of business in the Commons. It is the function of the Leader of the House to announce the parliamentary business for the following week. The Leader of the House is a Minister of the Crown.[34] When the Prime Minister is unavailable, it is the Leader of the House who represents the House of Commons.

The party whips

The party political control of Members of Parliament is in the hands of the party whips. On the government side, all whips receive salaries[35] and are Ministers of the Crown. The Chief Whip[36] is assisted by up to 12 other Members. The Chief Whip organises the details of business of the House. The Opposition has a Chief Whip, two salaried assistants and eight to 10 non-salaried assistants. The task of the government Chief Whip is to act as contact between the Prime Minister, the Leader of the House (to both of whom he is

---

32 An officer of the House responsible for order.

33 *Op cit*, Erskine May, fn 12, pp 381–82.

34 House of Commons (Administration) Act 1978, s 1.

35 Ministerial and other Salaries Act 1975, s 1(1)(a) and Sched 1.

36 Who holds office as Parliamentary or Patronage Secretary to the Treasury.

responsible) and Members. The whips (of all parties) keep Members informed about the House's business, and inform Members when they are obliged to attend the House. The degree of coercion of Members will depend on the importance of the matter in hand. When attendance is required – and when political consequences will flow from non-attendance – a 'three line whip' is announced. Where attendance is necessary, but not essential, a 'two line whip' is applied. In order that Members are not unduly pressured by the need for attendance in Parliament, the whips arrange 'pairing'. Pairing is the arrangement whereby Members of government and opposition parties will be linked together: if one is absent the other may abstain from voting. Thus, the non-attendance of one Member will be off-set – in the counting of votes – by the absence of the other. It is this arrangement which is most frequently threatened when relationships between the government and Opposition break down.

Much of the organisation of the business of the House is in the hands of the whips, including planning the parliamentary timetable and advising on practice and procedure. Whips of all parties are also responsible for recommending candidates for membership of parliamentary committees.

Members of Parliament

Front- and backbenchers

Business in the House is conducted on adversarial lines. The adversarial nature of the Commons is reflected in the layout of the House. The House is divided into two sections which face each other, separated by the Table of the House, behind which the Speaker sits. Each side has a front-bench and several rows of backbenches. On the side to the right of the Speaker sit Members of the government party, Ministers of the government occupying the front-bench. Opposite, on the front-bench, will sit the shadow Ministers of the Opposition Party. All other Members of both the government and Opposition will sit on the backbenches: hence the term 'backbenchers'.

The representation of women in the Commons

The 1992 election resulted in 60 women Members of Parliament: 9.2 per cent of the total of 651 Members. The Parliament (Qualification of Women) Act 1918 made women eligible to stand as Members of Parliament. Of 1,613 candidates at the 1918 election, only 17 were women. The first female candidate to take her seat in the House of Commons was Lady Astor, elected in 1919 in a by-election. The representation of women has always been poor in the Commons, as a sampling of the figures shows. In 1918, there was just one woman Member; in 1929, this figure had risen to 14; and, in 1945, 24 women were elected to Parliament. The figures remain between 17 and 29 until 1987, when 41 women were elected. All the major political parties are committed to increasing the representation of women in the Commons. The 1997 general election resulted in a significantly improved proportion of women Members of Parliament. The total number elected was 120 (18 per cent of 659 seats), with 101 Labour, 14 Conservative, three Liberal Democrat and two Scottish National Party Members, plus the Speaker of the House of Commons, the Right Honourable Betty Boothroyd, MP.[37]

The first woman to hold ministerial office was Margaret Bondfield. She became the first female Member of Cabinet in 1929. Two women have held the office of Speaker: the Rt Hon Betty Harview in 1970, and Miss Betty Boothroyd from 1987. The first female Prime Minister was the Rt Hon Margaret Thatcher MP (as she then was), who held office from 1979–90, the longest premiership this century.

Salaries and allowances of Members of Parliament

As far back as the thirteenth century, representatives attending Parliament were paid – either in cash or kind – and, in addition, had travelling expenses. Payment by electors had ceased by the end of the seventeenth century. In the eighteenth and nineteenth centuries, though unpaid, a seat in the House of Commons was valuable, and could attract large sums of money for its purchase. Members of Parliament remained formally unpaid until 1911, despite numerous previous attempts to introduce payment. In 1911, the salary amounted to £400 per annum. In 1996, the Review Body on Senior Salaries, successor to the Top Salaries Review Board, recommended that Member's pay should be increased by 26 per cent to £43,000 per annum. The government, however, proposed an increase of a mere three per cent. The House rejected the government's proposal and agreed to the Review Body's recommendation. The House also agreed that, from 1997, the yearly rate would be increased by the average percentage of Senior Civil Service pay bands. Accordingly, with effect from April 1997, the annual salary was £43,860.

Members also receive allowances for secretarial and research assistance, car mileage allowance, and for limited travel between the constituency and Parliament. The Office Costs Allowance, as it is called, in April 1997 amounted to up to £47,568. In addition, Members whose constituencies are within inner London are entitled to claim a London Supplement payment, which in April 1997 amounted to £1,358.

---

37 A by-election in November 1997 increased the number of women Members to 121. Note that there is to be an election for the office of Speaker in 2000.

Members' Code of conduct

Members of Parliament are governed by a Code of Conduct setting out general principles to guide members on the standards of conduct that the House and the public have a right to expect.[38] See, further, Chapter 16.

The size of the House of Commons

Prior to the 1997 general election, the number of seats in Parliament was increased from 651 to 659, as a result of constituency boundary changes. Over the past 40 years, the number of parliamentary seats has increased by 10 per cent. In protest over the increasing number of constituencies, one Member of Parliament has resigned.[39] If the number of parliamentary representatives is compared with the total population of the country, it can be seen that there is a wide discrepancy in the representativeness of differing legislatures. In Ireland, for example, there are 166 Members of Parliament, each representing 24,000 citizens. By contrast, in Australia, there are 147 Members, each representing 122,000 citizens. In the United Kingdom, there are 659 Members of Parliament, each representing approximately 89,000 citizens.

Resignation of Members of Parliament

A Member, once duly elected, cannot relinquish his seat.[40] However, provision is made whereby a Member may retire under differing procedures,[41] each of which involves accepting office under the Crown, which obliges the Member to relinquish his seat on the basis of disqualification from membership[42] and a Writ to be issued for a by-election. Application for the office is normally granted,[43] although power remains for the application to be refused. The offices are nowadays purely nominal and retained as a device to avoid the absence of any resignation procedure.

---

38 As recommended by the Committee on Standards and Privileges: *Third Report of the Committee on Standards and Privileges*, HC 604 (1995–96), London: HMSO; HC Deb Vol 282 Col 392, 24 July 1996.

39 (1995) *The Times*, 31 July.

40 Commons' Journal (1547–1628) 724.

41 Most usually accepting the office of steward or bailiff of Her Majesty's Three Chiltern Hundreds of Stoke, Desborough and Burnham or steward of the Manor of Northstead.

42 Under the House of Commons Disqualification Act 1975, s 4.

43 By the Chancellor of the Exchequer.

The political parties

The major political parties have a similar organisational structure in Parliament. The Conservative and Labour Parties (and Liberal Democrats) have a system of election for the party leader, and are organised into front and backbench Members. Looking at the Commons as a whole, we see that it comprises the government, elected on the basis of the simple majority vote,[44] Her Majesty's Loyal Opposition, being the second largest party in the House, and minority parties – Liberal Democrat, Ulster Unionist, Scottish Nationalist, Plaid Cymru.

Composition of the House of Commons by political party

The 1997 general election resulted in the House of Commons being made up of 418 Labour Members, 165 Conservative Members, 46 Liberal Democrat Members, and 30 Members from other minority parties. The total number of Members of Parliament is currently 659.

GOVERNMENT AND OPPOSITION

It is the government which controls the majority of Parliament's time. On 75 per cent of sitting days, government business takes priority and it is the government which determines the business to be undertaken (subject to established practices as to Opposition Days, days set aside for Private Members' Bills, etc). From scrutinising the work of Parliament, it may be tempting to underplay the importance of Parliament as a whole, and the Opposition in particular, in comparison with the power of the government. Such a view is implicit in the pejorative labelling of government as an 'elective dictatorship'.[45] Such charges need to be viewed with some caution. In 1947, Sir Ivor Jennings described the role of the Opposition as 'at once the alternative to the government and a focus for the discontent of the people. Its function is almost as important as that of the government'.[46]

---

44 See Chapter 13.
45 Hailsham (Lord), *The Dilemma of Democracy*, 1978, London: Collins, p 21.
46 Jennings, I (Sir), *Cabinet Government*, 3rd edn, 1959, Cambridge: CUP, Chapter XV.

In its constitutional role, the Opposition must constantly be questioning, probing and calling government to account. Viewed in this light, notwithstanding the government's control over the timetable and business of the House, it can be said that all parliamentary time is as much 'Opposition time' as 'government time'.

The constitutional importance of the official Opposition is reflected in the fact that the Leader of the Opposition draws a substantial salary in both the House of Commons and Lords, which is drawn on the Consolidated Fund.[47] In addition, since 1975, financial assistance has been provided to all opposition parties to enable them to carry out their role effectively. Each party is entitled to a fixed sum per annum per seat won by the party, plus an amount for every 200 votes cast in the previous election.

The Opposition is allocated 20 days per session in which it can determine the business of the day, representing in an average session 11.6 per cent of parliamentary time. Following the Queen's Speech at the opening of a new parliamentary session, the Opposition has the right to determine the subjects for debate on the second of the six days set aside for debate on the Speech.

In addition to normal parliamentary procedure for debate, questions, etc, and opposition time, the Opposition has the weapon of the motion of censure – or vote of no confidence. The motion takes the form of 'the House has no confidence in Her Majesty's government'. By convention, the government always makes time for debate on the motion, a three line whip will be employed, and a division (see below, p 579) invariably takes place. While fairly infrequent and confined to serious matters of policy, the loss of a motion of confidence can, as in 1979, lead to the resignation of the government, and such motions are always regarded as important parliamentary occasions.

47 See Chapter 15.

TABLE I: OPPOSITION DAYS 1998–99: SUBJECT MATTER[48]

DATE	DAY NO	SUBJECT OF DEBATE
13.1.99	1	(a) Government information (LD)* (b) Role of the UK in Europe (LD)
18.1.99	2	(a) Rationing in the NHS (b) Pensioners and dividend tax credits
27.1.99	3	(a) Terrorist mutilations in Northern Ireland (b) London Underground
3.2.99	4	(a) Governments record on pensions (b) Planning and green belt
2.3.99	5	(a) Sierra Leone (b) Burdens on schools
18.3.99	6	(a) Reduction in strength of police (b) Governments roads policy
22.3.99	7	(a) Council tax increases (LD) Europe, America and World Trade Organisation (LD)
21.4.99	8	(a) Taxation of road haulage industry (b) State of British livestock farming
29.4.99	9	(a) Government policies on housing and the green belt (b) job loss, the state of industry and the new deal
11.5.99	10	(a) Government pensions policy (b) Implications of Scottish and Welsh devolution for the Westminster Parliament
13.5.99	11	(a) American food exports and European trade policy (LD) (b) Parliamentary democracy
19.5.99	12	(a) Fraud in the European Union budget (b) Conditions of service in NHS personnel
23.6.99	13	(a) Proportional representation (b) Planning
24.6.99	14	(a) Governments policy for widows (LD) (b) Food and supermarkets (LD)
26.6.99	15	(a) Delays in issue of passports (b) Planning and transport congestion
7.7.99	16	(a) Dairy industry (b) Choice and diversity in education
15.7.99	17	(a) Impact of Governments policies on motorists (b) Future of post offices
20.7.99	18	(a) Health care provision in UK (b) Governments proposed energy tax
20.10.99	19	(a) Food and farming (LD) (b) Transport safety (LD)
26.10.99	20	(a) Home Office issues (b) National Health Service

*   Liberal Democrat motions.
48   *House of Commons Sessional Information Digest 1998–99*, 2000, London: HMSO.

VOTING IN THE COMMONS

A 'division' is the name for the counting of votes on important issues where conflict is apparent. Not every debate will result in a division: divisions are reserved for instances when it is important to register formally the number of votes for and against a particularly important issue. On average, between 1979 and 1987 there were 320 divisions per parliamentary session. In the 1992–93 session, 401 divisions were ordered. For the observer, there is something archaic and humourous about the procedure. The Speaker orders 'Division: clear the lobbies'. Division bells sound throughout Parliament and in the division district immediately surrounding Parliament. Members will interrupt whatever they are doing in response to the bell and return to Parliament for the vote. Members crowd into the 'Aye' or 'Noe' lobby, and as they exit the lobby their attendance is checked. The Speaker then announces the result of the division. Votes are recorded by name in the Official Journal of the House of Commons.

Pairing

Not every Member must be present for every division. Provided that the Member has agreed with a Member of an opposing party not to participate in the division, he or she is excused since the absence of both Members will not affect the overall result. Pairing arrangements must be registered with the Party Whips. Pairing is not permitted in relation to divisions on the most important matters.

PARLIAMENTARY PUBLICATIONS AND PAPERS

The House of Commons

The Commons' Journal

The Commons' Journal contains the official record of the proceedings of the House. The Journal dates back to 1547 and is published annually. The Journal contains rulings from the Speaker on procedural matters.

The Commons' Official Report

The Report contains the records of speeches made in the House and written answers to Parliamentary Questions. It is a substantially verbatim report of the proceedings.

The Vote

The Vote is the collective name of a bundle of papers delivered to Members daily during a parliamentary session. It contains the record of the previous day's proceedings together with the Order Paper for the day which lists the business of the House.

The Order Book

A daily publication setting out the future business of the House.

The House of Lords

Minutes of proceedings

The record of the proceedings in the House of Lords together with details of forthcoming business.

The Lords' Journal

Since 1461, the Journals have been kept, providing details of attendance and voting.

Televised proceedings in Parliament

Radio broadcasting of Ministerial Question Time[49] began in 1978. Televised broadcasts of the House of Lords have been transmitted since 1985. In 1988, the House of Commons resolved that:

> ... this House approves in principle the holding of an experiment in the public broadcasting of its proceedings by television.[50]

The Select Committee on Televising of Proceedings was established to make recommendations as to the rules of coverage.[51] Broadcasting commenced in 1989. The Journals of the House of Commons and Lords remain the official record of proceedings in Parliament.

---

49 See Chapter 16.

50 HC 141 (1988–89), London: HMSO, and *Votes and Proceedings 1988–89*, 12 June 1989. And see Norton, P, 'Televising the House of Commons' (1991) 44 Parl Aff 185.

51 *Votes and Proceedings 1987–88*, 7 February and 9 March 1988.

CHAPTER 15

THE LEGISLATIVE PROCESS[1]

THE HOUSE OF COMMONS

Approximately two-thirds of the time of the House of Commons is devoted to the consideration of proposals for legislation.[2] In order to effect changes in the law, any proposal must receive the authority of Parliament. Parliament legitimises policy objectives. A mere decision of Parliament, in the form of a Resolution of the Commons, cannot change the law of the land.[3] In order to become law, a legislative proposal must receive the consent of the three component parts of Parliament: the Commons, the Lords[4] and the Crown through the giving of the royal assent. In this chapter the process of scrutiny in the House of Commons is considered. Discussion of the legislative role of the House of Lords is to be found in Chapter 17.

Before examining the process of scrutiny in the Commons, the various types of legislation must be considered. Legislative proposals fall under two main categories: primary and delegated (or secondary) legislation. Primary legislation refers to Acts of Parliament. Delegated or secondary legislation refers to legislation drafted by authorised persons or bodies under the authority of a 'parent' statute.

WESTMINSTER AND DEVOLUTION

As seen in Chapter 12, devolution to the Northern Ireland Assembly, Scottish Parliament and, to a lesser extent, the Welsh Assembly (which has no power to enact primary legislation), represents a diminution in Westminster's

---

1   See Norton, P, *The Commons in Perspective*, 2nd edn, 1985, Oxford: Blackwells, Chapter 5; Miers, DR and Page, AC, *Legislation*, 2nd edn, 1990, London: Sweet & Maxwell; Ryle, M and Richards, G (eds), *The Commons Under Scrutiny*, 3rd edn, 1988, London: Routledge and Kegan Paul, Chapter 7; Silk, P and Walters, R, *How Parliament Works*, 1987, London: Longman, Chapter 6; Norton, P, *Does Parliament Matter?*, 1993, Hemel Hempstead: Harvester, Chapter 5; Griffith, JAG and Ryle, M, *Parliament: Functions, Practice and Procedures*, 1989, London: Sweet & Maxwell, Chapter 8.

2   For details of allocation of time in the Commons, see Chapter 14.

3   *Stockdale v Hansard* (1839) 9 Ad & E 1.

4   Other than where the Parliament Act procedure is employed. See Chapter 17.

legislative role. Under devolution, in practical terms, the United Kingdom Parliament retains power to enact primary legislation only to the extent to which this power has not passed to the regional legislature.

PRIMARY LEGISLATION[5]

The classification of Bills

The majority of Bills will be those put forward by the government to implement its policy. Bills fall into four categories: Public Bills, Private Bills, Hybrid Bills and Money Bills. The procedure for passing the Bill differs according to the classification of a Bill. Most attention is here devoted to the legislative procedure for Public Bills.

A Public Bill is one which has general application to all members of society, for example, Road Traffic Acts, Environmental Protection Acts, National Health Service Acts. A Private Bill is one which affects only an individual or bodies in society, such as local authorities.

A Hybrid Bill is one of general application, that is to say a Public Bill, which also affects particular private interests in a manner different from the private interests of other persons or bodies of the same category or class. The Bill regulating the development of the Channel Tunnel is an example of a Hybrid Bill, since it affected the private rights of landowners whose land would be compulsorily purchased.[6]

A Money Bill is one which is certified by the Speaker as such, and is one which contains nothing other than financial measures.

A Private Members' Bill is one promoted by an individual Member of Parliament, as opposed to the government[7] or, alternatively, a matter which the government has been unable to fit into its legislative programme but will subsequently adopt and provide time – and support – for the passage of the Bill. Most often, such Bills involve sensitive issues of particular interest to their promoters. The Abortion Act 1967, for example, originated from a Private Members' Bill. Private Members' Bills follow the same legislative process as government Bills, but the time available for their consideration is restricted. Normally, 10 (although, occasionally more) Fridays each session will be set aside for Private Members' Bills, and it is rare for a Bill to succeed unless the government is prepared to provide additional time for its consideration.

---

5   See Rose, R, 'Law as a resource of public policy' (1986) 39 Parl Aff 297; Hansard Society, *Making the Law*, 1993, London: Hansard.

6   See, also, London (Transport) Bill 1968–69; Norfolk and Suffolk Broads Bill 1986–87.

7   See *op cit*, Griffith and Ryle, fn 1, pp 385–400; Marsh, D and Read, M, *Private Members' Bills*, 1988, Cambridge: CUP.

Consolidation Bills represent a re-enactment of legislation in a comprehensive manner and they enable previous legislation – which will generally exist in several statutes – to be repealed. Consolidation Bills do not, for the most part, represent any change in the law; rather, they represent the chance to 'consolidate' all the law on a particular matter within one statute. Consolidation Bills are normally introduced in the House of Lords and then scrutinised by a Joint Committee on Consolidation Bills, comprised of Members of both the House of Commons and the House of Lords. Since there is no change being made in the substantive law, parliamentary time devoted to Consolidation Bills is short and it is rare for a Consolidation Bill to be debated more than briefly on the floor of the Commons. In 1994, the House of Commons agreed that, in order to save further time, Consolidated Bills would no longer require a committee stage. Finally, there are Consolidated Fund and Appropriation Bills which provide statutory authority for government expenditure and which are not debated in Parliament.

The legislative picture cannot be complete without consideration of delegated or subordinate legislation. In the decade 1980–90, an average of 62 Bills were enacted each session, and the average number of statutory instruments[8] amounted to 2,000 per session. In addition, administrative rules drafted by government departments must be considered. These include Codes of Practice, Circulars and Guidances and, while they do not have the force of law, they nevertheless have an impact on the manner in which laws are implemented.[9]

The origins of legislation

The majority of Bills considered by Parliament will be introduced by the government of the day. This does not mean that the source of the proposal is one emanating from government policy, still less from the party manifesto on which the election was fought. Between 1970–74, only eight per cent of Bills were attributable to the Conservative Party Manifesto, and between 1974–79, only 13 per cent of Bills were attributable to the Labour Party *Manifesto*.[10] In 1981, 75 per cent of Bills originated within government departments, and the remainder were responses to particular events. Illustrations of reactive legislative proposals include the War Damage Bill 1964–65, introduced rapidly to nullify the effect of the House of Lords' decision in *Burmah Oil v Lord*

---

8   See, further, below.
9   Eg, Guidance to Local Authorities on the Provision of Sites for Gypsies under the Caravan Sites Act 1968; Guidance on Allocation of Local Authority Housing under the Housing Act 1985. See Baldwin, R and Houghton, J, 'Circular arguments: the status and legitimacy of administrative rules' [1986] PL 239; Ganz, G, *Quasi-legislation: Some Recent Developments in Secondary Legislation*, 1987, London: Sweet & Maxwell.
10   Rose, R, *Do Parties Make a Difference?*, 2nd edn, 1984, London: Macmillan.

Advocate;[11] the Prevention of Terrorism Act 1974, passed in response to the Birmingham Pub bombing by the Irish Republican Army; the Dangerous Dogs Act 1990, a response to the increased numbers of dogs causing serious injury, particularly to children.

Consideration of the origins of legislative proposals is important in evaluating the extent to which government and the House of Commons interacts with the society it is elected to serve. As John Stuart Mill said, Parliament is 'the sounding board of the nation'.[12] JAG Griffith and M Ryle express the same idea when they observe that Parliament is 'the recipient of a wide range of external pressures and proposals':[13]

> It is a central feature of Parliament, however, that it performs a responsive rather than initiating function within the constitution. The government – at different levels – initiates policy, formulates its policy on legislation and other proposals, exercises powers under the prerogative or granted by statute and, in all these aspects, performs the governing role in the State. Both Houses of Parliament spend most of their time responding, in a variety of ways, to these initiatives, proposals or executive actions.

The government, however, is not the only source of input of business for Parliament. Much business originates from the Opposition front-bench, and from backbenchers on either side of the two Houses. The inspiration for their input is largely found in general public opinion, outside pressures or interest groups, newspapers, radio and television, and in the minds and attitudes of millions of citizens represented in the Commons by Members.

Parliament, therefore, finds itself the recipient of a wide range of external pressures and proposals, broadly divided in origin between the government of the day on the one hand and the outside world – the public – on the other.[14]

Professor Finer[15] labels the forces external to Parliament which have an impact on its working as the 'anonymous empire'. Finer is here referring to all those individuals and organisations, lobby groups and interest groups whose aim is to influence the content of legislation. Finer claims that the detailed programme of government legislation 'owes a great deal to sectional groups'. Amongst these groups, we can include such organisations as the Confederation of British Industry, Trades Union Congress, National Farmers' Unions, National Union of Teachers, the British Medical Association, and the Law Society, each of which is engaged in promoting its own sectional interests. Other pressure groups pursue particular causes: for example, the Royal Society for the Prevention of Cruelty to Animals, JUSTICE (the

---

11 [1964] AC 75. See, further, Chapter 7.
12 Mill, JS, *Representative Government* (1865), 1958, Indianapolis: Bobbs-Merrill.
13 *Op cit*, Griffith and Ryle, fn 1, p 5.
14 *Op cit*, Griffith and Ryle, fn 1, p 5.
15 Finer, SE, *Anonymous Empire*, 1958, London: Pall Mall.

International Commission of Jurists), Howard League for Penal Reform, Friends of the Earth (environmental issues), Shelter (housing).

In addition to these and many other groups, the law reform bodies provide a source of legislation. The Law Commission, established under the Law Commissions Act 1965, is under a duty to keep the law under review with a view to its systematic development and reform, including codification of law, and simplification and modernisation of law.[16] If we take, by way of example, the Law Commission's work on family law, the Commission has reviewed the law of legitimacy, custody, wardship, divorce, domestic violence and occupation of the matrimonial home. In conjunction with inter-departmental committees, the Law Commission has been engaged in a comprehensive review of adoption law. Between 1965–88 the Law Commission had published 111 reports, 71 of which were given legal effect in full or in part.

Commissions of inquiry may be established by the government to examine and report on particular issues, often culminating in a change in the law. For example, the Committee of Inquiry into Child Abuse in Cleveland (in part) resulted in changes implemented in the Children Act 1989 which represented a major overhaul of the law relating to children. The Criminal Law Revision Committee, has examined the law relating, *inter alia*, to conspiracy, contempt, arrest and detention, and criminal deception.

Each of these sources may result in proposals for changes in the law. The success of these proposals in terms of becoming law is largely dependent upon the government of the day and its willingness to provide parliamentary time for the consideration of Bills.

The preparation of a Bill

Once the government has decided to implement a particular measure, the aims of government must be translated effectively into language which will achieve those objectives. That task is entrusted to parliamentary draftsmen, or Parliamentary Counsel, attached to the Management and Personnel Office of the Treasury.[17] Drafting involves five stages: understanding, analysis, design, composition and revision.[18] Once a draft Bill is in being, it is examined by the Cabinet Home Affairs Committee before being formally submitted to Parliament for scrutiny and enactment.

---

16 Law Commissions Act 1965, s 3.

17 SI 1981/1670.

18 Thornton, GC, *Legislative Drafting*, 3rd edn, 1987, London: Butterworths, pp 116–17.

The structure of a Bill

Each Bill has a short title, for example, the Transport Bill, which indicates the general area of policy involved, together with a long title which summarises the main objectives of the Bill. The Bill is made up of Chapters or Parts which encompass groups of related clauses, and Schedules which contain details supplementary to the primary clauses. The Bill may grant powers to make delegated legislation to Ministers or other specified bodies, such as local authorities. There is, necessarily, no uniformity as to the length of Bills, which may range from one clause (Abortion Amendment Bill 1988–89), to 27 Parts, 747 clauses and 25 Schedules (Companies Bill 1985).

The legislative stages: Public Bills

First reading

A Bill which is to be introduced will appear on the Order Paper of the relevant day. The Bill will be presented in 'dummy form' and is deemed to be read a 'first time'. Alternatively, a Bill may be introduced on order of the House, or after having been sent to the Commons following its passage by the House of Lords. Following the purely formal introduction into Parliament, a date will be set for second reading and the Bill will be printed and published.

Second reading

It is at the second reading that a Bill will receive the first in depth scrutiny. The scrutiny occurs in the form of a debate, generally on the floor of the House, and is confined to matters of principle rather than detail. Exceptionally, the second reading debate may be referred to a committee for consideration, but may only be so referred if 20 or more Members of Parliament do not object and, accordingly, the procedure is reserved for non-controversial matters and not measures 'involving large questions of policy nor likely to give rise to differences on party lines'.[19] Where a Bill has been committed to a second reading committee, the committee considers the principles of the Bill, but the vote on the Bill is taken on the floor of the House.[20] It is at second reading stage that the Minister in charge of the Bill must explain and defend the contents of the Bill. The Opposition's task is to probe and question and set out reasons for opposing the Bill. It should not be assumed that the Opposition invariably opposes Bills. In many instances, the proposed legislation is uncontroversial and may even be welcomed by the

---

19   *First Report Select Committee on Procedure,* HC 149 (1964–65), London: HMSO, para 3.

20   Between 1965 and 1994, only 139 Bills were considered in a second reading committee. 105 of these had already been considered by the House of Lords.

Opposition. The Dangerous Dogs Bill and the Child Support Bill 1990 are illustrations of this phenomena. If the Bill is opposed, a vote will take place which determines the fate of the Bill. If the vote is lost, the Bill is rejected and the proposed legislation must either be abandoned or the Bill must be reintroduced at a later date.

Once a Bill has successfully completed the second reading stage, it 'stands committed' to a standing committee, unless, exceptionally, the House orders otherwise.[21] Bills of constitutional importance may 'stand committed' to a Committee of the Whole House, or the Bill may be divided and part considered by a Committee of the Whole House and part in standing committee. A Bill may also be referred to a special standing committee or to a select committee, although, as seen below, this is rare.

Public Bills which are to give effect to proposals contained in a report by either of the Law Commissions, other than a Private Members' Bill or a Consolidation Bill, when set down for second reading will be committed to a second reading committee, unless the House orders otherwise, or the Bill is referred to the Northern Ireland, Scottish or Welsh Grand Committee. If a Minister of the Crown moves a motion that a Bill not be referred to a second reading committee, the House will vote on the motion.

Committee stage

Standing committees are designed to scrutinise Bills in detail. The name is in fact a misnomer, for it implies that these are permanent committees, whereas in fact they are not. The committee will be established for the purpose of examining a particular Bill and will then stand down, a feature which, as will be seen, may have implications for the adequacy of scrutiny.

At any one time, there will be eight to 10 standing committees in operation. Committees may comprise between 16 and 50 Members of Parliament, and normally between 18 and 25.[22] Membership is drawn from Members of Parliament from all political parties and is proportionate to the overall strength of the party in the House, thus, the larger the government's majority in the House, the larger its majority in the standing committee. Appointments are made by a Committee of Selection who will take advice from party whips as to appropriate Members. The Speaker of the House appoints the Chairman of the standing committee, who may be a Member of either side of the House (government or Opposition). Once selected, the Chairman is impartial and enjoys the same powers as the Speaker of the House in relation to selection of amendments for discussion and imposition of the Closure Motion (see further, below, p 594).

---

21 Standing Order No 61.
22 Complex Bills may warrant a larger committee membership, as with the Finance Bill 1992.

The function of the standing committee is to examine the Bill clause by clause. The Minister in charge of the Bill has the task of steering it successfully through committee, aided by his Parliamentary Private Secretary and civil servants. Amendments may be proposed by Members giving notice to the Public Bill Office of the House of Commons. These amendments may take the form of linguistic details, adding or subtracting a word here or there; alternatively, amendments may be of major substance. Once the clauses of the Bill have been considered, the committee moves to consider any proposed new clauses. Proposals for amendment may be ruled out of order if they are irrelevant, beyond the scope of the Bill, conflict with other proposed amendments, conflict with the principle of the Bill or are unintelligible, ineffective, vague or spurious.[23]

The proceedings in standing committee are formal and ritualistic. A Member moves an amendment, the Minister responds, the Opposition speaks, other Members comment, and debate continues until a decision on a clause – 'that the clause do stand part of the Bill' – is reached. For the most part, deliberations will follow party political lines, and it follows that, provided the government has a majority on the committee, the chances of successfully moving amendments is slight. The Minister's task is to ensure a smooth passage for the Bill in the fastest possible time. Richard Crossman,[24] Minister of Housing and Local Government in the Labour government of 1974, commented that committee stage is tedious with the Minister 'being pinned to the wall' throughout the process.

Professor Griffith[25] examined the work of standing committees in three parliamentary sessions, 1967–68, 1968–69 and 1970–71. In these sessions, of 3,510 amendments moved by private members, only 171 were accepted by the government, 4.3 per cent of Opposition backbenchers, 9.2 per cent from government backbenchers. More recent research reveals that, between 1970–74, the government lost only 24 votes in standing committee and, between 1974–79, over 100 votes.

The low success rate of backbench proposals for amendment should not be given disproportionate weight. It has been seen above that Standing Orders set out a number of 'inadmissible' categories of proposed amendments. It must also be noted that Members may put forward amendments solely with a view to gaining a clearer picture of the Bill, or for more spurious reasons, such as delaying a Bill or embarrassing the government. Equally, it should be remembered that the composition of the committee reflects that of the House overall: governments with a firm majority will inevitably suffer fewer defeats in committee. Finally, recognition must be given to the fact that the

---

23   See Erskine May, T, *Parliamentary Practice*, 21st edn, 1989, London: Butterworths, pp 555–58 (see, now, 22nd edn, 1997); *op cit*, Griffith and Ryle, fn 1, p 232.

24   Crossman, R, *The Diaries of a Cabinet Minister*, 1977, London: Jonathan Cape.

25   Griffith, JAG, *Parliamentary Scrutiny of Government Bills*, 1973, London: Allen & Unwin.

government has gained a mandate in a general election and, whether or not a specific legislative proposal stems from that mandate, the government has a legitimate expectation of getting its legislative programme on the statute book. Equally, the principle of the Bill has been approved on second reading by the House. While Parliament as a whole, through its representative committee, has the equally legitimate expectation of being able to give adequate scrutiny to government proposals, that should not necessarily be understood to mean that standing committees should expect to be able to force their views on government.

That said, there have long been criticisms of the effectiveness of standing committees. It has been noted above that the Minister in charge of the Bill, together with his civil service advisers, steers the Bill through committee. Any Minister not totally in charge of his subject matter will have a short ministerial career, and it is essential that the Minister should have a command of his subject and the necessary advice to hand to fend off Opposition attacks. It is inevitable, therefore, that there will be a disparity of information and expertise between the Minister and other members of the committee, and that this will affect the adequacy of scrutiny. Further, the shortcomings of standing committees may be exacerbated by their non-specialist composition.

At first sight, it appears anomalous that there is no standing committee system organised on specialist lines. There is a *prima facie* case for committees to be geared to particular subjects, or groups of subjects. On this reasoning, a standing committee could be devised with the remit to consider transport matters, another to consider science and technology Bills, another to consider environmental issues and so on. If such committees were appointed for the life of the Parliament, or for a parliamentary session with Members appointed on the basis of their expertise and interests, the potential for improved scrutiny would be enhanced. However, there is a counter-argument to this. A specialist semi-permanent committee, while having the benefit of expertise, would lose the quality of the assortment of interests which is currently brought to bear on proposals. Members of the committee might become too familiar with each others' attitudes, and Ministers and the committee could suffer from becoming inward looking and overly concerned with one subject to the neglect of others. Committees are open to the public and their proceedings are recorded in the Official Report of the House, *Hansard*. For debate to become too narrow and technical might disadvantage other Members and the public in their capacity to understand proceedings.

One recognised shortcoming in standing committee procedure is the lack of power to send for 'persons and papers', in other words, witnesses and documents. For Members who are not specialists in the subject matter or in statutory drafting and interpretation, the task of understanding the content of a complex Bill, its implications for other aspects of the law and the relationship between various Parts and Clauses can be daunting. This was a procedural aspect examined by Professor Griffith, who recommended reform.

The Procedure Committee[26] examined this perceived difficulty and recommended that a hybrid committee displaying the normal features of a standing committee but adopting some of the procedures and powers of select committees be introduced.[27] Standing Order No 91, passed by the House in 1986, provides that within the first 28 days of a Bill being committed to the Special Standing Committee, written and oral evidence may be taken. A further committee sitting can be devoted to debate on the evidence given to the committee. At this preliminary stage, the committee is acting as a Committee of Inquiry, attempting to see the Bill in its entirety and to evaluate its substance and implications. Following the inquiry period, the committee reverts to ordinary standing committee procedure. In the experimental period from 1980–85, only five Bills were committed to Special Standing Committees. In 1985 in debate, the Leader of the House[28] reported that the views of Ministers on the new procedure were mixed, some finding it helpful, others considering it irksome. In light of the pressure on parliamentary time and the reluctance of Ministers to be 'tied up' in committee proceedings, it is unlikely that Special Standing Committees will become the standard form of procedure for the scrutiny of Bills.

Other Bills may be referred to Second Reading Committees, under the procedure outlined above. Neither major nor controversial Bills are referred to Second Reading Committees. Many of these Bills will already have passed through the House of Lords.

Report stage[29]

Once the Bill has been considered in standing committee, the Bill is reported back to the House of Commons[30] as a whole. If amendments have been made in committee, the Bill will be reprinted. Further amendments may be introduced at this stage, but the Speaker will be careful to avoid repetition of the debate in standing committee, so any proposed amendments previously considered will be rejected. The Speaker will accept amendments proposed by the government, proposals representing a compromise and amendments relating to new developments. Generally, the debate at this stage will be brief but, again, this will depend on the importance of the Bill. The Police and Criminal Evidence Bill, for example, was debated for eighteen and a half hours at report stage. Approximately nine per cent of time on the floor of the House is taken up with report.

---

26 See Chapter 16.
27 *Ibid*.
28 Mr John Biffen.
29 See *op cit*, Griffith and Ryle, fn 1, pp 235–36.
30 Standing Order No 71.

Third reading

Third reading represents the last chance for the House of Commons to examine a Bill before it is passed to the House of Lords. At this stage, the Bill cannot be amended, other than to correct small mistakes such as grammatical or printing errors. A Bill may pass through the report and third reading stages at the same time.

TABLE I: TIME SPENT ON GOVERNMENT BILLS ON THE FLOOR OF THE HOUSE OF COMMONS

1995–96 and 1998–99 (hours : minutes)

Session	Second reading (Standing Committee)	Committee of Whole House	Report	Third reading	Lords' amendments	Total
1995–96	101 : 17	19 : 56	98 : 04	12 : 58	16 : 37	248 : 52
1998–99	88 : 19	101 : 69	120 : 53	17 : 10	48 : 37	375 : 88

In any parliamentary session, approximately 50–60 Bills will be introduced, the vast majority of which will reach the statute book. In 1983–84, for example, 60 Bills were introduced and 60 passed; in 1985–86, 56 Bills were introduced and 54 passed; in 1992–93, 52 Bills were introduced and 52 passed. In 1995–96, 43 government Bills were introduced into the House of Commons, of which all passed on to the statute book. Eighty-nine Private Members' Bills were introduced, of which 17 received the royal assent. A total of 60 Bills received the royal assent.

PRIVATE MEMBERS' BILLS[31]

Introducing a Private Members' Bill

In addition to Public (and Private and Hybrid) Bills, a number of legislative proposals will be introduced by individual Members of Parliament. A Private Members' Bill may be introduced in one of four ways. The first procedure is that of the ballot.

---

31   See *op cit*, Marsh and Read, fn 7.

Introduction by ballot[32]

The House will agree, early in the session, for days to be appointed for the purpose of the Ballot. Members of Parliament may put their names on the Ballot Paper on that day. Over 400 Members normally enter the Ballot, although many will have no specific proposed legislation in mind. Twenty Members will be successful at the Ballot. If successful, the Member must then, within nine days, table the subject matter for his or her Bill. Six Fridays per session are allocated to Private Members' Bills, on which days the Bills take precedence over other parliamentary business.

Introduction under Standing Order procedure[33]

Any Member may present a Bill under this procedure by placing the long and short title of the Bill on the Order Paper of the House. The Bill will not be considered, but simply be deemed to have received a first reading and a date set for second reading.

Introduction under the 'Ten Minute Rule'[34]

A Member may give notice of a motion for leave to introduce a Bill. The motions will be considered at specific times allotted by the House, which permits the Member to raise an issue after Question Time on Tuesdays and Wednesdays, thus guaranteeing media attention.[35] Several rules apply. The Member may give one notice at any one time. No notice may be given for leave to bring in a Bill which relates to taxation or expenditure, or to bring in a Bill which covers matters which are substantially the same as those contained in Bills on which the House has already reached a decision in that session.

'Ordinary presentation' of a Bill[36]

Every Member is permitted to introduce a Bill after having given notice. These Bills, however, are not presented until after the Ballot Bills have been presented and put down for second reading. They therefore have little chance of success. Nor do they enjoy the publicity given to Bills introduced under the Ten Minute Rule.

---

32 In 1992–93, 20 Bills (of a total of 163) were introduced under this procedure of which six received the Royal Assent. Standing Order No 14.

33 In 1992–93, 63 (of 163) Bills were introduced under this procedure, of which three received the Royal Assent.

34 In 1992–93, 74 (of 163) Bills were introduced under this procedure, of which two received the Royal Assent. Standing Order No 23.

35 Usually, on Tuesdays or Wednesdays before the start of public business.

36 Standing Order No 57.

Introduction of a Bill after consideration in the House of Lords[37]

Most Private Members' Bills are introduced in the House of Commons, but a small number each session may have started their parliamentary life in the Lords. If the Bill passes the Lords, it then comes to the Commons. However, Bills introduced in the Lords are considered only after Bills introduced in the Commons and, accordingly, given the severe time constraints, few are likely even to receive a second reading in the Commons.

The enactment of Private Members' Bills

The success, or otherwise, of a Private Members' Bill is largely dependent upon it receiving government support. As has been seen in Chapter 14, the government controls the parliamentary timetable, and dominates parliamentary business. Since only six Fridays per session are allocated for consideration of Private Members' Bills, it will be necessary for the government to make additional time for the completion of its parliamentary stages. Whether or not the government is willing to do this will depend upon the political support which the Bill acquires. However, even if a Bill does not successfully pass all its legislative stages, it may have served the useful purpose of heightening parliamentary and public awareness of a particular issue. For example, the Rt Hon Tony Benn MP has introduced Private Members' Bills, *inter alia*, on placing the royal prerogative on a statutory basis,[38] and for enacting a written constitution.[39] Neither of these has succeeded, but represent matters in which there is widespread interest.

The volume of Private Members' Bills

In the 1979–80 session, 125 Private Members' Bills were introduced into the House of Commons. Of these, only 10 were given royal assent. In 1983–84, 118 were introduced, and 13 received the royal assent. In the 1992–93 session, 163 Private Members' Bills were introduced, of which 16 received the royal assent (compared with 52 government Bills, 52 of which received the royal assent). In the 1996–97 session, a total of 22 Private Members' Bills received the royal assent.

---

37 In 1992–93, eight (of 163) Bills were introduced under this procedure, of which four received the royal assent.

38 Crown Prerogatives (House of Commons Control) Bill 1988–89.

39 Commonwealth of Britain Bill.

Curtailing debate on legislative proposals

As a result of the pressure on parliamentary time, and the need for a Bill to pass through all its legislative stages in a single session, procedures exist to limit consideration of a Bill.

Closure Motions

The Closure Motion, introduced in 1881,[40] is a means of stopping debate, usually by agreement between government and Opposition, in order to ensure that debates end at times agreed by the parties. The Closure can be used in debate on the floor of the House or in standing committee. It is an instrument of control, and one which is used sparingly: rarely will it be used without agreement. In the 1987–88 session, however (a long session), it was used 20 times without inter-party agreement.

In terms of procedure, the motion for Closure is put to the Speaker who has discretion whether or not to accept the motion. In addition, at least 100 Members of Parliament must vote in favour of Closure.

Selection of amendments

This device is confined to legislative proposals and enables the procedure to be streamlined by the selection of amendments for discussion.

The Allocation of Time Motion

The most extreme form of control is the Allocation of Time Motion, colloquially called the Guillotine Motion, introduced in its present form in 1887. Erskine May[41] describes Guillotine Motions as representing:

> ... the extreme limit to which procedure goes in affirming the rights of the majority at the expense of the minorities of the House, and it cannot be denied that they are capable of being used in such a way as to upset the balance, generally so carefully preserved, between the claims of business, and the rights of debate.

The device, if approved by the House, enables the government to set a date by which a Bill is to be reported from standing committee to the House, or a date for third reading. If the government puts forward a motion for an Allocation of Time, Standing Orders provide that a debate of up to three hours may take place (which may be extended), unless otherwise proposed in the motion or decided by the Business Committee of the House. Once agreed, the Business

---

40   Standing Order No 51.
41   *Op cit*, Erskine May, fn 23, pp 480–89.

Committee of the House, or a business sub-committee of the Standing Committee will determine how many scrutiny sessions are to be held and the date by which the next procedural stage must be accomplished.

Between 1881–1921, 36 Bills were guillotined, between 1921–45, 30. The highest number of Bills guillotined in any one session, 10, was in the 1988–89 session. The table below shows the Bills guillotined between 1988 and 1999. In respect of many Bills, the guillotine will be applied more than once, and can apply to any stage of the legislative process. The Dangerous Dogs Bill 1990–91, for example, regarded by the government as an urgent matter, was guillotined twice with the effect that the second reading debate, the committee stage, report and third reading and the consideration of amendments from the House of Lords were all subject to strict time limits.

TABLE II: ALLOCATION OF TIME MOTIONS: 1988–89; 1998–99

Session	Title of Bill
1988–89	Prevention of Terrorism (Temporary Provisions) Bill Water Bill Official Secrets Bill Self-Governing Schools (Scotland) Bill Dock Work Bill Football Spectators Bill Companies Bill Children Bill Local Government and Housing Bill Employment Bill
1998–99	European Parliament Elections Bill Greater London Authority Bill Local Government Bill Welfare Reform and Pensions Bill Health Bill Immigration and Asylum bill Tax Credits Bill Access to Justice Bill Youth Justice and Criminal Evidence Bill Northern Ireland Bill Food Standards Bill Employment Relations Bill

Both sessions illustrated made particularly heavy use of the Allocation of Time Motion. In most sessions the Motion is only used on up to four Bills.

In the 1997–98 session to date, the Referendums (Scotland and Wales) Bill and the Finance Bill have been guillotined. Both were guillotined after second reading. In the case of the Referendums Bill, two further days were allocated. The Finance Bill was timetabled for two days debate in Committee of the Whole House.

For the most part, the Guillotine Motion is used sparingly and will, generally, be applied only after a considerable amount of time has been spent on the Bill in committee and the government is at risk of losing the Bill altogether.[42] For example, the Housing Bill of 1979–80 and the Social Security Bill of 1985–86 had both spent over 100 hours in committee before the Allocation of Time Motion was moved. Moreover, the Police and Criminal Evidence Bill 1983–84 had no Guillotine applied despite having 59 sittings in standing committee.

If the government chooses to move an Allocation of Time Motion, it is a rare occurrence for it to lose the vote. In 1977, the Labour government moved an Allocation of Time Motion on the Scotland and Wales Bill 1976–77 but, following a six hour debate, the vote was lost by 312 votes to 283 and the government withdrew the Bill.

In 1984, the Select Committee on Procedure examined the use of the Guillotine and, in April 1985, published a report[43] recommending that all controversial Bills should be timetabled at the start of the standing committee stage. The House rejected the proposal in February 1986. The greater certainty provided by some form of automatic timetabling must be set against the constraints that would be imposed on the Opposition's ability to delay a Bill and cause the government to reconsider a particular measure or make concessions.

The use of the Guillotine procedure undeniably limits the effectiveness of parliamentary scrutiny of Bills and may result in Bills leaving the House of Commons with significant portions unexamined. This point must be borne in mind when assessing the role and value of the House of Lords in the legislative process, which will be considered in Chapter 17.

---

42 See *op cit*, Griffith and Ryle, fn 1, Chapter 7.
43 HC 49 (1984–85), London: HMSO.

DELEGATED LEGISLATION

The picture of the law making process would be incomplete without a consideration of delegated, or subordinate, legislation.

In 1972, Parliament's Joint Committee on Delegated Legislation described subordinate legislation as covering 'every exercise of power to legislate conferred by or under an Act of Parliament'.[44] Some examples will make the scope of delegated legislation clearer.

Delegated legislation may be made by:

(a) *Ministers*, in the form of rules and regulations which supplement the provisions of an Act of Parliament;

(b) *local authorities*, in the form of bylaws to regulate their locality according to particular localised needs;

(c) *public bodies*, in the form of rules and regulations. Such bodies include the British Airways Authority (section 9 of the Airport Authorities Act 1975); British Railways Board (section 67 of the Transport Act 1962); and the Nature Conservancy Council (section 37 of the Wildlife and Countryside Act 1981);

(d) *judges*, in the form of rules of court made under the authority of section 75 of the Supreme Court Act 1981;

(e) *government departments*, in the form of codes of practice, circulars and guidance. These do not contain legal rules, but have a substantive effect on the manner in which the legal rules operate;

(f) *House of Commons*, in the form of Resolutions of the House. The Provisional Collection of Taxes Act 1968 makes possible the lawful imposition and collection of taxation between the Budget speech and the enactment of the Finance Bill in July/August. Whereas normal Resolutions of the House do not have the force of law, Resolutions enabling the impositions and collections of taxation – being authorised by statute – have legal effect.

The volume of delegated legislation also reveals its importance as a source of law.

---

44 *Report of the Joint Committee on Delegated Legislation*, HL 184, HC 475, 1971–72, London: HMSO, para 6.

TABLE III: The volume of delegated legislation

Year	Number
1901	156
1921	727
1951	2,335
1971	2,167
1991	1,892
1994	3,300[45]
1997	1,399[46]
1999	1,479[47]

The use of delegated law making power is not a purely modern phenomenon, arising from increasing legal regulation of all aspects of life. The power to make subordinate legislation was exercised as early as the sixteenth century.[48] The increase in the volume of delegated legislation derives from the early nineteenth century. AV Dicey approved of delegated legislation. In Dicey's view:

> The cumbersomeness and prolixity of English statute is due in no small measure to futile endeavours of Parliament to work out the details of large legislative changes ... the substance no less than the form of law would, it is probable, be a good deal improved if the executive government of England could, like that of France, by means of decrees, ordinances, or proclamations having the force of law, work out the detailed application of the general principles embodied in the Acts of the legislature.[49]

If satisfaction and approval of delegated legislation was widespread at the time of Dicey's writing, strongly opposing views were being expressed before long. Chief Justice Hewart, in *The New Despotism* (1929), argued that the increased use of delegated legislation, particularly during the First World War under the Defence of the Realm Act 1914, amounted to an effective usurpation of the sovereign law making powers of Parliament. Such criticisms led to the appointment, in 1929, of a committee[50] of inquiry to consider the powers

---

45 This figure includes many statutory instruments relating to local matters.

46 Of which, 1,241 were subject to the negative resolution procedure; 158 to the affirmative resolution procedure.

47 Of which, 1,266 were subject to the negative resolution procedure; 178 to the affirmative procedure. An additional 35 other instruments not subject to parliamentary proceedings were also passed.

48 Statute of Proclamations 1539 (31 Hen 8 c 26); and see Allen, CK, *Law and Orders*, 3rd edn, 1965, London: Stevens.

49 Dicey, AV, *Introduction to the Study of the Law of the Constitution*, 10th edn, 1959, London: Macmillan, pp 52–53.

50 The Donoughmore-Scott Committee.

exercised by Ministers by way of delegated legislation and to report what safeguards are desirable or necessary to secure the constitutional principles of the sovereignty of Parliament and the supremacy of the law.

The committee's report,[51] while recognising the need for improved parliamentary scrutiny of delegated legislation, nevertheless, emphasised the necessity of it in terms of legislative efficiency. It is efficiency which is the principal justification for the delegation of law making power. Put simply, Parliament, as currently constituted, struggles to give adequate scrutiny to primary legislation. To burden Parliament with the task of scrutinising every detail of legislation would overload the parliamentary timetable to the extent that the system would break under the strain. A related justification for delegated power lies in the need to supplement or amend the primary rules in light of new developments. Delegated legislation enables the fine tuning of the primary rules to take place, without encumbering Parliament as a whole. Further, it may be that the government is clear as to the broad policy to be pursued under an Act, and as to the primary legal rules necessary to achieve a particular goal. There may be less certainty as to the technical, detailed rules necessary: the delegation of law making power enables such rules to be worked out, often in consultation with specialist interest groups outside Parliament.

The justifications for subordinate legislation can hold good only if the powers granted are sufficiently clear and precise as to be adjudicated upon by the courts by way of judicial review[52] and if the parliamentary scrutiny accorded to it is adequate.

Under the doctrine of parliamentary sovereignty, the validity of Acts of Parliament cannot be questioned.[53] Subordinate legislation, however, can be reviewed, provided that the jurisdiction of the courts has not been excluded – or 'ousted' – in order to determine its compatibility with the enabling Act. Such exclusion of review is rare and, to ensure immunity from review, the exclusion clause would have to be unambiguous on the face of the parent Act. Of equal importance to the possibility of successful challenge in the courts is the breadth of discretion conferred on the delegate by the Act. If a statute conferred powers on a Minister to make regulations 'whenever the Minister thinks fit' or (say) to award compensation for injury 'under circumstances to be determined by the Minister', the grant of discretion is so wide as to be virtually unreviewable by the courts. Also important is that delegated legislation should not impose retrospective liability on citizens, or be so vague as to be unintelligible. Further, it is necessary that the power granted is conferred on an identifiable delegate in order that the exercise of power be

---

51 *Report on Ministers' Powers*, Cmnd 4060, 1932, London: HMSO.
52 See Chapters 24 and 25.
53 *Pickin v British Railways Board* [1974] AC 765. See Chapter 7.

challengeable. On this latter point, the Emergency Powers Act 1939 provided for differing levels of delegation. The Act provided that regulations might empower any authority on persons to make orders, rules and bylaws, for any of the purposes for which the Defence Regulations might themselves be made. Ministerial orders were issued under the regulations, directions issued under the regulations and licences issued under the directions. Such subdelegation breaches the rule that a person or body to whom powers are entrusted may not delegate them to another, *'delegatus non potest delegare'*.

The Statutory Instruments Act 1946

The vast majority of delegated legislation is in the form of statutory instruments governed by the Statutory Instruments Act 1946. Section 1 provides that where any Act confers power on His Majesty in Council or on any Minister of the Crown, where that power is expressed as a power exercisable by Order in Council or by statutory instrument, the provisions of this Act apply thereto.

Parliamentary scrutiny of delegated legislation[54]

The Statutory Instruments Act 1946 lays down the means by which an instrument may come into effect, but the method adopted will depend on that which is stipulated in the particular enabling Act. First, the parent Act may provide that the instrument be laid before Parliament[55] but that no parliamentary action is needed. Secondly, the parent Act may provide that the instrument is subject to the 'negative resolution procedure'.[56] Under this procedure, the instrument can be laid before Parliament in its final form and come into immediate effect subject only to there being a successful move to annul the instrument. This move takes the form of a motion, known here as a 'prayer' for annulment of the instrument, which can be made within 40 days of the instrument being laid. Thirdly, the enabling Act may stipulate that the instrument be laid in draft form and that it will come into effect only if a prayer for annulment is not moved successfully. The Statutory Instruments Act also provides for an 'affirmative resolution procedure'. If this is adopted, the instrument may either come into immediate effect, subject to subsequent approval by Parliament, or be laid in draft form to come into effect if approved by Parliament.

---

54 See Beith, A, 'Prayers unanswered: a jaundiced view of the parliamentary scrutiny of statutory instruments' (1981) 34 Parl Aff 165; Hayhurst, JD and Wallington, P, 'The parliamentary scrutiny of delegated legislation' [1988] PL 547; *op cit*, Hansard Society, fn 5, Annex A.

55 Statutory Instruments Act 1946, s 4.

56 *Ibid*, s 5.

The choice of the procedure to be adopted lies with the government. The problem posed for Parliament is again one of time and opportunity. The affirmative resolution procedure is rarely adopted by government; the negative resolution procedure requires that Members of Parliament must be vigilant and astute if they (usually the Opposition) are to be aware that a particular instrument has been laid and are to be able to move a prayer for annulment within the 40 day period. Instruments made under the European Communities Act 1972 to give effect to Community law may be subject to either the affirmative or negative procedure.[57]

Since 1994–95, instruments subject to affirmative resolution are automatically referred to a standing committee, unless the House orders otherwise. Instruments subject to the negative resolution procedure, to which a prayer has been tabled, may be referred to a standing committee on a Motion by a Minister of the Crown.

Supplementing the above scrutiny methods is the Joint Select Committee on Delegated Legislation The Joint Committee comprises seven Members of the House of Commons and seven Members of the House of Lords, and is chaired by a member of the House of Commons. The committee is charged with examining all instruments laid before Parliament and those instruments for which there is no laying requirement. The grounds on which the committee will report to Parliament are:

(a) that the instrument imposes a tax or charge;

(b) that the parent Act excludes review by the courts;

(c) that the instrument is to operate retrospectively;

(d) that there has been unjustifiable delay in publication or laying;

(e) that the instrument has come into effect in contravention of the rules of notice to the House;

(f) that there is doubt as to whether the instrument is *intra vires*;

(g) that the instrument requires clarification;

(h) that the instrument's drafting is defective.

The committee examines over 1,000 instruments per session. Less than one per cent are reported to Parliament and few are debated. The strength of the committee's work lies not in its reports to Parliament and any consequent action but rather in its scrutiny of instruments and drawing attention to defects in instruments to the relevant government department.

The *Report of the Committee on Ministers' Powers*, in 1932,[58] emphasised the importance of distinguishing between 'normal' delegation of powers, matters of technical detail, and 'exceptional' delegation of powers, which entailed the

---

57 European Communities Act 1972, Sched 2, para 2(2).

58 *Report on Ministers' Powers*, Cmnd 4060, 1932, London: HMSO.

delegation of power to make laws on matters of policy and principle. With regard to the latter category, concern was expressed as to 'whether Parliament was surrendering its own function in the process'.[59] Research conducted by JD Hayhurst and P Wallington[60] suggests that, while the volume of statutory instruments per session remains fairly stable, there has been a change in emphasis in the content of delegated legislation, an increasing volume of which entail the 'exceptional' delegation of powers. Statutes are becoming less detailed and granting broad enabling powers to delegates. The Education Reform Act 1988, Legal Aid Act 1988, Children Act 1989 and Child Support Act 1991 may all be cited in support of this proposition.

The Child Support Act 1991, which aims to ensure that absent parents, rather than the State, make financial provision for their natural children, by way of example, grants to the Secretary of State the power to prescribe, *inter alia*, those persons under a duty to disclose information, the purposes for which such disclosure shall be made and the mathematical formula to be employed in making maintenance assessments. Section 51(1) of the Act confers a further and more general power, namely that:

> The Secretary of State may by regulations make such incidental, supplementary and transitional provision as he considers appropriate in connection with any provision made by or under this Act.

At committee stage in the House of Lords, the Child Support Bill was criticised for its 'skeletal' nature and at second reading in the House of Commons the volume of proposed delegated legislation, estimated to amount to over 100 regulations, was described as a 'major flaw' in the Bill.[61] Given the constitutional importance that delegated legislation be capable of being scrutinised by the courts in order to ensure that it is *intra vires*, it is extremely difficult to envisage a successful challenge being made in the courts against such wide delegated powers as those granted under the Child Support Act 1991.

Standing Order 101 (Standing Committees on Delegated Legislation), approved by the House of Commons, provides that, from the 1996–97 session, one or more standing committees are appointed for consideration of delegated legislation. Where a member gives notice of intention to pray for the annulment of a statutory instrument, or draft thereof, the instrument may be referred to the standing committee.[62] In addition, a Joint Select Committee of both Houses scrutinises and reports if necessary on technical issues such as drafting or unexpected use of powers granted in the parent Act. If an instrument concerns finance, these may be considered by the House of

---

59 *Report on Ministers' Powers*, Cmnd 4060, 1932, London: HMSO.
60 *Op cit*, Hayhurst and Wallington, fn 54.
61 See Barnett, H, 'Reflections on the Child Support Act' [1993] 5 J of Child Law 77.
62 HC Deb Cols 405–45, 2 November 1995.

Commons Select Committee on Statutory Instruments. The House of Lords' Scrutiny Committee for delegated legislation is discussed in Chapter 17.

FINANCIAL PROCEDURES IN THE HOUSE OF COMMONS

Any evaluation of Parliament's role and the legislative process must incorporate discussion of the extent to which, and means by which, Parliament controls national finance, both in terms of taxation and expenditure. In part, this topic requires consideration both under the heading of the legislative process and the scrutiny of the executive.[63]

From a constitutional standpoint, the control over expenditure may be viewed as control over the government of the day and its policies. As WE Gladstone[64] remarked, 'expenditure flows from policy – to control expenditure one must control policy'. Constitutionally, therefore, Parliament's role in relation to spending is but one part of its wider role of scrutinising and calling the government to account. Hence, general debates, Question Time, and Select Committees are all germane to this matter.[65]

Expenditure (supply)

Historically, the need to summon Parliament arose from the financial needs of the Crown.[66] The authority of the House of Commons sprang from, and is based on, its power to approve both the raising of taxation and approve expenditure. The governing maxim was, and remains, that 'the Crown demands, the Commons grant and the Lords assent to the grant of monies'.[67]

Nowadays, for the 'Crown', must be inserted 'Ministers of the Crown'. Two propositions flow from this situation. First, that all charges – that is, proposals for the expenditure of monies – must be demanded by the Crown before they can be considered by Parliament. The demand for approval of monies comes today from Ministers, not backbenchers. Secondly, all charges must be considered by the House of Commons before they are approved. The proposals for charges come before the House in the form of resolutions which, once approved, must be embodied in legislation originating in the House of Commons but approved by both Houses.[68]

---

63 See, further, Chapter 16.
64 Prime Minister 1868–74; 1880–85; 1886; 1892–94.
65 See Chapter 16.
66 See Chapters 6 and 7 on the historic struggles between Crown and Parliament.
67 *Op cit*, Erskine May, fn 23, p 684 and see Standing Order No 46.
68 Subject to the Parliament Acts 1911–49.

National revenue to cover the cost of government is derived from three main sources: taxation, borrowing and revenue from Crown lands. All revenue, of whatever kind, is credited to the Exchequer Account at the Bank of England in the form of the Consolidated Fund. All withdrawals must be authorised by statute. Under the Consolidated Fund Acts, approximately one-third of expenditure is authorised in permanent form and does not require annual parliamentary approval. Charges which are immune from this scrutiny are those payments for service which it is deemed should not be constantly drawn into the political arena for debate.[69] For example, payment of interest on the national debt, salaries of judges of superior courts, the Speaker of the House of Commons, Leader of the Opposition, Comptroller and Auditor General, Parliamentary Commissioner for Administration, payments to meet European Community and Union obligations and the Queen's Civil List all fall under Consolidated Fund Services.

In contrast to Consolidated Fund Services are Supply Services. These cover the bulk of annual public expenditure and cover the needs of all government departments and the cost of the armed forces. Provision for Supply Services require annual approval. The following requirements must be satisfied. The government must lay before the House of Commons each year its estimates for the forthcoming financial year, in the form of resolutions. Once approved, these are translated into Bills – the Consolidated Fund Bills and Appropriation Bills. Money must be appropriated for specific purposes in the same session as that in which it is required by the government: thus, monies voted for one financial year cannot be applied to a subsequent year.

The Voting of Supply is announced in the Queen's Speech at the autumn opening of the parliamentary session: 'Members of the House of Commons, estimates for the Public Service will be laid before you.' The financial year for the purposes of national expenditure runs from 1 April to 31 March.

Prior to 1993, the Chancellor's Autumn Statement was made to Parliament, preceded by preparation of estimates by each government department for the forthcoming financial year, and the Budget was announced in the Spring. With effect from November 1993, the Budget is combined with the Autumn Statement, although this is not an invariable arrangement: the Budget in 1998 was presented to Parliament on 17 March 1998.[70]

Estimates

There exist six classes of estimates.

---

69 See Standing Orders Nos 46–57.
70 See the White Paper, *Budgetary Reform*, Cmnd 1867, 1992, London: HMSO.

Ordinary annual estimates

Ordinary annual estimates are the principal estimates. They set out the specific grants of money which will be required to fund the civil service, defence services, the cost of House of Commons administration and the National Audit Office. Control over the form in which estimates are presented is in the hands of the Treasury.[71] Before any change in the form of the estimates is made, approval must be obtained from the Treasury and Civil Service Committee.

Prior to estimates being settled, the Public Expenditure Survey Committee, under the responsibility of the Chief Secretary to the Treasury, will have reported on anticipated needs of departments, and settled any disagreements between departments. Its confidential report is sent to the Cabinet, which formalises expenditure plans.

Votes on account

Votes on account are designed to cover the problem caused by the lapse in time between the end of one financial year and the enactment of legislation authorising expenditure for the forthcoming year. A vote on account authorises up to 45 per cent of projected annual expenditure.

Supplementary estimates

Supplementary estimates may be presented to Parliament for approval in relation to increased sums needed for a particular service, or to meet a new situation.

Excess votes

Where a department has exceeded its budget, its administration and expenditure will be audited by the Comptroller and Auditor General who reports to the House. The Committee of Public Accounts will consider the Comptroller's report on the matter, which states its approval or objection to the proposed excess vote. If the Public Accounts Committee approves the additional expenditure, the matter is put to Parliament without debate.[72]

Votes of credit

An emergency situation – or unexpected need for supply – may give rise to an application for a vote of credit. Situations of war will give rise to such votes.[73]

---

71   Exchequer and Audit Departments Act 1866.
72   Standing Order No 53(3).
73   As occurred in both the First and Second World Wars.

Exceptional grants

An exceptional grant is one authorised by Parliament for expenditure for some particular objective, such as State funeral expenses or the erection of memorial statues.

Following parliamentary debate and approval, the Appropriation Bill will be drafted authorising withdrawal from the Exchequer Fund. In most parliamentary sessions, three regular Consolidated Fund and Appropriation Bills (and, where necessary, extra Consolidated Fund Bills) are put to Parliament for approval.

It will have been noticed that parliamentary approval for these financial Bills is 'without amendment or debate'. Thus far, it appears as if there is a virtual abandonment of Parliament's role in assenting to the 'demands of the Crown'.

Limited time for the scrutiny of expenditure estimates is provided under Standing Orders. Standing Order No 52[74] provides for three days per session to be allocated for the consideration of estimates. The estimates to be considered are selected by the Liaison Committee, under Standing Order No 131. The estimates selected for debate will generally be those into which the select committee has inquired and reported. Amendments may be tabled, including the reduction in the estimates.

Aside from this limited opportunity, any control which Parliament exercises is through the control of policy and the normal parliamentary mechanisms for the scrutiny of government policy and administration. Griffith and Ryle sum up the supply procedure as follows:

> The House has largely abandoned all opportunities for direct control of public expenditure by means of debate and vote on the estimates presented to the House. Except on the three Estimates Days, there is no opportunity to amend or negative any of the individual estimates, and the government secures formal approval for its expenditure, without debate, in three or four block votes each year. In place of formal direct control by Voting Supply, which for many years has become theoretical, the House has increasingly relied on informal indirect control through the exercise of its influence on policy, through scrutiny of policy, administration and expenditure by departmentally related select committees and by *ex post facto* scrutiny of actual spending by the Public Accounts Committee.[75]

As the Public Accounts Committee Report to the House in 1987 admits, 'Parliament's consideration of annual estimates – the key constitutional control – remains largely a formality'.[76] The Public Accounts Committee was established in 1861, for the purpose of examining accounts of departments

---

74 Adopted in 1982.
75 *Op cit*, Griffith and Ryle, fn 1, p 251.
76 HC 98 (1986–87), London: HMSO, para 2, cited in *op cit*, Griffith and Ryle, fn 1.

following the submission of reports from the National Audit Office. The work of the Audit Office and the Committee is considered in Chapter 16.

Taxation (ways and means)

In relation to taxation – ways and means – the role of parliamentary scrutiny is rather different. The initiative in tax policies lies with the Treasury, under the political direction of the Chancellor of the Exchequer.[77]

The starting point for the annual cycle is the Chancellor's Budget in the Spring or Autumn wherein, as Erskine May points out, 'the Chancellor develops his views of the resources of the country, communicates his calculations of probable income and expenditure and declares whether the burdens upon the people are to be increased or diminished'.

The Budget[78]

The Budget is the annual statement of tax proposals for the forthcoming year, together with the government's expenditure plans for the following three years. At the end of the Budget speech, the ways and means resolutions are tabled. These resolutions form the basis for the main debate on the Budget, which lasts for between three and five days. The Finance Bill is then introduced and, within three to four weeks, will receive its second reading. The Bill then stands committed, in part, to a Committee of the Whole House and to a standing committee. The size of the standing committee for consideration of the Finance Bill is larger than the normal composition, and will have about 30 to 40 Members. Hundreds of amendments are generally proposed to Finance Bills, although not all of these will be debated.

Income tax rates are effective only until the end of the tax year and require annual renewal under the Finance Act. The authority to collect taxes expires on 5 April each year. The Finance Act becomes law in July. In *Bowles v Bank of England*,[79] the legality of taxation was considered. On 2 April 1912, the House of Commons passed a resolution approving the income tax rate for the year beginning 6 April 1912. The plaintiff had purchased stocks. The Bank deducted income tax from dividends due on 1 July at the new tax rate before the Consolidated Fund Act authorising the new rate had been passed by Parliament. The plaintiff sought a declaration that the Bank was not entitled to deduct the tax until approved by Parliament. Parker J stated that:

---

77 Nominally, the Prime Minister as First Lord of the Treasury.
78 The name derives from French: the *bougette*, or little bag.
79 [1913] 1 Ch 57.

The question for decision is, does a resolution of the House of Commons authorise the Crown to levy on the subject an income tax assented to by such resolution but not yet imposed by Act of Parliament?

By the Statute of 1 William and Mary, usually known as the Bill of Rights, it was finally settled that there could be no taxation in this country except under the authority of Act of Parliament. The Bill of Rights remains unrepealed and no practice or custom can be relied on by the Crown as justifying any infringement of its provisions.

It follows, therefore, that no resolution ... has any legal effect whatsoever ... Such resolutions are necessitated by parliamentary procedure and adopted with a view to the protection of the subject against the hasty imposition of taxes, and it would be strange to find them relied on as justifying the Crown in levying a tax before such tax is actually imposed by Act of Parliament.

Bowles v Bank of England led to the Provisional Collection of Taxes Act 1913,[80] which gives statutory authority to resolutions, as if imposed by Act of Parliament. In *Attorney General v Wilts United Dairies Ltd*,[81] the Food Controller had, under a regulation of 1919, established a pricing structure for the issue of licences for milk purchase. The company claimed that the Food Controller had no power to impose conditions of payment in granting licences and that the condition amounted to a tax, which could not be imposed without clear and distinct legal authority. Lord Justice Atkin declared that:

> ... in view of the historic struggle of the Legislature to secure to itself the sole power to levy money on its subjects, its complete success in that struggle, the elaborate means adopted by the representative House to control the amount, the conditions and purposes of the levy, the circumstances would be remarkable indeed which would induce the court to believe that the Legislature had sacrificed all the well known checks and precautions and not in express words but, by mere implication, had entrusted a Minister of the Crown with undefined and unlimited powers of imposing charges upon the subject for purposes connected with his department.

The Provisional Collection of Taxes Act 1968 now requires that the resolutions passed be confirmed by the second reading of the Bill relating to the tax within 25 days of the House approving the resolution. It also provides that their statutory effect shall continue only until 5 August if passed in April or March, or for four months if passed at any other time. It is this, then, that sets the deadline for the passage of the Finance Act.

Note that the Finance Act is not usually a Money Bill for the purposes of the Parliament Act 1911, since it deals with wider matters than those listed in section 1(2) of the Act. Accordingly, unless certified by the Speaker to be a Money Bill, the Finance Bill will pass through the Lords in the usual manner.

---

80 Now, Provisional Collection of Taxes Act 1968.
81 (1921) 37 TLR 884.

By convention, however, in relation to a Finance Bill, the House of Lords has relinquished any effective role in relation to taxation or expenditure.

SCRUTINY OF LEGISLATION BY THE HOUSE OF LORDS

Some Bills will start their life in the House of Lords and, once successfully passed in the Lords, will pass to the Commons for debate and scrutiny. Law Reform Bills, in particular, are regularly introduced in the House of Lords, under the aegis of the Lord Chancellor. The majority of Bills, however, start their parliamentary life in the Commons. Detailed consideration will be given to the House of Lords' role in legislation in Chapter 17. Note, however, that, unless the Parliament Act procedure is used (which limits the role of the House of Lords in relation to legislation), Bills which have completed their passage in the Commons are passed to the House of Lords which employs, with some notable differences, the same legislative stages as the House of Commons. The House of Lords may propose amendments to Bills, the acceptance or rejection of which will be a matter for negotiation between the two Houses.

THE ROYAL ASSENT

Receiving the royal assent represents the final stage in the enactment of legislation. The royal assent is a prerogative act.[82] The giving of the royal assent is not a matter which involves the Monarch personally. No monarch since 1854 has given the royal assent, although the power to do so still remains. When royal assent is required, the Lord Chancellor submits a list of Bills ready for the Assent. In the House of Lords, attended by the Commons with the Speaker, the Clerk of the Parliaments reads the title of the Bills for assent and pronounces the assent in Norman French. Once assent has been given, it is notified to each House of Parliament by the Speaker of the House.[83]

PARLIAMENT AND EUROPEAN COMMUNITY LEGISLATION

The manner in which Community law is enacted and takes effect within the United Kingdom is considered in Chapters 8 and 9. Note here that some

---

82 For further discussion, see Chapter 6.
83 Royal Assent Act 1967.

Community legislation becomes directly applicable within the United Kingdom without any enactment by Parliament. Accordingly, it is of particular importance that Parliament has the opportunity to scrutinise both proposals for Community legislation and legislation which has been enacted.

In addition to periodic debates on Europe, Parliament sets aside time at Question Time for European Community matters to be considered. Furthermore, Ministers make regular statements to Parliament concerning decisions reached in the Council of Ministers.

The House of Commons has established a Select Committee on European Legislation. The House of Lords also has a Select Committee on the European Community.[84] Both committees consider delegated legislation which is being introduced to give effect to Community law and also scrutinise legislative proposals for future European Community law.

In addition to the select committees, the Commons has established two standing committees for the consideration of European matters.[85] The select committee may refer such documentation to the standing committees as it thinks fit. The standing committees, comprising 13 Members, report to the House on matters referred to them.

Finally, successive governments have undertaken not to agree to important European legislative proposals until these have been considered by the committees. However, the effectiveness of these undertakings must be put in doubt by the increasing use of majority voting in the Council of Ministers, which makes it difficult for individual Member States to 'block' any proposed legislation.

---

84 See, further, Chapter 17.
85 Standing Order Nos 102 and 127 (as amended).

CHAPTER 16

SCRUTINY OF THE EXECUTIVE

The concept of responsible government and the fundamental principle of ministerial responsibility were considered in Chapter 11. The structure of central government was considered in Chapter 10. In Chapter 14, the composition of the House of Commons was introduced. It will be recalled that the Commons comprises Her Majesty's government, which is drawn from the political party winning the largest number of seats at a general election, government backbenchers, Her Majesty's Loyal Opposition, comprising the Leader of the Opposition and Opposition spokesmen, who comprise the shadow Cabinet, and Opposition backbenchers, and Members of other minority political parties.

With the composition of the House of Commons in mind – and, to a lesser extent, that of the House of Lords[1] – and the functions which Parliament is designed to fulfil, the issue which must now be addressed is the procedures by which the House of Commons scrutinises government action in order that an evaluation may be made as to the quality of that scrutiny. Consistent with the doctrine of responsible government, the accountability of government towards the democratic legislature is of fundamental importance in ensuring that the government acts under the law and in accordance with the principles of constitutionalism and democracy. In order to evaluate the role of Parliament in ensuring compliance with these constitutional doctrines, the procedural mechanisms of the House must be examined.

QUESTION TIME[2]

Question Time in the House of Commons is one of the most publicised features of Parliament and represents one of the principal means by which information is obtained from Ministers by Members of Parliament and the public, and of underpinning individual ministerial responsibility.[3]

---

1   See Chapter 17.
2   See Chester, N and Bowring, N, *Questions in Parliament*, 1962, Oxford; OUP; Irwin, H, 'Opportunities for backbenchers', in Ryle, M and Richards, PG (eds), *The Commons Under Scrutiny*, 1988, London: Routledge; Griffith, JAG and Ryle, M, *Parliament: Functions, Practice and Procedures*, 1989, London: Sweet & Maxwell; Erskine May, T, *Parliamentary Practice*, 22nd edn, 1997, London: Butterworths.
3   See Chapter 11.

Standing Order No 17 provides that, from Monday to Thursday, the period from 2.35 pm to 3.30 pm is set aside for Question Time.[4] On Mondays, Tuesdays and Thursdays, Ministers from several departments may answer Questions, appearing on a rota, determined by the government,[5] which ensures that most departments feature in Question Time at least once every three to four weeks.

The Speaker calls the first Member listed on the Order Paper. The Minister then answers the question, and the Member is able to ask a supplementary question. When that has been answered, the Speaker may then call on other Members to ask their supplementary questions. The time allocated to supplementary questions is within the Speaker's discretion. Currently, about 15 to 20 questions are answered orally on each day.

Questions may be put to Ministers for either oral[6] or written answers. Questions requiring written answers, which are to be printed in the Official Journal, are marked with a 'W'.[7] Those questions tabled for oral answer are randomly ordered by the Table Office of the House and printed on the Order Paper of the day. Between 100 and 150 questions may be put to a Minister on a single day. As a result, only a few will receive an oral reply. However, those which do not receive an oral reply will receive a written reply published in the Official Report of the House. The number of questions which an individual Member of Parliament may have pending at any one time is eight during a period of 10 sitting days, and not more than two on any one day, of which not more than one may be addressed to any one Minister.[8] Questions put down for written answer – which may be for either a priority or non-priority answer – are less subject to restrictions and there is no limit on the number of questions which may be put down. In the 1995–96 session, 49,897 questions appeared on the Order Papers. Of these, 4,464 were for oral answer, 16,059 for written answer and 40,307 questions for a non-priority written answer. A total of 5,859 oral answers and 42,570 written answers appeared in *Hansard*.

Prime Ministerial Question Time

Prime Minister's Question Time has been moved from the conventional 15 minute sessions on Tuesdays and Thursdays, to Wednesdays, when the Prime

---

4   No question shall be taken after 3.30 pm (Standing Order No 17(3)), other than where the Speaker deems it to be a matter of urgency relating to matters of public importance or to the arrangement of business of the House.

5   HC Deb 898 (1975–76), London: HMSO. See *op cit*, Erskine May, fn 2, Chapter 16.

6   Indicated by an asterisk: Standing Order No 17(1).

7   Standing Order No 17(7).

8   *Op cit*, Erskine May, fn 2, p 285.

Minister answers questions for 30 minutes.[9] It is felt that more meaningful and indepth scrutiny is facilitated by the reform.

Questions put to the Prime Minister simply request that the Prime Minister list his engagements for the day. Over 100 such questions may appear on the Order Papers.[10] The purpose of this form of open question[11] is to avoid the possibility that the Prime Minister will simply refer the questioner to the Minister having responsibility for a particular matter. The open question also avoids the possibility – given the rules of notice for questions – that a question put to the Prime Minister will be politically stale. The open question, therefore, provides a neutral peg on which to hang a supplementary, and real, question. Only two supplementary questions per Member are allowed. Supplementary questions may concern any matter for which the Prime Minister carries responsibility or matters which do not fall within any individual Minister's responsibility. For example, if a question is addressed to the Prime Minister which should be addressed to the Secretary of State for Social Security, the Prime Minister will decline to answer and suggest that the matter be referred to the responsible Minister. Generally, however, the issue raised will be one of general government policy in relation to matters such as the economy, unemployment, European or other international affairs. The strength of Prime Ministerial Question Time lies in the lack of notice given and the need for the Prime Minister to demonstrate his competence across the full range of government policy.

The Leader of the Opposition does not table questions for oral answer to the Prime Minister. Instead, by convention, the Leader of the Opposition is given the opportunity to put one or more supplementary questions to the Prime Minister and, because of the open ended nature of the primary question, it is possible for the Opposition Leader to raise virtually any aspect of government policy. For the observer, this is frequently Parliament at its best, providing the opportunity – for Question Time is televised – to witness the leaders of the two main political parties in oral combat. As Griffith and Ryle observe:

> Here is experienced the direct confrontation of the Prime Minister and the Leader of the Opposition in its most concentrated and highly charged form. It is an opportunity no Leader of the Opposition can afford to neglect. It is also the occasion when the Prime Minister can be most critically tested, and various commentators or experienced observers have testified to how carefully the Prime Minister has to prepare for this ordeal. Success or failure on these occasions can greatly strengthen or seriously weaken the political standing of the two protagonists.[12]

---

9 See HC Deb Vol 295 Col 349, 4 June 1997.

10 On occasions, this number has risen to over 200.

11 Which has been adopted since the 1970s.

12 *Op cit*, Griffith and Ryle, fn 2, pp 356–57.

A selection of questions put to the Prime Minister on 21 May 1997 included the following matters:

- the Prime Minister's engagements;
- the EC ban on British beef;
- drug abuse;
- procedure at Prime Minister's Question Time;
- education;
- the government's reform programme;
- taxation;
- EC fishing quotas;
- land mines;
- the Irish Republican Army;
- pensioner's standard of living;
- the minimum wage.

The role of the Speaker

The rules concerning questions have been developed over time by the Speaker of the House, who is responsible for enforcing them. Only questions on matters which are directly within a Minister's responsibility may be put and in addition, by convention, there exists a range of issues which may not form the subject of questions in the House. The following matters are not subject to Question Time:

(a) questions bringing the Sovereign directly before Parliament, or questions reflecting on the Sovereign;

(b) questions concerning issues on which the Prime Minister has given advice to the Crown in relation to the royal prerogative: the grant of honours, ecclesiastical patronage, appointment and dismissal of Privy Councillors or the dissolution of Parliament;

(c) questions not relating to the individual responsibility of the relevant Minister. Accordingly, questions relating to organisations under the control of authorities other than Parliament (for example, the Stock Exchange, Trades Unions and nationalised industries) are not permitted.[13]

The following subjects are also excluded:

- local authorities and nationalised industries;
- personal powers of the Monarch;
- internal affairs of other countries;

---

13 *Op cit*, Erskine May, fn 2, Chapter 16.

- questions which have previously been put, or on which a Minister has previously refused to answer, or to which the answer is a matter of public record;
- defence and national security;
- Cabinet business, and advice given to Ministers by civil servants;
- questions seeking legal advice;
- questions which raise issues so broad as to be incapable of reply within the time constraints;
- trivial or irrelevant questions;
- questions aiming to criticise judges;
- questions on matters which are *sub judice*;
- questions posed in unparliamentary language.[14]

The volume of parliamentary questions

The volume of questions put down for oral or written answer on average amount to some 40,000 per parliamentary session. In 1986–87, a short session, an average of 313 questions were tabled per sitting day. In 1998–99, 5,008 questions were put down for oral answer and 32,149 were put down for a written answer, giving a total of 37,157 questions. Figures such as these emphasise one of the most important functions of Question Time: the accountability of government. A superficial observation of Question Time may prompt scepticism as to its value. The charge is frequently made that Question Time is no more than a theatrical occasion, with Ministers fully briefed by the Civil Service giving prepared answers to questions posed within the rules as to notice and substance. Questions are not limited to the Opposition parties and may, accordingly, come from the government's own supporters. This feature leads to the comment that questions are planted by government supporters in order to give a Minister the opportunity to promote the government's view or boast about its achievements. To exaggerate such claims would be to miss a point of prime importance about Question Time, that of the provision of information. Every answer given, oral or written, becomes a matter of public record, thus providing a wealth of data about the workings of government.

Question Time is not a spontaneous affair, and it should not necessarily be criticised for not being so. Members wishing to ask questions are required to give a minimum of two sitting days' notice, and a maximum of 10 days' notice. This time span for notice is designed to ensure both that there is

---

14   *Op cit*, Erskine May, fn 2, Chapter 17; See, also, Munro, CR, *Studies in Constitutional Law*, 1987, London: Butterworths, Chapter 7.

adequate opportunity for Ministers to prepare answers and that the issue being raised is still fresh and relevant.

Private notice questions

A private notice question[15] is an oral question put to a Minister without the need to observe the normal rules as to notice. Standing Order No 17(3) defines private notice questions as raising matters which are: '... in the Speaker's opinion, of an urgent character, and relate either to matters of public importance or to the arrangement of business.'

Private notice questions enable a matter of urgency to be raised for immediate discussion in the period following Question Time. Because private notice questions take priority over other parliamentary business, rules provide that a Member who wishes to put such a question must give notice to the Speaker before noon on the day he seeks to put the question, and the Speaker has absolute discretion as to whether to allow or disallow the question to be put.[16] Many applications for a private notice question are made, but few are granted. In 1998–99, a total of 12 private notice questions were put.

APPLICATIONS FOR EMERGENCY ADJOURNMENT DEBATES

Under Standing Order No 24,[17] any Member of Parliament may apply to the Speaker to raise an urgent matter for debate.[18] If granted, the matter will be raised immediately after Question Time and private notice questions, if any. At that time, the matter is briefly introduced and a substantive three hour debate will be arranged for the following day. Because emergency debates disrupt the parliamentary timetable, they are confined to matters deemed to be of urgent national importance, and applications are sparingly granted (normally only one or two per session). In the 1991–93 session, there were 19 unsuccessful applications for an emergency debate and one successful application,[19] whereas in 1998–99, there were a mere three unsuccessful applications.

---

15 See *op cit*, Erskine May, fn 2, Chapter 16.
16 See *op cit*, Erskine May, fn 2, p 296.
17 Dating from 1967.
18 See *op cit*, Erskine May, fn 2, Chapter 16(3).
19 On the effect of the supply for defence equipment on the Scottish economy.

DAILY ADJOURNMENT DEBATES

At the close of the parliamentary day, under Standing Order No 9, the opportunity is provided for backbenchers to initiate a short debate on a matter of their choosing. Competition for a debate is keen and Members take part in a ballot held in the Speaker's Office for the opportunity. If successful, the Member may speak for 15 minutes on the chosen subject and the relevant Minister is given 15 minutes for reply. The subject matter for debate is as varied as are Members' interests. The matter raised may be one of relevance solely to the Member's constituency or the matter may be related to a particular source of general concern.

EARLY DAY MOTIONS

Behind this curious colloquial term, lies one of the least well known or evaluated parliamentary processes. An Early Day Motion (EDM) is a written motion tabled in Parliament requesting a debate 'at an early day'. Any Member of Parliament may table an EDM, on any subject matter, subject to a few procedural rules.[20]

EDMs originated in the mid-nineteenth century. Before that time, the parliamentary timetable was relaxed and Members had adequate opportunity to raise matters for subsequent debate in the House. As pressure for time in the House increased, the practice developed of Members giving notice that they intended to raise a particular matter for debate at some future, unspecified, date. These notices were formally recorded from 1865 in the daily papers of the House and today appear on the Motions Notice Paper, which forms part of the daily 'Vote Bundle' – the working papers of the House.

The purpose of tabling an EDM is not only to express a view and request a debate, but also to test the strength of feeling in the House over the matter involved. An EDM may be tabled by one Member or by several, and other Members may add their names in support. Some EDMs are tabled by the Leader of the Opposition: for example, EDM No 351 of 1978–79, supported by five other senior Conservative Members led to a debate on 28 March 1979, which resulted in the resignation of the government and the subsequent general election. The Opposition may also table motions giving notice of a prayer to annul a statutory instrument.[21]

Many EDMs are tabled by Members of all parties on a particular issue. These 'all-party' EDMs are increasing, as is the volume of EDMs generally, and provide an important outlet for the expression of views across party lines.

---

20   See *op cit*, Griffith and Ryle, fn 2, Chapters 6 and 10.
21   See Chapter 15.

Once tabled, an EDM remains current for the duration of the parliamentary session and may or may not attract considerable support within the House. Between 1948–49 and 1990–91, 29 EDMs have attracted over 300 signatures.

The rules and restrictions on EDMs are few, and are consistent with the general rules concerning motions. Thus, the motion must be worded in parliamentary language, must not relate to a matter which is *sub judice* and is limited to 250 words. Within these limits, a Member may table an EDM on any subject.

The volume of EDMs tabled per parliamentary session reveals their increasing popularity as a means of expression of, primarily, backbench opinion.

TABLE I: NUMBER OF EARLY DAY MOTIONS TABLED IN SELECTED SESSIONS

1945–46	71
1965–66	164
1974–75	759
1983–84	1,058
1985–86	1,262
1987–88	1,601
1989–90	1,482
1990–91	1,289
1992–93	2,595
1995–96	1,246
1998–99	1,009

In terms of the number of debates which flow from EDMs, their success rate must be regarded as low. The EDM censuring the government tabled by the Rt Hon Mrs Thatcher in 1979 is a rarity, both in terms of securing a debate and in the dramatic effect of signalling the fall of a government. The occasional success of the EDM was again seen in 1988 in relation to the Education Reform Bill 1988. There, two senior Conservative front-bench Members, Norman Tebbit and Michael Heseltine, tabled a motion calling for the abolition of the Inner London Education Authority: a matter which was contrary to the then policy of the Secretary of State for Education, Kenneth Baker. The EDM was supported by 120 other Conservative backbenchers and caused the Secretary of State to amend the Bill.[22]

Notwithstanding such rare examples of EDMs having important political and legal effects, the overall significance of the EDM should not be

---

22 EDM 563; Notices of Motions, 1987–88, p 3519, cited in *op cit*, Griffith and Ryle, fn 2, p 383.

underestimated. Depending on the volume of support a particular EDM attracts, it represents an expression of the mood of the House across a whole spectrum of issues which places pressure on the government to respond. The dramatic rise in the number of EDMs per Session since the early 1980s to the current day attests to their popularity as a vehicle for the expression of views and concerns. The EDM has been described as the 'graffiti board' of Parliament, signalling to government the issues and concerns of Members. Where the rules of the House prevent a Member from expressing a view in Debate, perhaps because he cannot catch the Speaker's eye, or by means of a question, perhaps because of ministerial responsibility or because the subject matter falls within one of the excluded categories, the EDM may represent the only vehicle for expression.

SELECT COMMITTEES OF THE HOUSE OF COMMONS

Select committees in the House of Commons are of some antiquity, although the current structure of committees dates back only to 1979. Select committees take several forms, dealing with diverse matters such as public accounts, consolidation Bills, statutory instruments, standards and privileges, the Parliamentary Commissioner for Administration, European Community legislation, domestic matters relating to the House, procedure of the House, selection (of Members to committees of the House), administration, broadcasting, deregulation, environmental audit, finance and services ʳmation, public administration, delegated legislation, ad hoc committees hed to enquire into a particular subject and, most importantly, the ᵗally-related select committees and the Liaison Committees which them. In 1997, a Modernisation Committee of the House of established to consider how practices and procedures should ᵗe Committee has 15 members, the quorum being five. The ᵐmittees are established under Standing Orders of the

ᵗ of departmentally-related select committees was result of dissatisfaction with the then current ʳing of government departments.[23] The report oᶠ ᵉdure[24] recommended that 12 new committ∈ ∋ as being one of enabling the House as a w⸱ ⸠ and stewardship over Ministers a∩ odern State for which they are answeʳ

d backbench power', in Jowell, ᵗ n, 1994, Oxford: Clarendon, anᵈ ⸱ OUP.

rocedure (1977–78), Londoᵖ

Following debate in the House,[26] the proposals were approved and implemented. In debate, the Leader of the House,[27] described the proposals as:

> ... a necessary preliminary to the more effective scrutiny of government ... and opportunity for closer examination of departmental policy ... an important contribution to greater openness in government, of a kind that is in accord with our parliamentary arrangements and our constitutional tradition.

Functions of select committees

Standing Order No 130 defines the functions of departmentally-related committees as being:

(a) to send for persons, papers and records, to sit notwithstanding any adjournments of the House, to adjourn from place to place and to report from time to time;

(b) to appoint specialist advisers, either to supply information which is not readily available or to elucidate matters of complexity within the committee's order of reference;

(c) to report from time to time the minutes of evidence taken before sub-committees; and

(d) to report to the House their opinion and observations upon any matters referred to them for their consideration, together with minutes of evidence taken before them, and also to make a special report of any matters which they may think fit to bring to the notice of the House.

The scope of power granted to select committees under Standing Order No 130 is very broad. It is for the committee to determine, within the confines of the work of the department, what subject matter to examine and to determine what evidence the committee needs to assist in its examination. To facilitate the working of select committees, each has a permanent staff of some three to four, and some committees have the power, under Standing Orders, to establish sub-committees.

The committee structure

• departmental select committees and their related departme

ˈs:

ˈ979.

ˈn St John-Stevas, MP (subsequently, Lord St

TABLE II: DEPARTMENTAL SELECT COMMITTEES

SELECT COMMITTEE	GOVERNMENT DEPARTMENTS	NUMBER OF MEMBERS
Agriculture	Ministry of Agriculture, Fisheries and Food	11
Culture, Media and Sport	Heritage Department	11
Defence	Ministry of Defence	11
Education and Employment	Department of Education and Employment	17
Environment, Transport and Regional Affairs	Department of Environment, Transport and Regional Affairs	17
Foreign Affairs	Foreign and Commonwealth Office	12
Health	Department of Health	11
Home Affairs	Home Office, Lord Chancellor's Department, Attorney General's Office, Crown Prosecution Service, Serious Fraud Office	11
International Development	Department for International Development	11
Northern Ireland Affairs	Northern Ireland Office	13
Science and Technology	Office of Science and Technology	11
Scottish Affairs	Scottish Office, Lord Advocate's Department	11
Social Security	Department of Social Security	11
Trade and Industry	Department of Trade and Industry	11
Treasury	Treasury Office, Office of Public Service and Science, Board of Customs and Excise, Inland Revenue	12
Welsh Affairs	Welsh Office	11

The Liaison Committee

The task of co-ordinating the work of select committees falls to t
Committee, first established in 1967, the membership of which
the Chairmen of the departmentally-related select commi
Chairmen of the Public Accounts Committee and the Euro
Select Committee. Standing Order No 131 defines its role a
(a) to consider general matters relating to the work of sel

(b) to give such advice relating to the work of select committees as may be sought by the House of Commons Commission.[28]

Membership of select committees

Membership of select committees, unlike that of standing committees,[29] lasts for the life of a Parliament, thus providing stability of membership[30] and the opportunity for Members to develop a degree of expertise in the subject matter. Membership is largely limited, by convention, to backbenchers. The only Ministers who are members are the Leader of the House,[31] the government Deputy Chief Whip[32] and the Financial Secretary to the Treasury.[33] Opposition front-bench spokesmen are not appointed to select committees.

Competition for membership of select committees is keen, particularly for the high profile committees. The political party whips have great influence, if not total control, over membership. The Committee of Selection, itself a select committee, is made up of senior Members of the House drawn from all political parties. The party whips make nominations to the committee which in turn reports to the House for approval. The strength of each political party overall in the House is reflected, largely but not totally accurately, in the membership of select committees, thus giving to the committee an legitimacy approximate to that of the House as a whole. In July 2000, the Liaison Committee recommended that control over membership of Select Committees by the whips should be ended and appointments be placed in the hands of a panel of Members of Parliament. The government rejected the proposal.

Committee chairmanship

It might reasonably be assumed that the chairmanship of the committees always fell to Members of the government's own party, but this is not the case, and select committees may be chaired by a Member of any political party. The decision as to which party should chair a particular committee is a matter for negotiation between government and Opposition. Once that decision has been reached, it is for the committee members, under the 'advice' of the whips, rmally to elect the chairman. In 1998, the Conservative Party Members chaired e Committees – Agriculture, Northern Ireland Affairs and Science and ology. The Liberal Democrat Party chaired the Social Security Committee. aining Committees were chaired by government Members.

riffith and Ryle, fn 2, pp 160–61.

5.

from 0–27% per annum.

e.

nittee.

Following debate in the House,[26] the proposals were approved and implemented. In debate, the Leader of the House,[27] described the proposals as:

... a necessary preliminary to the more effective scrutiny of government ... and opportunity for closer examination of departmental policy ... an important contribution to greater openness in government, of a kind that is in accord with our parliamentary arrangements and our constitutional tradition.

Functions of select committees

Standing Order No 130 defines the functions of departmentally-related committees as being:

(a) to send for persons, papers and records, to sit notwithstanding any adjournments of the House, to adjourn from place to place and to report from time to time;

(b) to appoint specialist advisers, either to supply information which is not readily available or to elucidate matters of complexity within the committee's order of reference;

(c) to report from time to time the minutes of evidence taken before sub-committees; and

(d) to report to the House their opinion and observations upon any matters referred to them for their consideration, together with minutes of evidence taken before them, and also to make a special report of any matters which they may think fit to bring to the notice of the House.

The scope of power granted to select committees under Standing Order No 130 is very broad. It is for the committee to determine, within the confines of the work of the department, what subject matter to examine and to determine what evidence the committee needs to assist in its examination. To facilitate the working of select committees, each has a permanent staff of some three to four, and some committees have the power, under Standing Orders, to establish sub-committees.

The committee structure

The departmental select committees and their related departments are as follows:

---

26 19, 20 February 1979.
27 The Rt Hon Norman St John-Stevas, MP (subsequently, Lord St John of Fawsley).

underestimated. Depending on the volume of support a particular EDM attracts, it represents an expression of the mood of the House across a whole spectrum of issues which places pressure on the government to respond. The dramatic rise in the number of EDMs per Session since the early 1980s to the current day attests to their popularity as a vehicle for the expression of views and concerns. The EDM has been described as the 'graffiti board' of Parliament, signalling to government the issues and concerns of Members. Where the rules of the House prevent a Member from expressing a view in Debate, perhaps because he cannot catch the Speaker's eye, or by means of a question, perhaps because of ministerial responsibility or because the subject matter falls within one of the excluded categories, the EDM may represent the only vehicle for expression.

SELECT COMMITTEES OF THE HOUSE OF COMMONS

Select committees in the House of Commons are of some antiquity, although the current structure of committees dates back only to 1979. Select committees take several forms, dealing with diverse matters such as public accounts, consolidation Bills, statutory instruments, standards and privileges, the Parliamentary Commissioner for Administration, European Community legislation, domestic matters relating to the House, procedure of the House, selection (of Members to committees of the House), administration, broadcasting, deregulation, environmental audit, finance and services information, public administration, delegated legislation, ad hoc committees established to enquire into a particular subject and, most importantly, the departmentally-related select committees and the Liaison Committees which is related to them. In 1997, a Modernisation Committee of the House of Commons was established to consider how practices and procedures should be modernised. The Committee has 15 members, the quorum being five. The majority of these committees are established under Standing Orders of the House.

The current system of departmentally-related select committees was established in 1979 as a result of dissatisfaction with the then current arrangements for the monitoring of government departments.[23] The report of the Select Committee on Procedure[24] recommended that 12 new committees be established, seeing their role as being one of enabling the House as a whole to exercise effective control and stewardship over Ministers and the expanding bureaucracy of the modern State for which they are answerable.[25]

---

23 See Drewry, G, 'Select committees and backbench power', in Jowell, J and Oliver, D (eds), *The Changing Constitution*, 3rd edn, 1994, Oxford: Clarendon, and Drewry, G (ed), *The New Select Committees*, 1989, Oxford: OUP.

24 HC 588 (1977–78), London: HMSO.
   First Report of the Select Committee on Procedure (1977–78), London: HMSO.

25

TABLE II: DEPARTMENTAL SELECT COMMITTEES

SELECT COMMITTEE	GOVERNMENT DEPARTMENTS	NUMBER OF MEMBERS
Agriculture	Ministry of Agriculture, Fisheries and Food	11
Culture, Media and Sport	Heritage Department	11
Defence	Ministry of Defence	11
Education and Employment	Department of Education and Employment	17
Environment, Transport and Regional Affairs	Department of Environment, Transport and Regional Affairs	17
Foreign Affairs	Foreign and Commonwealth Office	12
Health	Department of Health	11
Home Affairs	Home Office, Lord Chancellor's Department, Attorney General's Office, Crown Prosecution Service, Serious Fraud Office	11
International Development	Department for International Development	11
Northern Ireland Affairs	Northern Ireland Office	13
Science and Technology	Office of Science and Technology	11
Scottish Affairs	Scottish Office, Lord Advocate's Department	11
Social Security	Department of Social Security	11
Trade and Industry	Department of Trade and Industry	11
Treasury	Treasury Office, Office of Public Service and Science, Board of Customs and Excise, Inland Revenue	12
Welsh Affairs	Welsh Office	11

The Liaison Committee

The task of co-ordinating the work of select committees falls to the Liaison Committee, first established in 1967, the membership of which comprises all the Chairmen of the departmentally-related select committees, and the Chairmen of the Public Accounts Committee and the European Legislation Select Committee. Standing Order No 131 defines its role as being:

(a) to consider general matters relating to the work of select committees; and

(b) to give such advice relating to the work of select committees as may be sought by the House of Commons Commission.[28]

Membership of select committees

Membership of select committees, unlike that of standing committees,[29] lasts for the life of a Parliament, thus providing stability of membership[30] and the opportunity for Members to develop a degree of expertise in the subject matter. Membership is largely limited, by convention, to backbenchers. The only Ministers who are members are the Leader of the House,[31] the government Deputy Chief Whip[32] and the Financial Secretary to the Treasury.[33] Opposition front-bench spokesmen are not appointed to select committees.

Competition for membership of select committees is keen, particularly for the high profile committees. The political party whips have great influence, if not total control, over membership. The Committee of Selection, itself a select committee, is made up of senior Members of the House drawn from all political parties. The party whips make nominations to the committee which in turn reports to the House for approval. The strength of each political party overall in the House is reflected, largely but not totally accurately, in the membership of select committees, thus giving to the committee an legitimacy approximate to that of the House as a whole. In July 2000, the Liaison Committee recommended that control over membership of Select Committees by the whips should be ended and appointments be placed in the hands of a panel of Members of Parliament. The government rejected the proposal.

Committee chairmanship

It might reasonably be assumed that the chairmanship of the committees always fell to Members of the government's own party, but this is not the case, and select committees may be chaired by a Member of any political party. The decision as to which party should chair a particular committee is a matter for negotiation between government and Opposition. Once that decision has been reached, it is for the committee members, under the 'advice' of the whips, formally to elect the chairman. In 1998, the Conservative Party Members chaired three Committees – Agriculture, Northern Ireland Affairs and Science and Technology. The Liberal Democrat Party chaired the Social Security Committee. The remaining Committees were chaired by government Members.

---

28 See *op cit*, Griffith and Ryle, fn 2, pp 160–61.
29 See Chapter 15.
30 Turnover ranges from 0–27% per annum.
31 Services Committee.
32 *Ibid*.
33 Public Accounts Committee.

The significance of the sharing of chairs between government and opposition parties lies in the attempt to minimise party political conflict, in order to increase the effectiveness and efficiency of the scrutiny to be brought to bear on government departments. Once appointed, the chairman acts with complete impartiality. Select committees are designed to operate on the basis of broad consensus as to aims and objectives, and to produce a single authoritative report to Parliament as a whole. It is not usual for the committee to vote on party lines although, in highly controversial matters, this may occasionally be inevitable. If the committee intends to be critical of the government in its report, it is necessary for at least one Member of the government party to agree with the criticism(s).

The work of select committees illustrated

The inquiries undertaken by select committees are both broad ranging and in depth. It is entirely a matter for the committee to determine what subject to investigate and, accordingly, every aspect of government administration is potentially susceptible to inquiry. In the past, for example, select committees have inquired into the conduct of the Falklands War[34] and the banning of trades union membership at the Government's Communication Headquarters (GCHQ).[35] The committees have investigated such matters as the Westland Helicopter affair; arms to Iraq; salmonella in eggs; and the loss of the Maxwell pension funds.[36] The wide ranging nature of inquiries undertaken is illustrated in the subject matter chosen by just two of the committees in the 1998–99 session:

Inquiries undertaken by the Foreign Affairs Committee 1998–99

- Foreign Policy and Human Rights;[37]
- Sierra Leone;[38]
- European Union Enlargement;[39]
- Gibraltar;[40]
- Foreign and Commonwealth Office Resources;[41]

---

34 HC 11 (1984–85), London: HMSO.
35 HC 238 (1983–84), London: HMSO.
36 On which, see, further, below.
37 Paper No HC 100; Government reply Cm 4299.
38 Paper No HC 116; Government reply Cm 4325.
39 Paper No HC 86; Government reply Cm 4348.
40 Paper No HC 366; Government reply Cm 4470.
41 Paper No HC 271; Government reply Cm 4462.

- South Caucasus and Central Asia;[42]
- Kosovo: Interim Report.[43]

Inquiries undertaken by the Home Affairs Committee 1998–99

- Relationship between Health and Social Services;[44]
- Primary Care Groups;[45]
- Future NHS Staffing Requirements;[46]
- Long Term Care of the Elderly;[47]
- The Regulation of Private and other Independent Healthcare;[48]
- Procedures Related to Adverse Clinical Incidents and Outcomes in Medical Care.[49]

The co-operation of government

It has been seen above that Standing Order 130 gives the committees power to send for 'persons and papers'. The work of select committees would be much impaired if the committee was obstructed in its attempt to gain access to evidence. The Select Committee on Procedure had suggested, *inter alia*, that there should be power to compel Ministers to attend and to give evidence. That recommendation was rejected by the government, on the basis that select committees should not have power to issue orders to Ministers – such a power lay with the House alone. Accordingly, there is no formal requirement that the government co-operate with select committees. However, the Leader of the House has undertaken that:

> ... every Minister, from the most senior Cabinet Minister to the most junior Under Secretary, will do all in his or her power to co-operate with the new system of committees and to make it a success.[50]

For the most part, governments do co-operate with the committees, but limits to this co-operation can be perceived through an examination of four instances.

---

42 Paper No HC 349; Government reply Cm 4458.
43 Paper No HC 188.
44 Paper No HC 74; Government reply Cm 4320.
45 Paper No HC 153; Government reply Cm 4468.
46 Paper No HC 38; Government reply Cm 4379.
47 Paper No HC 318; Government reply Cm 4414.
48 Paper No HC 281.
49 Paper No HC 549.
50 HC Deb Col 45, 25 June 1979; Col 1677, 16 January 1981.

The Westland affair

In the aftermath of the Westland Helicopter affair,[51] during which both the Secretary of State for Defence, Michael Heseltine, and the Secretary of State for Trade and Industry, Leon Brittan, resigned,[52] three select committees inquired into the matter.[53] When the Select Committee on Defence announced its intention to inquire into the matter, the government refused to allow witnesses from the Department of Trade and Industry, in particular the Director of Information, to whom a leak of the Solicitor General's letter had been attributed, to give evidence to the committee. The government's justification for this refusal was that the giving of evidence by a senior civil servant to a parliamentary committee would have major implications for the conduct of government and for relations between Ministers and their civil servants. This refusal had two implications. First, it meant that Parliament was unable to check the accuracy of statements made by the Prime Minister in the House, or those made by Leon Brittan in relation to the leaked letter. The second implication was that the civil servants concerned were neither able to explain nor to defend their actions.

Salmonella in eggs

In 1988, a junior Health Minister, Edwina Currie, resigned office, subsequent to public comments made about alleged contamination of eggs. Her remarks that 'most eggs produced in the country' were infected with salmonella had an immediate impact on the sale and consumption of eggs, causing financial damage to egg producers. The Select Committee on Agriculture invited Mrs Currie to give evidence to the committee, but Mrs Currie declined. Following an exchange of letters which involved the select committee chairman insisting that it was for the committee, and not Mrs Currie, to decide whether or not she should give evidence, Mrs Currie grudgingly agreed to appear. In the event, her evidence proved, as she had indicated that it would, unhelpful.

The Maxwell pension fund

During the 1991–92 session, the Social Services Select Committee was enquiring into the mismanagement of pension funds by the Mirror

---

51 See the discussion in Chapter 9.

52 See Hennessy, P, 'Helicopter crashes into Cabinet: Prime Minister and constitution hurt' (1986) 13 JLS 423; Oliver, D and Austin, R, 'Political and constitutional aspects of the *Westland* affair' (1987) 40 Parl Aff 20; Linklater, M, Leigh, D with Mather, I, *Not Without Honour: The Inside Story of the Westland Scandal*, 1986, London: Sphere, Chapter 11; Marshall, G, 'Cabinet government and the *Westland* affair' [1986] PL 181.

53 Defence Committee, HC 518, 519 (1985–86), London: HMSO; Trade and Industry Committee, HC 176 (1986–87), London: HMSO; Treasury and Civil Service Committee, HC 92 (1985–86), London: HMSO.

Newspaper Group's recently deceased Chairman, Mr Robert Maxwell. Mr Maxwell's sons, both holding prominent positions in the Group before their father's death, and subsequently assuming control of the companies, were summoned to give evidence. The Maxwells refused, relying on a claimed right to silence in the light of imminent criminal charges and the risk of jeopardising their own fair trial. The committee chairman wanted the Maxwells to be charged with contempt of Parliament,[54] but no action was taken.

Arms to Iraq

In February 1992, the Select Committee on Trade and Industry examined the sale of equipment to Iraq during the conflict in the Gulf.[55] The equipment involved was piping which allegedly could be used to manufacture a missile launcher – a 'supergun'. That inquiry was frustrated by the alleged refusal of the Attorney General and others to give details of the information known to the Department of Trade and Industry when the export licence was granted. Subsequently, three directors of the company Matrix Churchill were prosecuted by Customs and Excise for breach of the restrictions on the export of military equipment contrary to the Import, Exports and Customs Powers (Defence) Act 1939 by obtaining export licences by deception. The prosecution was halted when Alan Clark[56] revealed in court that there had been no deception, since the government was fully aware of the exports and their intended usage. The trial collapsed and prompted a judicial inquiry headed by Sir Richard Scott. The affair has involved allegations of a cover up on the part of the government and has given rise to serious questions concerning the role and use of public interest immunity certificates, by the use of which, information may be withheld from the courts 'in the public interest'.[57]

The power of select committees to compel witnesses to give evidence

The extent to which Ministers and civil servants can be made to give evidence detracts from the effectiveness of select committee inquiries and from effective parliamentary scrutiny of the administration of government. The Select Committee on Procedure had examined its powers to call for 'persons and

---

54 See Chapter 18.

55 See Phythian, M and Little, W, 'Parliament and arms sales: lessons of the Matrix Churchill affair' (1993) 46 Parl Aff 293; Leigh, I, 'Matrix Churchill, supergun and the Scott Inquiry' [1993] PL 630.

56 Former Minister of State at the Department of Trade and Industry and Defence Procurement Minister.

57 See, further, Chapter 11.

papers' in 1977–78.[58] The committee accepted that
Commons could be invited, but not compelled, to
attendance could only be effected by an Order of the Hou.
limitations, the committee recommended that their powers
include the right to order the attendance of Ministers to give evi.
order the production of papers and records by all Ministers,
Secretaries of State.[60] Were the Minister not to co-operate, the co.
proposed that it should make a special report to the House and to ta.
motion for an address for parliamentary debate on the Minister's conduct. 1.
recommendation was not, however, implemented.

Reform of parliamentary evidence rules

The problem of witnesses who attend but who give evidence which is either
untruthful or which paints only half the picture – a problem faced by
Parliament in its committee inquiries into the Arms to Iraq affair, about which
Sir Richard Scott was particularly critical – has been addressed in Chapter 11.
In a further attempt to strengthen Parliament's powers over its Members, and
witnesses giving evidence to its committees, since January 1997, new rules
have applied. Persons giving evidence are now required to take a formal oath.
Anyone found to have lied to Parliament may be reported to the Crown
Prosecution Service with a view to prosecution for perjury, which, in the event
of conviction, could lead to a maximum prison sentence of seven years. Where
the person is a Member of Parliament, the committee will ask the Commons to
vote to remove the Member's immunity from prosecution.

The move was in part presaged by the David Willett's affair, in which the
former Paymaster General was accused by the Committee on Standards and
Privileges of having 'dissembled' in his evidence over whether he had tried to
influence a parliamentary inquiry into the cash for questions affair.[61] As
discussed in Chapter 18, the Joint Committee on Parliamentary Privileges
recommended in 1999 that a new Parliamentary Privileges Act be introduced
and that the failure to answer questions or produce necessary evidence to
committees should be made a criminal offence.

---

58 *First Report from the Select Committee on Procedure*, HC 588 (1977–78), London: HMSO,
    paras 7.5–7.9, 7.19–7.27.
59 See, further, Chapter 11.
60 HC 588 (1977–78), London: HMSO, paras 7.21 and 7.22.
61 See, further, Chapters 11 and 18.

ct committee reports

the conclusion of a select committee inquiry, a report will be drawn up. he committee aims to produce an authoritative, unanimous report which is presented to Parliament. The degree of consensus over a particular issue within the committee membership will dictate the extent to which unanimity can be achieved. Griffith and Ryle[62] comment that 'the committees have managed to achieve a high degree of unanimity in their finding and recommendations'. This 'high degree' is recognised by Griffith and Ryle to be one achieved where the matter is not politically controversial between the parties, and that the need for unanimity may result in committees avoiding 'some of the big issues of the day'. Two illustrations are offered by Griffith and Ryle. The first relates to the Foreign Affairs Committee investigation[63] into the sinking of the *General Belgrano* during the Falklands War.[64] In the inquiry, the membership of the committee had divided cleanly along party lines and the end result was a 'dissenting' report by four Opposition Members. On the other hand, the Defence Committee investigation into the Westland affair, despite political disagreement during the investigation, nonetheless resulted in a unanimous report.

Between 1979–80 and 1987–88, 116 reports were debated on the floor of the House, representing nearly 25 per cent of all reports published during that period. This fact is one which also gives rise to criticism of select committee effectiveness, although it must be conceded that the time given for debate on reports has increased in recent years. Parliamentary procedure does not make specific provision for debate on reports. The Procedure Committee has suggested that eight days per session should be devoted to such debates but this proposal has not been acted upon. Sufficient, but not too much, weight should be attached to this alleged defect, and four arguments may be advanced which limit its impact. The first relates to the commitment undertaken by successive governments to respond to select committee reports. Such an undertaking does not, of itself, ensure that the recommendations of the committee will be implemented but it does ensure that the government will react to any criticisms made and proposals put forward. Members of the committee and other interested Members of Parliament, particularly the Opposition, will be slow to let an opportunity to criticise government pass. The second argument centres on the information gained through the process of the inquiry. It has been seen that Ministers may decline or refuse to answer questions fully, and that they can restrict the extent to which civil servants may give evidence. Where a Minister refuses to co-operate with a select committee he will inevitably find media attention

---

62 *Op cit*, Griffith and Ryle, fn 2, pp 520–21.

63 Session 1984–85.

64 In May 1982. See, further, Chapter 23.

focused upon him and some cogent justification for his reticence will have to be forthcoming. For the most part, evidence suggests that there is a high degree of ministerial co-operation with committees; this need not be seen as being necessarily willing participation but, rather, a matter of political prudence.

Thirdly, it must be recognised that the reports emanating from select committee inquiries are matters of public record, available both to Members of Parliament and to the interested press and public. The information gathered in the course of an inquiry becomes public information, information which, before the introduction of the new committee structure, was often hidden from the public gaze. Finally, the absence of debate on the floor of the House in many cases will be justified by the pressure on the parliamentary timetable. It may well be the case that debate on all reports is desirable in principle, but, since 1979, over 900 reports have been published by select committees, of varying significance and on a plethora of matters. On many matters, opening debate to all Members of the House may involve a duplication of effort, with non-specialist Members of Parliament inexpertly attempting to reanalyse the information examined by the more specialised select committee Members.

Evaluation

An evaluation of the work of select committees in relation to the fundamentally important question concerning the accountability of government must be approached with caution. The outcome of an appraisal is inevitably related to the expectations which the appraiser holds and, as a consequence, the evaluation of one commentator may not be the same as another's. Caution is also urged against the making of sweeping generalisations as to the effectiveness of select committees which are diverse in nature and operation. Many factors are involved in the analysis: the extent to which media, and hence public, attention is focused on a particular enquiry; the sensitivity of the subject matter; the degree of political consensus within the committee; the extent to which governments are prepared to make time on the floor of the House to debate select committee reports; the extent to which select committee inquiries result in improved efficiency in government; and the extent to which government and other witnesses co-operate with the committees in the provision of information. All of these factors, and more, must be put in the balance before any reasoned conclusions can be reached.

Griffith and Ryle[65] state that:

> If we compare these committees with their predecessors, there is little doubt that the new committees present a more formidable critical presence to Ministers and departments.

---

65 *Op cit*, Griffith and Ryle, fn 2, p 520.

Philip Norton[66] comments that:

> Committees are thus able to ensure that Ministers and civil servants are subjected to scrutiny in a public authoritative forum, eking out explanations and data that otherwise may not be forthcoming. In so doing, they have ensured ... a greater transparency of departments, ensuring that their actions are more visible to Parliament and to the public and outside groups. Through issuing reports and recommendations, they also serve to have some impact on departmental thinking.

Nevil Johnson[67] draws five general conclusions regarding select committees:

1   there can be no doubt that the range of scrutiny has been significantly widened;

2   ... the system has operated to strengthen the sense of accountability to Parliament on the part of the executive, and indeed has added a new dimension to the traditional procedures on the floor of the House for asserting the accountability of government;

3   ... the committees have for the most part recognised that partisan politics have as a rule got to be held in check if they are to achieve anything;

4   ... the new committees have as a rule gained a satisfactory degree of co-operation from the government, and this embraces both Ministers and officials;

5   ... the committees can plausibly be regarded as making a contribution to the desire felt by many backbenchers to specialise in particular areas of government activity and to demonstrate their own professionalism.

These various strengths must be borne in mind when considering the alleged deficiencies of the committees. At the heart of any evaluation must lie the recognition of the inherent tension – already stressed in relation to the scrutiny of legislation[68] – between the legitimate right of the government to govern and the equally legitimate right of Parliament as a whole to ensure the collective accountability of government and the individual responsibility of Ministers.

SCRUTINY OF NATIONAL FINANCE

In Chapter 15, the means by which the House of Commons scrutinises proposals for taxation and expenditure was examined. In this section, the manner in which Parliament scrutinises the manner in which public money has been spent is discussed. The responsibility for, and control over,

---

66   Norton, P, *Does Parliament Matter?*, 1993, Hemel Hempstead: Harvester, p 100.
67   Johnson, N, 'Departmental Select Committees', in *op cit*, Ryle and Richards, fn 2, pp 166–70.
68   Chapter 15.

expenditure lies with the Chancellor of the Exchequer. The manner in which Parliament scrutinises public expenditure is through the Public Accounts Select Committee which examines reports of audits conducted by the Comptroller and Auditor General, who is head of the National Audit Office.[69]

The Public Accounts Committee (PAC)

The committee was first established in 1861. The committee has the power to examine the accounts 'showing the appropriation of the sums granted by Parliament to meet the public expenditure, and of such other accounts laid before Parliament, as the committee may think fit'.[70] The committee consists of not more than 15 Members, of whom four represents a quorum. While the composition of the committee represents (as does that of all select committees) the party-political strength of the House, the PAC functions in a non-partisan manner. By convention, the PAC's Chairman is a Member of the Opposition. The committee has the power to 'send for persons, papers and records' and to report from time to time.[71] The PAC issues approximately 30 to 40 reports per session.[72]

The principal function of the committee is to ensure that money is spent for the purposes intended by Parliament, and that money is spent effectively and economically. The committee holds many meetings in public. One day per session is set aside for debate of its reports. By critically examining the expenditure of departments and assessing the extent to which expenditure produces value for money, the PAC exerts considerable influence on government.

The Comptroller and Auditor General (CAG)

The CAG is an officer of the House of Commons, appointed by the Crown, and can be removed from office for misbehaviour only on the successful moving of an address to both Houses of Parliament. As head of the National Audit Office, the CAG's function is to examine the economy, efficiency and effectiveness with which bodies have used their resources in the pursuit of policy.[73] The CAG appoints his own staff, who are not civil servants. The

---

69 National Audit Act 1983.
70 Standing Order No 122.
71 *Ibid*, para 2.
72 In May 1995, the PAC issued a highly critical report concerning delays and overspending by the Ministry of Defence in relation to defence equipment.
73 National Audit Act 1983, ss 6 and 7.

reports of the National Audit Office[74] are recorded in the Weekly Information Bulletin of the House of Commons and are available to the public.

The CAG audits and certifies the accounts of over 450 departments and bodies. Three significant areas of administration lie outside his jurisdiction: nationalised industries, local authorities and private bodies.

During the 1992–93 parliamentary session, the National Audit Office and the Northern Ireland Audit Office published 67 reports, of which 21 formed the basis of Public Accounts Committee reports in that session. Matters on which the Public Accounts Committee reported in that session included the sale of regional electricity companies, National Power, PowerGen and Girobank plc; health service facilities for physically disabled persons; the administration of legal aid in England and Wales, coastal defences in England; overseas aid; and water and the environment.

The independence of the CAG from government, backed by the non-partisan Public Accounts Committee, provides powerful watchdog over the administration of government and the expenditure of public money. It must, however, be conceded that where serious overspending or the misuse of public monies has already taken place, the scrutiny and report can only be made *ex post facto*.

---

74   And the corresponding Office for Northern Ireland.

CHAPTER 17

THE HOUSE OF LORDS

INTRODUCTION

The majority of liberal democracies have bicameral legislatures, or legislatures with two 'chambers' or 'houses'.[1] In the United Kingdom, the second chamber, the Upper House – or House of Lords – is currently an unelected chamber which has judicial, legislative, scrutinising and debating functions.[2] The justifications for, and advantages of, a second chamber, irrespective of the merits of the actual second chamber, are twofold. First, a second chamber provides a forum for reflection, and for 'second thoughts' on policies and legislative proposals. A second chamber provides for a *diffusion* rather than *concentration* of power within Parliament. Secondly, depending on the allocation of power between the two chambers,[3] the Upper House plays a valuable role in the revision of legislation which has passed through the Lower House. Such revision is of particular significance where the Lower House is dominated by a government with a strong majority and also when – irrespective of the political make up of the Lower House – procedures for curtailing debate have been employed.[4] The scrutiny, and amendment, of Bills is equally important in improving the quality of the statute book. As will be seen below, the House of Lords plays a major role in statute revision. On occasion, such revision is contrary to the wish of the Commons, which may choose to acquiesce in the Lords' amendments rather than employ the Parliament Act procedure which regulates the respective powers of the two Houses of Parliament. On other occasions, however, the revision undertaken in the Lords is either at the instance of the government itself, which may choose to introduce amendments to Bills in the Lords, or by Members of the House of Lords in order to improve the drafting of the Act.

Until 1999, when the first stage of a major reform to the composition of the House of Lords was implemented, the House of Lords was unique among second legislative chambers. A majority of parliamentary democracies have elected second chambers, or a second chamber which is part elected and part

---

1   Denmark, Sweden and New Zealand have unicameral Parliaments.
2   See Bromhead, PA, *The House of Lords and Contemporary Politics*, 1958, London: Routledge and Kegan Paul; Morgan, JP, *The House of Lords and the Labour Government 1964–1970*, 1975, Oxford: OUP; Shell, D, *The House of Lords*, 2nd edn, 1992, London: Harvester.
3   See, further, below.
4   See Chapter 15.

nominated. By contrast, until 1999, the House of Lords was comprised of a majority of unelected hereditary members and a minority of nominated members. In 1999, the right of most hereditary peers to sit and vote in the Lords was abolished, leaving the Lords with a majority of nominated and no democratically elected members. Only Canada and Ireland have a predominantly nominated second chamber. Before the 1997 general election, the Labour Party had pledged to reform the House of Lords, regarding the role of the unelected House as incompatible with modern democracy. Rather than introduce wholesale reform immediately, however, the government decided on a two stage reform. The first, which is largely but not wholly accomplished (see, further, below), was to remove the right of the hereditaries to participate in Parliament. The second, which remains for the future, was to decide precisely what form of composition was needed – whether fully elected or partly elected and partly nominated – and the powers which the reformed second chamber should have. In order to reach this decision, the government established a Royal Commission, chaired by Lord Wakeham, to consider the issue and make recommendations. While this second stage of reform was expected to be implemented during the Labour government's first Parliament, it was decided to postpone the second stage until after the general election widely expected to be held in 2001. Details of the reforms, achieved and proposed, are discussed below.

HISTORICAL OVERVIEW[5]

The origins of the House of Lords lie in the councils summoned by English Kings in the eleventh, twelfth and thirteenth centuries, in order to give advice, decide on appeal cases and, under certain circumstances, to make financial grants to the King. These 'King's Councils' had developed into a form which is recognisable today by 1295, then being an assembly of the 'three estates of the realm', the clergy, barons and commons – 'those who pray, those who fight, those who work'.[6] From the earliest times, both spiritual and secular hereditary peers formed the membership of the House of Lords, by which name it became known in the sixteenth century. Maitland asserts that the separation into two Houses occurred around the middle of the fourteenth century,[7] although Stubbs contends that the two bodies were separate from the earliest time.[8] The functions of the two Houses also differed: it was for the

---

5   See Powell, E and Wallis, K, *The House of Lords in the Middle Ages*, 1968, London: Weidenfeld & Nicolson; Maitland, FW, *The Constitutional History of England*, 1908, Cambridge: CUP. See, also, Chapter 6.

6   *Ibid*, Maitland, p 75.

7   *Ibid*, Maitland, p 175.

8   Stubbs, W, *The Constitutional History of England: In its Origin and Development*, 1880, Oxford: Clarendon.

Lords to advise the King, and it was for the Commons to consent to the King's proposals. By 1330, Parliament was to meet annually,[9] at least once but more times as summonsed. Nevertheless, as seen in Chapter 6, the sitting of Parliament was a matter for the King to determine and, between 1364 and 1689, there were many years in which no Parliament met, the longest period being 11 years, during which time Charles I ruled under the prerogative.

The House of Lords, until 1999, comprised a majority of hereditary non-spiritual (secular or temporal) peers,[10] along with life peers (nominated members) and 26 Archbishops and Bishops. Before the seventeenth century, the power of the Lords Spiritual was great. In the 1453–54 parliamentary session, to take but one typical example of historical membership, the membership of the House of Lords was two Archbishops, 18 Bishops, 27 abbots and priors, five dukes, 11 earls, three viscounts and 44 barons: a total of 111. With the suppression of the monasteries, spiritual peers were excluded from Parliament and, from this time, the Upper House became a predominantly secular body. The growth in the number of secular, or temporal, peers stems from the reign of James I,[11] with 96 sitting in his last Parliament. By 1685,[12] the number had increased to 145. The Lords Spiritual were totally excluded from Parliament between 1642 and 1661.

An early conflict between the House of Commons and House of Lords and the King occurred in 1649, when by a vote of the Commons it was declared that neither the consent of the House of Lords, nor that of the King, was necessary to enact valid law:

> The commons of England in Parliament assembled do declare that the People are under God the original of all just power, and that whatsoever is enacted or declared for law by the commons in Parliament assembled, hath the force of law ... although the consent and concurrence of the King or the House of Peers be not had thereunto.

In March 1649, the Commons – under the leadership of Oliver Cromwell – abolished both the Monarchy and the House of Lords – an Act which was regarded as of no effect once the Restoration of the Monarchy took place in 1660. In 1661, Bishops were restored to the House of Lords.[13] The Acts of

---

9 4 Edw III c 14.

10 The Lords Temporal (secular peers) comprise in order of precedence after the Prince of Wales (from 1302), Dukes (from 1337), Marquesses (from 1385), Earls, Viscounts and Barons. Other members of the Royal Family entitled to sit are the Duke of Edinburgh, Duke of Gloucester, Duke of Kent and Duke of York.

11 1603–25.

12 In the reign of James II.

13 Under the Clergy Act 1661.

Union, with Scotland in 1707, and Ireland in 1800, provided for Scottish and Irish representation in the House of Lords.[14]

THE CURRENT COMPOSITION OF THE HOUSE OF LORDS

The House of Lords – almost uniquely amongst democratic legislatures – is unelected. While this situation is anomalous, undemocratic and anachronistic in an otherwise democratic society, there are some advantages in the arrangement which are too often overlooked. In essence, the theoretical value of an unelected chamber paradoxically lies in its lack of accountability to either the government of the day or to the electorate, giving it an independence without which the value of its work would be diminished. However, whether such advantages actually flow from the House of Lords can only be evaluated through examining the impact which the House has, in its revising role, on government legislation. Prior to the removal of the majority of hereditary peers from the House, they represented a majority of peers and, being dominated by Conservative Members, had the ability to act in a party political preferential manner – both to support a Conservative government's legislation and to frustrate that of a Labour government. It was perceptions such as this which caused, in part, the current Labour government to act swiftly to remove the hereditary element as a first stage of reform. In the event, some 92 hereditary peers remained in the Lords, and will so remain until the second stage of reform takes place. Historically, there has also been a political imbalance in the allegiance of life peers, with the Conservative peers outnumbering Labour peers. This imbalance is also being redressed, with the government increasing the number of appointed Labour life peers. However, the uncompleted reform has led to the criticism that the government holds, through its selection of appointees, excessive powers of patronage, capable of undermining the independence of the Lords. A further factor in the composition of the House, which renders evaluation of its work more complex, is the considerable proportion of independent peers, or 'cross benchers', who owe no political allegiance to any party.

The House of Lords also has, under the Parliament Act 1911, the power to block any Bill attempting to extend the life of a Parliament.[15] This may be seen as no more than a constitutional 'backstop' against a potential abuse of power by government, and the life of a Parliament has indeed been extended in

---

14 Numbering 16 and 28, respectively. Scottish peers continue to sit in the House; Irish peers continued to sit in the House of Lords after 1922 (see Chapter 3), but were not replaced on their deaths. The last Irish peer entitled to sit in the Lords died in 1961. See Lysaght, CE, 'Irish peers and the House of Lords' (1967) 18 NILQ 277.

15 Limited to five years: Parliament Act 1911, s 7, amending Septennial Act 1715, previously regulated under the Meeting of Parliament Act 1694.

recent history in times of national emergency.[16] Such extensions, however, have been with the consent of the Lords. Any attempt by a government to suspend elections in order to protect its own political power would be blocked by the Lords without whose consent such a Bill could not become law. On the other hand, any advantages which flow from the current composition of the Lords must be weighed in the balance against the demands of democracy. While an unelected second chamber having no role in the passage of legislation might be acceptable to some, an unelected second chamber with real – although ultimately limited – legislative power represents an affront to the idea of democratic government. It is for this reason that the issue of reform of the House of Lords has been for so long on the political agenda.[17]

Hereditary peers

Hereditary peers are created under the prerogative of the Crown on the advice on the Prime Minister. A peerage is created either by a Writ of Summons to the House or, more recently, under Letters Patent from the Sovereign which will define the line of succession, which invariably falls to the male heirs. A peerage created by a Writ of Summons will devolve to all heirs, thus enabling female successors to the title. Disputes concerning succession to a title are resolved by the House of Lords, through the Committee for Privileges. The evidence of blood tests is admissible in evidence.[18] A peerage cannot be surrendered other than under the disclaimer for life under the Peerage Act 1963,[19] on which, see below. The disclaimer does not prevent the conferment of a life peerage:[20] Both Lord Hume and Lord Hailsham were subsequently awarded a life peerage.

In January 1998, there were 759 hereditary peers, out of a total membership of 1,272, comprising just under 60 per cent of the total.[21] The number of hereditary peers had been gradually declining in relation to the number of life peers. In 1965, for example, the respective number of hereditary and life peers was 875 and 117. By 1975, the respective figures were 823 and 272; in 1985, 789 and 358; and, in 1994, 773 and 402. All this changed, however, in 1999. Under the House of Lords Act 1999, the rights of most hereditary peers have been removed. While it had been intended to remove the rights of

---

16 Eg, during the two World Wars.
17 For previous attempts to reform the Lords, and current reform proposals, see below.
18 See *The Ampthill Peerage Case* [1977] AC 547; *Barony of Moynihan* (1997) *The Times*, 28 March.
19 *Re Parliamentary Election for Bristol South East* [1964] 2 QB 257.
20 See below.
21 This figure excludes the 78 peers who had applied for leave of absence and 86 who had not applied for Writs of Summons.

all hereditary peers to sit and vote, threats of opposition to the House of Lords Bill from the majority of Conservative hereditary peers persuaded the government to allow 92 peers to remain. In the deal brokered by Viscount Cranborne, the then Conservative Leader in the Lords, the remaining hereditaries would be elected by the hereditary peers themselves. A further seven former hereditary peers were returned to the House of Lords as life peers appointed by the Prime Minister, Tony Blair, in March 2000.

Life peers

Non-judicial life peers were not introduced until the Life Peerages Act 1958. In 1998, there were 461 peers appointed under the 1958 Act: 81 female life peers and 380 male life peers. The award of a peerage is one of the highest honours conferred in the United Kingdom. Approximately one third of former government Ministers will receive life peerages. Some former Prime Ministers – such as Sir Winston Churchill and Sir Edward Heath – refused the award of a peerage in order to remain in the House of Commons. Others will decline on point of political principle. Peerages are conferred by the Crown on the advice of the Prime Minister. Twice a year – at New Year and on the Queen's birthday – honours are awarded.[22] Honours are also awarded on the dissolution of Parliament and, if there is a change of government, the outgoing Prime Minister will draw up a special honours list. However, there is much evidence to suggest that the system of appointment is used politically by governments, a factor which further undermines the legitimacy of the House of Lords, and there currently exists no formal mechanism by which a balance between the parties can be established and maintained against the wishes of a Prime Minister. If the Prime Minister insists that the working life peers should reflect party-political strength in the House of Commons, as did Margaret Thatcher, and if, as was the case with the Conservative government, that government is in power for a continuous period of 18 years, there is an inbuilt bias in appointments.

This was the legacy inherited by the Labour Government in 1997. In order to redress the political imbalance, the Prime Minister appointed an unprecedented number of life peers, intended to be 'working peers', actively participating in the work of the upper House. Of the 33 appointed in March 2000, 20 are Labour, nine Liberal Democrat and four Conservatives. Whereas Mrs Thatcher appointed 203 peers in her 11 years of office, Tony Blair appointed 209 peers in under three years.

Once appointed, life peers tend to be more active in the House of Lords – both in terms of attendance in the House and of participation in debate – than hereditary peers.

---

22   There are, occasionally, honours lists announced to mark special occasions.

Indeed, the Prime Minister made it clear that the appointment of new Labour life peers carried with it the responsibility to attend the House at least three nights a week for late night votes which carry 'three line whips' in order to ensure that the government gets its key legislation through Parliament.[23]

Judicial peers

In 1856, for the first time, a life peerage was granted to a retired judge, although he was allowed neither to sit nor to vote in Parliament. In 1876, the Appellate Jurisdiction Act[24] provided that two Lords of Appeal in Ordinary could be appointed as life peers, with both sitting and voting rights.

The Lords of Appeal in Ordinary were originally appointed to add legal expertise to the House. In their judicial capacity, the Judicial Committee of the House of Lords represents the highest domestic court[25] for civil appeals in the United Kingdom and for criminal appeals from England, Wales and Northern Ireland.[26] The Law Lords also sit as Members of the judicial Privy Council which has jurisdiction to hear appeals from a limited number of Commonwealth countries. Consideration of the judicial work of the Law Lords should be kept distinct from consideration of their role in the other functions of the House of Lords.

The Law Lords play a role in the legislative and other functions but, by convention, do not participate in purely political debate. To do so would detract from the judicial impartiality which must be evident when acting in a judicial capacity, and would have implications for the delicate balance maintained in the separation of powers.[27]

In relation to legislation, the Law Lords' role is at times both significant and valuable, although it cannot be assumed that they act in a united manner.[28] Their contributions express personal – not official judicial – opinions. It is notable that Bills on family law matters – divorce,[29] domestic violence, the law relating to children – are introduced in the House of Lords under the auspices of the Lord Chancellor. Other Law Lords make significant contributions on controversial matters, some of which can bring them into conflict with the government. D Shell, for example, instances the influence

---

23 On the whip system, see Chapter 14.
24 39 and 40 Vic c 59.
25 Consideration is given to the European Court of Justice in Chapters 8 and 9.
26 No appeal lies from the highest Scottish criminal court, the High Court of Justiciary. Criminal Procedure (Scotland) Act 1887.
27 See Chapter 5.
28 See *op cit*, Shell, fn 2, Chapter 2 and references therein.
29 Children Bill 1988; Family Home and Domestic Violence Bill 1995; White Paper on *Divorce Reform*, April 1995.

exerted by Lord Chief Justice Parker on the issue of abolition of the death penalty,[30] and over the War Damage Bill 1965.[31]

Lords Spiritual

In addition to the hereditary and life peers, 26 Archbishops and Bishops of the Church of England sit in the Lords, and up to 12 Lords of Appeal in Ordinary (Law Lords). The explanation for the presence of Anglican Archbishops and Bishops is historical. As seen above, until the dissolution of the monasteries, spiritual peers represented a majority in the House of Lords. Today, their presence is explained both on the basis of tradition and on the basis of the close links between the established Church of England and the State. There are arguments for reform in this regard,[32] but it should be recognised that the Spiritual Peers owe no allegiance to any political party and, while by convention not speaking or voting on purely political issues, make a significant contribution to debate on many, often sensitive, moral and social issues, such as housing, divorce, abortion, homosexuality, embryology and human fertilisation.

The oath of allegiance

Before becoming a full Member of the House, the new peer is formally introduced and takes the oath of allegiance to the Crown.[33]

Government members in the Lords

In 1998, 23 peers were members of the government. The government is represented in the House by the Lord Chancellor, Leader of the House (Lord Privy Seal), Lord Advocate, five Ministers of State, seven Under Secretaries of State, the Chief Whip and Deputy Chief Whip and seven whips.

---

30 Homicide Act 1957.
31 On which, see Chapter 7.
32 See, further, below.
33 Promissory Oaths Act 1868, s 2; Oaths Act 1978, s 1.

Disqualification from membership of the Lords

Aliens

Aliens are disqualified from membership of the Lords under section 3 of the Act of Settlement 1700, which provides that membership of the House excludes:

> ... person[s] born out of the Kingdoms of England, Scotland or Ireland, or the Dominions thereunto belonging ... (except such as are born of English parents).

The British Nationality Act 1981[34] amends the Act of Settlement to the effect that Commonwealth citizens or citizens of the Republic of Ireland are excluded from its provisions.

Persons under the age of 21

While the age of majority has been reduced from the age of 21 to the age of 18 years,[35] no person succeeding to a peerage below the age of 21 may take his or her seat in the House.[36] Technically, persons under the age of 21 are not disqualified, but merely ineligible to take their seats until they reach the age of 21.

Bankrupts

Under the Bankruptcy and Insolvency Acts,[37] no peer may sit whilst adjudicated bankrupt. The disqualification ceases in accordance with the Acts.[38] It is a breach of privilege to sit whilst disqualified.

Treason

Any peer convicted of treason is disqualified from sitting or voting as a Member of the House unless and until he has either completed his term of imprisonment or received a pardon.

---

34   British Nationality Act 1981, Sched 7.
35   Family Law Reform Act 1969, s 1.
36   Standing Order No 2, 1685. In 1994, the youngest peer was aged five.
37   Bankruptcy Disqualification Act 1871; Bankruptcy Act 1883; Bankruptcy Act 1890; Bankruptcy (Scotland) Act 1913; Bankruptcy Act 1914; Insolvency Act 1986.
38   Insolvency Act 1986, s 427.

The disclaimer of hereditary peerages[39]

Under the Peerage Act 1963, it became possible to disclaim a peerage.[40] A peer who disclaims his or her title does so irrevocably, but the disclaimer will not affect the succession of the title to the next generation. Under the Act, a peer succeeding to a title before the passing of the Act had 12 months in which to disclaim the title. Peers succeeding to titles subsequently have one year within which to disclaim succession, or, in the case of a person under the age of 21, a year from the date of attaining the age of 21 years. One exception exists to this rule. If the successor is a Member of the House of Commons, or a candidate for election to the House of Commons, at the date on which he inherits the title, the period for disclaimer is one month.[41] A total of 11 peers (including Viscount Stansgate, now Tony Benn, Lord Hume and Lord Hailsham) have disclaimed titles under the Act.

Leave of absence

Leave of absence from the House of Lords may be granted at any time during a Parliament by applying to the Clerk of the Parliaments.[42] At the start of each new Parliament peers who have previously obtained leave of absence will be asked whether they wish it to continue. Where leave of absence is granted it is expected that the peer will not attend the House. Should he or she wish to do so, he may give one month's notice of his intention to attend. However, there is no mechanism by which the House can exclude a peer who has leave of absence but nevertheless attends the House.[43]

Attendance in the House

All peers are entitled to attend and vote in the House. Before becoming eligible to sit in the Lords, it is necessary to apply for and receive a Writ of Summons.[44] It is expected that Lords who have not taken leave of absence will attend as regularly as possible.

---

39 See Hailsham (Lord), *The Door Wherein I Went*, 1975, London: Collins.
40 See *Report of Joint Committee on House of Lords Reform*, HL 23 (1962–63) and HC 38 (1962–63), London: HMSO.
41 Peerage Act 1963, s 2.
42 Standing Order No 20. In 1994, 78 peers had applied for leave.
43 See, further, below.
44 In 1994, 86 peers had not applied for or received Writs.

TABLE I: MEMBERSHIP OF THE HOUSE OF LORDS: APRIL 1998

Archbishops and Bishops	26
Peers by succession	750 (16 women)
Hereditary peers of first creation	9
Life peers under the Appellate Jurisdiction Act 1876	26
Life peers under the Life Peerages Act 1958	462 (80 women)
TOTAL	1,273*

*   This figure includes 68 Lords without Writs of Summons and 60 peers on leave of absence.

TABLE II: MEMBERSHIP OF THE HOUSE OF LORDS: 31 JULY 2000

Archbishops and Bishops	26
Peers under House of Lords Act 1999	92
Life peers under the Appellate Jurisdiction Act 1876	28
Life peers under the Life Peerages Act 1958	552
TOTAL	698

It can be seen from Table I that the hereditary peers outnumbered the life peers by two to one. One of the vehement arguments of some reformers was that the House of Lords was dominated by hereditary peers who were, by virtue of their background and upbringing, innately conservative and hence supported the Conservative Party. If this was true, then the natural implication which followed was that the House of Lords was naturally sympathetic towards a Conservative government and naturally hostile towards a Labour government. The bare statistics of membership, however, leave out an important dimension – that of the political allegiance of those who actually attended the House regularly and played a significant role in the law making process.

Political allegiance in the House of Lords

The political allegiance within the House overall, that is, taking into account the full membership of the House[45] in January 1998 was as follows:

TABLE III: POLITICAL ALLEGIANCE IN THE HOUSE OF LORDS: JANUARY 1998 (FIGURES EXCLUDE PEERS WITHOUT WRITS OF SUMMONS OR ON LEAVE OF ABSENCE)

PARTY	LIFE PEERS	HEREDITARY PEERS OF FIRST CREATION	HEREDITARY PEERS BY SUCCESSION	LORDS SPIRITUAL	TOTAL
Conservative	172	4	319	0	495
Labour	140	1	16	0	157
Liberal Democrat	44	0	24	0	68
Cross bench *	118	4	200	0	322
Other	8	0	71	25	104
TOTAL	482	9	630	25	1,146

*   Cross bench peers are those peers who are independent of any political party.

The party political position had now changed, with Conservative peers being outnumbered by 647 to 475. However, not all of these peers were regular attenders at Parliament. The most meaningful statistics are those revealing the political allegiance of those peers who attended over 50 per cent of all parliamentary sittings.

TABLE IV: SESSION 1996–97: PEERS ATTENDING 36 OR MORE SITTINGS (MAXIMUM SITTING DAYS 79)

Conservative	195	49%
Labour	83	21%
Liberal Democrat	37	9%
Cross bench	81	21%
TOTAL	396	100%

---

45   Excluding Lords on leave of absence.

From Table IV, it can be seen that the Conservative Party peers, whilst numerically the largest group, did not, when compared with the number of peers of other parties (or none), command a majority.

Lords' expenses

No salary is payable to Members of the House of Lords. They are entitled to expenses to cover the cost of travel, overnight accommodation, subsistence and secretarial and other expenses pertaining to their parliamentary duties. In 1996, the amounts which might be claimed were £74 for overnight subsistence; £33 daily allowance and £32 for secretarial assistance for each day's attendance at the House.

Salaried Members of the House of Lords

The Lord Chancellor receives part of his annual salary for acting as Speaker of the House. The Chairman and Principal Deputy Chairman of Committees, government Ministers and whips and Lords of Appeal in Ordinary are salaried. The Leader of the Opposition and the Chief Opposition Whip also receive salaries.

Functions of the House of Lords

Until 1911, the powers of the Lords were equal to those of the Commons, with the exception that the Lords recognised – by convention – the supremacy of the Commons in relation to financial matters and accepted that they had no right to initiate or amend Bills relating to finance. The Lords nevertheless claimed the power to reject outright financial legislation, a power which, when exercised, led to a curtailment of their powers.

In the White Paper of 1968,[46] which formed the basis for the Labour government's attempt further to reform the House of Lords, the following functions of the House of Lords were recorded:

(a) the provision of a forum for debate on matters of public interest;

(b) the revision of Bills brought from the House of Commons;

(c) the initiation of Public Bills and Private Members' Bills;

(d) the consideration of delegated legislation;

(e) the scrutiny of the executive;

(f) the scrutiny of private legislation;

---

46 *House of Lords Reform*, Cmnd 3799, 1968, London: HMSO, para 8.

(g) select committee work;

(h) the Supreme Court of Appeal.

Before considering the manner in which the House of Lords allocates its time, it is useful to look at the overall time available to the House in a parliamentary session.

TABLE V: TIME AVAILABLE AND ATTENDANCE IN THE HOUSE OF LORDS

Session	1982–83	1991–92	1998–99
Total sitting days	123	194	154
Total sitting hours	798	765	1,171.28
Average length of sitting	6.29	7.18	7.36
Average daily attendance	303	379	446
Late sittings (after 10 pm)	45	67	89

What is most apparent from the above figures is the overall increase in both the time spent on the work of the House and the number of peers regularly attending. When compared with statistics from earlier decades, the increased activity in the Lords seems all the more remarkable.

In the 1940s, of a membership of some 800, only 100 attended regularly and, of these, only 60 played an active part in the business of the House. The introduction of life peers under the Life Peerage Act 1958 was intended to increase the membership of the House without extending the hereditary element. The Act also enabled governments to put forward to the Crown nominations of men and women from all walks of life who had achieved prominence in their careers.

The House of Lords contains a wealth of specialism and experience which is unmatched by the House of Commons. It is in part the introduction of life peers which explains the revival of the House of Lords. Perhaps the major factor explaining the resurgence of activity in the Upper House lies in the sheer volume of legislative work introduced by governments in recent years.

ALLOCATION OF TIME IN THE HOUSE OF LORDS

The time spent on various aspects of the business of the House over recent years is shown in percentages:

TABLE VI: ALLOCATION OF TIME IN THE HOUSE OF LORDS
(AS PERCENTAGE OF AVAILABLE TIME)

Session	1982–83	1991–92	1998–99
General debates	25.0	20.3	17.0
Debates on select committee reports	4.6	1.4	3.1
Delegated legislation	5.7	3.2	3.2
Ministerial statements	3.8	1.7	4.4
Public Bills	42.0	55.3	56.1
Miscellaneous	4.4	5.9	1.2
Starred questions	6.0	6.4	5.9
Unstarred questions	8.5	5.8	7.6

The most remarkable changes in the allocation of time which are evident from the statistics on time allocation is the decrease in the time spent on general debates from 25 per cent in 1982–83 to 17 per cent in 1998–99, and the correlative increase in time spent on the consideration of legislation, primary and secondary. In 1982–83, legislation occupied some 47 per cent of the House's time; in 1998–99, this had risen to 56.1 per cent. The pressure of legislation caused a major review of procedure in the Lords,[47] details of which are outlined below.

Procedure in the House of Lords

To some extent, the procedure in the House of Lords mirrors that of the Lower House, although significant differences must be noted. The control of procedure lies within the Privileges[48] of the House, and is regulated by the Leader of the House, the government Chief Whip and by the House as a whole. The Speaker of the House, the Lord Chancellor,[49] has no formal

---

47 *Report from the Select Committee on the Committee Work of the House*, HL 35-1 (1991–92), London: HMSO.

48 See Chapter 18.

49 See Gardiner (Lord), *The Trials of a Lord Chancellor*, 1968, Birmingham: Holdsworth Club, University of Birmingham; *op cit*, Hailsham, fn 39; Heuston, RFV, *Lives of Lord Chancellors, 1885–1940*, 1964, Oxford: Clarendon and *1940–70*, 1987, Oxford: Clarendon; Mackay (Lord), *The Administration of Justice*, 1994, London: Sweet & Maxwell.

powers to control the House, but is under a duty to attend the House and to sit on the Woolsack. The duty to attend derives from a Standing Order of the House made on 9 June 1660: '... that it is the duty of the Lord Chancellor or the Lord keeper of the great Seale of England ordinarily to attend the Lords house of Parlyament.' That Standing Order, slightly amended, is still in force, and the Lord Chancellor attends all sittings of the House unless absent by reason of illness. His role, as Speaker of the House, however, has been described as 'ornamental and symbolic',[50] for the Lord Chancellor does not have the same powers as the Speaker of the House of Commons. In the passage of legislation, for example, there is no power to select amendments for debate or to curtail debate. Whereas the Speaker in the Commons may rule that certain proposed amendments cannot be debated – perhaps because they are not strictly relevant to the content of the Bill – the House of Lords may decide to debate any and all amendments.

The Leader of the House is a political appointment in the hands of the Prime Minister, and the Leader of the House is a Member of Cabinet. It is his or her principal duty to advise on matters of procedure and order. The government Chief Whip is responsible for the arrangement of government business and consultation with other parties as to its arrangement. As with the Whip in the Commons, the Chief Whip sends out a weekly indication of the need for Member's attendance at particular items of business.

Having examined the composition of the House, the allocation of time and the principal officials of the House, we can now turn our attention to examining the actual business of the House.

GENERAL DEBATES

The importance of debates in the House of Lords, although occupying a decreasing percentage of the time of the House, should not be underestimated. Wednesdays are generally devoted to debates on matters of general public importance. One Wednesday per month is set aside for two short debates limited to two and a half hours, when the subject matter is chosen by backbench peers selected by ballot. Other debates take place as a result of consultation between the political parties, and will be generally timetabled to last for a maximum of either five hours or two and a half hours. In the 1998–99 Session, 74 general debates on matters of public interest occupied 198 hours, or 17 per cent of available time in the Lords.

The subject matter for debate is wide ranging, and it is often commented that the quality of debate in the House of Lords attains a higher standard than

---

50 *Report by the Group on the Working of the House*, HL 9 (1987–88), London: HMSO, para 13. But see the discussion of the role of the Lord Chancellor in Chapter 5.

that in the House of Commons. In part, this is due to the less partisan nature of the House of Lords and, paradoxically, their very lack of accountability enhances their capacity for independence and openness. Since the introduction of life peers in 1958, the quality of debate is enriched by the diverse backgrounds and experience of Members.

Questions in the House of Lords

Four types of questions are provided for under Standing Orders: starred, unstarred, written and private notice questions.

The daily business of the House commences with up to four starred questions[51] addressed to the government on four days per week. Notice must be given of the question to be asked, and each peer is restricted to two questions per day. The purpose of the question is not to initiate debate but to secure information from the government. In the 1998–99 session, 539 starred questions were asked and they occupied 5.9 per cent of the time of the House overall.

Unstarred questions are asked at the end of the day's business and may initiate debate. They may be likened to daily adjournment debates in the Lower House.[52] These are popular with Members, providing an opportunity to initiate debate on a matter of public interest. In the 1976–77 session, 36 were asked; in 1987–88, 51 were asked, taking up 5.3 per cent of the time of the House. In the 1991–92 session, there were 276 starred questions, 22 unstarred questions and 664 questions put down for written answer. In the 1998–99 session, there were 539 starred questions, 83 unstarred questions and 4,322 questions put down for written answer.

Questions for written answer are printed on the Order Paper of the day and a government Minister will reply within 14 days. The questions and replies are printed in *Hansard*, the official journal of the House. There is no limit on the number of questions which may be asked.

Private notice questions fulfil the same function as in the Lower House, that is, to raise matters for urgent debate without the need to observe the strict rules of notice for other questions. Notice must be given to the Leader of the House by noon on the day on which the question is to be put, and the Leader has absolute discretion as to whether to allow the question to be put. In 1987–88, only three such questions were allowed and, in the 1998–99 session, only two.

---

51 Standing Order No 32.
52 See Chapter 14.

TABLE VII: QUESTIONS IN THE HOUSE OF LORDS

SESSION	1994–95	1995–96	1996–97 *	1998–99
Number of starred questions	515	498	262	539
Number of unstarred questions	42	26	27	83
Number of questions for written answer	12,172	2,471	1,349	4,322
Number of private notice questions	1	0	1	2

*   Short session, running from October to March, rather than November to October.

THE SCRUTINY OF LEGISLATION

As has been seen above, the scrutiny of legislation occupies the largest, and an increasing, proportion of the time of the House, and it is to this aspect of the work of the House that most attention must be paid. The allocation of time for the scrutiny of legislation, and the distribution of that time between differing types of Bills is shown below:

TABLE VIII: TIME SPENT ON PUBLIC BILLS (IN HOURS AND AS A PERCENTAGE OF TIME AVAILABLE)

SESSION	1994–95	1995–96	1996–97 *	1998–99
Public Bills	486.44 (53.8%)	487.27 (52.1%)	278.14 (52.8%)	657.32 (56.1%)
Government Bills	426.50 (47.2%)	447.25 (47.2%)	234.28 (44.5%)	622.45 (53.2%)
Private Members' Bills	59.54 (6.6%)	40.02 (4.3%)	43.56 (8.3%)	34.47 (3.0%)

*   Short session, running from October to March, rather than November to October.

Bills, other than financial Bills, which fall within the exclusive powers of the House of Commons, can be introduced in either the Commons or the Lords. The majority of government Bills will be introduced in the Commons and, having passed the Commons' stages of scrutiny, will be passed to the House of Lords, although many Bills are introduced in the Lords. The process of scrutiny in the Lords in many respects mirrors that in the Commons, and Bills receive a formal first reading, followed by the second reading debate and then 'stand committed' for the committee stage, after which the Bill is reported back to the House and then receives its third reading.

Legislative committees in the House of Lords

There are significant differences between the two Houses in the scrutiny of legislation. First, in the House of Lords, there is no regular use of standing committees, and Bills will be considered in the Chamber by a Committee of the Whole House. In the 1991–92 session, a Select Committee of the House of Lords reviewed the role of committees in the House.[53] The committee considered extending the use of Public Bill Committees – the equivalent of standing committees in the House of Commons – but rejected the proposal. A majority of witnesses to the committee opposed their introduction. In the words of the committee, such committees were:

> ... unrepresentative of a non-partisan House; they increased the time required on report; and breadth of experience and participation at committee stage was considered desirable.[54]

However, the House of Lords did make provision for Bills to be read off the floor of the House. All peers are entitled to attend and participate. The measure facilitates greater efficiency by freeing time in the chamber itself.[55] The introduction of Special Public Bill Committees was, also, favourably considered in relation to a limited number of Bills and first used in the 1994–95 session.[56] The procedure reflects that of the special standing committees in the Commons,[57] with a limited period of time set aside for consideration of the Bill, where the committee takes written and oral evidence on the provisions of the Bill. The committee then reverts to standard standing committee procedure and examines the Bill clause by clause. The committees are used to scrutinise Law Commission Bills which are introduced by the Lord Chancellor in the House of Lords. Note that select committees may also be used for the committee stage.[58]

---

53 *Report from the Select Committee on the Committee Work of the House*, HL 35-1 (1991–92), London: HMSO.

54 *Ibid*, para 48. Public Bill Committees had been established to consider the Pilotage Bill of 1986 and the Charities Bill 1991. The Select Committee felt that consideration of the former Bill had been less than satisfactory.

55 The committee was first used in the 1994–95 session for the Children (Scotland) Bill.

56 For the Law of Property (Miscellaneous Provisions) Bill.

57 Standing Order No 91. See Chapter 15.

58 House of Lords Procedure Committee, *Third Report*, 1993–94.

Curtailment of debate

A further difference between procedure in the Commons and the Lords lies in the absence of procedures in the Lords for the curtailment of debate. The absence of the Closure Motion or the Allocation of Time Motion (Guillotine) in the Lords ensures that the contents of Bills are fully debated.[59]

Party discipline in the House of Lords

There exists a system of 'whipping' which ensures some party political control over Members, although the extent of that control is far less than the control exerted by the whips in the Commons. The House of Lords is generally a far less party-political forum than the elected House of Commons. It must also be remembered that the House of Lords contains some 322 cross benchers, or independents, who do not owe allegiance to any particular political party. This group represents a potentially significant force in so far as the way in which cross benchers will vote cannot necessarily be foreseen in advance, let alone guaranteed. These factors, together with the independence the House and not being accountable to an electorate, results in a scrutinising body which can review legislation in depth and largely free from the political and procedural controls which are prevalent in the House of Commons.

THE AMENDMENT OF LEGISLATION

The House of Lords has the power to delay enactment of a Bill under the Parliament Acts 1911–49, but not to veto a Bill. As will be seen, the democratically elected Lower House has the ultimate right to enact legislation in the face of opposition from the Upper House. The House of Lords does, however, have the power to propose amendments to Bills and it is their success or otherwise in this regard which requires examination. At the outset, it must be recognised that amendments proposed are of differing types and are put forward in response to a variety of circumstances. Not all amendments proposed in the Lords and accepted by the House of Commons stem from principled opposition in the House of Lords. Griffith and Ryle[60] identify the sources and explanations for Lords' amendments as follows.

---

59   For details, see Chapter 15.
60   Griffith, JAG, and Ryle, M, *Parliament: Functions, Practice and Procedures*, 1989, London: Sweet & Maxwell, pp 508–10.

Drafting and technical amendments

These amendments account for a large proportion of all amendments accepted. They amount to no more than the tidying up of statutory language, and do not occupy much time. Citing the Channel Tunnel Bill 1987, Griffith and Ryle state that, of 204 amendments made in the Lords, 54 were drafting amendments and 65 were technical amendments.

Fulfilment of pledges made in the Commons

In order to expedite the passage of a Bill, the government frequently undertakes to implement a proposed Commons' amendment in the Lords, often after consulting various interest groups outside Parliament. For example, when the House of Lords considered the Banking Bill 1986, 11 amendments arose from Commons' undertakings and, when considering the Agriculture Bill 1986, 15 Lords' amendments were introduced to reflect undertakings made in the House of Commons.

Policy amendments from departmental or external sources

Such amendments arise out of the government's willingness to rethink an aspect of the Bill in the light of considerations in the Commons or within the department concerned with the legislation. The Lords here acts as a convenient forum for proposing the relevant amendments.

Policy amendments due to pressure in Parliament

It may be the case that there has been opposition in the Commons to a particular proposal which the government has resisted, and has used its majority to that effect. If the government is prepared to concede a point, particularly where it foresees opposition in the Lords, it may prefer to give way than to risk losing part of the Bill on a vote in the Lords. Negotiations will frequently take place between the government department and those intending to oppose the measure in order to secure a satisfactory compromise which will ensure the smooth passage of the Bill into law.

Policy changes as a result of pressure in the House of Lords

Some amendments arise purely as a result of objections voiced in the House of Lords. One recent example of principled opposition in the Lords, not apparent in the Lower House, is offered by the Child Support Bill 1991.[61] In that Bill, unmarried separated mothers on State benefit were to be placed under a statutory duty to reveal the identity of the fathers of their children in order that the Child Support Agency could enforce the financial duty of fathers to support their children. When the Bill arrived in the Lords, clause 46, which offered no defence to the mother who declined to give the information, was rejected by the Lords. The Bill returned to the Commons and the government reinstated the clause but made a concession to the Lords and inserted a defence of reasonably withholding information.

It has been seen above that, over recent years, the House of Lords has spent an increasing amount of time on the scrutiny of legislation. Of the overall time spent on legislation, some 20 per cent of time is devoted to the second reading debates; nearly 50 per cent of time is spent on committee stage; 22.5 per cent is spent on report; and seven per cent is spent on third reading.[62] Committee stage normally takes place on the floor of the House, but the Lords may utilise select committees for the committee stage where a Bill is deemed to be of a particularly sensitive nature and the House wishes to be able to summon experts and take evidence on the Bill. If that route is adopted, the select committee reports back to the House as a whole with its recommendations.

In addition to the increasing time spent on legislative work, there has also been a marked increase in the number of amendments put forward in the House of Lords. The reasons for amendments have been considered above. Attention can now be turned to the level of amendments introduced in the Lords.

Bills in differing sessions have attracted an unusually large number of amendments. By way of illustration, in the Nationalisation Bill of 1946–47, 1,200 amendments were put down, 95 per cent of which were accepted by the Commons. In considering the Criminal Justice Bill 1967, 300 amendments were made, of which only six were rejected by the Commons. In relation to the Industrial Relations Bill 1971, 341 amendments were proposed, of which 50 per cent were accepted by the Commons and, when considering the Local Government Bill 1972, 610 amendments were proposed, the majority of which were introduced by government Members in the Lords.

In the 1992–93 session, a total of 79 government Bills were scrutinised by the House of Lords, of which 23 were amended. The total number of amendments made by the House of Lords amounted to 2,097. The government suffered 16 defeats on divisions on public Bills in the House of Lords in that session.

---

61 See Barnett, H, 'Reflections on the Child Support Act' [1993] 5 J of Child Law 77.
62 *Op cit*, Griffith and Ryle, fn 60, p 483.

The bald figures on amendments give no indication of the quality of the amendments and their substantive impact on legislation. For example, the House of Lords put forward amendments to the Education (No 2) Bill 1980 which resulted in the government abandoning a proposal to impose charges for school transport; amendments to the Local Government (Interim Provisions) Bill 1984 resulted in the government revising plans governing local government prior to the abolition of the Greater London Council and amendments to the 1992 Education (Schools) Bill resulted in changes made to inspections of schools.[63]

From these figures, it can be seen that the House of Lords is both very active in relation to legislation and makes a substantial impact on many legislative proposals. Most often, the House of Commons will give way to the Lords and accept their amendments, rather than risk losing a Bill for lack of parliamentary time. It must be remembered that, if a Bill fails to pass all of its stages within a session, the Bill will be lost and the government must make time to reintroduce it in the next session. Accordingly, the later in a session a Bill is considered by the Lords, the greater will be the inclination of the House of Commons to accept Lords' amendments. (On Suspension Motions, however, see p 664.)

In the run-up to the reform of the Lords, the House exercised its revising powers robustly, opposing government measures, *inter alia*, relating to the closed list system of proportional representation for the 1999 European parliamentary elections,[64] welfare and pensions reform,[65] immigration and asylum,[66] and the establishment of a London Authority and Mayor.[67] The House also threatened to exercise its powers to the full in relation to the House of Lords Bill, in defiance of the Salisbury convention that peers would not block a government measure which had formed part of its manifesto programme. As noted above, negotiations between the then Conservative Leader of the Lords, Viscount Cranborne, and the Prime Minister resulted in a compromise measure in which 92 hereditary peers would remain in the Lords following the removal of the majority of hereditaries.

---

63 See Norton, P, *Does Parliament Matter?*, 1993, Hemel Hempstead: Harvester, Chapter 5; and, for an analysis of the treatment of government legislation 1979–87, see *op cit*, Shell, fn 2, Chapter 6. For a case study of the role of the House of Lords, see Clarke, DN and Shell, D, 'Revision and amendment of legislation by the House of Lords – a case study' [1994] PL 409.

64 European Parliamentary Elections Bill 1998.

65 Welfare Reform and Pensions Bill 1999.

66 Immigration and Asylum Bill 1999.

67 Greater London Authority Bill 1998.

The House of Lords post-reform

When parliamentary business resumed in January 2000, the majority of hereditary peers had been ousted. It soon became clear, however, that the 'new' House of Lords was not prepared to be more acquiescent towards government legislative proposals. Even before the new year started, the Lords were proclaiming their renewed 'legitimacy' as a revising chamber. The Conservative Leader in the Lords, Lord Strathclyde, had in December 1999 called for a strengthening of the Lords' powers vis à vis the Commons, suggesting that the Lords abandon the convention whereby delegated legislation is not opposed in the Lords, and warning that the House would not give way easily when it came to disagreement over a Bill. The Labour Leader in the Lords also referred to the Lords, post-reform, as 'more legitimate'. With the second stage of reform of the Lords postponed by the government which has proposed establishing a Joint Committee of both Houses of Parliament to consider the details of further reform, the revised House of Lords soon made an impact on the government's legislative programme. The Criminal Justice (Mode of Trial) Bill, which in part removes the right of defendants charged with 'either way offences', such as theft and burglary, to choose their mode of trial, was introduced in the Lords. The effect of this is that the Parliament Act procedures do not apply, thus making it easier for the Lords to press home its objections to the Bill successfully. The Lords rejected the Bill, forcing the government to reintroduce the Bill in the Commons where at second reading the government secured a substantial majority. The government also suffered a defeat of its proposals to introduce a new executive structure for local government.[68] Most controversially, the Lords opposed the government's proposal to repeal 'Section 28', which prohibits the promotion of homosexuality in education. This caused the government to delay enactment until the summer of 2000 when more Labour life peers had been appointed, which it was hoped would secure a majority for the government in the Lords to ensure the passage of the Local Government Bill. Difficulty was also caused by the Lords over the government's proposal to lower the age of consent for homosexual sex to 16 years, opposing the Sexual Offences (Amendment) Bill, and forcing the government to employ the Parliament Act procedure. The Care Standards Bill, which would introduce regulation of private hospitals and establish two bodies to inspect and impose standards, one for National Health Service hospitals, one for private hospitals, was also opposed by the Lords, which inflicted its tenth defeat on government legislative proposals since the removal of the hereditary peers in 1999.

---

68   Local Government Bill 2000.

The House of Lords and delegated legislation

The House of Lords' Delegated Powers Scrutiny Committee's principal concern is to scrutinise Bills with a view to establishing the extent of legislative powers which Parliament intends to delegate to government ministers. Prior to the establishment of the committee, Bills with potentially or actually contentious delegated powers took up a large amount of time in the House of Lords' legislative debates. The committee's prior scrutiny of Bills presaging delegated powers, and its approval thereof, means that this issue no longer occupies legislative time in the consideration of the Bill by the House. The role of the Committee is 'to report whether the provision of any Bill inappropriately delegates legislative power, or whether they subject the exercise of legislative power to an inappropriate degree of parliamentary scrutiny'. The committee reports to the House, which decides whether or not to accept the committee's recommendations. The committee has eight members and meets as needs require. The committee hears oral evidence in public, and takes evidence in writing on each public Bill from the relevant government department.

The committee, in the examination of a Bill, considers four principal matters. First, the committee considers whether the power to make delegated, or secondary, legislation is appropriate, or whether the grant of power is so important that it should only be granted in primary legislation. Secondly, the committee pays special attention to *Henry VIII powers*. A Henry VIII power is a power to change the law without parliamentary action, that is to say, the primary legislation may be amended or repealed by subordinate legislation with or without further parliamentary scrutiny. Thirdly, the committee considers which form of parliamentary scrutiny of delegated legislation is appropriate, and in particular whether the power specifies the use of the affirmative or negative resolution procedure.[69] Fourthly, the committee considers whether the legislation should provide for consultation in draft form before the regulation is laid before Parliament, and whether its operation should be governed by a Code of Conduct.

The Deregulation Committee

The Deregulation and Contracting Out Act 1994 introduced a new form of delegated legislation. Under the Act, a Minister may issue a deregulation order to amend or repeal any enactment of primary legislation with a view to removing or reducing any administrative or bureaucratic element. The aim is towards greater efficiency in administration. The power is exercisable provided that no necessary protection is removed from the law. The 1994 Act

---

69   On which, see, further, Chapter 15.

provides for parliamentary scrutiny. The two stage process involves, first, the proposal being laid before Parliament as a draft order. The Lords' committee, and the House of Commons equivalent committee have 60 days in which to report. Secondly, the government then lays a draft order before Parliament, either in its original form or amended to take account of the two committees' opinions, for approval by a resolution of each House. The House of Lords can only approve the draft order after the committee has made a second report on the order.

The committee is concerned with four principal matters. First, whether the measure is *intra vires*; secondly, that the measure removes the relevant administrative burden; thirdly, whether the order removes any required 'necessary protection'; and, fourthly, whether the consultation required under the Act has been adequate. The committee takes oral and written evidence. In 1995, the committee rejected a proposed draft deregulation order in relation to charges being permitted for public dances held on Sundays. The Sunday Observance Act 1780 prohibits charging for public dances. The deregulation proposal aimed to exempt dances from the 1780 Act and allow premises to be licensed for Sunday dancing, and to extend the permitted hours for the sale of alcohol at dances on Sunday nights. Having heard oral evidence and considered written evidence, the committee rejected the proposal. In the committee's opinion, the subject matter was unsuitable for such an expedited procedure and, further, the prior consultation had been inadequate.

THE BALANCE OF POWER BETWEEN THE HOUSE OF LORDS AND THE HOUSE OF COMMONS

The Parliament Acts 1911 and 1949

Where the House of Commons is not prepared to accept Lords' amendments, or where the House of Lords rejects a Bill outright, the role of the Parliament Acts must be considered. The Parliament Act 1911 altered the balance of power between the House of Commons and the House of Lords, restricting the powers of the Upper House. Until that Act, the House of Lords enjoyed equal power with the Commons over legislation, with the exception of financial measures which, by convention, the Lords recognised as falling under the authority of the elected Lower House. However, in 1909, the Finance Bill containing Lloyd George's Budget was rejected, in breach of convention, by the House of Lords. As a consequence, the House of Commons passed a Resolution declaring that there had been a breach of the constitution and a usurpation of the rights of the Commons and calling for the power of the House of Lords to be restricted. King Edward VII was called upon to create sufficient new peers to guarantee the passage of the Finance Bill but refused to do so until the Budget was approved by the electorate. Parliament was dissolved and, in the election in January 1910, the government secured a majority of seats only with the help of minor parties. The House of Lords then passed the Finance Bill.

This conflict between the House of Commons and House of Lords resulted in the Parliament Act 1911, passed by both Houses of Parliament but with the House of Lords being threatened with the creation of more peers to ensure the Bill's safe passage. The Act abolished the Lords' right to reject Money Bills,[70] and imposed a one month time limit during which the Lords may consider such Bills and suggest amendments. If the Bill has not been approved without amendment within one month, provided it has been sent to the Lords within one month before the end of the session, the Bill will proceed to receive the royal assent without the approval of the Lords. Not all financial bills are Money Bills. Where a Bill contains provision dealing with other subjects it will not be a money Bill. The Finance Bill is not automatically a Money Bill, and over half of the Finance Bills sent to the Lords since the 1911 Act have not been certified as Money Bills. Similarly, the Local Government Finance Bill 1988, which introduced the Poll Tax, was not certified as a Money Bill and, accordingly, was considered by the House of Lords. While the purpose of the 1911 Act is to prevent amendment or delay in Money Bills, should the Lords propose amendments, these can be either accepted or rejected by the Commons. By way of example, the Commons accepted Lords' amendments to the following certified Bills: the China Indemnity Bill 1925; the Unemployment Assistance (Temporary Provisions) Extension Bill 1935–36; the Inshore Fishing Industry Bill 1947; and the Industrial Development (Ships) Bill 1969–70.

Regarding non-Money Bills, the power of the House of Lords was curtailed, their right to reject legislation replaced by a power to delay Bills for a two year period spread over three parliamentary sessions.

Conflict between the two Houses resurfaced over the Labour government's nationalisation programme following the Second World War. The Labour government, fearful that the Lords would reject the Iron and Steel Bill, introduced the Parliament Bill in 1947. In 1948, a conference between party leaders from both Houses met to attempt to reach agreement on the terms of the Parliament Bill. In the event, the conference broke down and the Parliament Bill was rejected by the House of Lords at second reading, only to be passed by the Commons under the Parliament Act 1911. The 1949 Act reduced the House of Lords' power of delay over non-Money Bills from two years over three sessions to one year over two sessions. No amendment was made to the provisions of the Parliament Act 1911 regarding Money Bills.

---

70   Bills certified by the Speaker as Money Bills, defined by the Parliament Act 1911, s 1(2).

Exclusions from the Parliament Acts

The Parliament Acts do not apply to private Bills, Bills originating in the House of Lords, Bills containing financial measures but not certified as Money Bills (because they contain other non-money provisions), statutory instruments or Bills purporting to extend the life of a Parliament beyond the five years laid down in the Septennial Act 1715, as amended by section 7 of the Parliament Act 1911.

The use of the Parliament Acts

It is notable that the Parliament Acts have been used infrequently. Aside from the Parliament Act 1949, which was passed under the 1911 Act, only the Government of Ireland Act 1914, the Welsh Church Act 1914 and the War Crimes Act 1991 have been passed under this procedure. The explanation for this fact largely lies in conventional practices regulating the relationship between the two Houses. First, as has been seen above, the House of Commons accepts a great many Lords' amendments, for a variety of reasons. Secondly, the House of Lords exercises its delaying powers with some caution. In debate on the War Damage Bill 1965, Lord Salisbury stated that the House of Lords should insist on amendments under two circumstances:

(a) if a matter raises issues important enough to justify such 'drastic' action;

(b) if the issue is such that the electorate can understand it and express approval for the House of Lord's position. In this regard, the House of Lords acts as a 'watchdog of the people'.

In 1975, in debate, Lord Carrington[71] stated that:

(a) the House of Lords should not insist on opposing a government Bill for which there is a mandate from the people (the 'Salisbury doctrine');[72]

(b) but that the House of Lords may impose delay if the constitution otherwise would be at risk; or

(c) if public opinion was against the government.

Lord Carrington asserted that, in rare cases, the Lords could legitimately enforce a delay so as to cause a reassessment by the government and the people. Thirdly, if the House of Lords strongly disapproves of a measure but does not wish to defeat the Bill, it may move a resolution deploring parts of the Bill, as occurred in relation to the Immigration Bill 1971 and the British Nationality Act 1981. Fourthly, many disagreements between the House of Commons and the House of Lords will be resolved by negotiations between the two Houses which generally will result in the avoidance of ultimate

---

71 HL Deb Vol 365 Col 1742, 11 November 1975.
72 HL Deb Vol 261 Col 66, 4 November 1964.

deadlock. Finally, the Parliament Act procedure may be avoided under the amendment procedure laid down in s 2(4) of the Parliament Act 1911. Under that section, the Acts may only be used if the House of Lords, over two successive sessions, rejects the same Bill. A Bill will be deemed to be the same Bill if it is identical with the former Bill 'or contains only such alterations as are certified by the Speaker to be necessary owing to the time which has elapsed since the date of the former Bill, or to represent any amendments which have been made by the House of Lords in the former Bill in the preceding session'.[73] If amendments have been made which are not agreed to by the Commons, the Bill is deemed to be rejected. This formulation facilitates agreements between the two Houses, yet preserves the ultimate possible use of the Parliament Act procedure. Three Bills over which conflict was ultimately avoided by this process were the Temperance (Scotland) Bill 1913; the Trades Union and Labour Relations Bill 1975–76 and the Shipbuilding Industry Bill 1976–77.

A contemporary illustration of the working of the amendment procedure is provided by the Teaching and Higher Education Bill 1997 which was introduced into the House of Lords and thus not susceptible to the Parliament Act procedure. The government intended to introduce tuition fees for students at Scottish universities which would have the effect of penalising students attending those universities from England, Wales and Northern Ireland, but not Scottish students. The House of Lords, objecting on principle to this discriminatory treatment between Scottish and other students, amended the offending section. The House of Commons rejected the amendment. On the Bill's return to the House of Lords, on two further occasions, the House of Lords introduced a newly worded amendment – an amendment *in lieu* – which had the same substantive effect of removing the alleged discrimination.[74] The House of Lords had thus rejected the government's proposal three times, risking the loss of the Bill in the 1997–98 session. The Secretary of State for Education, David Blunkett, rejected the House of Lords' view, and claimed that, while 'it is right that the Lords should scrutinise it [the Bill]', having had 'its advice rejected three times by the elected House – on a matter with financial consequences – it cannot be right for the unelected House, yet again, to refuse to accept that decision'.[75] Compromise was, however, reached. The House of Lords finally agreed to accept the will of the Commons, but only after securing the government's agreement to 'consider the recommendations ... very seriously' made by a

---

73 Erskine May, T, *Parliamentary Practice*, 21st edn, 1989, London: Butterworths, p 533 (see, now, 22nd edn, 1997).

74 The Parliament Act 1911, as amended by the Parliament Act 1949, s 2(4), provides for this 'ping pong' procedure, by (in part) deeming a Bill to be the same Bill only where 'it is identical with the former Bill ...'.

75 (1998) *The Times*, 14 July.

newly established independent review body which is to examine fee arrangements.

Conflict between the House of Commons and House of Lords also arose in July 1998 over proposed provisions in the Crime and Disorder Bill 1998, which lowered the age of consent for sexual intercourse between males from 18 to 16. The rejection of the clause by the House of Lords, on a vote of 290 to 122 against the reform, came within two weeks of the end of the parliamentary session. However, with the session so near to its end, the government chose to drop the provision rather than risk the loss of the Bill.

Suspension Motions

The Suspension Motion is a device currently available in relation to Private Bills which facilitates their passage through Parliament. Where the Suspension Motion is agreed by the House of Commons, a Private Bill may be carried over form one session to another, without the loss of that Bill.

The House of Commons Procedure Committee and the House of Lords Procedure Committee have recently agreed to extend the procedure to Public Bills. Where a Bill is in the Commons at the end of one session, and a Suspension Motion is agreed, that Bill will be able to continue its life into the next session. However, the procedure is not designed to 'rescue' contentious Bills over which the two Houses disagree.[76] Rather, the procedure will apply to those Bills which the government notifies to the House of Commons as candidates for the 'carry over' procedure. It will be for the Commons to agree the motion to suspend the Bill, should the need arise.

The House of Lords and Conservative and Labour governments – pre-1999

It is frequently asserted by proponents of reform of the House of Lords that the House of Lords is dominated by Conservative Members and, accordingly, is ideologically opposed to the Labour Party and will be more active in revising or rejecting Bills during a Labour government.

Such preconceptions should be treated with caution. Research evidence suggests that the House of Lords does not act in a predictable fashion in relation to legislative proposals of either Labour or Conservative governments. In part, this is due to the fluctuating membership of the Lords, from which it is seen that there is no overall majority for any one political party – still less a dominance of Conservatives – at any particular point in

---

76 Eg, the Crime and Disorder Bill 1998, which provided for the lowering of the age of consent to sexual intercourse between men .

time. It is unsurprising, therefore, to find that, for the most part, the House of Lords cannot be relied upon to exhibit any one particular party-political bias.

If the House of Lords were – as has been claimed by some – ideologically opposed to Labour governments, it might be expected that Labour's legislation is amended to a greater extent than that of the Conservative governments. However, whereas the picture presented by statistics reveal that, prior to 1979, the Labour government's legislative proposals fared particularly badly in the House of Lords,[77] since 1979, the House of Lords has actively amended – with much success – Conservative legislative proposals. The Thatcher government between 1979 and 1989 was forced to accept 125 amended Bills rather than risk the possible damage to its legislative programme. In the three years between March 1980 and April 1983, the Conservative government suffered 10 major defeats at the hands of the Lords.[78] The government's attempt to abolish elections to the Greater London Council under the Local Government (Interim Provisions Bill) 1984 in advance of its abolition was rejected by the House of Lords and the government was forced to accept the House of Lord's 'wrecking' amendment. The Community Charge Bill 1988, introducing the Poll Tax as a substitute for the local government rating system, aroused such public hostility that there was rioting in the streets. The House of Lords, mindful of public opinion, opposed the Bill, which was passed ultimately only by the government bringing in the 'backwoodsmen'[79] to ensure a vote in favour of the Bill, which was secured by 317 to 183 votes. The House of Lords rejected outright the War Crimes Bill 1990.[80] When the Bill was rejected at second reading for the second time in the Lords, the government resorted to the Parliament Act procedure for the first time in over 70 years.[81] This record of activity against Conservative legislation seems difficult, indeed impossible, to reconcile with the image of a complacent, Conservative minded and dominated Upper House.

It may be argued, although there is no evidence, that the House of Lords is less likely to oppose Labour legislation for fear of reactivating the traditional hostility of the Labour Party towards the unelected House.[82] Conversely, the argument runs that, under a Conservative government, the House of Lords

---

77 Suffering 116 defeats between 1964 and 1970, 355 defeats between 1974 and 1979.

78 On the Education Bill; Housing Bill; British Nationality Bill; BBC External Services (Motion); Oil and Gas Enterprise Bill; Employment Bill; Ordnance Survey (Motion); Housing and Building Control Bill. See Shell, D, 'The House of Lords and the Thatcher government' (1983) 38 Parl Aff 16.

79 Those peers entitled to sit and vote in the Upper House, but who normally play no role in the Lords.

80 On 4 June 1990, the Lords rejected the Bill by 207 votes to 74, a majority of 133.

81 Second Reading of the Bill occurred in the second Session on 18 March 1991, where it was approved by 254 votes to 88, a majority of 166.

82 This argument is not substantiated by recent evidence. The House of Lords has opposed the Labour government, elected in May 1997, by inflicting 28 defeats on legislative proposals within 14 months.

has greater confidence, which reflects itself in more robust criticism and opposition to legislative proposals. Certainly, the evidence makes it clear that a Conservative government cannot rely on the quiet acquiescence of the Upper House.

SELECT COMMITTEES IN THE HOUSE OF LORDS

The House of Lords has no structured system of select committees as exists in the House of Commons. However, three types of select committees exist in the Lords. The House may establish *ad hoc* committees to consider a matter of public importance: such committees have considered Sport and Leisure (1971–72), Unemployment (1979–82), Overseas Trade (1984–85), Murder and Life Imprisonment (1988–89). Domestic select committees exist to consider matters of procedure and privileges of the House. In addition, as has been seen, Bills may be committed to select committee for in depth consideration and report.

Seventeen sessional committees exist.[83] The most significant of these are the European Community Select Committee and the Science and Technology Committee. The former was established in 1974 to consider Commission[84] proposals for European legislation. The committee has acquired a reputation for authoritative scrutiny of the proposals. The committee has a salaried chairman and 24 permanent Members, a considerable staff of clerks and legal advisers and has the right to appoint expert advisers as and when needed. The committee also has the power to appoint sub-committees.[85] Each year, the select committee produces some 20 reports, all of which (unlike those of the House of Commons) are debated in the Chamber. The government undertakes to respond to the reports within two months, and not later than three months, of a report's publication. The European Community Select Committee's terms of reference are:

> To consider Community proposals whether in draft or otherwise, to obtain all necessary information about them, and to make reports on those which, in the opinion of the committee, raise important questions to which the committee considers that the special attention of the House should be drawn.

---

83 Two Appeal Committees; two Appellate Committees; Leave of Absence and Expenses Committee; Personal Bills; Hybrid Instruments; Standing Orders (Private Bills); Joint Select Committees on Consolidation Bill; Statutory Instruments; European Communities; House of Lords Offices; Committee for Privileges; Procedure; Science and Technology, Committee of Selection; Committee on Broadcasting: see, further, *op cit*, Erskine May, fn 75, pp 582–85.

84 See Chapter 8.

85 Six sub-committees have been established, considering such diverse matters as Law and Institutions, Energy, Transport and Technology, Environment, Finance, Trade and External Relations.

The committee has seven sub-committees: Economic and Financial Affairs; Trade and External Relations; Energy, Industry and Transport; Environment, Public Health and Consumer Protection; Agriculture, Fisheries and Food; Law and Institutions; Social Affairs, Education and Home Affairs. In addition, *ad hoc* committees are established to deal with specific proposals.

With the establishment of the European Union in 1992, the House of Lords' European Communities Committee took the view that aspects of the Union's work should be scrutinised by the national Parliament.[86] The Common Foreign and Security Policy pillar of the Union, and the Justice and Home Affairs pillar do not involve legislation, but inter-governmental co-operation. The committee took the view that documents should be provided to Parliament if they qualify under one of three tests, namely: significance; eventual need for United Kingdom legislation or the imposition of legal commitments on the United Kingdom.[87]

The Science and Technology Select Committee of the House of Lords was set up in 1980. The committee is unique in that it provides a forum for inquiry, examination, debate and recommendation over an important subject which is not represented in any one House of Commons committee. Subjects which have been given in depth examination include Hazardous Waste Disposal (1980–81), Civil Research and Development (1986–87) and Priorities in Medical Research (1987–88). The government undertakes to respond to reports of the committee in writing. Reports are debated in the Chamber of the House of Lords.

The Steering Committee

In order to co-ordinate better the work of committees in the Lords, a Steering Committee has been introduced. The committee serves functions similar to those of the Liaison Committee in the Commons – namely, deciding on subjects for investigation by ad hoc select committees, allocating resources between differing select committees and monitoring the work of the committees.

Members' interests in the Lords

In November 1995, a Register of Members' Interests was established, in which a number of interests must be recorded. The requirements are that three categories of interests must be registered, namely:

---

86 House of Lords, *Twenty-Eighth Report*, 1992–93.
87 The government agreed: see Cm 2471, 1994, London: HMSO.

(a) consultancies or other similar arrangements involving payment or other incentive or reward for providing parliamentary advice or services. Registration under this category is mandatory;

(b) financial interests in businesses involved in parliamentary lobbying on behalf of clients. This requirement is also mandatory;

(c) other particulars relating to matters which the Lords consider may affect the public perception of the way in which they discharge their parliamentary duties. Registration under this category is discretionary.

Interests should be declared in debate whenever Lords have a direct financial interest in a subject, along with any other interest which might affect the judgment of the House. The Committee on Lords' Interests has power to investigate allegations of failure to comply with the requirements. The register is published annually.

REFORM OF THE HOUSE OF LORDS

> With a perfect Lower House it is certain that an Upper House would be scarcely of any value ... But though beside an ideal House of Commons the Lords would be unnecessary, and therefore pernicious, beside the actual House a revising and leisured legislature is extremely useful ...[88]

From the earliest times, the granting of a peerage – and the right to sit in the House of Lords – has been a political act. The House of Lords, itself mindful of the Crown's power to manipulate the membership of the House, tried in the past to limit the number of peerages which could be created by the Crown by setting a maximum number of Members of the House.[89]

Both the Labour and Liberal Democrat Parties have long had proposals to reform the House of Lords. As see above, the current Labour government is translating its commitment into reality, as a first step removing the right of the majority of hereditary peers to sit and vote. In the past, the Labour Party has advocated total abolition of the Upper House. Much of the antagonism to the Lords stems from basic principles of democracy, its opponents centering on the fundamental paradox of a sophisticated democratic State having, as part of its legislative body, an unelected and democratically unaccountable institution. Before the issue of principle and its implications for reform can be addressed, it is essential to understand the actual working of the House. A note of caution regarding these important matters should be observed at this early stage. SA de Smith and R Brazier[90] make the pertinent observation that:

---

88 Bagehot, W, *The English Constitution* (1867), 1993, London: Fontana, pp 133–34.

89 In 1719 and 1720: the Bills were rejected by the Commons.

90 de Smith, SA and Brazier, R, *Constitutional and Administrative Law*, 6th edn, 1989, London: Penguin, p 311 (see, now, 8th edn, 1998).

Agreement in principle amongst the sophisticated tends to be less than whole hearted and to beget new disagreements when principle is translated into detail. Real enthusiasm for Lords' reform is too often to be found among the eccentric and the naive, who may have little idea of the mediocre performance of second chambers in so many other countries or of the limited expectations that can reasonably be reposed in a reconstituted British second chamber.

As noted above, the preamble to the Parliament Act 1911 envisaged replacing the House of Lords with an elected House:

And whereas it is intended to substitute for the House of Lords as it at present exists a Second Chamber constituted on a popular instead of hereditary basis, but such substitution cannot be immediately brought into operation ...

This did not represent the first proposal to reform the House of Lords. As early as 1886 and 1888, debate took place in the House of Commons on the desirability or otherwise of an hereditary element in the legislature. As has been seen above, the constitutional conflict between the House of Lords and Commons in 1908–10 resulted in the restriction on the Lords' powers and the intent to replace the House of Lords.

In 1917, a conference comprising 15 Members of each House was established, under the chairmanship of Viscount Bryce, to consider the composition and powers of the Upper House. Reporting in 1918, the conference recommended that the Upper House should consist of 246 Members indirectly elected by Members of Parliament grouped into regional units, plus 81 Members chosen by a joint standing committee of both Houses of Parliament. The conference regarded the appropriate functions of this revised chamber to be the examination and revision of Commons Bills, the initiation of non-controversial Bills, the discussion of policy, and the 'interposition of so much delay (and no more) in the passing of a Bill into law as may be needed to enable the opinion of the nation to be adequately expressed upon it'. No action was taken on the recommendations.

Following the First World War, reform of the House of Lords remained on the political agenda. A Cabinet committee established to consider the matter rejected the Bryce conference proposals as unacceptable. In 1922, the government put forward proposals for a House of Lords made up of 350 Members. The majority of these were to be either directly or indirectly elected 'from the outside', with the remainder comprising some hereditary peers elected by peers, plus Members nominated by the Crown. The precise numbers of these latter categories were to be laid down in statute. No action resulted from these proposals. Between 1924 and 1935 one further set of Cabinet committee proposals was rejected, as were three Private Members' Bills introduced by Conservative peers in 1929, 1933 and 1935. The Parliament Act 1949, discussed above, was passed by the Labour government and remains the basis for the relationship between the Houses of Commons and Lords today.

Reform remained on the agenda in the 1950s, the Conservative Party *Manifesto* of 1951 promising a further all-party conference on reform. The Labour Party in 1953 declined to co-operate and no further action was taken. In 1958, two significant reforms were introduced by the Conservative government. The first of these related to the problem of the 'backwoodsmen': those peers who make no contribution to the work of the House but nevertheless retain the right to sit and vote when called upon to do so by the government. The report of a House of Lords select committee recommended that Standing Orders be amended to enable those peers who did not regularly attend the House to take leave of absence. This recommendation was adopted but, as has been noted earlier, it has not produced an effective solution to the problem posed by the 'backwoodsmen'. The remaining defect lies in the fact that, even where leave of absence has been obtained, there is no mechanism existing whereby a peer can be denied the right to enter the House, even if he has not complied with the requirement to give once month's notice of his intention to return to the House.

The Life Peerage Act 1958

The second reform of 1958 was the introduction of the Life Peerage Act. This Act enables the Crown, on the advice of the Prime Minister, to confer peerages for life on men and women who have reached prominence in public life. This single reform has effectively revitalised the Upper House, providing an increased resource of specialisation and experience. By convention, life peerages are conferred on Members of any political party, and on those who have no particular political affiliation. Towards this end, the leaders of the major political parties put forward nominations to the Prime Minister on an annual basis. The Labour Party in the 1980s refused to make any nominations at all, basing their refusal on principled objection to the elitist nature of the House of Lords. This stance has proven to be something of an 'own goal' for the Labour Party, whose membership of the House of Lords is now smaller than it might otherwise have been.

The Peerage Act 1963

In 1963, a more limited, but nonetheless important, reform was implemented. The Peerage Act 1963 has its origins in the succession to a peerage by Anthony Wedgwood-Benn (as he then was), a Member of the House of Commons. As a result of succeeding to the title of Viscount Stansgate, Tony Benn, the Member for Bristol South East[91] was barred from taking his seat in the Commons. A

---

91 See *Re Parliamentary Election for Bristol South-East* [1964] 2 QB 257; [1961] 3 WLR 577.

joint committee of the Houses of Commons and Lords reported on this matter in 1962 and recommended reform. As noted earlier, the Peerage Act 1963 provides that a person succeeding to a peerage may disclaim his peerage within one year of his succession,[92] and that a Member of the House of Commons may disclaim within a one month period from succession. The disclaimer is irrevocable, but operates only for the lifetime of the peer disclaiming the title: the title will devolve to his heir upon his death. Section 6 of the the Peerage Act 1963 provides for the first time that peeresses in their own right are entitled to sit and vote in the House of Lords.

The 1968 reform proposals

The Labour government of 1967–69 again turned its attention to reform of the composition of the House of Lords. The party *Manifesto* of 1966 declared the intention to introduce reforms to safeguard measures approved by the House of Commons against delay or defeat in the House of Lords. An all-party conference took place in 1967–68, at which substantial cross-party agreement was reached on the proposals for reform. The resultant government White Paper of 1968[93] proposed that there should be a two tier House. The first tier would consist of 230 voting peers who satisfied a test of attendance on a regular basis. The second tier would consist of peers who remained entitled to attend and to participate in debate, but would not be entitled to vote. The right to a seat in the House of Lords by virtue of succession to a peerage would be removed but existing peers (who did not satisfy the attendance criteria) would either become non-voting peers or might be conferred a life peerage with entitlement to vote. It was recommended that the government of the day should have a small, but not overall, majority of voting peers in the House. The White Paper also recommended that the power of delay by the House of Lords be reduced to a six month period. The White Paper was approved by the House of Lords by 251 votes to 56. An alliance of the far right of the Conservative Party and the left wing of the Labour Party in the House of Commons caused the White Paper to be rejected by 270 votes to 159.

The government proceeded to introduce the Parliament (No 2) Bill 1968 to give effect to the White Paper. The Bill received a Second Reading by 285 votes to 185, but the committee stage, taken as a committee of the Whole House, became protracted and, after over 80 hours of consideration, the Prime Minister announced the withdrawal of the Bill.

---

92 Or on attaining the age of majority.
93 Cmnd 3799, 1968, London: HMSO.

OPTIONS FOR REFORM OF THE HOUSE OF LORDS

Outright abolition of the House of Lords?

The vast majority of States have a bicameral legislature comprised of elected Members. If a unicameral Parliament were adopted in the United Kingdom a number of important consequences would follow. First, the volume of legislation and the role of the House of Lords has been examined above. With a unicameral Parliament, means would have to be found to reform procedures in such a manner as to cope adequately with the volume of work currently undertaken by the Lords.

Secondly, the Parliament Act 1911 does not apply to a Bill attempting to extend the life of a Parliament and, hence, the House of Lords acts as a constitutional safeguard against a government seeking to avoid the judgment of the electorate. The life of Parliament has been extended in the past: during both the First and Second World Wars, elections were suspended. These times, however, were exceptional, and the life of Parliament was extended only with all-party agreement, and the agreement of the Lords.

Thirdly, the second chamber, with its revising powers, is able to delay, if not defeat, proposed legislation. As has been seen above, the power to delay is exercised with circumspection, and under understood conditions. This power is of particular constitutional significance in the United Kingdom, which currently employs an electoral system which invariably, but not inevitably, results in a government having a strong majority in the Commons. The knowledge that its legislation may be delayed, and ultimately defeated, unless the government is willing to invoke the Parliament Act procedure, acts as an important psychological restraint on government.

Fourthly, a second chamber, constituted differently from the House of Commons, is able to make a valuable contribution to the revision of legislation and scrutiny of government. To abolish the Upper House would be to deprive Parliament as a whole of this contribution. Abolition, for these reasons, is not a viable option in the United Kingdom.

Reform of the composition of the Lords

The aspect of the House of Lords' composition today which attracts most opposition is the hereditary element. As has been seen, such objections have been being voiced for over 100 years. It is unarguable that, in a twentieth century democracy, it is anomalous (at least) and, in principle, objectionable that the legislative proposals of the elected government, approved by the elected House of Commons, can be amended or defeated by an unelected, unaccountable Upper House.

The Labour government's reform agenda

The first commitment made in relation to the House of Lords by the Labour Party before its election to office in 1997, was to abolish, as a first measure, the voting rights of hereditary peers. Consistent with this proposal is the removal of the right of members of the Royal Family to vote in the House of Lords. The government's ultimate objective, as stated in its election *Manifesto*, was to replace the current House of Lords with a new elected second chamber, elected under a system of proportional representation. The elected House, according to the *Manifesto*, would have the power to delay, for the lifetime of a Parliament, changes to 'designated legislation reducing individual or constitutional rights'. However, as will be seen below, the Labour Party's plans for reforming the Lords changed significantly once elected to government.

The Liberal Democrat Party also favoured an elected second chamber. The Liberal Democrat proposals are for a directly elected Senate of 225 Members, elected by proportional representation in the form of the single transferable vote.[94] The Senate would have a fixed six year term of office. In addition, provision would be made for 60 nominated Members to be chosen, not by the Prime Minister, but by a committee of the Senate. The Senate would have full power to delay Bills, other than Money Bills, for up to two years. It would also have special powers in relation to constitutional matters.[95]

Once in office, the Labour government moved cautiously. Removing the right of hereditary peers was the first step towards reform. A Royal Commission was established to consider the next phase in reform and to make recommendations. However, the second stage was postponed until after the general election (expected in 2001) with no clear commitment as to the government's ultimate preference for reform.

All reform of the House of Lords is problematic. The 1968 reforms failed to be implemented, not because of opposition in the House of Lords, but through opposition in the House of Commons, which crossed party lines. The opposition arose from the Commons' perception that removing the right of hereditary peers to vote would enhance the authority of the House of Lords, and would risk the Lords becoming more bold in its dealing with the House of Commons. One key question for the Royal Commission and the government, therefore, is how to move forward to the second reform stage in order to produce an effective and valuable second chamber without threatening the supremacy of the democratically elected House of Commons.

---

94 On which, see Chapter 13.

95 It should be noted that the Liberal Democrat proposals exist within the context of wider constitutional change, resulting in a written Constitution, changes to which would require a two-thirds majority in both Houses of Parliament.

The problem of legitimacy remains after the removal of the hereditary peers' right to vote. Given the fact of political patronage, for services rendered to the Party or country, the life peers have no more constitutional legitimacy than do hereditary peers.[96] Thus, removing the hereditary peers from the House of Lords does not effect any constitutional change of real value, and certainly does not mark a move towards greater democratic legitimacy, but represents no more than a starting point for further, largely undefined, future reform, the consequences of which, in terms of the distribution of power between the two Houses, will depend on both the nature and scope of the reform, and will remain uncertain until specified. Until the government reveals its intentions in relation to the final composition and role of the House of Lords, even the relatively modest issue of removing the right of hereditary peers remains contentious.

In the absence of the government finalising its proposals for the second phase of reform of the House of Lords, two Conservative Party groups published their own proposals and urged the party to adopt a more constructive stance in relation to reform of the Lords. Both called for a second chamber with a membership comprising a mix of appointed and elected members, and both agreed that to leave the House of Lords with an entirely appointed composition secures an unacceptable level of power to the Prime Minister. Each expressed scepticism as to the government's announced intention to move to a second phase of reform. The Conservative Policy Forum paper suggested a House with approximately 300 paid members, part elected by proportional representation and part appointed. The Tory Reform Group paper called for a House having 160 regionally elected members, serving nine year terms of office, 91 independent life peers and 50 non-voting hereditary peers representing rural communities.

The Royal Commission Report: a House for the future

The Royal Commission Report was published in January 2000. To the disappointment of those advocating radical reform, the Commission recommended that the Upper House, having around 550 members, comprise a majority of nominated members and a minority of selected or elected members representing regional interests. However, despite widespread consultation, the Commission reached no consensus on the most difficult issue: the number of selected or elected members and the method by which members would be selected.

The powers of the second chamber would remain broadly as they are at present, with the second chamber being able to delay, but ultimately not to

96 The Labour government is redressing the party political imbalance between life peers by appointing Labour 'working peers' to the House.

defeat, primary legislation. The Salisbury convention should continue to be respected. The report recommends that there be greater use of pre-legislative scrutiny of Bills. In relation to secondary legislation, the second chamber should be given power to delay their implementation and to voice its concerns. The power to defeat secondary legislation – in practice, never used – would be removed.

In relation to composition, three options were put forward. Model A provided for 65 members selected by dividing up a regional allocation of seats according to each party's share of the vote in that region at general elections, with one third of the regions selecting regional members at each general election. Model B, supported by a majority of the Commission, proposes 87 members, directly elected at the same time as the European Parliament elections under a system of proportional representation. Model C provides for 195 regional members directly elected at the same time as the European Parliament elections.

On the system of nominations for the House, the Commission recommended that an independent Appointments Commission be established. The Commission would have eight members, three nominated by the main political parties, one nominated by cross benchers (independents), and four independents, one of which should be chairman or woman. Establishing the Commission would sever the link between the granting of honours and the political patronage of the Prime Minister and government. Members of the House of Lords – the new name for which the Commission did not decide – would not be known as 'peers'. The current system of granting of honours would remain, but would not result in membership of the House of Lords. The granting of a peerage is therefore no longer to be a precondition for membership of the second chamber. The remaining hereditary peers will cease to be entitled to sit and vote once the regional members join the second chamber. Hereditary peers will, however, be eligible to seek nomination as regional members or apply for appointment by the Appointments Commission. The Commission will be under a duty to maintain balance in the composition of the House of Lords. The Commission should ensure that at least 20 per cent of the members are not affiliated to one of the major parties; it should be under a statutory duty to ensure that a minimum of 30 per cent of new members are female, with the aim of gradually achieving gender balance within the House. It will also be required to attempt to ensure a representative level of membership from ethnic minority groups, and appropriate representation for all religious faiths. Regional members would serve for the equivalent of 'three electoral cycles' and appointed members should serve for a fixed 15 year term. The earliest the new system for regional members would operate be 2004.

The Commission recommended that existing life peers, appointed before the publication of the report, who wish to remain in the second chamber should be deemed to have been appointed for life, whereas life peers appointed between the publication of the report and the necessary legislation implementing the report's recommendations should be deemed to be appointed for a 15 year term from the date of the award of the life peerage.

On remuneration, the Commission recommended that the financial arrangements be adequate to make regular attendance economically viable, and that remuneration should be linked to attendance in Parliament. Payments made, however, for time and lost income should be less than the basic salary of a Member of Parliament over an average session.

The report's recommendations are far removed from the aspirations of those seeking a democratically elected second chamber. That radical option foundered on the problem of the constitutional balance of power between two elected chambers, and the fear – which has always dogged reform of the House of Lords – that the Commons might lose its supremacy. But the Wakeham Report does foresee a second chamber with at least the same powers as the current House of Lords, and one which is broadly representative of British society. In breaking the link between peerages and membership of the second chamber, the Commission has removed one of the most contentious aspects of the political honours system in which membership of the second chamber is seen to be conferred for political services to the governing party. Instead, the Commission seeks a second chamber which 'should be authoritative, confident, and broadly representative of the whole of British society', and its members should have a breadth of experience outside the world of politics, skills and knowledge relevant to the careful assessment of constitutional matters. The Commission stated that its intention was to recommend proposals which were not only 'persuasive and intellectually coherent but also workable, durable and politically realistic'.

The government signalled its acceptance in principle of the Wakeham Report. A Joint Committee of both Houses of Parliament is to consider the details of the report. The Leader of the House of Lords, Baroness Jay, made it clear that no legislation would be introduced before the next general election.

The Life Peerages (Appointments Commission) Bill 2000 provides for the establishment of a Commission to made proposals for the conferment of life peerages under the Life Peerages Act 1958. Under clause 1(1), the Commission will make proposals to the Prime Minister for recommendations to Her Majesty for the conferment of life peerages. The Commission has the status of an advisory non-departmental public body and will be appointed in accordance with the rules of the Commissioner for Public Appointments, from whom the Commission may seek advice concerning attracting and assessing potential nominees. The Commission is to consist of eight members of the Privy Council, of whom four shall be appointed by a special Commission of the Prime Minister, the Speaker of the House of Commons, and the Lord

Chairman of Committees of the House of Lords.[97] Each of the three largest parties in the House of Commons shall appoint one Commissioner on the nomination of the Leader of each party, and one Commissioner shall be appointed from the cross bench members on the nomination of the Convenor of the cross bench peers.[98]

The Commission is to operate 'an open and transparent nominations system for members of the House of Lords not belonging to, or recommended by, any political party', and actively invite nominations from the general public, professional associations, charities and other public bodies. The Commission will also reinforce the function of the Political Honours Scrutiny Committee in vetting the suitability of all nominations, and in particular scrutinise all nominations for life peerages on the grounds of propriety in relation to political donations.[99]

Nominations as cross bench members (independents) are to be proposed to the Prime Minister at least once a year, and at most every six months, 'at least to fill any vacancies ... that may occur through death, disqualification or a decision to join a political party' represented in the House of Lords.[100] The Prime Minister may not refuse to submit nominations for cross bench members to the Queen, and must not seek to influence such nominations, 'save in exceptional circumstances, such as those endangering the security of the realm'.[101] When considering nominations as cross bench members, the Commission is not to give any additional weight to recommendations from the Prime Minister or leaders of other political parties.[102]

An annual report is to be made by the Commission to Parliament on recommendations made to the Queen, and the report will declare if the following criteria are being observed, namely that:

(a) no one political party commands a majority in the House of Lords;

(b) there is broad parity of numbers between the number of members of the House of Lord who support Her Majesty's Government and the number of those who support the main opposition party in the House of Lords; and

(c) the proportion of the cross bench members to the total number of members of the House of Lords holding life peerages under the 1958 Act remains as it was on the day before the passing of the House of Lords Act 1999.[103]

---

97 Life Peerages (Appointments Commission) Bill 2000 , cl 1(8).
98 *Ibid*, cl 1(9).
99 *Ibid*, cl 1(2).
100 *Ibid*, cl 1(4).
101 *Ibid*, cl 1(5).
102 *Ibid*, cl 1(6).
103 *Ibid*, cl 1(7).

CHAPTER 18

PARLIAMENTARY PRIVILEGE

DEFINITION AND CONSTITUTIONAL SIGNIFICANCE OF PRIVILEGE

The privileges of Parliament are those rules of both Houses of Parliament which offer protection from outside interference – from whatever source – to the Houses collectively, and to individual Members.[1] Erskine May defines privilege as being:

> ... the sum of the peculiar rights enjoyed by each House collectively as a constituent part of the High Court of Parliament, and by Members of each House individually, without which they could not discharge their functions, and which exceed those possessed by other bodies or individuals. Thus, privilege, though part of the law of the land, is to a certain extent an exemption from the general law.[2]

Parliamentary privilege provides protection for Members of Parliament against accusations of defamation from outside Parliament and also protects the individual Member – in the exercise of his or her freedom of speech – from the executive.

Parliamentary privilege presents some intriguing constitutional issues. In some respects, privilege may be compared with the royal prerogative,[3] in so far as both privilege and the prerogative represent a unique aspect of legal power reserved exclusively for a special class of persons. Moreover, parliamentary privilege is a legal power in respect of which the courts – mindful of the doctrine of separation of powers[4] – will be cautious in accepting jurisdiction to regulate. By asserting special powers and immunities for Parliament as a whole, and for its Members individually, Parliament throws around itself a cloak of protection which provides rights and immunities not accorded to individual citizens. The balance which is – and ought to be – struck between legitimate and necessary safeguards for Parliament and its Members in the exercise of parliamentary duties and the

---

1   See Erskine May, T, *Parliamentary Practice*, 22nd edn, 1997, London: Butterworths; Wilson, G, *Cases and Materials on Constitutional and Administrative Law*, 2nd edn 1976, Cambridge: CUP; Munro, CR, *Studies in Constitutional Law*, 2nd edn, 1999, London: Butterworths; Griffith, JAG, and Ryle, M, *Parliament: Functions, Practice and Procedures*, 1989, London: Sweet & Maxwell.

2   *Ibid*, Erskine May, p 69.

3   See Chapter 6.

4   See Chapter 5.

rights of individuals to the protection of the general law is not always satisfactorily achieved.

The law and practice of privilege reveals the extent to which individual Members and Parliament as a body are free from outside pressure – whether from interest groups, sponsoring bodies and institutions or the media – a freedom which is central to ensure an independent Parliament. However, as Marshall and Moodie point out, 'the boundary lines between free comment, legitimate pressure, and improper interference are obviously not easy to formulate in principle'.[5] This issue came to the fore in 1994, and was the subject of a judicial inquiry, the details of which are given below.

The issue of privilege rose in prominence as a result of numerous allegations of improper conduct made against a small number of Members of Parliament in the last few years of Conservative government rule, which ended in 1997. Partly as a consequence of these allegations and the resultant loss of public confidence in the probity of Members of Parliament, a Joint Committee of both Houses of Parliament undertook a wide ranging inquiry into privilege and made a number of recommendations for significant reform.[6]

The law and custom of Parliament

The privileges enjoyed form part of the 'law and custom of Parliament' – *lex et consuetudo parliamenti* – and, as such, it is for Parliament to adjudicate on matters of privilege, not the courts.[7] Privileges are embodied in rules of the Houses of Parliament. The United Kingdom Parliament, however, is not free to extend existing privileges by a mere resolution of the House: only statute can create new privileges.[8] Privileges derive from practice and tradition; they are thus customary in origin. Nevertheless, they are recognised as having the status of law, being the 'law and custom of Parliament'. Parliament itself can – in the exercise of its sovereign power – place privileges on a statutory basis. For example, in 1770, the Parliamentary Privilege Act withdrew the privilege of freedom from arrest from servants of Members of Parliament. Further, in 1689, Article IX of the Bill of Rights gave statutory recognition to the freedom of speech in Parliament. In 1868, Parliament ended its own jurisdiction to determine disputed elections, conferring jurisdiction on the courts.[9]

---

5   Marshall, G and Moodie, G, *Some Problems of the Constitution*, 5th edn, 1971, London: Hutchinson, p 112.
6   See below.
7   Coke, 1 Inst 15.
8   *Stockdale v Hansard* (1839) 9 Ad & E 1.
9   Administration of Justice Act 1868.

The role of the courts

The role of the courts in matters of privilege is confined to determining whether a privilege exists, and its scope. If the court rules that a disputed matter falls within parliamentary privilege the court will decline jurisdiction. This relationship between Parliament and the courts may be viewed in two ways. First, it could be viewed as the courts giving recognition to the supremacy – or sovereignty – of Parliament. Historically, Parliament was established as the High Court of Parliament, having legislative *and* judicial powers.[10] Accordingly, it was appropriate for the ordinary courts of law to defer to the highest court in the land. Nowadays, this justification is less well founded. It is unconvincing to portray Parliament, except when exercising its judicial function in enforcing and upholding privilege, as a judicial body.[11] The relationship between Parliament and the courts may also be explained by reference to the doctrine of the separation of powers. For the judiciary to rule on the legality of actions of Members of Parliament acting in their parliamentary capacity or on the actions of the House as a whole would, under current constitutional arrangements, place judges in a potentially dangerous position, exercising a controlling power over both the legislature and the executive within it.

THE PRINCIPAL PRIVILEGES

The principal individual privileges are freedom of speech in Parliament and freedom of Members from arrest in civil matters. The collective privileges of Parliament include the exclusive right to regulate composition and procedure, right of access to the Sovereign, the right to the 'favourable construction' by the Sovereign in relation to its actions. These are formally claimed by the Speaker, in the form of a Speaker's Petition to Her Majesty, at the opening of each new parliamentary session.

The privileges are substantially the same for both Houses of Parliament.[12] Each House has the sole right to regulate the privileges it enjoys – although neither House is free to extend its own privileges other than by statute – and, as a result, some minor differences may be discerned between the two Houses.

---

10 See McIlwain, CH, *The High Court of Parliament and its Supremacy*, 1910, New Haven: Yale UP.

11 See below for a discussion of recent criticism of the Committee of Privileges and the decision making process of the House of Commons in disciplining Members.

12 But see below on the 'privilege of peerage'.

Historical overview

Originally designed to protect the right of the King to the services of his advisers, the right to freedom from molestation and arrest was established early. By the sixteenth century, Parliament itself was assuming jurisdiction to regulate privilege, and privilege was increasingly being used to protect the fledgling Parliament from the power of the Crown. Nowadays, while a few privileges are principally of historical interest, the majority remain central to the working of Parliament.

Freedom from arrest

The first recorded statement of the right to freedom from arrest dates from 1340.[13] In 1404, the Commons formally claimed that members were privileged against arrest 'for debt, contract, or trespass of any kind according to the custom of the realm'.[14] The King, however, paid little heed and the matter was not finally resolved. In 1512, Strode, a Member of the Commons, was imprisoned under a court order for proposing certain Bills in Parliament. Parliament reacted by passing an Act declaring the proceedings against him void, and also that any future proceedings against its Members would be void.[15] In 1627, when King Charles I arrested and detained five knights, his action was challenged by an application for habeas corpus. The application failed, the court accepting the certificate of the Crown stating that they had been detained by special order of the King: *per speciale mandatum regis*.[16] In 1629, three Members were charged with uttering seditious words in debate and violence against the Speaker of the House. The Crown contended, and the court accepted, that privilege did not attach to seditious words or assault.[17] The Petition of Right 1628 declared the arbitrary power of detention unlawful. In 1640, the Habeas Corpus Act placed protection by writ of habeas corpus from the Crown on a statutory basis and, in 1641, the House declared that arrests of its Members were contrary to the law and privilege of Parliament.[18]

---

13 *Bulletin of the Institute of Historical Research*, 1970, Vol 43, pp 214–15, cited in *op cit*, Erskine May, fn 1, p 74.

14 *Ibid*.

15 *Strode's Case*, see Maitland, FW, *The Constitutional History of England*, 1908, Cambridge: CUP.

16 *Darnel's Case* (the *Five Knights' Case*) (1627) 3 St Tr 1.

17 *Eliot's Case* (1629) 3 St Tr 309.

18 CJ (1640–42) 203, 3 St Tr 235; 1 Hatsell 250–80, cited in *op cit*, Erskine May, fn 1, p 73.

Freedom of speech

An early example of the Commons protecting its own against the King is that of Thomas Haxey,[19] who, in 1397, laid a Bill before Parliament criticising Richard II. The House of Lords condemned Haxey to die as a traitor, but an Archbishop claimed he was a clerk, thereby giving him the protection of the clergy. He was later pardoned. The Commons subsequently declared that the action against him was contrary to their privileges.

Erskine May reports that the first recorded claim of privilege of speech was contained in the petition of Sir Thomas More in 1523, asking Henry VIII:

> ... to take all in good part, interpreting every man's words, how uncunningly soever they may be couched, to proceed yeat of a good zeale towards the profit of your Realme.[20]

This bold assertion met with no recorded reply, but it is thought that Henry was generally tolerant of the Commons since he had little to fear from it. Nevertheless, between that time and 1689, freedom of speech in Parliament remained a contended matter. In 1571, Elizabeth I warned the Commons that they would 'do well to meddle with no matters of State but such as should be propounded unto them, and to occupy themselves in other matters concerning the Commonwealth'.[21] Elizabeth maintained her grudging attitude to free speech, reminding the Speaker in 1593 that it was her prerogative not only to summon and dissolve Parliament but also to dictate what Members could discuss.[22] James I reasserted the supremacy of the Monarchy, stating in 1621 that the privileges of the Commons were derived from the 'grace and permission of our ancestors and us', and that privileges would be respected only to the extent that Members acted 'within their duty' – as the King saw it. Parliament's response was to draw up a protestation formally asserting, *inter alia*, that:

> Every Member of the House of Parliament hath, and of right ought to have, freedom of speech, to propound, treat, reason and bring to conclusion the same.[23]

The King's reaction was to remove the protestation from the Commons' Journal and dissolve Parliament.

The reign of Charles I[24] was dominated by the struggle between the King and Parliament, culminating in the Civil Wars of 1642–48 and the execution of

---

19 (1397) Rot Parl, iii 434.

20 *Op cit*, Erskine May, fn 1, p 72.

21 Cited in Lockyer, R, *Tudor and Stuart Britain 1471–1714*, 2nd edn, 1985, Harlow: Longman.

22 The penalty for flouting the Queen's will was either to be barred from the House or to be imprisoned: *ibid*, Lockyer, p 190.

23 *Ibid*, Lockyer, p 226.

24 1625–49.

Charles I in 1646. The Petition of Right asserted Parliament's power over the King in matters of taxation, imprisonment without good cause and the imposition of martial law. Charles I dissolved Parliament in 1629 and ruled for 11 years without Parliament.[25]

The Glorious Revolution of 1688 and the Declaration of Right was finally to settle the conflicts between Parliament and the Crown. The issue of free speech in Parliament was to be resolved by Article IX of the Bill of Rights 1689,[26] which conferred absolute protection – or legal immunity – for words spoken by Members of Parliament during the course of proceedings in Parliament.

THE CURRENT SCOPE AND ROLE OF PRIVILEGE

Freedom from arrest

For Members of the House of Commons, the freedom extends for 40 days before the start of and 40 days after the end of the session. For peers, the privilege protects from arrest in civil matters at all times. The freedom from arrest does not extend to criminal charges or convictions.[27]

Where the criminal law is concerned, there is no immunity, and the re-arrest of a Member of the House of Commons who had escaped from prison, in the Chamber of the House, was not contrary to privilege.[28] In 1939, a Member of Parliament – Captain Ramsay – was detained under defence regulations. His detention did not amount to a breach of privilege, although it would have done so had he been detained for words spoken in Parliament.[29]

Where a Member is arrested on a criminal charge, the Speaker of the House is notified and in turn will report to the House either orally or in writing. If a Member is detained on grounds of mental illness under the Mental Health Act 1983 then – following specialists' reports to the Speaker confirming the Member's illness and detention – his seat will be declared vacant.[30]

Nowadays, the freedom relates only to civil matters and is generally of little significance, given that, with one important exception, imprisonment for

---

25 On this reign under the royal prerogative, see Chapter 6.

26 See, further, below.

27 4 Rot Parl 357; 1 Hatsell 17–22, *Thorpe's Case* (1452) 5 Rot Parl 239; 1 Hatsell 28–34, cited in *op cit*, Erskine May, fn 1, Chapter 5, p 75; *John Wilke's Case* LJ (1760–64) 426; CJ (1761–64) 674; 15 Parl Hist 1362–78.

28 Lord Cochrane, 1815: CJ (1814–16) 186; Parl Deb (1814–15) 30, c 309, 336; Colchester ii, 534, 536, cited in *op cit*, Erskine May, fn 1, Chapter 7, p 95.

29 HC 164 (1939–40), London: HMSO.

30 See, further, Chapter 14.

debt has been abolished. The exception concerns the availability of imprisonment as a penalty for the non-payment of financial provision during marriage, upon divorce, and for children born outside marriage. In 1963, in the case of *Stourton v Stourton*,[31] a Member of the House of Lords was able to escape the sanction of prison for maintenance default by pleading privilege. It is anomalous that Members of Parliament should be immune from the law in even this limited manner. The Committee on Parliamentary Privilege recommended, in 1967, that the freedom be abolished,[32] but no action was taken.

Freedom of speech and 'proceedings in Parliament'

At the present day, it is more important to notice that this freedom of speech holds good not only against the Crown, but against private individuals also. A Member speaking in either House is quite outside the law of defamation:

> He may accuse any person of the basest crimes, may do so knowing that his words are false, and yet that person will be unable to take any action against him.[33, 34]

The most important privilege claimed by Parliament is freedom of speech. Article IX raises a question which has caused much difficulty for the courts.[35] It has been seen above that, if a matter falls within the privileges of Parliament, the courts will have no jurisdiction over the matter, other than to determine whether or not a matter of alleged privilege falls within the ambit of privilege. If a positive determination is made, jurisdiction to rule on the matter falls to Parliament and not the courts. In order to make such a determination in relation to freedom of speech, the courts are obliged to interpret Article IX of the Bill of Rights, and the phrase 'proceedings in Parliament'.

Some matters are settled. The Bill of Rights makes clear that freedom of speech in debate is protected from legal action and redress under the law of defamation. Debates and questions on the floor of the House and in standing and select committees are therefore clearly protected. Other situations are, or have been, less straightforward. For example, what is the situation where a Member of Parliament is discussing parliamentary matters outside the precincts of Parliament, or where a Member of Parliament writes to a Minister on such a matter? Moreover, what is the position where a Member writes to the Minister or another Member with regard to a matter which he wishes to

---

31   [1963] P 302.
32   HC 34 (1967–68), London: HMSO, p xxix.
33   *Op cit*, Maitland, fn 15, p 375.
34   On the Defamation Act 1996, see, further, p 691, below.
35   See Leopold, P, '"Proceedings in Parliament": the grey area' [1991] PL 475.

raise in Parliament, or which involves allegations made against bodies or persons outside Parliament, on which he requires further information before raising the issue in Parliament? Despite numerous suggestions for reform to inject greater clarity into the law, many matters remain unclear. The most recent consideration of the scope of proceedings in Parliament is discussed below.

The case law is instructive. In *Rivlin v Bilainkin*,[36] the plaintiff in an action for defamation had been granted an interim injunction to restrain the defendant from repeating the alleged defamation. The defendant repeated the defamatory remarks in letters and took them to the House of Commons, giving one to a messenger to deliver to a Member of Parliament and posting the other four, addressed to other Members, in the House of Commons' post office. In an action for an order committing the defendant for a breach of the injunction, the defendant argued that publication of the repetition of the libel was committed within the precincts of the House of Commons and was accordingly not actionable in a court of law. Mr Justice McNair declared himself:

> ... satisfied that no question of privilege arises, for a variety of reasons, and particularly I rely on the fact that the publication was not connected in any way with any proceedings in that House ...

In *Duncan Sandys's* case, in 1938, Mr Duncan Sandys had sent to the Secretary of State for War the draft of a parliamentary question in which he drew attention to a shortage of military equipment. Within the draft, Mr Sandys quoted figures which, in the view of the War Office, could have been obtained only as a result of a breach of the Official Secrets Acts 1911–20. The Attorney General interviewed Mr Sandys, who later complained that he was being threatened with prosecution – in breach of privilege – for failing to disclose the source of his information. A select committee was established to consider the relevance of the Official Secrets Acts to Members acting in their parliamentary capacity. The Committee Report considered Article IX of the Bill of Rights, and it observed that:

> ... the privilege is not confined to words spoken in debate or to spoken words, but extends to all proceedings in Parliament. While the term 'proceedings in Parliament' has never been construed by the courts, it covers both the asking of a question and the giving written notice of such question, and includes everything said or done by a Member in the exercise of his functions as a Member in a committee of either House, as well as everything said or done in either House in the transaction of parliamentary business.

The Committee went on to assert that:

> ... words spoken or things done by a Member beyond the walls of Parliament will generally not be protected. Cases may, however, easily be imagined of

---

36 [1953] 1 QB 485.

communications between one Member and another, or between a Member and a Minister, so closely related to some matter pending in, or expected to be brought before, the House, that though they do not take place in the chamber or a committee room they form part of the business of the House, as, for example, where a Member sends to the Minister the draft of the Question he is thinking of putting down or shows it to another Member with a view to obtaining advice as to the propriety of putting it down or as to the manner in which it should be framed ...

... on the other hand, a casual conversation in the House cannot be said to be a proceeding in Parliament, and a Member who discloses information in the course of such a conversation would not, in their view, be protected by privilege ...

The privileges of Parliament ... are indefinite in their nature and stated in general and sometimes vague terms. The elasticity thus secured has made it possible to apply existing privileges in new circumstances from time to time. Any attempt to translate them into precise rules must deprive them of the very quality which renders them adaptable to new and varying conditions, and new or unusual combinations of circumstances and, indeed, might have the effect of restricting rather than safeguarding Members' privileges ...

The Committee ruled that if it were necessary, in order to prove the charge alleged, to produce evidence of what the defendant had said in the House:

... it would be in the power of the House to protect him by withholding permission for the evidence to be given.[37]

The response of the House differed markedly in the case of *Strauss and the London Electricity Board* in 1958.[38] At issue was whether or not communication in written form between a MP and a Minister was protected by privilege. George Strauss MP had forwarded a letter from a constituent to the relevant Minister, in which criticism was made of the manner in which the Board disposed of scrap metal. The Minister passed the letter to the Board for comment, whereupon the Board threatened to sue Mr Strauss for libel. The Member believed that this was a matter concerned with his parliamentary duties and that he should be covered by privilege. The Committee of Privileges concluded that the letter written was a proceeding in Parliament and that, accordingly, the Board had committed a breach of the privilege of the House. The committee was undecided as to whether the Parliamentary Privilege Act 1770 (which provides that legal action taken against Members is in itself a breach of the privilege of the House) applied. It was recommended that the House seek a ruling from the Judicial Committee of the Privy Council on the matter. The Judicial Committee ruled that the Act referred only to legal

---

37 *Report from the Select Committee on the Official Secrets Act*, HC 146 (1938–39), London: HMSO.

38 HC 305 (1956–57), HC 227 (1957–58), 591, HC Official Report, 5th Ser, Col 208, London: HMSO; [1958] AC 331; Cmnd 431, 1958, London: HMSO; Denning (Lord), 'The *Strauss* case' [1985] PL 80.

action taken against a Member in his private capacity, and not as a result of his conduct as a Member of Parliament.[39] The committee so reported to the House which, following debate, surprisingly rejected the finding of the committee. The London Electricity Board subsequently withdrew its action for libel, and an independent inquiry set up by the Minister exonerated the Board.[40]

The case raises two important questions for consideration. First, a great many important negotiations and communications take place through informal discussion between Members outside the precincts of the House. Much of this business is as important as matters raised for formal debate in the House, yet they are not covered by parliamentary privilege unless so closely associated to actual or pending proceedings in Parliament as to be brought within that phrase.

Secondly, many of the matters dealt with by Members of Parliament involve, as did the *Strauss* case, alleged grievances reported by constituents against government departments and associated public bodies. Inevitably, such grievances may entail actual or potentially libellous statements, but they are not protected by privilege. Where such a matter falls within the jurisdiction of the Parliamentary Commissioner, protection is now afforded by section 10(5) of the Parliamentary Commissioner Act 1967, which provides that such communications are absolutely privileged.[41] Uncertainty remains, however, where it is unclear as to whether or not the matter falls within his jurisdiction. It is unsatisfactory that neither members of the public, nor of Parliament, are clear as to the potential scope of liability under the law of defamation.

Two further cases illustrate the scope of the privilege. *R v Rule*[42] entailed a letter written by a constituent to his Member of Parliament complaining about the conduct of a police officer and a magistrate. In an action for libel, the court held that, where a communication was one made under a duty or common interest, the matter would attract qualified privilege: that is to say, it would be protected from liability unless malice were proven. A similar conclusion was reached in *Beach v Freeson*,[43] where a Member of Parliament was sued by a firm of solicitors, concerning whom the Member had received complaints from a constituent and forwarded the letter, with a covering letter, to the Lord Chancellor and the Law Society. That the letters were defamatory was not contested, but the court nevertheless held that publication of the letters (to the

---

39 HC 305 (1956–57), London: HMSO; *Re Parliamentary Privilege Act 1770* [1958] AC 331; HC 227 (1957–58), London: HMSO.

40 Cmnd 605, 1958, London: HMSO.

41 On the jurisdiction of the Commissioner, see Chapter 26.

42 [1937] 2 KB 375.

43 [1972] 1 QB 14.

Lord Chancellor and Law Society) was protected by qualified privilege on the basis of public interest.

Freedom of speech: its use and misuse

In the Committee of Privileges report of 1986–87,[44] the Committee had endorsed the view expressed by the Speaker[45] that:

> We should use our freedom of speech ... with the greatest care, particularly if we impute any motives or dishonourable conduct to those outside the House who have no right of reply.

The Committee recognised that there is 'no clear dividing line between statements which represent a legitimate exercise of freedom of speech, on the one hand, and those which constitute an abuse, on the other' and called on Members to exercise self-restraint.

In 1955, Kim Philby was named in the House as a Soviet spy, an allegation which surely would not have been made without the protection of privilege. In the 1960s, the Minister of War's association with Christine Keeler, who also had a relationship with a Soviet Attaché was revealed under the cloak of privilege. Also, in the 1960s, a London property racketeer, Peter Rachmann, was identified in the House. In 1980, Jeff Rooker MP made a number of false accusations against a Director of Rolls Royce: the allegations were withdrawn only after the lapse of five weeks. In the 1985–86 session, Ministers were accused in Parliament of improper involvement with the Johnson Matthey Bank following its collapse. In 1986, Geoffrey Dickins MP accused an Essex doctor of the sexual abuse of children, following a decision of the Director of Public Prosecutions not to prosecute the doctor on the basis that there was insufficient evidence to secure a conviction. Which of these exercises of freedom of speech represented a legitimate exercise of the freedom and which represented an abuse is a matter for individual judgment.

The House relies heavily on the notion of the self-restraint of its Members, and is slow to use its disciplinary powers against offending Members. The Committee on Procedure in its First Report urged Members to exercise caution, and to avoid misusing their freedom. Where Members insist on using privilege as a protective device and cause damage to the reputations and livelihoods of citizens, the advice of the Procedure Committee will give little comfort.[46] Individuals may try to rebut any allegations, may petition Parliament and may try to persuade a Member of Parliament to retract a damaging allegation, but such forms of redress are wholly unsatisfactory in comparison with the right to legal redress.

---

44 *Third Report of the Committee of Privileges 1986–87,* HC 604 (1995–96), London: HMSO.
45 HC 110, Official Report, Col 1084.
46 Given that 'advice' is less compelling than binding rules.

A Joint Committee on Parliamentary Privilege issued its First Report in 1999. In relation to members of the public, the Committee considered whether a 'right of reply' should be introduced but decided against it. A right of reply would do nothing to prove the truth or falsity of any allegation and no financial redress could be made, nor would a statement published in *Hansard* attract the same degree of publicity as the offending allegation.

The courts and privilege

More recent case law further illustrates the meaning of Article IX and the role of the courts in relation to matters of privilege. In *Rost v Edwards*,[47] a Member of Parliament sued *The Guardian* newspaper for alleged libel.[48] *The Guardian* article had stated that the Member, who was a Member of the Energy Select Committee and a nominee for selection to the standing committee, considering an Energy Bill, had not registered his interests – as a consultant with two organisations concerned with energy. Subsequent to publication of the article, the Member was informed that he was no longer being considered for membership of the standing committee and, further, that he had not been given the chair of the Energy Select Committee. The Member instituted libel proceedings, which were adjourned by the court in order to determine the issue of parliamentary privilege. The Member wished to adduce evidence before the court which comprised correspondence between himself and a clerk of the House and the Register of Members' Interests.

Mr Justice Popplewell ruled that the correspondence could not be submitted in evidence: that clearly fell within the exclusive domain of Parliament and not the court. As to the Register, the judge took the view that it was a public document and, accordingly, could be put in evidence. Mr Justice Popplewell, recognising the respective jurisdictions of Parliament and the courts, declared that the courts should nevertheless be slow to refuse to admit in evidence documents which could affect the outcome of legal proceedings and hence individual rights. *Rost v Edwards* was doubted by the Privy Council in *Prebble v Television New Zealand Ltd*.[49] In *Prebble*, a Member of the New Zealand House of Representatives sued the television company for libel for publishing an article alleging that State assets had been sold off, contrary to stated policy, and that the Member had been involved in a conspiracy to effect the sale. In its defence, the company wished to introduce in evidence parliamentary papers which substantiated its claim. The Member pleaded privilege. The House of Representatives ruled that it had no power to waive its own privileges and thereby allow the papers to be considered in

---

47 [1990] 2 WLR 1280; [1990] 2 All ER 641.
48 See *op cit*, Leopold, fn 35.
49 [1994] 3 WLR 970.

court. The Privy Council ruled that to adduce such evidence – without the House's waiver of privilege – contravened privilege and the protection given to parliamentary proceedings under Article IX of the Bill of Rights 1689.

In *Pepper v Hart*,[50] the question considered by the House of Lords was whether judges may refer to *Hansard* as an aid to the interpretation of statutes. This issue has long been one of some controversy, and the orthodox view has hitherto been that judges may not under any circumstances refer to *Hansard*. In *Davis v Johnson*,[51] Lord Denning MR stated openly that he privately referred to *Hansard* as an aid to interpretation, only to be criticised for so doing by the House of Lords.[52] However, in *Black-Clawson International Ltd v Papierwerke AG*,[53] all five judges in the House of Lords had agreed that official reports could be consulted to discern the 'mischief' with which the legislation was intended to deal, although their Lordships differed over the extent to which they could be used. Further, in *Pickstone v Freeman*,[54] three Members of the House of Lords made reference to a parliamentary speech of the Secretary of State (the other two judges were silent on this matter).

In *Pepper v Hart*,[55] six of the seven judges hearing the case ruled in favour of admitting parliamentary debates before the court in some circumstances (the Lord Chancellor dissented on this point). Arguments were advanced by the Attorney General against such a decision – not least that, by consulting parliamentary debates, the courts would be acting contrary to Article IX of the Bill of Rights 1689, which prohibits the courts from questioning proceedings in Parliament. The court rejected those views, concluding that there were no constitutional reasons which outweighed the merits of a 'limited modification' of the rule. Lord Browne-Wilkinson, giving the leading judgment of the court, stated that the rule should be relaxed where:

(a) legislation is ambiguous or obscure, or leads to an absurdity;

(b) the material relied on consists of one or more statements by a minister or other promoter of the Bill together, if necessary, with such other parliamentary material as is necessary to understand such statements and their effect; and

(c) the statements relied on are clear.

The House of Lords in *Pepper v Hart* revealed a marked change in attitude, although the right to refer to *Hansard* is not an unqualified right. The significance of this judgment from the point of view of parliamentary

---

50 [1993] 1 All ER 1; and see Oliver, D, '*Pepper v Hart*: a suitable case for reference to *Hansard*?' [1993] PL 5.
51 [1979] AC 264.
52 [1979] AC 317.
53 [1975] AC 591.
54 [1988] 2 All ER 803.
55 [1993] 1 All ER 1.

privilege lies in the court's consideration of the scope of Article IX of the Bill of Rights 1689. The Attorney General had argued strongly before the court that for judges to refer to *Hansard* infringed Article IX, amounting to an inquiry into the proceedings in Parliament. This submission was rejected by the court, Lord Templeman declaring that reference to *Hansard*, under limited circumstances, involved no questioning of Parliament, but merely clarification as to Parliament's intention.[56]

In *R v Deegan*,[57] however, the Court of Appeal ruled that recourse to *Hansard* was not justified. The court below had referred to *Hansard* in order to clarify Parliament's intentions as to the meaning of the phrase 'folding pocketknife', the possession of which had led to the appellant's conviction. The Court of Appeal, however, ruled that the conditions laid down in *Pepper v Hart* had not been satisfied, and that, for the court to rely on parliamentary records of debate, on a term which was inherently open to interpretation, was unjustified. The appeal was dismissed.

The case of *Prebble v Television New Zealand Ltd*[58] was reconsidered by the Queen's Bench Division in *Allason v Haines*.[59] Joe Haines, a political journalist, and Mr Richard Stott, editor of *Today*, applied to have a libel action brought against them by the plaintiff, Mr Rupert Allason, MP, stayed. The court held that where, in order to defend a libel action, it was necessary to bring evidence of a Member of Parliament's behaviour in the House of Commons, and such a defence would be in breach of parliamentary privilege, the action would be stayed, for it would be unjust to deprive the defendants of their defence. The defendants had sought to show that Early Day Motions were inspired to improper motives or were activated upon a failure to take proper care. Such evidence would be in contravention of Article IX of the Bill of Rights 1689. To enforce parliamentary privilege in this case would be to cause injustice to the defendants. A stay was granted.

Rost v Edwards was also critically considered by the Joint Committee on Parliamentary Privilege which reported in 1999, which stated baldly that 'we are in no doubt that if this decision is correct, the law should be changed'.[60] In the Committee's opinion, it is quite wrong for a court of law to be free to investigate and adjudicate upon matters relating to the Register. If there are allegations of wrongful failure to register, that matter should be 'a matter for

---

56 In *Three Rivers District Council v Bank of England (No 2)* [1996] 2 All ER 363; *(No 3)* [1996] 3 All ER 558, it was held that references to Ministers' speeches in *Hansard* may be made not only to construe a particular statutory provision whose meaning was ambiguous or unclear, but also in a case where the purpose or object of the statute as a whole is in issue.

57 (1998) *The Times*, 17 February.

58 [1995] 1 AC 321; (1994) *The Times*, 13 July.

59 (1995) *The Times*, 14 July; (1995) 145 NLJ Rep 1576.

60 First Report of the Joint Committee on Parliamentary Privilege, 1999, para 123.

Parliament alone'. The Committee recommended that legislation be introduced to make clear that the Register and matters relating thereto are 'proceedings in Parliament'.

The Defamation Act 1996 and Article IX of the Bill of Rights

The Defamation Act 1996 came into being as a result of the Rupert Allason case and Neil Hamilton's intended libel suit against *The Guardian* newspaper over its allegations that he had accepted rewards in relation to his parliamentary duties.[61] Section 13 of the Defamation Act provides that a person may waive, for the purpose of defamation proceedings in which his conduct in relation to proceedings in Parliament is in issue, the protection of any enactment or rule of law which prevents proceedings in Parliament being impeached or questioned in any court or place outside Parliament. As a result, a Member of Parliament may bring an action for defamation to defend his or her actions, provided that he or she waives the Article IX protection and thereby enables the defence to adduce evidence which otherwise would be excluded on the basis of privilege. If, however, the Member of Parliament is not willing to waive the Article IX privilege, then, on the authority of *Prebble v Television New Zealand Ltd*, the defamation action may be stayed in order to enable the newspaper to adduce evidence which proves the truth of its allegation.

The Hamilton saga continued with Mr Hamilton suing Mohamed Al Fayed for defamation. Mr Al Fayed sought to have the action struck out on the basis that, since the Committee on Standards and Privileges and the Parliamentary Commissioner for Standards had already investigated the allegation, the trial would breach parliamentary privilege. It was argued that section 13 of the Defamation Act 1996 was addressed at the individual privilege of the Member concerned and did not apply to Parliament's collective privilege of exclusive jurisdiction over its internal regulation. The judge at first instance refused to strike out the action, as did the Court of Appeal.[62] On appeal to the House of Lords, the decision of the Court of Appeal was affirmed. Section 13 applied. Its effect was that the defendant's waiver of his parliamentary protection in relation to the parliamentary inquiry into his conduct overrode any privilege belonging to Parliament as a whole and thus allowed the parties in the libel proceedings to challenge the veracity of evidence given to the parliamentary committee.[63]

---

61 *Hamilton v Hencke; Greer v Hencke* (1995) unreported, 21 July. On which, see, further, below.
62 [1999] 1 WLR 1569.
63 Judgment 23 March 2000.

First Report of the Joint Committee on Parliamentary Privilege (1999)

The 1999 report offers an in depth analysis of the contemporary law and practice relating to privilege. On the issues raised in *Pepper v Hart*[64] and related cases, the report endorses the decision, stating that this 'use of parliamentary proceedings is benign'.[65] The Committee did, however, also stress that, where the courts depart from accepted practice, that departure 'must be scrutinised thoroughly to see whether *as a matter of principle and practice*, it is justified',[66] and that there should be no 'general weakening of the prohibition contained in Article IX'.

In similar vein, the Committee considered the use of parliamentary proceedings made in judicial review proceedings. Accepting the legitimacy of reference to *Hansard* in judicial review proceedings, the Committee accepted that both parliamentary scrutiny and judicial review have an important role to play in ensuring both democratic and legal control over the executive. Whereas Parliament had the sole right to ensure ministerial accountability to Parliament, 'only the courts can set aside an unlawful ministerial decision'.[67]

On the circumstances surrounding the *Hamilton* case, and section 13 of the Defamation Act 1996 enacted to remedy the defect which flowed from Article IX, namely, a plaintiff being unable to pursue his action for defamation because the defendant newspaper was prevented, by Article IX, from justifying what it had written, the Committee was extremely critical and recommended reform of the law. Section 13, allowing a Member of Parliament to waive Article IX, but preventing non-Members from doing so, which had the effect of making newspapers (and others) unable to establish the truth of their allegations, had 'created indefensible anomalies of its own which should not be allowed to continue.[68] Having reviewed alternatives for reform, the Committee recommended that the individual Member should no longer have the right to waive the protection of Article IX, and that this right should be given to the House as a whole, subject to the overriding consideration that such waiver was in the interests of justice and would not result in a Member attracting legal liability in a court of law. In considering the mechanism for reaching such a decision, the Committee recommended that, in the House of Lords, the Committee of Privileges always contained four Law Lords and was therefore the appropriate forum for decision, whereas, in the Commons, it would be appropriate for such decisions to be reached by the Speaker, assisted

---

64 [1993] AC 593. See, also, Erskine May, T, *Parliamentary Practice*, 22nd edn, 1997, London: Butterworths, p 91.

65 First Report of the Joint Committee on Parliamentary Privilege, 1999, para 45.

66 *Ibid*, emphasis in original.

67 *Ibid*, para 50.

68 *Ibid*, paras 68 and 69.

with advice from a small committee of Members to include the Leader and Shadow Leader of the House with the Attorney General and representatives of the political parties.[69]

The composition and procedure of Parliament

The Houses of Parliament have an inherent right to regulate their own composition and procedure. For example, in *Ashby v White*,[70] the plaintiff – a qualified voter – had been denied the right to exercise his vote by the Mayor of Aylesbury. The House of Lords awarded Ashby damages. The case gave rise to a significant constitutional conflict between Parliament and the courts. The House of Commons – which at the time had jurisdiction to hear matters on disputed elections – regarded the decision of the House of Lords as interfering with the exclusive right of the House of Commons to adjudicate on disputed elections. Other voters, similarly denied the right to vote, instigated legal proceedings and were committed to prison by the House of Commons. They brought an application for habeas corpus to test the legality of their detention. In *Paty's Case*,[71] in 1704, the court refused the writ of habeas corpus. Counsel for the applicants, intending to appeal to the House of Lords, was committed to prison. The majority of the court refused to grant the application, deferring to the Commons. The dissenting judge, Lord Holt, declared that the courts had the power to decide that a writ of habeas corpus could effect the release of those detained for contempt by the House of Commons. In judgment, Lord Holt stated that:

> I will suppose, that the bringing of such actions was declared by the House of Commons to be a breach of their privilege; that that declaration will not make that a breach of privilege that was not so before. But if they have any such privilege, they ought to shew precedent of it. The privileges of the House of Commons are well known, and are founded upon the law of the land, and are nothing but the law ... And if they declare themselves to have privileges, which they have no legal claim to, the people of England will not be estopped by that declaration. This privilege of theirs concerns the liberty of the people in a high degree, by subjecting them to imprisonment for the infringement of them, which is what the people cannot be subjected to without an Act of Parliament.[72]

In *Bradlaugh v Gosset*,[73] Bradlaugh had been duly elected as a Member of Parliament. On arriving to take his seat, Bradlaugh refused to swear the requisite oath on the Bible, offering instead to swear an oath of allegiance to

---

69 For other recommendations for reform, see, further, pp 719–20.
70 (1703) 2 Ld Raym 938; (1703) 3 Ld Raym 320; (1703) 14 St Tr 695.
71 (1704) 2 Ld Raym 1105.
72 *Ibid*, p 1113.
73 (1884) 12 QBD 271.

the Crown. The House of Commons resolved to exclude Bradlaugh from the House. The plaintiff sought a declaration from the court that the resolution was invalid and an injunction to prevent the House of Commons from excluding him. The Court of Queen's Bench declared that it had no jurisdiction to interfere with a matter concerning the internal regulation of Parliament's procedures.

The right of the House to regulate its own procedure is further demonstrated in the case of the *British Railways Board v Pickin*.[74] There the court declined to inquire into the manner of the passage of a Bill even though the plaintiff alleged that he had been denied his right to make representations on a matter adversely affecting his rights in breach of convention. The Court of Appeal held that the procedure used in relation to a Private – but not Public – Bill could be examined. Lord Denning MR took a bold approach, arguing that it was for the court to ensure that 'the procedure of Parliament itself is not abused, and that undue advantage is not taken of it. In so doing, the court is not trespassing on the jurisdiction of Parliament itself. It is acting in aid of Parliament and, I might add, in aid of justice.' The House of Lords disagreed and adopted its traditional stance: the court will not look 'behind the Parliamentary Roll'.[75] See, also, the case of *Re Parliamentary Election for Bristol South East*,[76] discussed in Chapter 17. There Mr Tony Benn was refused the right to enter and sit in the Commons, despite being duly elected, because he had succeeded to a peerage on the death of his father, Viscount Stansgate. Only by the passage of the Peerage Act 1963 was Tony Benn able to renounce his peerage and take his seat in the Commons.

On a lighter note, the exclusive rights of the Commons were tested in *R v Campbell ex parte Herbert*.[77] Three Members of the Kitchen Committee of the House of Commons were accused of breaching the licensing laws. The action failed, the court holding that the House was not governed by the ordinary laws relating to licensing, which would only apply if it could be shown that they were expressly intended to apply to Westminster. It is for this reason that the House remains free to open its bars at any time of day or night. Sir AP Herbert once speculated whether the immunity conceded in *R v Cambell ex parte Herbert* could be extended by analogy to permit other licentious behaviour in the Commons.

---

74 [1974] AC 765.

75 Following, *inter alia, Edinburgh and Dalkeith Rly Co v Wauchope* (1842) 8 Cl & Fin 710; (1842) 1 Bell 252; *Lee v Bude and Torrington Junction Rly Co* (1871) LR 6 CP 576.

76 [1964] QB 257.

77 [1935] 1 KB 594.

An early conflict between Parliament and the courts

In *Stockdale v Hansard*,[78] a prison inspector made a written report to the Secretary of State alleging that 'improper books' were being circulated in Newgate prison. The report was subsequently published by *Hansard*, on order of the House of Commons. Stockdale, the publisher of the 'improper book', sued *Hansard* as publishers of the report, which he regarded to be libellous. In defence, *Hansard* argued that the publication had been by an order of the House of Commons and was, accordingly, covered by the privilege of the House. The Court of Queen's Bench ruled that such publication was not covered by privilege and, moreover, that the House of Commons could not by a resolution deprive the courts of jurisdiction to protect the rights of individuals. Stockdale was awarded damages. The Sheriff of Middlesex levied execution on *Hansard's* property to satisfy the award of damages to Stockdale and the House of Commons responded by passing a resolution to commit the Sheriff for breach of privilege and contempt of Parliament. The Sheriff applied for a writ of habeas corpus to test the legality of his detention.[79] The Sergeant at Arms produced a certificate from the Speaker stating simply that the Sheriff was 'guilty of a contempt and a breach of the privileges of this House'. The court refused to examine the lawfulness of the Sheriff's detention, stating that, since the Speaker's warrant did not specify the facts justifying the detention, it was not for the court to inquire into Parliament's business. Mr Justice Littledale stated that:

> If the warrant returned be good on the face of it, we can inquire no further. The principal objection is, that it does not sufficiently express the cause of commitment ... If the warrant declares the grounds of adjudication, this Court, in many instances, will examine into their validity; but, if it does not, we cannot get into such an inquiry.[80]

Accordingly, the court conceded jurisdiction to the House of Commons and rendered itself powerless to provide a remedy for a individual who, acting as an agent for the courts in enforcing the court's order for damages, found himself incarcerated on the order of the Commons. While such an outcome hardly inspires confidence in the judicial system, it nevertheless illustrates clearly the judges' reluctance to cross the boundary into matters of privilege.

Breach of privilege and contempt of Parliament

A breach of privilege is conduct offending against one of the known privileges of Parliament. Contempt is a far wider concept than this and has been defined as:

---

78   (1839) 9 Ad & E 1.
79   *Sheriff of Middlesex's Case* (1840) 11 Ad & E 273.
80   *Ibid*, p 293.

... any act or omission which obstructs or impedes either House of Parliament in the performance of its functions, or which obstructs or impedes any Member or Officer of the House in the discharge of his duty or which has a tendency, directly or indirectly, to produce such results.[81]

The main types of contempts dealt with by the House of Commons, with illustrations, are listed by Erskine May as being:

(a) Misconduct in the presence of the House or its committees:

- interrupting the proceedings of a committee;
- a witness persistently misleading a committee.

(b) Disobedience to rules or orders of the House or its committees:

- refusal to attend as a witness;
- refusing an order to withdraw from the House.

(c) Presenting a forged or falsified document to the House or its committees:

- forging signatures to petitions;

(d) Misconduct by Members or officers as such:

- deliberately misleading the House;
- corruption by acceptance of bribes.

(e) Constructive contempts:

- speeches or writing reflecting on the House;
- wilful misrepresentation of debates;
- premature disclosure of committee proceedings of evidence;
- other indignities offered to the House, such as fighting in the lobbies, using the badge and the name of the House in connection with an unofficial publication; and serving a writ on a Member in the precincts, while the House was sitting, without leave of the House.

(f) Obstructing Members in the discharge of their duty:

- molesting or insulting Members attending, coming to, or going from the House;
- attempted intimidation of Members, including publishing threatening posters regarding Members voting in a forthcoming debate and threatening to stop public investment in a Member's constituency if that Member persisted in making speeches of the kind he had made in a recent debate;
- molesting Members on account of their conduct in Parliament, for example, by inciting newspaper readers to telephone a Member to complain of a question he had tabled;
- speeches or writings reflecting on Members' conduct in the House, for example, accusing the Speaker of partiality in the Chair.

---

81 *Op cit*, Erskine May, fn 1, Chapter 9.

(g) Obstructing officers of the House while in the execution of their duty:

- resisting the Serjeant at Arms when enforcing an order of the House.

(h) Obstructing witnesses:

- calling a person to account or censuring him for evidence given by him to a committee of the House.[82]

The 1999 Report of the Joint Committee on Parliamentary Privilege recommends that contempt of Parliament be defined in statute as part of its proposal for a new Parliamentary Privileges Act and an accompanying code.[83]

MEMBERS' INTERESTS AND MEMBERS' INDEPENDENCE

Freedom from interference in Parliament's work is a foundational principle of privilege. Accordingly, it is essential that all Members of Parliament are under no external pressure which could pose an actual or potential threat to their independence. However, from a constitutional standpoint, this issue represents one of the most troublesome aspects of privilege. This remains a topic of much contemporary significance and is one which raises difficult questions. In 1994, this issue came to the fore and, as a result of a number of allegations concerning Members' interests – on which, see further below – an inquiry headed by Lord Justice Nolan was established by the Prime Minister to examine the issue.[84] The findings of the inquiry are discussed below.

A majority of Members of the House of Commons are in paid employment in addition to being salaried Members of the House.[85] Many Members are also sponsored by outside bodies who contribute to their election expenses and may contribute towards the cost of secretarial and/or research staff employed by a Member.[86] It may be argued as a point of principle that Members of Parliament should not receive any financial or other assistance from any outside party, whether a company or a trades union, since the very fact of receipt of such support potentially undermines the independence and integrity of the recipient.[87] This is not, however, the view adopted by the House of Commons itself although, from time to time, the House is troubled

---

82 *Op cit*, Erskine May, fn 1, Chapter 9.

83 See, further, pp 719–20.

84 Committee of Inquiry on Standards in Public Life.

85 Non-ministerial salaries have only been payable since 1911. For the background, see *op cit*, Erskine May, fn 1, Chapter 1.

86 The trade unions have a statutory right to sponsor Members of Parliament from separate political funds (Trade Union and Labour Relations (Consolidation) Act 1992).

87 A view expressed by Dennis Skinner MP: 'One Member, one salary' (*BBC Television News*, 20 April 1995).

by such issues. The traditionally accepted view is that such sponsorship or remuneration is perfectly proper, provided that it does not impede the Member's independence in the actual exercise of his parliamentary duties.

However, there is a fine line to be drawn between legitimate payments to Members and payments designed to impede a Member's independence, which may amount to bribery and corruption. On the Joint Committee on Parliamentary Privilege Report on bribery and corruption see further below, p 715.

Rules regulating Members' interests

In 1695, by a resolution of the House, the 'offer of money or other advantage' to a Member of Parliament for the purpose of persuading him or her to promote any matter in Parliament was ruled to be 'a high crime and misdemeanour'. Further, in 1858, a resolution declared it to be 'improper for any Member to promote any matter' in relation to which he or she had received a financial reward.[88] Specifically in relation to the asking of parliamentary questions, the Committee of Privileges in 1945 ruled that it was a breach of the privileges of the House to 'offer money or other advantage' to induce Members to take up questions with Ministers.[89] Members of Parliament found guilty of corruption may be expelled from the House.[90]

When speaking in debate or in any proceedings in the House or its committees, or when communicating with other Members or Ministers, a resolution of 1974 requires that Members shall disclose 'any relevant pecuniary interest or benefit ... whether direct or indirect, that he may have had, may have or may be expecting to have'.[91]

In 1947, the Committee of Privileges had the opportunity to examine the issue of contracts made between Members and outside bodies. Mr WJ Brown was elected the Member for Rugby in 1942. He had previously held the post of General Secretary of the Civil Service Clerical Association and, following his election, agreed to become its Parliamentary General Secretary. Following disagreements between Mr Brown and the Association, it was resolved that Mr Brown's appointment should be terminated. The matter was raised in the Commons, the argument being advanced that the Association's threat to terminate Mr Brown's contract was calculated to influence the Member in the exercise of his parliamentary duties and, accordingly, amounted to a breach of privilege. The committee reported that:

88   CJ (1857–58) 247.

89   *Henderson's Case*, HC 63 (1944–45), London: HMSO.

90   See *op cit*, Erskine May, fn 1, p 119.

91   Adopting recommendations of the Select Committee on Members; Interests (Declaration), HC 57 (1969–70), London: HMSO.

It is a breach of privilege to take or threaten action which is not merely calculated to affect the Member's course of action in Parliament, but is of a kind against which it is absolutely necessary that Members should be protected if they are to discharge their duties as such independently and without fear of punishment or hope of reward.

The relationship between a Member and an outside body with which he is in contractual relationship and from which he receives financial payments is, however, one of great difficulty and delicacy in which there must often be a danger that the rules of privilege may be infringed. Thus it would certainly be improper for a Member to enter into any arrangement fettering his complete independence as a Member of Parliament by undertaking to press some particular point of view on behalf of an outside interest, whether for reward or not. Equally it might be a breach of privilege for an outside body to use the fact that a Member had entered into an agreement with it or was receiving payments from it as a means of exerting pressure upon that Member to follow a particular course of conduct in his capacity as a Member.

It would also be clearly improper to attempt to punish a Member pecuniarily because of his actions as a Member.

On the facts of the case, the Committee ruled that the making of such payments in itself did not involve any breach of privilege, and that:

On the other hand, your committee regard it as an inevitable corollary that if an outside body may properly enter into contractual relationships with and make payments to a Member as such, it must in general be entitled to terminate that relationship if it lawfully can where it considers it necessary for the protection of its own interest so to do. What, on the other hand, an outside body is certainly not entitled to do is to use the agreement or the payment as an instrument by which it controls, or seeks to control the conduct of a Member or to punish him for what he has done as a Member.[92]

A further instance of alleged improper pressure being brought to bear on Members of Parliament occurred in 1975. The Yorkshire Area Council of the National Union of Mineworkers who sponsored a number of Labour Members of Parliament, resolved that it would withdraw its sponsorship from any Member who voted in the House in a manner which conflicted with Union policy. The Committee of Privileges found this threat to be a serious contempt of the House, amounting as it did to an attempt to force a Member to vote in a particular way thus threatening a Member's freedom of speech.[93] In the event, the National Executive of the Union nullified the resolution and no action was taken against the Union.

---

92 See HC Deb 15 Col 284, July 1947; HC 118 (1946–47), London: HMSO.
93 See HC 634 (1974–75), London: HMSO.

The Register of Members' Interests

On the wider question of the financial interests of Members of Parliament, under the rules of the House, all Members are required to declare their interests, these being recorded in the Register of Members' Interests. A resolution[94] of the House of Commons provided that:

> ... in any debate or proceeding of the House or its committees or transactions or communications which a Member may have with other Members or with Ministers or servants of the Crown, he shall disclose any relevant pecuniary interest or benefit of whatever nature, whether direct or indirect, that he may have had, may have or may be expecting to have.

The practice was considered by the Select Committee on Members' Interests in 1968–69 and 1969–70. On the relevance of interests, the Committee reported that:

> The judgment on whether an interest is relevant and should be declared is in the first instance a matter for the Member concerned ... The main criterion for declaration should be relevant to debate or other activity in which a Member is taking part. An interest should be declared whenever a specific and relevant financial connection exists which might reasonably be thought to affect the expression of a Member's views on the matter under debate or other activity ... If the interest is not relevant there is no need to declare it. Nor need an interest be declared which does not entail an actual or potential benefit.[95]

The Register of Members' Interests is published annually.[96] The following classes of interests are required to be registered:[97]

(a) remunerated directorships of companies, public or private;

(b) remunerated employments, trades, professions, offices or vocations;

(c) the names and details of clients of a lobbying company in relation to which a Member plays a parliamentary role;

(d) gifts, benefits or hospitality received. Sums in excess of £125 cash or material benefit must be registered, as must hospitality over £160;

(e) financial sponsorships either as a parliamentary candidate where, to the knowledge of the Member, the sponsorship in any case exceeds 25 per cent of the candidate's election expenses; or as a Member of Parliament, by any person or organisation, stating whether any such sponsorship includes any payment to the Member or any material benefit or advantage, direct or indirect, such as the services of a research assistant;

---

94 22 May 1974.

95 See HC 57 (1969–70), London: HMSO, pp viii–x.

96 See below for data published in the *First Report of the Committee on Standards in Public Life* (the 'Nolan Report'), Cm 2850-I, 1995, London: HMSO.

97 1995 revised Register.

(f) overseas visits, relating to or arising out of membership of the House, where the cost of any such visit has not been borne wholly by the Member or by public funds;

(g) any payments or any material benefits or advantages received from or on behalf of foreign governments, organisations or persons;

(h) land or property of substantial value (excluding a Member's home) or from which a substantial income is derived;

(i) names of companies or other bodies in which a Member has, to his knowledge, either himself or with or on behalf of his spouse or infant children, a beneficial interest in share holdings of a nominal value greater than one hundredth of the issued share capital;

(j) miscellaneous and unremunerated interests. Registration of such interests is voluntary.[98]

The rules relating to Ministers are more strict than those relating to ordinary Members of Parliament.[99] Ministers are required to resign directorships in all companies other than those dealing with family estates, to divest themselves of any investments which might involve a conflict of interest with their ministerial position and to avoid speculative investments which might be seen to be made with the benefit of information acquired as a result of their ministerial office. A Minister may only continue to act as a Member of Lloyd's with Prime Ministerial permission.[100]

Failure to register an interest may be regarded as a contempt of the House. The only Member who consistently refused to enter any interests on the Register was Mr Enoch Powell. Mr Powell adopted the constitutional stance that, since only statute could impose legal duties on individuals, the House could not – through the use of resolutions – lawfully require him to register. The select committee, having tried persuasion and inviting the House to take action to enforce the duty to register, took no further action.

The seriousness with which the House regards matters of interests which come to its attention may be seen in the case of Mr Michael Mates, a senior Conservative Party Member. Mr Mates was chairman of the Select Committee on Defence, which was considering low flying exercises by the airforce, which entailed consideration of the use of flight simulation equipment. Mr Dale Campbell-Savours MP complained to the select committee that Mr Mates had failed properly to register and declare certain financial interests in the defence industry. Mr Mates had financial interests in a defence consultancy business, and in a manufacturer of flight simulation equipment, for whom Mr Mates acted as general adviser. It was not disputed that Mr Mates had never spoken

---

98 Register of Members' Interests as at 31 October 1997 is at HC 291 (1997–98), London: HMSO.

99 See *Questions of Procedure for Ministers*, 1992, London: Cabinet Office, para 8.

100 *Ibid*, paras 118–23. See, further, Chapter 11 on the issue of ministerial conduct.

on behalf of either company in the House or in committee, and there was no allegation that Mr Mates had used his parliamentary position to further the interests of either company.

Mr Mates's defence was that his interests had no relevance to the deliberations of the committee and that, in any event, the interests appearance on the Register of Members' Interests ensured that Members of the select committee were fully aware of his interests. The select committee was highly critical of Mr Mates's conduct, asserting that 'we do not believe that Mr Mates's judgement was sound on this point'.[101]

The committee took the view that Mr Mates was in error in not declaring his interests when asking, as Chairman of the Defence Select Committee, questions relating to flight simulators. It was accepted that Mr Mates had made no personal gain nor had he made any effort to conceal his interests. Nevertheless, his conduct fell below the high standard of disclosure expected by the select committee. In the event, the committee decided not to ask the House to take any action, but recommended that all Members of Parliament take serious note of the findings in the report.

Cash for questions[102]

The cash for questions affair began in 1993, when political lobbyist Ian Greer advised Mohamed Al Fayed to bribe Members of Parliament to pursue his interests in Parliament. In 1994, Al Fayed publicly claimed that Tory MPs were paid to plant questions. *The Guardian* newspaper pursued the story, leading to a libel action by Mr Hamilton and Mr Greer. That action was dropped when it became apparent that *The Guardian* had damning evidence which would cause the action to fail.[103]

In 1994, a number of allegations were made against Members of Parliament in relation to accepting money for the tabling of parliamentary questions to Ministers. Allegations were also made in relation to improper payments being accepted by Members from outsiders, in the form of payment for hotel bills. Further, allegations were made in respect of the failure of a number of Members of Parliament who allegedly failed to record benefits received and other relationships in which Members received financial reward for services in the Register of Members' Interests.

In 1994, two Parliamentary Private Secretaries resigned (from the government but not from Parliament) following allegations into the receipt of

---

101 *Second Report of the Select Committee on Members' Interests*, HC 506, July 1990, London: HMSO, para 20.

102 See, also, Chapter 11 on fitness for public office.

103 For an entertaining account, see Leigh, D and Vulliamy, E, *Sleaze: The Corruption of Parliament*, 1997, London: Fourth Estate.

money in exchange for tabling parliamentary questions. Furthermore, in 1994, two Junior Ministers faced allegations that they received payments and/or gifts in exchange for tabling parliamentary questions. On 20 October 1994, *The Guardian* alleged that Tim Smith MP and Neil Hamilton MP had each received £2,000 for tabling questions in Parliament concerning the take over of Harrods by the Al Fayed brothers. Tim Smith resigned on the day of the report. Neil Hamilton remained in office, claiming that he enjoyed the continued support of the Prime Minister. On 21 October, however, *The Guardian* newspaper published details of a bill from the Ritz Hotel in Paris, totalling an estimated £4,000, paid for by Mr Al Fayed. The then Prime Minister subsequently demanded Mr Hamilton's resignation.

The matter was referred to the Committee of Privileges. The rapidly accelerating and intensifying atmosphere of suspected corruption – or 'sleaze' – in public life caused the Prime Minister to appoint a judicial inquiry into standards of conduct in public life.[104]

The cash for questions affair also raises issues concerning the press. Journalists from *The Sunday Times*, working undercover, offered payment of £1,000 to two Conservative Parliamentary Private Secretaries, Graham Riddick and David Tredinnick. The offers were made by telephone and the conversations recorded by the journalists. The Committee of Privileges inquired into the allegations in July 1994 and, in April 1995, recommended that the two Members be suspended from Parliament for 20 days and 10 days respectively for conduct which 'fell below the standards of the House'. In April 1995, the House, following debate, adopted the committee's recommendation. The Members also lost their parliamentary salaries for the periods of suspension. Concerning the role of *The Sunday Times*, the committee was highly critical of the manner in which their investigation was conducted, but no action has been taken against the newspaper.

The Committee on Standards in Public Life: the Nolan Inquiry

The Committee on Standards in Public Life, chaired by Lord Nolan,[105] was established as a standing body, with membership being held for three years. The Committee's terms of reference are:

> To examine current concerns about standards of conduct of all holders of public office, including arrangements relating to financial and commercial activities, and to make recommendations as to any changes in present arrangements which might be required to ensure the highest standards of probity in public life.

---

104 Committee on Standards in Public Life.
105 The current Chairman is Lord Neill.

For these purposes, public life should include Ministers, civil servants and advisers, Members of Parliament and United Kingdom Members of the European Parliament, members and senior officers of all non-departmental public bodies and of national health service bodies, non-ministerial office holders, members and other senior officers of other bodies discharging publicly funded function, and elected members and senior officers of local authorities.

Individual allegations of impropriety do not fall within the committee's terms of reference.

The Committee has investigated and reported on three matters: issues relating to Members of Parliament; issues relating to Ministers and civil servants; and issues relating to non-departmental public bodies (NDPBs or quangos).[106] In this chapter, the findings relating to Members of Parliament are discussed. The conduct of Ministers and civil servants is considered in Chapter 11.

In May 1995, the committee published its First Report.[107] While finding that, in general, 'there is no evidence ... of a growth in actual corruption',[108] the committee records a widespread loss of public confidence in the probity of Members of Parliament. Evidence to the committee revealed that 64 per cent of the public believed that Members of Parliament made money by using their office improperly, a figure which had risen from 46 per cent in 1984.[109]

The committee set out the general principles of conduct which apply to public life as being selflessness, integrity, objectivity, accountability, openness, honesty and leadership.

Members of Parliament

The Nolan Report recorded that the 1995 Register of Members' Interests suggest that 26 Members had entered into agreements with public relations or lobbying firms. A further 142 Members had consultancies 'with other types of company or with trade associations'.[110] The 168 Members between them held a total of 356 consultancies. When Ministers and the Speaker are excluded from the analysis, almost 30 per cent of Members of Parliament held some form of consultancy agreement. In relation to associations with trades unions, a total of 184 Members had sponsorship agreements, 27 had paid consultancies, and a further 10 received some form of financial assistance from trades unions. Accordingly, the committee concluded that almost 70 per cent

---

106 Quasi-autonomous non-governmental organisations.
107 *Op cit*, Nolan Report, fn 96.
108 *Op cit*, Nolan Report, fn 96, para 6.
109 Professor Ivor Crewe citing a Gallup survey.
110 *Op cit*, Nolan Report, fn 96, para 13.

of Members of Parliament (excluding Ministers and the Speaker) had some form of financial relationship with outside bodies.

Despite the evidence of witnesses and persons writing to the committee, the committee did not conclude from this evidence that such arrangements should be banned. Indeed, the involvement of Members of Parliament in outside work was regarded by the committee as a benefit to Parliament as a whole. As the committee viewed the matter:

> ... a Parliament composed entirely of full time professional politicians would not serve the best interests of democracy. The House needs if possible to contain people with a wide range of current experience which can contribute to its expertise.[111]

The committee was also concerned that a ban on outside financial interests would act as a deterrent to people who would otherwise stand for election to Parliament. The committee recommended, therefore, that Members of Parliament should continue to have the right to engage in outside employment. The matter which remained was how best to protect the integrity of Members and the House as a whole in light of such continuing outside employment.

Having reviewed the early resolutions of the House, and the later resolution of 1947,[112] and the rules regulating the registration of Members' interests, the committee found that the Register had worked unsatisfactorily. The committee invited the House of Commons to review the statement of principle which governed the registration of interests.

Paid consultancies

Three fifths of all Members of the House have arrangements with clients or sponsors. While appreciating that paid consultancies enable 'many entirely respectable, and in some cases highly deserving, organisations' to 'gain a voice in the nation's affairs',[113] the Committee recognised that there was a fine – and difficult – line to be drawn between paid advice and paid advocacy, the latter of which is a matter of concern. To remove the right to engage in such arrangements would be 'impracticable' and was, accordingly, not recommended. There was, however, one area – the issue of 'general consultancies' – in which the committee wanted to see firm and immediate action.

---

111 *Op cit*, Nolan Report, fn 96, para 19.
112 See the case of Mr Brown, discussed above, pp 698–99.
113 *Op cit*, Nolan Report, fn 96, para 46.

General consultancies

Public relations and lobbying firms are engaged in acting as advisers and advocates to a wide range of clients, each of which is pursuing its own objective in terms of exerting pressure on Parliament. The problem posed by such companies is that registration of an agreement with the company does not necessarily disclose the actual client for whom, in fact, the Member is acting in a parliamentary capacity. The committee recommended that there be an immediate ban introduced on such relationships, but Parliament did not act specifically on this proposal but, rather, tightened the rules relating to registration and the declaration of interests.

Clarifying the Register of Members' Interests

The committee acknowledged that the 1995 Register was an improvement on previous Registers. However, there still remained areas of doubt and uncertainty as to the precise requirements of disclosure of interests, and an unacceptable degree of laxity in the enforcement of registration. The committee recommended that the entry requirements be clarified. Since the beginning of the 1995 session, Members have been required to deposit in full any contracts which involve the Member acting in a parliamentary capacity on behalf of any organisation, and these contracts are available for public inspection. In addition, Members are required to reveal their annual remuneration, and also estimated monetary benefits received of any kind. Furthermore, all agreements which do not involve the Member acting in a parliamentary capacity for an organisation and, therefore, do not need to be deposited, should contain clear terms stating that the agreement does not involve the Member acting for the organisation in a parliamentary capacity.[114]

The committee also emphasised the requirement that Members of Parliament disclose their interests on 'each and every occasion when a Member approaches other Members or Ministers on a subject where a financial interest exists'.[115] The onus is on the Members to disclose the interest, and he or she should not assume that the interest is one known about by the other party.[116]

The rules on conflicts of interest should be further developed, and clarification provided on the circumstances under which a Member of Parliament should withdraw from, or refrain from taking part in, proceedings in Parliament.

---

114 *Op cit*, Nolan Report, fn 96, para 70.
115 *Op cit*, Nolan Report, fn 96, para 63.
116 As occurred in the case of Michael Mates, discussed above, p 701–02.

Gifts and hospitality

In relation to gifts and hospitality, the committee found that the rules set out in *Questions of Procedure for Ministers*,[117] are sufficiently detailed and that no further elaboration is required. The committee endorsed the important principle set out in *Questions of Procedure*:

> It is a well established and recognised rule that no Minister or public servant should accept gifts, hospitality or services from anyone which would, or might appear to, place him or her under an obligation.[118]

Enforcing Members' obligations

The Nolan Committee considered that Members of Parliament are insufficiently aware of the binding nature of resolutions of the House, and that this climate of laxity is one of the contributory factors to poor compliance. Furthermore, the committee regarded the respective roles of the Select Committee on Members' Interests and the Committee of Privileges of the House as unclear. The committee proposed the appointment of an independent Parliamentary Commissioner for Standards, responsible for maintaining the Register of Members' Interests and for providing guidance on standards of 'conduct, propriety and ethics'. The Commissioner fulfils a similar function to that of the Comptroller and Auditor General[119] and the Parliamentary Commissioner for Administration.[120] The Commissioner has power to receive and investigate complaints concerning Members' conduct. Where the Commissioner considers that further action should be taken, he would refer the matter for investigation by a newly established sub-committee of the Committee of Privileges. The sub-committee, the committee recommended, should sit in public and be able to call specialist advisers. Any Member appearing before the sub-committee should be able to be accompanied by an adviser.

The sub-committee would report to the full Committee of Privileges.[121] In order to bolster the Commissioner's authority, a select committee should be established. Political reaction to the Nolan Report was mixed. In a six hour debate on the Nolan Report,[122] some curious alliances between right wing and left wing politicians of both the Conservative Party and Labour Party were formed to oppose the recommendations. Many Conservative Members

---

117 *Op cit*, Nolan Report, fn 96, paras 80–81.
118 *Op cit*, Nolan Report, fn 96, para 126. See Chapter 3, para 40 of the report.
119 See Chapter 16.
120 See Chapter 26.
121 Now, the Standards and Privileges Committee.
122 19 May 1995.

opposed, in particular, the introduction of a Commissioner. The former Prime Minister, Edward Heath, attacked the proposal on the basis that a Commissioner would be a parliamentary 'outsider' unable to detect poor standards of conduct in the House. A former senior Conservative Member of Parliament, Enoch Powell,[123] warned that questions of Members' conduct cannot be legislated for.

The *First Report of the Committee on Standards in Public Life* (the 'Nolan Report'), was published in July 1995.[124] The Nolan Report recommended the following:

(a) that all new Members of Parliament should undertake a training course in ethics;

(b) that there should be established the office of Commissioner for Standards – an ethics ombudsman – to investigate allegations of breaches of the rules. The Commissioner for Standards would be responsible solely to the House of Commons, and should not enjoy independent legal status – as recommended by the Nolan Inquiry – similar to that enjoyed by the Comptroller and Auditor General and the Parliamentary Commissioner for Administration. The Commissioner will investigate allegations and recommend whether the matter should be heard by the Select Committee on Standards and Privileges;

(c) the Committee on Standards and Privileges will replace the current Privileges Committee of the House;

(d) Members of Parliament against whom allegations have been made should be entitled to legal representation;

(e) Members of Parliament are to be required to declare financial interests when tabling parliamentary questions.

The proposal that Members of Parliament should be forbidden from working for multi-client lobbying companies is also subject to further consideration.

Members of the House of Commons were given a free vote (a vote free from any party-political pressure) on the recommendations. Following an acrimonious Commons' debate, the proposal that Members of Parliament should declare the size of their outside earnings was rejected by 282 votes to 248 votes.[125]

In relation to Ministers, the Nolan Report was critical of the present position, whereby Ministers may leave government office and assume senior positions with – in particular – companies which have recently been privatised by the government.

---

123 Who consistently refused to sign the Register of Members' Interests. Mr Powell lost his seat in the 1987 general election.

124 Cm 2931; (1995) *The Times*, 11 July.

125 (1995) *The Times*, 20 July.

In July 1995, the government announced that a seven point Code of Conduct was to be published in response to aspects of the Nolan Report.[126] Ministers leaving office will no longer be permitted to take employment in the private sector without the appointment being vetted by an independent committee. From the parliamentary session 1995–96, all Cabinet Ministers have to wait at least three months before taking outside paid employment. In addition, a two year waiting period may be imposed. In relation to appointments to non-governmental public bodies, a Commissioner for Public Appointments has been established to ensure that there is no political bias in such appointments.[127]

The House of Commons, in response to the Nolan Report, passed resolutions which (a) introduce a rule against paid advocacy and (b) require Members entering into agreements for the provision of services in their capacity of members to deposit the terms of their agreements with the Parliamentary Commissioner for Standards at the same time as they are registered in the Register of Members' Interests. Furthermore, the House resolved to revise the 1947 resolution by inserting the requirement that no Member of Parliament (nor member of his or her family) shall receive remuneration of any kind in relation to raising an issue in Parliament by means of any speech, question, motion, introduction of a Bill or amendment to a motion or Bill. In addition, the House resolved that the rules on declaration of interests be amended to make it clear that Members are required to declare any relevant interest when tabling questions for oral or written answer or when preparing amendments to a Bill. Further, a Committee on Standards and Privileges has been established; and the office of Parliamentary Commissioner for Standards. The first Commissioner is Sir Gordon Downey.

The Committee on Standards and Privileges' first investigation concerned allegations that David Willetts, the Paymaster General, attempted to influence a 1994 investigation into whether Neil Hamilton had broken House of Commons rules. A finding that he had tried improperly to influence an inquiry could have lead to a reprimand or suspension or expulsion from the House of Commons. Any recommendation for action made by the committee must be approved by the House of Commons. In December 1996, it was reported that Mr Willetts was to be rebuked by the committee and that he would apologise, but that no further action would be taken. As a result of the committee's report, Mr Willetts resigned from office.[128]

---

126 (1995) *The Times*, 19 July.

127 The first Commissioner is Sir Leonard Peach. See HC Deb Vol 267 Col 234, 23 November 1995.

128 (1996) *The Times*, 11 and 12 December. Allegations concerning the current Paymaster General, Geoffrey Robinson, have been referred to the Commissioner on Standards. It is alleged that the Paymaster General failed to register interests relating to his chairmanship of a machine tools company between 1983 and 1987: (1998) *The Times*, 26 February. The Commissioner cleared Robinson of any breach of the rules.

A Code of Conduct for Members of Parliament

It was recommended that a code be introduced, specifying the general principles underlying public office, and specifying clearly the rules relating to financial interests, registration and the need to avoid any semblance of doubt concerning conflicts of interest. The House of Commons approved the *Third Report from the Committee on Standards and Privileges*,[129] and the *Code of Conduct* setting out the general principles to guide Members on standards of conduct that the House and the public have a right to expect, together with a *Guide to the Rules relating to the Conduct of Members*.[130] These include matters relating to the registration of interests and their declaration and the advocacy rule (see, further, below). In relation to registration, interests to be registered are directorships; remunerated employment; sponsorships which amount to 25 per cent or more of election expenses, or other funds related to a candidate's election campaign; free or subsidised research assistance; gifts, benefits or hospitality; overseas visits; overseas gifts and benefits; land and property; shareholdings; and miscellaneous interests. Where Members have entered into agreements which are relevant to their parliamentary duties, these are to be deposited with the Parliamentary Commissioner for Standards in addition to being registered. Where an informal, unwritten agreement, has been entered into, it must also be deposited with the Commissioner in written form. In relation to paid advocacy, this is banned in relation to a number of important matters. In particular, paid advocacy is banned in relation to initiating parliamentary proceedings, including the presentation of Bills, presentation of petitions, the asking of parliamentary questions, tabling or moving motions, or moving amendments to Bills. Any Member of Parliament, or member of the public, may lay a complaint, alleging breach of the Code, with the Commissioner for investigation. The Commissioner has a discretion whether or not to investigate. It is this tightening of the rules which has led to recent investigations into allegations including the Prime Minister, Deputy Prime Minister, Paymaster General and Leader of the Liberal Democrat Party, discussed in Chapter 11. The Commissioner reports his findings to the Select Committee on Standards and Privileges, which examines the findings. If no *prima facie* case is disclosed, this is reported to the Commons. If there is a *prima facie* case disclosed, the committee, following its examination, will report to the Commons, detailing its findings. The final decision on the matter lies with the House of Commons.

Subsequent to the *cash for questions* affair, the House of Commons re-stated the resolution of 1947[131] and added the following:

---

129 HC 604 (1995–96), London: HMSO.
130 HC Deb Vol 282 Col 392, 24 July 1996.
131 HC Deb Col 284, 15 July 1947; HC 118 (1946–47), London: HMSO.

... in particular, no Member shall, in consideration of any remuneration, fee, payment, reward or benefit in kind, direct or indirect ...

(a) advocate or initiate any cause or matter on behalf of any outside body or individual; or

(b) urge any other Member of either House ... including Ministers, to do so, by means of any speech, question, motion, introduction of a Bill or amendment to a motion or Bill.[132]

Cash for questions: the Downey Report

The *Report of the Parliamentary Commissioner for Standards* (the 'Downey Report') was published in July 1997. The 898 page report, which had taken 10 months to complete, makes it clear that the five former Ministers and Members of Parliament involved in accusations of accepting financial rewards, which were not recorded as required in the Register of Members' Interests, and were denied by the MPs, were guilty of breaking the parliamentary rules. The former Ministers involved were Tim Smith, former Northern Ireland Minister, and Neil Hamilton, former Minister at the Department of Trade and Industry. Tim Smith had admitted impropriety and resigned office before the 1997 general election, while Neil Hamilton has consistently denied the allegations. The other Members of Parliament involved in the affair, Sir Andrew Bowden, Sir Michael Grylls and Michael Brown were defeated in the general election, as was Neil Hamilton. It is probable that, had the former Ministers remained in Parliament, they would have faced expulsion from Parliament. Five other MPs who faced allegations of taking cash for questions were exonerated.[133] The Downey Report found the evidence against Neil Hamilton, who continues to declare his innocence, 'compelling':

> The evidence that Mr Hamilton received cash payments from Mr Al Fayed in return for lobbying services is compelling: and I so conclude.

The Downey Report also found that Neil Hamilton had mislead the former President of the Board of Trade, Michael Heseltine, and had 'enriched himself at the indirect expense of a constituent', and 'persistently and deliberately failed to declare his interests in dealings with Ministers and officials'.

The insistence that Parliament remain a self-regulatory body has come under question in light of this Downey Report. While early analyses of the Downey Report all praised the painstakingly detailed approach of the Commissioner, there were suggestions that such allegations should perhaps

---

132 HC Deb Cols 604, 661, 6 November 1995.

133 Lady Olga Maitland, Norman Lamont, Nirj Deva and Gerald Malone, all of whom were defeated at the General Election, and Sir Peter Hordern who stood down before the election.

be investigated by a statutory tribunal, headed by a judge, and holding public, rather than private, hearings.[134]

In *R v Commissioner for Standards and Privileges ex parte Al Fayed*,[135] the Court of Appeal ruled that the court had no jurisdiction to review decisions of the Commissioner, on the basis that the Commissioner was concerned with activities within Parliament, and the Commissioner was accountable to the special standing committee in the House of Commons, which alone had the power to perform supervisory functions over the Commissioner.

Penalties for breach of privilege and contempt

Historically, the most important power available to the House was to commit the offender to prison. Erskine May describes this power as the 'keystone of parliamentary privilege', but it is little used and has not been used since *Bradlaugh's Case*[136] in 1880. The House can vote to allow the offender to be prosecuted by the police, as happened in 1970, when a stranger threw a CS gas canister into the Chamber.[137] The most regularly employed sanction is the reprimand. The reprimand was used against Mr Tam Dalyell in 1968.[138] The House may order that a Member be suspended from the House or expelled. In 1948, Garry Allighan MP was found to have lied to a committee, falsely accusing other Members of taking money. The House ordered his expulsion from Parliament.[139] In 1988, Ron Brown MP was suspended from the House for the contempt of damaging the Mace. In 1994, the House suspended two Members, with loss of salary, for 20 days and 10 days respectively, for accepting payment for putting down parliamentary questions.[140] Following a report from the Standards and Privileges Committee,[141] a Member of Parliament, the Member for Liverpool (Mr Wareing) was also suspended for failing to register a shareholding interest in the Register of Members' Interests. The House of Commons has also considered the reports of the Standards and Privileges Committee[142] in relation to 25 investigations of allegations of breach of the rules. The committee had upheld findings on allegations in relation to 25 Members and former Members made by the Parliamentary Commissioner for Standards. Allegations were proved against five Members,

---

134 See Professor Vernon Bogdanor (1997) *The Guardian*, 4 July.
135 [1998] 1 WLR 669.
136 (1884) 12 QBD 271.
137 CJ (1970–71).
138 HC Deb Vol 769 Cols 587–666, 24 July 1968.
139 HC Deb Vol 443 Cols 1094–1198, 30 October 1947.
140 See, further, below.
141 HC 182 (1997–98), London: HMSO; and see the MP's complaint concerning procedure, HC Deb Vol 299 Col 1051, 30 October 1997.
142 HC 240 and 261 (1997–98), London: HMSO.

but all had failed to be re-elected in the 1997 general election. Each would, but for their failure to be re-elected to Parliament, have faced suspension.

The House of Lords has the power to impose fines on offenders but, curiously, the House of Commons does not have that power although, historically, it did. The last occasion on which a fine was imposed was in 1666.[143] The power to impose fines was denied in *R v Mead*.[144] Recommendations of the Select Committee on Parliamentary Privilege in 1967 and 1977 that such a power be introduced by statute have not been implemented. Where newspapers breach the rules of privilege or commit contempt of Parliament, the editor may be called to the bar of the House to explain and apologise, and journalists may be excluded from the precincts of the House for a specified period.

With regard to maintaining order in the House, the Speaker has a range of available disciplinary powers. The Speaker will firstly warn a Member about his conduct. If this does not ensure order, the Speaker may request the Member to leave the Chamber. If the Member refuses to leave, the Speaker may direct him to withdraw[145] immediately, and the Member must leave the precincts of Parliament for the remainder of the day. In the rare event that a Member refuses to comply with the order to withdraw, the Speaker may formally 'name' the Member[146] and put down a motion that the Member be suspended from the service of the House. The suspension on a first offence will last for five sitting days, on a second occasion, for 20 sitting days and on any subsequent occasion, for as long as the House shall determine.

The Select Committee on Procedure,[147] which in 1988 considered the standard of conduct of Members, found a sharp increase in the use of the Speaker's formal disciplinary powers, in particular the number of namings. The Parliament of 1979–83 saw 12 cases, of which five involved naming, the 1983–87 Parliament saw nine cases, including five namings, but, in the 1988–89 session, nine cases occurred, eight of which led to namings. The committee recommended that everything possible should be done to maintain order in the House. The House of Commons is, however, powerless in relation to the punishment of former Members of Parliament in respect of breaches of privilege while Members.

The Joint Committee on Parliamentary Privilege Report of 1999 had considered in depth the issue of bribery of a Member of Parliament, subsequent to the Law Commission's investigation into the law relating to

---

143 *White's Case* (1666).
144 (1762) 3 Burr 1335.
145 Standing Order No 42.
146 Standing Order No 43.
147 *First Report of the Select Committee on Procedure*, 1988–89.

bribery and corruption.[148] Four options exist. The first is to rely solely on parliamentary privilege to deal with allegations of bribery; the second, to subject Members of Parliament to the same corruption laws as other people; the third, to distinguish between conduct to be dealt with by Parliament and that to be dealt with under the criminal law; and the fourth, to make criminal proceedings against Members subject to the approval of the relevant House of Parliament. Each of these, in the Committee's view, was attended by difficulties in relation to parliamentary privilege and Article IX. Nevertheless, the Committee favoured the second option – namely, bringing Members of both Houses of Parliament within the ambit of the criminal law of bribery. The necessary legislation would need to be drafted to make clear that evidence relating to an alleged offence would be admissible in a court of law notwithstanding Article IX.

In 2000, the Committee on Standards in Public Life made recommendations designed to improve discipline over Members of Parliament. In *Reinforcing Standards*, Lord Neill of Bladen recommended that legislation be introduced to bring Members of Parliament, and those who offered bribes to Members, within the reach of bribery laws. The report also recommended that there should be an appeal mechanism against findings of misconduct by the Committee on Standards and Privileges. Serious allegations of misconduct would be heard by a new tribunal, chaired by an independent legal expert and senior backbenchers, rather than the Standards and Privileges Committee. Before a case is referred to the tribunal, it would be considered by the Committee on Standards and Privileges and the accused Member would be able to make representations to the Committee. Financial assistance would be made available to fund legal representation before the tribunal. The tribunal's findings would be reported back to the Committee which would decide what penalty should be recommended to the House of Commons. The Neill Committee also recommended that an appeals procedure should be introduced to enable a Member to appeal against the decision to refer his or her case to the tribunal, and against the tribunal ruling. The appeal would be heard by a retired senior judge. Proceedings before the Committee should be held in public. The government is considering the report, but is unlikely to introduce legislation before the next general election.

PUBLICATION OF PARLIAMENTARY PROCEEDINGS

The publication of proceedings in Parliament is covered by the same rules as the reporting of proceedings in court. The underlying principle is that

---

148 Law Commission, *Legislating the Criminal Code: Corruption, A Consultation Paper*, Law Com No 145, 1997, London: HMSO; and *Legislating the Criminal Code: Corruption*, Law Com No 248, 1998 (HC 524 (1997–98)), London: HMSO.

publication is in the public interest and generally outweighs any disadvantage to individuals.

On the extent to which the reporting and publication of parliamentary proceedings is protected, section 1 of the Parliamentary Papers Act 1840 provides that, where civil or criminal proceedings are commenced, the defendant may present to the court a certificate stating that the publication in question was made under the authority of the House of Lords or House of Commons, and that the 'judge or court shall thereupon immediately stay such civil or criminal proceeding'.

Section 2 provides that similar protection exists for correct copies of official reports and authorised papers. Section 3 provides that extracts or abstracts from such reports or papers, for example, in newspapers, are protected provided that such extracts are published *bona fide* and without malice. Thus papers of the House, or papers ordered to be published by the House, plus fair and accurate, but unauthorised, reports of proceedings are covered by qualified privilege, and an action for damages for injury allegedly caused by their publication would only lie if malice could be proven.

The Parliamentary Papers Act was passed as a direct result of two cases in which the courts and Parliament came into conflict, namely *Stockdale v Hansard*[149] and the *Sheriff of Middlesex's Case* (discussed above, p 695). While the passing of the Parliamentary Papers Act 1840 gives statutory authority to publication of official papers and authorised reports, uncertainty still remains as to the scope of the protection.

Privilege and the media

Publications which reflect on the dignity of the House as a whole are classified as 'constructive contempts', as are reflections on individual Members.[150] Illustrations of adverse comments published in the press include that of *The Sunday Express* which, in 1953, commented that two Members were asleep during an all night sitting of the House. Further, in 1956, *The Sunday Express* criticised Members of Parliament for exempting themselves from the petrol rationing which had been imposed as a result of the Suez crises. The report of the Committee of Privileges held that the editor had been:

> ... guilty of a serious contempt in reflecting upon all Members of the House and so upon the House itself by alleging that Members of the House had been guilty of contemptible conduct in failing, owing to self interest, to protest at an unfair discrimination in their favour. Such an attack on Members is calculated to diminish the respect due to the House and so to lessen its authority.[151]

---

149 (1839) 9 Ad & E 1.

150 *Op cit*, Erskine May, fn 1, p 121.

151 *Second Report from the Committee of Privileges*, HC 38 (1956–57), London: HMSO.

The issue of media pressure again fell for consideration by the Committee of Privileges in 1956. A Member of Parliament, Mr Arthur Lewis, gave notice of a forthcoming Prime Ministerial parliamentary question, which asked:

> ... whether he will arrange for part of the money contributed by the government for relief in Hungary to be allocated to the relief of the several thousand Egyptian people who have been rendered homeless and destitute by British shelling and rocket fire in Egypt.

In a scathing editorial in *The Sunday Graphic*, readers were invited to telephone Mr Lewis and give him their views. To assist this task, the newspaper published the Member's telephone number. As a consequence, the Member received thousands of irate telephone calls before the Post Office was able to change his number. The committee ruled that:

> ... the principle that to molest a Member of Parliament on account of his conduct in Parliament is a breach of privilege is well established ... In our view, the principle clearly applies to the circumstances of this case and, in our opinion, the Editor of *The Sunday Graphic* was guilty of a breach of privilege in that he instigated the molestation to which Mr Lewis was subjected.[152]

In both cases, the editors were called to the Bar of the House and apologised.

Unauthorised disclosure of parliamentary proceedings

The unauthorised disclosure of proceedings conducted in private and of draft reports of committees which have not been reported to the House is governed by a resolution of the House of 1837, as amended in 1980.[153] The resolution makes such disclosure a contempt of the House.[154] The House resolved in 1978 that its penal jurisdiction should only be used where the action complained of was likely to cause a 'substantial interference' with a committee's work.[155] The Committee of Privileges recommended in its 1985 report that 'substantial interference' with regard to leaked documents should be confined to confidential or classified information or deliberate attempts to undermine the work of the committee.[156]

Between 1971 and 1988, six incidents of unauthorised disclosure were recorded.[157] In no case was the source of the leak – presumed to be a Member of the select committee – identifiable and, in each case, the journalists concerned had refused to reveal their sources. The House has shown itself to

---

152 *First Report from the Committee of Privileges*, HC 27 (1956–57), London: HMSO.
153 Standing Order No 94.
154 See Leopold, P, 'Leaks and squeaks in the Palace of Westminster' [1980] PL 368.
155 HC Deb Vol 943 Col 1198, 6 February 1978.
156 *Second Report from the Committee of Privileges: Premature Disclosure of Proceedings of Select Committee*, HC 555 (1984–85), London: HMSO, paras 51–55.
157 *Op cit*, Griffith and Ryle, fn 1, p 101.

be unwilling to punish publishers when it cannot identify and punish the source of the leak.

In 1985, *The Times* newspaper published a leaked draft report of the Home Affairs Select Committee and a draft report on the Environment Select Committee on the disposal of radioactive waste. The Committee of Privileges recommended that both the Member responsible for the leak and the journalist should be punished but, when the matter was put to the House, it declined to follow the committee's recommendation.[158]

A fresh issue arose in 1999 with the leak of select committee reports to Ministers. In July 1999, a senior Labour Member of Parliament, Earnest Ross, was forced to resign from the Foreign Affairs Select Committee after he had been found responsible for leaking a critical report over the Foreign Office's role in allegedly breaching a United Nations' arms embargo in Sierra Leone to the Foreign Secretary, Robin Cook. The leak had the potential, if used by the Foreign Secretary, of interfering with the work of the Select Committee. After criticism by the Standards and Privileges Committee, Mr Ross apologised to the House and was suspended for 10 days. Subsequently, two Labour Members, one who had leaked a Social Security Select Committee Report and one who had received the report, were suspended from the Commons for three and five days, respectively. The Prime Minister and the Cabinet Secretary then issued directions to Ministers and senior civil servants that any leaked documents were to be returned immediately and without use having been made of them, and that the Ministerial Code of Practice would be amended to cover the leaking of such reports which potentially undermine the authority of Select Committees.

The procedure for determining issues of privilege and contempt

If an allegation of breach of privilege or contempt is made, the complaint is communicated to the Speaker. The Member will be given written notice of the complaint. The Speaker must be satisfied, first, that the matter is one involving privilege and, secondly, that the complaint is substantial. If he or she so finds, the Speaker advises the complainant that he may put down a Motion which will be debated the following day. For the most part, the matter will then be referred by the House to the Committee on Standards and Privileges (formerly, the Committee of Privileges). The committee is made up of 17 senior Members of the House from all political parties, chaired by the Leader of the House. Although acting in a quasi-judicial capacity, the committee is not bound to follow strict rules of procedure. The legal rules of evidence do not apply and there is normally no legal representation. The Committee sits in

---

158 HC Deb Vol 98 Cols 293–330, 20 May 1986.

private.[159] If the Committee finds that there has been a breach, it will make recommendations as to punishment, but has no power to apply the sanction: that is for the House as a whole, who will vote on the matter following a debate. The House is not bound by the Committee's recommendations and may, as happened in the case of *Strauss*,[160] reject them.

Members' interests in the House of Lords

Privilege in the House of Lords

The House of Lords enjoys the same privilege of freedom from arrest[161] and freedom of speech as the Commons. Freedom of access to the Sovereign is enjoyed by the House collectively and by each peer individually. This privilege of peerage extends to all peers, irrespective of whether they sit in the House of Lords. The House of Lords has the same right as the Commons to determine its own procedure. In the event of a disputed peerage, the House of Lords has jurisdiction to determine the matter.[162] The House of Lords has the power to commit persons for breach of privilege or contempt and also the power to impose fines. The House of Lords may also summon judges to attend in order to give advice on points of law.

Members' interests in the House of Lords

In July 1995, Lord Griffiths published his report on outside interests of peers. The report was submitted to the Lords' Procedure Committee. The recommendations included the introduction of a Register of Members' Interests on which all remunerated positions are to be declared. Peers will no longer be permitted to act as advocates for companies or organisations from whom they receive remuneration. They will, however, continue to be allowed to act as advisers to outside groups. Peers will no longer be free to ask questions or to table amendments where their sponsoring organisation stands to gain benefit.

An estimated 100 of approximately 1,200 peers act as consultants. Peers acting as parliamentary advisers are estimated to receive between less than £8,000 per annum and £25,000 per annum. Lord Bethell defended the right of peers to accept paid positions, pointing out that, if a peer attended the House

---

159 Demands by the Rt Hon Tony Benn MP that the Committee sit in public were rejected in 1994. Moreover, his announced intention to disclose details of the Committee's hearings resulted in his deselection from the Committee.

160 [1985] PL 80.

161 (1995) *The Sunday Times*, 16 July.

162 See *Stourton v Stourton* [1963] P 303.

every sitting day, the remuneration in expenses would amount to only some £8,000 per year.[163]

In 1996, in response to increased concerns over Members' interests, a Register of Members' Interests was established in the House of Lords. In addition, the House has approved a motion that Lords should always act on their personal honour and should never accept any financial inducement as an incentive or reward for exercising parliamentary influence.

Further reform of parliamentary privilege

In addition to the reforms considered above, there remains a need to clarify the definition given to the phrase 'proceedings in Parliament' in Article IX of the Bill of Rights in order that both Members and other individuals may better understand the scope of the protection given by privilege.

The Joint Committee on Parliamentary Privilege considered the question of the definition of parliamentary proceedings in its 1999 report. The Committee recommended that there should be enacted a Parliamentary Privileges Act to cover this and a number of other reforms.

Defining 'proceedings in Parliament'

Rejecting earlier suggested definitions of parliamentary proceedings as too wide, the Committee proposed the following statutory definition:

(1) For the purposes of Article IX of the Bill of Rights 1689 'proceedings in Parliament' means all words spoken and acts done in the course of, or for the purposes of, or necessarily incidental to, transacting the business of either House of Parliament or of a committee.

(2) Without limiting (1), this includes:

(a) the giving of evidence before a House or a committee or an officer appointed by a House to receive such evidence;

(b) the presentation or submission of a document to a House or a committee or an officer appointed by a House to receive it, once the document is accepted;

(c) the preparation of a document for the purposes of transacting the business of a House or a committee, provided any drafts, notes, advice or the like are not circulated more widely than is reasonable for the purposes of preparation;

---

163 (1995) *The Sunday Times*, 16 July.

(d) the formulation, making or publication of a document by a House or a committee;

(e) the maintenance of any register of the interests of the members of a House and any other register of interests prescribed by resolution of a House.

(3) A 'committee' means a committee appointed by either House or a joint committee appointed by both Houses of Parliament and includes a sub-committee.

(4) A document includes any disc, tape or device in which data are embodied so as to be capable of being reproduced therefrom.

In addition, there should be a statutory definition of 'place out of Parliament', and the scope of the prohibition on 'questioning'. Article IX should not apply to court proceedings in so far as they relate to interpretation of Acts of Parliament or subordinate legislation (the *Pepper v Hart* principle), or to judicial review. Tribunals appointed under the Tribunals of Inquiry (Evidence) Act 1921 could also be excluded from Article IX. The legislation should make it clear that the application of Article IX extends to Scotland and Northern Ireland. Disputes as to the meaning of 'proceedings in Parliament' arising in court proceedings should continue to be resolved by the trial judge, whereas those arising in the House should be dealt with there.

Other suggested reforms

The Committee recommends that 'contempt of Parliament' be statutorily defined. In relation to immunity from arrest in civil matters, the Committee recommends that this be abolished. On sanctions, it is recommended that the statute state the power to fine offenders and that the power to imprison be abolished, other than for the temporary detention of persons misconducting themselves within the precincts of Parliament. On contempt of Parliament by non-Members, the courts should be given concurrent jurisdiction. Failure to attend proceedings or to answer questions or produce required documents should constitute criminal offences, punishable with an unlimited fine or up to three months' imprisonment. In relation to the reporting of parliamentary proceedings, the Parliamentary Papers Act 1840 should be replaced by a modern statute.

To complement statute, the Committee recommends that there should be a statutory code. Notwithstanding the difficulties of codification, such as reduced flexibility for the future, the advantages of clarification for both Members and non-Members of Parliament would outweigh such problems, particularly if the code were to include definitive statements of principle followed by illustrative, but not exhaustive, examples.

PART VI

THE INDIVIDUAL AND THE STATE

CHAPTER 19

FREEDOM FROM DISCRIMINATION AND FREEDOM OF EXPRESSION

THE ORIGINS OF THE IDEA OF RIGHTS

In Chapter 4, the rule of law, a concept which portrays the idea of governmental power limited by law and the democratic process, was discussed. It was seen that from early times the sovereignty of law over man was proclaimed in order to safeguard citizens from the abuse of power by Monarchs and governments. The protection of individual rights and freedoms by the State is an essential feature of the rule of law. With that discussion in mind, in this chapter, the extent to which rights and freedoms are protected in the United Kingdom is considered and, in Chapter 22, the protection of rights under the European Convention on Human Rights is examined. The focus of study in this chapter is domestic statutory and common law protection. Before turning to the law, it is useful to review the theoretical approaches which underlie the contemporary constitutional position.

EARLY CONCEPTIONS OF LIMITED GOVERNMENTAL POWER

John Locke

In *Two Treatises of Government*,[1] John Locke claimed that sovereign power was limited and that the people had the right to resort to revolution against the sovereign if power was abused. Such writing was both revolutionary and seditious – challenging the very basis of State authority. Locke went into exile in 1683.[2] With the accession of William of Orange to the throne in 1689, Locke returned to England and his work – previously unpublished – reached the light of day, albeit anonymously. The timing of publication could not have been more forceful. An historic settlement between Parliament and Crown had finally and recently been reached, resulting in the Bill of Rights 1689,[3] thus ending centuries of conflict. However, Locke's writing presented a theory which challenged the basis of sovereign power by asserting the rights of man

---

1   Assumed to have been in manuscript form by 1683.
2   Whilst in exile, John Locke wrote *Essay Concerning Human Understanding* and *Letter on Toleration*, both 1990, Oxford: Clarendon.
3   See Chapters 6 and 7.

against the sovereign. Much of the first *Treatise* is an argument directed against absolute monarchical power and the use of the prerogative. By insisting that government held its power on trust, Locke was indirectly claiming the sovereignty of the people over the sovereignty of government. Government had a legitimate right to rule, and to use the law for the good of the people; but that right was conditional and limited by the ultimate power of the people to overthrow a government which violated its trust. As Locke observed:

> ... acting for the preservation of the community, there can be but one supreme power, which is the legislative, to which all the rest are and must be subordinate, yet the legislative being only a fiduciary power to act for certain ends, there remains still in the people a supreme power to remove or alter the legislative, when they find the legislative acts contrary to the trust reposed in them. For all power given with trust for the attaining an end being limited by that end, whenever that end is manifestly neglected or opposed, the trust must necessarily be forfeited, and the power devolve into the hands of those that gave it, who may place it anew where they shall think best for their safety and security. And thus the community perpetually retains a supreme power of saving themselves from the attempts and designs of anybody, even of their legislators, whenever they shall be so foolish or so wicked as to lay and carry on designs against the liberties and properties of the subject. For no man or society of men having a power to deliver up their preservation, or consequently the means of it, to the absolute will and arbitrary dominion of another, whenever any one shall go about to bring them into such slavish condition, they will always have a right to preserve what they have not a power to part with, and to rid themselves of those who invade this fundamental, sacred, and unalterable law of self-preservation for which they entered into society. And thus the community may be said in this respect to be always the supreme power, but not as considered under any form of government, because this power of the people can never take place till the government be dissolved.[4]

Thomas Paine

Thomas Paine,[5] who claimed not to have read Locke's works, was to echo many of Locke's radical and revolutionary sentiments. Paine was involved in two revolutions: that of the United States of America, in 1775, and that of France, in 1789.[6] The background of the two men could not have been more different. Whereas John Locke had a privileged upbringing, being educated at Westminster School, and Christ Church, Oxford, where he remained for some

---

4   Locke, J, *Two Treatises of Government* (1690), 1977, London: JM Dent, Bk II, Chapter XIII, para 149.

5   1737–1809.

6   An involvement which he claimed made his life 'truly useful'.

15 years, before entering into service with the Earl of Shaftsbury,[7] Thomas Paine was largely self-educated. In 1773, he issued a pamphlet,[8] the radical nature of which caused him to be discharged from his position as an exciseman (customs officer). In the course of his political lobbying for higher pay for fellow excise officers, he met Benjamin Franklin.[9] With Franklin's support, Paine emigrated to North America.

While John Locke had been writing against the background of the constitutional struggles in the United Kingdom, which were to culminate in the assertion of Parliament's sovereignty over the King, Paine was writing in the midst of the struggle for independence in America against the sovereign English King George III. In 1775, Paine, working as a journalist on the *Pennsylvania Journal*, was supporting the right of colonists to control their own affairs. In criticising England for her treatment of, among others, American Indians and black slaves, Paine predicted the eventual separation of America from Britain. In 1776, he published *Common Sense*, which not only attacked the policy of the King towards the colony, but also attacked the institution of monarchy itself. *Common Sense* exerted a profound influence on the course of political events, and the Declaration of Independence[10] echoed Paine's sentiments. In both *Common Sense* and *Rights of Man*, arbitrary power is decried and the freedom of the individual declared to be sovereign. Paine distinguished between the natural and civil rights of individuals:

> Natural rights are those which appertain to man in right of his existence. Of this kind are all the intellectual rights, or rights of the mind, and also those rights of acting as an individual for his own comfort and happiness, which are not injurious to the natural rights of others. Civil rights are those which appertain to man in right of his being a member of society. Every civil right has for its foundation, some natural right pre-existing in the individual, but to the enjoyment of which his individual power is not, in all cases, sufficiently competent.[11]

Civil rights, for Paine, are entailed in, and grow out of, individual natural rights and are, accordingly, antecedent to any form of government. When man entered into society:

> ... the individuals themselves, each in his own personal and sovereign right, entered into a compact with each other to produce a government: and this is the only mode in which governments have a right to arise, and the only principle on which they have a right to exist.[12]

---

7   Lord Ashley, one of the most powerful figures in the court of Charles II.

8   The Case of the Officers of the Excise.

9   1706–90. American statesman; a draughtsman of the American Constitution and Ambassador to France 1776–85.

10   4 July 1776.

11   Paine, T, *Rights of Man* (1791–92) 1984, rep 1998, Collins, H (ed), New York: Penguin, p 90.

12   *Ibid*, p 92.

Furthermore:

> The rights of men in society, are neither devisable, nor transferable, nor annihilable, but are descendable only; and it is not in the power of any generation to intercept finally, and cut off the descent.

The American constitution reflected these views, the preamble declaring that:

> We the People of the United States, in order to form a more perfect Union, establish Justice, ensure Domestic Tranquillity, provide for the Common Defence, promote the general Welfare, and secure the Blessings of Liberty to ourselves and our Posterity, do ordain and establish this CONSTITUTION for the United States of America.

THE EMERGENCE OF THE CONSTITUTIONAL PROTECTION OF RIGHTS

These early expressions of an emergent notion of individual rights can be seen today in most written constitutions in the world, whether or not the constitution is 'autochthonous'.[13]

The attempt to protect human rights on an international level began with the founding of the League of Nations after World War I and the imposition of certain safeguards of human rights in peace treaties negotiated after the war for the protection of minorities. It was not to be, however, until after the Second World War that the international community became convinced of the real and pressing need to protect and promote human rights as an integral and essential element for the preservation of world peace and co-operation. The United Nations[14] provided the appropriate forum for international quasi-legislative activity. In 1948, the Universal Declaration on Human Rights was adopted, supplemented by two implementing international covenants in 1966: the International Covenant on Civil and Political Rights and the International Covenant on Economic, Social and Cultural Rights. Taken together, these documents represent an international Bill of Human Rights. Inspired by the United Nations Declaration and Covenants, many other regional conventions were drafted, for example, the American Convention of Human Rights 1969 and the African Charter of 1987.[15]

---

13 Defined as a constitution originating from, and having the authority of, the people it governs: it springs from the people and is not conferred upon the people from any higher authority. See Wheare, KC, *Modern Constitutions*, 2nd edn, 1966, Oxford: OUP.

14 Which superceded the League of Nations in 1945.

15 See, also, the Hong Kong Bill of Rights based on the UN Covenant on Civil and Political Rights.

Natural law and positive law[16]

The ancient concept of natural law, as discussed in Chapter 4, concerns an evaluation of the validity of human law against some higher source of authority, whether theological or secular, which is both eternal and universal. The demands of natural law challenge the law of human rulers – demanding that law conform to higher principles. One such principle is the respect for individual rights and freedoms, and it may therefore be argued that the protection of human rights is a natural law concept. It should not be assumed, however, that the assertions that the rights of man derive from natural law has been completely or unequivocally accepted.

In the nineteenth century, for example, the rise of nationalism in the West challenged doctrines of natural law. The same century also witnessed the rise in positivism – the legal-theoretical schools of thought concerned solely to identify and define the concept of valid human law. These two developments – nationalism and positivism – shifted the focus of attention away from individual rights towards an analysis of State power. By way of illustration, Hegel's *Philosophy of Right*[17] portrayed the picture of the State as absolutely sovereign, its form and content being determined by history, but its existence and power being unrestricted by any form of natural law.

In the United Kingdom, the Scottish philosopher David Hume laid the foundations for positivism.[18] Positivism, in its many forms, concerns the endeavour of isolating the law laid down by human superior (the sovereign power) to human inferior (the subject).[19] In essence, Hume's thesis was that, in logic, it is not possible to derive a statement of fact (an existential statement) – from a statement of what ought to be (a normative statement). By this reasoning, only by keeping statements of fact and statements of 'ought' – or moral statements – separate can there be a true understanding of reality, and law. The implication of such a distinction for law and legal theory is that no moral statement as to what 'ought to be' can be inferred from a purely factual statement. This essential logical separation of the factual from the normative underlies the positivist endeavour: the attempt to provide a coherent logical structure of legal rules, and legal rules alone, unaffected by morality. For the positivist, whatever is enacted according to the accepted constitutional procedure employed within the State is valid law and entails an absolute obligation of obedience.[20] As such, there can be no claim to freedoms or

---

16 See Finnis, JM, *Natural Law and Natural Rights*, 1980, Oxford: Clarendon; Hart, HLA, *The Concept of Law*, 1961, Oxford: Clarendon.

17 1821.

18 See Hume, D, *An Enquiry Concerning the Principles of Morals* (1751) 1957, Indianapolis: Bobbs-Merrill, *Political Discourses* (1752), 1769, Edinburgh: Kineald and Donaldson.

19 See, eg, Austin, J, *The Province of Jurisprudence Determined* (1832), 1954, London: Weidenfeld & Nicolson; and *ibid*, Hart, Chapters 1–4.

20 See Chapter 4.

human rights which are capable of overriding the positive law. According to positivist theories of law, while in a perfect world the positive law may – and ideally should – conform to moral precepts, should it fail so to do, the individual is powerless to confront the law.

The nineteenth century rise in positivism represented both an attack on the claims of natural law and an attempt to analyse scientifically the law as it exists in fact. The doctrine of natural law for which so much had been claimed in relation to human rights and freedoms was placed on the defensive. The protection of rights based on natural law was further damaged by the utilitarians. Having rejected natural law as providing the lodestar for enactment of positive law, the utilitarians adopted the principle of utility. By utility is meant that the proper guidance in the formation of laws is the overall effect of a legislative proposal on society as a whole. A proposal for legislation will be in conformity with the doctrine of utility if it increases the sum of happiness in society overall. The leading exponent of the utilitarian school was Jeremy Bentham[21] whose *An Introduction to the Principles of Morals and Legislation*[22] was to exert enduring influence. Bentham dismissed the idea of natural law and natural rights: natural rights were 'nonsense' – and, worse – 'nonsense on stilts'.

Despite the attacks from nationalists, positivists and utilitarians, the quest for the protection of rights – from wheresoever derived – continued; a quest which became reinvigorated by the horrors of the Second World War.

Rights and freedoms under an unwritten constitution

In the absence of a written constitution enshrining the rights of individuals and limiting the power of government and Parliament, Parliament is supreme. The constitution of the United Kingdom adopts the positivist approach to law, admitting no 'higher' source of authority for law than Parliament itself. Accordingly, it is the duty of the judges to implement Parliament's will, and the courts have no power to rule on the validity of an Act of Parliament on the basis that the Act is contrary to 'right reason' or some other dictate of morality.[23] The Human Rights Act 1998, which incorporates the European Convention on Human Rights into English law preserves this conventional sovereignty: judges in the superior courts will be empowered to make declarations of incompatibility of domestic law with Convention requirements, but not to invalidate statute: that power is preserved for Parliament.

---

21 1748–1832.

22 Bentham, J, *An Introduction to the Principles of Morals and Legislation*, 1970, Burns, JH and Hart, HLA (eds), London: Athlone.

23 *Pickin v British Railways Board* [1974] AC 765. See, further, Chapter 7.

It is a paradox that the United Kingdom – viewed as a liberal democratic State – should have no comprehensive written Bill of Rights.[24] This is especially so, given that the United Kingdom has been responsible for restoring independence to many former colonies and dominions and, in so doing, has conferred upon those States both a written constitution and a Bill of Rights. In order to ascertain what rights exist, and the scope of such rights, it is necessary in the United Kingdom to turn to Acts of Parliament and the common law and, increasingly, to the European Convention on Human Rights and European Community law. Accordingly, such rights as exist in the United Kingdom have been both fragmentary and uncertain. However, the Human Rights Act 1998, discussed further in Chapter 22, will provide a yardstick against which to measure current law and proposals for new legislation, and will mark a significant conceptual change in the manner in which rights and liberties are regarded in the United Kingdom.

It is a cardinal maxim of English law that there is 'no remedy without a right': *ubi jus ibi remedium*. For this reason, it is, in large measure, inaccurate to speak of 'rights' and more appropriate – for the most part and until incorporation of the Convention – to speak of freedoms. A freedom exists unless, and to the extent that, its exercise is constrained by law. As Sir Ivor Jennings states:

> There is no more a 'right of free speech' than there is a 'right to tie up my shoe lace'; or, if there is a right of free speech, there is also a right to tie up my shoe lace. The question to be discussed in each case is the nature of the legal restrictions.[25]

It has been seen throughout this text, that the fundamental characteristic of the constitution lies in its largely unwritten nature, from which flows the capacity for evolution. *Par excellence*, the United Kingdom constitution is flexible.[26] It has been seen that many – indeed most – other countries have achieved their current status by way of revolution or the grant of independence, and that such States invariably adopt a written constitution as the cornerstone of their new constitutional arrangements. In the majority of States, a formal part of the constitution will be devoted to the rights of individuals. The United States of America, for example, following the French model of 1789, enacted provisions relating to freedoms in the first 10 amendments to the constitution, including: the right to free speech; the right to security of the person, property and effects; freedom from unreasonable search and seizures; freedom from being compelled to give evidence against oneself in a criminal case; the right to speedy public trial; and the right not to be deprived of life, limb or property without the due process of law.

---

24 The Bill of Rights 1689, it will be recalled, was concerned with constitutional arrangements between the Crown and Parliament, not with the rights of individuals.

25 Jennings, I (Sir), *The Law and the Constitution*, 5th edn, 1959, London: Hodder & Stoughton, pp 262–63.

26 See Chapters 1 and 3.

The United Kingdom possesses rules of law relating to each of these 'rights' but they are contained in measures very different from a written Bill of Rights. Whereas, under a written constitution, there will generally be a Supreme Court with powers to test the constitutionality of legislation[27] and, if necessary, to strike legislation down, under the United Kingdom's unwritten constitution, that situation does not exist. Citizens in the United Kingdom, therefore, have traditionally been dependent upon the elected Parliament to protect rights, or on the judiciary to protect rights through the common law.

There are disadvantages with such an arrangement, both in psychological and practical terms. In practical terms, the law books must be studied in order to establish whether an alleged right exists and, if new situations arise which are not covered by existing legal authorities, citizens remain in doubt as to their rights. There has hitherto been, for example, no single written authoritative document which can be used as either a sword or a shield against government action. The Human Rights Act 1998 will, for the first time, provide both sword and shield. The point about the significance of Bills of Rights should not, however, be exaggerated for, even under written constitutions, doubts may exist as to the scope of rights until the issue is tested and decided by the highest court in a legal system. However, as will be discussed in Chapter 22, the effectiveness of the protection given by the domestic courts will turn largely on the robustness of the judges in interpreting statutes and secondary legislation in accordance with the requirements of the Convention. At the current time, it is difficult to speculate as to the likely impact and effectiveness of the Convention in the domestic courts, although its incorporation should mark a sea change in citizen's perceptions of rights.

The protection of rights and freedoms traditionally emanate from differing sources, and at differing levels. They may be protected, under domestic law, by statute or the common law and, under international law, rights are protected by conventions and treaties. Hitherto, the prevailing attitude of governments to individual rights in the United Kingdom today has been much the same as it was in Dicey's day. Dicey,[28] writing on the rule of law,[29] stated that the rights and freedoms of citizens were best protected not by written constitutions or special courts but by the judges under the common law. However, there is much evidence against this view, which must be regarded as an outdated and complacent attitude, as will be revealed by discussion of the case law. Moreover, under the Human Rights Act 1998, every aspect of law to which Convention rights apply, will be scrutinised to

---

27 See, for the position in the United States of America, *Marbury v Madison* 1 Cranch 103 (1803).

28 Dicey, AV, *Introduction to the Study of the Law of the Constitution* (1885), 10th edn, 1959, London: Macmillan.

29 See Chapter 4.

ascertain whether or not, and to what extent, it is consistent with the standards which have been set by the European Court of Human Rights. With the Act coming into effect in 2000 in England and Wales, considerable litigation is expected as domestic law is evaluated in relation to Convention rights.

FREEDOM FROM DISCRIMINATION: RACIAL AND SEXUAL EQUALITY

The common law proved inadequate to protect individuals against discrimination on the basis of either race or sex. Parliament has intervened, passing originally the Race Relations Act 1965 (now, the Race Relations Act 1976) and the Sex Discrimination Act 1975 (as subsequently amended). The two Acts employ similar concepts and are enforced by similar machinery.

The Human Rights Act 1998 incorporates Article 14 of the European Convention on Human Rights, which provides for non-discrimination on the grounds of sex, race, colour, language, religion, political or other opinion, national or social origin, association with a national minority, property, birth or other status. However, Article 14 protects against discrimination only in respect of 'the enjoyment of the rights and freedoms set forth in [the] Convention': it is not, therefore, a blanket prohibition on discrimination in all circumstances.

RACIAL DISCRIMINATION

Race Relations Acts[30]

In 1965, Parliament, for the first time, considered legal protection against racial discrimination to be necessary. The Race Relations Act 1965, however, proved to provide only limited value in protection.[31] The Act provided not for access to the courts for protection from discrimination, but for an application to be made to the Race Relations Board established under the 1965 Act. The Race Relations Act 1968 strengthened the powers of the Board, but protection from discrimination remained limited. The law is now found in the Race Relations Act 1976.

---

30 See Lustgarten, L, *The Legal Control of Racial Discrimination*, 1980, London: Macmillan and 'Racial inequality and the limits of law' (1981) 44 MLR 68.

31 The Race Relations Act 1968 extended the 1965 Act, but effectiveness remained unsatisfactory.

Racial discrimination is defined under the Act as being discrimination based on the grounds of colour, race, nationality, ethnic or national origins. Discrimination may be direct or indirect.[32] The Act does not, however, prohibit all forms of racial discrimination, and confines protection to discrimination in the field of employment, including service of the Crown, such as the armed forces,[33] the police and local authorities, and to education, housing and the provision of goods and services.

The definition of racial discrimination

The courts have encountered problems with the definition of racial discrimination which is linked to discrimination of the grounds of colour, race, nationality, ethnic or national origins. In *Seide v Gillette Industries*,[34] for example, it was held that people of Jewish origin and culture fell within the definition. In *Mandla v Dowell Lee*,[35] the House of Lords ruled that Sikhs fell within the definition of a racial group and were thus protected under the Act.[36] Gypsies have also held to be within the definition,[37] although Rastafarians have not. The tests propounded by the court in *Dawkins v Department of the Environment*,[38] in relation to whether a group constitutes a racial group for the purposes of the Act, is whether there is a long shared history and a cultural tradition and customs. In *Mandla v Dowell Lee*,[39] the House of Lords ruled that the characteristics of an ethnic group included a long shared distinctive history and a distinctive cultural tradition. Further common characteristics included a common geographical origin, common language and religion, common literature, and being a minority within a larger society.

In *Commission for Racial Equality v Dutton*,[40] the Court of Appeal had to decide whether Gypsies constituted a racial group. The court reviewed the variety of meanings given to 'Gypsies'. Applying the tests propounded by the House of Lords in *Mandla v Dowell Lee*,[41] Nicholls LJ stated that:

> ... Gypsies are a minority, with a long shared history and a common geographical origin ... having certain, albeit limited, customs of their own ... a

---

32 See, further, below.
33 Including the armed forces: see *R v Army Board of Defence Council ex parte Anderson* [1992] QB 169.
34 [1980] IRLR 427.
35 [1983] 2 AC 548.
36 Race Relations Act 1976, s 3(1).
37 *Commission for Racial Equality v Dutton* [1989] IRLR 8.
38 (1993) *The Times*, 4 February.
39 [1983] 2 AC 548.
40 [1989] IRLR 8.
41 [1983] 2 AC 548.

distinctive style of dressing, ... a language or dialect, ... a repertoire of folktales and music passed on from one generation to the next.

The court accepted that many Gypsies no longer derive from a 'common stock', but that of itself did not prevent them from being a racial group within the wide definition in the Act.[42] By distinction, the court ruled, in *Dawkins v Department of Environment*, that Rastafarians, while enjoying distinctive cultural features, having their own music and hair styles, do not fall within the meaning of a racial group, for their 'shared history' is only of some 60 years duration (compared with that of Gypsies, whose history is of over 700 years duration).

Direct and indirect discrimination

Direct discrimination

Under section 1(1) of the Act, direct discrimination involves the treatment of a person less favourably than another, on the basis of racial grounds. For an offence to be proven, there is no need to establish that the person discriminating on racial grounds intended so to do.[43] Direct discrimination includes segregation on the grounds of race, and to provide separate facilities for differing races, irrespective of the quality of the facilities, is an offence.[44] Proving direct discrimination – whether on grounds of race or sex – is difficult: there will usually be a number of other grounds for, say, rejecting an application for employment, other than pure racial or sexual discrimination.[45] In order to minimise the difficulties of proof, it has been established that, once the inference has been raised that discrimination has occurred, the burden of proof shifts to the alleged discriminator to prove that the decision was not racially or sexually discriminatory.[46] In *Sidhu v Aerospace Composite Technology Ltd*,[47] the Court of Appeal ruled that an employer's policy in relation to violence and abusive language which applied to all employees, irrespective of race, was not direct discrimination when applied to an employee who had suffered racial abuse and retaliated with violence.

---

42 [1989] IRLR 8, p 27G. See Barnett, H, 'The end of the road for Gypsies?' (1995) 24 Anglo-American L Rev 133 and 'A privileged position? Gypsies, land and planning law' [1994] Conveyancer 454.

43 *R v Council for Racial Equality ex parte Westminster City Council* [1984] ICR 770.

44 Race Relations Act 1976, s 1(2).

45 See Cotterrell, RBM, 'The impact of sex discrimination legislation' [1981] PL 469; Millar, E and Phillips, P, 'Evaluating anti-discrimination legislation in the United Kingdom: some issues and approaches' (1983) 11 Int J Soc L 417.

46 *Dornan v Belfast County Council* [1990] IRLR 179.

47 (2000) *The Times*, 21 June.

In *Nagarajan v London Regional Transport*,[48] the House of Lords considered the meaning of discrimination by way of victimisation under section 2 of the Race Relations Act 1976. Nagarajan had applied unsuccessfully for a post, and alleged that he had been treated less favourably than other applicants because he had previously brought proceedings under the Race Relations Act, and that, as a result, he had been discriminated against. The issue turned on whether or not it was necessary to establish that there was conscious motivation to discriminate, as was held by the appeal tribunal and the Court of Appeal. The House of Lords ruled that conscious motivation was not a prerequisite for a finding of direct discrimination under section 1 of the Act, and that section 2 had to be read in that context. If a job applicant's previous complaint under the Act had a significant influence on the decision not to offer him a job, the case fell within section 2(1), even though the interviewee did not consciously realise that he was prejudiced by that knowledge.

Indirect discrimination

Indirect discrimination occurs when a person conducts him or herself in a manner which is not directly discriminatory, but which has the indirect effect of being discriminatory. Indirect discrimination may affect individuals or a group of persons. Accordingly, if, for example, an employer attaches conditions of employment to an advertised post which a member of a particular racial group cannot fulfil, there will be indirect discrimination. The proof of indirect discrimination is again a difficult one to establish. Once a *prima facie* case of discrimination has been made out, it is for the defendant to rebut the presumption that there has been discrimination. To do so, the defendant must establish to the satisfaction of the court that any conditions of employment are justifiable. By way of example, in *Mandla v Dowell Lee*,[49] the House of Lords ruled that the rules relating to school uniform, which prohibited the wearing of a turban, which the pupil was required to wear on religious grounds, were discriminatory. The House of Lords ruled that the statutory words 'can comply' meant 'can in practice comply' or 'can consistently with customs and cultural conditions of the racial group comply', not 'can physically comply'.[50] Conversely, in *Singh v British Railway Engineers*,[51] a condition of employment was the wearing of protective headgear – a condition with which the applicant could not comply by virtue of wearing a turban in accordance with the requirements of his faith. The court here held that the condition was justifiable on the basis of the requirements of safety. In *Bilka-Kaufhaus GmbH v Weber von Hartz*,[52] however, the European Court of

---

48 [1999] 3 WLR 425.

49 [1983] 2 AC 548.

50 *Ibid*, pp 565–66, *per* Lord Fraser.

51 [1986] ICR 22.

52 [1986] IRLR 317; [1986] CMLR 701.

Justice ruled that conditions of employment must be justifiable, *inter alia*, according to the extent to which they are appropriate to achieving a necessary objective.[53] This test has made it more difficult for employers to argue that conditions are non-discriminatory. However, the position remains uncertain and unsatisfactory, and the Equal Opportunities Commission advocates reforming the meaning of the phrase 'conditions of employment'.[54]

Section 33(1) of the Race Relations Act 1976 provides that a person is to be treated as a person committing an unlawful act if that person knowingly aids another person to do an unlawful act. In *Anyanwu v South Bank Students' Union*,[55] two students had been expelled from the university and debarred from entering university premises, including the Students' Union, by which they were employed. The Union then dismissed the students from their employment. The students brought proceedings alleging that they had been discriminated against on racial grounds by the Union and that the university had knowingly aided the Union in their unlawful dismissal. The Court of Appeal held, by a majority, that, although the university had taken action against the students, and that action brought about their dismissal from employment, the university had not aided or helped the Union to dismiss the students.

Where there is an allegation of unfair dismissal by virtue of racial discrimination, what had to be compared was how the employer had treated the complainant and how that employer would have treated another employee, not how a hypothetical reasonable employer would have treated another employee. The House of Lords so ruled in *City of Glasgow Council v Zafar*,[56] holding that it was not legitimate to infer from the unreasonableness of the dismissal that it had been racially motivated.

Exceptions to protection

Exceptions are made to the protection of the Act. Residential accommodation in small premises is excepted, as is foster accommodation for the care of children.[57] Businesses with less than six partners are also exempted, as are associations with less than 25 members. Further limitations in the protection given lie in the areas of employment. For example, it is justifiable for an employer to insist on candidates for employment being of a particular race in order to ensure authenticity. Accordingly, it is lawful for an Indian restaurant to advertise for, and employ, only Indian staff.[58]

---

53   See *Hampson v Department of Education and Science* [1991] AC 171.
54   Equal Opportunities Commission, *Equal Treatment for Men and Women*.
55   [2000] 1 All ER 1.
56   1988 SLT 135.
57   Race Relations Act 1976, s 23(2).
58   *Ibid*, s 29.

A regrettable exception to the protection against racial discrimination under the Race Relations Act 1976 was considered by the Court of Appeal in *Post Office v Adekeye*.[59] The Court of Appeal ruled that racial discrimination against an employee in the course of an appeal against dismissal was not unlawful under section 4(2) of the Act, since that section applied only to a person in employment. The plaintiff had been dismissed from her position at the Post Office, and her appeal against dismissal was unsuccessful. In her appeal, the plaintiff argued that the rejection of her appeal was based on racial grounds. The tribunal decided that her appeal had been brought out of time and declined jurisdiction. That decision was reversed by the Employment Appeal Tribunal and the case remitted to the Industrial Tribunal. At that point, the Post Office argued that she could not complain of racial discrimination under section 4(2) of the Race Relations Act 1976 because that section related only to persons in employment, and not to persons dismissed from employment. That view was not accepted by the Industrial Tribunal, and the Post Office successfully appealed to the Employment Appeal Tribunal. Ms Adekeye then appealed to the Court of Appeal. Lord Justice Peter Gibson commented that it was unsatisfactory that the 1976 Act did not extend to give a remedy to an ex-employee pursuing an appeal against dismissal.

An employer may be guilty of discrimination contrary to the Race Relations Act 1976 where the employer allows a third party to abuse employees racially in circumstances over which the employer had power to control the third party. In *Burton and Another v De Vere Hotels*,[60] the Employment Appeal Tribunal ruled that the hotel, in allowing a guest speaker to make racially abusive remarks in the presence of its employees, acted unlawfully. An employer is under a duty to protect its employees from the detriment of racial abuse and harassment. If an employer had sufficient control over an event, and it was reasonably foreseeable that offence or harassment would occur, the employer is guilty of subjecting employees to racial abuse or harassment, contrary to section 4 of the 1976 Act.

The Commission for Racial Equality

Under the former Race Relations Acts,[61] the Race Relations Board – a statutory body which had no powers of initiative to initiate investigations – and the Community Relations Commission were established. Under the 1976 Act, these bodies have been replaced by the Commission for Racial Equality (CRE). The chairperson and members of the Commission are appointed by the Home Secretary, and the Commission lays an annual report before

---

59   (1996) *The Times*, 3 December.
60   (1996) *The Times*, 3 October.
61   Of 1965 and 1968.

Parliament. The Commission can assist claimants in the preparation of their case. The Commission also has the power to initiate investigations, provided that it has a reasonable suspicion that acts of discrimination have occurred.[62] The Home Secretary may direct the Commission to undertake investigations. If the Commission finds that discrimination has occurred, it has powers to issue a 'non-discrimination notice'. A right of appeal against a non-discrimination notice is available.[63] Further, for a period of five years from the issue of the notice, the Commission may seek an injunction from the county court. In relation to individual complaints of racial discrimination in employment, complaints may be made to an Industrial Tribunal.[64] The tribunal has the power to make an order for compensation and to make orders as to the manner in which the discrimination should be alleviated.[65] Complaints relating to other areas may be made to the county court, and the court may award damages.[66]

There are perceived weaknesses in the jurisdiction of the Commission. The House of Lords has ruled that the Commission is not entitled to investigate a person or a company unless it has a strong reason to believe that discrimination has occurred. Accordingly, the Commission may not investigate on a mere suspicion that discrimination is occurring.[67]

SEXUAL DISCRIMINATION

Sexual equality[68]

Factual and legal inequalities between the sexes have bedevilled history, and the issue is one which is firmly on the agenda for reform. Feminist legal theory, which seeks to unmask and eradicate legal discrimination based on gender, has moved from being a minority interest subject and become a popular field of study. It is often assumed that the feminist movement is a fairly recent phenomenon, dating from the liberalising 1960s. Whilst the struggle for women's rights dates only from the eighteenth century, the debate concerning the position of women in society has a far longer history

---

62 *R v Commission for Racial Equality ex parte Hillingdon Council* [1982] AC 868; *Race Relations Board v Dockers' Labour Club* [1976] AC 285.

63 *Council for Racial Equality v Amari Plastics* [1982] QB 265.

64 Appeal from which lies to the Employment Appeal Tribunal.

65 Race Relations Act 1976, ss 53–55.

66 See *Alexander v Home Office* [1988] 2 All ER 118.

67 *Prestige Group plc, Re; CRE v Prestige Group plc* [1984] 1 WLR 335; [1984] ICR 473.

68 See, *inter alia*, Atkins, E and Hoggett, B, *Women and the Law*, 1984, Oxford: Blackwells; Pannick, D, *Sex Discrimination Law*, 1985, Oxford: Clarendon; Fredman, S, *Women and the Law*, 1997, Oxford: Clarendon; Barnett, H, *Introduction to Feminist Jurisprudence*, 1998, London: Cavendish Publishing.

than that. It is possible, for example, to trace the issue back to ancient Greece and to the writings of Plato and Aristotle. In Plato's *Republic*, Socrates argues that children, wives and property should be owned in common. Aristotle[69] rejects such a notion in relation to both wives and property. Instead, we find that Aristotle favours private ownership of the wife – by the husband. Nothing had changed at the time William Blackstone was writing his *Commentaries on the Laws of England* (1765–69). For Blackstone, in marriage, the husband and wife are 'one person in law: that is, the very being or legal existence of the woman is suspended during the marriage, or at least is incorporated into that of the husband: under whose wing, protection, and cover she performs every thing'. While Blackstone insisted on human freedom and the protection of the individual by law; on the priority of the individual over the community and on the protection of private property, this free, autonomous individual was a property owning man having dominion over his wife and children.

The 'feminist campaign' began in the eighteenth century. Mary Wollstonecraft[70] argued for equality in treatment between men and women. In *The Vindication of the Rights of Women*, Wollstonecraft argued for educational and political equality. Socio-economic changes in the eighteenth century resulted in the emergence of middle class society, in which women became a 'leisured class'. Thus, the differences between men and women became more, rather than less, defined. Excluded from public affairs and the world of work, femininity became an objective and a goal. It was a dangerous development for women, for femininity emphasised the idea of both difference and fragility – and dependence.

The legal disabilities under which women laboured, analysed by John Stuart Mill over a century ago, have been slow to pass.[71] On marriage, a wife traditionally and effectively became the property of the husband: the doctrine was that of 'one flesh' created by the spiritual, legal and physical union within – in the United Kingdom – a Christian marriage. Three consequences, at least, flowed from this doctrine. First, a married woman was, until 1882, effectively incapable of owning property. Secondly, by marriage, a woman impliedly consented to sexual intercourse with her husband whenever he so required. It was, until the House of Lords decision in *R v R* in 1991 (see below, p 740), impossible in law for a married man to rape his wife. As Archbold stated: 'It is a clear and well settled law that a man cannot rape his wife.'[72] Thirdly, the husband had sole control, or custody, of the children of the marriage. Mothers, until 1839, had no custody rights whatsoever – and then only to the

---

69 384–322 BC.

70 1759–97.

71 Mill, JS, *The Subjection of Women* (1869), 1989, Cambridge: CUP.

72 See Archbold, *Criminal Law, Practice and Proceedings*, 1989, London: Sweet & Maxwell.

age of seven years. The 'right', such as it was, would be lost through committing adultery. Equality in parental rights was not to be achieved until 1973.[73]

This power of dominion of husbands over wives – unchanged from the fourth century BC to the late nineteenth century – arose, as John Stuart Mill observed:

> ... simply from the fact that from the very earliest twilight of human society, every woman (owing to the value attached to her by men, combined with her inferiority in muscular strength) was found in a state of bondage to some man. Laws and systems of polity always begin by recognising the relations they find already existing between individuals. They convert what was a mere physical fact into a legal right, give it the sanction of society, and principally aim at the substitution of public and organised means of asserting and protecting these rights, instead of the irregular and lawless conflict of physical strength.[74]

Furthermore:

> ... this dependence, as it exists at present, is not an original institution, taking a fresh start from considerations of justice and social expediency – it is the primitive state of slavery lasting on, through successive mitigations and modifications occasioned by the same causes which have softened the general manners, and brought all human relations more under the control of justice and the influence of humanity. It has not lost the taint of its brutal origin.[75]

It followed from its natural origins that, in the minds of men – and probably many women – this was the natural position and, accordingly, raised some sort of presumption that the position was right and just. In short, the presumption needed to be rebutted by those seeking so to do – by women themselves, or such rare men as Mill.

General male attitudes towards the inferior status of women have been reflected in legal judgments. By way of example, in *Meacher v Meacher*,[76] Henn Collins J held that a husband was within his rights in assaulting his wife because she refused to obey his orders to visit her relations.[77] While smacking a woman as punishment amounted to cruelty under the old law of divorce, it would not have been cruel if the husband had punished her 'as one would a naughty child'.[78]

---

73 Guardianship Act 1973.
74 *Op cit*, Mill, fn 71, Chapter 1.
75 *Op cit*, Mill, fn 71, Chapter 1.
76 [1946] P 216.
77 The Court of Appeal reversed his decision.
78 *McKenzie v McKenzie* (1959) *The Times*, 5 June.

Marital rape

Until 1991, it was impossible, in law, for a husband to rape his wife,[79] because the fact of marriage entailed implied consent to intercourse. This anachronism was only removed in *R v R*,[80] when the House of Lords ruled that rape within marriage did not constitute lawful intercourse and, accordingly, fell within the prohibition laid down in section 1 of the Sexual Offences Act 1956, which provided that 'it is a felony for a man to rape a woman'.

The Law Commission recommended that 'the law should continue to be that there is no immunity for husbands in the crime of rape.[81] The response has been equivocal. Professor Glanville Williams, for example, argues, in relation to intercourse without consent, that 'what is wrong with this demand is not so much the act requested but its timing, or the manner of the demand' and that the 'fearsome stigma of rape is too great a punishment for husbands who use their strength in these circumstances'.[82] Feminists have argued that the criminalising of rape provides the mask of protection, but not its reality, a view supported by evidence from Australia, where rape within marriage has been a criminal offence for over 20 years but few prosecutions are brought.[83]

It is against this broad background that legal protection from overt discrimination on the basis of sex must be evaluated.

Statutory protection from sexual discrimination

In 1919, Parliament enacted legislation to remove some legal disabilities in the field of property and contract, the vote and employment.[84] However, in the field of employment, many exceptions existed to a right to equal treatment. The Sex Discrimination Act 1975 attempted to redress the factual inequalities which remained. Much still remains to be achieved: the average pay for women has traditionally been lower than that of men; women form the

---

79 See *op cit*, Archbold, fn 72.

80 [1991] 3 WLR 767. See, on this, Naffine, N, 'Possession: erotic love in the law of rape' (1994) 57 MLR 10.

81 Report No 205, *Rape Within Marriage*, 1992. The Criminal Justice and Public Order Act 1994, s 142.1(2), defines rape, in part, as: (a) sexual intercourse with a person (whether vaginal or anal) who at the time of the intercourse does not consent to it; and (b) at the time he knows that the person does not consent to the intercourse or is reckless as to whether that person consents to it. Section 142.1(1) makes it an offence for a man to rape a woman or another man.

82 Williams, G, 'The problem of domestic rape' (1991) 141 NLJ 205 and (1991) 141 NLJ 246; but see *op cit*, Barnett, fn 68, Chapter 11.

83 See Naffine, N, 'Windows on the legal mind: evocations of rape in legal writing' (1992) 18 Melbourne UL Rev 741 and *Law and the Sexes*, 1990, Sydney: Allen & Unwin.

84 Sex Disqualification (Removal) Act 1919.

majority of part time, low paid workers.[85] Moreover, the demands of child care continue to reduce the opportunities for women in employment, and the State has not been robust in insisting that employers provide child care facilities. The law of the European Community has had a significant impact on the issue of equal pay for women, and domestic legal protection must be seen nowadays in light of Community law.[86]

The Equal Pay Act 1970 and Sex Discrimination Act 1975[87]

Employment and dismissal

Contractual employment rights are regulated under the Equal Pay Act 1970, whilst other aspects of employment are governed by the Sex Discrimination Act 1975. The two Acts are thus designed to provide protection in all fields of employment. It is unlawful to discriminate on the basis of sex or marital status in the context of employment, education and the provision of goods and services.[88] Sexual discrimination – as with racial discrimination – may be direct or indirect. Indirect discrimination may arise through unjustified conditions for employment, for example, through stipulating that applicants be of a certain height or age, where height or age is irrelevant to the particular job. On the other hand, some conditions of employment will be fully justified, for example, particular academic qualifications. As with racial discrimination, once an inference of discrimination has been raised, it is for the allegedly discriminatory person to disprove that he or she has in fact discriminated on the grounds of sex or marital status.[89] The issue of justifiable qualifications arose in *Price v Civil Service Commission*,[90] where a condition was applied that applicants be under the age of 28 years. Mrs Price, aged 35, alleged discrimination and her claim was upheld. However, in *Saunders v Richmond upon Thames LBC*,[91] a female qualified applicant was refused employment as a golf professional, although her qualifications were higher than that of the man

---

85   See, eg, *R v Secretary of State for Employment ex parte Equal Opportunities Commission* (1994) *The Times*, 4 March, in which English employment legislation was declared to be incompatible with the requirements of European Community law (see, further, Chapter 9).

86   EC Treaty, Art 119; Equal Pay Directive 75/117; Equal Treatment Directive 76/207; Pregnancy Directive 92/85; Parental Leave Directive 96/34/EC (OJ L145/4, 1996) and see 96/34/EC (OJ L19/24, 1998); Working Time Directive 93/104/EC (OJ L307/18, 1993).

87   The domestic employment legislation must be viewed in light of the substantial development of case law under the law of the European Community, discussed in Chapters 8 and 9.

88   Sex Discrimination Act 1975, ss 6, 22 and 29.

89   *Dornan v Belfast County Council* [1990] IRLR 179.

90   [1978] 1 WLR 1417.

91   [1978] IRLR 362.

who was appointed. Despite her qualifications, the Employment Appeal Tribunal ruled that there was insufficient evidence that she had in fact been discriminated against on the basis of her sex.

In order to establish sexual discrimination, a women must prove that – but for her sex – she would have been treated more favourably. In order to establish this requirement, the 1975 Act provides that a woman's treatment must be evaluated against that of a 'comparable man'.[92] Accordingly, the curious and regrettable consequence arises whereby, if an employer only employs women – and does so at a lower rate of pay than he would have paid to men – no discrimination can be proven, for there is no comparator.

In *Glasgow City Council v Marshall*,[93] the House of Lords had to determine whether employers who paid employees different rates in respect of their duties as teachers and instructors (the teachers being paid more) had acted lawfully. Proceedings were brought under the Equal Pay Act 1970 by one male and seven female instructors, claiming that they were entitled to equal pay. The employers relied on the absence of sexual discrimination. The House of Lords ruled that the employer had established a defence under section 1(3) of the Act, and that the inequality of pay was due not to sexual discrimination but to some other material fact. The House of Lords also considered the section 1(3) defence in *Strathclyde Regional Council v Wallace*.[94] In that case, female teachers did the same work as principal teachers but were paid at a lower rate. The House of Lords ruled that, if a difference in pay was explained by genuine factors – in the instant case, by financial constraints and a promotion structure established by statute – and not tainted by discrimination, that was sufficient to raise a defence. If, however, the factor was tainted by sexual discrimination, the defence would not succeed unless such discrimination could be objectively justified.

The position of pregnant women in employment causes particular difficulties and, again, the idea of the comparator is utilised.[95] The Trades Union Reform and Employment Rights Act 1993 provides that dismissal on the grounds of pregnancy is unfair.[96] However, in *Webb v EMO Cargo (UK) Ltd*,[97] the Court of Appeal ruled, and the House of Lords affirmed, that a woman who was dismissed from employment because of her pregnancy was not unlawfully dismissed, since – comparing her to a man with a temporary physical disability who would also have been unable to work – the man

---

92 Sex Discrimination Act 1975, s 5; and see *James v Eastleigh Borough Council* [1990] 2 AC 751.

93 [2000] 1 WLR 333.

94 [1998] 1 WLR 259.

95 See, eg, *Turley v Allders* [1980] ICR 66; *Hayes v Malleable WMC* [1985] ICR 703.

96 Trades Union Reform and Employment Rights Act 1993, ss 23–25 and Scheds 2 and 3; EC Pregnancy Directive 92/85.

97 [1992] ICR 445.

would also have been dismissed.[98] The House of Lords, however, referred the issue to the European Court of Justice for a ruling under Article 177 of the EC Treaty (now, Article 234 of the EC Treaty), with the following questions:

Is it discrimination on grounds of sex, contrary to the Equal Treatment Directive, for an employer to dismiss a female employee:

(a) whom it engaged for the specific purpose of replacing another female employee during the latter's forthcoming maternity leave,

(b) when, very shortly after appointment, the employer discovers that the appellant herself will be absent on maternity leave during the maternity period of the other employee and the employer dismisses her because it needs the jobholder to be at work during that period, and

(c) had the employer known of the pregnancy of the appellant at the date of appointment, she would not have been appointed, and

(d) the employer would similarly have dismissed a male employee engaged for this purpose who required leave of absence at the relevant time for medical or other reasons?

Under European Community law, it has been held that a pregnant woman whose application for employment was rejected on the basis of her pregnancy was a victim of discrimination.

The Court of Justice ruled in favour of the appellant on two grounds. First, the Court ruled that pregnancy could not be compared with a male illness, since pregnancy was not pathological. Secondly, the appellant could not be dismissed, because her inability to perform the terms of her employment was temporary, not permanent. The dismissal of the appellant therefore constituted sex discrimination. The House of Lords remitted the case to the Industrial Tribunal to consider the question of compensation.[99] While the ruling of the European Court is welcome, it does not answer the question as to the lawfulness of dismissing a temporary employee on the basis of pregnancy.

The Trade Union Reform and Employment Rights Act 1993 provides that a woman is protected from dismissal on the grounds of pregnancy and is entitled to 14 weeks of maternity leave. Where that employee has been in continuous employment for two years, she is entitled to return to work within 29 weeks of the birth.[100] The position in relation to women with less than two years' continuous service remains uncertain although, in *O'Neill*,[101] the court followed *Webb* and ruled that dismissal on the grounds of pregnancy was unlawful.

---

98 *Dekker v VJV Centrum* [1991] IRLR 27; [1990] ECR I-3941. On the European Court's ruling in *Webb*, see [1994] 2 CMLR 729.

99 *Webb v Emo Cargo (UK) Ltd (No 2)* [1995] 1 WLR 1454.

100 Employment Protection Consolidation Act 1978, s 39(1)(b).

101 (1996) *The Times*, 7 June.

The right to return to work has been further protected by the Court of Appeal in *Crees v Royal London Mutual Insurance Society Ltd* and *Greaves v Kwik Save Stores Ltd*.[102] Both employees had taken extended maternity leave. However, at the date on which they were due to return to work, the employees were unwell. The employers took the view that they had failed to exercise their right to return to work and that, accordingly, their contracts of employment were terminated, and that, accordingly, there had been no dismissal which could be construed as unfair. The employees appealed to the Employment Appeal Tribunal on the basis of unfair dismissal. The tribunal held that they had not been unfairly dismissed.[103] On appeal to the Court of Appeal, the court ruled that the employees had been unfairly dismissed. The employees qualified for the right to return to work,[104] and had given the necessary notices. However, the court ruled that the right to return to work was a right which had to be exercised. Nevertheless, section 42 of the 1978 Act did not expressly require an actual presence at work on the notified day. The provisions did not expressly say, either, that the right to return would be 'terminated, divested or avoided' by non-attendance. There were circumstances where it would be impossible to return to work – for example, during a period when her place of work was closed for an annual holiday. Under section 42(1) of the 1978 Act, what was required was that the employee gave written notice of a return to work. This the employees had done. To require the physical presence of the employee, in order for the right to return to work to remain, would result in absurdities. Situations such as an employee who worked from home or who had had an accident, or where a natural disaster had occurred, would all result in the employee being vulnerable to dismissal. Under the circumstances the only conclusion which could be reached was that the employees had, in effect, been unfairly dismissed.[105]

The right to non-discrimination applies equally to men and women.[106] The Court of Appeal so confirmed in *Hammersmith and Fulham London Borough Council v Jesuthasan*.[107] In this case, a part time worker employed in the public sector was held to be equally entitled as a female employee to claim redundancy payments and compensation for unfair dismissal. Jesuthasan had originally alleged that he had been the victim of racial discrimination. He subsequently sought to amend his original application to include claims for unfair dismissal and redundancy. The Employment Appeal Tribunal refused

---

102 (1998) *The Times*, 5 March.

103 [1997] ICR 629.

104 Under the Employment Protection (Consolidation) Act 1978, s 39, as substituted by the Trade Union Reform and Employment Rights Act 1993, s 23.

105 On equality of treatment in relation to redundancy payments, see *Barry v Midland Bank plc* [1999] 1 WLR 1465, HL. See, also, *Halfpenny v IGE Medical Systems Ltd* (1999) *The Times*, 4 January, CA.

106 Sex Discrimination Act 1975, preamble.

107 (1998) *The Times*, 5 March; [1998] ICR 640.

to allow him to amend his application.[108] The Employment Protection (Consolidation) Act 1978 had been amended by the 1995 Employment Protection (Part time Employees) Regulations,[109] in order to conform to the House of Lords decision in *R v Secretary of State for Employment ex parte Equal Opportunities Commission and Another*.[110] The novel point for decision was whether a male part time worker employed in the public sector was entitled to claim a redundancy payment and compensation for unfair dismissal, in relation to a dismissal occurring before the 1978 Act was amended. It was common ground that, had the employee been a female part time worker, she could have claimed redundancy payment and compensation for unfair dismissal. In the *Equal Opportunities Commission (EOC)* case, the House of Lords had ruled that the qualifying periods for entitlement[111] were incompatible with European Community law. In the present case, the employee was in exactly the same position as the female employee in the *EOC* case. It was argued for the Council that the *EOC* case was distinguishable, in that the objective of Community law was to protect women against indirect discrimination arising out of the fact that more women than men were part time workers. Mummery LJ was unable to accept that proposition. The general proposition of law in the *EOC* case was that discriminatory provisions should be disapplied irrespective of sex and, further, the employee did not complain of sexual discrimination but unfair dismissal and redundancy under the 1978 Act, subject to the disapplication of qualifying provisions declared in the *EOC* case to be incompatible with European Community law. The employer was an 'emanation of the State' and bound by the direct effect of Article 119 (now, Article 141 of the EC Treaty) and relevant directives. The appeal was allowed.

In *Hill and Stapleton v Revenue Commissioners and the Department of Finance*,[112] the Court considered the legality of provisions relating to remuneration of job sharing staff and the requirements of equality when job sharing staff returned to full time employment. In the instant case, whereas the job sharers were paid the strict proportional equivalent as full time staff, when the employee chose to return to full time work, she was placed on a point on the pay scale lower than that of other full time employees. The purpose of the job sharing scheme was to promote employment and enable women with family responsibilities to participate in the employment sphere. The Court ruled that the protection of women within family life and in the

---

108 [1996] ICR 991.

109 SI 1995/31.

110 [1995] 1 AC 1. The *EOC* case is discussed in Chapter 9.

111 Namely, two years of continuous employment for employees who worked for 16 or more hours a week, and five years of continuous employment for employees who worked between eight and 16 hours a week.

112 Case C-243/95: judgment 17 June 1998.

course of their professional activities is a principle widely regarded as being the natural corollary to the equality between men and women. Article 119 precluded legislation which provided for allocation to a lower point on the pay scale, unless such legislation could be justified by objective criteria unrelated to any discrimination on grounds of sex, which in the instant case it could not.[113]

The House of Lords has ruled that it was not discriminatory under the Equal Pay Act 1970 and Article 119 of the EC Treaty to calculate severance pay according to length of service and terminal salary even though more women than men would end their service working part time and thus have lower terminal salaries. On the facts, there was no direct discrimination, and the appellant accordingly had to prove indirect discrimination by showing that she belonged to a group of employees differently and less well treated than others and that that difference affected considerably more women than men. The purpose of the severance payment in question was to provide support for lost income during periods after redundancy, not to remunerate for past service. Accordingly, it was not a relevant difference for the purposes of the 1970 Act and Article 119 of the Treaty.[114] It has been held that discrimination on the ground of sexuality, which does not fall within the concept of sex discrimination under the Sex Discrimination Act 1975, can be unlawful. Discrimination based on a man's homosexuality might still be discrimination against him if the same discrimination would not have been directed against a homosexual woman.[115]

Indirect discrimination was found in *London Underground Ltd v Edwards*,[116] in which the Court of Appeal ruled that London Underground had discriminated against female train operators by introducing new rostering arrangements which were such that all 2,023 male train operators and 20 of the 21 female operators could comply. There was indirect discrimination against the one woman under section 1(1)(b) of the Sex Discrimination Act 1975.

Sexual harassment

Sexual harassment is defined as 'conduct of a sexual nature or other conduct based on sex affecting the dignity of men and women at work'.[117] Section 6(6)(b) of the Sex Discrimination Act 1975 and section 4 of the Race Relations

---

113 On Art 119 and pay and conditions of work of pregnant women, see Case C-66/96: judgment 19 November 1998.
114 *Barry v Midland Bank plc* (1999) unreported, 22 July.
115 *Smith v Gardner Merchant Ltd* [1998] 3 All ER 852, CA.
116 [1998] *The Times*, 1 June.
117 OJ C157/2.

Act 1976 refer to conduct which has detrimental effect on the victim. In *Hereford and Worcester County Council v Clayton*,[118] it was held that a sexist comment directed against a woman firefighter was detrimental to women in the message which it conveyed. The European Commission has drafted a Code of Practice on sexual harassment giving guidance to employees and employers.[119] Sexual harassment, as a form of sexual discrimination, is, again, difficult both to define and to prove.

However, the Court of Appeal took a robust approach to the issue of harassment in *Tower Boot Company v Jones*,[120] holding that employers were under a duty to make themselves aware of any harassment in the workplace and take steps to prevent harassment. This was the approach taken in *Burton and Another v De Vere Hotels*,[121] in which the hotel management was held liable for avoidable racial abuse on the part of hotel guests against female staff.

The Protection from Harassment Act 1997 provides for civil remedies for harassment. The Act provides that a person must not pursue a course of conduct which amounts to harassment of another, and which he knows, or ought to know, amounts to harassment.[122] Harassment is not further defined. The Act creates a criminal offence of harassment in addition to providing for civil remedies in the form of a restraining order.[123] The Act is not designed to inhibit journalists or photographers, but is aimed to stop 'stalking'. However, where an individual reporter or photographer repeatedly follows and causes harassment, that conduct may fall within the scope of the Act.

Formerly, the courts had found difficulty in protecting individuals from harassment where they fell outside the scope of the domestic violence legislation.[124] The former legislation, now repealed and replaced by the Family Law Act 1996, provided for relief only where the parties were either married to each other, or living together as husband and wife in a cohabiting relationship.[125] In *Patel v Patel*,[126] for example, the courts were powerless to grant relief in a situation where a family member (a father in law) was being harassed by another family member (his son in law), because the relationship

---

118 (1996) *The Times*, 9 October.
119 *On the Protection of the Dignity of Men and Women at Work*, 35 OJ L49/3, 1992.
120 [1997] ICR 254; [1997] IRLR 168.
121 (1996) *The Times*, 3 October.
122 Protection from Harassment Act 1997, s 1 and, in relation to Scotland, s 8(1).
123 *Ibid*, s 3.
124 As contained in the Domestic Violence and Matrimonial Proceedings Act 1976 and the Domestic Proceedings and Magistrates' Courts Act 1978. The former statute has been repealed, the latter repealed in part in so far as it relates to domestic violence.
125 The 1978 Act covered only married couples.
126 [1988] 2 FLR 179.

fell outside the definitions of the domestic violence legislation. In *Khorasandjian v Bush*,[127] however, the Court of Appeal controversially extended the law of tort to provide a remedy against unwanted intrusions into privacy through persistent telephone calls. In that case, a former boyfriend was unable to accept that the relationship was over. There had been no cohabitation. While it is unclear whether there existed a separate head of tortious liability for harassment, the Court ruled that the occupier of property, in addition to the owner of the property, had the right to relief under the law of nuisance. The Family Law Act 1996 extends the scope of eligible applicants to include relatives and former partners, although the circumstances in *Khorasandjian* would still fall outside the scope of the Family Law Act 1996, in the absence of a sexual relationship and cohabitation. The Protection from Harassment Act 1997 would, on the other hand, provide a remedy.

Effectiveness

In an area of regulation which is both complex and sensitive, the law inevitably falls short of achieving the ideal of a racially or sexually non-discriminatory society.[128] Much remains to be achieved – in law and practice – before claims to real equality can be made.

Sexual equality under European Community law

In the field of employment, the law of the European Community has greatly extended the equality of men and women. The law of the Community has been discussed in Chapters 8 and 9 but, for present purposes, it is helpful briefly to review the law of equality here. Article 119 of the EC Treaty (now, Article 141)[129] provides that Member States will ensure and maintain the application of the principle that men and women should receive equal pay for equal work. Equal pay without discrimination based on sex, means that pay for work at piece rates shall be calculated on the basis of the same unit of measurement and that pay for work at time rates shall be the same for the same job.[130] In addition to this provision, secondary legislation also extends protection.[131]

---

127 [1993] 3 All ER 669. See, however, *Hunter v Canary Wharf* [1997] 2 All ER 426, HL.

128 See *op cit*, Lustgarten, fn 30.

129 The Treaty on European Union 1997 renumbered individual EC Treaty Articles. For this reason, both the former and revised Article numbers are given in the text. See, further, Chapters 8 and 9.

130 EC Treaty, Art 119(a) and (b).

131 See Council Directive 75/117/EEC (OJ L45/19, 1975); Council Directive 76/207/EEC (OJ L39/40, 1976); Council Directive 77/187/EEC (OJ L61/26, 1977); Council Directive 79/8/EEC (OJ L6/24, 1979); Council Directive 86/378/EEC (OJ L225/40, 1986).

In relation to English law, the European Court of Justice (ECJ) has ruled that women must be paid the same amount as men, irrespective of whether the women is employed at the same time as a man, or succeeds him in his job.[132] Benefits to which retired employees are entitled must be the same for men and women.[133] Furthermore, the ECJ has ruled that unequal retirement ages for men and women are discriminatory.[134] The House of Lords has ruled that domestic Regulations amending the Equal Pay Act 1970 must be interpreted so as to give them the meaning compatible with EC law.[135]

However, there are limits to this protection as seen in *Duke v Reliance Systems Ltd*,[136] in which the House of Lords ruled that, while interpretation of domestic legislation must favour Community law, if Parliament has deliberately chosen not to amend law in line with the requirements of Community law, the House of Lords must respect Parliament's will. However, in *R v Secretary of State for Employment ex parte Equal Opportunities Commission*,[137] the House of Lords granted a declaration stating that the provisions of English law relating to the employment and benefits of part time female workers[138] were incompatible with the requirements of EC law. Furthermore, in the case of *Marleasing*,[139] the ECJ ruled that national courts have a duty to interpret law in line with the requirements of Community law, on the basis that Article 5 of the EC Treaty (now, Article 10) imposes an obligation on national authorities to take all appropriate measures to ensure the fulfilment of Community obligations.

The net effect of the case law on equality appears to be that, currently, the English courts will interpret legislation in line with the more stringent requirements of EC law but, should Parliament choose deliberately to enact measures contrary to EC law, the courts will give effect to the Act of Parliament. Whether this position can sustain in the future is subject to doubt, as the law of the Community becomes ever more significant and the ECJ becomes ever more insistent that Member States, including judges, give appropriate effect to Community law. This is particularly the case since the European Court ruled in *Von Colson v Land Nordrhein-Westfalen*,[140] and subsequent cases, that Article 5 of the EC Treaty (now, Article 10) imposes a duty not only on Member States to take all necessary steps to comply with

---

132 *Macarthys Ltd v Smith* [1981] 1 All ER 111; [1980] 2 CMLR 205.

133 *Garland v British Rail Engineering Ltd* [1983] AC 751; [1982] 1 CMLR 696.

134 *Marshall v Southampton and South West Hampshire Area Health Authority* [1986] 1 QB 401; [1986] 1 CMLR 688.

135 *Pickstone v Freemans plc* [1989] AC 66.

136 [1988] 1 AC 618.

137 [1994] 2 WLR 409.

138 Employment Protection (Consolidation) Act 1978.

139 *Marleasing SA v La Commercial Internacional de Alimentacion SA* [1992] 1 CMLR 305.

140 [1984] ECR 1891; [1986] 2 CMLR 430.

Community law, and to refrain from taking any adverse steps which would limit Community law objectives, but that the duty also falls on the courts to interpret domestic law in line with Community law.[141]

Furthermore, as will be discussed more fully in Chapter 9, while the European Court of Justice has held that national provisions which give special priority to female workers, in order to redress historical imbalances in equality in employment, contravene the EEC Equal Treatment Directive,[142] the Treaty on European Union 1997 (the Treaty of Amsterdam) extends the scope of the former Article 119. Article 141 of the EC Treaty (formerly, Article 119 of the EC Treaty), amplifies the principle of equality. Most significantly, Article 141(4) now provides that:

> With a view to ensuring full equality in practice between men and women in working life, the principle of equal treatment shall not prevent any Member State from maintaining or adopting measure providing for specific advantages in order to make it easier for the under-represented sex to pursue a vocational activity or to prevent or compensate for disadvantages in professional careers.[143]

EQUALITY AND DISABILITY

In 1995, Parliament passed the Disability Discrimination Act, under which the National Disability Council was established as an advisory body. The Council had no investigative powers in relation to allegations of discrimination nor did it have enforcement powers. The Disability Rights Commission Act 1999 amends the 1995 Act and provides for the establishment of the Disability Rights Commission, modelled on the EOC and the Commission for Racial Equality. The government has confirmed that the Act is compatible with the European Convention on Human Rights, as required by section 19 of the Human Rights Act 1998.

Under the 1995 Act, a person has a disability for the purposes of the Act if he has a physical or mental impairment which has a substantial and long term adverse effect on his ability to carry out normal day to day activities.[144] The provisions of the Act relate both to persons with current disability and to persons who have previously suffered a disability. It is unlawful for an employer to discriminate against a disabled person in relation to

---

141 See, further, Chapter 9.

142 Council Directive 76/207/EEC of 9 February 1976. See Case 318/86: *Commission v France* [1988] ECR 3559; Case 222/84: *Johnston v Chief Constable of the RUC* [1986] ECR 1651; Case 450/93: *Kalanke v Freie Hansestadt Bremen* [1995] IRLR 660.

143 Note, however, that this Article is facilitating; it does not impose a legal duty on Member States to adopt such measures.

144 Disability Discrimination Act 1995, s 1.

arrangements for interviews, the terms of an offer of employment, or refusing to offer or deliberately not offering the disabled person employment. It is equally unlawful to discriminate against a disabled employee. The meaning of discrimination in section 5 is modelled on the Race Relations Act 1976 and Sex Discrimination Act 1975. However, the Court of Appeal has ruled that discrimination in relation to disability is different from discrimination based on race and sex, and that cases under the legislation relating to racial and sexual discrimination are not a satisfactory guide to interpretation of the 1995 Act. If less favourable treatment of a disabled person is shown to be justified, it is not discrimination.[145] Where any arrangements made by the employer, or any physical feature of the relevant premises place the disabled person at a 'substantial' disadvantage, the employer is under a duty to make adjustments to premises, reallocate work, transfer the employee to another post, alter working hours, assign him or her to a different place of work, allow him or her to be absent for the purposes of rehabilitation, assessment or treatment, providing training, acquiring or modifying equipment or instruction or reference manuals, modifying procedures for testing or assessment, providing a reader or interpreter and providing supervision.[146] Section 7 makes detailed provision for matters to be taken into consideration when determining whether an employer has complied with the duty imposed, and provides for the making of regulations to amplify the specific requirements of the Act. Small businesses are exempt from the provisions of the Act, and Part I does not apply to an employer having less than 20 employees.

Complaints under the Act are made to an industrial tribunal, which has the power to make a declaration as to the rights of the complainant and the respondent in relation to the complaint, to order the respondent to pay compensation to the complainant and to make recommendations to the respondent as to the actions required to be taken to obviate or reduce the adverse effect on the complainant. Compensation is calculated by applying the principles applicable to the calculation of damages in claims of tort or, in Scotland, reparation for breach of statutory duty, and may include compensation for injury to feelings.[147]

Part III of the Act relates to discrimination in other areas, including the provision of goods or services, accommodation and facilities. Part V regulates public transport and provides that the Secretary of State may make regulations relating to the accessibility of taxis, public service vehicles and rail vehicles.

Under Part VI, the National Disability Council was established (now, the Disability Rights Commission, see below), with advisory, but not investigatory powers. Section 55 of the Act makes it unlawful to discriminate

---

145 *Clark v TDG Ltd* (1999) *The Times*, 1 April.
146 Disability Discrimination Act 1995, s 6.
147 *Ibid*, s 8.

against another by way of victimisation. Victimisation is interpreted as meaning treating a disabled person less favourably than another person whose circumstances are the same as the disabled person, and the relevant person is treated less favourably because the relevant person has brought proceedings under the Act, or given evidence or information or otherwise done anything under the Act in relation to the discriminator, or alleged that the other person has contravened the Act, or the person believes or suspects that the disabled person has done or intends to do any of those things. It is unlawful for a person to knowingly aid another person to do an act made unlawful under the Act.[148]

The Disability Rights Commission is a non-departmental public body. It consists of between 10 and 15 members, a majority of whom must be disabled or be people who have had a disability. The general functions of the Commission are to work towards the elimination of discrimination against disabled persons; to promote the equalisation of opportunities for disabled persons; to take such steps as it considers appropriate with a view to encouraging good practice in the treatment of disabled persons and to keep under review the working of the 1995 and the 1999 Acts.[149] The Commission may make proposals or give advice to Ministers as to any aspect of the law or a proposed change to the law, and advise government agencies and other public authorities as to the practical application of the law and undertake the carrying out of research.[150]

The Act also imposes a number of specific duties on the Commission. Under section 4, the Commission may issue non-discrimination notices if it is satisfied, in the course of a formal investigation, that a person has committed an unlawful act. In lieu of enforcement notices, agreements may be entered into between the Commission and the relevant person, in writing and binding on both parties, detailing the steps to be taken to ensure no unlawful act is committed.[151] The Commission may assist persons bringing or contemplating bringing legal proceedings under the 1995 Act.[152] Where such assistance is given and the Commission incurs costs, those costs are recoverable from costs awarded to the complainant, but not from any award of damages or compensation.[153]

The Disability Rights Commission has power to issue Codes of Practice, and when requested by the Secretary of State to do so, must prepare a Code of Practice dealing with specified matters. Draft Codes are to be approved by the Secretary of State.[154]

---

148 Disability Discrimination Act 1995, s 57.
149 Disability Rights Commission Act 1999, s 2(1).
150 *Ibid*, s 2(2).
151 *Ibid*, s 5.
152 *Ibid*, s 7.
153 *Ibid*, s 8.
154 *Ibid*, s 9.

FREEDOM OF EXPRESSION

Freedom of expression entails many aspects: an individual's freedom to express any view he or she wishes, however offensive to others, in private or public; freedom of the press to express any view; freedom of authors to write and publish; and freedom of film makers to record and distribute films/videos for private and public consumption. Blackstone[155] said of freedom of the press that:

> ... the liberty of the press is indeed essential to the nature of a free State. Every free man has an undoubted right to lay what sentiments he pleases before the public; to forbid this is to destroy the freedom the press; but if he publishes what is improper, mischievous or illegal, he must take the consequences of his own temerity.

In the United Kingdom, there is no right to free speech but, in a negative way, there is a freedom of expression subject to the limitations imposed by law. Lord Wellington's maxim 'publish and be dammed' must be viewed with caution, for freedom of speech is subject to, *inter alia*, the laws of defamation and blasphemy and other restrictions. In short, it is a freedom governed by law. By way of contrast, the First Amendment to the United States' Constitution guarantees the freedom of the press. Even here, however, limitations on free speech have been incorporated into the law by judicial decisions. For example, in *Roth v United States*,[156] on the issue of the right to publish and distribute pornographic literature, the Supreme Court held that the right was not unqualified; freedom of speech could be restrained in relation to pornography, which fell outside the meaning of speech as interpreted by the Supreme Court. Freedom of expression is regulated under Article 10 of the European Convention on Human Rights, which is to be incorporated into domestic law under the Human Rights Act 1998. However, even here, as with the United States' Supreme Court, the right is limited by restrictions. For discussion of Article 10, see Chapter 22.

Restrictions on freedom of speech

Defamation[157]

Defamation – slander or libel – may be defined as the publication, whether oral or written, of a falsehood which damages the reputation of the person concerned and lowers the victim's reputation in the eyes of 'right thinking

---

155 Blackstone, W (Sir), *Commentaries on the Laws of England* (1765–69), Chicago: Chicago UP.
156 354 US 476 (1957).
157 For details, see textbooks on the law of tort.

members of society generally'.[158] Slander is defamation in the form of the spoken word; libel is defamation in some permanent form, such as publication in books or newspapers. Publication via radio or television broadcasting, or in the course of public theatre performances, is defined as libel rather than slander.[159]

Defamation may attract criminal or civil liability. Criminal libel[160] is rare, and proceedings may not be brought without leave of a High Court judge, which will be granted only where the libel is *prima facie* very serious and the public interest justifies the prosecution. In 1976, a private prosecution was brought against the publishers of *Private Eye* in respect of allegations that Sir James Goldsmith was involved in a conspiracy to obstruct the course of justice.[161] The Law Commission has recommended that criminal libel should be abolished.[162]

Civil liability for defamation is more frequent and poses difficult questions concerning the extent to which freedom of expression is to be balanced against protection of the reputation of others – whether individuals or organisations. Relaxation of the restrictions on reporting imposed by the law of defamation in the United Kingdom were considered, but rejected, by the Faulks Committee.[163]

Freedom of expression is essential in a free and democratic society, and restrictions which inhibit criticism of public authorities, in particular, undermine the potential for scrutiny of official action. For this reason, in *Derbyshire County Council v Times Newspapers*,[164] the House of Lords has ruled that neither local nor central government had standing to sue for defamation. Lord Keith stated that 'it is of the highest importance that a democratically elected governmental body ... should be open to uninhibited public criticism'.[165]

---

158 *Sim v Stretch* (1936) 52 TLR 669, p 671.

159 Theatres Act 1968, s 4; Broadcasting Act 1990, s 166.

160 An offence at common law but, in part, regulated by statute: see Libel Act 1843; Law of Libel Amendment Act 1888.

161 *Goldsmith v Pressdram Ltd* [1977] QB 83 (the prosecution was withdrawn after a settlement was reached with the publishers). See, also, *Desmond v Thorne* [1982] 3 All ER 268.

162 Working Paper No 84, 1982, London: HMSO. See, also, *Report of the Committee on Defamation*, Cmnd 5909, 1975, London: HMSO.

163 Cmnd 5909, 1975; cf the Justice Report, *The Law and the Press*, 1965.

164 [1993] AC 534.

165 *Ibid*, p 547.

Defences to an action for defamation

The defence of truth

If a statement is damaging to the reputation of another but nevertheless justified on the basis that it is true, no liability will arise. It is not essential that every aspect of a statement must be absolutely true, but it must be true in most material respects.[166] Section 5 of the Defamation Act 1952 provides a statutory defence of truth.[167]

Fair comment

Expressions of opinion on matters of public interest – even though unfair or biased – may be protected under the defence of fair comment. The defence will not succeed if there are factual inaccuracies in the statement or if the statement was motivated by malice. The defence is important in giving limited protection to the publication of comments about public figures whose actions are matters of public interest.[168]

Unintentional defamation

Under section 4 of the Defamation Act 1952, the unintentional, or innocent, publication of statements which are defamatory may be defended. It must be shown that the publisher of the defamation has genuinely tried to make amends either by way of an apology and by correcting the false statement.

Absolute privilege

Some speech is absolutely privileged. That is to say, the words, however libellous, are protected from the law of defamation. An example of such protection is parliamentary privilege.[169] As we have seen, Article IX of the Bill of Rights 1689 gives absolute protection to words spoken in proceedings in Parliament. Statements made in the course of judicial proceedings also attract absolute privilege; as do statements by the Parliamentary Commissioner for Administration.[170]

---

166 See, eg, *Bookbinder v Tebbit* [1989] 1 All ER 1169.

167 The protection is not absolute and is restricted, for example, in relation to publications regarding records of former (spent) criminal convictions: Rehabilitation of Offenders Act 1974, s 8.

168 See *Silkin v Beaverbrook Newspapers Ltd* [1958] 2 All ER 516; *Slim v Daily Telegraph Ltd* [1968] 2 QB 157.

169 See Chapter 18.

170 Parliamentary Commissioner Act 1967, s 10(5).

Qualified privilege

This offers a more limited protection. A statement will attract qualified privilege provided that the defamatory statement is made without malice. The Parliamentary Papers Act 1840 gives privilege from defamation laws to fair and accurate reports of proceedings in Parliament. Qualified privilege has been held to attach to a communication between a Member of Parliament – who forwarded a constituent's complaint – and the Lord Chancellor and the Law Society where the matter is held to be in the public interest.[171]

Newspapers radio and television broadcasts also attract qualified privilege. Under the Defamation Act 1952, protection extends to fair and accurate reports of judicial proceedings and international organisations; fair and accurate reports of public meetings; local authority meetings; meetings of public companies; proceedings before statutory tribunals and inquiries and public election meetings.[172]

Qualified privilege was considered by the House of Lords in *Reynolds v Times Newspapers Ltd*.[173] The former Prime Minister of the Republic of Ireland brought libel proceedings against *The Times* newspaper in relation to an article which, he alleged, suggested that he had lied to Parliament and to Cabinet colleagues. No account of the Prime Minister's explanation was given. On qualified privilege, the House of Lords ruled, *inter alia*, that there should be no defence of generic qualified privilege for political information. The article had made serious allegations without giving the former Prime Minister's explanation, and the defence of qualified privilege was not made out and could not be argued by the defendants at the re-trial of the issue.

SEDITION, INCITEMENT TO DISAFFECTION AND TREASON[174]

Sedition

Sedition includes words or conduct directed against the peace or authority of the State. Sedition is a common law offence which may involve the spoken word or written materials which are libellous. The intention which must be proven in relation to sedition is that the accused intended to bring 'into hatred or contempt', or to 'excite disaffection' against, the Crown or government.[175]

---

171 *Beach v Freeson* [1972] 1 QB 14.

172 Defamation Act 1952, ss 7 and 10.

173 [1999] 3 WLR 1010.

174 See Robertson, G, *Freedom, the Individual and the Law*, 6th edn, 1989, London: Penguin, Chapter 4 (see, now, 7th edn, 2001).

175 *R v Burns* (1886) 16 Cos CC 355.

The words used must be such that they are intended to promote violence or public disorder. Merely strong criticism, therefore, which is not intended to be inflammatory will not result in liability. Recent use of the law of sedition is seen in *R v Chief Metropolitan Stipendiary Magistrate ex parte Choudhury*,[176] in which the Divisional Court,[177] adopting the test laid down by the Canadian Supreme Court,[178] ruled that the correct test for seditious intention is 'an intention to incite to violence or to create public disturbance or disorder against His Majesty or the institutions of government'.

Incitement to disaffection

The Incitement to Disaffection Act 1934 provides that it is an offence intentionally to attempt to dissuade a member of the armed forces from complying with his duty. It is also an offence to aid, counsel or procure commission of the principal offence. In *R v Arrowsmith*,[179] the defendant was accused and convicted of distributing leaflets to soldiers urging them not to serve in Northern Ireland, and the conviction was upheld by the Court of Appeal.[180] A similar offence exists in relation to causing disaffection within the police force.[181] There also remains on the statute book the Aliens Restriction (Amendment) Act 1919, section 3 of which prohibits aliens from causing sedition or disaffection among the population and the armed forces, and makes it a summary offence to cause industrial unrest in an industry in which he has not been employed for two years.

Treason

Treason represents the only criminal offence for which the death penalty still exists in the United Kingdom. The Treason Act 1351 makes it a capital offence to give 'aid and comfort to the King's enemies'. In *Joyce v Director of Public Prosecutions*,[182] William Joyce was convicted of making propaganda broadcasts on behalf of the Nazis during the Second World War. The Law Commission has recommended repeal of the Treason Acts and replacement with an offence of assisting an enemy country with which the United Kingdom is at war.[183]

---

176 [1991] 1 QB 429.

177 On an application for judicial review of a magistrate's refusal to issue summonses against Mr Salman Rushdie, author of *The Satanic Verses*.

178 *Boucher v R* [1951] SCR 265.

179 [1975] QB 678.

180 An application under the European Convention on Human Rights failed: see *Arrowsmith v United Kingdom* (1978) 3 EHRR 218.

181 Police Act 1964, s 53.

182 [1946] AC 347.

183 Working Paper No 72, *Treason, Sedition and Allied Offences* (1977).

Incitement to racial hatred

The first attempt at protecting persons from racial hatred was contained in the Race Relations Act 1965. The justification for restricting offensive racist speech – and hence freedom of expression – lies in the greater need to protect individual minority groups from demeaning and discriminatory speech. Incitement to racial hatred is now regulated under sections 17 to 22 of the Public Order Act 1986.[184] Section 17 defines racial hatred as meaning 'hatred against any group of persons in Great Britain defined by reference to colour, race, nationality (including citizenship) or ethnic or national origins'.

There are two basic requirements which relate to the offences in the Act. First, that the words used, or behaviour, must be 'threatening, abusive or insulting'. Secondly, the words or behaviour must either have been intended to incite racial hatred or be likely to do so. Under the Act, it is an offence to use words or behaviour, or display written material, which have the above elements. Publication of or distributing such material is also an offence.[185] The performance of plays,[186] showing of films or videos or playing of records or broadcasts intended to or likely to incite racial hatred is an offence.[187] The Act also creates the offence of possession of such materials.[188] Prosecutions may only be commenced with the consent of the Attorney General.

OBSCENITY, INDECENCY, CENSORSHIP AND PORNOGRAPHY[189]

Obscenity[190] and indecency[191] raise difficult constitutional issues for freedom of expression. Whilst pornographic material will be encompassed within the meaning of obscenity, obscenity represents a wider class of material. Thus, books or cards depicting the effects of drug taking, or scenes of violence, and sold to children may be obscene.[192]

John Stuart Mill, writing in 1869, argued for the sovereignty of the free individual exercising freedom of conscience, thought and expression 'without

---

184 As amended by the Criminal Justice and Public Order Act 1994, s 155.

185 Public Order Act 1986, s 19.

186 *Ibid*, s 20.

187 *Ibid*, ss 21 and 22.

188 *Ibid*, s 23.

189 See *op cit*, Robertson, fn 174, Chapter 5.

190 Defined as that which is offensive or outrageous to accepted standards of decency or modesty: Adams, D (ed), *Collins English Dictionary*, 3rd edn, 1991, London: Collins.

191 Writings, pictures, films designed to stimulate sexual excitement: *ibid*, Adams.

192 See, eg, *Calder (Publications) Ltd v Powell* [1965] 1 QB 509; *R v Skirving* [1985] QB 819.

impediment from our fellow creatures, so long as what he does does not harm them, even though they should think our conduct foolish perverse, or wrong'.[193] The role of the law, for Mill, should be confined to the prevention of harm to others:

> ... the sole end for which mankind are warranted, individually or collectively, in interfering with the liberty of action of any of their number, is self-protection. That the only purpose for which power can be rightfully exercised over any member of a civilised community, against his will, is to prevent harm to others. His own good, either physical or moral, is not a sufficient warrant.[194]

One question raised is whether restrictions on freedom of expression should be allowed on the basis that it causes harm to others. This harm principle was adopted by the Williams Committee in its review of obscenity and censorship.[195] The problem with the harm principle in relation to pornography lies in establishing whether harm is caused, and to whom. The evidence itself is equivocal and provides no clear basis on which to draw conclusions.[196]

Arguments of principle against pornographic material are advanced by writers of differing theoretical persuasions. Feminist legal theorists such as Catharine MacKinnon[197] and Andrea Dworkin[198] argue the case against pornography on the basis that it demeans women by 'objectifying' them – portraying women as merely objects to be used by men.[199] The Canadian Supreme Court in *R v Butler*[200] adopted similar reasoning. Arguing from the point of equality between the sexes, Sopinka J observed that:

> ... we cannot ignore the threat to equality resulting from the exposure of audiences to certain types of violent and degrading material. Materials portraying women as a class of objects for sexual exploitation and abuse have a negative impact on the individual's sense of self-worth and acceptance.[201]

---

193 Mill, JS, *On Liberty* (1859), 1989, Cambridge: CUP, p 15.

194 *Ibid*, p 13.

195 *Report of the Committee on Obscenity and Film Censorship*, Cmnd 7772, 1979, London: HMSO.

196 Howitt, D and Cumberbatch, G, *Pornography: Impacts and Influences*, 1990, London: Home Office.

197 MacKinnon, C, *Feminism Unmodified: Discourses on Life and Law*, 1987, Cambridge, Mass: Harvard UP.

198 Dworkin, A, *Pornography: Men Possessing Women*, 1981, London: The Women's Press.

199 The literature is now extensive. See Dworkin, A, 'Against the male flood' and Wolgast, E, 'Pornography', in White, P (ed), *Feminist Jurisprudence*, Oxford: OUP. See, also, Smart, C, *Feminism and the Power of Law*, 1989, London: Routledge, especially Chapter 6; Itzin, C (ed), *Pornography: Women, Violence and Civil Liberties*, 1992, Oxford: OUP; *op cit*, Barnett, fn 68, Chapter 12.

200 (1992) 89 DLR (4th) 449.

201 *Ibid*, p 479.

The United States' Supreme Court has also justified restrictions on freedom of speech in the form of pornography on the basis that pornographic literature is not truly a matter of freedom of speech at all.[202]

The Obscene Publications Act 1959

The Obscene Publications Act 1959 creates the offence of publication of an obscene article, whether or not for gain. Further, it is an offence to have such articles in ownership, possession or control for the purpose of publication for gain or with a view to publication.[203] An article[204] is 'obscene' if 'its effect ... is ... such as to tend to deprave and corrupt persons who are likely, having regard to all relevant circumstances, to read, see or hear the matter contained or embodied in it'.[205]

An article will be 'published', according to section 1(3), if a person:

(a) distributes, circulates, sells, lets on hire, gives or lends it, or who offers it for sale or for letting on hire; or

(b) in the case of an article containing or embodying matter to be looked at or a record, shows, plays or projects it.

The Criminal Justice and Public Order Act 1994 amends section 1(3) by adding the words 'or where the matter is stored electronically, transmits that data'.[206]

The tendency to 'deprave and corrupt'

It is not sufficient that an article disgusts, or is 'filthy', 'loathsome' or 'lewd'.[207] What must be established is that the article will 'deprave or corrupt'.[208] Nor is it sufficient that the article is capable of depraving or corrupting just one person: the test is whether or not a significant proportion of persons likely to read or see the article would be depraved or corrupted by it.[209] The fact that the persons likely to read the article regularly read such materials is irrelevant to whether or not the material can deprave or corrupt,[210] although the same argument may not hold if the likely audience is to be police officers experienced with dealing with pornography.[211]

---

202 *US v Roth* 354 US 476 (1957).
203 Obscene Publications Act 1959, s 2(1), as amended.
204 Which covers books, pictures, films, records and video cassettes.
205 Obscene Publications Act 1959, s 1(1).
206 Criminal Justice and Public Order Act 1994, s 84.
207 *R v Anderson* [1972] 1 QB 304.
208 *R v Martin Secker and Warburg* [1954] 2 All ER 683.
209 *DPP v Whyte* [1972] AC 849, p 860, *per* Lord Wilberforce.
210 *Shaw v DPP* [1962] AC 220.
211 *R v Clayton and Halsey* [1963] 1 QB 163.

There exists a defence of public good[212] but the defence is interpreted narrowly.[213] For example, in *Director of Public Prosecutions v Jordan*,[214] where the defendant argued the psychotherapeutic benefit of 'soft porn' for the consumer, the judge rejected the defence, holding that what was for the public good was art, literature or science.

Broadcasting, cinemas, theatres and video recordings

Section 2 of the Theatres Act 1968 prohibits obscenity in theatrical performances. The law relating to obscenity applies to live performances, subject to the defence of public good, although the former requirement that plays should be licensed before performance has been abolished by the Theatres Act 1968. Legal regulation of live performances also exists in the form of section 20 of the Public Order Act 1986, which prohibits the use of threatening, abusive or insulting words or behaviour intended or likely to stir up racial hatred. Section 6 of the Theatres Act prohibits words or behaviour likely to cause a breach of the peace. Offences which relates to gross indecency between males can also be committed under section 13 of the Sexual Offences Act 1956. In order to avoid frivolous or censorious legal action, the consent of the Attorney General is required in relation to prosecutions under the Theatres Act, Public Order Act and Sexual Offences Act.

The Broadcasting Act 1990 and Video Recordings Act 1984 each prohibit obscenity on local radio services, television and video. In relation to broadcasting, the British Broadcasting Corporation (BBC), established under the royal prerogative,[215] is under a duty not to adopt its own political stance on current affairs, and may only broadcast party political programmes with the consent of the major political parties. In relation to television companies and radio services financed through advertising, the Broadcasting Act 1990 provides statutory regulation. An Independent Television Commission (ITC),[216] whose members are appointed by the Home Secretary, is under a duty to ensure effective competition in the provision of services. The Commission licenses programme makers. Under section 6 of the Broadcasting Act, a number of duties are imposed on the Commission. Section 6 provides, in part, that:

---

212 Obscene Publications Act 1959, s 4.

213 See, eg, *R v Penguin Books Ltd* [1973] QB 241.

214 [1977] AC 699; and see *Attorney General's Reference (No 3 of 1977)* [1978] 3 All ER 1166.

215 The BBC was established by Royal Charter. Its chairman and governors are appointed by the Crown on the advice of the Prime Minister. The BBC operates under licence from the government issued under the Wireless Telegraphy Acts 1904–67.

216 Broadcasting Act 1990, s 1.

(1) The Commission shall do all that they can to secure that every licensed service compiles with the following requirements, namely:

    (a) that nothing is included in its programmes which offends against good taste or decency or is likely to encourage or incite to crime or to lead to disorder or to be offensive to public feeling;

    (b) that any news given (in whatever form) in its programmes is presented with due accuracy and impartiality;

    (c) that due impartiality is preserved on the part of the person providing the service as respects matters of political or industrial controversy or relating to current public policy;

    (d) that due responsibility is exercised with respect to the content of any of its programmes which are religious programmes, and that, in particular, any such programmes do not involve:

        (i) any improper exploitation of any susceptibilities of those watching the programmes, or

        (ii) any abusive treatment of the religious views and beliefs of those belonging to a particular religion or religious denomination ...

Under section 143 of the Broadcasting Act 1990, the Broadcasting Complaints Commission was under a duty to adjudicate upon complaints concerning:

    (a) unjust or unfair treatment in programmes ...; or

    (b) unwarranted infringement of privacy in, or in connection with the obtaining of material included in, such programmes ...

The Broadcasting Act 1996 established the Broadcasting Standards Commission, amalgamating the Broadcasting Standards Council and the Broadcasting Complaints Commission. The Broadcasting Standards Commission is under a statutory duty to draw up codes of guidance in relation to the portrayal of violence in programmes, and in connection with the portrayal of sexual conduct in programmes, and 'standards of taste and decency for such programmes generally'.[217] In addition, the Commission is under a duty to monitor programmes and to report of such matters as the portrayal of violence, sexual conduct, and standards of taste and decency in programmes[218] and to consider complaints.[219] The Commission also has the power to make reports on standards and, in particular, may make an assessment of the attitudes of the public at large in relation to violence or sexual conduct in programmes, and standards of taste and decency.

The Broadcasting Act 1990 also conferred power on the Secretary of State to proscribe foreign satellite services, where the Independent Television Commission, or Radio Authority, consider that a satellite service is 'unacceptable' on the basis that it repeatedly contains material which 'offends

---

217 Broadcasting Act 1996, ss 107, 108.
218 *Ibid*, s 109.
219 *Ibid*, s 110.

against good taste or decency or is likely to incite to crime or to lead to disorder or to be offensive to public feeling'.[220]

The Broadcasting Act 1996 extends the functions of the Broadcasting Standards Commission to include monitoring:

> ... so far as practicable, all television and sound programmes which are transmitted or sent from outside the United Kingdom but are capable of being received there, with a view to ascertaining:
>
> (a) how violence and sexual conduct are portrayed in those programmes; and
>
> (b) the extent to which those programmes meet standards of taste and decency.[221]

The regulation of films falls to the British Board of Film Classification (BBFC), and their availability for viewing by the public controlled by local authorities. The BBFC operates a system of classification by age: 'U' for general circulation, 'PG' (parental guidance), 12, 15, and 18 certificate films, and R18 films which are for restricted viewing only on segregated premises. The BBFC may refuse a certificate if the film contravenes the Obscene Publications Act 1959, and may insist on cuts to a film before a certificate is granted. Local authorities exercise control through the granting of licences for a particular film to be shown in its area.[222]

The BBFC also classifies videos for private viewing.[223] The Video Recordings Act 1984 requires that the BBFC should have 'special regard to the likelihood of video works being viewed in the home'.[224] The BBFC must also pay 'special regard' to the harm caused potential viewers by the depiction of criminal activity, illegal drugs, violence and sexual behaviour.[225] The growth in Internet availability led to the transmission of electronically stored data being included within the Obscene Publication Act 1959 definition of 'publication'.[226] However, the likelihood of enforcement is slim, given the nature of the Internet and the ability of anyone, worldwide, to place items on it.

Conspiracy to corrupt public morals

Under the common law, publishers may be liable for the offence of conspiracy to corrupt public morals. In *Shaw v Director of Public Prosecutions*,[227] Shaw, the

---

220 Broadcasting Act 1990, s 177.
221 Broadcasting Act 1996, s 109.
222 Under the Cinemas Act 1985.
223 Under the Video Recordings Act 1984.
224 *Ibid*, s 4.
225 Under the Criminal Justice and Public Order Act 1994, s 90.
226 Under *ibid*, s 168.
227 [1961] AC 220.

publisher of a directory giving the names and details of prostitutes was prosecuted for conspiracy to corrupt public morals.[228] The House of Lords (Lord Reid dissenting) held that the courts have a 'residual power to enforce the supreme and fundamental purpose of the law, to conserve not only the safety and order but also the moral welfare of the State'.[229]

Shaw v Director of Public Prosecutions was upheld in *Knuller Ltd v Director of Public Prosecutions*.[230] The publishers had produced a magazine containing advertisements for male homosexuals. The House of Lords upheld *Shaw*, rejecting as a defence the fact that the Sexual Offences Act 1967 provided that homosexual acts between adult males, in private, were no longer an offence. The use of this common law offence is rare; nevertheless, it remains an available offence which enables the State to avoid statutory offences which provide defences such as that of the 'public good'.[231]

Blasphemy[232]

Blasphemy is a common law offence which prohibits words which cause outrage to the feelings of a Christian by abusing Christ or by denying or attacking the established church. Between 1922 and 1977, there were no prosecutions brought and it was thought that the offence had fallen into disuse. In 1976, however, the magazine *Gay News* published a poem and illustration depicting Christ at the Crucifixion. A private prosecution against the editor and publisher was instigated,[233] alleging that the poem and illustration 'vilified Christ in His Life and His Crucifixion'. The resulting case was *R v Lemon*,[234] in which the jury, by a majority verdict, found the words and drawing blasphemous.[235] On appeal to the House of Lords, the question of law concerned the mental element required for a conviction of blasphemy. By a majority, the House of Lords held that there was no need to prove an intention to blaspheme, but rather that it was sufficient to prove that a blasphemous libel – a publication calculated to outrage and insult a Christian's religious beliefs – had been published. The majority[236] dismissed the appeal against conviction, holding that the law required no more than an

---

228 Shaw was also found guilty of an offence under the Obscene Publications Act 1959. See, further, above.

229 [1962] AC 220, p 268. Seaborne Davies, D, 'The House of Lords and the criminal law' (1962) 6 JSPTL 104.

230 [1973] AC 435.

231 Obscene Publications Act 1959, s 4.

232 See Kenny, CS, 'The evolution of the law of blasphemy' [1992] CLJ 127.

233 By Mrs Mary Whitehouse.

234 [1979] AC 617.

235 See, also, *Gay News Ltd v United Kingdom* (1982) 5 EHRR 123.

236 Lords Scarman, Dilhorne and Russell.

intention to publish words found by the jury to be blasphemous. It was unnecessary to hold[237] that there was intention to offend, or reckless indifference to whether or not offence was caused.

In Lord Scarman's opinion, the law should be extended to protect the religious beliefs and feelings of non-Christians. Lord Scarman stated that:

> ... the offence belongs to a group of criminal offences designed to safeguard the internal tranquillity of the kingdom. In an increasingly plural society such as that of modern Britain it is necessary not only to respect the differing religious beliefs, feelings and practices of all but also to protect them from scurrility, vilification, ridicule and contempt.[238]

Furthermore:

> It would be intolerable if by allowing an author or publisher to plead the excellence of his motives and the right of free speech he could evade the penalties of the law even though his words were blasphemous in the sense of constituting an outrage upon the religious feelings of his fellow citizens. This is no way forward for a successful plural society.[239]

This view was not to prevail, however. In *R v Chief Metropolitan Stipendiary Magistrate ex parte Choudhury*,[240] it was held that blasphemy remained confined to protection of the Christian religion as exemplified by the established Church of England, and did not extend to the protection of the Islamic faith. That the law should offer such limited and discriminatory protection is both anachronistic and offensive to the principle of equality in a pluralistic society. The Law Commission in 1985 recommended that the offence be abolished,[241] but the government has not acted on this recommendation.[242]

Contempt of court

The law relating to contempt of court developed in order to protect the judiciary and judicial proceedings from actions or words which would impede or adversely affect the administration of justice, or 'tends to obstruct, prejudice or abuse the administration of justice'.[243] Contempt of court may be

---

237 As did Lords Diplock and Edmund-Davies.

238 [1979] AC 617, p 658.

239 *Ibid*, p 665.

240 [1991] 1 QB 429.

241 See Report No 145; also Working Paper No 79, *Offences Against Religion and Public Worship* (1981) and Robilliard, StJ, 'Offences against religion and public worship' (1981) 44 MLR 556.

242 HC Deb Col 395, 27 June 1989.

243 *Report of the Phillimore Committee on Contempt of Court*, Cmnd 5794, 1974, p 2. See Dhavan, R, 'Contempt of court and the *Phillimore Committee Report*' (1976) 5 Anglo-American L Rev 186.

criminal or civil. In relation to criminal contempt, which may be dealt with in both the civil and criminal courts, the action relates to conduct which is designed to interfere with the administration of justice, which may of itself involve a criminal offence. The court has the power to rule on the existence of a contempt and to punish the guilty party. Where the judge finds the person guilty of contempt, he may commit the person instantly to prison. Two principal forms of criminal contempt exist.

Scandalising the court

The need to maintain public confidence in the judiciary underpins this offence. Criticism of a judge, or a court's decision, may be a contempt if it suggests bias or unfairness on the part of the judge or court.[244]

Contempt in the face of the court

Conduct in court which impedes the judicial process may be a contempt. A demonstration which interrupts proceedings,[245] or insulting behaviour, or refusal of a witness to answer questions or give evidence, or comply with a court order to disclose information may amount to contempt.[246]

Publications prejudicing the course of justice

The balance to be struck between freedom of expression and the protection of judicial proceedings is a matter for debate. The Contempt of Court Act 1981, which reformed the common law of contempt, sought to achieve the appropriate balance. Before that Act, the law relating to contempt proved capable of inhibiting freedom of the press for an extensive period of time, where judicial proceedings became protracted. The leading case which presaged reform of the law is that of *The Sunday Times v United Kingdom*.[247] In 1974, the House of Lords restored an injunction[248] prohibiting *The Sunday Times* from publishing articles relating to the drug Thalidomide, manufactured by Distillers Ltd, which, it was alleged, caused serious deformities in babies. The parents of the affected children intended to sue Distillers for compensation. The company entered into protracted negotiations

---

244 See *R v New Statesman (Editor) ex parte DPP* (1928) 44 TLR 301; *Ambard v Attorney General for Trinidad and Tobago* [1936] AC 322; *R v Metropolitan Police Commissioner ex parte Blackburn (No 2)* [1968] 2 QB 150.

245 See *Morris v Crown Office* [1970] 2 QB 114.

246 See *Attorney General v Mulholland and Foster* [1970] 1 QB 114; *British Steel Corporation v Granada Television Ltd* [1963] 2 QB 477.

247 (1979) 2 EHRR 245. See, further, Chapter 22.

248 *Attorney General v Times Newspapers Ltd* [1974] AC 273. The injunction had been discharged by the Court of Appeal.

with the families' solicitors. The injunction restrained any further publication on the matter by the newspaper. *The Sunday Times* made an application under the Article 10 of the European Convention on Human Rights, which protects freedom of expression, alleging that the common law of contempt violated Article 10. The European Court of Human Rights held that there had been a violation of Article 10.

The Contempt of Court Act 1981

Section 1 of the Contempt of Court Act provides for the 'strict liability rule'. The rule is defined as 'the rule of law whereby conduct may be treated as a contempt of court as tending to interfere with the course of justice in particular legal proceedings *regardless of intent to do so*' (emphasis added). In order for the strict liability rule to be established, a number of issues need to be satisfied. First, the test relates only to publications falling within section 2 of the Act. Publications are defined in section 2(1) as including 'any speech, writing [programme included in a programme service][249] or other communication in whatever form, which is addressed to the public at large or any section of the public'. Secondly, the publication must be such that it 'creates a substantial risk that the course of justice in the proceedings in question will be seriously impeded or prejudiced'. Thirdly, the strict liability rule applies only if the proceedings in question are 'active', as defined by Schedule 2 of the Act. In relation to appellate proceedings, these are active from the time when they are commenced, by an application for leave to appeal or apply for review, or by notice of appeal or of application to review or by other originating process, 'until disposed of or abandoned, discontinued or withdrawn'.[250] In relation to criminal proceedings, the starting point is the issue of a warrant for arrest, arrest without warrant or the service of an indictment.[251] The end point is acquittal, sentence, any other verdict or discontinuance of the trial. In relation to civil proceedings, the start point is when the case is set down for a hearing in the High Court. The end point is when the proceedings are disposed of, discontinued or withdrawn.[252]

It is a defence to prove that, at the time of publication, or distribution of the publication, he or she does not know, and has no reason to suspect, that relevant proceedings are active.[253] Fair and accurate reports of legal proceedings, held in public, and published 'contemporaneously and in good faith' do not attract the strict liability rule.[254] In addition, if publication is

---

249 Added by the Broadcasting Act, s 203.

250 Contempt of Court Act 1981, Sched 2, para 15.

251 *Ibid*, Sched 1, para 4.

252 Contempt of Court Act 1981, Sched 1, paras 12 and 13. See *Attorney General v Hislop and Pressdam* [1991] 1 QB 514; [1991] 1 WLR 219, CA.

253 *Ibid*, s 3(1), (2).

254 *Ibid*, s 4.

made as, or as part of, a discussion in 'good faith of public affairs or other matters of general public interest', it is not to be treated as contempt of court, 'if the risk of impediment or prejudice to particular legal proceedings is merely incidental to the discussion'.[255]

Section 10 of the Contempt of Court Act regulates the disclosure of sources. The court may not require disclosure, and a person will not be guilty of contempt as a result of non-disclosure, unless the court is satisfied that 'disclosure is necessary in the interests of justice or national security or for the prevention of disorder or crime'. The leading case is *X Ltd v Morgan Grampian*,[256] in which the House of Lords ruled on the decision making process entailed in section 10. In that case, a confidential plan was stolen from the plaintiffs and information from the plan given to a journalist. The plaintiffs applied for an order requiring the journalist, William Goodwin, to disclose the source and sought discovery of his notes of the telephone conversation in order to discover the identity of the source. The House of Lords, in balancing the competing interests – the applicant's right to take legal action against the source and the journalist's interest in maintaining confidentiality with the source – that the interests of the plaintiffs outweighed the interests of the journalist. This decision led to an application under the European Convention under Article 10 – the right to freedom of expression. In *Goodwin v United Kingdom*,[257] the Court ruled that the order against the journalist violated his right to freedom of expression which was central to a free press.[258]

It is for the court to determine whether a particular decision making forum is a 'court' for the purposes of the law as to contempt of court. In *General Medical Council v British Broadcasting Corporation*,[259] the Court of Appeal ruled that the Professional Conduct Committee (PCC) of the General Medical Council was not part of the judicial process of the State and accordingly was not subject to the Contempt of Court Act 1981. The PCC was a statutory committee under the Medical Act 1983, with power to remove the registration of a medical practitioner if found guilty of a criminal offence or judged to be guilty of serious professional misconduct. The PCC sat in public and had the assistance of a legally qualified assessor to advise on questions of law. All parties were entitled to be heard and represented by solicitors and counsel. Evidence was given on oath and witnesses could be summonsed and documents called for. The PCC was therefore exercising a sort of judicial power, but it was not the judicial power of the State. It has a recognisable

---

255 See *Attorney General v English* [1983] 1 AC 116; [1982] 2 All ER 903; *Attorney General v TVS Television; Attorney General v HW Southey & Sons* (1989) *The Times*, 7 July; *Pickering v Liverpool Daily Post and Echo Newspapers plc* [1991] 2 AC 370; 1 All ER 622.

256 [1991] AC 1; [1991] 2 All ER 1.

257 (1996) 22 EHRR 123.

258 On freedom of expression under the Convention, see Chapter 22.

259 [1998] 3 All ER 426; [1998] 1 WLR 1573; [1998] EMLR 833.

judicial function, but was not part of the judicial system of the State. Accordingly, the PCC did not constitute a court for contempt of court purposes.

Where the judge considers that disclosure is necessary in the interests of justice, a discretion remains as to whether disclosure should be ordered. That involved weighing up the competing interests of the need for disclosure and the need for protection of sources. In *John and Others v Express Newspapers and Others*,[260] the Court of Appeal ruled that the need to protect journalistic sources overrode the need for disclosure of the source of a confidential document which had come into the hands of a journalist by a breach of confidentiality in relation to legal advice given by a firm of solicitors.[261] However, the exercise of discretion led to a different conclusion in *Camelot Group plc v Centaur*.[262] In that case, a disloyal employee of Camelot sent a copy of draft accounts to a journalist employed by the defendant. The Court of Appeal ruled that the public interest in enabling the plaintiffs to discover a disloyal employee who leaked confidential information was greater than the public interest in enabling the employee to escape detection. The order for disclosure was upheld.

Law of confidence

Injunctions may be sought in order to restrain the publication of information. Injunctions are orders of a court, which can be either permanent or interim. Injunctions impose what is called a 'prior restraint', that is to say, they prevent disclosure of information in advance to avoid publication. An injunction can be granted on the basis that the proposed item is libellous (defamatory) or in breach of the common law duty of confidence. In the case of alleged libel, judges are reluctant to impose a 'prior restraint' by way of injunction and will not grant it if the defendant swears that they can prove the truth of the defamatory statement or can defend it on the basis of 'fair comment'. In cases of breach of confidence, the judges are more willing to grant the injunction. An example of this is seen in *Schering Chemical v Falkman Ltd*.[263] In *Schering*, a Thames Television documentary regarding a pregnancy drug was scheduled for transmission. The programme's producer had been engaged as a consultant to the drug manufacturers and the programme revealed material obtained by him during his consultancy. The court held that a duty of confidence existed, which should be enforced by injunction. In 1987, the

---

260 (2000) *The Times*, 26 April.

261 See, most recently, the Court of Appeal's refusal to order disclosure to the police of supposed evidence relating to former MI5 officer, David Shayler, held by *The Guardian* and *The Observer* newspapers: (2000) *The Guardian*, 21 July.

262 [1999] QB 124.

263 [1981] 2 All ER 321.

British Broadcasting Corporation (BBC) intended to transmit a television documentary *My Country Right or Wrong* in which former security officers were interviewed. An injunction was granted on the basis that there had occurred a breach of confidence in the course of interviews.[264] The BBC was vetted by the Attorney General, who then withdrew the action but, nevertheless, the transmission of the programme had been delayed for six months.

In the *Thalidomide* case (which resulted in *The Sunday Times v United Kingdom*),[265] injunctions were used to restrain newspapers from publishing material which might have been prejudicial to forthcoming judicial proceedings. For discussion of the case, see, further, Chapter 22. The book *Spycatcher*, written by a former member of the Security Services, was also restrained by way of an injunction based on breach of confidence owed to the Service. See Chapter 23 for a discussion of *Spycatcher*. One objectionable aspect of the use of such prior restraint is that there exists no trial of the merits of the work which is being restrained: an injunction is issued, and the trial of the facts may occur much later, when it may transpire that there has been an unjustified, and often lengthy, restriction on freedom of expression.

The notion of breach of confidence, originally relevant mainly to trade secrets and unfair competition and industrial espionage, has expanded over two decades in no particularly logical way, proceeding on a case by case basis. Disclosure of information may amount to breach of confidence if the relationship is based on marriage,[266] contracts of employment, consultancies and potentially any situation involving a 'confidential relationship'. A duty of confidence is owed to Cabinet by individual Ministers,[267] and by members of the Security Services and civil servants to the Crown.[268] Where such a relationship is held to exist, an obligation is imposed to keep information confidential and a proposed disclosure will found an action for breach of confidence. Defences to an action for breach of confidence include the following:

Staleness

In *Attorney General v Jonathan Cape Ltd*[269] (the *Crossman Diaries* case) the information disclosed in breach of confidence was some 10 years old and no harm would follow from its publication. Accordingly, the court held that, in

---

264 (1987) *The Times*, 5 and 18 December.

265 (1980) 2 EHHR 245. See Chapter 22.

266 See *Duke of Argyll v Duchess* [1967] Ch 302.

267 See Chapter 11.

268 See Chapters 23 and 11, respectively. On members of the Security Services, see, also, *Attorney General v Blake* (1996) *The Times*, 23 April, below p 946, fn 34.

269 [1976] QB 752.

the absence of a breach of national security, further restraint was not justified. However, in the *Spycatcher* case, *Attorney General v Guardian (No 2)*,[270] while the injunction was eventually lifted, the government claimed that the duty of former Security Service personnel is lifelong and that no publication of any matter concerning their employment may be disclosed. Section 1 of the Official Secrets Act 1989 now reflects this duty and imposes criminal sanctions on any revelations made in relation to security matters.

The material is in the public domain

While there may be found to be a duty of confidence, this duty does not necessarily result in an injunction being permanently imposed to restrain publication. In addition to the material being 'stale', it may be that the material has already been published elsewhere, and is thus in the 'public domain'. In relation to the book *Spycatcher*, this matter weighed with the court. The book had been published in Australia and the United States of America and was, in fact, freely available anywhere outside the United Kingdom.

Revealing true information to correct falsity

Irrespective of the existence of a duty of confidence, there may be situations where material has been published which is false and which justifies a breach of confidence in order to rectify the falsehood. In *Woodward v Hutchins*,[271] for example, a falsehood concerning a pop star had been published. Notwithstanding a duty of confidence, there was a justified and legitimate need for rebuttal of the untruths.

Iniquity: to reveal evidence crime/fraud

Breach of confidence may be excused by the court if the defence of revealing criminal or fraudulent activities is made out.

Public interest

The defence of public interest was considered in *Lion Laboratories v Evans and Express Newspapers*.[272] *The Express* newspaper revealed information concerning faulty intoximeters used to measure the extent of alcohol in an individual's bloodstream. Deficiencies in the breathalyser equipment could have resulted in wrongful convictions for driving under the influence of alcohol. The disclosure of confidential information was justified. There was no

---

270 [1990] 1 AC 109; [1988] 3 All ER 545.
271 [1977] 2 All ER 751.
272 [1984] 2 All ER 417.

question of the manufacturer having been guilty of any 'iniquity' or wrongdoing. However, the matter was one of public interest which overrode any claim to confidentiality of the information.

PRIVACY AND THE MEDIA

The invasion of privacy by the media has also become a matter of rising concern. In 1953, the Press Council was established.[273] This self-regulatory body proved woefully inadequate at controlling the press, not least because it had no powers to fine newspapers. In 1972, the Younger Committee was established to consider reforms in relation to press freedom. The Committee recommended that a tort of disclosure of information unlawfully acquired and a tort and crime of unlawful surveillance by technical devices be introduced.[274] The proposed reforms were not implemented. Concern over intrusions into individual privacy have increased with the media attention given to the Royal Family in recent years. The case of *Kaye v Robertson and Another*[275] heightened public interest in the respective right of an individual to privacy and the right of the public to information. In *Kaye*, journalists entered a hospital room in which the well known actor, Gordon Kaye, was being treated for severe injuries sustained in a car accident. Kaye agreed neither to be photographed nor interviewed. An injunction was sought, and granted, to restrain the newspaper from publishing the 'interview' and photographs. On appeal, the Court of Appeal ruled that there was no right to privacy under English law which could found the basis for an injunction.

In 1990, the Committee on Privacy and Related Matters (the Calcutt committee) was established, which led to the creation of another self-regulatory body in 1991, the Press Complaints Commission.[276] A review of the working of the Commission by Sir David Calcutt[277] found the protection accorded to individuals inadequate. It has been recommended, therefore, that a statutory body be established. That recommendation has not been favoured.[278]

---

273 The Broadcasting Complaints Commission plays a similar role in relation to broadcasting: Broadcasting Act 1990, s 142.

274 *Report of the Younger Committee*, Cmnd 5012, 1972; and see MacCormick, DN, 'A note on privacy' (1973) 84 LQR 23.

275 (1991) *The Times*, 21 March.

276 *Report of the Committee on Privacy and Related Matters*, Cmnd 1102, 1990. See Munro, CR, 'Press freedom: how the beast was tamed' (1991) 54 MLR 104.

277 *Review of Press Self-Regulation*, Cmnd 2135, 1993, London: HMSO.

278 *Fourth Report of the National Heritage Select Committee Privacy and Media Intrusion*, 294-I (March 1993).

A statutory tort of or criminal liability for invasion of privacy?

The Younger Committee in 1972 recommended the introduction of a statutory tort to provide individuals with an action for the protection of privacy. The Calcutt Report of 1990 rejected this recommendation, but recommended the introduction of a criminal offence, creating liability if personal information, or photographs, are obtained by entering onto private property without consent, using surveillance devices, taking photographs, or recording the voice of an individual without consent. Damages could be granted in respect of the liability. Defences to an action would include: actions taken for the purpose of preventing, detecting or exposing criminal activity; actions taken for the purpose of disclosing information about an individual acting in his or her official capacity; and actions taken for the protection of public health or safety or acting under lawful authority.

Subsequently, both the National Heritage Select Committee and the Lord Chancellor's Department recommended that a tort of invasion of privacy be introduced. The difficulties with these proposals lie in the extent to which there would be a defence of public interest or justified disclosure. There is a very difficult balance here to be struck between freedom of information, freedom of expression and the right of individuals not to have their privacy invaded by the press. Particularly in respect of public figures, there remains the problematic issue of whether protection should be given in relation to matters which are purely private or just matters which relate to the lives and behaviour of individuals in their public capacity. It has become particularly evident over recent years that the press wields considerable power over the lives of public figures, such as the Royal Family and politicians, to the extent that the press can play the role of accuser, judge and jury.[279] Proposals to curb the power of the media, in order to tilt the balance away from the public's right to know, and towards greater respect for individual privacy, have, however, come under critical scrutiny. The incorporation of the European Convention on Human Rights, under the Human Rights Act 1998, will, as discussed in Chapter 22, provide the judges with a code against which to interpret domestic legislation. Article 8 of the Convention provides that: '... everyone has the right to respect for his private and family life, his home and his correspondence', and that there shall be no interference with this right save on specified grounds. By contrast, Article 10 of the Convention provides for the right to freedom of expression, a right which again may be circumscribed only on specific grounds. Once the Convention is enacted into domestic law under the Human Rights Act 1998, it will be for domestic judges, subject to an application to the Court in Strasbourg, to strike the balance between the two provisions. However, in an amendment to the

---

279 See, for examples, the discussion on resignations of Ministers in Chapter 11.

Human Rights Bill introduced in the House of Commons, in an attempt to inhibit judges from developing a domestic privacy law which would delimit press freedom, judges are directed to interpret Article 8 in light of Article 10, and not vice versa.

CHAPTER 20

FREEDOM OF ASSOCIATION AND ASSEMBLY, PUBLIC ORDER AND POLICE POWERS[1]

PART I – ASSOCIATION AND ASSEMBLY

While the detection and prosecution of crime and the preservation of public order are of first importance in any State, the extent to which police powers reflect a legitimate interference with the liberty and security of citizens is a problematic question which involves evaluating the balance struck between the rights of the individual and the powers of the police.

In any society, it is essential that there be a balance effected between the legitimate rights of individual citizens to conduct their lives in maximum freedom and the equally important need to protect order in society, without which no citizen would enjoy freedom. In this chapter, the organisation of the police forces is considered. Further, the manner in which law regulates associations and assemblies – whether meetings or processions – is examined. In addition, it is necessary to consider the manner in which law regulates an individual's freedom to move around, and the conditions under which it is or is not lawful to enter into and remain on land, both private and public. The powers of the police in relation to these issues and public order offences are also considered, as are the powers of the police in relation to arrest and detention in the course of the investigation of crime.

FREEDOM OF ASSOCIATION

While citizens are generally free to join any club, society or trades union, two statutory restrictions exist. The first restriction relates to membership of military or quasi-military organisations. The Public Order Act 1936 provides, in part, that the wearing of uniforms in public with the intention of promoting a political objective is unlawful, and that membership of groups organised and trained for the purpose of displaying physical force is unlawful.[2]

---

1   See, *inter alia*, Robertson, G, *Freedom, the Individual and the Law*, 6th edn, 1993 (7th edn, 2001), London: Penguin; Ewing, KD and Gearty, CA, *Freedom Under Thatcher*, 1990, Oxford: Clarendon; Feldman, D, *Civil Liberties and Human Rights in England and Wales*, 1993, Oxford: OUP; Fenwick, H, *Civil Liberties*, 2nd edn, 1998 (3rd edn, 2001), London: Cavendish Publishing.

2   See, now, the Terrorism Act 2000, discussed in Chapter 23.

In *R v Jordan and Tyndall*,[3] the defendants were members of a fascist group, Spearhead. They exercised in military fashion and were known to be storing chemicals capable of being used for the manufacture of bombs. They were convicted under section 2(1)(b) of the Public Order Act 1936. In *Director of Public Prosecutions v Whelan*,[4] the defendants were charged under section 1 of the Act. Participating in a *Sinn Fein* march in Northern Ireland, the defendants wore black berets, dark clothing and carried the Irish flag. It was held that the wearing of similar clothing could amount to a 'uniform'.

Specific groups are proscribed. Under the Prevention of Terrorism (Temporary Provisions) Act 1989, it is an offence to belong to a proscribed group. Section 1 and Schedule 1 of the Act proscribes the Irish Republican Army (IRA) and the Irish National Liberation Army (INLA). In Northern Ireland, the Northern Ireland (Emergency Provisions) Act 1991 proscribes membership of a number of groups.[5] To be a member of such a group, or to solicit or invite financial or other support for the group, is an offence. Schedule 2 of the Terrorism Act 2000 replaces the 1989 Act in relation to proscribed organisations. See Chapter 23.

FREEDOM OF ASSEMBLY[6]

... it can hardly be said that our constitution knows of such a thing as any specific right of public meeting.[7]

Freedom of assembly is closely related to freedom of speech. An individual is free to assemble with others to the extent that the law does not prohibit such assemblies or the assembly does not involve unlawful actions. In 1885, Dicey was to record that 'the police have with us no special authority to control open air assemblies'.[8] Today much has changed. Under common law, a number of restraints were placed on this freedom, and the Public Order Acts 1936 and 1986 and the Criminal Justice and Public Order Act 1994 restrict rights of assembly. While there is a general freedom to assemble on private property or on public land, in the case of the former, it will be a trespass to do so without the consent of the landowner. In relation to land to which the public have the

---

3   [1963] Crim LR 124.

4   [1975] QB 864.

5   The IRA, INLA, Irish People's Liberation Organisation, *Cumann na mBan, Fianna na Eireann, Saor Eire,* Red Hand Commandos, Ulster Freedom Fighters, Ulster Volunteer Force, Ulster Defence Association.

6   See Williams, DGT, *Keeping the Peace,* 1967, London: Hutchinson; Supperstone, M (ed), *Brownlie's Law of Public Order and National Security,* 2nd edn, 1981, London: Butterworths; *op cit,* Ewing and Gearty, fn 1; Bevan, V, 'Protest and public disorder' [1979] PL 163; Smith, ATH, 'The Public Order Act, Part I' [1987] Crim LR 156.

7   Dicey, AV, *Introduction to the Study of the Law of the Constitution,* 10th edn, 1959, London: Macmillan, p 271.

8   *Ibid,* p 270.

right of access, the right of assembly is controlled by local authority bylaws, and a criminal offence is committed if these are breached. Further, the right of assembly may be controlled by statute. By way of example, the right to assemble in Trafalgar Square is regulated under statute, under which, permission must be granted by the Secretary of State for the Environment.[9] Hyde Park is equally regulated.[10] The law relating to freedom of assembly must be viewed in the light of Article 11 of the European Convention on Human Rights which, *inter alia*, provides a right to freedom of peaceful assembly and to freedom of association with others. See, further, Chapter 22.

The duty to facilitate meetings

The constitutional importance of freedom of expression and involvement in civic life is reflected in the right to use schools and other public rooms for meetings in local elections, by-elections and general elections.[11] In addition, under the Education (No 2) Act 1986, the governing bodies of universities and colleges are under a duty to 'take such steps as are reasonably practicable to ensure that freedom of speech within the law is secured for members, students and employees of the establishment and for visiting speakers'.[12] This requirement gave rise to a challenge in *R v University of Liverpool ex parte Caesar-Gordon*.[13] In that case, the university had refused permission for a meeting at which two diplomats from the South African Embassy were due to speak. The decision was based on the fear that the meeting would cause public unrest in the surrounding area. The Divisional Court ruled that the university had acted *ultra vires* its powers. The university authorities were not entitled to take into account threats of violence outside its precincts. Only where the risk of violence would relate to university precincts, would the university be justified in imposing restrictions.

INDIRECT RESTRICTIONS ON THE RIGHT OF ASSEMBLY

A number of indirect means may be employed in order to restrain public meetings. Such means include breach of the peace, obstruction of police officers and obstruction of the highway.

---

9   SI 1952/776.
10 Royal and Other Parks and Gardens Regulations 1988 SI 1988/217, and see *Bailey v Williamson* (1873) LR 8 QB 118.
11 Representation of the People Act 1983, ss 95, 96.
12 Education (No 2) Act 1986, s 43.
13 [1991] 1 QB 124.

Breach of the peace

In *Beatty v Gillbanks*,[14] the Salvation Army met knowing that there would be an opposing meeting. The magistrates' court issued an order preventing the meeting. When the meeting assembled in defiance of the order, the police ordered the meeting to disband and arrested one of the members. On the defendant's appeal against conviction, the Queen's Bench Division refused to accept the restriction on freedom of assembly based on the threatened unlawful acts of others. Where, however, participants in a meeting engage in unlawful conduct which provokes others and results in a breach of the peace – or a reasonable apprehension of a breach of the peace – the meeting may be held to be unlawful. Further, if the meeting is conducted lawfully and yet provokes an actual breach of the peace, the police may order the meeting to disband. Failure to comply with an order to leave an assembly on the grounds of an officer's reasonable belief that it is necessary to avoid a breach of the peace is a criminal offence.[15]

The *Beatty v Gillbanks* principle – namely, that a person acting lawfully was not responsible for the unlawful reaction of others – has been undermined in a number of cases. In *Jordan v Burgoyne*,[16] the court ruled that a person addressing an audience would be found guilty of a breach of the peace if his or her words were likely to inflame the audience and lead to violence. Equally, in *Percy v Director of Public Prosecutions*,[17] the court ruled that conduct which was not itself unlawful could amount to a breach of the peace if the words spoken were likely to cause disorder among those listening, even if member of the audience had attended with the express intent of causing trouble. Further, in *Morpeth Ward Justices ex parte Ward*,[18] the issue was not so much the conduct of the protesters but, rather, whether or not the conduct had the effect of provoking violent behaviour, even where the reaction to the protest was unreasonable. However, in *Nicol v Director of Public Prosecutions*,[19] the court adopted a more restrictive approach. The protest in question concerned an attempt to stop anglers from fishing. The protesters blew horns and provoked the anglers. It was held that, although there was nothing unlawful in the protesters' actions, the provocation of the anglers was likely to cause a breach of the peace because it was unreasonable action.

In *Redman-Bate v Director of Public Prosecutions*[20] three women preachers, who were preaching on the steps of a cathedral, were approached by a police

---

14 (1882) 9 QB 308.
15 *Duncan v Jones* [1936] 1 KB 218.
16 [1963] 1 KB 218.
17 [1995] 3 All ER 124.
18 (1992) 95 Cr App R 215.
19 (1996) 1 J Civ Lib 75.
20 (1999) *The Times*, 28 July.

constable and warned not to stop people. Later, he returned to find that a crowd had gathered, some of whom were hostile to the speakers. The constable asked the women to stop preaching, but when they refused arrested them for a breach of the peace. They were convicted of obstructing a police officer in the execution of his duty. On appeal, it was held that there was no lawful basis for the arrest. Free speech, provided that it did not tend to provoke violence, irrespective of its content (unless contrary to law), was to be respected. There were no grounds on which the constable could apprehend a breach of the peace, much less one for which the preachers would be responsible.

Breach of the peace is a concept which traditionally has involved a degree of proximity and immediacy between the conduct of individuals and the anticipated breach of the peace. However, in *Moss v McLachlan*,[21] in the course of the miners' strike 1984–85, the defendants were ordered to turn back on a journey to another colliery some four miles away. The police suspected that they were intending to join the picket line in support of fellow miners and that a breach of the peace might occur. When the miners refused to obey the order to turn back, they were arrested for obstruction. The judge conceded a wide discretion to the police and ruled that, provided a senior police officer 'honestly and reasonably formed the opinion' that there was a real risk of a breach of the peace, in an area proximate to the point of arrest, they could take whatever measures were reasonably necessary to prevent it.

This decision, whilst understandable from the police's point of view, is regrettable for it introduces a dangerous breadth to the offence. Furthermore, uncertainty is created as to the precise scope of the police's power to interfere with freedom of movement.[22]

Obstructing the police

Under the Police Act 1996,[23] it is a criminal offence to obstruct the police in the execution of their duty. Section 89 provides that:

(1) Any person who assaults a constable in the execution of his duty, or a person assisting a constable in the execution of his duty, shall be guilty of an offence ...

(2) Any person who resists or wilfully obstructs a constable in the execution of his duty, or a person assisting a constable in the execution of his duty, shall be guilty of an offence ...

---

21 [1985] IRLR 76.

22 See *Nicol v Director of Public Prosecutions* (1996) 1 J Civ Lib 75.

23 Formerly, Police Act 1964, s 51.

In *Duncan v Jones*,[24] the defendant had intended to hold a public meeting at a place previously used for that purpose. The police, aware that a disturbance had previously occurred in that place, instructed Mrs Duncan to hold the meeting on an alternative site. Mrs Duncan refused and started the meeting on the highway. She was arrested and charged under section 51 of the Police Act. The defendant could have been charged with obstruction of the highway (see below) or with inciting a breach of the peace. However, in the alternative the police charged her with obstructing a police officer. The court held that, once the police officer reasonably considered that a breach of the peace could occur, any action which impeded him in the course of preventing such an occurrence, amounted to an obstruction of the police. In *Piddington v Bates*,[25] in the course of an industrial dispute, the police directed that no more than two pickets should be allowed at each entrance to the factory. The defendant joined the picket line in defiance of the order, regarding the restriction as unreasonable, and was charged with obstruction. On appeal, the Divisional Court upheld his conviction.

Obstructing the highway

The Highways Act 1980

A citizen is free to move along the highway. It is, however, a criminal offence to obstruct the highway. Obstructing the highway also represents a public nuisance, which may be prosecuted on indictment under common law.[26] Under section 137 of the Highways Act 1980, 'if a person, without lawful authority or excuse, in any way wilfully obstructs the free passage along a highway he is guilty of an offence'. In *Hirst v Chief Constable for West Yorkshire*,[27] animal rights demonstrators protesting outside a store selling animal fur products were charged with obstructing the highway. The magistrates' court convicted them of obstruction. However, on appeal, the Divisional Court held that the justices should have considered the reasonableness of the action and weighed in the balance the right to protest and demonstrate and the need for public order. The magistrates' court had failed to consider this and, accordingly, failed to respect the freedom to protest on matters of public concern. See, also, *Director of Public Prosecutions v Jones*, discussed below, p 784.

---

24   [1935] 2 KB 249.
25   [1960] 3 All ER 660.
26   *R v Clark (No 2)* [1964] 2 QB 315.
27   (1986) 85 Cr App R 143.

The Public Order Act 1986 and Criminal Justice and Public Order Act 1994

The Public Order Act 1986 was passed after growing concern over demonstrations, industrial disputes, riots and football hooliganism. The Red Lion Square riot in 1974 led to an inquiry chaired by Lord Scarman,[28] as did the Brixton riots in 1981.[29] In 1983, the Law Commission reviewed public order law[30] and, in 1985, the government published a White Paper.[31] The resulting Public Order Act 1986 had two principal objectives. The first was to provide a comprehensive code as to the organisation and control of processions and demonstrations. The second was to provide a code relating to disorderly conduct, which can range from behaviour which causes alarm or distress to riot. In addition, the Act creates offences relating to football hooliganism and to control of persons unlawfully camping on private land.

The law relating to public order was further reformed substantially by the Criminal Justice and Public Order Act 1994.[32] The Criminal Justice and Public Order Act made major reforms across a wide spectrum of criminal justice matters and matters relating to sexual offences. New sentences for young offenders were introduced; the right to silence of defendants has been curtailed; and the powers of police to take body samples increased. In relation to public order,[33] the Act increased the powers of the police and local authorities in respect of trespass, 'rave parties', squatters and campers, and marked a significant shift away from individual liberties towards increasing State regulation in favour of maintaining public order. The Act had a stormy passage through Parliament, and its eventual implementation was delayed for several months due to major amendments being introduced in the House of Lords.

The regulation of processions

A procession is not defined in the Public Order Act. Processions were originally regulated under the Public Order Act 1936 and the powers were extended under the Public Order Act 1986. In *Flockhart v Robinson*,[34] a procession was said to be 'not a mere body of persons: it is a body of persons moving along a route'. Accordingly, a procession must involve more than one person. To be regulated by the Act, a procession must be public. A public place is defined in section 16 as being:

---

28 *Report on the Red Lion Square Disorders*, Cmnd 5919, 1975, London: HMSO.
29 *Report on the Brixton Disorders*, Cmnd 8427, 1981, London: HMSO.
30 *Criminal Law: Offences Relating to Public Order*, Law Com No 123, 1983, London: HMSO.
31 *Review of Public Order Law*, Cmnd 9510, 1985, London: HMSO.
32 *Implementing the Report of the Royal Commission on Criminal Justice*, Cmnd 2263, 1993, London: HMSO.
33 Criminal Justice and Public Order Act 1994, Pt V.
34 [1950] 2 KB 498, p 502

(a) any highway ...; and

(b) any place to which at the material time the public or any section of the public has access, on payment or otherwise, as of right or by virtue of express or implied permission.

The requirement of notice

Under section 11, notice must be given to the police of a procession which is designed to express or oppose the views of another, to publicise or encourage support for a campaign, or to commemorate an event. Processions which are regularly held within a particular area need not be notified to the police. Where it is impracticable to give notice in advance, the requirement may be waived. This exception enables spontaneous demonstrations to take place.

Six clear days' notice must be given, except where it is impracticable to do so[35] Failure to give notice, or organising a procession different from the one notified, is a summary offence. In Scotland, similar requirements exist. Under the Civil Government (Scotland) Act 1982, as amended,[36] the police must receive at least seven days' notice. Where a ban is imposed on a particular march, a right of appeal exists.[37]

The power to impose conditions

Where notice has been given in accordance with section 11, then a senior police office (Chief Constable or Commissioner) may impose conditions, under section 12. If a procession is under way, then a senior officer on the scene may impose conditions. The basis on which conditions may be attached include situations where the senior police officer reasonably believes that a procession may result in serious public disorder, serious damage to property or serious disruption of the life of the community.[38] An alternative basis for conditions is where it is reasonably believed that the procession is taking place for an illegitimate purpose. Intimidation, for example, would be an 'illegitimate purpose'. Under section 14 of the Act, conditions may also – on the same grounds as those stated in section 12 – be imposed on assemblies.

If the requirements for the imposition of conditions are met, the senior officer has a wide discretion as to the conditions which may in fact be imposed. Section 12(1) merely states that he may impose conditions 'as appear to him necessary'. Under section 12, there is power to impose conditions as to the route to be followed, and to prohibit entry into particular public places.

---

35 Public Order Act 1986, s 11(6).
36 By the Local Government (Scotland) Act 1994.
37 Civil Government (Scotland) Act 1982, ss 62 and 64.
38 Public Order Act 1986, s 12(1).

Failure to comply with the conditions, or to incite others not to comply, is an offence.[39]

The power to ban processions

Under section 13, the Chief Officer of Police[40] may issue a banning order, which may only be issued if the power to impose conditions is insufficient to prevent serious public disorder. In London, the banning order must be with the consent of the Home Secretary, elsewhere, with the consent of the local authority. The power to ban processions represents a power to ban all processions, rather than to ban a particular procession, and can cover all or part of a police area and last for up to three months.[41] Organising or participating in, or inciting participation in, a banned procession is a summary offence.[42]

The power to enter meetings on private premises

Where a private meeting is held, the police have power to enter and remain on the premises under certain circumstances. A meeting is defined as a private meeting if it is held in entirely enclosed premises. Thus, even if the meeting is held in publicly owned and managed premises, such as a school or town hall, it will be a private meeting. In *Thomas v Sawkins*,[43] a police officer entered a private meeting which was held to protest against the Incitement to Disaffection Bill. The organiser of the meeting brought an action based on trespass, and argued that, as a result of trespass by the police, he had the right to evict the officers. The meeting had not given rise to a breach of the peace. However, the court held that notwithstanding its peaceful nature, the police had grounds for reasonably suspecting that a breach of the peace might occur and were therefore entitled to enter and remain on the premises.

The regulation of public assemblies[44]

While there is power to regulate a public assembly, there was no power to issue a banning order under the 1986 Act. However, section 70 of the Criminal Justice and Public Order Act 1994 inserted section 14A into the 1986 Act which

---

39 Public Order Act 1986, s 12(4), (5).

40 In London, the Commission for the City of London for Commissioner for the Metropolis.

41 The power to ban a procession is subject to judicial review: *Kent v Metropolitan Police Commissioners* (1981) *The Times*, 15 May.

42 Public Order Act 1986, s 13(7), (8), (9).

43 [1935] 2 KB 249.

44 See Bonner, D and Stone, R, 'The Public Order Act 1986: steps in the wrong direction' [1987] PL 202.

provided a power to ban assemblies. A public assembly is defined as 'an assembly of 20 or more persons in a public place which is wholly or partly open to the air'.[45] The basis on which the conditions which may be attached[46] are the same as those for conditions imposed on processions. Intimidation, as a ground for imposing a condition, has been interpreted to mean more than 'causing discomfort'.[47]

Trespassory assemblies

A Chief Officer of Police may apply for a banning order if he reasonably believes that an assembly is likely to involve trespass or might result in serious disruption to community life or cause damage to buildings and structures. This power must be seen within the context of section 14(c) of the Public Order Act 1986,[48] discussed below, p 786, which confers power on the police to stop persons within a five mile radius of the assembly, if the police reasonably believe that they are on their way to the assembly, and the assembly is subject to a section 14A order.

In *Director of Public Prosecutions v Jones*,[49] section 14 was considered. A section 14A order had been issued, which prohibited the holding of a trespassory assembly within a four mile radius of Stonehenge, between 29 May and 1 June 1995. The assembly was heading for Stonehenge, and was within the four mile radius, and on the public highway. The court held that the highway was for passing and repassing only, and that assembling on the highway was outside the purpose for which the implied licence to use the highway was granted. The respondents argued that they were both peaceful and not obstructive and were making 'reasonable use' of the highway. The House of Lords ruled, by a majority of three to two, that the public had the right to use the highway for such reasonable and usual activities, *inter alia*, including peaceful assembly, as was consistent with the primary use for passage and repassage. It was a question of fact and degree in each case whether the user was reasonable and not inconsistent with that primary right.

The right to move freely along the highway, for a minority group such as Gypsies, entails the need for a lawful place to stop. While local authorities had been under a duty to provide sites under the Caravan Sites Act 1968,[50] the government has now removed that statutory duty.[51] This is of particular

---

45 Public Order Act 1986, s 16.
46 *Ibid*, s 14(1).
47 *Police v Reid* [1987] Crim LR 702.
48 Inserted by the Criminal Justice and Public Order Act 1994, 1994, s 71.
49 [1999] 2 WLR 625; [1997] 2 All ER 119, HL.
50 Caravan Sites Act 1968, s 6.
51 Criminal Justice and Public Order Act 1994, s 80.

concern, given that Gypsies – a recognised racial group protected under the Race Relations Act 1976 and under international law[52] – traditionally travel with caravans from area to area, usually in search of seasonal work.

The problems encountered in the 1970s and 1980s with groups of New Age Travellers combining for the summer solstice at Stonehenge and the problems caused by 'rave parties' resulted in the criminalisation of trespass for the first time under English Law. Section 39 of the Public Order Act 1986 provided the police with powers to direct persons to leave land where they had entered land as trespassers, with a common purpose of remaining there, where steps had been taken by the occupier[53] to ask them to leave. A further requirement, under section 39, was that the trespasser had caused damage to property on the land or had used threatening, abusive or insulting words or behaviour towards the occupier and his associates, or that the trespassers had brought 12 or more vehicles onto the land. Failure to obey the instruction of the police to leave the land as soon 'as reasonably practicable'[54] amounted to a criminal offence. A number of difficulties arose with the interpretation of section 39, and that section has been repealed and replaced by section 61 of the Criminal Justice and Public Order Act 1994. A number of significant amendments have been made to the powers of the police.

First, whereas, under the 1986 Act, persons could be directed to leave where they had entered the land as trespassers, the 1994 Act makes it possible to remove persons who are in fact trespassing, whether or not they entered the land as trespassers.[55] Thus, even where persons originally entered land at the invitation of the occupier, if they have subsequently become trespassers they can be directed to leave the land. Secondly, whereas the 1986 Act provided for damage to property on land as a criterion for a direction to leave, the 1994 Act has extended the concept of damage to include damage to the land itself. Thirdly, the 1986 Act applied in relation to persons having 12 or more vehicles on the land: the 1994 Act reduces the number of vehicles to six. This is a major change and one of great disadvantage for the minority Gypsy population which traditionally migrates in convoys of caravans.

Fourthly, the Act extends the land to which the provisions apply. Common land[56] is now included, as are footpaths, bridleways, byways, public paths and cycletracks.[57] Fifthly, the 1994 Act has given the police new powers to remove 'vehicles and other property' on land.[58] The power to seize vehicles and property arises where the trespasser fails to comply with a direction to

---

52 *Commission for Racial Equality v Dutton* [1989] 2 WLR 17, discussed above.
53 Or on behalf of the occupier.
54 Public Order Act 1986, s 39(2).
55 Criminal Justice and Public Order Act 1994, s 61(2).
56 As defined in the Commons Registration Act 1965, s 22.
57 Criminal Justice and Public Order Act 1994, s 61(9)(b)(i).
58 *Ibid*, s 62.

leave within a reasonable time. Reasonableness is an objective test and will depend on all the circumstances of the case, including the road worthiness of vehicles.[59] Where vehicles are seized, powers are given for the safe keeping, disposal and destruction of the vehicles, the powers to be exercised according to Regulations to be drafted by the Secretary of State.[60]

The power of seizure and destruction was introduced by the government, which was aware of the limitations of fines for non-compliance, and recommended the seizure of caravans as a sanction 'as a last resort'. Circumspection is appropriate here. The potential for harrowing scenes of families being physically wrenched from their homes and removal of those homes until 'the offender(s) satisfied the court that he (they) either had a legal place to camp or alternative accommodation'[61] is great and chilling in its contemplation. The cumulative effect will be that Gypsy families comply with the request to leave, only to find themselves – in the absence of official sites – with no lawful place to stop. As Baroness Mallalieu stated in debate 'we are in very real danger of putting people in Britain in 1994 in the position of the road sweeper in *Bleak House* in the last century who was forever being told to move on but had nowhere to go'. The only alternative will be to submit to seizure of their homes, leaving them without a roof over their heads until rehoused under the Housing Act 1985 provisions. Failure to leave land as directed amounts to a criminal offence, for which arrest without warrant is provided.[62]

Rave parties

The Criminal Justice and Public Order Act 1994 introduces new police powers to order persons to leave gatherings, creates a new criminal offence of failing to leave within a reasonable time and provides for arrest without warrant. The provisions govern open air gatherings of 100 or more persons, where amplified music is played at night time. Failure to comply with a police direction may result in the power to seize and remove vehicles and sound equipment.[63]

The Act gives the police power to regulate the movement of persons to a gathering. Where a direction has been made under section 63, the police may stop persons and order them not to proceed to the gathering. The exercise of this sweeping new power is confined to an area within a five mile radius of the gathering.

---

59 See *Krumpa v Director of Public Prosecutions* [1989] Crim LR 295.

60 Public Order Act 1986, s 67(3).

61 Consultation Paper, para 21.

62 Criminal Justice and Public Order Act 1994, s 61(4), (5).

63 *Ibid*, s 64.

Other public order offences under the 1986 Act

The Act has rationalised a number of common law offences. The Law Commission considered, for example, that the offence of breach of the peace was too vague a concept and that it should be replaced with more specific offences. In its place, the concept of unlawful violence is used, which encompasses a number of situations. Violent conduct is defined as meaning any violent conduct, whether or not intended to cause injury or damage.[64]

Riot

Riot is the most serious offence created under the Act. 'Riot' is defined in section 1 as being where 12 or more persons who are present together use or threaten unlawful violence for a common purpose and the conduct of them (taken together) is such as would cause a person of reasonable firmness present at the scene to fear for his personal safety; each of the persons using unlawful violence for the common purpose is guilty of riot.

A riot may be committed in private as well as public places.[65] The common purpose may be inferred from the conduct, and does not need to be articulated.[66] The purpose itself need not be unlawful – a perfectly legitimate demonstration may turn into a riot if the conditions for a riot are satisfied, namely the use of unlawful violence for a common purpose which is such as to cause persons 'of reasonable firmness' present to fear for their personal safety, although it is not necessary that such persons actually be present at the scene.[67] The mental element required for liability is that a person 'intends to use violence or is aware that his conduct may be violent'.[68] The seriousness with which the offence is viewed is reflected in the requirement of trial on indictment (trial by jury) and the liability on conviction to imprisonment for a term not exceeding 10 years or a fine or both.[69]

Violent disorder

Section 2 of the Public Order Act 1986 creates a new statutory offence of violent disorder, which replaces the common law offence of unlawful assembly. The offence shares similarities with the offence of riot, but differs in several respects. First, for the offence to be committed, there needs to be only three people, rather than 12 as required for a riot, involved in the violent

---

64 Public Order Act 1986, s 8.
65 *Ibid*, s 1(5).
66 *Ibid*, s 1(3).
67 *Ibid*, s 1(4).
68 *Ibid*, s 6(1).
69 *Ibid*, s 1(6).

conduct. Secondly, there needs to be no common purpose, as is required for the offence of riot. It is sufficient for an offence of violent disorder to be committed that the persons be involved in the use or threat of violent conduct. It is necessary that the conduct be such that it causes a person 'of reasonable firmness' to 'fear for his personal safety', although such persons need not actually be present.[70] The offence can be committed in private or public.[71] The mental element required is that the person intends to use or to threaten violence, or is aware that his conduct may be violent or threaten violence.[72] Self-induced intoxication, other than through prescribed medication in a course of medical treatment, is not an excuse.[73]

The requirement of three person's involvement in the violent disorder has caused difficulties. In *R v Fleming*,[74] for example, four persons were charged, one was acquitted and the jury failed to reach a decision on a second. Accordingly, the conviction of the remaining two defendants was quashed.[75] The Court of Appeal in *Fleming* noted that it was possible for less than three persons to be convicted where, for example, there was sufficient evidence as to the involvement of more than three persons but some of the greater number evaded arrest or lacked the required mental element for the offence. The jury must be correctly directed on the matter, and failure to direct appropriately will cause a conviction to be quashed. This occurred in *R v Whorton*,[76] where there was evidence that eight to 10 people were involved in the violence, but only four were charged and only two convicted. Their appeal against conviction was successful, on the basis that the judge had not directed the jury that they could only convict if there were either three defendants before them, or if a lesser number, that a greater number had in fact been involved in the violent disorder.

The offence is triable on indictment (by the Crown Court) or summarily (by a magistrates' court), and carries a term of imprisonment of up to five years on indictment or a fine or both and, on summary conviction, imprisonment of up to six months or a fine or both.[77]

---

70 Public Order Act 1986, s 2(3).
71 *Ibid*, s 2(4).
72 *Ibid*, s 6(2).
73 *Ibid*, s 6(5).
74 [1989] Crim LR 658.
75 See, also, *R v Abdul Mahroof* (1988) 88 Cr App R 317.
76 [1990] Crim LR 124.
77 Public Order Act 1986, s 2(5).

Affray

A person is guilty of an affray if he uses or threatens unlawful violence towards another and his conduct is such as would cause a person of reasonable firmness present at the scene to fear for his personal safety.[78]

Two or more persons may be involved in the offence, in which case it is necessary that their conduct be considered together for the purpose of section 1. A verbal threat of unlawful violence is not sufficient for the offence to be committed.[79] The offence may take place in private or in public[80] and, again, the test for unlawful violence is whether a person of reasonable firmness, who need not in fact be present,[81] is put in fear for his personal safety. The mental element is the same as that required for violent disorder. Police constables may arrest without warrant, and the offence is triable on indictment or summarily. On indictment, the offence carries a term of imprisonment not exceeding three years or a fine or both; on summary conviction, there is liability to imprisonment of up to six months or a fine or both.[82]

The definition of affray was considered by the Court of Appeal in *R v Sanchez*.[83] On the charge of affray, the trial judge directed the jury on the requirement for a 'person of reasonable firmness' and said that the victim was such a person and that he was to be believed when he said that he was frightened. The Court of Appeal held that there was a misdirection, in that the judge's directions overlooked the need to direct the jury to consider not only the victim but also the putative third person, the hypothetical bystander; affray was a public order offence and there were other offences for the protection of persons at whom the violence was aimed.

Fear or provocation of violence

A person is guilty of an offence if he:

(a) uses towards another person threatening, abusive or insulting words or behaviour; or

(b) distributes or displays to another person any writing, sign or other visible representation which is threatening, abusive or insulting, with the intent to cause that person to believe that immediate unlawful violence will be used against him or another by any person, or to provoke the immediate use of unlawful violence by that person or another, or whereby that person is

---

78 Public Order Act 1986, s 3(1).
79 *Ibid*, s 3(3).
80 *Ibid*, s 3(5).
81 *Ibid*, s 3(4).
82 *Ibid*, s 3(7).
83 (1996) *The Times*, 6 March.

likely to believe that such violence will be used or it is likely that such violence will be provoked.[84]

The offence is one which may be committed by a single person. For a prosecution to succeed, it is necessary to establish that threatening, abusive or insulting words or behaviour have been directed towards a specific person. Rude or offensive words or behaviour may not necessarily be insulting, and swearing may not be abusive.[85] It is also necessary to establish that the person affected is caused to believe that immediate unlawful violence is about to be used against him. In *Horseferry Road Metropolitan Stipendiary Magistrate ex parte Siadatan*,[86] it was held that the violence feared must be both immediate and unlawful. A threat of violence at some future time will not suffice for this offence to be proven. The mental element required is that the person intends his words or behaviour (or signs, etc) to be threatening, abusive or insulting or that he is aware that it may be threatening, abusive or insulting.[87]

Harassment, alarm or distress[88]

A person is guilty of an offence if he:

(a) uses threatening, abusive or insulting words or behaviour, or disorderly behaviour; or

(b) displays any writing, sign or other visible representation which is threatening, abusive or insulting, within the hearing or sight of a person likely to be caused harassment, alarm or distress thereby.[89]

The introduction of this offence,[90] and the use to which it is put by the police, raises controversy. The offence was designed to provide powers to deal with relatively minor acts of antisocial, unruly or disorderly conduct which, while of itself not serious, cause fear in others. In its White Paper, the government illustrated the sort of behaviour which was being targeted:[91]

(a) hooligans on housing estates causing disturbances in the common parts of blocks of flats ...;

(b) groups of youths persistently shouting abuse and obscenities or pestering people waiting to catch public transport or to enter a hall or cinema; someone turning out the lights in a crowded dance hall, in a way likely to cause panic;

---

84 Public Order Act 1986, s 4(1).

85 *R v Ambrose* (1973) Cr App R 538.

86 [1990] 3 WLR 1006; [1991] 1 All ER 324, and see, further, p 791, below.

87 Public Order Act 1986, s 6(3).

88 See *Criminal Law: Offences Relating to Public Order*, Law Com No 123, 1983, and Williams, DGT, 'Public order and common law' [1984] PL 12.

89 Public Order Act 1986, s 5.

90 There existed a predecessor offence, but the Public Order Act 1986, s 5, broadens the scope of the offence.

91 *Review of Public Order Law*, Cmnd 9510, 1985, London: HMSO, para 3.22.

(c) rowdy behaviour in the streets late at night which alarms local residents.

For the offence to be proven, it is necessary that the words or behaviour, or signs etc, are uttered or displayed within the sight of a person who is likely to be harassed or alarmed or distressed – it is not necessary to prove actual harassment, alarm or distress. However, the mental element required is that the person using the words, behaviour or signs either intended his conduct to be threatening, abusive or insulting or be aware that it might be. Thus, words uttered in a public place (for example, by demonstrators or persons attending football matches) which might in fact be threatening or abusive, and might in fact cause alarm or distress to someone hearing the words will not be sufficient for a prosecution to succeed.[92]

In *Jordan v Borgoyne*,[93] the accused made an inflammatory racist speech in Trafalgar Square. He was prosecuted under the forerunner to section 4 of the Public Order Act 1986, section 5 of the Public Order Act 1936. It was held that the speech went beyond the limits of tolerance. The defendant could not argue that the words used were not likely to cause ordinary persons to commit breaches of the peace. The defendant had to 'take his audience as he found them'. If the words used were likely to provoke that audience, or part thereof, to commit a breach of the peace, the defendant was guilty of an offence.

Insulting words were the subject of judicial scrutiny in *Brutus v Cozens*.[94] In *Brutus*, the defendant and other anti-apartheid protesters interrupted play at a Wimbledon tennis match. The audience resented the interruption. Brutus was charged with insulting behaviour likely to cause a breach of the peace. In the Divisional Court, it was held that an offence occurred where the behaviour affronted other people, and reflected a contempt for their rights. The House of Lords, however, allowed Brutus's appeal. Not all speech or conduct fell within the meaning of the section. It must be conduct or speech which the ordinary person would recognise as insulting – a term which was deemed incapable of precise definition. The mere resentment of the crowd, as opposed to violence, did not suffice to make the actions insulting.

The issue of violent reaction to provocative words was considered in *R v Horseferry Road Magistrate ex parte Siadatan*.[95] The case concerned Salman Rushdie's novel, *The Satanic Verses*. An application was laid against the publishers and the author it was argued that distribution of the book offended against section 4 of the 1986 Act, in so far as it contained abusive and insulting language which was likely to provoke violence amongst devote Muslims. The magistrate refused to issue a summons. The issue went to the Divisional Court

---

92   See *Director of Public Prosecutions v Clarke* [1992] Crim LR 60.

93   [1963] 2 QB 744.

94   [1973] AC 854.

95   [1991] 1 QB 260.

for judicial review. It was there held that the violence which was apprehended by the words must be immediate violence, not some distant act of violence.

In *R v Stephen Miller*[96] the defendant appealed against sentence for racially aggravated threatening words. The defendant had pleaded guilty to two offences, first, aggravated threatening words and behaviour contrary to section 4 of the Public Order Act 1986, as amended by section 31 of the Crime and Disorder Act 1998, and, secondly, travelling on a railway without a ticket. He was sentenced to 18 months' imprisonment with one month concurrent, and appealed. The Court of Appeal dismissed his appeal. His conduct towards the conductor on the train was particularly bad. The sentence was designed to reflect public concern about conduct which damaged good racial relations within the community.

The mental element on the part of the accused must be satisfied. KA Ewing and CA Gearty provide illustrations of the uses to which section 5 has been put.[97] The Act has been used to curb the use of obscene T-shirts and hats; to suppress a satirical poster of the former Prime Minister Mrs Thatcher; and to prosecute protesters outside abortion clinics in Ireland.[98] In Gearty and Ewing's assessment, section 5 of the Act represents a 'mechanism for punishing non-violent non-conformity for the crime of being itself'.[99] It must be conceded that section 5 represents a serious, and hitherto uncontemplated, limitation of freedom of expression and an alteration of the balance between individual liberty and the legitimate expectations of citizens to be protected from the consequences of another person's words and actions. The extent to which the balance has been correctly struck is a matter for personal judgment.

The Crime and Disorder Act 1998

The Crime and Disorder Act 1998 introduces significant changes to the law relating to sentencing and criminal procedure in England and Wales. The Act also abolishes the death penalty for treason and piracy.[100] The Act makes special provisions creating racially aggravated offences.

---

96 [1999] Crim LR 590.

97 *Op cit*, Ewing and Gearty, fn 1, Chapter 4.

98 *Director of Public Prosecutions v Fidler* [1992] 1 WLR 91; *Director of Public Prosecutions v Clarke* [1992] Crim LR 60.

99 *Op cit*, Ewing and Gearty, fn 1, p 123.

100 Repealing the Treason Acts 1790, 1795, the Treason by Women Act (Ireland) 1796, the Treason Act 1817 and the Sentence of Death (Expectant Mothers) Act 1931, and repealing the Treason Felony Act 1848, section 2.

PART II – THE POLICE AND POLICE POWERS

THE ORGANISATION OF THE POLICE[101]

The United Kingdom has no national police force. Instead, the police are organised on a basis which links the police to the locality. There now exist 43 police forces: the City of London Police, the Metropolitan Police and 41 forces outside London. The Police Act 1996 provides that the Home Secretary may alter police areas 'in the interest of efficiency or effectiveness'.[102]

In 1962, a Royal Commission examined the question whether there should be a national police force under central government control, but concluded that the status quo should be maintained, subject to supervision by central government.[103] The Police Act 1964 was enacted which, as amended, regulated the organisation of the police in England and Wales. In 1994, the Police and Magistrates' Courts Act conferred additional powers on the Home Secretary, enabling him or her to play a role in the membership of local police authorities. The Police Act 1996 consolidates the Police Act 1964, Part IX of the Police and Criminal Evidence Act 1984, Chapter 1 of Part I of the Police and Magistrates' Courts Act 1994 and other minor enactments. The Police Act 1996 further extends Home Office control, providing that the Home Secretary may direct police authorities to set performance targets, and give directions concerning police budgets. The Police Act 1996 has consolidated the Police Act 1964 and relevant parts of the Police and Magistrates' Courts Act 1994, and now provides the statutory regime concerning the organisation and discipline of the police. The Police Act 1997 provides for further centralisation, with the establishment of a National Criminal Intelligence Service which provides criminal intelligence to local forces and a National Crime Squad, with power to detect and prevent serious crime which affects more than one police area.

The regulation of the police represents a tri-partite arrangement involving the Home Secretary, local police authorities and Chief Constables of Police.

---

101 See Zander, M, *The Police and Criminal Evidence Act 1984*, 3rd edn, 1995, London: Sweet & Maxwell; Levenson, H and Fairweather, F, *Police Powers*, 1990, London: Legal Action Group.

102 Police Act 1996, s 32.

103 Cmd 1728.

THE HOME SECRETARY

The Home Secretary and Metropolitan Police

Until 1999, the Home Secretary was the police authority for the Metropolitan Police. Under the Greater London Authority Act 1999, on which see Chapter 12, there is established a Metropolitan Police Authority, which replaces the Home Secretary as police authority.[104] The 1999 Act amends the Police Act 1996, section 310 of the 1999 Act amending section 5 of the 1996 Act and introducing a Police Authority for the Metropolitan Police District and specifying membership of the Authority. The Authority is headed by the Commissioner of Police of the Metropolis, appointed by the Crown and holding office at Her Majesty's pleasure.[105] The Metropolitan Police Force is under the direction and control of the Commissioner. There is established a Deputy Commissioner who has the power to exercise any or all of the powers and duties of the Commissioner during any absence from duty of the Commission, any vacancy in the office of the Commissioner or at any other time with the consent of the Commissioner.[106]

The Home Secretary and other police authorities

Each of the local police forces has its own police authority, the role of which is discussed below. The Home Secretary, however, has a number of powers in relation to local forces. The Home Secretary may, in consultation with the police authority and Chief Constable, determine policy objectives for the policy authority.[107] The Home Secretary may issue Codes of Practice which regulate the manner in which the police authority pursues policy objectives,[108] may direct the authority to establish performance targets and may impose conditions on police authorities.[109] In addition, section 57 of the 1994 Act extends previous powers[110] of the Home Secretary to provide and maintain 'such organisations, facilities and services' as the Home Secretary thinks necessary for promoting the efficiency and effectiveness of the police.[111] The Police Act 1996 also extends the powers of the Home Secretary,

---

104 Greater London Authority Act 1999, ss 310, 312.

105 *Ibid*, ss 314 and 315 amending the Police Act 1996, ss 9 and 9A.

106 *Ibid*, s 316 amending the Police Act 1996, s 9.

107 Police and Magistrates' Courts Act 1994, s 37.

108 *Ibid*, s 39.

109 *Ibid*, s 39.

110 Under the Police Act 1964, s 41.

111 See *R v Home Secretary ex parte Northumbria Police Authority* [1989] QB 26; [1988] 1 All ER 556.

and provides that the Home Secretary may make regulations for the government, administration and conditions of service of police forces.[112]

Police authorities are funded by central government. The annual grant is determined by the Home Secretary with the approval of the Treasury. Formerly, the grant amounted to 51 per cent of approved expenses. Now, the Home Secretary has a wide discretion as to the amount of the grant.[113] The efficiency of police forces is under the jurisdiction of Her Majesty's Inspectors of Constabulary appointed by the Home Secretary and accountable to him.[114]

Codes of Practice, notes for guidance and Home Office circulars

Under the Police and Criminal Evidence Act 1984, a number of Codes of Practice have been issued. The Codes do not have the force of law, but represent an administrative means of regulating differing aspects of police powers. Breach of the Codes does not give rise to civil or criminal liability.[115] Under the 1984 Act, there are five Codes of Practice. Code A relates to stop and search procedures; Code B to the search of premises; Code C relates to interviews and conditions of detention; Code D regulates identification procedures; and Code E regulates the tape recording of interviews. The notes for guidance are not part of the Codes, but represent interpretative guidelines. Home Office circulars are designed to supplement the provisions of the Police and Criminal Evidence Act and other statutes.

The functions of police authorities

Local police authorities are responsible for setting policy objectives for the police, subject to the Home Secretary's power to determine the objectives for police authorities.[116] The police authority is responsible for ensuring the efficiency of the local force.[117] The composition of the police authority is now regulated by the Police and Magistrates' Courts Act 1994. The standard membership of the authority is 17, of which nine are local authority councillors. Five further members are appointed from a shortlist drawn up by the Home Secretary. The remaining three members are local magistrates and appointed by the magistrates collectively.[118] The police authority has control over the police budget.

---

112 Police Act 1996, s 50.
113 *Ibid*, s 46.
114 *Ibid*, s 54.
115 PACE 1984, s 67(10).
116 Police Act 1996, s 37.
117 *Ibid*, s 6.
118 Police and Magistrates' Courts Act 1994, Sched 2, para 1(1)(a).

The police authority has the power to order a Chief Constable or Assistant Chief Constable to retire 'in the interests of efficiency and effectiveness', following consultation with, and the approval of, the Home Secretary.[119] The Home Secretary also has power to require a police authority to exercise the powers. The police authority reports annually to the Home Secretary.[120]

Chief Constables of Police

Outside the Metropolitan area, which is headed by the Metropolitan Commissioner of Police, police forces are under the operational control of Chief Constables.[121] The Chief Constable is responsible for recruitment and promotions to the ranks below that of Assistant Chief Constable, and exercises disciplinary powers over the police. The Chief Constable makes annual reports to the police authority,[122] and the Home Secretary can require the Chief Constable to submit reports.[123]

Section 88[124] of the Police Act 1996 makes it clear that Chief Constables are liable for torts committed by constables under his direction and control:

> The chief officer of police for a police area shall be liable in respect of torts committed by constables under his direction and control in the performance or purported performance of their functions in like manner as a master is liable in respect of torts committed by his servants in the course of their employment, and accordingly shall in respect of any such tort be treated for all purposes as a joint tortfeasor.

The legal status of police officers

A police officer is a servant of the State.[125] He or she is not employed under a contract of employment, but is a holder of public office. In *Attorney General for New South Wales v Perpetual Trustee Company Ltd*,[126] the Privy Council stated that:

> ... he is to be regarded as a servant or minister of the King because ... the administration of justice, both criminal and civil, and the preservation of order and prevention of crime by means of what is now called police, are among the most important functions of government, and by the constitution of this country these functions do of common right belong to the Crown.

---

119 Police Act 1996, ss 11 and 12.
120 *Ibid*, s 9.
121 *Ibid*, s 10.
122 *Ibid*, s 22.
123 *Ibid*, s 44.
124 Formerly, Police Act 1964, s 48.
125 *Fisher v Oldham Corporation* [1930] 2 KB 364.
126 [1955] 1 All ER 846.

Prior to the enactment of section 88 of the Police Act 1996, the liability of a police officer for wrongful actions was personal. While a servant of the Crown, the Crown was not, at common law, vicariously liable for wrongful actions of officers because, being neither appointed nor paid by the Crown, the officer was not 'in the employment of the Crown'. Where damages or costs are ordered in legal action, these are awarded against the Chief Constable and paid out of the local police budget.

Police officers hold office under statute, and are subject to the police disciplinary code. Police officers are not allowed to belong to trades unions, or any other association concerned with levels of pay or conditions of employment. Police Federations represent police officers in matters relating to welfare, and have restricted powers in relation to police discipline.[127] Police officers are not permitted to take any active part in politics, nor participate in any other activity which could actually impede, or give the suggestion that it could impede the officer's impartiality.[128]

Co-operation between police forces

Co-operation between police forces is facilitated by the Association of Chief Police Officers. Further, the Mutual Aid Co-ordination Centre (formerly the National Reporting Centre), which operates from Scotland Yard, enables co-ordinated policing policy in times of unrest, and the deployment of officers on a national basis. These powers were used in the miners' strike of 1984–85, and add weight to the argument that centralised control of policing is a feature of modern police work. In addition, the Police Act 1997 establishes a National Intelligence Service and National Crime Squad, the former to gather and disseminate information concerning serious crime to local forces, the latter of which has powers in relation to the prevention and detection of serious crime which may affect more than one police area.

Judicial control and police policy

The exercise of police discretion is reviewable by the courts, although the courts confer a great deal of latitude in relation to that discretion. In *R v Commissioner of Police for the Metropolis ex parte Blackburn (No 1)*,[129] the Court of Appeal made it clear that an order of mandamus would lie against the Metropolitan Police Commissioner. The Commissioner had issued a policy statement in which he made it clear that supervision of gambling clubs would

---

127 Police Act 1996, s 59.
128 Police Regulations 1995 SI 1995/215.
129 [1968] 2 QB 118.

not take place, other than where there was a suspicion that the clubs were being frequented by criminals. The applicant, Blackburn, claimed that illegal gambling was taking place and applied to the courts for an order of mandamus to compel the Commissioner to reverse his policy. The court insisted that the Commissioner had a public duty to enforce the law, and that his discretion could be controlled by the courts. Nevertheless, since the Commissioner had undertaken to reverse his former policy, the order would not be granted. Neither was mandamus ordered in *R v Commissioner of Police for the Metropolis ex parte Blackburn (No 3)*.[130] In that case, the applicant sought to compel, by order of the court, enforcement of the Obscene Publication Act 1959. However, the Chief Office had increased the numbers in the vice squad, and reorganised its working methods.

Police discretion returned for consideration in *R v Chief Constable of Sussex ex parte International Trader's Ferry Ltd*.[131] In that case, animal rights protesters, concerned about the welfare of live animal exports, blockaded ports in order to stop the exports. International Trader's Ferry Ltd exported animals from Shoreham in Sussex, a port run by the Shoreham Port Authority. Exports were due to be made in January 1995 and, to assist the company, the police mounted operation 'Ferndown'. The total number of police officers employed to keep the port open mounted to 1,125 police officers, a level of policing which was maintained for some 10 days. In order to maintain the operation, seven other police forces assisted.[132] The cost of the operation amounted to £1.25 million. The Home Office refused to make a special grant to assist with the financial cost of the operation. In April, the Chief Constable indicated that new arrangements would have to be made, which would involve the company having to reduce its shipments. The company sought judicial review of the Chief Constable's decision. The Court of Appeal upheld the Divisional Court's refusal to interfere with the decision of the Chief Constable. In light of the circumstances, the Chief Constable's decision could not be 'regarded as so unreasonable as to enable a court to interfere'. The Court approved the statement of Neill LJ in *Harris v Sheffield United Football Club Ltd*:[133]

> I see the force of the argument that the court must be very slow before it interferes in any way with a decision of a chief constable about the disposition of his forces.

The House of Lords affirmed the decision of the Court of Appeal.[134]

---

130 [1973] 1 All ER 324.
131 [1997] 2 All ER 65, CA.
132 Under the Police Act 1964 (now the Police Act 1996, s 24).
133 [1987] 2 All ER 838.
134 [1998] 3 WLR 1260; [1999] 1 All ER 186; (1968) *The Times*, 16 November.

Complaints against the police

Part IV of the Police Act 1996 regulates police complaints and discipline. Where a complaint is made against a police officer below the rank of Chief Superintendent, these are submitted to the Chief Officer of the force, who has powers to investigate.[135] Where a complaint is made regarding an officer of the rank of Chief Superintendent or above, the complaint is submitted to the Police Complaints Authority and the Authority supervises the investigation of the complaint, which is conducted by a police officer from a different police force than that to which the officer who is subject to the complaint belongs.[136]

In relation to the powers and duties of the Chief Officer, the procedure to be followed is dependent upon the categorisation of the complaint. If a complaint is classified as relatively minor, the Chief Officer may decide that the complaint may be resolved informally. No complaint can be dealt with under the informal procedure unless the complainant agrees, and the complaint does not involve conduct which would justify a criminal or disciplinary charge.[137] Where the complaint is more serious and cannot be resolved under the informal procedure, the Chief Officer must have the complaint investigated, either by a member of his or her own force, or by a member of a different force. If the investigation reveals that a criminal offence might have been committed and the officer should be charged with that offence, the report is sent to the Director of Public Prosecutions.[138] If the Director of Public Prosecutions decides that prosecution is justified, the matter will go to trial. Irrespective of whether the defendant is convicted or acquitted, no disciplinary charge can then be brought against the officer relating to matters substantially the same as those raised in the prosecution.[139]

The third category of cases involves allegation of serious crime. Where there is an allegation that an officer has caused death or serious injury, the complaint must be referred to the police authority.[140] Other allegations involving assault occasioning serious bodily harm, corruption, or a serious arrestable offence (on which, see below, p 809) must also be referred to the authority.[141] Where a matter is referred to the authority, the authority appoints an investigating officer and supervises the investigation. In 1995–96, the number of complaints referred to the authority was 2,761, of which 1,142

---

135 Police Act 1996, s 69.

136 *Ibid*, s 68.

137 *Ibid*, s 69.

138 *Ibid*, s 73, in relation to junior officers, s 74 in relation to senior officers, and s 75 on the procedure to be followed after investigation on complaints against junior officers.

139 *Ibid*, s 67(5).

140 *Ibid*, s 70.

141 SI 1985/673.

were settled informally.[142] Disciplinary proceedings may result in a reprimand, fine, reduction in rank, the requirement to resign or dismissal.

Legal liability of the police[143]

In addition to making complaints about police conduct, the police are liable in law in actions for assault, wrongful arrest,[144] false imprisonment, trespass, public misfeasance, negligence or an action for the return of property which has been wrongfully taken. An action for malicious prosecution is available where a person believes that the police have maliciously and, without reasonable cause, abused their powers in recommending prosecution to the Crown Prosecution Service. Further, the police are liable in law for the care of those in their custody.[145]

POLICE POWERS IN RELATION TO THE DETECTION AND INVESTIGATION OF CRIME

Questioning by the police

It is a fundamental rule that the citizen is not obliged to answer police questions, unless there is lawful justification for official interference with the citizen's liberty. The rule was endorsed in *Rice v Connolly*.[146] There, the appellant was questioned by the police. He refused to answer questions and was, accordingly, arrested for obstructing a police officer in the execution of his duty contrary to section 51(3) of the Police Act 1964.[147] On appeal, Lord Parker CJ stated that a citizen has every right to refuse to answer questions; generally the citizen has a 'right to silence'.

In *Kenlin v Gardiner*,[148] the issue in question concerned whether a person could lawfully be stopped in the street by the police. Police officers attempted to question two boys. One of the boys tried to run away, whereupon a police constable tried physically to stop him and a scuffle broke out. The boys were charged with assaulting a police constable in the execution of his duty. There

---

142 HC 469 (1995–96), London: HMSO.

143 See Clayton, R and Tomlinson, H, *Civil Actions against the Police*, 2nd edn, 1992, London: Sweet & Maxwell.

144 See, eg, *Wershof v Metropolitan Police Commissioner* [1978] 3 All ER 540.

145 See *Kirkham v Chief Constable of Greater Manchester* [1990] 2 QB 283; *Treadway v Chief Constable of West Midlands* (1994) *The Times*, 25 October.

146 [1966] 3 WLR 17.

147 Now, Police Act 1996, s 89.

148 [1967] 2 QB 510.

was no question that an assault on the police had occurred. The question for decision was whether the assault by the boys was justified. The Divisional Court held that the attempt to restrain the boy amounted to an assault by the police officer, and was, accordingly, an unlawful attempt to detain him. As such, the police officer was not acting in the course of his duty and, as a result, the boys were not guilty of assaulting a police officer 'in the execution of his duty'. A distinction must be made between a refusal to answer questions and conduct which amounts to obstruction of the police.[149]

There are, however, situations in which a citizen is under a duty to answer questions. For example, under road traffic law,[150] there is a duty to give information as to one's name and address, and a refusal to do so and to give up one's driving licence and other motoring documents is an offence. Other than under statutory authority, however, there is a right to silence.[151]

Power exists to stop motorists on any ground,[152] and failure to stop is an offence.[153] A police officer is entitled to immobilise a car by removing the ignition keys. The vehicle owner may be detained in order to allow the officer sufficient time to determine whether an arrest is to be made, to effect arrest, and to give reasons for the arrest. Moreover, the police have the power to detain a motorist in order to administer a breathalyser test.[154] Powers also exist under the Official Secrets Act 1911, whereby the Home Secretary can grant the police permission to question suspects. Refusal to answer questions in respect of inquiries made under the Companies Act 1985 and under the Criminal Justice Act 1987 in respect of investigations into fraud amount to a criminal offence, as can refusal to disclose information under the Prevention of Terrorism Acts[155] and the Drug Trafficking Offences Act 1984.

Stop and search powers

Under the Police and Criminal Evidence Act 1984, the police have been given the power to stop and search a person reasonably suspected of carrying prohibited articles such as offensive weapons and/or housebreaking equipment or stolen goods.[156] The police also have the power to set up road blocks[157] if there are reasonable grounds for suspicion that a person in the

---

149 See, further, below.

150 See Road Traffic Act 1988, s 163.

151 *Lodwick v Sanders* [1985] 1 All ER 577.

152 Road Traffic Act 1988, s 163.

153 *Ibid*, s 163.

154 *Lodwick v Sanders* [1985] 1 All ER 577.

155 See Chapter 23. See, also, the Official Secrets Act, s 6, which imposes a duty to provide information as to offences under the 1911 Act.

156 PACE 1984, s 1.

157 Road Traffic Act 1988 and PACE 1984, s 4.

area has committed a serious arrestable offence (see further, below, p 809), or that a serious arrestable offence is about to be committed, or that a person is unlawfully 'at large'.[158] Section 60 of the Criminal Justice and Public Order Act 1994 provides that powers may be given to the police, by a police officer of the rank of superintendent or above, to stop and search persons and vehicles, where that officer reasonably believes that incidents involving serious violence may take place in any locality in his area, and that it is expedient so to do to prevent their occurrence. The authorisation lasts for up to 24 hours. If no superintendent is available, a Chief Inspector or Inspector may grant authorisation for the stop and search, if 'he reasonably believes that incidents involving serious violence are imminent'.[159]

The Police Act 1997

The Police Act 1997 places the power to interfere with property and plant surveillance devices. Modelled on the Interception of Communications Act 1985,[160] the Act provides that authorisation for the bugging of property may be given on the basis that it would facilitate the 'prevention and detection of serious crime', which cannot 'reasonably be achieved by other means'.[161] No exemptions from the provisions are made: thus, solicitor's offices, doctor's surgeries and even Roman Catholic confessionals may fall victims of bugging by the police. No judicial scrutiny for bugging warrants is provided. Instead, and as a reaction to the House of Lords' objections to the Bill, authorisation must be given by the Chief Officer of Police[162] or, if he is unavailable, by an officer of Chief Constable rank.[163] Written authorisations remain in effect for three months whereas, in cases of emergency, oral authorisation may be made which will remain in force for 72 hours. Following opposition to the Bill, the government accepted that independent commissioners[164] should review the authorisations. Such review does not, however, necessarily precede police action on the warrant. In cases where private dwellings, hotel bedrooms or offices are involved, a commissioner's prior approval for the authorisation is required. Prior approval is also required where the surveillance may result in the revealing of confidential personal information, confidential journalistic material or matters which are subject to legal privilege.[165]

---

158 PACE 1984, s 4.

159 *Ibid*, s 60(2).

160 See, now, the Regulation of Investigatory Powers Act 2000, discussed in Chapter 23.

161 Police Act 1997, s 93(2).

162 *Ibid*, s 93(5).

163 *Ibid*, s 94.

164 *Ibid*, s 91(1).

165 *Ibid*, s 97. On surveillance under the Security Services Act 1989, see Chapter 23.

THE PROTECTION OF SUSPECTS

Helping the police with inquiries[166]

In law, the police have no power to detain a person in order to make inquiries. Section 29 of the Police and Criminal Evidence Act clarifies this rule. A person is either at will to leave a police station where he voluntarily attends to assist the police, or the police must arrest him. If a person is detained by the police, he must be informed immediately that he is under arrest, and given reasons for the arrest, the absence of which may render the arrest unlawful.

The identification of suspects

One of the principal causes of wrongful conviction lies in the wrongful identification of suspects.[167] Identification may take place by witnessing, or by fingerprinting and the taking of bodily samples. Code of Practice D governs the procedures to be followed, although Code D does not regulate those detained as terrorist suspects under section 14 or Schedule 5 of the Prevention of Terrorism Act 1989, save for the provisions relating to fingerprinting and bodily samples.

Identification by identity parade is the most reliable means of identification, and will be carried out if the defendant requests it or consents to it. If it is impracticable to hold an identity parade,[168] perhaps because there is a large number of suspects or because there are insufficient people with relevant characteristics to the suspect,[169] the police may then turn to alternative means of identification. Identification by witness may be effected by arranging for the witness to see the suspect in a group, generally in a public place away from the police station. The consent of the suspect is required, but his or her failure to consent does not prohibit the use of group identification. Alternatively, identification may be by video identification. Face to face confrontation of the witness and accused may take place provided identification is not possible by any other means.

---

166 See Zander, M, 'When is an arrest not an arrest?' (1997) 147 NLJ 379; Clarke, DN and Feldman, D, 'Arrest by any other name' [1979] Crim LR 702.

167 *Report of the Criminal Law Revision Committee*, Cmnd 4991, 1972, London: HMSO, para 196.

168 Cf *R v Ladlow, Moss, Green and Jackson* [1989] Crim LR 219 and *R v Penny* (1991) *The Times*, 17 October.

169 See *Campbell and Another* [1993] Crim LR 47.

Search of the person

Before 1984, there was considerable doubt about the breadth of power to search an arrested person. The police had a common law power to search a person if they reasonably believed that he was carrying a weapon or evidence relevant to the crime of which he was suspected. Resisting a lawful search would amount to obstruction of the police. In *Lindley v Rutter*,[170] the police, having arrested the defendant while drunk, insisted on searching her person and attempted to remove her bra. Ms Lindley resisted the attempt and scratched and bit a police woman. On a charge of obstruction of the police, the magistrates' court convicted Ms Lindley. On appeal, however, the conviction was quashed. While it was conceded that the police were under a duty not to allow a person to escape, or to destroy evidence, the lawfulness of their action depended upon the circumstances of the case. This personal search, which was highly unlikely to yield any evidence, required strong justification. Under the circumstances the police had exceeded their powers. In *Brazil v Chief Constable of Surrey*,[171] the police also attempted to search a woman, in the course of which she assaulted the officers. The police claimed that the search was necessary, first, to ensure the detainee's own safety and, secondly, to discover whether she was carrying drugs. The search was ruled unlawful. There was no need for the search and, in relation to the search for drugs, the detainee had not been informed of the police's reasons for the search. Her conviction for assaulting a police officer in the execution of his duty was quashed.

Search of an arrested person under the Police and Criminal Evidence Act 1984

Section 32 of the Police and Criminal Evidence Act 1984 provides that searches may be made of an arrested person, the premises on which he or she was arrested and any vehicle in which the suspect was arrested. The grounds for the search are for evidence relating to any offence, or for evidence which may assist the escape of the suspect.[172]

Intimate body searches are also permitted under section 55 of the 1984 Act. The search must be carried out by a doctor, unless a senior officer believes that that is impracticable. The search may only be made for articles which may cause injury or for class 'A' drugs. The powers to search the person, and personal samples which may be taken, have been extended by the Criminal Justice and Public Order Act 1994. Section 58 extends the definition of intimate

---

170 [1980] 3 WLR 660.
171 [1983] 3 All ER 537.
172 PACE 1984, s 32(2).

and non-intimate samples which may be taken. An intimate sample is one of blood; semen or any other tissue fluid; urine; pubic hair; a dental impression; or a swab taken from a person's orifice other than the mouth.[173] A non-intimate sample means a sample of hair other than pubic hair; a sample taken from a nail or from under the nail; a swab taken from any part of a person's body including the mouth but not other body orifice; saliva; or a footprint or a similar impression of any part of a person's body other than a part of his hand.[174]

The conditions of interviews

The Code of Practice on the Detention, Treatment, and Questioning of Persons by Police Officers (Code C) provides that a suspect should be given eight hours in any 24 hours free of questioning. Breaks for refreshment should be given regularly (every two hours), unless such breaks would adversely affect the inquiries. Persons who are mentally disordered and children should be interviewed in the presence of a competent adult. The detention must be reviewed regularly, the first taking place after six hours from the time of lawful detention; subsequent reviews to be conducted at intervals of no more than nine hours.

Tape recording of interviews[175]

The tape recording of police interviews acts as a protection for the person being questioned, and as protection for the police against accusations of oppression. Tape recording is regulated by a code of practice.[176] Both the defence and prosecution have the right to listen to tape recordings, although the police provide summaries of the recordings.[177]

Video recording experiments are being conducted in Australia, Canada and the United States of America, and in the United Kingdom. The police must maintain proper records of any interview, including the time of commencement and ending and any breaks in questioning. The person interviewed must be allowed to read the record.

---

173 Criminal Justice and Public Order Act 1994, s 58.

174 *Ibid*, s 58(3).

175 See Baldwin, J, 'The police and tape recorders' [1985] Crim LR 659.

176 Code of Practice for the Detention, Treatment and Questioning of Persons by Police Officers, Code C.

177 See Baldwin, J and Bedward, J, 'Summarising tape recordings of police interviews' [1991] Crim LR 671.

The caution

The caution to be administered to a suspect has been amended by the Criminal Justice and Public Order Act 1994. Previously, the caution given was 'You do not have to say anything unless you wish to do so, but what you say may be given in evidence'. The caution now reads:

> You do not have to say anything. But, if you do not mention now something which you later use in your defence, the court may decide that your failure to mention it now strengthens the case against you. A record will be made of anything you say and it may be given in evidence if you are brought to trial.[178]

Arrest

A lawful arrest is an arrest for which there is legal authority. Three categories of lawful arrest exist: arrest under warrant; arrest without warrant under common law and arrest without a warrant under statute. Where a person has been wrongly arrested and detained under statute,[179] the person detained in entitled to damages: *Roberts v Chief Constable of Cheshire Constabulary*;[180] *Woodward v Chief Constable, Fife Constabulary*.[181]

Arrest under warrant

Section 1(1) of the Magistrates' Courts Act 1980 provides that a warrant for arrest may be made on the basis that a 'person has, or is suspected of having, committed an offence'. The warrant should not be issued unless the offence is indictable[182] or punishable by imprisonment.[183]

Arrest without warrant: common law

The only common law power to arrest without warrant is where there are reasonable grounds for suspicion that a breach of the peace is about to occur, or has been committed and is likely to continue or to reoccur.[184] If violence has occurred, or is about to occur to persons or property, a police officer may

---

178 Criminal Justice and Public Order Act 1994, s 34; Code C, para 10.4.
179 PACE 1984, s 34, Criminal Justice (Scotland) Act 1980.
180 (1999) *The Times*, 27 January.
181 1998 SLT 1342.
182 A serious offence triable by jury in the Crown Court.
183 Criminal Justice Act 1967, s 24(1).
184 See *R v Howell* [1982] QB 416; [1981] 3 All ER 383.

reasonably believe that a breach of the peace is about to occur. If a breach of the peace has occurred, but has ceased, the power to arrest ceases.

In *Trevor Foulkes v Chief Constable of Merseyside Police*,[185] the Court of Appeal considered the issue of reasonable grounds in law for the arrest and subsequent detention of a person in relation to an apprehended breach of the peace. The police officer had arrested the appellant in the course of a domestic incident, honestly believing that arrest was necessary to prevent a breach of the peace. The Court of Appeal ruled that, where there was no actual breach of the peace but only an apprehended breach, the power of arrest was only to be exercised in the clearest of circumstances where the officer was satisfied that a breach of the peace was imminent. The arresting officer in this case acted honestly but did not have reasonable grounds for the arrest. Arrest was an inappropriate management of a dispute between husband and wife in the family home.

An apprehended breach of the peace was also central to the decision in *Bibby v Chief Constable of Essex Police*.[186] A bailiff had gone to a debtor's premises for the purpose of seizing assets due under a liability order issued by a Magistrates' Court. The debtor threatened to call his friends to prevent the removal of goods. Fearing a breach of the peace a police constable, who had been called to the premises, ordered the bailiff to leave. When the bailiff refused, he was arrested and led away to the police station in handcuffs. He was later released without charge. The bailiff sued the police for assault and wrongful imprisonment. The Court of Appeal considered the conditions to be met in order to exercise the 'now exceptional' common law power of arrest. These included:

> There must be the clearest of circumstances and a sufficiently real and present threat to the peace to justify the extreme step of depriving of his liberty a citizen who is not at the time acting unlawfully.[187]
>
> The threat must be coming from the person who is to be arrested.[188]
>
> The conduct must clearly interfere with the rights of others.[189]
>
> The natural consequence of the conduct must be violence from a third party.[190]
>
> The violence from the third party must not be wholly unreasonable.[191]
>
> The conduct of the person to be arrested must be unreasonable.[192]

---

185 [1998] 3 All ER 714; (1998) 2 FLR 789.
186 (2000) *The Times*, 24 April; (2000) 164 JP 297.
187 *Foulkes v Chief Constable of Merseyside Police* [1998] 3 All ER 714; (1998) 2 FLR 789.
188 *Redmond-Bate v Director of Public Prosecutions* (1999) *The Times*, 28 July.
189 *Ibid.*
190 *Ibid.*
191 *Ibid.*
192 *Nicol v Director of Public Prosecutions* (1996) 1 J Civ Lib 75.

In the instant case, the bailiff was acting lawfully and attempting to enforce an order of a court. Although the constable reasonably came to the conclusion that a breach of the peace was imminent he had failed to consider where the threat was coming from. Accordingly, neither the arrest, nor the use of handcuffs was justified.[193]

Arrest without warrant under statute

Section 24 of the Police and Criminal Evidence Act 1984 defines the power of arrest without warrant for serious offences.

A person may be arrested without warrant under the following circumstances:

(a) he or she is conspiring to commit, or attempting to commit, or inciting, aiding, abetting, counselling or procuring the commission of an offence under section 24(2);

(b) he or she is in the act of committing an arrestable offence;

(c) where the arrestable offence has been committed, the person who is guilty may be arrested;

(d) where the arrestable offence has been committed, the person who is reasonably suspected of having committed the offence;

(e) where a constable reasonably believes that an arrestable offence has been committed, any person whom he has reasonable grounds for suspecting to be guilty of the offence;

(f) any person is about to commit an arrestable offence;

(g) any person whom the police officer reasonably believes is about to commit an arrestable offence.[194]

Arrestable offences

Section 24 applies:

(a) to offences for which the sentence is fixed by law;

(b) to offences for which a person of over 21 years of age or over (not previously convicted) may be sentenced to imprisonment for a term of five years (or might be so sentenced but for the restrictions imposed by section 33 of the Magistrates' Courts Act 1980); and

---

193 See, also, *Redmond-Bate v Director of Public Prosecutions* (1999) *The Times*, 28 July, above.

194 PACE 1984, s 24(4), (5), (6), (7). The Immigration and Asylum Act 1999, section 50, provides for the arrest without warrant of a person reasonably suspected of have broken or being likely to break any bail condition.

(c) to the offences to which section 24(2) applies and in this Act 'arrestable offence' means any such offence.

Offences for which a person may be arrested under section 24 may also be classified as 'serious arrestable offences' under section 116 and Schedule 5, Part I of the Police and Criminal Evidence Act.[195] Where that is the case, the power of arrest is unaffected, but the safeguards and powers exercisable under detention conditions are affected. Helen Fenwick analyses the importance of the distinction between the two categories as follow:

> The section 24 offences which may also fall into this category fall into two groups as defined under section 116 – first, those which are so serious (such as murder, manslaughter, indecent assault which amounts to gross indecency) that they will always be serious arrestable offences and secondly, those which will be so classified only if their commission has led to certain specified consequences, namely, serious harm to the security of the state or public order, serious interference with the administration of justice or investigation of offences, death or serious injury, substantial financial gain or serious financial loss.[196]

An arrestable offence is a serious offence which carries a sentence fixed by law. Thus, for example, offences for which a person over the age of 21 years may be imprisoned for a term of five years, offences under the Customs and Excise Management Act 1979; offences under the Official Secrets Acts 1911 and 1989; offences under the Sexual Offences Act 1956 as amended;[197] offences under the Drug Trafficking Offences Act 1986; offences of taking a motor vehicle or going equipped for stealing under the Theft Act 1968; and offences under the Public Bodies Corrupt Practices Act 1889 and Prevention of Corruption Act 1906 are all arrestable offences. Causing death by dangerous driving,[198] intercourse with a girl under the age of 13,[199] possession of firearms with intent to injure, the use of firearms and imitation firearms to resist arrest and carrying firearms with criminal intent are arrestable offences.[200] Hostage-taking and hijacking of aircraft are also arrestable offences.[201] Conspiracy to commit such offences, or attempts or incitement,

---

195 Offences include treason, murder, manslaughter, rape, kidnapping, incest with a girl under the age of 13, buggery with a boy under the age of 16 or a person who has not consented, and an indecent assault which constitutes an act of gross indecency. The Criminal Justice and Public Order Act 1994, s 85, extends the list to include an offence under the Protection of Children Act 1978, s 1 (indecent photographs and pseudo-photographs of children) and an offence under the Obscene Publications Act 1959, s 2 (publication of obscene matter).

196 *Op cit*, Fenwick, fn 1, p 407.

197 By the Criminal Justice and Public Order Act 1994.

198 Road Traffic Act 1972, s 1.

199 Sexual Offences Act 1956.

200 Firearms Act 1968, ss 16, 17 and 18.

201 Taking of Hostages Act 1982, s 1, Aviation Security Act 1982, s 1, respectively.

aiding, abetting, counselling or procuring such offences are all arrestable offences.[202]

Where an arrestable offence has occurred, or the police reasonably suspect someone is committing such an offence, or about to commit such an offence, the police may arrest without a warrant.[203] In these circumstances, there is no need for the police to establish the 'general arrest conditions' which apply to arrest for less serious offences.

The police may arrest without warrant for any non-arrestable offence – that is to say, less serious offences – where the 'general arrest conditions' are satisfied.[204] The 'general arrest conditions' are:

(a) that the name of the relevant person is unknown, and cannot be readily ascertained by, the constable;

(b) that the constable has reasonable grounds for doubting whether a name furnished by the relevant person as his name is his real name;

(c) that:

(i) the relevant person has failed to furnish a satisfactory address for service; or

(ii) the constable has reasonable grounds for doubting whether an address furnished by the relevant person is a satisfactory address for service;

(d) that the constable has reasonable grounds for believing that the arrest is necessary to prevent the relevant person:

(i) causing physical injury to himself or any other person;

(ii) suffering physical injury;

(iii) causing loss of or damage to property;

(iv) committing an offence against public decency; or

(v) causing an unlawful obstruction of the highway;

(e) that the constable has reasonable grounds for believing that the arrest is necessary to protect a child or other vulnerable person from the relevant person.[205]

Section 1 of the Offensive Weapons Act 1996 confers a new power of arrest under the Police and Criminal Evidence Act 1984 for the offence of carrying an offensive weapon in a public place contrary to section 1(1) of the Prevention of Crimes Act 1953, and of having an article with a blade or point in a public place contrary to section 139(1) of the Criminal Justice Act 1988. A power of arrest is also conferred in relation to a new offence created under section 4, namely, having an article with a blade or point or an offensive weapon in school premises.

---

202 PACE 1984, s 24(3).
203 *Ibid*, s 24(4), (5).
204 *Ibid*, s 25.
205 *Ibid*, s 25(3).

Giving reasons for the arrest

A failure to give reasons for an arrest will cause the arrest to be unlawful. In *Christie v Leachinsky*,[206] the House of Lords ruled that a person must be told of the fact of his or her arrest and the grounds for arrest, although this need not be done if the circumstances are obvious or it is difficult to communicate with the arrested person. Section 28 of the Police and Criminal Evidence Act 1984 places the requirements on a statutory basis and makes them more stringent. Subject to a person escaping before the information can be communicated, section 28 requires that:

(a) the person making the arrest must inform the arrested person of the fact of, and reasons for, arrest, either immediately or as soon as is reasonably practicable afterwards;[207]

(b) a police officer making an arrest must inform the person arrested of these matters even if they are obvious.[208]

No particular form of words need be used, but they must be in sufficient detail to enable the arrested person to understand the issue and, if possible, to deny the allegation and be released. Where it is not possible to state reasons immediately, for example, because the arrestee is reacting violently, reasons must be stated as soon as practicable. This requirement is illustrated in *Director of Public Prosecutions v Hawkins*.[209] In that case, a violent struggle prevented reasons being given immediately. However, when the arrestee was subdued, reasons for the arrest were still not given. The arrest became unlawful when the opportunity to give reasons arose, and reasons were not given. However, in *Murray v Ministry of Defence*,[210] the House of Lords held that an arrest was lawful, even though reasons were not immediately given. In that case, which involved the use of arrest powers by the army in Northern Ireland, a patrol entered Mrs Murray's house, intending to arrest her. When she asked whether she was under arrest, she was not answered. It was only 30 minutes after the patrol's entry that she was informed that she was under arrest. However, the House of Lords ruled that the arrest was lawful since, from the time of the patrol's entry, it must have been obvious to Mrs Murray that she was no longer at liberty. A similarly sympathetic attitude to the arresting authorities was seen in *Lewis v Chief Constable of the South Wales Constabulary*.[211] There, two people were arrested and not immediately informed of the reasons for arrest. In an action for false imprisonment, the

---

206 [1947] AC 573.
207 PACE 1984, s 28(1), (3).
208 *Ibid*, s 28(2), (3).
209 [1988] 1 WLR 1166.
210 [1988] 1 WLR 692.
211 [1991] 1 All ER 206.

Court of Appeal upheld the decision of the circuit judge, that the arrests were unlawful until the reasons were given but, once the reasons were given, the arrests became lawful.

The giving of reasons for arrest is also a requirement under the European Convention on Human Rights, discussed in Chapter 22. In *Fox, Campbell and Hartley v United Kingdom*,[212] the applicants were arrested on suspected terrorist offences, but were not informed of the reason for the arrest, although they were told they were being arrested under a specified statutory provision. When later interviewed, they were asked about specific criminal offences. The Court of Human Rights held that paragraph 5(2) of Article 5 had not been satisfied at the time of the arrest, but that the defect was later rectified. The case of Murray, discussed above, also went to the European Court. The Court again found no breach of Article 5. Although she was denied reasons for some half an hour, she was eventually informed of the reason for arrest during interrogation.

Detention following arrest

Once a person has been arrested, he or she may be detained by the police for questioning before a charge is laid. There exists a fine balance to be achieved here between permitting the police to question a suspect in order to determine whether there exist sufficient grounds on which to make a charge, and the need to protect persons from unwarranted detention by the police. Section 41(1) of the Police and Criminal Evidence Act 1984 provides that a person shall not be kept in police detention for more than 24 hours without being charged. The time runs from the time of the person's arrest or, in the case of a person's arrest outside the relevant police area, from the time at which he arrives in the police station.[213]

The 24 hour period is extendable. The grounds on which detention beyond 24 hours may be authorised are as follows. For authorisation by a senior officer of police, there must be reasonable grounds for believing that the detention is necessary in order to secure or preserve evidence or obtain evidence by questioning; that the offence in question is a 'serious arrestable offence'; and that the police investigation is being conducted 'diligently and expeditiously'.[214] A review of detention must be made after 24 hours.[215] On application to the senior officer, authorisation may be given to detain him for up to 36 hours.[216] After 36 hours of detention, a person must be brought

---

212 (1990) 13 EHRR 157.
213 PACE 1984, s 41(2)(a)(i), (ii).
214 *Ibid*, s 42(1)(a), (b), (c).
215 *Ibid*, s 42(4).
216 *Ibid*, s 42(2).

before the magistrates' court for a hearing. The authorised period of further detention is at the magistrates' discretion, but shall not be longer than 36 hours,[217] but the police may apply for a further period of detention which, if granted, may extend the period of detention to a possible maximum of 96 hours.[218]

Bail

Section 41(7) provides that, if a person has not been charged at the expiry of 24 hours, he shall, subject to sub-section 8, be released, either on bail or without bail.[219] The 24 hour time limit does not apply to persons whose detention for more than 24 hours has been authorised by a senior officer[220] or where a successful application has been made to a magistrates' court by the police for continued detention.[221]

Conditions of detention

The Codes of Practice detail the conditions under which persons may be held. These include no more than one person in a cell, access to toilet and washing facilities, the provision of adequate food and daily exercise. The police may not use more than 'reasonable force' in relation to detainees in preventing escape, or causing damage to property. Appropriate medical treatment must be given where necessary.

In *R v Commissioner of Police of the Metropolis*,[222] the House of Lords considered the liability of the police. In 1990, Martin Lynch, who had been remanded in custody on criminal charges, hanged himself in his cell in Kentish Town police station. He had made previous attempts at suicide and the police had noted that he was a suicide risk. The House of Lords ruled that authorities, such as the police or prison service, who were entrusted with holding prisoners in custody, had a duty to take reasonable care to prevent them from harming themselves or committing suicide. Where there was a breach of that duty and a suicide occurred, the authorities were not entitled to rely on the defences of *volenti non fit injuria* or *novus actus interveniens* in an action for negligence brought by the estate of the deceased.

---

217 PACE 1984, ss 43(11), (12) and 44.
218 *Ibid*, ss 43 and 44.
219 See, further, below.
220 PACE 1984, s 42(1).
221 *Ibid*, s 43.
222 (1999) *The Times*, 16 July.

The right to legal advice[223]

Under section 58(1) of the Police and Criminal Evidence Act 1984, 'a person arrested and held in custody in a police station or other premises shall be entitled, if he so requests, to consult a solicitor privately at any time'.

Delay in complying with a request to consult a lawyer is only permitted where the person is being held in connection with a serious arrestable offence and where a senior officer has authorised the delay. The grounds on which delay may be authorised include reasonable grounds for believing that there will be interference with or harm to evidence; that exercising the right would lead to alerting other suspects who have not yet been arrested; or that exercising the right would hinder the recovery of any property obtained as a result of the offence.[224]

Legal representation may be crucial to the protection of the suspect from oppressive questioning by the police. Where confessions are obtained by oppression, a guilty verdict may subsequently be set aside.[225] Guidelines laid down for solicitors who attend interviews are published by The Law Society. The guidelines for intervening in questioning include, *inter alia*, the following:

> ... you may need to intervene if the questions are: ... oppressive, threatening or insulting;
>
> ... you should intervene if the officer is not asking questions but only making his/her own comments ...
>
> ... if questions are improper or improperly put, you should intervene and be prepared to explain your objections ...
>
> ... if improprieties remain uncorrected or continue, advise the suspect of his/her right to remain silent.[226]

When a person has been arrested and is being held in custody at a police station, he or she has the right to communicate with one other person 'as soon as practicable'.[227] A delay is only permitted, where an officer of the rank of superintendent authorises it, on the basis that 'he has reasonable grounds to believe' that the communication will lead to interference with evidence connected with a serious arrestable office, or physical injury to other persons, or will lead to alerting of other suspects connected with the offence, and will hinder the recovery of property obtained as a result of the offence.[228] Section 58(1) of the Police and Criminal Evidence Act 1984 also provides that a person

---

223 See Baldwin, J, *The Role of Legal Representatives at the Police Station*, RCCJ Research Study No 3, 1993, London: HMSO.

224 PACE 1984, s 58(8).

225 See *R v Paris, Abdullahi and Miller* (1992) 97 Cr App Rep 99.

226 *Guidelines*, 1991, London: The Law Society, para 6.

227 PACE 1984, s 56.

228 *Ibid*, s 56(5)(a), (b), (c).

who is in police detention 'shall be entitled, if he so requests, to consult a solicitor privately at any time'. In addition, section 59 inserts into the Legal Aid Act 1982 a provision which is capable of preventing a solicitor from providing advice and legal representation under the Legal Aid scheme if 'they do not also provide advice and assistance ... for persons ... held in custody'. Under Code of Practice C,[229] a detainee is to be informed of the right to legal advice,[230] and given the name of a duty solicitor if he or she requires it.[231] The detainee is also entitled to have a solicitor present during questioning.[232] However, where a person is arrested for a serious arrestable offence, and an officer of the rank of superintendent or above so authorises, access to a solicitor may be delayed for up to 36 hours. Such a delay may be authorised where the officer is concerned that there is a risk to witnesses or to evidence relating to the case, or would hinder the recovery of any property obtained as a result of the offence.[233] In cases of suspected terrorism, the right to consult a solicitor is conditioned by the requirement that the interview is conducted within 'the sight and hearing' of a uniformed officer.[234] The Court of Appeal has construed section 58(8) narrowly. In *R v Samuel*,[235] it was held that delay in access to legal advice can only be justified on specific grounds which must be substantiated to the satisfaction of the court.

The right to have a solicitor attend during police interviews has been held not to apply to a suspect arrested in Northern Ireland under section 14 of the Prevention of Terrorism (Temporary Provisions) Act 1989, since section 58 of the Police and Criminal Evidence Act 1984 was not applicable to a person arrested or detained under the terrorism provisions.[236] The House of Lords so held in *R v Chief Constable of the Royal Ulster Constabulary ex parte Begley*.[237]

The right to legal advice must also be considered in relation to Article 6 of the European Convention on Human Rights. See, *inter alia*, the discussion of *Magee v United Kingdom*[238] in Chapter 22.

The right to inform someone of arrest and detention

A person held in a police station is entitled to inform a relative or friend 'or other person concerned with his welfare' of his arrest without delay, unless

229 Code C, fn 175.
230 Code C, para 3.1(ii).
231 Code C, Note 6B.
232 Code C, para 6.5.
233 PACE 1984, s 58(8).
234 *Ibid*, s 58(15).
235 [1988] 2 WLR 920.
236 Police and Criminal Evidence (Northern Ireland) Order SI 1989/1341, Art 59(2).
237 [1997] 1 WLR 1475.
238 Application No 28135/95, Judgment 6 June 2000.

such notification would prejudice the investigation of crime or the arrest of other suspects.[239]

The right to silence: the Criminal Justice and Public Order Act 1994 reforms[240]

In relation to the right to silence, the position of a person who has been arrested is different from that of a citizen before arrest, and the Criminal Justice and Public Order Act 1994 made substantial amendments to this right.[241]

The reforms introduced under the Criminal Justice and Public Order Act are amongst the most controversial reforms of the protection of an accused for many years. Those who oppose a weakening of the right to silence base their arguments on the relative vulnerability of the accused, and the need to protect the accused from making statements which might falsely incriminate him.[242] Against this concern must be set the argument that when individuals are permitted to remain silent when questioned by the police, advantage of this right is taken by 'professional criminals' who are familiar with the process. The concern has been that such persons will conceal information under questioning and then 'ambush' the prosecution by revealing the information in court.[243] The government's view was that the balance had shifted too far in the favour of the defendant, and that reform was necessary.

Sections 34 to 38 of the Criminal Justice and Public Order Act 1994 effect the reforms. Under section 34, where an accused is being questioned under caution and fails to mention any fact later relied on in his evidence or, where the accused has been officially charged with an offence[244] or officially informed that he might be prosecuted for it,[245] fails to mention any fact which, in the circumstances existing at the time, 'the accused could reasonably have been expected to mention' when questioned, charged or informed, then the court, in determining whether there is a case to answer,[246] and the court of

---

239 PACE 1984, s 56.

240 See McConville, M and Hodgson, J, *Custodial Legal Advice and the Right to Silence*, RCCJ Research Study No 16, 1993, London: HMSO.

241 See, further, below.

242 The reform was opposed by, *inter alia*, The Law Society, the Bar Council and the Magistrates' Association. On the other side, those in favour included the Police Service, the Crown Prosecution Service, HM Council of Circuit Judges and many senior judges.

243 See *R v Zuckerman* [1989] Crim LR 855.

244 Criminal Justice and Public Order Act 1994, s 34(1)(a).

245 *Ibid*, s 34(1)(b).

246 *Ibid*, s 34(2)(c).

jury, in determining whether the accused is guilty of the offence charged,[247] may 'draw such inferences from the failure as appear proper.'

M Wasik and R Taylor argue that the reforms are of a more restricted nature than has been otherwise claimed.[248] First, the fact which the accused fails to mention must be one on which he subsequently relies on for his defence in court. Secondly, the non-disclosed fact must be one which, in the circumstances at the time, 'the accused could reasonably have been expected to mention'. The reasonableness of the non-disclosure is an objective criteria to be determined by the court. Thirdly, only such inferences may be drawn as appear 'proper'. If, therefore, the accused had a genuine and reasonably explained reason for non-disclosure (perhaps fear of possible consequences of disclosure), it may not be 'proper' to draw inferences from his or her silence. Fourthly, the fact of silence cannot itself establish a *prima facie* case against the accused, although it may contribute to establishing such a case. The most important restriction on section 34 is that it does not apply until the accused has been charged or cautioned. Accordingly, the right to silence remains until that point in time, when the person concerned is clear that official proceedings are in motion.

Section 35 relates to the accused's silence at trial. Other than where a person's guilt is not in issue, or where the court considers that the physical or mental condition of the accused 'makes it undesirable for him to give evidence', the court must satisfy itself that the accused is aware that the stage has been reached where he or she can give evidence in defence. If the accused then chooses not to give evidence, or without good cause refuses to answer questions, it is then permissible for the court or jury to draw such inferences 'as appear proper from his failure to give evidence or his refusal, without good cause, to answer any question'.[249] Section 35 relates to persons who have attained the age of 14 years[250] and, where the age of the person is 'material', his age 'shall for those purposes be taken to be that which appears to the court to be his age'.[251]

Section 36 relates to the effect of an accused's failure to account for objects, substances or marks. Where a person has been arrested by a constable, and the police reasonably believe that the presence of the object, substance or mark may be attributable to the accused participating in the commission of a specific offence, the police are entitled to ask for an explanation as to the

---

247 Criminal Justice and Public Order Act 1994, s 34(2)(d).
248 Wasik, M and Taylor, R, *Blackstone's Guide to the Criminal Justice Act 1994*, 1995, London: Blackstone, Chapter 3; and see Lord Taylor of Gosforth CJ, *Hansard*, Lords Cols 519–23, 23 May 1994.
249 Criminal Justice and Public Order Act 1994, s 35(2).
250 *Ibid*, s 35(1).
251 *Ibid*, s 35(6).

object, etc.[252] If the person fails to account for it, then the court, when (a) considering whether to dismiss the charge, or (b) deciding whether there is a case to answer, or (c) whether the accused is guilty of the offence charged, is entitled to 'draw such inferences from the failure or refusal as appear proper'.[253]

Section 37 relates to the accused's failure to account for his or her presence at a particular place. If a person arrested by a constable was found at a place where the offence was committed, and the officer reasonably believes that his presence was attributable to participation in the offence, and the constable requests him to account for his presence, then, if that person fails to do so, a court, or court or jury, in circumstances (a), (b) and (c) in relation to section 36, may draw 'such inferences from the failure or refusal as appear proper'.[254]

The Court of Appeal has interpreted these provisions. In *R v Condron and Another*,[255] the accused were suspected on being involved in the supply and possession of heroin. Acting on the advice of their solicitor, the accused refused to answer questions on the basis that their solicitor felt they were suffering withdrawal symptoms. At trial, the prosecution submitted that they should at interview have mentioned the facts on which they now relied in court. The judge directed the jury that it was for them to decide whether adverse inferences should be drawn from their silence. The defendants were found guilty and appealed. The Court of Appeal ruled that remaining silent on the basis of legal advice was not sufficient reason for not mentioning relevant matters which would later be relied on in their defence. The reason for the advice must also be given, not just a bare statement that the advice has been given. However, in *Condron v United Kingdom*, the Court of Human Rights ruled that Article 6 – the right to a fair trial – had been violated. *Condron* is discussed in Chapter 22.

In *R v Argent*,[256] the Court of Appeal ruled that six formal conditions had to be met before the jury could draw adverse inferences under section 34 of the Criminal Justice and Public Order Act 1994. The accused had been convicted for manslaughter and sentenced to 10 years in prison. The defendant appealed against conviction. The Lord Chief Justice stated that the formal conditions to be met were:

(1) there had to be proceedings against a person for an offence. That condition had necessarily to be satisfied before section 34 could bite;

(2) the alleged failure had to occur before a defendant was charged;

---

252 Criminal Justice and Public Order Act 1994, s 36(1).

253 *Ibid*, s 36(2).

254 *Ibid*, s 37(1), (2), (3).

255 (1997) 1 Cr App R 185. See, also, *R v Cowan* [1995] All ER 939.

256 (1996) *The Times*, 19 December.

(3) the alleged failure had to occur during questioning under caution by a constable, or any other person within section 34(4);

(4) the questioning had to be directed to trying to discover whether or by whom the alleged offence had been committed;

(5) the alleged failure by the defendant had to be to mention any fact relied on in his defence to those proceedings. That raised two questions of fact:
(a) was there some fact which the defendant had relied on in his defence?;
(b) did the defendant, when he was being questioned in accordance with section 34, fail to mention it?;

(6) the fact that the appellant failed to mention was a fact which, in the circumstances existing at the time, he could reasonably have been expected to mention when so questioned.

The relevant time was the time of questioning and account had to be taken of all the relevant circumstances existing at that time.

The court should not construe the expression 'in the circumstances' restrictively; matters such as time of day, the defendant's age, experience, mental capacity, state of health, sobriety, tiredness, personality and legal advice were all part of the relevant circumstances. Those were only examples of the things which might be relevant.

The Court of Appeal turned to section 35 of the Criminal Justice and Public Order Act 1994 in *R v Cowan*.[257] In that case, it had been argued that section 35 should be permitted to operate in exceptional cases only. The court ruled that the effect of section 35 was simply to 'add a further evidential factor in support of the prosecution case'. The accused's silence could not be the only factor on which a conviction was based, and the prosecution remained under an obligation to establish a *prima facie* case before any question of the defendant testifying is raised. The jury, accordingly, must be convinced that a *prima facie* case exists before drawing adverse inferences from an accused's silence. The Court of Appeal returned to section 35 in *R v Friend*.[258] In that case, the defendant, aged 15, had a mental age of a nine year old. The judge at trial had not ruled at the defendant's condition made it undesirable for him to give evidence. Children as young as eight give evidence, the defendant had given a coherent account to the police, and he was not abnormally suggestible. The defendant did not give evidence at his trial, and the judge directed that it was open to the jury to draw an adverse inference from that fact. The defendant was convicted of murder and appealed against conviction. The Court of Appeal ruled that the defendant fell within section 35, being over 14 years of age, and the fact that he had a mental age of a younger person did not provide him the same immunity as it would to a person under the age of 14.

---

257 [1996] QB 373; [1995] 4 All ER 939.
258 [1997] 2 All ER 1011.

The court ruled that the trial judge had exercised his powers correctly: he had considered all relevant facts and not considered irrelevant facts. The trial judge's decision could only be impugned if it came within the meaning of 'unreasonable' in the *Wednesbury Corporation* sense,[259] 'that no judge faced with this evidence could rationally have reached this conclusion'.[260] The Court of Appeal took the opportunity to consider whether or not there was an 'appropriate test' to be applied in reaching such decisions, and concluded that there was not, stating that 'we do not consider it appropriate to spell out a test to be applied in such a situation'.[261] The language of the section was 'simple and clear'. 'It is for the judge in a given case to determine whether or not it is undesirable for the accused to give evidence.'[262]

The 'right to silence' and serious fraud trials

Different provisions apply to serious fraud trials. Under the Criminal Justice Act 1987, where the Serious Fraud Office issues a 'section 2 notice', the person to whom the notice is addressed commits a criminal offence if he or she does not attend for interview and answer questions. In addition, under section 432(2) of the Companies Act 1985, where a company is under investigation, a person is under a legal obligation to answer questions. By these means, any 'right to silence' is effectively negatived.[263] In *Saunders v United Kingdom*,[264] the Court of Human Rights ruled that the provisions were in violation of Article 6 of the European Convention on Human Rights.[265]

The reliability of evidence[266]

It is central to the protection of the individual that evidence be obtained in a lawful manner. The question arises as to how the law can secure a balance

---

259 *Associated Provincial Picture Houses Ltd v Wednesbury Corporation* [1948] 1 KB 223. See Chapter 25.

260 [1997] 2 All ER 1011, p 1021.

261 *Ibid*, p 1020.

262 *Ibid*, p 1020.

263 See *Director of the Serious Fraud Office ex parte Smith* [1993] AC 1; [1992] 3 WLR 66; *R v Saunders* (1995) *The Times*, 28 November.

264 (1997) 23 EHRR 313.

265 See, further, Chapter 22.

266 The law of evidence is complex and outside the scope of this chapter other than by way of introduction. See, generally, Tapper, C, *Cross and Tapper on Evidence*, 8th edn, 1995, London: Butterworths; *op cit*, Fenwick, fn 1, Chapter 11, pp 469–99. On the balance between controlling police powers and admitting evidence, see Ashworth, A, 'Involuntary confessions and illegally obtained evidence in criminal cases – Part I' [1963] Crim LR 15 and 'Part II' [1963] Crim LR 77; Birch, D, 'The pace hots up: confessions and confusions under the 1984 Act' [1989] Crim LR 95; Birch, D, 'Excluding evidence from entrapment: what is a "fair cop"?' (1994) 47 CLP 73.

between ensuring that the police operate within the law, and the Codes of Practice which supplement the law, and allowing evidence to be used which may have been obtained in a manner not strictly in accordance with the rules but which does prove that a suspect committed a particular crime. If evidence is made inadmissible, on the basis of a procedural irregularity, a guilty suspect may go free. On the other hand, if the evidence – however obtained – is admitted, and proves false, there is a danger of innocent suspects being wrongfully convicted.

Prior to the Police and Criminal Evidence Act 1984, the admissibility of evidence was regulated under the common law. A distinction was drawn between illegally obtained evidence which was admissible, and involuntary confessions which were inadmissible on the basis that they might be unreliable.[267] The Police and Criminal Evidence Act 1984 places the admissibility of evidence on a statutory basis. In relation to confessions, there are four criteria to be employed in determining whether they should be admissible in court. Section 76 regulates confessions.[268] Confessions are admissible into court unless the confession has been obtained by (a) oppression,[269] or (b) in consequence of anything said or done which was likely, in the circumstances existing at the time, to render unreliable any confession which might be made by him in consequence thereof.[270] In those circumstances, the court 'shall not allow the confession to be given in evidence against him except in so far as the prosecution proves to the court beyond reasonable doubt that the confession (notwithstanding that it may be true) was not obtained as aforesaid'.[271] Moreover, in any case where the prosecution proposes to give in evidence a confession, the court may, of its own motion, require the prosecution to prove that the confession has not been obtained in the circumstances above.[272] However, where a confession has been partly or wholly excluded on the grounds above, that fact does not affect the admissibility in evidence (a) of any facts discovered as a result of the confession, or (b) where the confession is relevant as showing that the accused speaks, writes or expresses himself in a particular way, of so much of the confession as is necessary to show that he does so.[273]

In relation to the exclusion of 'unfair evidence', section 78 of the Police and

---

267 See *R v Isequilla* [1975] All ER 77; *R v Ping Lin* [1976] AC 574; *R v Sang* [1980] AC 402; [1979] 2 All ER 1222.

268 Confessions are defined to include 'any statement wholly or partly adverse to the person who made it, whether made to a person in authority or not and whether made in words or otherwise': PACE 1984, s 82.

269 'Oppression' is defined to include torture, inhuman or degrading treatment, and the use or threat of violence (whether or not amounting to torture): PACE 1984, s 76(8).

270 PACE 1984, s 76(1)(a), (b).

271 *Ibid*, s 76(2).

272 *Ibid*, s 76(3).

273 *Ibid*, s 76(4).

Criminal Evidence Act 1984 provides that:

> In any proceedings, the court may refuse to allow evidence on which the
> prosecution proposes to rely to be given if it appears to the court that, having
> regard to all the circumstances, including the circumstances in which the
> evidence was obtained, the admission of the evidence would have such an
> adverse effect on the fairness of the proceedings that the court ought not to
> admit it.[274]

Section 78 of the Police and Criminal Evidence Act 1984 is far wider than
section 76, and may be relevant to confessions obtained which do not fall
within the requirements of section 76.[275] Thus, for example, if a confession is
fabricated, the defence will argue that the accused did not make a confession
and, accordingly, that 'confession' could not fall under section 76. The power
to refuse to allow evidence is discretionary. Where there has been a breach of
the rules under the Police and Criminal Evidence Act, and that breach is
substantiated to the satisfaction of the court, the question to be determined is
whether the breach is substantial or significant,[276] other than where the police
had acted in bad faith.[277] Having established whether a breach of the rules is
substantial or significant, the court will then look to the nature of the rule in
question in relation to the circumstances of the case. Thus, for example, the
right to have a legal adviser present will be deemed the more important in
relation to a vulnerable suspect who could be easily confused by police
questioning.

Habeas corpus

The ancient writ of habeas corpus is available to test the legality of a person's
detention.[278] The writ can be issued either by the person imprisoned or by
someone acting on his behalf. If it is established that there is a *prima facie*
ground for believing the detention to be unlawful, the writ will be issued.
Originally a common law power, the right to a writ was placed on a statutory
basis under the Habeas Corpus Act 1679. The Act of 1679 relates to persons
imprisoned on a criminal charge. The Habeas Corpus Act 1816 relates to
persons detained other than on a criminal charge.[279] AV Dicey instructed that:

---

274 PACE 1984, s 82(3), preserves the common law power to exclude evidence at the court's
discretion.

275 *R v Mason* [1987] Crim LR 119; [1987] All ER 481. See, also, *R v Khan* (1996) 146 NLJ 1024,
HL; and *Khan v UK*, discussed in Chapter 22. See, also, *R v Chalkley* [1998] QB 848, CA.

276 *R v Keenan* [1989] 3 WLR 1193; [1989] All ER 598.

277 *R v Walsh* [1989] Crim LR 822; [1989] 19 Cr App R 161.

278 See, also, Chapter 6.

279 The Habeas Corpus Act 1862 prohibits the courts from issuing writs in respect of
colonies or dominions where those jurisdictions have power to issue the writ.

... if, in short, any man, woman, or child is deprived of liberty, the court will always issue a writ of habeas corpus to any one who has the aggrieved person in his custody to have such person brought before the court, and if he is suffering restraint without lawful cause, set him free.[280]

In the case of *Wolfe Tone*,[281] Tone was tried and found guilty of high treason by a court-martial and sentenced to death. A writ was issued on the basis that, since Wolfe Tone was not under commission to the English army, but rather held a commission from the French Republic, there was no jurisdiction for his trial by court-martial in Ireland. The Lord Chief Justice instructed the sheriff to go immediately to the army barracks and demand that Tone not be executed. When the officers refused to comply with the order, the Lord Chief Justice ordered that Tone, and the detaining officers, be taken into the custody of the sheriff. On seeking to recover Tone from detention, it was found that he had cut his throat and could not be moved. On this case, Dicey wrote, seemingly without irony, that 'it will be admitted that no more splendid assertion of the supremacy of law can be found than the protection of Wolfe Tone by the Irish Bench'.[282]

Stockdale v Hansard[283] and *Sheriff of Middlesex's Case*[284] also reveal the power – and limits – of habeas corpus. There, it will be recalled from the discussion in Chapter 18, the Sheriff had been directed to enforce the order of the court against *Hansard* and recover damages due to Stockdale. On attempting to execute the order, the Sheriff was imprisoned by the House of Commons. A writ of habeas corpus was issued. The Speaker of the House issued a certificate stating that the Sheriff had been detained on the order of the House for contempt. The court declared that it was unable to look behind the face of the certificate: since it revealed nothing *prima facie* unlawful on its face, the court had no jurisdiction to intervene.

The writ has also been used to test the legality of detention of slaves: *Sommersett's Case*[285] and of students: *Ex parte Daisy Hopkins*.[286] In *Board of Control ex parte Rutty*,[287] a writ was issued to test the legality of the detention of a mentally defective patient who had been detained for eight years without an order of a court.

Nowadays, the writ of habeas corpus is most often used to test the legality of the detention of immigrants. However, in *R v Home Secretary ex parte*

---

280 *Op cit*, Dicey, fn 7, p 219.

281 (1798) 27 St Tr 614.

282 *Op cit*, Dicey, fn 7, p 294. See, also, Heuston, RFV, *Essays in Constitutional Law*, 2nd edn, 1964, London: Stevens, Chapter 2.

283 (1839) 9 Ad & E 1.

284 (1840) 11 Ad & E 273. See, further, Chapter 18.

285 (1771) 20 St Tr 1.

286 (1891) 61 LJ QB 240.

287 [1956] 2 QB 109.

Mughal[288] and *R v Home Secretary ex parte Zamir,*[289] the court refused to allow habeas corpus to be used to question the decision to remove an illegal immigrant from the country. Conversely, in *R v Home Secretary ex parte Khawaja,*[290] the House of Lords ruled that the question as to whether a person was an illegal immigrant was not within the exclusive jurisdiction of the Home Secretary to decide. Rather it was a matter of fact, which the courts would decide. Before Khawaja could be removed from the country, the court had to be satisfied on the evidence that he was in fact an illegal immigrant. Only if he was an illegal immigrant would the court permit deportation.

There exists an overlap between habeas corpus and judicial review[291] which causes uncertainty. In *R v Home Secretary ex parte Cheblak,*[292] the Court of Appeal held that habeas corpus is not a substitute for judicial review proceedings. However, where an application for judicial review is pending, a writ may be used to ensure that the applicant is not prematurely removed from the country.[293]

The writ of habeas corpus – once so roundly applauded by Dicey – has been so encroached upon by legislative enactments as to be regarded as of limited value nowadays.[294] In the face of legislative supremacy – exemplified most starkly by the Prevention of Terrorism Acts, which permit detention without recourse to a court of law for up to seven days – the force of the action has been weakened. More protection may be given nowadays under Article 5 of the European Convention on Human Rights which provides for protection against unlawful detention, than the protection afforded by habeas corpus,[295] although, as will be seen in Chapter 22, the United Kingdom government has derogated from Article 5 in relation to persons detained under the Prevention of Terrorism Acts.

PROTECTION OF PERSONAL PROPERTY

In *Semayne's Case,*[296] the principle was judicially declared that an 'Englishman's home is his castle'. Two early cases reveal judicial boldness in the protection from unlawful entry into property. In *Wilkes v Wood,*[297] an

---

288 [1974] 1 QB 313.
289 [1980] AC 930.
290 [1984] AC 74.
291 See Chapters 24 and 25.
292 [1991] 2 All ER 319.
293 *R v Home Secretary ex parte Muboyayi* [1991] 1 QB 244.
294 See Le Sueur, AP, 'Should we abolish the writ of habeas corpus?' [1992] PL 13.
295 See, further, Chapter 22.
296 (1605) 5 Co Rep 91a.
297 (1763) 19 St Tr 1153.

Under Secretary of State, accompanied by police, entered into Wilkes's home, broke open his desk and seized papers. In an action for trespass against the Under Secretary, Lord Pratt CJ stated that the power claimed would affect 'the person and property of every man in this kingdom, and is totally subversive of the liberty of the subject'. Moreover, such action, being without justification and unlawful, was 'contrary to the fundamental principles of the constitution'.

In the seminal case of *Entick v Carrington*,[298] the Secretary of State, under a general warrant, authorised the entry into property and the seizure of property of Entick, suspected of publishing seditious literature. In an action for trespass against Carrington, Lord Camden CJ declared:

> This power, so claimed by the Secretary of State, is not supported by a single citation from any law book extant ...
>
> If it is law, it will be found in our books. If it is not to be found there, it is not law.
>
> By the laws of England, every invasion of private property, be it ever so minute, is a trespass. No man can set his foot upon my ground without my licence, but he is liable to an action, though the damages be nothing ...
>
> According to this reasoning, it is now incumbent upon the defendants to show the law by which this seizure is warranted. If that cannot be done it is a trespass ... Where is the written law that gives any magistrate such a power? I can safely answer, there is none; and therefore it is too much for us without such authority to pronounce a practice legal, which would be subversive of all the comforts of society.

Every entry into the property of the citizen must be authorised by law. However, such freedom from arbitrary intrusion is – in the absence of a written guarantee of rights – subject always to the sovereignty of Parliament. It may also be that the royal prerogative will confer legitimacy on what might otherwise be deemed an invasion of property. The doctrine that 'a man's home is his castle'[299] has many exceptions. As seen in Chapter 6, statutory rights of entry are conferred on employees of the Gas Board, Electricity Board, and others. A right of entry has also been conferred upon Child Support Inspectors to enter into premises – other than purely private premises – to search for evidence in relation to claims for child maintenance.[300]

In addition to rights of physical entry into property, the issue of warrants to intercept communications[301] authorises a non-physical but nevertheless real intrusion into a person's private property. In *Malone v Metropolitan Police Commissioner*,[302] however, the English court ruled that such intrusions did not

---

298 (1765) 19 St Tr 1030. See, further, Chapters 6 and 7.

299 *Semayne's Case* (1605) 5 Co Rep 91a.

300 Child Support Act 1991, s 15.

301 Under the Interception of Communications Act 1985. See, further, Chapter 23.

302 [1979] Ch 344; and see *Malone v United Kingdom* (1984) 7 EHRR 14. See, also, *R v Khan* (1996) 146 NLJ 1024, HL; and *Khan v UK*, discussed in Chapter 22.

amount to a trespass to property. Warrants to enter into and search premises are also provided for under the Security Services Act 1989.

Rights of entry under common law

The courts have considered rights of entry under common law. In *Thomas v Sawkins*,[303] it was held that the police are entitled to be present at a public meeting on private premises even where organisers asked them to leave. The officers had reasonably believed that a breach of the peace would occur and, hence, were justified in remaining and were not trespassing.[304]

In *R v Inland Revenue Commissioners ex parte Rossminster Ltd*,[305] Lord Denning MR, in the Court of Appeal, had declared that:

> Once great power is granted, there is a danger of it being abused. Rather than risk such abuse, it is, as I see it, the duty of the courts to construe the statute so as to see that it encroaches as little as possible upon the liberties of the people of England.

> ... it seems to me, as a matter of construction of the statute and therefore of the warrant [the legality of which was in issue] – in pursuance of our traditional role to protect the liberty of the individual – it is our duty to say that the warrant must particularise the specific offence which is charged as being fraud on the revenue.[306]

That bold view was not, however, to prevail in the House of Lords. While Lords Wilberforce and Scarman both insisted on the primacy of protecting the individual's right to privacy in his home, that right had been overridden by clear words of the statute. Lord Wilberforce succinctly expressed the view of the court:

> The courts have the duty to supervise, I would say critically, even jealously, the legality of any purported exercise of these powers. They are the guardians of the citizens' right to privacy. But they must do this in the context of the times, that is, of increasing parliamentary intervention, and of the modern power of judicial review. In my respectful opinion, appeals to eighteenth century precedents of arbitrary action by Secretaries of State[307] and references to general warrants do nothing to throw light on the issue. Furthermore, while the courts may look critically at legislation which impairs the rights of citizens and should resolve any doubt in interpretation in their favour, it is no part of their duty, or power, to restrict or impede the working of legislation, even of

---

303 [1935] 2 KB 249.
304 See Goodhart, AL, '*Thomas v Sawkins*: a constitutional innovation' [1936–38] CLJ 22.
305 [1980] AC 952, HL.
306 *Ibid*, pp 972, 974.
307 The reference here is to *Entick v Carrington* (1765) 19 St Tr 1030.

unpopular legislation; to do so would be to weaken rather than to advance the democratic process.[308]

Police powers of entry came into conflict with Article 8 of the European Convention in *McLeod v United Kingdom*.[309] The applicant was required by a court order to surrender certain items to her former husband. The former husband entered the premises, with members of his family and a solicitor's clerk, with the permission of the applicant's mother, but in the applicant's absence. The police had been called because of fears of a breach of the peace and entered the premises and checked the list of items to be removed. Following the applicant's return, the police insisted that the husband leave with the property. The applicant's action against the police was dismissed by the Court of Appeal. The Court of Human Rights ruled that although the police's action was lawful and had the legitimate aim of preventing a breach of the peace, their entry in the applicant's absence and their failure to check the terms of the court order rendered their conduct disproportionate and in violation of the right to privacy.

Police powers of entry, search and seizure

The police have special powers of entry and search, recognised under common law, but now clarified under the Police and Criminal Evidence Act 1984. For the most part, entry is authorised under a warrant authorised by a magistrate.[310] Over and above entry under warrant, however, there exists a class of cases under which the police may enter without warrant under sections 17 and 18 of the Act. Included in this class, are entry to arrest for an arrestable offence or for offences under the Public Order Act 1936, or Criminal Law Act 1977. Entry without warrant is also lawful if exercised to recover a prison, court or mental hospital detainee and to save life or prevent serious damage to property. The Immigration and Asylum Act 1999 permits the detention of a vehicle, small ship and small aircraft (each of which is defined in the Act), until all charges for carrying clandestine entrants have been paid. See, further, Chapter 21.

Under sections 18 and 19 of the Police and Criminal Evidence Act 1984, the police have the power to seize and retain a vehicle and not just parts of it or its contents, although those sections relate to 'premises'. The Court of Appeal so held in *Cowan v Commissioner of Police of the Metropolis*,[311] in which the court

---

308 [1980] AC 952, p 997.
309 Case No 72/1997/856/1065: (1998) *The Times*, 1 October; [1998] 2 FLR 1048; [1999] 27 EHRR 493.
310 PACE 1984, s 8.
311 (1999) *The Times*, 31 August.

also ruled that a vehicle was 'premises' for the purpose of the Act and the Act did not give power to seize premises but only contents, that rule applied where the premises were immoveable and could not physically be removed. Where premises were moveable there was no reason not to interpret 'anything' in sections 18 and 19 as including 'everything'. When exercising a search warrant under section 8(1) of the Police and Criminal Evidence Act 1984, however, a police officer was not entitled to remove items from the premises in order to sift through them for the purpose of deciding whether they fell within the scope of the warrant.[312] In *Webb v Chief Constable of Merseyside Police*,[313] the Court of Appeal ruled that there was no statutory power for the police to retain money seized by the police in the investigation of drug trafficking, where the person entitled to possession of the money was not convicted of a drug trafficking offence, and there was no general power to retain the money on public interest grounds. It might be lawful for the police to retain goods of a kind that it was unlawful to deal in them at all, but money was not of this character.

Where police exercise statutory powers of entry by the use of reasonable force, unless circumstances make it impossible, impracticable or undesirable, the police should give any occupant present the reason for his seeking to exercise that power of entry. The police had entered premises under section 17 of the Police and Criminal Evidence Act 1984, for the purpose of arrest. The Court of Appeal, dismissing an appeal by the Chief Constable of Essex against an order of the county court granting damages and costs to the defendant for, *inter alia*, assault by the defendant's officers, so held in *O'Loughlin v Chief Constable of Essex*.[314]

Under section 32 of the Police and Criminal Evidence Act 1984, where a person is arrested at a place other than a police station, a police constable may search the arrested person for anything which might assist him to escape from lawful custody or for anything which might be evidence relating to an offence, and to enter and search any premises in which he was when arrested or immediately before he was arrested for evidence relating to the offence for which he has been arrested.[315] The power is subject to the requirement that the 'constable has reasonable grounds for believing that the arrested person may present a danger to himself or others'.[316] The power to search is limited to what is 'reasonably required' for the purpose of discovery.[317] Search of the person is restricted: a person may not be required to remove any of his or her clothing in public, other than an outer coat, jacket or gloves, and the search

312 *R v Chesterfield Justices and Others ex parte Bramley* (1999) *The Times*, 10 November, QBD.
313 [2000] 1 All ER 209.
314 [1998] 1 WLR 374.
315 PACE 1984, s 32(2).
316 *Ibid*, s 32(1).
317 *Ibid*, s 32(3).

may only be conducted if the constable 'has reasonable grounds for believing' that the person concerned has concealed on his or her person anything for which a search is permitted.[318] If the permitted search discloses anything which might be used to cause physical injury to the person or any other person, the officer may seize and retain anything found, other than an item subject to legal privilege, if there are reasonable grounds for believing that the item may be used to assist escape from lawful custody, or is evidence of an offence, or has been obtained in consequence of the commission of an offence.[319]

Searching a suspect's property

At common law, the legality of searches of a person's property was doubtful. In *Ghani v Jones*,[320] police officers investigating a woman's disappearance, searched, without a warrant, her father-in-law's house. At the request of the police, passports and documents were handed over. When the return of the passports was requested, the police refused. The plaintiffs then brought an action for an order to deliver up the passports, an injunction restraining their detention and damages. Lord Denning MR, while recognising that an individual's privacy was 'not to be invaded except for the most compelling reasons', nevertheless ruled that the police had not acted unlawfully. Where no one had been arrested, the police were justified in taking an article if, first, 'there were reasonable grounds for believing that a serious offence had been committed'; secondly, that there were reasonable grounds 'for believing that the article in question is either a fruit of the crime ... or is the instruments by which the crime was committed ... or is material evidence to prove the commission of the crime'; thirdly, the police must reasonably believe that the person in possession of the article has 'himself committed the crime, or is implicated in it, or is accessory to it, or at any rate his refusal must be quite unreasonable'; fourthly, the police must not keep the article longer than reasonably necessary; and finally, the 'lawfulness of the conduct of the police must be judged at the time, and not by what happens afterwards.' This decision tipped the balance very much in favour of the powers of the police, to the detriment of individual citizens. However, in *Jeffrey v Black*,[321] where the defendant was arrested for allegedly stealing a sandwich, and the police subsequently searched his home and found drugs, the court ruled that, whereas the search might have been lawful if the police were looking for evidence connected with the theft, it was unlawful to search for evidence of

---

318 PACE 1984, s 32(4), (5).
319 *Ibid*, s 32(8), (9).
320 [1969] 3 All ER 1700.
321 [1978] 1 All ER 555.

another offence. In *McLorie v Oxford*,[322] the court disapproved of lenient attitudes to police searches. Lord Justice Donaldson confirmed that there was no common law right to enter into a dwelling house to search for 'the instruments of crime, even of serious crime'.

Police powers to enter into property other than after arrest

At common law, the police have no right to enter into private property without a warrant. Accordingly, if they so enter and are asked to leave – even where reasonable force is used to evict them – the police are not acting in the execution of their duty and an individual cannot be convicted for assaulting a police officer executing his duty.[323] There are a number of conditions under which a police officer might enter property, each of which is founded on the basis of a 'lawful excuse'. In the absence of a lawful excuse for entry, the police committed a trespass. At common law, entry was lawful to prevent a breach of the peace,[324] or in the case of actions designed to save life or prevent injury. Under the Criminal Law Act 1967, there was statutory power to enter premises in order to execute an arrest.

In *Khazanchi v Faircharm Investments Ltd; McLeod v Butterwick*,[325] the Court of Appeal held that the police have no right to forcibly enter property for lawful purposes, even where the owner had previously consented to their entry, when the owner, not aware of the police's intention to visit at a particular time, locked his house on leaving.

The right to search premises under the Police and Criminal Evidence Act 1984

Under section 18, a police officer may enter premises of a person arrested for an arrestable offence and search for evidence of the offence for which he has been arrested or for related offences. There must be reasonable grounds for believing that the evidence is on the premises. Authorisation for the search must be given by a senior officer, and a written record of the grounds for the search and the evidence sought made. Under the Prevention of Terrorism Act (Temporary Provisions) Act 1989,[326] a senior police officer may authorise a

---

322 [1982] 3 WLR 423.
323 *Davis v Lisle* [1936] 2 KB 434.
324 See *Thomas v Sawkins* [1935] 2 KB 249, above.
325 (1998) *The Times*, 25 March
326 See, further, Chapter 23.

search if there are reasonable grounds for believing that the case is 'one of great emergency' and that in the 'interests of the State, immediate action is necessary'.[327] Powers of entry, search and seizure are also granted under the Police Act 1997, on which, see Chapter 23.

[327] Prevention of Terrorism (Temporary Provisions) Act 1989, Sched 7, para 7(1). See, now, Terrorism Act 2000, discussed on Chapter 23.

CHAPTER 21

CITIZENSHIP, IMMIGRATION AND EXTRADITION[1]

INTRODUCTION

The concept of citizenship is fundamental to the question of rights of residence and freedom of movement of the individual. Historically, at common law, any individual lawfully within the realm owed a duty of allegiance to the Crown, in return for which the Crown owed a duty of protection to the individual.[2] This reciprocal relationship, in the eighteenth century, came to be dubbed the social contract under which citizens conceded power to government to rule, the government holding its powers as a trustee of the individual's rights and freedoms.[3] The Crown had the right to control rights of entry to the country, and the duty to protect the country's borders. Being an island, from a historical point of view, the task of controlling the external boundaries of the State was a relatively easy matter.

The Magna Carta of 1215 recognised the right of merchants, other than those from enemy countries in time of war, to enter, leave, stay and travel in England.[4] The Magna Carta also expressed the right of other individuals who owed allegiance to the King, to enter, leave and re-enter the realm.[5] In times of emergency, the King could prevent persons from leaving the realm.[6] Classes of persons could be denied entry and those already present ordered to leave the land, where their remaining constituted a perceived threat to the 'public good'. In 1530, for example, a statute[7] provided that Gypsies could no longer

---

1 See Macdonald, IA and Blake, NJ, *Macdonald's Immigration Law and Practice*, 4th edn, 1997, London: Butterworths; Dummett, A and Nichol, A, *Subjects, Citizens, Aliens and Others – Nationality and Immigration Law*, 1990, London: Weidenfeld & Nicolson; Supperstone, M and Cavanagh, J, *Immigration*, 3rd edn, 1994, London: Longman.

2 See Chitty, J, *Law of the Prerogatives of the Crown*, 1820, London: Butterworths.

3 See Locke, J, *Two Treatises on Government* (1960) 1977, London: JM Dent; Paine, T, *Rights of Man* (1791, Pt I), 1984, rep 1998, Collins, H (ed), New York: Penguin; Rousseau, J, *The Social Contract and Discourses* (1762), 1977, London: JM Dent.

4 Chapter 41.

5 Excepting those who had been lawfully convicted, or outlawed, or who were enemy aliens: Chapter 42. The right to leave one's country is an international law right under the International Covenant on Civil and Political Rights, Art 12(2), which provides that 'everyone shall be free to leave any country, including his own'. The making of exclusion orders against suspected terrorists under the Prevention of Terrorism Acts, which confines that person to his own country, violates that international law right. See, further, Chapter 23.

6 Under the prerogative writ of *ne exeat regno*.

7 An Act concerning outlandifh People, calling themfelves Egyptians.

enter the country and, in 1547, statute provided that Gypsies over the age of 14 born in England had one month in which to leave the realm.[8] In the Victorian era, immigration was legally uncontrolled. From the 1880s, large numbers of East European Jews fleeing from persecution entered the country, and a political campaign for restrictions to be introduced resulted in the enactment of the Aliens Act 1905. Not all aliens were barred, and controls were aimed at those arriving at certain ports and travelling on the cheapest class of ticket. The Act also introduced power to curb the entry of certain groups – powers which were on one occasion used to restrict entry of Chinese and Gypsy people. The aliens inspectorate was the forerunner to the immigration service, and came under the control of the Home Office. The First World War marked a tightening of immigration control under the Aliens Restriction Act 1914 and the Defence of the Realm Acts. From 1919, all aliens were subject to controls on entry. The Aliens Restriction (Amendment) Act 1919 confirmed the restrictions and remained in force until 1973.

With the expansion of the British Empire, the status of British subject was conferred on all citizens within the Empire. With the growth in independence of formerly dependent territories, the newly independent States exerted their own right to control nationality and immigration. In 1948, the British Nationality Act created a new classification – that of citizens of the United Kingdom and Colonies. All such citizens, and citizens of other Commonwealth nations, became British subjects or Commonwealth citizens, and enjoyed the same rights of entry and residence into the United Kingdom. These extensive rights to enter and reside were, by the 1960s, put under great strain as increasing numbers of overseas subjects sought to enter and reside in the United Kingdom. The Commonwealth Immigration Acts of 1962 and 1968 imposed restrictions on entry. Discrimination entered into the law.[9] Under the Commonwealth Immigrants Act 1962, controls were introduced which distinguished between the rights of entry of citizens from Commonwealth countries who had familial and ancestral links with the United Kingdom and those who did not. The 1968[10] Act further tightened rights of immigration, limiting the rights of entry of those who had no parental or grandparental links with the United Kingdom. The Immigration Act 1971 further distinguished between subjects who were free to enter the United Kingdom and those who needed permission to enter. The 1971 Act, which came into force on 1 January 1973, also provided the criteria for rights of residence in the United Kingdom. Under the Act, the distinction between aliens and

---

8   The Act of Elizabeth 1547. See Barnett, H, 'The end of the road for gypsies?' (1995) 24 Anglo-American L Rev 133.

9   See Martin, I, 'Racism in immigration law and practice', in Wallington, P (ed), *Civil Liberties*, 1984, Oxford: Martin Robertson, pp 245–57.

10 The Act was regarded as racially discriminatory by the European Commission on Human Rights: the *East African Asian* cases (1973) 3 EHRR 76. See, further, Chapter 22.

Commonwealth citizens was reduced, and the important distinction became between those with rights of abode in the United Kingdom and others, whether aliens or Commonwealth immigrants, who were subject to immigration control and required permission to enter and remain. Also in 1973, the United Kingdom became a member of the European Communities, now the European Community and Union, and distinctions arose between the rights of citizens of Member States of the Community and citizens from non-EC countries. Section 1 of the Act lays down general principles. Section 1(1) of the Immigration Act 1971 provides that:

> All those who are in this Act expressed to have the right of abode in the United Kingdom shall be free to live in, and to come and go into and from, the United Kingdom without let or hindrance except such as may be required under and in accordance with this Act to enable their right to be established or as may be otherwise lawfully imposed on any person.

Section 2 of the 1971 Act stipulates who has the right of abode. A person has a right of abode in the United Kingdom if (a) he is a British citizen; or (b) he is a Commonwealth citizen who (i) immediately before the commencement of the British Nationality Act 1981 was a Commonwealth citizen having the right of abode in the United Kingdom by virtue of section 2(1)(d) or section 2(2) of this Act as then in force; and (ii) he has not ceased to be a Commonwealth citizen in the meanwhile.

The 1971 Act also created the status of patriality and non-patriality – non-patrials having lesser rights of entry than patrials. The classification scheme was complex and much criticised. One consequence of the concept was that some Commonwealth and United Kingdom citizens were not conferred a right of entry by virtue of patriality, notwithstanding that they had no other country to go to. In particular, in relation to East African Asians, the rules worked harshly, and resulted in condemnation by the Court of Human Rights on the basis that it represented degrading treatment contrary to Article 3 of the European Convention on Human Rights.[11]

The need to bring the law relating to nationality and immigration law into conformity led to the Immigration Act 1981. Immigration law was substantially reformed by the British Nationality Act 1971, with a tightening of the rules on rights of appeal against deportation orders and making it a criminal offence to overstay leave to enter.[12] It is also from the Immigration Act 1981 that current citizenship status flows. The Act replaced the former categories of citizenship of the United Kingdom and Colonies with three

---

11 The *East African Asian* cases (1973) 3 EHRR 76. The matter was referred to the Committee of Ministers which failed to reach a decision by the required two-thirds majority.

12 The problems caused by refugees seeking to enter and remain in the United Kingdom led to further reforms under the Asylum and Immigration Appeals Act 1993 and the Asylum and Immigration Act 1996, both of which have, in turn, been substantially reformed by the Immigration and Asylum Act 1999.

classes of persons: British citizenship, British Dependent Territories citizenship and British Overseas citizenship. In addition to these categories, there exists the status of British National (Overseas) citizens, Commonwealth citizens, and citizens of the European Union.

BRITISH CITIZENSHIP

British citizenship may be acquired by birth, adoption, descent, registration or naturalisation.

Birth

A legitimate child born in the United Kingdom, one of whose parents is a British citizen or is 'settled'[13] in the United Kingdom at the time of its birth assumes British citizenship. A child born outside marriage acquires citizenship through his or her mother, unless the child is legitimated by the subsequent marriage of his or her parents. Prior to the 1981 Act, any person (with minor exceptions) born in the United Kingdom became a British citizen.

Adoption and legitimation

A child[14] adopted by a British citizen becomes a British citizen from the date of the adoption order. Where the adopters are married, the child becomes a British citizen provided that one of the adoptive parents is a citizen. A child born out of wedlock and subsequently legitimated by the marriage of his or her parents shall be treated as legitimate for the purposes of the British Nationality Act 1981.[15]

Descent

A child born outside the United Kingdom becomes a citizen if one of his or her parents is a British citizen, provided that that parent has not also acquired citizenship through descent. Where the child is born to a parent who acquired citizenship through descent, the child will only acquire citizenship if the parent is an employee of the Crown, or other designated services.[16]

---

13 Being ordinarily resident in the United Kingdom and not subject to restrictions on the time a person may remain under immigration law: Immigration Act 1971, s 50(2).

14 Under the age of 18 years: Family Law Reform Act 1969.

15 British Nationality Act 1981, s 47.

16 *Ibid*, ss 14 and 2(1)(b), (c).

In *R v Secretary of State for the Home Department ex parte Rahman*,[17] the Court of Appeal ruled that, where a court had to establish the truth relating to a precedent fact on which the Secretary of State formed the opinion that a person had entered the country by deception and was an illegal entrant, the court was entitled to take into account all the material on which the decision maker had relied, even though that might be hearsay. The onus was on the Secretary of State to establish, to a level of proof appropriate to a crime in civil proceedings, that the person was an illegal entrant. On the facts, by a majority, the court ruled that the Secretary of State had done so.

Registration

After a period of residence in the United Kingdom, a person may acquire citizenship through residence. Children born in the United Kingdom, who are not automatically entitled to citizenship through birth, have a right to be registered as citizens at the age of 10 years, provided that the child has not been absent from the United Kingdom for more than 90 days in each of the first 10 years.[18] A child is also entitled to registration if one of his or her parents acquires citizenship or becomes settled in the United Kingdom during his or her minority.[19] British Dependent Territories citizens, British Overseas citizens and British Protected Persons[20] resident for five years in the United Kingdom are also entitled to registration.[21] The Home Secretary has a general discretion to register any child as a British citizen.[22]

Naturalisation

Persons not covered by the provisions of the 1981 British Nationality Act may acquire citizenship through naturalisation. A five year residence period is a precondition for applying for naturalisation, which is granted at the discretion of the Home Secretary. The Home Secretary, in deciding whether to grant naturalisation must be satisfied that the applicant is of 'good character', has a command of the English, Welsh or Gaelic language, and intends to have his or her principal residence in the United Kingdom, unless employed in a designated form of employment as specified in the Act.[23] Naturalisation may

---

17 [1997] 3 WLR 990.
18 British Nationality Act 1981, s 1(4).
19 *Ibid*, s 1(3).
20 A British Protected Person is one so declared by Order in Council or by virtue of the Soloman Islands Act 1978.
21 British Nationality Act 1981, s 4.
22 *Ibid*, s 3(1).
23 *Ibid*, s 6(1) and Sched 1.

also confer citizenship on the spouse of a British citizen.[24] Where citizenship is conferred through naturalisation, the Home Secretary's decision is final and is not subject to appeal.[25]

BRITISH DEPENDENT TERRITORIES CITIZENSHIP

Part II of the 1981 British Nationality Act governs Dependent Territories[26] citizenship. A person may acquire citizenship through birth, adoption, descent, registration as a minor or naturalisation, concepts which follow the same formula as that discussed above.[27]

The Falkland Islands

The British Nationality (Falkland Islands) Act 1983 confers British citizenship on persons born in the Falklands to parents who are settled there.

Hong Kong

The Hong Kong Act 1985 created the status of British Nationals (Overseas) for Hong Kong citizens after the transfer of sovereignty from the United Kingdom to China in 1997. Under the British Nationality (Hong Kong) Act 1990, the Home Secretary could confer citizenship on up to 50,000 Hong Kong residents, nominated by the Governor of Hong Kong, to enable them to live in the United Kingdom in the future if they wish to leave Hong Kong after the transfer of power.[28]

British overseas citizenship

Any person who was a citizen of the United Kingdom and Colonies immediately before the commencement of the Act, and who does not become

---

24 British Nationality Act 1981, s 6(2) and Sched 1.

25 *Ibid*, s 44(2).

26 Dependent Territories are Anguilla, Bermuda, British Antarctic Territory, British Indian Ocean Territory, Cayman Islands, Falkland Islands and Dependencies, Gibraltar, Montserrat, Pitcairn, Henderson, Ducie and Oeno Islands, St Christopher and Nevis, St Helena and Dependencies, the Sovereign Base areas of Akrotiri and Dhekelia (Cyprus), Turks and Caicos Islands, Virgin Islands: *ibid*, Sched 6.

27 *Ibid*, ss 15, 16, 17, 18.

28 British Nationality (Hong Kong) (Selection Scheme) Order 1990 SI 1990/14. The British Nationality (Hong Kong) Act 1997 provides that the Secretary of State shall on application register as a British citizen any person who was ordinarily resident in Hong Kong and satisfied certain conditions immediately before 4 February 1997.

either a British citizen or British Dependent Territories citizen by virtue of the Act, becomes a British Overseas citizen. Overseas citizenship may otherwise be acquired through registration during a child's minority[29] and registration through marriage.[30]

COMMONWEALTH CITIZENSHIP

Every person who is a British citizen, British Dependent Territories citizen, a British Overseas citizen or a British subject, or is a subject in a country listed in Schedule 3,[31] has the status of a Commonwealth citizen.[32]

EUROPEAN UNION CITIZENSHIP

The Treaty on European Union 1992, as amended by the Treaty on European Union 1997 (TEU), confers Union citizenship on the citizens of all Member States.[33] Under the 1992 Treaty, asylum policy, immigration, control over external borders and policies relating to nationals of third countries, was one of the designated areas of common interest between Member States, and fell within the Justice and Home Affairs pillar.[34] Member States were under a duty to co-operate in these matters, and to act in compliance with the European Convention on Human Rights and the 1951 Convention on the Status of Refugees. There was common agreement that the working of third pillar of the Union structure – Justice and home Affairs – was unsatisfactory. As a result, under the Treaty on European Union 1997 (the Treaty of Amsterdam), as discussed in Chapter 8, all issues relating to the free movement of persons within the Union, including asylum, visas and immigration, have now been placed under Community law and its law making processes, while issues relating to crime and the police remain in the Justice and Home Affairs pillar.

---

29 British Nationality Act 1981, s 27.

30 *Ibid*, s 28.

31 Antigua and Barbuda, Australia, Bahamas, Bangladesh, Barbados, Canada, Republic of Cyprus, Dominica, Fiji, The Gambia, Ghana, Grenada, Guyana, India, Jamaica, Kenya, Kiribati, Lesotho, Malawi, Malaysia, Malta, Mauritius, Nauru, New Zealand, Nigeria, Papua New Guinea, Saint Lucia, Saint Vincent and the Grenadines, Seychelles, Sierra Leone, Singapore, Solomon Islands, Sri Lanka, Swaziland, Tanzania, Tonga, Trinidad and Tobago, Tuvalu, Uganda, Vanuatu, Western Samoa, Zambia, Zimbabwe.

32 British Nationality Act 1981, s 36.

33 See, further, Chapter 8. Note that the TEU 1997 renumbers all the EC Treaty Articles. Both the former and current Article numbers are given in the text.

34 It was thus outside the European Community structure. On the distinction, see, further, Chapter 8.

Freedom of movement and rights of establishment are a central feature of the European Union and Community. The elimination of border controls between Member States – which the United Kingdom government is currently resisting – further extends the freedom of movement for persons within the territorial boundaries of the European Union.

Article 4(4) of Council Directive of 1968, on the abolition of restrictions on movement and residence within the European Community for workers of Member States and their families[35] provides that:

> A member of the family who is not a national of a member state shall be issued with a residence document which shall have the same validity as that issued to the worker on whom he is dependent.

The Treaty on European Union 1992 (the Maastricht Treaty), Article B, introduced the concept of European citizenship. This is reaffirmed in Article 2 of the Treaty on European Union 1997 (the Amsterdam Treaty), which states that, among the objectives of the Union, is the aim to:

> ... to strengthen the protection of the rights and interests of national of its Member States through the introduction of a citizenship of the Union.

Part 2 of the revised EC Treaty provides that:

> Article 17 (formerly, Article 8)
>
> Citizenship of the Union is hereby established. Every person holding the nationality of a Member State shall be a citizen of the Union. Citizenship of the Union shall complement and not replace national citizenship.
>
> Citizens of the Union shall enjoy the rights conferred by this Treaty and shall be subject to the duties imposed thereby.
>
> Article 18 (formerly, Article 8a)
>
> Every citizen of the Union shall have the right to move and reside freely within the territory of the Member States, subject to the limitations and conditions laid down in this Treaty and by the measures adopted to give it effect.

In addition to rights of residence, every citizen of the Union has the right to stand as a candidate and to vote in municipal elections in the Member State in which he or she resides,[36] and to stand as a candidate and vote in elections for the European Parliament.[37] Union citizens are entitled to protection from the diplomatic or consular authorities of any Member State.[38] Citizens of the Union have the right to petition the European Parliament under Article 194 of

---

35 68/360/EEC (OJ Special English edn, 11, 1968, p 485), as amended by Dec 95/1/EC (OJ L1/1, 1995).

36 EC Treaty, Art 19 (formerly, Art 8b).

37 *Ibid*, Art 19 (formerly, Art 8b).

38 *Ibid*, Art 20 (formerly, Art 8c).

the Treaty, and have the right also to apply to the European Union Ombudsman under Article 195.[39]

The free movement of persons provisions under the EC Treaty founded the basis for the development of the idea of European citizenship. The ideas of free movement of persons and rights of establishment within the common market were essentially linked to the economic aspects of the Community. The concept of citizenship now adopted under the TEU is far broader than this, and reflects the wider political and social union which is aspired to. The Commission has the duty to develop further the concept of citizenship and to report to the European Parliament, and the Council on developments. The Council has the power to adopt the proposals of the Commission, following consultation with the European Parliament, and acting unanimously, which the Council will recommend for adoption by Member States.

HUMAN RIGHTS AND THE EUROPEAN COMMUNITY[40]

Under the Schengen Agreement of 1985–95, several Member States agreed to remove all forms of border controls between their countries. This agreement is now formally incorporated, under the Treaty on European Union 1997, into the EC Treaty.[41] In respect of the United Kingdom and Ireland, however, opt outs have been negotiated, in order to allow these Member States to preserve border controls, in light of their particular geographical characteristics.[42]

Although Article 8 confers citizenship, and the EC Treaty provides for the free movement of workers and rights of establishment, this does not give an unqualified right for residents of other Member States to enter and remain in the United Kingdom. In *R v Secretary of State for the Home Department ex parte Vitale*,[43] for example, the Court of Appeal ruled that it was clear from the case law of the European Court of Justice that Article 48 of the EC Treaty (now, Article 39), which confers freedom of movement for work, does not confer unlimited freedom in relation to residence. Article 48 (now, Article 39) protects those who are actively seeking work, and a Member State is justified in requiring the person to leave the country where he had been unsuccessful in securing employment for six months, unless he could demonstrate that he

---

39 EC Treaty, Art 21 (formerly, Art 8d).

40 The literature is extensive. In the context of the Convention and the European Union, see Twomey, PM, 'The European Union: three pillars without a human rights foundation', in O'Keefe, D and Twomey, PM (eds), *Legal Issues in the Maastricht Treaty*, 1994, London: Chancery, Chapter 8. See, also, Lenaerts, K, 'Fundamental rights to be included in the Community catalogue' (1991) 16 EL Rev 367.

41 See, further, Chapter 8.

42 Special arrangements also exist in relation to Denmark.

43 (1996) *The Times*, 26 January.

was actively continuing to seek employment, and that he had a real chance of being engaged. The Treaty on European Union had not affected that legal position.

Further, in *Sahota v Secretary of State for the Home Department; Zeghraba v Same*,[44] on appeal by the Secretary of State against decisions of the Immigration Appeal Tribunal granting indefinite leave to remain in the United Kingdom to Sahota and Zeghraba, the Court of Appeal ruled that a person who was not a citizen of a Member State of the European Community but was married to a British citizen, was not entitled under Community law to the same rights of residence in the United Kingdom as those enjoyed by his spouse under UK law when they returned to live and work in the United Kingdom.

The wives of the applicants were British citizens, with rights of abode in the United Kingdom and citizens of the European Community. In 1989, Mrs Sahota exercised her rights under Article 48 of the EC Treaty and went to live and work in Germany. There she married the applicant, an Indian citizen. Mr Zeghraba, an Algerian citizen, had twice been removed from the United Kingdom. While in the United Kingdom on a false passport, he entered into a marriage under Islamic law. He and his wife returned to Algeria. On their return to the United Kingdom, the applicant applied for indefinite leave to remain as the husband of an EC worker exercising her right of free movement.

The Court of Appeal ruled that spouses of United Kingdom citizens did not on marriage automatically become entitled to identical rights. Their entry into the UK was subject to immigration controls. The rights under Community law were not to be amalgamated with those which arose under domestic law within the territory of Member States for their own nationals and spouses. National law continued to distinguish between British citizens with a right of abode and citizens of the Community exercising Community rights. The Secretary of State's appeal was allowed.

The distinction between entry into the United Kingdom under Community law and national rights of residence was also considered, by the Court of Appeal, in *Boukssid v Secretary of State for the Home Department*.[45] In that case, the spouse of a British citizen had been admitted under Community law. Whereas, under national law, she would have had a right to indefinite leave to remain, that was not the position when she had entered the United Kingdom under Community law. Counsel for the applicant argued that, provided the applicant had entered the country lawfully, the basis on which she had entered was irrelevant. Further, he argued that the length of residency requirements which applied to the applicant, but not to a national, were

---

44 (1997) *The Times*, 30 April.
45 (1998) *The Times*, 6 March.

discriminatory and contrary to Article 6 of the EC Treaty (now, Article 12). Both arguments were rejected.

Rights of entry and residence

Rights of entry and residence are inextricably linked to the question of citizenship. The United Nations' International Covenant on Civil and Political Rights, to which the United Kingdom is a signatory, provides that 'No one shall be arbitrarily deprived of the right to enter his own country'.[46] The United Kingdom entered a reservation in respect of this broadly phrased right under international law, by which it reserved the right to 'continue to apply such immigration legislation governing entry into, stay in and departure from the United Kingdom' as it deems necessary.[47]

Establishing the right to enter

The holding of a valid British passport identifying that person as a British citizen or as a citizen of the United Kingdom and Colonies having the right of abode in the United Kingdom, or travel document of a European Union Member State entitles the holder to entry. Passports may be issued by the Passport Agency for a full 10 year period, or for a lesser period, or a British visitor's passport may be issued. Full passports are only issued once the Passport Agency is satisfied as to the accuracy of the application and supporting documentation. Section 3 of the Immigration Act 1971, as amended by the British Nationality Act 1981 and the Immigration and Asylum Act 1999, provides that:

> (8) When any question arises under this Act whether or not a person is a British citizen ... it shall lie on the person asserting it to prove that he is.

> (9) A person seeking to enter the United Kingdom and claiming to have the right of abode there shall prove that he has that right by means of either:

>> (a) a United Kingdom passport describing him as a British citizen or as a citizen of the United Kingdom and Colonies having the right of abode in the United Kingdom; or

>> (b) a certificate of entitlement issued by or on behalf of the government of the United Kingdom certifying that he has such a right of abode.

The holding of a passport, however, is not conclusive proof of the right to enter. Where as passport has been obtained as a result of fraud, or theft, then an immigration officer who suspects that this is the case is entitled to require that the passport holder substantiate his or her claim to be the legitimate

---

46 United Nations' International Covenant on Civil and Political Rights, Art 12(4).
47 Reservation of 20 May 1976.

holder of the passport. In these situations, therefore, the burden of proof as to identity rests with the passport holder. However, where the Passport Agency has indisputably issued a passport to the holder, albeit one of a limited duration, the issue arises – should a dispute occur over the matter – as to where the burden of proof lies over the issue of the validity of that passport and the right of its holder to enter. A British Visitor's passport is distinguishable from a full passport, albeit of limited duration. A visitor's passport does not qualify for section 3(9) purposes.[48]

The issue was tested in the Queen's Bench Division in *R v Home Secretary ex parte Obi*.[49] In *Obi*, the passport agency had issued a passport limited to six month's duration. When he applied for a renewal of the passport, he was arrested and served with a notice directed to him as an illegal immigrant, on the basis that, notwithstanding the passport, the Secretary of State was not satisfied that the applicant was Obi, and that the onus of proof of identity, once queried, lay with the applicant to prove that he was the person whom the passport described as a British citizen. The applicant sought judicial review of the Home Secretary's decision. The issue was one of precedent fact.[50] However, Sedley J ruled that the most important question which fell for answer was the question as to who was under the duty to satisfy the burden of proof: the applicant or the Home Secretary:

> ... the principal question I have to decide is, however, one of pure law: is it for the Secretary of State to satisfy the court that the applicant is an illegal entrant or for the applicant to satisfy the court that he is not?[51]

Sedley J ruled that on the balance of probabilities in light of the evidence as to identity of the applicant, and the evidence which the applicant refused to disclose, the applicant had not proven that he was the person for whom the passport had been issued. However, that finding was not determinative of the issue. The Secretary of State was unable to discharge the burden of proof which the statute placed upon him, showing that the passport issued, naming him as Mr Obi and describing him as a British citizen, does not entitle him to a right of abode. The application for judicial review accordingly succeeded.

Rights of entry and abode: immigration policy and citizenship status

Immigration, asylum and deportation law is a complex web of statutes, with Acts of Parliament being enacted in piecemeal fashion and no attempt being made to consolidate the law in a manageable, comprehensive form. The

---

48 *Minta v Secretary of State for the Home Department* [1992] Imm AR 380.

49 [1997] 1 WLR 1498.

50 On which, see, further, Chapter 25.

51 [1997] 1 WLR 1498, p 1499.

Immigration Act 1971, Immigration Act 1988, Asylum and Immigration Appeals Act 1993, the Asylum and Immigration Act 1996 and the Immigration and Asylum Act 1999 are the Immigration Acts regulating the area. In order to determine rights of entry for other than British citizens and others referred to above, it is necessary to consider immigration law and policy in light of citizenship status to which the policy is linked.

Immigration policy

The first modern statutory control over immigration was provided by the Aliens Act 1905, which permitted the refusal of entry to persons regarded as 'undesirable'. By the Commonwealth Immigrants Act 1962, more favourable treatment was given to descendants of white immigrants than to citizens of the New Commonwealth.[52] The Immigration Act 1971, as amended,[53] together with the Immigration Rules, provides the structure of immigration law. Rights of entry are determined by citizenship status under the British Nationality Act 1981. As noted above, section 1 of the Immigration Act 1971 provides that those who 'have a right of abode shall be free to live in, and to come and go into and from, the United Kingdom without let or hindrance' subject to restrictions enabling their status to be determined.[54] Those who do not have the right of abode, may live, work and settle in the United Kingdom 'by permission and subject to such regulation and control of their entry into, stay in and departure from the United Kingdom'.[55]

A person who has the right of abode is a person who is a British citizen, or a Commonwealth citizen who was a Commonwealth citizen having the right of abode immediately before the commencement of the British Nationality Act 1981, and who has not ceased meanwhile to be a Commonwealth citizen.[56] Where a person is not a British citizen (or a Commonwealth citizen as defined above), a person 'shall not enter the United Kingdom unless given leave to do so under this Act'.[57] Leave may be given to enter the United Kingdom either for a limited period or for an indefinite period.[58] Where limited leave is given for entry into the United Kingdom, the leave may be subject to conditions restricting an individual's right of employment or occupation, or requirements to register with the police, or both.[59] The leave to enter may be

---

52 See Evans, JM, *Immigration Law*, 1983, London: Sweet & Maxwell, p 3.
53 By the British Nationality Act 1981.
54 Immigration Act 1971, s 1(1).
55 *Ibid*, s 1(2).
56 *Ibid*, s 2.
57 *Ibid*, s 3.
58 *Ibid*, s 3(1)(b).
59 *Ibid*, s 3(1)(c).

varied. The leave may be restricted or enlarged, or added to by varying or revoking conditions.[60]

The general provision relating to regulation and control is section 3 of the Immigration Act 1971, as amended, which provides in part that:

(1) Except as otherwise provided by or under this Act, where is person is not [a British citizen]:

   (a) he shall not enter the United Kingdom unless given leave to do so in accordance with this Act;

   (b) he may be given leave to enter the United Kingdom (or, when already there, leave to remain in the United Kingdom) either for a limited or for an indefinite period;

   (c) if he is given limited leave to enter or remain in the United Kingdom, it may be given subject to all or any of the following conditions, namely –

      (i) a condition restricting his employment or occupation in the United Kingdom;

      (ii) a condition requiring him to maintain and accommodate himself, and any dependants of his, without recourse to public funds; and

      (iii) a condition requiring him to register with the police.

The Home Secretary has the power to lay down rules for the regulation of entry and stay in the United Kingdom, and these must be laid before Parliament. The rules are subject to nullification by Parliament within 40 days of being laid.

Section 3(5) of the 1971 Act, as amended by the Immigration and Asylum Act 1999,[61] provides that a person who is not a British citizen is liable to deportation from the United Kingdom if:

   (a) the Secretary of State deems his deportation to be conducive to the public good; or

   (b) another person to whose family he belongs is or has been ordered to be deported.

Where a person is given leave to enter and remain, that leave may be indefinite or limited. Where it is limited, that leave may be varied, whether by restricting, enlarging or removing the limit on its duration, or by adding, varying or revoking conditions.[62] The Immigration and Asylum Act 1999 makes further provision in relation to the giving, refusing or varying of leave to enter the United Kingdom, and the Secretary of State may make orders by statutory instrument which must be laid before Parliament and approved by a resolution of each House. Provision may be made for leave to be given or refused before a person arrives in the United Kingdom, for the manner or

---

60 Immigration Act 1971, s 3(3).
61 Sched 14, para 44.
62 Immigration Act 1971, s 3(3).

form in which leave may be given, refused or varied, for the imposition of conditions, and that a person's leave to enter not lapse on his leaving the common travel area (as per section 3 of the 1971 Act).[63] The Secretary of State also has power to make statutory instruments, subject to parliamentary approval, regulating leave to remain in the United Kingdom, including the form or manner in which leave may be given, refused or varied, the imposition of conditions and providing that a person's leave to remain does not lapse on his leaving the common travel area.[64]

The Immigration Act 1971, as amended, created a number of criminal offences relating to immigration matters. Under the Act, it is a criminal offence to enter the country illegally;[65] to fail to observe conditions of leave; to assist illegal immigrants; or to obtain leave to remain by deception. A person who is not a British citizen is liable for deportation from the United Kingdom if he or she has a limited leave to enter does and not observe conditions attached, or remains beyond the time limited by the leave, or if the Secretary of State deems his deportation to be conducive to the public good, or if a member of his or her family has been ordered to be deported.[66] A person may also be deported if, when over the age of 17, he is convicted of an offence for which he is punishable by imprisonment, and on conviction, there is a recommendation by the court for deportation.[67] The Act provides that any person claiming entitlement to British citizenship bears the onus of proof that he is a citizen.[68] Such proof may be established either by the production of a British passport, or a certificate of entitlement certifying that a person has a right of abode issued by, or on behalf of, the government of the United Kingdom.[69]

The powers to control immigration are under the responsibility of the Home Secretary, but, in practice, are entrusted to immigration officers. Powers to give leave to remain in the United Kingdom, or to vary conditions of leave, are exercisable by the Secretary of State.[70] Deportation orders are the responsibility of the Secretary of State for the Home Office (the Home Secretary). The effect of a deportation order is to invalidate any leave to enter

---

63 Immigration and Asylum Act 1999, s 1, inserting s 3A into the 1971 Act.
64 *Ibid*, s 2, inserting s 3B into the 1971 Act.
65 Under the Asylum and Immigration Act 1996, s 5, it is a criminal offence to assist the entry of asylum claimants, other than for employment purposes by an organisation for the assistance of refugees.
66 Immigration Act 1971, s 5.
67 *Ibid*, ss 3(6) and 6.
68 *Ibid*, s 3(8).
69 *Ibid*, s 3(9).
70 *Ibid*, s 4.

or remain in the United Kingdom.[71] A deportation order may be made against members of a deportee's family, but shall not be made against a family member if eight weeks have elapsed since the deportee left the country, or if a person has ceased to be a member of the deportee's family.[72] The making of a deportation order while a claim for asylum is outstanding is invalid.[73]

Commonwealth citizens, or citizens of the Republic of Ireland who were ordinarily resident in the United Kingdom at the time the Act came into force are not liable to deportation, provided that they have remained ordinarily resident in the United Kingdom or British Islands since the Act came into force, or have for the five years previous to the Secretary of State's decision been resident in the United Kingdom and Islands, or upon conviction for an offence, if they have been ordinarily resident for the previous five years.[74]

Appeals against immigration decisions and deportation orders

The immigration appeal structure was established by the Immigration Appeals Act 1969, and now falls under the Immigration Act 1971. Adjudicators are appointed by the Lord Chancellor. Above the adjudicators is the Immigration Appeal Tribunal, whose President is a lawyer of not less than seven years' standing. Members of the Tribunal, which sits in two divisions, each having three members, are also appointed by the Lord Chancellor.[75] The system is subject to the supervision of the Council on Tribunals. Before 1993, there was no further right of appeal against the decision of the Immigration Appeal Tribunal, although judicial review proceedings were available. Section 9 of the Asylum and Immigration Appeals Act 1993 provides a right of appeal on point of law, with leave, to the Court of Appeal or to the Scottish Court of Session. Additionally, the Home Secretary has the power to uphold or reverse a decision.

A person who has been refused leave to enter has a right of appeal to an adjudicator against the decision.[76] No right of appeal lies against a decision regarding leave to enter unless the person has a passport or certificate as required by section 3(9). Under the 1971 Act, no person had a right of appeal unless he was refused entry at a port of entry and at a time when he held a

---

71 Immigration Act 1971, s 5; the power to regulate entry into the United Kingdom under the Prevention of Terrorism Act is discussed below.

72 *Ibid*, s 5(3).

73 *R v Secretary of State for the Home Department, ex parte Sanusi* (1999) *The Times*, 6 January.

74 Immigration Act 1971, s 7.

75 In 1995–96, 136 adjudicators heard just under 21,000 cases, the Tribunal decided over 9,900 appeals: *Annual Report of the Council of Tribunals*, 1995–96, London: HMSO, p 105.

76 Immigration Act 1971, s 13(1).

current entry clearance.[77] A person entering the United Kingdom as a visitor, or as a student or as a dependent person is not entitled to appeal against a refusal of an entry clearance or against a refusal of leave to enter unless he held a current entry clearance at the time of the refusal.[78]

Appeals against conditions lie to an adjudicator. A person is not entitled to appeal against a variation of his leave which reduces its duration, or against any refusal to enlarge or remove the limits of its duration if the Secretary of State certifies that the person's departure from the United Kingdom would be 'to the public good'.[79] The adjudicator also has jurisdiction to hear appeals against deportation orders.[80] No deportation order shall be made while an appeal may be lodged, or while the appeal is pending.[81] The adjudicator may allow the appeal on the basis that a decision taken was not in accordance with the law, or with applicable immigration rules or, where the decision involved the exercise of discretion by the Home Secretary, the discretion has been improperly exercised.[82] Appeals against the decision of an adjudicator may be made to an Appeal Tribunal which may affirm the determination, or vary it.[83]

Extradition

Extradition is the means by which a fugitive from another country is returned to that country. The Extradition Act 1989[84] now governs the law. The law applies to all persons, irrespective of citizenship and extends extradition to all foreign countries, Commonwealth States and colonies. An exception exists in the relation to the Republic of Ireland, which is regulated by the Backing of Warrants (Republic of Ireland) Act 1965. Whereas deportation is at the instance of the Home Secretary, extradition is commenced by way of a request from another country to the United Kingdom's Home Secretary for the return of the person.[85] Only countries with whom a bilateral Treaty has been entered into, may request extradition. If the Home Secretary is satisfied as to the request, the matter is referred to a metropolitan stipendiary magistrate who

---

77 Immigration Act 1971, s 13(3).

78 *Ibid*, s 13(3A).

79 *Ibid*, s 14(3).

80 *Ibid*, s 15(1).

81 *Ibid*, s 15(2).

82 *Ibid*, s 19.

83 *Ibid*, s 20.

84 Formerly, the Criminal Justice Act 1988; and see the Green Paper, *Extradition*, Cmnd 9421, 1985, London: HMSO, and *Criminal Justice: Plans for Legislation*, Cmnd 9658, 1986, London: HMSO.

85 Extradition Act 1989, s 7.

may issue an arrest warrant.[86] On arrest, the person is brought before the magistrate for committal into the custody of the Home Secretary.[87]

An offence for which extradition may be ordered is one which, if committed in the United Kingdom, would carry a term of imprisonment of 12 months or more and carries the same punishment in the requesting State and where, if committed outside the United Kingdom, would amount to an extra-territorial offence against the United Kingdom or, in a case where the requesting State's jurisdiction is dependent upon the nationality of the offender, the offence would be an offence under the law of the United Kingdom.[88] No extradition may be granted for a purely political offence, or where the request for the return of the person is based on race, religion, nationality or political opinions.[89] The question of what amounts to a political offence is one for the court to determine, and the categories are not closed. However, terrorist acts will not be regarded as 'political offences'. The Suppression of Terrorism Act 1978 and the European Convention on the Suppression of Terrorism[90] aim to preclude terrorists pleading that their actions are political and, accordingly, offences for which extradition will be allowed include murder, kidnapping and the use of imitation firearms.

A person detained must be notified of his right to make representations to the Home Secretary as to why he should not be extradited. The detainee has the right to institute judicial review proceedings to test the lawfulness of the Home Secretary's decision, and may apply for habeas corpus to review the legality of his detention. If the decision is challenged unsuccessfully, the Home Secretary may extradite the person. If there are no legal proceedings undertaken, the person may be returned after 15 days from the date of committal. If the requesting State is not satisfied with the Home Secretary's decision not to commit the person, it may apply for a review.[91]

Extradition arrangements between the United Kingdom and the Republic of Ireland are governed by the Backing of Warrants (Republic of Ireland) Act 1965, which in part provides for an extradition order to be made where an offence has been committed in the Republic of Ireland which corresponds to an offence in the United Kingdom which is an indictable offence or punishable on summary conviction with imprisonment for six months. In *R v Governor of Belmarsh Prison ex parte Gilligan*,[92] the House of Lords, on an application for habeas corpus, ruled that the word 'correspond' in relation to

---

86 Extradition Act 1989, s 9.
87 *Ibid*, s 8.
88 *Ibid*, s 2.
89 *Ibid*, s 6(1).
90 See Cmnd 7031, 1977, London: HMSO.
91 Extradition Act 1989, s 11.
92 [1999] 3 WLR 1244.

relevant offences was not used in any technical sense and should be understood in its ordinary meaning. There was, on the facts, sufficient correspondence between charges of murder and of unlawful carnal knowledge. The meaning of the 'accused' in section 1 of the Extradition Act 1989 was also held not to be a term of art in *Re Ismail*.[93] The applicant had applied for habeas corpus challenging the decision to commit him on bail to await the Secretary of State's decision whether to extradite him to Germany. He argued that he was not an accused within the meaning of section 1 of the Extradition Act 1989. The House of Lords held that, given the differences between the criminal procedures of various countries and, in particular, between those of England and civil law countries, the word 'accused' should be given a broad, general and purposive construction. A person was accused of an extradition crime in a foreign State if the competent authorities there had commenced prosecution.

In *R v Bow Street Metropolitan Stipendiary Magistrate ex parte Government of the United States of America*,[94] the House of Lords considered the concept of an extradition crime. The Extradition Act 1989 preserved Orders in Council made under section 2 of the Extradition Act 1870, relating to giving effect to extradition treaties and the power to amend them. The Treaty between the United Kingdom and the United States provided, *inter alia*, for extradition for offences listed in the Schedule to the Treaty or any other offence if the offence was extraditable under the law of the United Kingdom. Section 15 of the Computer Misuse Act 1990 provided that extraditable offences included offences relating to computer crime, offences not listed in the Schedule to the Treaty. The House of Lords ruled that the 1990 Act clearly intended to make such offences extraditable for the purposes of the Order in Council giving effect to the Treaty, even though neither the Treaty nor the Order in Council had been amended.

The House of Lords also considered the scope of extradition crimes under the Extradition Act 1989 in *R v Bow Street Metropolitan Stipendiary Magistrate ex parte Pinochet Ugarte (No 3)*.[95] The applicant, the former president of the government junta of Chile from 1973 to 1974, and subsequently head of State of the Chilean Republic until 1980, had been subject to an international warrant for his arrest in respect of murder, genocide and terrorism, and the stipendiary magistrates had issued arrest warrants. On an application for judicial review, both warrants were quashed on the ground, *inter alia*, of sovereign immunity. The Commissioner of Police for the Metropolis and the Government of Spain appealed. Since the first hearing before the House of Lords, which was set aside on grounds of judicial bias,[96] the crimes alleged

---

93   [1998] 3 WLR 495.
94   [1999] 3 WLR 620.
95   [1999] 2 WLR 827.
96   See, further, Chapters 5 and 26.

had been widened to include offences allegedly committed before Pinochet became head of State. Counsel for the defence claimed that, irrespective of the issue of sovereign immunity, a number of the alleged offences were not extradition crimes. On that point, the House of Lords ruled that, under section 2 of the Extradition Act 1989, the alleged conduct had to be a crime in the United Kingdom at the time at which the crimes took place. Extraterritorial torture did not become an offence until September 1998 when section 134 of the Criminal Justice Act 1988 came into force. On sovereign immunity, the House of Lords ruled that, by section 20 of the State Immunity Act 1978, a former head of State enjoyed immunity for acts done in his official capacity, but that torture was an international crime against humanity for which there could be no immunity under customary international law, or there could be no immunity after December 1988 when the International Convention against Torture 1984 had been ratified by Chile, Spain and the United Kingdom.

THE ASYLUM AND IMMIGRATION ACTS 1996 AND 1999[97]

The 1996 Asylum and Immigration Act, according to the then Home Secretary, the Right Honourable Michael Howard, had three objectives, namely:

> First, to strengthen our asylum procedures so that bogus claims and appeals can be dealt with more quickly; secondly, to combat immigration racketeering through stronger powers, new offences and higher penalties; and, thirdly, to reduce economic incentives which attract people to come to this country in breach of our immigration laws.[98]

The Act was brought into force in 1996. The Act amended the administrative procedures for dealing with asylum and immigration as contained in the Immigration Act 1971 and the Asylum and Immigration Appeals Act 1993. The Act must be seen in light of developments within the European Union, and also in light of international law obligations under the United Nation's Convention Relating to the Status of Refugees 1951 and the Convention Against Torture, Cruel, Inhuman or Degrading Treatment 1981 and the European Convention on Human Rights and Fundamental Freedoms 1951.

As discussed in Chapter 8, protection of the borders of the United Kingdom from illegal immigrants is a major concern of the United Kingdom government. The Schengen Agreement and the Maastricht Treaty on European Union provide for the free movement of persons within the countries of the European Union without national controls. The 1996 Act is in

---

97 See the White Paper, *Fairer, Faster and Firmer – A Modern Approach to Immigration and Asylum*, 1998, Cm 4018, London: The Stationery Office.

98 *Hansard*, 11 December, 1995, Col 699.

part aimed at extending national controls, by providing safeguards for genuine refugees, and providing for appeals for those refused asylum before deportation, but expediting the processing of cases which represent bogus claims and tightening up on immigration racketeering.

THE IMMIGRATION AND ASYLUM ACT 1999[99]

The Labour government sought to reform the law in the face of substantial pressure imposed on the administrative system by escalating numbers of persons seeking asylum in the United Kingdom. The Home Secretary stated that the 1999 Act was intended to make the 'system fairer, faster and firmer'.[100] The 1999 Act makes provision covering most areas of immigration and asylum. The Act is intended to enable genuine travellers to enter more quickly while also combating illegal entry and strengthening powers to deal with other persons not entitled to enter or remain in the United Kingdom.

Immigration: general

Section 1 of the 1999 Act amends section 3 of the Immigration Act 1971 (the 1971 Act), and is designed to make more flexible and streamlined the granting of leave to enter. Leave to enter may now be granted, refused or varied outside the United Kingdom, thus relieving the pressure on immigration officers at points of entry and giving greater certainty to travellers intending to enter the United Kingdom. Under section 2, the Secretary of State may, by statutory instruments, make further provision in relation to the giving, refusing or varying of leave to remain in the United Kingdom, including the imposition of conditions. Where a person has limited leave to enter or remain and applies to the Secretary of State, before the leave expires, for it to be varied and no decision has been taken on the application when leave expires, the leave is to be treated as continuing until the end of the period allowed under the rules relating to appeals against a decision on an application.[101] A person who has overstayed their leave to enter or remain in the United Kingdom may, during the regularisation period (during 2000), which is to be not less than three months, apply for leave to remain in the United Kingdom.[102] However, whereas previously, overstayers who were liable to deportation had a right of appeal against deportation which could be

---

99 The government certificated the Bill as being in conformity with the European Convention on Human Rights.
100 Hansard, HC Vol 326, Col 37.
101 Immigration and Asylum Act 1999, s 3.
102 *Ibid*, s 9.

exercised before any action was taken to remove them from the United Kingdom, the right of appeal has been removed by the 1999 Act, although persons removed have a right of appeal against removal on the ground that there was no lawful basis for their removal under section 66 (see below, p 862). Section 10 provides that a person who is not a British citizen may be removed from the United Kingdom in accordance with directions given by an immigration official if the person having limited leave to enter or remain does not observe conditions attached to the leave or remains beyond the time limit, or has obtained leave to remain by deception. The only protection remaining for such persons is to appeal to an adjudicator under section 65 alleging that the Immigration Authority has acted in breach of human rights, or to make a claim for asylum under the 1971 Act.

Section 11 of the Act reduces the possibility of challenges by judicial review (on which see below) to decisions to remove asylum seekers to third countries which are Member States of the European Union. Whereas in *R v Secretary of State for the Home Department ex parte Besnik Gashi*[103] and in *R v Secretary of State for the Home Department ex parte Lul Omar Adan, Sittampalan Subaskarant and Hamid Aitesegeur*[104] the claimants argued that Germany was not a safe third country, section 11 introduces the presumption that all Member States are safe and are to be regarded as places where a person's life and liberty is not threatened by reason of his race, religion, nationality, membership of a particular social group or political opinion, and as places from which a person will not be sent to another country otherwise than in accordance with the Refugee Convention. The remaining avenue for such persons is to appeal to an adjudicator under section 65 alleging violation of Convention rights. Where the Secretary of State intends to remove an asylum claimant to a third country other than a Member State of the European Union, section 12 applies. Section 12, *inter alia*, provides that section 15 (restrictions on removal of asylum claimants while the application is pending) shall not prevent the removal of a claimant if the Secretary of State has certified that the claimant is not a national or citizen of the country to which he is to be sent, that his life and liberty would not be threatened there as above in relation to section 11, and that the government of that country would not send him to another country otherwise than in accordance with the Convention on Refugees.[105] Unless such a certificate has been issued, the claimant is not to be removed from the United Kingdom if he has an appeal pending under section 65, or before the time for giving notice of such an appeal has expired.[106]

Section 22 of the 1999 Act amends section 8 of the Asylum and Immigration Act 1996, and provides that the Secretary of State must issue a

---

103 [1999] INLR 276, discussed below.
104 [1999] INLR 362, discussed below.
105 Immigration and Asylum Act 1999, s 12(1), (2), (7).
106 *Ibid*, s 12(3).

Code of Practice for employers, advising on the measures to be taken to avoid the commission of an offence under section 8 (employing a person subject to immigration control), and also to avoid racial discrimination contrary to the Race Relations Act 1976.

Sections 28 to 30 of the 1999 Act relate to criminal offences in relation to immigration control. Section 24 of the Immigration Act 1971 provides that it is a criminal offence to knowingly enter the United Kingdom in breach of a deportation order or without leave, to use deception in order to obtain leave to enter or remain, or to breach time limits or conditions of limited leave and related offences. Section 28 amends section 24 of the 1971 Act, and relates to deception in relation to obtaining or seeking to obtain leave to enter or remain in the United Kingdom, or securing or seeking to secure the avoidance, postponement or revocation of enforcement action against him (the giving of directions for removal under Schedule 2 to the 1971 Act or section 10 of the 1999 Act). Section 25 of the 1971 Act makes it a criminal offence to assist unlawful entry and harbouring an unlawful entrant. Section 29 of the 1999 Act increases the maximum penalty for facilitating illegal entry. Making false statements to an immigration officer or obstructing an immigration officer acting lawfully is an offence under section 26 of the 1971 Act, which is amended by section 30 of the 1999 Act to make clear that making false statements under any of the post-1971 Immigration Acts is an offence.

Section 31 of the 1999 Act reflects the prohibition in Article 31(1) of the 1951 Convention against penalising refugees for their method of entry to a country to seek asylum,[107] and provides that it is a defence for a refugee charged with an offence to which this section applies to show that, having come to the United Kingdom directly from a country where his life or freedom was threatened, he presented himself to the authorities in the United Kingdom without delay, showed good cause for his illegal entry or presence and made a claim for asylum as soon as was reasonably practicable. If the refugee has stopped in a third country in transit from a country where his life or freedom was threatened en route to the United Kingdom, the defence in sub-section (1) only applies if he shows that he could not reasonably have expected to be given protection under the Refugee Convention in that other country.[108]

The Immigration Services Commissioner and Immigration Services Tribunal

The 1999 Act introduces an Immigration Services Commissioner, appointed by the Secretary of State, in consultation with the Lord Chancellor and Scottish Ministers.[109] It is the general duty of the Commissioner to promote

---

107 See *Adimi, Sorani and Kaziu* (1999) TLR 596.
108 Immigration and Asylum Act 1999, s 31(2).
109 *Ibid*, s 83.

good practice by those who provide immigration advice or immigration services.[110] The Commissioner will issue a Code of Standards and rules. The Commissioner will have responsibility for registering those persons or bodies qualified to provide immigration advice or services.[111] The Immigration Services Tribunal has jurisdiction to consider appeals by persons aggrieved by decisions of the Commissioner in relation to registration,[112] and to consider disciplinary charges laid by the Commissioner in relation to registered persons or bodies providing immigration advice or services.[113]

Carriers' liability

Part II of the Act imposes civil liability on persons responsible for the transport of 'clandestine entrants' to the United Kingdom and repeals and replaces the Immigration (Carriers' Liability) Act 1987.[114] Civil liability covers all vehicles, trains, ships or aircraft bringing clandestine entrants to the United Kingdom, and provides power to detain such vehicles, ships or aircraft as security until all charges for the carriage of illegal entrants have been paid. The definition of clandestine entrant is broad.

Section 32(1) provides that a person is a clandestine entrant if:

(a) he arrives in the United Kingdom concealed in a vehicle, ship or aircraft,

(b) he passes, or attempt to pass, through immigration control concealed in a vehicle, or

(c) he arrives in the United Kingdom on a ship or aircraft, having embarked:

(i) concealed in a vehicle;

(ii) at a time when the ship or aircraft was outside the United Kingdom, and claims, or indicated that he intends to seek, asylum in the United Kingdom or evades, or attempts to evade, immigration control.

'Immigration control' means United Kingdom immigration control and includes any United Kingdom immigration control operated in a prescribed control zone outside the United Kingdom,[115] with the effect that a person may

---

110 On functions, see, also, Sched 5.

111 See Immigration and Asylum Act 1999, s 84.

112 *Ibid*, s 87. On the Tribunal, see, also, Scheds 2 and 7.

113 *Ibid*, s 89. On offences relating to the provision of immigration advice and services see ss 91 and 92.

114 It is a criminal offence to knowingly make or carry out arrangements facilitating or assisting illegal entrants: Immigration Act 1971, s 25.

115 Immigration and Asylum Act 1999, s 32(10).

be a clandestine entrant even though he or she does not arrive in the United Kingdom. The prescribed control zones will be defined by regulation.

The 'responsible person', defined in section 32(5) and (6), is liable to a penalty for each clandestine entrant, irrespective of whether the responsible person knew or suspected that a clandestine entrant was concealed in the transporter, or that there were one or more other persons concealed with the clandestine entrant in the same transporter.[116] Liability is fixed at £2,000 per clandestine entrant. It is a defence for the carrier to show that he or an employee was acting under duress, and for the carrier to show that he did not know and had no reasonable grounds for suspecting that a clandestine entrant was or might be concealed in the transporters or that an effective system for preventing the carriage of clandestine entrants was in operation and that, on the occasion in question, the responsible person was operating that system properly.[117] If the Secretary of State decides that a person is liable, he must issue a penalty notice stating the reasons for deciding that the person is liable, the amount of the penalty or penalties, the date before which the penalty must be paid, and include an explanation of the steps to be taken if the person objects to the penalty.[118] If a penalty notice has been issued, a senior officer (which means an officer not below the rank of Chief Immigration Officer)[119] may detain the relevant vehicle, small ship or small aircraft, as defined in section 43, until all penalties have been paid, but the power may only be exercised if there is a significant risk that the penalty will not be paid in the prescribed time if the transporter is not detained, and may not be exercised if alternative security has been given. The detention of the transporter is lawful, even though it is subsequently established that the penalty notice was ill founded,[120] unless the Secretary of State was acting unreasonably in issuing the penalty notice.[121] Where a transporter is detained, the owner or responsible persons or any person with an interest in the transporter may apply to the court for its release. The court may order its release if satisfactory security has been tendered, there is no significant risk that the penalty will not be paid or there is significant doubt whether the penalty is payable and the applicant has a compelling need to have the transporter released.[122] If the court does not order release, the Secretary of State may sell the transporter if the penalty is not paid before the end of a period of 84 days beginning on the date on which the detention began.[123] Provision is also made for the detention

---

116 Defined as a ship, vehicle or aircraft: Immigration and Asylum Act 1999, s 43.
117 *Ibid*, s 34.
118 *Ibid*, s 35.
119 *Ibid*, s 38(8)
120 *Ibid*, s 36(4).
121 *Ibid*, s 36(5).
122 *Ibid*, s 37.
123 *Ibid*, s 37(4).

of ships, aircraft and vehicles following the arrest of a person in connection with offences relating to assisting illegal entry and harbouring an unlawful entrant.[124]

Where an owner of a ship, aircraft or vehicle, or train operator transports a passenger without proper immigration documents, that carrier is liable to a charge of £2,000 or such other sum as may be prescribed. The charge is payable to the Secretary of State on demand.[125] No charge is payable if the person is shown to have produced the required documentation, or, in relation to a train operator or owner of a road passenger vehicle, if the law applicable to the place where the person embarked prohibits the production of documentation or satisfactory arrangements designed to ensure that such passengers were not carried were in place, or, where all steps were taken to ensure that the person had the required documents, or where that person refused to produce the documentation, that all practicable steps were taken to prevent his or her arrival in the United Kingdom.[126] Where payment of a charge is pending, a senior officer may detain the transporter, the release of which may be ordered by a court on the same grounds as under section 37.[127]

Bail

Under the Immigration Acts,[128] persons seeking leave to enter the United Kingdom, persons who are illegal entrants and those subject to deportation proceedings may be detained. Persons suspected of offences under the Immigration Acts may also be detained, although in those cases the rules relating to bail on criminal charges apply. Previously, decisions to detain persons had not been attended by independent judicial supervision. The 1999 Act seeks to remedy this situation by providing for bail hearings for those persons detained under the 1971 Act. The 1999 Act does not amend the right to bail, but provides that the Secretary of State may do so by way of regulations.[129] The Secretary of State must arrange a reference to the court for it to determine whether the detained person should be released on bail.[130] Such a reference must be made no later than the eighth day following which the person was detained. Where the detained person remains in detention, the

---

124 Immigration and Asylum Act 1999, s 38, amending the Immigration Act 1971, s 25.

125 *Ibid*, s 40.

126 *Ibid*, s 40.

127 *Ibid*, s 42.

128 Immigration Act 1971, Immigration Act 1988, Asylum and Immigration Appeals Act 1993, Asylum and Immigration Act 1996.

129 Immigration and Asylum Act 1999, s 53.

130 *Ibid*, s 44(1), (2).

Secretary of State must arrange for a second reference to the court no later than the 36th day following the date of detention. Exceptions to the section 44(2) duty to refer apply in relation to persons detained other than under a provision of the 1971 Act, or where a person is liable to deportation as a result of a recommendation of a court or if the person concerned has given written notice to the Secretary of State that he does not wish his or her case to be referred to the court.[131] Section 46 provides that the court must release the detained person on bail, subject to exceptions. These exceptions include where the court is satisfied that there are substantial grounds for believing that, if released, he or she would fail to comply with bail conditions, or commit an offence while on bail, or be likely to cause danger to public health, or be a serious threat to the maintenance of public order.[132] Also, the detained person need not be granted bail if the court is satisfied that he or she is or has been knowingly involved in a concerted attempt to enter the United Kingdom in breach of immigration law, or he or she is suffering from a mental disorder and his or her detention is necessary in his or her own interests or for the protection of others, or he or she is under the age of 18 and no satisfactory arrangements have been made for his or her care on release, or he or she is required to submit to an examination by immigration officers or medical examiners,[133] or there are directions in force for his or her removal from the United Kingdom. A detained person also need not be granted bail if the court is satisfied that he or she falls within the national security provisions of section 3(2) of the Special Immigration Appeals Commission Act 1997, which provides that the Secretary of State has certified that his or her detention is necessary in the interests of national security, or that he or she is detained following a decision to refuse him or her leave to enter on the basis of national security or that he or she is detained following a decision to make a deportation order on the grounds of national security. Where granted, conditions may be attached to bail.[134] Where a condition is attached and has been broken, any recognisance or security may be forfeited.[135] A power of arrest without warrant applies where an immigration officer or constable has reasonable grounds for believing that a released person has broken or is likely to break a bail condition.[136]

---

131 Immigration and Asylum Act 1999, s 44.
132 *Ibid*, s 46(2).
133 Under the Immigration Act 1971, Sched 2.
134 Immigration and Asylum Act 1999, s 48.
135 *Ibid*, ss 48 and 49.
136 *Ibid*, s 50.

Immigration and asylum appeals

Part IV and Schedules 2, 3 and 4 of the 1999 Act reform the system of immigration and asylum appeals with a view to providing a comprehensive right of appeal replacing the multiplicity of appeal mechanisms formerly in place. Other than in relation to national security cases, where the person may appeal to the Special Immigration Appeals Commission under the 1997 Special Immigration Appeals Commission Act 1997,[137] all other persons may appeal under the 1999 Act, which repeals appeal provisions under earlier legislation. The right of appeal extends to decisions requiring a person to seek leave or the refusal of leave to enter the United Kingdom under the 1971 Act.[138] Where, before an appeal is lodged, directions have been given for the person's removal from the United Kingdom, or before or after he or she appeals, the Secretary of State or an immigration officer serves notice that directions for his removal will be for removal to a country or one of several countries specified in the notice, the appellant may object to the country to which he or she would be removed and claim that he or she ought to be removed, if at all, to a different country specified by him or her.[139] Section 60 of the 1999 Act makes detailed provisions limiting rights of appeal under section 59, largely replicating the provisions of the Immigration Act 1971. There is the right to appeal decisions to vary, or refuse to vary any limited leave to enter or remain if, as a result of that decision, the person may be required to leave the United Kingdom within 28 days of being notified of the decision.[140] The right of appeal under section 61 is limited by the provisions of section 62. Less detailed than the restrictions in section 60, section 62 provides for four situations to which the right to appeal does not apply. A person may not appeal against a refusal to vary leave if the refusal is on the ground that the relevant document which is required by the Immigration Rules has not been issued, or if the person does not satisfy a requirement of the Immigration Rules as to age or nationality or citizenship, or the variation would result in the duration of a person's leave exceeding that permitted by the Immigration Rules, or where any required fee has not been paid. The right to appeal against a decision to deport a person under the 1971 Act, or the refusal of the Secretary of State to revoke a deportation order, is regulated under sections 62 and 63. A person is entitled to appeal against the making of a deportation order by the Secretary of State under section 5(1) of the Immigration Act 1971 as a result of his liability to deportation under section 3(5) of that Act, or the refusal to revoke a deportation order. Under the 1999 Act, deportation appeals are limited to cases where deportation is deemed by

---

137 Immigration and Asylum Act 1999, Sched 14, para 119.
138 *Ibid*, s 59.
139 *Ibid*, s 59(3), (4).
140 *Ibid*, s 60.

the Secretary of State to be 'conducive to the public good' and cases where 'another person to whose family he belongs is or has been ordered to be deported'.[141] Where the Secretary of State serves notice that directions will be given for his or her removal to a country, or one of several specified countries, the person may object to the specified country and claim that he or she ought to be removed, if at all, to a different country specified by him or her. A deportation order is not to be made under section 5(1) of the 1971 Act against a person while an appeal may be brought against the decision to make it.[142] Section 64 restricts the right of appeal under section 63, providing that the right to appeal is not available where deportation is ordered as being conducive to the public good, in the interests of national security or of relations between the United Kingdom and any other country, or 'for other reasons of a political nature'. No right of appeal lies against a refusal to revoke a deportation order if the Secretary of State has certified that the appellant's exclusion from the United Kingdom is conducive to the public good.

Section 65 of the 1999 Act makes provision in relation to Convention rights under section 6(1) of the Human Rights Act 1998. If, under the Immigration Acts, a public authority acts in breach of a person's human rights, by acting or failing to act in a way made unlawful by section 6(1), the person may appeal to an adjudicator, unless he or she has grounds for appealing against the decision under the Special Immigration Appeals Commission Act 1997.

Where directions are given for the removal of a person on being refused leave to enter, or on a deportation order being made against him or her, or that person entering the United Kingdom in breach of a deportation order, an appeal lies to an adjudicator on the ground that he or she ought to be removed, if at all, to a different country specified by him or her.[143] Section 68 restricts the right of appeal under section 67, *inter alia*, providing that, where a person has objected to a specified country and has stipulated another country of destination, if he or she is not a national or citizen of that other country, he or she must prove that the country will admit him or her.

Appeals in relation to asylum claims are regulated under section 69 of the 1999 Act. A person who is refused leave to enter may appeal on the ground that his or her removal would be contrary to the Convention on Refugees. A decision varying or refusing to vary a person's limited leave to enter or remain may also be appealed against to an adjudicator, on the ground that such a requirement would be contrary to the Convention on Refugees, if it results in the person being required to leave the United Kingdom within 28

---

141 Immigration and Asylum Act 1999, Sched 14, para 44, amending the Immigration Act 1971, s (5). Other persons liable to removal from the United Kingdom by virtue of breaching conditions of leave to enter or remain or exceeding the time limit, or obtaining leave to remain by deception are liable to removal under the 1999 Act, s 10.

142 *Ibid*, s 63(3), (4).

143 *Ibid*, s 67.

days. Further, a person who has been refused leave to enter or remain, but has been granted limited leave to enter or remain, may, if that limited leave will not expire within 28 days of notification, appeal on Convention grounds to an adjudicator. Where the Secretary of State has decided to make a deportation order or refused to revoke such an order, an appeal lies to an adjudicator on Convention grounds, as it does if directions are given under section 66(1) for the removal of the person from the United Kingdom. The right of appeal is restricted by section 70 of the 1999 Act, and section 69 does not entitle a person to appeal against refusal of leave to enter if the Secretary of State certifies, personally, that the exclusion is in the interests of national security. A person is not entitled to appeal against a variation of leave which reduces its duration or a refusal to enlarge to remove the limit on its duration if the Secretary of State has certified that the appellant's departure would be in the interests of national security, or that the decision questioned by the appeal was taken on that ground by the Secretary of State personally. Where a person has been refused leave to enter or remain on the basis of a claim for asylum, but has been granted limited leave to enter or remain, no right of appeal lies if the reason for the refusal was that he or she was a person to whom the Convention did not apply and the Secretary of State has certified that the disclosure of material on which the refusal was based is not in the interests of national security. A person is not entitled to appeal against a refusal to revoke a deportation order where the Secretary of State has certified that exclusion is in the interests of national security, or where revocation was refused on that ground.[144]

Support for asylum seekers

Part VI of the 1999 Act provides support for asylum seekers and their dependants. Asylum seekers are taken out of the benefits system[145] and detailed provision is made for their support under the Act. Support may be given through the provision of accommodation which is 'adequate', providing for the essential living needs of the supported person, enabling the person to meet expenses (other than legal and other prescribed expenses) in relation to asylum claims, enabling the asylum seeker to attend bail proceedings.[146] If the circumstances of a particular case are 'exceptional', the Secretary of State may provide such support as he considers necessary to enable the supported

---

144 On procedures relating to appeal, see Immigration and Asylum Act 1999, ss 74–76.

145 The exclusion from benefits covers jobseeker's allowance, attendance allowance, severe disablement allowance, invalid care allowance, disability living allowance, income support, working families' tax credit, disabled person's tax credit, social fund payments, child benefit, housing benefit, council tax benefit: s 115.

146 *Ibid*, s 96, specifying the types of support which may be given to eligible persons defined in s 95.

person to be supported.[147] Local authorities may also provide support in accordance with arrangements made by the Secretary of State.[148] Where the Secretary of State asks a local authority to assist him in providing support under section 95, the local authority must co-operate in the provision of accommodation.[149] In order to spread the burden of providing for asylum seekers throughout the country in an equitable manner, the Secretary of State has power to designate reception zones in relation to the provision of support, including accommodation.[150] Where the Secretary of State decides that an applicant for support under section 95 is not qualified for support, the applicant may appeal to an Asylum Support Adjudicator.[151] The Act introduces a number of offences relating to support. It is an offence to make false representations, dishonest representations, or to delay or obstruct, without reasonable excuse, a person exercising functions relating to support, or to refuse or neglect to undertake an obligation to maintain a supported person, having given a written undertaking to do so.[152]

Powers of arrest, search and fingerprinting

Part VII of the 1999 Act increases the powers of immigration officers in relation to entry of premises, arrest and search of suspects, and introduces a power to fingerprint persons suspected of immigration offences. Arrest without warrant is regulated by section 128, amending section 28 of the 1971 Act, and provides for the arrest of a person who has committed or attempted to commit an offence under section 24 or 24A (illegal entry and deception), or offences under section 25(1) (assisting illegal entry) and obstruction of an immigration officer under section 26(1)(g). Search and arrest by warrant is governed by section 129, amending section 28 of the 1971 Act. For the purpose of arresting a person for an offence under section 25(1) (assisting illegal entry), an immigration officer may enter and search any premises, but the power may be exercised only to the extent that it is reasonably required for that purpose and only if the officer has reasonable grounds for believing that the person whom he is seeking is on the premises. The power to enter and search premises for evidence is under warrant.[153] Following arrest at a place other than a police station, an immigration officer may enter and search any premises in which the person was when arrested, or in which he was immediately before he was arrested for evidence relating to the offence for

---

147 Immigration and Asylum Act 1999, s 96(2).

148 *Ibid*, s 99.

149 *Ibid*, s 100.

150 *Ibid*, s 101.

151 *Ibid*, s 102.

152 *Ibid*, ss 106, 107, 108, respectively.

153 *Ibid*, s 131, amending the Immigration Act 1971, s 28.

which the arrest was made. The power may only be exercised if the officer has reasonable grounds for believing that there is relevant evidence on the premises and only to the extent that it is reasonably required for the purpose of discovering the relevant evidence.[154] Similar powers of entry and search of premises following arrest under section 25(1) of the 1971 Act are provided by section 133, amending section 28 of the Act. Where a person is arrested at a place other than a police station, an immigration officer may search the arrested person if he has reasonable grounds for believing that the arrested person may present a danger to him or herself or others. The search may be conducted to search for anything which might be used to escape from lawful custody, and anything which might be evidence relating to the offence for which he or she was arrested. The power may only be exercised on reasonable grounds and to the extent reasonably required. The power conferred does not authorise an officer to require a person to remove any clothing in public other than an outer coat, jacket or gloves, but does authorise the search of a person's mouth. Evidence discovered may be seized.[155] Where a person is arrested under Schedule 2, an immigration officer may search the person on similar grounds to those above, save that the immigration officer may also search for any document which might establish his or her identity, nationality or citizenship, or indicate the place from which he or she has travelled to the United Kingdom or to which he or she is proposing to go.[156] Similar powers relate to the search of persons in police custody, and provide that an immigration officer may search to see if the arrested person has anything with him or her which might be used to cause physical injury to him or herself or others, damage property, interfere with evidence or assist his or her escape.[157] Fingerprinting is regulated by section 141 of the 1999 Act. Fingerprints may be taken from adults arriving without proof of identity, those granted temporary entry where there is a suspicion that they may break entry conditions, illegal entrants subject to removal, a person who has been arrested about whom a decision to give leave to enter has not yet been reached, asylum seekers and dependants of the above.[158] The fingerprinting of children under the age of 16 is subject to restrictions. Where there is doubt as to the age of the person, fingerprints may be taken if a senior officer (Chief Constable, Chief Immigration Officer, Prison Governor) reasonably believes that the person is aged 16 or over.[159] Provision is made for requiring attendance for fingerprinting, and for the subsequent destruction of fingerprints.[160] Codes of

---

154 Immigration and Asylum Act 1999, s 132, amending the Immigration Act 1971, s 28.
155 *Ibid*, s 134, amending the Immigration Act 1971, s 28.
156 *Ibid*, s 134, amending the Immigration Act 1971, Sched 2, para 25.
157 *Ibid*, s 135, amending the Immigration Act 1971, s 28.
158 *Ibid*, s 141.
159 *Ibid*, s 141(13).
160 *Ibid*, ss 142 and 143, respectively.

Practice, based on the Codes issued under the Police and Criminal Evidence Act 1984, must be complied with by immigration officers and those authorised to take fingerprints. An immigration officer exercising any power conferred under the 1971 Act or the 1999 Act may, if necessary, use reasonable force.[161]

Detention centres for detained persons

Part VIII of the 1999 Act provides for arrangements for the management of detention centres for the accommodation of immigration and asylum detainess, and provides for the contracting out of the provision and running of detention centres.

Marriage regulations

Part IX of the 1999 Act tightens up the law relating to abuse of marriage for the purposes of immigration.[162] Registrars have the power to request evidence of name, age, marital status and nationality from couples, and to refuse to give authority for the marriage where the Registrar is not satisfied that a person is free, legally, to contract the marriage. The existing procedure for authorising marriage by a certificate with a licence is abolished, and the existing period of notice for the Superintendent Registrar to issue a certificate without a licence reduced from 21 to 15 days. The law is amended to ensure that notice of intent to marry is given personally by each party before the Superintendent Registrar in the registration district where they reside, and the notice will have to state their nationality. Under section 24, Registrars are under a duty to report to the Home Office those marriages suspected of having been arranged for the purpose of evading immigration controls.

Judicial review and immigration

Immigration raises difficult questions for the courts, particularly in light of the wide powers conferred on the Home Secretary. Exercise of the Home Secretary's powers which resulted in judicial criticism occurred in *M v Home Office*.[163] The Home Secretary, Kenneth Baker, had ignored an order of the court that M should not be returned to Zaire, where he feared torture.

---

161 Immigration and Asylum Act 1999, s 146.
162 The Act amends the Marriage Act 1949, the Marriage (Registrar General's Licence) Act 1970 and the Marriage Act 1983: Sched 14.
163 [1992] 4 All ER 97; [1993] 3 All ER 537, HL.

Immigration officials put M on a plane, which the Home Secretary refused to have turned back. The House of Lords held that an injunction could lie against Ministers of the Crown, and that they would be guilty of contempt of court – in their official capacity – for defiance of orders of the court.

Where the Home Secretary has rejected an application for asylum, and the applicant submits a fresh application based on 'new, apparently credible evidence', the Home Secretary has a duty to consider that application afresh: *R v Secretary of State for the Home Department ex parte Boybeyi*.[164] The Court of Appeal so held, dismissing the Home Secretary's appeal against the judgment of the lower court in judicial review proceedings. An unsuccessful application for asylum does not preclude the making of a second application, based on fresh evidence.[165] However, where no fresh application is submitted, there is no right of appeal against the Home Secretary's decision to deny asylum: *R v Special Adjudicator ex parte Secretary of State for the Home Department*.[166]

Moreover, where a repeat application for asylum is made to the Home Secretary, which the Home Secretary regards as repetitious as opposed to an application based on fresh evidence, judicial review of that decision – that the application is not a fresh application – will only lie if the Home Secretary's decision is 'perverse' within the *Wednesbury* grounds.[167] The Court of Appeal so held in *R v Special Adjudicator ex parte Secretary of State for the Home Department; R v Secretary of State for the Home Department ex parte Cakabay*.[168] The decision of the Home Secretary was not analogous to the refusal by an immigration officer of leave to enter, for which an appeal would lie. Section 8 of the 1996 Act (which is now repealed by the 1999 Act) provided for appeals. Parliament had not made provision in section 8 for the decision of the Home Secretary over whether or not a repeat application amounted to a fresh claim. The only right of appeal was under section 8 of the Act, and that did not encompass the decision of the Home Secretary that there had been no fresh application for asylum.

In *R v Secretary of State for the Home Department ex parte Salem*,[169] the Court of Appeal ruled, by a majority, that the Home Secretary's decision is 'final' once it is made and recorded. Accordingly, where an asylum applicant is

---

164 (1997) *The Times*, 5 June.

165 *R v Secretary of State for the Home Department ex parte Onibiyo* [1996] 1 WLR 490.

166 (1997) *The Times*, 25 November.

167 *Associated Provincial Picture Houses Ltd v Wednesbury Corporation* [1948] 1 KB 223. On *Wednesbury* grounds, see, further, Chapter 25.

168 (1988) *The Times*, 13 July. See, also, *R v Special Adjudicator ex p Secretary of State for the Home Department* [1999] Imm AR 176, CA.

169 (1998) *The Times*, 18 March.

reliant on income support benefits, the Home Secretary had the right to order the Benefits Agency to stop income support benefits from the date of his decision.[170] The fact that the Home Secretary could subsequently consider representations made on behalf of the asylum seeker did not mean that his decision was not final, and represented 'no more than a recognition' that the Home Secretary has a continuing duty to observe the Geneva Convention and Protocol relating to the Status of Refugees 1951 and 1967.[171]

The Convention Relating to the Status of Refugees

In *R v Home Secretary ex parte Bugdaycay and Musisi*,[172] the House of Lords took a more robust approach. In judicial review proceedings, the House of Lords ruled that the Home Secretary had failed to take into account relevant considerations in his decision to deport a Ugandan refugee to Kenya (in which the applicant had lived previously). Evidence existed that Kenya had previously returned refugees to Uganda. The court had the aid of the Convention Relating to the Status of Refugees 1954, Article 33 of which provides that no one should be returned to a territory where his life or freedom would be threatened, which the court boldly held should govern the interpretation of the Immigration Rules.

Under the Convention Relating to the Status of Refugees,[173] which came into force in 1954, the United Kingdom has undertaken certain obligations. The United Nations' Office of High Commissioner for Refugees is the umbrella office responsible for providing advice and guidance as to the interpretation and implementation of the Convention. A person is defined under the Convention as a refugee if he:

(a) is outside the country of his nationality;

(b) has a well founded fear of being persecuted for reasons of race, religion, nationality, membership of a particular social group, or political opinions; and

(c) is unable or, because of that fear, unwilling to avail himself of the protection of that country.[174]

---

170 Income Support (General) Regulations SI 1987/1967, reg 70(3A), as amended by the Income Support (General) Amendment Regulations SI 1996/606, provides that a person: '... (b) ... ceases to be an asylum seeker (i) in the case of a claim for asylum which, on or after 5 February 1996, is recorded by the Secretary of State as having been determined (other than on appeal) ... on the date on which it is so recorded ...'

171 Cmd 9171, 1951, London: HMSO; and Cmnd 3906, 1967, London: HMSO, respectively.

172 [1987] AC 514.

173 See UK Treaty Series No 39, Cmnd 9171, 1954, London: HMSO. The Convention was amended in 1966 by the Protocol Relating to the Status of Refugees.

174 Convention Relating to the Status of Refugees, Art 1A(2).

If a person is found to be a refugee, that person is entitled not to be expelled or returned to the country from which he fears persecution. If, however, the person has come to the United Kingdom from a third country, he may be returned to that third country, provided that that third country will not return him to the country from which he has fled.[175]

If a person is deemed to be a refugee, and has not come from a safe third country, he is entitled to remain. However, he may be deported on the basis of the requirements of national security or public order, although only if some country in which he would be safe will accept him.[176]

The test for deciding whether a person has a well founded fear is both subjective and objective. In *R v Secretary of State for the Home Department ex parte Sivakumaran*,[177] the House of Lords ruled that, whilst the fear is subjective, the reasonableness of that fear is an objective test. Moreover, the House of Lords ruled that the test was one to be applied by the Home Secretary. If the Home Secretary decides that there is a 'reasonable chance', a 'serious possibility' or 'substantial grounds for thinking' that the person will be persecuted, the objective test will be satisfied.

In *R v Secretary of State for the Home Department ex parte Gashi (Besnik)*,[178] the Secretary of State made an order to return the applicant to Germany, which he had previously been required to leave, having fled there from Kosovo. The applicant sought to challenge the decision to remove him on the basis that Germany was not a safe third country, alleging that the German courts were returning ethnic Albanians to Kosovo. The Queen's Bench Division ruled, however, that the German courts respected the demands of the Convention, and that the Secretary of State had taken all reasonable and necessary steps to remain abreast of the German courts' approach. Accordingly, his decision was not unlawful because of unreasonableness. The Court of Appeal, however, allowed the applicant's appeal. The Home Secretary was not entitled to assume that Germany properly applied the Refugee Convention, and evidence suggested disparities in treatment between asylum seekers which the Home Secretary had a duty to investigate. In *R v Secretary of State for the Home Department ex parte Lul Omar Adan, Sittampalan Subaskaran and Hamid Aitsegeur*,[179] the Court of Appeal also found that the interpretation of the Convention in Germany and France, in relation to refugees from Somalia, Sri Lanka and Algeria respectively, was inconsistent

---

175 See *R v Secretary of State for the Home Office ex parte Bugdaycay* [1987] AC 514; [1987] 1 All ER 940.

176 Convention Relating to the Status of Refugees, Arts 32, 33(2).

177 [1988] AC 958; 1 All ER 193.

178 [1999] Imm AR 231; [1999] INLR 276.

179 [1999] INLR 362.

with the requirements of the Convention, and that neither country applied the Convention in their approach to persecution by non-State agents.[180]

In determining whether a person is suffering a well founded fear of persecution, past persecution is relevant for the purposes of determining a person's refugee status. It is a question of fact and degree whether a single beating amounts to persecution and, in that determination, a court or tribunal should consider not only the seriousness of the beating but also the risk of repetition if that person was returned to his or her country of origin.[181] A person does not forfeit the right to the protection of the Convention on the Status of Refugees even where an asylum seeker had in bad faith and for the sole purpose of obtaining refugee status acted in such a manner in this country as to put himself at risk of persecution in his country of origin. While his claim would need careful scrutiny and his credibility would be low, nevertheless, he would still be entitled to protection in this country if he could establish a genuine and well founded fear of persecution if returned to his home country.[182] Moreover, it did not follow that an asylum seeker must be refused asylum because the asylum seeker, albeit unreasonably, would engage in certain political or religious activities on his return which would put him or her at greater risk. The Court of Appeal insisted that a single question arose in all asylum cases, namely, 'was there a serious risk that on return the applicant would be persecuted ...'.[183] The adequacy of the protection which State authorities would provide for a person if returned to his or her country, from the activities of third parties who posed a risk to a person or group, is also a relevant consideration in determining whether a person should be granted asylum. Where the State was unwilling or unable to protect the person from acts of ill treatment, that factor formed part of the consideration as to whether the applicant's fear of persecution was well founded.[184] In *R v Immigration Appeal Tribunal ex parte Shokar*,[185] the Queen's Bench Division ruled that, where a person had suffered ill treatment at the hands of the Punjabi police, and the authorities would not tolerate police misconduct, the police could not be termed agents of persecution under the Convention.

In *R v Immigration Appeal Tribunal and Another ex parte Shah; Islam and Others v Secretary of State for the Home Department*,[186] the House of Lords ruled

---

180 The Court of Appeal, however, upheld the entitlement of the Secretary of State to determine the credibility of any fresh evidence adduced by an applicant for asylum in *R v Secretary of State for the Home Department ex parte Nkereuwen* [1999] Imm AR 267.

181 *Demirkaya v Secretary of State for the Home Department* (1999) *The Times*, 29 June, CA.

182 *Danian v Secretary of State for the Home Department* (1999) *The Times*, 9 November, CA.

183 *Ahmed (Iftikhar) v Secretary of State for the Home Department* (1999) *The Times*, 8 December, CA.

184 *Horvath v Secretary of State for the Home Department* (1999) *The Times*, 8 December, CA.

185 [1998] Imm AR 447.

186 (1997) *The Times*, 13 October; (1999) *The Times*, 26 March.

on the meaning of 'membership of a particular social group', within Article 1A of the Geneva Convention and Protocol Relating to the Status of Refugees,[187] for the purposes of refugee status. The appellants were two Pakistani women, who had been accused of adultery and disobedience to their husbands, and who had no protection from their families and faced persecution under Sharia law, and possibly death by stoning, if returned to Pakistan. The Court of Appeal ruled that they were not members of a 'particular social group' for asylum purposes under the Convention. 'Membership, etc' meant that 'members of the group had to share a common uniting attribute which set them apart from the rest of society, which was recognised as such by society generally, and which existed independently of the feared persecution', and that women did not form such a group. The House of Lords, however, ruled that the fact that some women in Pakistan escaped the effects of systematic discrimination was not sufficient ground to deny Convention protection to particular women. Women in Pakistan were a social group in that 'society discriminated on the basis of sex' and were not 'entitled to the same fundamental rights as men'.

In *Ouanes v Secretary of State for the Home Department*,[188] the Court of Appeal also considered the characteristics defining social groups for asylum. The characteristic 'which defined the social group had to be one which the members should not be required to change because it was so fundamental to their individual identities or conscience'. Shared identities by virtue of employment did not constitute the requisite characteristics for asylum purposes within the Convention. The application for review by a member of a group of Algerian government employed midwives was rejected.

In *Adan v Secretary of State for the Home Department; Noor v Same; Lazarevic v Same; Radivojevic v Same*,[189] the Court of Appeal was called upon, for the first time in 46 years, to consider the definition of 'refugee' in Article 1A(2) of the Convention and Protocol relating to the Status of Refugees 1951 and 1967.[190]

Under Article 1A(2) of the Convention, an asylum seeker unable to return to his country of origin might be entitled to recognition as a refugee provided only that the fear or actuality of past persecution still played a causative part in his presence in the United Kingdom. In the case of each applicant, the Immigration Appeal Tribunal decided, in 1996, that the asylum seeker was not entitled to refugee status. The Court of Appeal considered that what was in issue was whether it was always necessary for a person unable to return to his country of origin to show a current well founded fear of persecution, or whether a historical fear might sometimes suffice. The Home Secretary argued that there must be a currently well founded fear of persecution.

---

187 Cmd 9171, 1951, London: HMSO; and Cmnd 3906, 1967, London: HMSO.

188 (1997) *The Times*, 26 November.

189 (1997) *The Times*, 7 March.

190 Cmd 9171, 1951, London: HMSO; and Cmnd 3906, 1967, London: HMSO, respectively.

Under Article 1A(2), a refugee was someone who:

1   (a) owing to well founded fear of being persecuted for [a Convention reason] was outside the country of his nationality, and (b)(i) was unable to avail himself of the protection of that country, or (ii) owing to such fear, was unwilling to avail himself of the protection of that country; or who

2   (a) not having a nationality and being outside the country of his former habitual residence, (b)(i) was unable to return to it, or (ii) owing to a well founded fear of being persecuted for [a Convention reason] was unwilling to return to it.

Lord Justice Simon Brown ruled that that Article was capable of three meanings, namely: (a) that the applicant was outside owing to a well founded fear of persecution still current at the time of the asylum application; or (b) has at some time, however long in the past, come to be outside on account of such fear and, for whatever reason, had ever thereafter left; or (c) had come to be outside or, being already outside, not to return, owing to past persecution and still remained abroad on that account, in the sense that the causal link remained operative and had never been broken. It was the latter interpretation which was to be preferred.

However, the House of Lords, in a unanimous decision on appeal from the Court of appeal, tightened the interpretation of 'refugee'. In *Adan v Secretary of State for the Home Department*,[191] the House of Lords ruled that it was insufficient for an asylum seeker to ground his or her claim to asylum on potential persecution if returned to his or her home country, unless that claim could demonstrate that that person would be specifically discriminated against. Accordingly, where the applicant claimed that he or she would be persecuted because of membership of a particular group involved in a civil war – in this case in Somalia – the applicant was not to be accorded refugee status. Unless the applicant could prove that he or she was in particular danger, over and above that of others in society, the claim would fail. In this case, every person claiming refugee status had to demonstrate a 'well founded fear of persecution, above the risk to life and liberty involved in being caught in a civil war'. Additionally, the House of Lords ruled, the fear of persecution must exist at the time they apply for asylum – a fear founded on the time at which they left the country was not sufficient.

Section 2 of the Asylum and Immigration Act 1996 (now repealed by the 1999 Act), provided that, in reaching decisions as to whether to return an asylum seeker to a third country, the Home Secretary had to be satisfied that the third country presented no risk which would breach international obligations, namely, that the third country would not send the detainee to another country, other than in accordance with the Convention and Protocol relating to the Status of Refugees 1951 and 1967.[192]

---

191 (1998) *The Times*, 6 April.
192 Cmd 9171, 1951, London: HMSO; and Cmnd 3906, 1967, London: HMSO, respectively.

In *R v Secretary of State for the Home Department and Another ex parte Canbolat*,[193] an application for judicial review of the decisions of the Home Secretary to issue a certificate under section 2 of the 1996 Act, authorising the applicant's removal from the United Kingdom to France as a safe country for the purposes of adjudication of her claim for asylum, and of the immigration officer refusing her leave to enter and removing her from the United Kingdom to France. The applicant, a Turkish citizen of Kurdish origin, had arrived in the United Kingdom in 1996 and claimed political asylum. The application for judicial review was dismissed and the applicant appealed to the Court of Appeal.

Prior to the 1996 Act, special adjudicators had expressed concerns about the safety of France as a third country, on the basis that there was a risk that an asylum seeker would be deported prior to his or her claim being heard. However, the Home Secretary had made enquiries concerning French laws and procedures, and had satisfied himself that the government of France would not send the applicant to another country other than in accordance with the Convention. It was not for the court, in an application for judicial review, to assess the merits of the case, but to determine whether the Home Secretary was entitled to come to the opinion he did. Only if the Home Secretary had reached a decision to which he could not properly have come, on the material before him, could the court interfere. The appeal was dismissed.

The wide discretion of the Home Secretary in decision making diminishes the prospect of successful judicial review proceedings. In *R v Secretary of State for the Home Department ex parte Abdie; Secretary of State for Home Affairs ex parte Gawe*,[194] the Home Secretary had issued certificates to the effect that the applicants' claim to asylum was without foundation. The applicants had left the United Kingdom for Spain. The Home Secretary believed that Spain would honour its Convention obligations. The applicants appealed to the Special Adjudicator. In subsequent judicial review proceedings, it was held that the Home Secretary was not obliged to reveal all the information on which he had based his decision, and that the Home Secretary's letters were sufficient evidence on which the Special Adjudicator could reach a decision.[195]

In *R v Secretary of State for the Home Department ex parte Launder*,[196] the House of Lords ruled that the Home Secretary had not acted with procedural impropriety, illegality or irrationality, in deciding to issue an extradition warrant under the Extradition Act 1989. The Home Secretary had decided that

---

193 (1997) *The Times*, 9 May.
194 (1996) *The Times*, 17 February.
195 See, also, *R v Secretary of State for Home Affairs ex parte Chahal* (1993) *The Times*, 12 March.
196 [1997] 1 WLR 839; [1997] 3 All ER 961; (1997) *The Times*, 26 May.

the person to be returned to Hong Kong would, in light of the Sino-British Declaration and implementation of the basic law, receive a fair trial and not be exposed to injustice or repression.

The House of Lords considered the meaning of 'particular social group' in *Islam v Secretary of State for the Home Department*.[197] The asylum applicants, who were citizens of Pakistan and had suffered violence there as a result of allegations of adultery, sought asylum on the basis that, if they returned to Pakistan, they would suffer persecution and would be unprotected by the authorities, and might be liable to death by stoning. They argued that their return would be contrary to the Convention, and that the persecution they would suffer would be 'for reasons of membership of a particular social group'. The House of Lords held that a particular social group had to exist independently of the Convention. Women in Pakistan constituted a particular social group because they were discriminated against as a group and the State gave them no protection.

In *Kriba v Secretary of State for the Home Department*,[198] it was held that, where an asylum applicant had relied on a letter from Amnesty International based on an Algerian newspaper report, and that evidence was unchallenged and uncontradicted, came from an apparently responsible source and was a vital element in the applicant's case, it was procedurally unfair to reject the evidence without giving the applicant the chance to adduce support for it.

National security and the public interest

In 1962, Dr Soblen, an American citizen who had been convicted of espionage in the United States, fled from the country before being sentenced. Whilst on an aeroplane, Dr Soblen cut his wrists, and was landed in London for hospital treatment. The Home Secretary issued a deportation order on the basis that his continued presence was 'not conducive to the public good'. When Dr Soblen applied for habeas corpus, the Court of Appeal ruled that Dr Soblen had no right to make representations, and that deportation was an administrative matter for the Home Secretary.[199]

In *R v Home Secretary ex parte Hosenball*,[200] two American journalists, Philip Agee and Mark Hosenball, were detained with a view to deportation, on the basis that their work involved obtaining and publishing information prejudicial to national security. There is no appeal against the Home

---

197 [1999] 2 WLR 1015.
198 1998 SLT 1113.
199 See *R v Home Secretary ex parte Soblen* [1963] 2 QB 243. See, also, Thornberry, CHR, 'Dr Soblen and the alien law of the United Kingdom' (1963) 12 ICLQ 414.
200 [1977] 3 All ER 452.

Secretary's decision where national security[201] is pleaded.[202] Instead, there is a right of a hearing before a panel of three advisers to the Home Secretary. When Hosenball tried to challenge the Home Secretary's decision in the courts, the Court of Appeal upheld the deportation order. While recognising that the rules of natural justice[203] had not been complied with in the decision to deport Hosenball, the Court of Appeal nevertheless ruled that the requirements of national security prevailed and that, in matters of national security, the Home Secretary was responsible to Parliament, and not to the courts.

In *Rehman v Secretary of State for the Home Department*,[204] the Special Immigration Appeals Commission considered the Secretary of State's decision to refuse an application for indefinite leave to remain in the United Kingdom on the basis that the applicant represented a threat to national security, in that he was allegedly involved in an Islamic terrorist organisation. The applicant appealed against notice of intention to make a deportation order.[205] The Commission allowed his appeal. The Commission ruled that its jurisdiction was not restricted to reviewing the Secretary of State's decision on grounds of *Wednesbury* unreasonableness, but rather had a duty to decide all matters of law and fact raised by an appeal. The definition of national security was a 'matter of fact' to be decided by the Commission, which was entitled to substitute its own view for that of the Secretary of State. National security should be construed narrowly. A person offending against national security was one who engaged in, promoted or encouraged violent activity targeted at the United Kingdom, its system of government, or its people. A person also offended against national security if he engaged in activity directed at the destabilisation or overthrow of a foreign government which was likely to take reprisals against the United Kingdom affecting its security or that of its nationals. The Secretary of State had not established that the applicant was or was likely to be a threat to national security.

The case of *R v Home Secretary ex parte Cheblak*[206] also reveals the extensive powers of the Home Secretary to detain persons 'in the interests of national security'. During the Gulf War, 160 Iraqi and Palestinian citizens were detained with a view to deportation, on the basis that their presence was not 'conducive to the public good'. Abbas Cheblak and his family had been resident in the United Kingdom for 16 years. In an application for habeas corpus, the Court of Appeal accepted the Home Secretary's explanation that

---

201 See Chapter 23.
202 Immigration Act 1971, s 15(3).
203 See Chapter 25.
204 [1999] INLR 517.
205 Under the Special Immigration Appeals Commission Act 1997.
206 [1991] 2 All ER 319.

Cheblak had associations with an unspecified organisation which supported the Iraqi government, and refused to press the Home Secretary for further information.[207]

In *R v Secretary of State for the Home Department ex parte Jahromi*,[208] the Court of Appeal clarified the information to be provided to potential deportees by the Home Secretary which will be deemed sufficient. Mr Jahromi, an Iranian citizen, had received refugee status in Kuwait and entered the United Kingdom in 1985 for study purposes. The Home Secretary had issued a deportation order on the basis of national security, following the arrest of Mr Jahromi. The Home Secretary's 'bare assertion' of the 'likelihood of your involvement in terrorist activity' did not amount to an adequate reason for making a deportation order under the Immigration Act 1971. However, the fact that the Home Secretary had submitted affidavit evidence that he had seen materials suggesting involvement in the planning of terrorist activities was held to be sufficient to prevent a potential deportee from challenging the decision. The Court of Appeal accepted the affidavit evidence in support of the Home Secretary's claim that deportation was being ordered on the basis of evidence concerning alleged terrorist activity, and that to give further reasons would in itself be damaging to national security. The applicant has the right to make representations to the Independent Advisory Panel.

EXCLUSION ORDERS AND BORDER CONTROLS

Prior to the Terrorism Act 2000, the State also had the power to prevent persons from entering into the country on specified grounds. Under the Prevention of Terrorism (Temporary Provisions) Act 1989,[209] a person could be detained for up to 12 hours when entering or leaving Britain or Northern Ireland (or travelling between the Republic of Ireland and Northern Ireland), in order to establish whether that person was, or had been, involved in the preparation, commission or instigation of acts of terrorism, was subject to an exclusion order or had committed an offence contrary to an exclusion order.[210] There was no concept of 'reasonable suspicion' involved in the detention. Under section 5, the Home Secretary could make an exclusion order if he was satisfied that any person:

---

207 Mr Cheblak was subsequently released from detention following a hearing before the Home Secretary's panel.

208 (1995) *The Times*, 6 July.

209 See, further, Chapter 23. Note that the Terrorism Act 2000 repeals the 1989 Act.

210 Prevention of Terrorism (Temporary Provisions) Act 1989, s 16 and Sched 5.

(a) is or has been concerned in the commission, preparation or instigation of acts of terrorism to which this Part of this Act applies; or

(b) is attempting or may attempt to enter Great Britain with a view to being concerned in the commission, preparation or instigation of such acts of terrorism.

An exclusion order had the effect of prohibiting a person from being in, or entering, Great Britain.[211] An exclusion order could not be made against a British citizen who was ordinarily resident in Great Britain and had been so resident for the three previous years, or who was subject to an exclusion order from Northern Ireland.[212] A person could be excluded from Northern Ireland on the same grounds as for an exclusion order under section 5, but no exclusion order could be made against a British citizen who was, and had been for the previous three years, ordinarily resident in Northern Ireland, or who was subject to an exclusion order under section 5 above.[213] Section 7 provided for exclusion orders to be granted, prohibiting a person – on the grounds set out above – from entering the United Kingdom. An exclusion order could not be made under this section against a person who was a British citizen.

Not only did exclusion orders substantially impair liberty, but the means by which they operated were also deficient from the civil liberties perspective. The Home Secretary had no duty to provide reasons for the exclusion order.[214] The only 'appeal' mechanism against the order was to apply for an interview with a person designated by the Home Secretary, and accountable to him. Judicial review was also likely to fail. In *Secretary of State for Home Affairs ex parte McQuillan*,[215] for example, the court upheld the Home Secretary's decision to exclude the applicant from Great Britain on the basis of national security and refused to quash the decision of the Home Secretary not to review the applicant's case, in spite of new evidence being adduced as to non-involvement with terrorist activities and the danger to his life if he remained in Northern Ireland.

In *R v Secretary of State for the Home Department ex parte Gallagher*,[216] the European Court of Justice considered the procedure employed under the Prevention of Terrorism (Temporary Provisions) Act 1989 for the making of exclusion orders. Gallagher, an Irish citizen, had been arrested and served with an order under section 7 excluding him from the United Kingdom. When interviewed at the British Embassy in Dublin, the interview did not reveal his

---

211 Prevention of Terrorism (Temporary Provisions) Act 1989, s 5(2).

212 *Ibid*, s 5(4).

213 *Ibid*, s 6.

214 See *Secretary of State for Home Affairs ex parte Stitt* (1987) *The Times*, 3 February.

215 [1995] 4 All ER 400.

216 Case C-175/94: (1995) *The Times*, 13 December.

identity or provide information on the grounds of the exclusion. The Court of appeal referred the matter to the European Court of Justice for consideration of Article 9(1) of Directive 64/221. The Court of Justice ruled that, save in cases of urgency, the administrative authority could not make an exclusion order before a competent authority had given its opinion. The Court also ruled that Article 9(1) did not preclude the competent authority from being appointed by the same administrative authority as took the decision ordering expulsion, provided that the competent authority could perform its duties in absolute independence.

As noted above, the 1989 Act is repealed by the Terrorism Act 2000. The 2000 Act now regulates port and border controls in relation to Great Britain, the Republic of Ireland and Northern Ireland.[217] See, further, Chapter 23.

217 Terrorism Act 2000, s 53 and Sched 7.

CHAPTER 22

THE PROTECTION OF HUMAN RIGHTS

INTRODUCTION

The conventional constitutional position of civil liberties, as discussed in Chapters 19 to 21, is one of individual freedom, save where circumscribed by law, and rights which have developed in an ad hoc manner under common law and statute. Over and above such freedoms and rights is the European Convention on Human Rights and Fundamental Freedoms, which provides a code of human rights, enforceable by the individual citizen against his or her State.

As will be seen from the discussion below, there has long been a demand that this Convention be incorporated into English law, in order that its provisions be directly enforceable in the domestic courts. In the Labour Party's 1996 general election *Manifesto*, the Party undertook to incorporate Convention rights.[1] Following the Labour government's significant election victory in 1997, a White Paper was published, together with the Human Rights Bill which gave effect to the government's commitment. The Human Rights Act 1998 marks a significant constitutional change in relation to citizen's awareness about rights, and their protection by judges in the domestic courts. The Act and its implications are considered later in this chapter. Prior to incorporation of Convention rights, the judges used the Convention as an aid to interpretation to assist in resolving ambiguities in domestic law. However, given the supremacy of Parliament, the judges previously had no jurisdictional basis on which directly to employ the Convention to protect rights. The Human Rights Act confers this jurisdiction, requiring the courts not only to protect Convention rights, but to make 'declarations of incompatibility' wherever domestic law is judicially seen to conflict with Convention rights. By this means, Parliament preserves its supremacy over changes in the law which may be required by judicial evaluation of domestic law against the provisions of the Convention. Before considering the Human Rights Act, however, it is necessary to understand the scope and application of the Convention rights which the Act incorporates.

Not only is the Convention a fertile resource for the enforcement of rights in the European arena, but also the jurisprudence of the Commission and

---

1   See the Consultation Paper, *Bringing Rights Home: Labour's Plans to Incorporate the European Convention on Human Rights into United Kingdom Law*, 1996, London: Labour Party. Note that technically the Human Rights Act 1998 does not incorporate the Convention, but rather makes Convention rights enforceable before the domestic courts.

Court of Human Rights must be applied by the domestic courts under the Human Rights Act 1998, by the government and by public bodies.

THE EUROPEAN CONVENTION ON HUMAN RIGHTS AND FUNDAMENTAL FREEDOMS[2]

Introduction

Europe was one of the principal theatres of the Second World War, following which there was felt to be a great need for European political, social and economic unity. Those objectives were perceived to be promoted, in part, by the adoption a uniform Convention designed to protect human rights and fundamental freedoms.[3] In 1949, the Council of Europe was established and the Convention on Human Rights ratified by Member States in 1951, coming into force in 1953.[4] Despite having been instrumental in the drafting of the text of the Convention, the British government had strong reservations about the Convention and its impact on British constitutional law. As a result of such reservations, it was not until 1965 that the government gave individuals the right to petition under the Convention.

The status of the Convention under English law prior to the Human Rights Act 1998[5]

The attitude of the United Kingdom courts towards the Convention has, in the past, been the traditional one adopted in relation to treaties. Treaties form part of international law and have no place within the domestic legal order unless and until incorporated into law.[6] The courts regarded the Convention as an aid to interpretation but had no jurisdiction directly to enforce the rights and

---

2   The literature on the Convention is extensive. See, *inter alia*, Fawcett, J, *The Application of the European Convention on Human Rights*, 1987, Oxford: Clarendon; Jacobs, FG, *The European Convention on Human Rights*, 1975, Oxford: Clarendon; Van Dijk, P and Van Hoof, G, *Theory and Practice of the European Convention on Human Rights*, 2nd edn, 1990, Deventer, Netherlands: Kluwer; Palley, C, *The United Kingdom and Human Rights*, 1991, London: Sweet & Maxwell; Harris, DJ, O'Boyle, M and Warbrick, C, *Law of the Convention on Human Rights*, 1995, Edinburgh: Butterworths.

3   See Robertson, AH, *Human Rights in Europe*, 2nd edn, 1977, Manchester: Manchester UP.

4   For a succinct history of the Convention, see Lester (Lord), 'European human rights and the British constitution', in Jowell, J and Oliver, D (eds), *The Changing Constitution*, 3rd edn, 1994, Oxford: Clarendon.

5   See Browne-Wilkinson (Lord), 'The infiltration of a Bill of Rights' [1992] PL 405; Bingham, TH (Sir), 'The European Convention on Human Rights: time to incorporate' (1993) 109 LQR 390; Laws, J (Sir), 'Is the High Court the guardian of fundamental constitutional rights?' [1993] PL 60.

6   See *Kaur v Lord Advocate* [1980] 3 CMLR 79.

freedoms under the Convention.[7] This could, however, of itself be significant. For example, in *Waddington v Miah,* Lord Reid stated – having referred to Article 7 of the Convention which prohibits retrospective legislation – that 'it is hardly credible that any government department would promote, or that Parliament would pass, retrospective criminal legislation'.[8]

The influence of the Convention before the Human Rights Act 1998

While previously lacking the jurisdiction to enforce Convention rights. the English courts were nevertheless influenced by Convention provisions. By way of example of the influence of the Convention, in *R v Secretary of State for the Home Department ex parte Brind,*[9] the Home Secretary had exercised his discretionary power under section 19(3) of the Broadcasting Act 1981 to issue a notice requiring the Independent Broadcasting Authority 'to refrain from broadcasting any matter or classes of matter specified in the notice'. In 1988, with the aim of depriving those connected directly or indirectly with terrorist activity related to Northern Ireland of the 'oxygen of publicity', the Home Secretary issued a notice prohibiting the broadcasting on television or radio of the voices of any person speaking on behalf of a 'proscribed organisation'. The words used could be reported through the medium of an actor, provided that the voice of the spokesperson was not broadcast. The challenge to this prohibition was, in the House of Lords, based primarily on the argument that it was contrary to the United Kingdom's obligations under Article 10 of the Convention, guaranteeing freedom of expression. It was argued that the Home Secretary should have had regard to the Convention in exercising his discretion under the Broadcasting Act.

The House of Lords was prepared to accept that there was a presumption that Parliament would enact laws that were in conformity with the Convention. Accordingly, it was accepted that, where a statute permits two interpretations, one in line with the Convention, the other contrary to it, the interpretation which fitted with the Convention should be preferred. The House of Lords, however, was not prepared to accept that where a discretion could be exercised, the presumption that Parliament intended that it should be exercised having regard to the Convention must be applied. Lord Bridge stated that to do so would go beyond the resolution of ambiguity and would, in effect, compel the courts to enforce conformity with the Convention. In *Brind,* the court could find no ambiguity in section 29(3) of the Broadcasting Act. The only basis for challenge therefore was that the Home Secretary's

---

7   *Waddington v Miah* [1974] 2 All ER 377.
8   [1974] 2 All ER 377, p 379. See, further, below for the (retrospective) War Crimes Act 1991.
9   [1991] 1 All ER 720.

decision was unreasonable in the *Wednesbury*[10] sense, that is to say, that the decision was so irrational or unreasonable that no rational or reasonable person could have reached the same decision.

A rather different approach to the Convention was adopted in *Derbyshire County Council v Times Newspapers Ltd*, concerning the question of whether a local council could bring an action in libel against newspapers,[11] Lord Justice Balcome stated that Article 10 of the Convention could be used to resolve ambiguities in legislation and also as guidance to the court in considering the principles on which the court should exercise a discretion and also as a guide when the common law is uncertain. The Court of Appeal found that common law was uncertain with respect to the right of central or local government to sue in defamation, and that the court was entitled to rely on the Convention as an aid to interpretation. As a result, the court held that a right to sue newspaper editors in defamation would endanger freedom of expression as protected by Article 10 of the Convention. In the Court of Appeal, Butler-Sloss LJ was forthright in declaring that 'where there is ambiguity, or the law is otherwise unclear as so far undeclared by an appellate court, the English court is not only entitled but ... obliged to consider the implications of Article 10'.

The House of Lords, however, while arriving at the result achieved in the Court of Appeal – namely that local authorities enjoyed no standing to sue in defamation – did so without relying on Article 10 of the Convention. Lord Keith said:

> I have reached my conclusion upon the common law of England without finding any need to rely on the European Convention. Lord Goff in *Attorney General v Guardian Newspapers* [1990] 1 AC 109 expressed the opinion that in the field of freedom of speech there was no difference in principle between the English law on the subject and Article 10 of the Convention. I agree, and can only add that I find it satisfactory to be able to conclude that the common law of England is consistent with the obligations assumed by the Crown under the Treaty in this particular field.[12]

Accordingly, there existed (before the Human Rights Act 1998 came into force) no obligation for courts to rely on the Convention if a source of authority can be found within domestic law. Increasingly, however, it appeared that – within certain limits – the judiciary expressed willingness to protect individual liberties and, where a statute was ambiguous, or silent, to construe the statute strictly and in favour of the liberty of the citizen.

However, there were limits to the extent to which judges were able to protect rights, as the case of *R v Inland Revenue Commissioners ex parte*

---

10 *Associated Provincial Picture Houses Ltd v Wednesbury Corporation* [1948] 1 KB 223. See, further, Chapter 25.

11 See, further, below.

12 [1993] 1 All ER 1011, p 1012.

Rossminster Ltd[13] revealed. In *Rossminster*, the House of Lords ruled that, where the meaning of a statute is clear and unambiguous, the court possessed no jurisdiction to go against its unambiguous words, and was under a duty to uphold the will of Parliament by giving effect to its words. In both *Attorney General v BBC*[14] and *Attorney General v Guardian Newspapers (No 2)*,[15] however, the House of Lords confirmed that it was the duty of the courts to have regard to the international obligations assumed under the Convention, and to interpret the law in accordance with those obligations.

The application of Convention provisions in the interim period between the passing of the Human Rights Act 1998 and its coming into effect in England and Wales was considered by the House of Lords in *R v DPP ex p Kebiline and Others*.[16] The House of Lords ruled, on an appeal by the Director of Public Prosecutions from a decision of the Divisional Court,[17] that the decision of the Director of Public Prosecutions to proceed with a prosecution under section 16A of the Prevention of Terrorism (Temporary Provisions) Act 1989, which reverses the burden of proof in relation to the possession of articles for purposes connected with terrorist activities and which is, arguably, contrary to Article 6 of the Convention, was not unlawful. In light of Article 6 and its impending incorporation under the Human Rights Act 1998, the applicants had argued that the Director of Public Prosecutions should have had regard to Article 6 in relation to his decision to prosecute, and sought judicial review of his decision to prosecute. The House of Lords ruled that the decision to prosecute, notwithstanding the reversal of the burden of proof in the Prevention of Terrorism Act, was not amenable to judicial review. Such challenges as will arise when the Human Rights Act is in force should be brought within the context of trial or appeal proceedings.

Cases against the United Kingdom[18]

It has been recorded that, between 1975 and 1990, the European Court of Human Rights decided 30 cases involving the United Kingdom, 21 of these case resulting in a finding of a violation of the Convention: a 70:30 ratio of

---

13 [1980] AC 952. See also *R v Kelly*, *R v Sandford* (1998) *The Times*, 29 December, CA; and *R v Secretary of State for the Home Department ex parte Hussain Ahmed* (1998) *The Times*, 15 October.

14 [1981] AC 303; [1981] 3 WLR 109.

15 [1990] 1 AC 109.

16 (1999) *The Times*, 31 March.

17 [1999] 3 WLR 175.

18 See Bradley, AW, 'The United Kingdom before the Strasbourg Court 1975–90', in Finnie, W, Himsworth, C and Walker, N (eds), *Edinburgh Essays in Public Law*, 1991, Edinburgh: Edinburgh UP.

success.[19] By 1997, a total of 50 successful applications had been made, alleging violations under the Convention, against the United Kingdom. The significance of the figures should not be exaggerated. In all other European countries,[20] either the Convention is enshrined in law or the constitution of the State provides a Bill of Rights. The United Kingdom was thus in the minority of Member States of the Council of Europe in not previously having such protective legislation.

The European Convention on Human Rights: the substantive rights

ARTICLE 1

The High Contracting Parties shall secure to everyone within jurisdiction the rights and freedoms defined in Section 1 of this Convention.

ARTICLE 2

1   Everyone's right to life shall be protected by law. No one shall be deprived of his life intentionally save in the execution of a sentence of a court following his conviction of a crime for which this penalty is provided by law.

2   Deprivation of life shall not be regarded as inflicted in contravention of this Article when it results from the use of force which is not more than absolutely necessary:

    (a) in defence of any person from unlawful violence;

    (b) in order to effect a lawful arrest or to prevent the escape of a person lawfully detained;

    (c) in action lawfully taken for the purpose of quelling a riot or insurrection.

The scope of this Article is broad but vague. It is clear that imposition of the death penalty is not *per se* contrary to the Convention, although there may be situations where the circumstances leading up to imposition of the death penalty amount to a violation of Article 3, which prohibits torture or inhuman or degrading punishment or treatment. However, it is much less clear as to the duty, if any, which is imposed on States to sustain life by providing, for example, the economic and social conditions under which the right to life is meaningfully upheld. In *Simon-Herald v Austria*,[21] for example, allegations that the State had failed to provide adequate medical care to prisoners was

---

19   See Churchill, RR and Young, JR, 'Compliance with judgments of the European Court of Human Rights' [1991] BYIL 283.

20   The Republic of Ireland and Denmark have not incorporated the Convention, but each has its own Bill of Rights.

21   (1971) 14 YB 351.

ruled admissible, although a friendly settlement was reached thus avoiding the need for a judicial analysis.

Issues are also raised under Article 2 as to the legality of euthanasia and abortion. Under domestic law, euthanasia – the act of facilitating a person's death when suffering from an incurable illness – amounts to murder and would also appear to be a violation of Article 2, if sanctioned by the State. In relation to abortion, under United Kingdom law, there is a restricted right to abortion under the Abortion Act 1967.[22] Whether such provisions violate Article 2 depends on the interpretation given to the word 'everyone' in Article 1. Domestic law has consistently ruled that legal protection of the person commences at birth, and not before, a view supported in *Paton v United Kingdom*,[23] although whether the right to unrestricted abortion would violate the Article was mooted in *Open Door Counselling and Well Woman v Ireland*.[24]

The allowable exceptions to the protection of Article 2 are designed to excuse unintentional causes of death in violent situations. Thus the use of plastic bullets in a riot will not violate Article 2,[25] nor will measures taken to prevent possible future terrorist activities.[26] There are, however, limits to the lawful use of force. In *Kelly v United Kingdom*,[27] an application under Article 2 was rejected as manifestly ill founded. Soldiers had shot dead a joyrider who had attempted to avoid an army checkpoint, and the use of force was held to be justifiable. The killing of three Irish Republican Army members by members of the SAS in Gibraltar[28] was challenged under the European Convention on Human Rights.[29] In *McGann, Farrell and Savage v United Kingdom*,[30] the Court ruled that, given the information which the security forces had received regarding the movements of the suspected terrorists, their shooting did not violate Article 2 of the Convention. Nevertheless, the Court ruled that there had been inadequate control over the security forces operation and that, as a result, the killing of the suspected terrorists was 'more than absolutely necessary' as provided within Article 2. Thus the action taken, to be lawful, must be proportionate to the circumstances of the case. A violation of Article 2 was also found in *Andronicus and Constantinou v Cyprus*,[31] a case arising when the police, in a siege operation, fired at the hostage taker but

---

22 As amended.
23 (1980) 3 EHRR 408.
24 (1992) 15 EHRR 244.
25 *Stewart v United Kingdom* (1985) 7 EHRR 453.
26 *Kelly v United Kingdom* (1993) 16 EHRR 20.
27 Appl 17579/90: (1993) 16 EHRR 20; (1993) 74 D & R 139.
28 For further details on the circumstances, see Chapter 23.
29 Case 17/1994/464/545: (1995) *The Times*, 9 October.
30 (1995) 21 EHRR 97, A.324, Council of Europe Report.
31 (1996) 22 EHRR CD 18.

killed the hostage. It was held that the number of bullets fired reflected a lack of caution in the operation.

ARTICLE 3

No one shall be subjected to torture or to inhuman or degrading treatment or punishment.

In *Ireland v United Kingdom*,[32] the Republic of Ireland[33] alleged that the United Kingdom had, *inter alia*, violated Article 3 of the Convention, which proscribes 'inhuman or degrading treatment or punishment'. In 1966, the United Kingdom had declared that there was a state of emergency in Northern Ireland. In 1971, acting under the Civil Authorities (Special Powers) Act 1922,[34] the government introduced new powers of detention and internment of suspected Irish Republican Army terrorists. Some 354 men were initially arrested. Within 48 hours, 104 were released. Of the remainder, 14 were singled out for interrogation, during which time such techniques as hooding, wall-standing for between 23 and 29 hours, noise intrusions and deprivation of sleep, food and water were employed. There was evidence that the men subjected to these practices suffered a loss of weight and pain. Between August and November 1971, a total of some 980 suspects were arrested[35] and further allegations of ill treatment made. The Compton Committee of Inquiry,[36] ruled that the interrogation techniques amounted to ill treatment. The government of the Republic of Ireland alleged violations of Articles 3, 5 and 14. The Commission on Human Rights held that the Convention requirements had been violated by administrative practices. The Commission sought to reach a 'friendly settlement' with the government of the United Kingdom but the negotiations broke down. The Commission reported under Article 31, stating the facts and its opinion as to whether the facts disclosed a breach of the standards set by the Convention.

For the purposes of its report, the Commission was required to define Article 3: what was the meaning of the terms 'torture, inhuman or degrading treatment or punishment'? Further, was the State liable for the acts of its agents? The Commission held that, regardless of the rank of those carrying out the techniques, the actions were those authorised by, and the responsibility of, the government. Despite the techniques having been abandoned, the Commission went on to rule on the justifiability of ill treatment under the circumstances.

---

32 (1976) 2 EHRR 25.

33 Under ECHR, Art 24, which provides for inter-State applications.

34 See, now, the Northern Ireland (Emergency Provisions) Act 1991, Pt IV and Sched 3.

35 See Spjut, RJ, 'Internment and detention without trial in Northern Ireland' (1986) 49 MLR 712.

36 Cmnd 4823, 1971, London: HMSO.

The matter was referred to the Court under Article 48. On its judicial role, the Court declared that it had jurisdiction not just to decide issues but also to elucidate, safeguard and develop rules and thereby contribute to the observance of obligations of States.

In the instant case, no derogation was permitted under Article 15 (see, further, below). The techniques, applied in combination and with premeditation for hours at a time caused, if not actual bodily injury, at least intense physical and mental suffering and led to acute psychiatric disturbances. The treatment fell within the meaning of inhuman treatment; it was also degrading, arousing feelings of fear, anguish and inferiority capable of humiliating and debasing them and breaking their physical or moral resistance. To amount to torture, however, comparison must be made with inhuman and degrading treatment. The distinction, ruled the Court, derives from the difference in the intensity of suffering inflicted. In this case it did not occasion suffering of a particular intensity and cruelty implied by the word torture as understood by the Court.[37]

In *Tyrer v United Kingdom*,[38] the Court ruled on the compatibility of birching as a judicial punishment in the Isle of Man[39] with the requirements of Article 3. Tyrer, then aged 15, was given three strokes of the birch as punishment for an assault on a school prefect. The question raised was whether the punishment amounted to a violation of Article 3.

The Commission decided that the treatment did not fall within the meaning of torture as defined in the *Ireland* case, nor inhuman treatment, but questioned whether it amounted to degrading treatment. It was held that judicial birching humiliates and disgraces the offender, and can therefore be said to be degrading treatment. The government tried to argue the benefit of birching as a deterrent, but the Commission found no 'social value' and, moreover, that, once there was a finding of a breach under Article 3, the issue of social value was irrelevant. The Court held that, while a conviction for a criminal offence itself could humiliate, for a finding to be sustained under Article 3, there needed to be found a humiliation deriving from the execution of punishment imposed. The treatment must attain a particular level and the assessment was relative: the assessment turns on the nature and context of the punishment and the method of its execution. Corporal punishment, the Court stated in *Tyrer*, may be undesirable without necessarily being degrading. When inflicted with proper safeguards and when traditionally sanctioned for

---

37 There was no violation of Art 14 (the harsher treatment given to the IRA suspects was justified by their greater menace), and no violation of Art 1 (which cannot be a head for a separate breach of the ECHR).

38 (1978); (1980) 2 EHRR 1.

39 See Chapter 2.

offences in the society to which the offender belongs, it may not be degrading. The mere fact that the punishment being inflicted was distasteful was not enough. Under the circumstances, with the victim having to undress, the treatment reached a level of degrading punishment.

In *Campbell and Cozens*,[40] the issue of corporal punishment in United Kingdom state schools was raised and declared incompatible with the Convention.[41] Children had been suspended from school as a result of their parents' opposition to corporal punishment: a policy contrary to Article 2 of Protocol Number 1 to the Convention. However, in *Costello-Roberts v United Kingdom*,[42] the Court indicated that there is a distinction to be drawn between ordinary physical punishment, which may not violate the Convention, and corporal punishment, which is degrading. The determination as to whether or not the requirements of the Convention have been breached will depend upon the conditions under which the punishment is inflicted. In *A v United Kingdom*,[43] the stepfather of a child had beaten him with a stick, resulting in bruising which a paediatrician considered to indicate that he had been beaten with considerable force on more than one occasion. The stepfather was acquitted by a majority verdict of charges of assault occasioning actual bodily harm. The Court of Human Rights held that domestic law did not provide adequate protection for children in relation to treatment or punishment contrary to Article 3 of the Convention.

The law relating to immigration, race and citizenship has also been tested under Article 3. In *East African Asians v United Kingdom*,[44] the immigration legislation[45] restricted immigration of British passport holders in East Africa, preventing those who had neither a parent or grandparent born or naturalised in the United Kingdom from entering the country. The Commission ruled that racial discrimination of this type constituted a form of affront to human dignity and amounted to degrading treatment.

Issues are also raised as to the lawfulness of the conditions under which a prisoner is detained.[46] The rights of persons to remain in the United Kingdom may also be raised under Article 3. If an individual is returned to his homeland in the knowledge that he will there suffer certain imprisonment or death, a State may violate Article 3 by refusing to allow him to remain. Two illustrative cases may be cited. In *Soering v United Kingdom*,[47] the applicant

---

40 (1982) 4 EHRR 293.

41 Education (No 2) Act 1986.

42 Judgment, 25 March 1993.

43 Case No 100/1997/884/1096: (1998) *The Times*, 1 October; [1998] 2 FLR 959; [1999] 27 EHRR 611.

44 (1973) 3 EHRR 76.

45 Commonwealth Immigrants Act 1968.

46 See *Krocher and Moller v Switzerland* (1984) 6 EHRR 345.

47 Judgment, 7 July 1989.

successfully alleged that his extradition to the United States on a charge of capital murder, which would result in his detention on Death Row prior to execution, would amount to a breach of Article 3. Conversely, in *Vilvarajah and Four Others v United Kingdom*,[48] the applicants had applied for political asylum in the United Kingdom, fearing persecution if they returned to Sri Lanka. Following deportation four of them were arrested and ill treated. No breach of Article 3 was established, since the court held that there was no clear risk of ill treatment proven, only a possibility of ill treatment.

The issue was tested in *Chahal v United Kingdom*,[49] in which the Court of Human Rights ruled that the United Kingdom violated Article 3 of the Convention[50] and that there had been a violation of Article 13 in conjunction with Article 3, in that effective remedies did not exist before the courts in England.[51] In addition, there was also a violation of Article 5(4), in that Mr Chahal had been denied the opportunity to have the lawfulness of his detention decided by a national court.[52]

Mr Chahal, a Sikh, had been politically active in Sikh affairs. In 1990, the Home Secretary decided to deport him from the United Kingdom on the ground of national security and the international fight against terrorism. He was arrested in 1990 and detained. Mr Chahal applied for political asylum, claiming he would be a victim of torture if deported to India. The Home Secretary refused his request in 1991. There was no right of appeal to an independent tribunal because of the claim to national security. The matter was considered by an advisory panel including a Court of Appeal judge. Mr Chahal was not informed of allegations against him, nor allowed to be represented by a lawyer. The deportation order was signed in 1991. He applied to judicial review, which was granted on the basis of inadequate reasons having been given. In 1992, the Home Secretary again refused asylum. Mr Chahal sought judicial review, which was denied. He appealed to the Court of Appeal.[53] Mr Chahal had been subject to torture in India on a visit in 1984. The Court was appraised of substantiated allegations of torture by the authorities in India. By refusing Mr Chahal asylum and threatening to deport him, the United Kingdom authorities violated Article 3. Mr Chahal's detention on the basis of national security was not a violation of Article 5(1), since there was *prima facie* evidence that national security would be threatened by his release.

---

48 (1991) 14 EHRR 248; A.215.
49 (1997) 23 EHRR 413; (1996) *The Times*, 28 November.
50 By 12 votes to seven.
51 Unanimously.
52 Case 70/1995: (1996) *The Times*, 28 November.
53 *R v Secretary of State for the Home Department ex parte Chahal* [1995] 1 WLR 526; (1993) *The Times*, 27 October.

Following the decision of the European Court,[54] Mr Chahal sought compensation from the Secretary of State. His application was refused. He then sought judicial review of the Home Secretary's decision. In *R v Secretary of State for the Home Department ex p Chahal (No 2)*,[55] the Court of Appeal ruled that a person detained on the ground of national security, whose deportation would be a breach of his Convention rights and whose detention was otherwise lawful, had not been unlawfully or irrationally refused compensation.

The threat to remove was retested in *D v United Kingdom*.[56] D had arrived in the United Kingdom in 1993 from his country of origin, St Kitts. On arrival, he was found to have in his possession a substantial quantity of cocaine. Rather than being deported, he was arrested and charged with illegally importing a controlled drug. He was convicted and sentenced to six years imprisonment. In 1994, the applicant was diagnosed as HIV positive and suffering from AIDS. A medical report of 1996 indicated that his life expectancy was limited to eight to 12 months. In January 1996, shortly before the applicant was due to be released from prison on licence, the immigration authorities ordered his removal to St Kitts. D applied unsuccessfully for judicial review. His appeal was dismissed by the Court of Appeal. An application was lodged under the Convention.

The Court of Human Rights heard the case in February 1997. The Commission had decided that there would be a violation of Article 3 if the applicant were to be removed to St Kitts. On the alleged violation of Article 3, the Court ruled that whereas States had the right to control residence and expel aliens, and whereas the applicant had been guilty of drug trafficking, nevertheless, the State must exercise its powers in the light of Article 3 of the Convention. Article 3 prohibited in absolute terms torture or inhuman or degrading treatment or punishment, and its guarantees applied, irrespective of the reprehensible nature of the conduct of the person in question. The Court was not limited to considering Article 3 within the context of anticipated torture or inhuman treatment on the part of the public authorities of the recipient country. The applicant's condition was deteriorating. To remove him to St Kitts, where he had no family willing to care for him or home of his own, and no guarantee of adequate medical treatment, would expose him to 'a real risk of dying in the most distressing circumstances and thus to inhuman treatment contrary to Article 3'.

ARTICLE 4

1   No one shall be held in slavery or servitude.

2   No one shall be required to perform forced or compulsory labour.

---

54   (1996) 23 EHRR 413; (1996) *The Times*, 28 November.

55   (1999) *The Times*, 10 November.

56   Case 146/1996/767/964: (1997) *The Times*, 12 May.

3   For the purpose of this Article the term 'forced or compulsory labour' shall not include:

   (a) any work required to be done in the ordinary course of detention imposed according to the provisions of Article 5 of this Convention or during conditional release from such detention;

   (b) any service of a military character or, in the case of conscientious objectors in countries where they are recognised, service exacted instead of compulsory military service;

   (c) any service exacted in case of any emergency or calamity threatening the life or well being of the community;

   (d) any work or service which forms part of normal civic obligations.

This provision has little relevance in the majority of Western democracies and has given rise to little case law. Challenges have been made relating to the requirement that German lawyers undertake compulsory legal aid work, but these have failed.[57]

ARTICLE 5

1   Everyone has the right to liberty and security of person.

   No one shall be deprived of his liberty save in the following cases and in accordance with a procedure prescribed by law:

   (a) the lawful detention of a person after conviction by a competent court;[58]

   (b) the lawful arrest or detention of a person for non-compliance with the lawful order of a court or in order to secure the fulfilment of any obligation prescribed by law;

   (c) the lawful arrest or detention of a person effected for the purpose of bringing him before the competent legal authority on reasonable suspicion of having committed an offence or when it is reasonably considered necessary to prevent his committing an offence or fleeing after having done so;[59]

   (d) the detention of a minor by lawful order for the purpose of educational supervision or his lawful detention for the purpose of bringing him before the competent legal authority;[60]

   (e) the lawful detention of persons for the prevention of the spreading of infectious diseases, of persons of unsound mind, alcoholics or drug addicts, or vagrants;[61]

---

57   *Van der Mussele v Germany*, judgment 23 November 1983.

58   See *Van Droogenbroeck v Belgium* (1982) 4 EHRR 443; *Weeks v United Kingdom* (1987) 10 EHRR 293.

59   See *Lawless v Republic of Ireland* (1960) 1 EHRR 1; *Brogan v United Kingdom* (1988) 11 EHRR 117; *Fox, Campbell and Hartley v United Kingdom* (1990) 13 EHRR 157; *McKee v Chief Constable for Northern Ireland* [1985] 1 All ER 1; *Ciulla v Italy* (1989) 13 EHRR 346.

60   See *Bouamar v Belgium* (1988) 11 EHRR 1.

61   See *X v United Kingdom* (1981) 4 EHRR 188; *Brogan v United Kingdom* (1988) 11 EHRR 117; *De Wilde, Ooms and Versyp v Belgium* (1971) 1 EHRR 373 (the vagrancy cases).

(f) the lawful arrest or detention of a person to prevent his effecting an unauthorised entry into the country or of a person against whom action is being taken with a view to deportation or extradition.

2 Everyone who is arrested shall be informed promptly, in a language which he understands, of the reasons for his arrest and of any charge against him.[62]

3 Everyone arrested or detained in accordance with the provisions of paragraph 1(c) of this article shall be brought promptly before a judge[63] or other officer authorised by law to exercise judicial power and shall be entitled to trial within a reasonable time[64] or to release pending trial. Release may be conditioned by guarantees to appear for trial.[65]

4 Everyone who is deprived of his liberty by arrest or detention shall be entitled to take proceedings by which the lawfulness of his detention shall be decided speedily by a court and his release ordered if the detention is not lawful.[66]

5 Everyone who has been the victim of arrest or detention in contravention of the provisions of this article shall have an enforceable right to compensation.[67]

This long and intricate Article has provided the platform for many challenges on behalf of persons detained and is in many cases linked to Article 6 (on which, see below). The first requirement to be met in relation to Article 5 is that, where a person is deprived of his liberty, the deprivation must be in consequence of a lawful detention (paragraph 1(a)–(f)).

In *Van Droogenbroeck v Belgium*,[68] the applicant was convicted and sentenced to imprisonment for theft. He was ordered by the court to be 'placed at the government's disposal' for 10 years. On his release, on conditional terms, the applicant disappeared and committed further offences for which he was acquitted. Nevertheless, he was detained in premises used for the detention of reoffenders. The Court held that, since his original sentence involved decisions to be taken by the Minister of Justice, the applicant was not unlawfully detained. A similar situation arose in the *Weeks* case.[69] The issue raised, under Article 5(1)(a), was whether the revocation of a

---

62 See *Murray v United Kingdom* (1995) 19 EHRR 193; (1994) *The Times*, 1 November.

63 *Brogan v United Kingdom* (1988) 11 EHRR 117; *Brannigan and McBride v United Kingdom* (1994) 17 EHRR 539; (1993) *The Times*, 28 May.

64 See *Wemhoff v Federal Republic of Germany* 7 YB 280 and 11 YB 796; (1979–80) 1 EHRR 55.

65 See *Neumeister* (1968) 1 EHRR 91; *De Jong, Baljet and van den Brik v Netherlands* (1983) 8 EHRR 20.

66 See *X v United Kingdom* (1981) 4 EHRR 188; *Brogan v United Kingdom* (1988) 11 EHRR 117; *De Wilde, Ooms and Versyp v Belgium* (1971) 1 EHRR 373 (the vagrancy cases).

67 *Wemhoff v Federal Republic of Germany* 7 YB 280 and 11 YB 796; (1979–80) 1 EHRR 55; Appl 6821/74: *Huber v Austria*.

68 (1982) 4 EHRR 443.

69 (1987) 10 EHRR 293.

life licence deprives a person of his liberty without the conviction of a court of law. In that case, the applicant had been sentenced to life imprisonment but, after 10 years, was released on licence. The Home Secretary revoked the licence after Weeks had failed to stay out of trouble. The Court held, however, that the original sentence was passed in the knowledge that the Home Secretary enjoyed a discretion as to the liberty of prisoners under sentence and that, accordingly, there was a sufficient link between the original sentence passed, the granting of a licence, and the revocation of the licence.

The lawfulness of arrest was also tested in *Steel and Others v United Kingdom*.[70] In a case involving five applicants, allegations of breaches of Articles 5, 6, 10, 11 and 13 were made. The applicants had been involved in animal rights and other protests, and had been arrested and charged with breach of the peace. In relation to Article 5(1), while the concept of breach of the peace was sufficiently clear and formulated 'with the degree of precision required by the Convention', where, as in the case of three of the applicants, the protest had been entirely peaceful and there had been no obstruction of others or any provocation of others to violence, the Court ruled that their arrest and subsequent detention was not lawful within the meaning of Article 5(1).

Article 5(1) was also violated in the case of *Johnson v United Kingdom*.[71] In this case, the applicant had been convicted of a number of assaults and, having been found to be suffering from mental illness within the Mental Health Act 1983, was in 1984 ordered to be detained indefinitely. In 1989, the Mental Health Review Tribunal decided that the applicant was no longer suffering from mental illness. However, since no suitable accommodation for the applicant could be found, he was detained until 1993. That detention violated the requirements of lawful detention.

The second group of requirements is that, where a person is arrested, that person must be informed of the grounds for the arrest (paragraph 2), be brought 'promptly' before a court of law and, moreover, is entitled to a trial within a reasonable time, or to be released on bail (paragraph 3). In *Wemhoff v Federal Republic of Germany*,[72] the Court ruled that the reasonableness of a person's detention depended upon whether or not that detention was 'unreasonably prolonged'. In *Neumeister v Austria*,[73] the applicants had been held on remand for over three years, pending trial. The Commission ruled that there had been no violation of Article 5(3) in light of the circumstances and complexity of the case (involving allegations of terrorist activities). In other cases, the requirement for a prompt trial will be more demanding and

---

70   Appl 67/1997/851/1058 1998: judgment 23 September 1998.
71   Case 119/1996/738/937.
72   7 YB 280 and 11 YB 796; (1979–80) 1 EHRR 55.
73   (1968) 1 EHRR 91.

immediate, as in *Stogmuller v Austria*,[74] where detention pending trial was less than 24 months but, nevertheless, unreasonably long.

These requirements were tested in *Murray v United Kingdom*.[75] The applicant alleged a breach of Article 5 and a breach of Article 8, on the basis that she had been detained by soldiers in Northern Ireland who suspected that they had grounds for arrest. Despite there being a period of a few hours between the time of arrest and informing the applicant of the reason for arrest, this was insufficient to amount to a violation of Article 5.[76] In *Brogan v United Kingdom*,[77] a challenge was lodged to the lawfulness of detention for up to seven days, at the Home Secretary's discretion, under the Prevention of Terrorism Act. The Court ruled that such detention represented a violation of the requirements of Article 5.[78]

Articles 5 and 6 of the Convention were considered by the Court of Human Rights in *Yagci and Sargin v Turkey* and *Mansur v Turkey*.[79] Yagci and Sargin, respectively, general secretaries of the Turkish Workers' Party and the Turkish Communist Party, had been arrested on their return to Turkey in November 1987 and kept in custody pending trial for charges relating to their organisations, for approximately two and a half years. In the case of Mr Mansur, the applicant had been convicted of a drug trafficking offence committed in 1980. On his release in 1984, he returned to Turkey in order to acquire Turkish nationality, which was granted in 1989. In 1984, Mr Mansur was arrested in Turkey and placed in detention by a police court 44 times. In 1991, Mr Mansur was found guilty of exporting drugs and sentenced to 30 years imprisonment. His sentence was later reduced to 10 years and he was released from detention in 1991.

Each of the applicants' alleged breaches of Articles 5 and 6 in respect of the length of their detention pending trial and of the criminal proceedings against them. The Commission, having found their applications admissible, failed to secure a friendly settlement with the Turkish government.

In the case of *Yagci and Sargin*, the Court ruled that their detention violated the Convention. The State's claim that the seriousness of the offences alleged and the risk of the defendant's absconding before trial justified the detention was not accepted. The applicants had been detained from November 1987, when they were arrested, until their acquittal in October 1991. In *Mansur's*

---

74 (1969) 1 EHRR 155.

75 (1995) 19 EHRR 193; (1994) *The Times*, 1 November.

76 There was also a finding that no violation of Art 8 had occurred. The arrest and detention were justified under Art 8(2). See, further, below.

77 (1989) 11 EHRR 117 and see *Brannigan and McBride v United Kingdom* (1994) 17 EHRR 539; (1993) *The Times*, 28 May.

78 The government in response issued a derogation notice and re-enacted the provisions.

79 (1995) *The Times*, 25 June.

case, proceedings had commenced in April 1984 and were determined only in April 1991. The Court ruled, in *Yagci and Sargin* by eight votes to one and in *Mansur* unanimously, that there had been violations of Articles 5(3) and 6(1) of the Convention. The Court awarded 30,000 French francs damages to each of the applicants and a sum to cover legal expenses.

Paragraph 4 provides for the right to test the lawfulness of the detention. In essence, this represents a form of habeas corpus under the Convention. In the *Vagrancy* cases,[80] the applicants had been detained on the order of magistrates on the basis that they were vagrants within the meaning of Article 5(1)(e). The Court ruled that, in order for Article 5(4) to be satisfied, the applicants should have been allowed to test the lawfulness of their detention before a court of law. In relation to the detention of mental patients, the Court has held that, where there is no periodic judicial review of their detention, the detainee must have the opportunity periodically to have his detention reviewed by a judicial body.[81] Paragraph 5 provides for a right to compensation for violation of Article 5.

In *Benham v United Kingdom*,[82] the Court of Human Rights[83] ruled that there was no violation of Article 5(1) of the Convention. Magistrates had committed Benham to prison for thirty days pursuant to his failure to pay his community charge, the reason for which the magistrates found to be his culpable neglect. Benham had not been legally represented before the magistrates. On an application under the Convention alleging breaches of Articles 5 and 6, the Court ruled that, under national law, the order was valid; that the detention was not arbitrary as the magistrates had not acted in bad faith or failed to apply the relevant legislation. There was, however, a violation of Article 6 since, given the complexity of the legal issues and the fact that these were criminal proceedings, Benham should have been entitled to legal representation.

In *Hussain v United Kingdom; Singh v United Kingdom*,[84] the European Court of Human Rights ruled that the United Kingdom had violated Article 5(4) of the Convention. The applicants, who had been sentenced to be detained during Her Majesty's pleasure, were unable to have the lawfulness of their continued detention reviewed by a court.[85]

Articles 5 and 6 have also provided the basis for recent challenges in relation to military proceedings in *Hood v United Kingdom*[86] and *Jordan v*

---

80 *De Wilde, Ooms and Versyp v Belgium* (1971) 1 EHRR 373.
81 *X v United Kingdom* (1982) 4 EHRR 188.
82 Case 7/1995/513/597: (1996) *The Times*, 24 June.
83 By a majority of 17 votes to four.
84 Cases 55/1994/502/584; 56/1994/503/585: (1996) *The Times*, 26 February.
85 See, also, *Curley v United Kingdom* (2000) *The Times*, 17 March.
86 (1999) *The Times*, 11 March.

United Kingdom.[87] In *Hood's* case, the applicant had been tried and convicted of criminal charges under the Army Act 1955. The applicant's commanding officer had decided on pre-trial detention, and had subsequently played a role in hearing the case against the applicant. Accordingly, he could not be impartial, and the proceedings did not meet the requirements of independence and impartiality required by Article 6(1). In *Jordan's* case,[88] the applicant had completed a sentence of imprisonment, but continued to be detained, under close arrest, on the basis of further suspected offences under investigation by military police. Jordan had been released following habeas corpus proceedings and had brought proceedings against the Ministry of Defence, claiming unlawful detention. The commanding officer, who had been involved in Jordan's case since 1995, could not be considered impartial, and there was a violation of Article 5(3) and (5).[89]

Provisions relating to the prosecution of juveniles for criminal offences have also been subject to the scrutiny of the Court of Human Rights. In *T and V v United Kingdom*,[90] the Court ruled that there were violations of Article 5(4) and one violation of Article 6(1). Two boys, aged 10 when they killed a two year old child, were convicted of murder. Following their conviction, the Home Secretary had set the tariff period to be served for retribution and deterrence. Accordingly, there was no opportunity for the lawfulness of their detention to be assessed by a judicial body and, thereby, Article 5(4) was violated. In addition, the adult trial process, although specially adapted in light of the defendants' young age to reduce its formality, caused the defendants stress and, thereby, violated the right to fair trial guaranteed by Article 6.

ARTICLE 6

1   In the determination of his civil rights and obligations or of any criminal charge against him, everyone is entitled to a fair and public hearing within a reasonable time by an independent and impartial tribunal established by law. Judgment shall be pronounced publicly but the press and public may be excluded from all or part of the trial in the interest of morals, public order or national security in a democratic society, where the interests of juveniles or the protection of the private life of the parties so require, or to the extent strictly necessary in the opinion of the court in special circumstances where publicity would prejudice the interests of justice.

---

87   (2000) *The Times*, 17 March. See, also, *Findlay v United Kingdom* (1997) *The Times*, 27 February.

88   See, also, Case 124/1996/743/942: *Coyne v United Kingdom*, in which a court martial conducted before the Armed Forces Act 1996 came into force was not an independent and impartial tribunal.

89   See, now, the Armed Forces Discipline Act 2000.

90   (1999) *The Times*, 17 December.

2 Everyone charged with a criminal offence shall be presumed innocent until proved guilty according to law.

3 Everyone charged with a criminal offence has the following minimum rights:

   (a) to be informed promptly, in a language which he understands and in detail, of the nature and cause of the accusation against him;

   (b) to have adequate time and facilities for the preparation of his defence;

   (c) to defend himself in person or through legal assistance of his own choosing or, if he has not sufficient means to pay for legal assistance, to be given it free when the interests of justice so require;

   (d) to examine or have examined witnesses against him and to obtain the attendance and examination of witnesses on his behalf under the same conditions as witnesses against him;

   (e) to have the free assistance of an interpreter if he cannot understand or speak the language used in court.

Article 6 is the most frequently cited Article. Up to the end of 1989, 63 violations had been found. The protection given relates to the 'determination of ... civil rights and obligations' and 'of any criminal charge'. The Court has had to determine the meaning and scope of these phrases. A 'criminal charge' has been interpreted to mean 'the official notification given to an individual by the competent authority of an allegation that he has committed a criminal offence'.[91]

The former category – 'civil rights and obligations' – has given rise to extensive interpretation. The Article has been held to apply to proceedings before an administrative tribunal – the Regional Land Commission – in Austria.[92] The decisions of most public authorities are outside the scope of the phrase. If, however, the consequence of an administrative decision is one which affects the civil rights of individuals, then Article 6 may be held to apply.[93] For example, in *Konig*, Dr Konig's licence to practise as a doctor in his own clinic was withdrawn. The Court ruled that the decision affected Dr Konig's civil rights and that, therefore, the protection of Article 6 applied.

Particular difficulties arise in disciplinary proceedings for criminal offences in the armed services. The consequence of trying the matter under disciplinary regulations is to remove the normal application of Article 6. The Court has ruled that whether an offence is classified as criminal or disciplinary is less important than the nature of the offence. In *Campbell and Fell v United Kingdom*,[94] following involvement in a prison riot, the applicants had been punished by the Board of Prison Visitors with loss of remission of

---

91 *Eckle v Federal Republic of Germany* (1982) 5 EHRR 1, para 73.
92 *Ringeisen v Austria* (1971) 1 EHRR 455.
93 *Konig v Federal Republic of Germany* (1980) 2 EHRR 170.
94 (1984) 7 EHRR 165.

sentence. The Court held that Article 6 applied to the decision making process of the Board of Visitors.[95]

A 'fair and public hearing' has been interpreted to include the right to legal advice before the judicial hearing. In *Golder v United Kingdom*,[96] Golder, serving a prison sentence, wanted to sue a prison officer for defamation. His request to the Home Secretary to consult a solicitor was denied. The Court held that Article 6 had been violated. The Court has further ruled that not only must access to law not be impeded (by the denial of legal advice or other means), but that the State has a duty to ensure effective access to law.[97] The right of access to law is not absolute, but any restrictions which are imposed must not be such as to impair 'the very essence of the right'. Limitations will be incompatible with the Convention, if they do not pursue a legitimate aim and are not proportional to the objective being sought.[98]

The Court of Human Rights ruled that the United Kingdom authorities had violated Article 6(1) in the case of *Saunders v United Kingdom*.[99] The case concerned the prosecution of Ernest Saunders, formerly chief executive officer of Guinness plc, for corporate fraud. The investigating authorities (inspectors appointed by the Department of Trade and Industry) interviewed Mr Saunders on nine occasions in 1987, using their powers under sections 532(2) and 436(3) of the Companies Act 1985. By law, Mr Saunders was compelled to answer questions put by the inspectors, under threat of contempt of court and the imposition of a fine or a prison sentence. In 1996, the inspectors notified the Secretary of State that they had evidence of possible criminal offences. These were passed to the Crown Prosecution Service which, in turn, made them available to the police, who began their own investigations into the matter in May 1987. As a result, the applicant was charged on 15 counts. The trial commenced in 1989, and Mr Saunders pleaded not guilty. The prosecution sought to prove the case against Mr Saunders by using the transcripts of statements made by him to the Department of Trade and Industry inspectors. In 1990, the applicant was convicted on 12 counts of conspiracy, false accounting and theft. He received a five year term of imprisonment, a term reduced by the Court of Appeal in 1991. In 1994, as a result of new evidence, the Secretary of State referred the case back to the Court of Appeal. In 1995, however, the Court of Appeal rejected the appeal and refused to certify a point of law of general public importance for appeal to the House of Lords.

In 1994, the Commission on Human Rights ruled, by 14 votes to one, that there had been a violation of the Convention. In its judgment, the Court

---

95   Cf *Engel et al v Netherlands* 15 YB 508; (1976) 1 EHRR 647.
96   (1975) 1 EHRR 524.
97   *Airey v Ireland* (1979) 2 EHRR 305.
98   *Ashingdane v United Kingdom* (1985) 7 EHRR 528.
99   Case 43/1994/490/572: (1996) *The Times*, 18 December.

confined itself to the issue of the use by the prosecution of evidence in court which had been obtained by the inspectors under legal compulsion. The Court ruled, by a majority of 16 votes to four, that there had been a violation of the fundamental right not to incriminate oneself, as guaranteed by Article 6(1). The Court held that whether or not evidence obtained under legal compulsion was, or was not, incriminating, was not relevant. The evidence given by Mr Saunders had been read out in court over a three day period, despite the defence's objections. The public interest in combating fraud could not be allowed to override the defendant's right not to incriminate himself. The Court awarded Mr Saunders £75,000 to cover his legal costs in bringing the application, but declined to award compensation.

The right to legal advice was considered by the Court of Human Rights in *Magee v United Kingdom*.[100] The applicant had been arrested in 1988 under the Prevention of Terrorism Act 1984 in connection with an attempted bomb attack on military personnel. He had been held for more than 48 hours without access to legal advice, despite his specific request to see a solicitor on arrival at the Police Office. He signed a confession statement at his seventh interview, and was only subsequently allowed to consult his solicitor. The Court of Human Rights considered that the central issue raised by the applicant's complaint was that: '... he had been prevailed upon in a coercive environment to incriminate himself without the benefit of legal advice.'[101] Although the right to legal advice is not expressly stated in Article 6 and may be subject to restriction for 'good cause', Article 6 normally requires that the accused by allowed access to a lawyer at the initial stages of police interrogation. The Court ruled that there had been a violation of Article 6, stating that 'to deny access to a lawyer for such a long period and in a situation where the rights of the defence were irretrievably prejudiced is – whatever the justification for such denial – incompatible with the rights of the accused under Article 6'. However, in the earlier case of *Murray (John) v United Kingdom*,[102] where the applicant refused to give evidence at trial and adverse inferences were drawn as a result, the Court ruled that there was no violation of Article 6. Unlike *Magee's* case, where the only evidence against him was the confession, in *Murray's* case there existed a formidable body of other evidence against him.

100 Appl 28135/95: judgment 6 June 2000; (2000) *The Times*, 20 June.
101 *Ibid.*
102 (1996) *The Times*, 9 February; and see Munday, R [1996] Crim LR 370.

See, also, *Averill v United Kingdom*,[103] in which the Court of Human Rights ruled that Article 6(1) was violated when access to a lawyer was denied before the applicant was interrogated by the police.

The right to silence was also considered in *Condron v United Kingdom*.[104] In *Condron*, the applicants had been under police surveillance and were charged with drug offences. Following conviction, by a decision of the jury by a majority of nine to one, the two applicants were sentenced to four and three years' imprisonment respectively. When interviewed by the police, the applicants, acting on the advice of their solicitor who was concerned that their state of withdrawal from drugs made them unfit to answer questions, had remained silent, only offering 'no comment' to questions. The applicants were cautioned that the jury could draw adverse inferences from their silence. At trial, the judge failed to give a proper direction to the jury on the correct approach to be taken to the drawing of inferences. Nevertheless, on appeal the Court of Appeal ruled that the convictions were safe. However, what the Court of Appeal did not consider – which was of the essence of consideration before the Court of Human Rights – was whether the trial of the defendants was *fair* in accordance with the requirements of Article 6 of the Convention.

The Court ruled that there was a violation of Article 6. The defendants had given evidence at their trial, and had explained that they had declined to answer questions at interview on the advice of their solicitor. It was the function of the jury, properly directed, to decide whether or not to draw an adverse inference from the applicants' silence.[105] They therefore had a discretion. However, the judge in his direction did not restrict that discretion, since he failed to advise the jury that it should only draw an adverse inference if it concluded that their silence was attributed to their having no answer to the charges or none that would stand up to cross-examination. The right to silence, according to the Court, 'lies at the heart of the notion of a fair procedure guaranteed by Article 6'. Accordingly, the applicants did not receive a fair trial.

The requirement of an 'independent and impartial tribunal established by law' has been closely examined. The essential characteristics which must be respected are that the body is independent of the executive, free from pressure and free from bias. The process adopted at a hearing must be fair. Article 6(1) requires that the accused be able to put their case, and to hear and challenge witnesses. Judgment should be given in public, and reason given for the decision. In 1995, 12 cases involving courts-martial operated by the Royal Air Force, Royal Navy and army, and alleging violations of Article 6, were declared admissible.[106]

---

103 (2000) *The Times*, 20 June.
104 Appl 35718/97: judgment 2 May 2000; (2000) *The Times*, 9 May.
105 Under the Criminal Justice and Public Order Act 1994, s 34.
106 See, also, *Brozicek v Italy* (1989) 12 EHRR 371. See, now, the Armed Forces Discipline Bill 2000.

Article 6(1) also requires that the hearing take place 'within a reasonable time'. The reasonableness of the length of the proceedings will depend upon their complexity. In *Huber v Austria*,[107] the proceedings took over 12 years, and this was held to be unreasonable.

The availability of free legal representation is essential to the fairness of a trial, and denial of legal aid, where the interest of justice demand that it should be made available, violates the Convention. In *Granger v United Kingdom*,[108] for example, Granger was refused legal aid for his appeal against conviction on a charge of perjury. The Crown was represented by the Solicitor General for Scotland and junior counsel, whereas Granger was obliged to represent himself. The Court held that there was a violation of Article 6. Granger had no available remedy, and no right to make a fresh application for legal aid once his original application had been rejected, and he had no means to pay for representation. The sole question for determination was whether the interests of justice required him to be given free assistance. The appeal raised complex issues, and the consequences of the appeal – involving a five year sentence – were serious. Granger was awarded compensation. The denial of legal aid also resulted in a violation of the Convention in *Benham v United Kingdom*.[109]

The European Court of Human Rights ruled, in *Osman v United Kingdom*,[110] that Article 6 had been violated in respect of the effect of the police's immunity from civil actions under the rule formulated in *Hill v Chief Constable of West Yorkshire Police*.[111] The applicant alleged that there had been violations relating to Articles 2, 6 and 8 of the Convention. The applicant's son had become the object of attachment on the part of a schoolteacher. The family had suffered criminal damage to their home. The police visited the school but took no further action. Subsequently, the teacher was questioned by police in relation to missing school files. Following damage to their home and other incidents, the police again questioned the teacher. In 1988, the teacher went to the Osmans' home, where he shot and killed the applicant's husband and injured her son. He then shot and injured the deputy headmaster and shot and killed his son.

In 1989, the applicant commenced a civil action against the police. In 1992, the Court of Appeal upheld the request of the police that the statement of claim be struck out, on the basis that, according to the ruling in *Hill*, no action could lie for public policy reasons against the police for their negligence in the investigation and suppression of crime.

---

107 Appl 4517/70: 18 YB 324.
108 (1990) 12 EHRR 469.
109 (1995) *The Times*, 28 January.
110 Case No 87/1997/871/1083: (1998) *The Times*, 5 November.
111 [1989] AC 53.

The Court of Human Rights ruled that, in relation to Article 2, there was no violation of the Convention, *inter alia*, because of the difficulty in policing modern societies, the unpredictability of human conduct and the operational choices which the police had to make. Any obligation to protect the right to life of the applicant's husband had to be interpreted in a way which did not impose an impossible or disproportionate burden on the authorities. In respect of Article 8, which was allegedly breached by the failure of the police to protect the family, no violation was found. The Court ruled that, given the finding in relation to Article 2, it followed that there had been no violation of any implied positive obligation under Article 8. In relation to Article 6, however, the Court ruled unanimously that the application of the exclusionary rule constituted a disproportionate restriction on the applicant's right of access to a court.

In addition to those cases alleging breaches of Articles 5 and 6 simultaneously, Article 6 has been subject to further scrutiny. The requirement of judicial impartiality was recently tested before the European Court of Human Rights, in a judgment which has implications for the role of Lord Chancellor. In *McGonnell v United Kingdom*,[112] a case relating to the position of the Deputy Bailiff of Guernsey as President of the States of Deliberation, Guernsey's legislative body, and subsequently as the sole judge of law in proceedings relating to the applicant's planning application which had been refused, the Court of Human Rights held that the Deputy Bailiff's position was 'capable of casting doubt' as to his 'impartiality' and, as a result, was in violation of Article 6(1) of the European Convention of Human Rights, which guarantees 'a fair and public hearing ... by an independent and impartial tribunal established by law'.

The Bailiff in Guernsey occupies a number of positions. He is a senior judge of the Royal Court and is *ex officio* President of the Guernsey Court of Appeal. In his non-judicial capacity, the Bailiff is President of the States of Election, of the States of Deliberation and of four States committees (the Appointments Board, the Emergency Council, the Legislation Committee and the Rules of Procedure Committee). He also has a role in communications between the Guernsey authorities and the United Kingdom Government and the Privy Council. Referring to its earlier decision in *Findlay v United Kingdom*,[113] the Court restated the requirements of 'independence' and 'impartiality'. On independence, the Court declared that, in establishing whether the court or tribunal was independent, regard had to be had, *inter alia*, to the 'manner of appointment of its members and their term of office, the existence of guarantees against outside pressures and the question whether the body presented an appearance of independence'. On impartiality, the Court restated the proposition that:

---

112 (2000) *The Times*, 22 February.
113 (1997) *The Times*, 27 February.

... [the tribunal] must be subjectively free of personal prejudice or bias. Secondly, it must also be impartial from an objective viewpoint, that is, it must offer sufficient guarantees to exclude any legitimate doubt in this respect ...

In the instant case, there was no question of actual bias on the part of the Bailiff; nevertheless, the Court considered that:

... any direct involvement in the passage of legislation, or of executive rules, was likely to be sufficient to cast doubt on the judicial impartiality of a person subsequently called on to determine a dispute over whether reasons exist to permit a variation from the wording of the legislation or rules at issue.

Accordingly, 'the mere fact that the Deputy Bailiff presided over the court ... was capable of casting doubt on his impartiality...'. There was, therefore, a violation of the requirements of fair trial before an independent and impartial tribunal.

The position of the Lord Chancellor has again come under question, most particularly in relation to the judicial appointments system. In *Starrs v Procurator Fiscal, Linlithgow*,[114] the issue of an impartial tribunal was tested. It should be noted that this case arose in Scotland, where the Human Rights Act 1998 is already in force. The challenge arose over the position of temporary sheriffs, appointed by the Lord Advocate, who hold office for one year renewable terms 'at pleasure' and who enjoy no security of tenure. The High Court of Justiciary ruled that the appointment system and lack of security created a situation of 'dependence', which was 'objectionable' and contrary to the fundamental requirement of judicial independence from the Executive, of which the Lord Advocate is a member. Accordingly, the appointment system was contrary to Article 6 of the European Convention, which requires a fair hearing before an independent and impartial tribunal.

The case raises questions about both the Lord Chancellor's powers of appointment over magistrates and part time recorders in England and Wales and his disciplinary powers. The system of appointment to the judiciary is also under question. While defending the current system, Lord Irvine of Lairg has also indicated that a judicial appointments commission, involving laypersons, may be needed to ensure greater openness in the system.

The question of impartiality as required by Article 6 was also considered in *Sander v United Kingdom*.[115] The applicant was on trial on allegations of conspiracy to defraud. Towards the end of the trial, when the judge had commenced summing up, a juror complained to the judge that fellow jurors had been making racist remarks, and that he feared that the defendant would not receive a fair verdict. The defence asked the judge to dismiss the jury on the ground that there was a real danger of bias. The judge, however, decided

---

114 (1999) *The Times*, 17 November.
115 (2000) *The Times*, 12 May.

to direct the jury in relation to their duties, and advised that, should any of them, following consideration, find that they could not put aside their prejudices, they should so indicate to the court. A subsequent collective letter from the jury to the court refuted the allegations of racial bias, and one juror, who felt that he had been the cause of the complaint, apologised for making jokes but insisted that he was not biased. In light of the assurances, the judge allowed the trial to continue. The defendant was found guilty and sentenced to five years imprisonment.

The applicant complained of a violation of Article 6(1) of the Convention. The Court of Human Rights ruled that the judge should have discharged the jury. The Court held that the issue of whether a court was impartial had to be viewed objectively, and that the direction given by the judge to the jury could not dispel the reasonable impression and fear of a lack of impartiality. The allegations about racism were capable of causing the applicant and any objective observer legitimate doubts as to the impartiality of the court, which neither the collective letter nor the redirection of the jury by the judge could have dispelled. By failing to discharge the jury, the judge did not provide sufficient guarantees to exclude any objectively justified or legitimate doubts as to the impartiality of the court, and it followed that there was a violation of Article 6(1).

In *Rowe and Others v United Kingdom*,[116] the failure by the prosecution to lay Public Interest Immunity Certificates before the judge in a trial for murder deprived the applicants of a fair trial, as required by Article 6. The withholding of evidence from the court breached the fundamental principle that there should be 'equality of arms' between prosecution and defence. While there was no absolute right to disclosure, and the rights of the accused must be weighed against the interests of, *inter alia*, national security, it was for the judge to control the release or otherwise of material.

ARTICLE 7

1 No one shall be held guilty of any criminal offence on account of any act or omission which did not constitute a criminal offence under national or international law at the time when it was committed. Nor shall a heavier penalty be imposed than the one that was applicable at the time the criminal offence was committed.

2 The article shall not prejudice the trial and punishment of any person for any act or omission which, at the time when it was committed, was criminal according to the general principles of law recognised by civilised nations.

There is little case law under Article 7. It is an accepted presumption of statutory interpretation under English law that Parliament does not intend – in the absence of clear words – to legislate with retrospective effect. Lord

---

116 (2000) *The Times*, 1 March.

Reid's observation in *Waddington v Miah*,[117] to the effect that 'it is hardly credible' that Parliament would pass retrospective criminal legislation[118] must now be seen in light of the War Crimes Act 1991 which does, however, have retrospective effect, making it a criminal offence to have participated in war crimes during the Second World War. However, this Act would appear not to violate Article 7 of the Convention, given that such activities fall within paragraph 2 of Article 7, being crimes against the 'general principles of law recognised by civilised nations'.

A challenge lodged under the Convention, claiming a violation of Article 7, for a penalty imposed which could not have been foreseen occurred in *Harman and Hewitt v United Kingdom*.[119] Ms Harman showed confidential documents to a journalist after these had been read out in court, as a result of which she was found guilty of contempt. Previously, no liability had been imposed in such situations – the information had been regarded as having entered the 'public domain' through disclosure in court. Ms Harman's application was ruled admissible, but a friendly settlement was reached with the government.

The European Court of Human Rights has ruled on the compatibility of a conviction for marital rape with Article 7 of the Convention: *SW v United Kingdom; CR v United Kingdom*.[120] In *R v R*,[121] the House of Lords ruled that the exemption of husbands from the law of rape against their wives was obsolete. Two men were convicted of rape or attempted rape of their wives in 1989 and 1990, following the decision in *R v R* (above). The applicants alleged that their conviction amounted to a violation of Article 7 which prohibits a retrospective change in the criminal law. The Court ruled that the convictions did not violate the Convention: the judicial decisions had done no more than continue a line of reasoning which diminished a husband's immunity; the decisions had become a reasonably foreseeable development of the law and the decisions were not in contravention of the aims of Article 7. A different conclusion was reached in *Welch v United Kingdom*.[122] In *Welch*, the applicant was awaiting trial for drug offences. Before the trial, the Drug Trafficking Offences Act 1996 came into force, under which there was provision made for confiscation orders. A confiscation order was made, even though the provision was not in force at the time the applicant committed the offences.

---

117 [1974] 2 All ER 377.
118 *Ibid*, p 379.
119 (1989) 14 EHRR 657.
120 Cases 47/1994/494/576; 48/1994/495/577: (1995) *The Times*, 5 December.
121 [1992] 1 AC 599.
122 Ser A.307-A; (1995) 20 EHRR 247.

ARTICLE 8

1   Everyone has the right to respect for his private and family life, his home and his correspondence.

2   There shall be no interference by a public authority with the exercise of this right except such as is in accordance with the law and is necessary in a democratic society in the interests of national security, public safety or the economic well being of the country, for the prevention of disorder or crime, for the protection of health or morals, or for the protection of the rights and freedoms of others.

Article 8 has provided the legal means by which to challenge domestic law and practice in two principal areas – the respect for privacy and non-intervention by the State (including the keeping of personal records), and the respect for the individual's private life in terms of his or her own personal relationships.

Respect for individual privacy

As can be seen from the text of Article 8, the right to privacy is subject to several exceptions, and the protection which can in fact be accorded to privacy is limited.

The interception of communications has given rise to challenges under the Convention. For example, in *Klass v Federal Republic of Germany*,[123] lawyers challenged German legislation which authorised the interception of mail and telecommunications. The Court held that, whilst the right to privacy was undoubtedly infringed, the interceptions were justified under paragraph 2 of Article 8. The Court ruled that any surveillance of citizens could be legitimate only to the extent that it was necessary for 'safeguarding the democratic institutions' of the State. Provided that there exist adequate guarantees against abuse, Article 8 was not violated.

In *Foxley v United Kingdom*,[124] the Court of Human Rights ruled that Article 8 was violated by the interception of correspondence which included correspondence between the applicant and his solicitors. The legal basis for the interception was the Insolvency Act 1986, under which a court ordered the redirection of the applicant's mail to a trustee in bankruptcy. However, the intercepts continued after the expiry of the court order and involved communications between the applicant and his lawyer. That was unjustified and violated Article 8.

In *Malone v Metropolitan Police Commissioner*,[125] a different conclusion was reached by the Court. The Court found that the law was unclear, and that,

---

123 (1978) 1 EHRR 214.
124 (2000) *The Times*, 4 July.
125 (1985) 7 EHRR 14.

accordingly, 'the minimum degree of legal protection to which citizens are entitled under the rule of law in a democratic society is lacking'.[126] The government's response to the judgment was to introduce the Interception of Communication Act 1985,[127] which places the granting of warrants for interception of communication on a statutory basis. In *Kruslin v France*[128] and *Huvig v France*,[129] the Court also ruled that insufficient safeguards existed in law, and that the Convention was, accordingly, violated.[130]

In *X, Y and Z v United Kingdom*,[131] a female to male transsexual applied to have his name registered on 'his' child's birth certificate. The child had been conceived after artificial insemination by donor. His application was refused, on the basis that a female to male transsexual was not a 'man' within the meaning of that term under the Human Fertilisation and Embryology Act 1990. The Commission of Human Rights expressed the view that this position violates Article 8.

In *Halford v United Kingdom*,[132] Alison Halford, a former Assistant Chief Constable, won a significant victory in the European Court of Human Rights. Whilst in her post in Merseyside, Ms Halford's telephone calls were intercepted by senior police officers. Ms Halford applied under the European Convention, alleging a breach of her right to privacy, as guaranteed under Article 8. Nine judges of the Court of Human Rights on 25 June 1997 ruled unanimously that there had been a violation of the Convention. The Court also ruled that domestic law provided no avenue for a complaint such as this to be determined. Ms Halford was awarded £10,000 compensation. This case raises, for the first time, the issue of the right to privacy of employees at work. Government lawyers had argued, unsuccessfully, that there was no protection under the Convention on the basis that the telephones which had been tapped were government property.

The requirements of the Births and Deaths Registration Act 1953 have also been challenged under Article 8. In this case, however, no formal ruling was handed down by either the Commission or the Court of Human Rights because the British government agreed to amend the Act as a result of the case. In *AV v United Kingdom*,[133] a married woman had registered her husband as the father of T, her child, at a time when the parties were going through divorce proceedings. Later, the mother told her husband that he was

---

126 (1985) 7 EHRR 14, para 79.

127 See Chapter 23.

128 (1990) 12 EHRR 528.

129 (1990) 12 EHRR 547.

130 See, also, *McLeod v United Kingdom* (1998) *The Times*, 1 October, discussed in Chapter 20.

131 Appl 21830/93: (1997) 24 EHRR 143.

132 [1997] IRLR 471; (1997) *The Times*, 26 June.

133 Appl 34546/97: 20 May 1998. See Leach, P, 'Birth certificates, privacy and human rights' (1998) 142 SJ 628.

not the father of the child. The mother then took affiliation proceedings against the natural father, and a maintenance order was granted to her. Despite the mother's admission that her husband was not the child's father, and the existence of a court order against the natural father, her husband was unable to amend the birth certificate as a result of the regulations contained in the Births and Deaths Registration Act, which required statutory declarations from two 'qualified informants' of the birth, or persons who are 'credible persons having knowledge of the truth of the case'. The husband provided his own statutory declaration, but his wife refused, as did the natural father of the child. The government agreed to amend the 1953 Act to enable the correction of a birth certificate on the presentation of either two statutory declarations, or one declaration and an 'unequivocal' order of the court.

Covert surveillance by the police prior to the enactment of the Police Act 1997, which provided for statutory authority for such surveillance, violated the right to respect for private and family life, as guaranteed by Article 8. The Court of Human Rights so held in *Khan v United Kingdom*.[134] The applicant had been convicted for drug dealing, on the basis of evidence improperly obtained by a secret listening device installed by the police. The evidence so gained was the sole evidence against the accused. The applicant had appealed to the Court of Appeal and to the House of Lords, both of which had dismissed his appeal, the House of Lords ruling that, although the evidence had been obtained in circumstances which amounted to a breach of Article 8, that was not determinative of a judge's discretion to admit or exclude such evidence under section 78 of the Police and Criminal Evidence Act 1984.

The applicant alleged that his trial was unfair and in breach of Article 6, that his right to respect for private life under Article 8 had been breached and that his right to an effective remedy under Article 13 had also been breached. On Article 6, the Court of Human Rights ruled that the applicant had had ample opportunity to challenge the use of the evidence and had done so before the trial court, the Court of Appeal and House of Lords, and that the domestic courts had considered the question of admissibility. Accordingly, there was no violation of Article 6. There was, however, a violation of Article 8. The principal issue was whether the action of the police was justified under Article 8(2) as being 'in accordance with the law' and 'necessary in a democratic society'. The law had to be sufficiently clear and certain to give individuals adequate indication as to the circumstances and conditions in which public authorities were entitled to resort to such measures. In the absence of statutory authority, the interference could not be considered to be in accordance with law and, accordingly, violated Article 8.

On Article 13, the Court considered the avenues open to the applicant, principally the police complaints mechanism. Having considered the

---

134 (2000) *The Times*, 23 May.

respective roles of Chief Constables, the Police Complaints Authority and that of the Home Secretary in relation to the appointment, remuneration and dismissal of members of the Police Complaints Authority, the Court ruled that the system of investigation of complaints did not meet the requisite standards of independence needed 'to constitute sufficient protection against the abuse of authority and thus provide an effective remedy'. Accordingly, there was a violation of Article 13.[135]

Privacy of the family

In *Hoffman v Austria*,[136] the Court ruled that Ms Hoffman had been discriminated against (contrary to Article 14) and her respect for family life violated (Article 8) by the Supreme Court of Austria, which had denied her the custody of her children on divorce, principally because she had become a Jehovah's Witness. In *Marckx v Belgium*,[137] a complaint was lodged on the basis that Articles 12 and 14 had been violated by discriminatory inheritance rules for illegitimate children. Belgian law provided that there was no automatic legal relationship between a mother and her illegitimate child. The law provided that a mother could give legal recognition to her child which would entitle the child to inherit on her death, but with lesser inheritance rights than any legitimate children. Moreover, even if the mother adopted her own child, the child could not inherit – as could legitimate children – from grandparents if they died intestate. As a result, Belgian law,[138] and that of the United Kingdom, was amended to bring domestic law in line with the requirements of Article 8.[139] English law relating to care proceedings and the powers of local authorities to control access of parents to children in local authority care have also been successfully challenged under the Convention, leading to changes to the rights of parents to access to a court of law in order to challenge a local authority's decision to terminate contact between children and their parents.[140]

The rights to Gypsies to live on their own land without planning permissions was considered by the Court of Human Rights in *Buckley v United*

---

135 On the admissiblity of evidence gained through foreign intercepts and consideration of *Khan v United Kingdom*, see *R v X, Y and Z* (2000) *The Times*, 23 May, Court of Appeal, Criminal Division.

136 (1993) *The Times*, 27 July; (1994) 17 EHRR 293.

137 Judgment 13 June 1979, Ser A.31; (1979) 2 EHRR 33.

138 By an Act of 1987.

139 See the Family Law Reform Act 1987; see, also, the Inheritance (Provision for Family and Dependants) Act 1975 and the Fatal Accidents Act 1976, as amended, both of which place the illegitimate child in the same position as legitimate children.

140 *WRO v United Kingdom* [1988] 2 FLR 445; (1987) 10 EHRR 29, which resulted in the Child Care Act 1980, s 12.

Kingdom.[141] The Court ruled that the United Kingdom authorities had not violated Article 8 (respect for private and family life, home and correspondence) or Article 14 (enjoyment of substantive rights without discrimination) of the Convention. Mrs Buckley had purchased land, and had sought and been refused planning permission.

The Court ruled, by a majority, that the protected right to a home may be limited 'in accordance with law' as 'necessary in a democratic society.' However, the Court ruled that the measures taken by national authorities must be proportionate to the legitimate aim pursued. Two dissenting judges ruled that there was a violation of Article 8 and one dissenting judge, that there had also been a violation of Article 14 of the Convention. There are a number of Gypsy cases pending under the Convention and it is likely that the Court will re-examine this issue in the foreseeable future.

Respect for private sexual life

In *Dudgeon v United Kingdom*,[142] the right to respect for privacy was examined against the claim that legislation in force in Northern Ireland prohibited homosexual conduct between adult males. As a result, the Homosexual Offences (Northern Ireland) Order 1982 was passed to bring domestic law into line with the requirements of the Convention. See, also, *Lustig-Praen and Beckett v United Kingdom*[143] and *Smith and Grady v United Kingdom*,[144] in which the Court of Human Rights ruled that the ban on homosexuals in the armed forces violated Article 8 of the Convention.

The prosecution and conviction of a man, for engaging in non-violent homosexual acts in private with up to four other men, was a violation of Article 8. The Court of Human Rights so held in *ADT v United Kingdom*.[145] The applicant had been arrested and charged with gross indecency between men, contrary to section 13 of the Sexual Offences Act 1956. The government had argued that the sexual activity concerned fell outside the scope of 'private life' within the meaning of Article 8(1). The activities had been recorded on video tapes which were seized by the police when conducting a search under warrant. The Court ruled that there was no likelihood of the contents of the tapes being rendered public, deliberately or inadvertently, nor had the applicant been prosecuted in relation to offences involved in the making or distribution of the tapes. The Court ruled that the applicant was a victim of an interference with his right to respect for his private life, both as to the

---

141 (1996) *The Times*, 26 September; (1997) 23 EHRR 101. See Barnett, H, '*Buckley v United Kingdom*: landmark or signpost?' (1996) 146 NLJ 1628.

142 (1982) 4 EHRR 149.

143 Appl 31417/96: judgment of the Chamber of the Court 25 July 2000.

144 (1999) *The Times*, 11 October.

145 Appl 35765/97: judgment 31 July 2000; (2000) *The Times*, 8 August.

existence of legislation prohibiting consensual sexual acts between more than two men in private, and as to the conviction for gross indecency. The interference was not justified as being 'necessary in a democratic society' in the protection of morals and rights and freedoms of others.

ARTICLE 9

1   Everyone has the right to freedom of thought, conscience and religion; this right includes freedom to change his religion or belief, and freedom, either alone or in community with others and in public or private, to manifest his religion or belief, in worship, teaching, practice and observance.

2   Freedom to manifest one's religion or beliefs shall be subject only to such limitations as are prescribed by law and are necessary in a democratic society in the interests of public safety, for the protection of public order, health or morals, or for the protection of the rights and freedoms of others.

Freedom of thought, conscience and religion have founded the basis for few cases under the Convention. Applications which have been made under this Article relate primarily to the conditions under which an individual may exercise his rights. In the case of prisoners detained following a criminal conviction, the prison authorities are entitled to prescribe limits to the exercise of religious and other rights, simply because such restrictions represent 'an inherent feature of lawful imprisonment'. In X v Austria,[146] refusal by prison authorities to allow a Buddhist prisoner to grow a beard was held not to violate the Convention.

ARTICLE 10

1   Everyone has the right to freedom of expression. This right shall include freedom to hold opinions and to receive and impart information and ideas without interference by public authority and regardless of frontiers. This article shall not prevent States from requiring the licensing of broadcasting, television or cinema enterprises.

2   The exercise of these freedoms, since it carries with it duties and responsibilities, may be subject to such formalities, conditions, restrictions or penalties as are prescribed by law and are necessary in a democratic society, in the interests of national security, territorial integrity or public safety, for the prevention of disorder or crime, for the protection of health or morals, for the protection of the reputation or rights of others, for preventing the disclosure of information received in confidence, or for maintaining the authority and impartiality of the judiciary.

In a significant case relating to the responsibility of the State towards citizens affected by industrial and manufacturing hazards, the Court of Human Rights ruled in *Guerra v Italy*[147] that the failure of State authorities to advise citizens of the threat posed by environmental pollution violated their right of

---

146 (1965) YB VIII.
147 (1998) 26 EHRR 357; [1998] HRDC 277.

enjoyment of their homes in such a way as to affect their private and family life adversely.

Freedom of expression has given rise to several cases under the Convention. In *The Sunday Times v United Kingdom*,[148] the English law of contempt was considered in the light of Article 10. In 1972, *The Sunday Times* published an article concerning children born deformed as a result of their mothers taking the drug Thalidomide during pregnancy. The manufacturers, Distillers, were involved in pending court proceedings between the claimants for compensation. In October 1972, Distillers made representations to the Attorney General, claiming *The Sunday Times* article would prejudice negotiations and would amount to contempt of court. The Attorney General sought and was granted an injunction. The Court of Appeal reversed the decision but, in July 1973, the House of Lords confirmed the injunction. As a result, *The Sunday Times* turned to Article 10.

At issue was whether Article 10, paragraph 2, justified the restriction of the injunction. The Court held that Article 10(2) – since it limited freedom of expression – should be strictly construed and that no implied limits should be read into it. The English law of contempt, imposing a restriction of over three years, was ruled to be uncertain and unsatisfactory. The Court was required to decide whether the restriction imposed by the injunction was really necessary in the circumstances and, moreover, whether the restriction was proportionate to the objective being sought. The government claimed that the law of contempt was a necessary device whereby the authority and impartiality of the judiciary was upheld. However, given that the trial was not in sight in 1972 (when the injunction was granted) and that the authority of the judiciary was unlikely to be at risk from journalistic articles, the restriction imposed violated Article 10. As a result, the Contempt of Court Act 1981 was enacted, clarifying the law on pre-trial publicity.[149]

The Court of Human Rights reached a different conclusion in *Handyside v United Kingdom*,[150] in which a publication entitled *The Little Red Schoolbook* had been seized under the Obscene Publications Act 1959. The publishers claimed that the Obscene Publications Act represented a violation of Article 10 in several respects. The Act was claimed to be obscure, to provide inadequate defences and to entail a discretion to prosecute; it was also claimed that the United Kingdom failed to secure the rights to which the publisher was entitled under the Convention or to provide him with an effective remedy for the violation of his rights, as required by Article 13. The government argued that Article 10(2) gave them a discretion – a margin of appreciation. In 1976, the Court ruled there was no breach of the Convention. The 'protection of

---

148 (1979) 2 EHRR 245.
149 See, further, Chapter 19.
150 (1976) 1 EHRR 737. See, also, *Muller v Switzerland* (1991) 13 EHRR 212.

morals' clause in Article 10(2) entitled the government to impose restrictions on freedom of expression, provided that the restrictions were proportional to the aim pursued. It was for the Court to decide whether the restrictions were necessary and sufficient. In this case, the book was aimed at under 18 year olds and encouraged promiscuity. Accordingly, there was no violation of Article 10.

In *Open Door Counselling and Dublin Well Woman v Ireland*,[151] the Court ruled that restrictions – an injunction – placed on the dissemination of any information regarding the availability of abortion advice and treatment represented an unlawful restriction and was therefore contrary to Article 10.

Article 10 of the Convention came under renewed scrutiny by the Court of Human Rights in *Tolstoy Miloslavsky v United Kingdom*.[152] In a libel action against Count Nikolai Tolstoy Miloslavsky, damages of £1.5 million had been awarded. The size of the award was accepted to be three times the size of the highest libel award previously made in England. The English court had not employed the concept of proportionality in order to establish whether the award was commensurate to the damage inflicted on the plaintiff's reputation. Under English law, the Court of Appeal could only set aside an award of the jury if the court regarded the amount of the award to have been so unreasonable that no reasonable person would have made it and that, accordingly, it had been made 'capriciously, unconscionably or irrationally'. The Court of Human Rights held, unanimously, that the English court's power to control the award by the jury was inadequate, and did not give adequate and effective safeguards to the defendant against a disproportionately large award. Accordingly, there had been a violation of the applicant's rights under Article 10.

The European Court of Human Rights again considered Article 10 of the Convention in *Wingrove v United Kingdom*.[153] The British Board of Film Classification, exercising its powers under section 4(1) of the Video Recordings Act 1984, had refused to grant a certificate for a video film *Visions of Ecstasy*. The applicant alleged that the refusal of the certificate and the statutory provisions making it a criminal offence to distribute a video work without a certificate amounted to a violation of Article 10 (freedom of expression). The Court ruled by seven votes to two that there had been no violation of Article 10, and that the refusal was justified under Article 10(2) as being necessary in a democratic society. The video film concerned the life and writings of St Theresa of Avila, a sixteenth century Carmelite nun who experienced powerful ecstatic visions of Jesus Christ. The Board of Film Classification took the view that the film would infringe the criminal law of blasphemy.

---

151 (1992) 15 EHRR 244.
152 Case 8/1994/455/536: (1995) *The Times*, 19 July.
153 Case 19/1995: (1996) *The Times*, 5 December.

The European Commission of Human Rights had previously found that there had been a violation of Article 10.[154] The Court accepted that the refusal of a certificate undoubtedly infringed the applicant's right to freedom of expression. In order to establish whether the interference was contrary to the Convention the Court had to consider Article 10(2). The English law of blasphemy was consistent with the aims of Article 9 of the Convention (freedom of thought, conscience and religion). The fact that the law of blasphemy did not treat all religions equally did not detract from the legitimacy of the aim pursued. In relation to the 'necessity' of the interference, the Court ruled that, while blasphemy law was invoked increasingly rarely, there was not yet sufficient consensus within Member States of the Council of Europe to conclude that the blasphemy legislation was 'unnecessary in a democratic society and incompatible with the Convention'. However, the Court would look at such restrictions very closely in order to ensure the absence of arbitrariness or excessive interferences. In the present case, the restriction was justified on the basis that the film could cause 'outrage and insult' to believing Christians, which would amount to blasphemy. The national authorities had not exceeded their margin of appreciation and there had been no violation of Article 10.

The margin of appreciation had also dictated the outcome in the case of *Otto-Preminger Institut v Austria*.[155] In that case, a satirical film depicting Christ was seized by the authorities and a prosecution brought against the manager of the Institute which intended to show the film. It was held that, in the absence of European consensus on blasphemy, the State had a wide margin of appreciation, and had not therefore infringed the applicant's right to freedom of expression.[156]

The rights of protesters to freedom of expression was considered by the Court in *Steel and Others v United Kingdom*[157] and *Hashman and Harrup v United Kingdom*.[158] In *Steel*, the Court distinguished between the actions and treatment of the applicants. The first applicant, Steel, had been arrested during a protest, detained by the police and cautioned and charged with breach of the peace, and was later charged with an offence under section 5 of the Public Order Act 1986. In total, she was detained for approximately 44 hours. She was later convicted on the section 5 charge, and the complaint regarding the alleged breach of the peace was proved. On appeal, she was fined for the

---

154 By 14 votes to two.

155 (1994) 19 EHRR 34.

156 On Art 10, see, also, *Ahmed and Others v United Kingdom* (1998) *The Times*, 2 October, in which the Court of Human Rights ruled that restrictions on senior council officers in relation to political activity did not violate Art 10 since the objective of the restriction was to underpin the principle of political neutrality and the effectiveness of local political democracy.

157 [1998] Crim LR 893; (1999) 28 EHRR 603. Also discussed in relation to Arts 5 and 6, above.

158 (1999) *The Times*, 1 December; [2000] Crim LR 185.

public order offence and ordered to agree to be bound over to keep the peace for 12 months. She refused to be bound over and was committed to prison for 28 days. The protest was regarded by the Court as a legitimate expression of opinion within Article 10. By refusing to be bound over, the applicant challenged the authority of the court. The committal to prison was intended to deter future breaches of the peace but also pursued the aim under Article 10 of maintaining the authority of the judiciary.

Although the measures taken amounted to serious interferences with freedom of expression, regard had to be had to the dangers inherent in such protest activity and the risk of disorder arising from it: the actions of the police in arresting Steel were not disproportionate, nor was it disproportionate for the applicant to be committed to prison for refusing to comply with the order of the court. Equally, in relation to the second applicant, there was no violation of Article 10. However, in relation to the three remaining applicants, the interference with the exercise of their right to freedom of expression was disproportionate to the aims of preventing disorder and protecting the rights of others and was not necessary in a democratic society. Their protest had been entirely peaceful. In the absence of obstruction or provocation of others to violence, their arrest and detention was unlawful under Article 5 and also amounted to a violation of Article 10.

In *Hashman and Harrup*, the issue was freedom of expression relating to hunt saboteurs who disturbed the hunt by blowing a hunting horn and shouting at hounds. The Crown Court to which they appealed found that, as there had been no violence or threat of violence, there had been no breach of the peace. Nevertheless, their actions had been unlawful and exposed hounds to danger and were *contra bona mores*. The applicants were bound over 'to be of good behaviour' for one year. The applicants claimed that the concept of behaviour *contra bona mores* was so broadly defined that it did not comply with Article 10(2) of the Convention, the requirement that any interference with freedom of expression must be 'prescribed by law'. The Court of Human Rights ruled that the definition of *contra bona mores*, as behaviour which was 'wrong rather than right in the judgment of the majority of contemporary fellow citizens', was particularly imprecise and failed to give the applicants sufficiently clear guidance as to how they should behave in future. Accordingly, the interference with the freedom of expression was not 'prescribed by law' and there had been a violation of Article 10.[159]

The House of Lords upheld the right of prisoners to freedom of expression in *R v Secretary of State for the Home Department ex p Simms; Same v Same ex parte O'Brien*.[160] The Court ruled that an indiscriminate ban on all visits to

---

159 See, also, *Alison Redmond-Bate v DPP* (1999) *The Times*, 28 July; [1999] Crim LR 998, in which free expression under Art 10 was considered in relation to obstruction a police officer in the execution of his duty, discussed in Chapter 19.

160 (1999) *The Times*, 9 July.

prisoners by journalists or authors in their professional capacity was unlawful. A prisoner had a right to seek through oral interviews, to persuade a journalist to investigate his allegations of miscarriage of justice in the hope that his case might be re-opened. The Court of Appeal had allowed an appeal by the Secretary of State from the decision of the High Court, granting judicial review of the Home Secretary's decision that the applicant could receive visits in prison from journalists only if the journalists signed written undertakings not to publish any part of the interviews, as laid down in the Prison Rules issued by the Home Secretary.[161] The applicants were serving life sentences for murder and, having had their renewed applications for leave to appeal against conviction turned down, continued to protest their innocence. The Home Office had adopted a blanket policy that no prisoners had a right to oral interviews with journalists. Lord Steyn stated that the applicants wished to challenge the safety of their convictions, and that, 'in principle, it was not easy to conceive of a more important function which free speech might fulfil'. His Lordship was satisfied that it was administratively workable, and consistent with prison order and discipline, to allow prisoners to be interviewed for the purpose here at stake. The Home Secretary's policy and the governor's administrative decisions pursuant to that policy were unlawful.

ARTICLE 11

1   Everyone has the right to freedom of peaceful assembly and to freedom of association with others, including the right to form and to join trades union for the protection of his interests.

2   No restriction shall be placed on the exercise of these rights other than such as are prescribed by law and are necessary in a democratic society in the interests of national security or public safety, for the prevention of disorder or crime, or the protection of health or morals or for the protection of the rights and freedoms of others. This Article shall not prevent the imposition of lawful restrictions on the exercise of these rights by members of the armed forces, of the police or of the administration of the State.

The right to a peaceful assembly is more limited than a right to assemble. Where a State seeks to regulate assemblies which are not peaceful – or unlikely to be peaceful – no violation of the right occurs.

The right to join a trades union has been interpreted to incorporate the right not to join a trades union. In *Young, James and Webster*,[162] the Court interpreted Article 11 to mean that there is a measure of choice left to individual workers whether or not to join a trades union.

Deprivation of the right to be a member of a trade union was considered by the Court in *Council of Civil Service Unions v United Kingdom* (the *GCHQ*

---

161 [1999] QB 349.
162 (1981) 4 EHRR 38.

case).[163] It will be recalled that the Minister for the Civil Service, the Prime Minister, had, following industrial unrest, by Order in Council ruled that workers at Government Communications Headquarters (GCHQ) would no longer be entitled to membership of a trade union. The ban was challenged by judicial review proceedings, which were ultimately unsuccessful in the House of Lords. The applicants argued that rights under Article 11 had been infringed, and also rights under Article 13, which provides for an effective domestic remedy. In answer, the government argued that the order was justified, *inter alia*, under Article 11(2) on the basis of the protection of national security. The Commission found a clear violation of Article 11. However, the ban on union membership was justifiable under Article 11(2) and therefore there was no violation of the Convention.

ARTICLE 12

Men and women of marriageable age have the right to marry and to found a family, according to the national laws governing the exercise of this right.

The right to marry and to found a family has formed the basis on which transsexuals have challenged the law. In *Rees v United Kingdom*[164] and *Cossey v United Kingdom*,[165] the applicants both argued that English law, which prohibited them from entering into a valid marriage, was contrary to the Convention. The Court, while expressing some sympathy for the plight of transsexuals, in both cases declined to find English law in breach of the Convention. In *B v France*,[166] the Court heard a complaint by B, who had been born male but underwent surgery to become female, that French law prohibited her from entering into a valid marriage. The Court refused to overturn the *Rees* and *Cossey* decisions on the right to marry but, nevertheless, did find a violation of Article 8, in that B had been prohibited from altering the civil register and official identity documents and had suffered distress and humiliation.

The right to marry and found a family does not entail a right to a termination of marriage by divorce. In *Johnston v Ireland*,[167] the applicant claimed that his right under Article 12 was violated by the government through its failure to provide for divorce in Ireland which would enable him to marry and found a family with the woman with whom he was now living.

Challenges have been lodged by prisoners denied the right to marry by virtue of their imprisonment. In *Hamer v United Kingdom*[168] and *Draper v*

---

163 [1985] AC 374; (1988) 10 EHRR 269. For further discussion, see Chapters 6 and 23.
164 [1987] 2 FLR 111.
165 [1992] 2 FLR 249.
166 Judgment 25 March 1992, Ser A.232-C.
167 (1987) 9 EHRR 203.
168 Appl 7114/75: Report of 13 December; (1981) D & R 24.

United Kingdom,[169] the Commission ruled that it was for the individual – and not governments – to determine whether he or she would enter into marriage. However, the right of prisoners to marry does not entail a right to conjugal relations whilst in prison.[170]

ARTICLE 13[171]

Everyone whose rights and freedoms as set forth in this Convention are violated shall have an effective remedy before a national authority notwithstanding that the violation has been committed by persons acting in an official capacity.

Article 13 imposes a duty on Member States to provide effective remedies for any violation of the substantive rights protected by the Convention. Article 13 has been interpreted to mean that an effective remedy before a national authority is guaranteed to 'everyone who claims that his rights and freedoms under the Convention have been violated'.[172]

Judicial review[173] provides an effective means by which to ensure that government complies with the requirements of the law.[174] In *Klass v Federal Republic of Germany*,[175] the applicant argued, in relation to telephone tapping, that there was no effective way in which to challenge the decision to intercept communications and that the only method of control was through a parliamentary committee. The Court adopted the doctrine of margin of appreciation and ruled that under the circumstances – where national security was involved – no better remedy could be given.

ARTICLE 14

The enjoyment of the rights and freedoms set forth in this Convention shall be secured without discrimination on any ground such as sex, race, colour, language, religion, political or other opinion, national or social origin, association with a national minority, property, birth or other status.

Article 14 provides for non-discrimination in the enjoyment of the substantive rights and freedoms protected by the Convention. There is not, therefore, a right to non-discrimination *per se* but, rather, a right not to be discriminated against in relation to any of the other rights and freedoms. Thus, Article 14 enjoys no independent existence; it is tied to other Articles in the

---

169 Appl 8186/78.
170 Appl 6564/74: *X v United Kingdom* [1975] D & R 2.
171 Human Rights Act 1998.
172 *Klass v Federal Republic of Germany* (1978) 2 EHRR 214.
173 See Chapters 24 and 25.
174 *Vilvarajah and Four Others v United Kingdom* (1991) 14 EHRR 248; and see *Leander v Sweden* (1987) 9 EHRR 433.
175 (1978) 2 EHRR 214.

Convention.[176] However, it is possible that a violation of Article 14 is found, even where a claim that a breach of another Article has occurred fails. For example, in *Abdulaziz, Cabales and Balkandali*,[177] three foreign wives residing in England complained that their husbands were not allowed to enter into the country. The applicants alleged a violation of Articles 8 and 14. The Court rejected the complaint concerning Article 8, adopting the view that the right to family life does not entail the right to establish a home wheresoever people choose. However, there was a violation of Article 14, in so far as the rules provided easier conditions under which men could bring in their wives than those which existed for wives trying to bring their husbands into the country.[178]

ARTICLE 16

Nothing in Articles 10, 11 and 14 shall be regarded as preventing the High Contracting Parties from imposing restrictions on the political activity of aliens.

Article 16 affects all Articles in the Convention in so far as they relate to the political activities of aliens. Article 16 does not mean that there can be no violation of other substantive Articles in respect of aliens.

ARTICLE 17

Nothing in this Convention may be interpreted as implying for any State, group or person any right to engage in any activity or perform any act aimed at the destruction of any of the rights and freedoms set forth herein or at their limitation to a greater extent than is provided for in the Convention.

According to the Commission, the purpose of Article 17 is to:

> ... prevent totalitarian groups from exploiting in their own interests the principle enunciated by the Convention ... Article 17 covers essentially those rights which, if invoked, will facilitate the attempt to derive therefrom a right to engage personally in activities aimed at the destruction of any of the rights and freedoms set forth in the Convention.[179]

Accordingly, convictions before a domestic court – as in the case of *Glimmerveen and Hagenbeek v Netherlands*[180] – for possessing racially discriminatory literature was not a violation of Article 10. The conviction was justified both by Article 10(2) and by Article 17 of the Convention.

---

176 Appl 4045/69: *X v Federal Republic of Germany* (1970) YB XIII.
177 (1985) 7 EHRR 471.
178 The Immigration Rules were amended in 1985 as a result of this case.
179 *Glimmerveen and Hagenbeek v Netherlands* (1982) 4 EHRR 260.
180 *Ibid.*

The Convention protocols

In addition to the substantive Articles of the Convention, there exists a series of nine Protocols on matters ranging from the right to peaceful enjoyment of possessions (First Protocol, Article 1), education (First Protocol, Article 2), the holding of regular free elections (First Protocol, Article 3), freedom of movement (Fourth Protocol), abolition of the death penalty (Sixth Protocol), the rights of aliens and sexual equality (Seventh Protocol), procedural matters under the Convention (Ninth Protocol) and minority rights (Tenth Protocol). The United Kingdom is not a party to the Fourth, Sixth or Seventh Protocols. In relation to Article 2 of the First Protocol, the government has entered a reservation to the effect that the rights of parents to determine the education of their children are respected in the United Kingdom only to the extent that such respect is compatible with the requirements of the Education Acts.

INSTITUTIONS AND PROCEDURE
UNDER THE CONVENTION

The Council of Europe, under which the Convention operates, is constitutionally distinct from the European Community. The Council was founded in 1949, inspired by the United Nation's Universal Declaration of Human Rights of 1948. The Committee of Ministers is the political body, consisting of one representative from each Member State government.[181] The Commission, comprising one member from each country, is elected by the Committee of Ministers, but acts independently, 'serving in their individual capacity'.[182] The Court of Human Rights – elected by the Consultative Assembly of the Council of Europe – represents the judicial body.[183] Judges are elected for a renewable nine year term of office,[184] and need not be drawn exclusively from the judiciary in Member States. The qualifications for appointment are defined as being persons 'of high moral character' who must either possess the qualifications required for appointment of high judicial office or be jurisconsults of recognised competence.[185]

Prior to 1998, the role of the Commission was to act as a filter for applications. By employing the rules on admissibility,[186] the Commission exercised a quasi-judicial function. The effect of an application being declared

---

181 Usually, Foreign Ministers.

182 ECHR, Art 23.

183 *Ibid*, Arts 38–43. On the role of the Court, see Gearty, CA, 'The European Court of Human Rights and the protection of civil liberties' [1993] CLJ 89.

184 *Ibid*, Art 40.

185 *Ibid*, Art 38.

186 *Ibid*, Arts 26 and 27.

inadmissible was that the matter would never reach the Court of Human Rights. If declared admissible, the Commission investigated the case fully and attempted to reach a friendly settlement between the parties,[187] namely, the State and the aggrieved individual. If negotiations for the friendly settlement failed, a report was sent by the Commission to the State concerned and to the Council of Ministers.[188] The matter could then be determined by the Council of Ministers – deciding by a two-thirds majority – thus conferring on the political institution a judicial function. Alternatively, the case could be referred to the Court by the Commission or by the State concerned.[189] Originally, the complainant had no involvement in the proceedings, let alone the right to insist that the matter be referred to the Court. Since 1983, the complainant has a right to be represented before the Court and, by an amendment to Article 48, a limited right to refer the case to the Court.[190] The decision of the Court is final[191] and binding on Member States.[192] Between 1955 and 1991, 11 inter-State cases, but 17,116 complaints from individuals, had been considered by the Commission.

In May 1993, the Committee of Ministers of the Council of Europe agreed to move towards replacing the existing machinery with a single Court of Human Rights.[193] From November 1998, the Commission and Court are merged into a single Court performing the tasks of both the Commission and the Court.[194] The objectives sought are greater clarity for the citizen in terms of organisation and better control of cases. By this means, the Court is able to scrutinise applications and determine the admissibility of a complaint. Speed and cost are also factors in the reformed procedures. On average, when cases go to the Court, it takes some four to five years before a final decision is reached.

Further, in October 1993, the 32 European nations agreed to strengthen the powers of the Council of Europe. It was reported that nine nations had joined since 1989 and that, by the end of 1992, the number of cases before the Courts was 1,861, compared with only 404 in 1981. Most recently joined as candidate members are Russia, the Ukraine, Belorussia, Moldavia, Latvia, Albania and Croatia. The summit recorded disquiet over resurging nationalism – especially in the Balkans. Full membership of the Council for these countries will depend upon their record in the protection of minorities.

---

187 ECHR, Art 28.

188 *Ibid*, Art 31.

189 *Ibid*, Arts 47 and 48.

190 *Ibid*, Art 48, amended by the Ninth Protocol to the Convention.

191 *Ibid*, Art 52.

192 *Ibid*, Art 48.

193 Mowbray, A, 'Reform of the control system of the ECHR' [1993] PL 419.

194 Protocol 11 of the ECHR.

The right of application

Inter-State applications[195]

By 1994, only 18 inter-State complaints had been recorded, and many of these involved the same factual situation. In relation to the United Kingdom, *Republic of Ireland v United Kingdom*[196] is the most significant.

Complaints from individuals[197]

The right of individual petition to a body outside the jurisdiction of Member States was a constitutional innovation. As noted above, the British government was exceedingly cautious about conceding such a right and only in 1965 did the right of individual application become available to citizens of the United Kingdom. Applications may be from individuals, groups of individuals or non-governmental organisations. The applicant(s) must be personally affected by the issue: complaints involving alleged conduct which does not personally affect the individual complainant are not admissible.[198]

The procedure

Exhaustion of domestic remedies

Any domestic remedies which are available must be exhausted.[199] Thus, if a remedy is available within domestic law, it must first be sought. Only where there exists no remedy in law, or where the pursuit of a remedy would be unequivocally certain to fail,[200] may an individual lodge a petition.

The time limit

The application must be made within six months of the final decision of the highest court having jurisdiction within the domestic legal system.[201]

Admissibility

A number of hurdles face the applicant in having his application declared admissible:

---

195 ECHR, Art 33.
196 (1976) 2 EHRR 25, discussed above.
197 ECHR, Art 34.
198 *X v Norway* (1960) YB IV 270. See, also, *Vijayanathan v France* (1991) 15 EHRR 62.
199 ECHR, Art 35.
200 Eg, where there are strong precedents established.
201 ECHR, Art 35.

(a) a complaint must not constitute an 'abuse of right of complaint'.[202] In essence, this means that the complainant should not be pursuing a remedy out of improper motives – such as political advantage. In short, the complaint must be brought for genuine reasons;

(b) a complaint must not be anonymous;[203]

(c) a complaint must not relate to a matter which has been investigated and ruled upon previously;[204]

(d) a complaint must not relate to a right which is not protected under the Convention;[205]

(e) a complaint is inadmissible if, although the application relates to a protected right, the State against which the complaint is made has derogated[206] from that provision, or lodged a reservation;[207]

(f) the application must relate to violation of the Convention by a State which is bound by the Convention, or to an organisation for which the State has responsibility;

(g) the application must not be such that it represents an attack on another right protected by the Convention. Article 17 provides that there is no right to 'engage in any activity or perform any act' which is aimed at the destruction of protected rights;

(h) a complaint must not be 'manifestly ill founded'.[208] By this is meant that the application must be plausible – there must be *prima facie* evidence of a violation.

Once an application is declared admissible, the examination of the merits will commence. The complainant has a limited right to appear where the Court requires further evidence. The Court's decision must be reasoned and, if not unanimous, there is a right for individual judges to give a separate opinion. Under Article 43(1) of the Convention, any party to the case may, within three months from the date of the judgment of a Chamber (effectively the 'court of first instance' hearing the case), request that the case be referred to the Grand Chamber. If it is not so referred, the judgment becomes final. Alternatively, if referred, the judgment of the Grand Chamber is final and Member States undertake to abide by the decision of the Court. Compensation can be awarded by the Court.

---

202 ECHR, Art 35(3).
203 *Ibid*, Art 35(2)(a).
204 *Ibid*, Art 35(2)(b).
205 *Ibid*, Art 35(3).
206 *Ibid*, Art 15.
207 Derogations and reservations are discussed, further, below.
208 ECHR, Art 35(3).

Enforcing the judgment

The task of ensuring that the judgment is complied with is for the Committee of Ministers: the matter is thus returned to the political arena. If a State refuses to comply with the judgment, its membership of the Council of Europe can be suspended or, ultimately, it may be expelled from the Council. Where exercised, this ultimate power has regrettable implications and would remove the protection of the Convention from individuals within the State and thus further damage the protection of rights. Greece withdrew from the Council of Europe following five allegations of persecution against it between 1967 and 1970. In 1974, a new Greek government ratified the Convention once more. However, failure to comply with a judgment will cause adverse publicity for the State and there is thus great political pressure to conform. Following the judgment in *Brogan v United Kingdom*,[209] concerning the seven day detention provisions in the Prevention of Terrorism Acts, however, the British government announced its intention to derogate from the protection given in Article 5 to the right to liberty and freedom and access to a court of law for the determination of the legality of detention.

THE 'MARGIN OF APPRECIATION'

In respect of almost all Articles of the Convention, there is an area of discretion left to Member States as to the means by which they protect the substantive rights. This margin of appreciation is necessary in order that the Convention can apply in a workable fashion in very differing societies. It also means, however, that application to the Convention will not be uniform throughout the legal systems of Member States, and that States may be able to deviate from the protection given.

Whether the State has a margin of appreciation – and the scope of it – is a matter to be determined under the Convention. The doctrine is unpredictable in operation and has become, over the years, applicable to all Articles. Accordingly, it is a concept which is capable of significantly undermining the protection given by the Convention, and has been criticised for so doing.[210]

DEROGATION AND RESERVATION

Where a State finds it impossible or undesirable to comply with specific Articles, it is possible for the State to derogate,[211] or enter a reservation[212] as

---

209 (1989) 11 EHRR 117.
210 See *op cit*, Van Dijk and Van Hoof, fn 2, p 604.
211 ECHR, Art 15.
212 *Ibid*, Art 64.

to the matter. No derogation is permitted in relation to Article 2 (the right to life), other than in war situations. Derogation is not allowed in respect of Articles 3 (freedom from torture), 4(1) (slavery or servitude), and 7 (freedom from retrospective criminal liability).[213] The right of derogation is limited. Article 15 provides that:

1. In time of war or other public emergency threatening the life of the nation any High Contracting Party may take measures derogating from its obligations under this Convention to the extent strictly required by the exigencies of the situation, provided that such measures are not inconsistent with its other obligations under international law.

2. No derogation from Article 2, except in respect of deaths resulting from lawful acts of war, or from Articles 3, 4 (paragraph 1) and 7 shall be made under this provision.

3. Any High Contracting Party availing himself of this right of derogation shall keep the Secretary General of the Council of Europe fully informed of the measures which it has taken and the reasons therefor. It shall also inform the Secretary General of the Council of Europe when such measures have ceased to operate and the provisions of the Convention are again being fully executed.

A challenge can be made to the lawfulness of derogation. Following the United Kingdom's derogation after the decision in *Brogan v United Kingdom*,[214] a challenge was lodged, but failed when it was held that the situation in Northern Ireland did amount to a public emergency[215] and was thus within the terms of Article 15.

INCORPORATION OF THE EUROPEAN CONVENTION ON HUMAN RIGHTS

The debate about whether to incorporate the European Convention on Human Rights into domestic law hitherto is now laid firmly to rest with the Human Rights Act 1998, which effects incorporation of Convention rights. It is nevertheless instructive to reflect on the principal arguments which have formerly been advanced for and against incorporation, if only to set the reforms within context and to provide markers for the potential success of the Convention before the domestic courts.[216]

---

213 Note, however, the War Crimes Act 1991, s 1 of which provides for the prosecution of war crimes committed between 1939 and 1945.

214 (1988) 11 EHRR 117.

215 *Brannigan and McBride v United Kingdom* (1993) *The Times*, 28 May; (1994) 17 EHRR 539.

216 The Human Rights Act 1998 came into force in Scotland in 1998 and in England and Wales in October 2000.

The arguments for incorporation

The Convention has proved to be immensely significant in extending the protection given to rights and freedoms within Member States. In terms of practicalities, incorporation of the Convention, as opposed to drafting a Bill of Rights tailor-made for the United Kingdom, was the most simple option. The Convention has an impressive track record in the protection of rights, and the judiciary is well versed in the jurisprudence of the Court of Human Rights. Incorporation also avoids what would be very difficult questions of politics and substance if the alternative of drafting a new Bill of Rights specifically for the United Kingdom were to be adopted.

The arguments against incorporation

The substantive limits of the Convention

On the other hand, it has been argued that the Convention is out dated,[217] and is not tailored to meet the distinctive needs of the United Kingdom.[218] As noted above, one of the major substantive limitations of the Convention, for example, lies in the absence of a general non-discrimination provision. Moreover, while Article 3 guarantees protection against 'torture ... inhuman or degrading treatment or punishment', it does not guarantee any right to decent treatment *per se* for, for example, persons serving custodial sentences in prison, or patients detained in mental hospitals, or elderly persons living in residential homes. Nor does the Convention guarantee economic or social rights – a matter which has recently become of central concern within the European Community, but remains politically contentious within the United Kingdom. The Convention omissions have been described as 'extensive'.[219]

The role of the judiciary[220]

The judges in the United Kingdom are unelected[221] and, accordingly, enjoy no 'mandate of democracy'. Under the constitution, judges are subordinate to the will of the elected legislature and, mindful of this subordination and the doctrine of separation of powers, exercise caution concerning the appropriate scope of the jurisdiction of the courts.

---

217 See Zander, M, *A Bill of Rights*, 3rd edn, 1985, London: Sweet & Maxwell, Chapter 4.

218 See, eg, Denning (Lord), *What Next in the Law?*, 1982, London: Butterworths, Pt 7.5.

219 By Thornberry, CHR, *Minutes of Evidence taken before the Select Committee on the Bill of Rights*, House of Lords, 1977, para 13.

220 See, *inter alia*, Pannick, D, *Judges*, 1988, Oxford: OUP; Lee, S, *Judging Judges*, 1989, London: Faber & Faber; Griffith, JAG, *The Politics of the Judiciary*, 5th edn, 1997, London: Fontana.

221 On appointment, see Chapter 5.

Moreover, Professor JAG Griffith has argued cogently that the judges are ill equipped to assume the mantle of guardian of individual rights in the face of executive power and parliamentary sovereignty.[222] Judges are traditionally selected, he argues, from a cohesive and limited socio-economic class. Judges are predominantly white, male, middle or upper class and middle aged. Judges, by virtue of their background and training, it is argued from this perspective, are not suited to the task of protecting the rights of the poor, socially and economically disadvantaged, or members of groups and associations in society whose outlook and background is so very different from that of the elite judges. Nevertheless, as discussed in Chapter 5, it must be recognised that the judiciary, once appointed, enjoys security of tenure and, while subordinate to Parliament's sovereignty, is independent of the government, whatever the government's political persuasion. In its role in relation to judicial review of administrative action[223] and in relation to the interpretation and application of European Community law,[224] the judges have increasingly displayed a robustness which undermines the arguments about an ideological alignment with the interests of the executive, especially an executive with a conservative complexion. Furthermore, while the appointment of judges lies, and remains, in the hands of the executive, there have been proposals for change in the system of judicial appointments in order to open the judiciary up to men and woman with more diverse backgrounds. In a modest reform, since 1994, the Lord Chancellor's Department has been advertising for applications to posts in the lower rungs of the judiciary, and the current Lord Chancellor has announced that this will be extended to vacancies for High Court judges. This falls far short of the establishment of an independent Judicial Appointments and Training Commission, although the Labour Party's pre-election statement on constitutional reform did provide for such a Commission.[225]

There is also a difficulty perceived in so far as interpretation and application of a Bill of Rights would involve essentially complex political issues, thus drawing the judiciary increasingly into the political arena, from which they have traditionally steered clear. The 'politicisation of the judiciary' is a real and difficult issue but one which should not be, and has not been, allowed to determine the outcome of the Bill of Rights debate.

The difficulties also should not be exaggerated. Lord Lester of Herne Hill has argued that the judges to date have been very successful in interpreting the fundamental provisions of European Community law.[226] However, the

---

222 See *op cit*, Griffith, fn 220.
223 See Chapters 24 and 25.
224 See Chapters 8 and 9.
225 *A New Agenda for Democracy: Labour's Proposals for Constitutional Reform*, 1997, Labour Party.
226 Lester (Lord), 'Fundamental rights' [1994] PL 70.

success of judges in treading the fine line between adequately respecting the provisions of the Convention and respecting the traditional balance of power between Parliament and the judiciary is a matter which is dependent upon the manner in which incorporation is effected (see below, pp 929–39).

The seeming traditional ambivalence towards extending the courts' jurisdiction to protect Convention requirements has been removed by incorporation of the Convention under the Human Rights Act 1998. Lord Lester QC, recognising the 'radical departure from traditional canons of statutory interpretation' which the Act will require, has expressed cautious optimism:

> Would they [the judges] use it [the Convention] to go much further than the traditional position in which the courts seek to interpret ambiguous legislation so as to be in accordance with rather than in breach of the Treaty obligations undertaken by the United Kingdom? I hope and believe that they would indeed do so, seeking to avoid inconsistencies by limiting statutory provisions that encroach upon Convention rights, and implying the necessary procedural and other safeguards into legislation ...[227]

The question of parliamentary sovereignty

The principal difficulty in enacting a Bill of Rights which enjoys fundamental and supreme authority lies in the traditional Diceyan concept of sovereignty.[228] Under the constitution, Parliament – subject to moral and social, but not legal, restraints – may enact law on any matter and no one, including a court of law, may challenge the validity of an Act of Parliament. Entrenchment, as has been discussed, is not possible under the constitution without a radical realignment of power between Parliament and the judiciary, whereby the judges would be given the power to rule that an Act of Parliament was null and void on the basis of offending the Bill of Rights. The paradox must be faced that a Bill of Rights could not be given the legal sanctity it deserves without a written constitution which redefines the power within the State.

However, to argue that a written constitution is a prerequisite for a Bill of Rights is to overstate the constitutional difficulties posed by parliamentary sovereignty. A precedent for according a 'special status' to law has already been established with the incorporation of European Community (EC) law into domestic law. Section 2(4) of the European Communities Act 1972 operates as a directive to the judges to give effect to EC law and to interpret domestic law in the light of the requirements of EC law. As discussed in

---

227 Lester (Lord), 'First steps towards a constitutional Bill of Rights' (1997) 2 EHRLR 124, p 127.
228 See Chapter 7.

Chapter 9,[229] while the judges have been faced with difficulties in this respect, and have identified clear limits to the power to interpret domestic law as required by EC law, the judiciary has nevertheless been largely successful in complying with the section 2(4) duty. It has been seen that the doctrine of implied repeal does not apply to EC law and that the judges have adapted to the need to interpret law according to EC requirements, but that where Parliament expressly legislates inadvertent contravention of EC requirements, the judiciary will respect the will of Parliament.

One possible model for incorporation, therefore, would have been to follow the precedent set by section 2(4) of the European Communities Act 1972. An alternative would have been to adopt the Canadian formulation. In Canada, the Bill of Rights 1960 provided that every law of Canada should be interpreted and applied so as to avoid limiting or infringing the rights protected in the Bill of Rights and the Canadian Charter of Rights and Freedoms of 1982.[230] Section 2 of the Canadian Bill of Rights provides that the Canadian Parliament may enact legislation contrary to the Bill of Rights but that, in the absence of a clear direction to the judges, contained in a 'notwithstanding clause', all legislation must be construed in conformity with the Bill. By virtue of adopting such a legislative device, a special status is given to the Bill of Rights, whilst the ultimate sovereignty of the elected legislature is preserved. However, as discussed below, neither of these possible devices have been favoured, and the Human Rights Act 1998 makes it clear that the judges have no power to set aside statutes which contravene Convention rights.

THE HUMAN RIGHTS ACT 1998

The incorporation of Convention rights into domestic law under the 1998 Act, as a first step towards the better protection of rights, puts an end, finally, to the debate over whether or not to incorporate. What remains to be considered, however, is the manner of incorporation and the scope of the Act.

The Human Rights Act 1998 provides that public authorities exercising executive powers must comply with the requirements of the Convention. As the White Paper stated:

---

229 Which should be referred to for discussion of the case law.

230 See the Canada Act 1982. See, generally, Hogg, PW, *Constitutional Law of Canada*, 2nd edn, 1985, Toronto: Carswell; Russell, PH, Knopff, R and Morton, E, 'The Canadian Bill of Rights', in Russell, PH, Rainer, K and Morton, T (eds), *Federalism and the Charter: Leading Constitutional Decisions*, 1989, Ottawa: Carleton UP; Finkelstein, N, 'Note on the Canadian Bill of Rights', in Laskin, B (ed), *Canadian Constitutional Law*, 5th edn, 1986, Toronto: Carswell, Vol 1.

Although the United Kingdom has an international obligation to comply with the Convention, there at present is no requirement in our domestic law on central or local government, or others exercising similar executive powers, to exercise those powers in a way which is compatible with the Convention. This Bill will change that by making it unlawful for public authorities to act in a way which is incompatible with the Convention rights.[231]

Included within the definition of public authorities is central government, including executive agencies, local government, the police, immigration officers, prisons, courts and tribunals, and companies exercising functions which otherwise would be exercised by government – for example, privatised utility companies. The definition of public authorities is not, however, exhaustive and will depend upon the courts' evaluation of their role and functions. The actions of Parliament are, however, excluded.

Section 6 of the Act makes provisions relating to public authorities. Section 6(1) provides that it is unlawful for public authorities to act in a way which is incompatible with one or more of the Convention rights. However, section 6(1) does not apply to an act if the authority could not have acted differently because of a provision in an Act of Parliament. A public authority includes a court, a tribunal exercising functions in relation to legal proceedings and any 'person certain' of whose functions are of a public nature,[232] but does not include either House of Parliament or a person exercising functions in connection with proceedings in Parliament.

Accordingly, where a public authority acts in contravention of a Convention right, that right may be relied on in judicial review proceedings. It may also be relied on in other legal proceedings as a defence. As further discussed in Chapter 25, the Convention extends the scope of judicial review, not just in relation to actions and decisions of bodies which are reviewable under the current rules of judicial review, but also in relation to those affecting Convention rights. The concepts employed in judicial review will also extend to the doctrine of proportionality, which, as will be seen, is wider than the conventional doctrines of irrationality, illegality, and procedural impropriety. The doctrine of proportionality is one utilised by the European Court of Human Rights when determining the legality of acts and decisions, in order to determine whether action taken which restricts a Convention right is proportionate to the legitimate aim being pursued, under, for example, paragraph two of the many Articles which provide for restrictions 'in the public interest', 'in the interests of public health and safety' or 'in the interests of national security'.

However, a Convention right cannot be given protection against actions by public authorities, as section 6(2)(a), makes clear, where that action –

---

231 White Paper, *Rights Brought Home: The Human Rights Bill*, Cm 3782, 1997, London: HMSO, para 2.2.

232 On the definition of 'public bodies', see, further, Chapter 25.

notwithstanding a Convention right – is consistent with primary domestic legislation. For example, Article 8 confers the right to privacy in respect of 'private and family life, home and correspondence'. If the police, acting under the lawful authority of a warrant, place a surveillance device in a person's home in order to detect and investigate serious crime under the Police Act 1997, that action – having statutory authority – will be lawful. In any subsequent criminal proceedings against the individual, the evidence procured by the surveillance, being lawfully acquired, may be admitted in evidence. Furthermore, no court which falls outside the definition of a 'court' in section 4(5), of the Act, may make a declaration of incompatibility with the Convention. In order, therefore, for the issue to be tested by a court which has jurisdiction to make a declaration of incompatibility, it would be necessary for the aggrieved individual to appeal to a higher court and, although that court could make a declaration, the declaration would be of no benefit to the individual, given that, as section 4(6)(a) and (b), makes clear, the declaration has no effect on the 'validity, continuing operation or enforcement of the provision' and is not binding on the parties to the proceedings in which it is made.

The potential problems of enforcement of Convention rights also extend to civil proceedings. Since private individuals and purely private bodies are not bound by the Convention, the majority of cases in which Convention rights will be invoked are likely to be criminal proceedings. However, if an individual finds that his or her Convention right is breached by a civil law statute, once again, the problem of having to appeal to a higher court is apparent. This problem is exacerbated by the absence of legal aid for such appeals, even if the individual were to qualify under the stringent and limited eligibility rules for legal aid.

Where an issue is governed not by statute but by common law, it will fall to the judges to develop the law in line with Convention rights. Section 6(3), specifies that a public authority includes courts and tribunals and, accordingly, the court or tribunal must act in a manner compatible with Convention rights. Not to construe the common law in line with the Convention would render a decision susceptible to appeal to a higher court. The extent to which this duty will enhance Convention rights under the common law will depend very much on the willingness of the superior courts to adopt a positive developmental approach to rights, and must remain, at this time, a matter for speculation.

In an amendment to the Bill, special consideration was given to the position of religion and the churches. Section 13 of the Act provides for freedom of thought, conscience and religion, and states that:

> 13(1) If a court's determination of any question arising under this Act might affect the exercise by a religious organisation (itself or its members collectively) of the Convention right to freedom of thought, conscience and religion, it must have a particular regard to the importance of that right.

The section was included to protect the churches from liability under the Convention. Thus, for example, if a person alleges that he or she is the victim of a breach of the Convention right to marry (Article 12) or the right to respect for private and family life (Article 8) by the beliefs, rules and practices of a religious faith, the court, in determining the issue, must have special regard to the importance of those beliefs and practices.

The status of the Convention under the Human Rights Act 1998

As noted above, the Canadian Charter of Rights and Freedoms 1982 provides the courts with power to invalidate legislation which is contrary to the Charter, subject only to the requirement that legislation which has been expressly passed to contravene the Charter should not be invalidated. This is the 'notwithstanding clause' approach which represented one model for the United Kingdom Parliament to follow. The Hong Kong Bill of Rights Ordinance of 1991 distinguished between legislation enacted before the Ordinance took effect, and legislation subsequent to the Ordinance. In the case of previous legislation, it must be construed consistently with the Ordinance. In relation to subsequent legislation, however, the legislation takes precedence over the Ordinance. Yet another alternative approach, employed in New Zealand, under the New Zealand Bill of Rights Act 1990, is to state that the interpretation of statutes should, as far as possible, be consistent with the Bill of Rights. The courts do not, however, have the power to strike down statutes, and the Act provides that, where consistent interpretation is impossible, the validity of the statute is unaffected. This is a far weaker model than that adopted in Canada, and represents the model on which the Human Rights Act 1998 has been introduced.

As discussed in Chapter 7, under the constitution of the United Kingdom, and consistent with the doctrine of parliamentary sovereignty, legislation cannot be entrenched. That is to say, it cannot be given a 'special' or 'higher' status than other Acts of Parliament. This traditional doctrine has been preserved in relation to the Human Rights Act.

In its White Paper, the government announced that it did not intend to permit the courts to strike down Acts of Parliament, whether that legislation preceded the Act or was introduced subsequently. Thus the Convention has a status subordinate to ordinary primary legislation. Thereby, Parliament's sovereignty and, to the extent possible, the separation of powers, is preserved. The Convention, in the government's view, is 'intended to provide a new basis for judicial interpretation of all legislation, not a basis for striking down any part of it'.[233] However, the courts are given power over delegated, or

---

233 White Paper, *Rights Brought Home: The Human Rights Bill*, Cm 3782, 1997, London: HMSO, para 2.14.

secondary, legislation. Unless the parent Act stipulates that the courts do not have power to invalidate a piece of secondary legislation, its validity will depend on the court's interpretation of its compatibility with the Convention.

Accordingly, section 3 of the Human Rights Act 1998 requires that primary and secondary legislation, whenever enacted, must be interpreted and applied in a manner consistent with Convention rights. However, section 3(2) makes it clear that this requirement does not affect the validity, continuing operation or enforcement of any incompatible primary legislation, and does not affect the validity, continuing operation or enforcement of incompatible subordinate legislation, if the primary legislation prevents removal of the incompatibility.

Declarations of incompatibility are regulated under section 4, which provides that, if a court is satisfied that a provision of primary or subordinate legislation is incompatible with one or more Convention rights, it may make a declaration of incompatibility. The courts with the jurisdiction to make declarations of incompatibility are the House of Lords, the Judicial Committee of the Privy Council, the Courts-Martial Appeal Court; in Scotland, the High Court of Justiciary, sitting as a court of criminal appeal, or the Court of Session; and, in England, Wales and Northern Ireland, the High Court or Court of Appeal. Section 4(6), however, contains a vital limitation, in that a declaration of incompatibility does not affect the validity, continuing operation or enforcement of the provision in question, and is not binding on the parties to the proceedings in which it is made.

As is evident from section 4, it is only the superior courts which have jurisdiction to make declarations of incompatibility and, further, a declaration of incompatibility, as emphasised in sub-section (6)(a) and (b), the declaration will have no effect on the validity of the primary legislation in question, nor will the declaration affect the legal position of the parties to the litigation. The power to amend the law has thereby been preserved for Parliament, although a fast track legislative procedure, discussed below, will be employed to facilitate rapid parliamentary action in relation to the declaration.

Making an application under the Act

The Act provides that an individual may make an application to the courts if, and only if, he or she 'is (or would be) a victim of an unlawful act'. Accordingly, pressure groups and other interest groups will not be able to use the Convention procedure to challenge government actions. Section 7 stipulates the procedures.

A person claiming that a public authority has acted, or proposes to act, in a way made unlawful by section 6(1) may bring proceedings against the authority, or may rely on the Convention right concerned in any legal proceedings. In relation to judicial review proceedings, the victim test is also applied, giving a narrower meaning to 'sufficient interest' than that applied under other judicial review proceedings.[234] Proceedings must be brought within one year of the date on which the act complained of took place, but this limit may be extended by the court if it considers it 'equitable', having regard to any stricter time limit imposed on the proceedings in question.[235] 'Legal proceedings' is defined to mean proceedings brought by a public authority and appeals against the decision of a court or tribunal.[236]

Section 2 of the Human Rights Act 1998 provides interpretative provisions, and requires a court or tribunal determining a question arising under the Act to take into account any judgment, decision, declaration or advisory opinion of the European Court of Human Rights, opinions of the Commission, decisions of the Commission under Article 26 or 27 and decisions of the Committee of Ministers taken under Article 46.[237]

The judicial remedies

Article 13 of the Convention, which provides that everyone shall have an effective remedy before a national authority, notwithstanding that the violation has been committed by persons acting in an official capacity, is not being incorporated. Instead, section 8 of the Human Rights Act regulates remedies.

Section 8 provides that, where a court finds that a public authority has acted unlawfully, it may grant 'such relief or remedy, or make such order within its jurisdiction as it considers just and appropriate'. Damages may only be awarded by a court which has power to award damages or to order the payment of compensation in civil proceedings, and no award of damages is to be made unless, taking into account all the circumstances of the case and any other relief or remedy available, the court is satisfied that the award is necessary to afford just satisfaction to the complainant. The court must take into account the principles applied by the Court of Human Rights in relation to the award of compensation under Article 41.

One question which arises for future determination is the issue whether or not section 8 provides an adequate remedy according to the jurisprudence of the European Court of Human Rights. For example, in *Chahal v United Kingdom*,[238] the Court ruled that there had been a violation of Article 13 in

---

234 Human Rights Act 1998, s 7(3).

235 *Ibid*, s 7(5).

236 *Ibid*, s 7(6).

237 Which relates to the binding nature of judgments and the supervision of the Court's judgment by the Committee of Ministers.

238 (1996) 23 EHRR 413, discussed above, p 890.

conjunction with Article 3. A complainant's deportation would violate Article 3, and, because there was no review mechanism for the decision of the Home Secretary in relation to deportation, there was a violation of Article 13. The courts are under a duty, under section 2, to take into account the case law developed in Strasbourg. Accordingly, there is the potential for considerable case law on the relationship between section 8 of the Human Rights Act 1998 and Article 13 of the Convention.

Ensuring legislative conformity with Convention rights

Ensuring that domestic legislation conforms to Convention requirements involves two procedures. The first relates to the enactment of legislation generally, and the second relates to legislative action taken after a declaration of incompatibility has been issued by the courts.

In relation to non-remedial legislation, the Act provides for declarations to be made to Parliament that the proposed legislation conforms to Convention requirements. Section 19 requires that a Minister in charge of a Bill in either House of Parliament must, before second reading, make a statement either to the effect that a Bill does comply with Convention rights or that, although such a statement cannot be made, the government nevertheless wishes to proceed with the Bill.

In relation to remedial legislation, the courts are not given the power under the Act to invalidate or set aside primary legislation which is incompatible with Convention rights. Instead, the power to reform the law is preserved for the executive and Parliament. The Act introduces a special legislative procedure for reform. While this mechanism preserves the principle that it is Parliament, as the democratically elected legislature, which is sovereign in making, and reforming, law, it also opens the door to the possibility that governments of differing political persuasions may react with greater or lesser enthusiasm to declarations of incompatibility. The extent to which successive governments respond to the ruling of the courts thus lies in the *moral* rather than *legal* authority of the Convention.

The fast track legislative procedure

Where a higher court[239] makes a declaration of incompatibility, or where the Court of Human Rights in Strasbourg declares that the Convention has been violated, the relevant government Minister will have power to enact amending legislation by Order in Council (a 'remedial order'). Other than where it is necessary for the Order to have immediate effect, the Order will be

---

239 As interpreted by the Human Rights Act 1998, s 6.

subject to the approval of both Houses of Parliament, and will only come into effect once approval has been secured. Section 10 and Schedule 2 regulate remedial action and remedial orders.

Section 10, which was considerably amended in Standing Committee in the House of Commons, provides for the amendment of legislation to make it compatible with Convention rights. The remedial procedure can be used either following a declaration of incompatibility or in response to a decision of the European Court of Human Rights, whether or not the decision in question related to United Kingdom law. Two procedures are provided for. Under the standard procedure,[240] a draft of the order must be laid before Parliament for a 60 day period before it is approved by resolution of each House. When laying the draft instrument, the Minister must also provide the 'required information', which entails an explanation of:

> ... the incompatibility which the proposed order seeks to remove, including particulars of the court declaration, finding or order which caused the Minister to propose a remedial order; and a statement of the reasons for proceeding under section 10 and for making an order in the terms proposed.[241]

During the period in which the draft is laid before Parliament, representations may be made to the Minister, either by Parliament or by any other person. If representations are made, the draft must be accompanied by a statement containing a summary of the representations and details of any changes introduced into the proposed order as a result of the representations.[242] Section 10 and Schedule 2 also provide that, if a Minister considers that there are compelling reasons, he may make such amendments to legislation as he considers necessary to remove the incompatibility, by means of a statutory instrument. The power applies to both primary and subordinate legislation. In debate on the Bill, the Lord Chancellor stated that, 'if legislation has been declared to be incompatible, a prompt parliamentary remedy should be available'.[243]

The Human Rights Act 1998 makes provision for derogations and reservations. Sections 14 to 17 regulate designations and reservations. Section 14, in part, provides that:

(1) In this Act, a 'designated derogation' means:

(a) the United Kingdom's derogation from Article 5(3) of the Convention [which provides for the right to be brought promptly before a court]; and

---

240 Human Rights Act 1998, Sched 2.
241 *Ibid*, para 3.
242 *Ibid*, para 2.
243 *Hansard*, House of Lords, 3 November 1997, Col 1231.

   (b) any derogation by the United Kingdom from an Article of the Convention, or of any protocol to the Convention, which is designated for the purposes of this Act in an order made by the Secretary of State.

(6) A designation order may be made in anticipation of the making by the United Kingdom of a proposed derogation.

In relation to reservations, section 15, in part, provides that:

(1) In this Act, 'designated reservation' means:

   (a) the United Kingdom's reservation to Article 2 of the first protocol to the Convention [the right to education in conformity with parents' religious and philosophical convictions]; and

   (b) any other reservation by the United Kingdom to an Article of the Convention or of any protocol to the Convention, which is designated for the purposes of this Act in an order made by the Secretary of State.

The Human Rights Act 1998 came into effect in Scotland in 1998. As seen above, an early challenge arose in *Starrs v Procurator Fiscal, Linlithgow*, in which the position of temporary sheriffs enjoying no security of tenure was incompatible with Article 6, which provides, *inter alia*, for a fair and impartial tribunal. Compatibility with Article 6 requirements also fell for consideration in *Brown v Procurator Fiscal, Dunfermline*,[244] in relation to self-incrimination. There, a police officer who suspected a person of driving while drunk required him to say whether he had been driving his car. The response 'it was me', and evidence of that reply, was given to the court by the prosecution on a charge of driving whilst drunk. That evidence violated the driver's right to silence and rights against self-incrimination under Article 6. The relevant statutory provision, section 172 of the Road Traffic Act 1972, had to be interpreted subject to the requirements of Article 6. Article 6 was also examined by the High Court of Justiciary in *Hoekstra v Her Majesty's Advocate*.[245] In that case, the right to an impartial tribunal was violated by a judge sitting in a case of criminal appeal, who wrote a newspaper article strongly critical of the Convention. The article, which *inter alia* suggested that persons suspected of drug dealing should not have the right to privacy (under Article 8) against covert surveillance, would create in the mind of an informed observer 'an apprehension of bias' on the part of its author against the Convention and its rights. The Court ordered that fresh appeal proceedings should be heard by three different judges. A violation of Article 6 also arose in *R v Her Majesty's Advocate*,[246] where a nine month delay between an original interview of a suspect and the suspect being charged rendered a prosecution unlawful. The delay had been unreasonable and contrary to Article 6(3).

---

244 (2000) *The Times*, 14 February.
245 (2000) *The Times*, 14 April.
246 (2000) *The Times*, 14 April.

CONCLUSION

The European Convention on Human Rights has provided vital protection for citizens against the power of the State. As has been seen, the case law against the United Kingdom is substantial and, in many instances, has led to considerable reform of the law. Nevertheless, the right of individual petition, conferred in 1965, has meant long delays and high costs for litigants. To be set against that is the benefits which have accrued from a judicial forum which employs European criteria in its interpretation of the meaning and scope of rights – a forum which avoids the often insuperable difficulties of the subordinate position of domestic judges to the 'will of Parliament' and, moreover, any perceptions of partiality on the part of the domestic judges for aligning themselves with the executive.

The Convention has for the most part, and despite its limitations in scope, served individuals well in the protection of fundamental rights. The incorporation of Convention rights into domestic law was a logical step forward for a government seriously committed to individual rights and freedoms. Incorporation also may change the traditional public conception of individual freedoms in favour of rights, and bring a greater clarity to the law relating both to civil liberties and human rights. It may be argued that the manner of the Convention rights' incorporation is deficient: that it represents 'half a loaf' by allowing for express repeal and for the retention of legislative control by the executive and Parliament. Perhaps, however, to state the obvious, half a loaf is better than none.

The effectiveness of the Human Rights Act 1998 rests on three foundations: the willingness of the judges robustly to defend rights and to interpret Convention rights in a manner favouring individual protection against governmental encroachment; the government's willingness to make remedial orders to ensure compliance with declarations of incompatibility with Convention rights; and, finally, the energy with which individual citizens are prepared to assert their rights in courts of law.

As exemplified by the recent application under the Convention, *AV v United Kingdom*,[247] discussed above, the applicant had been unable to secure a remedy within the United Kingdom, because the primary legislation, the Births and Deaths Registration Act 1953, laid down procedures to be followed. The applicant, had he proceeded under the Human Rights Act 1998, rather than applying to the Commission in Strasbourg, would not have had a judicial remedy in the courts but, rather, remain in the unenviable position of having to await remedial action by the relevant Minister and Parliament. Furthermore, section 7, which confines the right to bring proceedings against

---

247 Appl 34546/97: 20 May 1998; (1998) 142 SJ 628. See *op cit*, Leach, fn 133.

a public authority, and the right to rely on Convention rights in any legal proceedings, including judicial review, to persons who are, or would be, a victim of that act, is particularly restrictive and precludes applications by interest groups and representative bodies acting on behalf of their members and supporters. As will be seen in Chapter 24, in judicial review proceedings, the 'standing' of applicants is far broader than that provided for under the Human Rights Act 1998, and whereas, *inter alia*, the courts have ruled that various organisations such as the Equal Opportunities Commission have sufficient interest to undertake judicial review proceedings, enforcement of Convention rights under the 1998 Act will rely purely on the individual victim of an alleged violation. To have utilised the 'sufficient interest' test, rather than the 'victim' test, would have lessened the onus on the individual victim and facilitated applications from interest groups and those with special expertise in particular areas.

CHAPTER 23

STATE SECURITY[1]

INTRODUCTION

The security of the State is of the utmost importance to the integrity and well being of a nation and to individual citizens whose rights and freedoms are protected by the security of the State. On the other hand the rights of citizens may be adversely affected by the exercise of such powers and there exists the potential for governments to hide behind the doctrine of national security in order to prevent scrutiny of executive action. Two principal constitutional questions arise from State security. The first concerns the extent to which arrangements secure some form of balance between the competing needs of State security and protection of the individual. The second issue relates to the manner in which – and extent to which – the government is held accountable for powers exercised in the name of State security, either through supervision of the courts or through the democratic process.

Legal regulation of State security matters is relatively recent. Although the original Official Secrets Act dates from 1911, it has only been in the past two decades that statute has regulated the interception of communications,[2] and the security and intelligence services, MI5 and SIS or MI6, and the government's signals intelligence organisation, Government Communications Headquarters (GCHQ). Incorporation of Convention rights under the Human Rights Act 1998 necessitated further clarity in the law, provided by the Regulation of Investigatory Powers Act 2000, the main purpose of which is to ensure that relevant investigatory powers are used in accordance with human rights.

---

1   See, *inter alia*, Bulloch, J, *MI5: The Origin and History of the British Counter-Espionage Service*, 1963, London: Arthur Barker; Deacon, R, *A History of the British Secret Service*, 1969, London: Frederick Muller (updated, 1980, London: Panther); Pincher, C, *Their Trade is Treachery*, 1981, London: Sidgwick and Jackson; West, N, *MI5: British Security Service Operations 1909–45*, 1981, London: Bodley Head; West, N, *A Matter of Trust: MI5 1945–72*, 1983, London: Hodder & Stoughton; Williams, DGT, *Not in the Public Interest*, 1965, London: Hutchinson; Andrew, C, *Secret Service: The Making of the British Intelligence Community*, 1985, London: Heinemann; Lustgarten, L and Leigh, I, *In From the Cold: National Security and Parliamentary Democracy*, 1994, Oxford: Clarendon; Garton Ash, T, *The File: A Personal History*, 1997, London: HarperCollins.

2   Interception of Communication Act 1985, State Security Act 1989, Intelligence Services Act 1994.

The revival of public and academic interest in security matters

Public and academic interest in the role of the Security Services has been heightened in recent years by, *inter alia*, the banning of trades union membership at the GCHQ;[3] the litigation concerning the publication of an autobiography of a former Security Service officer, Peter Wright, and, more recently, the arms to Iraq affair, in the course of which the government used public immunity certificates,[4] apparently to suppress evidence which would have led to an earlier abandonment of the prosecution of Matrix Churchill directors for alleged breaches of export regulations during the Iran-Iraq War. The arms to Iraq affair resulted in the appointment of a judicial inquiry into the matter, the details of which are discussed in Chapter 11.

THE SECURITY SERVICES

The terminology

The United Kingdom's internal Security Service is known as MI5.[5] The Security Service dealing with matters overseas is the Secret Intelligence Service, or MI6. The government's signals intelligence gathering headquarters is Government Communications Headquarters, or GCHQ. Special Branch is part of the police forces and has special duties in relation to public order, the gathering of intelligence and combating subversion and terrorism. The operations of MI5 and MI6 are co-ordinated by the Intelligence Co-ordinator, based in the Cabinet Office. In addition, there is the armed forces wing of military intelligence which, nowadays, is operative principally, but not exclusively, in Northern Ireland (see, further, below, p 974 *et seq*).

The Security Service (MI5)

Until 1989, the internal Security Service, MI5, was unknown to law.[6] It was not regulated by statute and the Service did not enjoy any special common law powers. MI5 was established in 1909,[7] under the royal prerogative as part of the defence forces of the realm. The Service is headed by a Director General[8] who is responsible to the Secretary of State for the Home Office. The Service is not, however, formally a part of the Home Office and thus occupies

---

3   See, further, Chapters 6 and 25.
4   See, further, Chapter 11.
5   MI stands for Military Intelligence.
6   See, now, the Security Services Act 1989; Intelligence Services Act 1994.
7   As part of the War Office. The Service was originally known as MO5.
8   Stephen Lander.

a curious constitutional status. The Director General has access to the Prime Minister on matters of importance. The Service employs some 2,000 personnel. Since the ending of the Cold War, approximately 70 per cent of the Service's resources are devoted to gathering intelligence about terrorism.[9] Moreover, the Security Services Act 1996 now extends the role of the Service in relation to investigations relating to 'serious crime', particularly the drugs trade.[10]

Functions of the Service

In 1952, the then Home Secretary, Sir David Maxwell-Fyfe, issued a directive to the Director General outlining the functions of the Service:

> The Security Service is part of the defence forces of the country. Its task is the defence of the Realm as a whole, from external and internal dangers arising from attempts at espionage and sabotage, or from actions of persons and organisations whether directed from within or without the country, which may be judged to be subversive of the State.[11]

The Profumo affair[12]

In 1963, the Secretary of State for War, the Rt Hon John Profumo resigned from office as a result of his lying to the House of Commons over press disclosures concerning an alleged affair with Christine Keeler, who had associations with a Russian Naval Attaché. The Prime Minister, Harold Macmillan, appointed Lord Denning to inquire into the security aspects of the affair. In his report, Lord Denning stressed that the function of the Security Service:

> ... is to defend the Realm from dangers which would threaten it as a whole, such as espionage on behalf of a foreign power, or internal organisations subversive of the State. For this purpose it must collect information about individuals and give it to those concerned. But it must not, even at the behest of a Minister or a government department, take part in investigating the private lives of individuals except in a matter bearing on the defence of the Realm as a whole.[13]

---

9   The Home Secretary revealed in July 1998 that M15 currently holds approximately 440,000 files, but that only 13,000 are 'active' dossiers on British citizens, over half of which were suspected of terrorist activities. Of the remainder, 35,000 files related to the Service's administration; 40,000 related to subjects and organisations studied by M15; 290,000 files related to individuals who had been subject a Service inquiry in the past 90 years. A further 230,000 files were 'closed'. Active files included about 20,000 of which one third related to foreign nationals: *Hansard*, HC Vol 317 Col 251.

10 On the 1996 Act, see, further, below.

11 Reproduced in Lord Denning MR's judgment in *R v Home Secretary ex parte Hosenball* [1977] 3 All ER 452.

12 See Denning (Lord), *The Due Process of Law*, 1980, London: Butterworths, Chapter 3.

13 The *Report on the Security Aspects of the Circumstances leading up to the Resignation of Mr JD Profumo*, Cmnd 2152, 1963, London: HMSO, caused disquiet. One outcome was the establishment of the Security Commission in 1964. See Leigh, I and Lustgarten, L, 'The Security Commission: constitutional achievement or curiosity?' [1991] PL 215.

Further judicial expression of the role of the Service is found in the judgment of Taylor J in *R v Secretary of State for the Home Department ex parte Ruddock*.[14]

> The function of the Security Service is the defence of the realm as a whole from, *inter alia*, the actions of persons who and organisations which may be subversive of the State ... A warrant to intercept should only issue where there is reasonable cause to believe that major subversive activity is already being carried on and is likely to injure the national interest. The material reasonably likely to be obtained by the interception must be of direct use to the Security Service in its functions ...
>
> Normal methods of investigation must either have failed or be unlikely to succeed. Interception must be strictly limited to what is necessary to the Security Service's defined functions and must not be used for party political purposes ...[15]

Despite such strictures, there have been many charges made against the Service from journalists and from members of the Service themselves.[16]

Spycatcher[17]

The most celebrated exposure of the Service came in the form of Peter Wright's book, *Spycatcher*.[18] Among many allegations made by Wright in *Spycatcher* was the claim that MI5 had 'bugged and burgled its way across London' without lawful authority.

As an electrical engineer with MI5, Peter Wright's expertise included bugging embassies, diplomatic residences and international conferences. In 1963, Wright was promoted to an interrogator and to the post of Chairman of an internal committee inquiring into Soviet infiltration of the Security Services. Wright believed that MI5's perceived poor performance in the Cold War years of the 1950s and 1960s was in part due to Soviet infiltration at the highest point of the Security Service. The defections of two security agents, Donald Maclean and Guy Burgess, in 1951, and the confession and defection of Kim Philby, in 1963,[19] gave added weight to the security fears. Wright was further convinced that the then head of MI5, Roger Hollis, was a Soviet agent:

---

14 [1987] 2 All ER 518.

15 *Ibid*, p 522.

16 See, *inter alia*, *op cit*, Pincher, fn 1; *op cit*, West, 1983, fn 1.

17 See Watt, D, 'Fallout from treachery: Peter Wright and the *Spycatcher* case' [1988] Political Quarterly 206; Pannick, D, '*Spycatcher*: two years of legal indignation', in Kingsford-Smith, D and Oliver, D (eds), *Economic With the Truth: The Law and Media in a Democratic Society*, 1990, Oxford: OUP.

18 Wright, P, *Spycatcher: The Candid Autobiography of a Senior Intelligence Officer*, 1987, New York: Viking.

19 An MI6 officer, appointed to MI6 Head of Station in Washington. See Trevor-Roper, H, *The Philby Affair: Espionage, Treason and the Secret Service*, 1968, London: Kimber; Philby, K, *My Silent War*, 1968, London: MacGibbon and Kee.

a matter officially denied but never categorically proven.[20] The revelation in 1979 that Anthony Blunt, surveyor of the Queen's art collection and knight of the realm, had been a KGB[21] spy since his recruitment by the Russians whilst a student at Cambridge University[22] revealed the extent to which the Security Services had become vulnerable to Russian infiltration.

Wright became convinced that Harold Wilson, leader of the Labour Party and Prime Minister 1964–70 and 1974–76, was planted by the KGB, which Wright claimed had poisoned the former Labour Party leader Hugh Gaitskell.[23] Wright claimed that MI5 viewed the Labour Party's electoral victory of 1974 as against the national interest and instigated a plot to feed anti-Labour Party information from MI5 files to pro-Conservative newspapers.[24] In 1976, Wright retired and Lord Rothschild introduced him to the journalist Chapman Pincher. In collaboration with Pincher, *Spycatcher* was written, a book which launched one of the most farcical chapters in recent legal and political history, revealing as much about the secrecy of government as about the working of the Security Service.

The government, intent on stopping circulation of *Spycatcher*, sought an injunction to restrain publication.[25] The basis for the injunction was an alleged breach of confidence by Wright. Breach of confidence had been employed in *Attorney General v Jonathan Cape Ltd*,[26] in the attempt to prevent publication of Richard Crossman's *Diaries*.[27] As was seen there,[28] the court accepted that revelations of Cabinet discussions could be restrained by an action for breach of confidence but, when weighed against the public interest in freedom of information, the action failed.

In *Spycatcher*, Wright alleged that the Service had, over the years, in addition to 'bugging and burglary', interrogated and hounded hundreds of individuals in an inquiry into the membership of the Communist Party rivalling that of the McCarthy Inquiry in the United States of America in the

---

20 See *op cit*, Pincher, fn 1. Pincher relied heavily on information obtained from Wright. An official inquiry chaired by Lord Trend in 1974–75 failed to establish Hollis's innocence. See HC Deb Vol 1 Cols 1079–85, 26 March 1981. Hollis retired from MI5 in 1965. The Security Commission investigated the charges: its report was never published. Instead, a government statement was issued outlining measures taken as a result of the report: see Cmnd 8450, 1982, London: HMSO.

21 The Russian secret service.

22 From 1926. Following Blunt's exposure, Blunt was stripped of his knighthood.

23 For Lord Wilson's views on the Security Service, see Wilson, H, *The Governance of Britain*, 1976, London: Weidenfeld & Nicolson.

24 See Wilson, H, *The Labour Government 1964–70: A Personal Record*, 1971, London: Weidenfeld and Nicolson.

25 See Turnbull, M, *The Spycatcher Trial*, 1988, London: Heinemann.

26 [1976] QB 752.

27 See Young, H, *The Crossman Affair*, 1976, London: Hamish Hamilton.

28 See Chapters 2 and 11.

1930s. The allegations made by Wright became a matter of intense political and legal interest.

The litigation against *Spycatcher* commenced in Australia in 1985,[29] and ultimately failed.[30] In 1986, both *The Guardian* and *The Observer* newspapers carried reports of the pending hearing and reproduced some of the *Spycatcher* material. Temporary injunctions were obtained by the Attorney General. The following month, *The Sunday Times* began serialisation of *Spycatcher* against which a further injunction was granted. In 1987, the book was published in the United States of America. The House of Lords, however, decided that the injunctions against the press should be continued.[31] The matter returned to the courts for consideration of whether permanent injunctions against the publication of *Spycatcher* should be granted. The House of Lords held that the wide availability of the information and the public interest in freedom of speech and the right to receive information outweighed the interests of the Crown in preserving government secrecy.[32] Nonetheless, by this time, there had been suppression of the information for some four years.[33] The issue of the temporary injunctions was taken to the European Court of Human Rights, wherein it was held that the injunctions granted violated Article 10 of the Convention: *The Observer, The Guardian and The Sunday Times v United Kingdom.*[34]

One outcome of the *Spycatcher* affair was the enactment of the Security Services Act 1989, which placed the Security Service on a statutory basis. The Regulation of Investigatory Powers Act 2000 reforms the law relating to the security services and the interception of communications.

The Security Services Act 1989[35]

The Act defines the functions of the Service and places the issuing of warrants under statutory authority. The Act also provided, for the first time, a complaints procedure for individuals who are aggrieved by actions of the

---

29 (1987) 8 NSWLR 341.

30 HC of Australia (1988) 165 CLR 30.

31 *Attorney General v Guardian Newspapers Ltd* [1987] 3 All ER 316.

32 *Attorney General v Guardian Newspapers Ltd (No 2)* [1990] 1 AC 109.

33 See Bindman, G, '*Spycatcher*: judging the judges' (1989) 139 NLJ 94.

34 [1991] 14 EHRR 229. See, further, Chapter 22; and see Leigh, I, '*Spycatcher* in Strasbourg' [1992] PL 200. In *Attorney General v Blake* (1996) *The Times*, 23 April, Sir Richard Scott VC ruled that the Crown was not entitled to the profits gained by Blake, a former Secret Intelligence Officer who became a Soviet Agent in 1951 through the publication of his autobiography. By 1989, when the autobiography was published, none of the information was any longer confidential and, therefore, there was no breach of the lifelong duty imposed on former security service officers not to disclose confidential information. Furthermore, it was ruled that to grant relief would entail an infringement of Blake's rights under ECHR, Art 10.

35 See Leigh, I and Lustgarten, L, 'The Security Services Act 1989' (1989) 52 MLR 801.

Security Service and a Commissioner charged with the task of reviewing the procedure by which the Home Secretary issues warrants. Section 1 defines the functions of the Service as being:

> (2) ... the protection of national security and, in particular, its protection against threats from espionage, terrorism and sabotage, from the activities of agents of foreign powers and from actions intended to overthrow or undermine Parliamentary democracy by political, industrial or violent means.
>
> (3) It shall also be the function of the Service to safeguard the economic well being of the United Kingdom against threats posed by the actions or intentions of persons outside the British Islands.

In 1992, the Security Service assumed responsibility for terrorism related to Northern Ireland. This had previously been under the jurisdiction of Special Branch.

The Security Service itself is not defined in the Act. The Secret Intelligence Service – M16 – did not fall under the control of the Act. Other agencies, such as Special Branch, which carries out many of the functions of the Security Service,[36] and GCHQ, are not mentioned in the Act.[37] National security is not defined in the Act. In debate on the Bill, the Home Secretary stated that the 'phrase refers – and can only refer – to matters relating to the survival or well being of the nation as a whole, and not to party-political or sectional or lesser interests'.[38]

The duties of the Director General of the Service are set out in section 2. These are primarily the responsibility 'for the efficiency of the Service',[39] and for ensuring that the Service only collects information necessary for the proper discharge of its functions,[40] and that the Service does not take any action to further the interests of any political party.[41] The Director General is required to report annually to the Prime Minister and the Secretary of State for the Home Department, and may otherwise report to them at any time the Director General so decides.[42]

While the Director General is under a duty to report to the Prime Minister, there is no duty imposed on the Prime Minister to lay that report before Parliament. There is thus no Parliamentary scrutiny of the Director General's exercise of power. Attempts in both the House of Commons and the House of

---

36   See, further, below.
37   This omission is remedied by the Intelligence Services Act 1994, on which, see, further, below.
38   *Hansard*, HC Vol 143 Col 1113; see, also, Vol 145 Col 217, and see *Hansard*, HL Vol 357 Col 947.
39   Security Services Act 1989, s 2(2).
40   *Ibid*, s 2(2)(a).
41   *Ibid*, s 2(2)(b).
42   *Ibid*, s 2(4).

Lords to introduce such scrutiny failed. However, the Intelligence Services Act 1994,[43] for the first time, brings Parliamentary scrutiny to the work of the Security Services, both MI5 and MI6 – and to GCHQ. Under the Act, a Parliamentary Intelligence and Security Committee is established. As discussed below, the Committee is not a select committee, and is not given the powers of a select committee. Furthermore, under the Act, information may be withheld from the Committee on the basis that 'the Secretary of State has determined that it should not be disclosed'.[44]

The Security Services Act 1996

The Security Services Act 1996 extends the function of the Security Service into matters concerning 'serious crime'. The government's objective was to enable the Service to investigate 'organised crime' and 'drug trafficking, money launderers and racketeers'. The Service acts in a supportive role, and the principal responsibility lies with the conventional law enforcement agencies.[45]However, 'serious crime' is not itself defined in the Act. Nor is the scope of the Service's jurisdiction entirely clear. Moreover, the Service will remain under the operation control of the Director General, and will not be accountable to local police authorities, nor will their operations be supervised by the Police Complaints Authority.

Warrants

Section 3 of the Security Services Act 1989 deals with warrants for the 'interference with property', and provided that no interference with property shall be unlawful if it is authorised by the Secretary of State.[46] 'Interference with property' includes, at least, breaking and entering and bugging. The Secretary of State may issue a warrant, on an application from the Service, on the basis that he thinks it necessary to take action in order to obtain information which:

(i)   is likely to be of substantial value in assisting the Service to discharge any of its functions; and

(ii) cannot reasonably be obtained by other means ...[47]

The Secretary of State must be satisfied that the warrant relates to the proper function of the Service. Where the warrant is signed by the Secretary of State, the warrant ceases to have effect at the end of a six month period.[48] Warrants

---

43   See Supperstone, M, 'The Intelligence Services Act 1994' [1994] PL 329.
44   Intelligence Services Act 1994, Sched 3, para 3(1)(b)(ii).
45   See HL Deb Cols 398–99, 14 May 1996.
46   Security Services Act 1989, s 3(1).
47   *Ibid*, s 3(2)(a).
48   *Ibid*, s 3(4).

may be issued on the Secretary of State's behalf, by a senior civil servant, where the Secretary of State so authorises, and where the matter is one of urgency.[49] Warrants issued on behalf of the Secretary of State have effect only for two working days. Section 3 is now repealed under the Intelligence Services Act 1994, and replaced by sections 5 and 6 of that Act which also now extends statutory control to MI6 and GCHQ. The procedural provisions, however, remain unaltered, although the safeguard in section 3 of the 1989 Act has been removed. Under the 1994 Act, a warrant may be issued not just on the basis that the information will be of 'substantial value' to the work of the Security Service, but merely on the basis that the information will directly assist them in carrying out their statutory functions.[50]

Prior to the Security Services Act 1989, warrants for 'interference with property' were issued (it is presumed) under the royal prerogative. The lawfulness of such warrants was questioned in *Malone v Metropolitan Police Commissioner*[51] (on which see, further, below, p 954). As to whether there were any lawful grounds on which the Home Secretary could previously have issued warrants for entry and search of property there is some doubt. In *Attorney General v Guardian Newspapers (No 2)*, Lord Donaldson MR doubted whether there was any lawful authority for such warrants, but appeared to excuse an individual's 'invasion of privacy' by the Security Services on the basis of the defence of the realm.[52]

The Intelligence Services Act 1994 provides for a similar procedure for the authorising of warrants for the interference of property as that contained in the 1989 Act. Once again, it is the Secretary of State who has the power to issue warrants, and not a court of law.[53]

The Commissioner and Tribunal

The 1989 Act established a Commissioner to oversee the granting of warrants, and a Tribunal to consider complaints against the Service. These provisions are now repealed and replaced by the Regulation of Investigatory Powers Act 2000, discussed below, pp 993–1003.

---

49 Intelligence Services Act 1994, s 3(3).
50 *Ibid*, s 5(2)(a).
51 [1979] Ch 344. See, further, Chapter 22.
52 [1990] AC 109, p 190.
53 Intelligence Services Act 1994, ss 5–7.

The Secret Intelligence Service (MI6)[54]

MI6 is the branch of the Security Services which deals with information gathering and operations outside the United Kingdom. Whereas a degree of openness has been established concerning the work of MI5, the work of MI6 remains closely guarded. It was only in 1992 that the Prime Minister acknowledged publicly for the first time that the Service existed. It is MI6 operations – together with military intelligence and the work of GCHQ – which gathers intelligence from around the world through espionage and covert action. In times of war – whether 'hot' or 'cold' – the Service is of inestimable value to the protection of the State against outside threats.[55] MI6 is under the control of the Foreign and Commonwealth Office, and requires its approval before launching operations. Any politically sensitive matters require the personal approval of the Foreign Secretary. While, in theory, MI6 is confined to operations outside the United Kingdom, and hands responsibility over to MI5 once a matter becomes 'internal', there have been doubts expressed as to whether the boundaries are, or indeed can be, so clearly drawn.

The functions of MI6

The Intelligence Services Act 1994 defines, for the first time, the statutory functions of the Service. Section 1 provides that the function of MI6 is to obtain and provide information relating to the actions or intentions of persons outside the British Islands, and to perform other tasks relating to the actions or intentions of such persons. Such actions must be related to the objectives defined in the Act, namely in the interest of national security 'with particular reference to defence and foreign policies'; the interests of the national's economic well being and assisting in the 'prevention or detection of serious crime'.[56]

Operations are authorised by the Secretary of State for Foreign and Commonwealth Affairs, and agent's activities are regulated by administrative internal rules. Where action within the British Islands is required, MI5 may apply to the Home Secretary for a warrant to carry out operations on behalf of MI6. Under the Act, the office of Commissioner and a Tribunal were established, along the same lines as the Commissioner and Tribunal established in relation to the work of MI5, as discussed above. These provisions have been repealed and replaced by the Regulation of Investigatory Powers Act 2000.

---

54 See *op cit*, West, 1981, fn 1; Bloch, J and Fitzgerald, P, *British Intelligence and Covert Action*, 1983, Dingle, Co Kerry: Brandon.

55 It was with MI6 that Paul Henderson, Managing Director of Matrix Churchill worked during the Iran-Iraq War – a matter which has led to a judicial inquiry. See, further, Chapter 11.

56 Intelligence Services Act 1994, s 2.

Authorisation and liability for actions of the Security and Intelligence Services

As seen above, Security Service personnel require warrants for the 'interference with property'.[57] Provided that a warrant has been issued, which specifies the action which may be taken in relation to specified property, no interference with that property – whether real or personal – is unlawful. The Act does not define the meaning of 'interference with property', but it clearly means more than mere trespass to property and will provide immunity from suit in relation, for example, to negligence, and/or the removal and detention of any property covered by the warrant.

Actions of the Intelligence Service require authorisation from the Secretary of State. The authorisation must relate to an operation related to the 'proper discharge of the function of the Intelligence Service', and not exceed the action necessary for that purpose. Authorisation under the hand of the Secretary of State shall cease to have effect after a six months period. The period is renewable for a further six months.[58] Where urgent authorisation is required, and the Secretary of State has authorised such action, the authorisation may be signed by a senior official of his Department. In such a case, the authorisation only has effect for two working days.[59]

Provided that actions outside the British Islands are authorised by the Secretary of State, such actions will render the authorised person immune from civil or criminal liability in the United Kingdom.[60]

Government Communications Headquarters (GCHQ)[61]

The Government's Communication Headquarters at Cheltenham[62] was established under the royal prerogative, as part of the Foreign and Commonwealth Office.[63] The principal tasks of GCHQ include the security of military and official communications and the provision of signals intelligence (SIGINT) for the government. GCHQ has an annual budget of about £500 million and a staff of some 6,000 personnel,[64] making it the largest of the three intelligence services in the United Kingdom.

---

57 Security Services Act 1989, s 3.
58 *Ibid*, s 7.
59 *Ibid*, s 6.
60 *Ibid*, s 7.
61 See *op cit*, Andrew, fn 1; West, N, *GCHQ: The Secret Wireless War 1900–86*, 1986, London: Weidenfeld & Nicolson (rep 1987, Sevenoaks: Coronet); *op cit*, Lustgarten and Leigh, fn 1.
62 GCHQ has stations abroad including Cyprus.
63 Its original title was the Government Code and Cipher School.
64 (1995) *The Times*, 31 January.

Legal authority for the interception of international communications was first provided under the Official Secrets Act 1920, section 4 of which provided for the interception of 'telegrams' under the warrant of the Home Secretary on the basis of the public interest. The Regulation of Investigatory Powers Act 2000 now provides statutory authority for external warrants issued by the Secretary of State.[65] No warrant may be issued for interference with individual communications within the United Kingdom, unless the interception is designed to uncover information relating to the prevention or detection of terrorism.[66] GCHQ co-operates in signals intelligence matters with its counterparts in Australia, Canada, New Zealand and the United States.

From 1947 until 1984, employees at GCHQ were entitled to belong to trades unions. In January 1984, the Foreign Secretary announced, without warning, that this right was to be removed. GCHQ had experienced disruption for some two years, with a loss of 10,000 working days. In 1983, a GCHQ employee, Geoffrey Prime,[67] was arrested and convicted of spying for the Soviet Union. Both factors – and the government's general desire to curb the power of trades unions – contributed to the banning of unions at GCHQ[68] The legal outcome of the exercise of the prerogative[69] in banning union membership at GCHQ led to *Council of Civil Service Unions v Minister for the Civil Service*,[70] in which the House of Lords ruled in favour of the government on the basis of national security.[71]

The Intelligence Services Act 1994 placed GCHQ on a statutory basis.[72] The statutory duty of the Secret Intelligence Service and GCHQ is to exercise its functions 'in the interests of national security, with particular reference to the defence and foreign policies of Her Majesty's government in the United Kingdom'.[73] The Director of GCHQ is responsible for the 'efficiency of the

---

65   Interception of Communications Act 1985, ss 3(2) and 10(1).

66   *Ibid*, s 3(3).

67   See *Report of the Security Commission: GA Prime*, Cmnd 8876, 1981, London: HMSO.

68   See Young, H, *One of Us*, 1989, London: Macmillan, Chapter 16.

69   Under the Civil Service Order in Council 1982, Art 4, which empowers the Minister to make regulations and issue instructions regarding the conditions of service of civil service employees. See Forsyth, C, 'Judicial review, the royal prerogative' (1985) 36 NILQ 25; cf Wade, HWR, 'Procedure and prerogative in public law' (1985) 101 LQR 180.

70   [1984] 3 All ER 935; [1985] AC 374. See, further, Chapters 6 and 22.

71   In 1995, the government amended the terms and conditions of employment of staff at GCHQ. Staff are to be restricted to membership of a body whose officers and representatives are appointed from, and answerable only to, GCHQ staff. The conditions of service continue to exclude any form of industrial action: HL Deb Vol 567 Col 147, 20 December 1995. Note that the incoming Labour government announced, in 1997, that trades union rights would be restored to employees at GCHQ.

72   The Australian and Canadian equivalents, the Defence Signals Directorate and Communication Security Executive respectively, remain regulated under the prerogative.

73   Intelligence Services Act 1994, ss 1(2)(a) and 3(2)(a).

agency'[74] and has a right of access to the Prime Minister and Secretary of State for Foreign and Commonwealth Affairs. The Director is under a duty to report annually to the Prime Minister.

The monitoring of communications is regulated by the Regulation of Investigatory Powers Act 2000, on which, see below.

As with the Interception of Communications Act 1985 and the Security Services Act 1989, a Commissioner[75] and Tribunal[76] were established to deal with complaints arising from GCHQ operations. See, now, the Regulation of Investigatory Powers Act 2000, discussed below.

Special Branch[77]

Established in 1883 to deal with problems of security in relation to Ireland, Special Branch rapidly expanded to deal with many security matters. Originally, Special Branch was confined to the Metropolitan Police Force; from 1945, other police forces established Special Branches. Nowadays, each provincial force has its own Special Branch. Special Branch is staffed by ordinary police officers under the direction of the Chief Constable. Much of their work is related to Security Service matters. Other functions include jury vetting in cases involving national security or terrorism, providing personal protection and assisting with immigration matters, including keeping watch at airports and seaports.

MILITARY INTELLIGENCE AND THE ARMED FORCES

In 1940, the Special Operations Executive (SOE) was formed to supplement the work of MI5 and MI6, which were geared principally to work in peace time. Subsequently, the need for special units to operate under military command, and under cover, became perceived as imperative. Originally known as L Detachment, Special Air Service Brigade and, later, simply the SAS, the service was introduced on the initiative of David Stirling of the Scots Guards, and approved by the Commander-in-Chief. Members of the SAS were recruited primarily from commandos. A parallel organisation, the Special Boat Service (SBS), was also established to complement the work of the SAS.

---

74 Intelligence Services Act 1994, s 4.
75 *Ibid*, s 5(3).
76 *Ibid*, s 9 and Scheds 1 and 2.
77 See Bunyan, T, *The History and Practice of the Political Police in Britain*, 1977, London: Quartet; Allason, R, *The Branch: A History of the Metropolitan Police Special Branch 1883–1983*, 1983, London: Secker & Warburg.

The SAS has been involved in many operations overseas, in Northern Ireland and on the mainland, principally working against terrorism. It was, for example, in 1980, the SAS which stormed the Iranian Embassy in London to free hostages from terrorists who had occupied the Embassy and, as discussed below, it was the SAS which was dispatched to Gibraltar to arrest suspected IRA terrorists.

The SAS is controlled at a political level and a practical, operational level. In relation to terrorism, a special committee, known as COBRA and chaired by the Home Secretary, meets with representatives from the Ministry of Defence, the Security Service (MI5), the Foreign and Commonwealth Office and the SAS to decide the appropriate political and military response. In relation to operational matters, a special unit within the Ministry of Defence, the Joint Operations Centre (JOC), comprising the Foreign Office, Home Office, intelligence services and the SAS, activates the SAS at home or overseas. Exceptionally, the Prime Minister may personally activate the SAS, as in the Iranian Embassy siege. When the SAS is operational, it exercises the powers of the police, although formal authority remains with the police, and the police resume their normal functions once the operation is complete.

THE INTERCEPTION OF COMMUNICATIONS[78]

In *Malone v Metropolitan Police Commissioner*,[79] the defendant in a criminal prosecution discovered that evidence had been acquired by the police, under a warrant issued by the Home Secretary, through the Post Office by means of a telephone intercept. Malone challenged the legality of the intercept on the basis that it amounted to a breach of his right to privacy and confidentiality and that the warrant was unlawful. The judge, however, felt powerless to find any breach of law. The Post Office Act 1969 gave statutory recognition to such warrants, and Malone had no right to privacy which could be protected by the courts. Malone made an application under Article 8 of the European Convention on Human Rights, which provides for the right to privacy. The European Court of Human Rights held that the United Kingdom practices were unlawful, because the powers used had no foundation which indicated with reasonable clarity the scope and manner of the exercise of discretion, and that 'the degree of legal protection to which citizens are entitled under the rule

---

78 See *Report of the Committee on the Interception of Communications* (the 'Birkett Report'), Cmnd 283, 1957, London: HMSO; *The Interception of Communications in Great Britain*, Cmnd 7873, 1980, London: HMSO; *The Interception of Communications in Great Britain* (the 'Diplock Report'), Cmnd 8191, 1981, London: HMSO; Williams, DGT, 'Telephone tapping' [1979] CLJ 225; Lambert, J, 'Executive authority to tap telephones' (1980) 43 MLR 59; *The Interception of Communications in the United Kingdom*, Cmnd 9438, 1985, London: HMSO; Leigh, I, 'A tapper's charter?' [1986] PL 8.

79 [1979] 2 All ER 620. See, also, Chapter 22.

of law in a democratic society is lacking'.[80] The Regulation of Investigatory Powers Bill 2000 when enacted repeals the 1985 Act.

The government's response to the outcome of *Malone v United Kingdom* was to pass the Interception of Communications Act 1985. The Act makes it a criminal offence to 'intentionally intercept a communication'.[81] Section 2 provides power for the Secretary of State to issue warrants. Section 2 provides that no warrant shall be issued by the Secretary of State unless 'he is satisfied that the warrant is necessary in the interests of national security, or for the purpose of preventing or detecting serious crime or for the purpose of safeguarding the economic well being of the United Kingdom'.[82] Before granting a warrant, the Secretary of State must consider whether the information could be obtained by other means.[83] In 1989, 522 warrants were issued.[84] By 1993, however, the number had increased to 1,005 telephone interceptions and 115 mail interceptions,[85] while in 1995, 1,135 warrants were issued.[86]

The absence of any judicial scrutiny of warrants has been a consistent feature of legislation relating to national security.[87] It is doubtful whether this arrangement is consistent with the European Convention on Human Rights, Article 8, which protects privacy and family life and 'home and correspondence' and prohibits interference with the exercise of the right 'except such as in accordance with the law and is necessary in a democratic society'. However, it can be argued that Article 8(2), by providing for interference 'in the interests of national security, public safety or the economic well being of the country, for the prevention of disorder or crime ...' is sufficiently broad to provide justification. In *Malone*, the objection expressed in the Court of Human Rights related to the absence of any clear and specific criteria in law for the issue of warrants.[88]

While it is clear that the Act legitimised communication intercepts, it did not appear to cover the use of electronic surveillance equipment.[89] The Intelligence

---

80 *Malone v United Kingdom* (1984) 7 EHRR 14.

81 Interception of Communications Act 1985, s 1.

82 *Ibid*, s 2(2)(a), (b), (c).

83 *Ibid*, s 2(3).

84 *Report of the Commissioner for 1989*, Cm 1063, 1989, London: HMSO, p 2.

85 *Report of the Commissioner for 1993*, Cm 2522, 1993, London: HMSO.

86 *Report of the Commissioner for 1996*, Cm 3254, 1996, London: HMSO.

87 See Duffy, PJ and Mulchlinski, P, 'The interception of communications in Great Britain' (1980) 130 NLJ 999; Bailey, SH, Harris, DJ and Jones, BL, *Civil Liberties – Cases and Materials*, 4th edn, 1995, London: Butterworths.

88 *Ibid*, Bailey, Harris and Jones record that 60 per cent of warrants requested by the police relate to the importation or distribution of drugs and that arrests have been effected in relation to 'just under 50 per cent of warrants issued'.

89 Eg, infra red cameras or long range microphones.

Services Act 1994 provided authority for the Security Services to apply for warrants to intercept by electronic and other means (see above). The relationship between the Interception of Communications Act 1985 and the Intelligence Services Act 1994 was uneasy and far from clear. Furthermore, from the point of view of a person aggrieved by the Security Services, the establishment of differing Tribunals to investigate complaints under the Interception of Communication Act 1985 and the Intelligence Services Act 1994 (and before that, the Security Services Act 1989) caused jurisdictional difficulties. There was no mechanism by which a complaint wrongly made to one Tribunal may be transferred automatically to the other Tribunal. Accordingly, an individual who wished to complain about an interference with his or her property or interceptions of communications needed to be clear as to which Tribunal to complain. Given the covert nature of such operations, it was unlikely that an individual would have any idea which personnel have been interfering with property through surveillance techniques. The problems have been removed by the Regulation of Investigatory Powers Act 2000 which rationalises the law relating to intercepts and the jurisdiction to hear complaints. See further, below.

Section 9 of the Interception of Communications Act proscribed the admission of evidence acquired through intercepts under warrant into court. The purpose of this prohibition was to prevent disclosure as to either the existence of a warrant or that a warrant had been applied for.[90] However, it has been held that evidence acquired through an interception which has been placed on a telephone line with the consent of a customer, did not preclude the admission of that evidence into court.[91] Moreover, the prohibition on the admissibility of evidence at trial was not to be extended to apply in the case of foreign telephone intercepts, notwithstanding the provisions of the Human Rights Act 1998 and the European Convention on Human Rights relating to privacy. The Court of Appeal, Criminal Division, so held in *R v X, Y and Z*.[92] Any alleged violation of Article 8 was not such that Article 6, the right to fair trial, was also violated.

Section 9 of the Interception of Communications Act 1985 was considered by the Court of Appeal in *R v Owen* and *R v Stephen*.[93] At issue was whether the prohibition in section 9 precluded any investigation into whether an intercept was consensual under section 1(2), which provides that a person shall not be guilty of an offence under section 1 if that person has reasonable grounds to believe that the person to whom, or the person by whom, the communication is sent had consented to the interception. That prohibition applied, even though the particular circumstances of the case did not fall

---

90 See *R v Preston* [1994] 2 AC 130.
91 *R v Choudhary* (1997) *The Times*, 17 February. See, also, *R v Effick* [1994] 3 WLR 583; (1994) 99 Cr App R 312; (1992) 95 Cr App R 427.
92 (2000) *The Times*, 23 May.
93 (1998) *The Times*, 11 November.

within the objective of the 1985 Act, namely, to avoid the embarrassment in terms of confidentiality if the authorities were challenged as to the lawfulness of their actions.

Prior to the Police Act 1997, the power of the police to effect surveillance remained obscure. In *R v Khan (Sultan)*,[94] the question of the admissibility of evidence acquired as a result of bugging devices was considered by the House of Lords. The defendant was suspected of being involved in the importation of drugs. The police installed a listening device in a house which Khan was visiting. The defence argued that the recording was inadmissible, there being no statutory authority for such an installation, which accordingly amounted to a trespass to property and a violation of Article 8 of the European Convention on Human Rights. The House of Lords rejected the defence arguments. While accepting that there had been a trespass, and an invasion of privacy, these factors were outweighed by the fact that the police had largely complied with the Home Secretary's Guidelines. Moreover, Convention rights, not at that time being incorporated into English law, could not found the basis for a defence. Accordingly, even if the evidence had been obtained improperly, on the authority of *R v Sang*,[95] the evidence was admissible. In *Khan v United Kingdom*,[96] on an application under the European Convention of Human Rights alleging violations of Articles 6, 8 and 13, the Court of Human Rights ruled that Articles 8 and 13, but not Article 6, had been breached.

Whereas the authority for police surveillance devices was formerly uncertain, the Police Act 1997 extends the scope of surveillance. Part I of the Police Act 1997 established a National Criminal Intelligence Service Authority to provide criminal intelligence to other police and law enforcement agencies, and placed surveillance techniques under statutory authority.[97] The Act is modelled on the Interception of Communications Act 1985, and places the Home Secretary's Guidelines on a statutory basis. Authorisation may be given, under section 93(2), for the use of surveillance devices if surveillance will be of substantial value in the prevention and detection of serious crime, and the objective cannot reasonably be achieved by other means. Serious crime is defined as including crimes of violence, crimes involving financial gain and crimes involving large numbers of persons, or crimes for which a person with no previous conviction could expect to receive a prison sentence of three or more years. Authorisation is given by a Chief Officer of Police, or an officer of rank of Assistant Chief Constable.[98] Prior authorisation by a

---

94 [1995] QB 27; [1996] 3 All ER 289.

95 [1980] AC 402; [1979] 2 All ER 1222, on which, see, further, Chapter 4.

96 (2000) *The Times*, 23 May. See, further, Chapter 22.

97 The Act also establishes a National Crime Squad, a Police Information Technology Organisation. The Act also makes provision for access to criminal records for employment and licensing purposes.

98 Police Act 1997, ss 93(5) and 94. Minor amendments to the Act are introduced under the Regulation of Investigatory Powers Act 2000.

commissioner, appointed under section 91 of the Act, must be obtained if the property involved is a private dwelling, a hotel bedroom or office premises, and also where the surveillance may result in the acquisition of confidential knowledge, or journalistic or other matters subject to legal privilege.

One unsuccessful attempt to challenge the legality of telephone interceptions was made in *R v Secretary of State for the Home Department ex parte Ruddock*.[99] On an application for judicial review, a member of the Campaign for Nuclear Disarmament sought a declaration to the effect that the Secretary of State had no power or authority to authorise the interception and monitoring of telephone communications. The warrant was issued on the ground that the applicant, Mr Cox, was a member of the Communist Party and a leading member of the CND, and that it was desirable to establish whether the Communist Party was secretly manipulating CND. There was affidavit evidence from a former MI5 officer[100] that a warrant had been applied for, and signed by the Home Secretary in 1983. The Home Secretary claimed that the court ought not to entertain the application for review 'because to do so would be detrimental to national security', and relied, according to Taylor J, 'on the long established policy that a Secretary of State does not disclose or discuss the existence of a warrant'.[101] Taylor J distinguished the situation where national security is used as a justification for action, from the instant case where national security was being employed to preclude the court from considering an action at all. The Home Secretary did not deny that the court had jurisdiction, but rather argued that the court had a discretion to decline to review, and that in such a matter it should exercise this discretion in the Minister's favour. This the judge would not accept either 'as a general proposition or in this particular case'. Taylor J went on to state that 'totally to oust the court's supervisory jurisdiction in a field where *ex hypothesi* the citizen can have no right to be consulted is a draconian and dangerous step indeed'.[102]

It was claimed by the applicants that they had a legitimate expectation that no warrant would be issued contrary to the published criteria for the issue of warrants. On this point, however, the application failed. The court held that the warrant had been issued within the criteria and that there was no evidence that the Home Secretary had flouted the guidelines for an improper purpose – namely for party-political purposes. Furthermore, it could not be said that the issue of the warrant was 'outrageous in its defiance of logic' within the *Wednesbury* principle.[103]

---

99 [1987] 2 All ER 518: the decision was reached prior to the Interception of Communications Act 1985.

100 Ms Cathy Massiter.

101 *R v Secretary of State for the Home Department ex parte Ruddock* [1987] 2 All ER 518, pp 524–25.

102 [1987] 2 All ER 518, p 527.

103 On which, see Chapter 25.

In *Halford v United Kingdom*,[104] however, in an application under the European Convention on Human Rights alleging a violation of Article 8 (the right to privacy), it was held that English law, under the Interception of Communications Act, violated the applicant's rights. The applicant was an Assistant Chief Constable of Police. She had applied for promotion on several occasions and had been refused. She alleged that she had been the victim of sexual discrimination. The proceedings on sexual discrimination were settled in 1992. The applicant had suspected that the police had been intercepting her telephone calls and complained. Her complaint was determined by the Interception of Communications Tribunal, which informed her that there had been no violation of the 1985 Act. The applicant was not informed, however, whether this was because there had been no interception, or because the interception was pursuant to an authorising warrant being issued. The applicant was also informed by the Home Office that, in any event, tapping the police's own telephone system fell outside the Act and did not require a warrant. In hearings before the European Court of Human Rights, the government conceded that there was a 'reasonable likelihood' that her telephone had been tapped. The Court ruled, first, that interference with telephone calls at work was capable of violating Article 8 and, secondly, that to intercept the applicant's calls in order to gather evidence in relation to the sex discrimination complaint violated the Convention and that, since English law provided the applicant with no remedy, there had also been a violation of Article 13 of the Convention.[105]

The Security Commission[106]

In 1964, following the *Profumo* affair, the Prime Minister, Sir Alec Douglas-Home announced the creation of a Security Commission. The Commission investigates and reports upon the circumstances in which a breach of security is known to have occurred in the public service, and upon any related failure of departmental security arrangements or neglect of duty; and, in the light of any such investigation, advises whether any change in security arrangements is desirable.[107]

The Commission meets at the request of the Prime Minister, who consults the Leader of the Opposition and the Chairman of the Commission before making a reference to the Commission. The Commission has no power of initiative in relation to the matters it investigates. The Chairman of the Commission is a senior judge, and the Commission has seven members. The

---

104 Case 73/1996/692/884: (1997) *The Times*, 3 July.
105 See, also, *Khan v United Kingdom*, discussed above and in Chapter 22.
106 On the role and work of the Commission, see *op cit*, Leigh and Lustgarten, fn 13.
107 See HC Deb Cols 1271–75, 23 January 1964,

Commission has undertaken inquiries, *inter alia*, into the conduct of former Ministers,[108] into allegations about the Head of MI5, Roger Hollis (on whom, see above, pp 944–45),[109] into investigations of security matters in Signals and Communication Units[110] and into the circumstances surrounding the conviction of Geoffrey Prime for espionage.[111] The Commission has power to call whomsoever it wishes as witnesses, and to summon documents. Prior to its hearings, the Commission will frequently have availed itself of the security services to investigate allegations. No legal representation is allowed for witnesses before the Commission. The Commission reports, with recommendations, to the Prime Minister.

Lustgarten and Leigh evaluate the Commission's success and future development. The Commission, in their view, is useful 'in its narrow and specific sphere of operation'.[112] The authors call for the Commission to be placed on a statutory basis, with independent powers of investigation, for the Commission's powers to be explicitly stated and for greater protection to be built in for individuals who come before the Commission.

PARLIAMENTARY SCRUTINY OF THE SECURITY SERVICES

Matters of national security and the work of the Security Services have traditionally been ones on which governments have declined to provide information to Parliament. Parliamentary Committees repeatedly have been denied the right to investigate the Security Service[113] although, since 1979, the Defence Committee has considered aspects of security. In 1989, the government again rejected proposals that a select committee be established to inquire into the Service.[114] In 1994, however, the Intelligence and Security Committee was established with limited powers to investigate security matters. The Committee, which has a membership of nine, is established to 'examine the expenditure, administration and policy of the Security Service, the Intelligence Service and GCHQ'.[115] Membership is confined to non-ministerial Members of the House of Lords and House of Commons. Members are appointed by the Prime Minister, after consultation with the Leader of the Opposition.[116] The establishment of the Committee, which is

---

108 *Earl Jellicoe and Lord Lambton,* Cmnd 5367, 1973, London: HMSO.
109 The report remained unpublished.
110 Cmnd 9923, 1986, London: HMSO.
111 Cmnd 8876, 1985, London: HMSO.
112 *Op cit*, Lustgarten and Leigh, fn 1, p 486.
113 See HC 773 (1979–80); HC 242 (1982–83); HC Deb Col 444, 12 May 1983.
114 See HC Deb Col 36, 16 January 1989.
115 Intelligence Services Act 1994, s 10.
116 *Ibid*, s 10(3).

based in Whitehall, rather than Parliament, brings both MI6 and GCHQ under a weak form of quasi-parliamentary scrutiny although, operating *ex post facto*, and lacking the openness of, for example, a select committee, its constitutional effectiveness must be questionable. The Committee must make an annual report to the Prime Minister, which must be laid before Parliament. However, should the Prime Minister feel that publication of any matter would be 'prejudicial to the continued discharge of the functions of the Services, or GCHQ', the Prime Minister may exclude such matters from the report.[117]

The Committee determines its own procedure.[118] Where the Committee requests information from the Director General of the Security Service, the Chief of the Intelligence Service or the Director of GCHQ, that information must be supplied unless the relevant person informs the Committee that it cannot be disclosed on the basis of sensitivity, or where the Secretary of State has determined that it should not be disclosed. The Secretary of State shall not refuse to disclose information to the Committee on the basis of national security alone: the criterion for non-disclosure is whether the Secretary of State would think it proper not to disclose the information if requested to do so by a departmental select committee of the House of Commons.[119] Schedule 3 defines sensitive information – for the purposes of paragraph 3 – as being:

(a) information which might lead to the identification of, or provide details of, sources of information, other assistance or operational methods available to the Security Service, the Intelligence Service or GCHQ;

(b) information about particular operations which have been, are being or are proposed to be undertaken in pursuance of any of the functions of those bodies; and

(c) information provided by, or by an agency of, the government of a territory outside the United Kingdom where that government does not consent to the disclosure of the information.

OFFICIAL SECRECY[120]

The Official Secrets Acts 1911–89

The 1911 Act

The first Official Secrets Act arrived on the statute book in 1889. The latest Act is that of 1989. The 1911 Act – which survived virtually untouched until 1989 –

---

117 Intelligence Services Act 1994, s 10(5), (6), (7).

118 *Ibid*, Sched 3, para 2.

119 *Ibid*, para 3(1), (4).

120 See Robertson, G, *Freedom, the Individual and the Law*, 7th edn, 1993, London: Penguin; Hooper, D, *Official Secrets: The Use and Abuse of the Act*, 1988, Sevenoaks: Coronet; Ewing, KD and Gearty, CA, *Freedom Under Thatcher*, 1990, Oxford: Clarendon.

was passed through Parliament with one hour's debate and within 24 hours. Motivation for the 1911 Act lay in alleged enemy agent activity in the country.[121] The motives behind the 1989 Act were formed largely from the failure of the earlier Act. As will be seen, section 2 of the Act provided for numerous offences based on vague criteria of disclosure of information and juries have on occasion refused to convict, even where it was clear from the facts and the law that a guilty verdict should have been returned.[122] Official inquiries into the working of the Act revealed deficiencies.[123]

The *Spycatcher* case also provided motivation for the government to reform the law. In the government's view, members and ex-members of the Security Services should be under a life long duty of confidentiality in respect of their work. One defect in the 1911 Act lay in the duty of – and hence liability for – non-disclosure enduring only for the duration of their employment.

Section 1 of the 1911 Act provides penalties for spying. It is an offence to enter into top-secret establishments or to collect, publish or communicate any official document (which includes official code words, passwords, sketches, plans, models, articles or notes) or information which might be useful to a potential enemy, if the actions are carried out 'for any purpose prejudicial to the safety or interest of the State'. The accused has no 'right to silence' and a trial may be held in secret, or partly in secret. Section 2 of the Act reverses the normal burden of proof from the prosecution to the defence. It is not necessary for the prosecution to prove that the accused is guilty of any particular act 'tending to show a purpose prejudicial to the safety or interest of the State'. Guilt may be established if 'from the circumstances of the case, or his conduct, or his known character as proved, it appears that his purpose was a purpose prejudicial to the safety or interest of the State'. Moreover, any information or document handed over to another person, without lawful authority, shall 'be deemed to have been made, obtained, collected, recorded or communicated for a purpose prejudicial to the safety or interests of the State unless the contrary is proved'. Penalties for espionage are swingeing. George Blake, a former MI6 officer convicted of espionage, was sentenced to 42 years' imprisonment.[124] In 1985, Michael Bettany, a former MI5 officer, was convicted of attempting to pass official information to the Russians and sentenced to 23 years' imprisonment. Geoffrey Prime was sentenced to 35 years for disclosing material whilst employed at GCHQ.[125] Not all offences

---

121 See *op cit*, Andrew, fn 1; French, D, 'Spy fever in Britain 1900–15' (1978) 21 Historical Journal 355; Le Queux, W, *German Spies in England*, 1915, London: S Paul.

122 See *R v Ponting* [1985] Crim LR 318, discussed below.

123 See *Departmental Committee on Section 2 of the Official Secrets Act 1911*, Cmnd 5104, 1972, London: HMSO; White Paper, *Reform of Section 2 of the Official Secrets Act 1911*, Cmnd 7285, 1978, London: HMSO.

124 Blake subsequently escaped from prison after 25 years with the help of friends.

125 *R v Prime* (1983) 5 Cr App Rep 127.

will lead to a prosecution. Neither Kim Philby nor Anthony Blunt were prosecuted. Instead, each was offered immunity from prosecution in return for a confession, an offer declined by Kim Philby, who fled to Moscow.

Section 2 of the 1911 Act (now reformed under the Official Secrets Act 1989) prohibited the disclosure of any official information without authorisation to anyone not authorised to receive it, and covered some one million public servants and a further one million government contractors. It also covered the retention of any document by a person not entitled to retain the same, failure to take reasonable care of a document, and receiving any document without authority. Section 2 was capable of generating over 2,000 different criminal offences, including the disclosure of the number of cups of tea consumed in the MI5 canteen.[126] Five cases illustrate well the working of the 1911 Act: *Chandler v Director of Public Prosecutions*,[127] *R v Aitken*,[128] *R v Ponting*,[129] *R v Tisdall*[130] and the Zircon affair.

Chandler v Director of Public Prosecutions

In *Chandler v Director of Public Prosecutions,* the Committee of 100 of the Campaign for Nuclear Disarmament organised a demonstration on an operational airfield at Wethersfield. The defendants were charged under section 1 of the Official Secrets Act 1911 with the offence of approaching, entering or inspecting a prohibited place. Evidence was given as to the importance of the base for national security. In defence, it was put to the court that the defendants were trying to bring about an end to nuclear armaments, which would be in the interests of the State. It was held that their claim to be acting in the interests of the State was irrelevant. Intentionally to engage in prohibited conduct contrary to the Official Secrets Acts could not be condoned on the basis of an individual's belief in the interests of the State. Moreover, the policy, disposition and use of the armed forces was within the scope of the royal prerogative and not subject to judicial scrutiny.

R v Aitken[131]

In 1971, Jonathan Aitken, then a journalist, acquired Army documents which suggested that the government's version of events concerning the Biafran War

---

126 *Departmental Committee on Section 2 of the Official Secrets Act 1911*, Cmnd 5104, 1972, London: HMSO, para 16, and see *op cit*, Robertson, fn 120, p 132.

127 [1964] AC 763.

128 1971, unreported. For an account, see Aitken, J, *Officially Secret*, 1971, London: Weidenfeld & Nicolson.

129 [1985] Crim LR 318.

130 Unreported.

131 Unreported, but see *ibid*, Aitken.

were inaccurate. Aitkin, the colonel who had disclosed the information and the editor of *The Daily Telegraph* were prosecuted under section 2 of the Act. The defence argued that the prosecution was politically motivated and that they had a moral duty to reveal the truth. The defendants were acquitted, the trial judge having stated that it was time section 2 was 'pensioned off'. The acquittal of Aitken and others led directly to the establishment of a committee to examine section 2 (see further below).

R v Tisdall *and* R v Ponting[132]

In *R v Tisdall*,[133] the defendant had leaked documents relating to the arrival of Cruise missiles at Greenham Common Airbase to *The Guardian* newspaper, in breach of section 2. She was convicted and sentenced to six months' imprisonment, a sentence which was greeted with public disquiet at its severity. While Sarah Tisdall was imprisoned, Clive Ponting OBE was leaking secrets.[134] The background to this case, which, more than any other, discredited section 2 of the Official Secrets Act 1911, lay in the Falklands War. In May 1982, the Argentinian cruiser, the *General Belgrano*, was torpedoed – without prior warning – by the British submarine, *Conqueror*, with a loss of 368 lives.[135] The *Belgrano* was, at the time, outside the 200 mile exclusion zone set by the British and had been steaming away from the Falklands for some 11 hours. The government was evasive on the matter and the public was uneasy about the sinking without warning. Tam Dalyell[136] raised questions for written answer by the Secretary of State for Defence.

At the time, Ponting was head of a Ministry of Defence secretariat, and an adviser on naval operations. He investigated the sequence of events for the then Secretary of State, Michael Heseltine, in a high security classified document. Dalyell's quest for answers was unsuccessful. Ponting sent an unsigned note encouraging Dalyell to persevere, and indicating that he was 'on the right track'. Meanwhile, the House of Commons Foreign Affairs Committee was considering the conduct of the Falklands campaign. In response to questions, the Ministry of Defence advised the Committee that the rules of engagement frequently changed during the campaign. Ponting considered that this Memorandum was misleading and designed to block any

---

132 See Ponting, C, *The Right to Know*, 1985, London: Sphere Books and *R v Ponting* (1987) 14 JLS 366; Drewry, G, 'The *Ponting* case – leaking in the public interest' [1985] PL 203; Norton-Taylor, R, *The Ponting Affair*, 1985, London: Woolf.

133 (1984) *The Times*, 26 March.

134 See, *inter alia, op cit*, Robertson, fn 120, Chapter 4; *op cit*, Ewing and Gearty, fn 120.

135 See Foreign Affairs Committee: HC 3rd Report, *Events Surrounding the Weekend of 1–2 May 1982*, 1985, London: HMSO; Franks Committee, Falkland Islands Review, *Report of the Committee of Privy Councillors*, Cmnd 8787, 1983, London: HMSO; White Paper, *The Falklands Campaign: The Lessons*, 1982, London: HMSO; Rice, D and Gavshon, A, *The Sinking of the 'Belgrano'*, 1984, London: Secker & Warburg.

136 Labour MP for Linlithgow.

real inquiry. As a result, he sent a copy of a confidential Memorandum and his draft answers to Dalyell's questions to Dalyell who passed them to the Chairman of the Foreign Affairs Committee. Ponting was charged under section 2, as having communicated information to someone other than an authorised person, or someone to whom it would not be in the interest of the State to disclose the information.

In his defence, Ponting pleaded the 'public interest' in the disclosure of information to Parliament. Witnesses for the defence included Merlyn Rees, a former Home Secretary, and Professor HWR Wade.[137] Merlyn Rees argued that a civil servant's highest duty was to Parliament; Professor Wade asserted that if a civil servant was convinced that the truth was not being told to Parliament, it 'might be in the public interest for him to give the information direct to Parliament'.[138] The judge disagreed. A civil servant's duty was his official duty. In relation to the interests of the State, McCowan J stated that the interests of the State 'mean the policies of the State as they were in July 1984 ... and not the interests of the State as Mr Ponting, Mr Dalyell, you or I might think they ought to have been'. Despite the judge's clear indication to the jury that Ponting had breached the Act, the jury acquitted, thus fatally undermining the authority of the Act.

The Zircon affair

The Zircon affair further illustrates vividly a government's preoccupation with secrecy.[139] Allegations concerning the Security Service made by an MI5 officer, Cathy Massiter, were included in a Channel 4 television programme scheduled for transmission. The programme was withdrawn when it was believed that it would attract a prosecution under section 2 of the Official Secrets Act. The journalist who made the programme arranged for it to be shown to Members of Parliament within the precincts of the House of Commons in January 1987. The Attorney General sought an injunction restraining its screening which was refused on the basis that activities within the House of Commons were within the House's jurisdiction and not that of the courts. Following discussions between the Attorney General and the Speaker of the House, the Speaker ordered the film not to be shown. The Rt Hon Tony Benn MP – a senior Labour Party member – put forward an amendment to the motion for debate in Parliament calling for the matter to be referred to the Committee of Privileges,[140] which, after considering the matter, upheld the Speaker's right to restrict the film.

---

137 Professor HWR Wade QC, Fellow of the British Academy; former Professor of Law in the University of Oxford and Cambridge and Master of Gonville and Caius College, Cambridge.

138 Cited in *op cit*, Ewing and Gearty, fn 120, p 146.

139 See Bradley, AW, 'Parliamentary privilege and the *Zircon* affair' [1987] PL 1.

140 See Benn, T, *The End of an Era, Diaries 1980–90*, 1994, London: Arrow, p 491.

Warrants were issued under section 9 of the Official Secrets Act 1911 to search for documents, films and videos relating to the programme. The home of Duncan Campbell, a journalist, had been raided and documents removed. Two of the three warrants were subsequently held to be unlawful, and the third, lawful but questionable. The end result of the affair is described by KD Ewing and CA Gearty:

> In the end, however, the matter fizzled out, the Official Secrets Act having served its purpose of intimidation. The injunctions against Campbell were discharged, the Speaker lifted his ban on showing the film in Parliament and it was eventually transmitted by the BBC some two years later. Significantly, no charges were brought in connection with the incident, though the Special Branch did advise that Campbell be prosecuted under the Official Secrets Act.[141]

Reform of the Official Secrets Act 1911[142]

The pressure for reform had mounted after the *Aitken* affair in 1971. The government announced that a committee was to be set up to examine the workings of section 2 of the Act. The Committee of Inquiry, headed by Lord Franks, was highly critical of section 2 and recommended that it be reformed.[143] It was not, however, until 1989 that reform took place.[144]

The major provisions of the Official Secrets Act 1989

Section 2 of the Official Secrets Act 1911 is repealed and replaced by the 1989 Act. Rather than the catch-all section 2 of the 1911 Act, the 1989 Act creates offences directed to specific groups of people and information. In relation to most areas, the prosecution must prove both that the information has been unlawfully transmitted and that the disclosure of the information is 'damaging'. The concept of 'damaging disclosure' has, however, not been incorporated into section 1 which relates to security and intelligence matters. With this exception, there is a presumption of harm built into the Act. A further exception relates to those who are not Crown servants or government

---

141 *Op cit*, Ewing and Gearty, fn 120, pp 151–52.

142 See, *inter alia, op cit*, Hooper, fn 120; White Paper, *Reform of Section 2 of the Official Secrets Act 1911*, Cm 408, 1988, London: HMSO. See, also, White Paper, *Open Government*, Cm 2290, 1993, London: HMSO, discussed in Chapter 11.

143 *Departmental Committee on Section 2 of the Official Secrets Act 1911*, Cmnd 5104, 1972, London: HMSO.

144 See White Paper, *Reform of Section 2 of the Official Secrets Act 1911*, Cmnd 7285, 1978, London: HMSO; Green Paper, *Freedom of Information*, Cmnd 7520, 1979, London: HMSO; White Paper, *Reform of Section 2 of the Official Secrets Act 1911*, Cm 408, 1988, London: HMSO.

contractors in relation to whom the prosecution will have to prove – in addition to the harm test – that the defendant knew or had good reason to know that the specific harm was likely to have been caused. In relation to such information, the disclosure in itself is an offence. There is no longer a defence of 'public good' which applied under section 2 of the 1911 Act.

Security and intelligence

Under section 1, any person who is, or has been, a member of the Security and Intelligence Services, and any other person who is informed that the provision of the Act applies to him, is guilty of an offence if 'without lawful authority' he discloses 'any information, document or other article related to security or intelligence'. A person who is, or has been, a Crown servant or government contractor will be guilty of an offence if he makes a 'damaging disclosure of any information, document or other article relating to security or intelligence'.[145] Security and intelligence are defined as being the work of, or work in support of, the Security and Intelligence Services.[146] A disclosure is defined as damaging if 'it causes damage to the work of, or of any part of, the Security or Intelligence Services' or if unauthorised disclosure would be likely to cause such damage.[147] A charge may be defended if the person in question can prove that, at the time of the alleged offence, 'he did not know, and had no reasonable cause to believe' that the unauthorised disclosure related to security or intelligence or, in the case of an offence under sub-section (3), he did not know, or had no reasonable cause to believe, that the disclosure would be damaging.[148]

Defence

Any unauthorised damaging disclosure of information, documents or other articles relating to defence is an offence.[149] A disclosure is damaging if 'it damages the capability of any part of the armed forces, or leads to loss of life or injury to the forces, or endangers the interests of the United Kingdom abroad, or obstructs the promotion or protection of those interests, or is likely to have any of these effects'.[150] It is a defence to prove that the person did not know, and had no reasonable cause to believe, that such disclosure would be damaging.[151]

145 Official Secrets Act 1989, s 1(3).
146 *Ibid*, s 1(9).
147 *Ibid*, s 1(4)(a), (b).
148 *Ibid*, s 1(5).
149 *Ibid*, s 2(1).
150 *Ibid*, s 2(2).
151 *Ibid*, s 2(3).

Defence is defined as including the 'size, shape, organisation, logistics, order of battle, deployment, operations, state of readiness and training of the armed forces of the Crown; weapons, stores or other equipment of those forces; defence policy and strategy, and military planning and intelligence; and plans and measures for the maintenance of essential supplies and services that are, or would be, needed in time of war.[152]

International relations

An unauthorised damaging disclosure, by a person who is or has been a Crown servant or government contractor, of any information, document or other article relating to international relations, or confidential information obtained from another State or international organisation is an offence.[153] A disclosure is damaging if it 'endangers the interests of the United Kingdom abroad, or seriously obstructs the promotion or protection of those interests or endangers the safety of British citizens abroad', or 'is likely to have any of those effects'.[154] It is a defence to prove that the accused did not know, and had no reasonable cause to believe, that the information fell within sub-section (1), or that its disclosure would be damaging.[155]

Crime and special investigation powers

Section 4 of the Act makes it an offence to disclose, without lawful authority, information, documents or other articles which result in the commission of an offence, or facilitates an escape from legal custody or impedes the prevention or detection of offences or the apprehension or prosecution of suspected offenders, or disclosures which are likely to have those effects.[156] It is a defence to a charge to prove that the person did not know, and had no reasonable cause to believe, that the disclosure related to prohibited materials or that disclosure would have any of the damaging effects mentioned.[157]

Authorised disclosures under the Act

A disclosure by a Crown servant (or other notified person) is authorised, if it is made with lawful authority and if (and only if) the disclosure is made in accordance with a person's official duty.[158] In relation to government

---

152 Official Secrets Act 1989, s 4.
153 *Ibid*, s 3.
154 *Ibid*, s 3(2).
155 *Ibid*, s 3(4).
156 *Ibid*, s 4(2).
157 *Ibid*, s 4(4) and (5).
158 *Ibid*, s 7(1).

contractors, a disclosure is lawful only if it is made with official authorisation or for the purposes of his functions relating to the contract and without contravening an official restriction.[159] In relation to any other person, a disclosure is lawful only if it is made to a Crown servant for the purposes of his functions as such, or in accordance with official authorisation.[160] It is a defence to a charge to prove that, at the time of disclosure, he believed that he had lawful authority to make the disclosure in question.[161]

The duty to safeguard information

Crown servants and government contractors are under a duty to protect any information, document or other article, which it would be an offence to disclose under the Act.[162] It is an offence for a Crown servant to retain an article contrary to his or her official duty, and for a government contractor to fail to comply with a request for the return or disposal of the information or document, or to fail to take such care of the information or document as 'a person in his position may be reasonably expected to take'.[163] It is a defence for a Crown servant to prove that he believed he was acting in accordance with his official duty and 'had no reasonable cause to believe otherwise'.[164]

Prosecutions

No prosecution may be instituted other than with the consent of the Attorney General.[165]

Penalties

A person convicted of an offence under the Act, other than under section 8(1), (4) or (5), shall, on indictment, be liable to imprisonment for a two year term, or a fine, or both. On summary conviction, a person is liable to up to a six month's term of imprisonment, or a fine, or both. A person convicted under section 8(1), (4) or (5) is liable, on summary conviction, to a term of imprisonment of up to three months or a fine, or both.

The catch-all nature of section 2 of the Official Secrets Act 1911 has thus been reformed. Whether, in fact, the 1989 Act is less swingeing in scope is another matter. Geoffrey Robertson QC states that the scope of the 1989

---

159 Official Secrets Act 1989, s 7(2).
160 *Ibid*, s 7(3).
161 *Ibid*, s 7(4).
162 *Ibid*, s 8(1).
163 *Ibid*, s 8.
164 *Ibid*, s 8(2).
165 *Ibid*, s 9.

legislation, 'while not the theoretical dragnet of the old section 2, is none the less considerable'.[166]

Restrictions on the media: 'D' Notices[167]

The Official Secrets Acts of course apply to information which might be revealed by the press, and the doctrine of breach of confidence also represents a fetter on freedom of information. A further restriction on press freedom is the 'D' (Defence) Notice system, as it was called until 1992. 'D' Notices are requests to newspaper editors not to publish information. The basis for the system is entirely extralegal and voluntary. No formal sanction exists for failure to comply with a 'D' Notice. The system was established in 1912.[168] A 'D' Notice Committee was established, chaired by a Permanent Under Secretary of the Ministry of Defence, which comprised both newspaper editors and civil servants. At the request of a government department, the committee will draft a Notice, and advice as to its scope and meaning will be given to the press by the committee's secretary. Compliance with a 'D' Notice will not affect any right to bring legal action against a newspaper,[169] and neither will non-compliance. The system is vague and defective. It is also contrary to principle to have a non-legal system which effectively fetters the freedom of the press. 'D' Notices are mainly issued to restrict publication of information 'relating to defence plans and equipment, nuclear weaponry, codes and communication interception, the Security Services, civil defence and the photography of defence installations'.[170] The system was reviewed in both 1962 and 1980, when retention of the system was recommended. The 1980 inquiry by the Defence Committee of the House of Commons nevertheless expressed reservations about retaining the system.[171] Further review was carried out in 1992, when the number of notices was reduced to six and 'D' Notices renamed Defence Advisory Notices.

---

166 *Op cit*, Robertson, fn 120, p 142. See, also, Palmer, S, 'Tightening secrecy law' [1990] PL 243.

167 See *The 'D' Notice System*, Cmnd 3312, 1967, London: HMSO; *Report of the Committee of Privy Councillors Appointed to Inquire into 'D' Notice Matters*, Cmnd 3309, 1967, London: HMSO; *Third Report of the Defence Committee: The 'D' Notice System*, HC 773 (1979–80), London: HMSO; *Ministry of Defence: The Defence Advisory Notices: A Review of the 'D' Notice System*, MOD Open Government Document 93/1993.

168 Then known as the Admiralty, War Office and Press Committee; now, officially, the Defence, Press and Broadcasting Committee.

169 As occurred in 1970 when *The Sunday Telegraph* was prosecuted under the Official Secrets Act 1911 for disclosure of material supplied by Jonathan Aitken, discussed above.

170 *Op cit*, Robertson, fn 120, p 158.

171 HC 773 (1979–80), London: HMSO, and see Jaconelli, J, 'The "D notice" system' [1982] PL 37.

Judicial attitudes to pleas of national security

The principal avenue for legal redress of grievances against the executive in relation to actions undertaken in pursuit of protecting national security is that of judicial review, discussed in Chapters 24 and 25. It is apparent that the courts are exceedingly reluctant to challenge the executive where national security is pleaded by the government in judicial review proceedings. Whilst this is, *prima facie*, regrettable from the point of view of the aggrieved citizen, it is explained – although not necessarily justified – by the relationship between the executive, legislature and judiciary. As seen in Chapter 5, the doctrine of separation of powers, whilst not strictly adhered to under the United Kingdom's constitution, is respected by the courts. In no area of policy is this respect more clearly demonstrated than in matters of national security, which will frequently, but not inevitably, be linked to the exercise of the royal prerogative. In Chapter 6, the judiciary's cautious approach to review of the prerogative was examined, and it was there seen that the prerogative ensures for the executive a wide and inadequately defined area of power which is largely immune from judicial review. It will be recalled that in *Council of Civil Service Unions v Minister for Civil Service* (the *GCHQ* case),[172] the House of Lords ruled that the courts have jurisdiction to review the exercise of executive power irrespective of whether the source of power was statutory, or under the common law prerogative.

Notwithstanding that claim, the House of Lords conceded that matters of national security fell within the class of powers which were deemed 'non-justiciable' by the courts (by which is meant that the subject matter is one more appropriately controlled by the executive accountable to Parliament rather than the courts of law). Accordingly, despite the applicants having a 'legitimate expectation' to be consulted in the decision to terminate the right of employees to belong to trades unions, that expectation was effectively defeated by the government's plea of national security. Such a judicial attitude, and deference to the executive, was neither novel nor exceptional. A number of cases illustrate the court's position when national security is pleaded by government.

Detention in wartime

In *Liversidge v Anderson*,[173] the House of Lords refused[174] to review the Home Secretary's power of detention under the Defence of the Realm Acts. It will be

---

172 [1985] AC 374.

173 [1942] AC 206.

174 Lord Atkin dissenting. See [1942] AC 206, pp 225–46. Note that Lord Atkin's dissent was accepted as a correct statement of common law in *R v Inland Revenue Commissioners ex parte Rossminster Ltd* [1980] AC 952.

recalled[175] that the regulation provided that the Minister had power to order detention of persons whom he 'had reasonable cause to believe' to be of hostile origin or associations and 'in need of subjection to preventative control'.

Detention with a view to deportation in peace time[176]

In 1962, Dr Soblen, an American citizen who had been convicted of espionage in the United States, fled from the country before being sentenced. Whilst on an aeroplane, Dr Soblen cut his wrists, and was taken off the plane in London for hospital treatment. The Home Secretary issued a deportation order on the basis that Soblen's continued presence was 'not conducive to the public good'. When Dr Soblen applied for habeas corpus, the Court of Appeal ruled that Dr Soblen had no right to make representations, and that deportation was an administrative matter for the Home Secretary.[177]

In *R v Home Secretary ex parte Hosenball*,[178] two American journalists, Philip Agee and Mark Hosenball, were detained with a view to deportation, on the basis that their work involved obtaining and publishing information prejudicial to national security. In 1976, Mark Hosenball had co-authored, with Duncan Campbell, an article which appeared in *Time Out* magazine, entitled *The Eavesdroppers*. The article described the relationship between GCHQ and the United States National Security Agency (NSA), and the work of GCHQ, which, at the time, was not officially acknowledged. Meanwhile, Philip Agee, who had provided information for *The Eavesdroppers*, had written and had published a book on the work of the Central Intelligence Agency (CIA).[179] Later in 1976, Agee and Hosenball were informed by the government that they were to be deported on grounds of national security. No precise reasons were given. The Home Secretary, Merlyn Rees, established a committee of three to hear Agee's and Hosenball's submissions against deportation. However, without precise details being given – other than 'conducive to the public good' – the committee confirmed the Home Secretary's decision.

There is no appeal against the Home Secretary's decision where national security is pleaded as a basis for the deportation order.[180] Instead, there is a right of a hearing before a panel of three advisers to the Home Secretary.

---

175 See discussion in Chapter 6.

176 On deportation and extradition, see, further, Chapter 21.

177 See *R v Home Secretary ex parte Soblen* [1963] 2 QB 243. See, also, Thornberry, CHR, 'Dr Soblen and the alien law of the United Kingdom' (1963) 12 ICLQ 414.

178 [1977] 3 All ER 452.

179 Agee, P, *Inside the Company: CIA Diary*, 1975, Harmondsworth: Penguin.

180 Immigration Act 1971, s 15(3).

When Hosenball tried to challenge the Home Secretary's decision in the courts, the Court of Appeal upheld the deportation order. While recognising that the rules of natural justice had not been complied with, the Court of Appeal nevertheless ruled that the requirements of national security prevailed, and that the Home Secretary was responsible to Parliament, and not to the courts, for matters of security.

The case of *R v Home Secretary ex parte Cheblak*[181] also reveals the extensive powers of the Home Secretary to detain persons 'in the interests of national security'. In 1991, during the Gulf War, 160 Iraqi and Palestinian citizens were detained with a view to deportation, on the basis that their presence was not 'conducive to the public good'. Abbas Cheblak and his family had been resident in the United Kingdom for 16 years. In an application for habeas corpus, the Court of Appeal accepted the Home Secretary's explanation that Cheblak had associations with an unspecified organisation which supported the Iraqi government, and refused to press the Home Secretary for further information.[182]

Exercise of the Home Secretary's powers which did result in judicial criticism occurred in *M v Home Office*.[183] The Home Secretary, Kenneth Baker, had ignored an order of the court that M should not be returned to Zaire, where he feared torture. Immigration officials put M on a plane, which the Home Secretary, refused to have turned back. The House of Lords held that an injunction could lie against Ministers of the Crown, and that they would be guilty of contempt of court – in their official capacity – for defiance of orders of the court.

The Secretary of State also has the power to refuse admission to the United Kingdom on the grounds that their presence would not be conducive to the public good. Immigration and residency and extradition in the United Kingdom is considered in Chapter 21.

EMERGENCY POWERS

While, in peace time, the responsibility for maintaining order and detecting crime lies with the police forces, in times of emergency, further assistance will be needed if order is to be restored. In this section, the role of the armed forces in support of the police is considered.

---

181 [1991] 2 All ER 319.
182 Mr Cheblak was subsequently released from detention following a hearing before the Home Secretary's panel.
183 [1992] 4 All ER 97; [1993] 3 All ER 537, HL.

In peace time

Where serious civil unrest occurs, the government, acting in the name of the Crown, may issue a proclamation declaring a state of emergency under the Emergency Powers Act 1920, as amended by the Emergency Powers Act 1964. The proclamation, which has effect for a one month period, confers wide powers to govern by way of regulations. The grounds for making the order are stipulated in the Act. Section 1(1) provides that, 'if it appears to His Majesty that there have occurred, or are about to occur, events of such a nature as to be calculated, by interfering with the supply and distribution of food, water, fuel, or light, or with the means of locomotion, to deprive the community, or any substantial portion of the community, of the essentials of life, His Majesty may, by proclamation declare that a state of emergency exists'. Where a proclamation is made, Parliament must be immediately informed and, if in recess, must be recalled within five days for debate on the matter.

Where a Proclamation has been made, Orders in Council may confer on a Secretary of State or government department, or any person in the Crown's service, such powers and duties 'as His Majesty may deem necessary for the preservation of the peace, for securing and maintaining the means and distribution of food, water, fuel, light, and other necessities, for maintaining the means of transit or locomotion, and for any other purposes essential to the public safety and the life of the community ...'.[184] No power exists to impose compulsory military service or industrial conscription, or to make it an offence to take part in an industrial strike.[185] The powers conferred may continue in force for up to seven days, unless both Houses of Parliament resolve to extend the period.[186] Regulations may be made for the summary trial of persons guilty of offences against the regulations, conviction for which carries a maximum term of imprisonment of three months, or a fine, or both. Any goods or money obtained through breach of the regulations may be forfeited.[187]

The use of the armed forces in times of unrest

The use of troops in 1911 in South Wales is the only occasion on which troops have been brought in to assist the police. During the miner's strike 1984–85, the troops were not called in. Instead, the police forces co-ordinated their operations in order to contain the situation successfully. Where troops are

---

184 Emergency Powers Act 1920, s 2.
185 *Ibid*, s 2(1).
186 *Ibid*, s 2(1).
187 *Ibid*, s 2(3).

deemed necessary to aid the police, it is the Home Secretary, acting on the request of the Chief Officer of police, who has responsibility. As was seen in Chapter 6, the Home Secretary has the power to issue weapons to police forces for the quelling of civil disturbance.[188]

In time of war

The Defence of the Realm Acts 1914–15 conferred wide powers on the Crown to make Regulations for ensuring public safety and defence of the realm. The court have ruled that these broad powers include the power to detain a person without trial on the basis of his or her hostile associations.[189] The power to regulate supplies did not include, however, the power to impose a tax upon produce.[190] Specific power to impose charges in relation to matters regulated under Defence Regulations was conferred under the Emergency Powers (Defence) Act 1939. Under the regulations, the Home Secretary was given power to detain persons whom he had reasonable cause to believe came within certain categories. The power was regarded by the courts as reviewable.[191] Under the Emergency Powers (Defence) (No 2) Act 1940, powers were conferred compulsorily to direct labour in support of the war effort. Compulsory military service was introduced under National Service Acts.

Special powers in relation to Northern Ireland[192]

In Chapter 3, an outline history of the troubles in Northern Ireland is provided. It will be recalled that the partition of Ireland, with six counties of Ulster being separated from the rest of Ireland and becoming the newly created state of Northern Ireland, did not quell the centuries of disturbances between the mainly Catholic South of Ireland and the mainly Protestant newly created Northern Ireland. In order to contain the terrorist activities of the Irish Republican Army,[193] in 1922, the Civil Authorities (Special Powers)

---

188 See *R v Secretary of State for Home Affairs ex parte Northumbria Police Authority* [1988] 1 All ER 556.

189 See *R v Halliday ex parte Zadig* [1917] AC 260.

180 See *Attorney General v Wilts United Dairies Ltd* (1921) 37 TLR 884 and the War Charges Validity Act 1925.

191 See *Liversidge v Anderson* [1942] AC 206.

192 See Calvert, H, *Constitutional Law in Northern Ireland*, 1968, London: Stevens; Macdermott (Lord), 'Law and order in times of emergency' [1972] Juridical Review 1.

193 For a brief history, see Chapter 3.

Act[194] was passed by the Northern Ireland Parliament. From 1969, British troops have been used in Northern Ireland in support of the civil authorities. In 1971 – under this Act – the internment of suspected terrorists was introduced. In 1973, the Northern Ireland (Emergency Provisions) Act was passed at Westminster, amended in 1975 and re-enacted in 1978, 1987, 1991 and 1996.[195] In 1974, the Prevention of Terrorism Act was passed, initially for a five year renewable term. The Act was subsequently renewed, although the 1989 Act was not subject to the five year term, but was subject to annual renewal by Parliament, as are parts of the Northern Ireland (Emergency Provisions) Act 1996. The Prevention of Terrorism (Additional Powers) Act 1996 further extended the law. The law is substantially reformed by the Terrorism Act 2000, discussed below.

THE PREVENTION OF TERRORISM ACTS[196]

The law before the Terrorism Act 2000

The Birmingham pub bombings in 1974, believed to have been carried out by the Irish Republican Army, in which 16 people died and many more were injured, prompted the rapid passage of the Prevention of Terrorism (Temporary Provisions) Act 1974. The Terrorism Act 2000 supercedes the Prevention of Terrorism Acts and places the law on a permanent basis, no longer subject to annual renewal by Parliament.

Membership of terrorist organisations

Section 1 of the Prevention of Terrorism Act 1989 proscribed membership and support of the Irish Republican Army and the Irish National Liberation Army. It is an offence to belong to, solicit or invite support for, arrange or assist any meeting of three or more persons knowing that the meeting is to support a

---

194 Walsh, D, *The Use and Abuse of Emergency Legislation in Northern Ireland*, 1983, London: The Cobden Trust; Lord Diplock, *Report of the Commission to Consider Legal Procedures to Deal with Terrorist Activities in Northern Ireland*, Cmnd 5185, 1972, London: HMSO; Lord Gardiner, *Report of a Committee to Consider, in the Context of Civil Liberties and Human Rights, Measures to deal with Terrorism in Northern Ireland*, Cmnd 5847, 1975, London: HMSO.

195 Scarman J, *Government of Northern Ireland: Report of a Tribunal of Inquiry into Violence and Civil Disturbances in Northern Ireland in 1969*, (NI) Cmd 566, 1972, London: HMSO; Earl Jellicoe, *Review of the Operation of the Prevention of Terrorism (Temporary Provisions) Act 1976*, Cmnd 8803, 1983, London: HMSO. See, also, Chapter 20.

196 See, *inter alia*, Bell, JB, *The Secret Army: The IRA 1916–79*, 1979, Dublin: Academy; Bishop, P and Maillie, E, *The Provisional IRA*, 1987, London: Heinemann; Lord Shackleton, *Review of the Operation of the Prevention of Terrorism (Temporary Provisions) Acts 1974 and 1976*, Cmnd 7324, 1978, London: HMSO.

proscribed organisation. On conviction on indictment, 10 years imprisonment, unlimited fine, or both, may be imposed; on summary conviction, six months imprisonment or a fine, or both, may be imposed. It is a criminal offence to wear an item of dress or wear or display any article which arouses reasonable apprehension that the wearer is a member of a proscribed organisation.[197] On summary conviction, six months imprisonment and level 5 fine may be imposed. The consent of the Attorney General is required before a prosecution can proceed.

Financial contributions to terrorist funds

It was an offence under Part III of the Act to solicit, receive or make contributions in support of an organisation which is engaged in acts of terrorism. While, originally, the offence was confined to organisations involved in the Northern Ireland conflict, the 1989 Act extended the offence to include international terrorism.[198] The Act also covered financial dealings, in which an individual played no direct role, but which were designed to finance terrorist activities.[199] Money or property which was being contributed for terrorist organisations could be forfeited under the Act.[200]

Exclusion orders

Under section 5 of the Prevention of Terrorism Act 1989, the Home Secretary was empowered to make exclusion orders on particular people whom the Home Secretary was satisfied were concerned with the commission, preparation or instigation of acts of terrorism.[201] A named person could be excluded from Northern Ireland or the United Kingdom, and it was an offence to fail to comply with the order. The power applied to British citizens[202] who had been ordinarily resident in Britain for three years or less. The order prevented the named person from remaining in or entering Britain. Under section 6, an order could be made preventing a person from remaining in or entering Northern Ireland. Under section 7, non-British citizens could be excluded from either Britain or Northern Ireland.

---

197 Prevention of Terrorism (Temporary Provisions) Act 1974, s 3. See *Morgan v Director of Public Prosecutions* (1974) *The Times*, 12 December.

198 Prevention of Terrorism Act 1989, s 9.

199 *Ibid*, ss 10 and 11.

200 *Ibid*, s 13.

201 *Ibid*, ss 4–8. In March 1995, 56 exclusion orders were in effect: 16 of which were removed on 9 March 1995.

202 As defined under the British Nationality Act 1981, on which, see Chapter 21.

If the Home Secretary was satisfied that the person was involved in terrorism, a notice was served on the person concerned, who then had between seven and 14 days in which to make written representations to the Home Secretary, and to have an interview with an advisor nominated by the Home Secretary.[203] The Home Secretary was not under a duty to give reasons for issuing the exclusion order.[204] Once the order was in force, its duration was for a three year, renewable period and the order could not be suspended for a period of time.

Where an exclusion order was in force, the police had power to detain a person who was found to be in contravention of the order. In *Breen v Chief Constable for Dumfries and Galloway*,[205] it was held that the police could lawfully detain Breen while an exclusion order was being prepared, and that, provided that the police were not aware that there was no evidence for the making of an order, their action was lawful.

Because of the national security nature of the decision, the possibility for a successful application for judicial review was extremely limited. In *R v Secretary of State for Home Affairs ex parte McQuillan*,[206] the applicant challenged the Home Secretary's decision to exclude him from Great Britain, and the Home Secretary's decision not to review his case in light of changed circumstances. The applicant claimed that at no time had he been involved in terrorist activity and that, if he were forced to remain in Northern Ireland, his life would be in danger. The court, however, ruled that, given the lack of duty to state reasons for the decision to exclude, the court could not determine whether or not the Home Secretary's decision was rational.

Exclusion orders have been replaced under the Terrorism Act 2000 with border and port controls. See below.

Police powers of arrest, stop and search

Police powers in relation to suspected terrorists were governed by Part IV of the 1989 Act. A person suspected of terrorist activity could be arrested, without warrant, and detained for 48 hours, unlike arrest under the Police and Criminal Evidence Act 1984, where detention is initially limited to 24 hours. Section 81 of the Criminal Justice and Public Order Act 1994 amended the 1989 Act and conferred powers on the police to stop and search vehicles where 'it is expedient to do so' in order to prevent acts of terrorism. With the resumption of the Irish Republican Army's campaign of terrorism, the government decided that additional stop and search powers were needed.

---

203 Prevention of Terrorism Act 1989, Sched 2, para 4.
204 *R v Secretary of State for Home Affairs ex parte Stitt* (1987) *The Times*, 3 February.
205 (1997) *The Times*, 24 April.
206 See, further, Chapter 20.

The Prevention of Terrorism (Additional Powers) Act 1996 completed its passage through both Houses of Parliament in two days. Section 1 of the Prevention of Terrorism (Additional Powers) Act 1996 inserted a new section (section 13B) into the 1989 Act, and provided that a senior officer of police could authorise the stop and search of pedestrians at any place or within any locality within his area. Where that power was conferred, a police constable in uniform could stop any pedestrian and search him or anything carried by him for articles which could be used for a purpose concerned with the commission, preparation or instigation of acts of terrorism. The powers were exercisable whether or not the constable had 'any grounds for suspecting the presence of articles of that kind'. Where authorisation was given under section 13 of the 1989 Act, the authorisation had to be notified to the Secretary of State. If the Secretary of State confirmed the authorisation, it would continue in force for a period not exceeding 28 days from the date on which authorisation was given, or for a shorter period as directed by the Secretary of State.[207] If the Secretary of State did not confirm the authorisation within 48 hours, the authorisation lapsed.[208] Further, the Secretary of State could cancel the authorisation.[209]

Section 14(1) of the Prevention of Terrorism (Temporary Provisions) Act 1989 provided that:

> ... a constable may arrest without warrant a person whom he has reasonable grounds for suspecting to be:

> ... a person who is or has been concerned in the commission, preparation or instigation of acts of terrorism to which this Part of this Act applies ...

In *O'Hara v Chief Constable of the Royal Ulster Constabulary*,[210] the House of Lords interpreted the basis of 'reasonable suspicion'. A constable had arrested O'Hara and detained him, but he was not subsequently charged with any offence. In an action for false imprisonment, the constable stated that, as a result of a briefing given by a superior officer, he suspected that the plaintiff had been involved in acts of terrorism. The House of Lords ruled, on appeal, that the judge was entitled to conclude that the police had reasonable grounds for suspicion. What was in issue was not whether, at the time of the arrest, the constable thought that the grounds were reasonable, but rather whether a reasonable man would, in light of the circumstances, think that the grounds were reasonable. The officer was entitled to form a suspicion based on the briefing.

Powers of detention were laid down under section 14, which permitted detention without access to a court of law, where authorised by the Secretary

---

207 Prevention of Terrorism Act 1989, s 13B(9)(c).
208 *Ibid*, s 13B(9)(b).
209 *Ibid*, s 13B(9)(a).
210 [1997] 2 WLR 1.

of State, for up to seven days,[211] and powers of stop and search in relation to terrorism were contained in section 15. A senior police office could authorise the stop and search of vehicles and persons, for a specific period not exceeding 28 days. The power conferred was exercisable at any place within the police area. This broad power of stop and search empowered a constable in uniform to search for any 'articles which could be used for a purpose connected with the commission, preparation or instigation of acts of terrorism'.[212] Any person who failed to stop when required to do so by a constable, or who wilfully obstructed a constable in the exercise of his powers, was guilty of an offence.[213]

The Prevention of Terrorism (Additional Powers) Act 1996 inserted a new section 16B into the 1989 Act which provided power for the police to impose cordons. The power was exercisable by a police officer of at least the rank of superintendent. He could authorise a cordon to be imposed on an area specified by him, if 'it appeared' to him that 'it is expedient to do so' in connection with an investigation into the commission, preparation or instigation of an act of terrorism. A new Part IVB of the 1989 Act, inserted by the Prevention of Terrorism (Additional Powers) Act 1996, provided the police with the power to impose parking prohibitions and restrictions and to remove vehicles. The restrictions or prohibitions on parking may be for a specified period not exceeding 28 days. A number of criminal offences attended these powers.

In addition, the Chemical Weapons Act 1996 authorised the Secretary of State or a justice of the peace to authorise entry into premises and to remove, immobilise or destroy chemical weapons. Section 25 enables the Secretary of State to issue an authorisation where it is proposed to conduct an inspection of premises. Section 29 enables a justice of the peace to issue a warrant authorising inspection of premises where there are reasonable grounds for suspecting that an offence under the Act is being, has been or is about to be committed. Where a constable has reasonable grounds to believe that a person has been engaged in offences under the Act, a magistrate may grant a warrant for the search of premises to find that person.[214]

Information about acts of terrorism

Any person who failed, without reasonable excuse, to disclose information which might be material in preventing the commission of acts of terrorism, or

---

211 See *Brogan v United Kingdom* (1988) 11 EHRR 117.
212 Prevention of Terrorism Act 1989, s 13A(3).
213 *Ibid*, s 13A(6).
214 *Ibid*, s 15(1).

apprehending, prosecuting and convicting a person for terrorist offences, committed an offence.[215] The offence carried a term of imprisonment of up to five years or a fine, or both, on conviction on indictment. On summary conviction, the penalty was a term of imprisonment of up to six months, or a fine, or both. Further, persons who suspected that another person was providing financial assistance for terrorist activities, which came into their knowledge through trade, profession, business or employment, and who did not disclose that information to a constable, was guilty of an offence.[216] It was not an offence for a professional legal adviser to withhold information which had come to him in privileged circumstances.[217] It was a defence to prove that a person had a reasonable excuse for not disclosing the information.[218]

THE TERRORISM ACT 2000

The Terrorism Act 2000 reforms and extends existing terrorist legislation.[219] It repeals the Prevention of Terrorism (Temporary Provisions) Act 1989, the Prevention of Terrorism (Additional Powers) Act 1996, the Northern Ireland (Emergency Provisions) Act 1996 and the Northern Ireland (Emergency Provisions) Act 1998, and makes minor amendments to other relevant Acts. Whereas the Prevention of Terrorism Act 1989 required annual renewal, the Terrorism Act has permanent status. In relation to Northern Ireland, it had been hoped that special provision would no longer be required for Northern Ireland following the peace settlement. However, in light of the problems implementing full devolution to Northern Ireland, special provisions are included in Part VII of the Terrorism Act which are time-limited to five years.

Defining terrorism

Whereas under the Prevention of Terrorism Act 1989, terrorism was defined as the 'use of violence for political ends, and includes the use of violence for the purpose of putting the public or any section of the public in fear',[220] the Terrorism Act 2000 adopts a wider definition, namely:

> In this Act 'terrorism' means the use or threat, for the purpose of advancing a political, religious or ideological cause, of action which –

---

215 Prevention of Terrorism Act 1989, s 18.

216 *Ibid*, s 18A(1).

217 *Ibid*, s 18A(2).

218 *Ibid*, s 18A(3).

219 See *Inquiry into Legislation Against Terrorism*, 1996, Cm 3420, London: The Stationery Office; Legislation Against Terrorism, 1998, Cm 4178, London: The Stationery Office.

220 Prevention of Terrorism (Temporary Provisions) Act 1989, s 20.

(a) involves serious violence against any person or property,

(b) endangers the life of any person, or

(c) creates a serious risk to the health or safety of the public or a section of the public.[221]

Action includes action outside the United Kingdom, and references to any person or to property refer to any person or property wherever situated, and a reference to the public includes a reference to the public of a country other than the United Kingdom.[222] This definition is intended to cover not just terrorism for political ends, as in the case of Northern Ireland, but terrorism undertaken for religious or ideological motives, which, while not necessarily violent in themselves, are capable of having widespread adverse affects. Examples cited are of disruption to key computer systems or interference with the supply of water or power where life, health or safety may be put at risk.

Proscribed organisations

Part II of the Act relates to proscribed organisations, listed under Schedule 2.[223] The Secretary of State may add or remove)an organisation from Schedule 2 or otherwise amend it, but may only add an organisation if he believes that the organisation is concerned in terrorism.[224] An organisation is concerned in terrorism if it commits or participates in acts of terrorism, prepares for terrorism, promotes or encourages terrorism, or is otherwise concerned in terrorism.[225] The Act introduces a Proscribed Organisations Appeal Commission (POAC),[226] to which individuals or organisations may appeal, having first applied to the Secretary of State for deproscription and been refused.[227]

The Commission must allow an appeal if it considers that the Secretary of State's decision was flawed when considered in the light of the principles

---

221 Terrorism Act 2000, s 1.

222 *Ibid*, s 1(2). The Court of Appeal ruled in *Secretary of State for the Home Department v Rehman* (2000) *The Times*, 31 May, that the promotion of terrorism against any state by an individual in the United Kingdom was capable of being a threat to the national security of the United Kingdom, and accordingly the deportation in the interests of national security for terrorist activities where were not targeted against the United Kingdom or its citizens was lawful under the Immigration Act 1971.

223 The Irish Republican Army, *Cumann na mBan, Fianna na hEireann*, the Red Hand Commando, *Saor Eire*, the Ulster Freedom Fighters, the Ulster Volunteer Force, the Irish National Liberation Army, the Irish People's Liberation Organisation the Ulster Defence Association, the Loyalist Volunteer Force, the Continuity Army Council, the Orange Volunteers, the Red Hand Defenders.

224 Terrorism Act 2000, s 3.

225 *Ibid*, s 3(5).

226 *Ibid*, s 5.

227 *Ibid*, s 4.

applicable on an application for judicial review.[228] If the appeal is allowed, the Commission makes an order to that effect. Where an order is made, the Secretary of State must lay a draft order before Parliament or ,in urgent cases, make an order removing the organisation from the list in Schedule 2.[229] Appeals from the POAC, on a question of law, lie to the Court of Appeal, Court of Session or Court of Appeal in Northern Ireland. An appeal may only be brought with the consent of the Commission or, where the Commission refuses permission, the permission of the relevant court.[230] If an appeal to the POAC is successful, and an order made deproscribing the organisation, any individual convicted of an offence in relation to the organisation, provided the offence was committed after the date of the Secretary of State's refusal to deproscribe, may appeal against his conviction to the Court or Appeal or Crown Court and the court shall allow the appeal.[231] Section 8 makes equivalent provision for Scotland and Northern Ireland. Section 9 makes provision for the Human Rights Act 1998, section 7, to apply to appeal proceedings brought before the POAC, in relation to section 5(4) and (5), sections 6 and 7 (appeals to a court of law from a decision of the POAC), and paragraphs 4–8 of Schedule 3 (relating to procedure before the POAC, on which, see below). In relation to the above, reference to the Commission allowing an appeal shall be taken as a reference to the Commission determining that an action of the Secretary of State is incompatible with a Convention right, and reference to the refusal to deproscribe against which an appeal was brought shall be taken as a reference to the action of the Secretary of State which is found to be incompatible with a Convention right.[232] In order that individuals seeking deproscription should not be deterred from pursuing an appeal or from instituting proceedings under section 7 of the Human Rights Act 1998, through a risk of prosecution for offences in relation to a proscribed organisation, section 10 provides that evidence relating to anything done, and any documents submitted for these proceedings, cannot be relied on in criminal proceedings for such an offence except as part of the defence case.

Sections 11 to 13 relate to offences concerning membership of and support for a proscribed organisation, and are based on those in sections 2 and 3 of the Prevention of Terrorism Act 1989 and, in relation to Northern Ireland, sections 30 and 31 of the Emergency Provisions Act. A person guilty of an offence in relation to membership under section 11 shall be liable, on conviction on indictment, to a term of imprisonment not exceeding 10 years, to a fine or to both, and on summary conviction, to a term of imprisonment not exceeding

---

228 See Chapter 25.
229 Terrorism Act 2000, s 5.
230 *Ibid*, s 6.
231 *Ibid*, s 7.
232 *Ibid*, s 9(4).

six months, to a fine not exceeding the statutory maximum or to both. It is a defence for a person charged with an offence under section 11(1) to prove that the organisation was not proscribed on the last occasion on which he became a member or began to profess to be a member, and that he has not taken part in the activities of the organisation at any time while it was proscribed. Section 12 relates to the support for a proscribed organisation and makes it an offence to invite support, which is not restricted to the provision of money or other property. It is an offence to arrange, manage or assist in arranging or managing a meeting which he knows is to support or further the activities of a proscribed organisation, or one which he knows is to be addressed by a person who belongs or professes to belong to a proscribed organisation. It is also an offence to address such a meeting where the purpose is to support the organisation, or where he knows that the meeting is to be addressed by a person who belongs or professes to belong to a proscribed organisation. A meeting for these purposes means a meeting of three or more persons, whether or not the public are admitted. On conviction on indictment, a person guilty is liable to a term of imprisonment not exceeding 10 years, to a fine or to both, or on summary conviction to imprisonment for not longer than six months, a fine not exceeding the statutory maximum or both.

The wearing of an item of clothing, or wearing, carrying or displaying an article in a public place, in such a way or in such circumstances as to arouse reasonable suspicion that that person is a member or supporter of a proscribed organisation is an offence. On summary conviction, a person guilty under section 13 is liable to six months imprisonment, a fine not exceeding level 5 on the standard scale or to both.

Terrorist property

Part III of the Act relates to terrorist property, defined under section 14 to mean money or other property which is likely to be used for the purposes of terrorism (including any resources of a proscribed organisation), proceeds of the commission of acts of terrorism, and proceeds of acts carried out for the purposes of terrorism. It is an offence to partake in fundraising for the purposes of terrorism. Inviting others to provide, receiving or providing money or other property is an offence under section 15. In relation to inviting support from others or receiving money or other property, there must be an intention that it should be used, or reasonable cause to suspect that it may be used, for terrorist purposes. In relation to the provision of money or other property, knowledge or reasonable cause to suspect that it will or may be used for terrorism is required. The use or possession of money for terrorist purposes is an offence under section 16, and involvement in funding arrangements with knowledge or reasonable cause to suspect that it will be used for terrorist purposes is an offence under section 17. The concealment, removal, transfer or other mechanism for controlling terrorist property ('money laundering') is an offence under section 18. It is a defence to prove that the person did not know and had no reasonable cause to suspect that the arrangement related to terrorist property. Persons guilty of an offence under sections 15 to 18 are liable, on conviction on indictment to imprisonment for a term not exceeding 14 years, a fine or to both or, on summary conviction, for a term of imprisonment not exceeding six months, a fine not exceeding the statutory maximum, or to both.[233] A court before which a person is convicted of an offence under sections 15 to 18 may make a forfeiture order under section 23.

Section 19 is based on section 18A of the Prevention of Terrorism Act 1989 imposes a duty on banks and other businesses to report any suspicion that someone is laundering terrorist money or committing any other terrorist property offence to the police. Sub-section (5) exempts professional legal advisers in relation to information obtained in privileged circumstances. Section 20 relates to information disclosures to the police, and provides that a person so disclosing is not liable for breaching legal restrictions on disclosure. Section 21 covers those co-operating with the police, and provides that a person does not commit an offence under sections 15 to 18 if he is acting with the express consent of a constable.

Part III of the Act introduces new powers for the police, customs officers and immigration officers to seize cash[234] at borders and to seek forfeiture of cash in civil proceedings. This power enables cash being taken from Northern Ireland to Great Britain, and vice versa, to be seized, detained and forfeited. When cash is seized under section 25, the authorities have 48 hours in which to seek continued detention or forfeiture. If neither of these occurs, the cash must be returned. Continued detention is authorised under section 26, which provides for applications by authorised officers or Commissioners of Customs and Excise to a magistrates' court or, in Scotland, an application by the procurator fiscal to the sheriff. A person from whom the cash was seized, the person on whose behalf it was being transported and any other person may apply for the cash detained under section 25 to be returned.[235] The application will only be granted if the magistrates' court or the sheriff is satisfied that continued detention is no longer justified, for example, because investigations into the source and use of the cash have been concluded. The forfeiture of cash may be applied for by an authorised officer or Commissioners of Customs and Excise to the magistrates' court or, in Scotland, by the procurator fiscal to the sheriff. An order for forfeiture may

---

233 Terrorism Act 2000, s 22.
234 Defined as coins and notes in any currency, postal orders, travellers' cheques, bankers' drafts and such other kinds of monetary instrument as the Secretary of State may specify by order: *ibid*, s 24.
235 *Ibid*, s 27.

only be granted if the magistrates' court or sheriff is satisfied on the balance of probabilities that the cash is cash relating to terrorist purposes. No criminal proceedings for an offence under the Act are required.[236] Appeals must be lodged within 30 days, and if successful the cash returned.[237] If a forfeiture order has been made in relation to a proscribed organisation, and the organisation successfully appeals to the POAC for deproscription, cash which has been forfeited may be returned following an appeal.[238]

Terrorist investigations

Part IV of the Act regulates powers in relation to terrorist investigations, defined to include the commission, preparation or instigation of acts of terrorism, an act which appears to have been done for such purposes, the resources of a proscribed organisation, the possibility of making a proscription or deproscription order under section 3(3), or the commission, preparation or instigation of an offence under the Act.[239] Sections 33 to 36 give power to the police to designate and demarcate a specified area by cordons for the purposes of a terrorist investigation. It is an offence to fail to comply with an order, prohibition or restriction imposed, on summary conviction being liable to imprisonment for a term not exceeding three months, a fine not exceeding level four on the standard scale, or to both. It is a defence to prove that there is a reasonable excuse for failure to comply.[240]

Under section 39, where a person knows or has reasonable cause to suspect that a constable is conducting or proposes to conduct a terrorist investigation, it is an offence to disclose to another anything which is likely to prejudice the investigation or to interfere with material which is likely to be relevant to the investigation. Where a person knows or has reasonable cause to suspect that a disclosure has been or will be made under any of sections 19 to 21, it is an offence to disclose to another anything which is likely to prejudice an investigation resulting from the disclosure, or to interfere with material likely to be relevant to an investigation resulting from the disclosure. This deterrent measure carries on conviction on indictment, imprisonment for a term not exceeding five years, a fine or to both or, on summary conviction, imprisonment for a term not exceeding six months, a fine not exceeding the statutory maximum or to both.[241]

---

236 Terrorism Act 2000, s 28.
237 *Ibid*, s 29.
238 *Ibid*, s 29(6), (7).
239 *Ibid*, s 32.
240 *Ibid*, s 36(2), (3), (4).
241 *Ibid*, s 39(7).

It is also an offence for a person to collect, make a record of, publish, communicate or attempt to elicit information which is useful to a person committing or preparing an act of terrorism, or to possess a document or record containing information which would be useful.[242] The offence is confined to a person who is or has been a constable, a member of Her Majesty's Forces, the holder of a judicial office, an officer of any court or a full time employee of the prison service in Northern Ireland. If it is proved in criminal proceedings that a document or record was on any premises at the same time as the accused, or on premises of which the accused was the occupier or premises which he habitually used otherwise than as a member of the public, the court may assume that the accused possessed the document or records, unless he proves that he did not know of its presence on the premises or that he had no control over it. It is a defence to prove that he had a reasonable excuse for his action or possession. Conviction under section 103 on indictment carries a liability to a term of imprisonment not exceeding 10 years, a fine or to both or, on summary conviction, to imprisonment not exceeding six months, a fine not exceeding the statutory maximum or to both.

Counter-terrorist powers

A terrorist for the purposes of Part V of the Act is a person who has committed an offence under any of sections 11, 12 (membership or support for a proscribed organisation), 15 to 18 (fundraising and handling money), 54 (relating to weapons training) and 56 to 63 (directing a terrorist organisation and offences relating to committing or inciting terrorism wholly or partly outside the United Kingdom), or is or has been concerned in the commission, preparation or instigation of acts of terrorism.[243] A constable may arrest without a warrant a person whom he reasonably suspects to be a terrorist.[244] A person must be released, unless detained under any other power, within 48 hours. Where a review of a person's detention has taken place and the review officer does not authorise continued detention, the person shall be released. A police officer may make an application for a warrant extending a person's detention and, where the officer intends to make an application, the person may be detained pending the making of the application and conclusion of proceedings on the application. Where the application is granted, the person may be detained during the period specified in the warrant. A constable may apply for a warrant relating to specified premises if he is satisfied that there are reasonable grounds for suspecting that a person suspected of terrorism is

---

242 Terrorism Act 2000, s 103.
243 *Ibid*, s 40.
244 *Ibid*, s 41, Sched 8 relating to detention, treatment, review and extension applies.

to be found there. The warrant authorises entry and search for the purpose of arresting the person in question.[245]

Stop and search powers relating to suspected terrorists include the power to stop and search the person for evidence of being a terrorist, and an arrested person may be searched. Anything discovered in the course of a search which the constable reasonably suspects of being evidence that the person is a terrorist may be seized.[246] Specified senior police officers may authorise any constable in uniform to stop a vehicle in an area or at a place specified in the authorisation and to search the vehicle, its driver, a passenger and anything in the vehicle or carried by the driver or a passenger, and may also be granted to stop pedestrians.[247] The power may only be used for the purpose of searching for articles which could be used in connection with terrorism, and may be exercised whether or not the constable has grounds for suspecting the presence of articles of that kind. Where suspected items are discovered in the course of a search, they may be seized and retained.[248] Authorisations are for a maximum, renewable, 28 days. Authorisations must be confirmed or amended by the Secretary of State within 48 hours of their being made, or they cease to have effect.[249] It is an offence to fail to comply with an order to stop a vehicle, or to stop, or to wilfully obstruct a constable in the exercise of the power conferred by an authorisation under section 44. On summary conviction, a person guilty of an offence is liable to imprisonment for a term not exceeding six months, a fine not exceeding level five on the standard scale or to both.[250]

The Act makes weapons training for terrorist purposes an offence. Formerly relating only to Northern Ireland under the Emergency Provisions Act 1996, the 2000 Act applies throughout the United Kingdom. The Act covers conventional firearms and explosives and extends to cover chemical, biological and nuclear weapons and materials.[251] It is an offence to provide or receive instruction or invite another to receive instruction in the making or use of defined weapons. It is a defence to prove that the action or involvement was wholly for a purpose not concerned with terrorism. A person found guilty on indictment is liable to a term of imprisonment of up to 10 years, to a fine or to both or, on summary conviction, to a term of imprisonment not exceeding six months, to a fine not exceeding the statutory maximum or to both.[252]

---

245 Terrorism Act 2000, s 42.

246 *Ibid*, s 43.

247 *Ibid*, s 44. Authorisation may also be granted for the control of parking: ss 48–52.

248 *Ibid*, s 45.

249 *Ibid*, s 46.

250 *Ibid*, s 47.

251 *Ibid*, s 54.

252 *Ibid*, s 54.

It is an offence to possess articles in circumstances which give rise to a reasonable suspicion that such possession is for a purpose connected with the commission, preparation or instigation of an act of terrorism. Section 57 replicates section 16A of the Prevention of Terrorism Act 1989, and reverses the onus of proof, sub-section (2) providing that it is a defence for a person charged to prove that his possession of an article was not for a purpose connected with terrorism. Article 6(2) of the European Convention on Human Rights, provides for the presumption of innocence of the defendant in criminal trials, and presumes that the prosecution will need to prove guilt. However, the reversal of the burden of proof does not *per se* indicate a violation of the right to fair trial. The government certified that the Bill complied with the Convention. In *Kebilene's* case,[253] discussed in Chapter 22, the House of Lords refused to set aside a conviction under section 16A on the basis that the Attorney General should not have consented to the prosecution in light of the imminent implementation of the Human Rights Act 1998.

Terrorism overseas

Sections 59 to 64 regulate terrorism overseas. Under section 59, it is an offence to incite another person to commit an act of terrorism wholly or partly outside the United Kingdom, if that act would constitute an offence listed in sub-section (2) in England and Wales, namely, murder, wounding with intent, offences involving poison, explosions and endangering life by damaging property. A person found guilty shall be liable to any penalty to which he would be liable on conviction of the relevant offence. Sections 60 and 61 make equivalent provision in relation to Scotland and Northern Ireland. Section 62 regulates acts of terrorism outside the United Kingdom involving causing explosions,[254] the use of biological or chemical weapons, and provides that a person committing such an act is guilty of an offence. Equally, it is an offence to do anything outside the United Kingdom which would amount to an offence under sections 15 to 18 if it had been done in the United Kingdom. Section 64 amends the Extradition Act 1989 to include the Convention for the Suppression of Terrorist Bombings and the Convention for the Suppression of the Financing of Terrorism.

---

253 *R v Director of Public Prosecutions ex parte Kebeline and Others,* judgment 28 October 1999, HL.
254 An offence under the Explosive Substances Act 1883, ss 2, 3 or 5; an offence under the Biological Weapons Act 1974, s 1; an offence under the Chemical Weapons Act 1996, s 2.

Port and border controls

Section 53 and Schedule 7 regulate border controls. An 'examining officer', being a constable, immigration officer and customs officer designated for the purposes of Schedule 7 by the Secretary of State and Commissioners of Customs and Excise, has the power to stop, question and detain a person, at an airport, hoverport or port or border area, for the purposes of determining whether he or she is a person suspected of being concerned in the commission, preparation or instigation of acts of terrorism.[255] A place is within a border area if it is no more than one mile from the border between Northern Ireland and the Republic of Ireland.[256] In relation to a train travelling from the Republic of Ireland to Northern Ireland, the first place in Northern Ireland at which it stops for the purpose of allowing passengers to leave is within the border area. Owners or agents of ships or aircraft employed to carry passengers for reward on journeys between Great Britain, the Republic of Ireland and Northern Ireland must not dock or land for the purposes of embarking or disembarking passengers at any place other than a designated port as listed in the Act.[257] The Secretary of State may designate control areas in any port, and specify conditions for or restrictions on the embarkation or disembarkation of passengers in a control area. The captains of ships or aircraft travelling between Great Britain, the Republic of Ireland, Northern Ireland or any of the Islands are under a duty to ensure that passengers and members of crew do not disembark other than in accordance with arrangements approved by an examining officer. Section 16 introduces carding arrangements, which require persons embarking or disembarking in relation to journeys between Great Britain, the Republic of Ireland, Northern Ireland or any of the Islands to provide such information as the Secretary of State, by order, may require.

A person questioned is required to provide any information requested, and produce a valid passport or other document establishing his or her identity. A person may be removed from a ship, aircraft or vehicle for the purpose of detaining for questioning. A person detained for questioning must be released no later than the end of a nine hour period beginning with the time when the questioning begins, unless otherwise detained under any other power.[258]

Powers of search are granted to examining officers. The examining officer may 'for the purpose of satisfying himself whether there are any persons who

---

255 Defined in the Terrorism Act 2000, s 40(1)(b) and 40(2), as including a person who has been, whether before or after the passing of the Act, concerned in the commission, preparation or instigation of acts of terrorism within the meaning given in s 1.

256 *Ibid*, s 40(1).

257 *Ibid*, Sched 7, para 12.

258 *Ibid*, para 6.

he may wish to question' search a ship or aircraft; search anything on a ship or aircraft and search anything which he reasonably believes has been, or is about to be, on a ship or aircraft. In relation to the person questioned, the examining officer may search the person, his possessions or a ship or aircraft. In relation to questioning in border areas, the examining officer has the power to search vehicles, anything in or on the vehicle, or anything which he reasonably believes has been or is about to be in or on a vehicle. The search of a person in border searches must be carried out by a person of the same sex.[259] Property may be detained, for a period of seven days, for the purpose of deciding whether it may be needed for use as evidence in criminal proceedings, or in connection with decisions concerning deportation to be taken by the Secretary of State.[260] It is an offence knowingly to fail to comply, or contravene a prohibition imposed, or wilfully to obstruct or seek to frustrate a search or examination by an examining officer. On summary conviction, a person guilty of an offence is liable to imprisonment for a term not exceeding three months, a fine not exceeding level four on the standard scale, or both.[261]

The Prevention of Terrorism Acts and European law

The power of detention has been subject to successful challenge under the European Convention on Human Rights. In *Brogan v United Kingdom*,[262] the European Court on Human Rights declared the power a violation of Article 5. The government's response, however, was to enter a derogation from the Article in respect of the Prevention of Terrorism Act.

In *R v Secretary of State for the Home Department ex parte Gallagher*,[263] the European Court of Justice considered the procedure employed under the Prevention of Terrorism (Temporary Provisions) Act 1989 for the making of exclusion orders. Gallagher, an Irish citizen, had been arrested and served with an order under section 7 excluding him from the United Kingdom. When Gallagher was interviewed at the British Embassy in Dublin, the interviewer did not reveal his identity or provide information on the grounds of the exclusion. The Court of appeal referred the matter to the European Court of Justice for consideration of Article 9(1) of Directive 64/221. The Court of Justice ruled that, save in cases of urgency, the administrative authority could not make an exclusion order before a competent authority had given its opinion. The Court also ruled that Article 9(1) did not preclude the competent authority from being appointed by the same administrative authority as took

---

259 Terrorism Act 2000, Sched 7, paras 7 and 8.
260 *Ibid*, para 11.
261 *Ibid*, para 18.
262 (1988) 11 EHRR 117.
263 Case C-175-94: (1995) *The Times*, 13 December.

the decision ordering expulsion, provided that the competent authority could perform its duties in absolute independence. As noted above, exclusion orders have been replaced by border and port controls under the Terrorism Act 2000.

Operation Flavius[264]

In autumn 1987, the Army Council of the Irish Republican Army formed a special active service unit which was despatched to Gibraltar, a site used for rest and recreation by the British army following tours of duty in Ulster. Mairead Farrell, Danny McCann and Sean Savage were under surveillance by MI5 and observed watching a 'Changing of the Guard' ceremony. The Joint Intelligence Committee alerted the Joint Operations Centre manned by Home Office and Foreign Office personnel, the Ministry of Defence, Intelligence Service and an SAS Liaison Officer. Sixteen SAS men were deployed to Gibraltar to avert the anticipated terrorist operation. The team had been given inaccurate information as to whether suspects were armed and as to whether the suspects had brought a bomb onto the rock of Gibraltar, and that they were about to activate it. When the SAS team attempted to arrest the suspects, all three were shot dead. No prosecutions were brought against the servicemen.

The killings of the IRA members came before the Court of Human Rights and, in *McCann, Farrell and Savage v United Kingdom*,[265] the European Court of Human Rights considered Article 2 of the Convention. British forces had killed three terrorists in Gibraltar, believing that a terrorist attack was imminent. The Court ruled that the deprivation of life under Article 2 was justified only where 'absolutely necessary'. The Court ruled, *inter alia,* that allegations that the deaths were premeditated were not substantiated; that, given the information held by the soldiers relating to the likely terrorist attack, their reaction did not amount to a violation of Article 2. However, by 10 votes to nine, the Court ruled that there was a lack of appropriate care in the control and organisation of the arrest operation and that, accordingly, the use of force was greater than absolutely necessary in the defence of persons from unlawful violence within the meaning of Article 2. No compensation would be payable, however, given that the persons killed were terrorists.

The Convention on Human Rights was invoked in relation to the alleged use of excessive force in *Andronicus and Constantinou v Cyprus*.[266] In that case, Article 2 of the Convention was violated by the police when the police fired several rounds of bullets at a hostage taker, but instead killed the hostage. The police were found to have acted with excessive force in the circumstances.

---

264 See Kitchin, H, *Gibraltar Report: An Independent Observer's Report of the Inquest into the Deaths of Mairead Farrell, Daniel McCann and Sean Savage, Gibraltar, September 1988*, 1989, London: NCCL.

265 Case 17/1994/464/545: (1995) *The Times,* 9 October.

266 (1996) 22 EHRR CD 18.

THE REGULATION OF INVESTIGATORY POWERS ACT 2000[267]

As noted above, the main purpose of the Regulation of Investigatory Powers Act 2000 is to ensure that the relevant investigatory powers of differing agencies are exercised in accordance with human rights. The Act relates to powers concerning the interception of communications, intrusive surveillance on residential premises and in private vehicles, covert surveillance in the course of specific operations, the use of covert human intelligence sources (agents, informants, undercover officers), the acquisition of communications data and access to encrypted data. The Act is intended to ensure that the law clearly states the purposes for which such powers may be used, which authorities may exercise the powers, who should authorise the use of power, the use that can be made of material gained, independent judicial oversight of the exercise of powers and a means of redress for aggrieved individuals. The Act works in conjunction with existing legislation. The Act is in five parts: Part I dealing with interceptions of communications and the acquisition and disclosure of communications data. Part II deals with surveillance and covert human intelligence sources. Part III relates to the investigation of electronic data protected by encryption. Part IV governs the scrutiny of investigatory powers and Codes of Practice. Part V covers miscellaneous and supplemental matters.

The interception of communications

The Act repeals sections 1 to 10, section 11(2) to (5) and Schedule 1 of the Interception of Communications Act 1985. Section 1 creates the offences of unlawful interception and a separate tort of unlawful interception. The offence of unlawful interception is similar to that under section 1 of the 1985 Act, which is repealed by the 2000 Act. Unlawful interceptions relate to any communication in the course of its transmission by means of a public postal service or public telecommunications system. Conduct has lawful authority only if it is authorised under section 3 or 4, takes place in accordance with a warrant under section 5 or, in relation to any stored communication, if it is in exercise of any statutory power, other than this section, for the purpose of obtaining information or of taking possession of any document or other property. Conduct which has lawful authority shall also be taken to be lawful for all other purposes. A person having the right to control the operation or use of the system which is intercepted, or having the express or implied consent of such a person to make the interception, is excluded from criminal liability. A person found guilty of an offence is liable on conviction on indictment to a term of imprisonment not exceeding two years, or to a fine, or

---

267 The royal assent was granted on 28 July 2000.

to both. On summary conviction, there is liability to a fine not exceeding the statutory maximum. Proceedings may only be instituted with the consent of the Director of Public Prosecutions or, in Northern Ireland, with the consent of the Director of Public Prosecutions for Northern Ireland.

The circumstances in which conduct consisting of the interception, without a warrant, of a communication is lawful are defined in sections 3 and 4. Section 5 regulates interceptions under warrant. The Secretary of State may issue a warrant authorising or requiring interceptions, but shall not issue an interception warrant unless he believes that the warrant is necessary on the grounds of the interests of national security, or for the purpose of preventing or detecting serious crime, or for the purpose of safeguarding the economic well being of the United Kingdom, or for the purpose of preventing or detecting serious crime by giving effect to the provisions of any international mutual assistance agreement. The warrant shall not be issued unless the Secretary of State also believes that the conduct authorised by the warrant is *proportionate* to what is sought to be achieved by that conduct. In considering whether the requirements are satisfied in the case of any warrant, the Secretary of State must take into account whether the information which it is thought necessary to obtain under the warrant could reasonably be obtained by other means. The meaning of 'safeguarding the economic well being of the United Kingdom' under section 5(3)(c) must be read subject to section 5(5), which states that a warrant shall not be considered necessary unless the information which it is thought necessary to obtain is information relating to the acts or intentions of persons outside the British Islands.

Warrants may only be issued on the application of specified persons, namely, the Director General of the Security Service, the Chief of the Secret Intelligence Service, the Director of GCHQ, the Director General of the National Criminal Intelligence Service, the Commissioner of Police of the Metropolis, the Chief Constable of the Royal Ulster Constabulary, the chief constable of any police force under the Police (Scotland) Act 1967, the Commissioners of Customs and Excise, or a person who is the competent authority of a country outside the United Kingdom under any international mutual assistance agreement. Section 7 regulates the persons who may sign interception warrants and the circumstances in which they may do so. The warrant must be issued under the hand of the Secretary of State or, in urgent cases where the Secretary of State has expressly authorised the issue of the warrant and cases in which the warrant is for the purposes of a request for assistance made under an international mutual assistance agreement and either the subject is outside the United Kingdom or the interception relates to a place outside the United Kingdom, the warrant may be issued under the hand of a senior official. The senior official who signs the warrant must be expressly authorised by the Secretary of State to do so, which ensures that the

Secretary of State must give personal consideration to the application. A senior official is defined under section 7(1) as being a member of the Senior Civil Service. The warrant must name or describe either one person as the interception subject or a single set of premises as the premises in relation to which the interception is to take place.

Section 8 provides for two different forms which a warrant may take. Section 8(a) and (b) require that either the person or premises to be intercepted is named or described on the face of the warrant, and sub-section (2) provides that the warrant must include details setting out how the intercepted communications are to be identified. Sub-section (3) provides for certificated warrants and applies if the conditions in sub-sections (3)(a) and (b) and (4)(a) or (b) are met. Where a certificated warrant is required, there must be a certificate describing the intercepted material, the examination of which the Secretary of State considers necessary for the purposes for the issue of the warrant at the time when the Secretary of State issues the warrant, and which may be read, looked at or listened to by any other person. Any other intercepted material, though lawfully intercepted, may be so examined.

A warrant issued by a senior officer ceases to have effect at the end of the fifth working day following the day of the warrant's issue. A warrant ceases to have effect at the end of the relevant period, but is renewable. A warrant renewed under the signature of the Secretary of State shall have effect for six months. A warrant shall not be renewed unless the Secretary of State believes that the warrant continues to be necessary on grounds falling within section 5(3). A warrant must be cancelled if the Secretary of State is satisfied that it is no longer necessary. Where a warrant relates to a person outside the United Kingdom, and that person is in the United Kingdom, the warrant shall be cancelled. A warrant may be modified in the circumstances regulated by section 10. Under section 11, a warrant may be implemented by the person to whom it is addressed or by that person through or with such other persons as he may require to give assistance with giving effect to the warrant. A person required to give assistance under the section 11, who knowingly fails to comply with his or her duty, is guilty of an offence and liable on conviction on indictment to a term of imprisonment not exceeding two years, or to a fine, or to both and, on summary conviction, to a term of imprisonment not exceeding six months, or to a fine not exceeding the statutory limit, or to both.

Section 15 controls the dissemination of intercepted material. It is the duty of the Secretary of State to ensure that the number of persons to whom the material may be disclosed and the extent to which material may be disclosed or copied is limited to the minimum that is necessary for the authorised purposes. In relation to certificated warrants issued under section 8(3), which require a certificate certifying the description of intercepted material which the Secretary of State considers necessary for the purposes of the warrant, section 15 provides that such material so described may be read or looked at by any person, but that no other intercepted material, though lawfully intercepted, may be examined. The material authorised for examination is accordingly subject to ministerial control.

Section 16 provides that, subject to section 17, no evidence shall be adduced, question asked, assertion or disclosure made, or other thing done, for the purposes of, or in connection with, any legal proceedings which discloses any of the contents of an intercepted communication or any related communications data, or tends to suggest that anything falling within sub-section (2) has or may have occurred or be going to occur. The following fall within sub-section (2): conduct that was or would be an offence under section 1(1) or (2) of the Act, a breach of duty by the Secretary of State under section 1(4), the issue of a warrant under the Act or under the Interception of Communications Act 1985, the making of an application for an interception warrant or the imposition of any requirement on any person to give assistance in relation to the implementation of the warrant. The section 16 restrictions do not apply in relation to proceedings for a relevant offence,[268] civil proceedings under section 11(8) (proceedings by the Secretary of State for an injunction or other remedy to compel a person with a duty in respect of a warrant to give it effect), any proceedings before the Tribunal, proceedings on appeal or review, or proceedings before the Special Immigration Appeals Commission.

Investigation of electronic data protected by encryption

Part III of the Regulation of Investigatory Powers Act provides for the interception of data protected by encryption. The Home Secretary, commenting on the Regulation of Investigatory Powers Act, stated that it: '... will ensure that the United Kingdom's law enforcement and security agencies have the power they need to do their job effectively in a changed technological world. New communications tools such as the internet offer up huge legitimate benefits for us all. But serious criminals too have always been quick to jump on the latest technological bandwagon in their efforts to evade detection. The "e" prefix can apply to today's criminals as well as to commerce ...'[269]

Where protected information – defined as electronic data which, without the key to the data, cannot or cannot readily be accessed or cannot readily be put into an intelligible form'[270] – comes into the possession of 'any person'

---

268 Defined as being offences under the 2000 Act. The 1985 Interception of Communications Act, s 1, offences under the Official Secrets Acts 1911 and 1989 relating to documents of information, offences under the Telegraph and Post Offices Act and related offences: Regulation of Investigatory Powers Act 2000, s 17(11).

269 Home Office, *News Release*, 28 July 2000.

270 Regulation of Investigatory Powers Act 2000, s 56.

with statutory power to seize, detain, inspect, search or otherwise interfere with documents or property, or through the exercise of authorised interception powers in respect of national security matters, or through disclosure or through 'any other lawful means not involving the exercise of statutory powers' by the intelligence services, police or customs or excise, and it is necessary to decode the data through means of a key, a notice of requirement to disclose the key may be issued. The requirement to disclose a key may be made in the interests of national security, for the purpose of preventing or detecting crime or in the interests of the economic well being of the United Kingdom.[271] The Secretary of State is under a duty to ensure that arrangements are in force for requiring or authorising the section 49 notices.[272] Schedule 2 regulates authorisations. In relation to protected information, in England and Wales, written permission for the giving of section 49 notices, requiring the disclosure of a key, must be given by a circuit judge, in Scotland, a sheriff and, in Northern Ireland, a county court judge. The authorised notice must be in writing or in such a manner that produces a record of its having been given; describe the protected information to which the notice relates; specify the ground on which the information is required; specify the office, rank or position of the person giving the notice; specify the office, rank or position of the person who granted permission for the giving of the notice; specify the time by which the notice is to be complied with and must set out the disclosure that is required and the form and manner in which it is to be made.[273] Detailed provisions relate to the duty of persons given notice. Paragraph 53 of Schedule 2 relates to offences, and details of defences to proceedings, including that it was not reasonably practicable to make the disclosure required before the time in which he or she was required to make it but that the disclosure was made as soon as reasonably practicable to do so. On conviction on indictment, a person guilty of an offence is liable to imprisonment for a term of up to two years or to a fine, or both, or on summary conviction to a term of imprisonment not exceeding six months or to a fine not exceeding the statutory maximum or to both.

Safeguards relating to protected information are built into the Act and apply to the Secretary of State and all Ministers in charge of government departments, all Chief Officers of Police, Commissioners of Customs and Excise and all persons whose officers or employees include persons with duties that involve the giving of section 49 notices. These include the requirement that a key disclosed only be used for obtaining protected information in relation to which the notice was given, that the uses to which they key disclosed is put are reasonable and that the use and retention of the key are proportionate to what is sought to be achieved by its use or retention, that the key disclosed is stored securely and that all records of a key disclosed

---

271 Regulation of Investigatory Powers Act 2000, s 49.

272 *Ibid*, s 51.

273 *Ibid*, Sched 2, para 4.

are destroyed as soon as no longer needed for the purpose of enabling protected information to be put into an intelligible form. The number of persons to whom the key is disclosed or made available must be limited to the minimum necessary for enabling protected information to be put into intelligible form.[274]

Authorisation of surveillance and human intelligence sources

Part II of the Regulation of Investigatory Powers Act 2000 provides a statutory basis for the authorisation and use by the security and intelligence agencies, law enforcement and other public authorities, of covert surveillance, agents, informants and undercover officers. It is intended to regulate the use of such techniques and 'safeguard the public from unnecessary invasions of their privacy'. Section 26 defines the conduct regulated under Part II, and applies to directed surveillance, intrusive surveillance and the conduct and use of covert human intelligence sources. Surveillance is 'directed' if it is covert but not intrusive and is undertaken:

(a) for the purposes of a specific investigation or a specific operation;

(b) in such a manner as is likely to result in the obtaining of private information about a person (whether or not one specifically identified for the purposes of the investigation or operation); and

(c) otherwise than by way of an immediate response to events or circumstances the nature of which is such that it would not be reasonably practicable for an authorisation under this Part to be sought for the carrying out of the surveillance.

Surveillance is 'intrusive' if it is surveillance that either:

(a) involves the presence of an individual, or of any surveillance device, on any residential premises or in any private vehicle; or

(b) is carried out in relation to anything taking place on residential premises or in a private vehicle by means of any surveillance device that is not present on the premises or in the vehicle.

Surveillance is not intrusive if it is carried out by means of a device designed or adapted principally for the purposes of providing information about the location of a vehicle, or if it is surveillance consisting of any such interception of a communication. Surveillance which is carried out by means of a device in relation to residential premises or a private vehicle, but which is carried out without the device being present on the premises or in the vehicle, is not intrusive 'unless the device is such that it consistently provides information of the same quality and detail as might be expected to be obtained from a device actually present on the premises or in the vehicle'.

---

274 Regulation of Investigatory Powers Act 2000, para 55.

A person is defined as a 'covert human intelligence source' if he or she establishes or maintains a personal or other relationship with a person for the covert purpose of obtaining information or providing access to any information to another person, or the covert disclosure of information obtained by the use of such a relationship. The surveillance is covert if, and only if, it is carried out in a manner that is calculated to ensure that persons who are subject to the surveillance are unaware that it is or may be taking place. A purpose is covert if the relationship established or maintained is conducted in a manner calculated to ensure that one of the parties to the relationship is unaware of the purpose, and a relationship is used covertly, and information disclosed covertly, if it is used or disclosed in a manner calculated to ensure that one of the parties to the relationship is unaware of the use or disclosure.

Conduct is lawful for all purposes if an authorisation confers an entitlement to engage in that conduct on the person whose conduct it is, and his conduct is in accordance with the authorisation. No civil liability attaches to any conduct which is incidental to any conduct which is lawful as above, and is not conduct for which an authorisation or warrant is capable of being granted and might reasonably have been expected to have been sought in the case in question. The conduct authorised includes conduct outside the United Kingdom.

Those designated to have power to grant authorisations shall not grant an authorisation for the conduct or use of covert human intelligence sources unless he or she believes that the authorisation is necessary in the interests of national security; for the purpose of preventing or detecting crime or of preventing disorder; in the interest of the economic well being of the United Kingdom; in the interests of public safety; for the purpose of protecting public health; for the purpose of assessing or collecting taxes or charges due to a government department or for any purpose which is specified by an order made by the Secretary of State. An authorisation must not be granted unless the designated person believes that the authorised conduct is proportionate to what is sought to be achieved by that conduct or use. An authorisation must not be granted unless there are arrangements in place which satisfy the requirements of sub-section (5) of section 29. Those arrangements are such as are necessary for ensuring that there will be at all times a person having day to day responsibility for the agent on behalf of the relevant authority, that there is another person in the relevant authority having general oversight of the use made of the agent, that there is a person having responsibility for maintaining a record of the use made of the agent containing such particulars as may be specified in regulations made by the Secretary of State and that records that disclose the identity of the agent will not be available to persons except to the extent that such access to them is necessary.

Section 30 specifies the persons entitled to grant authorisations. The Secretary of State is a designated person for the purposes of authorisation for directed surveillance and the use of covert human intelligence sources combined with intrusive surveillance. Otherwise, the persons designated for the purposes of sections 28 and 29 are senior officers of relevant public authorities -- being the police, National Criminal Intelligence Service, National Crime Squad, the intelligence services, Ministry of Defence, Her Majesty's forces, Commissioners of Customs and Excise and any other such public authority granted power by order of the Secretary of State. In relation to Northern Ireland, the grant of authorisations is also exercisable by the First Minister and Deputy First Minister acting jointly. Neither the Secretary of State nor any senior authorising officer shall grant an authorisation for the carrying out of intrusive surveillance unless he or she believes that the authorisation is necessary in the interests of national security, for the purpose of preventing or detecting serious crime, or in the interests of the economic well being of the United Kingdom, and that the authorised surveillance is proportionate to what is sought to be achieved by carrying it out.

Commissioners and the Tribunal

The Regulation of Investigatory Powers Act 2000 repeals section 5 and Schedule 1 of the Security Services Act 1989 which provided for a Tribunal to investigate complaints. Section 9 and Schedules 1 and 2 to the Intelligence Services Act 1994, which also provided for a Tribunal, are repealed and replaced by the Regulation of Supervisory Powers Act 2000, Part IV. The Regulation of Supervisory Powers Act imposes additional functions on the Security Service Act Commissioner and the Intelligence Services Act Commissioner, requiring them to keep under review, respectively – so far as they are not required to be kept under review by the Interception of Communications Commissioner (on which office, see below) – the exercise and performance by the Secretary of State in relation to activities of the Security Service and activities of the Secret Intelligence Service and of GCHQ, and the activities in places other than Northern Ireland of officials of the Ministry of Defence and members of Her Majesty's forces. Additional functions are also conferred on the Chief Surveillance Commissioner whose powers derive from the Police Act 1997.

The Commissioner, known as the Interception of Communications Commissioner, is appointed by the Prime Minister. A person may only be appointed as Interception of Communications Commissioner if he or she holds or has held a high judicial office.[275] The Commissioner is under a duty to assist the Tribunal in connection with the investigation of any matter by the Tribunal, or otherwise for the purposes of the Tribunal's consideration or determination of any matter. It is not the Commissioner's function to keep

---

275 The current Commissioner is Lord Nolan.

under review the exercise of any power of the Secretary of State to make, amend or revoke any subordinate legislation. It is the duty of all persons employed by the Security and Intelligence Services and police to disclose or provide to the Commissioner all such documents and information as he or she may require for the purposes of enabling him or her to carry out his or her functions under Part IV. If it appears to the Commissioner that there has been a contravention of the provisions of the Act in relation to matters with which he is concerned, and that the contravention has not been the subject of a report made to the Prime Minister by the Tribunal, the Commissioner shall report to the Prime Minister. The Commissioner makes an annual report to the Prime Minister. The annual report is to be laid before each House of Parliament. If it appears to the Prime Minister, after consultation with the Interception of Communications Commissioner, that the publication of any matter in an annual report would be contrary to the public interest or prejudicial to national security, the prevention or detection of serious crime, the economic well being of the United Kingdom or the continued discharge of the functions of any public authority whose activities include activities that are subject to review by the Commissioner, the Prime Minister may exclude that matter from the report laid before each House.

The Tribunal is the only tribunal to which proceedings under section 7 of the Human Rights Act 1998 may be brought.[276] The relevant proceedings are those against any of the intelligence services, or any other person in relation to conduct by or on behalf of any of those services. The Tribunal is the appropriate forum for any complaint if it is a complaint by a person who is aggrieved by any conduct which he or she believes has taken place in relation to him or her or his or her property, to communications sent by or to or him or her, or his or her use of any postal service, telecommunications service or system and to have taken place in challengeable circumstances or to have been carried out by or on behalf of any of the intelligence services. Conduct to which proceedings relate is conduct by or on behalf of any of the intelligence services, conduct relating to the interception of communications, conduct relating to the acquisition and disclosure of communications data under Chapter II of Part I, conduct relating to surveillance under Part II, directed or intrusive surveillance in Scotland or the use of any agent in Scotland, conduct relating to protected information under section 46 and entrance into or interference with property or wireless telegraphy. The conduct in question must have been conduct by or on behalf of a person holding any office, rank or position with any of the intelligence services, any of Her Majesty's forces, any police force, the National Criminal Intelligence Service, National Crime Squad or Commissioners of Customs and Excise. The Secretary of State may by order allocate additional jurisdiction to the Tribunal, but may only do so

---

276 Section 7 proceedings relating to applications brought by victims of an alleged violation of Convention rights by a public authority.

having regard to the need to ensure that proceedings allocated to the Tribunal (from any court or tribunal) are properly heard and considered, and the need to ensure that information is not disclosed to an extent or in a manner that is contrary to the public interest or prejudicial to national security, the prevention or detection of serious crime, the economic well being of the United Kingdom or the continued discharge of the functions of any of the intelligence services. No order may be made unless a draft has been laid before Parliament and approved by a resolution of each House.

It is the duty of the Tribunal to hear and determine any proceedings brought, and to consider and determine any complaint or reference made to it. It is the duty of the Tribunal to investigate any alleged conduct, the authority for any conduct which it finds has been engaged in, and to determine the complaint by applying the same principles as would be applied by a court on an application for judicial review.[277] The Tribunal is not under a duty to hear or determine any complaint which is frivolous or vexatious. Complaints must be brought within one year after the taking place of the conduct to which it relates, but the Tribunal may, if it is equitable to do so, extend the time. The Tribunal has the power to make an award of compensation. In addition, the Tribunal may order the quashing or cancelling of any warrant or authorisation and/or the destruction of any records of information.

The extent to which the Commissioner is able to exercise any effective control over the Secretary of State is unclear. The weakness of the whole basis of the Tribunal's jurisdiction is reinforced by the absence of any appeal therefrom and the prohibition against questioning of the Tribunal and Commissioner before any court of law. With the exclusion of any form of judicial scrutiny of the Commissioner's and Tribunal's findings, the danger for the individual is all too apparent. This arrangement is far different from that pertaining in the United States, where security matters are regarded as being within the competence of the courts. In *United States v United District Court*,[278] the Supreme Court, in a unanimous judgment, declared that:

> We cannot accept the government's argument that internal security matters are too subtle and complex for judicial evaluation. There is no reason to believe that federal judges will be insensitive to or uncomprehending of the issues involved in domestic security cases ... If the threat is too subtle or complex for our senior enforcement officers to convey its significance to a court, one may question whether there is probable cause for surveillance.

---

277 See Chapter 25.
278 407 US 297 (1972).

The Canadian Security Intelligence Service Act 1984 involves judges and the Solicitor General in the process of granting warrants.[279]

In the ninth *Report of the Commissioner*,[280] it was recorded that there had been 18 complaints made against the Service which had been the subject for investigation by the Tribunal: in none of these cases were the complaints upheld.

---

279 See Burns, P, 'The law and privacy: the Canadian experience' (1976) 54 Canadian Bar Rev 1; Hazell, R, 'Freedom of information in Australia, Canada and New Zealand' (1989) 67 Public Admin 189; Hutchinson, A and Petter, A, 'Private rights/public wrongs: the liberal lie of the Charter' (1988) 38 Toronto ULJ 278.

280 *Security Services Act 1989: Report of the Commissioner for the Security Service for 1998*, Cm 4365, 1999, London: HMSO.

PART VII

INTRODUCTION TO ADMINISTRATIVE LAW

CHAPTER 24

JUDICIAL REVIEW: INTRODUCTION, JURISDICTION AND PROCEDURE[1]

THE CONSTITUTIONAL ROLE OF JUDICIAL REVIEW

Judicial review represents the means by which the courts control the exercise of governmental power. Government departments, local authorities, tribunals, State agencies and agencies exercising powers which are governmental in nature[2] must exercise their powers in a lawful manner. Judicial review has developed to ensure that public bodies which exercise law making power or adjudicatory powers are kept within the confines of the power conferred. Judicial review is concerned with the legality of the decision made, not with the merits of the particular decision. Accordingly, the task of the judges is to ensure that the exercise of any power which has been delegated to Ministers and administrative and adjudicatory bodies has been lawful according to the power given to that body by Act of Parliament. As will be seen below, there is currently academic debate concerning the appropriate basis on which the courts exercise their supervisory jurisdiction. The traditional view has been that the judge's task is to ensure that public bodies act within their powers – or *intra vires* – and that, provided that the body has acted within its powers as defined by statute, and according to the common law based rules of natural justice,[3] the body's decision will not be challengeable under the public law process of judicial review.

From this traditional perspective, judicial review is principally concerned with questions of jurisdiction and natural justice. The primary question to be asked is whether a particular person or body with delegated law making or adjudicatory powers had acted *intra vires* or *ultra vires*, and whether the decision making process entailed the application of natural justice. If the person or body was acting within its jurisdiction, and respecting the demands of natural justice, the courts would not interfere with the decision – even if the decision was in some respect wrong. Nowadays, although the judges still express their role in the traditional language of '*vires*', the approach taken is more robust than before. If a public body, as defined in law, makes an error of law, the courts – through the process of judicial review – will intervene to

---

1   See Craig, PP, *Administrative Law*, 3rd edn, 1994, London: Sweet & Maxwell; Wade, HWR and Forsyth, CF, *Administrative Law*, 7th edn, 1994, Oxford: Clarendon.

2   See, further, below.

3   On which, see Chapter 25.

ensure that the body in question reconsiders a matter and acts in a procedurally correct manner.[4]

The uncertain and expanding role of judicial review causes controversy.[5] Simply expressed, in any society regulated by a complex administrative machinery, an essential feature of that society is that administrators have a sphere of power within which, in the interests of certainty and efficiency, they should be free to operate. The doctrine of ministerial responsibility, discussed in Chapter 11, ensures that accountability for policy and administration lies with the relevant Secretary of State, who is accountable to the electorate through Parliament. However, against that argument for non-interference with matters of administration must be set the demands of individual justice and fairness. If an individual, or a body of persons, is aggrieved by an administrative decision, and their rights adversely affected, there exists a requirement that procedures exist whereby such decisions may be challenged in the courts. It is through judicial review that the requirements of legality of the exercise of powers by public bodies is tested. From this perspective, judicial review exemplifies the application of the rule of law[6] in a democratic society.[7] This raises a further question of constitutional significance. To what extent is it legitimate for a non-elected judiciary to intervene to correct the administrative process which is controlled through powers granted by the democratically elected Parliament? One response to this question is that judicial review – with respect to the review of delegated law making and adjudicatory powers – ensures that Parliament's will is observed, and judicial review may thus be regarded as an aspect of parliamentary sovereignty.[8]

As a result of extensive regulation, powers have been conferred by Parliament upon various government Departments, administrative bodies and tribunals – powers which must be exercised within the 'four corners' of the legislation. Traditionally, judicial review has been regarded as unconcerned with the merits of a particular case, or with the justice or injustice of the rules which are being applied, but rather as being concerned with the manner in which decisions have been taken: has this decision maker acted within the powers given? Most of the rules applied by administrators will be statutory, but the courts have also – under common law – developed rules which will apply to decision makers over and above the statutory rules. Thus, decision makers must not only exercise their powers in the correct

---

4   See Chapter 25 for further discussion of the concept of *ultra vires*.

5   See, eg, the differing views of Stephen Sedley J and Professor Ross Cranston expressed in Richardson, G and Genn, H (eds), *Administrative Law and Government*, 1994, Oxford: OUP, Chapters 2 and 3, respectively.

6   For an early expression of this view, see Dicey, AV, *Introduction to the Study of the Law of the Constitution*, 10th edn, 1959, London: Macmillan, Appendix 2.

7   See Allan, TRS, 'Legislative supremacy and the rule of law: democracy and constitutionalism' [1985] CLJ 111.

8   See Chapter 7.

manner as prescribed by the statute, but must also comply with the rules of reasonableness, natural justice and fairness.

In essence – and subject to changes which will be brought about by the Human Rights Act 1998, devolution to regional assemblies and the proposed Freedom of Information Act – the courts seek, by judicial review, to ensure three principal objectives:

(a) that Acts of Parliament have been correctly interpreted;

(b) that discretion conferred by statute has been lawfully exercised; and

(c) that the decision maker has acted fairly.

THE GROWTH IN PUBLIC ADMINISTRATION[9]

Judicial review derives from the historical power of the courts to keep inferior bodies within their legal powers. While 'public administration' may be traced back to Elizabethan times,[10] it was in the mid-nineteenth century that government expanded its legislative and administrative functions into areas hitherto untouched. The growth in the nineteenth century of industrialisation resulted in central regulation, for example, of town and country planning, the provision of housing and housing improvement,[11] public health,[12] regulation of the railways[13] and factory management[14] and schemes for compensation for injury.[15] One consequence of such regulation was the need for mechanisms for resolving disputes between individuals and the regulatory bodies. Statutory inquiries became the formal mechanism by which disputes were to be resolved.

The early twentieth century laid the foundations for the Welfare State. The introduction of health insurance[16] and measures to combat unemployment[17] led to the establishment of tribunals of administration and adjudication. The major reform came with the publication of the Beveridge Report,[18] which set out radical proposals for extensive reforms in social welfare and led to the introduction of the National Health Service.

---

9   See, *inter alia*, Dynes, M and Walker, D, *The Times Guide to the New British State: The Government Machine in the 1990s*, 1995, London: Times Books.

10 Eg, the Poor Relief Act 1601.

11 Artisans' and Labourers' Dwelling Improvement Act 1875; Housing of the Working Classes Act 1890.

12 Public Health Acts 1848, 1872, 1875.

13 From the 1840s.

14 Factory Act 1833.

15 Workmen's Compensations Acts 1897 and 1906.

16 National Insurance Act 1911.

17 Labour Exchanges Act 1909 and National Insurance Act 1911.

18 *Social Insurance and Allied Services*, Cmnd 6404, 1942, London: HMSO.

To portray succinctly the administrative system existing nowadays is not an easy task. As with so much of the institutional framework of the State, developments have proceeded in a pragmatic, ad hoc fashion. In 1980, the *Report on Non-Departmental Public Bodies*[19] classified administrative bodies into executive bodies, advisory bodies and tribunals. The Report cited 489 executive bodies. The work of tribunals and inquiries had earlier been investigated by the Franks Committee, whose report[20] led to the passing of the Tribunals and Inquiries Act 1958. Today, over 40 different tribunals exist, with jurisdiction over such diverse subject matters as commerce, economic matters, education, employment, Foreign Compensation, housing, physical and mental health, immigration, the National Health Service, pensions and residential homes.

What is a 'public body' for the purposes of judicial review?

Judicial review is only available to test the lawfulness of decisions made by public bodies. If judicial review is applied for, and the court rules that the body whose decision is being challenged is a private body, then the remedy of the aggrieved individual will lie in private law, not public law, proceedings. In determining whether or not the body whose decision is being challenged on an application for judicial review is a public, as opposed to private, body, the court will look at its functions. The test is not whether or not the authority is a government body as such but, rather, whether it is a body exercising powers analogous to those of government bodies. National public agencies have been a feature of administration since the Reform Act of 1832. The Poor Law Commissioners established in 1834, for whom there was no responsible Minister in Parliament (until 1847) are an early example of such an agency. The post Second World War nationalisation programmes of the Labour government[21] and the expansion of welfare provision, both then and subsequently, resulted in numerous public bodies being established which were not government bodies, nor were they part of local government. Examples of such bodies include the British Broadcasting Authority, Legal Aid Board, Atomic Energy Authority and British Airports Authority. It has been estimated that, by 1991, there were some 1,444 public bodies which were not related to government departments.[22] In 1979, the incoming Conservative government was firmly committed to privatisation. British Gas, British Airways, British Rail, British Telecom, the water supply industry and

---

19 Cmnd 7797, 1980, London: HMSO.
20 *Report of the Committee on Administrative Tribunals and Enquiries*, Cmnd 218, 1957, London: HMSO.
21 1945–51.
22 *Public Bodies*, 1991, London: HMSO.

electricity industry have all been privatised.[23] The drive towards privatisation and reduced State holdings in many other enterprises[24] has not, however, reduced the number of public bodies. Parallelling the privatisation movement has been the growth in standard setting and regulatory bodies designed to ensure appropriate accountability of providers to consumers. The Police Complaints Authority, Lord Chancellor's Advisory Committee on Legal Education and Conduct, Higher Education Funding Council, and Human Fertilisation and Embryology Authority are all examples of such bodies which have been created under statute.[25] Furthermore, there have been a number of regulatory bodies established on a voluntary basis. The Press Complaints Commission, the City Panel on Takeovers and Mergers, the Advertising Standards Authority, the Jockey Club and Football Association are all examples of such bodies. One question which arises is how the courts determine whether a body – howsoever established – is a public body and thus amenable to judicial review of its decisions. The City Panel on Takeovers and Mergers provided an opportunity for judicial analysis of public and private bodies.

THE COURTS' INTERPRETATION OF PUBLIC BODIES

In *R v City Panel on Takeovers and Mergers ex parte Datafin Ltd*,[26] the Takeover Panel had dismissed a complaint made by a bidder of 'acting in concert' contrary to the rules on takeovers. The bidder applied for judicial review. The court declined to grant the application on the basis that there were no grounds for judicial review[27] but, nevertheless, rejected the claim made by the City Panel that the court had no jurisdiction to consider the application. The Panel was subject to judicial review, despite its lack of statutory or prerogative source of power, because it was a body exercising public functions analogous to those which could be, or could have been in the absence of the Panel, exercised by a government department.[28] Lord Justice Lloyd stated that, for the most part, the source of the power will be decisive. Accordingly, if a body is set up under statute or by delegated legislation, then the source of the

---

23 Civil Aviation Act 1980, Gas Act 1986, Water Act 1989, Electricity Act 1989. Plans to privatise the Post Office were abandoned in 1994 after a backbench revolt against the plans.

24 Eg, British Petroleum, British Nuclear Fuels Ltd, Cable and Wireless, Rolls Royce, Jaguar.

25 Police and Criminal Evidence Act 1984, Courts and Legal Services Act 1990 and Higher Education Act 1992, Human Fertilisation and Embryology Act 1990.

26 [1987] 2 QB 815.

27 On which, see below.

28 See Lee, S, 'And so to school' (1987) 103 LQR 166; and see Jowell, J, 'The Takeover Panel: autonomy, flexibility and legality' [1991] PL 149.

power brings the body within the scope of judicial review. However, Lloyd LJ also recognised that in some cases the matter would be unclear. Where that situation existed, it was necessary to look beyond the source of the power and consider the 'nature of the power' being exercised. In Lloyd LJ's view, '[i]f a body in question is exercising public law functions, or if the exercise of its functions have public law consequences, then that may be sufficient to bring the body within the reach of judicial review'.

By contrast with the *City Panel on Takeover and Mergers* case, in *R v Disciplinary Committee of the Jockey Club ex parte Aga Khan*,[29] the Aga Khan sought judicial review of the Jockey Club's decision to disqualify his winning horse from a race for failing a dope test, and the court ruled that it had no jurisdiction. The relationship between racehorse owners and the Club, and the powers of the Club, derived from agreement between the parties and was a matter of private rather than public law.[30] The same principle will be applied whenever a matter is regulated by contract between two private parties – the matter is one of private and not public law. There is a fine distinction to be drawn here. The regulation of a private school, for example, has been held to be a matter of private law, whereas the regulation of City Technical Colleges, a non-fee paying publicly funded institution, is a matter of public law. However, where a pupil attends a private school under a publicly funded assisted places scheme, that school falls within the jurisdiction for judicial review in relation to the school's decision, in particular, the decision to expel a pupil.[31]

Review and appeal[32]

Judicial review must be distinguished from an appeal against a decision. The court and tribunal structure provides a more or less rational appeal structure for those aggrieved by a judicial decision. The appellate court will have the power to reconsider the case and to substitute its own decision for that of the lower court. An appeal may be made on both the law and the facts of the case, so that a full re-hearing may take place. Judicial review, by contrast, is concerned solely with the manner in which the decision maker has applied the relevant rules: it is thus procedural in nature. It is not for the court – in judicial review proceedings – to substitute its judgment for that of the decision

---

29 [1993] 1 WLR 909.

30 See, also, *R v Chief Rabbi ex parte Wachmann* [1993] 2 All ER 249; and Barendt, E, Baron, A, Herberg, JW and Jowell, J, 'Public law' (1993) 46 CLP Annual Review 101.

31 See *R v Governors of Haberdashers' Aske's Hatcham College Trust ex parte T* (1994) *The Times*, 19 October, *per* Dyson J.

32 See *Chief Constable of the North Wales Police v Evans* [1982] 1 WLR 1155.

making body to which powers have been delegated but, rather, to ensure that the adjudicator has kept within the rules laid down by statute and the common law. In short, the role of the courts in judicial review is to exercise a supervisory, not an appellate, jurisdiction. Judicial review 'is not an appeal from a decision, but a review of the manner in which the decision was made'.[33]

Judicial review derives from the courts' inherent powers to keep decision making bodies within the bounds of their powers, and to provide remedies for abuse of power, and its purpose is not to substitute a decision of the court for the decision of the administrative body.

Applying for leave for judicial review[34]

It must also be noted that there is no unfettered right to judicial review. The aggrieved individual must seek leave to apply for judicial review, and a number of criteria, which are discussed below, govern the exercise of the discretion to grant or refuse the application for judicial review.

The requirement to seek leave for judicial review is controversial, and there are cogent arguments for its repeal. For example, the JUSTICE-All Souls Report[35] argued for repeal on the basis, first, that the leave requirement is discriminatory; secondly, that the justification for leave based on eliminating 'groundless, unmeritorious or tardy harassment' on the part of applicants can be dealt with in the same manner as in ordinary litigation;[36] and, thirdly, that the issue of standing is no longer finally determined at the stage at which the application for leave is considered.[37] However, there is support for the view that, while the need to seek leave represents a procedural hurdle which does not exist in other areas of the law, there remains a need to filter out unmeritorious cases at an early stage. The Law Commission has re-examined the question of application for leave and concluded that it remains 'essential to filter out hopeless applications for judicial review by a requirement such as leave'.[38]

---

33 *Per* Lord Brightman in *Chief Constable of the North Wales Police v Evans* [1982] 1 WLR 1155, p 1174.

34 For the criteria, see, further, below.

35 *Administrative Law: Some Necessary Reforms*, 1988. See, also, Le Sueur, AP and Sunkin, M, 'Application for judicial review' [1992] PL 102; Law Commission, *Administrative Law: Judicial Review and Statutory Appeals*, Consultation Paper No 226/HC 669.

36 As provided for by RSC Ord 18 r 19.

37 See, further, below.

38 Law Commission, *Administrative Law: Judicial Review and Statutory Appeals*, Consultation Paper No 226/HC 669. The Law Commission recommends that the application for leave be renamed the 'preliminary consideration' stage.

The outcome of judicial review[39]

Differences also exist in the respective outcomes of appeal and judicial review. In the case of appeals, where the appeal is successful, it will usually result in a new decision being substituted for the previous decision.[40] In the case of review, a successful case will usually result in the previous decision being nullified – or quashed – but no new decision will be put in its place. Instead, the body in relation to which a successful application for judicial review has been made will be directed to redetermine the case according to the correct rules and procedure, and it is by no means inevitable that the decision reached according to the lawful procedure will be more favourable to the individual than the original decision.[41]

Furthermore, there is no automatic right to a remedy in judicial review proceedings: the remedy is discretionary. The matter is contentious.[42] In some cases, the court will decline to grant a remedy. The court may hold, for example, that, while the decision making process was defective, nevertheless, the applicant has suffered no injustice, or that, even if a remedy were granted, the decision maker would reach the same conclusion on the merits, or that the impact on administration would be too great if a remedy were granted.

THE CONCEPT OF JUSTICIABILITY

Justiciability is a concept which defines the judges' view of the suitability of the subject matter to be judicially reviewed. There are some matters in relation to which the courts – mindful of the doctrine of separation of powers – prove to be exceedingly reluctant to review. Matters such as the exercise of prerogative power and, most importantly, issues of national security, and matters of high policy, the courts may regard as non-justiciable.

Matters of public policy not for judicial review[43]

Where a matter complained of involves issues of high policy, the courts will decline to exercise a supervisory function over such decisions. Matters of public policy are for determination by the executive, and not the judiciary,

---

39 On remedies, see below.
40 In some instances, a new trial may have to be ordered in order for a fresh decision to be reached.
41 See Harlow, C, 'Administrative reaction to judicial review' [1976] PL 116.
42 See Bingham, TH (Sir), 'Should public law remedies be discretionary?' [1991] PL 64.
43 Hammond, AH, *Judicial Review: The Continuing Interplay between Law and Policy* [1998] PL 1.

and any purported attempt to control the decision would be regarded as a violation of the separation of powers and an intrusion into the proper decision making sphere of the executive. For example, in *Nottinghamshire County Council v Secretary of State for the Environment*,[44] it was held that the court should not intervene to quash guidance drafted by the Secretary of State, on the authority of Parliament, setting limits to public expenditure by local authorities. Lord Scarman ruled that:

> Unless and until a statute provides otherwise, or it is established that the Secretary of State has abused his power, these are matters of political judgment for him and for the House of Commons. They are not for the judges or your Lordships' House in its judicial capacity.

Similarly, in *Hammersmith and Fulham London Borough Council v Department of the Environment*,[45] concerning the lawfulness of 'charge capping' local authorities (penalising local authorities for exceeding their budgets), the House of Lords ruled that the decision was not open to challenge on the grounds of irrationality 'short of the extremes of bad faith, improper motive or manifest absurdity'.[46] Lord Bridge went on to rule that such decisions, relating to national economic policy, 'are matters depending essentially on political judgment' and that, in the absence of any evidence of bad faith or abuse of power, the courts would be 'exceeding their proper function if they presumed to condemn the policy as unreasonable'. More recently, in *R v Parliamentary Commission for Administration ex parte Dyer*,[47] Simon Brown LJ held that matters of national policy were not open to challenge before the courts other than on the basis of bad faith, improper motive or manifest absurdity. Matters of national economic policy were for political – not judicial – judgment.[48]

The royal prerogative and judicial review

The cautious attitude which judges adopt when it comes to reviewing the exercise of the royal prerogative has been discussed in Chapter 6 and 21.[49] It will be recalled from that discussion that the courts are slow to review the exercise of prerogative power, and will decline so to do in particular where issues of national security are involved. Many of the matters which the courts regard as non-justiciable – that is to say, not within judicial competence to determine – fall within the royal prerogative. However, as discussed in

---

44 [1986] AC 240.
45 [1990] 3 All ER 589; [1991] 1 AC 521.
46 *Per* Lord Bridge.
47 [1994] 1 All ER 375.
48 See, further, below.
49 For which, see discussion of the cases involving the prerogative.

Chapter 6, the courts will not decline to judicially review a matter simply because the source of the power exercised is the royal prerogative. The House of Lords made it clear in *Council of Civil Service Unions v Minister for Civil Service*[50] that the source of the power was not determinative of whether the courts would review, but rather the matter to be decided was whether the subject matter of the application was justiciable or not. It has also been seen that the courts will not allow the prerogative to be used when an Act of Parliament has been passed to regulate a matter previously governed by the prerogative,[51] or for the prerogative to be used to defeat a right arising under statute[52] or relied upon where a statutory duty to act has been imposed on a Minister,[53] and that the failure of a Minister to comply with a direction of the court not to deport an individual would render the Minister liable in his official capacity for contempt of court.[54]

However, anomalies continue to exist. It will be recalled that, in *R v Secretary of State for the Home Department ex parte Northumbria Police Authority*,[55] the Court of Appeal ruled that the Home Secretary, notwithstanding statutory powers under the Police Act 1964, also had prerogative power to keep the peace and to use that power as a supplement to his statutory powers.[56] However, the courts are insistent that, where statute regulates a matter previously regulated by the prerogative, or where statute coexists with prerogative powers, the statutory source of power should prevail over a claim to be acting under prerogative powers.[57]

In *R v Secretary of State for Home Department ex parte Fire Brigades' Union and Others*,[58] the Home Secretary had sought to amend the scheme of payments made under the Criminal Injuries Compensation Scheme (a scheme which was established under the prerogative rather than under statute) through the use of the prerogative. In 1988, the Criminal Justice Act provided that the Home Secretary had a statutory duty to introduce a new scheme of payments. The Home Secretary had taken no action to comply with that duty. On an application for judicial review by the Fire Brigades' Union, whose members would be adversely affected by the new scheme of payments, the Court of Appeal held that the Home Secretary could not – so long as the Criminal

---

50 [1985] AC 374.
51 *Attorney General v de Keyser's Royal Hotel Ltd* [1920] AC 508.
52 *Laker Airways v Department of Trade* [1977] QB 643.
53 *R v Secretary of State for the Home Department ex parte Fire Brigades' Union and Others* [1995] 2 WLR 1; 2 All ER 244, HL.
54 *M v Home Office* [1993] 3 WLR 433.
55 [1988] 1 All ER 556. For discussion, see Chapter 6.
56 *Council of Civil Service Unions v Minister for Civil Service* [1985] AC 374.
57 See *Attorney General v de Keyser's Royal Hotel Ltd* [1920] AC 508; and *Laker Airways v Department of Trade* [1977] QB 643.
58 [1995] 2 WLR 1.

Justice Act 1988 provisions remained on the statute book – exercise power under the prerogative to implement a new scheme. It was open to the government to seek to repeal the statutory provisions, or to amend them. However, it was not lawful to attempt to use a prerogative in order to avoid an existing statutory duty.[59]

THE EXCLUSION OF JUDICIAL REVIEW

It is a first principle of justice and the rule of law that public bodies are required to act within the scope of the powers allocated to them by Parliament and, accordingly, in principle, judicial review should lie wherever the *vires* of administrative action is in question. However, that principle must be set in the balance against the needs of certain administration, and the necessary restrictions which may be imposed on individuals or bodies seeking to disrupt the administrative process, without good cause. The balance to be struck between these often competing principles is a difficult matter. Where Parliament limits the availability of judicial review, the courts will adopt a restrictive interpretation to the statutory words, employing the presumption that Parliament did not intend – save in the most express manner – to exclude the jurisdiction of the courts. A number of different statutory means are employed in the attempt to limit the availability of judicial review. In summary, Parliament may adopt the following means:

(a) clauses which are intended to prevent any challenge;

(b) clauses which are designed to limit review to a specified time period;

(c) 'conclusive evidence' clauses.

Attempts to exclude judicial review totally

In *R v Medical Appeal Tribunal ex parte Gilmore*,[60] the statute provided that 'the decision on any medical question by a medical appeal tribunal ... is final'. Under an industrial injuries scheme, compensation for accidental industrial injuries was set under a tariff. Gilmore lost the sight of both eyes in two accidents and was assessed at a disablement of 20 per cent. The tariff provided that the loss of sight in both eyes entitled the applicant to a 100 per cent assessment. The tribunal had, accordingly, made an error of law. However, the opportunity for the court to redress the wrong turned on the exclusion of

---

59 The House of Lords upheld the decision of the Court of Appeal: [1995] 2 All ER 244. See, further, Chapter 6.

60 [1957] 1 QB 574.

review in the statute. The Court of Appeal held that the jurisdiction of the court was not ousted by the statutory words; Denning LJ, stating that:

> ... the remedy of certiorari is never to be taken away by any statute except by the most clear and explicit words. The word 'final' is not enough. That only means 'without appeal'. It does not mean 'without recourse to certiorari'. It makes the decision final on the facts, but not final on the law. Notwithstanding that the decision is by a statute made 'final', certiorari can still issue for excess of jurisdiction or for error of law on the face of the record ...[61]

However, in *South East Asia Firebricks v Non-Metallic Mineral Products Manufacturing Employees' Union*,[62] an 'ouster clause' succeeded. The Malaysian Industrial Court, in a successful legal challenge by trades unions, had ordered employers to take back employees after a strike. Statute[63] provided that an award of the Court shall be 'final and conclusive' and that '... no award shall be challenged, appealed against, reviewed, quashed or called into question in any court of law'.

The Privy Council, citing *Gilmore* with approval, nevertheless distinguished between an error which affected the jurisdiction of the court to make a determination[64] and decisions which, whilst in error, were not of such a fundamental nature as to deprive the court of jurisdiction. In this case, the error was within the jurisdiction of the court and, accordingly, the ouster clause was effective. According to Lord Fraser of Tullybelton:

> ... the Industrial Court applied its mind to the proper question for the purpose of making its award. The award was accordingly within the jurisdiction of that court, and neither party has contended to the contrary ... the error or errors did not affect the jurisdiction of the Industrial Court and their Lordships are therefore of the opinion that section 29(3)(a) effectively ousted the jurisdiction of the High Court to quash the decision by certiorari proceedings ...[65]

The seminal case on ouster clauses is *Anisminic v Foreign Compensation Commission*.[66] In 1956, property in Egypt belonging to an English company was sequestrated by the Egyptian authorities and subsequently sold to an Egyptian organisation, TEDO. Anisminic then sold to TEDO its mining business. In 1959, a Treaty signed by the United Kingdom and the United Arab Republic provided for the return of sequestrated property, other than property sequestrated in a period during which Anisminic's property was taken over. The Foreign Compensation Commission (FCC), established to make awards of compensation to companies adversely affected by

---

61 [1957] 1 QB 574, p 583.

62 [1981] AC 363.

63 Industrial Relations Act 1967, s 29(3)(a).

64 Relying on *Anisminic v Foreign Compensation Commission* [1968] 2 QB 862.

65 [1981] AC 363, pp 373–74.

66 [1969] 2 AC 147. See Wade, HWR, 'Constitutional and administrative aspects of the *Anisminic* case' (1969) 85 LQR 198.

sequestration of property, ruled that Anisminic did not qualify for compensation. The Foreign Compensation Order 1962,[67] Article 4(1)(b)(ii), provided that that both the applicant and the successor in title be British nationals. TEDO – the successor in title – was not a British national and, accordingly, Anisminic's claim failed. The Foreign Compensation Act 1950 provided that the decisions of the FCC 'shall not be called in question in any court of law'.[68]

Anisminic sought judicial review of the FCC's decision. The question for the court was whether the phrase 'shall not be questioned' succeeded in ousting the jurisdiction of the courts, or whether, notwithstanding that section, the courts had the power to rule on the lawfulness of the FCC's decision. The House of Lords ruled that the jurisdiction of the courts was not ousted. Accordingly the court had power to review the FCC's decision, which it declared to be null and void. The FCC had acted outside its jurisdiction by misinterpreting the Order in Council and reached a decision based on a ground which it was not entitled to take into account, namely the nationality of the successor in title. The nationality of the successor in title, according to the House of Lords, was not a relevant consideration when the applicant was the original owner of the sequestered property. The House of Lords ruled unanimously that section 4(4) did not protect decisions which were taken outside of jurisdiction.

The *Anisminic* decision raises complex issues. The House of Lords appeared to destroy the distinction between errors of law within the jurisdiction of the decision making body, which had previously been regarded as non-reviewable, and errors of law which took the decision maker outside its jurisdiction and were therefore reviewable. In effect, clauses which attempted to oust the jurisdiction of the courts appeared to have been rendered meaningless. The problem which remains is whether *Anisminic* provides clear guidelines as to how to distinguish between those elements of a tribunal's decision which, if decided incorrectly, cause the tribunal to exceed its jurisdiction, and those aspects of a tribunal's decision which, although decided incorrectly, do not cause the tribunal to exceed its jurisdiction — in other words the error is 'within jurisdiction'. The decision also reveals judicial emphasis on the rule of law – even in the face of apparently clear words that Parliament does not intend review to take place. In the view of Wade and Forsyth, the judges in *Anisminic* have ensured that the courts are 'the exclusive arbiters on all questions of law'.[69]

In *Pearlman v Keepers and Governors of Harrow School*,[70] the Court of Appeal ruled that the misinterpretation of provisions in the Housing Act 1974, by the

---

67   Egypt: Determination and Registration of Claims. An Order in Council.
68   Foreign Compensation Act 1950, s 4(4).
69   *Op cit*, Wade and Forsyth, fn 1, p 305.
70   [1979] QB 56.

county court, amounted to a 'jurisdictional error' which nullified the court's decision. Lord Denning MR, in *Pearlman*, stated that the distinction between errors which entail an excess of jurisdiction and an error made within jurisdiction should be abandoned.

The question of exactly which errors of law are 'jurisdictional' was considered in *Re Racal Communication Ltd*.[71] In *Racal*, the Director of Public Prosecutions (DPP) sought an order of the court[72] in order to obtain evidence relating to an alleged offence. The order was refused. Section 441(3) of the Companies Act provided that no appeal lay from a decision of the judge hearing the application. Nevertheless, the DPP appealed, and the Court of Appeal allowed the appeal, relying on *Anisminic* and *Pearlman*. Lord Denning ruled that the 'no appeal' clause was of no effect, for the judge had misconstrued the words in section 411 of the Act. The House of Lords overturned the Court of Appeal's decision, approving of Geoffrey Lane LJ's dissenting judgment in *Pearlman*, in which he had held that the judge had done nothing which was outside his scope of inquiry. A distinction was drawn between errors made by a tribunal or other administrative bodies, which would be reviewable, and errors made by a court of law. Lord Diplock, in *Racal*, supported the view expressed by Lord Denning MR in *Pearlman*, stating that:

> The breakthrough made by *Anisminic* was that, as respects administrative tribunals and authorities, the old distinction between errors of law that went to jurisdiction and errors of law that did not was for practical purposes abolished.[73]

A further distinction, and limitation to the *Anisminic* principle, is to be seen in *R v Lord President of the Privy Council ex parte Page*.[74] There, the issue concerned a decision made by a university Visitor, and whether such a decision was reviewable on the basis of *Anisminic*. The House of Lords ruled that it was not. The powers of Visitors were established by the founder of the university, who had established a body of law and the office of Visitor to enforce that 'domestic' law. Accordingly, *per* Lord Browne-Wilkinson, the Visitor could not 'err in law in reaching his decision since the general law is not the applicable law'. Accordingly the Visitor could not act *ultra vires* by applying his interpretation of the rules of the university. Jurisdiction to review did lie in cases where the Visitor acted outside his jurisdiction, or where he acted without regard to the rules of natural justice. However, there was no jurisdiction to review decisions taken within jurisdiction.

---

71   [1981] AC 374.
72   Under the Companies Act 1948, s 411.
73   *Re Racal Communications Ltd* [1981] AC 374, p 383.
74   [1992] 3 WLR 1112.

Parliament continues to insert exclusion clauses. See, for example, section 9 of the Interception of Communications Act 1985 and the Security Services Act 1989, discussed in Chapter 23.

Time limits on judicial review

In the attempt to protect decisions from challenges which may impede or otherwise affect their implementation, statute may provide that there should be no challenge by way of judicial review other than within a specified time period. *Smith v East Elloe Rural District Council*[75] illustrates the attitude of the courts to such time limits. In *Smith*, a challenge to the validity of a compulsory purchase order was limited, under statute, to a six week period following the date of confirmation of the order. If not challenged within that period the order 'shall not ... be questioned in any legal proceedings whatsoever'. Mrs Smith did not challenge the order within the time limit but, some six years later, sought to challenge the order on the basis that the clerk to the council had acted in bad faith, and that bad faith was a ground on which – despite the clear wording of the time limit in the statute – the order's validity could be impugned. The House of Lords, by a majority, rejected this view. It was, however, unanimously agreed that Mrs Smith could proceed against the clerk to the council, for damages, on the basis of bad faith in procuring the order. Viscount Simonds explained the attitude of the court:

> My Lords, I think that anyone bred in the tradition of the law is likely to regard with little sympathy legislative provisions for ousting the jurisdiction of the court ... But it is our plain duty to give the words of an Act their proper meaning, and ... I find it quite impossible to qualify the words ... in the manner suggested ... What is abundantly clear is that words are used which are wide enough to cover any kind of challenge which an aggrieved person may think fit to make. I cannot think of any wider words ... I come, then to the conclusion that the court cannot entertain this action in so far as it impugns the validity of the compulsory purchase order ...[76]

The Court of Appeal in *R v Secretary of State for the Environment ex parte Ostler*[77] followed the reasoning in *Smith*. In *Ostler*, the Highways Act 1959[78] provided that an aggrieved person had the right to challenge the validity of a compulsory purchase order – on the basis of *ultra vires* – within six weeks from the date of publication of the order. Subject to that right, the order 'shall not be questioned in any legal proceedings whatsoever'. The proposed road building scheme had two stages. The first involved the acquisition of the land for the main road; the second related to the acquisition of land for the side

---

75 [1956] AC 736.
76 *Ibid*, pp 750–52.
77 [1976] 3 All ER 90.
78 Highways Act 1959, Sched 2, paras 2 and 3.

roads which would give access to the main road. Two public inquiries were held, at the first of which there were allegations that an officer of the Department of the Environment had given assurances that vehicular access would be gained by a widening of the access road during the second phase of the development. Ostler's business would be affected by the widening of the access road, but he was unaware of the assurance allegedly given at the inquiry and did not challenge the decision. At the second inquiry, Ostler wished to object to the road widening, and wanted to give evidence that he would have objected at the first inquiry had he known of the secret undertaking. He was refused permission to give evidence on the basis that his objection related to the first stage of the development. Ostler subsequently learned of the undertakings and sought to challenge the compulsory order on the ground that natural justice had been denied and that the order had been made in bad faith amounting to fraud. The court accepted that, had Ostler challenged the order within six weeks, the court would have considered his complaint. The court was faced with the question as to whether *Anisminic* applied, or whether the decision in *Smith v East Elloe* was the relevant precedent. Lord Denning MR considered the two precedent decisions and distinguished between them in three respects. First, the limitation in the *Smith* case amounted to a time limitation for review, as opposed to a purported total ouster of jurisdiction as in *Anisminic*. Secondly, the decision by the Foreign Compensation Board in *Anisminic* was a 'truly judicial' decision, whereas that in *Smith* was an administrative decision. Thirdly, in *Anisminic*, the court was required to consider the 'actual determination of the tribunal', whereas, in *Smith*, the court was considering the process by which the decision was reached. Lord Denning concluded:

> ... the policy of the 1959 Act is that when a compulsory purchase order has been made, then if it has been wrongly obtained or made, a person aggrieved should have a remedy. But he must come promptly. He must come within six weeks. If he does so, the court can and will entertain his complaint. But if the six weeks expire without any application being made, the court cannot entertain it afterwards. The reason is because, as soon as that time has elapsed, the authority will take steps to acquire property, demolish it and so forth. The public interest demand that they should be safe in doing so.[79]

Exclusion of review by 'conclusive evidence clauses'

Parliament may effectively oust the jurisdiction of the courts by inserting a clause into statute which provides that a subordinate piece of legislation shall have effect 'as if enacted in this Act', or that confirmation of an order by a designated Minister shall be 'conclusive evidence that the requirements of this Act have been complied with, and that the order has been duly made and is

---

79 [1976] 3 All ER 90, pp 95–96.

within the powers of this Act'. Such clauses were strongly criticised in 1932 by the Committee on Ministers' Powers[80] but, nevertheless, they continue to be used and have been effective in ousting judicial review. In *R v Registrar of Companies ex parte Central Bank of India*,[81] for example, a clause in the Companies Act 1985 effectively ousted the jurisdiction of the courts. PP Craig comments that such clauses have 'passed out of fashion'.[82] Nevertheless, the potential for their use, and their effectiveness, provides the basis for a damaging exclusion of judicial review.

THE BASIS FOR JUDICIAL REVIEW

The Supreme Court Act 1981

The basis for review today lies in section 31 of the Supreme Court Act 1981 and the attendant Order 53 of the Rules of the Supreme Court.

Section 31 provides, in part, that:

(1) An application to the High Court for one or more of the following forms of relief, namely:

    (a) an order of mandamus, prohibition or certiorari;

    (b) a declaration or injunction under sub-section (2); or

    (c) an injunction under section 30 restraining a person not entitled to do so from acting in an office to which that section applies, shall be made in accordance with rules of court by a procedure to be known as an application for judicial review.

(2) A declaration may be made or an injunction granted under this subsection in any case where an application for judicial review, seeking that relief, has been made and the High Court considers that, having regard to:

    (a) the nature of the matters in respect of which relief may be granted by orders of mandamus, prohibition or certiorari;

    (b) the nature of the persons and bodies against whom relief may be granted by such orders; and

    (c) all the circumstances of the case, it would be just and convenient for the declaration to be made or for the injunction to be granted, as the case may be.

(3) No application for judicial review shall be made unless the leave of the High Court has been obtained in accordance with rules of court; and the court shall not grant leave to make such an application unless it considers that the applicant has a sufficient interest in the matter to which the application relates.

---

80   Cmd 4060, 1932, London: HMSO.
81   [1986] QB 1114.
82   *Op cit*, Craig, fn 1, p 604.

Under the Rules of the Supreme Court, an action must be brought within three months of the decision against which review is sought, although the period is extendable by the court:

> (4)   (1) An application for judicial review shall be made promptly and in any event within three months from the date when grounds for the application first arose unless the Court considers that there is good reason for extending he period within which the application shall be made ...
>
>   (3) Paragraph (1) is without prejudice to any statutory provision which has the effect of limiting the time within which an application for judicial review may be made.[83]

STANDING TO APPLY FOR JUDICIAL REVIEW[84]

The 'sufficient interest' test[85]

The Supreme Court Act 1981 provides that the court must not grant leave for an application for judicial review 'unless it considers that the applicant has a sufficient interest [otherwise expressed as "standing" or *locus standi*] in the matter to which the application relates'. The justification for such a requirement lies in the need to limit challenges to administrative decision making to genuine cases of grievance and to avoid unnecessary interference in the administrative process by those whose objectives are not authentic. The applicant may be an individual whose personal rights and interests have been affected by a decision, or an individual concerned with official decisions which affect the interests of society as a whole. Alternatively, the application may be brought by an interest or pressure group desiring to challenge a decision which affects the rights and interests of members of that group or society at large.

The manner in which the test is applied

The test of 'sufficient interest' was provided in *R v Inland Revenue Commissioners ex parte National Federation of Self-Employed and Small Businesses*.[86] The House of Lords' approach was as follows. The question as to whether there is standing should be examined in two stages. At the first

---

83 RSC Ord 53 SI 1977/1955, as amended by SI 1980/2000.
84 See Cane, P, 'The function of standing rules in administrative law' [1980] PL 303; Schiemann, K (Sir), '*Locus standi*' [1990] PL 342.
85 Supreme Court Act 1981, s 31(3).
86 [1982] AC 617.

instance, standing should be considered when leave to apply is sought. At that stage, the court is concerned, according to Lord Scarman, to ensure that 'it prevents abuse by busybodies, cranks and other mischief makers'. If leave is granted, the court may – at a second stage, when the merits of the case are known – revise its original decision and decide that after all the applicants do not have sufficient interest.

Individual standing: personal rights and interests

Given the breadth of administrative decision making in a heavily regulated society, individuals may have their rights or expectations affected in multifarious ways, as has been seen above. Two further examples from the case law illustrate the concept of individual standing. In *Schmidt v Secretary of State for Home Affairs*,[87] students who had entered the country as 'students of scientology' challenged the decision of the Home Office not to allow them to remain once the permitted period of stay had expired. The students had a 'legitimate expectation'[88] that they would be allowed to make representations to the Home Office, which they were denied, over a matter affecting their individual liberty. The students had 'sufficient interest' for leave to be granted.

In *R v Secretary of State for Foreign and Commonwealth Affairs ex parte Rees-Mogg*,[89] the applicant sought judicial review of the government's ratification of the Treaty on European Union without parliamentary consent. Rees-Mogg was held to have sufficient standing, but the application was dismissed on the basis that the issue was non-justiciable.[90]

The standing of interest and pressure groups

Actions in defence of the group's own interests

A group may have its interests adversely affected by administrative decision making. By way of illustration, in *R v Liverpool Corporation ex parte Liverpool Taxi Fleet Operators' Association*,[91] Liverpool Corporation had the duty of licensing taxis and fixing the number of licences to be granted. When the Corporation announced that the number of licences was to be increased,

---

87 [1969] 2 Ch 149.
88 See, further, below.
89 [1994] 2 WLR 115; [1994] 1 All ER 457.
90 For the meaning of 'justiciability', see above. See, also, *Blackburn v Attorney General* [1971] 1 WLR 1037, wherein a challenge to accession to the Treaty of Rome was unsuccessfully challenged.
91 [1972] 2 QB 299. Discussed above.

without consulting the Operators' Association, leave to apply for judicial review was sought. The Association had sufficient standing. Equally, in *Royal College of Nursing v Department for Health and Social Security*,[92] the Royal College had standing to challenge a departmental circular concerning the role of nurses in abortions.

Both these cases involve organisations seeking to challenge decisions which affect their own members. Accordingly, the standing requirement is relatively easy to satisfy, since each of their members would have individual standing. The position is less straightforward where a group seeks to defend what it regards as the wider interests of society.

The standing of interest and pressure groups acting in the public interest

Inland Revenue Commissioners v National Federation of Self-Employed and Small Businesses[93] provided the test for standing. The facts, in brief, entailed the employment of casual labour on newspapers, where the workers frequently adopted false names and paid no income tax. The Inland Revenue Commissioners (the IRC) entered into an agreement with the relevant trades unions, workers and employers, to the effect that, if the workers filled in tax returns for the previous two years, the IRC would not pursue tax due for previous years. The National Federation (an association of taxpayers) argued that the IRC had no power to enter into this agreement and sought judicial review. The IRC defended the action on the basis that the National Federation did not have sufficient interest – or standing (*locus standi*) – to apply for judicial review. The court upheld the IRC's claim. The House of Lords ruled that the court had been correct in granting leave at the first stage, but that on the facts – the second stage – the National Federation lacked sufficient interest to challenge the legality of the agreement. The House of Lords ruled that there was no standing to challenge the particular wrongdoing alleged but that, if the Revenue had in fact been acting with impropriety, there would have been standing in a taxpayer to challenge its unlawful acts. In *R v Her Majesty's Treasury ex parte Smedley*,[94] the applicant for review sought to challenge the decision of the Treasury to pay a sum of money from the Consolidated Fund, without express parliamentary approval, to meet European Community obligations. Smedley was thus applying in his own interest and in the interests of all British taxpayers and electors.[95] The court held that he had standing, although the challenge failed on its merits. A case to be distinguished from the *National Federation* case is that of *R v Attorney General ex*

---

92 [1981] AC 800.
93 [1982] AC 617.
94 [1985] 1 QB 657.
95 *Per* Sir John Donaldson MR.

parte ICI plc.[96] In the *ICI* case, the application was based on a complaint that four competitor companies had been assessed at too lenient a rate, contrary to the Oil Taxation Act 1975. The court held that the company had standing: it had a genuine and substantial complaint.

The judges are, however, not united in their approach to the 'sufficient interest' test, which confers on the courts a great deal of discretion. In *R v Secretary of State for the Environment ex parte Rose Theatre Trust Company Ltd*,[97] Schiemann J cited a number of propositions which he deduced from the *IRC* case. The *Rose Theatre* case concerned the question of whether a company which had been incorporated for the purpose of campaigning to save the historic Globe Theatre site in London had sufficient interest, or *locus standi*. Included in the guidelines were that the question of whether sufficient interest exists is not purely a matter within the discretion of the court; that sufficient interest did not necessarily entail a direct financial or legal interest; that the assertion of an interest by a person or a group does not mean that sufficient interest exists; and that, even where thousands of people joined together in a campaign, that was not conclusive that sufficient interest existed. The court ruled that the company did not have sufficient interest.[98] However, in *R v Poole Borough Council ex parte BeeBee*,[99] the same judge ruled that two pressure groups, The World Wildlife Fund (WWF) and the British Heperetological Society (BHS), had sufficient interest to challenge a decision of the Council which had granted planning permission to itself for the development of a heathland with designated 'special scientific interest' status. The BHS had a financial interest in the site, and the WWF had undertaken to pay any legal costs if necessary.[100]

A liberal approach to sufficient interest was also taken in *R v Secretary of State for the Environment ex parte Greenpeace Ltd (No 2)*.[101] Greenpeace applied for judicial review to challenge the decision of the Inspectorate of Pollution to allow the siting of a nuclear reprocessing plant (THORP) at Sellafield. It was held that the Inspectorate had not abused its powers in varying British Nuclear Fuel plc's licence. However, while Greenpeace lost the case, the court nevertheless ruled that Greenpeace did have standing to challenge the decision. It was in the interests of justice to allow Greenpeace – an organisation with over 400,000 supporters in the United Kingdom – to bring an action on behalf of all concerned with the project. The court declined to

---

96   (1986) 60 TC 1.

97   [1990] 2 WLR 186; 1 All ER 754.

98   And see *op cit*, Schiemann, fn 84.

99   [1991] 2 PLR 27.

100 But for another decision denying sufficient interest to interest groups, see *R v Darlington Borough Council ex parte Association of Darlington Taxi Owners* (1994) *The Times*, 21 January; [1994] COD 424.

101 [1994] 4 All ER 352.

follow the *Rose Theatre* decision, but warned that it should not be assumed that Greenpeace or other pressure groups would automatically be held to have sufficient interest in any future case.

Further cases involving successful challenges by pressure groups are that of *R v Secretary of State for Foreign and Commonwealth Affairs ex parte World Development Movement Ltd*,[102] *R v Secretary of State for Employment ex parte Equal Opportunities Commission*[103] (the *EOC* case) and *R v Secretary of State for the Environment ex parte the Royal Society for the Protection of Birds* (the *RSPB* case).[104] In the first case, the World Development Movement (WDM) sought judicial review of the Foreign Secretary's decision to grant financial aid to Malaysia for the building of the Pergau dam. The WDM argued that the Secretary of State had exceeded his powers. The court held that the WDM had sufficient interest. The WDM played a prominent role in giving advice and assistance in relation to aid and had consultative status with United Nation's bodies. Further, it was unlikely that there would be any other person or body with sufficient interest to challenge the decision. In the *EOC* case, the Equal Opportunities Commission (EOC) sought a declaration that the United Kingdom was in breach of European Community law obligations in relation to Article 119 of the EC Treaty and Equal Pay and Equal Treatment Directives of the Community. The alleged breach concerned the Employment Protection (Consolidation) Act 1978, which discriminated between full time and part time employees in relation to redundancy pay and compensation for unfair dismissal. The House of Lords confirmed that the EOC had sufficient interest and, moreover, that English law was incompatible with the requirements of European Community law. In the *RSPB* case, the Royal Society had sufficient interest to challenge the decision of the Secretary of State's decision affecting the development of land which had hitherto been a special site for the conservation of birds. Whilst the challenge was unsuccessful, the House of Lords referred questions to the European Court of Justice under Article 177 of the EC Treaty (now, Article 234 of the EC Treaty).

---

102 [1995] 1 All ER 111. See, further, Chapter 6.
103 [1994] 2 WLR 409. See, further, Chapter 9.
104 (1995) *The Times*, 10 February.

THE LAW COMMISSION REPORT 1994 AND REVIEW OF CIVIL JUSTICE REPORT 1995

The Law Commission, in its 1994 report,[105] recognised the uncertainty which surrounds the question of sufficient interest. The Commission recommended that there be two classes of cases. The first would include persons with a direct personal interest in the matter who should be granted standing. The second class of case would include those who did not necessarily have a direct personal interest in the decision, but who nevertheless should be granted standing on the basis that the court considered it 'in the public interest' for judicial review to be granted.

THE EXISTENCE OF ALTERNATIVE REMEDIES

The availability of alternative remedies is a relevant factor in deciding whether leave will be granted for judicial review. In *R v Inland Revenue Commissioners ex parte Preston*,[106] Lord Templeman stated that leave for an application for judicial review should not be granted 'where an alternative remedy was available'. Thus, by way of example, where Parliament had set up under statute a comprehensive appeals structure, judicial review cannot be used as a means of circumventing this.[107] Moreover, the statutory rights of appeal must be exhausted.[108] If, however, there are exceptional circumstances – for example, if inordinate delays are experienced in the proceedings – in which the court may grant leave to apply for judicial review.[109]

A MATTER OF PUBLIC – NOT PRIVATE – LAW

Judicial review is confined to matters of public – as opposed to private – law. The courts will not seize jurisdiction to review an administrative action or decision if the matter involved is one of private law. Accordingly, the respondent must be a public authority, and the right at issue must be a public right. If the matter is one of public law, the aggrieved person must apply by way of judicial review and not under any other procedure.

---

105 Law Commission, *Administrative Law: Judicial Review and Statutory Appeals*, Consultation Paper No 226/HC 669.
106 [1985] AC 835.
107 *R v Secretary of State for Social Services ex parte Connolly* [1986] 1 WLR 421.
108 *R v Secretary of State for the Home Department ex parte Swati* [1986] 1 WLR 477.
109 *R v Chief Constable of Merseyside Police ex parte Calveley* [1986] 2 WLR 144.

The 'exclusivity principle'

In *O'Reilly v Mackman*,[110] the applicants had taken part in a prison riot at Hull gaol and the Board of Visitors (who exercise disciplinary powers over prisoners) reduced the remission of sentence as punishment. The applicants tried to establish that the Board of Visitors had acted contrary to the rules of natural justice. This they attempted to do by means of an originating summons or writ.[111] It was not contested that the issue was a matter of public law and that they could have employed the judicial review procedure, provided that they applied for leave within the requisite three months. No leave from the court is needed in relation to private law proceedings. The issue for the court was whether it was an abuse of the process of the court to use the alternative basis to bring the action. Lord Diplock stated that:

> Order 53, since 1977, has provided a procedure by which every type of remedy for infringement of the rights of individuals that are entitled to protection in public law can be obtained in one and the same proceeding by way of an application for judicial review, and whichever remedy is found to be the most appropriate in the light of what has emerged upon the hearing of the application, can be granted to him. If what should emerge is that his complaint is not of an infringement of any of his rights that are entitled to protection in public law, but may be an infringement of his rights in private law and this is not a proper subject for judicial review, the court has power under rule 9(5), instead of refusing the application, to order the proceedings to continue as if they had begun by writ ...[112]

Referring to the procedural disadvantages which had existed prior to the reforms introduced in 1977 by the new Order 53, Lord Diplock went on to state that:

> ... now that those disadvantages to applicants have been removed and all remedies for infringement of rights protected by public law can be obtained upon an application for judicial review, as also can remedies for infringements of rights under private law if such infringement should also be involved, it would in my view as a general rule be contrary to public policy, and as such an abuse of the process of the court to permit a person seeking to establish that a decision of a public authority infringed rights to which he was entitled to protection under public law to proceed by way of an ordinary action and by this means evade the provisions of Order 53 for the protection of such authorities.[113]

---

110 [1983] 2 AC 237. See Wade, HWR, 'Public law, private law and judicial review' (1983) 99 LQR 166 and 'Procedure and prerogative in public law' (1985) 101 LQR 180; see, also, Friedman, S and Morris, G, 'Public and private? State employees and judicial review' (1991) 107 LQR 289.

111 The means by which private law proceedings are initiated.

112 [1983] 2 AC 237, pp 283–84.

113 *Ibid*, p 285.

The decision in *O'Reilly* has been trenchantly criticised by Professor HWR Wade.[114] The 'exclusivity principle' – keeping public and private law rigidly distinct – was introduced by Lord Diplock in *O'Reilly*, notwithstanding the Law Commission's intention that procedural reforms introduced in 1977 were not intended to create a rigid distinction between public and private law proceedings.[115] Before that time, although the distinction between public and private law was drawn, the system was not exclusive. Professor Wade regards the exclusivity principle, declared in *O'Reilly*, as amounting to a 'serious setback for administrative law'. He goes on to state that:

> ... it has caused many cases, which on their merits might have succeeded, to fail merely because of choice of the wrong form of action ... It has produced great uncertainty, which seems likely to continue, as to the boundary between public and private law, since these terms have no clear or settled meaning ...[116]

Professor Wade regards this as an unnecessary restriction on access to the courts, a restriction which has been avoided in Scotland, Australia, New Zealand and Canada. His assessment of the House of Lords' decision in *O'Reilly* is that:

> ... the House of Lords has expounded the new law as designed for the protection of public authorities rather than of the citizen. Such are the misfortunes which can flow from the best intentioned reforms.

Exceptions to the exclusivity principle

The harshness with which the exclusivity principle could operate, led Lord Diplock in *O'Reilly* to state that exceptions to the rule would exist, where the case involved both public and private law elements, particularly where the public law element was collateral (auxiliary or secondary) to the private law element. What is evident in this matter is that a balance needs to be struck between too rigid a rule, which denies individuals the protection of judicial review, and too lax an approach, which would enable individuals either to pursue a remedy in judicial review when other procedures are in fact more appropriate or, conversely, to pursue other remedies when judicial review would be appropriate, in order to evade the requirements of judicial review. It is also evident that the judges are struggling to find the correct balance.

---

114 *Op cit*, Wade and Forsyth, fn 1, p 682.

115 Cmnd 6407, 1976, London: HMSO.

116 *Op cit*, Wade and Forsyth, fn 1, p 682.

A public law issue used in defence in private law proceedings

In *Wandsworth London Borough Council v Winder*,[117] the House of Lords allowed a matter of public law (the lawfulness of the council's decision) to be used as a defence to private law proceedings (possession proceedings). Winder was a tenant of the local authority, which gave notice that rents were to be raised. Winder claimed that the increase was unreasonable and contrary to law. The local authority brought an action for possession of the premises. Winder defended this action on the basis that the rent increase was outside the powers of the local authority and void for unreasonableness. On appeal to the House of Lords, the question for the court was whether Winder could challenge the local authority's action by way of a defence based on judicial review grounds, or whether he should have instigated separate judicial review proceedings by way of an application to the High Court. The local authority submitted that Winder should have used judicial review but that, since he was by then out of time to do so, he could not challenge their decision by way of a defence to the possession proceedings.

Lord Fraser of Tullybelton, citing *O'Reilly*, acknowledged that it was in the interests of good administration to protect authorities from unmeritorious or late challenges, but that this factor had to be weighed in the balance against the argument for preserving the ordinary rights of private citizens to defend themselves against unfounded claims. In his opinion, Winder's action could not be described as an abuse of the process of the court. Winder had not selected the procedure, he was merely seeking to defend himself. If the public interest required that people should not have the right to defend themselves, then that was a matter for Parliament, not the courts.

Cases involving both public and private law issues

In *Roy v Kensington and Chelsea and Westminster Family Practitioner Committee*,[118] a further exception to the exclusivity principle emerged, whereby the House of Lords ruled that the principle did not apply where the proceedings involved matters of both public and private law. In *Roy*, a Family Practitioner Committee was responsible for making payments to general practitioners in respect of their National Health Service work.[119] Dr Roy's allowance was reduced by the committee on the basis that he had reduced the amount of his time spent on National Health Service work. Dr Roy litigated to recover the sum reduced. At first instance, the judge decided that the decision to reduce his payments was a matter of public law to be challenged under

---

117 [1985] AC 461.
118 [1992] 1 AC 624; [1992] 1 All ER 705.
119 Under the National Health Service (General Medical and Pharmaceutical) Regulations 1974.

judicial review proceedings. On appeal to the House of Lords, it was held that, when a litigant had a private law right – in relation to a matter which involved an issue of public law – he was not precluded from pursuing his private law right. Accordingly, the fact that the public law issue could have been determined under judicial review proceedings was not held to deny him a remedy under private law. In *Andreou v Institute of Chartered Accountants in England and Wales*,[120] the applicant had been granted leave to bring judicial review to challenge the validity of a bylaw of the Chartered Institute, but failed to observe the time limit. He then commenced a private law action alleging breach of contractual duty to exercise its bylaw making powers fairly and to act fairly in its disciplinary proceedings. The Court of Appeal ruled that the Institute was, in part, a public body. However, here it was appropriate to proceed under private law since there was a private law right at issue, even though there was also a public law issue involved.

Broad versus restrictive approaches to standing

O'Reilly and *Winder* were both considered extensively in *Roy v Kensington and Chelsea and Westminster Family Practitioner Committee*, in which Lord Lowry examined the 'broad' or 'liberal' approach to judicial review and the 'narrow' or 'restrictive' approach. A broad approach lessens the importance of the distinction between public and private law and would allow either the Order 53 procedure to be used or for the pursuit of a private law remedy. A narrow approach, however, would dictate that if the matter is primarily a matter of private law then the judicial review procedure is inappropriate. While Lord Lowry 'disclaimed any intention of discussing the scope of the rule in *O'Reilly*', he nevertheless went on to make a case for a more liberal approach. Lord Lowry stated that:

> ... the Law Commission, when recommending the new judicial review procedure, contemplated the continued co-existence of judicial review proceedings and actions for a declaration with regard to public law issues ...

> ... this House has expressly approved actions for a declaration of nullity as alternative to applications for certiorari to quash, where private law rights were concerned: *Wandsworth London Borough Council v Winder, per* Robert Goff LJ.[121]

Citing Goff LJ, Lord Lowry continued:

> The principle remains in fact that public authorities and public servants are, unless clearly exempted, answerable in the ordinary courts for wrongs done to individuals. But by an extension of remedies and a flexible procedure it can be said that something resembling a system of public law is being developed.

---

120 [1998] 1 All ER 14, CA.
121 [1992] 1 AC 624, p 655.

Before the expression 'public law' can be used to deny a subject a right of action in the court of his choice it must be related to a positive prescription of law, by statute or by statutory rules. We have not yet reached the point at which mere characterisation of a claim as a claim in public law is sufficient to exclude it from consideration by the ordinary courts: to permit this would be to create a dual system of law with the rigidity and procedural hardship for plaintiffs which it was the purpose of the recent reforms to remove': *Davy v Spelthorn Borough Council*,[122] *per* Lord Wilberforce.

In conclusion, my Lords, it seems to me that, unless the procedure adopted by the moving party is ill suited to dispose of the question at issue, there is much to be said in favour of the proposition that a court having jurisdiction ought to let a case be heard rather than entertain a debate concerning the form of the proceedings.[123]

Lord Slynn advanced the argument for a more flexible approach to the choice of proceedings in *Mercury Communications Ltd v Director General of Telecommunications*.[124] In that case, the effect of *O'Reilly v Mackman* was further limited. A dispute arose between Mercury Communications and British Telecom (BT), both of which are public limited companies licenced by the Secretary of State under the Telecommunications Act 1984. Mercury Communications was dependent upon the rental of part of BT's network. The Director General, exercising powers under the 1984 Act, determined the dispute, and his decision affected the terms of the contract between Mercury and BT. Mercury initiated private proceedings in the Commercial Court by originating summons. At first instance, the Director General and BT failed to have the proceeding struck out, the court applying the *O'Reilly* principle. On appeal, however, it was argued, successfully, that this was an abuse of process. The case went to the House of Lords, which reversed the decision of the Court of Appeal. Lord Slynn emphasised that when determining the issue of the choice of private or public law proceedings, flexibility must be retained. It was recognised that the Director General had statutory functions and performed public duties. However, this did not eliminate the possibility of private law proceedings. Since the Director General's decision had been imposed as part of a contract, this could be regarded as a contractual dispute. Accordingly, the commencement of private law proceedings was equally well suited to determine the issue as judicial review proceedings. The issue of the appropriateness of proceedings was a matter to be determined by the courts on a case by case basis. Lord Slynn stated that:

... when it comes to a question of striking out for abuse of process of the court the discretion exercised by the trial judge should stand unless the arguments

---

122 [1984] AC 262.
123 [1992] 1 AC 624, p 655.
124 [1996] 1 WLR 48; [1996] 1 All ER 575.

are clearly and strongly in favour of a different result to that to which he has come.[125]

The House of Lords reconsidered the question of the appropriate form of proceedings once more in *O'Rourke v Camden London Borough Council*.[126] In this case, the plaintiff had applied to the local authority for accommodation, under the Housing Act 1985, on his release from prison. Section 63(1) of the Housing Act provides that a local authority is under a duty to provide accommodation in respect of those who are 'homeless and [had] a priority need', and that includes persons who are 'vulnerable as a result of ... physical disability or other special reason'. Initially, the authority refused him accommodation, but subsequently provided accommodation for a 12 day period, after which the plaintiff was evicted and no alternative accommodation offered. The plaintiff brought a private action against the council for wrongful eviction without providing alternative accommodation, and claimed damages. The county court struck out the claim, on the grounds that the issue was a matter of public law which should be pursued under judicial review proceedings. The Court of Appeal restored the plaintiff's claim, on the basis that breach of section 63 was a tort. The authority appealed to the House of Lords.

The House of Lords reversed the decision of the Court of Appeal. The House of Lords ruled that the question of whether section 63 of the Housing Act gave rise to public or private law proceedings depended on the intention of Parliament. The duty to provide accommodation was a matter of public law and the Act 'was a scheme of social welfare, intended on grounds of public policy and public interest to confer benefits at the public expense not only for the private benefit of people who found themselves homeless but also for the benefit of society in general'. The provision of accommodation, and the type of accommodation, was 'largely dependent on the housing authority's judgment and discretion'. Accordingly, it was 'unlikely' that Parliament had intended section 63 to give rise to a private action.

The issue of the choice between public and private proceedings returned to the courts in *Trustees of the Dennis Rye Pension Fund and Another v Sheffield City Council*.[127] The plaintiffs were required by the local council to carry out repairs to certain houses to make them fit for human habitation,[128] and applied for improvement grants from the council under the Local Government and Housing Act 1989. When the work was complete, the council refused to pay the grant, on the basis that, *inter alia*, the repairs had not been carried out to the required standard. The plaintiff then commenced

125 [1996] 1 WLR 48, p 59.
126 [1997] 3 WLR 86; [1996] 3 All ER 23.
127 [1997] 4 All ER 747.
128 Under the Housing Act 1989, s 189.

private law proceedings for recovery of the money due. The council, however, argued that, if there were any grounds for complaint, the appropriate process was an application for judicial review. Accordingly, the council sought to have the plaintiff's claim struck out, on the grounds that the private law proceedings were an abuse of process. The issue went to the Court of Appeal. Lord Woolf MR regretted that the 'tactical' issue of the choice of proceedings had inevitably led to very substantial costs being incurred 'to little or no purpose'. He further criticised the narrow approach taken by the House of Lords in *O'Rourke v Camden London Borough Council*.

The Court of Appeal considered the choice between judicial review proceedings and other legal action against a public authority. In determining that question, the court should not be overly concerned with the distinction between public and private rights, but look to the practical consequences of pursuing the alternative actions. The court accepted that when a council was performing its role in relation to the making of grants, it was performing a public function which did not give rise to private rights. If the choice made had 'no significant disadvantages' for the parties, the public or the courts, it should not normally be regarded as an abuse of process. The court applied *O'Reilly v Mackman*[129] and *Roy v Kensington and Chelsea and Westminster Family Practitioner Committee*.[130] Lord Woolf MR, after a consideration of these, and other cases, ruled that as a general rule it is contrary to public policy, and as a result an abuse of the process of the court:

> ... to permit a person seeking to establish that a decision of a public authority infringed rights to which he was entitled to protection under public law to proceed by way of an ordinary action and by this means to evade the provisions of Order 53 for the protection of such authorities.

However, Lord Woolf made three 'pragmatic suggestions' and stated that it is to be remembered that:

> If it is not clear whether judicial review or an ordinary action is the correct procedure it will be safer to make an application for judicial review than commence an ordinary action since there then should be no question of being treated as abusing the process of the court by avoiding the protection provided by judicial review ...

> If a case is brought by an ordinary action and there is an application to strike out the case, the court should, at least if it is unclear whether the case should have been brought by judicial review, ask itself whether, if the case had been brought by judicial review when the action was commenced, it is clear leave would have been granted. If it would, then that is at least an indication that there has been no harm to the interests judicial review is designed to protect ...

---

129 [1982] 3 All ER 1124.
130 [1992] 1 AC 624; [1992] 1 All ER 705.

Finally, in cases where it is unclear whether proceedings have been correctly brought by an ordinary action, it should be remembered that, after consulting the Crown Office, a case can always be transferred to the Crown Office List as an alternative to being struck out.[131]

In *R v Peter Edward Wicks*[132] the House of Lords ruled that the validity of an enforcement notice under the Town and Country Planning Act 1990 could not be impugned in criminal proceedings, but only by the High Court on an application for judicial review. The defendant appealed against the Court of Appeal decision, dismissing his appeal against conviction for failure to comply with the enforcement notice. So long as the enforcement notice was not a nullity or patently defective on its face, it was valid and would remain so until quashed. No criminal court had the power to quash, and it was not open to the defence to go behind the notice and seek to investigate its validity. The proper course to take was to apply for an adjournment of the criminal proceedings and apply to the High Court for judicial review in which the validity of the notice could be attacked.

A challenge to the *vires* of subordinate legislation or an administrative act could be raised in criminal proceedings. The House of Lords so held in *Boddington v British Transport Police*.[133] The defendant, in criminal proceedings on charges of smoking a cigarette in a railway carriage where smoking was prohibited, sought to argue that the Network South Central's decision to post notices banning smoking was *ultra vires* its powers to bring the relevant bylaw into force. On appeal, the court had ruled that it was not open to the defendant to raise that public law defence in criminal proceedings against him. The House of Lords, however, stated that a defendant was so entitled, and that, if the defendant managed to rebut the presumption in favour of the lawfulness of the subordinate legislation or administrative act, the legislation or act had no legal effect at all and could not found a prosecution. In the instant case, there was noting in the bylaws or the relevant Act to rebut the presumption that the defendant was entitled to defend himself against a criminal charge on the basis of the validity of the decision to put no smoking notices in carriages. However, the manner in which the relevant bylaw had been brought into force was not *ultra vires* and accordingly the appeal was dismissed.

---

131 *Trustees of the Dennis Rye Pension Fund and Another v Sheffield City Council* [1997] 4 All ER 747, p 755.

132 [1997] 2 All ER 801; [1997] 2 WLR 876.

133 [1998] 10 Admin LR 321; (1998) 148 NLJ 515.

REMEDIES[134]

Certiorari

This remedy overlaps with that of prohibition (below). An order of certiorari is one which 'quashes' the original decision: accordingly it is both negative and retrospective in nature: *R v Criminal Injuries Compensation Board ex parte Lain*;[135] *O'Reilly v Mackman*.[136] The classic *dictum* is that of Lord Atkin:[137]

> ... whenever any body of persons having legal authority to determine questions affecting the rights of subjects, and having the duty to act judicially, act in excess of their legal authority, they are subject to the controlling jurisdiction of the King's Bench Division exercised in these writs.

Neither certiorari, nor prohibition lie against decisions of the higher courts.

Prohibition

Prohibition is an order which prevents a body from making a decision which would be capable of being quashed by certiorari. It is thus protective in nature.

Mandamus

This order is one which compels an authority to act. An order of mandamus does not lie against an authority which has complete discretion to act.

Declarations

A declaration is a statement of the legal position of the parties, and is not accordingly a remedy *per se*. Declarations are not prerogative orders, and may be useful as an alternative to an application for a prerogative order. The effect of granting a declaration is to nullify any previous decision which is incompatible with the statement of law made by the court.

---

134 See *op cit*, Bingham, fn 42.
135 [1967] 2 QB 864.
136 [1983] 2 AC 237.
137 *R v Electricity Commissioners ex parte London Electricity Joint Committee Company (1920) Ltd* [1924] 1 KB 194.

Injunctions

Injunctions may be interim or permanent, and positive or negative. Injunctions may be used to prevent a Minister or administrative body from acting unlawfully. In *M v Home Office*,[138] the House of Lords held that injunctions could lie against Ministers of the Crown, and that breach of an injunction could lead to a Minister, in his official capacity as representative of the Crown, being held in contempt of court.[139]

DEFAULT POWERS

Statute may provide that a Minister has powers to act in order to oblige a decision making body to comply with their statutory duty. For example, section 9 of the Caravan Sites Act 1968 provided that the Secretary of State had the power to give directions to local authorities to comply with their statutory duty to provide adequate sites for Gypsies residing in, or resorting to their area.[140] Other examples of similar powers are found in the Public Health Act 1936, the Education Act 1944, the National Health Service Act 1977, the Housing Act 1985, the Local Government Act 1985 and the Town and Country Planning Act 1990. In respect of the Housing Act provisions, in *R v Secretary of State for the Environment ex parte Norwich City Council*,[141] the Secretary of State had the power to act as he 'thinks necessary' to ensure that tenants are able to exercise their 'right to buy' from local authorities. His failure to enforce the local authorities' duty was itself subject to the control of the courts through judicial review. Default powers are a backstop, but an important weapon in ensuring that local authorities and other bodies comply with the requirements of statute.

---

138 [1993] 3 All ER 537.

139 See, further, Chapters 6 and 11.

140 The duty to provide sites has been repealed: Criminal Justice and Public Order Act 1994, s 80.

141 [1982] QB 808.

CHAPTER 25

THE GROUNDS FOR JUDICIAL REVIEW

With the procedural aspects of judicial review proceedings in mind, attention can now be turned to the grounds on which judicial review may be sought. Two principal classes of action may be pursued: those which allege that there has been a breach of statutory requirements, and those alleging that a decision has been reached in an unreasonable manner or in disregard of the rules of natural justice. These broad headings have traditionally been divided into a number of subheadings. In *Council of Civil Service Unions v Minister of State for Civil Service* (the *GCHQ* case),[1] the House of Lords took the opportunity to offer a rationalisation of the grounds for judicial review and ruled that the bases for judicial review could be subsumed under three principal heads, namely, illegality, irrationality and procedural impropriety. It was accepted that further grounds for review, such as 'proportionality' might emerge. Lord Diplock elucidated the concepts:

> By 'illegality' as a ground for judicial review, I mean that the decision maker must understand correctly the law that regulates his decision making power and give effect to it. Whether he had or not is *par excellence* a justiciable question to be decided, in the event of dispute, by those persons, the judges, by whom the judicial power of the State is exercisable.

> By 'irrationality', I mean what can now be succinctly referred to as *Wednesbury* unreasonableness.[2] It applies to a decision which is so outrageous in its defiance of logic or of accepted moral standards that no sensible person who had applied his mind to the question to be decided could have arrived at it. Whether a decision falls within this category is a question that judges by their training and experience should be well equipped to answer ...

> I have described the third head as 'procedural impropriety' rather than failure to observe basic rules of natural justice or failure to act with procedural fairness towards the person who will be affected by the decision. This is because susceptibility to judicial review under this head covers also failure by an administrative tribunal to observe the procedural rules that are expressly laid down in the legislative instrument by which its jurisdiction is conferred, even though such failure does not involve any denial of natural justice.

> That is not to say that further development on a case by case basis may not in course of time add further grounds. I have in mind particularly the possible adoption in the future of the principle of 'proportionality' which is recognised

---

1 [1985] AC 374.

2 *Associated Provincial Picture Houses Ltd v Wednesbury Corporation* [1948] 1 KB 223. See, further, below, p 1039.

in the administrative law of several of our fellow members of the European [Economic] Community ...[3]

The court's traditional attitude to proportionality is discussed later in this chapter, when consideration is given to the Human Rights Act 1998, which incorporates the European Convention on Human Rights into domestic law.

THE TRADITIONAL DOCTRINE OF *ULTRA VIRES*

Ultra vires refers to action which is outside – or in excess of – powers of decision making bodies. While judges continue to use the term *ultra vires*, it is nowadays too limited a term to encompass the whole ambit of judicial review. It may be preferable, therefore, to regard judicial review as the control of discretion and the regulation of the decision making process by the courts. By way of example, in *R v Hull University Visitor ex parte Page*,[4] Lord Browne-Wilkinson adopted the traditional language of *ultra vires*:

> If the decision maker exercises his powers outside the jurisdiction conferred, in a manner which is procedurally irregular or is *Wednesbury* unreasonable, he is acting *ultra vires* his powers and therefore unlawfully.

Two cases illustrate this rule. In *R v Richmond upon Thames Council ex parte McCarthy and Stone Ltd*,[5] the local planning authority implemented a scheme of charging £25.00 for informal consultation between corporation officers and property developers. The House of Lords held that the imposition of the charge was unlawful. Such a charge was neither incidental to the planning function of the local authority, nor could a charge be levied on the public without statutory authority. The council had misconstrued its powers and, accordingly, acted *ultra vires*. Further, in *Hazell v Hammersmith and Fulham Council*,[6] the council attempted to increase its revenue through financial investments which, for success, were dependent upon the fluctuation in interest rates. The House of Lords ruled that the council had no power to enter into 'interest rate swaps' which were purely speculative in nature. Such speculation was inconsistent with the statutory borrowing powers conferred on local authorities and neither conducive to nor incidental to the exercise of those powers.

---

3   [1948] 1 KB 223, pp 410–11.
4   [1993] 2 AC 237.
5   [1992] AC 48.
6   [1992] 2 AC 1.

Difficulties with the traditional *ultra vires* doctrine[7]

The *ultra vires* principle is consistent with the doctrine of parliamentary sovereignty and, to some extent, with the concept of the rule of law. However, there are objections to the courts holding so tenaciously to a concept which, in some respects, is inappropriate to describe what the courts actually do in the control of administrative powers.[8] The judges cling to the *ultra vires* doctrine as a means of protecting their constitutional position. As has been seen in Chapters 5 and 7, the judges are not entrusted with constitutional powers to invalidate Acts of Parliament, and judicial decisions are susceptible to being overruled by Acts of Parliament.[9] With the supremacy of Parliament in mind, the judges exercise care to maintain a sufficient separation of powers. It is for this reason that judges are cautious about reviewing the exercise of prerogative powers[10] and limit their role in relation to parliamentary privileges[11] to ruling on the existence and scope of privilege. Keen awareness of this constitutional position explains the hold which the traditional doctrine of *ultra vires* has for judges. *Ultra vires* is entirely consistent with the supremacy of Parliament and the rule of law. However, the doctrine of *ultra vires* cannot explain adequately the judges' power to rule, as they do, on certain aspects of decision making. While the judges declare that matters of 'high policy' are not for them to decide,[12] when judges rule on 'unreasonableness' or, as Lord Diplock classifies the concept, 'irrationality',[13] the judges come close to ruling on the merits of a particular decision. Furthermore, as shall be seen below, the concept of 'error of law' fits uneasily with the concept of *ultra vires*.

For reasons such as these, the concept of *ultra vires* is nowadays regarded by many as an inadequate rationale for judicial review. The preferred view is that the courts need not resort to fictions such as the 'intention of Parliament' or the technicalities of 'jurisdictional facts' and 'errors of law' (on which, see below), but that rather the courts will intervene wherever there has been an unlawful exercise of power. As Dawn Oliver expresses the matter, 'judicial review has moved on from the *ultra vires* rule to a concern for the protection of individuals, and for the control of power'.[14]

---

7   See Laws, J (Sir), 'Illegality: the problem of jurisdiction', in Supperstone, M and Goudie, J (eds), *Judicial Review*, 1988, London: Butterworths, Chapter 4.

8   See Oliver, D, 'Is the *ultra vires* rule the basis of judicial review?' [1987] PL 543; and see *ibid*, Laws.

9   See, eg, *Burmah Oil v Lord Advocate* [1965] AC 75 and the War Damage Act 1965.

10   See Chapter 7.

11   See Chapter 18.

12   See above.

13   See, further, below.

14   *Ibid*, Oliver.

Traditional terminological and classificatory difficulties in judicial review

While Lord Diplock, in the *GCHQ* case,[15] offered a rationalisation of the headings of review, the question of terminology and classification remains difficult and sometimes obscure. This problem should be recognised at the outset. It should also be borne in mind that the categories are by no means watertight and discrete: in many instances, there will appear overlaps between the headings. By way of illustration, a decision maker may act *ultra vires* by taking into account irrelevant considerations. Depending upon the magnitude of the irrelevant consideration, he or she may also be acting irrationally.

Irrationality: *Wednesbury* unreasonableness

Acting for improper motives, failing to take account of relevant considerations, failing to respect the requirements of natural justice and fettering a discretion by adopting a rigid policy will all amount to unreasonableness as understood by the courts. The term 'unreasonableness' may thus be seen as an 'umbrella concept' which subsumes all the major headings of review.

'Irrationality' is a concept which takes the courts further from reviewing the procedures by which a decision has been made and testing its legality, and closer to substituting the court's own view of the merits of the decision. The terms 'irrationality' and '*Wednesbury* unreasonableness' appear to be used at the judge's own preference.[16] Alternative expressions such as 'arbitrary and capricious', 'frivolous or vexatious' and 'capricious and vexatious' are also used on occasion to express the same concept.[17] 'Acting perversely' has also been used to judicially express the idea of unreasonableness.[18]

Early expression was given to the concept in two cases, *Rooke's Case*[19] and *Keighley's Case*.[20] In *Rooke's Case*, Coke LJ proclaimed that:

---

15 [1948] 1 KB 223.

16 See, eg, Lord Donaldson MR in *R v Devon County Council ex parte G* [1989] AC 573, p 577.

17 *Per* Wade, HWR and Forsyth, CF, *Administrative Law*, 7th edn, 1994, Oxford: Clarendon, p 391 and references therein.

18 *Per* Lord Brightman in *R v Hillingdon London Borough Council ex parte Pulhofer* [1986] AC 484. The test of *Wednesbury* unreasonableness is the foundation of the jurisdiction of University Visitors, who should only intervene in academic matters in exceptional circumstances: *Jhamat v Inns of Court School of Law (Visitors to the Inns of Court)* [1999] ELR 450.

19 (1598) 5 Co Rep 99b.

20 (1609) 10 Co Rep 139a.

... and notwithstanding the words of the commission give authority to the commissioners to do according to their discretions, yet their proceedings ought to be limited and bound with the rule of reason and law. For discretion is a science or understanding to discern between falsity and truth, between wrong and right, between shadows and substances, between equity and colourable glosses and pretences, and not to do according to their wills and private affections ...

The classic case of more recent times is that of *Associated Provincial Picture Houses Ltd v Wednesbury Corporation*.[21] The local authority had the power to grant licences for the opening of cinemas subject to such conditions as the authority 'thought fit' to impose. The authority, when granting a Sunday licence, imposed a condition that no children under the age of 15 years should be admitted. The applicants argued that the imposition of the condition was unreasonable and *ultra vires* the corporation's powers. The authority argued that there were no limits on the conditions which could be imposed in the statute. Lord Greene MR alluded to the many grounds of attack which could be made against a decision, citing unreasonableness, bad faith, dishonesty, paying attention to irrelevant circumstances, disregard of the proper decision making procedure and held that each of these could be encompassed within the umbrella term 'unreasonableness'. The test propounded in that case was whether an authority had acted, or reached a decision, in a manner 'so unreasonable that no reasonable authority could ever have come to it':

> Lawyers familiar with the phraseology commonly used in relation to exercise of statutory discretion often use the word 'unreasonable' in a rather comprehensive sense. It has frequently been used and is frequently used as a general description of the things that must not be done. For instance, a person entrusted with a discretion must, so to speak, direct himself properly in law. He must call his own attention to the matters which he is bound to consider. He must exclude from his consideration matters which are irrelevant to what he has to consider. If he does not obey those rules, he may truly be said, and often is said, to be acting 'unreasonably'. Similarly, there may be something so absurd that no sensible person could ever dream that it lay within the powers of the authority ...
>
> The court is entitled to investigate the action of the local authority with a view to seeing whether they have taken into account matters which they ought not to take into account, or, conversely, have refused to take into account and once that question is answered in favour of the local authority, it may still be possible to say that, although the local authority have kept within the four corners of the matters which they ought to consider, they have nevertheless come to a conclusion so unreasonable that no reasonable authority could ever have come to it. In such a case, again, I think the court can interfere.[22]

---

21 [1948] 1 KB 223.
22 *Ibid*, p 229.

'Unreasonableness' was employed to challenge a bylaw which prohibited singing 'in any public place or highway within fifty yards of any dwelling house' although, on the merits of the case, the challenge failed.[23] In *Roberts v Hopwood*,[24] the council, in adopting a policy of paying higher wages than the national average for its workers, was unreasonable, for the discretion of the council was limited by law – it was not free to pursue a socialist policy at the expense of its rate payers. The House of Lords ruled that, irrespective of the wording of the statute, the council had a duty to act 'reasonably'; its discretion was limited by law.[25]

The standard of reasonableness imposed by the courts is high: to impose too low a standard would in effect mean the substitution of judicial discretion for administrative discretion. It is for this reason that Lord Greene, cited above, states that a decision is unreasonable if it is 'so absurd that no sensible person could ever dream that it lay within the powers of the authority', and Lord Diplock, in *Council of Civil Service Unions v Minister for the Civil Service*,[26] regarded unreasonableness as entailing a decision '... so outrageous in its defiance of logic or of accepted moral standards that no sensible person who had applied his mind to the question to be decided could have arrived at it'.

In *Secretary of State for Education and Science v Tameside Metropolitan Borough Council*,[27] the Secretary of State for Education directed a newly elected local authority to implement plans, devised by the predecessor council, to introduce comprehensive schooling and abolish grammar schools.[28] At the election, there had been a change in the political composition of the council, which resulted in the change of policy. The Secretary of State's power was to direct an authority as to the exercise of its powers if he was satisfied that the authority was acting unreasonably. The Secretary of State argued that the new council would not be able to organise the necessary system of selective entry required for grammar schools in time for the new academic year, and that the authority was therefore unreasonable.

The matter went to the House of Lords. The court had to determine the extent of the Secretary of State's discretion under section 68 of the Education Act. The wording of the section was subjective: '... if the Secretary of State is satisfied.' It fell to the court to determine whether, in the circumstances of the case, the Secretary of State had acted lawfully according to the court's interpretation of whether the Secretary of State did in fact have reasonable grounds for believing that the authority had acted unreasonably. Applying

---

23   *Kruse v Johnson* [1898] 2 QB 91.
24   [1925] AC 578, discussed above.
25   See Lord Wrenbury's judgment [1925] AC 578, p 613.
26   [1985] AC 374, p 410.
27   [1977] AC 1014.
28   Under powers conferred by the Education Act 1944, s 68.

the *Wednesbury* reasonableness test to the decision of the local authority to retain grammar schools, the House of Lords ruled that the authority had not been unreasonable and, as a result, the Secretary of State's directions were unlawful.

In *R v Secretary of State for the Home Department ex parte Brind*,[29] the House of Lords re-examined the reasonableness of the exercise of the Home Secretary's discretion to issue a notice banning the transmission of speech by representatives of the Irish Republican Army and its political party, Sinn Fein. Despite the issue involving a denial of freedom of expression, the court ruled that the exercise of the Home Secretary's power[30] did not amount to an unreasonable exercise of discretion.

In *R v Radio Authority ex parte Bull*,[31] Amnesty International (British section) sought judicial review of the Radio Authority's decision to refuse to accept advertisements 'inserted by or on behalf of any body whose objects are wholly or mainly of a political nature' or an advertisement which 'is directed towards any political end' under section 92(2)(a) of the Broadcasting Act 1990. The Divisional Court ruled that the authority had a wide measure of discretion and that the court would not interfere with its decision so long as it was not unreasonable. The Court ruled, further, that Article 10 of the European Convention did not significantly affect the construction of section 92; that the authority had to strike a balance between competing interests including freedom of speech; that the authority's interpretation had been in accordance with the purposes of the Act.

Dismissal from the armed forces on the basis that homosexuality was incompatible with service in the forces was the subject of an application for judicial review in *R v Secretary of State for Defence ex parte Smith*.[32] The applicants were administratively discharged from the armed forces pursuant to a Ministry of Defence policy of 1994. The policy, formulated under the royal prerogative, prohibited homosexual men and women from serving in the armed forces and required the discharge of any man or woman found to be of homosexual orientation. The applicants claimed that the policy was discriminatory and in breach of the European Convention on Human Rights[33] and a breach of the European Community Council Directive on the implementation of the principle of equal treatment for men and women in relation to access to employment, vocational training and promotion and working conditions.[34] The Court of Appeal held that, at the time when the

---

29 [1991] 1 All ER 720.
30 Under the Broadcasting Act 1981. See, further, Chapter 19.
31 [1995] 3 WLR 572.
32 [1996] 1 All ER 257.
33 ECHR, Art 8, the right to privacy.
34 Directive 76/207.

dismissals took place, it was not possible to say that the policy, which was supported by both Houses of Parliament, was irrational. The court also ruled that the question whether the dismissals violated the European Convention on Human rights was a matter to be answered by the European Court of Human Rights, and not the domestic courts. Further, nothing in the EC Treaty or the Equal Treatment Directive 76/207/EEC appeared to relate to discrimination on the grounds of sexual orientation. However, the Court of Appeal also considered the human rights' dimension of the case, stating that, in judging whether 'the decision maker had exceeded that margin of appreciation', the human rights' context was important. Moreover, the more substantial the interference with human rights, the more the court would require by way of justification before it was satisfied that the decision was reasonable.

In *R v Broadmoor Special Hospital Authority ex parte S*,[35] the Court of Appeal, dismissing an appeal from an application for judicial review, ruled that the hospital's policy of conducting routine and random searches of patients without their consent was lawful. The applicants had claimed that the power to search could not be implied into the Mental Health Act 1983, and that, if such power existed, it was irrational and its exercise unlawfully fettered the hospital's discretion because it was not subject to any exception on medical grounds. The Court of Appeal upheld the finding of an implied power of search, ruling that it was consistent with a 'self-evident and pressing need'[36] to enable the hospital to fulfil its primary function of treating patients and ensuring a safe and therapeutic environment for both patients and staff. Since the hospital's policy was in the interests of all, it had to be permitted to override medical objections raised in individual cases.

The importance of protecting human rights was also evident in *R v Lord Saville of Newdigate ex parte B (No 2)*.[37] A tribunal of enquiry into the Bloody Sunday shootings in Northern Ireland decided to withdraw the anonymity of soldiers giving evidence to the enquiry, on the basis that the enquiry should be open and public. The soldiers affected applied for judicial review. Allowing the application, the court ruled that, where an interference with human rights was alleged, the court had jurisdiction to employ a stricter test than in other *Wednesbury* cases. The risk to the soldiers' fundamental rights to life, security of the person and respect for family life was extreme. The High Court ordered that anonymity be continued.[38]

---

35 (1998) *The Times*, 17 February.

36 The test laid down in *R v Secretary of State for the Home Department ex parte Leech (No 2)* [1994] QB 198; [1994] CLJ 3849.

37 (1999) 149 NLJ 965; (1999) *The Times*, 22 June.

38 See also *Re Austin's Application* [1998] NI 327, in which the court ruled that the more extensive the administrative decision maker's interference with human rights, the more the court would require in terms of justification.

Judicial review of Home Secretary's powers in relation to penal elements in mandatory life sentences

In *R v Secretary of State for the Home Department ex parte Pierson*,[39] the Court of Appeal ruled on the legality of the Home Secretary's decision to fix the penal element of a mandatory life sentence at twenty years, having rejected the recommendation of the judges that the term should be fifteen years. An incoming Home Secretary adhered to his predecessor's decision. The Home Secretary had the power, under section 35 of the Criminal Justice Act 1991, to release on licence a prisoner serving a mandatory life sentence which he could exercise after consulting the trial judge and the Lord Chief Justice and if release was recommended by the Parole Board. On an application for judicial review, the Court held that the decision was not irrational and that there was nothing in law to stop the Secretary of State exceptionally revising upwards the period originally determined, on the ground that it did not adequately meet the requirement of retribution and deterrence. On appeal to the House of Lords, however,[40] the decision of the Court of Appeal was reversed. By a majority of three to two, Lord Browne-Wilkinson and Lord Lloyd of Berwick dissenting, the House of Lords ruled that the Home Secretary had not been entitled to set the appellant's tariff period at 20 years when it had been shown that his predecessor in office had proceeded on the wrong basis by taking into account aggravating circumstances, in particular premeditation, when originally fixing the tariff. In doing so, the former Home Secretary had exceeded his powers for, by taking into account aggravating circumstances, the Home Secretary had not left the tariff period unchanged but had, in effect, increased the penal element in the sentence. Lord Steyn and Lord Hope of Craighead asserted that, once the tariff is set and communicated to the prisoner, the tariff cannot be raised. Lord Hope stated that:

> ... there is a clear, if narrow, difference between these decisions [concerning release on licence] on grounds of policy and decisions which are concerned purely and solely with the question of punishment. If the only reasons which the Home Secretary can give for setting a minimum period which differs from that which has been recommended by the judiciary, or which has been set by him or by his predecessor, are reasons concerned with the appropriate punishment for the particular crime which the prisoner her committed, he has moved into an areas of decision making which normally belongs to the courts. He is not disabled from taking a different view from the judges about the minimum period, because the power resides with him alone to decide on the release date. But he is bound by considerations of substantive fairness to observe the same rules as the judges if the view which he takes about the

---

39 (1995) *The Times*, 8 December.
40 [1997] 3 All ER 577; [1997] 3 WLR 492.

length of the minimum period is concerned solely with the question of punishment.[41]

... [the decision] was made in the belief, which I consider to be erroneous, that it was within the power of the Home Secretary to increase the minimum period simply because he disagreed with the view formed by his predecessor about the appropriate level of punishment.[42]

Lord Goff asserted that the Home Secretary had exceeded his powers because the policy statement relied on by the Home Secretary could not have retrospective effect and, therefore, could not apply to the appellant's case where the tariff period for retribution and deterrence had already been fixed and under the earlier policy statement was not liable to be increased. Given the differing bases for the decision, and the narrow majority in the House of Lords, there is no firm proposition as to the Home Secretary's right to increase the tariff. The current Home Secretary[43] has restated that in his view he still has this power.

The Home Secretary's power to set a tariff period of imprisonment[44] came under scrutiny in *R v Secretary of State for the Home Department ex parte Venables; R v Same ex parte Thompson*.[45] In this case, two child killers of a child aged two and a half applied for judicial review of the Home Secretary's decision to fix a tariff period of 15 years for each child, on the basis that this reflected the requirements of retribution and deterrence. The two boys had been detained at Her Majesty's pleasure following their conviction. The Master of the Rolls stated that the purpose of detention of the boys (who were aged 10 at the time of the offence) was not retribution or deterrence but reformation. The Home Secretary's decision amounted to the fixing of a term in line with mandatory adult life imprisonment, rather than discretionary detention at Her Majesty's pleasure. The Home Secretary's decision amounted to an overly rigid policy and was, accordingly, unfair. The decision was quashed. On appeal to the House of Lords, the decision of the Court of Appeal was affirmed. First, the House of Lords ruled, by a majority of three to two, Lords Goff and Lloyd dissenting, that there was a distinction between a sentence of detention at Her Majesty's pleasure and a life sentence imposed on an adult murderer. The order for detention concerned the authority to detain indefinitely and, accordingly, the Home Secretary had to decide from time to time, taking into account the punitive element, whether detention was still justified. A mandatory life sentence, on the other hand, involved an order of

---

41 [1997] 3 All ER 577, p 671g, j.

42 *Ibid*, p 619a.

43 Jack Straw.

44 See, also, *R v Secretary of State for the Home Department ex parte Pierson* (1995) *The Times*, 8 December, discussed above.

45 (1996) *The Times*, 7 August, but see *V and T v United Kingdom*, wherein the Court of Human Rights found Convention violations, discussed in Chapter 22.

custody for life which meant that the Home Secretary had to decide whether and when release was justified. Furthermore, according to Lord Browne-Wilkinson and Lord Hope, the Home Secretary was under a duty[46] to take into account the welfare of the child when exercising his discretion in relation to child offenders. It was, accordingly, unlawful for the Home Secretary to adopt a policy which treated as irrelevant the progress and development of the detained child. Secondly, the court ruled by a majority of three, Lord Lloyd dissenting, that, in fixing a tariff, the Home Secretary was under the same duty as a judge, and was required to remain detached from public opinion. The Home Secretary had accordingly misdirected himself and his decision was tainted with procedural unfairness as a result.

The Court of Appeal ruled, in *R v Secretary of State for the Home Department ex parte Furber*,[47] on an application for judicial review of the Home Secretary's decision, that the applicant's sentence should be set at seven years imprisonment, and that that period, for a juvenile offender, was excessive. The court ruled that, had the Secretary of State directed himself in accordance with the ruling in *R v Secretary of State for the Home Department ex parte Venables*,[48] he could not have arrived at the decision he did. A half, rather than two-thirds, of the determinate sentence was the appropriate period for a young person to serve.

In *R v Secretary of State for the Home Department ex parte Hindley*, however, the right of the Home Secretary to determine the length of the penal element of a prison sentence to be served by a person convicted of murder was upheld by the House of Lords.[49] As noted above, the Home Secretary's powers derive from the Criminal Justice Act 1991, which makes it clear that the Home Secretary has discretion as to the length of the penal element. The question which arose was whether the Home Secretary had the right to set a whole life tariff, which had the effect that Hindley's case could not be considered by the Parole Board. Hindley had been convicted in 1965. In 1982, the then Lord Chief Justice stated that a term of not less than 25 years was appropriate. In 1985, the Home Secretary reached the decision that the applicant should serve 30 years. In 1990, the Home Secretary decided that the applicant's sentence should be for her whole life, a decision upheld in 1997 by the new Home Secretary. The House of Lords ruled that there was no reason of principle which stated that crimes which were 'sufficiently heinous' should not be met with a whole life tariff. The Home Secretary was prepared to constantly re-assess the decision in light of further information and it could not be said that he had unlawfully fettered his discretion.

---

46 Imposed under the Children and Young Persons Act 1933, s 44(1).
47 (1997) *The Times*, 11 July.
48 [1997] 3 WLR 23; (1997) *The Times*, 13 June.
49 [2000] 2 WLR 730; [2000] 2 All ER 385.

In *R v Secretary of State for the Home Department ex parte Stafford*,[50] the Court of Appeal ruled that section 29 of the Crime (Sentences) Act 1997, conferred an 'extraordinary, wide discretion' on the Home Secretary. That discretion permitted the Home Secretary to refuse to release a mandatory life sentence prisoner, after the expiry of the term of imprisonment imposed, on the basis that the prisoner, once released, might commit some imprisonable offence, or not comply with the terms of his life sentence, even though the risk of him committing serious sexual offences for which he had been sentenced, was thought to be low. The court declared that the imposition, in effect, of a further substantial term of imprisonment, by the exercise of executive discretion, without trial, 'lay uneasily with ordinary concepts of the rule of law'. On appeal to the House of Lords, the Court of Appeal's decision was affirmed.[51]

Onerous conditions attached to decision

A decision by an authority may also be unreasonable if conditions are attached to the decision which are difficult or impossible to perform. For example, in *Pyx Granite Co Ltd v Ministry of Housing and Local Government*, Lord Denning MR in the Court of Appeal held that planning conditions '... must fairly and reasonably relate to the permitted development'[52] and must not be so unreasonable that it can be said that Parliament clearly cannot have intended that they should be imposed.

Accordingly, in the *Pyx Granite* case, the condition that permission be conditional upon the company constructing a road ancillary to the development at its own expense when so required by the authority and to grant a public right of passage over it was *ultra vires. Pyx Granite* was followed in *Hall and Co Ltd v Shoreham-by-Sea Urban District Council and Another*.[53] The defendant council granted planning permission for a development, subject to conditions, which included the requirement to construct an ancillary road over the entire frontage of the site and subject to the right of public passage. While the objective of the council was viewed as 'reasonable', the terms of the conditions requiring the plaintiffs to construct a road at their own expense, for public use and without compensation, were not reasonable. The *ultra vires* conditions were fundamental to the whole planning permission which was, accordingly, void. Equally, in *R v Hillingdon London Borough Council ex parte Royco Homes Ltd*,[54] planning permission was also tied to conditions. The

---

50   (1997) *The Times*, 28 November.
51   [1998] 3 WLR 372.
52   [1958] 1 QB 554, p 572.
53   [1964] 1 WLR 240.
54   [1974] QB 720.

conditions were that Royco Homes make properties constructed available for occupation by those on the council's housing waiting list and, further, that for 10 years the houses be occupied by persons subject to security of tenure under the Rent Acts. The conditions were unreasonable and *ultra vires*.

According to Lord Widgery CJ, the conditions represented:

> ... the equivalent of requiring the applicants to take on at their own expense a significant part of the duty of the council as housing authority. However well intentioned and however sensible such a desire on the part of the council may have been, it seems to me that it is unreasonable ...[55]

Where an authority makes a decision which is in part good, but in part bad – perhaps because of attaching onerous conditions to planning permission – the court may either invalidate the entire decision or sever the bad part of the decision from the good. The decision in *Agricultural Horticultural and Forestry Industry Training Board v Aylesbury Mushrooms Ltd*[56] illustrates the principle. There, the Training Board was under a mandatory statutory duty to consult certain organisations and trades unions before reaching a decision. The Board failed to consult the Mushroom Growers Association. The court held that the decision was good, and could remain, in relation to those associations which had been consulted, but bad in relation to the Mushroom Growers Association, and that the Board had a duty to reconsider their decision after consultations with the Association.

In some cases, it will not be possible to sever a part of a decision from the whole decision, in which case, the entire decision may be invalidated.[57] For example, in *Director of Public Prosecutions v Hutchinson*,[58] the local authority passed a bylaw which prohibited unauthorised access to Greenham Common air force base. The Act of Parliament, under which the authority purported to exercise its powers, provided that no bylaw should be passed which affected the rights of registered commoners in the area. In an action for trespass against anti-nuclear protesters, the defendants pleaded the invalidity of the bylaw. The House of Lords ruled that the bylaw was invalid and, as a result, the protesters escaped conviction for trespass.

---

55 [1974] QB 720, p 732.
56 [1972] 1 WLR 190.
57 As in *Hall and Co Ltd v Shoreham-by-Sea Urban District Council and Another*, discussed above.
58 [1990] 2 AC 783.

ACTING WRONGLY

Errors of law and errors of fact[59]

The problem concerning the role of the courts and the extent to which it is appropriate for there to be judicial intervention in administration, discussed in Chapter 24, is clearly illustrated in relation to errors of law and errors of fact. The question for determination is whether, and to what extent, administrators enjoy a measure of discretion in decision making, which empowers them to make determinations of fact which are immune from judicial review. Before considering the courts approach, it is necessary to define the terms error of law and error of fact.

An error of law may take several forms. An authority may wrongly interpret a word to which a legal meaning is attributed. For example, where an authority is under a duty to provide 'accommodation', the question arises as to whether the quality of what they have, in fact, provided amounts, in law, to accommodation. Does the accommodation have to be of a particular quality, or be particularly suited to what the applicant needs?[60] Questions may also arise as to whether there has been a legal exercise of power in relation to the objectives of relevant legislation, or whether a discretion has been properly exercised, or whether relevant considerations have been taken into account, or irrelevant considerations excluded from the decision making process. An error of law will be reviewed by the courts. An error of fact is an error which the courts will be more reluctant to review. Administrators are given powers to exercise in relation to their specialised area, and it is the decision maker who has all the factual information to hand on which to base a decision. For the courts to intervene in this matter, would – unless some caution is exercised – amount to the courts taking over the very role of the administrators. Nevertheless, there may be some errors of fact which are of such a fundamental nature that they cause a decision to be unlawful. Ian Yeats offers the following illustrative example of the role of fact in administrative decision making. He writes:

> In the simplest situations, the facts which have to be found and the law which has to be determined can be presented as a series of preconditions which have to exist before the duty can be performed or the power exercised. A board is empowered (or obliged) to take some action in respect of 'dilapidated dwelling houses in Greater London'. The ability (or duty) to act in respect of a particular building depends on establishing that it is (1) in Greater London, (2) a dwelling house and (3) dilapidated. If the board finds that the three conditions are satisfied, it may (or must) proceed. If it finds that any one of them is not satisfied, then it cannot.

---

59 See Yeats, IM, 'Errors of fact: the role of the courts law', in Richardson, G and Genn, H (eds), *Administrative Law and Government Action*, 1994, Oxford: OUP.

60 See *R v Hillingdon London Borough Council ex parte Pulhofer* [1986] AC 484.

A disgruntled property owner invites a court to review the board's findings: the court has to decide whether, and how far, it should defer to the board's views. If the complaint is that the premises are not in Greater London, the court is likely to intervene. The question defines in the most literal way the area in which the board has competence, can easily be resolved by a court, and is unlikely to occur frequently. The question is not about the correctness of the decision on the building's fate, but about whether the board whose decision is under review had the function of determining it. If the complaint is that the house is not dilapidated, the court will be reluctant to intervene. That is a question involving elements of judgment which naturally appear to have been remitted to the board and which it, rather than the court, has the facilities and probably the specialised expertise to answer; if the court were to agree to answer it, every decision of the board would be potentially reviewable. If the complaint is that the premises do not constitute a dwelling house, the issue is less clear-cut. The court might think it proper to impose its view, partly because the problem might be posed in a narrowly legal form, that of identifying the correct sense in which the expression 'dwelling house' was used in the legislation.[61]

When the court considers whether there has been an error of law, it is seeking to discover the correct definition of the legal words in the relevant statute. When the court is considering whether there has been an error of fact, the court is trying to determine whether the facts of the case 'fit' with the interpretation of the statute.

Historically, the judges have assumed the power to adjudicate on matters which are termed 'errors on the face of the record'. Errors on the face of the record – that is to say, evidence from the documentation that the decision maker has made a wrong decision in law – will cause the judges to rule that the decision was defective, even if the decision maker was acting inside jurisdiction (*intra vires*). Such a power does not sit easily alongside the concept of *ultra vires*, the very basis of which is to strike down decisions which have been taken *ultra vires* (outside jurisdiction).

As has been seen, if an authority is to act *intra vires*, it must conduct itself according to a correct interpretation of the law. However, what is of the essence in relation to error of law is that the authority misinterprets or misunderstands the powers which it has been granted and, accordingly, acts *ultra vires* whereas, when an authority uses powers for the wrong purpose, the authority has correctly interpreted its powers but used them towards the wrong objective. As has been said, an error of law may manifest itself in several ways. It may be that an authority misinterprets its legal powers, as in *Perilly v Tower Hamlets Borough Council*,[62] where the local authority believed – erroneously – that it was obliged to consider applications for stall licences in a

---

61 *Op cit*, Yeats, fn 59, pp 131–32.
62 [1973] QB 9.

street market in the order in which they were received. The effect of this was to deny a licence to Perilly even though his mother, by then deceased, had held a licence for some 30 years. The licence granted to an incoming applicant in preference to Perilly was set aside by the court.

The seminal case is that of *Anisminic Ltd v Foreign Compensation Commission*, discussed in Chapter 24.[63] It will be recalled that the House of Lords held the decision of the Commission to be *ultra vires*. The decision made by the Commission was so wrong that, in law, it did not amount to a decision at all. As a result, the section preventing the questioning of the Commission's decision in a court of law was not relevant or binding on the court, for the ruling of the Commission – being so wrong in law – resulted in the Commission acting outside its jurisdiction, and nothing in the Act prohibited a court of law from reviewing what was, in law and in effect, a nullity. The House of Lords ruled that:

> If the inferior tribunal, as a result of its misconstruing the statutory description of the kind of case in which it has jurisdiction to inquire, makes a purported determination in a case of a kind into which it has no jurisdiction to inquire, its purported determination is a nullity.

Anisminic Ltd v Foreign Compensation Commission[64] destroyed the distinction between errors of law which 'went to jurisdiction' (that is, deprived the decision making body of power to determine the question) and errors of law within jurisdiction. In *Anisminic*, the House of Lords ruled that, in effect, the old distinctions were obsolete in relation to the decisions of administrative and other bodies (but not necessarily inferior courts of law).[65] Lord Diplock has reasserted his support for this view in *Re Racal Communications Ltd*[66] and *O'Reilly v Mackmann*.[67] In the former case, Lord Diplock confirmed the 'breakthrough' achieved in *Anisminic*. In *O'Reilly*, Lord Diplock went further and asserted that the distinction had been rendered obsolete in relation both to tribunals and inferior courts.[68] This approach was confirmed by the House of Lords in *R v Hull University Visitor ex parte Page*.[69] Professor HWR Wade's evaluation of these cases is that 'it is clear now that they made an important extension of judicial review in English law ...'.[70]

---

63 [1969] 2 AC 147.

64 *Ibid*.

65 See Diplock (Lord), 'Administrative law: judicial review reviewed' [1974] CLJ 223; Wade, HWR, 'Constitutional and administrative aspects of the *Anisminic* case' (1969) 85 LQR 198; Gould, BC, '*Anisminic* and judicial review' [1970] PL 358; Gordon, DM, 'What did the *Anisminic* case decide?' (1971) 34 MLR 1.

66 [1981] AC 374.

67 [1983] 2 AC 237.

68 *Ibid*, p 278.

69 [1993] AC 682.

70 *Op cit*, Wade and Forsyth, fn 17, p 304.

The House of Lords returned to the questions of jurisdictional errors in *R v Monopolies and Mergers Commission ex parte South Yorkshire Transport Ltd.*[71] Under the Fair Trading Act 1973,[72] the Secretary of State has power to refer a merger of companies to the Monopolies and Mergers Commission (MMC). The jurisdiction of the MMC was to consider mergers which result in more than 25 per cent of services being supplied by one company 'in a substantial part of the United Kingdom'. The merger between two bus companies resulted in services being provided in an area which comprised 1.65 per cent of the United Kingdom, with a population of 3.2 per cent of the total United Kingdom population. The companies sought judicial review of the MMC's investigation, on the basis that the facts relating to the land area did not amount to a 'substantial part of the United Kingdom'. The House of Lords found in favour of the MMC. The court ruled that the MMC had directed itself properly as to the meaning of 'substantial'. However, it was also recognised that what amounted to 'substantial' could be interpreted in different ways, and that persons might reasonably disagree about that interpretation. Lord Mustill ruled that, in such a situation, a decision would only be ruled unlawful if the decision 'is so aberrant that it cannot be classed as rational'. Thus, where the statute provides broad criteria, over the meaning of which reasonable persons might reasonably disagree, the court will be slow to step in and substitute its judgment, unless the decision maker's decision falls outside what the court regards as a reasonable interpretation of a word which is essentially imprecise.

Applying the *South Yorkshire* case, the Court of Appeal in *R v Ministry of Defence ex parte Walker*[73] ruled that the court should respect a Ministry's interpretation of what constituted military activity for the purpose of excluding soldiers from criminal injuries compensation for injuries while in service. Only if the interpretation was irrational would the court intervene, and there was no irrationality in choosing to exclude from the scheme a feature peculiar to army life abroad. There was also no unfairness in not having informed soldiers going into active service of the exclusionary rule.

Errors of fact raise difficult questions. As has been seen, an error of law will be made when the decision maker acts contrary to the requirements of legality – or, in other words, he has broken one of the rules for lawful decision making. Errors of fact are more complex. If a decision maker bases his decision on a misunderstanding of the factual situation of the case, he will reach a decision which is wrong. The question which then arises is whether the courts will review such an error in judicial review proceedings. In general, the answer to that question is that the courts will be very cautious. After all,

---

71 [1993] 1 All ER 289.
72 Fair Trading Act 1973, s 64(1)(a).
73 (1999) *The Times*, 11 February.

the courts will often not have the expertise to assess the factual situation, and may have great difficulty in deciding whether a factual error has resulted in the wrong decision. The courts have traditionally approached this matter by dividing errors of fact into two categories. The first relates to reviewable errors of facts, which are jurisdictional, and the other category is that of non-reviewable, non-jurisdictional facts.

Professor Wade illustrates a jurisdictional fact as follows:

> A rent tribunal ... may have power to reduce the rent of a dwelling house. If it mistakenly finds that the property is a dwelling house when in fact it is let for business purposes, and then purports to reduce the rent, its order will be *ultra vires* and void, for its jurisdiction depends upon the facts which must exist objectively before the tribunal has power to act.[74]

On the other hand, other mistakes will not have this effect. Professor Wade illustrates as follows:

> Many facts on the other hand will not be jurisdictional, since they will have no bearing on the limits of the power. A rent tribunal's findings as to the state of repair of the property, the terms of the tenancy, and the defaults of landlord or tenant will probably not affect its jurisdiction in any way and will therefore be immune from jurisdictional challenge.[75]

The question to be asked, therefore, is whether the mistake of fact is one which is central to the decision maker's power of decision. Only such crucial errors of fact will be reviewed by the court. In addition, if a decision is reached on the basis of facts for which there is no evidence, or based on essential facts which have been proven wrong, or been misunderstood or ignored, the court will quash the decision.[76]

Two cases further illustrate the courts' approach to law and fact, and demonstrate that the judges will – depending upon the circumstances of the case – adopt either a strict approach or a more lenient approach to the matter. In *R v Secretary of State for the Home Department ex parte Khawaja*,[77] the House of Lords was required to rule on two questions. The first question was whether the phrase 'illegal immigrant' in the Immigration Act 1971, covered a person who had been granted permission to enter the country through fraud or deception as well as a person who secretly entered the country without any leave. On this point, the House of Lords held that it could. The second question concerned the standard of proof which the immigration officer had to apply. It was argued that the correct standard to be applied was whether the immigration officer had reasonable grounds for his decision. The House of Lords rejected that view, holding that, because the liberty of the person was

---

74 *Op cit*, Wade and Forsyth, fn 17, p 286.
75 *Op cit*, Wade and Forsyth, fn 17, p 287.
76 *Op cit*, Wade and Forsyth, fn 17, p 320.
77 [1984] AC 74.

involved, the standard of proof that deception had taken place was one of a high degree of probability.

In *R v Hillingdon London Borough Council ex parte Pulhofer*,[78] the House of Lords approached the matter rather differently. Under the Housing Act 1985,[79] local authorities are under a duty to provide accommodation for homeless persons as defined by the Act. For the purposes of decision, the House of Lords had to interpret the meaning of 'accommodation'. The House of Lords adopted a very broad interpretation of the word, refusing to import a standard of reasonableness of accommodation which would protect the individual from being placed in unsuitable housing. Unlike the decision in *Khawaja*, where the House of Lords introduced a standard of proof which was protective of the individual against the administration, in *Pulhofer*, the court's ruling protected the administration – the housing authority – and not the individual. The Housing and Planning Act 1986 reverses the House of Lords' decision in *Pulhofer*, and requires that 'accommodation' be accommodation which it is reasonable for a person to continue to occupy. It can be seen from these two cases, that the interpretation of the question of law can dictate a very different outcome, depending upon the judicial approach taken.

When the issue concerns individual rights, for example, the courts will be slow to adopt an approach which has the effect of delimiting those rights. *Tan Te Lam and Others v Superintendent of Tai A Chau Detention Centre and Another*,[80] decided by the Privy Council, illustrates the point well.[81] The applicants were detainees in Hong Kong, having arrived there by boat from Vietnam. They were detained in detention centres, pending decisions as to whether to grant or refuse permission to remain in Hong Kong, or, if a decision to refuse permission were made, pending their removal from Hong Kong and repatriation to Vietnam. The applied for writs of habeas corpus to test the legality of their detention. By the time the appeal reached the Privy Council, the applicants had been detained for long periods of time, the longest being 24 months, pending determination of refugee status, followed by a further 44 months. Citing Woolf J, as he then was, in *R v Governor of Durham Prison ex parte Singh*,[82] the Privy Council endorsed the view, first, that the power to detain could only be exercised during the period necessary, in all the circumstances, to effect removal; secondly, that, if it becomes clear that removal is not going to be possible within a reasonable time, further detention is not authorised; thirdly, that the person seeking to exercise the power of

---

78 [1986] AC 484.
79 Originally, the Housing (Homeless Persons) Act 1977.
80 [1996] 4 All ER 256.
81 Following the transfer of sovereignty in 1997, appeals no longer lie to the Privy Council from the Hong Kong courts.
82 [1984] 1 WLR 704; [1984] 1 All ER 983.

detention must take all reasonable steps to ensure removal within a reasonable time.

In *Khawaja v Secretary of State for the Home Department*,[83] discussed above, the House of Lords had earlier considered the legality of a detention order pending removal, as an illegal immigrant, from the United Kingdom.[84] There was a dispute of fact as to whether the applicant had obtained leave to enter as a result of fraud. The House of Lords ruled that the issue of whether the applicant was an illegal immigrant was a matter which had to be established before it could be determined whether there was any power to detain with a view to deportation. That question 'was a precedent or jurisdictional fact which, in the case of deprivation of liberty, had to be proved to exist before any power to detain was exercisable at all'.

In relation to *Tan Te Lam and Others*, the question was analogous to that in *Khawaja*. As Lord Browne-Wilkinson stated:

> The issue therefore in the present case is whether the determination of the facts relevant to the question whether the applicants were being detained 'pending removal' goes to the jurisdiction of the director to detain or to the exercise of the discretion to detain. In their Lordships' view the facts are *prima facie* jurisdictional. If removal is not pending, within the meaning of section 13D, the director has no power at all [to detain].

Further, as Lord Browne-Wilkinson said:

> The case is analogous to one where a continuing discretion to detain is conferred on A if a notice has been served on B and no counternotice has been served by B. If there was a dispute as to whether a notice or counternotice had been served, it must *prima facie* be for the court to determine the question: if no notice has been served, A's power has never arisen; if a counternotice has been served, A's power has come to an end.[85]

The detainees were ordered to be released.

Using powers for the wrong purpose

Powers conferred must be used for the purpose for which they were granted. In *Attorney General v Fulham Corporation*,[86] the authority was empowered under statute to establish washhouses for the non-commercial use of local residents. The Corporation decided to open a laundry on a commercial basis. The Corporation was held to have acted *ultra vires* the statute. *Westminster*

---

83   [1984] AC 74; [1983] 2 WLR 321; [1983] 1 All ER 765.
84   The power to detain in *Khawaja* arose from the Immigration Act 1971, Sched 2, paras 9 and 16.
85   *Tan Te Lam and Others v Superintendent of Tai A Chau Detention Centre and Another* [1996] 4 All ER 256, p 267c, *per* Lord Browne-Wilkinson.
86   [1921] 1 Ch 440.

Corporation v London and Northern Western Railway Company,[87] however, represents a case where a charge of wrong purpose failed. The Corporation had power[88] to provide public conveniences and had constructed them midway under the street with access gained by means of a subway. The Railway Company which owned stock in adjacent buildings claimed that the power had been used improperly. The House of Lords disagreed, stating that 'the primary object of the council was the construction of the conveniences with the requisite and proper means of approach thereto and exit therefrom'.

Thus, where a public authority uses a power for the purpose intended by Parliament and reasonably provides a facility incidental to – or complementary to – the power conferred, the authority is acting within its powers. It can of course be argued that the Corporation's prime objective was, in fact, the provision of a subway; nevertheless, that objective – if it was the primary objective – did not invalidate the action.

The *Westminster Corporation* case was further considered in *R v Inner London Education Authority ex parte Westminster City Council,*[89] which provided an opportunity for the Divisional Court to consider the issue of two purposes being pursued under one power. On the facts of the case, it was held that, in pursuing two purposes,[90] the Council had allowed an 'irrelevant consideration' to dominate its decision making and that, accordingly, it had acted *ultra vires*. On the question of 'two purposes', Lord Justice Glidewell cited both Professor Wade[91] and Professor Evans.[92] Professor Wade writes:

> Sometimes, an act may serve two or more purposes, some authorised and some not, and it may be a question whether the public authority may kill two birds with one stone. The general rule is that its action will be lawful provided the permitted purpose is the true and dominant purpose behind the act, even though some secondary or incidental advantage may be gained for some purpose which is outside the authority's powers. There is a clear distinction between this situation and its opposite, where the permitted purpose is a mere pretext and a dominant purpose is *ultra vires*.[93]

The test which Professor Evans prescribes is:

> What is the true purpose for which the power was exercised? If the actor has in truth used his power for the purposes for which it was conferred, it is immaterial that he was thus enabled to achieve a subsidiary object ...

---

87 [1905] AC 426.
88 Under the Public Health Act 1891, s 44.
89 [1986] 1 WLR 28.
90 In relation to education funding.
91 *Op cit*, Wade and Forsyth, fn 17, p 388.
92 Cited in de Smith, SA, *Judicial Review of Administrative Action*, 4th edn, 1980, London: Penguin.
93 *Op cit*, Wade and Forsyth, fn 17, p 436.

Were any of the purposes pursuing an unauthorised purpose? If so, and if the unauthorised purpose has materially influenced the actor's conduct, the power has been invalidly exercised because irrelevant considerations have been taken into account.[94]

Acting in a manner inconsistent with the purpose of an Act was seen in *Padfield v Minister for Agriculture, Fisheries and Food*.[95] Under the Agricultural Marketing Act 1958, a Committee of Investigation was established to make inquiries, if the Minister 'so directed', into complaints made to the Minister concerning the operation of, amongst other products, milk. South Eastern dairy farmers complained that the Milk Marketing Board had fixed prices in a manner prejudicial to farmers in the South Eastern region of the country. The Minister refused to refer the matter to the Committee of Investigation. The farmers challenged the Minister's decision. The House of Lords granted an order of mandamus, requiring the Minister to consider properly whether he should exercise his discretion to refer. The House of Lords ruled by a majority[96] that, while the Minister was not obliged to refer every complaint made, neither did he have an unfettered discretion to refuse to refer a case. Lord Reid declared that:

> In a matter of this kind, it is not possible to draw a hard and fast line but, if the Minister, by reason of his having misconstrued the Act or for any other reason, so uses his discretion so as to thwart or run counter to the policy and objects of the Act, then our law would be very defective if persons aggrieved were not entitled to the protection of the court.

Lord Reid further declared that:

> ... the Act imposes on the Minister a responsibility whenever there is a relevant and substantial complaint that the board (the Milk Marketing Board) are acting in a manner inconsistent with the public interest, and that has been relevantly alleged in this case.[97]

The result was something of a hollow victory for the farmers, since the incoming Minister, having referred the matter to the committee, which upheld the complaint, rejected the committee's recommendations.[98]

In *R v Secretary of State for Foreign and Commonwealth Affairs ex parte World Development Movement*, the government was held to have acted unlawfully in relation to aid money paid to Malaysia.[99] In 1988,[100] the United Kingdom government signed an agreement with the Malaysian Prime Minister,

---

94 *Op cit*, de Smith, fn 92, pp 330–32.
95 [1968] AC 997.
96 Lord Morris of Borth-y-Gest dissenting.
97 [1968] AC 997, p 1030.
98 See Harlow, C, 'Administrative reaction to judicial review' [1976] PL 116.
99 [1995] 1 All ER 611; (1994) *The Times*, 11 November.
100 When Baroness Thatcher was Prime Minister.

Mahathir Mohamed, for the sale of arms valued £1.3 billion.[101] In 1989, Britain offered £234 million towards the building of the Pergau Dam. In 1991,[102] the deal went ahead, despite warnings from officials that the project was uneconomic and a waste of public funds. The monies were paid out of the Overseas Development Administration (ODA) budget. Under international law, any linkage between aid monies and arms sales is prohibited. While the government denied any such link, a House of Commons Foreign Affairs Committee inquiry concluded that the government had, in effect, made such a link. Furthermore, under section 1 of the Overseas Development and Co-operation Act 1980, the Foreign Secretary is empowered to authorise payments only 'for the purpose of promoting the development or maintaining the economy of a country or territory outside the United Kingdom or the welfare of its people'. Legal proceedings were instituted by the World Development Movement which believed that 'a vast sum of public money is being devoted to subsidising a project which is a misuse of funds that should properly be devoted to development and the relief of poverty'.[103]

The High Court ruled that the Foreign Secretary had acted unlawfully, in part because the project was 'economically unsound', and also because the aid did not promote the development of a country's economy as required by law. As a result, some £55 million already spent on the project had to be returned to the ODA.

Relevant and irrelevant considerations in decision making

The following section considers relevant and irrelevant considerations which are taken into account in decision making. To a large extent, there is at best a fine line between using powers for the wrong purpose and the relevancy of considerations. Categorisation is a limited, although organisationally useful, device: the essential point to remember is that the heart of the matter lies in whether or not discretionary powers have been exercised lawfully or not, irrespective of the headings under which cases may be grouped.[104] One case which straddles the boundaries of using powers for an improper purpose and taking irrelevant considerations into account is that of *R v Somerset County Council ex parte Fewings*.[105] The local authority decided to ban stag hunting on land owned by the council and designated for recreational purposes.[106] Laws

---

101 The agreement being signed by the then Secretary of State for Defence, George Younger.
102 Under the premiership of John Major.
103 (1994) *The Times*, 11 November.
104 See Taylor, GD, 'Judicial review of improper purposes and irrelevant considerations' [1976] CLJ 272.
105 [1995] 1 All ER 513.
106 Under the Local Government Act 1972, s 120.

J accepted that, in some circumstances, stag hunting could legitimately be banned – for example, where the hunt would damage rare flora, or if the animals themselves were rare. Here, however, the motivation behind the ban was the moral objection of the councillors to hunting. Laws J ruled that:

> If the activity in question is permissible under the general law, as is the practice of deer hunting, it is by no means to be prohibited on grounds only of the decision maker's distaste or ethical objection where the reach of his statutory function on its face requires no more than the making of objective judgments for the management of a particular regime.[107]

On appeal to the Court of Appeal, the decision was upheld, but on narrower grounds.[108] The Court ruled that the Council's mind had not been directed to relevant statutory provisions, and it had not considered, as it was required to do, whether a ban of hunting would be for the general public benefit.

A case which illustrates the intermingling of grounds for review is that of *Wheeler v Leicester City Council*.[109] In *Wheeler*, the House of Lords thoroughly examined the concepts of unreasonableness and of fairness, and here the interaction between bad faith, unreasonableness and procedural impropriety can be discerned. In 1984, the Rugby Football Union announced a tour to South Africa, with a team including three members of the Leicester Football Club. At the time, the government was opposed to any sporting links with South Africa. Leicester City Council – with a 25 per cent immigrant population – was virulently opposed to the proposed tour. The Leicester Club secretary attended a meeting with the leader of Leicester Council, at which he was asked to support the government's – and the council's – policy of opposition to the South African regime of apartheid. The club's response was to assert its opposition to apartheid but to stress that they were not constrained from playing in South Africa as a result of governmental opposition, which had neither made such tours illegal nor subject to sanctions on those who visited South Africa. As a result of the club's refusal to comply with the City Council's request that they withdraw from the tour, Leicester City Council resolved that the club would be suspended from using a local playing field for a 12 month period, the ban to be reviewed after a year and a new decision to be taken based on the club's attitude to South Africa at that time.

Lord Roskill summarised the essence of the debate as follows:

> To my mind the crucial question is whether the conduct of the council in trying by their four questions, whether taken individually or collectively, to force acceptance by the club of their own policy ... on their own terms, as for example, by forcing them to lend their considerable prestige to a public condemnation of the tour, can be said either to be so 'unreasonable' as to give rise to 'Wednesbury unreasonableness' or to be so fundamental a breach of the

---

107 [1995] 1 All ER 513, p 530.
108 [1995] 3 All ER 20.
109 [1985] AC 1054.

duty to act fairly which rests upon every local authority in matters of this kind and thus justify interference by the courts.[110]

Lord Roskill recognised both the strength and the sincerity of the council's opposition to apartheid but, nevertheless, went on to state that:

> Persuasion, even powerful persuasion, is always a permissible way of seeking to obtain an objective. But in a field where other views can equally legitimately be held, persuasion, however powerful, must not be allowed to cross that line where it moves into the field of illegitimate pressure coupled with the threat of sanction.[111]

Lord Templeman agreed:

> In my view, therefore, this is a case in which the court should interfere because of the unfair manner in which the council set about obtaining its objective.

> In my opinion, this use by the council of its statutory powers was a misuse of power. The council could not properly seek to use its statutory powers of management or any other statutory powers for the purposes of punishing the club when the club had done no wrong ...[112]

Accordingly, a political policy – however morally justified – could not provide the lawful basis on which to deprive the club of engaging in its lawful activities.

Acting in bad faith

In *Cannock Chase District Council v Kelly*,[113] Megaw LJ cited Lord Greene in *Wednesbury*: '... bad faith, dishonesty – those of course stand by themselves.' Megaw LJ went on to say that:

> ... bad faith or, as it is sometimes put, 'lack of good faith', means dishonesty; not necessarily for a financial motive, but still dishonesty. It always involves a grave charge. It must not be treated as a synonym for an honest, though mistaken, taking into consideration of a factor which is in law irrelevant ...[114]

To some extent, any decision which is *ultra vires* may involve 'bad faith' whenever there has been a failure to decide a case in the manner required by law. Some decisions however, may have inadvertently breached the requirements of legality, whereas others will reveal an improper motive and unreasonableness, and more clearly demonstrate that the decision maker acted in 'bad faith'.

---

110 [1985] AC 1054, p 1078.
111 *Ibid*, p 1078.
112 *Ibid*, p 1081.
113 [1978] 1 WLR 1.
114 *Ibid*, p 6.

FAILING TO ACT

Fettering discretion

An authority may act *ultra vires* if, in the exercise of its powers, it adopts a policy which effectively means that it is not truly exercising its discretion at all. This principle is explained in *R v Port of London Authority ex parte Kynoch*,[115] in which it was held that an authority could not adopt a rigid policy which had the effect of ensuring that applications of a certain category would invariably be refused. In *Kynoch*, the applicant sought judicial review of the decision of the Port of London Authority to refuse him permission to construct a wharf on land he owned adjoining the Thames river. Permission was refused on the basis that the Authority itself had a duty to provide the facilities. The challenge to the Authority's decision failed, on the basis that it appeared to the court that the Authority had given genuine consideration to the application on its merits.

Compare *Kynoch* with *British Oxygen Co v Board of Trade*[116] in which *Kynoch* was judicially considered. In *BOC*, the House of Lords upheld the right of the Board of Trade to have a general policy, provided that the policy did not preclude the Board from considering individual cases. Lord Reid considered the scope of discretion, asserting that:

> There are two general grounds on which the exercise of an unqualified discretion can be attacked. It must not be exercised in bad faith, and it must not be so unreasonably exercised as to show that there cannot have been any real or genuine exercise of the discretion. But, apart from that, if the Minister thinks that policy or good administration requires the operation of some limiting rule, I find nothing to stop him ...
>
> What the authority must not do is to refuse to listen at all.[117]

The application failed. The Board of Trade had not adopted a rigid and invariable policy which rendered the consideration of applications a mere sham exercise in which there was no possibility of a fair consideration of the merits because of the adoption of a rigid policy.

However, in *H Lavender & Sons Ltd v Minister of Housing and Local Government*,[118] a different conclusion was reached. Lavender had applied for planning permission to extract sand and gravel from high grade agricultural land. The local planning authority refused permission and Lavender appealed to the Minister of Housing and Local Government. The appeal was dismissed,

---

115 [1919] 1 KB 176. See Galligan, DJ, 'The nature and functions of policies within discretionary power' [1976] PL 332.

116 [1971] AC 610.

117 *Ibid*, p 624.

118 [1970] 1 WLR 1231.

the Minister of Housing and Local Government being persuaded by the Minister of Agriculture that such land should be preserved for agricultural purposes. Accordingly, the Minister ruled that:

> It is the Minister's present policy that land should not be released for mineral working unless the Minister of Agriculture is not opposed. In the present case, the agricultural objection has not been waived and the Minister has therefore decided not to grant planning permission for the working of the site.

The decision was set aside. The Minister was entitled to have a policy but, in reality, in this instance, the Minister's decision had been based solely on another Minister's objection. The Minister, therefore, did not open his mind to Lavender's application and thereby fettered his discretion. In reality, the decision to refuse planning permission was that of the Minister of Agriculture who had no power to determine such matters.

In *Stringer v Minister of Housing and Local Government*,[119] the court considered the legality of a Minister's policy to restrict development of land which could interfere with the Jodrell Bank telescope. The court held that the Minister's general policy was lawful, provided that the policy did not result in his failing to take into account relevant issues in each individual application for planning permission.

Sagnata Investments v Norwich Corporation[120] illustrates the same point. The Betting, Gaming and Lotteries Act of 1963 provided that the grant or renewal of a permit to run amusement arcades was to be 'at the discretion of the local authority'. Sagnata Investments applied for a licence which was turned down on the basis that the council had a policy never to grant permits for arcades in Norwich. There was no objection to Sagnata Investments itself; rather, no application – whatever its merits – would have succeeded because of the council's policy. The court held that the council had failed to exercise its discretion under the Act and had paid no regard whatsoever to the merits of the application. The council's decision was therefore quashed.[121]

In *R v Chief Constable of North Wales Police and Others ex parte AB and Another*,[122] the Queen's Bench Division ruled that the policy of the North Wales police to disclose information to members of the public concerning the presence of a former paedophile offender was not unlawful. The court recognised that, in general, good public administration involved not disclosing damaging information about individuals unless there was sound justification for so doing. The applicants for judicial review, who were

---

119 [1970] 1 WLR 1281.

120 [1971] 2 QB 614.

121 See, also, *Stringer v Minister of Housing and Local Government* [1970] 1 WLR 1281, on fettering discretion.

122 [1997] 3 WLR 724; (1997) *The Times*, 14 July. See Barber, NW, 'Privacy and the police: private right, public right or human right? *R v Chief Constable of the North Wales Police ex parte AB*' [1998] PL 19.

married, had both been convicted of serious sexual offences against children, and had served long prison sentences. The Lord Chief Justice recognised the tension between the rights of former offenders and the interests of the community. The police had not adopted a policy of blanket disclosure, but had carefully considered the case on its merits, and accordingly had not fettered its discretion. The decision was upheld by the Court of Appeal.[123] The Master of the Rolls, Lord Woolf, recognised that, in such cases, there was a balance to be struck between providing protection for children who might be at risk, and the position of the offender who had already served his sentence and wished to re-establish himself in the community. There was also a need to avoid driving offenders 'underground'. The position of the police was 'difficult and sensitive'. Disclosure should only be made when there was a 'pressing need for such disclosure'. The action of the police had been neither irrational, nor was the policy unlawful.

In *R v Secretary of State for the Home Department ex parte Dinc*,[124] the applicant had been sentenced to five years' imprisonment and the judge had recommended that he be deported at the end of his term of imprisonment. In 1995, the Secretary of State accepted the recommendation and made the deportation order. The applicant sought judicial review of that decision. The court ruled that the Secretary of State had fettered his discretion by relying on the judge's view and had given disproportionate weight to it. This had led him to leave out of account relevant factors.[125] In *R v North West Lancashire Health Authority ex parte A*,[126] the Court of Appeal ruled that a health authority had adopted a policy which was invalid, by allocating low priority for the public funding of procedures which it considered to be clinically ineffective, which included gender re-assignment surgery. The Court of Appeal stated that the policy was over-rigid and did not amount to a genuine policy subject to individually determined exceptions.

Taking irrelevant considerations into account

As can be seen, the two purposes tests involves the issue of irrelevant considerations. That is to say, a subsidiary or secondary purpose being pursued may – if it dictates the decision making process – invalidate that process. Here, attention is turned to situations where an authority fails to take account of relevant considerations, or takes into account irrelevant

---

123 Reported as *R v Chief Constable of North Wales Police and Others ex parte Thorpe and Another* (1998) *The Times*, 23 March, and see the government's proposals for arrangements on release of paedophiles from prison, HL Deb, Vol 589, Col 479, 5 May 1998.

124 [1998] COD 326.

125 On judicial review of immigration and asylum decisions, see Chapter 21.

126 (1999) *The Times*, 24 August.

considerations which materially affect the decision reached, and may be held to be acting *ultra vires*. Many of the cases involve the fiduciary duty which is owed by local authorities to their rate payers. In *Roberts v Hopwood*,[127] for example, the local authority was empowered by statute to pay its workers 'as it thought fit'.[128] Nevertheless, when the council decided to pay wages which were higher than the national average and to pay men and women equally, it was held to have been acting beyond its powers. Its duty to its ratepayers overrode its desire to better the lot of its workers.[129] The court held that the council was pursuing a policy of 'philanthropic socialism' which was inconsistent with its duties to its ratepayers. Compare *Roberts v Hopwood* with *Pickwell v Camden London Borough Council*,[130] in which the council had paid additional monies to its manual workers in order to secure settlement of an industrial dispute. It was held that the payments were reasonable.

Similar considerations applied in *Bromley London Borough Council v Greater London Council*.[131] There, the Greater London Council, wishing to increase passenger numbers – and thereby reduce the traffic congestion on the roads – by decreasing fares on public transport, sought to pay for this by seeking a higher level of subsidy for London Transport by increasing the rates payable by ratepayers, the burden of which would fall on the residents of London boroughs. The House of Lords held the Greater London Council to be acting *ultra vires*.

The House of Lords ruled that, whilst section 3 of the Act[132] conferred a wide discretion on the authority, and that grants could be levied to supplement the income from transport fares, that discretion was limited by London Transport's basic obligation to run its operations on ordinary business principles, which their fare reduction policy contravened. As in *Roberts v Hopwood*,[133] the council could not use its grant making powers to achieve a social policy which was inconsistent with those obligations: the Greater London Council (GLC) was using its powers for the wrong purpose. Moreover, the rate reduction was also invalid in so far as it involved a breach of fiduciary duty owed by the council to its rate payers. The fact that the policy had been part of an election mandate was not sufficient justification for the policy. The members of the council were representatives of the people, not delegates thereof. Accordingly, they were not irrevocably bound to fulfil

---

127 [1925] AC 578.
128 Under the Metropolis Management Act 1855, s 62.
129 See, also, *Prescott v Birmingham Corporation* [1955] Ch 210; *Taylor v Munrow* [1960] 1 WLR 151.
130 [1983] 2 WLR 583.
131 [1983] 1 AC 768.
132 Transport (London) Act 1969.
133 [1925] AC 578.

election promises but, rather, must act in the interests of all constituents – not just those constituents who were users of London Transport.

This view on the doctrine of mandate – or responsibility to electors – may be contrasted with the decision in *Secretary of State for Education v Tameside Metropolitan Borough Council*, discussed above, p 1046.[134] It will be recalled that the Labour controlled Council in March 1975 proposed a scheme of comprehensive education to come into effect in 1976. In 1976, a Conservative Council was elected. The Party had conducted its election campaign in large part on the education platform. On entering office, the council reversed the education policy of the previous administration. The Secretary of State issued a direction under section 68 of the Education Act 1944, ordering the council to implement the comprehensive schooling policy of the previous local council. The House of Lords laid much emphasis on the wishes of the electorate. Lord Wilberforce declared that:

> ... if he [the Secretary of State] had exercised his judgment on the basis of the factual situation in which this newly elected authority were placed – with a policy approved by the electorate, and massively supported by the parents – there was no ground, however much he might disagree with the new policy and regret such administrative dislocation as was brought about by the change, on which he could find that the authority were acting or proposing to act unreasonably ...[135]

Where an irrelevant consideration does not affect the outcome of a decision, the court may hold that the authority is acting *intra vires*. For example, in *R v Broadcasting Complaints Commission ex parte Owen*,[136] the Broadcasting Authority – with the statutory responsibility of ensuring fairness in the allocation of broadcasting time for political parties at election time – refused to consider a complaint that a political party had been given too little broadcasting time. That decision was challenged in the courts. However, while the Commission had some good reasons for not considering the complaint, it had also erred by giving weight to an irrelevant consideration, namely, that the task would be burdensome. The court nevertheless held that the Commission was acting within its lawful discretion.

A local authority is entitled to take into account the social conditions in its area and the nature of the community in question when deciding to issue permits to install amusement machines with prizes in a shopping centre. The Court of Appeal so held in *R v Liverpool Crown Court ex parte Luxury Leisure Ltd*,[137] on application for judicial review against the decision of the local authority and the Crown Court, on appeal, of a decision refusing a permit under the Gaming Act 1968 and Lotteries and Amusements Act 1976.

---

134 [1977] AC 1014.
135 *Ibid*, p 1052.
136 [1985] QB 1153.
137 (1998) *The Times*, 26 October.

Whether or not a local authority may not take into account considerations relating to financial resources when assessing an individual's needs was considered by the Court of Appeal and House of Lords in *R v Gloucestershire County Council and Another ex parte Barry; R v Lancashire County Council ex parte Royal Association for Disability and Rehabilitation and Another*.[138] Under the Chronically Sick and Disabled Persons Act 1970, a local authority is under the duty to identify the needs of disabled persons, and to meet such needs. The Court of Appeal held that neither a third party's resources, nor the needs of others could be relevant to making the assessment of needs in relation to a disabled person. If that were to be the correct interpretation of the statute, a local authority with no funds to meet needs could avoid its duty to assess the needs and make the necessary provision. That would fly in the face of the plain language of the 1970 Act. In the House of Lords, however, that decision was reversed. By a majority of three to two, the House of Lords ruled that the resources of the authority were a relevant consideration. Lord Nicholls of Birkenhead conceded that the argument put forward by Lord Lloyd, dissenting, that a person's needs were unaffected by local authority resources was an 'alluring argument', but one which he could not accept. The argument, he stated, was flawed by a 'failure to recognise that needs for services cannot sensibly be assessed without having some regard to the cost of providing them'.[139]

The reasoning of the majority in the House of Lords in *Barry*, was followed in *R v Sefton Metropolitan Borough Council ex parte Help the Aged and Others*.[140] In that case, the needs of an elderly woman who was admitted to a nursing home, and the cost of meeting those needs, were in issue. Having considered the case of *Barry*, the Court of Appeal ruled that a local authority was entitled to have regard to its own limited financial resources. However, where a need existed, the authority was under a statutory duty to make arrangements to meet that need and lack of resources was no excuse. The authority could not, from the time that a person was assessed as being in need, fail to meet their statutory duty. Financial considerations were uppermost in the decision in *R v Cambridge Health Authority ex parte B*,[141] in which the Court of Appeal held that the courts could not make judgments about how health authorities decide to allocate a limited budget. The health authority had refused to fund further chemotherapy or a second bone marrow transplant for a 10 year old girl with only a few weeks to live. Notwithstanding that decisions relating to human life had to treated with the greatest seriousness, the court could not substitute

---

138 [1997] 2 All ER 1; (1996) *The Times*, 12 July.

139 *Ibid*, p 11e.

140 [1997] 4 All ER 532.

141 [1995] 2 All ER 129, CA. See James, R, and Longley, D, 'Judicial review and tragic choices' [1995] PL 367; and see O'Sullivan, D, 'The allocation of scarce resources and the right to life under the European Convention on Human Rights' [1998].

its judgment about the allocation of financial resources for that of the authority.

In *R v East Sussex County Council ex parte Tandy*,[142] the House of Lords ruled that, although a local education authority could have regard to its resources when deciding which of two alternative ways of providing suitable education should be chosen, resources were irrelevant when determining what sort of education was suitable under the Education Act 1993, section 298 of which defines suitable education as 'efficient education suitable to his age, ability and aptitude and to any special educational needs he may have'. The effect of taking resources into account would be to downgrade a statutory duty to a mere power.

In *B v Harrow London Borough Council*,[143] the House of Lords ruled that, when considering the impact of the cost of meeting special educational needs to the pupil's own local authority and another authority to which the parents had expressed a preference, it was to the home authority's resources that attention must be paid.

Unauthorised delegation

Where powers are conferred by statute, the general rule is that they may not be delegated unless that delegation is authorised by law. Not all delegations will be unlawful. The courts will not hold, for instance, that a Minister must exercise each and every power personally. It is accepted that that, where statute confers powers on Ministers, the powers are, in fact, exercisable on his behalf by the personnel of his department. As explained in *Local Government Board v Arlidge*,[144] 'a Minister cannot do everything himself'.[145] In *Arlidge* – an early and seminal case which ensured the conduct of government under the supervision of the courts – the court held that, whilst a Minister could lawfully delegate his power of determination to a subordinate, he, nevertheless, remained constitutionally and personally accountable to Parliament for the conduct of his department.[146]

This principle was well illustrated in *Carltona v Works Commissioners*.[147] The Commissioners were given powers, under wartime regulations, to requisition property. Carltona's property was requisitioned, the order for

---

142 [1998] 2 WLR 884.

143 [2000] 1 WLR 223.

144 [1915] AC 120.

145 Note, also, that this case is also an early authority for the proposition that the rules of natural justice do not necessarily require an oral hearing in every case: *per* Taylor LJ in *R v Army Board of the Defence Council ex parte Anderson* [1991] 3 WLR 42.

146 See Dicey, AV, *Introduction to the Study of the Law of the Constitution*, 10th edn, 1959, London: Macmillan, Appendix 2.

147 [1943] 2 All ER 560.

requisition being signed, for and on behalf of the Commissioners, by a civil servant with the rank of assistant secretary. Lord Greene MR stated that:

> It cannot be supposed that the particular statutory provision meant that in every case the Minister in person should direct his mind to the matter. Constitutionally the decision of such an officer is the decision of the Minister; the Minister is responsible to Parliament. If the Minister delegated to a junior official then he would have to answer to Parliament ...

The decision in *Arlidge* may be compared with that of *Barnard v National Dock Labour Board*.[148] In *Barnard*, disciplinary powers delegated by statute to the London Dock Board were subdelegated to a port manager. That delegation was held to be *ultra vires*, on the basis that such a disciplinary function could not lawfully be delegated to another and must be exercised by the Board to whom the power was granted. Similarly, in *R v Talbot Borough Council ex parte Jones*,[149] where a local councillor applied for local authority housing. The housing tenancy committee resolved that the applicant should be given priority status and that her rehousing, subsequent to divorce, should be decided by the chairman and vice chairman of the committee, according to the Council's Standing Orders,[150] in consultation with the Borough Housing Officer. In 1986, the Housing Officer allocated her a house. In proceedings for judicial review, it was held that the decision to allocate housing could not lawfully be subdelegated from the chairman and vice chairman of the committee to the Housing Officer. The decision was also void on the grounds that irrelevant considerations had been taken into account and that relevant considerations – the needs of others on the waiting list – had been ignored.

In *Oladehinde v Secretary of State for the Home Department*,[151] the question of authorised delegation came before the House of Lords. The applicants wished to challenge notices of intention to deport them. The notices were issued by immigration inspectors. The applicants argued that the powers under the Immigration Act 1971 were conferred upon the Secretary of State and could not be delegated. The House of Lords dismissed the appeal. The Act provided specific matters which could not be delegated by the Minister, and the court would not infer further restrictions. Provided that the decision was taken by officials of suitable grading and experience, they were unchallengeable.

Failure to act

An authority may be under a statutory duty to take action and, depending upon the specificity of that duty, may be held to be acting unlawfully if it fails

---

148 [1953] 2 QB 18.
149 [1988] 2 All ER 207.
150 Under the Local Government Act 1972, s 101.
151 [1990] 3 All ER 383.

to act. This is a difficult area of law, in that some duties imposed by statute are clear and precise, and hence enforceable by the courts, whereas others may be of a general, non-specific nature and thus not court-enforceable: all will turn on the wording of the statute. Statute may stipulate the objective to be achieved but leave it to a local authority or other public body to determine the manner in which the objective should be achieved. Furthermore, in many cases, statute will provide that the Secretary of State shall have default powers, by the use of which he can compel a local authority to act should it fail so to do, in which case, the courts may be reluctant to permit the pursuit of an alternative remedy.[152] In *R v Secretary of State for the Environment ex parte Norwich*,[153] the authority had the duty to sell council housing to tenants[154] at a discounted rate. If a tenant exercised his or her right to buy, and the council did not respect that right, the Minister could exercise his powers to ensure compliance with the legislation, if satisfied that a tenant's right had 'not effectively and expeditiously' been recognised. The council argued that this policy was reasonable. However, the Court of Appeal rejected that argument, since the council had no discretion in light of the statutory right to buy. The failure of the council to implement the 'right to buy' legislation was to be controlled by the Minister. Should the Minister, in the exercise of his powers, act *ultra vires*, the court will control the exercise of power by judicial review. However, the courts may not be willing to rule against the Minister merely because the court takes a different view of the merits of the case.[155]

An example of powers which are inextricably linked to resource availability can be seen in relation to health care provision. The Secretary of State for Health is under an obligation to provide hospital beds for those in need. If, in contravention of this clear requirement, a patient is denied a hospital bed, an action for judicial review will lie but, if the Minister claims inadequate resources, the judges may be reluctant to hold a Minister to be in breach of his duties. A more appropriate avenue of redress for a complainant may be to the Health Service Commissioners.[156]

---

152 See Cane, P, '*Ultra vires* breach of statutory duty' [1981] PL 11.

153 [1982] QB 808.

154 Housing Act 1980. The Housing Act 1985 confers default powers on the Minister to act where a local council fails to comply with the policy of the Act.

155 [1982] QB 808, *per* Lord Denning.

156 Established under the National Health Service Reorganisation Act 1973.

PROCEDURAL IMPROPRIETY

Under statute

Failure to comply with procedures laid down by statute may invalidate a decision. The courts distinguish between those procedural requirements which are mandatory, the breach of which will render a decision void, and those which are directory, which may not invalidate the decision taken. In *London and Clydesdale Estates Ltd v Aberdeen District Council*,[157] the House of Lords emphasised the inherent vagueness in the distinction and stressed that the court would not draw a hard and fast line: it is all a matter of degree and the particular circumstances of the case must be examined. However, in some cases, the requirement to adhere to procedural correctness is clear. For example, in *Bradbury v Enfield London Borough Council*,[158] the Education Act 1944 provided that, if a local education authority intends to establish new schools or cease to maintain existing schools, notice must be given to the Minister, following which, public notice must be given in order to allow interested parties to comment.[159] The Council breached the requirement of public notice and the plaintiffs sought an injunction. The Council claimed that educational chaos would occur if they were required to comply with the procedural requirements. That plea met with little sympathy in court. Lord Denning stated that:

> ... if a local authority does not fulfil the requirements of the law, this court will see that it does fulfil them. It will not listen readily to suggestions of 'chaos'. The department of education and the council are subject to the rule of law and must comply with it, just like everyone else ... I can well see that there may be a considerable upset for a number of people, but I think it far more important to uphold the rule of law. Parliament has laid down these requirements so as to ensure that the electors can make their objections and have them properly considered. We must see that their rights are upheld.[160]

Further, as has been seen earlier, in the *Aylesbury Mushroom* case,[161] the court ruled that the statutory requirements of consultation[162] with organisations or associations which represented substantial numbers of people could not be avoided by consultation with the largest representative body of all agricultural horticultural and forestry industry, workers – the National Farmers' Union. The Board claimed that consultation with the National

---

157 [1979] 2 All ER 876.
158 [1967] 1 WLR 1311.
159 Education Act 1944, s 13.
160 [1967] 1 WLR 1311, p 1324.
161 *Agricultural, Horticultural and Forestry Industry Training Board v Aylesbury Mushroom Ltd* [1972] 1 WLR 190.
162 Under the Industrial Training Act 1964, s 1(4).

Farmers' Union involved consultation with all smaller representative bodies; a claim rejected by the court. For true consultation to take place in accordance with law, there must be communication with the representative organisations and the opportunity given of responding thereto, without which 'there can be no consultation'.

However, on occasion, although an authority is under a duty to act, and fails to act, the court may nevertheless uphold the decision made, provided that the decision making process was otherwise fair and the failure to act does not affect the quality of the decision reached. This was the position in *Berkeley v Secretary of State for the Environment and Another*.[163] In this case, in a planning application by Fulham Football Club to redevelop part of its land to provide apartments and a riverside walk, the Secretary of State was required[164] to consider the environmental impact of the proposed development, and to issue an 'environmental statement'. Notwithstanding the failure of the Secretary of State to comply with the regulations, planning permission was granted. On appeal to the Court of Appeal against the refusal of the court below to quash the planning permission, the Court of Appeal ruled that the Secretary of State's failure to act did not invalidate the decision. The planning application had been referred to the Secretary of State who had appointed an inspector. A public hearing had been held, at which the applicant had been heard and at which the environmental impact of the proposed development had been fully considered. The court found that 'the procedures adopted, although flawed, had been thorough and effective [so as] to enable the inspector to make a comprehensive judgment on all the environmental issues'.

The Court of Appeal re-examined the effect of non-compliance with procedural requirements laid down in statute in *R v Secretary of State for the Home Department ex parte Jeyeanthan; Ravichandran v Secretary of State for the Home Department*.[165] The Home Secretary had failed to comply substantially with the requirements of the Asylum Appeals Rules by not including a declaration of truth in an application for leave to appeal from a special adjudicator to the Immigration Appeal Tribunal. However, the asylum seeker had not been affected by the omission, which was treated as an irregularity capable of being cured by the Tribunal. The court ruled that, in determining the effect of non-compliance with a procedural requirement, the court should consider what the legislator had intended to be the consequences of non-compliance, rather than merely whether the requirement was mandatory or directory. Neither of the applicants had in any way been affected by the omission and, other than to discipline the Secretary of State, there could be no reason to treat his successful application for leave as a nullity.

---

163 (1998) *The Times*, 2 March.
164 Under the Town and Country Planning (Assessment of Environmental Effects) Regulations SI 1988/1199, reg 4.
165 [1999] 3 All ER 231; (1999) *The Times*, 26 May.

Breach of natural justice

Of course, there is a wealth of authority on what are and what are not the rules of natural justice. The rules have been described in various ways, as an 'unruly horse', I think, in one decision, and there is no doubt that what may be the rules of natural justice in one case may well not be the rules of natural justice in another. As has frequently been said, and there is no harm in repeating it, all that the rules of natural justice mean is that the proceedings must be conducted in a way which is fair ... fair in all the circumstances.[166]

That the rules of natural justice are not rigid and determinate is emphasised by Lord Bridge in *Lloyd v McMahon*:[167]

... the so called rules of natural justice are not engraved on tablets of stone. To use the phrase which better expresses the underlying concept, what the requirements of fairness demand when any body, domestic, administrative or judicial, has to make a decision which will affect the rights of individuals depends on the character of the decision making body, the kind of question it has to make and the statutory or other framework in which it operates.

The rules of natural justice are common law rules – although, in many instances, their requirements may be made statutory. The fundamental dictate of justice is that those affected by decision makers should be dealt with in a fair manner. In order for this to be achieved, there may be several requirements which must be fulfilled.

The rule against bias: nemo iudex in causa sua[168]

The essence of justice lies in a fair hearing. The rule against bias is strict: it is not necessary to show that actual bias existed, the merest appearance or possibility of bias will suffice: '... justice should not only be done but should manifestly and undoubtedly be seen to be done.'[169] The suspicion of bias must, however, be a reasonable one. Both financial or personal interest in a case may disqualify a person from adjudicating.

Financial bias

In *Dr Bonham's Case*,[170] Lord Coke held that members of a board which determined the level of physicians' fines could not both impose and receive

---

166 Lord Lane CJ in *R v Commission for Racial Equality ex parte Cottrell and Rothon* [1980] 1 WLR 1580, p 1586.
167 [1987] 1 All ER 1118, p 1161.
168 See Rawlings, R, 'The test for the *nemo iudex* rule' [1980] PL 122. On the independence of the judiciary, see, also, Chapter 5.
169 See *R v Sussex Justices ex parte McCarthy* [1924] 1 KB 256, p 259, discussed below.
170 (1609) 77 ER 646.

the fines, thus giving early judicial expression for the requirement of freedom from bias. An early expression of the absolute requirement not only to be impartial in fact, but also to be demonstrably and clearly free from the merest suspicion of bias is found in *Dimes v Grand Junction Canal Ltd*.[171] In *Dimes*, Lord Cottenham LC held shares in the canal company involved in litigation. The House of Lords set aside the decision in which he had adjudicated despite the fact that:

> No one can suppose that Lord Cottenham could be in the remotest degree influenced by the interest ... It is of the last importance that the maxim that no man is to be judge in his own cause should be held sacred.[172]

Thus, the mere existence of a financial interest, even where it does not, in fact, result in actual bias but may present the appearance of bias will be sufficient to disqualify a judge from adjudication.[173]

In *R v Sussex Justices ex parte McCarthy*,[174] the applicant had been charged with dangerous driving and convicted. On discovering that the clerk to the magistrates' court was a solicitor who had represented the person suing McCarthy for damages, McCarthy applied for judicial review based on bias on the part of the clerk. The clerk had retired with the magistrates when they were considering their verdict. It was accepted that the magistrates neither sought advice nor were given advice by the clerk during their retirement. Nevertheless, McCarthy's conviction was invalidated on the basis of the possibility of bias.

The question of financial bias again arose in *Metropolitan Properties Co v Lannon*,[175] where an application was lodged by a property company in order to challenge a decision of a rent assessment committee on the basis that Lannon, a member of the committee had, in his professional capacity as a solicitor, given advice to tenants of a close business associate of the property company.[176] Lord Denning MR ruled that, while there was no actual bias:

> ... the court looks at the impression which would be given to other people. Even if he was as impartial as could be, nevertheless, if right minded persons would think that, in the circumstances, there was a real likelihood of bias on his part, then he should not sit. And, if he does sit, his decision cannot stand ...

> The court will not inquire whether he did, in fact, favour one side unfairly. Suffice it that reasonable people might think he did. The reason is plain enough. Justice must be rooted in confidence: and confidence is destroyed when right minded people go away thinking: 'The judge was biased.'[177]

---

171 (1852) 3 HL Cas 759.
172 *Ibid*, p 793.
173 See, further, Chapter 5.
174 [1924] 1 KB 256.
175 [1969] 1 QB 577.
176 [1968] 1 WLR 815. On the remedy of certiorari, see Chapter 24.
177 [1969] 1 QB 577, p 599.

A financial interest in a case which does not go beyond the financial interest of any citizen does not disqualify judges from sitting. Thus, for example, in *Bromley London Borough Council v Greater London Council*,[178] the fact that all the judges in the Court of Appeal were themselves both taxpayers and users of public transport in London did not disqualify them from hearing the case.

The same position prevails in the United States of America[179] but, there, the issue of the financial interests of federal judges is expressly covered by statute. The Ethics in Government Act 1978 requires that Supreme Court and Federal judges must make a public declaration of 'income, gifts, shares, liabilities and transactions in securities and real estate'.[180]

Other bias

Judges – as with any other person – may exhibit bias by virtue of race, sex, politics, background, association and opinions.[181] When adjudicating, however, they must be demonstrably impartial. This impartiality involves:

> ... the judge, listening to each side with equal attention, and coming to a decision on the argument, irrespective of his personal view about the litigants ...

and, further, a requirement that:

> Whatever his personal beliefs, the judge should seek to give effect to the common values of the community, rather than any sectional system of values to which he may adhere.[182]

The seminal recent case on bias if the *Pinochet* case.[183] This has been discussed in Chapters 5 and 21, which should be referred to for discussion.

The Court of Appeal reconsidered judicial bias in the *Locabail (UK) Ltd v Bayfield Properties Ltd* cases.[184] The court distinguished the two rules relating to disqualification, the first being where the judge had an interest in a case which he decided, as in *Dimes v Grand Junction Canal*,[185] and where he would be automatically disqualified. The second rule was that based on examination of all the relevant circumstances, where there was a real danger or possibility

---

178 [1983] 1 AC 768.

179 28 USC S455(b).

180 See Cranston, R, 'Disqualification of judges for interest or opinion' [1979] PL 237.

181 See Griffith, JAG, *The Politics of the Judiciary*, 4th edn, 1991, London: Fontana (see, now, 5th edn, 1997); Devlin (Lord), 'Judges, government and politics' (1978) 41 MLR 501.

182 Bell, J, *Policy Arguments in Judicial Decisions*, 1983, Oxford: Clarendon, pp 4 and 8.

183 *R v Bow Street Metropolitan and Stipendiary Magistrate and Others ex parte Pinochet Ugarte* [1999] 2 All ER 97; [1999] 2 WLR 827.

184 (1999) *The Times*, 19 November. See, also, Chapter 5.

185 (1852) 3 HL Cas 759.

of bias, as in *R v Gough*.[186] In relation to the circumstances surrounding *Timmins v Gormley*, one of the *Locabail* cases, which concerned the publication, by the Recorder who adjudicated in a personal injury case, of articles which were allegedly biased in favour of claimants and against insurers, the court ruled that, taking a broad common sense approach, a lay observer with knowledge of the facts could not have excluded the possibility that the Recorder was biased. While it was not inappropriate for a judge to publish in his area of expertise, and that such contributions could further rather than hinder the administration of justice, nevertheless, it was always inappropriate for a judge to use intemperate language about subjects on which he had adjudicated or would have to adjudicate. The appeal was allowed and a retrial ordered.[187]

Uncertainty in the test for bias

There has been uncertainty and inconsistency in the interpretation of 'bias'. In *R v Gough*,[188] opposing counsel presented two different tests for bias. The first suggested criterion was whether a reasonable and fair minded person sitting in the court and knowing all the relevant facts would have had a reasonable suspicion that a fair trial of the defendant was not possible – the 'reasonable suspicion' test. The second suggested test was whether there was a real likelihood of bias. The question to be asked is whether there was a 'real danger' that a trial may not have been fair as a result of bias – the 'real likelihood' test.[189] The House of Lords declared that the correct test was whether there was a real likelihood, in the sense of a real possibility, of bias of the part of a justice or member of a tribunal.

Where a judge feels that he has a bias against one of the parties to litigation he may disqualify himself from sitting on the case, as did Lord Denning MR in *Ex parte Church of Scientology of California*.[190] There, counsel for the Church requested that he disqualify himself as a result of eight previous cases involving the Church on which he had sat.

The right to a fair hearing:[191] audi alteram partem

It is a fundamental requirement of justice that, when a person's interests are affected by a judicial or administrative decision, he or she has the opportunity

---

186 [1993] 2 WLR 883.

187 See, also, *R v Local Commissioner for Administration in North and North East England ex parte Liverpool City Council* (2000) *The Times*, 3 February, CA, discussed in Chapter 26.

188 [1993] 2 All ER 724.

189 *Ibid*, p 727; see, also, *R v Spencer* [1987] AC 128.

190 (1978) *The Times*, 21 February.

191 See Rawlings, HF, 'Judicial review and the control of government' (1986) 64 Public Admin 135.

both to know and to understand any allegations made, and to make representations to the decision maker to meet the allegations. By way of example, a fair determination of a case may involve one or more of the following:

(a) the right to being given notification of a hearing;

(b) the right to be given indications of any adverse evidence;

(c) the right to be given an opportunity to respond to the evidence;

(d) the right to an oral hearing;

(e) the right to legal representation at a hearing;

(f) the right to question witnesses.

The basic requirement is that – irrespective of the decision making body, whether 'judicial', 'quasi-judicial' or 'administrative'[192] – the individual should be treated fairly in the decision making process.

'Judicial', 'quasi-judicial' and 'administrative' functions: the distinctions

The courts have long been struggling with the distinction between 'judicial', 'quasi-judicial' and 'administrative' functions in an attempt to bring the ever-expanding administration of government departments under judicial control. Two lines of thought were apparent. The first emphasised the distinction between a body which was exercising powers under restrictive rules and a body which was conferred with a wide measure of administrative discretionary power.[193] The second line of thought placed great weight on the absence of any true distinction between judicial and administrative functions, regarding the former as but a specialised form of the latter.[194] As a result of conceptual confusion, the phrase 'quasi-judicial' came to be used to cover those functions which were not easily compartmentalised into either one or other concept. As a result, differing legal consequences would follow from the classification: the rules of natural justice being less rigorous in the case of the exercise of power by those bodies which were deemed to exercise 'quasi-judicial' or 'administrative' functions.

An early expression of the requirement of a hearing is to be found in *Cooper v Wandsworth Board of Works*.[195] There, Cooper had – without giving notice to the Board, as required by law – started to erect a house. The Board had the power to demolish buildings built without the requisite permission, and exercised their power so to do. Cooper applied for – and recovered –

---

192 See, further, below.

193 See Gordon DM, '"Administrative" tribunals and the courts' (1933) 49 LQR 94.

194 See Jennings, I (Sir), *The Law and the Constitution*, 5th edn, 1959, London: Hodder & Stoughton, Appendix I.

195 (1893) 14 CB (NS) 180, p 194.

damages from the Board for trespass to his property. Byles J held that the plaintiff should have been given a hearing before the Board exercised their powers, even though there was no express statutory requirement that they do so:

> ... although there are no positive words in a statute requiring that the party shall be heard, yet the justice of the common law shall supply the omission of the legislature.[196]

However, such a dynamic and protective judicial attitude was not to be found, for example, in *Nakkuda Ali v Jayaratne*.[197] In *Nakkuda Ali*, the Privy Council held that there was no duty to give a hearing to a dealer when his licence was under consideration – and was revoked – because the statute made no such express provision and the court concluded that there was no duty on the licensing board to 'act judicially'.

Judicial rejection of the classifications

Ridge v Baldwin[198] represents a classic case which reveals judicial insistence on procedural fairness irrespective of the type of body determining a question.[199] Ridge, the Chief Constable of Brighton, had been suspended from duty following charges of conspiracy to obstruct the course of justice. Despite Ridge having been cleared of any allegations against him, the judge made comments which were critical of Ridge's conduct. Subsequently, Ridge was dismissed from the force.[200] Ridge was not invited to attend the meeting at which the decision to dismiss him was reached, although he was later given an opportunity to appear before the committee which confirmed its earlier decision. Ridge appealed to the Home Secretary,[201] who dismissed his appeal. Ridge then sought a declaration that the dismissal was *ultra vires*, on the basis that the committee had violated the rules of natural justice. The following extract is taken from Lord Reid's judgment, in which the opportunity was taken to review the doctrine.

> The principle of *audi alteram partem* goes back many centuries in our law and appears in a multitude of judgments of judges of the highest authority. In modern times opinions have sometimes been expressed to the effect that

---

196 See, also, *Steeple v Derbyshire County Council* [1984] 3 All ER 486; but cf *R v Amber Valley District Council ex parte Jackson* [1984] 3 All ER 501. See, also, *R v Hendon Rural District Council ex parte Chorley* [1933] 2 KB 696.

197 [1951] AC 66.

198 [1964] AC 40.

199 See, on this point, *R v Hillingdon Borough Council ex parte Royco Homes Ltd* [1974] QB 720; *R v Commission for Racial Equality ex parte Cottrell and Rothon* [1980] 3 All ER 265.

200 Under the Municipal Corporations Act 1882, s 191(4), which provides that a constable may be dismissed on the basis of either negligence in the discharge of his duty or being 'otherwise unfit' for duty.

201 Under the Police (Appeals) Act 1927.

natural justice is so vague as to be almost meaningless ... It appears to me that one reason why the authorities on natural justice have been found difficult to reconcile is that insufficient attention has been paid to the great difference between various kinds of cases in which it has been sought to apply the principle. What a Minister ought to do in considering objections to a scheme may be very different from what a watch committee ought to do in considering whether to dismiss a chief constable ...[202]

... I would think that the authority was wholly in favour of the appellant, but the respondent's argument was mainly based on what has been said in a number of fairly recent cases dealing with different subject matter. Those cases deal with the decisions of Ministers, officials and bodies of various kinds which adversely affected property rights or privileges of persons who had no opportunity or no proper opportunity of presenting their cases before the decisions were given ...[203]

Lord Reid proceeded to discuss the authorities in relation to differing functions which had led to the judicial conclusion that differing cases required different levels of respect for the requirement of a hearing, and concluded that:

... So I would hold that the power of dismissal in the Act of 1882 could not then have been exercised and cannot now be exercised until the watch committee have informed the constable of the grounds on which they propose to proceed and given him a proper opportunity to present his case in defence ...[204]

The right to a hearing founded a challenge in *Re Pergamon Press Ltd*,[205] in which the directors of two companies refused to answer questions unless given a judicial-style hearing. The court ruled, however, that, although the inspectors appointed to investigate the companies were under a duty to act fairly, this must be weighed against the interests of good administration.

The duty to act 'fairly' and concept of 'legitimate expectation'

Irrespective of the labelling attached to the body in question, there exists a duty to 'act fairly'. This principle can be clearly seen in the case of *Re HK (An Infant)*,[206] wherein it was held that, whilst immigration officers were not obliged to hold a hearing before deciding an immigrant's status, they were nevertheless under an obligation to act fairly. The duty to give a hearing will

---

202 [1964] AC 40, p 64.

203 *Ibid*, p 68.

204 *Ibid*, p 79. See, further, Craig, PP, *Administrative Law*, 3rd edn, 1994, London: Sweet & Maxwell, Chapter 8.3; *op cit*, Wade and Forsyth, fn 17, pp 494–575.

205 [1971] Ch 388. See, also, *Maxwell v Department of Trade* [1974] QB 523.

206 [1967] 2 QB 617.

be higher if a 'legitimate expectation' has been created in the mind of the complainant by the public body concerned.[207]

A legitimate expectation will arise in the mind of the complainant wherever he or she has been led to understand – by the words or actions of the decision maker – that certain procedures will be followed in reaching a decision. The complainant may have been led to believe, for example, that there would be an oral hearing, or that he would be able to make formal representations. Where such expectations have been created, the decision maker is not free simply to ignore the procedures which have been indicated. Two considerations apply to legitimate expectations. The first is where an individual or group has been led to believe that a certain procedure will apply. The second is where an individual or group rely upon a policy or guidelines which have previously governed an area of executive action. The Court of Appeal in *R v North and East Devon Health Authority ex parte Coughlan*[208] ruled that a decision by a health authority to close a home for the severely disabled at which the applicant resided, and to transfer her to the care of a local authority, was unlawful. The applicant had been assured by the predecessor to the health authority that the home was her home for life, thus creating a legitimate expectation which no public interest overrode. Furthermore, under Article 8 of the Convention on Human Rights, everyone had a right to respect for his home and the judge had been entitled to treat the case as one in which there would be an unjustifiable breach of Article 8.

However, while the concept of legitimate expectation has, according to the Court of Appeal, achieved an important place in developing the law of administrative fairness, whether such an expectation has been raised is dependent upon the circumstances in which statements are made, and whether in an instant case they could be taken as propounding a policy or merely statements applicable to particular cases. In *R v Secretary for the Home Department ex parte Behluli*,[209] the Home Secretary had ordered the removal of the applicant to Italy under section 2 of the Asylum and Immigration Act 1996. The applicant argued that he had a legitimate expectation that his case would be dealt with in accordance with the Dublin Convention.[210] The Court of Appeal ruled, however, that the statements relied on by the applicant fell short of the requirements necessary to establish to the requisite degree of clarity and certainty that the Secretary of State would deal with all

---

207 The courts are also concerned to ensure that government proposals which will affect individual citizens are fairly presented in order to enable objectors to address the issue in question. In *R v Secretary of State for Transport ex parte Richmond upon Thames London Borough Council and Others (No 4)* [1994] 1 All ER 577, the Court of Appeal ruled that the government's proposals to restrict night flights at Heathrow, Gatwick and Stansted had been fairly set out in consultations documents.

208 (1999) *The Times*, 20 July.

209 [1998] COD 328.

210 Relating to the removal of persons to safe third countries.

applications for asylum in accordance with the Convention and not in accordance with the Asylum and Immigration Act 1996 and rules made thereunder.

The giving of assurances

By way of illustration, in *Attorney General for Hong Kong v Ng Yuen Shiu*,[211] the applicant had been an illegal immigrant for some years. He was eventually detained and an order was made for his deportation. The Director of Immigration had given a public undertaking that illegal immigrants such as Ng Yuen Shiu would not be deported without first being interviewed. The assurance was also given that 'each case would be treated on its merits'. Lord Fraser of Tullybelton in the Privy Council ruled that there was no general right in an alien to have a hearing in accordance with the rules of natural justice. Nevertheless, a 'legitimate expectation' had been created in the mind of the immigrant and, accordingly, breach of the requirement of fairness justified the order for his removal from Hong Kong to be quashed.

Fairness may involve the due consultation of interested parties before their rights are affected by decisions. For example, in *R v Liverpool Corporation ex parte Liverpool Taxi Fleet Operators Association*,[212] the corporation had given undertakings to the taxi drivers to the effect that their licences would not be revoked without prior consultation. When the corporation acted in breach of this undertaking, the court ruled that it had a duty to comply with its commitment to consultation.

Acting in a manner so as to create an expectation

A public body may act in a manner which creates an expectation in the mind of a person or body. For example, in *R v Secretary of State for Health ex parte US Tobacco International Inc*,[213] the company had opened a factory in 1985, with a government grant, for the production of oral snuff. The government made the grant available notwithstanding its awareness of the health risks of the product. In 1988, however, the government – having received further advice from a committee – announced its intention to ban snuff. The company sought judicial review, relying on a legitimate expectation based on the government's action. The court ruled, however, that, even though the applicant had a legitimate expectation, that expectation could not override the public interest in banning a harmful substance.

---

211 [1983] 2 AC 629.
212 [1972] 2 QB 299.
213 [1992] QB 353.

The existence of policies and/or guidance

In *R v Secretary of State for the Home Department ex parte Asif Mahmood Khan*,[214] the Home Office had published a circular stating the criteria to be used for determining whether a child could enter the United Kingdom. When the applicant sought to bring his nephew into the United Kingdom from Pakistan, entry was refused. In judicial review proceedings, it was established that the immigration rules did not specify any particular criteria, but that the Home Department's circular did so specify. It was also established that the criteria used in determining whether to allow the child into the country were different from that provided under the circular. The Home Secretary had acted *ultra vires*: he had created legitimate expectation and was not free to employ different criteria.[215]

A further challenge to the powers of the Home Secretary can be seen in *R v Secretary of State for the Home Department ex parte Ruddock*.[216] The Home Secretary had authorised the interception of telephone calls without statutory authority.[217] The basis on which the Home Secretary decided to intercept calls was provided in a circular. The applicant claimed that the Home Secretary had failed to follow the criteria laid down in the circular. The court held that the applicant had a legitimate expectation that the criteria would be followed but, nevertheless, the applicant lost the case because it was held that the Minister could have come to the judgment that the criteria were applied and that he was not acting unreasonably. The decision, which appears to weaken the binding nature of legitimate expectations, is explainable in light of the alleged national security aspects of the case. The applicant had been a leading member of the Campaign for Nuclear Disarmament, which the government feared was being influenced by the Communist Party.

The concept of legitimate expectation based on the existence of procedural guidelines may also be seen in *Council of Civil Service Unions v Minister for Civil Service*,[218] where it was clear that, had issues of national security not been involved, the courts would have protected the legitimate expectations of employees at GCHQ not to have their right to be members of a trades union removed without consultation. However, there remains uncertainty about the extent to which judges will accept and apply the concept of legitimate expectation.

---

214 [1984] 1 WLR 1337.

215 Cf *Re Findlay* [1985] AC 318, wherein the doctrine was limited merely to an expectation that prisoners would have their cases individually considered according to whatever policy the Minister chose to adopt.

216 [1987] 1 WLR 1482, discussed, further, in Chapter 23.

217 The case was decided before the Interception of Communications Act 1985 was implemented.

218 [1985] AC 374.

A change made to a policy which had been embedded in an agreement between prison inmates and prison authorities was considered by the Court of Appeal in *R v Secretary of State for the Home Department and Another ex parte Hargreaves and Others*.[219] The agreement stated that prisoners could apply for home leave after serving one third of their sentence, subject to good behaviour. The Secretary of State decided, however, that only prisoners who had served half their sentence could apply for home leave. Hargreaves and others unsuccessfully applied for judicial review. They subsequently appealed to the Court of Appeal.

The Court of Appeal held that the agreement between the prison inmates and the prison authorities did not give rise to a legitimate expectation which could be enforced by judicial review. Furthermore, the Home Secretary's decision to change the policy was not to be tested against the overall fairness of that decision, but rather whether the policy was unreasonable in the *Wednesbury* sense.[220] On that test, the Home Secretary's decision was not unlawful. The Court of Appeal expressed regret, however, that the documents on which the prisoners relied were 'other than completely clear and unambiguous', and called for greater clarity in the future.

Uncertainty in the doctrine of fairness

The principles of fairness have not, as can be seen above, been given either universal or consistent interpretations. For example, in *McInnes v Onslow Fane*,[221] Megarry VC stated that:

> ... the further the situation is away from anything that resembles a judicial or quasi-judicial decision, and the further the question is removed from what may reasonably be called a justiciable question, the more appropriate it is to reject an expression which includes the word justice and to use instead terms such as 'fairness' or the 'duty to act fairly'.[222]

In *Council of Civil Service Unions v Minister for the Civil Service*,[223] the House of Lords once again turned to the apparent differences in the concepts, Lord Roskill seemingly rejecting the phrase 'natural justice' in favour of the duty to 'act fairly'. Lord Roskill asserted that:

> The phrase [natural justice] might now be allowed to find a permanent resting place and be better replaced by speaking of a duty to act fairly. But the latter phrase must not in its turn be misunderstood or misused. It is not for the courts to determine whether a particular policy or particular decisions taken in fulfilment of that policy are fair. They are only concerned with the manner in

---

219 (1996) *The Times*, 3 December.
220 [1948] 1 KB 223.
221 [1978] 1 WLR 1520.
222 [1978] 1 WLR 1520, p 1530.
223 [1985] AC 374.

which those decisions have been taken and the extent of the duty to act fairly will vary greatly from case to case as indeed the decided cases since 1950 consistently show. Many features will come into place including the nature of the decision and the relationship of those involved on either side before the decision was taken.[224]

In *Hardie v City of Edinburgh Council*,[225] a teacher who was informed that he would be removed from the list of supply teachers and not employed again following allegations by a pupil of professional misconduct, and consideration of reports concluding that such misconduct had taken place, was entitled to judicial review. Natural justice required that fair notice of the allegations made and an opportunity to comment on the reports should have been given, and that the report should have been communicated to the applicant before a decision was reached.

The right to make representations

Inevitably, the extent to which the individual is enabled to make representations to the decision making body will be inextricably linked to the question of the right to a hearing. Where there exists no right to an oral hearing, the question becomes one of the extent to which – and means by which – the view of the individual can be put to the decision making authority. It may well be the case that the opportunity to make written submissions will satisfy the requirements for justice and fairness. For example, in *Lloyd v McMahon*,[226] local government councillors were in breach of their statutory duty to set the level of local rates. When the district auditor came to determine the issue, the applicants claimed the right to an oral hearing, and that the absence of such a hearing amounted to a breach of the rules of natural justice and was, accordingly, *ultra vires*. The court disagreed, holding that, since the auditor had given notice of the case against them and had considered written representations from them, he had acted fairly and, accordingly, lawfully.

The right to question the 'other side'

It is not invariably the case that, where there is to be an oral hearing, it should be conducted according to the strict rules which would apply in a court of law. Accordingly, it should not be assumed that a party will be entitled to cross-examine the 'other side'. However, in *Errington v Wilson*,[227] it was made clear that Justices of the Peace must observe the rules of natural justice and, in

---

224 [1985] AC 374, p 414.
225 2000 SLT 130.
226 [1987] AC 625.
227 1995 SLT 1193.

particular, allow cross-examination under certain circumstances. A food authority had seized batches of cheese which it believed to be contaminated with listeria monocytogenes. The authority then sought a destruction order from the justice of the peace. The magistrate refused to allow cross-examination of witnesses called by the authority. The court held that, given the nature of the proceedings, the magistrate was required to allow cross-examination if the proceedings were to be fair; and that, given the difference of opinion between experts on crucial points, Errington had been denied natural justice.

The admissibility of evidence and attendance of witnesses

In *R v Board of Visitors of Hull Prison ex parte St Germain (No 2)*,[228] prisoners who had been involved in a prison riot were charged with breaches of the Prison Rules. In the course of the hearing, hearsay evidence was given to the court on behalf of a number of officers who were unable to attend the hearing. The decision of guilt on the charges was challenged by judicial review proceedings, on the basis that the Board of Visitors had breached the rules of natural justice. Lane LJ, while not ruling that hearsay evidence could never be admissible, nevertheless ruled that, in the particular circumstance of the case, the Board should have ruled the hearsay evidence inadmissible:

> ... it is clear that the entitlement of the board to admit hearsay evidence is subject to the overriding obligation to provide the accused with a fair hearing. Depending upon the facts of the particular case and the nature of the hearsay evidence provided to the board, the obligation to give the accused a fair chance to exculpate himself, or a fair opportunity to controvert the charge ... or a proper or full opportunity of presenting his case ... may oblige the board not only to inform the accused of the hearsay evidence but also to give the accused a sufficient opportunity to deal with the evidence. Again, depending upon the nature of that evidence and the particular circumstances of the case, a sufficient opportunity to deal with the hearsay evidence may well involve the cross-examination of the witness whose evidence is initially before the board in the form of hearsay.

> We appreciate that there may well be occasions when the burden of calling the witness whose hearsay evidence is readily available may impose a near impossible burden upon the board ... [however,] where a prisoner desires to dispute the hearsay evidence and for this purpose to question the witness, and where there are unsuperable or very grave difficulties in arranging for his attendance, the board should refuse to admit that evidence, or, if it has already come to their notice, should expressly dismiss it from their consideration ...[229]

The decision of the Board was quashed by order of certiorari. Similar issues were under scrutiny in *R v Commissioner for Racial Equality ex parte Cottrell and*

---

228 [1979] 1 WLR 1401.
229 *Ibid*, p 1409.

Rothon.[230] The Commissioner had received a complaint of unlawful discrimination by Messrs Cottrell and Rothon, a firm of estate agents. The company had been given the opportunity to make representations – both written and oral – to the commissioners. No witnesses were available at the hearing. Nevertheless, the Commission issued a non-discrimination notice.[231] The company sought to have the decision quashed, relying in part on *R v Board of Visitors of Hull Prison ex parte St Germain (No 2)*.[232] Noting the absence of any statutory requirement to provide an opportunity to cross-examine witnesses in the course of a hearing, and distinguishing between the facts of *St Germain*, the Court of Appeal ruled that there was no breach in the rules relating to fairness.

In *R v Panel on Takeovers and Mergers ex parte Guinness plc*[233] the Takeover Panel refused to grant an adjournment of the inquisitorial proceedings in order to allow witnesses to attend. The court expressed anxiety about this refusal, but declined to hold that the Panel had acted unlawfully.

A different conclusion was reached, in *R v Army Board of the Defence Council ex parte Anderson*.[234] The applicant for judicial review had made allegations of racial discrimination[235] which resulted in him taking absence without leave. Members of the Board considered his allegation of discrimination on the basis of circulated papers, and did not meet for the purpose of reaching its decision. The complainant had requested, but been refused, an oral hearing, and had also requested, but been refused, the disclosure of documents relating to his case. The Board decided that whilst there was some *prima facie* evidence of discrimination, it was insufficient to warrant either an apology or an award of compensation. Anderson sought judicial review of the Army Board's decision. Counsel for the Board reverted to the distinction between administrative and judicial functions. Taylor LJ, in the course of ruling that such a distinction was unnecessary, held that, should the distinction have been a necessary one, he would characterise the role of the Army Board, in connection with the complaint, as judicial rather than administrative. Applying the principles established in *Lloyd v McMahon*,[236] and rejecting the arguments advanced by the Army Board, Taylor LJ ruled that four principles applied to the standard of fairness required in a hearing such as that of the Board:

> (1) There must be a proper hearing of the complaint in the sense that the board must consider ... all the relevant evidence and contentions before

---

230 [1980] 1 WLR 1580.
231 Under the Race Relations Act 1976, s 58(5).
232 [1979] 1 WLR 1401.
233 [1990] 1 QB 146.
234 [1991] 3 WLR 42.
235 Under the Race Relations Act 1976.
236 [1987] 1 All ER 1118.

reaching its conclusion. This means, in my view, that the members of the Board must meet ...

(2) The hearing does not necessarily have to be an oral hearing in all cases ... Provided that they [the board] achieve the degree of fairness appropriate to their task it is for them to decide how they will proceed and there is no rule that fairness always requires an oral hearing ...

What it [the board] cannot do ... is to have an inflexible policy not to hold oral hearings.

The board fettered its discretion and failed to consider the requirements for an oral hearing in the present case on its own merits.

(3) The opportunity to have the evidence tested by cross-examination is again within the Army Board's discretion. The decision whether to allow it will usually be inseparable from the decision whether to have an oral hearing. The object of the latter will usually be to enable witnesses to be tested in cross-examination, although it would be possible to have an oral hearing simply to hear submissions.

(4) Whether oral or not, there must be what amounts to a hearing of any complaint under the 1976 Act. This means that the Army Board must have such a complaint investigated, consider all the material gathered in the investigation, give the complainant an opportunity to respond to it and consider his response.[237]

On the duty of disclosure of documents, Taylor LJ ruled that:

Because of the nature of the Army Board's function pursuant to the 1976 Act, ... I consider that a soldier complainant under that Act should be shown all the material seen by the board, apart from any documents for which public interest immunity[238] can properly be claimed.

The decision of the board was quashed by order of certiorari.

The rights of prisoners have also been scrutinised in relation to the requirement that they have sufficient information in order to challenge a Home Secretary's decision as to their detention or release. Under the Criminal Justice Act 1991,[239] the Home Secretary has a statutory duty to release, on the direction of the Parole Board, discretionary life prisoners after they have served a 'tariff period'.[240] The period to be served is considered by the trial judge. In *R v Secretary of State for the Home Department ex parte Doody*,[241] the House of Lords ruled that the prisoner was entitled to know the length of the tariff period recommended by the trial judge, and other relevant factors, in order that he may make written representation to the Home Secretary concerning the date fixed for consideration by the Parole Board of his

---

237 [1991] 3 WLR 42, pp 55–56.
238 On public interest immunity, see Chapter 11.
239 Criminal Justice Act 1991, ss 32–51.
240 *Ibid*, s 34.
241 [1993] 3 WLR 154.

sentence.[242] The failure to respect the entitlement to know the period recommended in order to make written submissions, led to the Home Secretary's decision being quashed.

In *R v Secretary of State for the Environment ex parte Slot*,[243] a property owner was denied natural justice where a planning authority determining her application did not allow her to make independent representations, and refused to give the applicant a copy of objections lodged. The decision was quashed. Further, in *R v Secretary of State for the Home Department ex parte McAvoy*,[244] a prisoner whose security status was under review, had the right to the 'gist' of the reports to the review body, in order that he could make representations knowing the case he had to meet.

The availability of legal representation

Whether or not legal representation is available as of right will also depend upon the nature of the hearing and the nature of the rights affected. There is no general right to legal representation and, in some cases, it may prove to be either unnecessary or counterproductive to the proceedings and, accordingly, the courts have been unwilling to concede a general right to representation.[245] Where the proceedings are before a tribunal, the right to be represented is at the discretion of the tribunal.[246] The general principle, according to the Royal Commission on Legal Services, is that 'it is desirable that every applicant before any tribunal should be able to present his case in person or to obtain representation'.[247]

Whereas legal representation is rarely denied before tribunals,[248] such representation is inextricably linked to the financial means of the applicant or to the availability of Legal Aid. It may be more appropriate, in many instances, for applicants to be represented by non-lawyers. A range of organisations offer representation. The Citizens Advice Bureaux, trades unions, social workers, specialist agencies,[249] the Free Representation Unit, friends or relatives may all be allowed to appear before tribunals. The

---

242 Where the trial judge does not make a recommendation, the Home Secretary may certify the length of the period of sentence which must be served: Criminal Justice Act 1991, Sched 12, para 9. See *R v Home Department ex parte McCartney* (1993) *The Times*, 28 October.

243 (1997) *The Times*, 11 December.

244 (1997) *The Times*, 12 December.

245 See, *inter alia, R v Secretary of State for the Home Department ex parte Tarrant* [1985] QB 251; *R v Board of Visitors of HM Prison, The Maze ex parte Hone* [1988] 1 AC 379.

246 See Alder, J, 'Representation before tribunals' [1972] 1 PL 278.

247 *Report of the Royal Commission*, 1979, Vol I, para 15.11, p 169.

248 Proceedings before the Family Practitioner Committee is an exception; National Health Service (Service Committees and Tribunal) Regulations SI 1974/455, reg 7.

249 Eg, the Child Poverty Action Group; the United Kingdom Immigration Advisory Service.

essential criteria for representation is that the tribunal should not adopt a rigid policy, but rather should exercise a genuine discretion in relation to the availability of representation.[250]

Failure to give reasons[251]

According to Lord Denning MR, the giving of reasons is 'one of the fundamentals of good administration'.[252] Unless a decision maker provides adequate information as to the basis on which a decision has been reached, any possible protection which could be given to an aggrieved person is adversely affected.

Under the Tribunals and Inquiries Act 1992, there exists a statutory duty to give reasons, on request, where decisions are reached by tribunals, public inquiries, or under specific statutes. Under common law, however, there is no such duty,[253] although the argument that there should be such a duty is strong. HWR Wade and CF Forsyth are critical of the lack of any general requirement to give reasons, and reason that:

> Although the lack of a general duty to give reasons is recognised as an outstanding deficiency of administrative law, the judges have gone far towards finding a remedy by holding that reasons must be given where fairness so demands; and the decisions show that that may now be the case more often than not. It has been held at first instance[254] that English law has now arrived at the point where the duty to act fairly imparts at least a general duty to give reasons, subject to necessary exceptions, and this conclusion seems well justified.[255]

Accordingly, a decision making body will be under a 'general duty' to give reasons, and any departure from the requirement to give reasons will require sound justification. Where an authority fails to give reasons for a decision which is challenged subsequently by judicial review proceedings, the failure to give reasons may cause the court to consider that there were no good reasons whatsoever for the decision. Lord Keith expressed it thus:

> ... if all other known facts and circumstances appear to point overwhelmingly in favour of a different decision, the decision maker who has given no reasons

---

250 *Per* Lord Denning MR in *Pett v Greyhound Racing Association (No 2)* [1970] 1 QB 46.

251 See Craig, PP, 'The common law, reasons and administrative justice' [1994] CLJ 282.

252 *Breen v AEU* [1971] 2 QB 175, p 191.

253 See *R v Secretary of State for the Home Department ex parte Doody* [1993] 3 All ER 92, p 111; and see, now, [1993] 3 WLR 154.

254 In *R v Lambeth London Borough Council ex parte Walters* (1993) *The Times*, 6 October.

255 *Op cit*, Wade and Forsyth, fn 17, pp 544–45.

cannot complain if the court draws the inference that he has no rational reason for his decision.[256]

The courts have developed a number of exceptions to the general rule that no reasons need be given at common law. The courts may hold, for example, that a failure to give reasons will prejudice an applicant's chances of successfully applying for judicial review,[257] or that a failure to give reasons amounts to arbitrariness,[258] or that legitimate expectations have been created which demand that any departure from that expectation be explained or, more sweepingly, that in the interests of fairness, reasons must be given.

In *R v Civil Service Appeal Board ex parte Cunningham*,[259] for example, the Court of Appeal, while again stating that there was no general duty to give reasons, held that the Civil Service Appeal Board – which determined the applicant's compensation for unfair dismissal – was under a duty to give reasons, for its powers were analogous to the judicial powers of an industrial tribunal. Fairness demanded that the Board give reasons, in the same manner as required for tribunals.[260]

The duty to give reasons must now be evaluated in light of the House of Lords' decision in *R v Secretary of State for the Home Department ex parte Doody*.[261] As seen above, p 1091, in *Doody*, the applicants, who were serving mandatory life sentences, sought information as to the basis on which the decision concerning the period for their mandatory detention had been reached. The House of Lords laid down two justifications for the requirement that information be given. First, if reasons were not given to the applicants, the possibility of their successfully applying for judicial review would be frustrated. Secondly, a failure to give reasons adversely affected the concept of fairness. Lord Mustill, while acknowledging that there remained no general duty to give reasons, stated that a duty would be implied under certain circumstances. Where, as in *Doody*, the applicant did not know the reasons for a decision, it was impossible to make any effective representations in support of his case. Without the knowledge of any case against him, the applicant was denied the very information which would found the basis of making representations in support of his case.[262] The Home Secretary was, accordingly, under a duty to provide reasons both on the basis that the giving

---

256 *R v Trade Secretary ex parte Lonrho plc* [1989] 2 All ER 609, p 620. See Bradley, AW, 'Openness, direction and judicial review' [1986] PL 508; and Herberg, J, 'The right to reasons – palm trees in retreat?' [1991] PL 340.

257 As in *Doody*'s case [1993] 3 All ER 92; 3 WLR 154.

258 See *Padfield v Minister of Agriculture, Fisheries and Food* [1968] AC 997.

259 [1991] 4 All ER 310.

260 See, also, *R v Parole Board ex parte Wilson* [1992] 1 QB 740.

261 [1993] 3 WLR 154.

262 [1993] 3 All ER 92, pp 106–11.

of reasons was a prerequisite to an application for judicial review, and on the basis of requirements of fairness.

In *R v Ministry of Defence ex parte Murray*,[263] the Divisional Court ruled that, although there was no general overriding principle of law which required decision makers to give reasons for their decisions, the duty of fairness required that reasons be given, where demanded by the circumstances of the case. The applicant had been convicted by court martial of wounding. The court martial reached its conclusion and passed sentence without giving reasons. The applicant's conduct, which was 'entirely out of character', and to which he pleaded guilty, was caused by ingestion of an anti-malarial drug. Where there was no explicit duty of fairness in statute, the courts would require that reasons be given where fairness demanded it. In this case, the applicant, his regiment and his family were entitled to reasons.

However, not all bodies will be under a duty to give reasons on the basis of fairness. In *R v Universities Funding Council ex parte Institute of Dental Surgery*,[264] for example, the Divisional Court ruled that the Higher Education Funding Council was not under a duty to give reasons as to why an academic institution was given a downgraded research grading which resulted in a loss to the Institute of research funds. Such matters were, in the court's opinion, matters of academic judgment, and a duty to give reasons for a decision could not, in this case, be founded on the requirements of fairness alone.[265] Sedley J stated that there were two classes of case emerging. The first class was exemplified in the *Doody* case, where the nature of the process requires, in the interests of fairness, reasons to be given. The second class is illustrated by *Ex parte Cunningham*,[266] in which the majority of the court held that there was something peculiar to the case which required reasons to be given in the interests of fairness. In the *Institute of Dental Surgery* case, provided the decision was based purely on academic judgment, and did not involve any irrelevant or improper factors being taken into account, the decision would not be impugned on the basis that reasons had not been given for the decision. TRS Allan is critical of the decision.[267] In his view, 'if the requirement of reasons, where it exists, reflects the demands of fairness and reasonableness, its denial in the present case must cause one to doubt whether the Institute was treated either fairly or reasonably'.[268]

---

263 (1997) *The Times*, 17 December.

264 [1994] 1 All ER 651.

265 See, also, *R v University College London ex parte Idriss* [1999] Ed CR 462, in which it was held that it was 'very doubtful' whether a university's refusal to admit an applicant for entry to a course was susceptible to judicial review and that there was no duty to give reasons either at common law or under the university's own statutes.

266 [1992] ICR 816.

267 See Allan, TRS, 'Requiring reasons for reasons of fairness and reasonableness' [1994] CLJ 207.

268 *Ibid*, p 210.

In *R v Secretary of State for the Home Department ex parte Al Fayed*,[269] the court of first instance ruled that there was no duty to give reasons for refusing applications for naturalisation under section 44(2) of the British Nationality Act 1981. On appeal, however, the Court of Appeal ruled that the Home Secretary had a duty to indicate to the applicant the area(s) of concern on which he was basing his refusal, in order that the applicant may have an opportunity to allay the Home Secretary's concerns.[270] The Home Secretary's decision was quashed. In *R v Secretary of State for the Home Department ex parte Moon*,[271] the court ruled that the Secretary of State's refusal to explain his reasons for concluding that the entry of the Reverend Sun Myung Moon would not be conducive to the public good was unfair and contrary to the rules of natural justice.

In the absence of compelling reasons to the contrary, and notwithstanding there being no general duty requiring the Director of Public Prosecutions to give reasons for a decision not to prosecute, he would be expected to do so where his refusal concerned a death in custody, in respect of which a coroner's inquest had returned a verdict of unlawful killing. The Court of Appeal so ruled in *R v Director of Public Prosecutions ex parte Manning and Another*.[272] Since judicial review of a refusal to prosecute was the only means of redress available to an aggrieved citizen, the standard of review should not be set too high since, although the court's power should be exercised sparingly, too exacting a test would deny him an effective remedy.

The giving of reasons, whether by courts or administrative bodies, assumes increased importance in light of the incorporation of Convention rights under the Human Rights Act 1998. Article 5 of the Convention (the right to liberty and security) expressly states that persons arrested shall be informed promptly, in a language which he or she understands, of the reasons for the arrest. Article 6 of the Convention protects the right to a fair trial in the determination of civil rights and obligations or of criminal charges. While the giving of reasons is not an explicit requirement in Article 6, it is implicit in facilitating the right of appeal. The duty of a professional judge to give reasons was upheld in *Flanner v Halifax Estate Agencies Ltd*,[273] in which the Court of Appeal so held, setting aside the judgment of the court in a claim for damages for professional negligence. In general, it was the duty of a judge to give reasons; the extent of the duty would depend on the circumstances, but, where the dispute involved opposing reasons and analysis, the judge must explain why he preferred one case over the other.[274] In *Stefan v General*

---

269 [1997] 1 All ER 228; (1996) *The Times*, 13 March.
270 (1996) *The Times*, 14 November.
271 (1995) *The Times*, 8 December.
272 (2000) *The Times*, 19 May.
273 (1999) *The Times*, 4 March.
274 See *Practice Direction* [1999] 1 WLR 2.

Medical Council,[275] the health committee of the General Medical Council had suspended the applicant indefinitely because of her medical condition. No reasons were given. The court stated that the common law rule against a general duty to give reasons was changing and might have to be reconsidered in light of the Human Rights Act 1998. Although there was no general duty to give reasons, nevertheless, in light of the nature of the appeal and the importance for the practitioner, they ought to have done so.

EXPANDING THE SCOPE OF JUDICIAL REVIEW

The freedom of information proposals and the Human Rights Act 1998

Freedom of information proposals

As discussed in Chapter 11, the proposed Freedom of Information Act will give legislative force to the Labour government's commitment to more open government. An Information Commissioner is to be appointed, with jurisdiction to investigate allegations that public authorities and bodies have failed to provide information and documents requested. The Act, it will be recalled, will introduce the principle that information and documents will be disclosed, subject to a test of harm which justifies official non-disclosure. The Commissioner's decisions will be published and will be subject to judicial review. While any prognosis is necessarily tentative and speculative at this point in time, the effect of the Freedom of Information Act on judicial review will, however, arguably be to reduce the number of applications for judicial review, in particular on the basis of failure to give reasons. This appears to be supported by the government's announcement that it did not intend to appeal against the decision in the *Al Fayed* case, but rather indicated that it would give reasons for refusing citizenship. Judicial review, as seen in the previous chapter, is concerned with the decision making process rather than the merits of the decision, and provides a discretionary remedy, which requires the decision maker to reconsider the matter in accordance with the correct procedure. Provided that the decision making process is in accordance with the requirements of law and the principles of natural justice, the decision will not be impugned. Under the Freedom of Information Act, however, where a public body – which is widely defined – fails to give reasons for its decision, recourse may be had to the Commissioner who has wide ranging powers to investigate, and has the power to order disclosure. Where a public body refuses to supply, for example, reasons for its decision, and the Commissioner orders it to disclose reasons, should the public body then continue to refuse to

---

275 [1999] 1 WLR 1293, PC.

disclose, with no justification, that refusal may be deemed to be analogous to contempt of court. Furthermore, should the body concerned reveal to the Commissioner that it had no rational basis for its decision, that decision may then be impugned on the basis of irrationality. The citizen may, accordingly, find a more efficient and effective remedy under the jurisdiction of the Commissioner than the courts.

The Human Rights Act 1998

From a judicial review perspective, the Human Rights Act 1998, which incorporates Convention rights into domestic law, presages significant developments.[276] The Convention, as it is referred to under the Human Rights Act, provides the basis on which to challenge primary and secondary legislation by those adversely affected by such legislation, and also provides a defence to legal action by public authorities. However, over and above these methods of challenging legislation on the basis of alleged incompatibility with the Convention, the Act also provides for judicial review to extend to the review of administrative action to determine its compatibility with Convention requirements. It is arguable that this will bring about not only a marked shift in judicial perceptions concerning individual rights, but also a change in juridical technique. As has been seen above, a fundamental concept utilised in domestic judicial review cases has conventionally been that of 'reasonableness':[277] at issue is whether a public body, in its exercise of administrative discretion, has acted within the bounds of reasonableness conferred by the legislation, under which are subsumed the concepts of illegality, irrationality and procedural impropriety. Both the European Court of Justice of the European Community and the European Court of Human Rights – which are separate institutions and operate under separate jurisdictions[278] – have long employed the concept of 'proportionality', and it is this concept, which has traditionally been regarded with some suspicion by domestic judges, which will now become applicable.[279] When the Human Rights Act is in force, therefore, not only will judicial review be available on the now conventional heads, but it will also be available to determine whether a particular administrative act has violated a right under the Convention.

---

276 On the status of the Convention before the Human Rights Act is fully in force, see Chapter 22. See, also, *R v Secretary of State for the Home Department ex parte Hussain Ahmed* [1999] COD 69; (1998) *The Times*, 15 October.

277 See *Associated Provincial Picture Houses Ltd v Wednesbury Corporation* [1948] 1 KB 223.

278 See, further, Chapter 8.

279 Proportionality has, however, been recognised by the Court of Appeal. See, eg, *Barnsley Metropolitan BC ex parte Hook* [1976] 1 WLR 1052; *Attorney General v Jonathan Cape Ltd* [1976] QB 752.

The doctrine of proportionality[280]

The doctrine of proportionality is one which confines the limits of the exercise of power to means which are proportional to the objective to be pursued. The doctrine has taken firm roots in the jurisprudence of, for example, the United States of America, Canada and the law of many European countries. It is also a concept which is increasingly adopted under European law. Both the European Court of Justice of the European Community[281] (ECJ) and the European Court of Human Rights[282] adopt proportionality as a test against which to measure the legality of actions of authorities.[283] In *R v Home Secretary ex parte Brind*,[284] the House of Lords was not prepared to accept that the concept yet represented a separate and distinct head of judicial review. Whilst recognising that proportionality was a distinctive head for review under the European Convention on Human Rights, Lord Ackner ruled that:

> Unless and until Parliament incorporates the Convention into domestic law ... there appears to me to be at present no basis upon which the proportionality doctrine applied by the European Court can be followed by the courts of this country.[285]

That time may now have been reached and, when the Act is in force, the doctrine of proportionality will become directly applicable in domestic courts of law.

In relation to the doctrine of proportionality, the judges appear to adopt differing approaches to the doctrine and, while it appears agreed that proportionality has not hitherto been part of English law, proportionality has been employed to determine whether a decision has been irrational or not. For example, in *Brind*,[286] Lord Ackner asked pithily whether the Secretary of State had 'used a sledgehammer to crack a nut'. In several cases, it is clear that the courts are using the doctrine of proportionality but without making explicit references thereto. For example, in *R v Barnsley Metropolitan Borough Council ex parte Hook*,[287] a market stall holder had had his licence revoked for urinating in public. Lord Denning MR quashed the decision, partly on the basis that the penalty – the loss of the licence – was disproportionate to the 'offence'.[288]

---

280 See Jowell, J and Lester, A, 'Proportionality: neither novel nor dangerous', in Jowell, J and Oliver, D (eds), *New Directions in Judicial Review*, 1988, London: Stevens and 'New directions in judicial review', in Jowell, J and Oliver, D (eds), *The Changing Constitution*, 3rd edn, 1994, Oxford: Clarendon.

281 See Chapters 8 and 9.

282 See Chapter 22.

283 See, eg, *Dudgeon v United Kingdom* (1981) 4 EHRR 149, discussed in Chapter 22.

284 [1991] 1 AC 696.

285 *Ibid*, p 763.

286 *Ibid*.

287 [1976] 1 WLR 1052.

288 Consider, also, *Wheeler v Leicester City Council* [1985] AC 1054, discussed below.

Where issues of European Community law or the European Convention on Human Rights are involved, the doctrine is one which must be considered if the English interpretation of European law is to be consistent with that of the European Court of Justice and the Court of Human Rights. In *Stoke-on-Trent City Council v B & Q plc*,[289] for example, Hoffmann J was prepared to adopt the ECJ's proportionality test when considering the compatibility of the Shops Act 1950 and the free trade provisions of the EC Treaty.

Consistent with the requirements of the Convention, any action which *prima facie* violates protected rights, must be justified on the basis that the infringement is justifiable on the grounds set out in the Convention Articles: thus, the action taken must be judged according to whether or not that action was proportionate to the objective behind the action. The Convention is replete with State discretion – the 'margin of appreciation' – allied to criteria such as 'necessary in a democratic society in the interests of national security, public safety or the economic well being of the country, for the prevention of disorder or crime for the protection of health or morals, or for the protection of rights and freedoms of others'.[290]

Of immense significance also is the duty imposed on public bodies to act in accordance with the requirements of the Convention. Hitherto, the courts have consistently denied that public authorities have a duty to act in accordance with the Convention requirements, although, increasingly, judges have also averred to the importance of the protection of human rights by public authorities. This represents something of a conundrum which requires unravelling.

In *R v Secretary of State for the Home Department ex parte Brind*,[291] discussed above, Lord Bridge stated:

> ... where Parliament has conferred on the executive an administrative discretion without indicating the precise limits within which it must be exercised, to presume that it must be exercised within Convention limits would be to go far beyond the resolution of an ambiguity. It would be to impute to Parliament an intention not only that the executive should exercise the discretion in conformity with the Convention, but also that the domestic courts should enforce that conformity by the importation into domestic administrative law of the text of the Convention and the jurisprudence of the European Court of Human Rights ... It would be surprising suddenly to find that the judiciary had, without Parliament's aid, the means to incorporate the Convention into such an important area of domestic law and I cannot escape the conclusion that this would be a judicial usurpation of the legislative function.

---

289 [1984] AC 754.

290 ECHR, Art 8(2).

291 [1991] 1 AC 696. See, further, Chapter 22.

From this passage, the former justification for not applying Convention standards and requirements to administrative decisions lies clearly within the concepts of parliamentary sovereignty and the doctrine of separation of powers. However, notwithstanding that position, the judges have, even in the absence of incorporation of the Convention, been alert to the protection of human rights in the face of administrative power. For example, in *Bugdaycay v Secretary of State for the Home Department*,[292] Lord Bridge asserted that:

> ... the courts are entitled to subject an administrative decision to the more rigorous examination ... according to the gravity of the issue which the decision determines. The most fundamental of all human rights is the individual's right to life and when an administrative decision under challenge is said to be one which may put the applicant's life at risk, the basis of the decision must surely call for the most anxious scrutiny.

Further, in *R v Secretary of State for Social Security ex parte Joint Council for the Welfare of Immigrants; R v Secretary of State for Social Security ex parte B*,[293] the Court of Appeal was to assert that, where basic human rights were at issue, there was no need to resort to the Convention to establish such a right, and that only primary legislation could undermine that right.[294]

However, when the Convention has the force of law under domestic law, not only will public bodies and administrative authorities have a duty to comply with its requirements, but the courts will also have to have recourse to the jurisprudence of the European Court of Human Rights and, in the absence of authority from that source, utilise the Convention as a standard by which to evaluate the actions of public bodies.

The definition of public bodies under the Human Rights Act 1998

Under section 6 of the Human Rights Act, public authorities are defined to include bodies 'whose functions are functions of a public nature'. Potentially, therefore, the scope for judicial review will broaden to encompass more bodies than hitherto defined by the courts.

One area of controversy which arose during the Bill's passage through the House of Lords concerned the right to privacy and the role of the media. There has long been a demand for the powers of the press to be curbed in order to provide respect for the private lives of, mainly, public figures, and arguments have been adduced to the effect that Article 8 of the Convention, once incorporated into domestic law, could provide the vehicle for the development of such a right. Moreover, with the wide definition of a public

---

292 [1987] AC 514.

293 [1997] 1 WLR 275.

294 See, also, *R v Ministry of Defence ex parte Smith; R v Admiralty Board of the Defence Council ex parte Lustig-Prean* [1995] 4 All ER 427.

authority under the Bill, it is argued that the Press Complaints Commission, the newspaper 'watchdog', would be obliged to comply with Article 8. However, when the Bill reached the House of Commons, amendments were introduced to exempt the Press Complaints Commission from the provisions of the Act, on the basis of the need for a free press in a democratic society. Accordingly, the hopes of some media critics that a privacy law would develop under the incorporated Convention, have been denied. Section 12 provides that no injunction preventing publication shall be issued unless the respondent is present or represented in court. Section 12(3) provides that no relief is to be granted so as to restrain publication before trial unless the court is satisfied that the applicant is likely to establish that publication should not be allowed. Further, that, when courts are considering allegations of breach of privacy enshrined in Article 8 (respect for private and family life, home and correspondence), they must have particular regard to freedom of expression which is protected under Article 10. In relation to journalistic, literary and artistic material, the court must consider also the extent to which the material is, or is about to become, available to the public and the extent to which it is in the public interest for the material to be published, and any relevant privacy code.

The Human Rights Act 1998: breach of the Convention as a heading for judicial review

Section 6 of the Act provides that 'it is unlawful for a public authority to act in a way which is incompatible with one or more of the Convention rights', unless the body in question is acting under provisions contained in legislation which is incompatible with the Convention. In addition to quashing a public body's decision, the courts are empowered to award up to £10,000 in damages.[295]

---

295 See, further, Chapter 22.

CHAPTER 26

COMMISSIONERS FOR ADMINISTRATION: 'OMBUDSMEN'[1]

INTRODUCTION

In the United Kingdom, the past 30 years has seen a major expansion in mechanisms for citizens to complain against government departments and other public bodies. Traditionally, when a citizen has a complaint against the administration of government, that complaint could be pursued in courts or tribunals or through Parliament via the constituency Member of Parliament. However, these means for the redress of grievances have been proven inadequate and, as a result, alternative and additional mechanisms have been introduced.

The word 'ombudsman' is Swedish, and means a representative of the people. In Sweden, the office of *Justitieombudsman* was established in 1809. Finland introduced a similar office in 1919, as did Denmark in 1955. In 1963, Norway followed, with a parliamentary ombudsman, the model which had been adopted by New Zealand in 1962. During the 1970s, countries throughout the world adopted some form of office of ombudsman.

COMMISSIONERS FOR ADMINISTRATION IN THE UNITED KINGDOM

The existing scheme of Commissioners for Administration is as follows:

---

1   See, *inter alia*, Gregory, R and Hutchesson, P, *The Parliamentary Ombudsman*, 1975, London: Allen & Unwin; Harlow, C and Rawlings, R, *Law and Administration*, 2nd edn, 1997, London: Weidenfeld & Nicolson; Rowat, D, *The Ombudsman: Citizen's Defender*, 1968, London: Allen & Unwin; Stacey, F, *Ombudsmen Compared*, 1978, Oxford: Clarendon; Williams, DW, *Maladministration: Remedies for Injustice*, 1976, London: Oyez; Birkinshaw, P, *Grievances, Remedies and the State*, 2nd edn, 1995, London: Sweet & Maxwell.

TABLE I: COMMISSIONERS FOR ADMINISTRATION

Commissioner	Date of introduction
Parliamentary Commissioner for Administration[2]	1967
Parliamentary Commissioner for Administration[3] and Commissioner for Complaints (Northern Ireland)[4]	1969
Health Service Commissioners: England, Wales and Scotland[5]	1972
Local Government Commissioners: England, Wales[6] and Scotland[7] (Scotland 1975)	1974
Legal Services Commissioner[8]	1990
European Union and Community Ombudsman[9]	1992

In addition, there exist a number of ombudsmen in the private sector, for example, the Banking Commissioner, Building Societies Commissioner, Corporate Estate Agents Commissioner, Pensions Commissioner,[10] Personal Investment Authority Ombudsman, Investment Commissioner, Insurance Commissioner, Commissioner for Trades Union Members and the press and media and telephone information services. Under the proposed Freedom of Information Act,[11] an Information Commissioner will be appointed to investigate complaints concerning non-disclosure of information.

---

2   Parliamentary Commissioner Act 1967. As amended by the Parliamentary and Health Service Commissioner Act 1987; Parliamentary Commissioner Act 1994.

3   Parliamentary Commissioner (Northern Ireland) Act 1969.

4   Commissioner for Complaints (Northern Ireland) Act 1969.

5   National Health Service (Scotland) Act 1972; National Health Service Reorganisation Act 1973; Parliamentary and Health Service Act 1987; Health Service Commissioners Act 1993.

6   Local Government Act 1974; Local Government and Housing Act 1989, s 23.

7   Local Government (Scotland) Act 1975.

8   Courts and Legal Services Act 1990.

9   EC Treaty, Art 138e, introduced under the Treaty on European Union 1992.

10 It has been held that the Pensions Ombudsman is required to observe the statutory procedure within the Pensions Schemes Act 1993 and the rules of natural justice: see *Seifert v Pensions Ombudsman and Others; Lynch and Another v Pensions Ombudsman and Another* (1996) *The Times*, 9 August. See, also, *Miller v Stapleton* [1996] 2 All ER 449; *Hamar v Pensions Ombudsman* (1997) *The Times*, 24 March.

11 Discussed in Chapter 11.

THE PARLIAMENTARY COMMISSIONER FOR ADMINISTRATION[12]

The movement towards establishing a Parliamentary Commissioner for Administration (or ombudsman) began in 1959. In that year, the British section of the International Commission of Jurists, JUSTICE, established an inquiry into grievances against the administration. The resultant report[13] advocated setting up an additional avenue for the redress of grievances, the office being modelled on the same lines as those of the ombudsmen in Scandinavian jurisdictions. As the report stated, there appeared to be:

> ... a continuous flow of relatively minor complaints, not sufficient in themselves to attract public interest, but nevertheless of great importance to the individuals concerned, which give rise to feelings of frustration and resentment because of the inadequacy of the existing means of seeking redress.[14]

The existing machinery was found wanting: parliamentary Question Time was inadequate to deal with the volume of problems arising; if a complaint was made directly to the government department, the department investigated the complaint; if a Member of Parliament attempted to investigate, he could not gain access to all departmental documentation. Accordingly, the report advocated establishing a permanent office, independent of the executive and accountable only to Parliament, removable from office only after a successful address had been moved to both Houses of Parliament. The report recommended that a select committee should be established to consider the Commissioner's reports and to give parliamentary authority to the work of the Commissioner. The report also recommended that the Parliamentary Commissioner for Administration's office should be one which supplemented, rather than undermined, existing procedures for complaint. Complaints, at least initially, concerning maladministration[15] should be routed through Members of Parliament, rather than directly addressed to the Parliamentary Commissioner. This would preserve to Members of Parliament the opportunity to resolve a matter of complaint but, failing their ability to do so, confer the right to refer the matter to the Parliamentary Commissioner for investigation and report.

The government's response to the report was cautious. Concern was expressed as to the interference in the running of government,[16] and that the

---

12 See Pugh, I (Sir), 'The ombudsman – jurisdiction, power and practice' (1978) 56 Public Admin 127. See, also, Clothier, C (Sir), 'Legal problems of an ombudsman' (1984) 81 Law Soc Gazette 3108 and 'The value of an ombudsman' [1986] PL 204.

13 *The Citizen and the Administration* (the 'Whyatt Report'), 1961.

14 *Ibid*, para 76.

15 On which, see below.

16 Lord Chancellor, HL Deb Vol 244 Cols 384–85.

Commissioner's role would be incompatible with the doctrine of ministerial responsibility. Furthermore, the government felt that:

> ... there is already adequate provision under our constitution and Parliamentary practice for the redress of any genuine complaint of maladministration, in particular by means of the citizen's rights of access to Members of Parliament.[17]

The incoming Labour government, however, accepted the need for an office to complement the existing complaints machinery.[18] Thus, in 1967, the Parliamentary Commissioner Act was passed. Being a constitutional innovation, the provisions as to procedure, jurisdiction and powers of enforcement were restrictive.

The constitutional position of the Commissioner

By 1983, the office of Parliamentary Commissioner for Administration had been operative for 15 years, and the Commissioner[19] took the opportunity to review the working of his office in his annual report. He described his office in the following manner:

> The office of Parliamentary Commissioner stands curiously poised between the legislature and the executive, while discharging an almost judicial function in the citizen's dispute with his government, and yet it forms no part of the judiciary. It is from the centre of that triangle that I have been able to appreciate the virtues of our unwritten and therefore flexible constitutional arrangements and still more the goodwill of those men and women, legislators and administrators who govern us.

THE COMPLAINTS PROCEDURE

Complaints must be in writing, and made to the constituency Member of Parliament.[20] The complaint must be made within 12 months of the day on which the person became aware of the matters alleged, unless the time period is extended by the Commissioner, on the basis that an investigation is necessary.[21] The complaint must relate to maladministration (see below, p 1111) and not the merits of a decision or the policy being pursued. This restriction has led to some 43 per cent of complaints made being rejected by the Commissioner.

---

17 Attorney General, 666 HC Col 1125.
18 *The Parliamentary Commissioner for Administration*, Cmnd 2767, 1965, London: HMSO.
19 Sir Cecil Clothier who held office from 1979–85.
20 Parliamentary Commissioner Act 1967, s 5(1)(a), but, on reform of this requirement, see below.
21 *Ibid*, s 6(3).

The requirement that complaints be made initially to Members of Parliament reinforces the view that the Commissioner is a supplement to the parliamentary process rather than a substitute. This restricted right of access, however, causes difficulties for complainants, and is not a model adopted elsewhere.[22] In the majority of countries having some form of parliamentary ombudsman, complaints are made directly to the ombudsman. Moreover, this filter mechanism has not been adopted in relation to the Health Service Commissioner, the Commissioners for Local Government or the Complaints Commissioner for Northern Ireland.[23]

In order to remedy this restriction on access to the Parliamentary Commissioner, the Parliamentary Commissioner (Amendment) Bill 2000 provides for the amendment of the Parliamentary Commissioner Act 1967 to enable members of the public to direct complaints to the Commissioner rather than to a Member of the House of Commons.

Jurisdiction

Section 5(1) of the Parliamentary Commissioner Act 1967 provides that a member of the public may make a complaint and the Commissioner may investigate that complaint where, subject to the rules on jurisdiction, the person 'claims to have sustained injustice in consequence of maladministration'.[24] Before examining that concept, it must be noted that there are a number of restrictions to the jurisdiction of the Parliamentary Commissioner, which result in a large number of complaints each year not being investigated.

Excluded matters

The work of the police,[25] of nationalised industries, the Cabinet Office, Prime Minister's Office, Parole Board, tribunals, Bank of England, Criminal Injuries Compensation Board and government commercial and contractual transactions are all excluded.[26] The Commissioner may not investigate any matter where the complainant has a right of 'appeal, reference or review' to a tribunal, or a remedy in any court of law, unless it would be unreasonable to expect the complainant to have resort to such a remedy.[27] The Commissioner

---

22 See the JUSTICE Report, *Our Fettered Ombudsman*, 1977, and the Select Committee Report, *Parliamentary Commissioner for Administration (Review of Access and Jurisdiction)*, HC 615 (1978–79), London: HMSO.

23 There is, however, a 'filter' procedure for the Parliamentary Commissioner for Northern Ireland.

24 See below for the meaning of 'maladministration'.

25 Which has its own internal complaints procedures.

26 See HC 322 (1983–84), London: HMSO.

27 Parliamentary Commissioner Act 1967, s 5(2).

thus has a discretion as to whether or not a complaint should be accepted. It has been indicated that, where the legal process would be too cumbersome, slow or expensive in relation to the objective to be gained, the complaint will be accepted.[28]

The interaction between legal proceedings and complaints to the Commissioner was well illustrated in 1975. The government decided to increase the licence fee for television sets. In advance of the fee increase, individuals renewed their licences at the existing rate. The Home Office then decided to revoke the 36,000 licences issued at the cheaper rate. A number of complaints were referred to the Commissioner, who found maladministration on the part of government, *inter alia*, for not giving sufficient warning of the increases and for inefficiency. The Commissioner, however, ruled that the government was acting on legal advice and therefore should not be sanctioned. Judicial review proceedings were commenced to determine the lawfulness of the Home Secretary's decision, as a result of which the complainants established a legal remedy.[29] It may be argued that the Commissioner was wrong in exercising his discretionary jurisdiction in this case, since it should have been foreseen that an action in judicial review would lie.

The departments and matters which the Commissioner is precluded from investigating are wide ranging. Schedule 3 of the Parliamentary Commissioner Act 1967 sets out the excluded matters, the most significant of which are:

1   Action taken in matters certified by a Secretary of State or other Minister of the Crown to affect relations or dealings between the government of the United Kingdom and any other government or any international organisation of States or government.

2   Action taken in connection with the administration of the government of any country or territory outside the United Kingdom which forms part of Her Majesty's dominions or in which Her Majesty has jurisdiction.

3   Action taken by the Secretary of State under the Fugitive Offenders Act 1967 or the Extradition Act 1989.

4   Action taken by or with the authority of the Secretary of State for the purposes of investigating crime or of protecting the security of the State, including action so taken with respect to passports.

5   The commencement or conduct of civil or criminal proceedings before any court of law in the United Kingdom.

6   Any exercise of the prerogative of mercy.

7   Action taken in matters relating to contractual or other commercial transactions ... being transactions of a government department.

---

28   See McMurtie, SN, 'The waiting game – the Parliamentary Commissioner's response to delay in administrative procedures' [1997] PL 159.

29   *Congreve v Home Office* [1976] QB 629.

8   Action taken in respect of appointments or removals, pay, discipline, superannuation or other personnel matters, in relation to:

the armed forces, any office or employment under the Crown.[30]

9   The grant of honours, awards or privileges within the gift of the Crown, including the grant of Royal Charters.

Departments and matters within the Commissioner's jurisdiction

Schedule 2 of the Act lays down those Departments subject to the jurisdiction of the Commissioner. The Parliamentary and Health Service Commissioners Act 1987 extended the Commissioner's jurisdiction to cover some non-departmental bodies, and the complete list of Departments and bodies within the Commissioner's jurisdiction is now found in Schedule 1 of the 1987 Act, as amended by the Parliamentary Commissioner Act 1994, which provides that the following bodies shall be subject to investigation by the Commissioner:

Advisory, Conciliation and Arbitration Service; Agricultural Wages Committee; Ministry of Agriculture, Fisheries and Food; Arts Council; British Council; British Film Institute; British Library Board; Building Societies Commission; Certification Officer; Central Statistical Office of the Chancellor of the Exchequer; Charity Commission; Office of the Minister for the Civil Service; Civil Service Commission; Co-operative Development Agency; Countryside Commission; Countryside Council for Wales; Crafts Council; Crofters Commission; Crown Estate Office; Customs and Excise; Data Protection Registrar; Ministry of Defence; Development Commission; Educational Assets Board; Department of Education and Science; Central Bureau for Educational Visits and Exchanges; Office of the Director General of Electricity Supply; Department of Employment; Department of Energy; Department of the Environment; Equal Opportunities Commission; Office of the Director of Fair Trading; English Heritage; Equal Opportunities Commission; Export Credits Guarantee Department; Foreign and Commonwealth Office; Forestry Commission; Register of Friendly Societies; Office of the Director General of Gas Supply; Health and Safety Commission; Health and Safety Executive; Department of Health; Highland and Islands Development Board; Historic Buildings and Monuments Commission; Home Office; Horseracing Betting Levy Board; Housing Corporation; Housing for Wales; Human Fertilisation and Embryology Authority; Central Office of Information; Inland Revenue; Intervention Board for Agricultural Produce; Land Registry; Legal Aid Board; Scottish Legal Aid Board; Lighthouse Authorities; Lord Chancellor's Department; Lord President of the Council's Office; Medical Practices Committee; Scottish Medical Practices Committee; Museums and Galleries Commission; National Debt Office; Department of National Heritage; Trustee of the National Heritage Memorial Fund; Department of National Savings; Nature Conservancy Council for England;

---

30   Commissioner for Complaints (Northern Ireland) Act 1969, s 5(1), provides that the Commissioner has jurisdiction over matters of employment in the public sector.

Commission for the New Towns; Development Corporations for New Towns; Northern Ireland Court Service; Northern Ireland Office; Ordnance Survey; Office of Population Censuses and Surveys; Registrar of Public Lending Rights; Office of Public Service and Science; Public Record Office; Scottish Record Office; Commission for Racial Equality; Red Deer Commission, Commission of the Registrars of Scotland; General Register Office, Scotland; Agricultural and Food Research Council; Economic and Social Research Council; Medical Research Council; Natural Environment Research Council; Science and Engineering Research Council; Residuary Bodies; Office of the Commissioner for the Rights of Trades Union Members; Royal Mint; Scottish Courts Administration; Scottish Legal Aid Board; Scottish Office; Central Council for Education and Training in Social Work; Department of Social Security; Sports Council; Sports Council for Wales; Office for Standards in Education; Stationery Office; Office of the Director General of Telecommunications; English Tourist Board; Scottish Tourist Board; Wales Tourist Board; Board of Trade; Department of Trade and Industry; Traffic Director for London; Agricultural Training Board; Clothing and Allied Products Industry Training Board; Construction Industry Training Board; Hotel and Catering Industry Training Board; Plastics Processing Industry Training Board; Road Transports Industry Training Board; Department of Transport; Treasury; Treasury Solicitor; Independent Tribunal Service; Urban Development Corporations; Development Board for Rural Wales; Office of the Director General of Water Services; Welsh Office.

The Commissioner's discretion

Where a matter falls within the Commissioner's jurisdiction, the Commissioner has discretion as to whether to accept the complaint.[31] Section 5(5) provides that the Commissioner shall act 'in accordance with his own discretion'. Because of the breadth of discretion conferred on the Commissioner, both in relation to accepting complaints and in the conduct of investigations, judicial review of his decisions is unlikely to succeed. For example, in *Re Fletcher*,[32] the applicant sought an order of mandamus to force the Commissioner to investigate a complaint. The House of Lords refused, relying on the broad discretion conferred on the Commissioner by statute. In *R v Parliamentary Commissioner for Administration ex parte Dyer*,[33] the applicant sought judicial review of the Commissioner's investigation into her complaints against the Department of Social Security. The applicant was dissatisfied with a report of the Commissioner and sought judicial review on four grounds. The allegations were, first, that the Commissioner had not investigated all her complaints; secondly, that she had not been given the

---

31 Parliamentary Commissioner Act 1967, s 5(1).
32 [1970] 2 All ER 527.
33 [1994] 1 All ER 375.

opportunity to comment on the draft reports; thirdly, that the Commissioner, having heard her complaints, refused to reopen the investigations; and, fourthly, that the Commissioner was wrong in holding that he could not reopen the inquiry. The Queen's Bench Division held that it had jurisdiction to review the work of the Commissioner. Lord Justice Simon Brown declared that he could see nothing in the Commissioner's role or the statutory framework in which he operated which is 'so singular as to take him wholly outside the purview of judicial review'. Nevertheless, the court would be slow to review given the breadth of discretion conferred under the Act.[34]

The meaning of 'maladministration'

Maladministration is the key concept relating to the Commissioner's jurisdiction, but it is not defined in the Act. The concept derives from the Whyatt Report of 1961, where it was described as a term which 'was not of precise meaning'. The failure to define the concept in the Act was deliberate. The Minister responsible for introducing the legislation, Mr Richard Crossman, felt that the Act was of such an innovatory nature that time would be needed to adjust to the Act's introduction and that no rigid criteria should be set. In the House of Commons, Mr Crossman[35] described maladministration as including 'bias, neglect, inattention, delay, incompetence, ineptitude, perversity, turpitude, arbitrariness and so on'.

The courts have examined the concept of maladministration in relation to the work of Local Government Commissioners. For example, in *R v Commissioners for Local Administration ex parte Bradford Metropolitan Borough Council*,[36] maladministration was described as 'faulty administration' and 'bad administration', whereas, in 1980, Lord Donaldson MR explained that maladministration is primarily concerned with the manner in which authorities reach or implement decisions, and is not concerned with the quality of the decision itself.[37] In *R v Local Commissioner for Administration in the North and North East England ex parte Liverpool City Council*,[38] the Court of Appeal ruled that the failure of local councillors to follow the National Code of Local Government Conduct, and failure to observe the requirement to declare financial interests when taking part in decisions relating to planning, was maladministration.

---

34 Cf *R v Parliamentary Commissioner for Administration ex parte Balchin* [1997] COD 146, in which judicial review was granted, and the Parliamentary Commissioner found to have fallen into error.

35 *Official Report* HC 734 Col 51.

36 [1979] QB 287.

37 *R v Commissioners for Local Administration ex parte Eastleigh Borough Council* [1980] QB 855.

38 (2000) *The Times*, 3 March.

Maladministration is a more restrictive concept than is employed in other jurisdictions. In Denmark, for example, the ombudsman may examine 'mistakes' and 'unreasonable decisions' and, in Norway, the ombudsman can investigate decisions which are 'clearly unreasonable'. In the United Kingdom, being tied to the concept of maladministration, the Commissioner is not concerned with the merits of any decision taken, nor the fairness or otherwise of the rules governing any situation, but rather with the manner of the application of the rules.

The Commissioner's investigation and report

In the exercise of his jurisdiction, the Commissioner is vested with strong powers. The Commissioner has the same powers as a court in respect of requiring the attendance of witnesses and the right of examination, and the production of documents, subject to the protections of Cabinet proceedings and documents and such information as a person would not be compelled to disclose to a court of law.[39] To obstruct the Commissioner in the performance of his duties under the Act, without lawful excuse, may be certified as a contempt.

Where the Commissioner accepts jurisdiction and investigates a complaint, a report of the findings are sent to the principal officer of the department concerned[40] and, if the matter has not been remedied, or is unlikely to be, he may lay a special report before each House of Parliament.[41] The Commissioner's *Annual General Report* is laid before Parliament.[42] The Commissioner has no power to grant a remedy or to grant compensation. He does, however, make recommendations as to the appropriate remedy, and as to levels of suitable compensation.

The volume of complaints

The number of complaints referred to the Parliamentary Commissioner in the period 1989–96 are as follows:

TABLE II

Year	Number of complaints
1989	677
1990	704
1991	801

---

39 Parliamentary Commissioner Act 1967, s 8.
40 *Ibid*, s 10(2).
41 *Ibid*, s 10(3).
42 *Ibid*, s 10(4).

1992	945
1993	986
1994	1,332
1995	1,706
1996	1,933

In the 1990 report, the Commissioner recorded that the average time for an investigation was 14 months. Twenty five per cent of all complaints referred were investigated: 42 per cent being wholly justified, 47 per cent partially justified and 11 per cent unjustified. In 1991, 183 investigations were completed, with findings that 47.5 per cent of complaints were wholly justified and 42.6 per cent partly justified. Just over 13 per cent of complaints were either not justified or discontinued. In 1992, the average length of time taken for an investigation was 12 months, 13 days. Of the 945 complaints received, 269 were accepted for investigation. Of the 1,679 cases dealt with in 1996, 1,419 were rejected as not involving maladministration; of the 260 cases investigated, 189 (73 per cent) were upheld in full and 57 (22 per cent) were upheld in part: in only 14 cases (five per cent) was no maladministration found. The evidence indicates that, whilst a high number of complaints are rejected (either because they relate to matters not within the Commissioner's jurisdiction, whether relating to an excluded department or relating to matters of policy, or because they reveal no *prima facie* case of maladministration), once a complaint is admitted for investigation, the prospect of a finding of maladministration – at least in part – is high. In 1992, for example, of 186 completed investigations, 177 (or 95 per cent) cases were found to reveal maladministration.

In terms of his investigations, the Commissioner has reported that 50 per cent of his time is consistently devoted to complaints about tax and social security – the two largest departments in terms of contact with, and effect on, individuals. In 1993, the Department of Social Security was the subject of 30 per cent of all referrals, the Inland Revenue the subject of 16 per cent. Of the problems encountered in terms of maladministration, these are put down to the sheer scale of the administrative function and the necessary complexity of laws. The impersonal nature of services, the forms and lack of access to administrators and problems of delay also feature highly.

As to the level of success achieved, the Commissioner reported that, in all cases where injustice had been found to have occurred through maladministration, the remedy proposed by the Commissioner had been accepted. Only twice in a 15 years' term were recommendations not accepted and in those instances a remedy had been effected through the select committee.

THE PROBLEM OF ACCESSIBILITY
AND PUBLIC AWARENESS

On accessibility, the Commissioner has questioned his own position.[43] As seen, prior to reform, discussed below, access to the Commissioner could only be gained through a Member of Parliament, and not directly. Of the 100 plus national ombudsmen around the world, the British Commissioner was unique in having no powers of initiative, being dependent upon references from the MP 'filter'. In the report for 1988, the Commissioner considered the difficulties in increasing public awareness about the Commissioner's role and powers,[44] despite regular press notices, press and radio and television interviews and the booklet available from Citizens Advice Bureaux and public libraries. In the Commissioner's report of 1990,[45] the problem of public awareness was again alluded to.

The Commissioner himself has noted that public awareness is most usually raised through some major issue or scandal. Two illustrations may be cited. The first major investigation arising out of a number of complaints was into the non-payment of compensation by the Foreign Office to 12 persons who had been prisoners of war in the Sachsenhausen camp.[46] Monies had been made available by the German government and distributed by the Foreign Office to former detainees. The Commissioner found there had been maladministration[47] and the government awarded compensation to the complainants.

The Barlow Clowes affair resulted in hundreds of complaints being made to the Commissioner concerning the collapse of the Barlow Clowes company.[48] In 1988, the group of companies collapsed, causing significant losses to shareholders. The Department of Trade and Industry has responsibility for licensing such investment companies.[49] Following the company's collapse, numerous shareholders complained to Members of Parliament, 159 of whom referred the complaints to the Parliamentary

---

43 *Parliamentary Commissioner for Administration Annual Report for 1983* (1983–84), London: HMSO. And see *Report of the Select Committee on the Parliamentary Commissioner for Administration: The Powers, Work and Jurisdiction of the Ombudsman* (1992–93), London: HMSO.

44 *Parliamentary Commissioner for Administration Annual Report for 1988* (1988–89), London: HMSO.

45 *Parliamentary Commissioner for Administration Annual Report for 1990* (1990–91), London: HMSO.

46 See Bradley, AW 'Sachsenhausen, Barlow Clowes – and then' [1992] PL 353.

47 *Third Report of the Parliamentary Commissioner for Administration*, HC 54 (1967–68), London: HMSO; and see Gregory, R and Drewry, G, 'Barlow Clowes and the ombudsman: Part I' [1991] PL 192 and 'Part II' [1991] PL 408.

48 See *ibid*, Gregory and Drewry.

49 Under the Prevention of Fraud (Investment) Act 1958; now, Financial Services Act 1986.

Commissioner. The Commissioner made five findings of maladministration on the part of the Department of Trade and Industry, including errors, lack of information before making decisions, delay in instigating a formal inquiry, a failure to appreciate that auditors would not find the relevant information and insufficient rigour in exercising its regulatory role – all of which resulted in injustice.

The government initially rejected the Commissioner's findings and recommendations as to compensation, arguing both that no investment is free of risk and that those with larger amounts of money should accept a higher level of responsibility and therefore loss. The Commissioner expressed disappointment that the government did not unreservedly accept his report. His recommendation was that compensation should be payable to investors at a rate of 90 per cent for losses incurred under £50,000, and 85 per cent for losses under £100,000. The Secretary of State for Trade and Industry accepted the recommendations, but maintained that the government had no legal liability to compensate investors, and claimed that the Department's handling of the case was 'within acceptable range of standards reasonably to be expected of regulators'. The Secretary of State went on to say that compensation was being made only because of the Parliamentary Commissioner's recommendations.[50]

The losses caused to egg manufacturers over allegations made by officials concerning the salmonella virus resulted in charges of maladministration and compensation of £600,000 being paid by the Ministry of Agriculture, Fisheries and Food.[51] The Animal Health Act 1981[52] provided that, where the salmonella virus was found in flocks, the flock should be slaughtered and compensation paid for the loss of the healthy birds. No compensation was payable for the diseased birds. The Ministry fixed the level of compensation – irrespective of the proportion of the flock infected by the virus – at 60 per cent of the value of the healthy birds. On investigation, the Commissioner found that inadequate compensation had been paid.[53]

It has been seen above that the government is, in general, prepared to accept the findings of the Commissioner and to implement his recommendations. In December 1991, the Financial Secretary to the Treasury[54] stated that 'I am not aware of any circumstances in which [the Parliamentary Ombudsman's] recommendations have been ignored. This is the basis on which the government has tended to work – and has, as far as I am aware, always worked – in that we do accept and implement the

---

50 In total, £150 million was paid in compensation.
51 HC 947 (1992–93), London: HMSO.
52 Animal Health Act 1981, Sched 3, para 5(2).
53 *Fourth Report: Compensation to Farmers for Slaughtered Poultry*, HC 519 (1992–93), London: HMSO.
54 Mr Francis Maude MP.

recommendations that are made'.[55] This commitment was reiterated by the Chancellor of the Duchy of Lancaster[56] in 1993, when he stated that 'invariably, in the end, [the government] accepted the Commissioner's say-so'.[57] However, it has also been seen above that, in relation to the Barlow Clowes affair, the government deviated from this normally accepted practice and, while prepared to offer compensation, did so 'without admission of fault or liability'.[58] The government has proved to be more obdurate in relation to the 1995 report of the Commissioner, relating to financial damage caused by the prolonged plans to build the Channel Tunnel Rail Link.

The Channel Tunnel Rail Link (the CTRL) is a new stretch of railway line, designed to take high speed cross-channel trains. The government's original intention was that the CTRL would be financed by the private sector. However, when private funding was not forthcoming, the project could not proceed. In 1990, the Secretary of State for Transport announced that the route was to be reconsidered. The project was thus kept alive, but uncertainty surrounded the area of south east England in which it was to built. As a result, thousands of properties were 'blighted' and owners unable to sell their homes. The route was finally decided in 1994.

In February 1995, the Commissioner[59] laid a special report before the House.[60] The special report was only the second such report to be made in the history of the office of Commissioner.[61] The basis for the laying of a special report is that the Commission considers that injustice has been caused to persons as a result of maladministration and that the injustice has not been, or will not be, remedied. In the Commissioner's report on the CTRL project, the Commissioner considered that maladministration had occurred in the Department of Transport between June 1990 and April 1994. The Commissioner's view was that the Department of Transport 'had a responsibility to consider the position of ... persons suffering exceptional or extreme hardship and to provide for redress where appropriate'[62] and that the government had a duty to consider the position not just of all citizens, but also of individual citizens harmed by its action. The Commissioner found that

---

55 *Second Report from the Select Committee on the PCA: The Implications of the Citizen's Charter for the Work of the Parliamentary Commissioner for Administration,* HC 159 (1991–92), London: HMSO, Q 11.

56 Then the Rt Hon William Waldegrave MP.

57 *First Report from the Select Committee on the PCA: The Powers, Work and Jurisdiction of the Ombudsman,* HC 33 (1993–94), London: HMSO, Q 733.

58 Observations by the government to the *Report of the PCA on Barlow Clowes,* HC 99 (1989–90), London: HMSO, para 43.

59 Mr William Reid CB.

60 Pursuant to the Parliamentary Commissioner Act 1967, s 10(3).

61 The first was in 1977–78, which also involved the Department of Transport.

62 *Fifth Report of the PCA: The Channel Tunnel Rail Link and Blight,* HC 193 (1994–95), London: HMSO, para 46.

'no special consideration was given to that aspect of good administration and it is on that basis that I criticise the department'.[63] The Commissioner recommended that individuals who had suffered exceptional hardship should receive compensation from the government. The government's reaction was to state that it was not its policy to compensate those affected by generalised blight, and that, in relation to those individuals who had suffered exceptional hardship, it was too difficult to define criteria to identify such individuals. With this, the Commissioner disagreed. While he accepted that there were definitional difficulties, he did not 'accept at all that it is technically beyond a government department's capabilities' to establish the relevant criteria.[64]

The Commissioner's report and the government's response was considered by the Select Committee on the Parliamentary Commissioner for Administration (see, further, p 1119). In its report,[65] the committee agreed with the Commissioner's assessment of the evidence. The committee stated that:

> The department failed to provide any material to contradict this finding when invited to do so by the committee. At no point was direct and comprehensive consideration given to the question of whether it was either desirable or possible to offer *ex gratia* compensation to those exceptionally afflicted by the generalised blight of the CTRL project.

The committee considered that at the heart of the matter lay the definition of maladministration. In his annual report for 1993, the Commissioner included in his definition 'failure to mitigate the effects of rigid adherence to the letter of the law where that produces manifestly inequitable treatment'.[66] Endorsing this definition, the committee stated that the definition implies:

> .... an expectation that when an individual citizen is faced with extraordinary hardship as a result of strict application of law or policy, the executive must be prepared to look again and consider whether help can be given. That the department did not do. It never considered the possibility of distinguishing cases of extreme hardship from the mass of those affected adversely by blight.[67]

The committee concluded that:

> 1(i) ... the Department of Transport should have considered whether any *ex gratia* payments were due when the CTRL project entered the period of uncertainty caused by problems of funding between June 1990 and April 1994;

---

63 *Fifth Report of the PCA: The Channel Tunnel Rail Link and Blight*, HC 193 (1994–95), London: HMSO, para 46, Q 1.

64 *Ibid*, Q 1.

65 *Sixth Report of the PCA: The Channel Tunnel Rail Link and Exceptional Hardship*, HC 270 (1994–95), London: HMSO.

66 *Report of the Parliamentary Commissioner for Administration Annual Report for 1993*, HC 345 (1993–94), London: HMSO, para 10.

67 *Ibid, Sixth Report*, para 20.

(ii) ... it is desirable to grant redress to those affected to an extreme and exceptional degree by generalised blight, in line with the principle that maladministration includes a failure to mitigate the effects of rigid adherence to the letter of the law where that produces manifestly inequitable treatment;

(iii) ... it should be possible to distinguish a small number of cases of exceptional hardship.

The committee recommended that:

> ... the Department of Transport reconsider its response to the Ombudsman's findings, accept his conclusion that maladministration has occurred and consider arrangements to determine whether there are householders who merit compensation on the grounds of exceptional hardship. That is very much a matter for the department's judgment, a point the Ombudsman emphasised. It would be most regrettable if the department were to remain obdurate. In such an event, we then recommend that as a matter of urgency a debate on this matter be held on the floor of the House on a substantive motion in government time.[68]

This highly critical report on the actions of the Department of Transport and the government's failure to respond positively to the Commissioner's report represents a landmark case in the complex tri-partite constitutional relationship between the Commissioner, his select committee and Parliament, and the executive. In 1997, the government finally agreed to pay compensation of £5,000 to property owners whose property value had been adversely affected by the delay in reaching decisions over the routing of the CTRL.[69]

The Child Support Agency has also attracted a significant volume of complaints.[70] The number of complaints was such that, in 1994, the Commissioner took the 'unprecedented step of declining to investigate fresh individual complaints' other than where they concerned aspects of the Agency's work which the Commissioner had not yet inquired into. In 1995, complaints against the Child Support Agency amounted to one quarter of all cases referred to the Commissioner.[71] In 1998, the government announced that the Child Support Agency was to be abolished, to be replaced by a more efficient body.

---

68 *Sixth Report of the PCA: The Channel Tunnel Rail Link and Exceptional Hardship*, HC 270 (1994–95), London: HMSO, paras 26 and 27.

69 See James, R and Longley, D, 'The Channel Tunnel Rail Link, the Ombudsman and the Select Committee' [1996] PL 38.

70 See *ibid*, Sixth Report, paras 29–32.

71 See *ibid*, Sixth Report, paras 17–18 and *Parliamentary Commissioner for Administration Annual Report for 1995*, Cm 296; and see HC 193 (1994–95), London: HMSO.

The Select Committee on the Parliamentary Commissioner[72]

The Parliamentary Commissioner is aided by a select committee, established under Standing Order Number 126(1), which provides that:

> There shall be a select committee to examine the reports of the Parliamentary Commissioner for Administration which are laid before this House, and matters in connection therewith; and the committee shall consist of nine Members of whom the quorum shall be three.

The select committee considers the annual and special reports of the Parliamentary Commissioner, the Health Service Commissioner and Northern Ireland Commissioner and takes evidence from the Commissioners and others, including government departments and health authorities on matters arising from reports in order to ensure that all reasonable efforts are made to tighten up procedures, prevent the repetition of faults and provide any appropriate remedies.

The select committee represents the formal link between the Commissioner and Parliament. The committee is able to exert pressure on government departments to comply with the recommendations of the Commissioner.

The Parliamentary Commissioner and ministerial responsibility

One aspect of the office of Commissioner which caused concern when the office was proposed was the relationship between the Commissioner and Ministers, and the impact of the Commissioner's office on the doctrine of ministerial responsibility. The view of the government at the time was that ministerial responsibility and the office of the Commissioner were irreconcilable. As noted above, in the Attorney General's view, there already existed 'adequate provision' under the constitution for the redress of grievances.

> JUSTICE replied that:

> The Commissioner would help to make ministerial responsibility more effective. He would penetrate the screen which Ministers interpose between Members of Parliament and government departments and he would keep Parliament informed about administrative practices which were open to criticism. The responsibility of the Minister would remain as it is – neither more nor less.

The Select Committee on the Parliamentary Commissioner in its report of 1967–68 considered this relationship between the Parliamentary Commissioner and ministerial responsibility, and took the view that:

---

72 See Gregory, R, 'The Select Committee on the Parliamentary Commissioner for Administration 1967–80' [1982] PL 49.

Your committee recognise that, by setting up the Office of the Parliamentary Commissioner for Administration, Parliament has undermined the doctrine to some extent, in that the power of the Commissioner to carry out an independent investigation within the department, and publish what he finds, is an encroachment upon the Minister's responsibility. The anonymity of civil servants may be infringed by the findings of the Commissioner, either because the complaint under investigation is directed against a specific official or because the Commissioner may identify an official in the course of his investigation.[73]

And, further:

In his evidence, the Attorney General recognised that under their Order of Reference there is no limitation upon the persons on whom your committee can call for evidence in discharge of their function of supporting the activities of the Parliamentary Commissioner. On the other hand, he suggested that the committee should organise their proceedings so as to maintain the balance between his function and the protection of ministerial responsibility upon which the efficiency of democratic government depends.

Your committee fully recognise that they have a responsibility for maintaining this balance ... Your committee feel confident that they will regulate their procedure so as to avoid the impression that they are in any way seeking to identify or blame individual officials where the finding of the Commission is that an administrative defect is the collective responsibility of the department or of officials in that department.

On the other hand, your committee do not agree with the suggestion that they should confine themselves to taking evidence from the Principal Officer of a department where they are considering what the department should do to remedy administrative defects disclosed by the Commissioner's investigation. As the Attorney General acknowledged, they have an undoubted right under their Order of Reference to call for evidence from any persons who they think can assist them in their inquiry. They agree that generally the appropriate witness will be the Principal Officer, in view of his responsibility and authority for the administrative systems of the department with which they are concerned. On the other hand, there may well be infrequent occasions when your committee will judge it necessary to inform themselves about the nature of the defect in the system as well as the measures taken to remedy that defect. For that and other purposes they may need to obtain the evidence of those officials who are concerned at first hand with the actions in question. Your committee are satisfied that they will be able to take evidence from subordinate officials for this purpose without exposing them to unfair publicity or criticism, and they feel that they can rely on department to indicate the appropriate witnesses ...[74]

---

73 *Report of the Select Committee*, HC 350 (1967–68), London: HMSO, para 24.
74 *Report of the Select Committee*, HC 350 (1967–68), London: HMSO, paras 28–30.

Developments in the organisation of government and other public bodies have implications for the future role of the Commissioner. In Chapter 11, the government's avowed intention to make government more accessible, open and accountable to citizens was considered. As there seen, three major developments reflected this commitment. The Citizen's Charter provided that public bodies must state their objectives, must publicise the standards of service to be expected by consumers and establish complaints procedures for dissatisfied customers.[75] Specific services must publish their own individuated Charter. By March 1994, there were 38 Charters in existence.[76] The establishment of 'Next Step Agencies',[77] the task of which is to achieve greater efficiency in the delivery of public services, also affects the role of the Commissioner. The setting up of Agencies, the head of which are responsible for operational matters and accountable to Parliament through select committee inquiries, has the effect of reducing the size of the central Civil Service and introducing greater management efficiency and accountability. The Minister remains responsible to Parliament for policy matters. In relation to the Parliamentary Commissioner,[78] his powers of investigation, report and recommendation continue to extend to Agencies. However, complaints made by the public to Members of Parliament about operational matters are to be directed to the chairman of the board of the Agency. Complaints regarding matters of policy remain within the political domain and the responsibility of Ministers.

REFORM OF THE OFFICE OF PARLIAMENTARY COMMISSIONER[79]

Before reform, as can be seen, the office of Commissioner suffered from a number of drawbacks. Individuals had – unlike in most other jurisdictions – no right of direct access to the Parliamentary Commissioner. Under the Parliamentary Commissioner (Amendment) Bill 2000, the right of direct access is provided, thereby removing one of the most problematic aspects of the Commissioner's jurisdiction. Moreover, the concept of maladministration is relatively narrow and is linked to injustice suffered as a result of a decision. Furthermore, while the 1987 Act has extended the bodies into which the

---

75 See Barron, A and Scott, C, 'The Citizen's Charter programme' (1992) 55 MLR 526.

76 See *op cit*, Birkinshaw, fn 1, Chapter 1.

77 See *Improving Management in Government: The Next Steps*, 1988, London: HMSO.

78 And Commissioner for Local Administration.

79 See Harlow, C, 'Ombudsmen in search of a role' (1978) 41 MLR 446; Woolf (Lord), *The Protection of the Public – A New Challenge*, 1990, London: Stevens; and Gregory, R and Pearson, J, 'The parliamentary ombudsman after twenty-five years: problems and solutions' (1992) 70 Public Admin 469.

Commissioner has jurisdiction to investigate, there remain a significant number of matters outside his jurisdiction. Many of these relate to matters which fall under the royal prerogative,[80] which, as has been seen, is subject to inadequate parliamentary scrutiny and to limited judicial review.

The question of direct access to the Commissioner was again considered by the Select Committee in 1993–94.[81] The committee conducted a survey of Members of Parliament in order to ascertain their views on the filter. Of the 333 Members who responded, the committee reported that 38.4 per cent were in favour of direct access to the Commissioners, whereas 58.0 per cent were against direct access.[82] The committee commented that:

> It is clear that many Members value their role as champions of their constituents' complaints and are unwilling to see this constitutional function in any way bypassed or diminished.[83]

The Commissioner himself, however, argued forcibly that the filter was 'potentially disadvantageous to complainants', in part because individuals may feel that their Member of Parliament would be unwilling to help them and because of the administrative burden on Members of Parliament in transmitting material to the Commissioner. JUSTICE and the National Consumer Council also argued for reform of the system. The committee summarised the objections to the MP filter as follows:

(a) The public should have direct access to the Commissioner as a matter of right.

(b) The filter is an anomaly, almost unknown in other ombudsman systems.[84] No such requirement exists, for instance, in the case of the Health Service Commissioner.

(c) Individuals with complaints may be unwilling to approach an MP, while desiring the ombudsman's assistance.

(d) The filter means that the likelihood of individuals' cases being referred to the Commissioner will largely depend on the views and practice of the particular constituency MP. Some look with more favour on the Office of the Commissioner than others.

(e) The filter acts as an obstacle to the Commissioner effectively promoting his services.

(f) The filter creates an unnecessary bureaucratic barrier between the complainant and the Commissioner, involving considerable paperwork for MPs and their offices.[85]

---

80 See Chapter 7.
81 HC 33 (1993–94), London: HMSO, paras 53–77.
82 See also Drewry, G and Harlow, C, 'A "cutting edge"? The Parliamentary Commissioner and MPs' (1990) 53 MLR 758.
83 HC 33 (1993–94), London: HMSO, para 58.
84 Only Sri Lanka and France employ similar filters.
85 HC 33 (1993–94), London: HMSO, para 65.

The committee concluded, however, that the advantages of retaining the filter system outweighed these significant disadvantages. The committee was particularly concerned to retain the role of the Member of Parliament in the investigation of complaints, and about the potentially vast increase in the number of complaints being received by the Commissioner if the filter was removed. As seen, the Parliamentary Commissioner (Amendment) Bill 2000 removes this anomalous feature of access to the Commissioner.

The question of the jurisdictional basis of maladministration has also been subject to consideration. The JUSTICE-All Souls report of 1988[86] recommended no change to the definition.

THE HEALTH SERVICE COMMISSIONER

The National Health Service (Scotland) Act 1972 and National Health Service Reorganisation Act 1973[87] introduced separate Health Service Commissioners for England, Wales and Scotland. The Parliamentary Commissioner for Administration undertakes the role of Health Service Commissioner. The Commissioner reports directly to the Secretary of State for Health, but his reports are laid before both Houses of Parliament and will be considered by the Parliamentary Commissioner Select Committee.

Jurisdiction

Section 109 of the Health Service Act 1977 provides that the following are subject to investigation by the Health Commissioner: regional, district and special health authorities; family health services authorities; Mental Health Act Commission; Dental Practice Board; and National Health Service Trusts.

The Commissioner may investigate any matter relating to an alleged failure to provide a service it is meant to provide, and any other action taken by or on behalf of the authority. The jurisdiction is thus much broader than 'maladministration'. However, the complaint must be one which involves injustice or hardship suffered as a result of failures under the two headings for complaint. Individuals have the right of direct access to the Commissioner.

---

86 JUSTICE-All Souls, *Administrative Law: Some Necessary Reforms*, 1988, London: HMSO.
87 As amended by the National Health Service Act 1977, Pt V. See, now, the Health Service Commissioners Act 1993.

Excluded matters

Section 116(2)(b) of the Health Service Act 1977 provides that the Commissioner shall not investigate complaints about services provided by family doctors, dentists, opticians and pharmacists. This broad exclusion was justified on the basis that the services provided are provided independently, under contracts with local family health services authorities which have jurisdiction to adjudicate on complaints. The most significant exclusion from jurisdiction related to clinical decisions. Part II of Schedule 13 of the 1977 Act provided that clinical decisions shall not be investigated, whether the complaint relates to diagnosis, care or treatment.[88] Such matters are for the judgment of the doctors, nurses or paramedics and not for the Commissioner. Accordingly, any complaint concerning clinical judgment must be rejected. The Health Service Commissioners (Amendment) Act 1996, however, extends the jurisdiction of health service commissioners. Section 6 removed the statutory bar which prevented the commissioner from investigating complaints concerning clinical judgment, thus correcting one of the most significant former jurisdictional exclusions.

Service committees which consider allegations against doctors, dentists, opticians and pharmacists originally could not be investigated by the Commissioner.[89] Personnel matters were also excluded,[90] as are commercial transactions,[91] and inquiries set up by the Secretary of State into aspects of the National Health Service.[92] Sections 1 and 2 of the Health Service Commissioners (Amendment) Act 1996, however, now bring the providers of general medical, dental, ophthalmic and pharmaceutical services and people in the independent sector who provide services to NHS patients within the Commissioners' jurisdiction.

The volume of complaints

In 1991–92, 1,176 complaints were received, of which 540 were rejected. In 1993–94, 1,384 complaints were received. The exclusion of matters relating to clinical judgment was a major factor in the rejection of complaints and a major flaw in the scrutiny of standards of practice in the health service. Opposition to extending the Commissioner's jurisdiction comes from the medical profession itself and insurance companies. Complaints concerning clinical judgment and practice in hospitals are regulated by the Hospital Complaints

---

88 National Health Service Act 1977, Sched 13, para 19(1).
89 *Ibid*, Sched 13, para 19(2).
90 *Ibid*, Sched 13, para 19(3).
91 *Ibid*, Sched 13, para 19(4).
92 *Ibid*, Sched 13, para 19(5).

Procedure Act 1985, and circulars. Complaints against individual General Practitioners are dealt with by Family Health Service Authorities, from which ultimately an appeal lies to the Secretary of State for Health.[93] The General Medical Council deals with complaints concerning serious professional misconduct of doctors. However, although 1,600 complaints are received by the General Medical Council each year, over half of these are rejected on the basis that the allegation is not one of 'serious professional misconduct'. A Patient's Charter exists to heighten the awareness of the public regarding complaints mechanisms.

LOCAL GOVERNMENT COMMISSIONERS[94]

The Local Government Act 1974 established Commissioners for Local Administration, for England and Wales. England is divided into three areas, each represented by one or more Commissioners.[95] The Scottish system is established under Part II of the Local Government (Scotland) Act 1975. Commissioners are appointed by the Crown and hold office 'during good behaviour'.

Jurisdiction

The Commissioners have jurisdiction to investigate any complaint of maladministration involving council committees, their Members and officers of the council. Police authorities and water boards are also subject to investigation.[96] The Local Government Act 1988[97] brings development corporations and the Commission for New Towns within the Commissioner's jurisdiction. Since 1989, the public has the right of direct access to the Commissioner, a reform which resulted in a 44 per cent increase in complaints by the year ending March 1989 and by March 1990 in a further 25 per cent increase in complaints.

---

93 NHS (Service Committee and Tribunal) Regulations SI 1992/664.

94 Recommended by the JUSTICE Report, *The Citizen and His Council: Ombudsmen for Local Government?*, 1969; and see the White Paper, *Reform of Local Government in England*, 1970, London: HMSO. See, also, Yardley, D, 'Local ombudsmen in England: recent trends and developments' [1983] PL 522; and *op cit*, Birkinshaw, fn 1.

95 Local Government Act 1974, s 23.

96 *Ibid*, ss 25, 34(1).

97 Local Government Act 1988, s 29, Sched 3.

Maladministration causing injustice

The concept of maladministration used for the Parliamentary Commissioner is adopted for the Local Commissioners. Maladministration resulting in injustice has been found to include incomplete record keeping and the failure to give reasons for decisions, and a finding of maladministration may be made where an authority fails to have adequate complaints procedures. Inadequate school places, and unreasonable delays in processing applications for improvement grants have also been found to amount to maladministration. Shortages of staff and financial resources will not excuse a council from a finding of maladministration.

Section 31 of the Act provides that an authority need only consider a Commissioner's report if it has been found that the maladministration in question has resulted in injustice. Mere maladministration is not enough.

Remedies

Where a finding of maladministration resulting in injustice has been made, section 31 of the Local Government Act 1974 imposes a duty on authorities to consider the report and to advise the Commissioner of any action taken to comply with the findings, or proposed action. Section 1 of the Local Government Act 1978 amends section 31 of the 1974 Act and provides that authorities may make 'any payment' to the aggrieved person that it thinks appropriate.

Not every decision of the Commissioners will be accepted. In 1986, for example, the Select Committee on the Parliamentary Commissioner noted that 19 per cent of local authorities who had adverse reports made by the Commissioners had ignored the recommendations.[98] The Local Government and Housing Act 1989 provides that local authorities have three months in which to respond to the Commissioner's report and that they should notify the Commissioner of any action taken, or action which they are proposing to take in response to his report.[99] If the Commissioner is not satisfied with the response he may issue a further report. Where the local authority proposes not to act in response to the report, the matter must be referred to a full council meeting.[100]

---

98 *Third Report from the Select Committee on the Parliamentary Commissioner for Administration: Local Government Cases: Enforcement of Remedies*, HC 448 (1985–86), London: HMSO.

99 Local Government and Housing Act 1989, s 26(2)–(2)(c).

100 See, further, Chapter 10.

Excluded matters

Schedule 5 of the Local Government Act excludes matters relating to the internal regulation of schools, personnel matters, action taken concerning the commencement of legal proceedings and criminal investigations, commercial and contractual matters.

Judicial review and Commissioners for Administration

Judicial review of decisions of Commissioners is an available form of redress, although the breadth of discretion conferred on Commissioners often renders their decisions beyond challenge. In *Law Debenture Trust Group plc v Pensions Ombudsman*,[101] the Chancery Division allowed an appeal against a finding of maladministration by the Pensions Ombudsman. The complainant had applied to trustees of his pension scheme for early retirement following an injury. The trustees concluded that he was not incapacitated, having carried out video surveillance. The court ruled that the only basis available to the Ombudsman for overturning the decision of the trustees was on the ground of perversity, and that such a finding would have to be expressed in clear terms in the Ombudsman's decision, which had not been done. Further, a finding of perversity could only be made after consideration of the *Wednesbury* criteria with respect to unreasonableness. The Ombudsman was wrong to find that surveillance *per se* amounted to maladministration.

In *R v Parliamentary Commissioner for Administration ex parte Balchin*,[102] the Queen's Bench Division quashed a decision of the Parliamentary Commissioner. The Commissioner had found maladministration in relation to property blighted by a road scheme in Norfolk, but following judicial review his decision was quashed, whereupon a second ombudsman investigated the matter. The second decision included fresh findings based on new evidence. It was disputed whether the Commissioner had made a finding as to whether, if there had been any maladministration, that had caused any injustice to the applicants. The court held that the decision on maladministration was flawed since his reasoning was inadequate, and that there had been a failure to give reasons for findings on the principal controversial issues. The application was granted and certiorari ordered.

---

101 (1999) *The Independent*, 25 October.
102 [1999] EGCS 78.

The volume of complaints

Between 1988 and 1993, the Local Government Commissioners received the following number of complaints:

TABLE III

Year	Number of complaints
1988–89	7,055
1989–90	8,733
1990–91	9,169
1991–92	12,123
1992–93	13,307

Housing matters form the basis for approximately 40 per cent of complaints each year, with complaints about planning accounting for approximately 30 per cent of complaints. Education, social services, local taxation and environmental health each comprise approximately five per cent of complaints. In 1992–93, 13,617 complaints were determined, 12,862 of which were concluded after initial inquiries. In 336 cases, complaints were determined when the investigation was discontinued. In 419 cases, 339 findings of maladministration with resulting injustice were made, 42 findings of maladministration were made and 38 of no maladministration.[103]

THE INFORMATION COMMISSIONER

The proposed Freedom of Information Act, discussed in Chapter 24, will represent a significant step in the direction of more open government by conferring on citizens a legal right, subject to limited exceptions, to access to information held by public bodies. An Information Commissioner will be appointed who will be independent of Parliament and accountable to the courts. The Commissioner's jurisdiction will normally come into play after there has been a complaint made to a department or other public body, and that body has conducted an internal inquiry which produces no satisfactory outcome. Complaints will be made by the public via a Member of Parliament. The Commissioner will have wide power of investigation of complaints, including the right of access, under warrant, to enter and search the records of public authorities and, where it is suspected that information is being, or will be suppressed, to remove that information. There will be no right of appeal from the Commissioner to the courts, but his or her decisions will be

---

103 See *op cit*, Birkinshaw, fn 1, p 225.

amenable to judicial review. The Commissioner will lay an annual report before Parliament, and will issue reports on investigations undertaken.

EUROPEAN UNION AND COMMUNITY OMBUDSMAN[104]

The Treaty on European Union 1992 introduced the office of ombudsman, appointed by the European Parliament.[105] The ombudsman is appointed for the life of a Parliament, and may be removed by the Court of Justice, at the request of the Parliament, on the basis that 'he no longer fulfils the conditions required for the performance of his duties or if he is guilty of serious misconduct'.[106] The ombudsman is completely independent in the exercise of his duties, and may not seek or take instructions from any body.[107]

Citizens of the European Union have the right of direct access to the ombudsman, and complaints may be referred by a Member of the European Parliament. The ombudsman has jurisdiction to hear complaints relating to institutions of the Community and to require national government bodies to provide information relating to complaints. Where a finding of maladministration is made, the matter is referred to the relevant institution which has a period of three months in which to respond. The ombudsman submits an annual report to the European Parliament. The complaint must relate to maladministration on the part of institutions of the Community. The Court of Justice and the Court of First Instance of the Community, acting in their judicial role, are excluded from the ombudsman's jurisdiction.

---

104 On the institutions of the Community, see Chapter 8.
105 EC Treaty, Art 195 (formerly, EC Treaty, Art 138e).
106 *Ibid.*
107 *Ibid.*

MONARCHS OF BRITAIN

NAME	LIVED	REIGNED
William the Conqueror	1027 – 1087	1066 – 1087
William II	1056 – 1100	1087 – 1100
Henry I	1068 – 1135	1100 – 1135
Stephen	?1097 – 1154	1135 – 1154
Henry II	1133 – 1189	1154 – 1189
Richard I	1157 – 1199	1189 – 1199
John	1167 – 1216	1199 – 1216
Henry III	1207 – 1272	1216 – 1272
Edward I	1239 – 1307	1272 – 1307
Edward II	1284 – 1327	1307 – 1327
Edward III	1312 – 1377	1327 – 1377
Richard II	1367 – 1400	1377 – 1399
Henry IV	1367 – 1413	1399 – 1413
Henry V	1387 – 1422	1413 – 1422
Henry VI	1421 – 1471	1422 – 1461
Edward IV	1442 – 1483	1461 – 1470 1471 – 1483 (Henry VI was briefly restored to the throne in 1470)
Edward V	1470 – ?1483	1483
Richard III	1452 – 1485	1483 – 1485
Henry VII	1457 – 1509	1485 – 1509
Henry VIII	1491 – 1547	1509 – 1547

Edward VI	1537 – 1553	1547 – 1553
Mary I	1516 – 1558	1553 – 1558
Elizabeth I	1533 – 1603	1558 – 1603
James I	1566 – 1625	King of Scotland: 1567 – 1625 (James VI); King of England: 1603 – 1625
Charles I	1600 – 1649	1625 – 1649
Interregnum	1649 – 1660	–
Charles II	1630 – 1685	1660 – 1685
James II	1633 – 1701	1685 – 1688
William and Mary	1650 – 1702	1689 – 1702
Anne	1665 – 1714	1702 – 1714
George I	1660 – 1727	1714 – 1727
George II	1683 – 1760	1727 – 1760
George III	1738 – 1820	1760 – 1820
George IV	1762 – 1830	1820 – 1830
William IV	1765 – 1837	1830 – 1837
Victoria	1819 – 1901	1837 – 1901
Edward VII	1841 – 1910	1901 – 1910
George V	1865 – 1936	1910 – 1936
Edward VIII	1894 – 1972	1936 (abdicated)
George VI	1895 – 1952	1936 – 1952
Elizabeth II	1926 –	1952 –

PRIME MINISTERS OF THE UNITED KINGDOM

NAME	PARTY	DATES
Sir Robert Walpole		3 April 1721 – 11 February 1742
The Earl of Wilmington		16 February 1742 – 2 July 1743
The Hon Henry Pelham		25 August 1743 – 10 February 1746
The Earl of Bath		10 – 12 February 1746
The Hon Henry Pelham		13 February 1746 – 6 March 1754
The Duke of Newcastle		6 March 1754 – 26 October 1756
William Pitt (the elder)		16 November 1756 – 6 April 1757
The Duke of Devonshire		6 April – 8 June 1757
Earl Waldegrave		8 – 12 June 1757
The Duke of Devonshire		12 – 29 June 1757
William Pitt (the elder)		19 June 1757 – 5 October 1761
The Duke of Newcastle		5 October 1761 – 26 May 1762
The Earl of Bute		26 May 1762 – 8 April 1763
George Grenville		10 April 1763 – 10 July 1765
Marquess of Rockingham		10 July 1765 – 12 July 1766

William Pitt (the elder)		30 July 1766 – 12 March 1767
The Duke of Grafton		12 March 1767 – 28 January 1770
Lord North		28 January 1770 – 20 March 1782
Marquess of Rockingham		27 March 1782 – 1 July 1782
The Earl of Shelburne		3 July 1782 – 24 February 1783
The Duke of Portland		2 April 1783 – 19 December 1783
The Hon William Pitt (the younger)	Tory	19 December 1783 – 14 March 1801
Henry Addington	Tory	14 March 1801 – 10 May 1804
The Hon William Pitt (the younger)	Tory	10 May 1804 – 23 January 1806
Lord Grenville	Whig	31 March 1807 – 6 September 1809
The Duke of Portland	Tory	31 March 1807 – 6 September 1809
Spencer Perceval	Tory	4 October 1809 – 11 May 1812
The Earl of Liverpool	Tory	8 June 1812 – 17 February 1827
George Canning	Tory	10 April 1827 – 8 August 1827
Viscount Goderich	Tory	31 August 1827 – 8 January 1828
The Duke of Wellington	Tory	22 January 1828 – 15 November 1830
Earl Grey	Whig	16 November 1830 – 9 July 1834
Viscount Melbourne	Whig	16 July 1834 – 17 November 1834

The Duke of Wellington	Tory	17 November 1834 – 10 December 1834
Sir Robert Peel	Conservative	10 December 1834 – 8 April 1835
Viscount Melbourne	Whig	18 April 1835 – 30 August 1841
Sir Robert Peel	Conservative	30 August 1841 – 30 June 1846
Lord John Russell	Whig	30 June 1846 – 23 February 1852
The Earl of Derby	Conservative	23 February 1852 – 19 December 1852
The Earl of Aberdeen	Coalition	19 December 1852 – 1 February 1855
Viscount Palmerston	Whig-Liberal	6 February 1855 – 19 February 1858
The Earl of Derby	Conservative	26 February 1858 – 10 June 1859
Viscount Palmerston	Whig-Liberal	12 June 1859 – 18 October 1865
Earl Russell	Whig-Liberal	29 October 1865 – 26 June 1866
The Earl of Derby	Conservative	6 July 1866 – 25 February 1868
Benjamin Disraeli	Conservative	28 February 1868 – 3 December 1868
William Gladstone	Liberal	3 December 1868 – 17 February 1874
Benjamin Disraeli	Conservative	20 February 1874 – 18 April 1880
William Gladstone	Liberal	23 April 1880 – 23 June 1885
Marquess of Salisbury	Conservative	23 June 1885 – 27 January 1886
William Gladstone	Liberal	1 February 1886 – 20 July 1886

Marquess of Salisbury	Conservative	25 July 1886 – 11 August 1892
William Gladstone	Liberal	15 August 1892 – 3 March 1894
Earl of Rosebery	Liberal	5 March 1894 – 25 June 1895
Marquess of Salisbury	Conservative	25 June 1895 – 12 July 1902
Arthur Balfour	Conservative	12 July 1902 – 4 December 1905
Sir Henry Campbell-Bannerman	Liberal	5 December 1905 – 7 April 1908
Herbert Asquith	Liberal	7 April 1908 – 26 May 1915
Herbert Asquith	Coalition	26 May 1915 – 7 December 1916
David Lloyd George	Coalition	7 December 1916 – 19 October 1922
Andrew Bonar Law	Conservative	23 October 1922 – 20 May 1923
Stanley Baldwin	Conservative	22 May 1923 – 22 January 1924
James Ramsey MacDonald	Labour	22 January 1924 – 4 November 1924
Stanley Baldwin	Conservative	4 November 1924 – 5 June 1929
James Ramsey MacDonald	Labour	5 June 1929 – 24 August 1931
James Ramsey MacDonald	National Government	25 August 1931 – 7 June 1935
Stanley Baldwin	National Government	7 June 1935 – 28 May 1937
Neville Chamberlain	National Government	28 May 1937 – 10 May 1940
Winston Churchill	Coalition	10 May 1940 – 23 May 1945

Winston Churchill	Conservative	23 May 1945 – 26 July 1945
Clement Attlee	Labour	26 July 1945 – 26 October 1951
Winston Churchill	Conservative	26 October 1951 – 5 April 1955
Sir Anthony Eden	Conservative	6 April 1955 – 9 January 1957
Harold Macmillan	Conservative	10 January 1957 – 13 October 1963
Sir Alec Douglas-Home	Conservative	18 October 1963 – 16 October 1964
Harold Wilson	Labour	16 October 1964 – 19 June 1970
Edward Heath	Conservative	19 June 1970 – 3 March 1974
Harold Wilson	Labour	3 March 1974 – 16 March 1976
James Callaghan	Labour	5 April 1976 – 28 March 1979
Margaret Thatcher	Conservative	4 May 1979 – 22 November 1990
John Major	Conservative	27 November 1990 – 2 May 1997
Anthony Blair	Labour	2 May 1997 to present

MEMBERSHIP OF THE COMMONWEALTH

MEMBER COUNTRY	STATUS
Antigua and Barbuda	Monarchy under Queen Elizabeth II
Australia	Monarchy under Queen Elizabeth II
The Bahamas	Monarchy under Queen Elizabeth II
Bangladesh	Republic
Barbados	Monarchy under Queen Elizabeth II
Belize	Monarchy under Queen Elizabeth II
Botswana	Republic
Britain	Monarchy under Queen Elizabeth II
Brunei Darussalam	National Monarchy
Cameroon	Republic
Canada	Monarchy under Queen Elizabeth II
Cyprus	Republic
Dominica	Republic
Fiji	Republic
The Gambia	Republic
Ghana	Republic
Grenada	Monarchy under Queen Elizabeth II
Guyana	Republic
India	Republic
Jamaica	Monarchy under Queen Elizabeth II
Kenya	Republic
Kiribati	Republic
Lesotho	National Monarchy
Malawi	Republic

Malaysia	National Monarchy
Maldives	Republic
Malta	Republic
Mauritius	Republic
Mozambique	Republic
Namibia	Republic
Nauru	Republic
New Zealand	Monarchy under Queen Elizabeth II
Nigeria* (Membership suspended 1995)	Republic
Pakistan	Republic
Papua New Guinea	Monarchy under Queen Elizabeth II
St Kitts and Nevis	Monarchy under Queen Elizabeth II
St Lucia	Monarchy under Queen Elizabeth II
St Vincent and the Grenadines	Monarchy under Queen Elizabeth II
Samoa	Republic
Seychelles	Republic
Sierra Leone	Republic
Singapore	Republic
Soloman Islands	Monarchy under Queen Elizabeth II
South Africa	Republic
Sri Lanka	Republic
Swaziland	National Monarchy
Tanzania	Republic
Tonga	National Monarchy
Trinidad and Tobago	Republic
Tuvalu	Monarchy under Queen Elizabeth II
Uganda	Republic
Vanuatu	Republic
Zambia	Republic
Zimbabwe	Republic

BIBLIOGRAPHY

Adams, D (ed), *Collins English Dictionary*, 3rd edn, 1991, London: Collins

Agee, P, *Inside the Company: CIA Diary*, 1975, Harmondsworth: Penguin

Aitken, J, *Officially Secret*, 1971, London: Weidenfeld & Nicolson

Alder, J, 'Representation before tribunals' [1972] 1 PL 278

Alderman, RK and Carter, N, 'A very Tory coup: the ousting of Mrs Thatcher' (1991) 44 Parl Aff 125

Alderman, RK and Smith, MJ, 'Can prime ministers be pushed out?' (1990) 43 Parl Aff 260

Allan, TRS, 'Law, convention, prerogative: reflections prompted by the Canadian constitutional case' [1986] CLJ 305

Allan, TRS, *Law, Liberty and Justice*, 1993, Oxford: Clarendon

Allan, TRS, 'Legislative supremacy and the rule of law: democracy and constitutionalism' [1985] CLJ 111

Allan, TRS, 'Parliamentary sovereignty: law, politics and revolution' (1997) 113 LQR 443

Allan, TRS, 'Requiring reasons for reasons of fairness and reasonableness' [1994] CLJ 207

Allan, TRS, 'The limits of parliamentary sovereignty' [1985] PL 614

Allason, R, *The Branch: A History of the Metropolitan Police Special Branch 1883–1983*, 1983, London: Secker & Warburg

Allen, CK, *Law and Orders*, 3rd edn, 1965, London: Stevens

Andrew, C, *Secret Service: The Making of the British Intelligence Community*, 1985, London: Heinemann

Anson, W (Sir), *Law and Custom of the Constitution*, 4th edn, 1933, Oxford: Clarendon

Aquinas, T (St), *Summa Theologica*, 1947–48, Fathers of the English Dominican Province (trans), London: Burns & Oates

Archbold, *Criminal Law, Practice and Proceedings*, 1989, London: Sweet & Maxwell

Aristotle, *The Politics*, 1962, Sinclair, TA (trans), London: Penguin

Arnull, A, 'National courts and the validity of Community acts' (1988) 13 EL Rev 125

Arnull, A, 'References to the European Court' (1990) 15 EL Rev 375

Arnull, A, 'The scope of Article 177' (1988) 13 EL Rev 40

Arnull, A, 'The uses and abuses of Article 177 EEC' (1989) 52 MLR 622

Ashworth, A, 'Excluding evidence and protecting rights' [1977] Crim LR 723

Ashworth, A, 'Involuntary confessions and illegally obtained evidence in criminal cases – Part I' [1963] Crim LR 15

Ashworth, A, 'Involuntary confessions and illegally obtained evidence in criminal cases – Part II' [1963] Crim LR 77

Atkins, E and Hoggett, B, *Women and the Law*, 1984, Oxford: Blackwells

Aubert, V, *In Search of Law*, 1983, Oxford: Martin Robertson

Austin, J, *The Province of Jurisprudence Determined* (1832), 1954, London: Weidenfeld & Nicolson

Bacon, F, *Advancement of Learning*, 1951, Oxford: OUP

Bagehot, W, *The English Constitution* (1867), 1993, London: Fontana

Bailey, S, *Cross on Principles of Local Government Law*, 2nd edn, 1997, London: Sweet & Maxwell

Bailey, SH and Gunn, M, *Smith & Bailey on The Modern English Legal System*, 3rd edn, 1996, London: Sweet & Maxwell

Bailey, SH, Harris, DJ and Jones, BL, *Civil Liberties – Cases and Materials*, 4th edn, 1995, London: Butterworths

Baldwin, J and Bedward, J, 'Summarising tape recordings of police interviews' [1991] Crim LR 671

Baldwin, J, 'The police and tape recorders' [1985] Crim LR 659

Baldwin, J, *The Role of Legal Representatives at the Police Station*, RCCJ Research Study No 3, 1993, London: HMSO

Baldwin, R and Houghton, J, 'Circular arguments: the status and legitimacy of administrative rules' [1986] PL 239

Barber, NW, 'Privacy and the police: private right, public right or human right? *R v Chief Constable of the North Wales Police ex parte AB*' [1998] PL 19

Barendt, E, Baron, A, Herberg, JW and Jowell, J, 'Public law' (1993) 46 CLP Annual Review 101

Barker, R, *Political Legitimacy and the State*, 1990, Oxford: Clarendon

Barnett, H, 'A privileged position? Gypsies, land and planning law' [1994] Conveyancer 454

Barnett, H, '*Buckley v United Kingdom*: landmark or signpost?' (1996) 146 NLJ 1628

Barnett, H, 'Reflections on the Child Support Act' [1993] 5 J of Child Law 77

Barnett, H, 'The end of the road for Gypsies?' (1995) 24 Anglo-American L Rev 133

Barnett, H, *Introduction to Feminist Jurisprudence*, 1998, London: Cavendish Publishing

Barron, A and Scott, C, 'The Citizen's Charter programme' (1992) 55 MLR 526

Bates, St JT, *Devolution to Scotland: The Legal Aspects*, 1997, Edinburgh: T & T Clark

Bebr, G, 'The reinforcement of the constitutional review of Community acts under Article 177 EEC Treaty' (1988) 25 CML Rev 667

Beith, A, 'Prayers unanswered: a jaundiced view of the parliamentary scrutiny of statutory instruments' (1981) 34 Parl Aff 165

Bell, J, *Policy Arguments in Judicial Decisions*, 1983, Oxford, Clarendon

Bell, JB, *The Secret Army: The IRA 1916–79*, 1979, Dublin: Academy

Benn, T, *The End of an Era, Diaries 1980–90*, 1994, London: Arrow

Bentham, J, *An Introduction to the Principles of Morals and Legislation*, 1970, Burns, JH and Hart, HLA (eds), London: Athlone

Bevan, V, 'Is anybody there?' [1980] PL 431

Bevan, V, 'Protest and public disorder' [1979] PL 163

Bindman, G, '*Spycatcher*: judging the judges' (1989) 139 NLJ 94

Bingham, TH (Sir), 'Should public law remedies be discretionary?' [1991] PL 64

Bingham, TH (Sir), 'The European Convention on Human Rights: time to incorporate' (1993) 109 LQR 390

Birch, D, 'Excluding evidence from entrapment: what is a "fair cop"?' (1994) 47 CLP 73

Birch, D, 'The pace hots up: confessions and confusions under the 1984 Act' [1989] Crim LR 95

Birkenhead (Lord), *Points of View*, Vol 1, 1922, London: Hodder & Stoughton

Birkinshaw, P, 'I only ask for information: the White Paper on *Open Government*' [1993] PL 557

Birkinshaw, P, *Grievances, Remedies and the State*, 2nd edn, 1994, London: Sweet & Maxwell

Bishop, P and Maillie, E, *The Provisional IRA*, 1987, London: Heinemann

Blackburn, RW, *Constitutional Studies*, 1992, London: Mansell

Blackburn, RW, *The Electoral System in Britain*, 1995, London: Macmillan

Blackstone, W (Sir), *Commentaries on the Laws of England* (1765–69), Chicago: Chicago UP

Blake (Lord), *The Office of Prime Minister*, 1975, Oxford: OUP

Bloch, J and Fitzgerald, P, *British Intelligence and Covert Action*, 1983, Dingle, Co Kerry: Brandon

Blom-Cooper, L and Drewry, G, *Final Appeal*, 1972, Oxford: Clarendon

Bogdanor, V (ed), *Constitutions in Democratic Politics*, 1988, London: Policy Studies Institute

Bogdanor, V and Butler, D, *Democracy and Elections*, 1983, Cambridge: CUP

Bogdanor, V, 'The forty per cent rule' (1980) 33 Parl Aff 249

Bogdanor, V, *Devolution*, 1979, Oxford: OUP

Bogdanor, V, *Multi-Party Politics and the Constitution*, 1983, Cambridge: CUP

Bogdanor, V, *Power and the People*, 1997, London: Gollancz

Bogdanor, V, *The People and the Party System*, 1981, Cambridge: CUP

Bolingbroke, H, *Remarks on the History of England*, 3rd edn, 1748, London: Francklin

Bonner, D and Stone, R, 'The Public Order Act 1986: steps in the wrong direction' [1987] PL 202

Bowen, CD, *The Lion and the Throne*, 1957, London: Hamish Hamilton

Boyle, K, Hadden, T and Hillyard, P, *Law and State*, 1975, London: Martin Robertson

Boyron, S, 'Proportionality in English administrative law: a faulty translation?' (1992) 12 OJLS 237

Bracton, H, *The Laws and Customs of England* (1200–68), 1968–77, Thorne, SE (trans), Cambridge, Mass: Harvard UP

Bradley, AW and Ewing, KD, *Constitutional and Administrative Law*, 12th edn, 1997, Harlow: Longman

Bradley, AW, 'Constitutional change and the Lord Chancellor' [1988] PL 165

Bradley, AW, 'Good government and public interest immunity' [1992] PL 514

Bradley, AW, 'Openness, direction and judicial review' [1986] PL 508

Bradley, AW, 'Parliamentary privilege and the Zircon affair' [1987] PL 1

Bradley, AW, 'Sachsenhausen, Barlow Clowes – and then' [1992] PL 353

Bradney, A, 'The judicial activity of the Lord Chancellor 1946–87' (1989) 16 JLS 360

Brazier, M, 'Judicial immunity and the independence of the judiciary' [1976] PL 397

Brazier, R, 'Choosing a prime minister' [1982] PL 395

Brazier, R, 'Government and the law' [1989] PL 64

Brazier, R, 'It is a constitutional issue: fitness for ministerial office in the 1990s' [1994] PL 431

Brazier, R, 'Ministers in court: the personal legal liability of ministers' (1993) 44 NILQ 317

Brazier, R, 'Regulating ministers' and ex-ministers' finances' (1992) 43 NILQ 19

Brazier, R, 'The downfall of Margaret Thatcher' (1991) 54 MLR 471

Brazier, R, *Constitutional Practice*, 2nd edn, 1994, Oxford: Clarendon

Brazier, R, *Constitutional Reform*, 1991, Oxford: Clarendon

Brazier, R, *Constitutional Texts*, 1990, Oxford: Clarendon

Bromhead, PA, *The House of Lords and Contemporary Politics*, 1958, London: Routledge and Kegan Paul

Brookfield, FM, 'The courts, Kelsen, and the Rhodesian revolution' (1969) 19 Toronto ULJ 326

Browne-Wilkinson (Lord), 'The independence of the judiciary in the 1980s' [1988] PL 44

Browne-Wilkinson (Lord), 'The infiltration of a Bill of Rights' [1992] PL 405

Bulloch, J, *MI5: The Origin and History of the British Counter-Espionage Service*, 1963, London: Arthur Barker

Bunyan, T, *The History and Practice of the Political Police in Britain*, 1977, London: Quartet

Burns, P, 'The law and privacy: the Canadian experience' (1976) 54 Canadian Bar Rev 1

Butler, D and Butler, G, *British Political Facts 1900–1985*, 1986, London: Macmillan

Butler, D and Ranney, A (eds), *Referendums around the World*, 1994, Basingstoke: Macmillan

Butler, D, 'The Australian crisis of 1975' (1976) 29 Parl Aff 201

Butler, D, *British General Elections since 1945*, 1989, Oxford: Blackwells

Butler, D, *Governing Without a Majority: Dilemmas for Hung Parliaments in Britain*, 1983, London: Collins

Butterworths European Information Services, *Butterworths' Annual European Review*, 1994, London: Butterworths

Byrne, A, *Local Government in Britain*, 6th edn, 1994, Harmondsworth: Penguin

Cain, M and Hunt, A, *Marx and Engels on Law*, 1979, London: Academic

Callaghan, J, *Time and Chance*, 1987, London: Collins

Calvert, H, *Constitutional Law in Northern Ireland*, 1968, London: Stevens

Campbell, A, 'The SEA and its implications' (1988) 35 ICLQ 932

Cane, P, 'The function of standing rules in administrative law' [1980] PL 303

Cane, P, '*Ultra vires* breach of statutory duty' [1981] PL 11

Chambers, G, *Equality and Inequality in Northern Ireland, Part 2: The Workplace*, 1987, London: Policy Studies Institute

Chandler, JA, 'The plurality vote: a reappraisal' (1982) 30 Political Studies 87

Charlesworth, A and Cullen, H, *European Community Law*, 1994, London: Pitman

Chester, N and Bowring, N, *Questions in Parliament*, 1962, Oxford; OUP

Chitty, J, *Law of the Prerogatives of the Crown*, 1820, London: Butterworths

Churchill, RR and Young, JR, 'Compliance with judgments of the European Court of Human Rights' [1991] BYIL 283

Clarke, DN and Feldman, D, 'Arrest by any other name' [1979] Crim LR 702

Clarke, DN and Shell, D, 'Revision and amendment of legislation by the House of Lords – a case study' [1994] PL 409

Clayton, R and Tomlinson, H, *Civil Actions against the Police*, 2nd edn, 1992, London: Sweet & Maxwell

Clothier, C (Sir), 'Legal problems of an ombudsman' (1984) 81 Law Soc Gazette 3108

Clothier, C (Sir), 'The value of an ombudsman' [1986] PL 204

Coke, E (Sir), *Institutes of the Laws of England; Concerning the Jurisdiction of the Courts*, 1644

Collins, H, *Marxism and Law*, 1982, Oxford: Clarendon

Connolly, M and Loughlin, J, 'Reflections on the Anglo-Irish Agreement' (1986) 21 Government and Opposition 146

Coppel, J, 'Horizontal effect of directives' [1997] Industrial LJ 69

Cotterrell, RBM, 'The impact of sex discrimination legislation' [1981] PL 469

Cowen, DV, *Parliamentary Sovereignty and the Entrenched Sections of the South Africa Act*, 1951, Cape Town: Juta

Craig, P and de Búrca, G, *European Community Law*, 2nd edn, 1998, Oxford: OUP

Craig, PP, 'Dicey: unitary, self-correcting democracy and public law' (1990) 106 LQR 105

Craig, PP, 'Directives: direct effect, indirect effect and the construction of national legislation' (1997) 22 EL Rev 519

Craig, PP, 'Sovereignty of the United Kingdom after *Factortame*' (1991) 11 YBEL 221

Craig, PP, 'The common law, reasons and administrative justice' [1994] CLJ 282

Craig, PP, *Administrative Law*, 3rd edn, 1994, London: Sweet & Maxwell

Cranston, R, 'Disqualification of judges for interest or opinion' [1979] PL 237

Crossman, R, *Introduction to the English Constitution*, 1993, London: Fontana

Crossman, R, *The Diaries of a Cabinet Minister*, 1977, London: Jonathan Cape

Curtin, D, 'The constitutional structure of the Union: a Europe of bits and pieces' (1993) 30 CML Rev 17

Curtin, D, 'The province of government: delimiting the direct effect of directives in the common law context' (1990) 15 EL Rev 195 d'Entrèves, AP, *Natural Law*, 2nd edn, 1970, London: Hutchinson

Dale, W, *The Modern Commonwealth*, 1983, London: Butterworths

Dauses, M, 'The protection of fundamental right in the Community legal order' (1985) 10 EL Rev 398

David, R and Brierley, JEC, *Major Legal Systems*, 1st edn, 1966, London: Stevens

David, R and Brierley, JEC, *Major Legal Systems*, 3rd edn, 1985, London: Sweet & Maxwell

Davies, K, *Local Government* Law, 1983, London: Butterworths

de Búrca, G and Scott, J (eds), *From Uniformity to Flexibility*, 2000, London: Hart.

de Búrca, G, 'A community of interests? Making the most of European law' (1992) 55 MLR 346

de Búrca, G, 'Giving effect to European Community directives' (1992) 55 MLR 215

de Búrca, G, 'The principle of proportionality and its application in EC law' [1993] 13 YBEL 105

de Búrca, G, 'The principle of subsidiarity and the Court of Justice as an institutional actor' (1998) 36(2) JCMS 217

de Smith, SA and Brazier, R, *Constitutional and Administrative Law*, 6th edn, 1989, London: Penguin

de Smith, SA and Brazier, R, *Constitutional and Administrative Law*, 8th edn, 1998, London: Penguin

de Smith, SA, *Judicial Review of Administrative Action*, 4th edn, 1980, London: Penguin

de Smith, SA, *The New Commonwealth and its Constitutions*, 1964, London: Stevens

Deacon, R, *A History of the British Secret Service*, 1969, London: Frederick Muller (updated, 1980, London: Panther)

Denning (Lord), 'The *Strauss* case' [1985] PL 80

Denning (Lord), *The Discipline of Law*, 1979, London: Butterworths

Denning (Lord), *The Due Process of Law*, 1980, London: Butterworths

Denning (Lord), *What Next in the Law?*, 1982, London: Butterworths

Devlin (Lord), 'Judges, government and politics' (1978) 41 MLR 501

Dhavan, R, 'Contempt of court and the *Phillimore Committee Report*' (1976) 5 Anglo-American L Rev 186

Dias, RWM, 'Legal politics: norms behind the grundnorm' [1968] CLJ 233

Dicey, AV, *Introduction to the Study of the Law of the Constitution*, 10th edn, 1959, London: Macmillan

Dickson, B, 'Northern Ireland's emergency legislation: the wrong medicine' [1993] PL 592

Diplock (Lord), 'Administrative law: judicial review reviewed' [1974] CLJ 223

Doherty, M, 'Prime ministerial power and ministerial responsibility in the Thatcher era' (1988) 41 Parl Aff 49

Donaldson, F, *The Marconi Scandal*, 1962, London: R Hart-Davis

Dremczewski, A, 'The domestic application of the European Human Rights Convention as European Community law' (1981) 30 ICLQ 118

Drewry, G (ed), *The New Select Committees*, 1989, Oxford: OUP

Drewry, G and Butcher, T, *The Civil Service Today*, 1988, Oxford: Blackwells

Drewry, G and Harlow, C, 'A "cutting edge"? The Parliamentary Commissioner and MPs' (1990) 53 MLR 758

Drewry, G, 'Judicial inquiries and public reassurance' [1996] PL 368

Drewry, G, 'Mr Major's Charter: empowering the consumer' [1993] PL 248

Drewry, G, 'The Lord Chancellor as judge' (1972) 122 NLJ 855

Drewry, G, 'The *Ponting* case – leaking in the public interest' [1985] PL 203

Driscoll, J, 'Excluding illegally obtained evidence in the United States' [1987] Crim LR 553

Driscoll, J, 'Excluding illegally obtained evidence – can we learn from the United States?', Legal Action Group Bulletin, June 1981

Duffy, PJ and Mulchlinski, P, 'The interception of communications in Great Britain' (1980) 130 NLJ 999

Dummett, A and Nichol, A, *Subjects, Citizens, Aliens and Others – Nationality and Immigration Law*, 1990, London: Weidenfeld & Nicolson

Dworkin, A, *Pornography: Men Possessing Women*, 1981, London: The Women's Press

Dworkin, R, *A Matter of Principle*, 1986, Oxford: Clarendon

Dworkin, R, *Taking Rights Seriously*, 1977, London: Duckworth

Dynes, M and Walker, D, *The Times Guide to the New British State: The Government Machine in the 1990s*, 1995, London: Times Books

Editorial, 'The Treaty of Amsterdam: neither a bang nor a whimper' (1997) 34 CML Rev 767

Eleftheriadis, P, 'The direct effect of Community law: conceptual issues' (1996) 16 YBEL 205

Emiliou, N, 'Subsidiarity: an effective barrier against "the enterprises of ambition"?' (1991) 17 EL Rev 383

Erskine May, T, *Parliamentary Practice*, 21st edn, 1989, London: Butterworths

Erskine May, T, *Parliamentary Practice*, 22nd edn, 1997, London: Butterworths

Esher, RBB, *The Influence of King Edward: and Essays on Other Subjects*, 1915, London: John Murray

Evans, JM, *Immigration Law*, 1983, London: Sweet & Maxwell

Ewing, K, *The Funding of Political Parties*, 1987, Cambridge: CUP

Ewing, KD and Gearty, CA, *Freedom Under Thatcher*, 1990, Oxford: Clarendon

Fawcett, J, *The Application of the European Convention on Human Rights*, 1987, Oxford: Clarendon

Feldman, D, *Civil Liberties and Human Rights in England and Wales*, 1993, Oxford: OUP

Fenwick, H, *Civil Liberties*, 2nd edn, 1998 (3rd edn, 2001), London: Cavendish Publishing

Fenwick, H and Phillipson, G, *Sourcebook on Public Law*, 1998, London: Cavendish Publishing

Fine, R, *Democracy and the Rule of Law: Liberal Ideals and Marxist Critiques*, 1984, London: Pluto

Finer, SE, 'The individual responsibility of ministers' (1956) 34 Public Admin 377

Finer, SE, *Adversary Politics and Electoral Reform*, 1975, London: Anthony Wigram

Finer, SE, *Anonymous Empire*, 1958, London: Pall Mall

Finer, SE, *The Changing British Party System*, 1980, Washington: AEI Studies

Finnie, W, Himsworth, C and Walker, N (eds), *Edinburgh Essays in Public Law*, 1991, Edinburgh: Edinburgh UP

Finnis, JM, *Natural Law and Natural Rights*, 1980, Oxford: Clarendon

Forsyth, C, 'Judicial review, the royal prerogative' (1985) 36 NILQ 25

Foster, RF (ed), *The Oxford History of Ireland*, 1989, Oxford: OUP

Foster, RF, *Modern Ireland 1600–1972*, 1989, London: Penguin

Fredman, S, *Women and the Law*, 1997, Oxford: Clarendon

Freedman, L, 'Even-handedness, guidelines and defence sales to Iraq' [1996] PL 391

French, D, 'Spy fever in Britain 1900–15' (1978) 21 Historical Journal 355

Friedman, S and Morris, G, 'Public and private? State employees and judicial review' (1991) 107 LQR 289

Fry, GK, 'The Sachsenhausen concentration camp case and the convention of ministerial responsibility?' [1970] PL 336

Fuller, L, 'Positivism and fidelity to law – a reply to Professor Hart' (1958) 11 Harv L Rev 630

Fuller, L, *The Morality of Law*, 1964, New Haven: Yale UP

Galligan, DJ, 'The nature and functions of policies within discretionary power' [1976] PL 332

Ganz, G, *Quasi-legislation: Some Recent Developments in Secondary Legislation*, 1987, London: Sweet & Maxwell

Gardiner (Lord), *The Trials of a Lord Chancellor*, 1968, Birmingham: Holdsworth Club, University of Birmingham

Garton Ash, T, *The File: A Personal History*, 1997, London: HarperCollins.

Gay, O and Winetrobe, B, 'Putting out the writs' [1997] PL 385

Gearty, CA, 'The European Court of Human Rights and the protection of civil liberties' [1993] CLJ 89

Gearty, G, *Terror*, 1991, London: Faber & Faber

Gibb, F, 'The Law Lord who took the rap over Pinochet' (1999) *The Times*, 19 October, p 3

Gilvarry, E, 'Selection changes to be urged' (1991) 88 Law Soc Gazette 6

Goodhart, AL, 'Thomas v Sawkins: a constitutional innovation' [1936–38] CLJ 22

Gordon DM, '"Administrative" tribunals and the courts' (1933) 49 LQR 94

Gordon, DM, 'What did the Anisminic case decide?' (1971) 34 MLR 1

Gould, BC, 'Anisminic and judicial review' [1970] PL 358

Gregory, R and Drewry, G, 'Barlow Clowes and the ombudsman: Part I' [1991] PL 192

Gregory, R and Drewry, G, 'Barlow Clowes and the ombudsman: Part II' [1991] PL 408

Gregory, R and Hutchesson, P, The Parliamentary Ombudsman, 1975, London: Allen & Unwin

Gregory, R and Pearson, J, 'The parliamentary ombudsman after twenty five years: problems and solutions' (1992) 70 Public Admin 469

Gregory, R, 'The Select Committee on the Parliamentary Commissioner for Administration 1967–80' [1982] PL 49

Griffith, JAG and Ryle, M, Parliament: Functions, Practice and Procedures, 1989, London: Sweet & Maxwell

Griffith, JAG, 'Crichel Down: the most famous farm in British constitutional history' (1987) 1 Contemporary Record 35

Griffith, JAG, 'Statutory restriction of judicial review' (1955) 18 MLR 557

Griffith, JAG, Parliamentary Scrutiny of Government Bills, 1973, London: Allen & Unwin

Griffith, JAG, The Politics of the Judiciary, 4th edn, 1991, London: Fontana

Griffith, JAG, The Politics of the Judiciary, 5th edn, 1997, London: Fontana

Guest, AG (ed), Oxford Essays in Jurisprudence, 1961, Oxford: OUP

Gwynn, SL, The Life of Walpole, 1932, London: Butterworths

Hadfield, B, 'The Anglo-Irish Agreement 1985 – blue print or green print' (1986) 37 NILQ 1

Hadfield, B, The Constitution of Northern Ireland, 1989, Belfast: SLS

Hailsham (Lord), The Dilemma of Democracy, 1978, London: Collins

Hailsham (Lord), The Door Wherein I Went, 1975, London: Collins

Hale, M (Sir), The History of the Pleas of the Crown, 1736, Emlyn, S (ed), London: E and R Nott and R Gosling

Hamilton, E, and Cairns, H (eds), Plato's Collected Dialogues, 1989, Ewing, New Jersey: Princeton UP

Hammond, AH, Judicial Review: The Continuing Interplay between Law and Policy [1998] PL 1

Hanks, PJ, Constitutional Law in Australia, 1991, Sydney: Butterworths

Hansard Society, Making the Law, 1993, London: Hansard

Harding, R, 'Caribbeans reject Privy Council jurisdiction' (1998) The Lawyer, 14 July

Harlow, C (ed), Public Law and Politics, 1986, London: Sweet & Maxwell

Harlow, C and Rawlings, R, Law and Administration, 1984, London: Weidenfeld & Nicolson

Harlow, C, 'Administrative reaction to judicial review' [1976] PL 116

Harlow, C, 'Comment' [1980] PL 1

Harlow, C, 'Ombudsmen in search of a role' (1978) 41 MLR 446

Harris, DJ, O'Boyle, M and Warbrick, C, *Law of the Convention on Human Rights*, 1995, Edinburgh: Butterworths

Harris, J, *Legal Philosophies*, 1980, London: Butterworths

Hart, HLA, 'Positivism and the separation of law and morals' (1958) 71 Harv L Rev 593

Hart, HLA, *The Concept of Law*, 1961, Oxford: Clarendon

Hartley, T, *The Foundations of European Community Law*, 4th edn, 1998, Oxford: Clarendon

Harvey Cox, W, 'The Anglo-Irish Agreement' (1987) 40 Parl Aff 80

Hayhurst, JD and Wallington, P, 'The parliamentary scrutiny of delegated legislation' [1988] PL 547

Hazell, R, 'Freedom of information in Australia, Canada and New Zealand' (1989) 67 Public Admin 189

Headey, BW, *British Cabinet Ministers: The Roles of Politicians in Executive Office*, 1974, London: Allen & Unwin

Hennessy, P, 'Helicopter crashes into Cabinet: Prime Minister and constitution hurt' (1986) 13 JLS 423

Hennessy, P, *Cabinet*, 1986: Oxford: Blackwells

Hennessy, P, *The Hidden Wiring: Unearthing the British Constitution*, 1996, London: Indigo

Hennessy, P, *Whitehall*, 1990, London: Fontana

Herberg, JW, 'The right to reasons – palm trees in retreat?' [1991] PL 340

Heuston, RFV, *Essays in Constitutional Law*, 2nd edn, 1964, London: Stevens

Heuston, RFV, *Lives of the Lord Chancellors, 1885–1940*, 1964, Oxford: Clarendon

Heuston, RFV, *Lives of the Lord Chancellors, 1940–70*, 1987, Oxford: Clarendon

Hewart, CJ, *The New Despotism*, 1929, London: Benn

Heydon, JD, 'Illegally obtained evidence' [1973] Crim LR 690

Hobbes, T, *The Leviathan* (1651), 1973, London: JM Dent

Hogg, PW, *Constitutional Law of Canada*, 2nd edn, 1985, Toronto: Carswell

Holdsworth, W, 'The treaty making power of the Crown' (1942) 58 LQR 177

Holt, J, *Magna Carta*, 1965, Cambridge: CUP

Hood-Phillips, O and Jackson, P, *Constitutional and Administrative Law*, 7th edn, 1987, London: Sweet & Maxwell

Hooper, D, *Official Secrets: The Use and Abuse of the Act*, 1988, Sevenoaks: Coronet

Howitt, D and Cumberbatch, G, *Pornography: Impacts and Influences*, 1990, London: Home Office

Hughes, M, *Ireland Divided: The Roots of the Modern Irish Problem*, 1994, Cardiff: Wales UP

Hume, D *Political Discourses* (1752), 1769, Edinburgh: Kineald and Donaldson

Hume, D, *An Enquiry Concerning the Principles of Morals* (1751) 1957, Indianapolis: Bobbs-Merrill

Hunt (Lord), 'Access to a previous government's papers' [1982] PL 514

Hutchinson, A and Petter, A, 'Private rights/public wrongs: the liberal lie of the Charter' (1988) 38 Toronto ULJ 278

Hutchinson, AP and Monahan, P (eds), *The Rule of Law: Ideal or Ideology*, 1987, Toronto: Carswell

IPPR and KPMG, *The Greater London Authority: Principles and Organisational Structure*, 1997, Corporation of London

Itzin, C (ed), *Pornography: Women, Violence and Civil Liberties*, 1992, Oxford: OUP

Iyer, TKK, 'Constitutional law in Pakistan: Kelsen in the courts' (1973) 21 AJCL 759

Jacob, JM, 'From privileged Crown to interested public' [1993] PL 121

Jacobs, FG, *The European Convention on Human Rights*, 1975, Oxford: Clarendon

Jaconelli, J, 'The "D notice" system' [1982] PL 37

Jalland, P, *The Liberals and Ireland: The Ulster Question in British Politics to 1914*, 1980, Hemel Hempstead: Harvester

James, R and Longley, D, 'The Channel Tunnel Rail Link, the Ombudsman and the Select Committee' [1996] PL 38

Jennings, I (Sir), *Cabinet Government*, 3rd edn, 1959, Cambridge: CUP

Jennings, I (Sir), *Parliament*, 2nd edn, 1969, Cambridge: CUP

Jennings, I (Sir), *The Law and the Constitution*, 5th edn, 1959, London: Hodder & Stoughton

Jones, G (ed), *The New Government Agenda*, 1997, Hemel Hempstead: ICSA

Jones, G and Stewart, J, *The Case for Local Government*, 2nd edn 1985, London: Allen & Unwin

Jowell, J and Oliver, D (eds), *New Directions in Judicial Review*, 1988, London: Stevens

Jowell, J and Oliver, D (eds), *The Changing Constitution*, 2nd edn, 1989, Oxford: Clarendon

Jowell, J and Oliver, D (eds), *The Changing Constitution*, 3rd edn, 1994, Oxford: Clarendon

Jowell, J, 'The Takeover Panel: autonomy, flexibility and legality' [1991] PL 149

Kafka, F, *Trial*, Muir, E and Muir, W (trans), 1956, London: Secker & Warburg

Keedy, ER, 'R v Sinnisiak: a remarkable murder trial' (1951) 100 Pennsylvania UL Rev 48

Keith, B, *The King, the Constitution, the Empire and Foreign Affairs: Letters and Essays 1936–37*, 1936, London: Longmans, Green

Keith-Lucas, B and Richards, PG, *A History of Local Government in the Twentieth Century*, 1979, London: Allen & Unwin

Kelsen, H, *The General Theory of Law and State*, 1961, New York: Russell

Kelsen, H, *The Pure Theory of Law*, 1967, Berkeley: California UP

Kenny, CS, 'The evolution of the law of blasphemy' [1992] CLJ 127

Kent, SK, *Sex and Suffrage in Britain 1860–1914*, 1987, Ewing, New Jersey: Princeton UP (rep 1990, London: Routledge)

King, ML, *Why We Can't Wait*, 1964, New York: Signet

Kingsford-Smith, D and Oliver, D (eds), *Economic With the Truth: The Law and Media in a Democratic Society*, 1990, Oxford: OUP

Kitchin, H, *Gibraltar Report: An Independent Observer's Report of the Inquest into the Deaths of Mairead Farrell, Daniel McCann and Sean Savage, Gibraltar, September 1988*, 1989, London: NCCL

Krämer, L, *The EEC Treaty and Environmental Protection*, 1992, London: Sweet & Maxwell

Labour Party, *Fairer, Faster and Firmer: a Modern Approach to Immigration and Asylum*, Cm 4018, 1998, London: The Stationery Office

Lambert, J, 'Executive authority to tap telephones' (1980) 43 MLR 59

Laski, H, *Reflections on the Constitution*, 1951, Manchester: Manchester UP

Laskin, B (ed), *Canadian Constitutional Law*, 5th edn, 1986, Toronto: Carswell

Laslett, P (ed), *Philosophy, Politics and Society*, 1975, Oxford: Blackwells

Lasok, P, '*Francovich* overrules *Bourgoin*: state liability for breach of Community law' [1992] ICCLR 186

Laws, J (Sir), 'Is the High Court the guardian of fundamental constitutional rights?' [1993] PL 60

Le Queux, W, *German Spies in England*, 1915, London: S Paul

Le Sueur, AP and Sunkin, M, 'Application for judicial review' [1992] PL 102

Le Sueur, AP, 'Should we abolish the writ of habeas corpus?' [1992] PL 13

Leach, P, 'Birth certificates, privacy and human rights' (1998) 142 SJ 628

Leach, S, Stewart, J and Walsh, K (eds), *The Changing Organisation and Management of Local Government*, 1994, Basingstoke: Macmillan

Lee, HP, 'Reforming the Australian Constitution – the frozen continent refuses to thaw' [1988] PL 535

Lee, JJ, *Ireland 1912–85: Politics and Society*, 1990, Cambridge: CUP

Lee, S, 'And so to school' (1987) 103 LQR 166

Lee, S, 'The limits of parliamentary sovereignty' [1985] PL 633

Lee, S, *Judging Judges*, 1989, London: Faber & Faber

Leigh, D and Vulliamy, E, *Sleaze: The Corruption of Parliament*, 1997, London: Fourth Estate

Leigh, D, *Betrayed: The Real Story of the Matrix Churchill Trial*, 1993, London: Bloomsbury

Leigh, I and Lustgarten, L, 'The Security Commission: constitutional achievement or curiosity?' [1991] PL 215

Leigh, I and Lustgarten, L, 'The Security Services Act 1989' (1989) 52 MLR 801

Leigh, I, 'A tapper's charter?' [1986] PL 8

Leigh, I, 'Matrix Churchill, supergun and the Scott Inquiry' [1993] PL 630

Leigh, I, '*Spycatcher* in Strasbourg' [1992] PL 200

Lenaerts, K, 'Fundamental rights to be included in the Community catalogue' (1991) 16 EL Rev 367

Leopold, P, '"Proceedings in Parliament": the grey area' [1991] PL 475

Leopold, P, 'Leaks and squeaks in the Palace of Westminster' [1980] PL 368

Leopold, PM, 'Freedom of speech in Parliament: its misuse and proposals for reform' [1981] PL 30

Lester (Lord), 'First steps towards a constitutional Bill of Rights' (1997) 2 EHRLR 124

Lester (Lord), 'Fundamental rights' [1994] PL 70

Levenson, H and Fairweather, F, *Police Powers*, 1990, London: Legal Action Group

Linklater, M, Leigh, D with Mather, I, *Not Without Honour: The Inside Story of the Westland Scandal*, 1986, London: Sphere

Locke, J, *Essay Concerning Human Understanding*, 1990, Oxford: Clarendon

Locke, J, *Letter on Toleration*, 1990, Oxford: Clarendon

Locke, J, *Two Treatises of Government* (1690), 1977, London: JM Dent

Lockyer, R, *Tudor and Stuart Britain 1471–1714*, 2nd edn, 1985, Harlow: Longman

Loughlin, M, 'Innovative financing in local government: the limits of legal instrumentalism: Part 2' [1991] PL 568

Loughlin, M, 'Innovative financing in local government: the limits of legal instrumentalism: Part 1' [1990] PL 372

Loughlin, M, 'The restructuring of central-local government legal relations' (1985) Local Government Studies 61

Loughlin, M, *Local Government in the Modern State*, 1986, London: Sweet & Maxwell

Lustgarten, L and Leigh, I, *In From the Cold: National Security and Parliamentary Democracy*, 1994, Oxford: Clarendon

Lustgarten, L, 'Racial inequality and the limits of law' (1981) 44 MLR 68

Lustgarten, L, 'Socialism and the rule of law' (1988) 15 JLS 25

Lustgarten, L, *The Legal Control of Racial Discrimination*, 1980, London: Macmillan

Lysaght, CE, 'Irish peers and the House of Lords' (1967) 18 NILQ 277

MacCormick, DN, 'A note on privacy' (1973) 84 LQR 23

MacCormick, N, 'Does the United Kingdom have a constitution? Reflections on *MacCormick v Lord Advocate*' (1978) 29 NILQ 1

MacCormick, N, 'The Maastricht-Urteil: sovereignty now' [1995] 1 ELJ 259

Macdermott (Lord), 'Law and order in times of emergency' [1972] Juridical Review 1

Macdonald, IA and Blak, NJ, *Macdonald's Immigration Law and Practice*, 3rd edn, 1991, London: Butterworths

Mackay (Lord), *The Administration of Justice*, 1994, London: Stevens

Mackenzie, R, *Free Elections*, 1967, London: Allen & Unwin

MacKinnon, C, *Feminism Unmodified: Discourses on Life and Law*, 1987, Cambridge, Mass: Harvard UP

Mackintosh, JP, *The British Cabinet*, 3rd edn, 1977, London: Stevens

MacMillan, CA, 'Burying treasure trove' (1996) 146 NLJ 1346

Macmillan, H, *At the End of the Day* (1961–63), 1973, London: Macmillan

Maitland, FW, *The Constitutional History of England*, 1908, Cambridge: CUP

Mancini, G and Keeling, D, 'From *CILFIT* to *ERTA*: the constitutional challenge facing the European Court' (1991) 11 YBEL 1

Markesinis, BS, *The Theory and Practice of Dissolution of Parliament*, 1972, Cambridge: CUP

Marsh, D and Read, M, *Private Members' Bills*, 1988, Cambridge: CUP

Marsh, NS, 'The declaration of Delhi' (1959) 2 J of the International Commission of Jurists 7

Marshall, G (ed), *Ministerial Responsibility*, 1989, Oxford: Clarendon

Marshall, G and Moodie, G, *Some Problems of the Constitution*, 5th edn, 1971, London: Hutchinson

Marshall, G, 'Cabinet Government and the Westland affair' [1986] PL 181

Marshall, G, 'The end of prime ministerial government?' [1991] PL 1

Marshall, G, 'The Queen's press relations' [1986] PL 505

Marshall, G, 'The referendum: what? when? how?' (1997) 50 Parl Aff 307

Marshall, G, *Constitutional Conventions*, 1984, Oxford: Clarendon

Marshall, G, *Constitutional Theory*, 1971, Oxford: Clarendon

Marshall, G, *Parliamentary Sovereignty and the Commonwealth*, 1957, Oxford: Clarendon

Martin, FX (ed), *Leaders and Men of the Easter Rising: Dublin 1916*, 1967, London: Methuen

Mathijsen, PSRF, *A Guide to European Union Law*, 1995, London: Sweet & Maxwell

Maude, A, *Why Electoral Change? Proportional Representation Examined*, 1982, London: Conservative Political Centre

McAuslan, P and McEldowney, JF, *Legitimacy and the Constitution: The Dissonance between Theory and Practice in Law*, 1985, London: Sweet & Maxwell

McAuslan, P, 'The Widdicombe Report: local government business or politics?' [1987] PL 154

McConville, M and Baldwin, J, 'Confessions: the dubious fruit of police interrogation' (1980) 130 NLJ 993

McConville, M and Hodgson, J, *Custodial Legal Advice and the Right to Silence*, RCCJ Research Study No 16, 1993, London: HMSO

McGarry, J, 'The Anglo-Irish Agreement and the prospects for power sharing in Northern Ireland' (1988) 59 Political Quarterly 236

McIlwain, CH, *Constitutionalism, Ancient and Modern*, 1958, Ithaca, New York: Great Seal

McIlwain, CH, *The High Court of Parliament and its Supremacy*, 1910, New Haven: Yale UP

McMurtie, SN, 'The waiting game – the Parliamentary Commissioner's response to delay in administrative procedures' [1997] PL 159

Mendelsen, M, 'The European Court of Justice and human rights' (1981) 1 YBEL 126

Miers, DR and Page, AC, *Legislation*, 2nd edn, 1990, London: Sweet & Maxwell

Mill, JS, *On Liberty* (1859), 1989, Cambridge: CUP

Mill, JS, *Representative Government* (1865), 1958, Indianapolis: Bobbs-Merrill

Mill, JS, *The Subjection of Women* (1869), 1989, Cambridge: CUP

Millar, E and Phillips, P, 'Evaluating anti-discrimination legislation in the United Kingdom: some issues and approaches' (1983) 11 Int J Soc L 417

Mitchell, JDB, 'Sovereignty of Parliament – yet again' (1963) 79 LQR 196

Mitchell, JDB, *Constitutional Law*, 2nd edn, 1968, Edinburgh: Green

Montesquieu, C, *De l'Esprit des Lois* (1748), 1989, Cambridge: CUP

Morgan, JP, *The House of Lords and the Labour Government 1964–1970*, 1975, Oxford: OUP

Morrison (Lord), *Government and Parliament*, 3rd edn, 1964, London: OUP

Morton, G, *Home Rule and the Irish Question*, 1980, Harlow: Longman

Mosley, RK, *The Story of the Cabinet Office*, 1969, London: Routledge and Kegan Paul

Mowbray, A, 'Reform of the control system of the ECHR' [1993] PL 419

Mummery, DR, 'The privilege of freedom of speech in Parliament' (1978) 94 LQR 276

Munro, CR, 'Laws and conventions distinguished' (1975) 91 LQR 224

Munro, CR, 'Power to the people' [1997] PL 579

Munro, CR, 'Press freedom: how the beast was tamed' (1991) 54 MLR 104

Munro, CR, *Studies in Constitutional Law*, 2nd edn, 1999, London: Butterworths

Naffine, N, 'Possession: erotic love in the law of rape' (1994) 57 MLR 10

Naffine, N, 'Windows on the legal mind: evocations of rape in legal writing' (1992) 18 Melbourne UL Rev 741

Naffine, N, *Law and the Sexes*, 1990, Sydney: Allen & Unwin

Neumann, F, *The Rule of Law: Political Theory and the Legal System in Modern Society*, 1986, Leamington Spa: Berg

Newton, K and Karran, TJ (eds), *The Politics of Local Expenditure*, 1985, London: Macmillan

Nicolson, IF, *The Mystery of Crichel Down*, 1986, Oxford: Clarendon

Norton, P, 'Televising the House of Commons' (1991) 44 Parl Aff 185

Norton, P, *Does Parliament Matter?*, 1993, Hemel Hempstead: Harvester

Norton, P, *Parliament in the 1980s*, 1985, Oxford: Blackwells

Norton, P, *The Commons in Perspective*, 2nd edn, 1985, Oxford: Blackwells

Norton-Taylor, R, *The Ponting Affair*, 1985, London: Woolf

Norton-Taylor, R, *Truth is a Difficult Concept: Inside the Scott Inquiry*, 1995, London: Fourth Estate

Nozick, R, *Anarchy, State and Utopia*, 1974, Oxford: Blackwells

O'Connor, U, *The Troubles: The Struggle for Irish Freedom 1912–1922*, 1989, London: Mandarin

O'Halpin, E, *The Decline of the Union: British Government in Ireland 1892–1920*, 1987, Dublin: Gill and Macmillan

O'Keefe, D and Twomey, PM (eds), *Legal Issues of the Maastricht Treaty*, 1994, London: Chancery

O'Sullivan, D, *The Allocation of Scarce Resource and the Right to Life under the European Convention on Human Rights* [1998] PL 1

Oliver, D and Austin, R, 'Political and constitutional aspects of the *Westland* affair' (1987) 40 Parl Aff 20

Oliver, D, 'Is the *ultra vires* rule the basis of judicial review?' [1987] PL 543

Oliver, D, '*Pepper v Hart*: a suitable case for reference to *Hansard*?' [1993] PL 5

Oliver, D, 'Reform of the electoral system' [1983] PL 108

Owen Dixon, J, 'The law and the constitution' (1935) 51 LQR 611

Paine, T, *Rights of Man* (1791, Pt I), 1984, rep 1998, Collins, H (ed), New York: Penguin

Paine, T, *Rights of Man* (1792, Pt II), 1984, rep 1998, Collins, H (ed), New York: Penguin

Palley, C, 'The evolution, disintegration and possible reconstruction of the Northern Ireland Constitution' (1972) 1 Anglo-American L Rev 368

Palley, C, *The United Kingdom and Human Rights*, 1991, London: Sweet & Maxwell

Palmer, S, 'Tightening secrecy law' [1990] PL 243

Pannick, D, *Judges*, 1988, Oxford: OUP

Pannick, D, *Sex Discrimination Law*, 1985, Oxford: Clarendon

Pennock, JR and Chapman, JW (eds), *Political and Legal Obligation*, 1970, New York: Atherton

Pescatore, P, 'Some critical remarks on the Single European Act' (1987) 24 CML Rev 9

Pescatore, P, 'The "doctrine of direct effect": an infant disease of Community law' (1983) 8 EL Rev 155

Petite, M, 'The Treaty of Amsterdam' (www.law.harvard.edu/programs/JeanMonnet/papers/98/98-14-The.html)

Philby, K, *My Silent War*, 1968, London: MacGibbon and Kee

Phythian, M and Little, W, 'Parliament and arms sales: lessons of the Matrix Churchill affair' (1993) 46 Parl Aff 293

Pincher, C, *Their Trade is Treachery*, 1981, London: Sidgwick and Jackson

Plamenatz, J, *Man and Society*, 1963, New York: Longman

Plato, *The Collected Dialogues*, Hamilton, E and Cairns, H (eds), 1989, Ewing, New Jersey: Princeton UP

Plucknett, TFT, '*Dr Bonham's Case* and judicial review' (1926) 40 Harv L Rev 30

Ponting, C, *R v Ponting* (1987) 14 JLS 366

Ponting, C, *The Right to Know*, 1985, London: Sphere

Poole, KP, 'The Northern Ireland Commissioner for Complaints' [1972] PL 131

Powell, E and Wallis, K, *The House of Lords in the Middle Ages*, 1968, London: Weidenfeld & Nicolson

Priestley, J, *An Essay on the First Principles of Government; and on the Nature of Political, Civil, and Religious Liberty, including remarks on Dr Brown's Code of Education, and on Dr Balguy's Sermon on Church Authority*, 2nd edn, 1771, London: J Johnson

Pugh, I (Sir), 'The ombudsman – jurisdiction, power and practice' (1978) 56 Public Admin 127

Ranelagh, J, *A Short History of Ireland*, 1983, Cambridge: CUP

Rasmussen, H, 'Between self-restraint and activism; a judicial policy for the European Court' (1988) 13 EL Rev 28

Rasmussen, H, 'The European Court's *acte clair* strategy in *CILFIT*' (1984) 9 EL Rev 242

Rawlings, HF, 'Judicial review and the control of government' (1986) 64 Public Admin 135

Rawlings, HF, *Law and the Electoral Process*, 1988, London: Sweet & Maxwell

Rawlings, R, 'The test for the *nemo iudex* rule' [1980] PL 122

Rawls, J, *A Theory of Justice*, 1973, Oxford: OUP

Raz, J, 'The rule of law and its virtue' (1977) 93 LQR 195

Raz, J, *The Authority of Law*, 1979, Oxford: OUP

Reed, C (ed), *Computer Law*, 2nd edn, 1993, London: Blackstone

Reid (Lord), 'The judge as lawmaker' [1972] JSPTL 22

Rice, D and Gavshon, A, *The Sinking of the 'Belgrano'*, 1984, London: Secker & Warburg

Richardson, G and Genn, H (eds), *Administrative Law and Government Action*, 1994, Oxford: OUP

Riddell, P, 'Quality control deficiency that lets down the law' (1994) *The Times*, 16 December

Ridley, FF, 'There is no British Constitution: a dangerous case of the Emperor's clothes (1988) 41 Parl Aff 340

Roberts-Wray, K, *Commonwealth and Colonial Law*, 1966, London: Stevens

Robertson, AH, *Human Rights in Europe*, 2nd edn, 1977, Manchester: Manchester UP

Robertson, G, *Freedom, the Individual and the Law*, 6th edn, 1989 (7th edn, 2001), London: Penguin

Robilliard, StJ, 'Offences against religion and public worship' (1981) 44 MLR 556

Rose, R, 'Law as a resource of public policy' (1986) 39 Parl Aff 297

Rose, R, *Do Parties Make a Difference?*, 2nd edn, 1984, London: Macmillan

Ross, M, 'Beyond *Francovich*' (1993) 56 MLR 55

Rousseau, J, *The Social Contract and Discourses* (1762), 1977, London: JM Dent

Rowat, D, *The Ombudsman: Citizen's Defender*, 1968, London: Allen & Unwin

Rudden, R and Wyatt, D, *Basic Community Laws*, 5th edn, 1994, Oxford: Clarendon

Russell, PH, Rainer, K and Morton, T (eds), *Federalism and the Charter: Leading Constitutional Decisions*, 1989, Ottawa: Carleton UP

Ryle, M and Richards, G (eds), *The Commons Under Scrutiny*, 3rd edn, 1988, London: Routledge and Kegan Paul

Sampford, CJG, '"Recognize and declare": an Australian experiment in codifying constitutional conventions' (1987) 7 OJLS 369

Savage, N and Edwards, C, *A Guide to the Data Protection Act 1985*, 1985, London: Financial Training

Sawer, G, *Australian Federalism in the Courts*, 1967, Melbourne: Melbourne UP

Sawer, G, *Federation Under Strain*, 1977, Melbourne: Melbourne UP

Schermers, HG, 'The European Community bound by fundamental human rights' (1990) 27 CML Rev 249

Schermers, HG, *Judicial Protection in the European Community*, 4th edn, 1987, Dordrecht: Kluwer

Schiemann, K (Sir), '*Locus standi*' [1990] PL 342

Schwarze, J, *European Administrative Law*, Luxembourg: Office for Official Publications of the European Communities

Scott, J, *Development Dilemmas in the EC: Rethinking Regional Development Policy*, 1995, Milton Keynes: OU Press

Scott, J, *European Community Environmental Law*, 1998, London: Longman

Scott, R (Sir), 'Ministerial accountability' [1996] PL 410

Scott, R (Sir), 'The acceptable and unacceptable use of public interest immunity' [1996] PL 427

Seaborne Davies, D, 'The House of Lords and the criminal law' (1962) 6 JSPTL 104

Sharpe, LG, 'Theories and values of local government' (1970) 18 Political Studies 153

Shell, D, 'The House of Lords and the Thatcher government' (1983) 38 Parl Aff 16

Shell, D, *The House of Lords*, 2nd edn 1992, London: Harvester

Silk, P and Walters, R, *How Parliament Works*, 1987, London: Longman

Simmonds, KR, 'The British Islands and the Community: II Isle of Man' (1970) 7 CMLR 454

Simmonds, KR, 'The British Islands and the Community: III Guernsey' (1971) 8 CMLR 475

Simon Brown LJ, 'Public interest immunity' [1994] PL 579

Slapper, G and Kelly, D, *The English Legal System*, 4th edn, 1999, London: Cavendish Publishing

Slot, PJ, 'Case C-194/94: *CIA Security International SA v Signalson SA and Securitel SPRL*' (1996) 33 CML Rev 1035

Slynn, G, 'The Court of Justice of the European Community' (1984) 33 ICLQ 409

Smart, C, *Feminism and the Power of Law*, 1989, London: Routledge

Smith, ATH, 'Dicey and civil liberties: comment' [1985] PL 608

Smith, ATH, 'The Public Order Act, Part I' [1987] Crim LR 156

Smith, DJ, 'Policy and research: employment discrimination in Northern Ireland' (1988) 9(1) Policy Studies 41

Smith, P and Bailey, SH, *The Modern English Legal System*, 2nd edn, 1991, London: Sweet & Maxwell

Spalin, E, 'Abortion, speech and the European Community' [1992] J of Social Welfare and Family Law 17

Spjut, RJ, 'Internment and detention without trial in Northern Ireland' (1986) 49 MLR 712

Stacey, F, *Ombudsmen Compared*, 1978, Oxford: Clarendon

Steiner, J, 'From direct effects to *Francovich*: shifting means of enforcement of Community law' (1993) 18(3) EL Rev 3

Steiner, J, *Enforcing EC Law*, 1995, London: Blackstone

Steiner, J, *Textbook on EEC Law*, 3rd edn, 1992, London: Blackstone

Steiner, J, *Textbook on EEC Law*, 5th edn, 1996, London: Blackstone

Stephens, L, *The Science of Ethics* (1882), 1972, Newton Abbot: David and Charles

Stewart, J and Stoker, J (eds), *The Future of Local Government*, 1989, Basingstoke: Macmillan

Stone, J, 'Mystery and mystique in the basic norm' (1963) 26 MLR 34

Stubbs, W, *The Constitutional History of England: In its Origin and Development*, 1880, Oxford: Clarendon

Supperstone, M (ed), *Brownlie's Law of Public Order and National Security*, 2nd edn, 1981, London: Butterworths

Supperstone, M and Cavanagh, J, *Immigration*, 3rd edn, 1994 London: Longman

Supperstone, M and Goudie, J (eds), *Judicial Review*, 1988, London: Butterworths

Supperstone, M, 'The Intelligence Services Act 1994' [1994] PL 329

Szyszczack, E, 'Sovereignty: crisis, compliance, confusion, complacency?' (1990) 15(6) EL Rev 483

Tapper, C, *Computer Law*, 4th edn, 1989, London: Longman

Tapper, C, *Cross and Tapper on Evidence*, 8th edn, 1995, London: Butterworths

Taylor, GD, 'Judicial review of improper purposes and irrelevant considerations' [1976] CLJ 272

Tebbitt, N, *Upwardly Mobile*, 1988, London, Weidenfeld & Nicolson

Temple-Lang, J, 'Community constitutional law: Article 5 EC Treaty' (1990) 27 CML Rev 645

Thatcher, M, *The Downing Street Years*, 1993, London: HarperCollins

Thompson, WI, *The Imagination of an Insurrection: Dublin, Easter 1916*, 1967, Oxford: OUP

Thoreau, HD, *Resistance to Civil Government* (1848), 2nd edn, 1992, Rossi, W (ed), London: Norton

Thornberry, CHR, 'Dr Soblen and the alien law of the United Kingdom' (1963) 12 ICLQ 414

Thorne, SE, '*Dr Bonham's Case*' (1938) 54 LQR 543

Thornton, GC, *Legislative Drafting*, 3rd edn, 1987, London: Butterworths

Tomkins, A, 'Government information and Parliament: misleading by design or by default?' [1996] PL 472

Tomkins, A, 'Public interest immunity after Matrix Churchill' [1993] PL 650

Tomkins, A, *The Constitution after Scott: Government Unwrapped*, 1998, Oxford: Clarendon

Toth, AG, 'The principle of subsidiarity in the Maastricht Treaty' (1992) CML Rev 1079

Trevor-Roper, H, *The Philby Affair: Espionage, Treason and Secret Service*, 1968, London: Kimber

Tur, R and Twining, W (eds), *Essays on Kelsen*, 1986, Oxford: Clarendon

Turnbull, M, *The Spycatcher Trial*, 1988, London: Heinemann

Upton, M, 'Marriage vows of the elephant: the constitution of 1707' (1989) 105 LQR 79

Van Dijk, P and Van Hoof, G, *Theory and Practice of the European Convention on Human Rights*, 2nd edn, 1990, Deventer, Netherlands: Kluwer

Vile, MJC, *Constitutionalism and the Separation of Powers*, 1967, Oxford: Clarendon

von Hayek, F, *The Constitution of Liberty*, 1960, London: Routledge and Kegan Paul

von Hayek, F, *The Road to Serfdom*, 1994, London: Routledge and Kegan Paul

Wade, ECS and Bradley, AW, *Constitutional and Administrative Law*, 11th edn, 1993, Harlow: Longman

Wade, ECS, 'Act of State in English law' (1934) 15 BYIL 98

Wade, HWR and Forsyth, CF, *Administrative Law*, 7th edn, 1994, Oxford: Clarendon

Wade, HWR, 'Constitutional and administrative aspects of the *Anisminic* case' (1969) 85 LQR 198

Wade, HWR, 'Procedure and prerogative in public law' (1985) 101 LQR 180

Wade, HWR, 'Public law, private law and judicial review' (1983) 99 LQR 166

Wade, HWR, 'Sovereignty – revolution or evolution' (1996) 112 LQR 568

Wade, HWR, 'The basis of legal sovereignty' [1955] CLJ 177

Wade, HWR, *Constitutional Fundamentals*, rev edn, 1989, London: Stevens

Wagner, A and Squibb, GD, 'Precedence and courtesy titles' (1973) 89 LQR 352

Walker, C, 'Review of the prerogative' [1987] PL 63

Wallington, P (ed), *Civil Liberties*, 1984, Oxford: Martin Robertson

Walsh, D, *The Use and Abuse of Emergency Legislation in Northern Ireland*, 1983, London: The Cobden Trust

Wasik, M and Taylor, R, *Blackstone's Guide to the Criminal Justice Act 1994*, 1995, London: Blackstone

Wasserstrom, R, 'The obligation to obey the law' (1963) California UL Rev 780

Watkins, A, *A Conservative Coup*, 1992, London: Duckworth

Watson, J, 'Experience and problems in applying Article 177 EEC' (1986) 23 CML Rev 207

Watt, D, 'Fallout from treachery: Peter Wright and the *Spycatcher* case' [1988] Political Quarterly 206

Weatherill, S and Beaumont, P, *EU Law*, 3rd edn, 1999, Harmondsworth: Penguin

West, N, *A Matter of Trust: MI5 1945–72*, 1983, London: Hodder & Stoughton

West, N, *GCHQ: The Secret Wireless War 1900–86*, 1986, London: Weidenfeld & Nicolson (rep 1987, Sevenoaks: Coronet)

West, N, *MI5: British Security Service Operations 1909–45*, 1981, London: Bodley Head

West, N, *MI5: British Security Service Operations 1909–45*, 1983, London: Weidenfeld & Nicolson

Wheare, KC, *Federal Government*, 4th edn, 1963, Oxford: OUP

Wheare, KC, *Modern Constitutions*, 2nd edn, 1966, Oxford: OUP

Wheare, KC, *The Constitutional Structure of the Commonwealth*, 1960, Oxford: Clarendon

White, P (ed), *Feminist Jurisprudence*, Oxford: OUP

Williams, DGT, 'Public order and common law' [1984] PL 12

Williams, DGT, 'Telephone tapping' [1979] CLJ 225

Williams, DGT, *Keeping the Peace*, 1967, London: Hutchinson

Williams, DGT, *Not in the Public Interest*, 1965, London: Hutchinson

Williams, DW, *Maladministration: Remedies for Injustice*, 1976, London: Oyez

Williams, G, 'The problem of domestic rape' (1991) 141 NLJ 205

Wilson, G, *Cases and Materials on Constitutional and Administrative Law*, 2nd edn 1976, Cambridge: CUP

Wilson, H, *The Governance of Britain*, 1976, London: Weidenfeld & Nicolson

Wilson, H, *The Labour Government 1964–70: A Personal Record*, 1971, London: Weidenfeld & Nicolson

Wilson, R (Sir), *The Civil Service in the New Millennium*, May 1999 (www.cabinet-office.gov.uk/1999/senior/rw_speech.htm)

Winter, JA, 'Direct applicability and direct effect: two distinct and different concepts in Community law' (1972) 9 CML Rev 425

Wolf-Phillips, L, 'A long look at the British Constitution' (1984) 37 Parl Aff 385

Woodhouse, D, 'Ministerial responsibility in the 1990s: when do ministers resign?' (1993) 46 Parl Aff 277

Woodhouse, D, 'Ministerial responsibility: something old, something new' [1997] PL 262

Woolf, H (Lord), *The Protection of the Public – A New Challenge*, 1990, London: Stevens

Wormald, J, 'James VI and I: two Kings or one?' (1983) 68 History 187

Wright, P, *Spycatcher: The Candid Autobiography of a Senior Intelligence Officer*, 1987, New York: Viking

Yardley, D, 'Local ombudsmen in England: recent trends and developments' [1983] PL 522

Young, H, *One of Us*, 1989, London: Macmillan

Young, H, *The Crossman Affair*, 1976, London: Hamish Hamilton

Zander, M, 'When is an arrest not an arrest?' (1997) 147 NLJ 379

Zander, M, *A Bill of Rights*, 3rd edn, 1985, London: Sweet & Maxwell

Zander, M, *Cases and Materials on the English Legal System*, 6th edn, 1993, London: Butterworths

Zander, M, *The Police and Criminal Evidence Act 1984*, 3rd edn, 1995, London: Sweet & Maxwell

Zellick, GJ, 'Government beyond law' [1985] PL 283

Zuckerman, AAS, 'Public interest immunity – a matter of prime judicial responsibility' (1994) 57 MLR 703

INDEX

Index